POPULAR MECHANICS

Guide To Basic Auto Repair And Maintenance

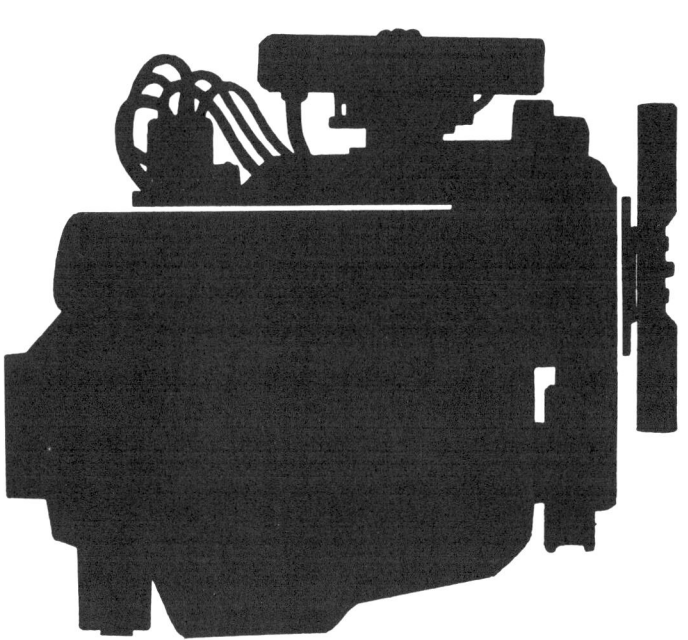

Book Division
The Hearst Corporation
New York, NY

Contents

HOW TO USE THIS BOOK 4

KNOW YOUR CAR 9
Orientation to the automobile and its component systems • Engine • Oil system • Cooling system • Fuel system • Exhaust system • Electrical system • Drivetrain system • Steering system • Suspension system • Brake system •

SETTING UP SHOP 105
Tools and equipment: wrenches, drives, ratchets, sockets, gauges, drills • Tuneup instruments • Power tools • Bare minimum setups • All-out setups • Tool and equipment price ranges • Typical garage layouts • Choosing and buying parts • How to get good deals • Inferior vs. quality items •

BASIC ENGINE TUNEUP 137
Importance of regular tuneups • Mileage vs. time • Safety precautions • Tools and equipment • 22 steps of a tuneup • Compression testing • Fuel system service • Ignition system service • Filter replacement • Test instruments • Electronic ignition systems • Tools and equipment for the job • Troubleshooting engine, ignition and fuel system problems •

PERIODIC MAINTENANCE 233
Whys of periodic maintenance • Items to be checked periodically • Periodic intervals: daily, weekly, monthly, seasonally • How to check for service needs • Checking for safety • Fluid leakage • Emergency equipment and supplies • Manufacturer's recommended service schedules • Manufacturer's new car warranties 1969-76 •

COOLING SYSTEM MAINTENANCE 265
Permanent-type coolants vs. alcohol or plain water • Flushing a system • Draining and refilling • Thermostats • Hoses and belts • Tools for the job • Troubleshooting cooling system problems •

EXHAUST SYSTEM MAINTENANCE 297
Dangers of faulty exhaust systems • Repairing vs. replacement • Exhaust pipes • Mufflers • Tailpipes • Hangers and brackets • Tools for the job • Troubleshooting exhaust system problems •

LUBRICATION GUIDE 329
Lubrication as preventive maintenance • Selecting proper engine oil • Grades and weights • Oil filters • Chassis lubrication • Long lube periods • Tools and equipment for the job •

TIRES 361
Why tire care is so important • Selecting tires for your needs • Buying tires without overbuying or overpaying • Bias-ply, bias-belted and radial ply tires • Aspect ratios • Size markings • Snow tires • Studs • Tire rotation • Troubleshooting abnormal wear patterns • Proper inflation • Tire problems • Mounting recommendations • Tire size interchangeability chart •

SHOCK ABSORBERS AND HANDLING 393
The hidden hazard • Safe vehicle control and handling • Testing shocks • Inspection • Replacement —front and rear • Standard vs. heavy duty • Air shocks • Overload shocks • Special applications • Tools and equipment for the job • Troubleshooting front end problems •

BRAKE SERVICE 425
Cautions for novice mechanic • Disc vs. drum brake service • Replacing disc pads • Adjusting drum brakes • Adjusting parking brakes • Tools for the job • Troubleshooting brake system problems •

GOOD VISION FOR SAFETY 489
You must see to drive • Replacing wiper blades and arms • Lighting • Sealed beams • Signal and parking lamps • Fuse and flasher replacement • Tools and equipment for the job •

BODY AND INTERIOR MAINTENANCE 521
Upping the resale value of your car • Washing • Waxing • Compounding • Repairing damaged paint • Maintaining weather strips • Cleaning upholstery • Repairing minor dings and dents • Paint touchup • Replacing broken radio antennas •

REFERENCE DATA 553
Specifications: 1969-76 U.S. cars, plus Volkswagen, Toyota, Datsun • Tuneup specs • Cooling system and fluid capacities • Metric/SAE equivalents • How to push and tow cars with automatic transmissions • Tap drill sizes • Car ride heights •

GLOSSARY 657
Automotive terminology explained. A complete glossary of automotive terms for the layman with clear definitions for each.

How To Use This Book

Ever since the first car owner donned cap, goggles and duster for a jaunt around town, there have been two distinct individuals who worked on automobiles—the professional mechanic and the do-it-yourself novice.

Early in its development stages, the automobile was little more than an expensive toy, a hobby for those who could afford to indulge their every whim. Tinkering with their own car, if they were so inclined, was merely an extension of the hobby.

Today, of course, the automobile has assumed enormous importance in our society. It is a basic means of transportation, a vital link in the commerce of the nation. Indeed, to some whose business depends entirely on motor vehicles, it *is* the commerce of the nation.

But through all the 75-odd years of development of the automobile, one fact has remained virtually unchanged. There are still two distinct individuals who work on cars—the professional mechanic and the do-it-yourself novice.

The motives of the professional mechanic have not changed one iota. He works on cars because that is how he earns his living.

The motives of the do-it-yourselfer, however, have changed perceptibly over the years. Where at first the novice tinkered with his automobile because it was fun and part of his hobby, gradually, repairing his own car became more and more an economic necessity. As the cost of auto repairs blasted through the roof along with everything else caught in the inflationary spiral, more and more people found that they could save significant amounts of money by doing their own auto repairs and maintenance.

Of course, there are still those who perform their own auto maintenance and repair simply because they like to, because it gives them pleasure and satisfaction when they complete a job, and because they think it is fun.

But even larger is the group of do-it-yourselfers who do their own repairs and maintenance strictly for a practical reason—to save money.

According to a recent survey by the Automotive Parts and Accessories Association, there are about 47 million individuals who perform some do-it-yourself tasks on their automobile. And this figure grows every day as the price of parts and labor continues upward.

Simply stated, you can save yourself a bundle of cash by doing it yourself. Just how much cash can be illustrated by a couple of typical job tickets comparing prices for certain repair and maintenance jobs. These are actual charges by a franchised new car dealer and an independent aftermarket facility for parts and labor. We have added a third column to show you approximately how much the same service would have cost you if you had done the work yourself and purchased the parts.

HOW MUCH MONEY CAN YOU SAVE BY DOING IT YOURSELF?

Comparison of charges by franchised car dealer (FCD) and independent aftermarket facility (IAF) for parts and labor. (Comparisons drawn from three invoices.) Car purchased new on June 9, 1973.

Invoice date			FCD	IAF	Do-It Yourself
10/30/73	Parts	Oil filter	$5.12	$2.99	$2.50
		5 quarts oil	4.75	3.45	2.50
		Shop materials	2.34	N/C	N/C
	Labor	Lubricate/change oil, change oil filter	4.80	3.50	N/C
		Rotate tires	6.00	4.00	N/C
		TOTAL:	$23.01	$13.94	$5.00
7/24/74	Parts	Oil filter	$8.74	$4.29	$3.25
		Gas filter	2.90	1.99	1.25
		PCV valve	2.32	1.99	1.50
		Points, condenser	8.25	3.99	3.75
		8 spark plugs	13.92	8.91	6.80
		Bulb	.90	.50	.40
	Labor	Tune engine	$27.60	$17.68	N/C
		Replace shifter light	2.40	1.00	N/C
		Replace canister filter	4.80	N/C	N/C
		Check service washer	4.00	4.00	N/C
		TOTAL:	$75.83	$44.35	$16.95
1/7/75	Parts	Thermostat	$4.18	$2.99	$2.50
		Gasket	.18	.18	.15
		Coolant	9.00	4.99	3.95
		Shop materials	.89	N/C	N/C
	Labor	Flush and check radiator, replace thermostat	14.00	10.00	N/C
		Service emission controls	8.40	5.00	N/C
		Repair defogger switch	14.00	11.00	N/C
		TOTALS:	$50.65	$34.16	$6.60

For comparison purposes, the independent aftermarket facility was selected in the same marketing area as was the franchised car dealer, assuring that overhead rates are generally comparable. Also, the parts used by the independent facility are designed and manufactured for identical applications for the specific 350 V-8 engine in the Oldsmobile Cutlass S. (In some instances the parts were made by the same manufacturer. Also, the prices quoted were the prevailing retail prices at the very time and in no case are they sale prices.)

As you can see with even a cursory inspection of the chart, when you do it yourself, your savings come from two sources. First, there is the amount saved on labor since you supply your own. Second, there is the amount saved on parts markup by the repair facility.

In total, the amounts become substantial. In fact, another survey indicates that every car in the United States that is out of warranty will require approximately $250-$300 in repairs and maintenance a year. Even forgetting about the savings in purchasing your own parts, your savings in labor charges alone should amount to about half that amount if you do the work yourself.

Even professionals need work aids

Customers are not allowed in the work areas of most repair facilities and that is too bad. If you were allowed to watch the professional mechanic at work, you would notice something immediately. Most professional mechanics are not geniuses. They do not have every fact and figure in their heads. With the myriad of makes and models on the road today, and with today's sophisticated automotive systems, it is virtually impossible for every mechanic to know every repair procedure and every specification he needs to complete a job.

So if you *were* allowed into the work area, you would see the professional mechanic constantly referring to reference books and repair manuals to help him through the day's chores. Auto repair manuals are widely used in the repair industry and are considered a necessity by most professionals.

Professional repair manuals cover procedures only for advanced repair jobs since a professional would know how to do the more elementary jobs without resorting to a reference book. A professional repair manual also contains complete specifications for almost all makes and models on the road so that the mechanic can make various settings according to manufacturer's specifications.

Your own repair guide

Up to now, this type of auto repair manual was not available for the novice mechanic—the do-it-yourselfer who wanted to save money by doing his own repairs and maintenance. Sure, you could buy a professional auto repair manual. But in most cases, a professional book is just too advanced for the novice. All professional repair manuals assume a certain level of mechanical competence in the user.

For instance, step one of a procedure might read: "Flush cooling system." But nowhere will it tell you *how* to flush a cooling system because the book assumes that every professional already knows how.

On the other hand, there have been a number of books written for the novice mechanic which purport to tell you how to do certain repairs and maintenance procedures on your car. The trouble with these books is that they have not been comprehensive enough to actually take you step-by-step through a job to completion. In addition, most of them read like novels instead of like repair manuals. So you cannot actually have the book open to follow the procedural steps as you actually perform them on your car.

This book is different

The *Popular Mechanics Guide to Basic Auto Repair and Maintenance* is meant to be a working manual, a manual that will be right there with you propped up on the fender or workbench, taking you step-by-step through scores of repair and maintenance procedures that you, the novice mechanic, *can* do.

It is a tool, just as a wrench is a tool, and it should be used like one whenever you have any work to do on your car. It might get dirty. But you will find that a little dirt will not diminish the book's usefulness. It is meant to work with you as you tackle an engine tuneup, oil change, shock absorber replacement, cooling system flush, muffler or tailpipe replacement or hundreds of other jobs on your car.

What you can and cannot do

As a novice mechanic, you have your limitations just as this book has its own limitation.

For instance, this book will *not* make you into a professional mechanic. It is not meant to. However, it *will* help you, the novice mechanic, save money by taking you step-by-step through hundreds of different repair and maintenance procedures on your car.

In compiling the information in this book, the editors have included only those jobs which we feel the novice mechanic can handle successfully. There are instances when a job is just too advanced for the novice. Or, a job may require highly sophisticated or expensive tools that the average novice mechanic would not have access to. In such cases, we will tell you to seek the services of a professional mechanic. Also, if a job is not included in this book, it is probably too difficult for a novice to handle.

Before you begin work

The first two chapters of this book deal with a general orientation to the automobile and a guide to setting up a toolbox and workshop.

Obviously, you should have at least an elementary knowledge of how the various systems in your car work. This will help you find components and locate parts once you begin the actual work. And you must have tools before you can do anything on a car.

The balance of the book is devoted to actual repair and maintenance procedures on your car. You will find instructions on how to tune up your engine, how to perform various periodic maintenance procedures, how to repair and maintain your cooling system, how to repair and replace exhaust system components, how to change oil and filters, how to inspect tires and how to buy new ones, how to replace shock absorbers, how to replace and adjust brake components, how to replace lights on your car, how to inspect and replace wipers and how to make your car look better both inside and out.

In the Periodic Maintenance chapter, you will find many pages of useful information on *when* to perform certain maintenance items. You will not find anything on *how* to do them, because that information is covered in the other chapters of the book.

For example, you may read in the Periodic Maintenance chapter that you should change the transmission oil in your automatic transmission every 22,000 miles. To find out *how* to change the oil, refer to the Lubrication chapter. If the Periodic Maintenance chapter tells you to flush the radiator, the Cooling System Maintenance chapter will tell you how to do it. And so on through the book.

Reference Data section

The Reference Data section contains thousands of specifications for all cars made in the U.S. plus the more popular imported cars. You probably will never use some of these specifications. But if you use this book as intended, there are some specs that are absolutely necessary. For instance, if you are using the Basic Engine Tuneup chapter and you come to a procedure that instructs you to set the spark plug gap according to manufacturer's specifications, you will find those specs in the Reference Data section. In fact, wherever you come to a reference to manufacturer's specifications in this book, you will find those specs in the Reference Data section.

The last chapter of the book is a glossary of automotive terminology that should prove invaluable in your work as a novice mechanic. You can use this section just like a dictionary, looking up terms that are unfamiliar to you as you come to them in the various other chapters.

Many individuals are intimidated by the complexity of today's modern automobile. As such, they never even get started on their own auto repairs and maintenance. With this book as your guide, you should have the confidence necessary to save yourself a substantial sum of money in the future by working on your own car. And who can possibly be against saving money? Good luck.

EDITOR JOE OLDHAM
ASSOCIATE EDITOR LYNNE P. KANTER
ART DIRECTOR MARVIN NUDELMAN
ILLUSTRATIONS JEFF MANGIAT
CONTRIBUTORS BOB BELL
BOB FENDELL
CLIFF GROMER
CHRIS LAIDLAW
MORTON J. SCHULTZ
PAUL WEISSLER

BOOK DIVISION
THE HEARST CORPORATION
NEW YORK, NY

No part of the text or illustrations in this work may be used without written permission by The Hearst Corporation.

Printed in the United States of America. ISBN 0-910990-64-6

© Copyright 1976 by The Hearst Corporation. All Rights Reserved.

The information herein has been compiled from authoritative sources. While every effort is made by the editors to attain accuracy, manufacturing changes as well as typographical errors and omissions may occur. The publisher cannot be responsible nor does it assume responsibility for such omissions, errors or changes.

ACKNOWLEDGMENTS

A book of this size and scope would be an impossibility were it not for the assistance of many different individuals and organizations. The editors of the *Popular Mechanics Guide to Basic Auto Repair and Maintenance* would like to specially thank the following organizations whose cooperation has been invaluable in the preparation of this book.

AC Delco Division
General Motors Corporation

American Motors Corporation

Automotive Information Council

Buick Division
General Motors Corporation

Cadillac Division
General Motors Corporation

Champion Spark Plug Company

Chevrolet Division
General Motors Corporation

Chrysler Corporation

Dayton Tire & Rubber Company

Dupont Company

Firestone Tire & Rubber Company

Ford Division
Ford Motor Company

Gabriel Division
Maremont Corporation

General Tire & Rubber Company

B.F. Goodrich Tire Company

Goodyear Tire & Rubber Company

Holley Carburetor Division
Colt Industries

Lincoln-Mercury Division
Ford Motor Company

Michelin Tire Corporation

Monroe Auto Equipment Company

National Bureau of Standards
US Department of Commerce

National Tire Dealers and
    Retreaders Association

Nissan Corporation, USA

Oldsmobile Division
General Motors Corporation

Pirelli Tire Corporation

Pontiac Division
General Motors Corporation

Rubber Manufacturers Association

Automotive Department
Sears, Roebuck & Company

Speedway Auto Radiator

Tire Industry Safety Council

Toyota Motor Sales Inc.

Union Carbide Corporation

Uniroyal Inc.

Volkswagen Division
Volkswagen of America

Know Your Car

Protecting your investment

An automobile is, ordinarily, the largest single personal investment you'll make, except for a home. Your investment will be more secure if you maintain your car properly.

If you are familiar with your automobile's systems, you'll be more able to identify problems and correct them or refer them to your serviceman. Better understanding of the car by its owner should result in better service at less cost.

Remember that the modern automobile is the product of advanced technology. The car makers are leaders in developing and adapting modern devices and systems. A repair serviceman must be familiar with dozens of makes and models of cars, each having about 15,000 parts. However, you only have to be familiar with one car—your own. There are many jobs you can perform yourself, thereby saving the labor charges that are added onto every repair bill. And labor charges are constantly on the rise, along with most other commodities.

This chapter is designed to acquaint you with the various parts of your automobile. You will learn where most systems and components are, why they are there, and how they work. Hopefully, this orientation will give you the knowledge and confidence to tackle the jobs in this book—jobs you can do yourself.

Your car is like the human body, composed of vital functioning systems, each with many operating parts. These parts wear from normal usage, deteriorate gradually from age and elements, and may become damaged or misaligned from hitting potholes and curbs or from minor accidents. And, as with the human body, checkups and repairs of your car are necessary from time to time.

Regular maintenance, as prescribed in your car owner's manual and this book, will help you obtain maximum car performance and safety, and reduce the possibility of unnecessary costs.

Thousands of parts

Each year you keep the car, its 15,000 parts grow older. Some wear out sooner than others because of their functions, but most last the lifetime of the car. The point to remember is that the performance of major systems like brakes, steering, suspension, ignition and carburetion depends on the condition of all the parts in each system. And most systems are dependent upon other systems working properly.

One reason major systems should be checked regularly is this: As parts within the systems gradually wear out and perform less effectively, most car owners tend, perhaps subconsciously, to adjust their driving habits to compensate for the change. For example: pumping the brake pedal when brakes are soft, or over-correcting the steering when the car pulls or wanders.

Remember, the operating systems can perform only as effectively as their condition permits.

Symptoms of trouble

Many symptoms of future trouble are visible. Others warn by sounds and noises, or can be identified by the way the car handles. After reading this chapter you will be able to do much of your own troubleshooting, and know when to take your car to a service facility for a thorough inspection.

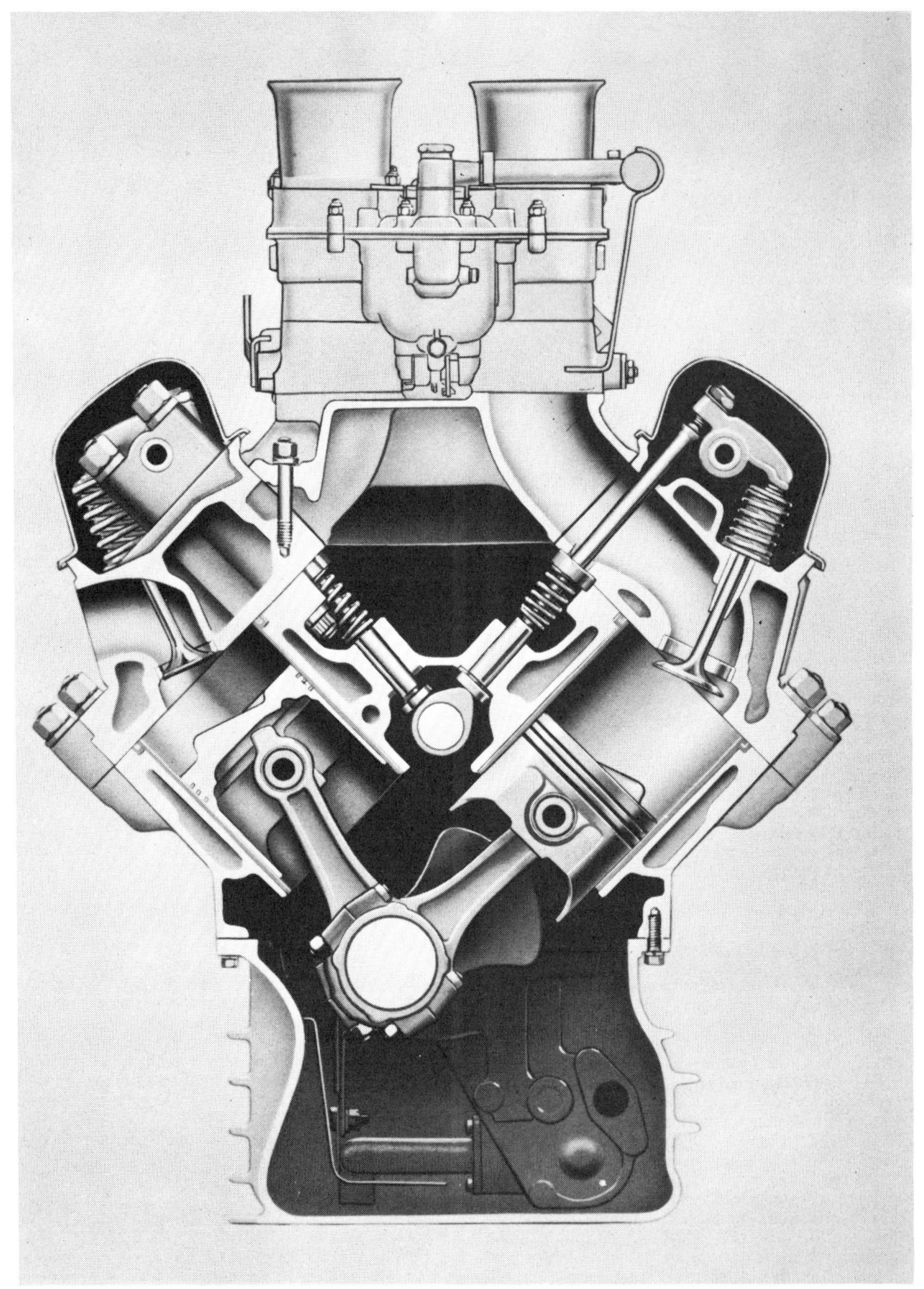

Today's modern automobile engine is a sophisticated piece of machinery that has been undergoing evolutionary change for at least 75 years.

THE ENGINE

When you start the engine you bring to life a machine that harnesses the energy of burning gasoline and air to drive the car and operate all the accessories.

WHAT IS AN INTERNAL COMBUSTION ENGINE?

What do we mean when we talk about internal combustion engines? "Internal combustion" is a rather cumbersome expression. But one thing can be said for it. It actually means what it says. "Internal" means "inside" or "enclosed." "Combustion" is an "act of burning." Thus an internal combustion engine is one in which the fuel burns inside. That is, it burns inside the same container which produces the power. In a steam engine the fuel can burn almost anywhere as long as it turns water into steam which can be led into the cylinder. That is "external combustion."

So an internal combustion engine is fundamentally a container into which we put air and fuel and start them burning.

Let us try a crude but simple experiment to illustrate this. Take an open glass beaker, like a drinking glass, and into it pour a few drops of gasoline—just one or two. Cover the top with a rubber diaphragm—a balloon will do. In the bottom of the beaker is a hole plugged with a cork, and running through the cork is a fuse—an ordinary firecracker fuse. We light the fuse and wait to see what will happen. The instant the fuse burns up into the beaker, the mixture of gasoline and air will be ignited and will burn very rapidly. The heat will make it try to expand, to grow larger and occupy a greater space. This will push against the diaphragm, which will bulge upward above the top of the beaker. As we might say, the balloon will be blown up. The important point is that, due to the combustion, pressure will be exerted against the diaphragm.

NOTE: This should be considered a theoretical experiment. It is not something to be tried in the kitchen. It actually does work as described, but the quantities are rather critical. A few too many drops of gasoline may cause a dangerous explosion under some conditions.

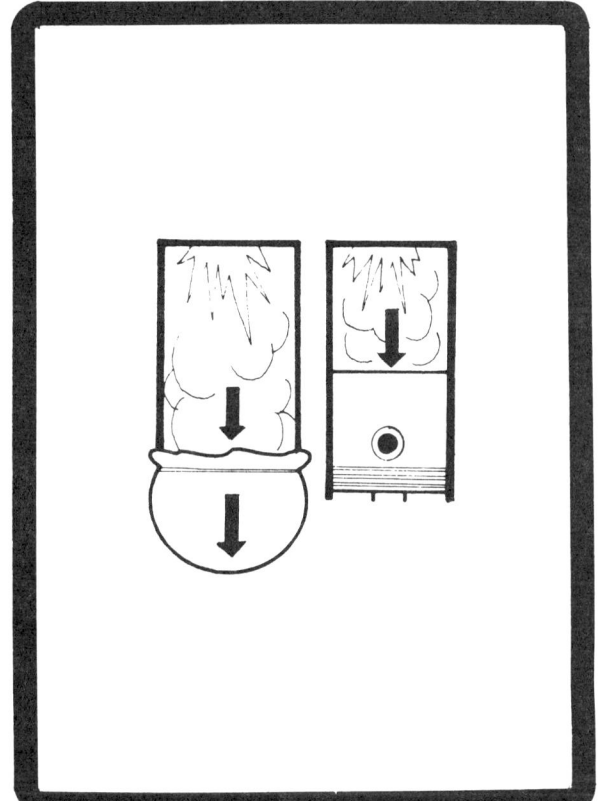

The combustion process within the cylinder forces the piston downward.

Now what do we have to do to make an engine out of this combustion? First, we need a cylinder, which is simply a hollow tube closed at one end. We will also need a piston, which is a cylindrical object which slides in the tube, and as it fits closely against the wall it thus seals the other end of the cylinder.

If combustion takes place in the cylinder, we will have expansion of the air and pressure will be exerted on the top of the piston. This will make the piston slide inside the cylinder. So all we have to do now is connect up that sliding piston in some way to get useful work from it.

For this we need a **connecting rod** and a **crankshaft**. The connecting rod is a straight rod with one end fastened to a pin or pivot in the piston so the lower end can swing. The crankshaft is a shaft with its ends mounted in oiled bearings so it can revolve, and thus the offset portion in the middle, the **crank,** describes a circle as the shaft turns around. The lower end of the connecting rod is fastened to the crank, so it must follow the same circular path.

We have probably all ridden a bicycle at some time during our lives. The lower part of the leg of a bicycle rider is a connecting rod. The knee moves approximately up and down in a straight line. The foot follows the pedal, and therefore goes around in a circle.

When the piston of our engine slides downward due to the pressure of the expanding gases, the upper end of the connecting rod moves downward with the piston, in a straight line. This is our knee. The lower end of the connecting rod must move down also, and the only path it can move in is the circular one prescribed by the crank. This is our foot. It moves the crank and rotates the shaft, which is what we wish to do. As often defined, the crankshaft and connecting rod combination is a mechanism for the purpose of changing straight-line, back-and-forth motion to circular, or rotary motion.

Here we have the basis for most of the engines in use today—cylinder, piston, connecting rod, and crankshaft.

THE 4-CYCLE ENGINE

Before we start adding parts, let us see what happens to the ones we already have during the actual running of an engine. They obviously must do the same things over and over again, so all we have to do is follow them through one series of events—until they begin to repeat themselves—and we know what they will be doing from then on. This one series of events we call a cycle.

Most engines today are what we call 4-cycle engines. What we really mean is 4-stroke cycle, but the American habit of abbreviating has eliminated the middle word, at least in ordinary conversation. It makes more sense when it is included however, as it means that there are four strokes of the piston, two up and two down, to each cycle. Then it starts over again on another cycle of the same four strokes.

We cannot see a piston at work in an engine. It must be surrounded by metal in order to work. But we will take some liberties in this book. We will show cross sections and cut-away sections of engines and other mechanisms. That simply means that we cut through an engine and take part of it away so we can see what is going on inside. Or we may consider some parts to be made of glass so we can see through them. But no matter how we do it, we assume that the mechanism keeps on running as usual.

A cylinder, piston, connecting rod and crankshaft are needed to convert the chemical energy of the burning gasoline to mechanical energy within the engine.

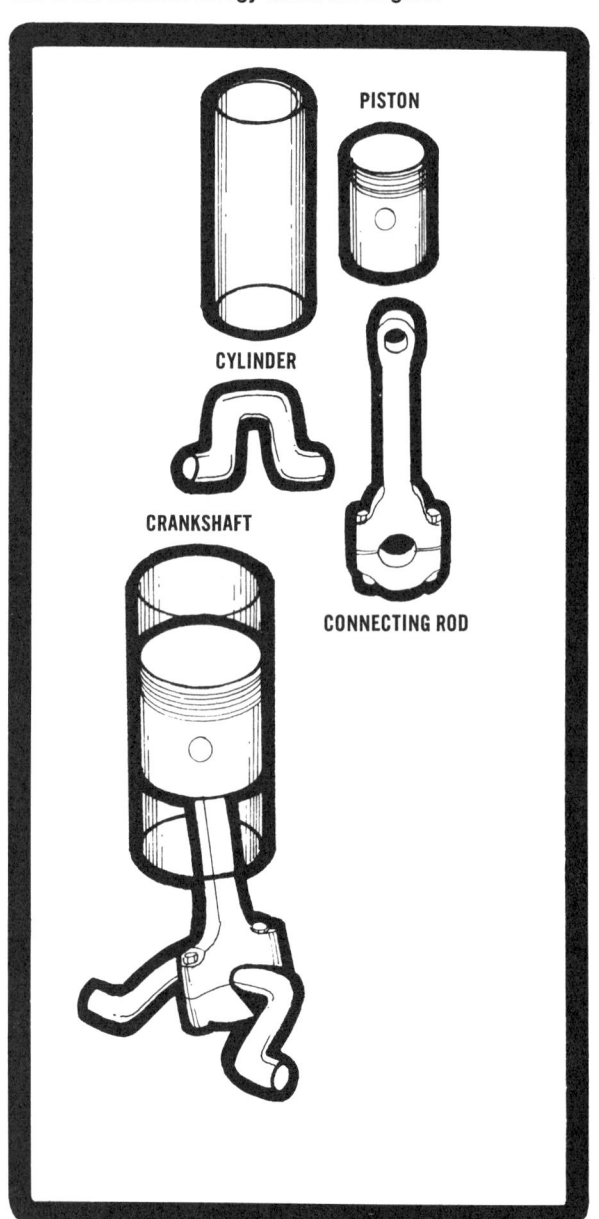

This is what the cylinder, piston, connecting rod and crankshaft look like when joined together inside the engine.

We start with the piston at the top of the cylinder, only a small space being left above it. This is as far as the crank and connecting rod will let it go. On the first stroke the piston moves down, or away from the closed end of the cylinder. This is called the **intake** stroke, because during it, air or a mixture of fuel and air is drawn into the cylinder. There are various ways of getting it in, but for the time being we will just assume that there is some kind of a "door" in the top of the cylinder which can be opened and closed as desired. When the piston is at the bottom of its stroke, that is, as far from the top of the cylinder as it can go, the cylinder is full of air or fuel-air mixture, depending on the type of engine. Note that the crankshaft has gone halfway around.

Then the intake "door" is closed and the piston starts to go up again. This second stroke is the **compression** stroke. It compresses the contents of the cylinder, so that instead of filling the whole cylinder it has all been squeezed up into that small space at the top. The piston is back where it started from, and the crankshaft has gone all the way around once. The ratio of the whole cylinder volume to the volume of that small space is called **compression ratio.** For example, suppose the cylinder held 80 cubic inches when the piston was at the bottom. We could measure this by filling it full of some liquid such as oil and measuring how much oil it took. Then we do the same thing with the piston in its uppermost position. Suppose it then took 10 cubic inches. We would say that the engine had a compression ratio of 8 to 1. That means that when the piston is at the top, the mixture in the cylinder has been squeezed to one-eighth its former volume.

In an engine that mixture is compressed before we ignite it. Then when it burns it expands a great deal more and a great deal faster, and develops more pressure. This means that we get much more power from it.

This whole matter of compression and compression ratio is an extremely important one, and we will keep running into it as we go along.

About the time the piston reaches the top of its second stroke, we ignite the mixture. It starts burning and expands, just as in the beaker. This pushes the piston down, and this third stroke is called the **power** stroke. It is what we really have been getting ready for all the time. It is what makes the engine run and gives it power. The pressure forces the piston down to its bottom position again.

The fourth stroke of the piston is called the **exhaust**, or scavenging stroke. Another "door" in the top of the cylinder has been opened, and the hot exhaust gases—the result of burning the air and fuel—start to escape through it. As the piston rises it helps them along, pushes them out the "door." At the end of this stroke the cylinder is practically clear of the burned gases, and the piston is in its top position ready to start on the first, or intake, stroke.

The crankshaft has now gone all the way around twice. This should be noted carefully. One of the principal features of the 4-cycle engine is that the crankshaft makes two revolutions during every cycle. To put it another way, there is only one power stroke to two revolutions of the engine.

The 4-stroke cycle is often called the Otto cycle, from the name of the man who built the first engine of this type over 75 years ago. To keep the essentials of this cycle straight in our minds, it is necessary

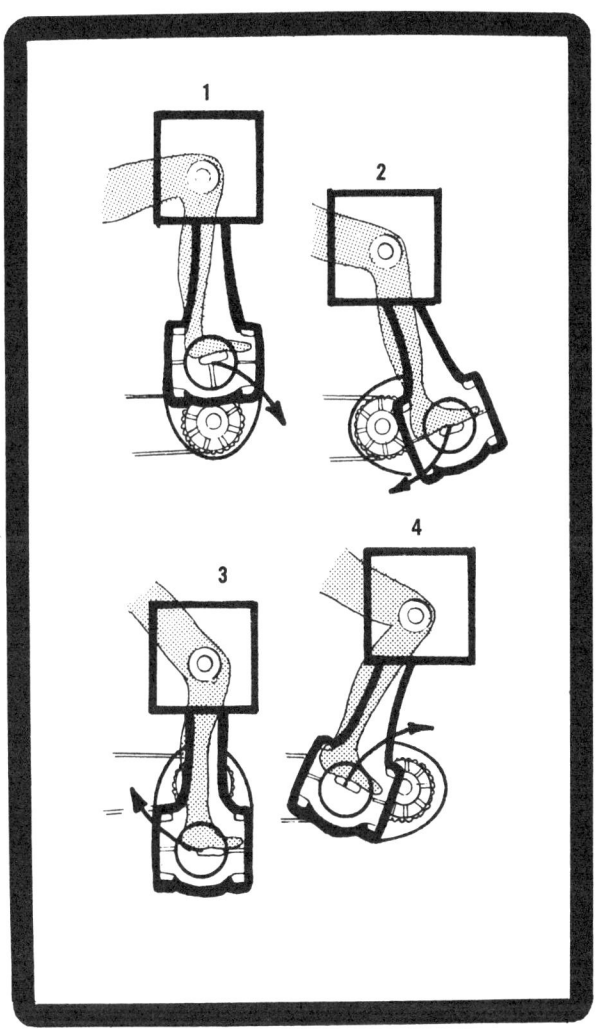

The 4-cycle engine goes through four distinct phases during its operation—intake phase, compression phase, power phase and exhaust phase.

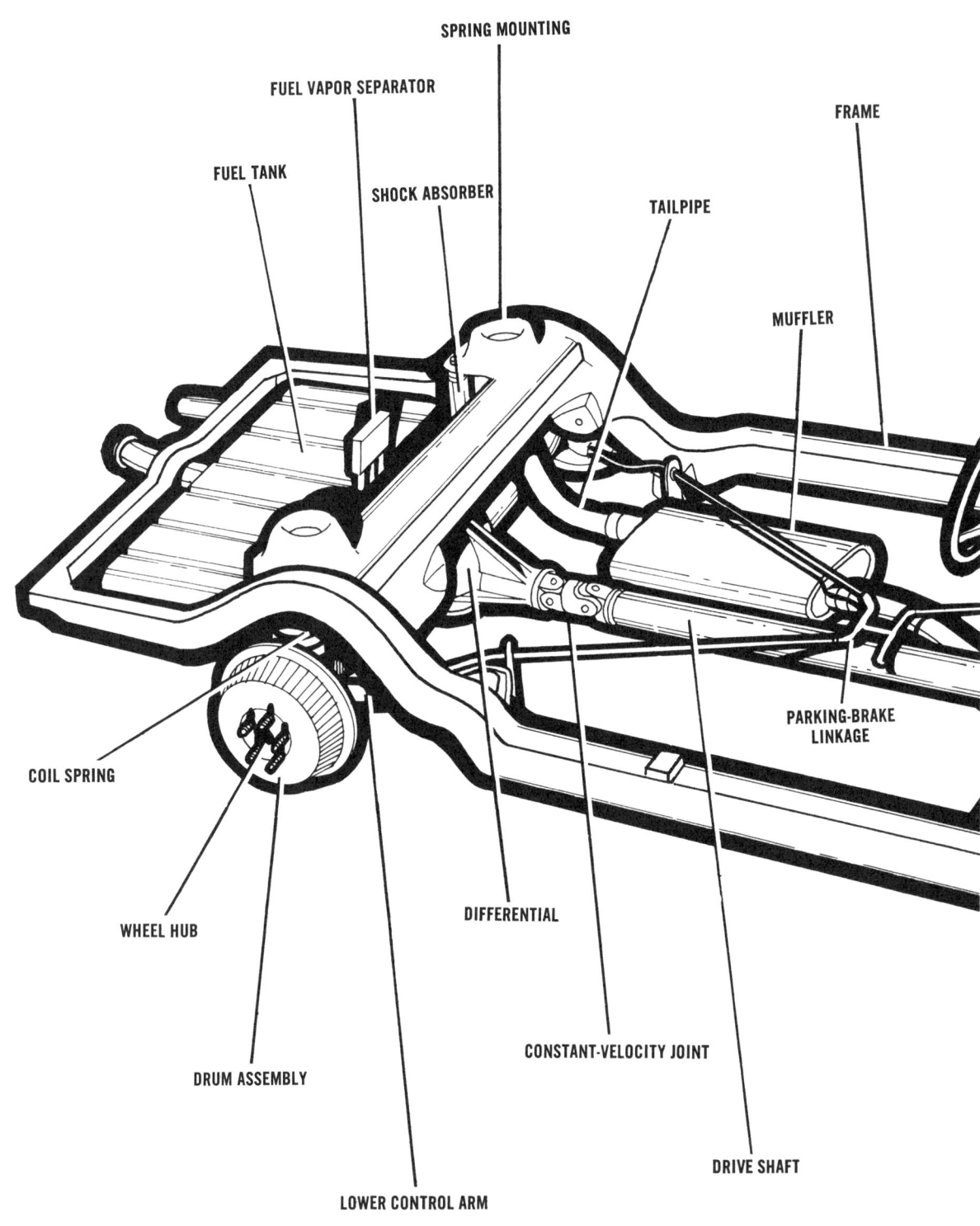

Today's automobile is made up of thousands of parts. In this illustration, just a few of the major components are shown.

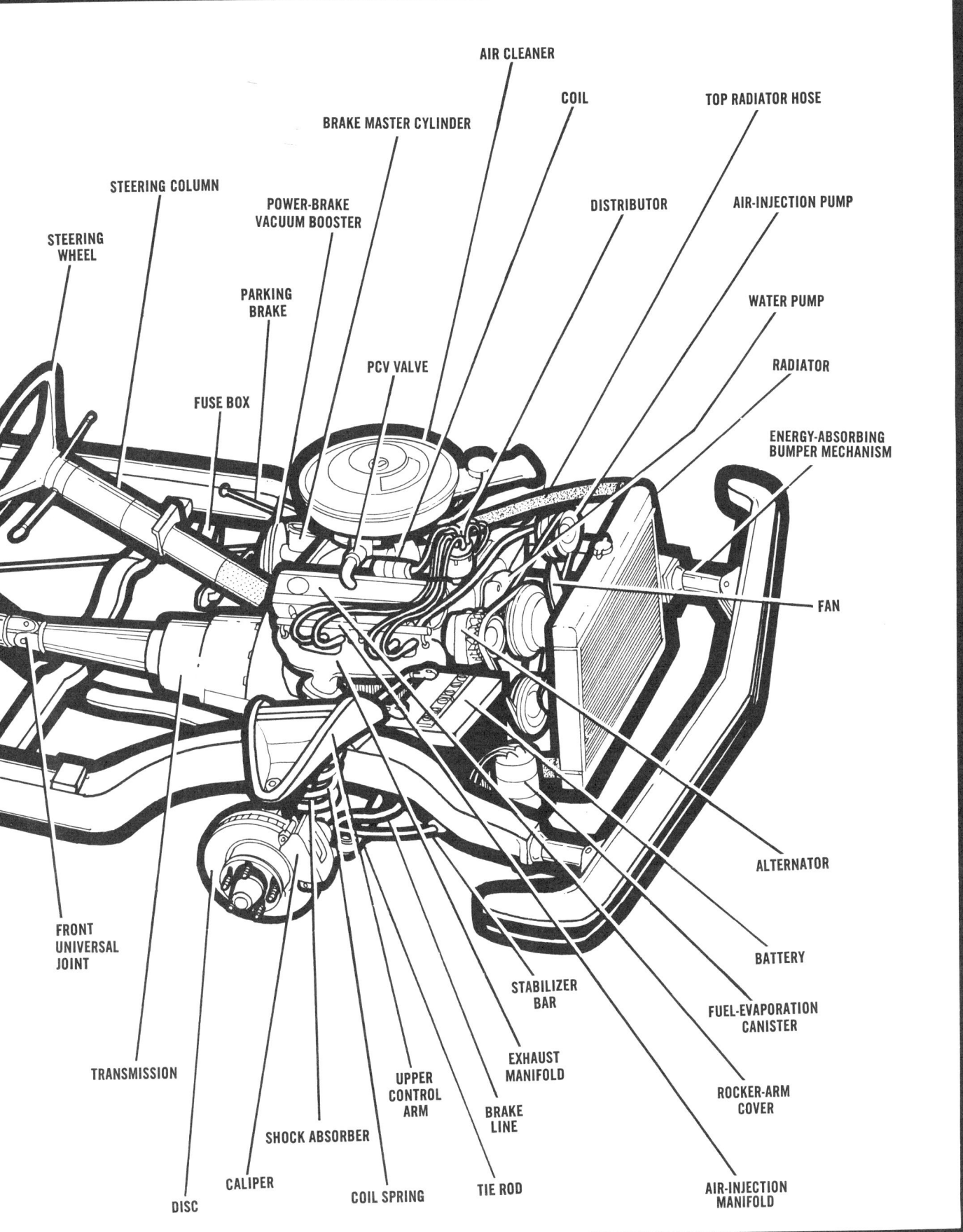

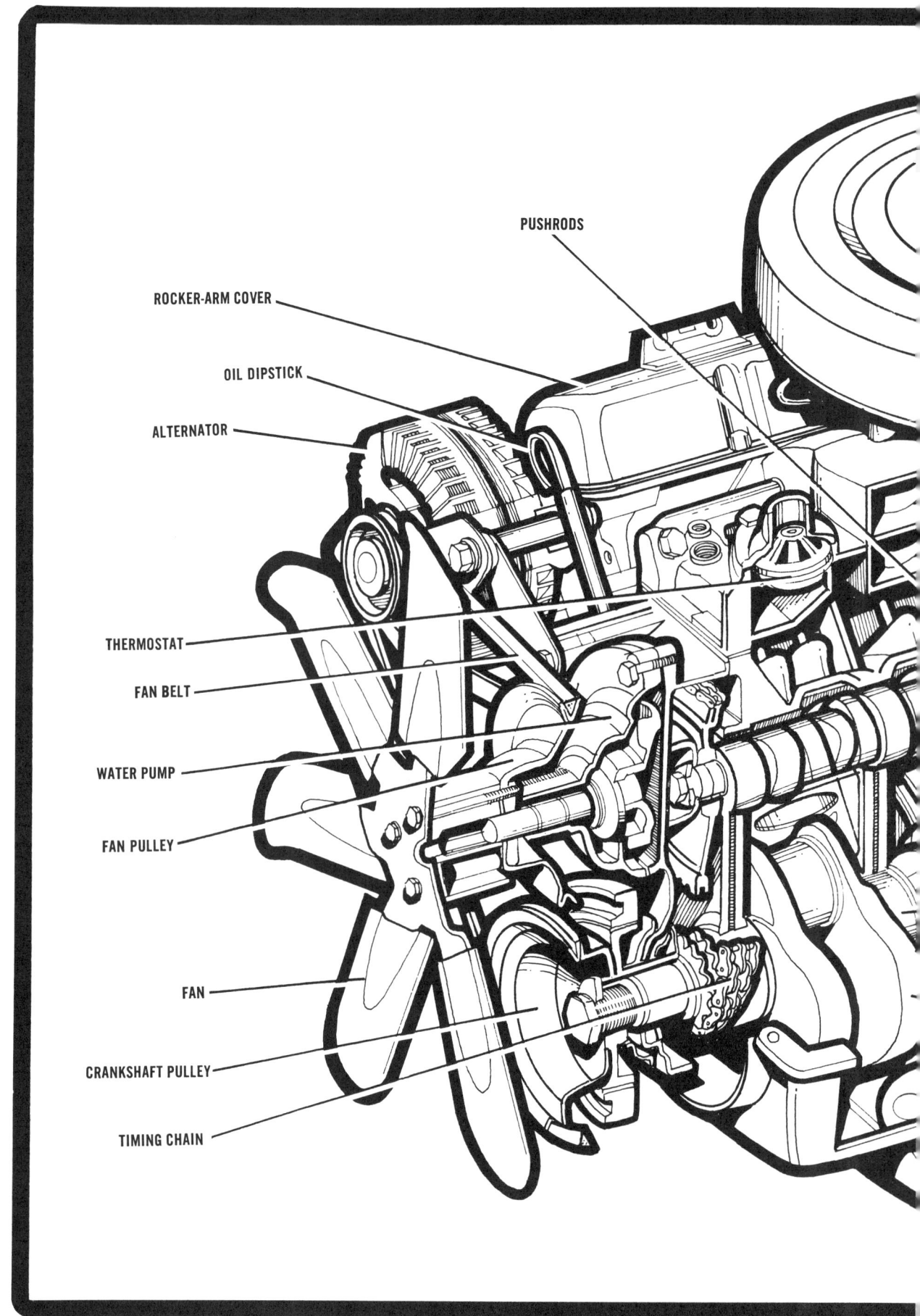

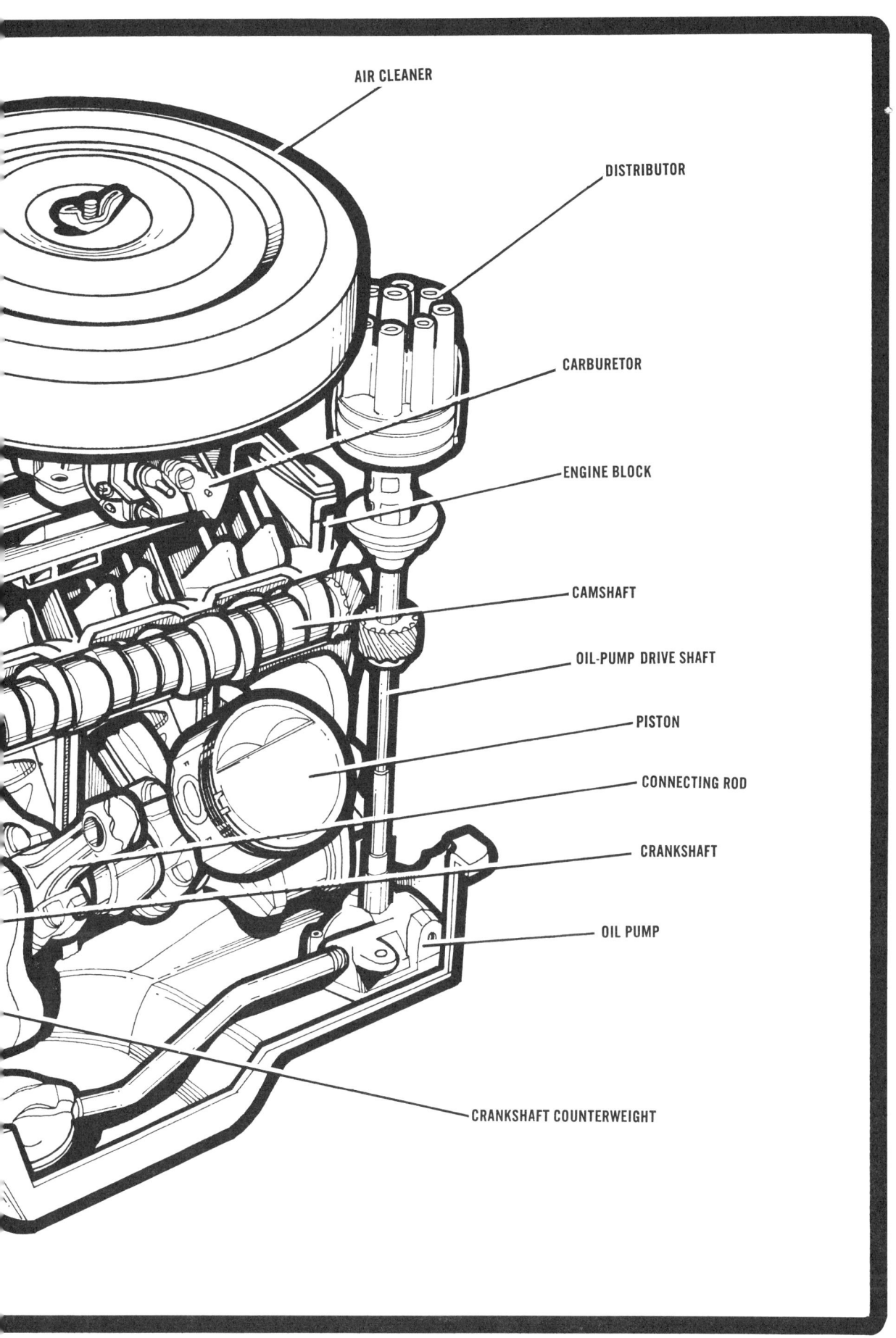

only to remember four words, in their proper order—intake, compression, power, exhaust.

If we analyze this to see what makes it all happen, we find there are just three things responsible for it. As we go along we will discover that those three things are the basis for all engines, and necessary to the operation of every engine.

They are AIR, FUEL, and IGNITION.

These three must all be present before we can have an internal combustion engine. Not one or two of them, but all three. If any one is lacking, we have a dead pile of metal. When they are all on hand, we have life and power.

Our human bodies have exactly the same requirements. In order to live, we must breathe, we must provide air for our system. We must eat, for the food is our fuel. There must be some means for burning this fuel, that is, for converting the food into energy. If we are deprived of air or food, or our ignition system gets out of adjustment, our body quickly becomes just as inert or useless as an engine which lacks one or more of these necessities.

So let us look at these three fundamentals in more detail.

Air

Everyone who has driven a car realizes that he must provide the engine with gasoline. But he may not have given much consideration to the necessity for air. That is entirely natural, as gasoline costs money, and air is there for the taking.

But in many ways, air is the more important of the two. Some people feel that the easiest way to

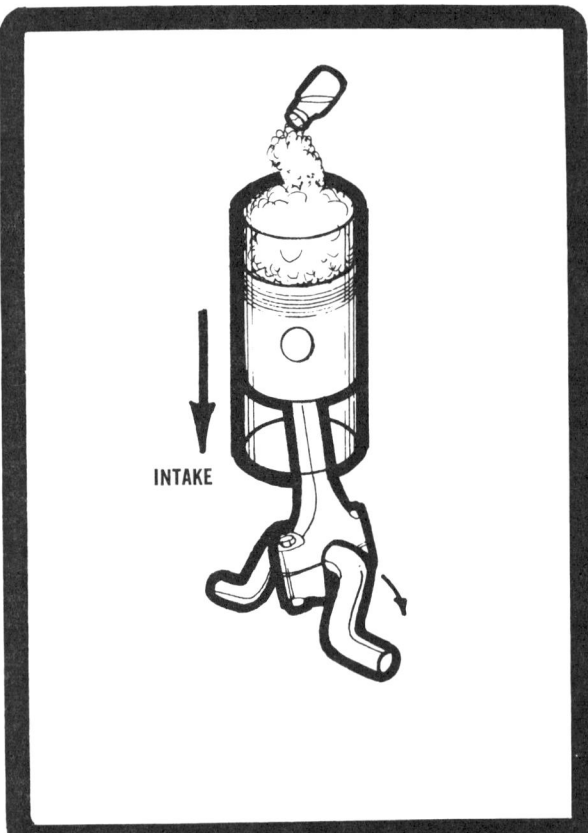

On the intake stroke, the air-fuel mixture is fed into the cylinder as the piston moves downward in the cylinder.

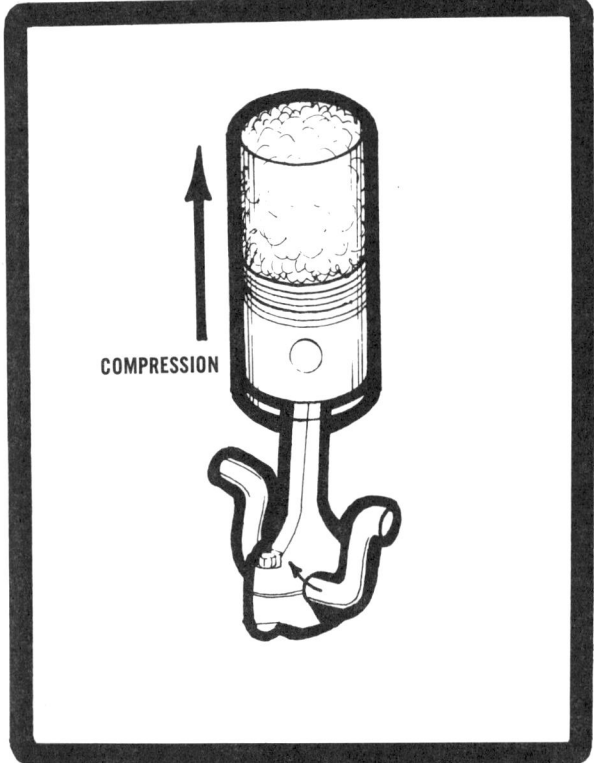

On the compression stroke, the piston moves upward in the cylinder to squeeze the air-fuel mixture, or, compress it.

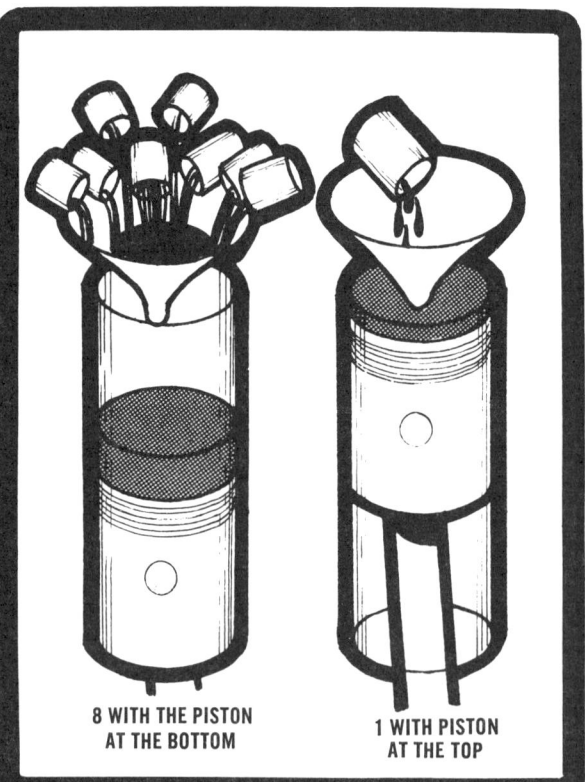

An 8 to 1 compression ratio is illustrated here. With the piston at the bottom of the cylinder, there is room for eight parts air-fuel mixture. With the piston at the top of its travel, the eight parts are squeezed to the equivalent of one part. The mixture in the cylinder has been squeezed to one-eighth its former volume.

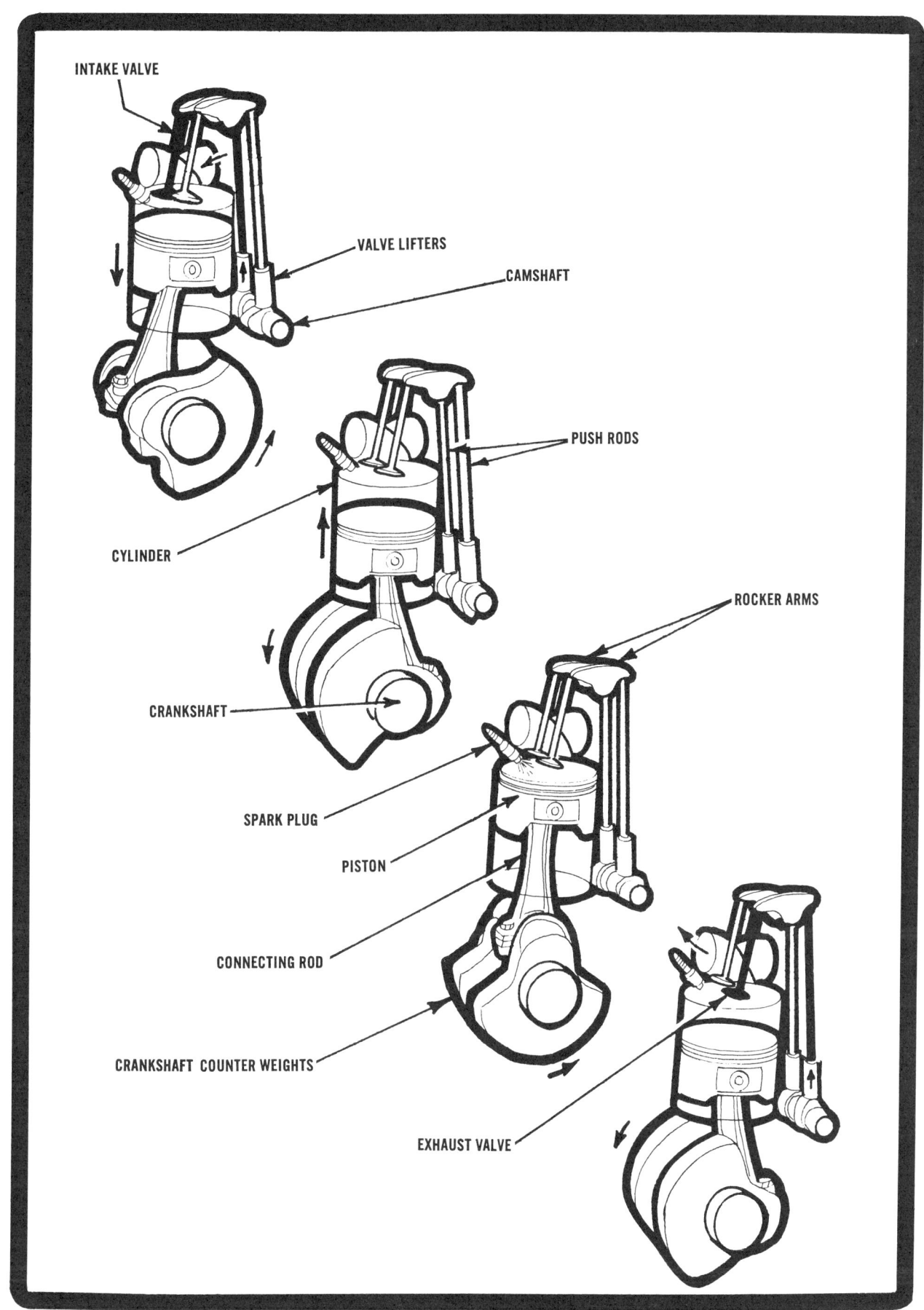

In slightly more detail, here is how the various valvetrain components interreact during the four phases of the 4-stroke engine.

To the engine designer air presents greater problems than does the fuel, which is largely due to the necessity for handling far greater quantities of it. Theoretically, in an automobile engine we should put about 15 parts of air to 1 part of gasoline into the cylinder—by weight. We may vary this somewhat either way, depending on whether we are more interested in power or fuel economy. So for every pound of gasoline we use, we must have 15 pounds of air. But gasoline weighs about 600 times as much as air at sea level—in other words, a pound of air takes up 600 times as much space as a pound of gasoline. So looking at it from the standpoint of volume, we must furnish 600 x 15, or 9000 cubic feet of air for every cubic foot of gasoline. This is enough air to fill an average small house. So it is easy to see that the air is bulky and hard to handle compared to the fuel.

We should mention here that it is not really the air we are so interested in. It is the oxygen in the air. Air is a mixture of 21% oxygen, 78% nitrogen, and 1% other gases. It is the oxygen which burns with the fuel. The nitrogen goes through the engine and out the exhaust unchanged. But inasmuch as air is the source of supply of the oxygen, and air is what we have to handle in designing or operating an engine, we will ignore the technicalities and continue to speak of air rather than oxygen.

There are various methods of getting this air into the cylinder, which we will show in more detail later. The most common is through holes or passages at the top of the cylinder which are opened and closed at the proper times by "doors" called **valves.** Another way is through holes or **ports** in the side of the cylinders, these being covered and uncovered automatically by the piston as it moves up and down. There have been numerous other arrangements tried, one of them, the sleeve valve, is still being used to some extent. In this, a sleeve, or sometimes two, slides between the piston and the cylinder wall, controlling the flow through ports in the side of the cylinder.

Some engines use a pump, called a **blower,** or **supercharger,** to force the air into the cylinder. Automobile type engines "suck" the air in. This is not strictly true but it is a simple way to think of it. What really happens is that the piston, moving down, creates a partial vacuum in the cylinder—that is, it lowers the pressure inside—and the atmospheric pressure outside pushes air in to fill it up.

As we know, air weighs something just as every other substance does. Sometimes we think of it as being nothing, mostly because we cannot see it. But it is real. The great mass of it surrounding the earth is pressing down on it and on us with a certain pressure at all times. It is similar to the terrific pressure on a diver or a submarine in deep water, increasing with each foot of depth. At the bottom of this ocean of air, that is, at sea level, this atmospheric pressure is about 14.7 pounds per square inch, and it is this pressure which forces air into the cylinder when the pressure inside is less than 14.7 pounds per square inch. If we ascend a mountain, or go up in an airplane, this atmospheric pressure decreases rapidly, just as the pressure in the ocean decreases as the diver approaches the surface. This brings many complications into the problem of supplying air to an engine.

understand an internal combustion engine is to consider it as an air pump. It is no problem to get enough fuel into an engine; its power usually depends on how much air one can crowd into it.

Intake valve moves to allow the air-fuel mixture into the cylinder. Then the intake valve seals the port to keep the mixture from escaping before it is ignited.

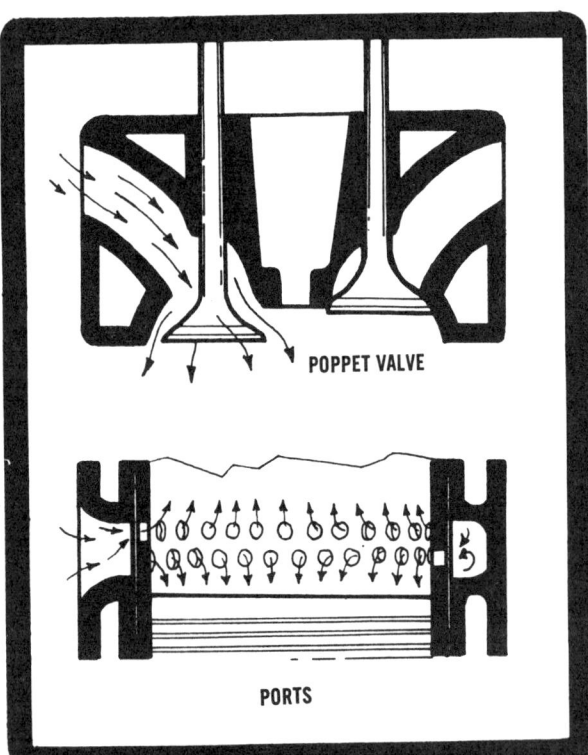

Engines other than the typical automobile engine use other methods of getting the air-fuel mixture into the cylinder. Some engines use a series of holes or ports in the side of the cylinder.

Fuel

Petroleum fuels are marvelous creations of Nature and Man. They are not always appreciated fully.

First, petroleum is the second most plentiful liquid in the world, which is a lucky thing for the internal combustion engine. Only water exceeds it in quantity. As for quality, it contains more energy—more "power"—than any explosive.

We think of dynamite or nitroglycerin as the ultimate in power or explosive force. We may even flatter a powerful engine by exclaiming, "Boy, that's dynamite!" But the potential energy in a gallon of dynamite would run a modern car less than three miles, as contrasted to perhaps 18 miles on a gallon of gasoline.

Gasoline and diesel fuel are what we call **hydrocarbons.** That is, they consist of hydrogen atoms and carbon atoms joined up together in various combinations. There are hundreds of these combinations, each with its own peculiar characteristics, and our fuel is a mixture of a great many of these. Nature made petroleum that way, and it is only in recent years that Man has begun to learn how to improve on it. Some of the hydrocarbons are good fuels, some are bad. We are just beginning to find out something about what we have to do to change the bad ones over to the good ones. But that involves molecules and chemistry and a lot of long words that we will not bother with here.

There are two principal methods of getting the fuel into the engine. One is to mix it with the air outside the cylinder and push the two in together as one mixture. The other is to inject it, squirt it into the cylinder after the air is already in there. There are some variations on these, such as injecting the fuel into the air intake passage just outside the cylinder, but most of the engines in this country fall definitely into one or the other of the two main classifications.

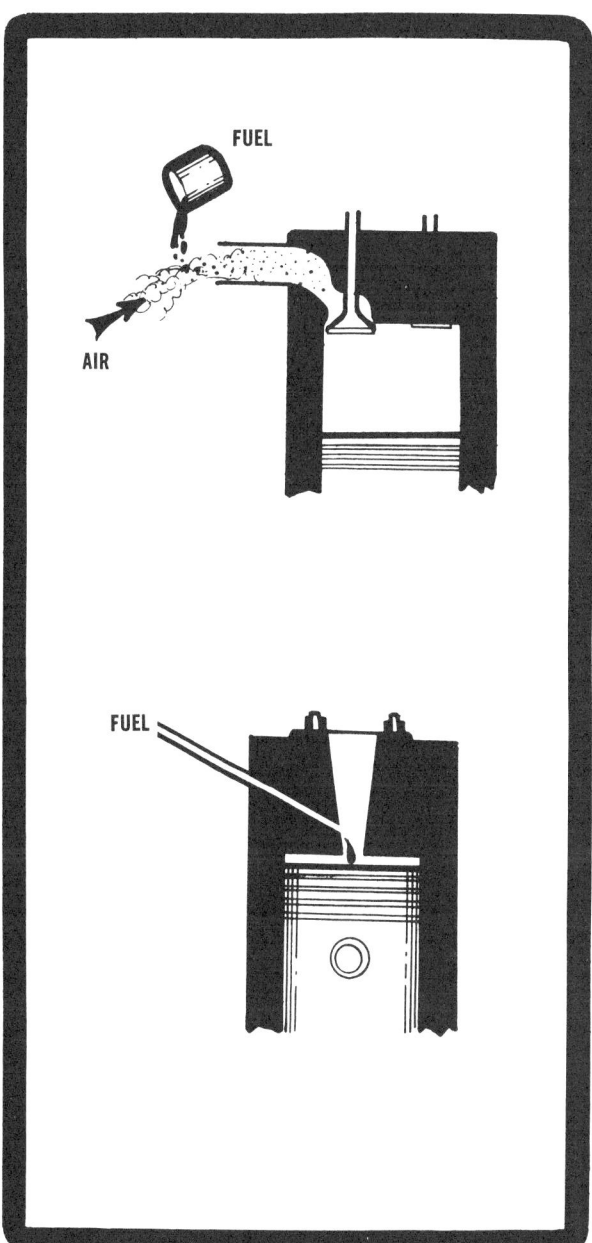

There are two general methods for getting the fuel into the engine. One is to mix the fuel with the air outside the cylinder and push the mixture into the cylinder. This is how an engine that utilizes a carburetor gets its fuel. The other method is to inject, or squirt, the fuel into the cylinder after the air is already in there. This is basically how a fuel injection system works.

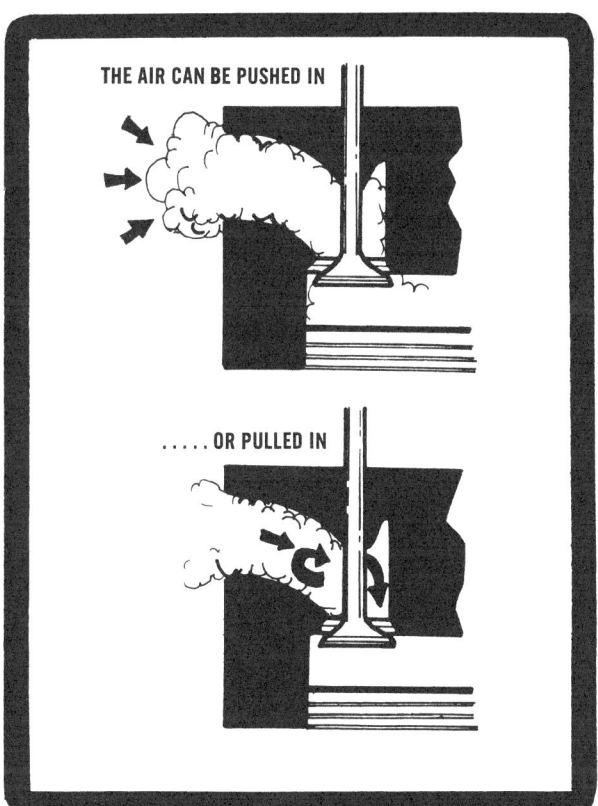

The air-fuel mixture is usually pulled into the cylinder under suction. It can be pushed in, too, by using a supercharger.

Engines using the first system are sometimes called "carburetor engines," as it is the **carburetor** which sees to it that the proper amount of fuel is mixed with the proper amount of air. After the two have been mixed, they may be forced into the engine in any of the ways we have already mentioned for getting air into the cylinder.

Most of the automobile engines in the United States use carburetors. It is possible and practical to use an injection system, however, and some manufacturers do currently use fuel injection.

All diesel engines use fuel injection. We will see later why this is necessary. There are various kinds of injection systems, but they all have one thing in common. The air is forced into the cylinder by itself and then the fuel is shot in just before ignition. The two are mixed inside the cylinder.

It is impossible to discuss fuels without getting into the subject of compression ratio. We said that by squeezing the mixture up into one end of the cylinder before igniting it, we got more power from it. We can go further and say that the more we compress it—the harder we squeeze it—the more power we get from it. The why's and wherefore's are rather complicated and technical, but it is a fundamental of internal combustion engines that the higher the compression ratio, the higher the efficiency. If we squeeze the mixture in an engine so hard that it exerts a pressure of 200 pounds per square inch before ignition, we will get several times the power which we would if we squeezed it to only 100 pounds per square inch. Twenty-five or 30 years ago, 4 to 1 was a common figure for the compression ratio of automobile engines. Today it is 8 or 8½ to 1. Most of the increase in power and economy which we now enjoy is due to that one fact.

Immediately the natural question is, "Why not raise the compression ratio a lot more? Why not make it 12 to 1, 15 to 1?"

There are two answers to that. First, we have done it—in the diesel engine. There compression ratios run as high as 22 to 1. We will go into that in more detail shortly, but for the present let us consider only the gasoline engine. The second answer, for the gasoline engine, is that the fuel of today will not let us.

For gasoline is not a perfect fuel—at least not yet. When we raise the compression ratio of an engine too high, the immediate result is detonation, or as we more commonly say, the engine knocks. This is an actual hammering inside the cylinder. It is not only annoying. It means loss of power and leads to damaged engines if carried too far. It was a mystery for many years, but was finally traced down to the fact that the fuel was not burning properly in the cylinder. Some of it was burning too fast—too much at one time. It would "explode" instead of burning smoothly. This caused the knock, or ping.

Then it was found that tetraethyl lead could be added to the gasoline which would help to prevent this too rapid burning and stop the knock. This quickly resulted in higher compression and better engines. Still later it was discovered that certain hydrocarbons were better than others from the anti-knock

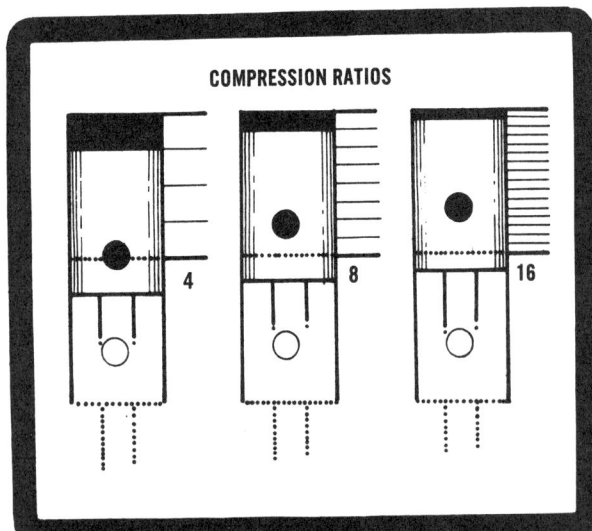

The compression ratio is determined by how much the air-fuel mixture is squeezed by the piston in the cylinder.

standpoint, and methods were developed for producing better gasoline from the same petroleum. It is these improvements in the fuel which have made possible the higher compression ratios we have today. And these in turn have meant more power and more miles per gallon, greater pay load and longer cruising range.

Today, though the catalytic converter has mandated that lead be taken out of fuel to prevent contamination of the catalyst. The converter, of course, is one of the prime emission control devices on the automobile.

You have probably heard the word "octane" in connection with gasoline. The actual basis for figuring the **octane rating** of gasoline is rather complicated, but it is enough to remember that the higher the octane number of a particular gasoline, the less it will knock. It is a measure of its anti-knock quality. A high octane gasoline can be used in a higher compression engine and other things being equal, it is a better gasoline. We used to have fuels of 50 octane or lower. Now the automobile gasolines are from 85 to 95 octane, and aviation fuel well over 100. The 100 figure was originally the end of the scale, but it is now just a station along the way, and there are expectations of fuels in the future far beyond this figure.

Now just a word about diesel fuels. They are hydrocarbons. They come from petroleum. They have many things in common with gasoline. But when it comes to knock, the diesel engine and carburetor engine are exactly opposite. The process of burning is different, so we want the fuels different. Instead of trying to slow down the rate of combustion, we do everything we can to make a diesel fuel burn as fast as possible. Therefore, while it starts with the same raw material, it goes through a different production process to make it better for the job it has to do. One of the greatest assets we now have is the knowledge of how to produce tailor-made fuels.

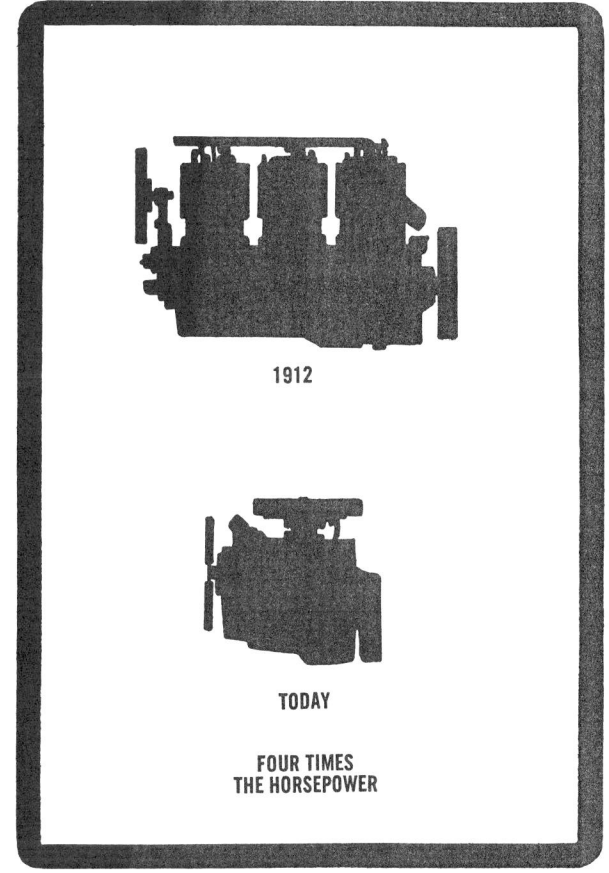

Today's modern engine can produce much more power and takes up a lot less room than an engine manufactured in the early 1900s.

Ignition

Our third necessity is ignition. By that we mean that something must start the fuel and air burning in the top of the cylinder, or **combustion chamber.**

In the gasoline engine the mixture is started burning by means of an electric spark. A **spark plug** fits into the wall of the combustion chamber. It has two wires, or electrodes, which extend slightly into the chamber, separated from each other by a narrow gap. High voltage electricity is led to the spark plug at the proper time, and jumps the gap from one electrode to the other. This causes a spark which starts the fuel and air burning.

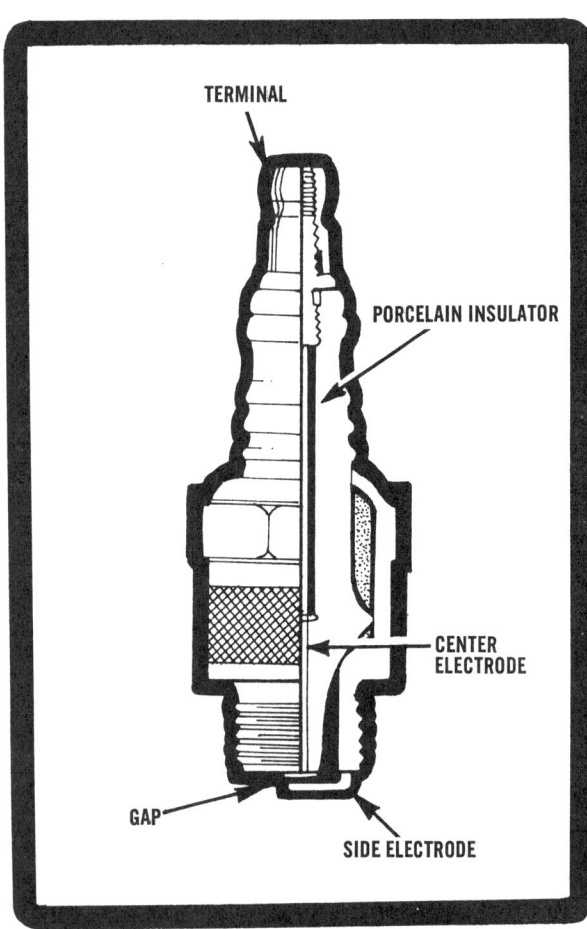

Cutaway of a typical spark plug.

The whole chamber of gas does not burn instantaneously. The flame spreads from the spark plug, moving across the combustion chamber like a fire moves across a dry meadow on a windy day. It takes about 1/350 of a second to complete this flame travel in an average automobile cylinder.

But if we raise the compression too much, we do not get this smooth, orderly combustion. The mixture has been heated up by squeezing it so hard, and parts of the metal combustion chamber may be very hot. Before the flame has completed its travel across the chamber, the remaining unburned mixture on the far side may get so hot that it will ignite by itself and burn all at once. This creates a sudden and very uneven rise in pressure which causes the knock.

If the compression is too high, we may have more trouble. We may get preignition. This means that the mixture gets so hot from compression that it starts burning before the spark occurs. We might say it is using the diesel ignition system. But the trouble is it does not do it at the proper time. It starts burning too soon, and may cause considerable trouble because the piston is still moving upward and is not yet ready to begin the power stroke.

That is why, in the diesel engine, we cannot mix the air and fuel outside the cylinder. We would have no control over the time of ignition. It would start burning much too soon. We must wait until the moment we want it to start burning, and then inject the fuel into the compressed air.

The automobile engine is the most familiar type of internal combustion engine. This is natural as there are something over 100,000,000 of them in this country. Practically everyone has some contact with them. The total horsepower represented by these engines is not only more than that of any other form of power plant—such as electrical central stations, locomotives, manufacturing plants—it is much more than all the rest put together.

Let us look at one of these engines. As installed in a car or truck, it may appear complicated at first glance. But if we go back to our basic engine unit, we find that we do not have to add a great many things in order to have all the essentials for this type of engine. We will not have everything that you will find in the car, but we will have a complete engine—one that will run.

As we have mentioned before, this is a carburetor type engine. So let us start there, and add a carburetor first of all. This will break the gasoline up into tiny drops and mix it with the air in just the proper proportions. Now we have to get the mixture over to the cylinder. So we add an **intake manifold,** which is a pipe from the carburetor opening into the combustion chamber. But we do not want this open all the time, so we put a valve in the hole which can be made to open and close at the proper times. This is the **intake valve.** We need something to ignite the mixture—a spark plug will take care of that. Now all we have to add is another poppet valve, the **exhaust valve,** which lets the hot gases out of the cylinder after they have finished their job.

There we have all the essentials of an automobile engine. We have provided it with air, fuel and ignition.

This is a 4-cycle engine. We start with the piston in its top-most position, commonly called top dead center (TDC). On the intake stroke, the piston moves down creating a vacuum in the cylinder. The intake valve is open, so the mixture of gasoline and air rushes through the opening, pushed by the atmospheric pressure outside. From its bottom position, bottom dead center (BDC), the piston starts up. The intake valve closes, and the mixture is compressed in the closed end of the cylinder. It is squeezed to a pressure of perhaps 200 pounds per square inch. Then the spark occurs. The burning mixture expands, and almost immediately the pressure jumps to 600 or 700 pounds per square inch, three or four times the pressure before ignition. With a piston 3½ inches in diameter, the total pressure on the top of it will be about three tons. This enormous force pushes the piston down, which of course makes the crankshaft turn and delivers power to whatever is connected to the shaft. Both valves have been closed during the compression and power strokes. But now the exhaust valve opens. As the piston moves up again it forces the exhaust gases out through the passage opened by the valve. As the piston gets to the top, the exhaust valve closes and the intake valve opens again, ready for the beginning of the next cycle.

We have pointed out earlier that the crankshaft goes around twice during each cycle. There is only one stroke out of four that the piston delivers power to the crankshaft. All the rest of the time this is reversed—the crankshaft is acting on the piston, pushing it up and pulling it down. In order to keep the crankshaft turning around more steadily between

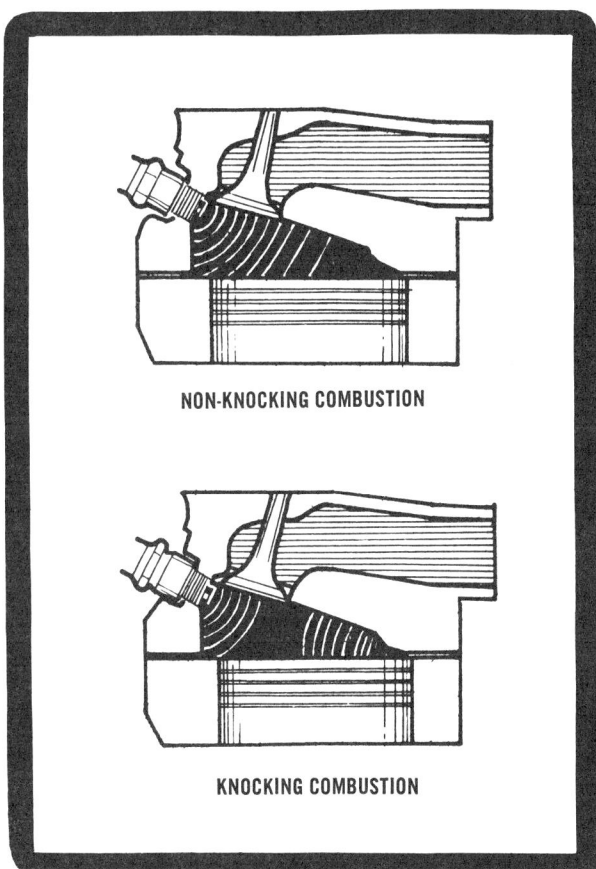

Top, a smooth combustion process results in a smooth power impulse from the cylinder. Bottom, pre-ignition in the combustion chamber produces an audible knock or metallic sound. Left unattended, knock could result in serious damage.

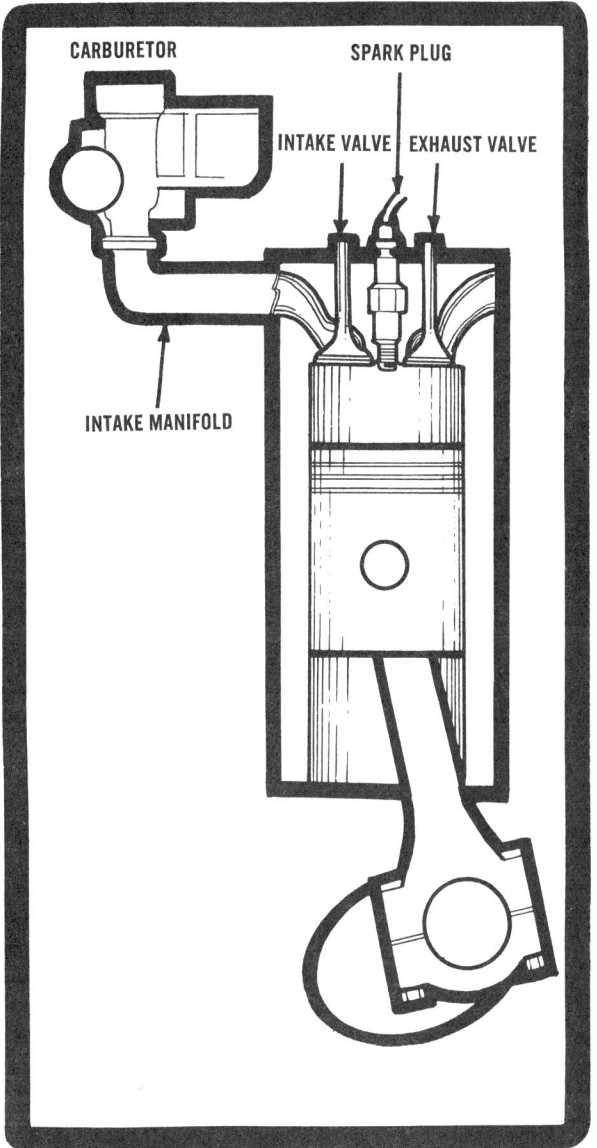

This oversimplified illustration shows the relationship between the various components in the combustion process.

power strokes, we fasten a **flywheel** to one end. This is simply a heavy metal disc, or wheel, which has considerable momentum when it has been gotten spinning. This tends to keep the shaft turning more smoothly. It is somewhat the same thing as spinning a short, stubby top rather than a long, thin stick.

In an automobile we have something else which helps this situation a great deal. Thus far we have been talking of engines on the basis of one single cylinder. But we do not have "one-lungers" in vehicles any more. We have put these 1-cylinder engines together, and now we have engines of four cylinders, six, eight, or even more cylinders. These may be arranged in different ways. But with all these various types of engines we must remember that we have not changed the fundamentals in any way. We have simply taken a number of the same single-cylinder engines and arranged them in different patterns. We can pick out one cylinder from any of these engines and it will operate just as we have been describing.

One way of combining these single-cylinder engines is to simply line them up, end to end. We put two together, add another one to the end, then a

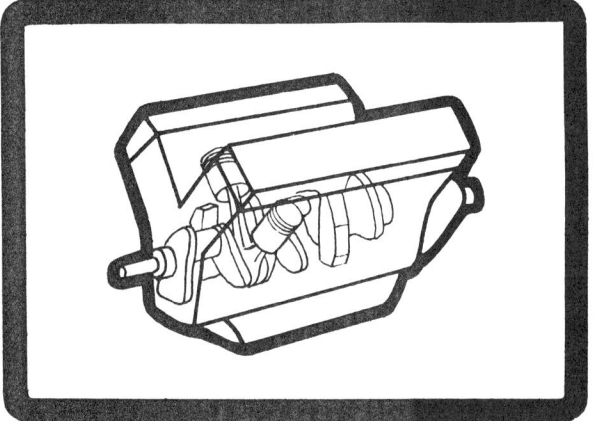

The pistons, cylinders, connecting rods and crankshafts are located inside the engine block. The **most common type of block is the V-type.**

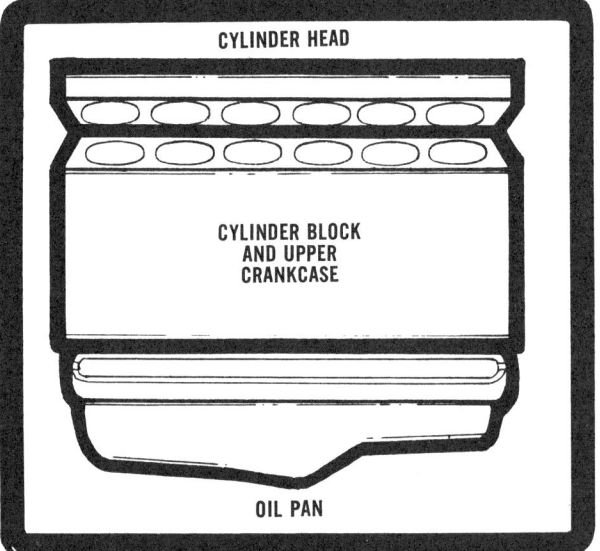

Other components that make up the engine are the cylinder head, cylinder block and oil pan.

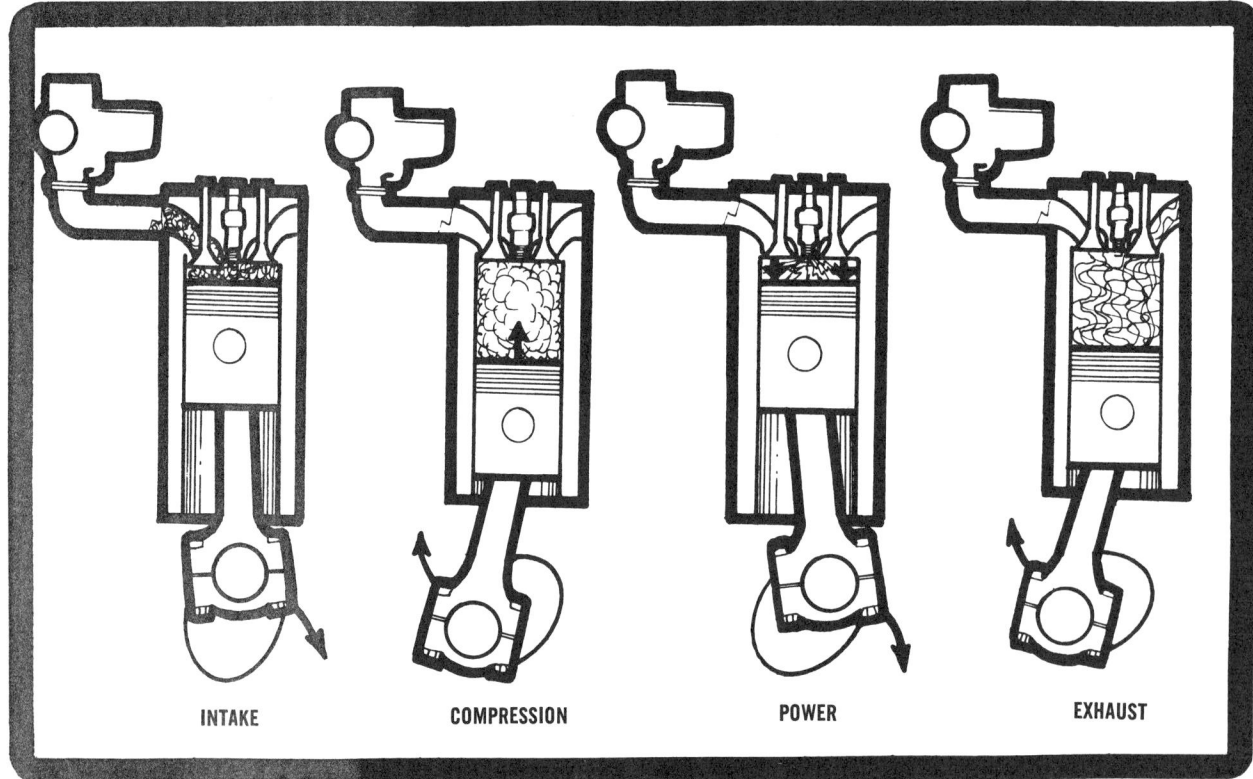

INTAKE   COMPRESSION   POWER   EXHAUST

The four strokes showing the relationship of all the components involved in the process.

fourth, and so on—just as we used to line up building blocks in a row on the floor. We can fasten the ends of the crankshafts together—in reality we use one long crankshaft with a crank, or throw, for each cylinder. These cranks are arranged so that when the power stroke is occurring in one cylinder, compression is going on in another, intake in a third, and exhaust in a fourth. Thus if we have four cylinders there is always one piston furnishing power to the crankshaft. With more than four cylinders there is actually an overlapping of power strokes. This makes the job of the flywheel much easier.

The other cylinder arrangement most often used in automobiles is the **V-type.** Here we have two rows of cylinders alongside each other. They are set at an angle, coming together at the bottom with the connecting rods all fastened to the same crankshaft. There are two pistons and two connecting rods for each crank. Thus in a V-8 engine we have a short crankshaft with only four cranks. It works much like two separate 4-cylinder engines, but of course they must be arranged so that the various events in one row of cylinders take place at the proper time in relation to those in the other row.

In an in-line automobile engine, the cylinders are not separate units. They are made all in one piece, the **cylinder block,** cast of a special alloy iron. We might consider this piece as just a block of metal with a line of holes running through it. The **cylinder head,** which forms the closed top of the cylinders and in the present case contains the valves, is a separate piece bolted to the block. The **crankcase** is that part of the engine below the cylinder block. It holds the crankshaft in place, encloses the whirling cranks, and acts as an oil reservoir. The upper half of this is usually made in one piece with the block, with the lower part just a thin pan to seal it up. This lower part is often called the **oil pan.**

Pistons are ordinarily made of cast iron (sometimes special alloys approaching the composition of steel) or aluminum. Light weight is important because pistons must travel so fast in modern high-speed engines. A piston must stop and reverse direction at the end of each stroke, and in between stops may reach speeds of 60 miles per hour.

It would be difficult to make a solid piston fit a cylinder accurately enough to form an efficient seal. With the variations in temperature encountered it is practically impossible. So we put **piston rings** in grooves in the piston. These are cast iron rings, split at one point and with enough spring in them so they constantly press against the wall of the cylinder. There are two types. Compression rings are to keep the gas from leaking down past the piston during the compression and power strokes. Oil control rings are to control the amount of oil on the cylinder wall and keep it from leaking up past the piston. There are usually several compression rings and one or more oil control rings on each piston.

The connecting rod is fastened to the piston by means of the **piston pin** or wrist pin. This is a tubular piece of hardened alloy steel which fits in the small end of the connecting rod. Its ends are fastened in the piston. The big end of the connecting rod has a separate cap which allows it to be bolted around the crank on the crankshaft. The connecting rod is usually of I-beam section and forged from a steel alloy to keep it as light and strong as possible.

Adding a flywheel keeps the crankshaft turning smoothly between engine pulses.

Simply by adding more sets of cylinders, pistons and connecting rods onto a longer crankshaft, we can build up 4-, 6- or 8-cylinder engines.

The crankshaft of an inline engine is a shaft with as many cranks as there are cylinders. We can think of it as that many single-cylinder crankshafts fastened end to end, although it may look somewhat different as there are not always bearings or supports for the shaft between each two throws. It also looks different from our first simple crank because of the counterweights. It has these weights opposite each crank throw to balance it, so the shaft will run smoothly. Otherwise it would be like trying to spin a lopsided top. The crankshaft is usually a forging of a nickel-steel alloy. There must be no question of its strength and durability, as it is literally the backbone of the engine.

FUEL SYSTEM

The fuel system starts with the **gasoline tank.** We must have a supply of fuel.

Then we have to get the gasoline from the tank to the carburetor. We ordinarily have only one carburetor for all the cylinders. The **fuel pump** gets the fuel there. It sucks the gasoline through a metal tube from the tank and forces it into the **float chamber** of the carburetor. This is a sort of store room for the fuel. It gets its name from the float in it, which floats on top of the gasoline and closes a valve when the gasoline reaches the proper level. This shuts off the fuel coming from the pump. Whenever the level begins to drop, the float opens the valve and lets more gasoline in.

Next to the float chamber is the carburetor proper. It is essentially a tube, something over an inch in diameter. It is open to the air at the top, with the intake manifold connected at the bottom. Air rushes down this tube at high speed, pulled in by the suction in the engine cylinders—or to be more accurate, pushed in by atmospheric pressure because of the lower pressure in the cylinders. It sometimes reaches a speed of 250 miles per hour. An **air cleaner** at the top of the tube takes out any dust or grit which might cause wear or injury to engine parts.

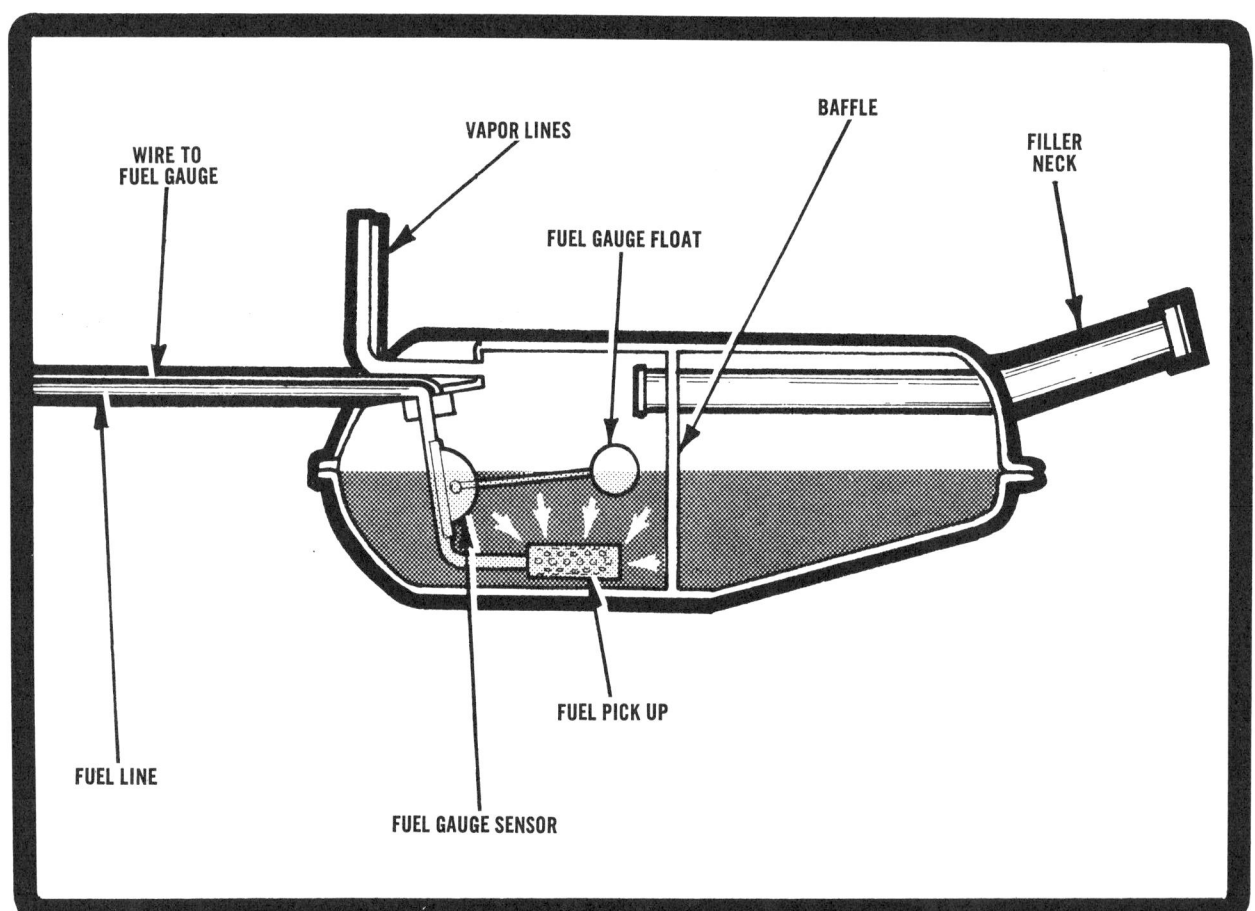

Gas tanks usually hold anywhere from 10 to 26 gallons. The gas is drawn from the tank by the fuel pump into the fuel pickup. Then the gas is drawn through the fuel line toward the engine. The float mechanism and sensor work through a wire to the dashboard gauge to let you know how much gas you have left. The baffle keeps the gas from sloshing around inside the tank during acceleration or braking.

At one point the tube narrows down, and then gradually tapers back to its original size. This shape as shown in the illustration is known as a **venturi.** It causes a decrease in air pressure at that particular point.

Into the side of the air tube right at that spot runs a small tube from the float chamber, its end sticking out slightly from the wall. This is almost full of gasoline, the level being the same as the level in the float chamber. As the air rushes by the opening, it sucks out fuel in very small drops and carries them along with it. It is exactly the same as an atomizer with which you spray your throat, or a sprayer for killing bugs in your garden. It might be likened to a gust of wind sucking dry leaves out of the end of a culvert and whirling them along with it.

The speed and power of an engine are determined by the amount of fuel-air mixture taken into the cylinders. This is controlled by the **throttle valve,** which in an automobile is connected to the accelerator pedal in the driver's compartment. The throttle valve is in the lower part of the carburetor, and simply varies the opening of the tube at that point. When it is part way closed, less air and fuel are pulled into the engine.

The carburetor has two jobs. One is to atomize the fuel, that is, to break it up into very tiny particles. This is fairly well done in sucking it out into the tube, and the process continues as it is whirled along in the miniature hurricane.

The second is to meter the fuel, that is, to see that it is mixed with the air in just the proper proportions. This is done primarily by having the proper size opening in the tube from the float chamber to the air tube. The proper proportions are then kept more or less automatically. When the throttle valve is opened wider, more air is pulled in and also more fuel, and the proportions—the mixture ratio—are kept about the same.

This is a very simplified example of a carburetor. In actual practice they have at least two jets or fuel passages from the float chamber to the carburetor proper. One is for idling and low speeds, the other for higher speeds or harder pulling. There are also various other auxiliary devices built in the carburetor. Most of them are for the purpose of changing the fuel-air ratio to take care of some special condition.

We have explained earlier that theoretically there should be 15 pounds of air to 1 pound of gasoline. We would call that a mixture ratio of 15 to 1. But gasoline will burn with a mixture ratio from about 18 to 1 down to 8 to 1. When there is more air than usual,

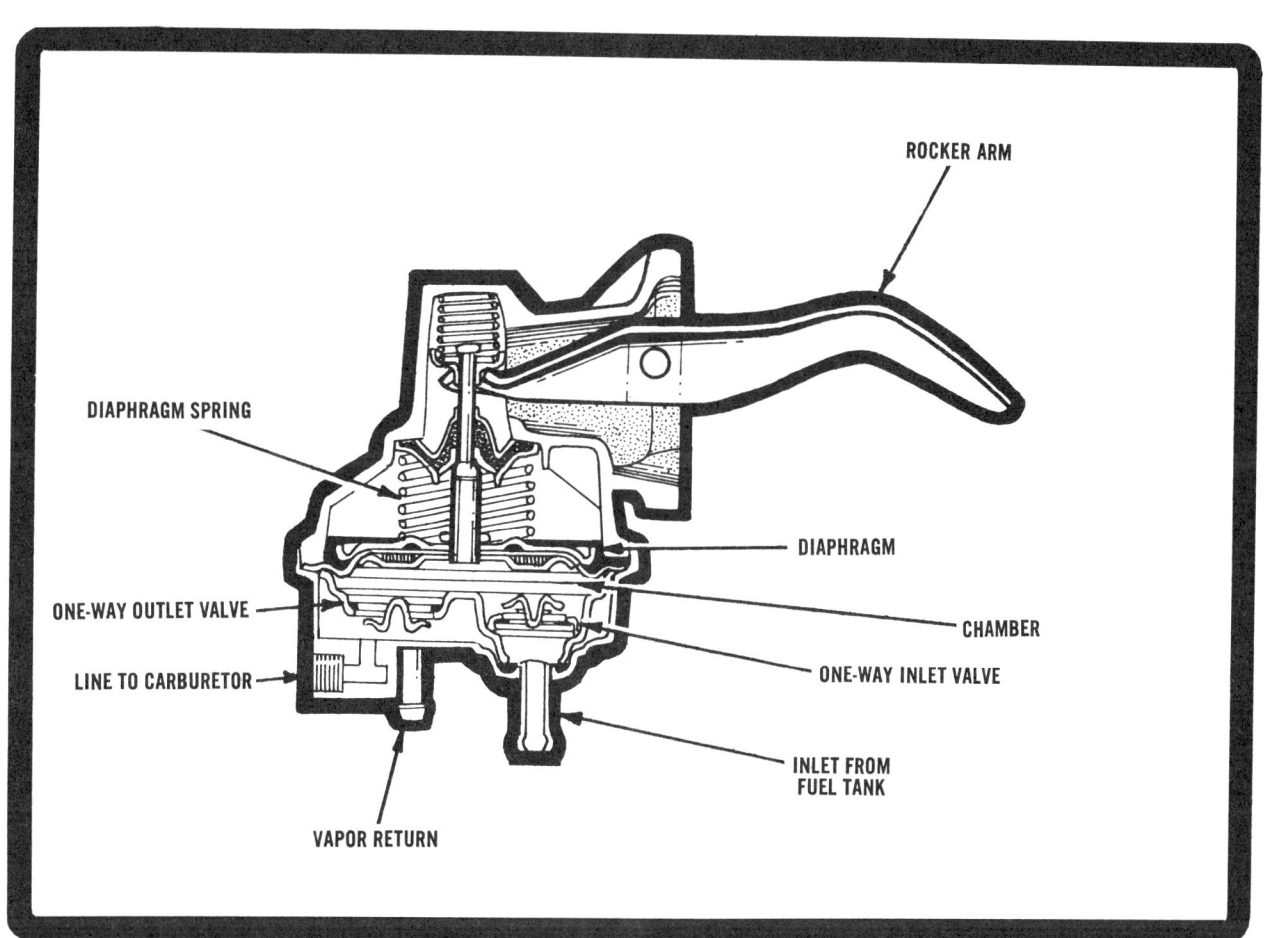

The typical fuel pump uses a pulsing diaphragm to draw gasoline from the fuel line to the carburetor. The camshaft activates a pushrod inside the pump to cause the diaphragm to rise and fall with each engine revolution. This creates a partial vacuum or suction, which is the force that moves the gasoline.

let us say a ratio of 16 to 1, we call it a "lean" mixture. When it is a low ratio, less than 14 to 1, we call it a "rich" mixture. Sometimes we want temporarily a mixture quite different from the theoretically correct one, such as for sudden acceleration or for the very highest speed. Most of the auxiliary devices on carburetors are to take care of such cases.

One of these deserves mention. When a car has been standing for some time, particularly in cold weather, it will not start with the ordinary mixture. It needs a rich mixture—more fuel in the air. To furnish this we have a **choke valve.** This looks much like the throttle valve, but is located in the tube above the carburetor. When it is partly closed, a high vacuum is formed beneath it. More fuel and less air are pulled in, giving the desired rich mixture. On most automobiles today, this choke valve is controlled automatically and the driver has nothing to do with it.

From the carburetor, the mixture of fuel and air enters the intake manifold. This is a carefully designed pipe with the branches leading to the tops of all the cylinders. When the engine is running, the mixture flows into the intake manifold in a continuous stream.

But we do not want it flowing into the cylinders continuously. Each cylinder should be open to the manifold only during its particular intake stroke. It is the intake valves which take care of this.

The same holds true for the exhaust. The exhaust manifold is a pipe quite similar to the intake manifold. This must be open to each cylinder only during its exhaust stroke to allow the hot gases to escape to the open air. The exhaust valves do this job.

Thus each cylinder must have at least one intake valve and one exhaust valve.

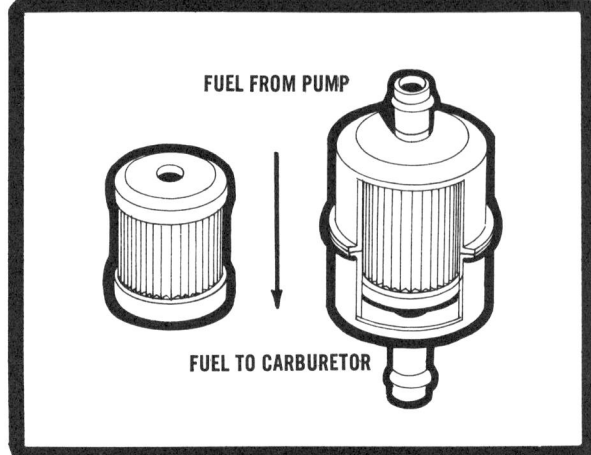

Two types of fuel filters are generally used today to remove foreign objects from the gasoline. Left, this type fits into the housing in the carburetor itself. Right, is an inline filter which is usually located in the fuel line somewhere before the carburetor and usually quite near it.

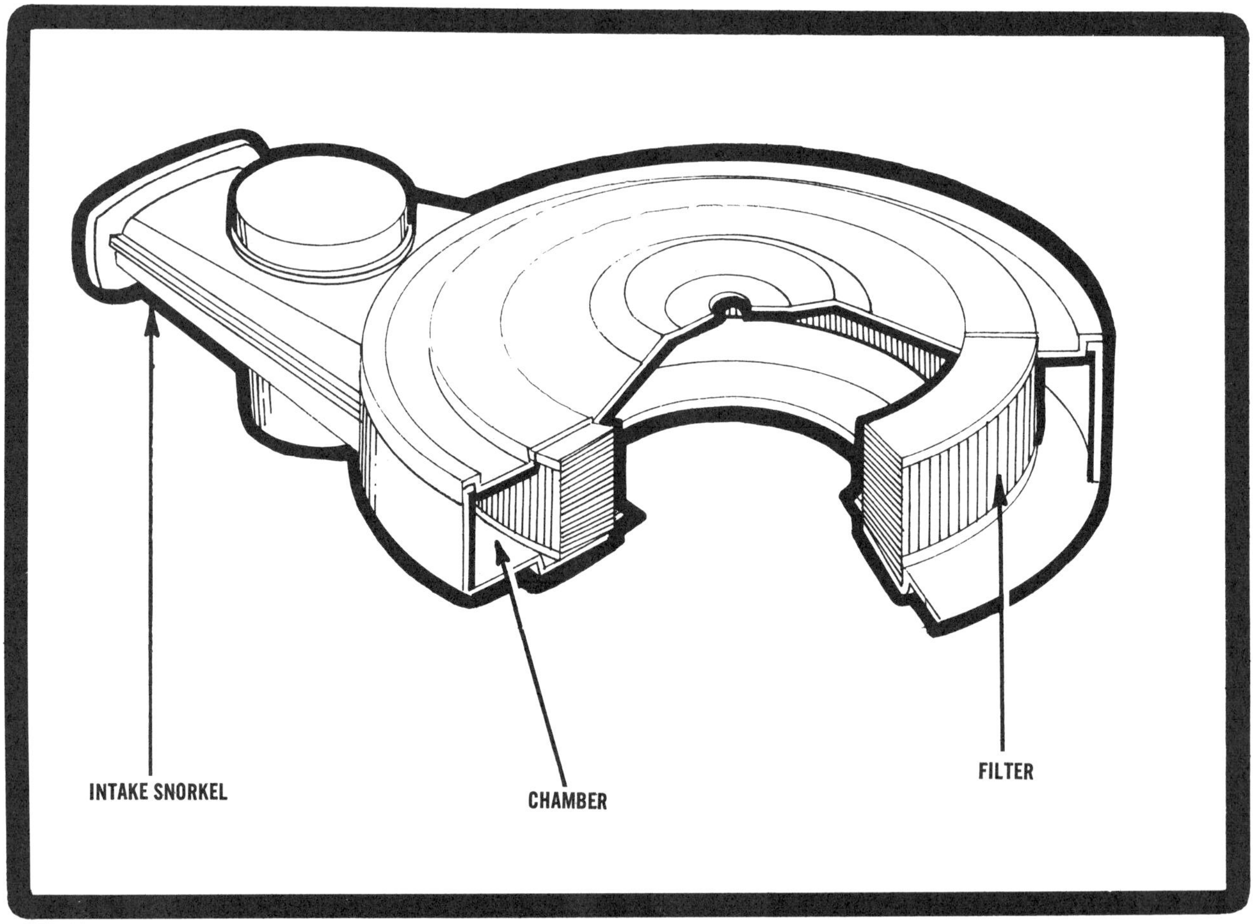

The typical modern air cleaner has a removable, serviceable filter element.

30

Automobile engines ordinarily use poppet valves. These are sometimes called "mushroom" valves, due to their shape. The outside edge of the circular head is cut at an angle, which must be exactly the same as the angle cut in the cylinder head where the two fit together. We do not want any leakage here. The valves are made of special alloy steels to withstand the high temperatures of the combustion chamber. This is especially true of the exhaust valve, as it does not have the benefits of being cooled by the incoming mixture passing over it.

The valves are controlled by the **camshaft.** This is a long straight shaft with knobs or projections on it called **cams.** There is one of these cams for each valve. As the shaft goes around, the **valve lifter** slides on the cam and is pushed up when the high part of the cam reaches it. This in turn lifts the **push rod** and one end of the **rocker arm.** The other end of the rocker arm moves down, like a teeter-totter, pushing open the valve against the pressure of the coil spring. As the cam goes on around, the spring closes the valve. The cam opens the valve and the spring closes it. A cam is really something like a crankshaft and connecting rod combination; it changes rotary motion to straight line motion.

The camshaft is connected to the crankshaft by gears or a chain at the front of the engine. Inasmuch as we want each valve to open only once for every two revolutions of the engine, the camshaft goes around at exactly half the speed of the crankshaft.

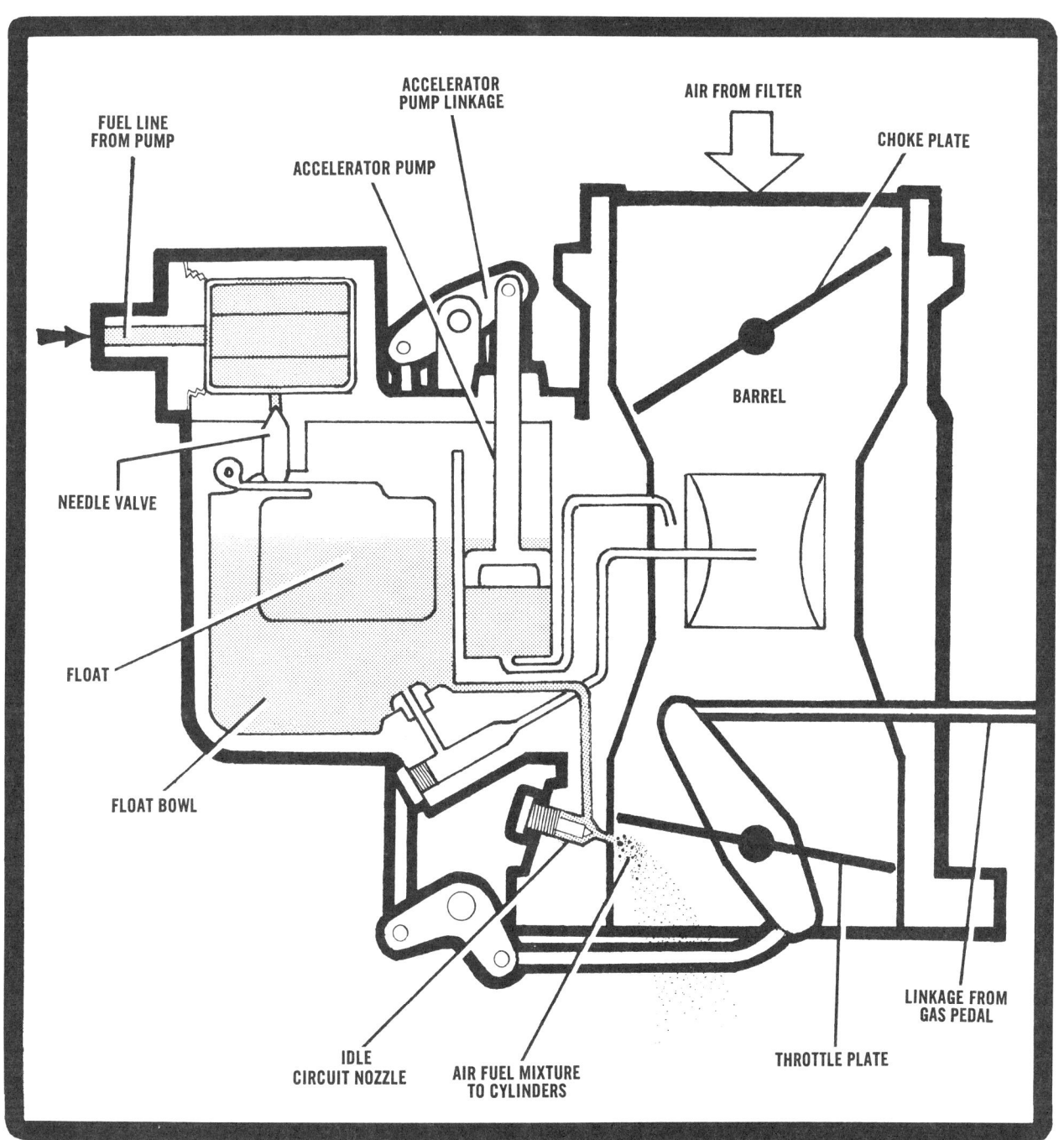

This internal cutaway of a typical carburetor at idle shows the location of the choke valve (or choke plate) which richens the air-fuel mixture, thereby making a cold engine easier to start.

The camshaft must be made with the cams in just the right places, and it must be connected with the crankshaft in exactly the right way. If these are not correct, the valves will not open and close at the right time in relation to the movement of the piston. The intake valve might open when the piston was going up on the compression stroke or down on the power stroke. The job of gearing the camshaft to the crankshaft so that the valves will open at just the right time is called timing the valves, and the gears on the two shafts are called **timing gears.**

The engine we have been discussing thus far is called an **overhead valve** engine, or **valve-in-head** engine. The reasons are obvious, as the valves are located in the cylinder head and are operated from above. The other common type of engine, when classifying them according to valve arrangement, is the **L-head** engine.

In the L-head engine, the combustion chamber is extended to one side beyond the cylinder, forming an upside down L. The valves are turned upside down and fit in ports in the bottom of that extension. They are in the cylinder block instead of in the cylinder head. They move upward to open the ports, and therefore there is no need of rocker arms to reverse the direction of movement. They can be opened directly by the camshaft and valve lifter. They are closed by the coil springs, and in general operate exactly the same as the overhead type.

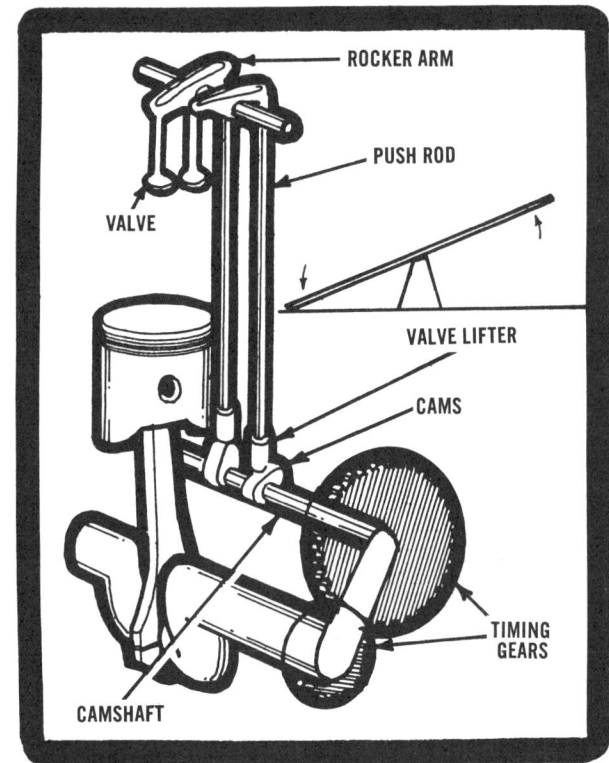

Here we have added other components to show you their interrelationship.

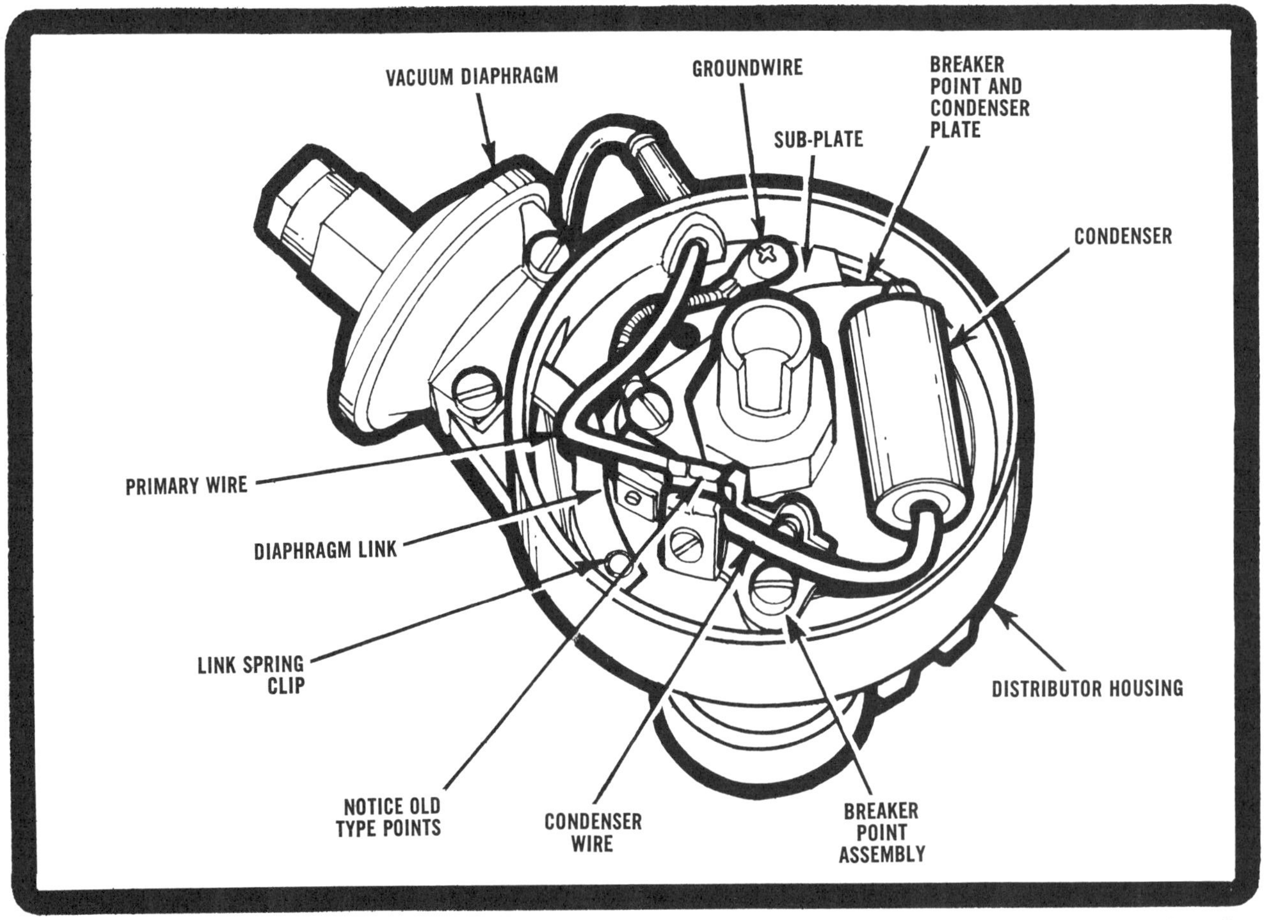

A look inside a typical V-8 distributor. The centrifugal advance weights are located below the ignition point breaker plate. On GM Delco-Remy distributors, the centrifugal advance weights are located above the ignition point breaker plate.

IGNITION SYSTEM

We have already explained that a spark plug ignites the mixture in an automobile type engine. The electricity travels down one electrode and jumps across the gap, or air space, to the other electrode. It jumps across in the form of a spark, which is just like any other kind of fire as far as the inflammable mixture in the cylinder is concerned.

We may wonder why it takes so many pieces of equipment just to make this spark. Suppose we see what the ignition system has to do.

There are two circuits in the ignition system, that is, two complete paths around which the electricity flows. These are the **primary,** or low voltage circuit, and the **secondary,** or high voltage circuit. If we think of electricity as water flowing through a pipe, voltage is the pressure pushing it through. Now it takes quite a bit of pressure to push that electricity across the space between the spark plug electrodes, much more than we have available in an automobile. One of the main jobs of the ignition system is to raise that voltage high enough to make sure that we have a hot, fiery spark in the combustion chamber.

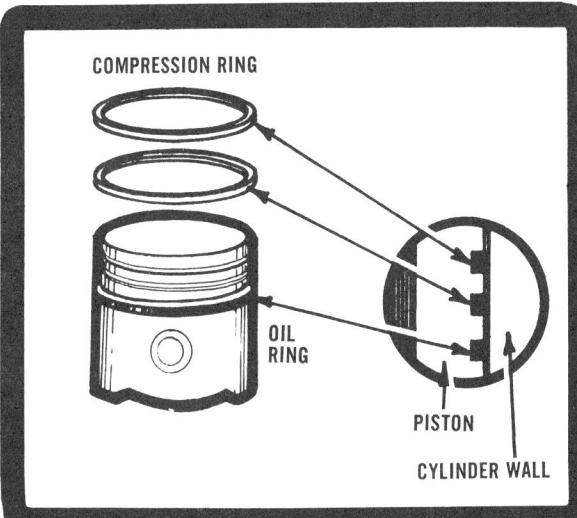

Piston rings seal the combustion process in the cylinder by forming a seal between the piston and cylinder wall.

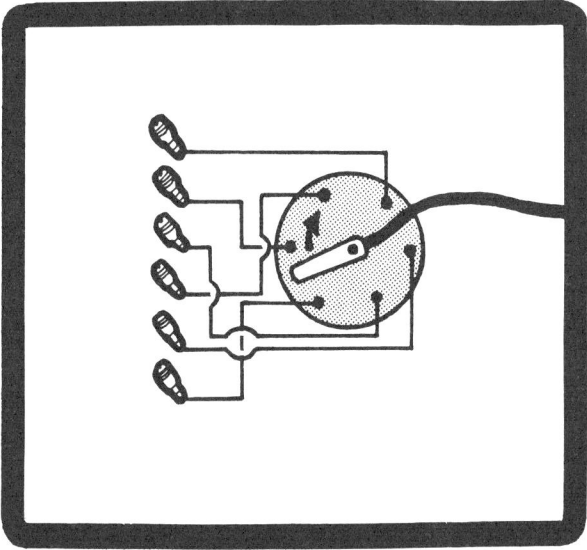

The timing gears are connected to the camshaft and crankshaft to time and control the occurrence of power impulses in the engine.

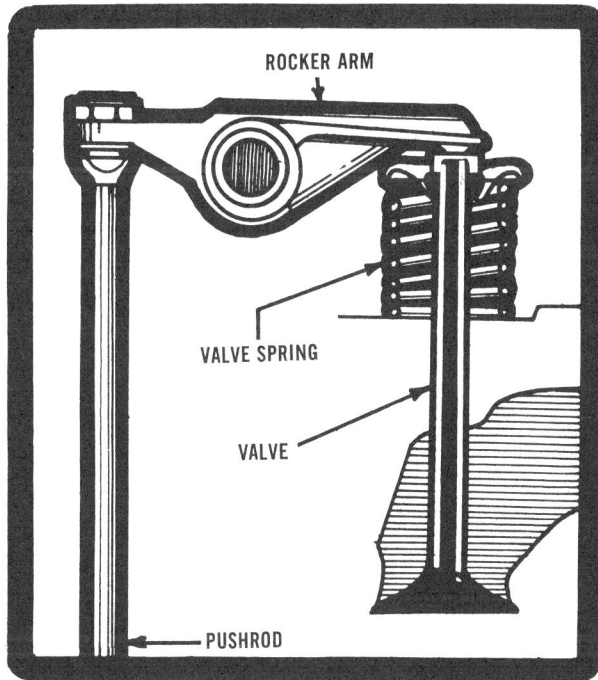

The relationship between an engine's pushrod, rocker arm, valve spring and valve is shown here.

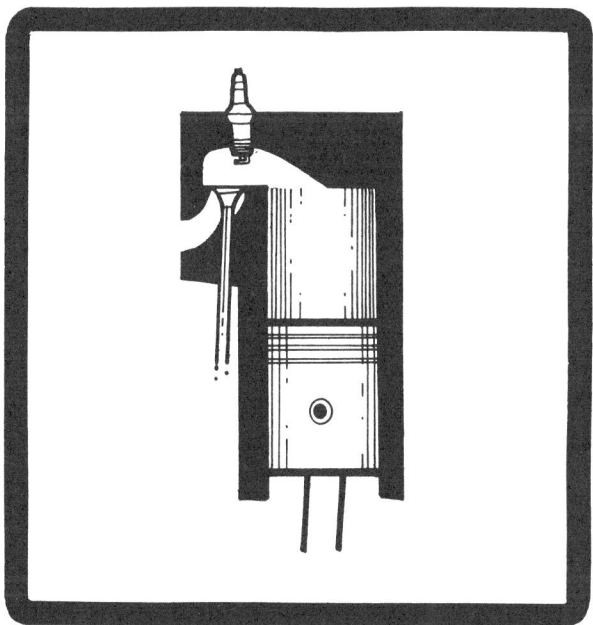

The spark plug fires the mixture in the combustion chamber after the valve opens to admit the air-fuel mixture.

Let us go around the primary circuit first. We will start with the **battery.** The battery supplies the electricity. It is sometimes called a device for changing chemical energy into electrical energy, or a storehouse for electricity. A dry cell, such as a flashlight battery, is much the same thing.

Electricity goes from the battery to the **coil.** It is the coil which raises the voltage. It consists of two coils of wire. The primary, which is connected to the battery, is several hundred turns of comparatively large wire. The secondary, which is wound over the primary but carefully separated, or insulated, from it, may have from 10,000 to 25,000 turns of fine wire, or more than a mile of wire.

As long as an electric current is flowing steadily in the primary circuit, nothing happens in the secondary. But if that current is suddenly stopped, if the primary circuit is broken, a momentary high voltage is set up in the secondary circuit. This may reach a value of 20,000 to 25,000 volts, as contrasted to the 6 or 12 volts furnished by the battery. We will not go into the scientific reason for this here, but will take the word of the electrical engineers that this is a fundamental characteristic of electricity.

Now what we need is something to break the primary circuit often enough to send that high voltage to each spark plug just when we want it to fire. So we put a **breaker** in the primary circuit. This is a pair of contacts which are opened and closed rapidly by a cam. The cam ordinarily has as many points as there are cylinders. It is driven from the engine, usually from the camshaft which operates the valves. The contacts are timed to open near the top of each piston's compression stroke. Thus the primary circuit is continually being broken and connected again, which sends a series of high voltage surges through the secondary circuit.

A **condenser** is incorporated in the breaker case. Its principal job is to help give a quick, clean electrical break without sparks when the breaker contact points separate. This is necessary to get a good spark in the combustion chamber.

These are all the parts of the primary circuit. To complete the path for the electricity, a wire is run from the circuit breaker to the frame of the vehicle. One terminal of the battery is always connected to the frame, which acts as a return path for all circuits in the car. This is called the **ground.**

For the secondary circuit we go back to the coil. The high voltage electricity starts there, in the winding of thousands of turns of small wire. To get this to the proper spark plug at the proper time, we have the **distributor.** This is a rotary switch. We might liken it to a clock—a clock with only one hand and with the hours marked in raised numerals which the hand rubs on as it moves around. Instead of the hand going around once an hour, it may go around more than two thousand times a minute. A wire from the coil goes to the center of the distributor, the point where the hand is fastened to the face of the clock. There is also a wire from each contact point—clock numeral—to a spark plug. Thus as the rotor—clock hand—goes around, electricity flows first to one contact point, then to another, and thus to one spark plug after another.

The spark plug itself consists of a steel shell in which is an insulator of porcelain or some similar material. An insulator is a body through which electricity will not flow. Through the center of this insulator runs a wire, or electrode, and another electrode extends out from the bottom of the steel shell to a point close to the center electrode. The shell is screwed into the cylinder head and the wire from the distributor is connected to the top of the center electrode. The electricity flows down and jumps the gap to the other electrode, hence to the engine block and to ground. This completes the secondary circuit and concludes the ignition cycle.

We should correct one false impression we have given. We have discussed the breaker and the distributor as if they were two separate and distinct units. One is in the primary circuit and one in the secondary circuit, and the jobs they have to do are quite different. But in an automobile they are combined in one housing, and the same shaft drives the distributor rotor and the cam which opens the breaker contacts. From the outside it looks like one unit. So when someone speaks of the distributor of an automobile engine, he is quite likely to mean the whole unit, including the breaker.

So we have all the parts necessary to start the mixture burning in the cylinder. There do not seem to be so many parts when we consider all that the ignition system has to do and the speed at which it must do it. In a 6-cylinder engine driving a car a 80 miles an hour, the coil must furnish about 12,000 sparks a minute, or 200 every second. The breaker contacts are closed for less than five thousandths of a second for each spark. On a thousand mile trip these contacts must open and close more than 9,000,000 times. And each of these millions of sparks must occur at exactly the right time and without a miss.

The ignition system has a real job to do. And if it fails—even in one part only—our engine is useless until it is fixed.

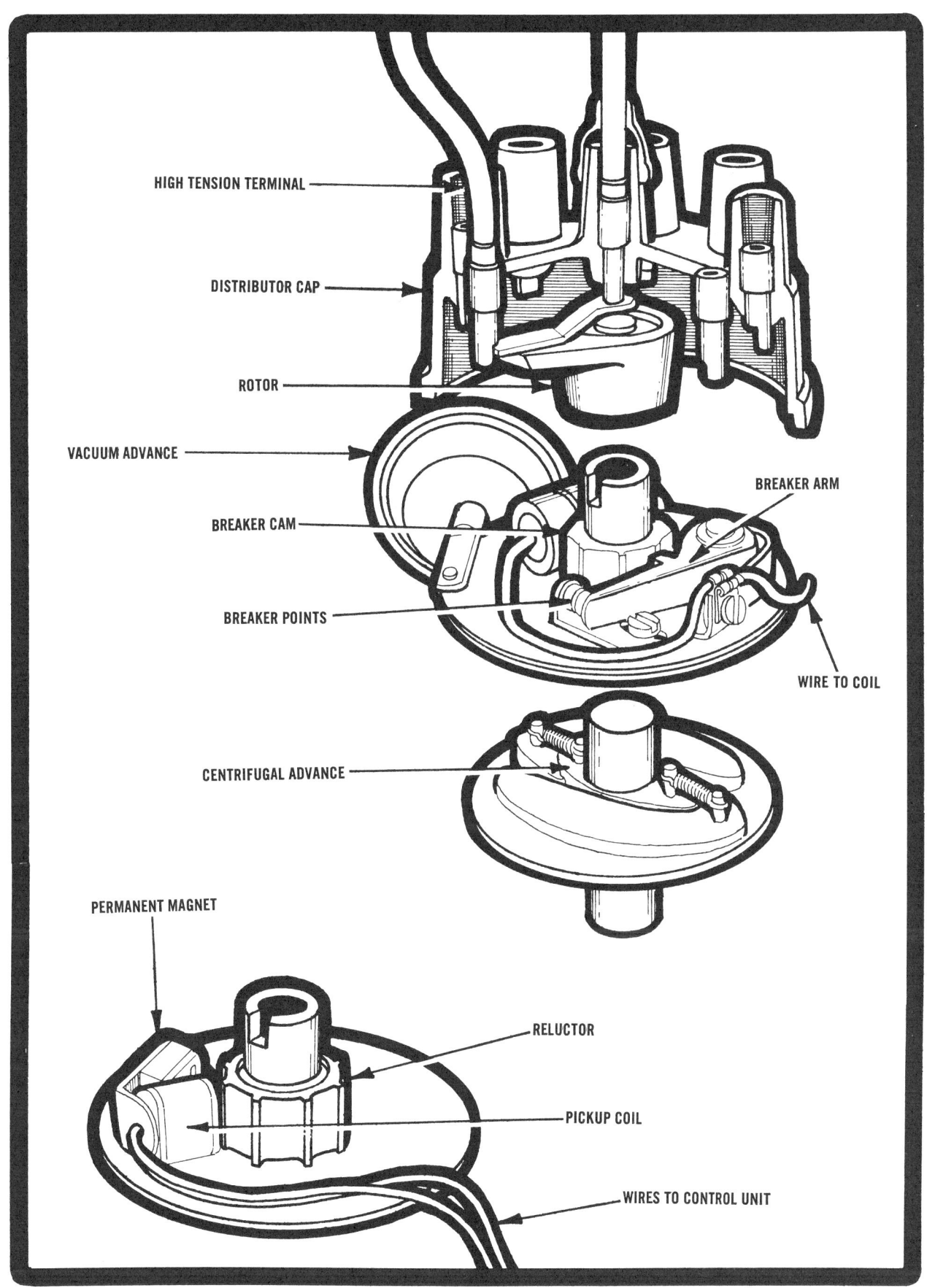

Upper right, the typical distributor has ignition breaker points which open and close to allow current to pass from the coil through a rotor and to the spark plug. Bottom left, the modern electronic ignition system replaces the traditional cam, breaker points and condenser with a rotating reluctor and magnetic pickup coil.

Other types of engines

There are two other types of engines found in automobiles. Neither are as prevalent as the 4-stroke internal combustion gasoline engine, but are becoming more popular for various reasons.

The rotary engine, also called the Wankel after its inventor, Felix Wankel, has been the subject of much attention the past few years.

Dispensing with separate cylinders, pistons, valves and crankshaft, the rotary applies power directly to the transmission. Its ingenious construction allows it to provide the power of a conventional engine that is twice its size and weight and that has twice as many parts. The Wankel burns as much as 20% more fuel than a conventional engine and is potentially a high polluter. But its reduced size means that bulky emission-control devices can be added more conveniently than to a piston engine.

The basic unit of the rotary engine is a large combustion chamber in the form of a pinched oval called an epitrochoid. Within this chamber all four functions of a piston take place simultaneously in the three pockets that are formed between the rotor and the chamber wall.

A main shaft, linked to the transmission, runs through the center of the chamber. It forms an axis for the three-sided rotor, which is geared to spin eccentrically along the chamber walls. As a result of this eccentric spinning, pockets are formed between the rotor's three surfaces and the chamber wall. Each pocket changes size four times in a single sweep of the rotor, and each change signals a new step in the continuous combustion cycle. In effect, each face of the rotor is performing the work of a piston inside a cylinder.

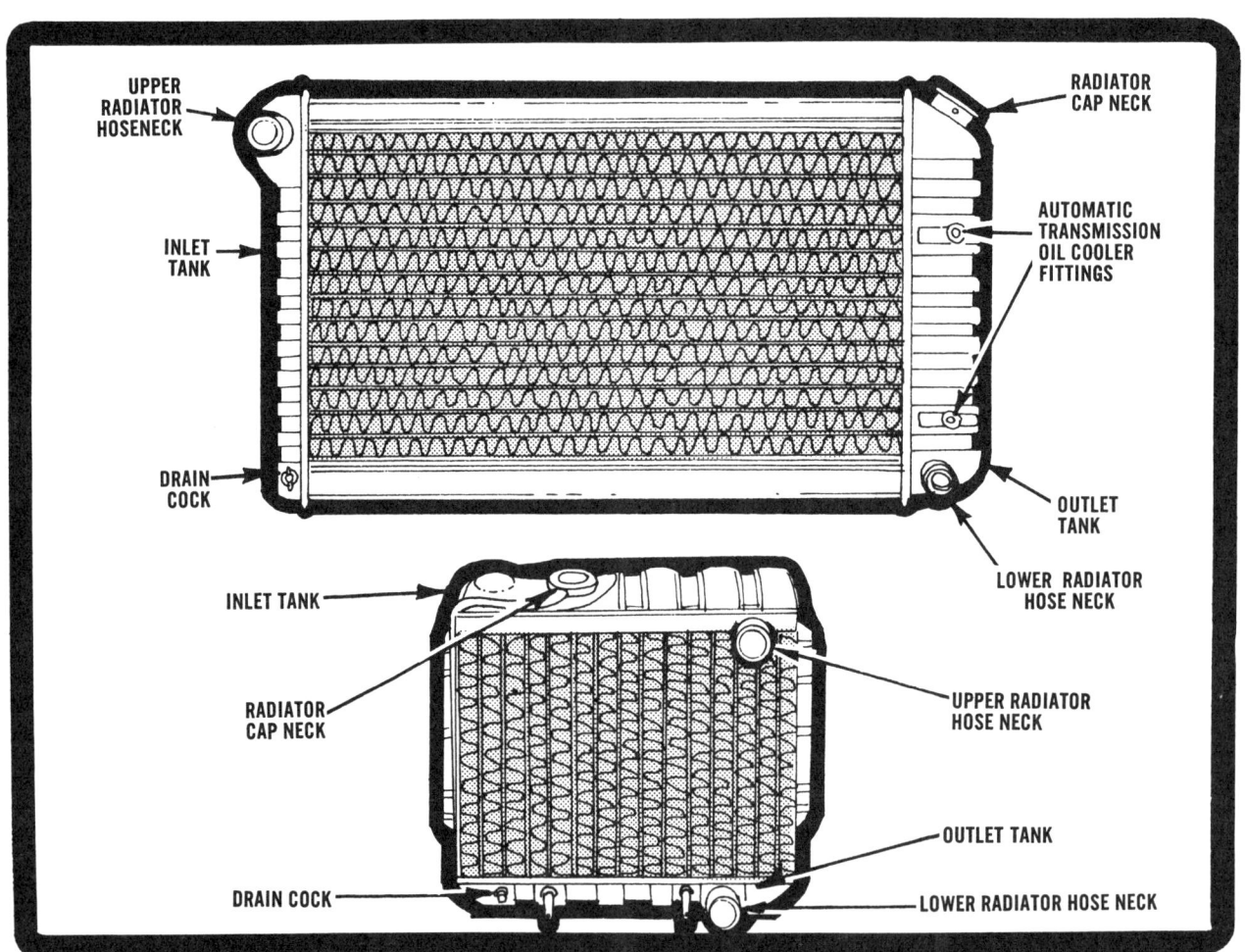

There are generally two types of radiators in use today. In the lower, wider crossflow radiator, top, the water flows from side to side for cooling exposure. In the more common downflow type, bottom, the hot water flows vertically through the core pipes which are surrounded by thin cooling fins which dissipate heat.

Just as the addition of cylinders increases the horsepower of a piston-powered engine, so the addition of combustion chambers increases the power of a rotary engine. The engine at left is similar to the two-chamber version being used in compact cars. Larger cars eventually may use rotaries with three or four chambers.

The other type of engine in general use is the diesel engine, again named after its inventor, Rudolph Diesel.

The diesel engine does not use a spark plug to ignite the fuel. Air is drawn into the cylinder and highly compressed. The compression is so high that the compressed air will reach temperatures of 1000° F. At the precise time the piston has completed the compression stroke, diesel fuel is sprayed into the combustion chamber. The intense heat of the compressed air ignites the fuel, and the power stroke follows.

The diesel fuel is sprayed by means of special injector nozzles. The pressure at the nozzle must be very high—3000 to 20,000 psi—depending on the system used.

The amount of fuel being delivered by the injector is controlled by means of a foot throttle connected to an actuating mechanism that in turn controls the pump output.

ENGINE COOLING, HEATING AND AIR CONDITIONING

Your engine needs a cooling system to protect it from self-destruction. Burning gases inside the cylinders can reach a temperature of 5000°F and produce enough heat to melt a 200 pound engine block in just 20 minutes.

About one-third of the heat produced in the engine must be carried away by the cooling system. Some is utilized for heating the passenger compartment. And, strange as it seems, your car's air conditioner produces heat in the process of cooling and dehumidifying the air.

The engine cooling, heating and air conditioning systems are interrelated and share some of the same components, so all three are covered in this chapter.

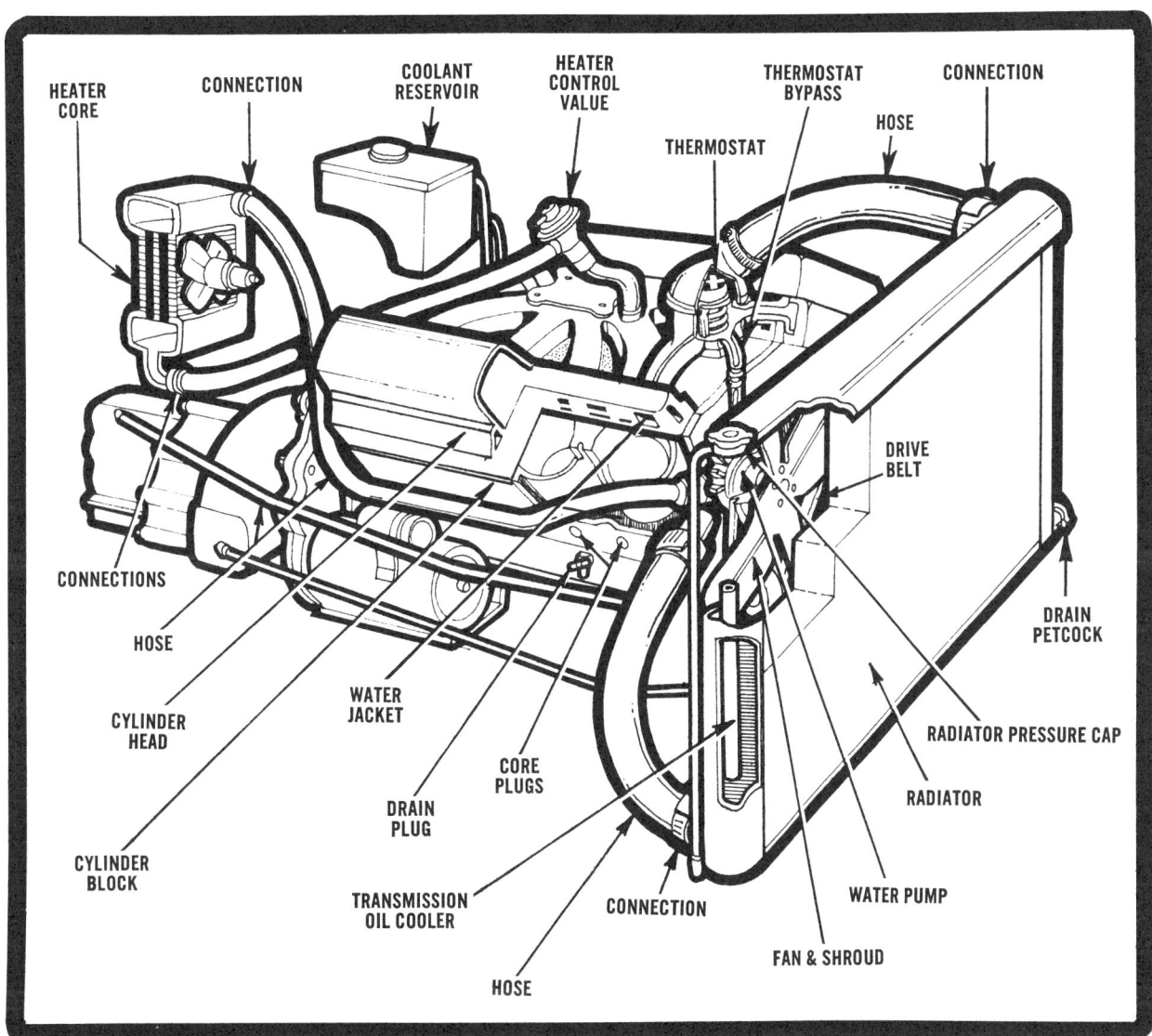

Typical cooling system components.

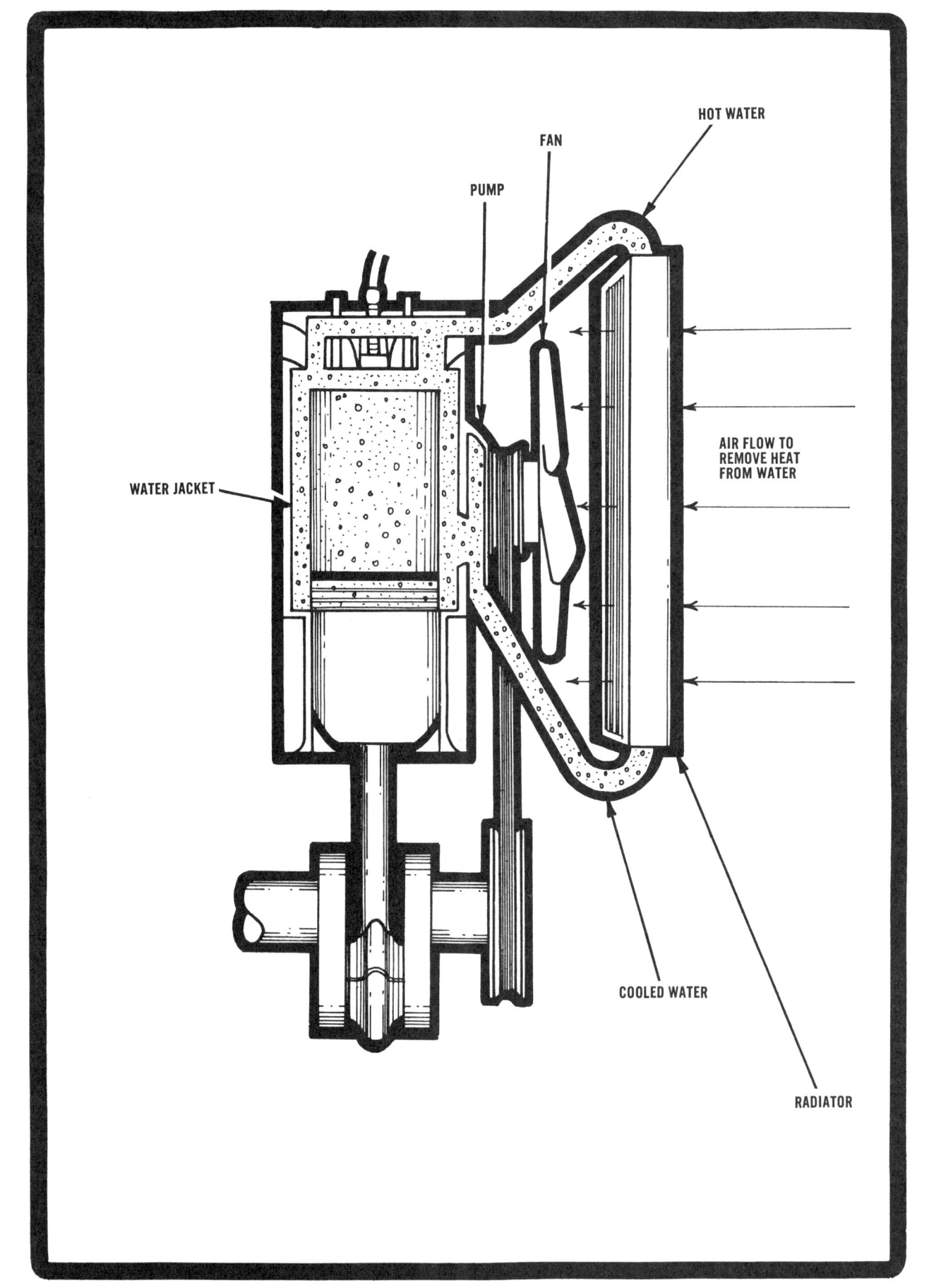

A simplified illustration of how the cooling system removes heat from the engine.

Engine cooling system

Most automotive engines are cooled by circulating water.

The main parts of the engine cooling system are the radiator, radiator pressure cap, hoses, thermostat, water pump, fan and fan belt. The system is filled with coolant, which should be a 50-50 mixture of antifreeze and water. No matter where you live or how hot or cold the weather becomes, the mixture should be maintained the year around.

The water pump and engine cooling fan are mounted on the same shaft and driven by a belt connected to the engine. The pump draws coolant from the bottom of the radiator and forces it through passages surrounding the hot area—the cylinders, combustion chambers, valves and spark plugs. From there the coolant flows through a hose into the top of the radiator, then downward through tubes attached to cooling fins and surrounded by air passages. Heat is transferred from the coolant to air forced through the radiator passages by the fan and the forward motion of the car.

The air cooled engine has proved to be a reliable and inexpensive alternative to the water cooled engine in some small cars such as the Volkswagen Beetle and all Porsches. In the rear engine cooling system air enters the compartment through ducts in a shroud covering the engine. A fan, powered by a belt and drive pulley attached to the crankshaft, sends air across the top of the engine. The air passes through a series of cooling fins cast into the engine block around each cylinder head. The engine heat, which has been absorbed by the fins, is picked up by the passing air. The fan then vents the hot air through ducts at the bottom of the engine.

Controlling the temperature

It's important to get the coolant up to normal operating temperature as quickly as possible to ensure smooth engine operation, free flow of oil and ample heat for the occupants. When the engine is cold, the thermostat blocks the passage from the cylinder head to the radiator and sends coolant on a shortcut to the water pump. The cooling fluid is not exposed to the blast of air from the radiator, so it warms up rapidly. As temperature increases, the thermostat gradually opens and allows coolant to flow through the radiator.

Cooling systems on older cars were limited to a maximum temperature of 212°F—the boiling point of water. To get rid of the extra heat generated by more powerful engines, automatic transmission and air conditioning, modern cars have pressurized systems using a 50-50 mixture of antifreeze and water, which enables them to operate at temperatures up to 263 degrees without boiling. At this temperature, plain water if used alone would boil over.

Transmission oil cooler

Automatic transmission fluid is cooled by a small, separate radiator, usually located in the lower tank of the main radiator. It serves the same purpose for the transmission as the main radiator does for the engine.

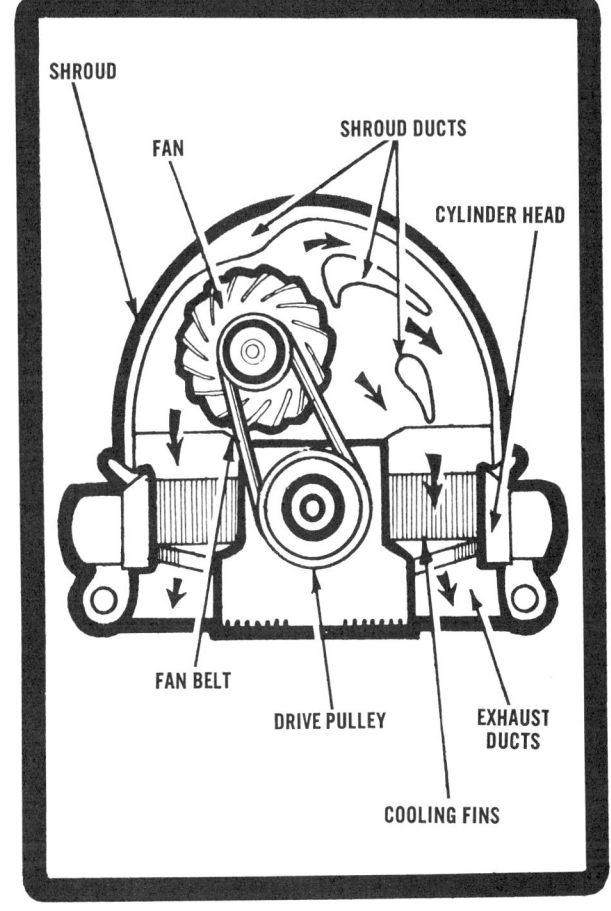

VW engine uses air circulation for cooling.

ment. Two outlets located inside and below the windshield shoot warm air streams against the glass when you need to remove ice or clear a fogged windshield. Temperature is controlled either by regulating the amount of coolant passing through the heater or by mixing heated and outside air.

Air conditioning

When a liquid vaporizes, it draws heat from its surroundings. That's the basic principle of your household refrigerator and your car's air conditioning system. For a practical demonstration, swab your forehead with rubbing alcohol on a hot day and feel the cooling effect as the liquid evaporates.

The air conditioning system is filled with refrigerant that boils at very low temperature. To cool the air, the refrigerant is alternately compressed, then allowed to expand. In the process, it changes back and forth between liquid and gaseous states. Each time it changes to a gas, it cools the coils in the evaporator, which is located in the passenger compartment. A blower forces air over the cold coils into the car's interior. To take moisture out of the air on cool days, many car coolers chill the air below the desired temperature, then force it through the heater to reach a comfortable temperature.

The heating system

You are kept warm during winter driving by the coolant mixture which is heated by the engine, and flows through the heater and back to the cooling system through special hoses. A blower forces air through ducts to outlets in the passenger compart-

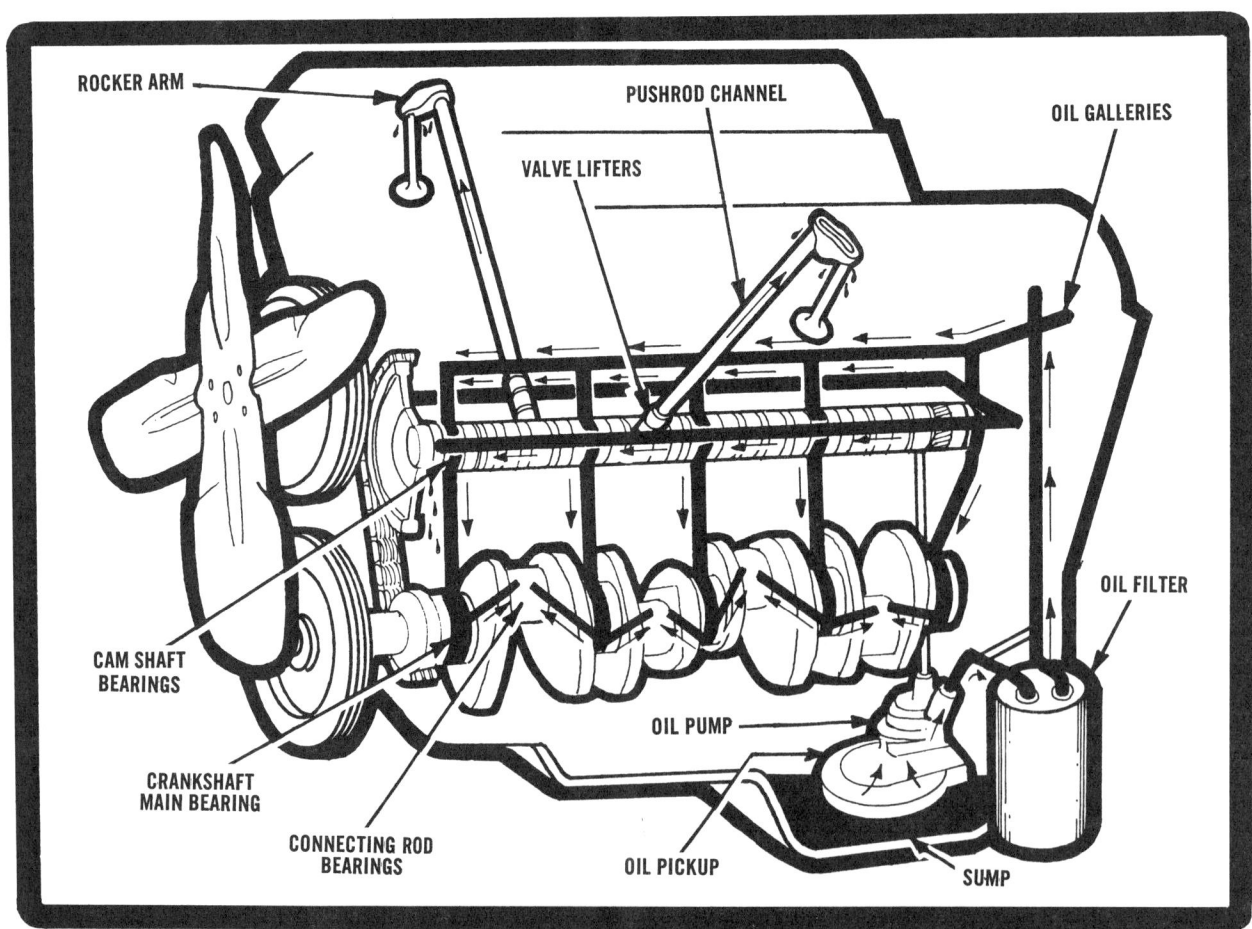

Typical lubrication system components.

Temperature control

In most units, temperature is controlled by varying the amount of cooled air that passes through the heater. In others, the compressor is turned on and off by a switch regulated by a thermostat.

LUBRICATION SYSTEM

Heat affects engine operation in another way also. Whenever we have two things rubbing against each other, or one turning inside another, we have friction. And when we have friction we have heat. So we need a **lubrication system** on an engine.

If we can keep oil between two rubbing surfaces, no matter how thin a film of it, the friction is very small. This not only prevents heating up, but makes it easier for the engine to run. Less power is wasted in moving the engine parts themselves, and thus more is available for useful work at the end of the crankshaft.

It is possible to run an engine without lubrication, but not for long. Almost immediately some part would get hot enough to seize or stick, and the engine would stop, probably with some broken pieces.

The oil is stored in the bottom of the crankcase, or oil pan. From there a pump forces it under pressure to some of the more critical points in the engine, particularly the crankshaft bearings. These **main bearings,** as they are often called, are inserts between the shaft and the members of the crankcase which support it. They are of special metal with good anti-friction qualities. A similar bearing is in the big end of each connecting rod where it goes around the crankshaft.

Usually the oil goes from the main bearings through passages drilled right in the crankshaft to the connecting rod bearings. Sometimes there is a passage the full length of the connecting rod, and the oil, still under pressure, is forced up through it to the piston pin. In some engines, the connecting rod bearings obtain oil by means of a dipper on the bottom of the rod which scoops oil out of a shallow pan.

It is very important that the piston and cylinder wall surfaces receive lubrication. But they do not need it under pressure. They, and many other parts, get their oil by the "splash" system. Oil is thrown off from some of the bearings, and the moving parts of the engine splash oil around. A mist of oil vapor fills the whole inside of the engine. This takes care of those places not included in the pressure system.

We might think of the lubrication system as the water system in our house. Water is forced under pressure to many different points, kitchen sink, wash bowl, and bath tub for example. If for some unknown reason we wanted to get the whole bathroom wet, we might turn on the hot water full force in the shower. The splashing and the steamy vapor would soon have moisture on everything in the room. Thus we would have a pressure system and a splash system just as in the engine.

We now have a complete engine. We have not attempted to discuss every part in detail, but we have put together an engine that will run and keep on running.

With proper provision for air, fuel, and ignition we have an engine that will run. We add cooling and lubrication to make sure that it keeps on running.

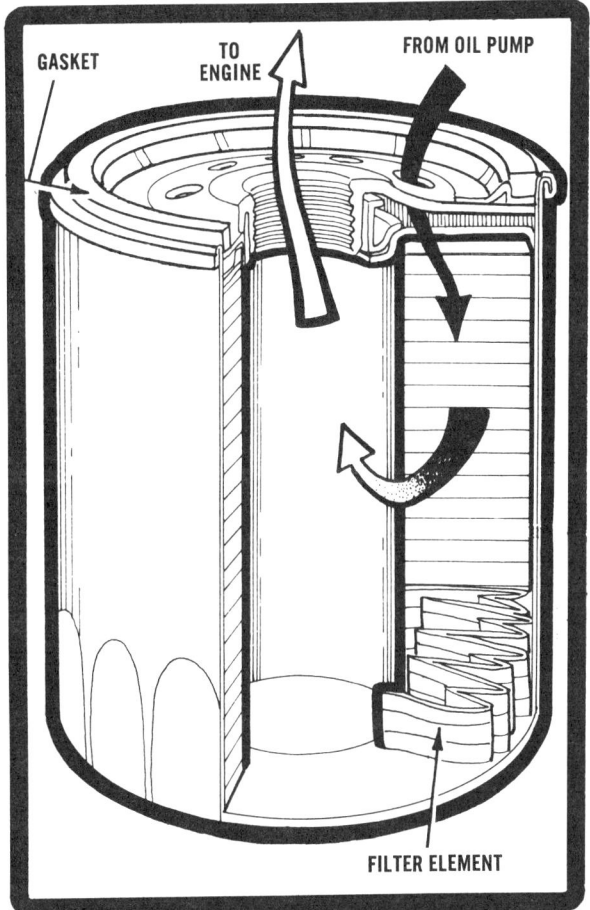

In the typical oil filter, oil from the oil pump passes into the filter where it is strained through the filtering element. The engine must have oil even if the oil is unfiltered. So if the filtering element gets clogged up, a bypass valve is forced open and the oil reaches the engine directly.

THE EXHAUST SYSTEM

The exhaust system's job is to get rid of the burned gases that remain in the engine after the combustion of gasoline and air, and to lower the engine noise to a socially acceptable level.

How it works

Burned gases escape from the cylinders through the exhaust valves and enter the exhaust manifold. Like the intake manifold, the exhaust manifold is a passage with openings at each cylinder. A V-8 engine has two exhaust manifolds—one for each side of the V. From the manifolds, the burned gases travel through a Y-shaped exhaust pipe to the muffler. Here the gases are channeled through perforated tubes to muffle the cracking sound of exploding gas. Gases then flow through the tailpipe and are discharged.

Noise reduction

To cut down noise still more, some cars also have resonators. These devices look like small mufflers and are mounted behind the main mufflers.

Many engines use a manifold heat valve to take hot exhaust gases to a passage around a section of the intake manifold. During starting and warmup, a thermostat holds the valve open. Exhaust gases warm the manifold and help vaporize the fuel. As the engine warms up, the valve closes and gases follow their normal path.

THE EMISSION CONTROL SYSTEM

To help clean up the air we breathe, auto makers install emission control systems to cut down air pollution from gases formed by burned fuel and air, and to prevent the evaporation of gasoline into the atmosphere. Currently, car makers are developing even more efficient systems.

Cleaning up the exhaust

The exhaust fumes—unburned hydrocarbons, carbon monoxide and oxides of nitrogen—must be controlled even though they are only a fraction of the total air pollution problem. Most exhaust systems include a modified ignition distributor which delays the spark in the cylinder when the engine is idling. This results in almost all the mixture being burned before it gets out of the cylinder. On some engines, a small air pump blows oxygen into the gases as they leave the cylinder, to afterburn any excess pollution.

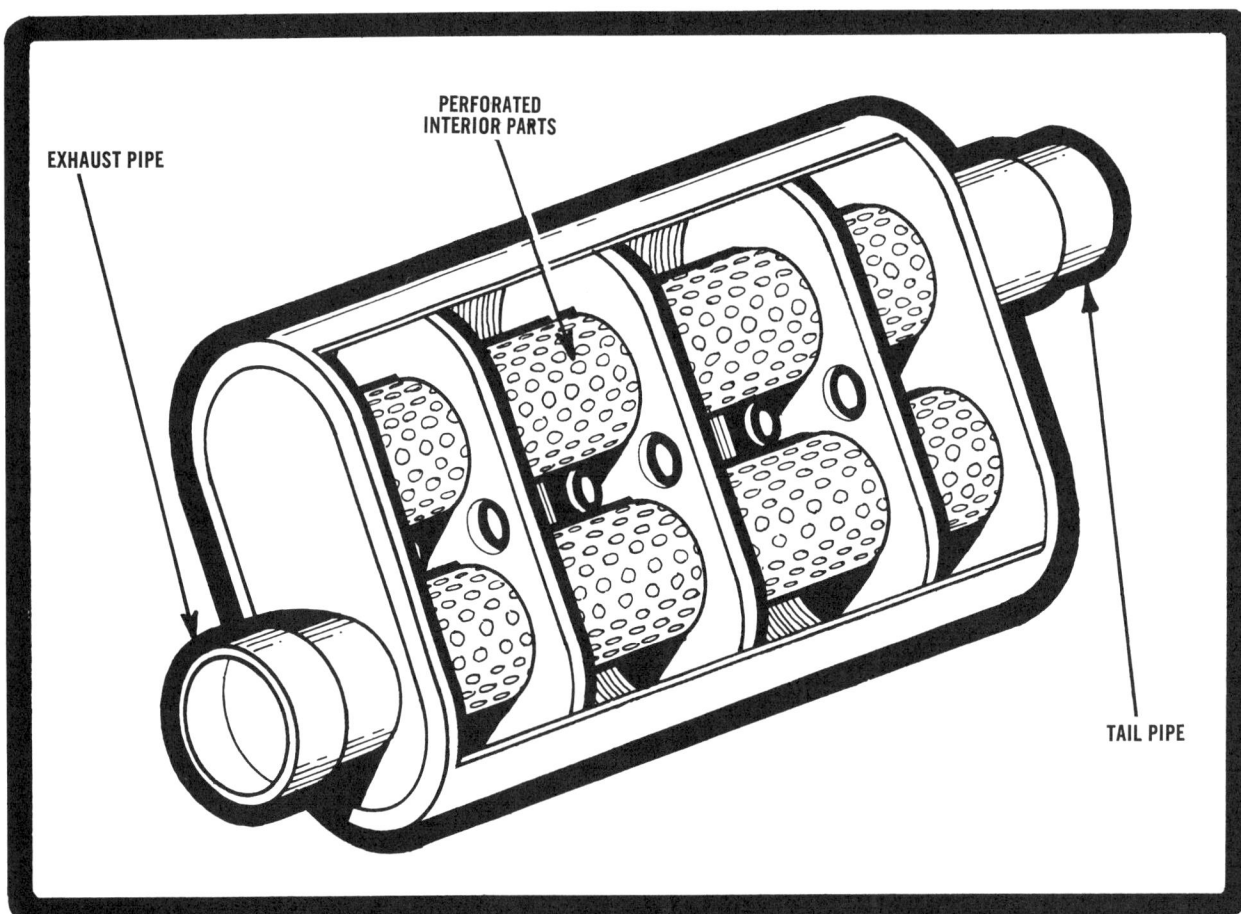

An internal view of a typical muffler illustrates how exhaust gases pass from the exhaust pipe to the tailpipe through sound deadening material. The gas flows through perforations, then through the sound deadener, which would normally be packed around the perforated pipes.

Many late model cars have an evaporative control system designed to prevent gasoline getting into the air through evaporation from the tank, fuel pump or carburetor.

Late model cars also have an exhaust gas recirculation system to accomplish the same purpose. The EGR system routes some of the exhaust gases back through the cylinders to burn up any pollutants that might have been missed the first time through.

Since 1974, most auto makers have been depending on a catalytic converter to help clean up the exhaust. A catalytic converter looks something like a muffler from the outside. It is mounted in the exhaust pipe usually ahead of the regular muffler. The converter does not muffle sound. Instead, it uses a chemical process to convert hydrocarbons and carbon monoxide into harmless carbon dioxide and water.

Positive crankcase ventilation

As a fireplace collects ashes, your engine collects waste material from the fire in the cylinders. Some unburned fuel, water vapor and other contaminants slip past the pistons and collect in the crankcase (the housing surrounding the crankshaft). If left there, these pollutants dilute engine oil and damage metal parts. So the crankcase must be ventilated to get rid of them. On older cars, a tube discharges fumes into the atmosphere. Modern cars have a system which recycles fumes back through the engine where they're burned off. The system is called positive crankcase ventilation, and the part that does this job is appropriately called the PCV valve. It's only the size of your thumb. But if it gets clogged, the system won't work. Rough idling, hard starting, and poor gas mileage can result.

These are the main emission control systems found on today's automobile. Of course, there are many other components and systems used to do the job of cleaning up exhaust emissions. However, they are so advanced technically that they are beyond the scope of this book.

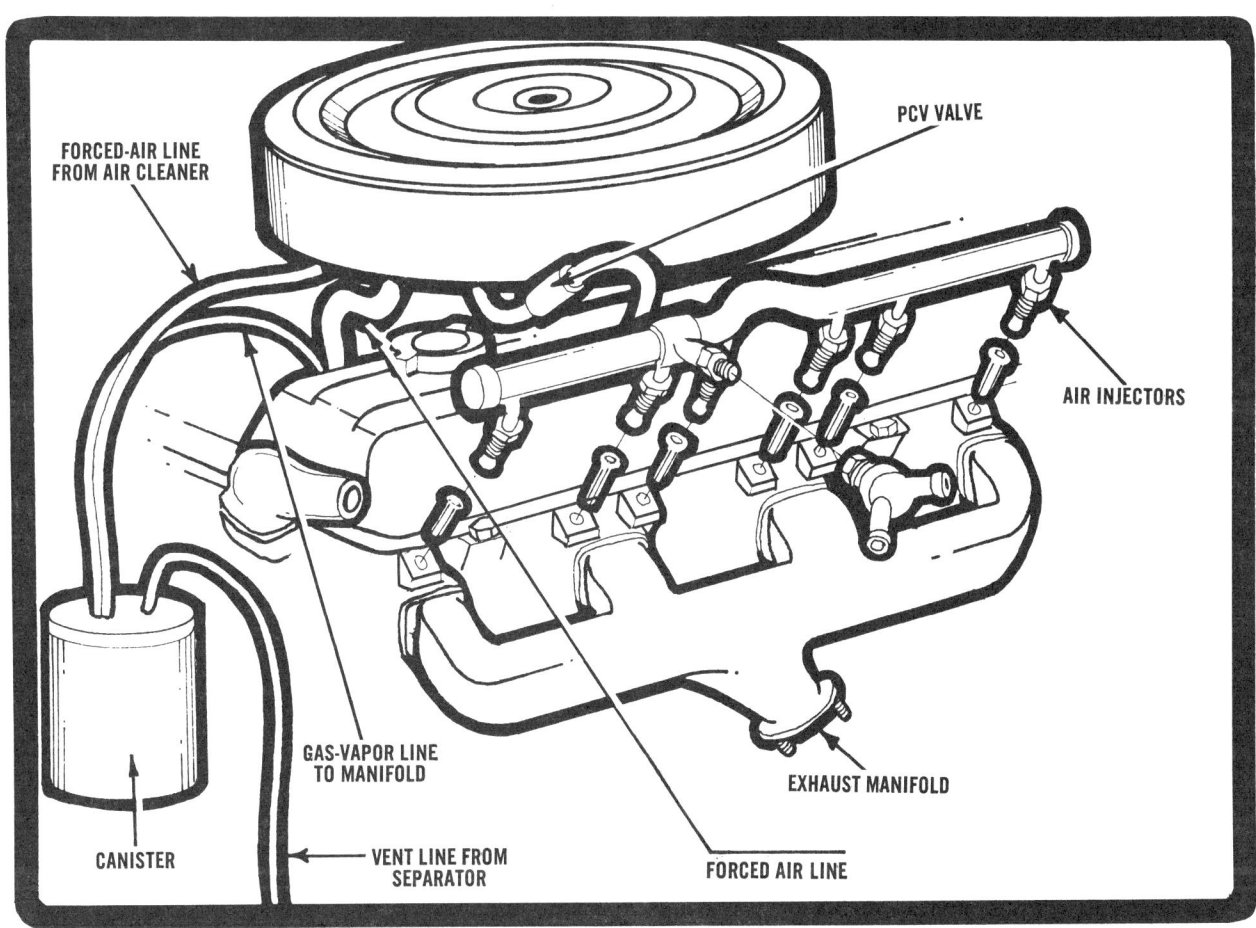

Typical exhaust emission controls found on many engines.

THE TRANSMISSION AND DRIVELINE SYSTEM

In this part of the chapter, we are going to try to explain what happens to the power after it leaves the engine. The engine furnishes us with a shaft turning around at a certain speed and with a certain force. What happens from there on? An automobile rolls itself along the ground. An airplane depends on the air to hold it up and make it move. A boat pushes on the water in order to go. They are all different but they all have much in common. They all start with power in one place and use it in another place. But a lot of things happen between the two places, and these are the things we are concerned with here.

Up until quite recently, about the only method of transmitting power to a vehicle was a shaft or straps to fasten it behind an animal. The wheels were only to make it easier to pull—they did not make it move. Not the earliest, but probably the simplest example of a vehicle carrying its own engine which turns a wheel to make it go is the bicycle. The engine of course is the rider. He makes the front sprocket, or gear, go around, which drives the chain, which makes the rear sprocket go around. This is fastened solidly to the wheel, so the wheel goes around, rolls along the ground, and moves the bicycle and rider with it. Here we have a familiar mechanism which is a definite example of generating power in one place and using it in another place.

But when the internal combustion engine, which has changed our lives in so many ways, came along, it brought some new problems with it. The internal combustion engine has certain fundamental characteristics which make it necessary to have rather complicated gearing in order to make an automobile do the things we want it to do. Power can be transmitted in various ways. But as it comes from the crankshaft of an engine, it is in the form of twist. The engine acts like a powerful giant turning a crank handle which exerts this twisting force on the shafts and gears which connect the engine to the wheels or propeller.

Let us see how this would work in a very simplified form of an automobile power transmission system. This system would not be very satisfactory for starting the car, or turning corners, or climbing hills, but for just driving along on a straight, level road it would be all right. There is a long shaft with one end fastened to the rear of the engine crankshaft, and on its other end, between the rear wheels, is a gear. Running from the center of one rear wheel to the other—fastened

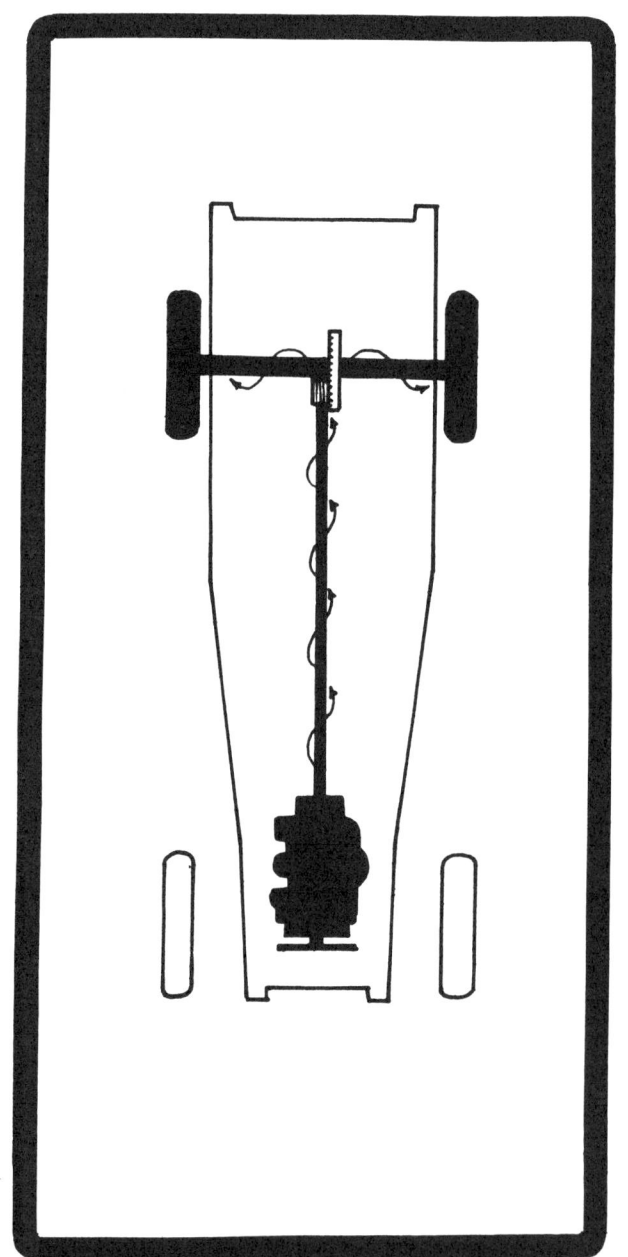

In a typical automobile, the engine's power must be transmitted from the engine to the rear wheels. Various components such as a driveshaft, gears and axles are used to do this job.

solidly to each—is the axle shaft. And at the center of this axle is fastened a circular gear with gear teeth on one side. The two gears fit together, so that as the propeller shaft turns, or twists, the axle turns also and causes the wheels to go around. As the wheels are resting solidly on the ground, we might say that they try to push the ground backward when they begin to turn. But the ground does not move—it is definitely going to stand still—so in order to turn, the wheels must roll forward. They necessarily move the car forward with them, and that is what we have been trying to do all the time.

As we said, this is a very much simplified arrangement. In fact about all we are doing is to make our path of power turn a corner. Or to be more accurate, perhaps we should say that our path splits and each half goes off at a right angle. Our only object is to get that twisting force of the crankshaft back to the rear of the vehicle and facing in a direction where it can twist the wheels. All we have been trying to do is get power from one place to another.

But that is only a part of most power transmission systems. And in many cases the least important part. We often use gears—or wheels, pulleys, etc.—for other purposes.

First, there is the question of **speed.** Suppose there is an engine running at one speed. But we have a machine we want to drive at half that speed. We can do this with gears. If we want the machine to run twice as fast as the engine, we can also do that—with different gears. We will see how a little later.

Second, there is **torque.** Webster says torque is "that which produces or tends to produce rotation or torsion." In everyday words, it is a force which tries to make something turn around. It is a **twist.** We can usually put the word "twist" in the place of "torque" and the meaning will be exactly the same. But the engineers prefer "torque."

We use gears to increase or reduce torque. We might have an engine connected directly to a machine by a solid shaft, and the engine could not produce enough torque, or twist, to turn that shaft and run the machine. By putting the right kind of gears between the engine and machine, we could increase the twisting force enough to run the machine.

Speed changes and torque changes are all mixed up together. Gear systems which change one will almost always change the other also. But before we get into the whys and wherefores of that, we are going to go back briefly to some of the fundamentals which form the basis for the whole thing. It may be old and familiar, but it will help explain a lot that follows.

Machines

There are a number of ways a man can increase the force he can apply with his own muscles. Some get to be rather complicated, but they are all made up of one or more simple machines. There are six of these machines. They are the lever, pully, wheel and axle, inclined plane, wedge, and screw. Let us look at them briefly, with particular attention to one or two which we are going to hear more about later.

We are all familiar with the **lever.** A teeter-totter furnishes an easy way to explain the principle of it. If a child is on one end and his father on the other, the child will go up and the heavier person down. But if his father moves closer to the center of the board, nearer and nearer the pivot point, there will come a time when the small weight of the child will raise the heavier person on the other side. If the father weighs twice as much as the child, they will just balance when the father is half as far from the pivot as the child is. That is **leverage,** or **mechanical advantage**—a weight in one place lifts a heavier weight in another place, or a force applied at one point of the lever produces a greater force at another point.

TORQUE IS TWIST

Torque is simply twisting energy.

The point of support, or the pivot point, is called the **fulcrum.** This may be between the two forces, as here, or at one end. And the forces or weights may be arranged in different ways.

We have examples of levers all around us. A pair of pliers pinches down on something with much more force than we apply with our fingers. With a crowbar we can lift more than we can lift direct. A nutcracker and a wheelbarrow are other levers in common use.

There are also examples of levers in which the force is decreased. We simply turn things the other way around. Fire tongs do not hold the chunk of coal as tightly as we are squeezing the handles. The fish end of a fish pole does not have the same force that we are supplying near the other end. Our own forearm is a good example of this type of lever. The muscle pulls at a point very close to the fulcrum, and the weight we are lifting is way out at the end.

There is one thing we should notice in all of these cases. When the force is increased, it does not move as far. We may move the handles of a pair of pliers an inch to get a movement of an eighth of an inch at the jaws. The long end of the crowbar moves several feet to move the weight a few inches. Looking at the other side of it, we can jerk a fish out of ten feet of water by moving our hands less than a foot. Whatever we gain in force, we sacrifice in distance, and vice versa.

There are many arrangements of **pulleys.** With the simple one shown here we can hold 100 pounds with a force of 50 pounds. Each rope supports 50 pounds. By arrangements of more pulleys and thus more supporting ropes, we can get a greater mechanical advantage than the 2 to 1 shown. However, we have the same condition we mentioned with the lever. If our 50 pound force moves 1 foot, it will raise the 100 pound weight only ½ foot.

The **wheel and axle** is usually just a wheel fastened to a rod, like the steering wheel of an automobile. A force applied to the outside of the big wheel produces a greater twisting force on the small rod than if we twisted the rod itself. Sometimes we use a handle instead of a wheel, a **crank,** but this does not change the principle. Take a crank and a rod with a rope around it and we have a windlass. The hand will move several feet in turning the crank once. This will turn the rod around once which will wind the rope up only a few inches. But it will lift a much greater weight than we could lift by pulling directly on the rope.

If a truck driver wants to get a barrel onto his truck, he lays a plank from the ground to the edge of the truck platform and rolls the barrel up. This plank is an **inclined plane.** He has to move the barrel a greater distance than he would by lifting it straight up, but it is a lot easier. He can get a barrel on the truck this way that he could not possibly lift.

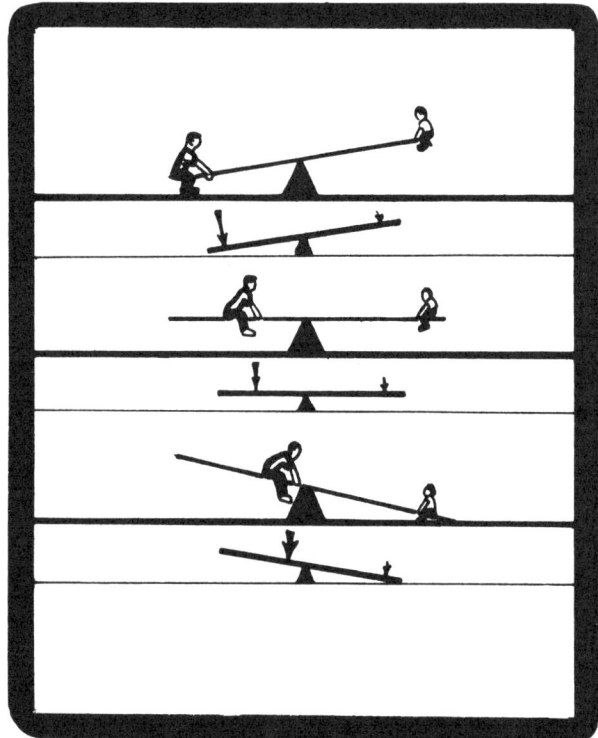

Positioning the fulcrum at various positions under the lever determines how much leverage or mechanical advantage can be derived.

A child's teeter-totter (see-saw) is an easy way to explain the principle of a lever.

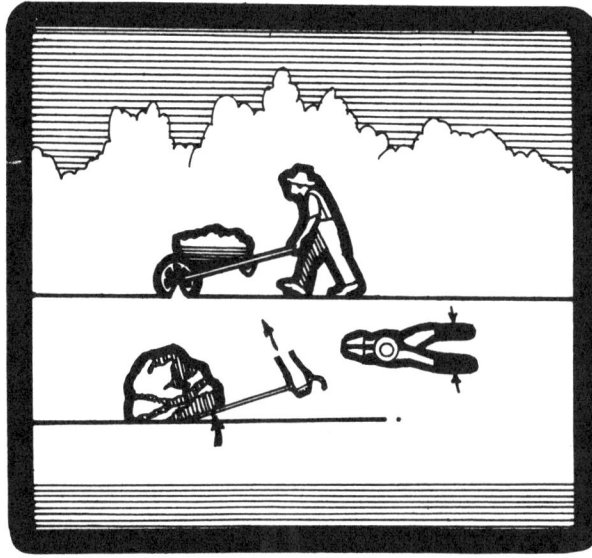

The lever principle is used constantly in our everyday lives.

The **wedge** is just a form of inclined plane. We push it under or between the objects to be moved instead of moving the object up the incline.

The **screw** is also a member of the same family. It is an inclined plane wrapped around a rod. As we follow the thread around the outside of the rod, we are continually going up hill. One complete turn of the screw moves the nut only the short distance between two threads. This distance is called the **pitch** of the screw. With a wood screw the action is just the same. Each turn of the screw moves it into the wood a distance equal to the pitch. The metal nut must have threads on the inside which will fit exactly the threads on the outside of the screw, but the wood screw cuts its own threads in the wood as it moves inward.

These few devices we have named are often combined in more complicated mechanisms, and sometimes it is difficult to recognize them as these same simple things. But if we take them apart and look them over carefully, we will find the familiar characteristics of the lever, the screw, or one of the others.

We will find also that these all really work on the same principle. That principle is that if we increase a force by means of one of these machines, that force cannot move as far as the original smaller force moves. As we have pointed out in each case, when we increase the force, we sacrifice distance. In text books, the formula says that *work equals force times distance.* And we cannot increase *work* by means of a lever. If we could, we would have perpetual motion. So the work remains the same, and if force increases, distance decreases, and vice versa.

The action of gears—the principle on which they work—is exactly the same as this. But before we get into that, let us see what a gear is, and what different kinds there are.

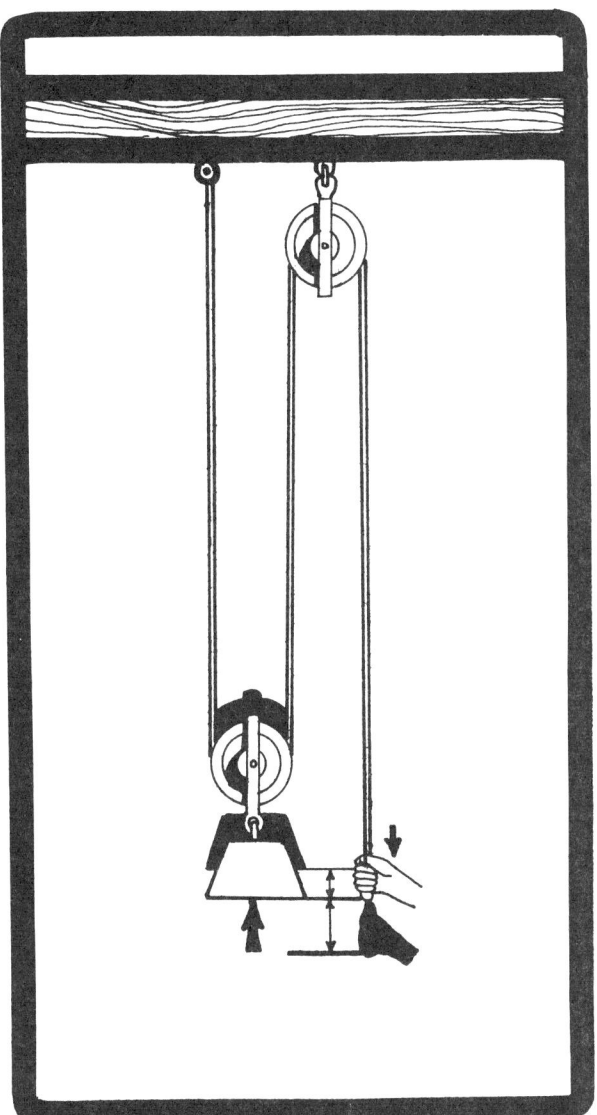

Pulleys are another method of gaining a mechanical advantage and making work easier.

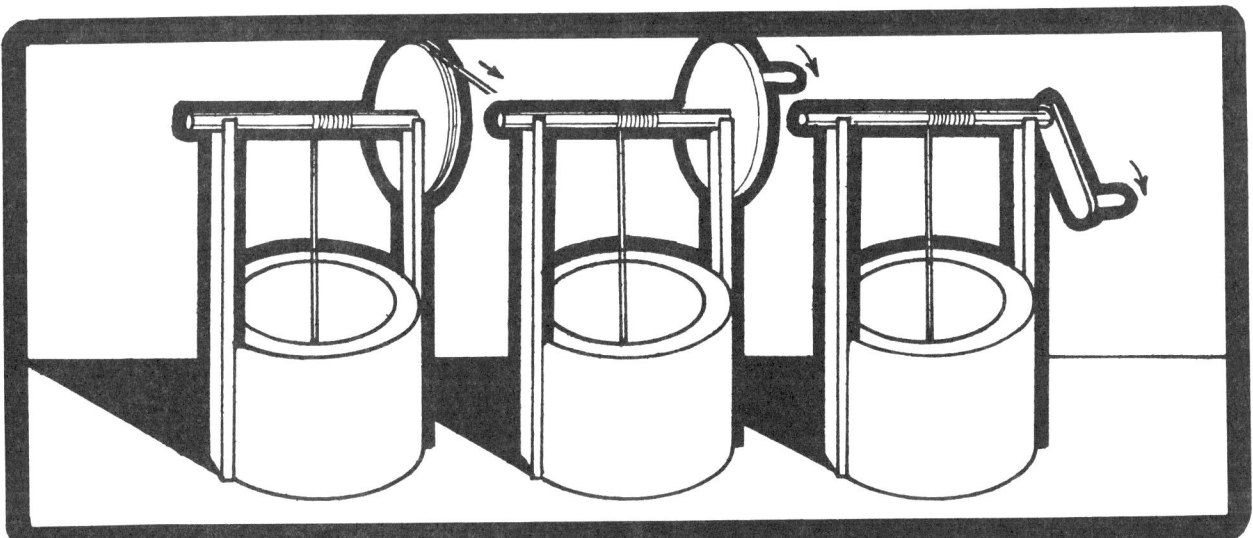

The wheel and axle is an ancient method of gaining a mechanical advantage. It is, of course, used on every automobile.

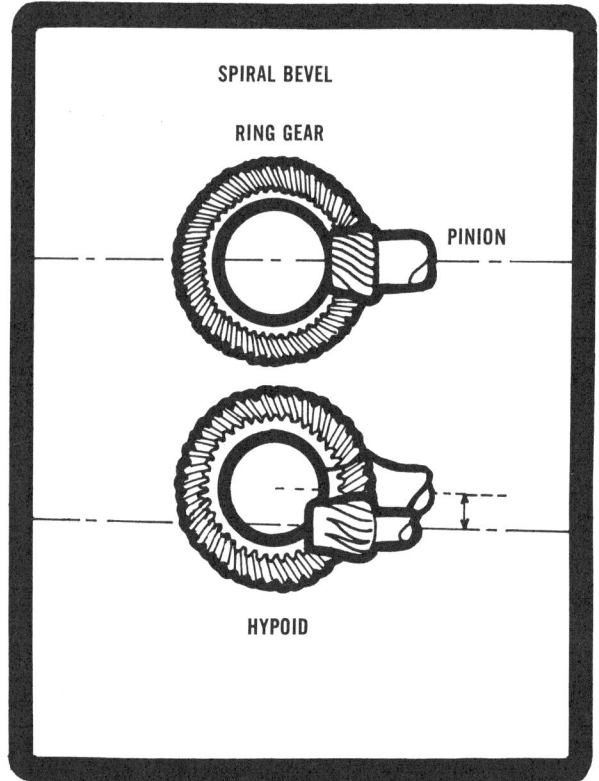

The wedge is just another form of an inclined plane.

Most final drives (commonly called rear axles) use hypoid, ring and pinion gears.

GEARS AND GEARING

What is a gear?

A gear is a wheel with bumps or projections on it called **teeth.** These teeth may be on the edge, on the side, or halfway between. Incidentally we no longer talk about **cog wheels** and **cogs**—they are **gears** and **gear teeth.** A gear is usually fastened to a shaft. Sometimes it turns and applies a twisting force to the shaft, and sometimes the shaft is turning and turns the gear with it.

The simplest type of gear is the **spur** gear. This has its teeth cut straight across the edge. For years it was almost universal, but recently other types have become more common in the transportation field.

Another type is the **helical** gear. This is the same as the spur gear, but its teeth are cut at an angle. The teeth of the gear it meshes with must of course be cut at the same angle. It is usually quieter than the ordinary spur gear, and for that reason is preferred for many uses. For the same reason we sometimes use **herringbone** gears. This is like two helical gears fastened together tightly side by side.

When our power must turn a corner, we ordinarily use a **bevel** gear. The teeth of this gear are not cut on the edge. They are cut, we might say, across the corner. Sometimes it is a spur bevel gear, with straight teeth, but it is more likely to be a **spiral bevel** gear. This is somewhat like a helical gear, except that the teeth, in addition to being set at an angle, are also curved.

We are going to leave out all the technical terms we can, but there is one we had better explain. **Pitch diameter** is the diameter of the **pitch circle.** The pitch circle is a purely imaginary line running through the gear teeth at a point usually a little outside the half way point of the tooth. The easiest way to define it is to suppose we have two smooth rollers running together instead of toothed gears. They are of such a size that they run at exactly the same speeds as the gears. In such a case the pitch diameter of a gear would be the same as the diameter of the corresponding roller. From now on, when we speak of the size of a gear we will mean the pitch diameter, as that is what really determines its speed and other characteristics.

There is still another way of classifying gears. They can be **external** or **internal.** To the ordinary person the word "gear" will always bring to mind a picture of an external gear, and he will be right ninety-nine times out of a hundred. But internal gears do play an important part in some mechanisms, as we will see later. An internal gear is simply a ring with teeth cut on the inside instead of the outside. To mesh with it we must have an external gear of smaller size.

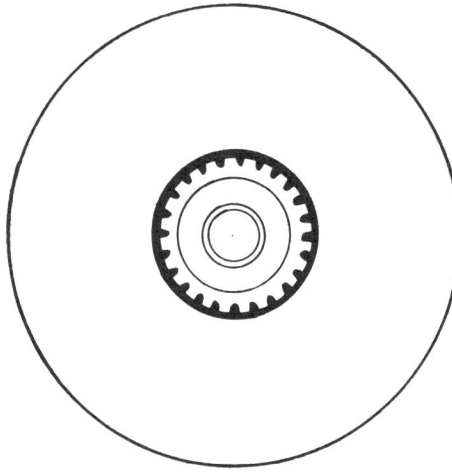

A gear is simply a wheel with bumps or projections on it. The projections are called gear teeth.

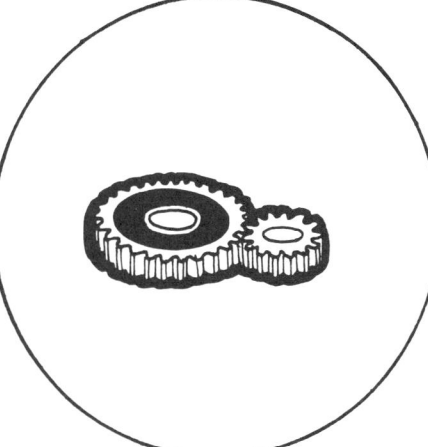

The simplest type of gear is the spur gear. The teeth are cut straight across the edge of the gear.

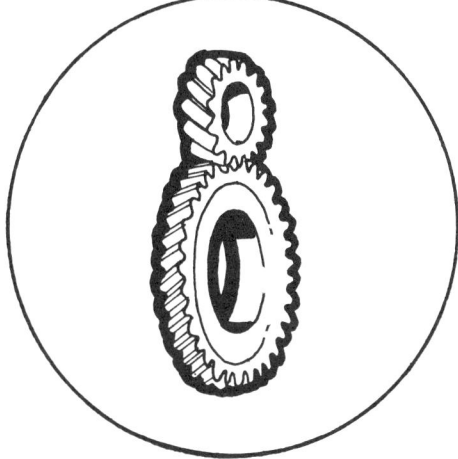

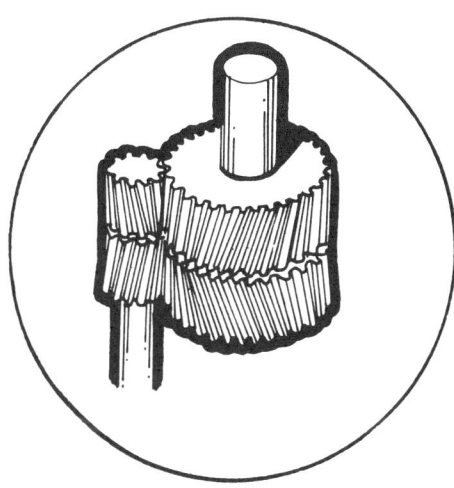

Helical gears have their teeth cut at an angle.

Herringbone gears are like two helical gears tightly fastened together side by side.

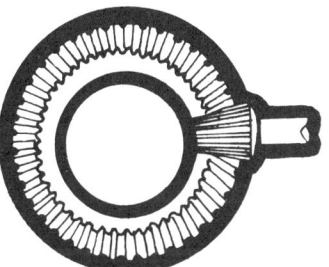

Bevel gears allow power to go around corners or change direction.

What does a gear do?

A gear is a spinning lever. It can increase or decrease torque in exactly the same way that a lever increases or decreases force. If you are interested in the explanation of this, more details are given further on. But these details are not necessary in order to understand what gears do and why we use them. The main thing to remember is that if we have a small gear fastened on one shaft driving a bigger gear on another shaft, the torque of the second shaft will be increased. The second shaft will have more twisting force than the first shaft. If we have an engine driving the small gear, our system now will be able to turn something—say a machine of some sort—that the engine could not turn when they were connected directly together.

The amount the torque is increased depends on the relative size of the gears. If the diameter—pitch diameter—of the second gear is twice the diameter of the first gear, the torque will be doubled. If the second gear is three times as big as the torque will be three times as much, etc. But if the *driving* gear is twice as big as the *driven* gear, the output torque will be cut down to ½ the input torque.

We can also think of a gear as another class of simple machine—the wheel and axle. A force applied at the outside edge of a gear, that is, where the teeth are, will exert a twist on the shaft. And the bigger the gear is, the greater will be this twist. With equal forces on the teeth of two gears, the shaft of the larger gear will have the greater torque. This is what we have when two gears are in mesh and one is driving the other.

In all this we have to remember one thing. We are not getting this increased torque for nothing. We are not discoverers of perpetual motion and claiming that we get more power out of the engine because we have added some gears to the system. We are still dealing with levers and they still follow the same rules. With levers we said that *whatever we gain in force we lose in distance.* When talking about gears and shafts we say, *whatever we gain in torque we lose in speed.* The two statements are not exactly the same, but we can think of them that way for the moment.

An internal gear is simply a ring with teeth cut on the inside instead of the outside.

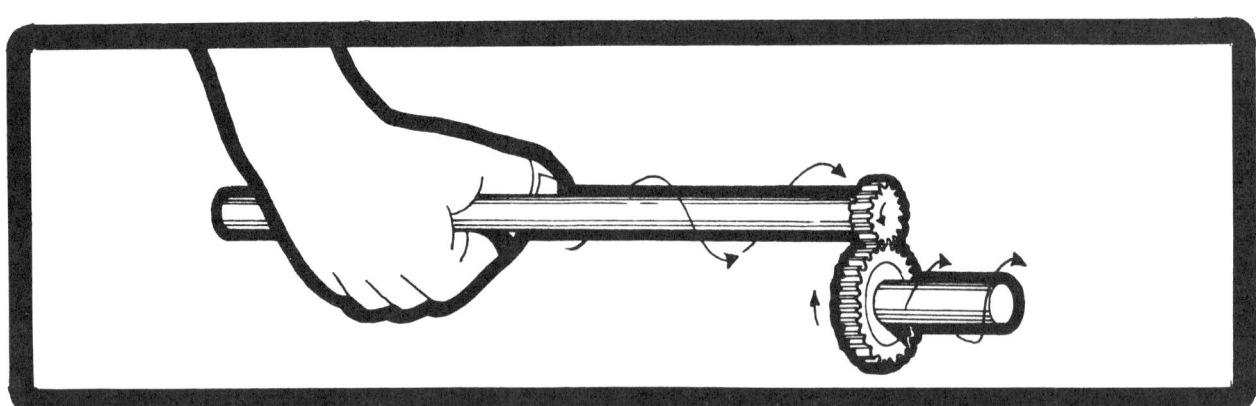

If small gear is fastened on shaft and drives larger gear on another shaft, the torque of second shaft will be increased.

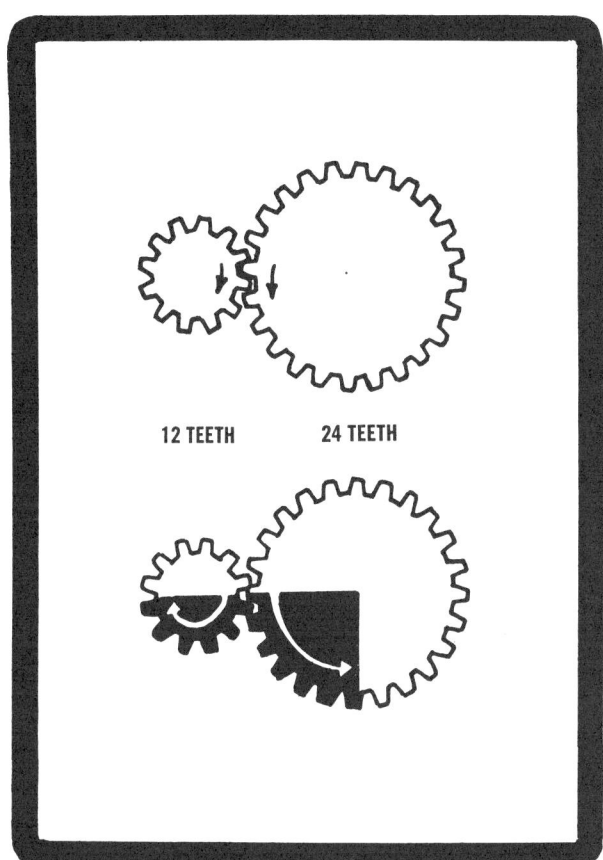

Whatever is gained in torque using gear multiplication, is lost in speed.

The best way to show this is to count the number of teeth on two gears. The teeth must all be the same size in order to fit together properly. Therefore if the diameter of one gear is twice the diameter of the other, the big one must have twice as many teeth as the small one. Let us say 24 and 12 teeth respectively. As the small one, the driving gear, goes all the way around once, its 12 teeth have meshed with 12 teeth of the larger gear. That means the large one has turned around only halfway. The small one has to go around again before the large one completes one revolution. So, for every two revolutions of the small driving gear the large driven gear revolves once. And for every 1000 revolutions of the small one the large one has made 500 revolutions. So, if an engine driving the small gear is running at a speed of 1000 revolutions per minute (rpm), the machine driven by the large gear is turning over only 500 rpm. We have doubled the torque furnished by the engine. We have increased the twist on the second shaft so now it can turn the machine when perhaps it could not before. But the machine turns only half as fast as it would if it were directly connected to the engine.

A force applied at the outside edge of a gear will exert a twist on the shaft. The bigger the gear, the greater will be this twist.

The gear with the greater number of teeth will always run more slowly and produce greater torque.

Counting the number of teeth on gears is usually easier than measuring the pitch diameter. And as we have just shown it will give us the same information concerning the gear ratio. That is, the amount of change in torque and speed. If the driving gear has 10 teeth and the driven gear 30 teeth, it will take three revolutions of the first to get the second all the way around through one revolution. Thus the speed of the driven gear will be ⅓ the speed of the driving gear, and we know from this that the torque will be multiplied by 3. We would say that the gear ratio was 30/10 or 3 to 1. This applies equally as well if we have an odd combination of numbers, such as 39 and 19, only it is not so easy to do the mathematics in our head. The gear ratio would be 39/19, or a little over 2 to 1.

The gear with the greater number of teeth will always run more slowly and will produce the greater torque.

Sometimes we are glad to have this reduction in speed along with the torque increase. In fact the main purpose of the gears in some mechanisms is to act as speed reducers. In other cases we need both more

In this example, the engine is connected to the top shaft and is running at 1000 rpm. The gearing cuts the speed of the second shaft to 500 rpm, which means that gear C is also turning at 500 rpm. Between gears C and D, the speed is halved again but the torque is doubled once more. So the last shaft, which is driving the machine, is turning at only 250 rpm. But the torque has been multiplied four times. So the overall ratio of the whole system is 4 to 1.

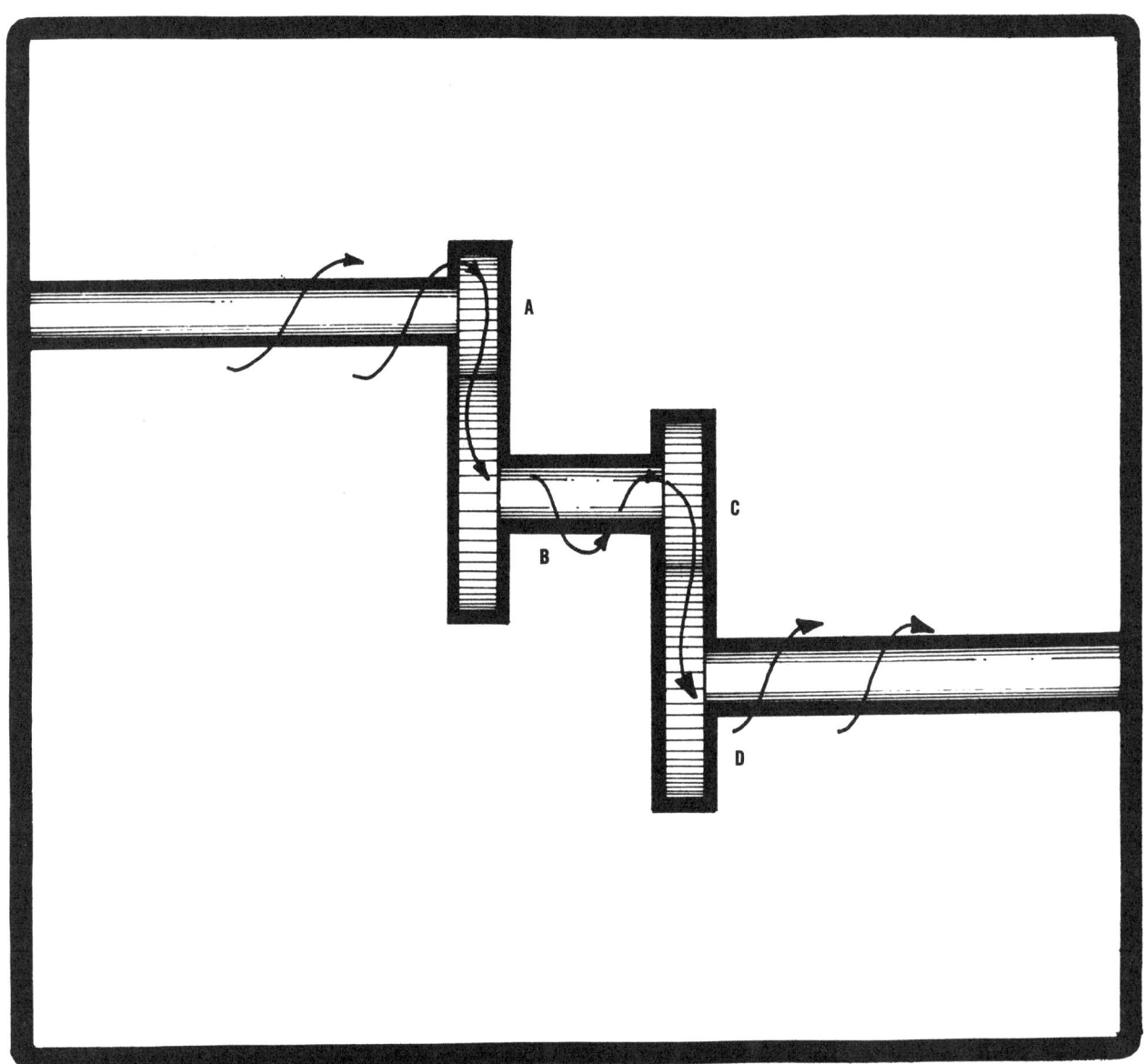

torque and less speed, so we gain both ways. On the other hand, sometimes we may wish to increase the speed. Maybe we have a machine that has to run at 2000 rpm and an engine running at 1000 rpm. In that case we use a gear ratio of 2 to 1 again, but we have to put the large gear on the engine shaft and the small one on the machine shaft. The torque will be cut in half, but if the engine has enough power to drive the machine under those conditions, the machine will run at the required speed of 2000 rpm. But we cannot eat our cake and have it too. If we need both more torque and more speed, there is nothing we can do about it—except get more power from the engine.

What we have been saying is really the same thing as is expressed by the formula found in textbooks— that *power equals torque times speed*. The gears cannot change the power. That stays the same. Therefore if the torque increases, the speed must decrease. If the speed goes up, the torque must go down.

NOTE: Everything said thus far has to do with gear mechanisms all by themselves, or we might say, with gear mechanisms driven by an engine which is running at *constant speed and constant power*. The statements are not necessarily true when applied to the overall mechanism as in an automobile where the speed and torque of the engine can change at any time. But even there, if we consider it at any one moment, the same rules apply.

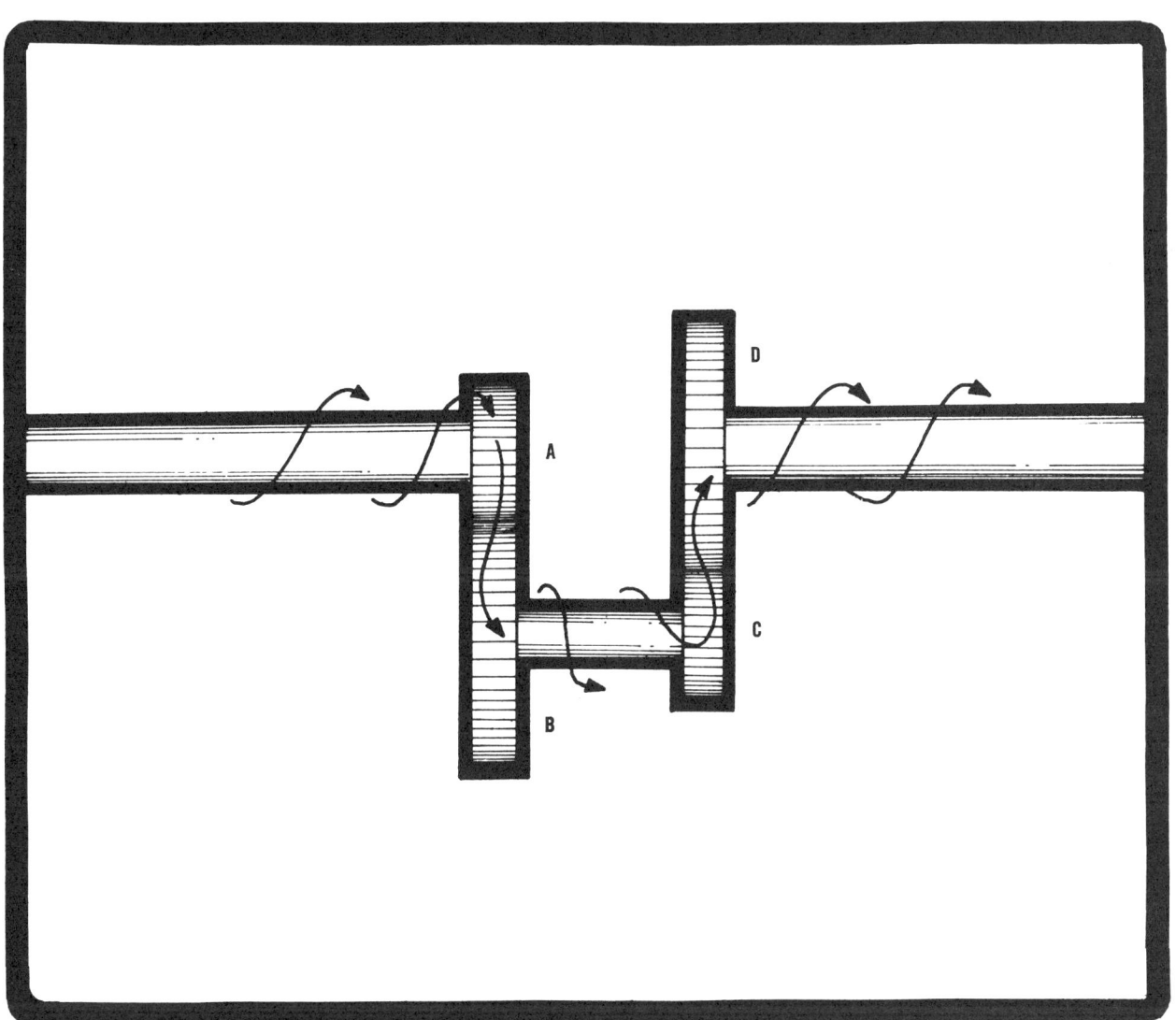

In actual practice, the gears would be arranged with the third shaft above the second, as in this illustration. This puts the first and third shafts directly in line. Since there is less wasted motion, it is a more efficient arrangement. What we have here now is really a simplified arrangement of a conventional automobile transmission.

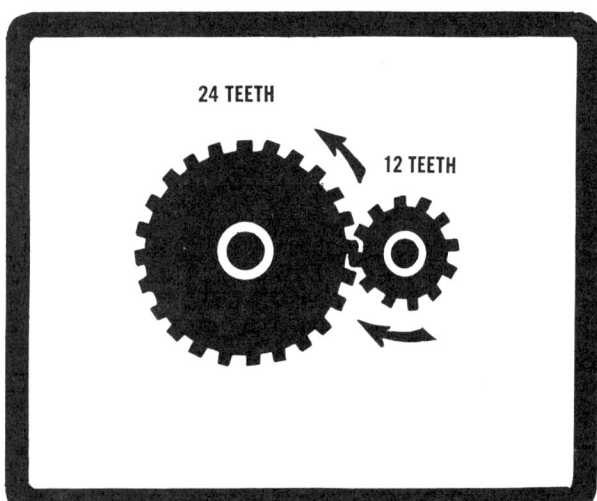

The large gear revolves at one-half speed of small gear.

In some mechanisms we have more than two gears between the input and output. A clock or watch—which incidentally was one of the very early users of gears—is a good example of multiple gears in series. Even the cheapest alarm clock sometimes astounds us by the number of gears inside it.

But suppose we look at something simpler to begin with. We will go back to our same two gears with 12 and 24 teeth and add another pair of gears to the system. These are just like the first two—12 and 24 teeth respectively—and the small gear C is fastened on the same shaft as large gear B. Now let us follow the path of the power flowing through this gear train. The engine is connected to the top shaft and is still running at 1000 rpm. We already know what happens with the first two gears. The speed is cut in half and the torque doubled. So our second shaft is turning only 500 rpm, which means that gear C is turning at that same speed. Now we can forget about the first two gears and consider only C and D. We know what happens there too, because they are just the same gears with a ratio of 2 to 1. Our speed will be halved again and the torque doubled once more. So our last shaft, which is driving the machine, is turning at only 250 rpm, but it is applying to the machine a torque or twist 4 times as much as that delivered by the engine. The over-all ratio of the whole system is 4 to 1.

In any simple case such as this we can get the same effect by using only two gears of the proper ratio. Sometimes, however, there is too great a difference to be efficient, and sometimes it is a matter of convenience or space saving. In actual practice we ordinarily would not arrange the gears as we have here. We would save room by moving the third shaft up above the second. The result would be exactly the same, and we would have the added advantage that the first and third shafts would be directly in line. What we really have here now is a simplified arrangement of a conventional automobile transmission. The third shaft would extend back to the rear axle to drive the wheels.

There is another feature using four gears here instead of two which is sometimes an advantage. And this brings up a characteristic of gears which has probably been self-evident but which we have not mentioned. It has to do with direction of rotation. Looking at a pair of gears it is easy to see that if one shaft rotates in one direction, the other must rotate in the opposite direction. If one runs clockwise, the other must go counter-clockwise. This may be a nuisance in some installations, and in some others it may be just what we want. Sometimes gears are used in order to reverse the direction of rotation and for no other reason. But if we want the output shaft to run the same way as the input shaft, we must use at least three gears. Or, we can use a combination of more gears such as we have just been discussing. To find out which way the final shaft runs in any complicated system of gearing, the best procedure is to go through the whole system and figure out which way each gear turns. And do not forget the exception to the above—when an ordinary external gear is driving an internal gear, both shafts will rotate in the same direction.

We should point out one more thing before we leave this subject. If we consider the gear system of any wheeled vehicle, we must consider the wheels themselves. The size of the wheels has just as much to do with the overall drive ratio as do the gears. It is the backward force the wheel exerts on the ground which makes the vehicle go, and if we have a certain torque or twist on the wheel shaft, this force at the ground depends on the size of the wheel. The larger the wheel, the less the force.

As an example, let us look at the bicycle. And let us look first at the bicycle as it was back in the 1890s. That was the great high front wheel with the rider perched on top of it. The size of the front wheel was a matter of much pride and argument in those days. A 56-inch wheel was fairly good. But a long-legged person who could straddle a 60-inch wheel really had something to brag about.

Why was the wheel made so big? It is very simple. They used a big wheel instead of using gears. The pedals were connected directly to the hub of the wheel, so every time the rider's feet went around once the wheel went around once. With a wheel of the size used today that would mean that the bicycle would move forward about 7 feet. But one revolution on that big wheel would roll it forward about 15 feet. This meant that pedalling at the same speed would make the high-wheeler go twice as fast. It might be harder to get started and tough-going on hills, but speed was what counted.

Eventually the "safety" bike became popular and is now the only kind of bicycle we know. It was objected to at first as being too complicated, but it was really very simple. The driving wheel was reduced to about half its former size and gears were used to give the rider the same effect he had before. Let us say we have 20 teeth on the front gear and 10 teeth on the back gear. We can disregard the chain because all that is for is to allow us to separate the gears. As far as the ratio is concerned we can think of the gears as meshing together directly. So we have a ratio of 1 to 2. The back gear will revolve twice as fast as the front gear, and thus the wheel will go around twice each time the pedals go around once. This gives us exactly the same result as if the wheel were twice as big and the pedals connected directly to it. The gears have cut the torque in half, but the driving wheel is only half the size of the big wheel, so the force between the wheel and the ground is the same in both cases.

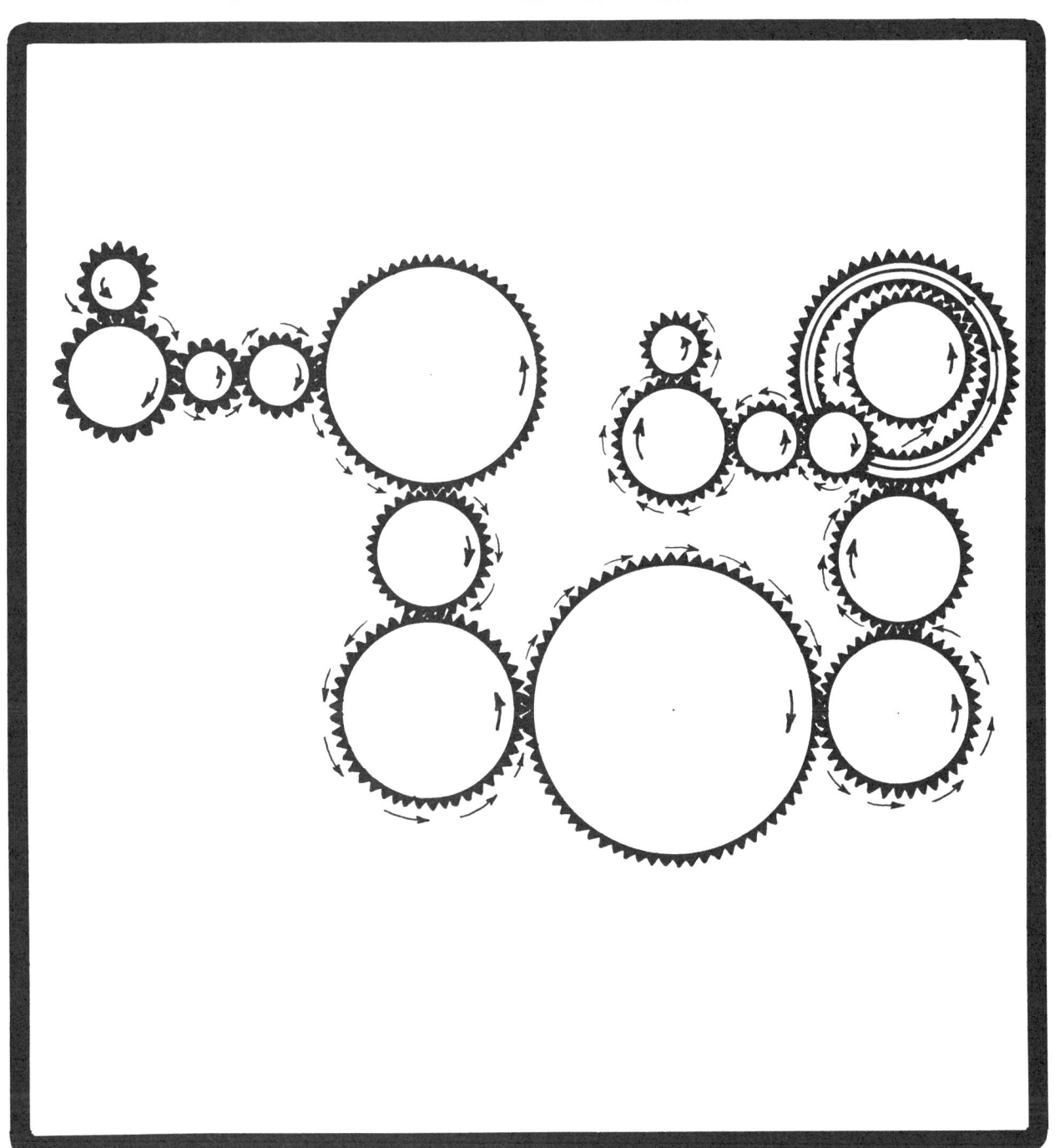

By using different combinations of different types of gears, the transmittal of power can be infinitely variable.

TRANSMISSIONS

The question might be raised, "Why use a transmission anyway? If any gain in torque is at the expense of speed, and vice versa, why not just put in an engine of the proper size and use only the gears necessary to get the power to where we need it?"

This argument might hold good for certain conditions. But where we have an internal combustion engine driving a vehicle, there are two things against it. One, the power necessary to make the vehicle go is very changeable. And two, the power delivered by the engine is also very changeable, depending on conditions.

When we are considering an automobile, quite a lot of force is used to get it started, to get it moving. Less force is needed to keep it moving at a moderate speed. A lot of force is needed again to drive it at very high speeds, force to overcome the resistance of the air and road. And of course, the hills. So it is easy to see that we never know from one moment to the next just what force is going to be necessary at the wheels.

And if we consider the characteristics of the engine, it is easy to see that we do not always get the power from it when we want it. We just said we needed a lot of force to get started, when the vehicle is standing still or moving very slowly. And that is just the time that the engine does not furnish very much power. One of the fundamentals of internal combustion engines is that they must run fairly fast before they can produce much power. They do not twist that shaft very hard when they are turning over slowly.

But if we put the right kind of gears in there we can kill two birds with one stone. The gears in an automobile let the engine run at high speed while the wheels are turning slowly, and at the same time they themselves increase the torque which is being delivered by the engine. Thus the transmission is responsible for more twist on the propeller shaft due to letting the engine run faster and deliver more power, and then it increases that twist still more by its multiplication of torque. So for starting, this arrangement is fine. But it is not so good for higher speeds, and that is why automobiles have some means for changing the gear ratio, depending on the load and speed of the car and the judgment of the driver.

It is possible to drive a car without ever shifting gears if we are careful to stay on hard level roads and if we do not object to other cars going by us and leaving us behind at traffic signals. But of course, conditions such as these do not exist in the real world. So we need a variable speed transmission to tailor the engine's torque to any given vehicle requirement.

Friction

There is one factor which always enters into the transmission of power which we have neglected thus far. That is **friction**. Friction has its good points and its bad points. We would have difficulty doing a great many things if there were no friction in the world. Try walking without it, for example. The only reason an automobile moves is because of the friction between the tires and the road. An automobile clutch depends entirely on friction.

But in transmitting power, most of the effects of friction that we think about and talk about are the troublesome ones. That is probably because they are the ones we have to do something about. Whenever two gears are running together, there is some friction. This means that some of the power is used up—wasted—in overcoming that friction. A shaft running in a bearing creates friction, which means more wasted power. And if there is too much of this friction in any one place, it means that the part will get very hot. And this may result in swelling up and sticking and all sorts of damage.

So we have to do the same things that are done in almost every moving mechanism. We have to use bearings to cut down the friction of all rotating shafts, and we have to furnish lubrication to these bearings and to the gears.

A little oil makes all the difference in the world in the amount of friction. A thin film of oil—no matter how thin—permits two metal surfaces of the right kind to rub against each other for very long periods with little wear and no damage. There are various ways used to get this lubricant to the right place. Sometimes a pump forces oil under pressure to the points needing it. It circulates all the time the mechanism is running. Many parts are oiled by the mist and spray splashed up by gears churning up the oil in the bottom of the case. Other points are packed permanently with grease, or have means to force grease into them every so often.

Plain bearings are used in many places—that is, bearings in which a metal shaft runs inside a metal ring of special bearing material. But in transmission systems we use a number of **anti-friction bearings.** These are **ball bearings, roller bearings**, and **needle bearings.** They have let us do things which without them would have been difficult and complicated, if not impossible. They have had a lot to do with the high speeds at which shafts and gears now run.

Early bicycles had extremely large front wheels. For every turn of the pedals, the wheel made one revolution. On more modern bicycles, the pedals revolve once for every two revolutions of the rear wheel.

In all our discussions so far we have not taken friction into account at all. All our mechanisms were perfect machines, with no losses due to friction. Friction is a variable factor and hard to pin down. Bearings and lubrication are a very important subject, but too large a subject to cover here. So in our discussion, we will just assume that the mechanism has proper bearings and is well lubricated in some way or other.

So far we have given just a general picture of the field of power transmission in vehicles using internal combustion engines, and have tried to point out the whys and wherefores of some of the arrangements. Essentially the problem is that we need a force to move the vehicle and we have an engine which must furnish that force. But the complication comes in because these are not always equal. The engine does not always furnish the right amount of torque at the right speed. So we must put something in between which can take the torque and speed of the engine and change them so they will come as close as possible to what the wheels or propeller need at that moment.

We compromise very often. Usually we do not try to make it too exact under all conditions because the mechanism becomes too complicated and expensive. And luckily the internal combustion engine is flexible enough to cover a wide range of conditions.

THE DRIVELINE

In an automobile there are a lot of things between the engine and the rear wheels. Some kinds of cars have more, others have less. Some have one thing, others have something else. They all have more than the simplified system we showed in the early part of this text. As we said, that might be all right for driving straight ahead on a level road. But there would be a lot of places where it would not be all right. So we will start out here with a complete power transmission system of a typical automobile. We will explain briefly what each part does, without much attention to how it does it, and we may take liberties with what it looks like. Later on we will take up the more important parts individually and go into greater detail.

Starting from the engine, the first thing we come to is the **clutch.** Its job is to disconnect the engine from the power transmission system when the driver so desires. When it is disengaged, the driving and driven plates are separated, and what the engine does has no effect on the rest of the drive system and what the wheels are doing has no effect on the engine. There are several reasons we want to be able to do that at certain times and under certain conditions.

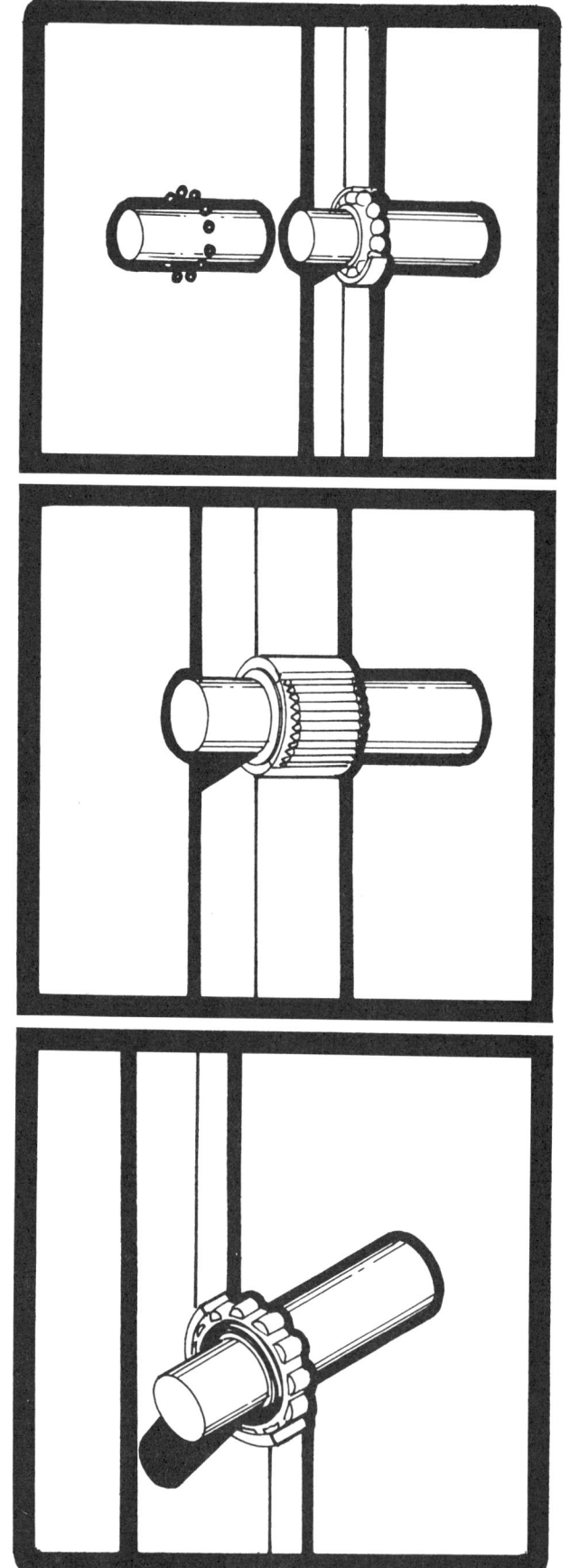

There are many different types of bearings used in transmissions to cut friction. Shown here, top to bottom, is a typical ball bearing, needle bearing and roller bearing.

Next is the **transmission.** The reason for calling it this is not too clear. "Torque converter" or the English expression "gear set" gives us a better idea of what it is and what it does. But everyone still calls it "transmission." Its purpose is to let us change the ratio between the engine and the rear wheels. When the car is starting we can run the engine fast and drive the wheels slowly, increasing the torque or driving force at the same time. When we are going faster we can change the ratio, so that the wheels are turning at more nearly the same speed as the engine. Finally, in direct drive, the shaft behind the transmission is connected directly to the shaft from the clutch, and it is just as if the transmission were not there at all. There is also a reverse gear in the transmission, so that we can make the car go backward, and a neutral position, in which no movement or power is transmitted.

From the transmission, the **propeller shaft,** or driveshaft, runs back to the rear of the car. This is a hollow or solid steel shaft, sometimes enclosed in an outer tube, sometimes left open. At the front end is a **universal joint,** and in many cars there is another universal joint at the rear end of the shaft.

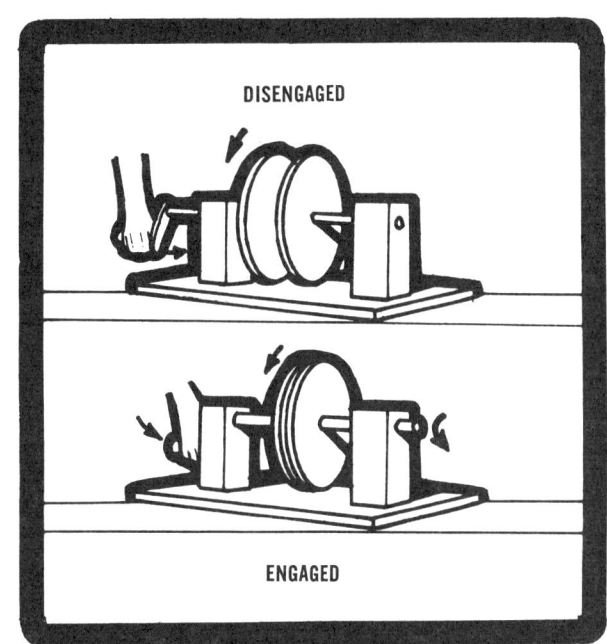

This simplified illustration shows how the component parts of a clutch interreact when disengaged and engaged.

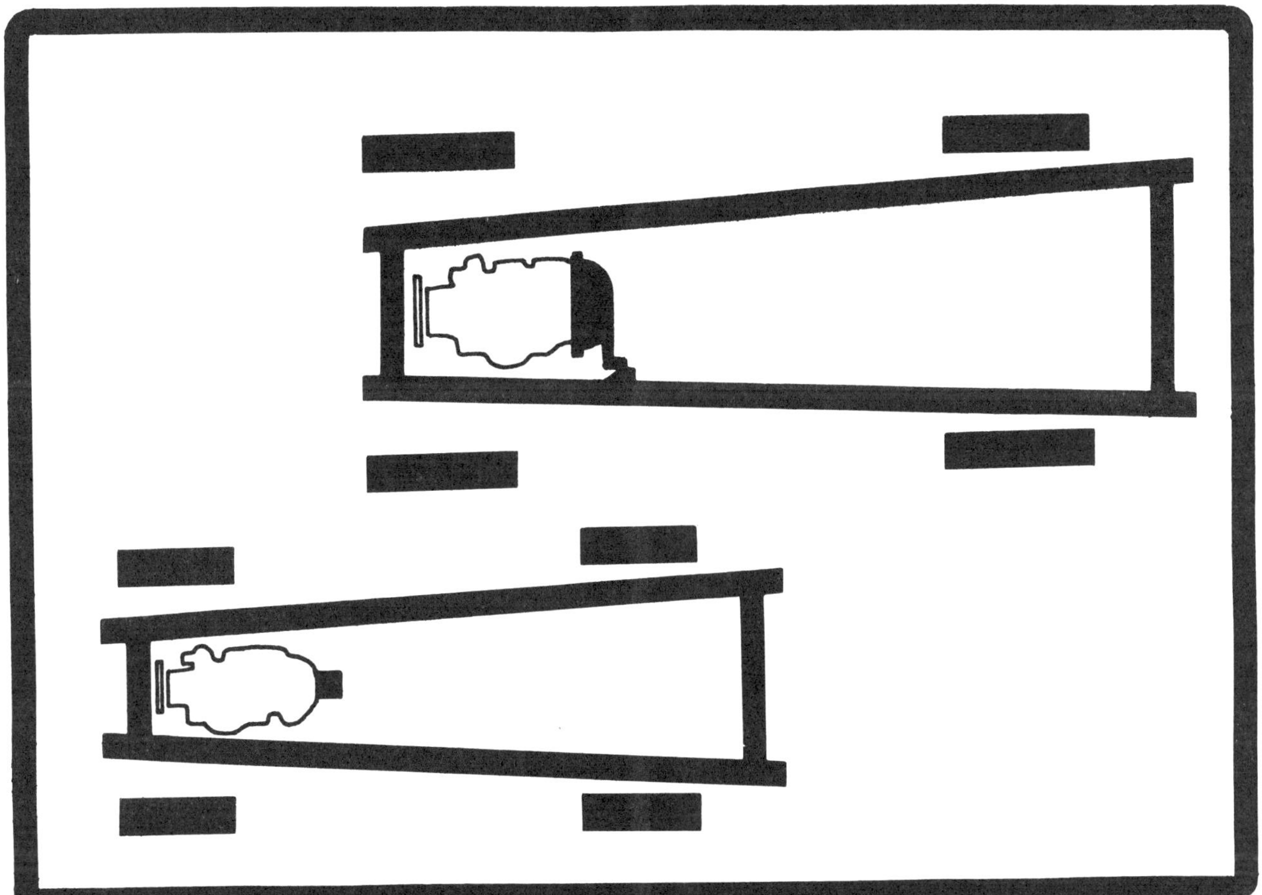

The clutch and transmission are connected to the engine and located directly behind it.

These are usually made up of two U-shaped pieces at right angles to each other and fastened together by a cross having arms at equal length. The U-shaped yokes can pivot on the arms of the cross, and inasmuch as there are two of these pivots, the two shafts can be at an angle to one another and can still turn around and transmit power. They do not have to be in a straight line. This is very important, because even if we could design the car to have them in a straight line to begin with, every time we went over a bump they would get out of line. The rear axle moves with the wheels, up and down with every bump, while the transmission does not move so much, being fastened to the frame. So the universal joint lets the propeller shaft keep on turning even though its two ends are moving around relative to each other.

At the rear end of the propeller shaft is fastened a short shaft carrying a gear on the end. This is a bevel gear and is called the **pinion.** It meshes with the **ring gear** which is mounted on the rear axle. Thus as the propeller shaft turns, the pinion drives the ring gear around which turns the rear axle and the wheels. This pinion and ring gear combination is often called the **final drive.**

For many years these rear axle gears were of the spiral bevel type. But now most cars use what are called **hypoid** gears. They are about the same as spiral bevel gears, except that the pinion does not meet the ring gear at its center line. It meets it at a lower point, which means that the shape of the teeth must be different. This allows us to lower the whole propeller shaft, which in turn lets us make the whole car lower.

It is easy to see that the pinion is much smaller than the ring gear so we know immediately that there is a speed reduction here, and an increase in torque. In most passenger cars, this ratio is somewhere around 4 to 1. The axles and wheels are turning only about a quarter as fast as the propeller shaft. It should be noted that this speed reduction and torque increase are always there and always stay the same. Even when we say we are in direct drive we are referring only to the transmission, and this rear axle ratio is still effective. And if the transmission is in low gear, say a ratio of 3 to 1, the overall ratio between the engine and rear wheels will be 3 x 4, or 12 to 1.

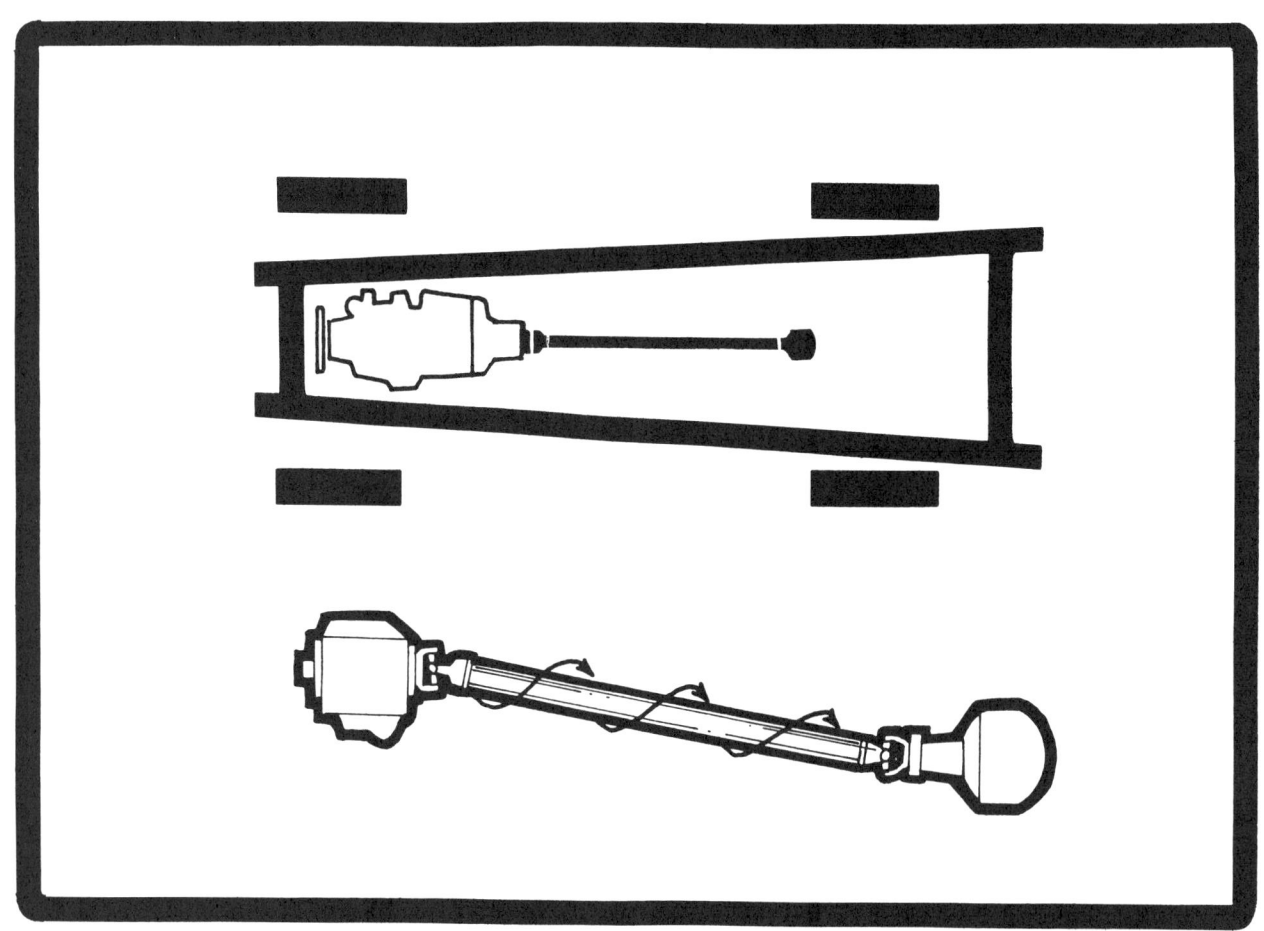

The driveshaft connects the transmission to the rear axle assembly and transmits the engine's power through it.

In the simplified automobile drive system which we showed in the first part of this text, the ring gear was fastened directly to a solid axle which ran from one wheel to the other. This would be all right for going straight. But when the car turns a corner, we have a problem. The wheel on the outside of the turn must travel farther than the inside wheel. It is like a horse race. The jockeys all try to get the inside position on the curves because the inside horse does not have to run as far as those on the outside. In an automobile we use a **differential** to take care of this. It allows one wheel to travel faster than the other, even though they are both driving.

Instead of fastening the ring gear to the axle, it is bolted to the differential case. There is a separate axle shaft for each wheel, which runs from the wheel into the differential. Thus as the ring gear turns, the differential case turns around with it and the differential gears inside drive the two axles. If the car is going straight ahead the two axles revolve at the same speed; if the car turns, the differential adjusts the speeds accordingly. Just how it does it, we will see later.

The **axles** are comparatively slender steel shafts. They have a flange at the outer end to which the wheel and brake drum are bolted. Around the axle is the axle housing. This holds the parts of the brake which do not turn with the wheel, and also supports the bearing in which the outer end of the axle shaft runs.

The **wheel** itself is probably familiar to everyone, as it is in plain sight on the outside of the car. It is essentially a metal disc with a rim around the outside which the tire fits into. A rubber tube inside the tire holds air under pressure. It is the outside surface of this tire which pushes on the ground and really makes the car move. But the engine furnishes this force, and all the other things we have just mentioned have a

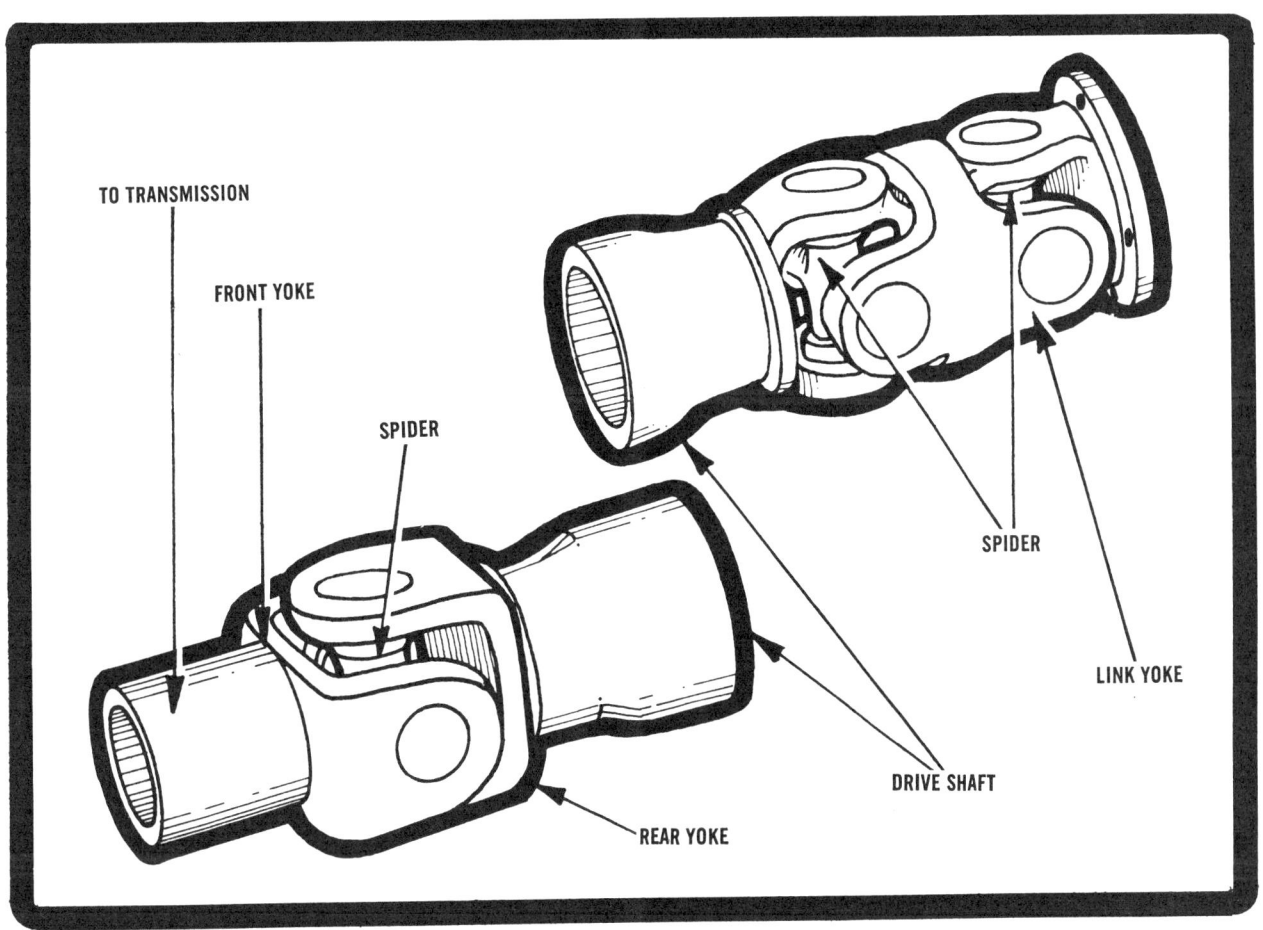

Universal joints are used to connect various drivetrain components.

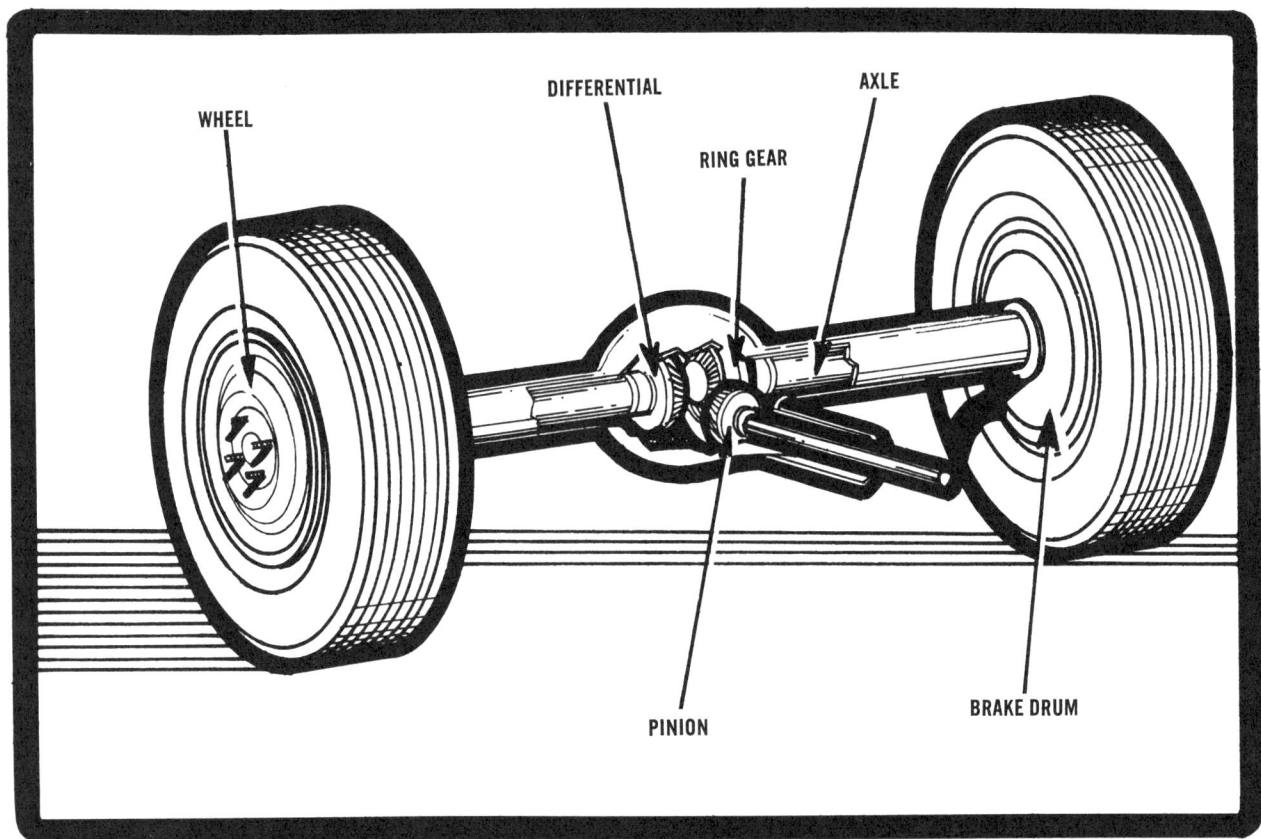

Components of typical final drive and rear axle assembly.

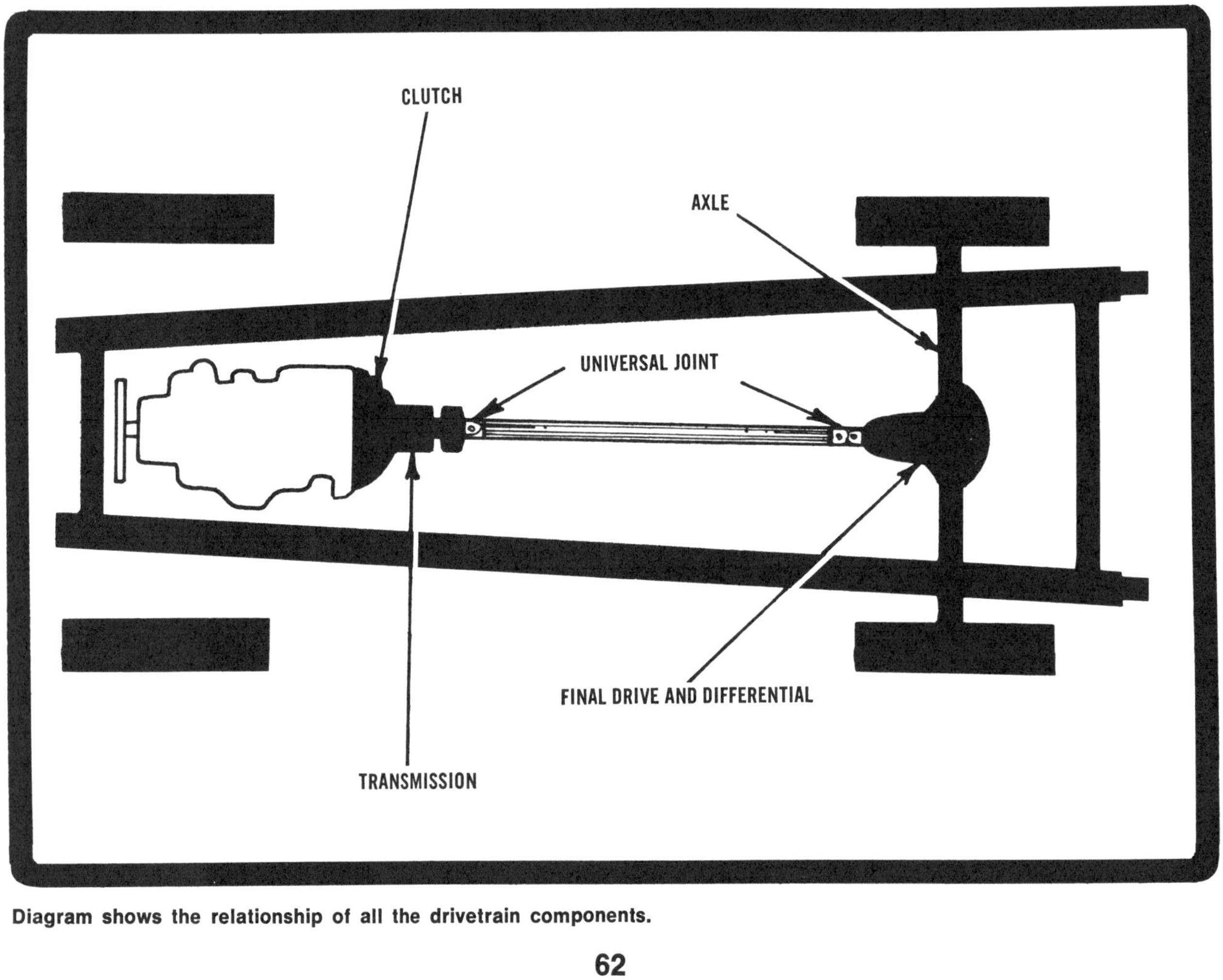

Diagram shows the relationship of all the drivetrain components.

certain part of the job to do in getting that force from one place to the other.

We said this was for a typical automobile. But they are not all like this. Some transmissions do not need a friction clutch. Others have both a friction clutch and hydraulic coupling or "fluid flywheel." In some trucks and buses we find quite a variety of additional features. We cannot try to show them all, but we will mention two arrangements used on special purpose trucks. These are for use in rough going where more than the usual traction is needed, where two wheels might get in a mud hole and not be able to pull out of it. So instead of having the engine drive just two wheels, it drives four wheels or six wheels. A four wheel vehicle driving on all four wheels is known as a 4 x 4, and one with six wheels, all driving, is a 6 x 6. A 4 x 6 is a 6-wheel truck with four driving wheels.

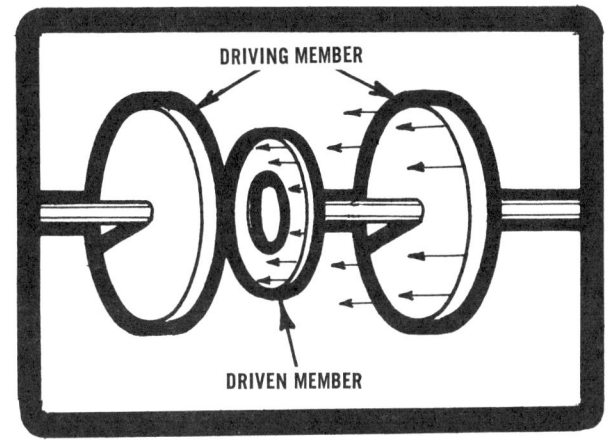

A clutch works through the frictional contact between its component parts.

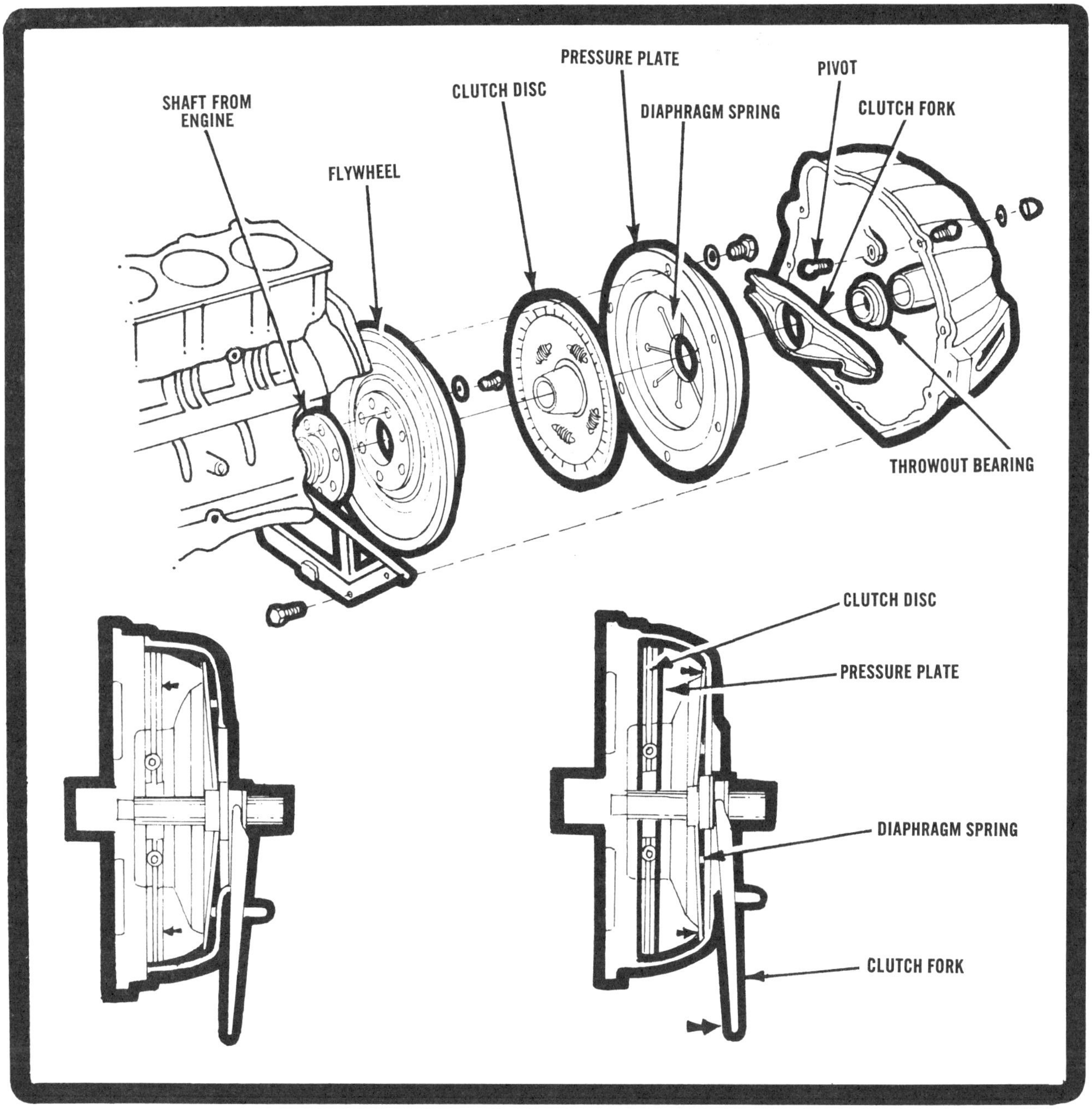

Typical clutch components consist of a flywheel, clutch disc (or drive plate) and pressure plate.

To get such a drive we use a **transfer case.** In back of the regular transmission is another set of gears. Essentially this consists of three gears meshing together in series, extending out to one side of the transmission. The first and third gears are the same size. From each side of the third gear a propeller shaft extends, one forward to the front axle, one back to the rear axle. Each axle is driven just as we have shown in the 2-wheel drive, except that in the front axle we must have some universal joints in order to steer.

For a 6-wheel drive a third propeller shaft extends straight back from the first gear in the transfer case; that is, in line with the regular transmission. Thus we have one input shaft into the transfer case and three output shafts.

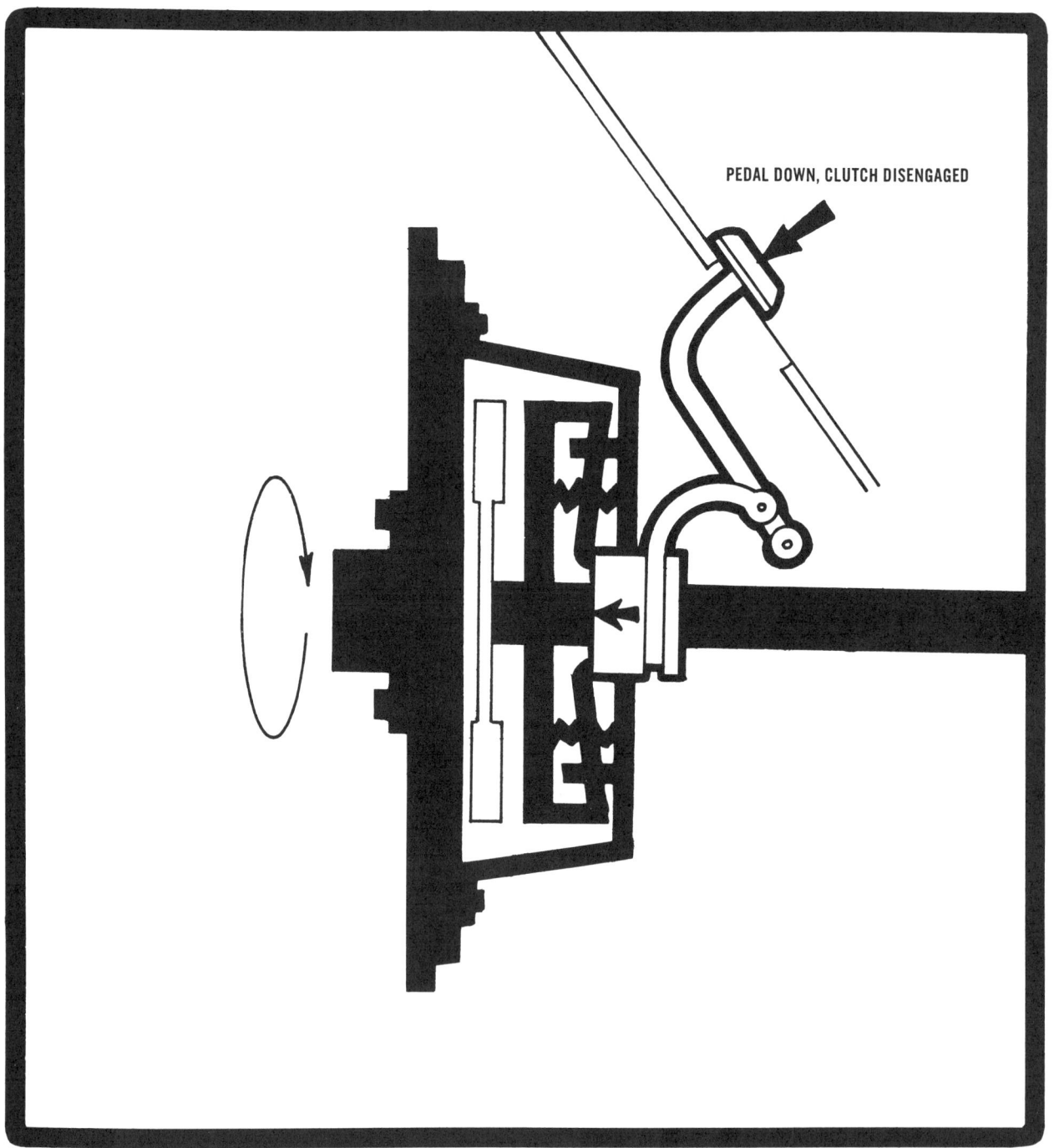

Clutch components with the pedal down and the clutch disengaged.

With the first and third gears the same size we have no change of speed or torque in the transfer case. Usually, however, there is another pair of gears in it which can be shifted to give us a different ratio. A 2-speed transfer case doubles the number of gear ratios available in the regular transmission.

CLUTCH

It is sometimes said that a good clutch *must slip* while being engaged and *must not slip* when it is engaged. This is almost a definition of a clutch. It is easy to see why when we consider what a clutch is for and what we want it to do.

First, we need something to disconnect the engine from the wheels, so that the engine can run while the car is standing still. Otherwise we would have to stop

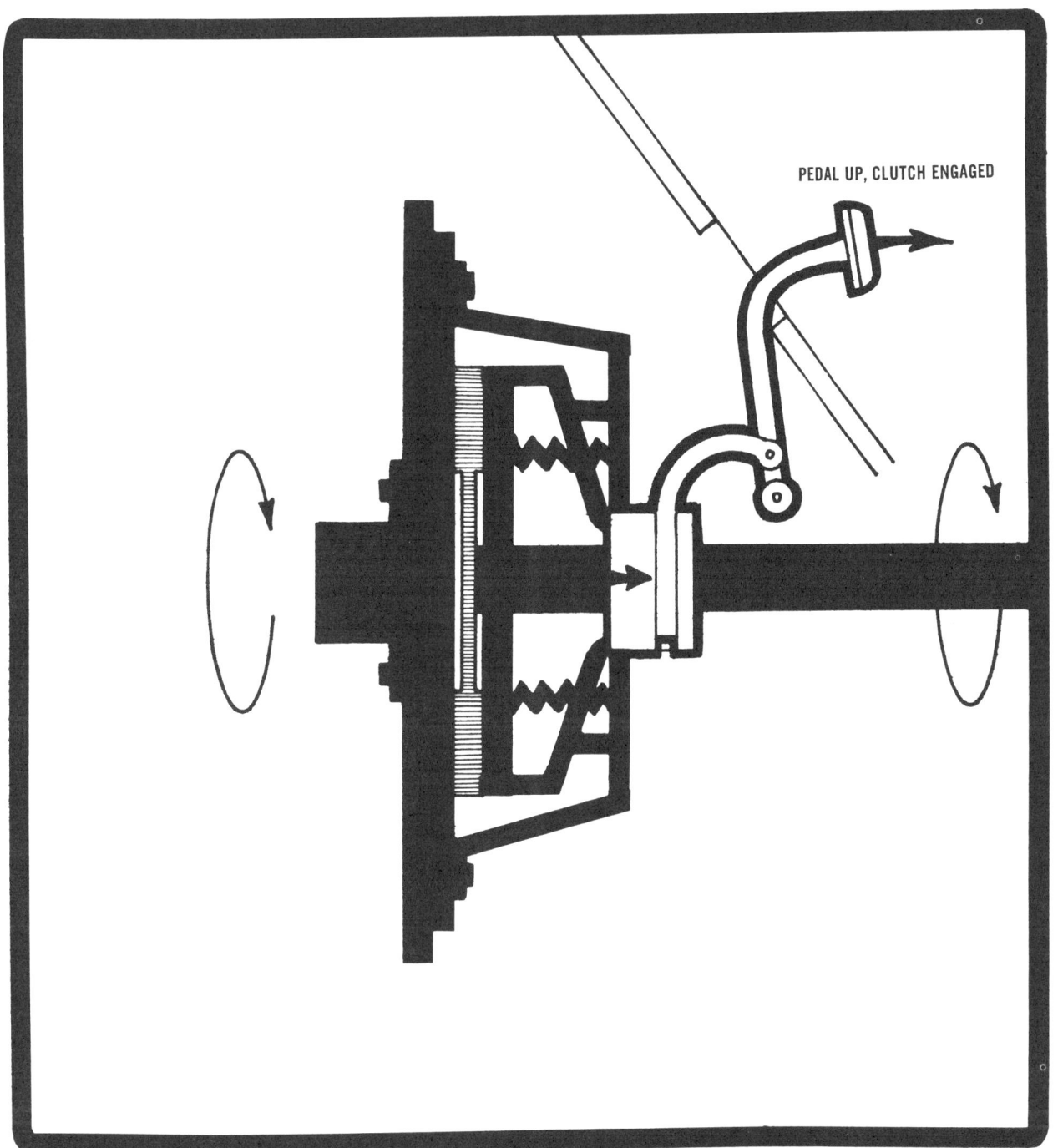

Clutch components with the pedal up and the clutch engaged.

the engine every time we came to a traffic light. And it would be a problem to start the engine while it was connected to the drive system. Also, with most transmissions, we have to disconnect it from the engine in order to shift gears easily.

There are various ways in which we could take care of these things, but we need something else. We need something which will take hold *gradually*, which will not jump abruptly from no connection at all to a direct, solid connection. When we want to start a car, we have to speed the engine up in order to get enough power to move it. At the same time the wheels are standing still. We cannot, in one moment, bring the speed of the wheels up to the speed of the engine. There would be a terrible jerk. And when we shift gears after the car is moving, we have almost the same situation—the wheels and propeller shaft are not turning at the same speed as the engine. So we want something which will slip a little, which will take hold gently at first and gradually grab harder and harder. Thus the rear wheels can start to move slowly and gradually pick up speed, until finally everything is turning at the same rate and the clutch is solidly engaged. From then on, of course, we do not want any slipping, because that is just wasting power and heating things up.

The kind of clutch we are talking about depends on friction for transmitting power. In fact, its full name is "friction clutch," as there are other types of devices commonly called clutches. In most automobile use it consists of one plate squeezed tightly between two other plates. The one in the middle is the **driven mem-**

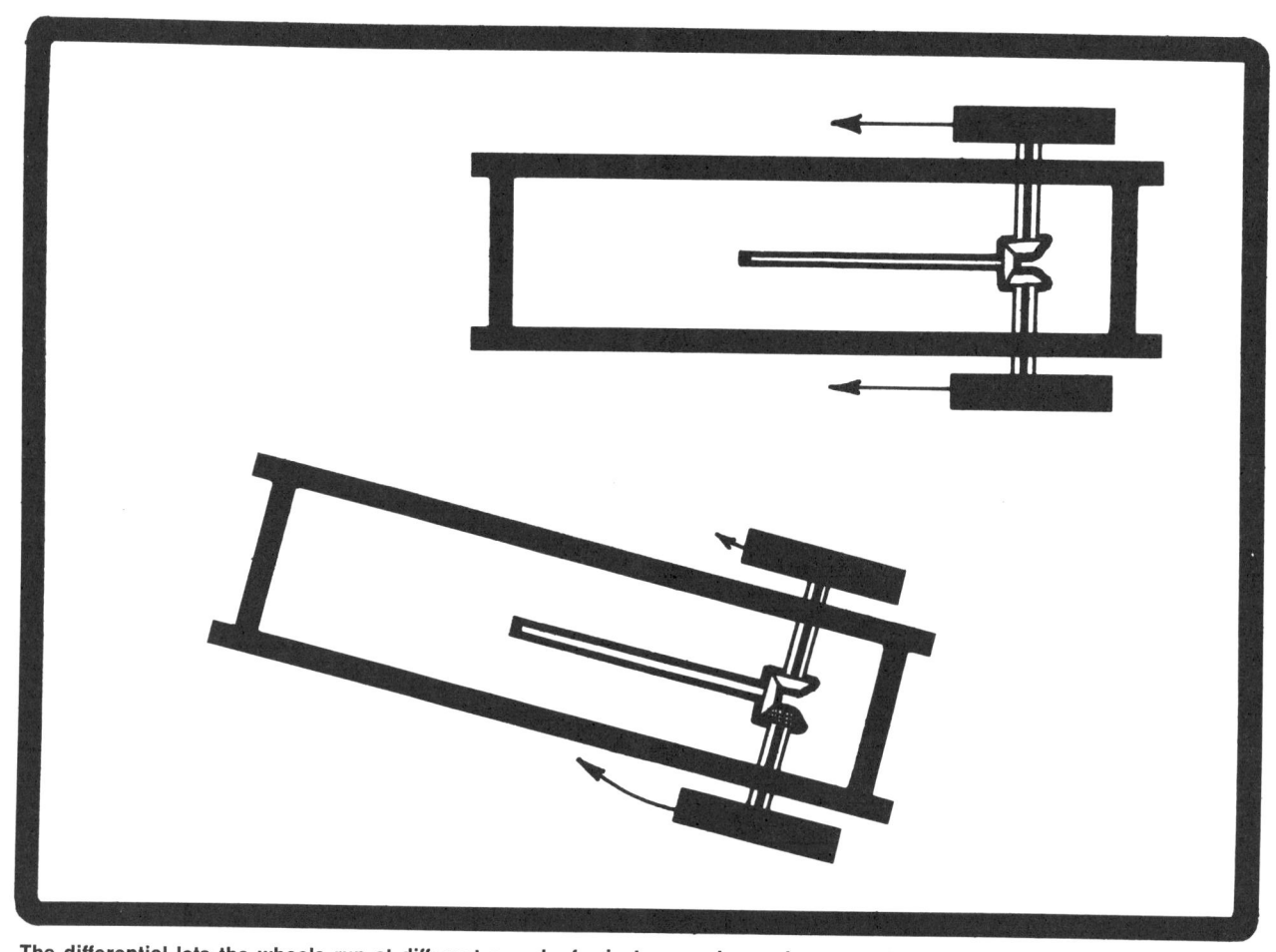

The differential lets the wheels run at different speeds, for instance, when going around a corner.

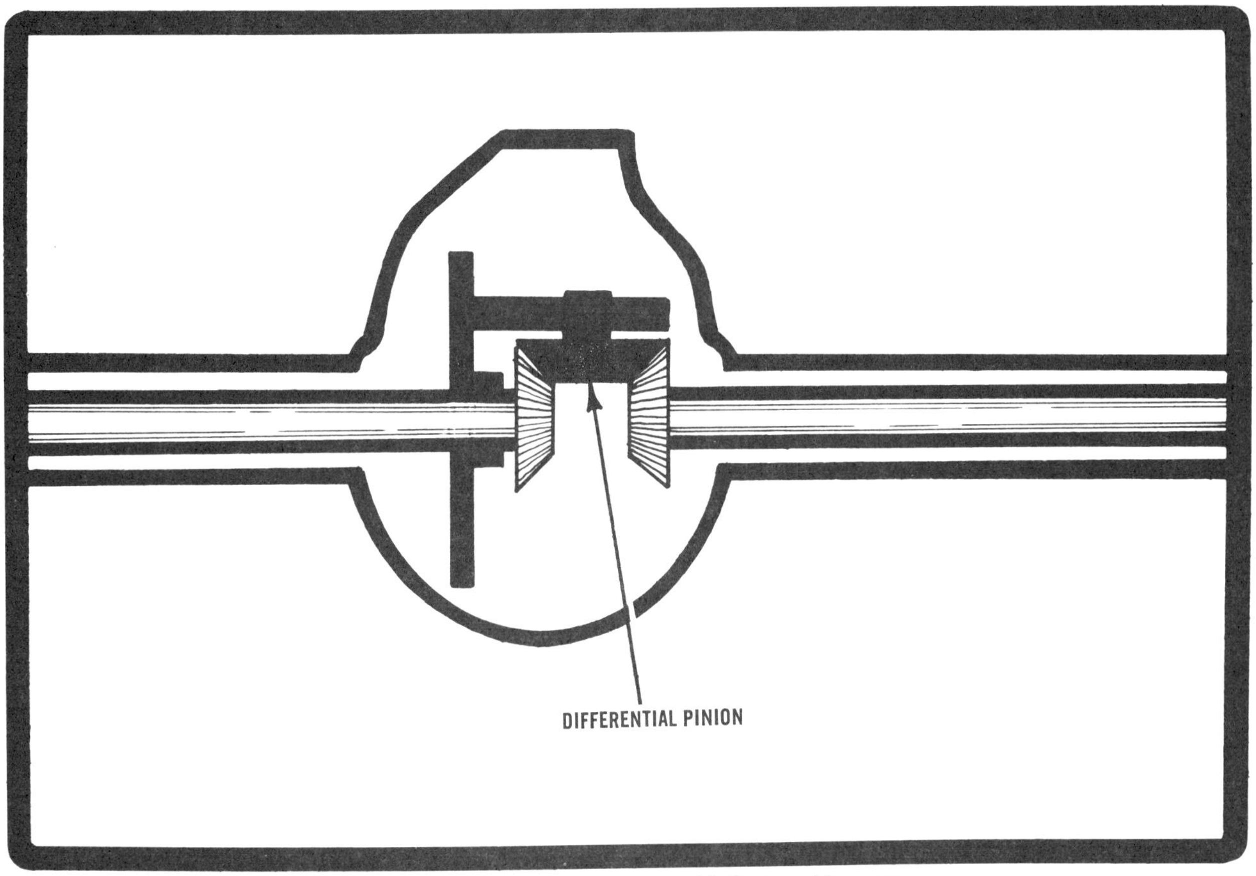

The differential pinion gear is a small bevel gear which meshes with the two side gears.

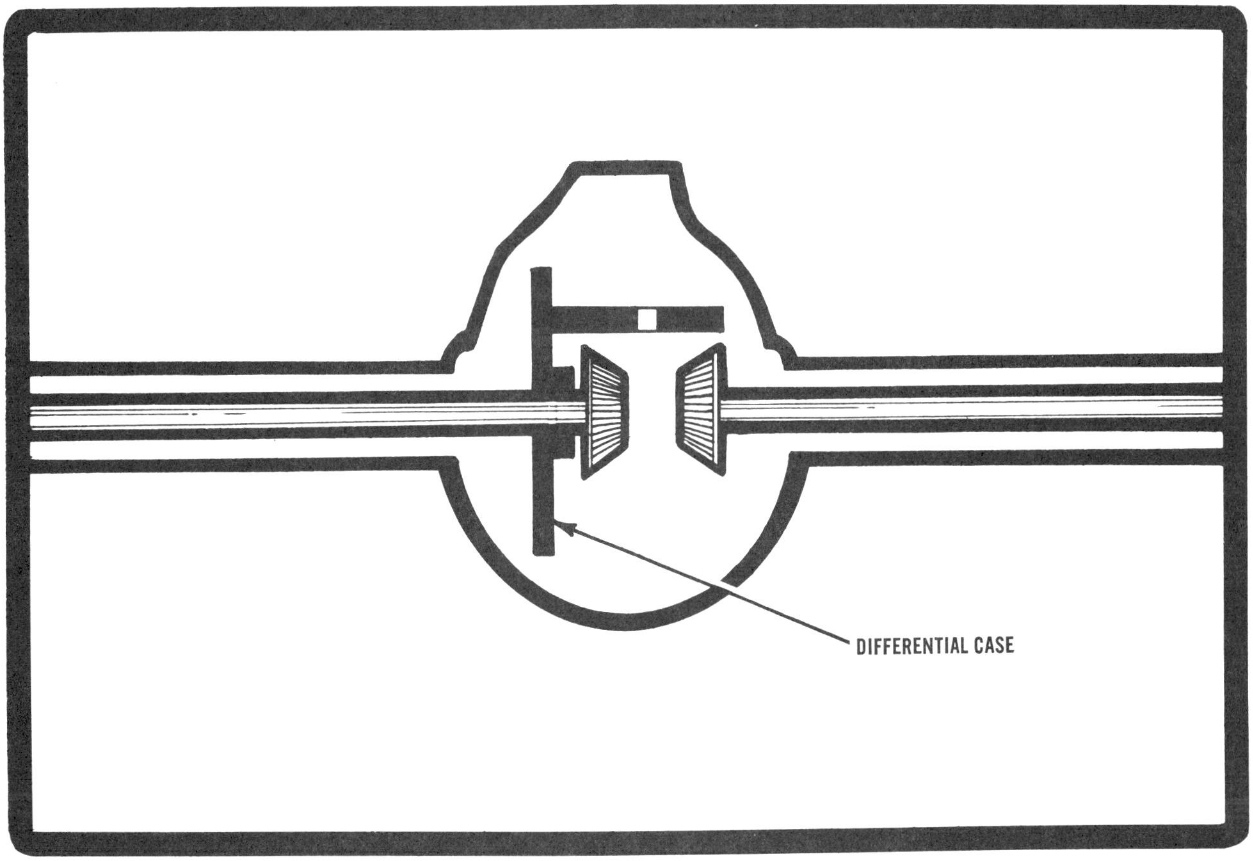

Typical layout of a differential case showing the differential gears (also called side gears) installed.

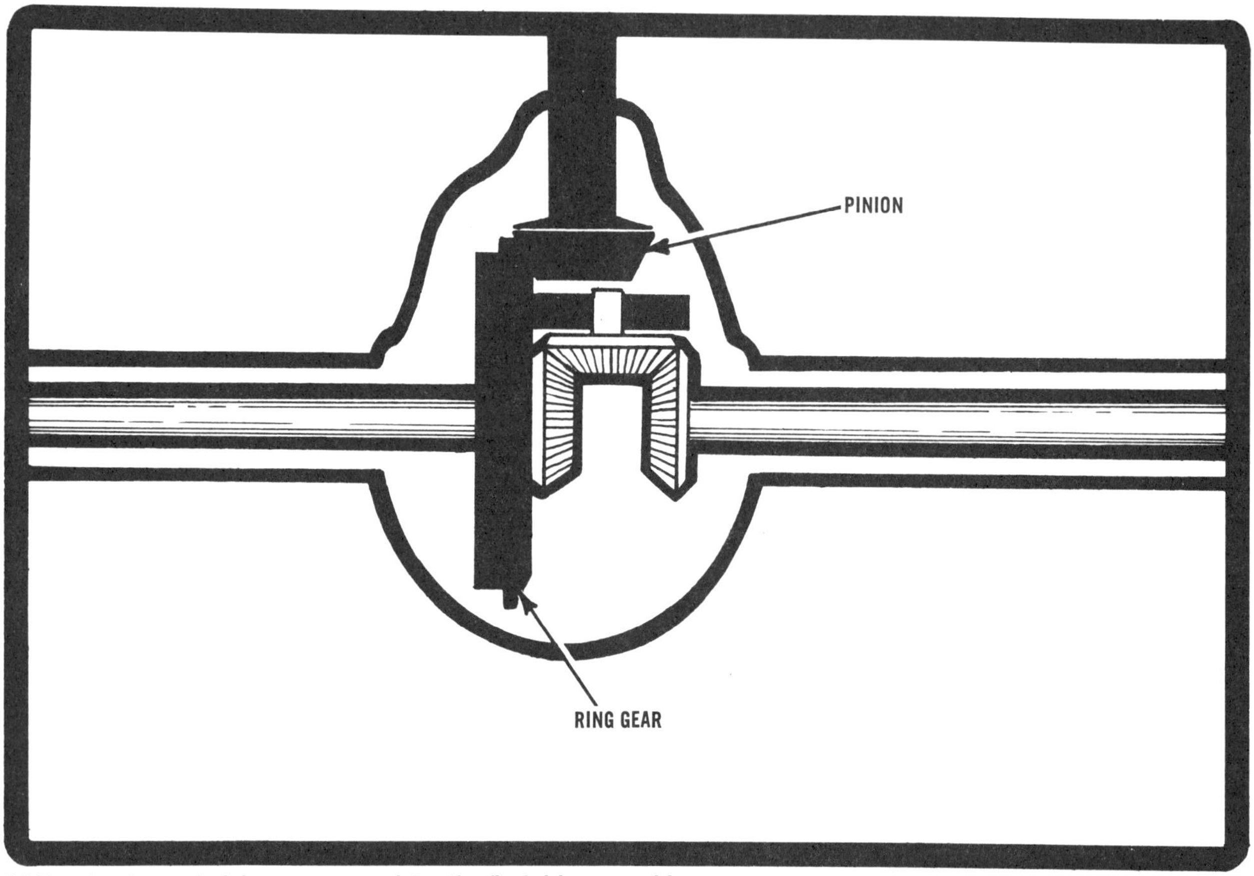

Adding the ring and pinion gears completes the final drive assembly.

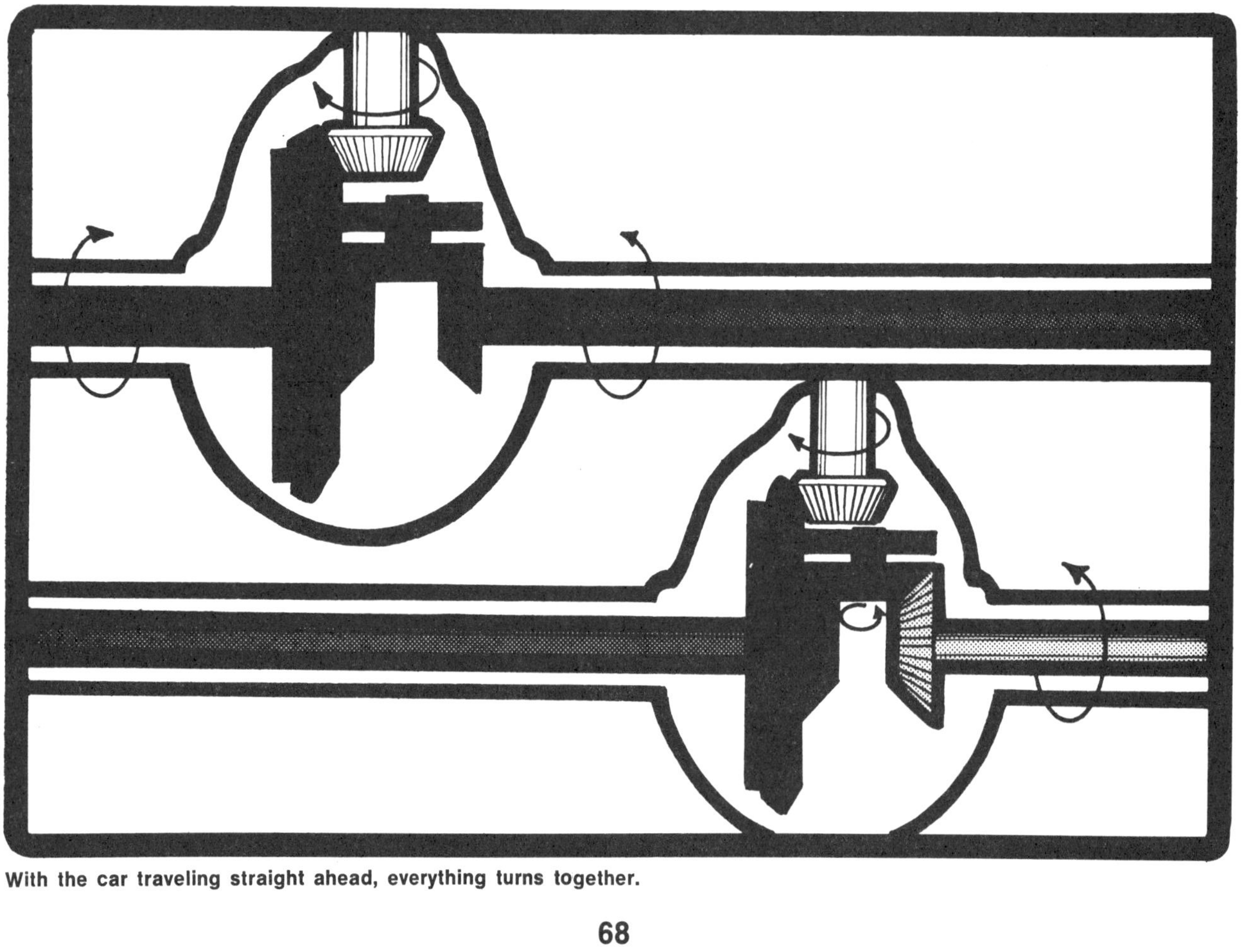

With the car traveling straight ahead, everything turns together.

68

ber. It is connected to the shaft leading back into the transmission. The other two are the **driving members.** They are connected directly to the engine. A strong spring, or springs, forces the two driving members together. This tightens their grip on the middle plate until they are all turning together as one unit.

The engine flywheel is used for the first driving member. Its surface is made very smooth where the driven plate pushes up against it.

The other driving member is called the **pressure plate.** It is a fairly heavy ring of cast iron, smooth on one side. It is fastened to the cover, which is bolted to the flywheel, so they all turn together. It is fastened in such a way that it can slide back and forth.

The **driven plate** is a flat disc of steel with friction facing fastened on each side. The plate is fastened by **splines** to a shaft going to the transmission. This means it fits into grooves on the shaft so that they must turn together but the plate can slide forward and backward on the shaft.

A series of coil springs, or sometimes one large flat spring, act between the clutch cover and the pressure plate. They push the pressure plate toward the flywheel, squeezing the driven plate between the two. The springs are always trying to engage the clutch, and they are strong enough to keep it from slipping under any ordinary conditions. To disengage the clutch, the driver pushes on the pedal. This works through levers to pull back the pressure plate against the force of the springs. This lets the driven plate loose and disconnects the transmission shaft from the engine crankshaft.

There have been many different designs of clutches in the past, and the present ones do not all look just like what we have shown. Sometimes more than one driven plate is used, with a corresponding increase in the number of driving plates. And there are other differences. But they all work on the same principle.

Various ways have been tried to make the clutch work automatically, that is to engage and disengage without effort on the part of the driver. Sometimes vacuum power is used to operate the linkage of a standard clutch. Sometimes the clutch itself is changed to operate centrifugally. We will not go into the details of it. The principle remains the same, but centrifugal weights are arranged to engage the clutch when the engine gets up to a certain speed and disengage it when it drops below a certain speed.

There is another more common type of clutch which is really a centrifugal clutch. This is the **hydraulic coupling,** or as it is more often called, the **fluid flywheel.** Sometimes this replaces the friction clutch entirely, taking its place between the engine and transmission. In other arrangements we have both—first the fluid flywheel behind the engine, then the friction clutch, then the transmission. The fluid flywheel does not do everything the friction clutch can do, and it does some things the friction clutch cannot do. But it is a centrifugal clutch in this way—if we run the engine slowly, it will not start the rear wheels turning. When we speed up the engine, it gradually takes hold until finally the engine is driving the rear wheels with practically no slip.

How does it work? Suppose we start with a simple example. If we shoot steel balls at the blades of this paddle wheel, each ball will give the wheel a little push, will try to turn it around. If we can shoot them fast enough and hard enough, the wheel will keep spinning. Now if we think of water or oil as being made up of a lot of small liquid balls, we can shoot these at the wheel and get the same results. You have probably seen water wheels which worked much like this, driven by the water falling over a dam or by the flow of a swift stream. That is about what we do in a fluid flywheel. But in an automobile we have to make an artificial stream. What it amounts to is a pump forcing oil against a turbine or hydraulic motor. Many years ago it was found that the most efficient way to do this was to get the pump and motor close together, to more or less combine them. The result was a hydraulic coupling essentially the same as the fluid flywheel we use today.

The working parts of a fluid flywheel look very much like a doughnut. But the doughnut is sliced down the middle, so there is no connection between the two halves. One half is fastened to the engine crankshaft; the other to the clutch, or transmission, or some part eventually leading to the rear wheels. The doughnut is hollow, but each half has a number of straight radial blades leading from the hub to the outside edge. Very often a section of each blade is cut away, and in that space is put a metal plate or guide ring shaped like half of another, smaller doughnut. The two halves of the fluid flywheel are just alike, and when we put them together we have what looks like a skinny doughnut inside a fat one, with thin blades connecting the two.

To make this complete we put a cover around it all, the cover often being fastened solidly to one of the rotating members. Then we fill it almost full of oil. Now if the engine is running, the first half of the fluid flywheel, the **driving member,** is turning with it. If it is turning fairly fast, the oil is being thrown toward the outside of the doughnut by centrifugal force, just like marbles on a phonograph turntable. When it gets to the outside it wants to keep on going, and the only place it can go is across into the other half of the doughnut, the **driven member.**

All this time that the oil is being forced outward, it is also being whirled around in the other direction by the blades of the driving member. Consequently, when it crosses over into the driven member, it hits against those blades just as in the water wheel we mentioned and pushes them around. This tends to slow up the drops of oil, and they travel toward the hub, or center, of the driven member, then across to the driving member and repeat the whole process. Thus we have the oil continually circulating, outward in the driving member, inward in the driven member. And at the same time it is traveling in a direction at right angles to this, being pushed by the blades of the driving member and pushing on the blades of the driven member.

The driven member can never go quite as fast as the driving member. There is always a certain amount of slip no matter how fast they are turning. But at ordinary driving speeds this may amount to less than one percent so it is not serious. When we get below a certain speed, however, this slip begins to get greater. Finally it gets down to the point where the driven member does not turn at all. There is still some torque being applied to it, but it is not enough to make the rear wheels turn and move the car. This means that we can stand at a traffic signal with the transmission in gear and the car will stand still just as if a friction clutch were disengaged. Then as we speed up the engine, the driven member begins to turn, gradually picks up speed and finally is running at approximately the same speed as the engine.

We mentioned that the driving member and driven member were just alike. There may be slight differences in them, but they are enough alike that a fluid flywheel can drive in one direction as well as the other. The oil just circulates in the opposite direction, from what was the driven member to the driving member. Thus if the car is coasting or being pushed, the wheels drive the engine just about the same as if there were a solid connection there.

The use of a fluid flywheel gives smoother pickup and makes it impossible to stall the engine when starting or climbing a hill. It also smooths out jerks, especially at low speeds, and in some ways acts as a centrifugal clutch. As we will see later, those characteristics let us use certain types of transmissions and shift gears in certain ways which would not be satisfactory without a fluid flywheel. But we must remember that this is just a clutch. It is not a transmission. It cannot replace the transmission because it does not increase the torque—it only transmits the torque which the engine delivers to it. We will see later on in this book some mechanisms which look very much like it and which do multiply torque. But they are different. We will point out just how they are different when we get there.

We have described the first items in back of the engine in the power train. The next major unit is the transmission, but we are going to skip that for the time being. The subject of transmissions includes several different varieties which we must consider separately to a certain extent, so we will leave them for the last. Now we will go back to the rear axle and try to show what a differential does and how it does it.

DIFFERENTIAL

When we look at the rear axle drive system of an automobile, the pinion and ring gear and various parts of the differential seem to be all mixed up together, just one mechanism. But when we consider what they do, we find there are two entirely different jobs being taken care of.

The job of the pinion and ring gear combination, or final drive, is to take the torque provided by the propeller shaft, increase it about four times, and turn it at right angles so it can twist the wheels and drive the car.

The differential is meant for just one thing. That is to let the wheels run at different speeds while still driving the car. It transmits equal torque to both wheels even when one is going faster than the other. If it was not necessary to have this difference in

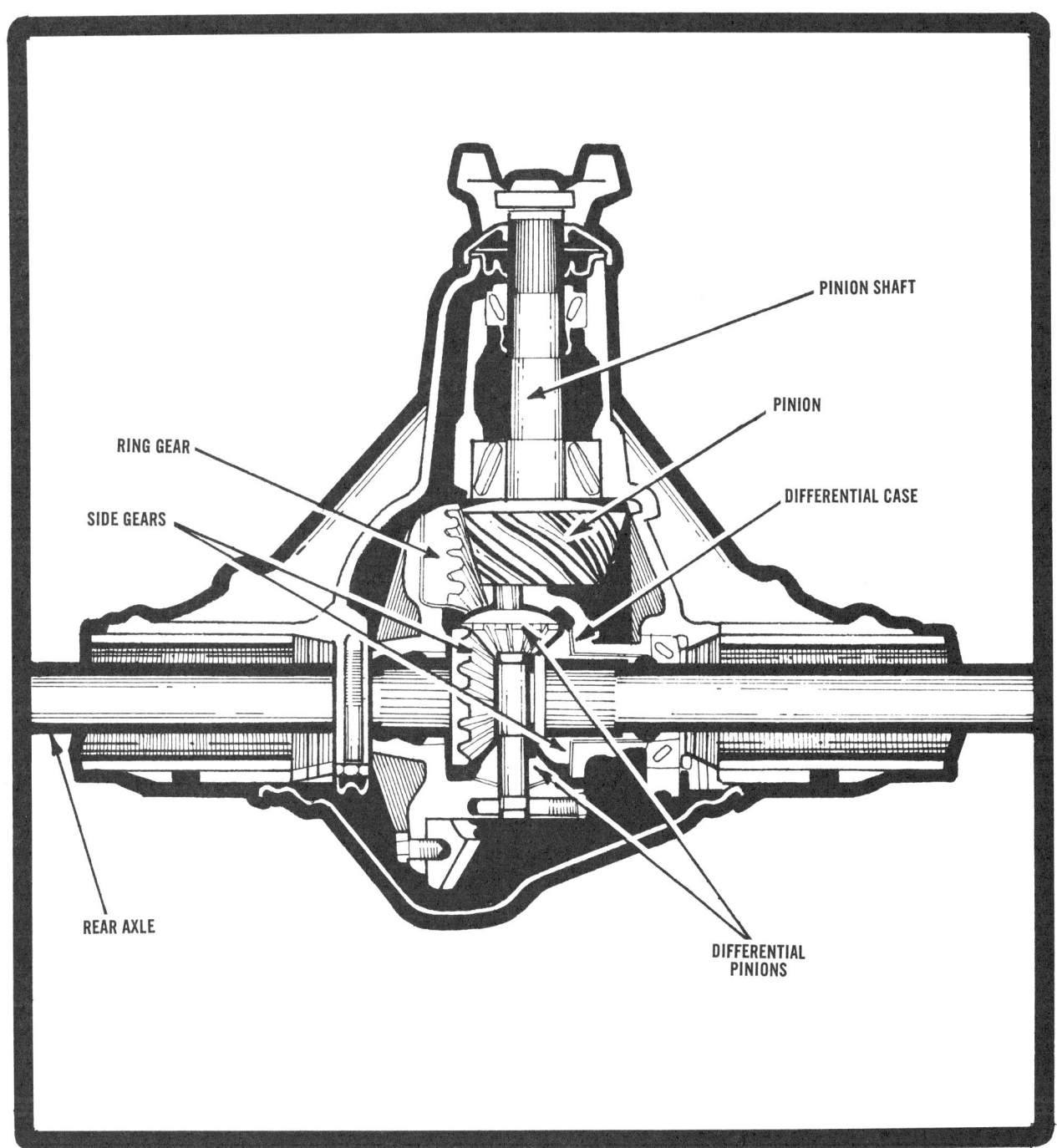

Internal view of a typical rear axle assembly and differential.

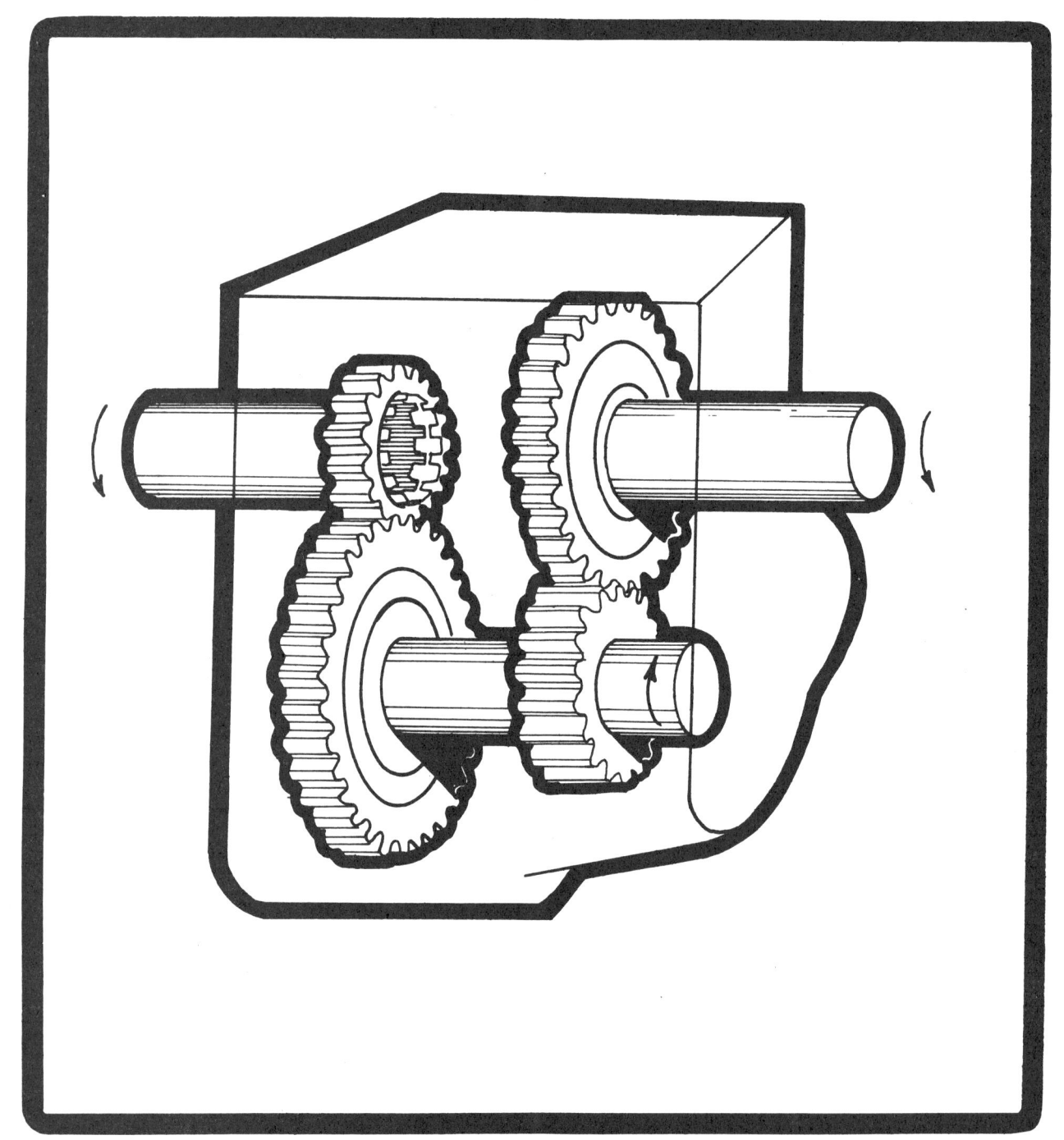

Typical First or low gear arrangement.

speed, we would throw away the differential and have a much simpler rear axle and drive system. Some cars have been built without one, but it is very hard on the tires. They have to slip or skid on the road whenever a corner is turned.

A differential is one of those mechanisms whose action is easy to see when it is working right in front of you, but it is not so easy to describe. We will build it up piece by piece, however, and try to show how simple it really is.

First we have the two axles, each with a wheel on one end and a gear on the other end. These are small spur bevel gears, and are called **differential gears** or **side gears.** Then we add what is called the **differential case,** but which we will show as just a crooked bar fastened around one of the axles. It is loose on the axle, however, so it can turn around on it. In this case we mount another gear, the **differential pinion.** This is a small bevel gear which fits in between the two side gears and meshes with both of them. There we have all the necessary parts for a differential—just three gears and a case.

We will add one more part, however, just to make it easier to tell the story. That is the ring gear. It is fastened solidly to the differential case. Thus the case is going around all the time, at the same speed as the ring gear. This should be noted carefully, as we are likely to think of a "case" as something stationary, just an enclosure for the working parts. But here what it is is the driving member of the differential. As long as the ring gear is revolving it goes around too, at the same speed. It carries the differential pinion around with it, but otherwise it knows nothing about what is going on in the differential. It just keeps going around.

Now suppose we are going straight ahead on a smooth road. The wheels should be turning at the same speed. Engine power is driving the ring gear, so the differential case is going around, carrying the pinion with it. This turns the two side gears, and the whole mechanism revolves as one solid unit. The gears are not turning on one another. The pinion is simply connecting the two side gears together. They could just as well be bolted together solidly. They are turning at the same speed as the differential case. It is the same as if we had no differential at all, because our wheels are traveling together and we do not need one.

Now let us take the other extreme. We will hold one wheel so it cannot turn. What happens in the differential? The case is turned as before, again carrying the pinion with it. But one axle is held, so its side gear cannot go around. Therefore, the pinion must turn. The pinion is being carried around by the case, but at the same time is revolving around its own short shaft. It must do so in order to stay meshed with the stationary side gear. It is running around the stationary gear.

But what is happening to the other side gear while this is going on? It is meshed with the pinion too, but it is free to turn. It is being turned just the same as it was in the first case, but *in addition* it is being turned more by the revolving of the pinion on its own shaft. The pinion is revolving in the right direction so that its motion is added to the movement of the differential case. So the second side gear is turning faster than before. In fact this axle and wheel are turning exactly twice as fast as when the two wheels were running at the same speed.

Now let us take a situation in between these two extremes. Both wheels are turning, but one is going faster than the other. This is the case we ordinarily have in an automobile turning a corner. The inside wheel travels a shorter distance than the outside wheel; therefore it must turn around more slowly.

The inside wheel—and thus the differential gear on its axle shaft—is revolving more slowly than the differential case. The differential gear is turning more slowly than the pinion is being carried around. So we have the same general effect as when it was held tight —the pinion must turn on its own shaft. It will not turn as fast as before but it will turn. And it again turns in a direction to add to the speed of the opposite differential gear. It adds to it exactly the amount taken away from the slower gear and wheel.

For example, suppose the differential case is being driven at 500 revolutions per minute. Then if the inside wheel is turning 400 rpm, the outer one must be turning 600 rpm. If one is turning 490 rpm, the other is 510 rpm. And in the extreme case we had, if one is standing still, which is 0 rpm, the other turns 1000 rpm. That is the way a differential must work—what is subtracted from one side must be added to the other. The ring gear speed always splits the difference between the two.

To make our mechanism look more like the real thing, we will add a little to it. This does not change its operation in any way, however. We will complete the case, and add another pinion to the bottom. This pinion simply does exactly the same thing as the first one, and helps it do the job we have just described.

The differential is a very necessary thing. It acts as a sort of balance between the rear wheels. But it can be a nuisance at times. This is usually when we have a situation giving us the result we mentioned earlier— one wheel standing still, the other going twice as fast as usual. It is easy to do this. All we have to do is stop the car so one rear wheel is on dry pavement or road, and the other is on a slick patch of ice. The differential will drive the wheel which is the easier to turn. So the wheel on the ice will just spin, the other one will stand still, and—which is usually more important—the car will stand still. We get the same effect when one wheel is stuck in deep sand or mud, and the other one is comparatively free to turn. To avoid this trouble, various kinds of differentials have been designed which will permit some difference in speed between the two wheels, but will not let one spin while the other stands still. This adds some complication, but it can be very helpful under many conditions.

We have described to some extent all the main parts of the power path except the transmission.

TRANSMISSION

The transmission is a box full of gears. It is located behind the clutch, and its case is usually fastened to the clutch housing, so the whole thing looks like an extension of the engine. The purpose of the transmission is as we have mentioned before—it is to let us vary the speed and torque of the rear axle in relation to the speed and torque of the engine.

For some years most passenger cars in this country have had three ratios or "speeds" in the transmission for forward driving. There have been several with four ratios, and some special transmissions which were different in many respects. We will leave all that until later however. And what we say here applies to the simple, three-speed, conventional transmission.

First speed, or **low gear,** is used for starting and for steep hills or heavy going in sand or mud. It lets the engine run fast while the car runs slowly. The engine runs 2½ to 3 times as fast as the propeller shaft. The exact figure varies in different cars. This means, of

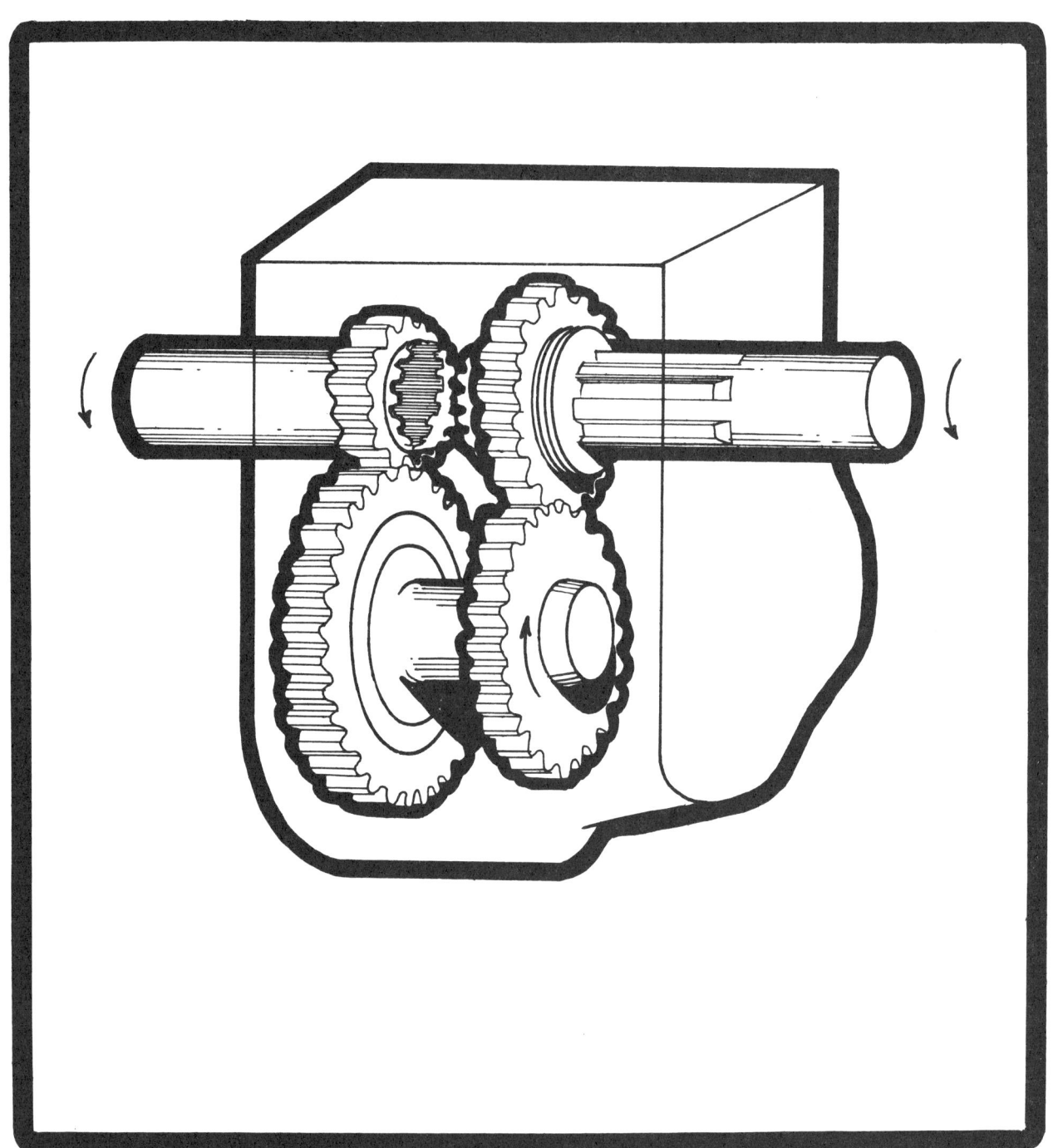

Second, or intermediate, gear arrangement.

course, that the torque of the propeller shaft is increased just as much as its speed is cut down. Thus we have a lot of twist on the rear wheels to get the car started from a standstill, or for use any other time we need it.

This is done with four gears and three shafts. A small gear on the shaft from the clutch drives a larger gear fastened to the transmission **countershaft.** Another smaller gear fastened on the countershaft drives a large gear on the third shaft. This last shaft goes to a universal joint on the front end of the propeller shaft. Thus we have the same arrangement we showed earlier. There is a certain speed reduction in the first two gears, and then some more reduction in the second set of two gears. The countershaft is running at a speed in between the speeds of the other two shafts. And the third shaft is of course running most slowly and with the greatest torque.

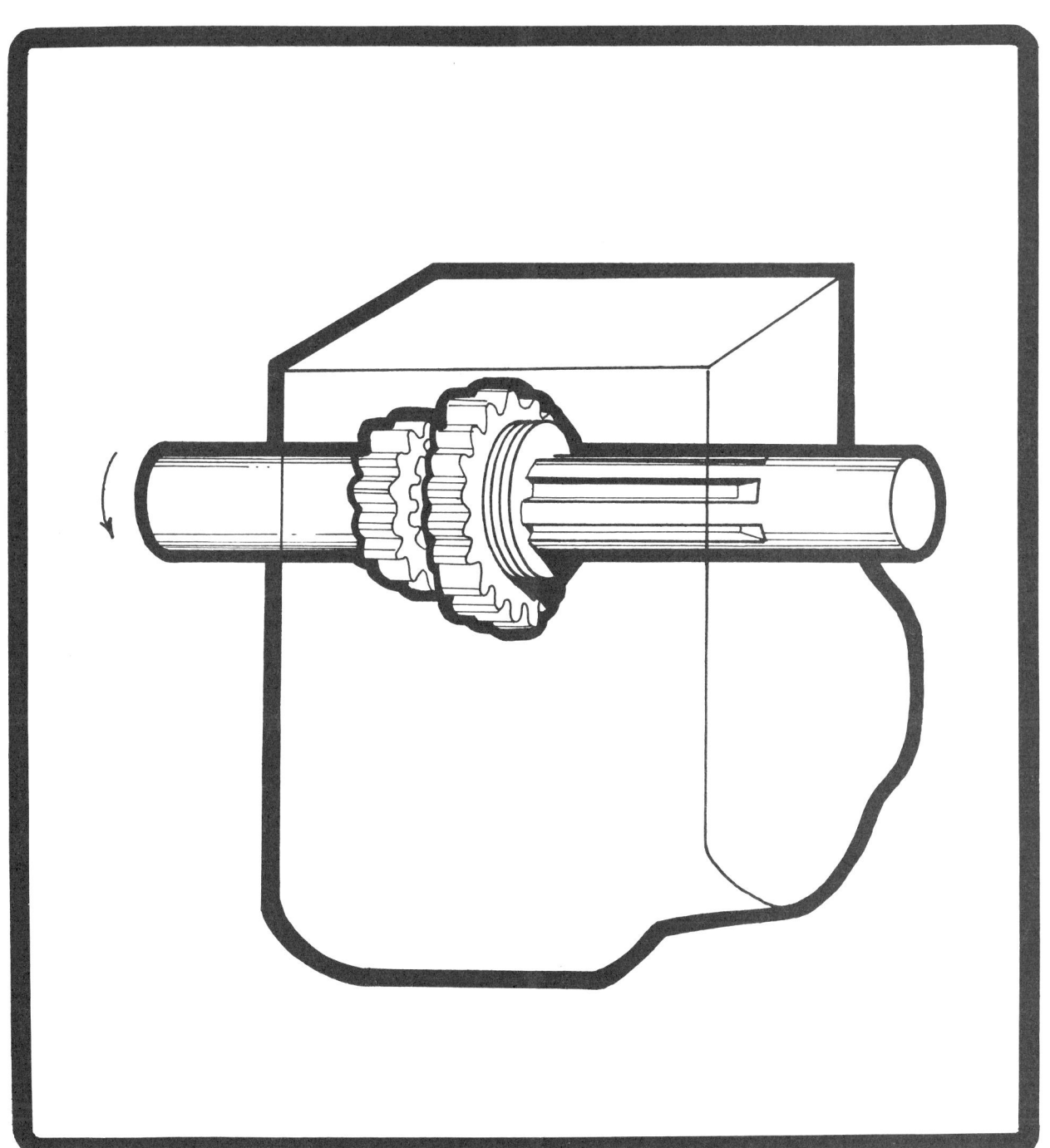

Third, or high, gear arrangement.

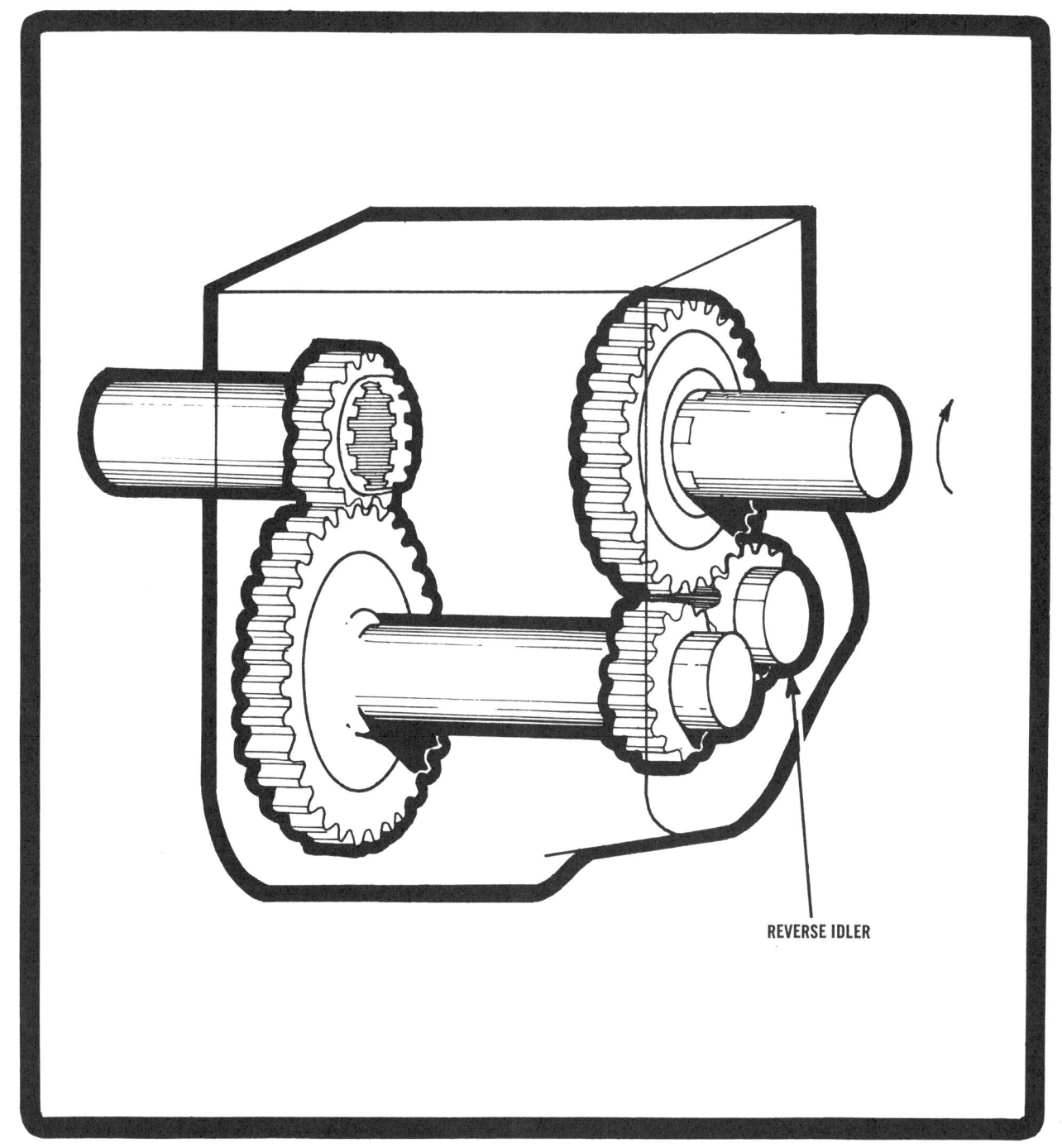

Reverse gear arrangement.

Second, or **intermediate gear,** works in about the same way. The first two gears are the same as we used in low gear. The next pair are different however. They are almost the same size, and sometimes the countershaft gear may be the larger. Thus the countershaft runs at the same speed as before, but there is little if any additional reduction from that to the third shaft. So the wheels will run faster for the same engine speed than they did in low gear. The usual ratio in second speed is around 1⅔ to 1. This means that the propeller shaft will run at 1000 rpm when the engine is running 1670 rpm.

Third, or **high speed,** is direct drive. The transmission does not do anything. We simply connect the first and third shafts together, and they turn as one. The propeller shaft turns the same speed as the engine, and delivers engine torque. Sticking to figures, we would say the ratio is 1 to 1.

Besides the three forward speeds, there are two other combinations we can get in a transmission. There is **neutral,** in which the transmission shaft is entirely disconnected from the clutch shaft, and the engine cannot drive the propeller shaft or anything beyond the transmission. It has about the same effect as disengaging the clutch. And there is **reverse.** It is a complicated matter to make an internal combustion engine run backwards, so we run it in one direction all the time and use gears to reverse the direction of rotation. We put an extra gear in between the countershaft and the final drive shaft. It is called the **reverse idler.** We drive the countershaft in the same way as before. It drives this reverse idler which in turn drives the low speed gear on the final drive shaft. The system is just like low gear which we described first except for this extra gear in between. This changes the direction of rotation, and we can see that the final shaft is turning opposite to what it was in all the previous cases. The ratio of reverse is about the same as low gear, or even lower. This is logical, because we may want to pull hard in reverse but we never want to back up very fast.

We have shown all the combinations found in an ordinary, 3-speed transmission. These can be put together in various ways to make a complete transmission. In earlier days, they used to slide the gears back and forth on the shafts to get them into mesh and out of mesh. This can be done by using a square shaft or a splined, or grooved, shaft. In this way a gear is fastened solidly to its shaft as far as revolving is concerned, but it can slide along it.

Now we commonly use the so-called **constant mesh** transmission. Some of the gears still slide, but some are constantly in mesh with each other and rotate all the time. But these gears do not necessarily drive the shaft. They are free to rotate on it until they are connected to it by a clutch. We should explain that this is not a friction clutch. It is a **positive clutch**—more like a gear—having teeth that fit into similar teeth on the gear. It is called a clutch because its only job is to connect or disconnect the gear and the shaft.

Let us look at a complete constant-mesh transmission, and note briefly what gears and shafts there are. There is the clutch shaft with gear A fastened solidly to it. There is the countershaft with all three gears, B, C, and D, fastened solidly to it. A and B are constant-mesh gears, so whenever the engine is running and the clutch engaged, the countershaft and its three gears are turning. Then there is the transmission main shaft, with the two gears E and F. E is in constant-mesh with C, but is free to rotate on its own shaft except when connected to it by a clutch arrangement. F is splined to the main shaft, so it turns with it but can slide back and forth. Finally we have the reverse idler, which is now a short shaft with the *two* gears G and H solidly fastened to it. G is always in mesh with D.

This may look rather complicated, but there is not really a great deal to it. And with this arrangement it is very simple to get any speed or gear we want. We can see that even in neutral the countershaft gears, gear E, and the reverse idler gears are all revolving. But the main shaft is standing still. Now suppose we slide gear F along the shaft. If we slide it in one direction it meshes with D and we have low gear. If we slide it the other way it meshes with H and we have reverse. We are using two gears on the reverse idler now, but as they are both fastened solidly on the same shaft and rotate in the same direction, the principle has not changed from that in our first example.

The other speeds we need are second and high. We get these by means of a positive clutch arrangement which slides between gears A and E. When it slides to the right it connects E to its shaft and we have second speed. When it slides to the left it connects the main shaft to the clutch shaft and we have

In passenger cars the common practice is to use all helical gears in the transmission. Most trucks use spur gears, and we have shown them here for convenience. The helical gears are quieter and are preferred for that reason, but this does not affect the principle of operation in any way.

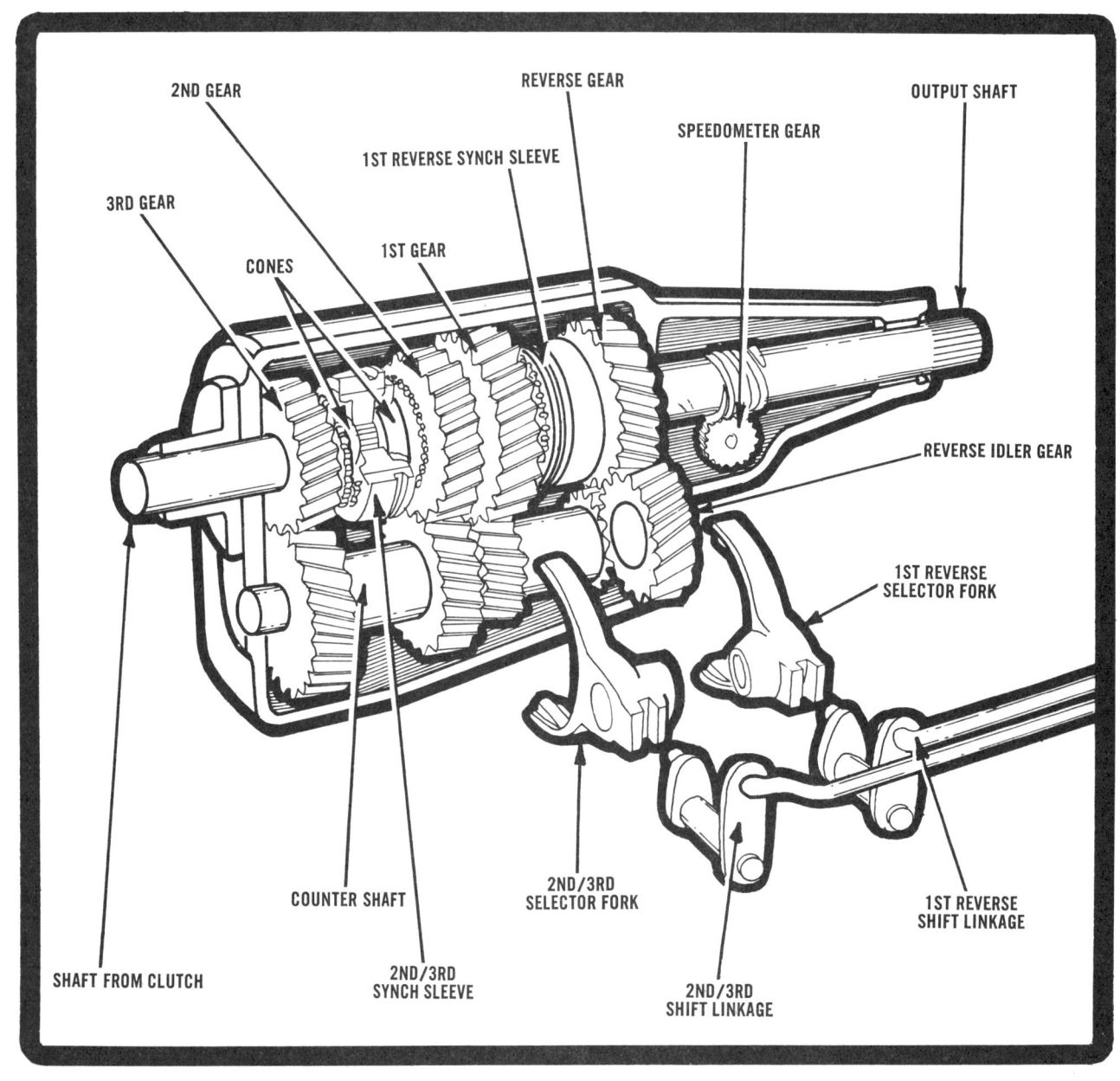

The transmission linkage allows you to select and change gears.

How do we shift these gears and clutches to get the different speeds? We have seen that we only have to move two things—the low speed gear and the double clutch. These both have grooves in them into which **shifting forks** fit loosely. The forks do not interfere with these parts turning around, but they can be used to slide them endwise.

Then we connect the forks to the gearshift lever in the driver's compartment in such a way that he can select either one and move it in either direction. Thus with the one lever he can take his choice of any one of the four positions of the gears—five, counting neutral.

We have to disengage the main friction clutch when we shift gears. Otherwise there would be jerks and much loud clashing of gears. Some gears are running and some are standing still, or they are running at different speeds. Also there is considerable pressure on the gear teeth when they are driving, so the gears do not slide apart easily. And of course it gives the clutch a chance to cushion the shock or jerk of suddenly changing the ratio between the engine and the rear wheels.

There has been a lot of work done to try to make it easier to shift gears. Probably the most successful result has been the development of gear synchronizers, or **synchronized transmissions.** This is a refinement of the constant mesh type we have described. Synchronizers are ordinarily used only for second and third speeds, inasmuch as that is when they are most needed. There are several types, but they all have the same object.

Most of the trouble in shifting gears is because the gears or clutches are running at different speeds. If we could synchronize them, get them running at approximately the same speed before we tried to mesh the teeth, there would be little clash or clatter. That is just what we do. When the second and high speed clutch slides on the shaft—in either direction—it does not mesh with the teeth on the other half of the clutch right away. Instead, a small friction clutch takes hold first. This is a cone-shaped clutch, with metal faces, but it acts like the friction clutches we have described. It can slip enough to prevent a shock, but it is almost immediately solidly engaged. In doing this it has brought the speed of the gear up to the speed of the shaft. As soon as they are turning at the same speed, it is easy to push in the toothed part of the clutch which gives a positive connection. The first part of the motion engages the friction clutch, and the second part engages the positive toothed clutch. This arrangement enables even a new driver to shift gears without trouble.

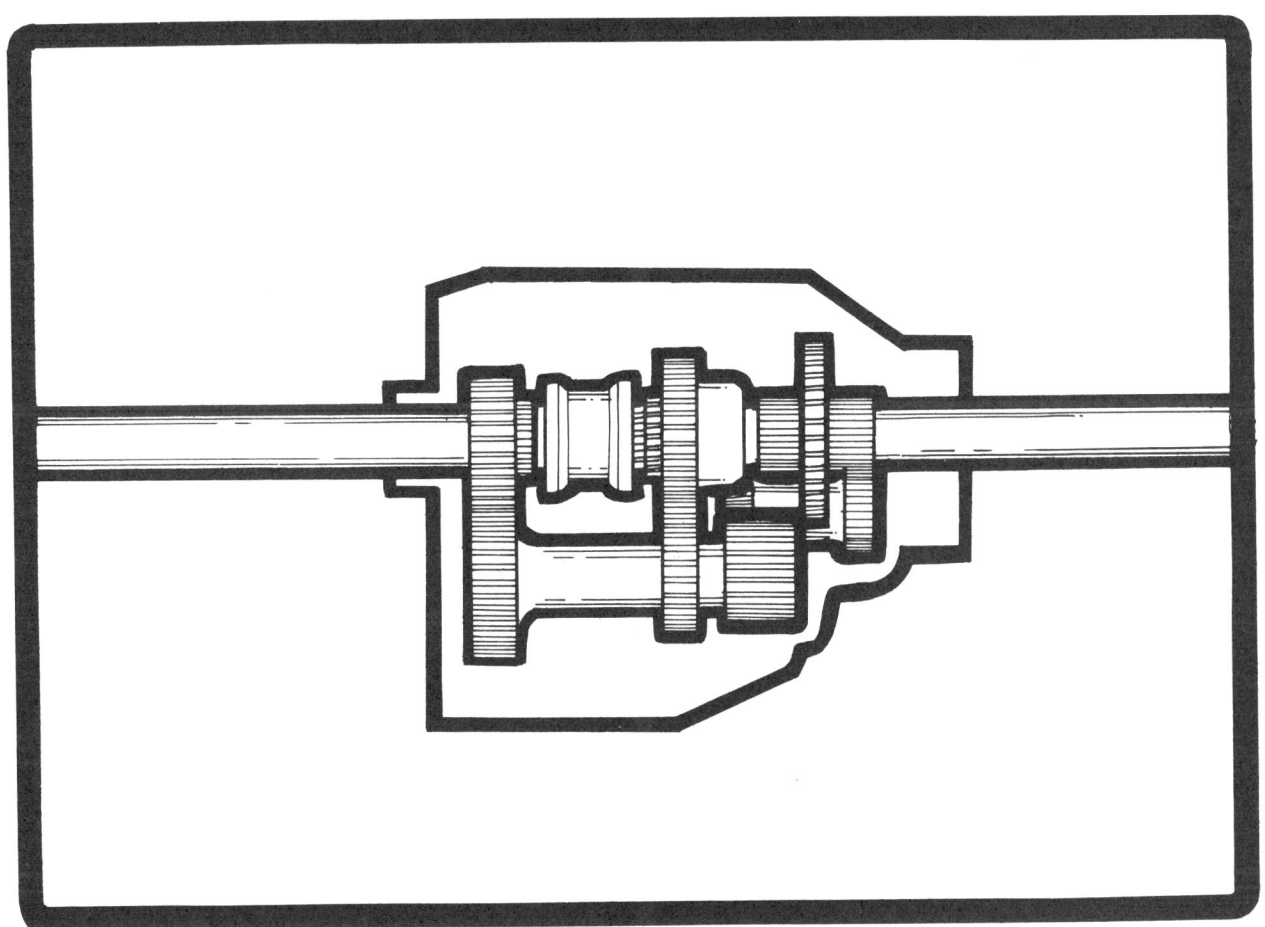

Typical constant mesh transmission in Neutral.

All transmissions do not look just like those we have shown. Some have a greater number of forward speeds, particularly trucks, and the gears may be arranged in a different order on the shafts. There are some entirely different types which we are going to discuss. But most transmissions operate on this same principle. There are a number of gears which can be connected together in different ways to give us the different ratios we want. Except when it is in direct drive, a certain amount of torque comes in at the front end from the clutch shaft, and a different amount goes out the back end to the propeller shaft.

THE AUTOMATIC TRANSMISSION

Planetary gears

Planetary gears are used in various arrangements in automobiles. And that is one of the interesting things about them. We can make them do a number of different things according to how we connect them into the power system. But first let us look at one and see what it is.

In its simplest form, it is essentially three gears. There is a **sun gear,** or pinion, in the center. Then there is a small **planet gear** meshing with it. On the outside is the **ring gear,** an internal gear meshing with the planets. The planet gears are fastened together by the **planet carrier.** This holds them in place but lets them rotate. Just how these gears and carriers are fastened to the shafts depends on what we want the mechanism to do.

Suppose we connect the sun gear to the input, or driving shaft, and the planet carrier to the output, or driven shaft. We put a brake band around the outside of the ring gear and hold it tight so it cannot move.

Then if the engine drives the sun gear, the planet gears must turn around. But they cannot stand still and rotate on their shafts because that would mean the ring gear must move, and we are holding that with the brake. So they have to move around the ring gear and the planet carrier moves with them. It is something like the differential we described. There are two motions to the planet gears. Each one is rotating about its own shaft, and at the same time they are all moving around in a circle on the teeth of the ring gear. This is where this type of gearing gets its name. The motion is much the same as the Earth and other planets around the sun. Each one rotates on its own axis, but they also continually circle around the sun.

The planet carrier, and thus the driven shaft, is turning much more slowly than the sun gear and drive shaft and in the same direction. Just what the ratio is depends on the size of the gears and we will not go into the details of how it is figured. As an example, however, with the smallest practical planets the ratio cannot be less than 2½ to 1. When the planets and the sun gear are the same size, the ratio is 4 to 1. This of course means that the speed is reduced to ¼, and the torque increased 4 times.

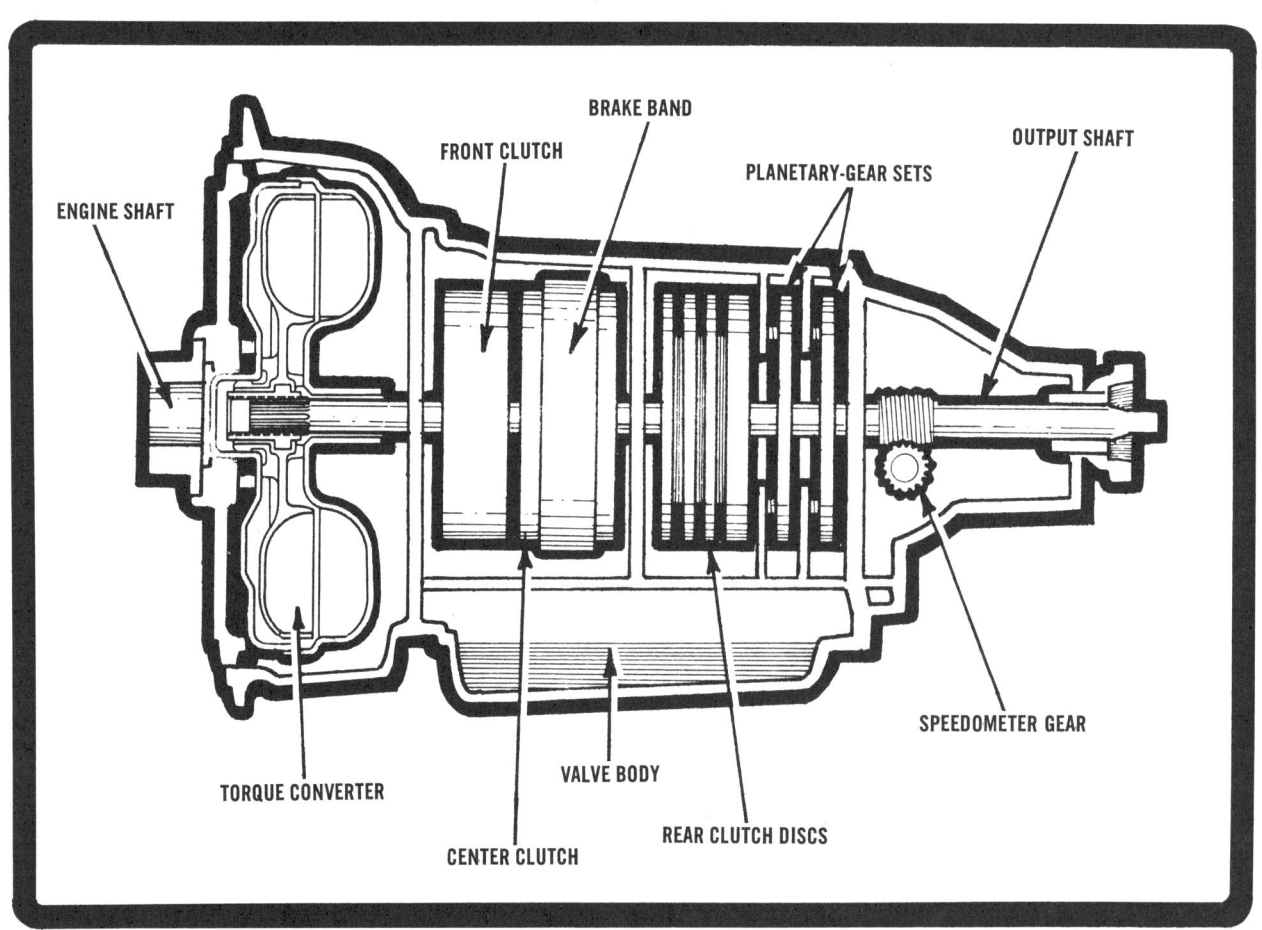

Cutaway of a typical automatic transmission.

In order to shift into direct drive, we release the brake on the ring gear and engage a clutch connecting the drive shaft directly to the driven shaft. If we wish, this can be done by clutching the planet carrier to either the sun gear or ring gear. In either case none of the gears can turn on each other, so the whole mechanism is locked and rotates all together without affecting the drive.

We mentioned that we can get various results with a planetary transmission by connecting it up in different ways. If we drive the ring gear and hold the sun gear still, we will still increase torque as we did in the case just described, but it will not be increased so much. By other arrangements we can increase the speed and reduce the torque, and by still other means we can get reverse. We have three units, any one of which we can hold stationary, and either of the other two can be the driving or driven member. So there are six possible combinations. Practically all of them are used in automobiles in one way or another.

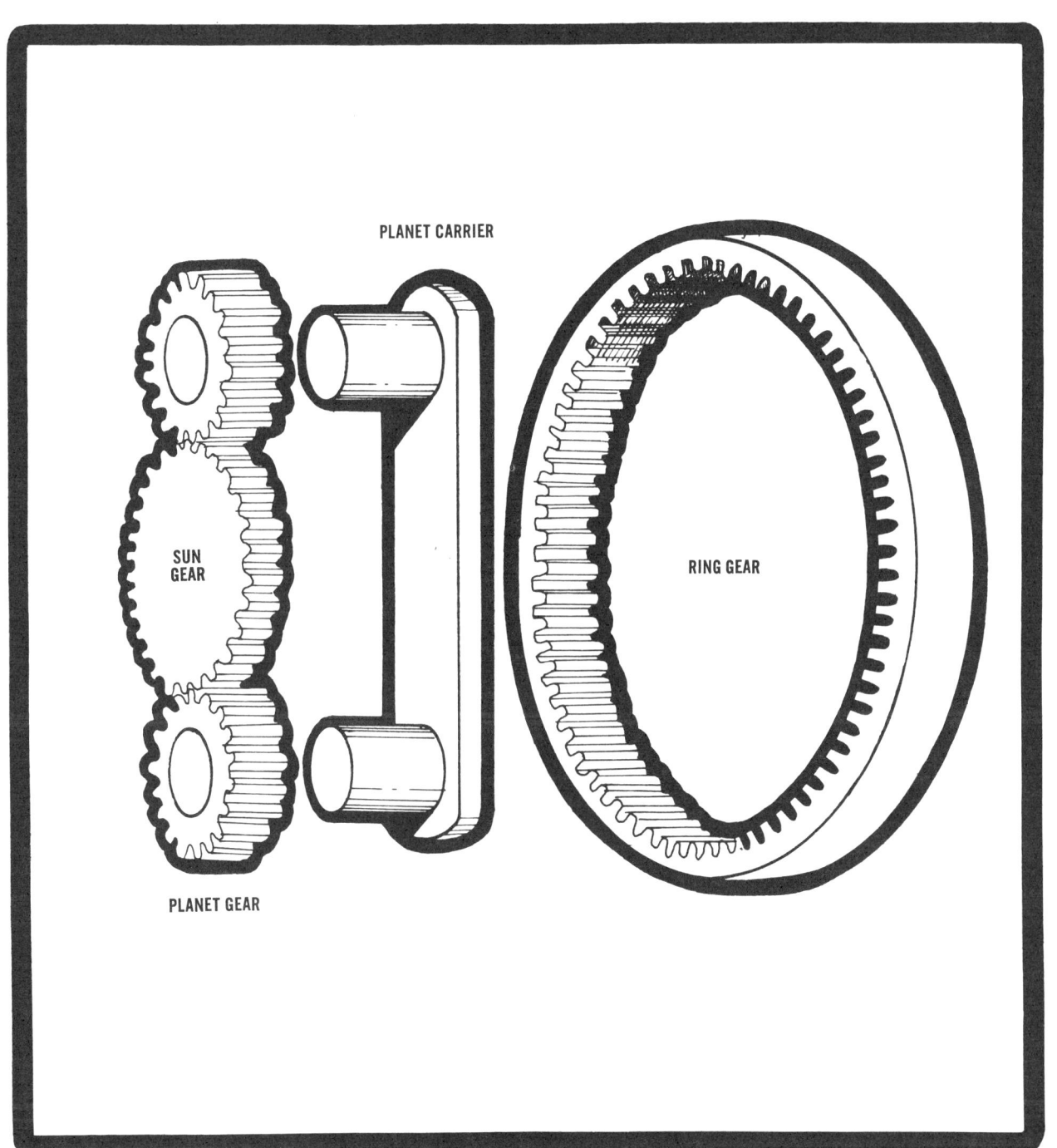

Typical planetary gearset which is the basis of operation for automatic transmissions.

There are various modifications of this simple planetary gear. There are some with double planets of different sizes, and there are compound planetary gears, which consist of two planetary gearsets with certain gears of one connected to certain gears of the other. These act in fundamentally the same way as the simple planetary, but following the power flow through them is rather complicated and figuring the gear ratio is not worth the trouble unless we are in the business of designing transmissions.

Planetary gears are used in automobiles largely as automatic or semi-automatic transmissions.

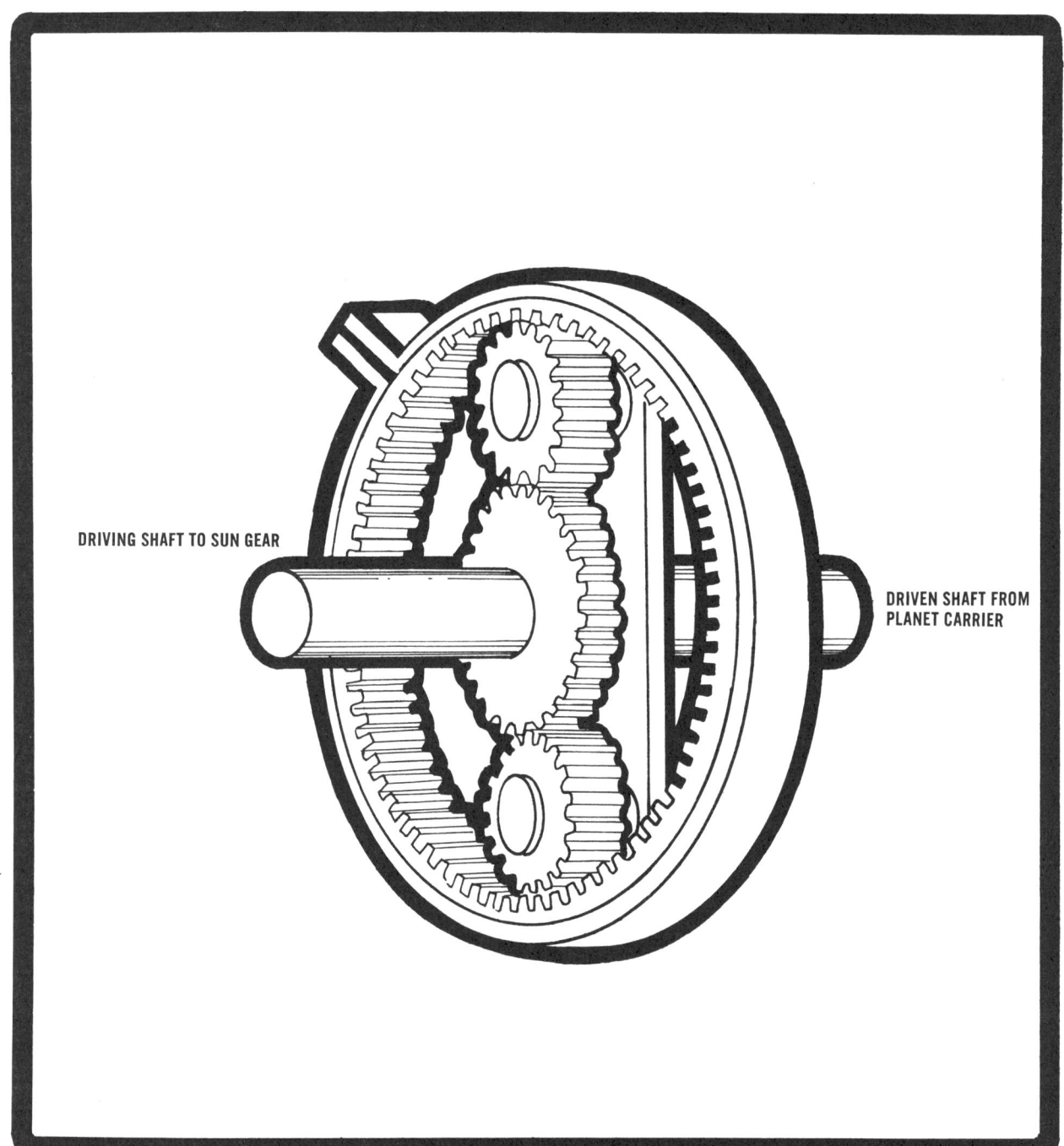

When the components are assembled together, this is how they mesh with one another.

PLANETARY GEAR COMBINATIONS

There are three units in a planetary gear—sun gear, planet gears and carrier, and ring gear. To get various results we can hold any one of these units stationary, and either of the other two can be the driving or driven member. So there are six possible combinations. We show them here, with colors indicating the driving, driven, and locked members, and the labels telling what kind of gear results from each arrangement.

They are all planetary gears, but a number of different results are obtained by hooking them up differently.

■ DRIVING   ▨ DRIVEN   ☐ LOCKED

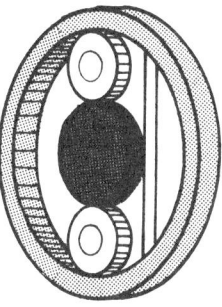

Reduction gear—less speed, more torque.

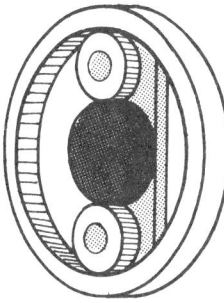

Reversing reduction gear—less speed, more torque, turns backward.

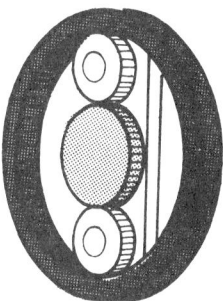

Reduction gear—less speed, more torque.

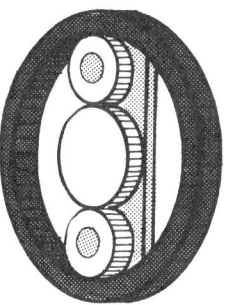

Reversing overdrive—more speed, less torque, turns backward.

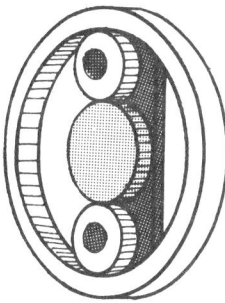

Overdrive—more speed, less torque.

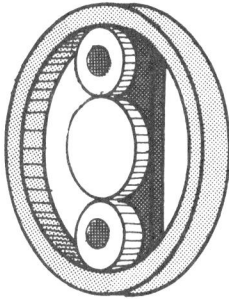

Overdrive—more speed, less torque.

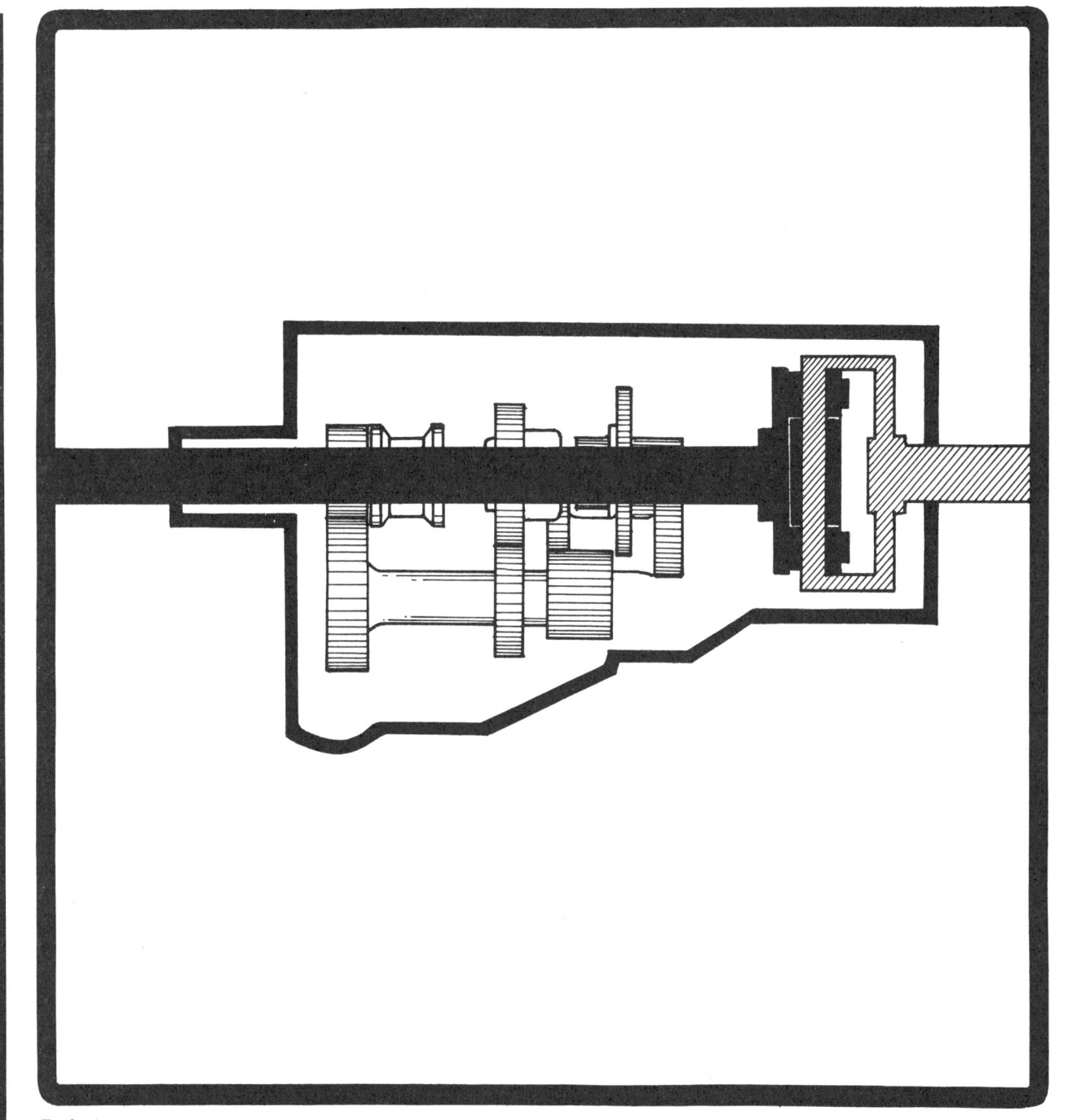

Typical power flow through an automatic transmission in high gear.

The name **automatic transmission** is used to cover a lot of different things. Ordinarily it means any arrangement which will change *by itself* the ratio between the engine and the wheels, change it without the driver having to do anything. Almost any transmission can be arranged to work automatically, or partially so. It is a question of the controls more than anything else. There must be something to think for the driver, to decide when the ratio should be changed. Various things have been used to control the time of shifting—car speed, engine speed, the torque required or load on the engine, and combinations of these. Automatic transmissions were invented almost as soon as there were automobiles, they have kept on being invented ever since, and what form they will take in the future is anybody's guess.

While almost any kind of transmission can be made to work automatically, some are easier than others to use this way. Some get into a lot of complications. Planetary gears have been popular for this purpose, one reason being that they are truly constant mesh gears. We do not have to shift gears. We only have to hold one member tight in some manner.

One use of planetary gears is in an automatic **overdrive.** This is not always thought of as an automatic transmission, but it really is. It is a 2-speed transmission in back of the regular 3-speed transmission, and it shifts automatically depending mostly on how fast the car is going. When we are cruising along the highway in the country, we do not need as much torque as when we are accelerating or driving in city traffic. We can afford to sacrifice some torque for speed. Or to say it another way, by changing the gear ratio we can get the same car speed with a lower engine speed. This means less noise and wear of engine parts, and usually less gasoline used. To do this we put a separate planetary transmission behind the regular transmission. At low speeds this is in direct drive and we do not even know it is there. We shift gears in the three-speed transmission in the ordinary way. But when we get above a certain speed in high gear, the planetary transmission comes into action. The sun gear is then grabbed and held stationary, power is applied to the planet carrier, and the ring gear is the driven member. As illustrated earlier, this gives us an overdrive. That is, we have more speed and less torque at the output shaft than we put into it. It is just opposite from first or second speed. We have come up from low gear to direct drive and now we go on through and beyond it. This ratio is usually about ¾ to 1. Or in other words, for the same miles per hour of the car, the engine is turning only three-quarters as fast as it would in direct drive.

There are a number of control devices mixed up with this which make it much less simple than it sounds. There are means to shift it automatically at certain speeds, to keep it from shifting when we do not want it to, to get back into direct drive even at high speeds, etc. Theoretically this can be used in combination with any gear of the regular transmission, giving us six speeds forward, but ordinarily it is used only with high gear.

We can get this same result by using a different ratio in the rear axle and going only to direct drive in the transmission. For example, if the rear axle—the ring gear and pinion—has a ratio of 4 to 1, and the overdrive ratio is ¾ to 1, the overall ratio from engine to wheels will be 4 x ¾, or 3 to 1. Now if we have a rear axle ratio of 3 to 1, the overall ratio in direct drive will again be 3 to 1. We should always bear in mind that the words **direct drive** and **overdrive** refer to the transmission only. There is still a reduction in the rear axle which we must take into account.

This general idea is used in one completely automatic transmission with which some cars have been equipped. It is a 4-speed transmission, the top gear being direct drive, and a low rear axle ratio is used. A low axle ratio usually means slower pickup or acceleration in high gear, so third speed is arranged so that it can be brought into use at almost any speed when more acceleration is desired.

The transmission consists of two planetary gear sets, one behind the other. Each planetary has two speeds, a reduction ratio and direct drive, but the reduction ratios are not the same. We can get the four speeds we want by choosing the proper ratios. In low gear, both planetaries are in action, giving us a double reduction. In second speed the front unit is in direct drive, and the rear unit alone gives a reduction of about 2½ to 1. In third speed we do just the opposite —the rear unit is in direct, and the front unit is working. This has a ratio of approximately 1½ to 1. In fourth speed, both units are in direct drive, so engine torque flows straight through to the rear axle. There is also a reverse gear, which is a third planetary unit behind the other two. It acts in combination with the other two units to furnish a low ratio in the reverse direction.

A fluid flywheel is a very important part of this combination. It is located between the engine and the transmission, but the flow of power from the engine actually goes first to the front planetary unit, then to the fluid coupling, and then to the second planetary unit. The effect is just the same, however, except that the coupling runs at a reduced speed at certain times, which has advantages. There is no friction clutch. The transmission shifts from one speed to another under load, without being disconnected from the engine. This is possible because the fluid flywheel cushions the shock, and is one of the big differences between this and most other transmissions, even some which use a fluid flywheel.

The planetary gears are controlled by brake bands and friction clutches. A brake band holds the proper member stationary in each unit when it is in low ratio, and a clutch locks each unit together when direct drive is needed in that unit. Oil pressure makes these brakes and clutches work at the right time, depending on how fast the car is going and how far the accelerator pedal is pushed down. All the driver has to do is control the speed of the engine, and the gear shifting will take care of itself.

All automatic transmissions are not of the planetary type. We could use a conventional 3-speed transmission if we wanted to, by adding the right kind of controls. It would probably be called a semi-automatic transmission. If we place the shift lever in one position it shifts automatically back and forth between first and second speed, depending on how fast the car is going. With the shift lever in another position it does the same thing between third and fourth. A fluid flywheel is provided, so the car can be started in third if desired and thus the driver does not need to do any shifting.

We will not try to explain the action of this transmission, but it is quite similar to that of the constant mesh type we described earlier. A positive clutch with synchronizers slides back and forth to make the shifts, but this is moved by a combination of vacuum and spring force instead of being shifted by hand.

As we said, these are only examples of automatic transmissions of various types. There are a great many others.

Hydraulic torque converter

In our discussion of the fluid flywheel, we pointed out that it was simply a clutch, a hydraulic clutch, which could not deliver any more torque than was put into it. It is a very useful addition to a transmission, but it cannot replace the transmission because it is not a torque multiplier.

But we can make a torque multiplier out of it, and the majority of automatic transmissions today use the multiplying type, commonly designated as **hydraulic torque converters.**

In principle, all we have to do to a fluid flywheel to make a torque converter is add another set of blades —**stationary** blades. You know the old rule that for every force there must be an equal and opposite reacting force. In transmissions this means that we cannot multiply torque unless we have some solid point to push on. We usually say we must have a reaction member, some stationary part connected to the frame of the vehicle. In a conventional transmission the whole casing is fastened solidly and this holds the shafts in place. In the planetary we have to grab hold of one of the three members before we can multiply torque—we have to hold it stationary in relation to the frame. And we have the same situation here. In a fluid flywheel the whole thing turns around together. But if we put in a new part, a set of blades tied solidly to the frame, we have something to take the reaction, to furnish the reacting force. Then it can multiply torque.

We show here the simplest arrangement. We have the pump, or driving element, and the turbine, or driven element, just as in the fluid flywheel. But between them we add a stator, the reaction element. The casing is filled with oil, which circulates in the usual manner, outward from the pump, inward through the turbine, and then through the stator back to the pump.

The blades are not straight and flat however. If we could spread the three members out flat and look down on them, we would get an idea of their shape and how the liquid flows through them. The pump pushes the oil in the direction it is turning, and this oil hits the turbine and forces it to turn in the same direction. In doing this the oil bounces off the turbine blades in the opposite direction, and is flowing somewhat backward when it reaches the stator. If this reaction member were free to turn it would turn backward, but it is held tight. So it straightens out the oil and gets it moving in a forward direction again before it returns to the pump. In this way the motion of the oil assists the pump, and that is why such an arrangement can multiply torque.

A hydraulic torque converter is completely automatic in itself. It furnishes the greatest multiplication of torque when the car is starting from standstill, and this becomes less as the car picks up speed. The torque converter does not shift. It just smoothly changes from one ratio to another and to another in a continuous fashion, without definite steps. It is what we know as a continuously variable transmission.

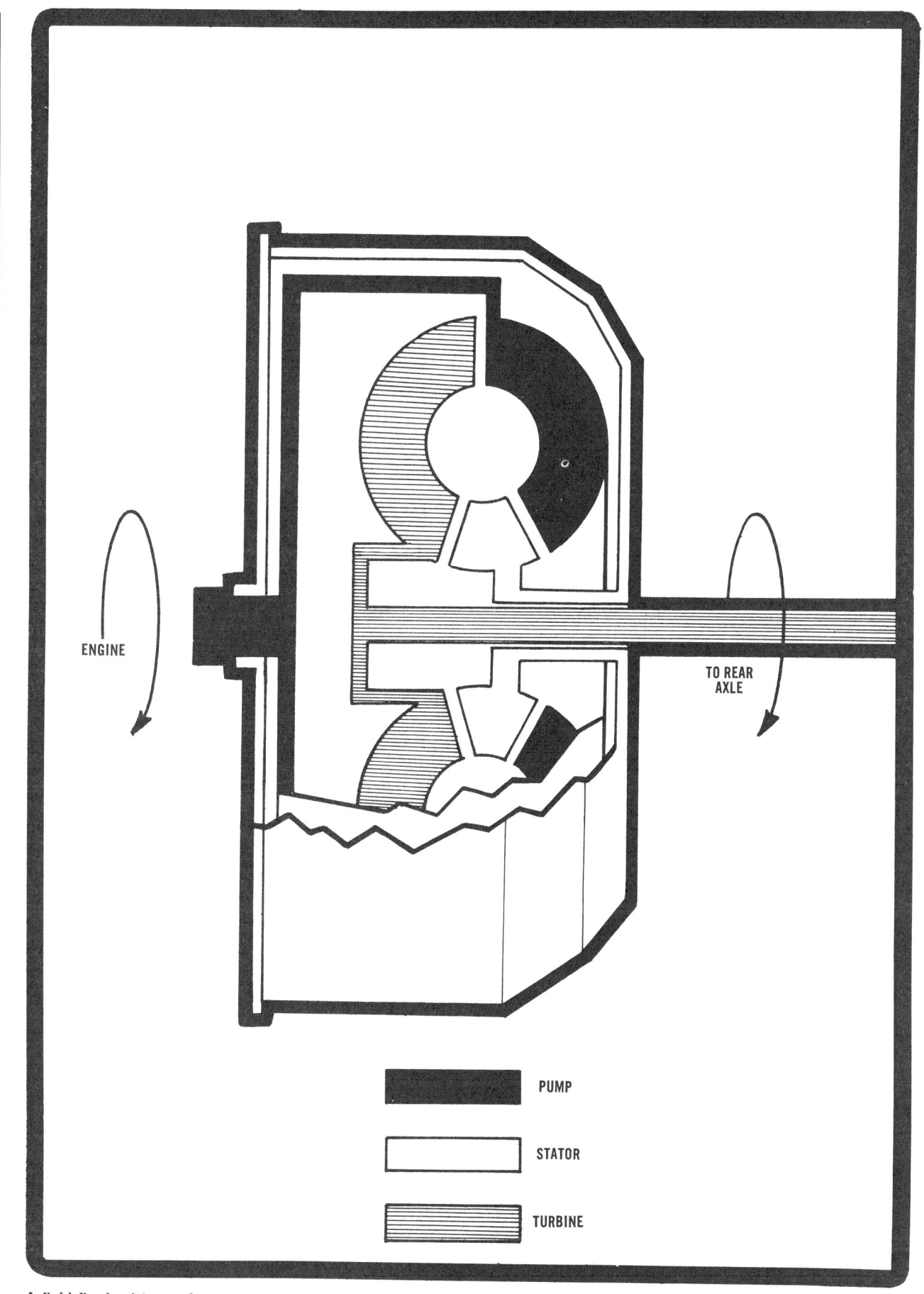

A fluid flywheel transmits power without any torque multiplication.

This seems like the perfect way to drive a car, but there are some problems. If we tried to use the simple design we have shown, the results would be disappointing. Such an arrangement gives maximum efficiency at only one speed, and a large part of the time we would be wasting fuel. The stationary blades are necessary for multiplying torque, but when we are cruising along they just get in the way and churn up the oil. The curvature of the blades in all three elements is important, and if we design them for one condition they may not be so good for others. It is difficult to get as much torque multiplication as we desire to give good performance in starting up, and if the designer concentrates on this problem, he must sacrifice something else.

But there are various things which can be done to overcome most of these difficulties. We lose some of the simplicity, but it is well worth it. For example, we might have two pumps instead of one—or two turbines or two stators. They would probably have different blade angles and operate more or less independently, usually one taking up where the other leaves off. There are many possible arrangements along this line, depending on conditions and what results are most desired.

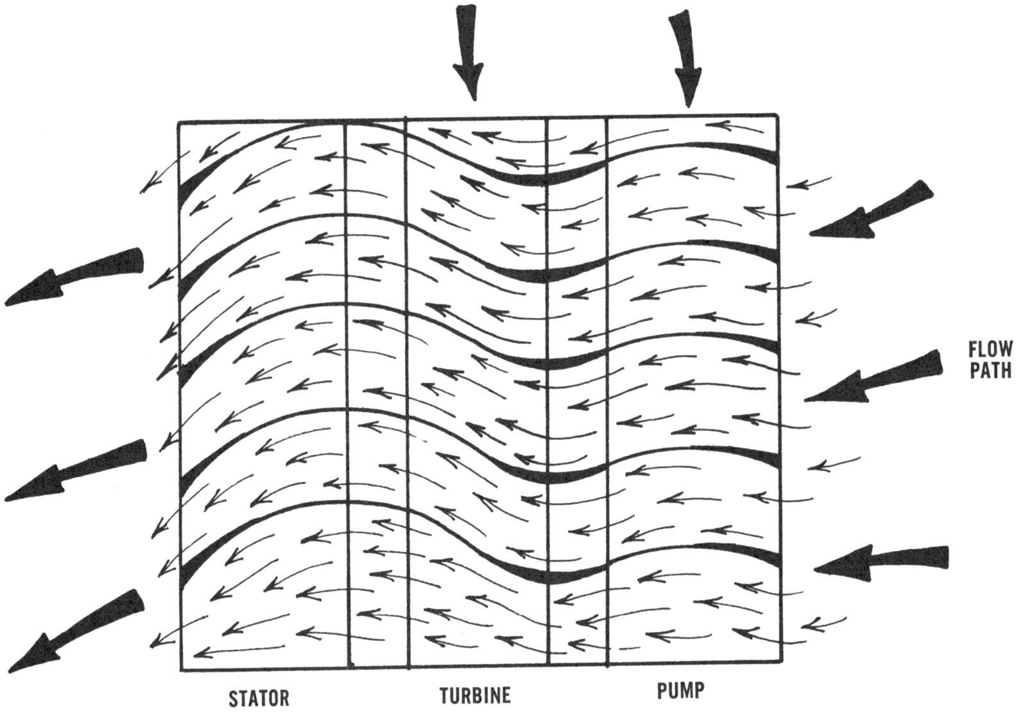

The flow path of transmission fluid through the torque converter.

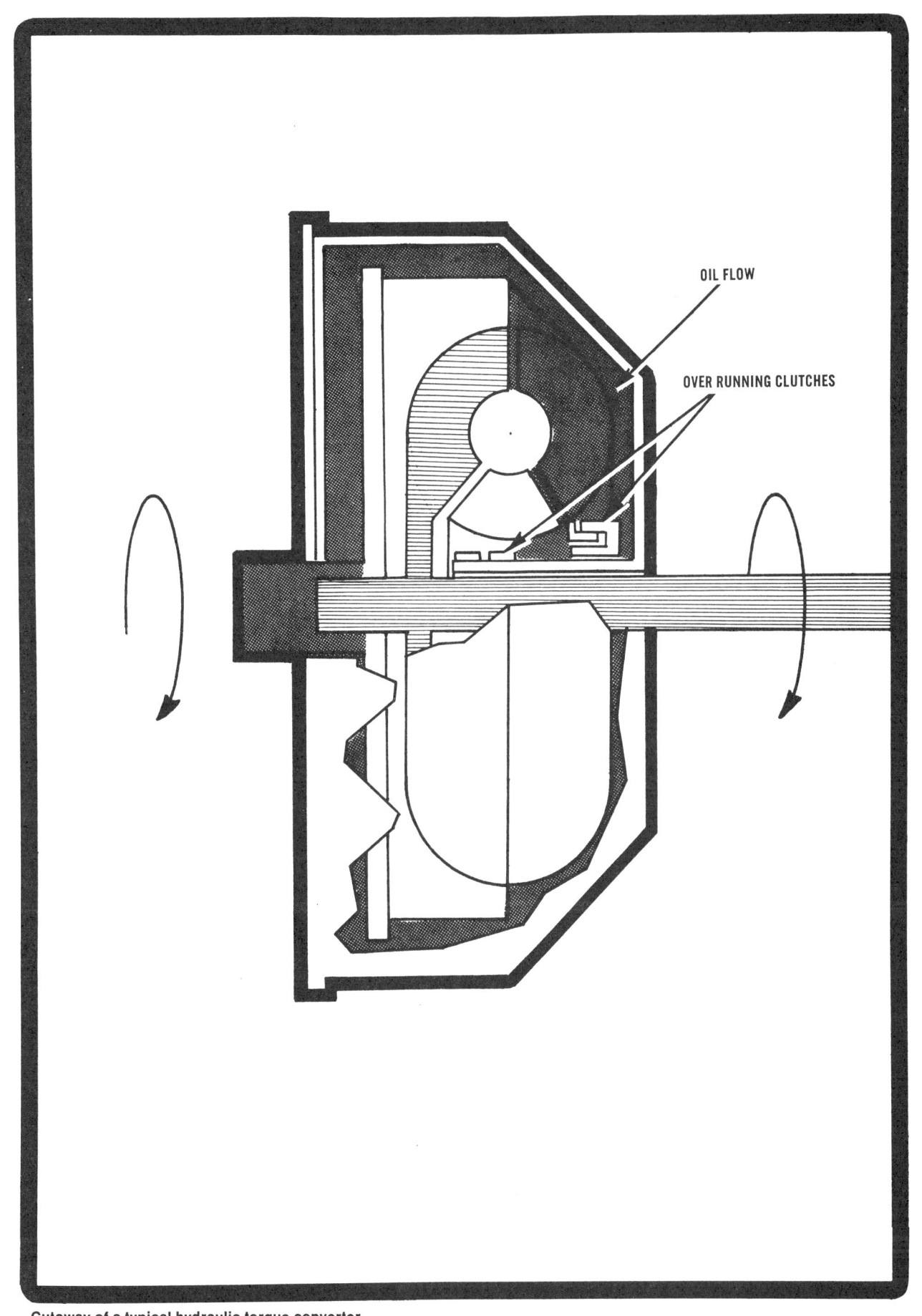
Cutaway of a typical hydraulic torque converter.

One thing which improves the efficiency is mounting the stator or stators on an overrunning, or one-way clutch. This prevents the stator from turning backward, and thus it can act as the reaction element for multiplying torque. When the car gets up to speed, however, there is no backward force on the blades, and they turn forward, or free-wheel, with the oil flow.

What this actually means is that the torque converter is now operating as a fluid coupling, which wastes very little power under these conditions.

In some cases the blades of the stator are mounted on pivots. Thus they can be shifted at the will of the driver from a low angle position giving economical cruising to a high angle for temporary increased acceleration or pull. This is known as variable pitch control.

With some automatic transmissions, gears are used to assist the torque multiplication of the torque converter. This means that the converter does not have to be designed to give a low range ratio and is therefore more efficient over the rest of the range. It is usually a planetary gear set behind the converter. It is sometimes used only as a manually selected "low" gear. In some transmissions it is controlled automatically and used regularly for starting. Various arrangements of gears and clutches may also be used to provide reverse, neutral and improved engine braking.

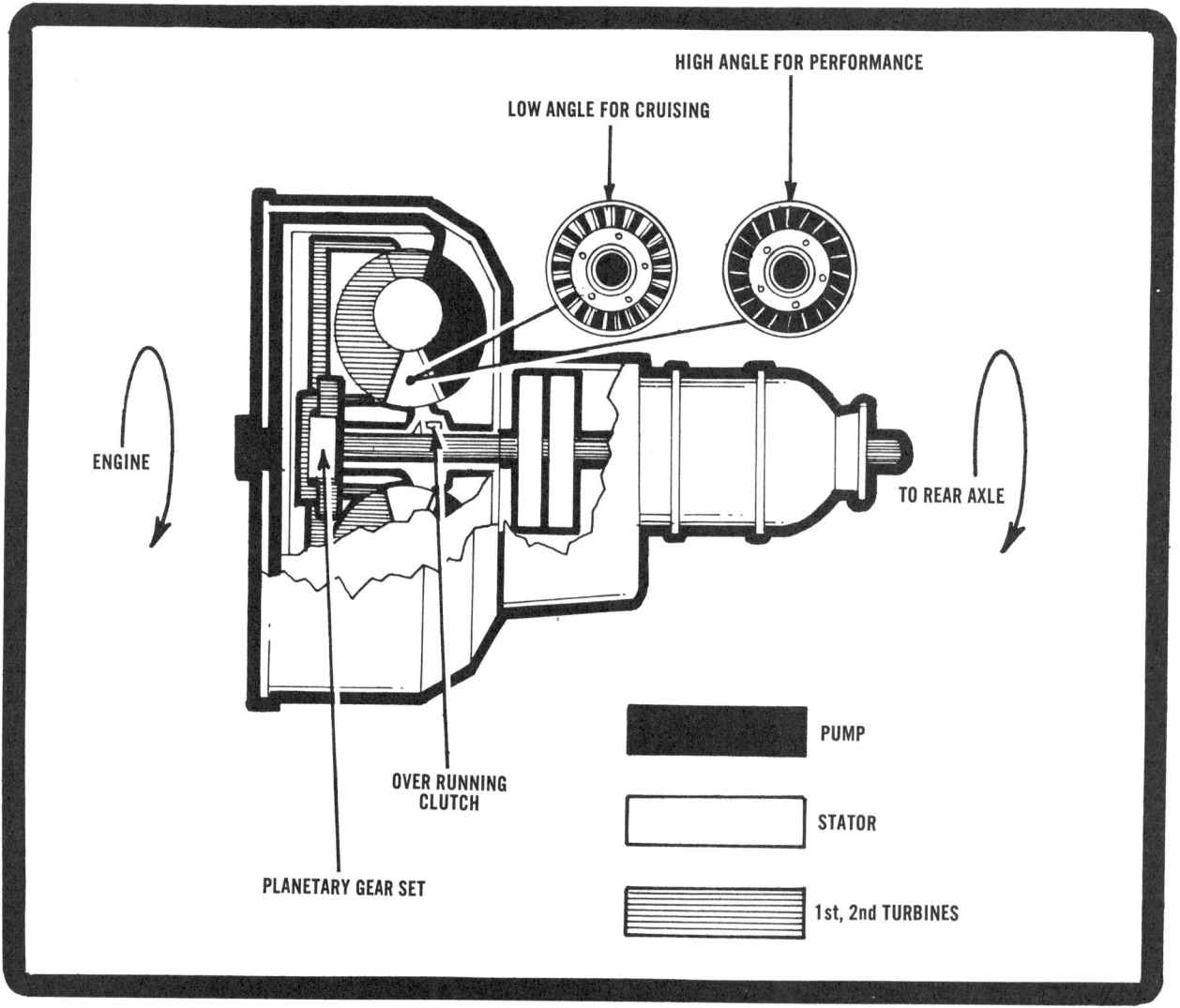

Typical operation of a torque converter and planetary gearset.

THE ELECTRICAL SYSTEM

BATTERY, CHARGING, STARTING AND IGNITION

Your car's electrical system starts the engine, supplies high voltage to the ignition system, and operates such important accessories as the lights, windshield wipers, heater, air conditioner and radio.

The storage battery is the heart of the system, and acts as a reservoir of energy. As the battery receives charges of electricity from the alternator, it converts this electrical energy into chemical energy, storing it for future use, and changes it back into electricity when needed.

The automobile battery is a lead-acid type in which two sets of different type lead plates are submerged in a solution of sulfuric acid and water. The plates are enclosed in the plastic or hard rubber container you see. A group of positive and negative plates forms a cell, which develops about two volts. Most automobile batteries have six cells and supply 12 volts, although some have three cells and supply six volts.

The terminals

The battery has two terminals, usually on the top of the case at opposite ends. One is positive (+) and the other negative (−). The negative terminal is usually connected to the car's steel frame, which acts as a ground. Another cable connects the positive terminal to the starter and other accessories.

When you turn on any of the car's electrical devices, you complete the circuit between the two terminals of the battery. This action immediately converts part of the chemical energy in the battery to electrical energy.

The charging system

Like any other reservoir, the battery energy must be constantly replenished or it won't function. A continuing supply of electrical current for storage in the battery is developed by either a generator or an alternator, which is driven by the fan belt. It works only when your car's engine is running. Older cars have a generator, which produces direct current (DC). Most newer models are equipped with alternators, which supply alternating current (AC), then convert it to DC before sending it to the battery. Alternators replaced generators because they can produce more current for the battery at low speeds in city driving.

The second important element in the charging system is the voltage regulator. This device makes sure the battery is not damaged by getting more electric current than it can store. When a battery is partially discharged, the alternator works at or near its maxi-

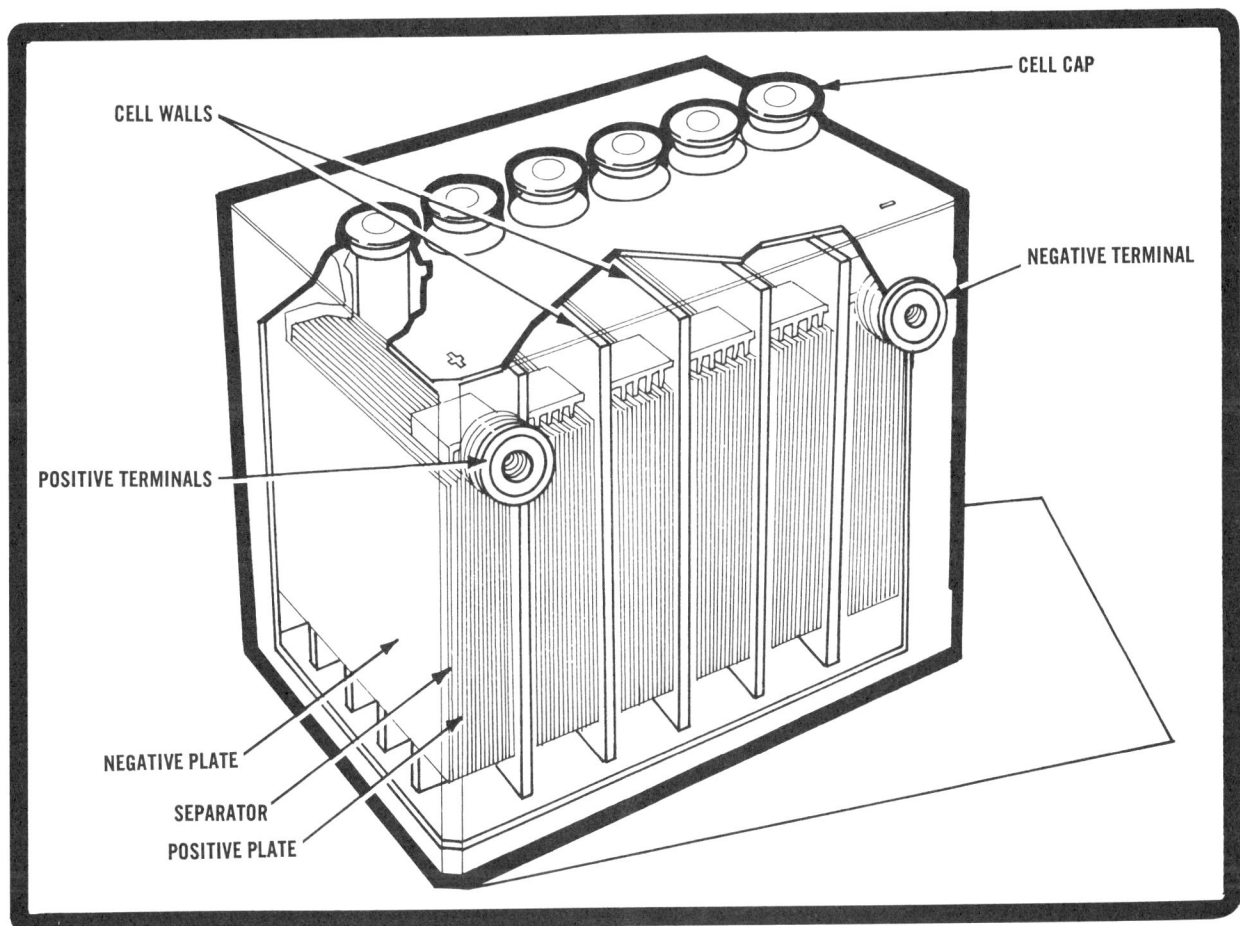

The heart of your car's electrical system is the battery.

mum capacity generating current. As the battery approaches full charge, the alternator's output must be cut to prevent damage from overcharging. The voltage regulator automatically adjusts the charging rate. If the system is functioning properly, the charge of electric current to the battery is kept just high enough to supply ignition and accessories without drawing off current from the battery. It's like living on your income without touching your savings.

Instrument panel

Your car's instrument panel contains either an ammeter or a warning light to alert you to conditions in the electrical system. The ammeter needle measures the rate of charge and discharge while a warning light merely registers discharge. If it lights up while the engine is running, you are taking more electricity out of the battery than you are putting in. If the warning stays on at any speed above idle, the alternator and regulator should be checked. The fan belt also should be checked. It may be loose or broken.

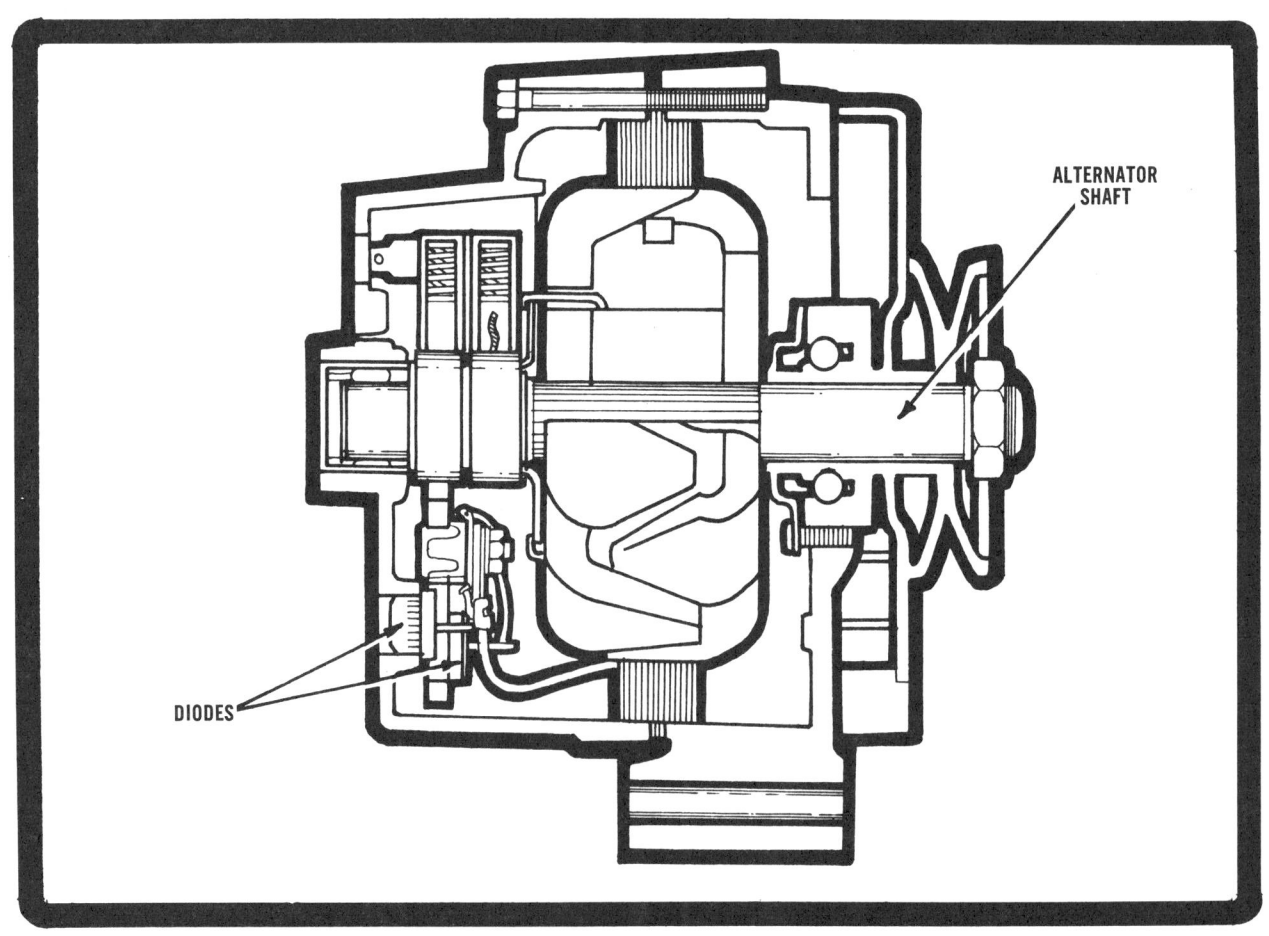

An alternator is really nothing more than an alternating current generator. It is the electrical system's chief source of power while the engine is running.

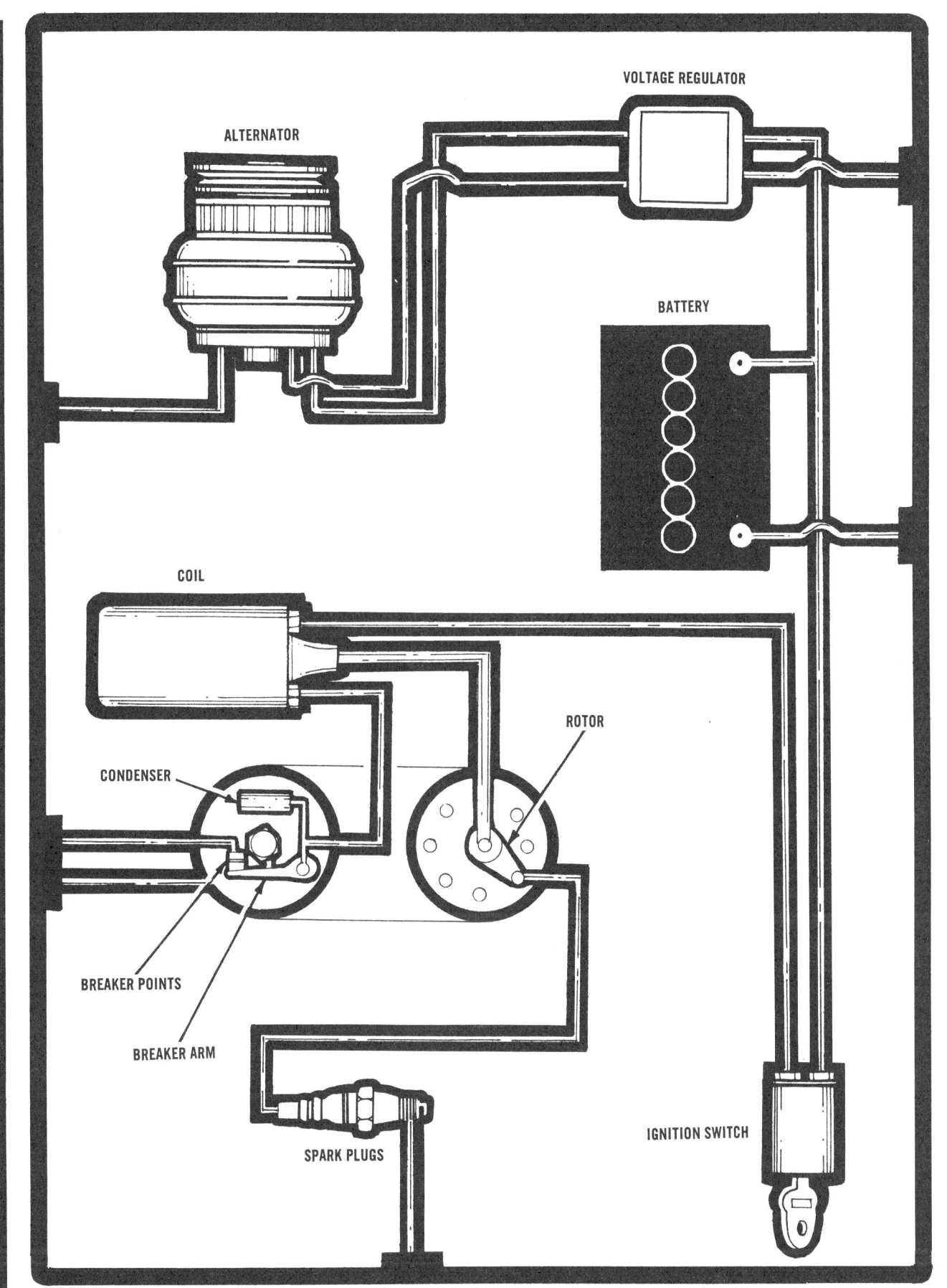

A simplified illustration of how various components in the ignition circuit of your car's electrical system are hooked up and work together.

The starting system

A gasoline engine cannot start without help. In the early days, that help was a strong arm and a crank. Now, the starter does the same job when you turn a key. The starter is an electric motor with a small gear on one end of its shaft. When you turn the key to the start position, the gear on the starter meshes with a larger gear on the engine, and the starter turns the engine until it catches and runs under its own power.

The starter draws more current than any other electrical device on the car. Therefore it drains the most energy from the battery. It requires heavy cables to carry the current from the battery with minimum loss. Electricity flows like water. You can pour more water through a large pipe than a small one. The large amount of current required by the starter, for example, could not be carried through the ignition switch and the electrical current load would burn out its contacts.

The solenoid

The problem is solved by a unit called the solenoid. When you turn the key to start the engine, a small amount of current is sent to the solenoid. Acting as a magnet, the solenoid draws the contacts of a large switch together, giving a wider passage for the large flow of current from the battery to the starter.

If your car has an automatic transmission, there is one other important part in the starting system. It is a neutral switch, and it prevents the motor from being started unless the transmission is in Neutral or Park.

The ignition system

Your car's engine develops its power from a rapid sequence of small explosions of the fuel-air mixture, driving the pistons up and down in the cylinders. All it takes to ignite these fires is an electric spark jumping a gap only a few thousandths of an inch wide in the spark plug of each cylinder. But it takes a ruggedly built ignition system to get the spark to the right place at the right time, several thousand times per mile.

The easiest way to understand how the ignition system works is to learn the function of each major part. The battery supplies the electric current. The ignition switch turns the whole system on or off when you turn the key. You have probably heard your serviceman refer to distributor points. They are also called breaker points, contact points or just plain points. There are two of them, shaped like discs and not much wider than the head of a match.

The points are located inside the distributor, which distributes electricity to each cylinder of the engine. As the distributor shaft turns, it pushes the distributor points apart and a spring pulls them back together.

When the points touch each other, they complete a circuit that sends electricity into the coil, which steps up the battery's 12 volts to the several thousand volts needed to fire the spark plugs. When the points open, the coil releases its high voltage to the cylinder scheduled to fire.

The electricity reaches the spark plugs by way of the distributor cap, rotor and ignition cables. The distributor cap is a round piece of plastic which holds the cables going to the spark plugs. The rotor is a small piece of plastic with a projecting metal tongue mounted on top of the distributor shaft. As the rotor turns, its metal tongue lines up with contacts in the distributor cap, and current flows through an ignition cable to the spark plug—where it jumps the gap between the two heavy wires, or electrodes, of the plug and creates the spark that starts the fire in the cylinder.

There's one other ignition part that plays an important role in the system: the condenser. It is located inside the distributor and connected to the points. Electric current, like anything that moves, builds up momentum, so it cannot be stopped instantly. Without a condenser, some current would jump the gap between the points as they start to open, creating a spark that would burn the points. The condenser traps this current before it can do any damage.

On most '74 and later cars, an electronic ignition system is used. A rotating reluctor and magnetic pickup coil replace the traditional cam, breaker points and condenser in the distributors of cars equipped for electronic ignition. This system reduces the time between tuneups. The high spots of the reluctor interrupt the magnetic field of the pickup coil and the permanent magnet. These interruptions, or pulses, are transmitted from the pickup to a nearby electronic control unit. There the pulses signal a transistor to break the low-voltage subcircuit and release high voltage from the coil to the spark plugs.

Timing the spark

If your engine ran at constant speed, it would be simple to set off the spark at precisely the right instant. However, as you speed up the engine, it's necessary to start the fire in the cylinder earlier.

An automatic spark advance mechanism in the distributor makes the points open sooner as engine speed increases.

THE STEERING AND SUSPENSION SYSTEM

Front end service, front end alignment, and wheel alignment are terms commonly used on signs or in advertising to describe the type of service for correcting problems of a car's steering control and tire wear. Wheel alignment angle adjustment or correction (explained later) is only part of the total service.

Several parts and operating systems are involved in your ability to steer the car and they are all connected or interrelated in some fashion. If one or more of the parts are bent, damaged, too loose or too tight, it can affect the entire steering system.

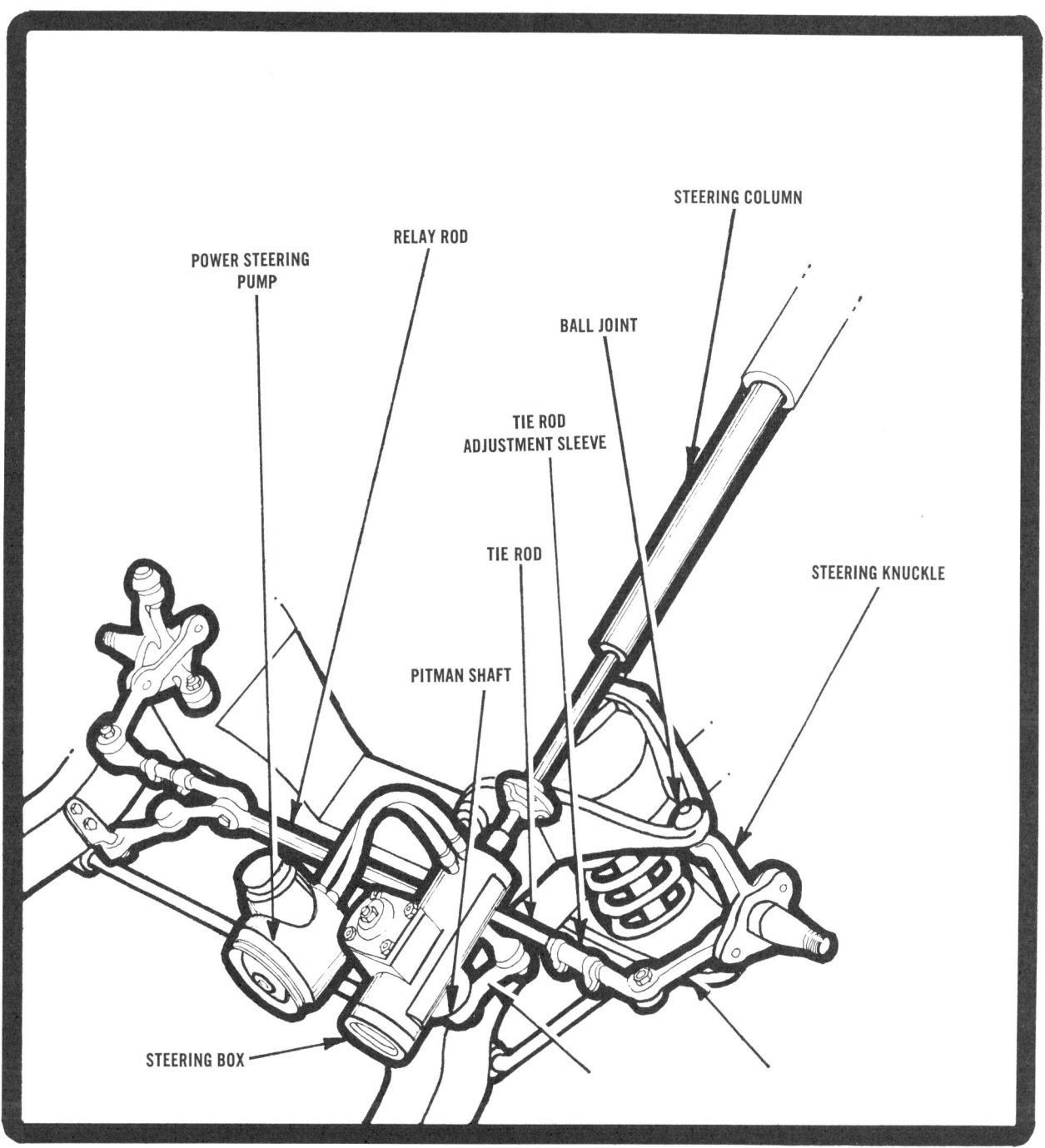

The interrelated parts of a steering system and how they interreact with each other each time the steering wheel is turned.

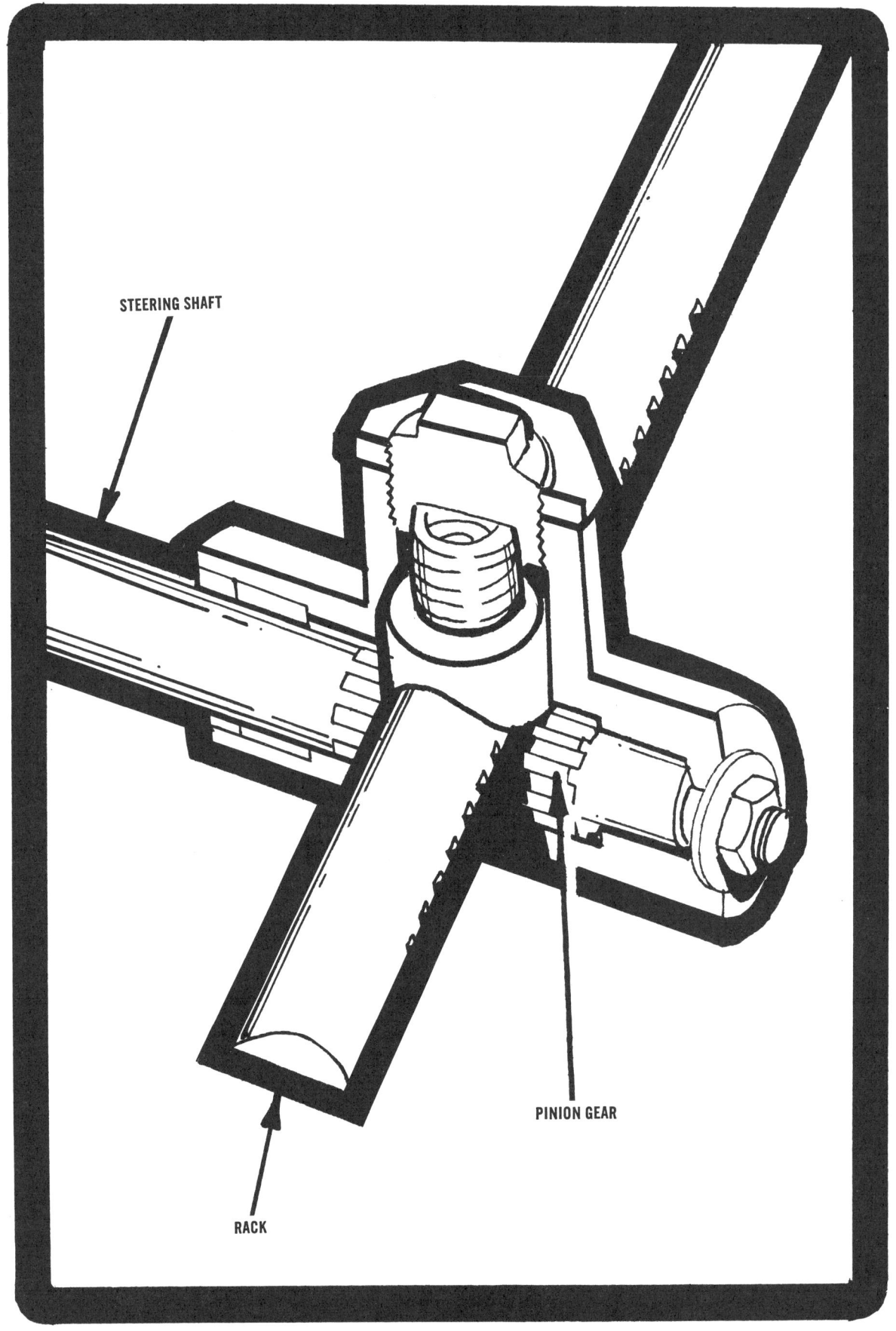

Rack and pinion steering, so popular with many of today's smaller cars, is a simple but precise system which transfers steering wheel movements almost directly to the steering linkage. When the steering shaft turns, it rotates a pinion gear meshed at right angles with a toothed rack which is connected to the Pitman arm.

What turns the car?

When you turn the steering wheel to change your car's direction, several things happen. The wheel turns the steering gear which is in the column extending down from the steering wheel. The gear is hooked to the steering linkage, a system of rods and levers which ties together the two front wheels. The steering gear pushes the steering linkage left or right which, in turn, swivels the front wheels, causing the car to turn.

Springs and shocks

The suspension system components attach the wheels to the frame of the car and permit each front wheel to turn and move up or down independently when going over bumps or dips in the road surface. Springs, either coil or leaf-type, suspend the body and allow the wheels to move up and dawn.

The term "shock absorber" is actually a misnomer. The car's springs actually absorb the shocks caused by road irregularities.

Inside a power steering box, the steering shaft turns a worm gear that is screwed into a large nut. The nut travels back and forth on friction-reducing ball bearings that are constantly recirculated by dropping into the nut's bored channels and emerging at the opposite side. Power to move the nut comes from pressurized fluid entering from a pump through rotary valves that open in response to the steering wheel. Depending on the turn direction, the fluid moves a piston forward or backward. This action moves the nut, which turns the Pitman shaft and steering linkage.

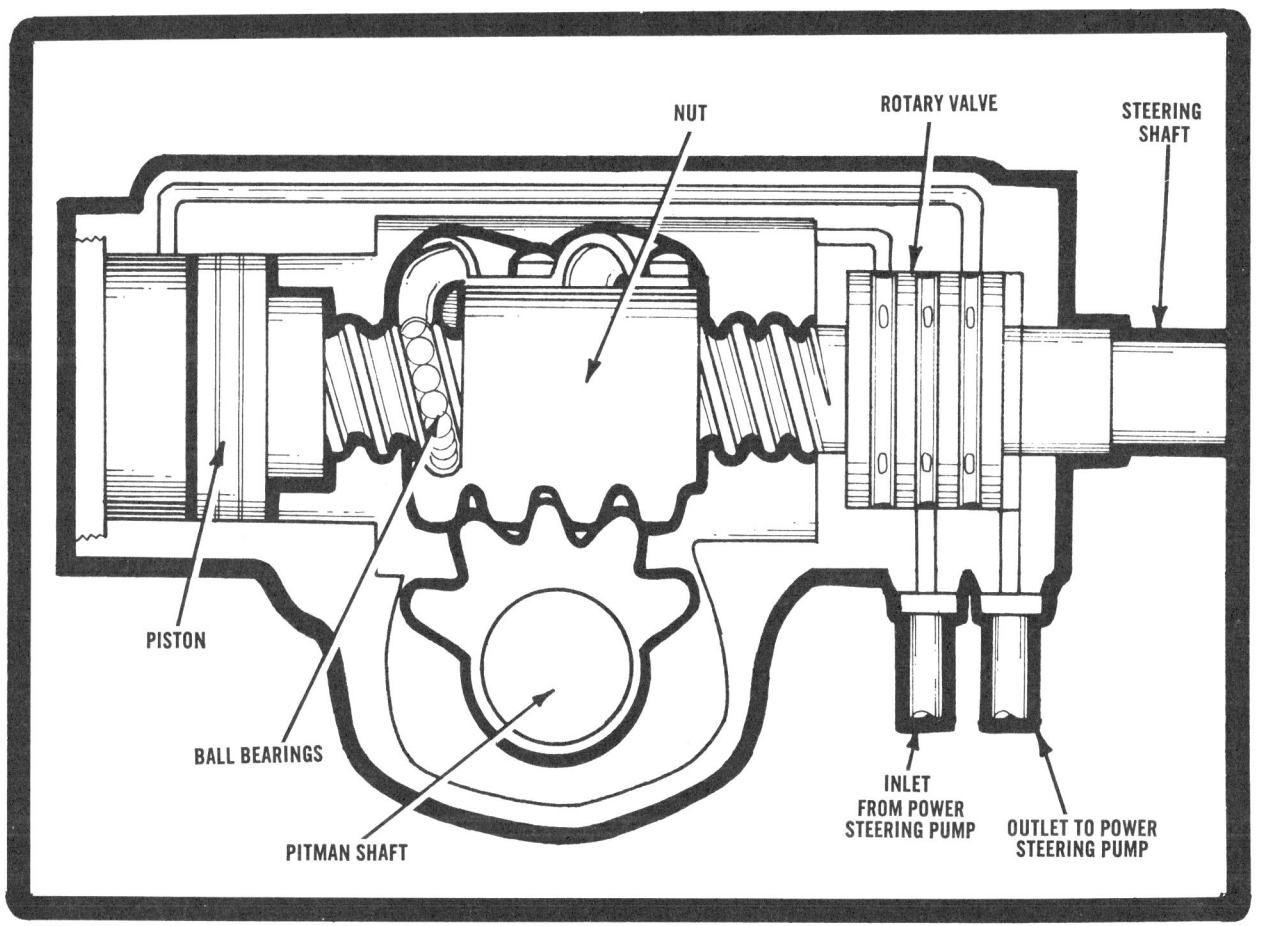

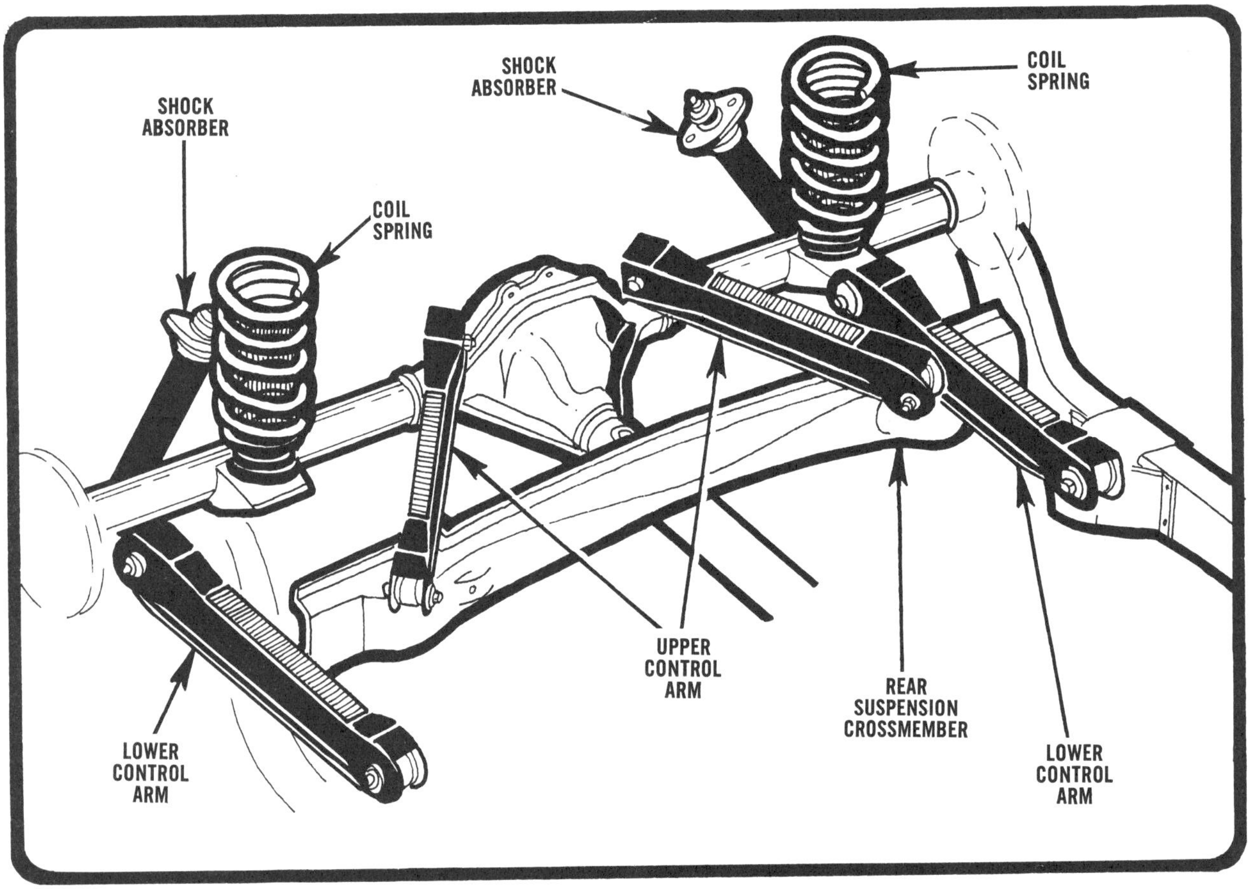

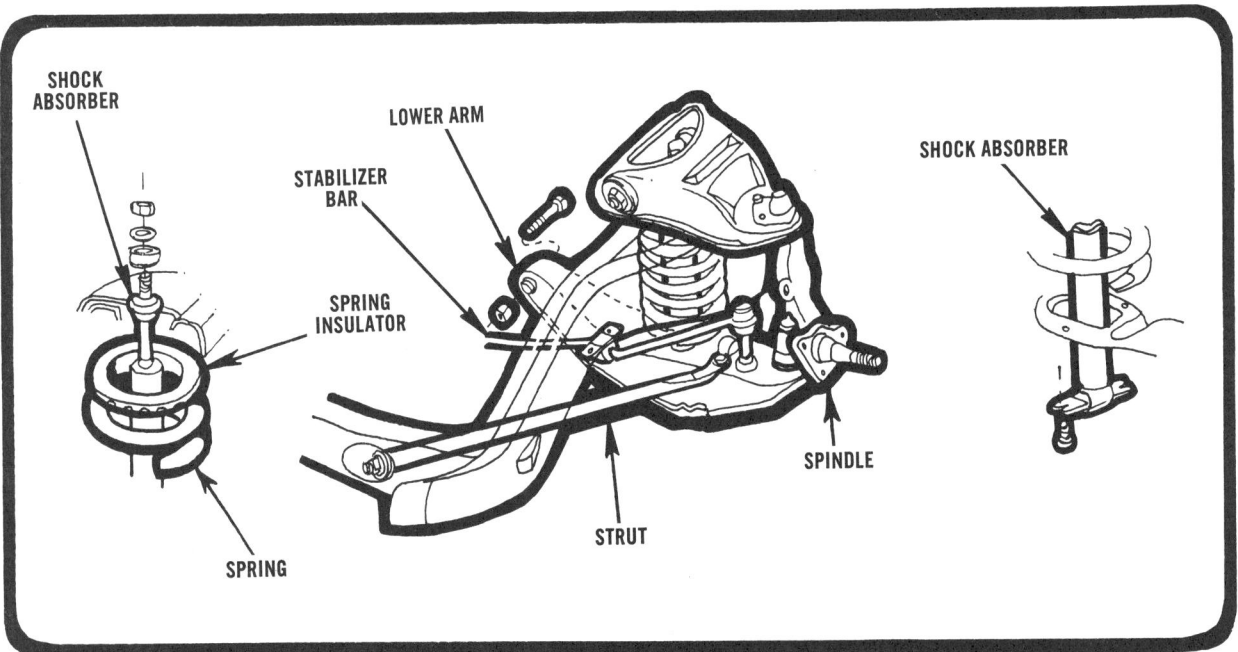

Typical rear suspension on cars using coil springs.

Typical front suspension on cars with coil springs located between control arms.

Shock absorbers are designed to damp, or control, the movements of the springs so that the movements up and down do not continue indefinitely. If there were no shock absorbers on a car, the springs would continue to bounce the body up and down unimpeded after contact with each bump in the road.

The car's weight on the front wheels is supported by ball joints, important in steering because the wheels pivot and turn on them, like human knee joints.

Wheel bearings (two on each wheel) are important because the wheels rotate on them, so they have to be adjusted properly—not too tight, not too loose.

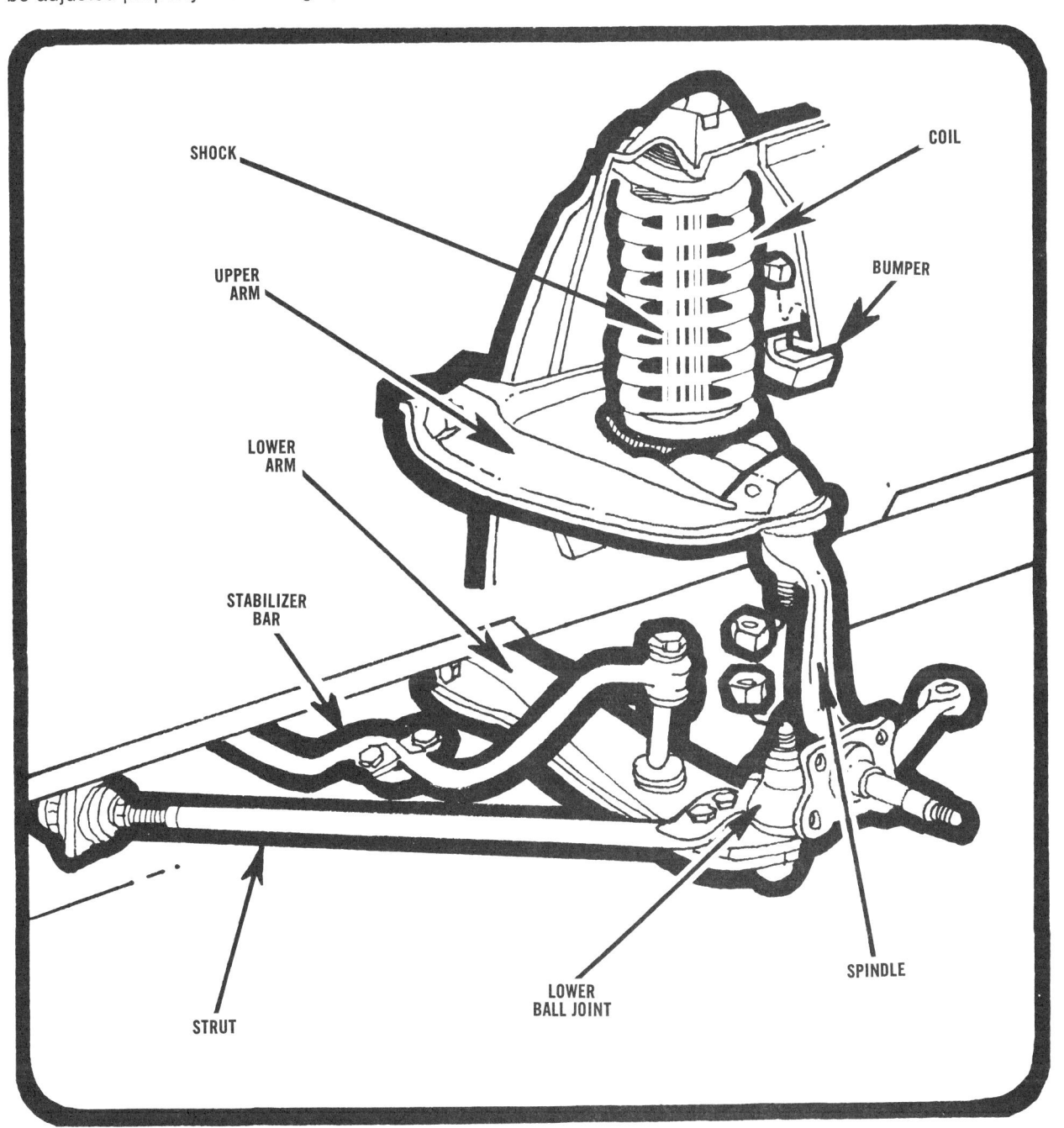

Typical front suspension on cars with the coil spring located on top of the upper control arm.

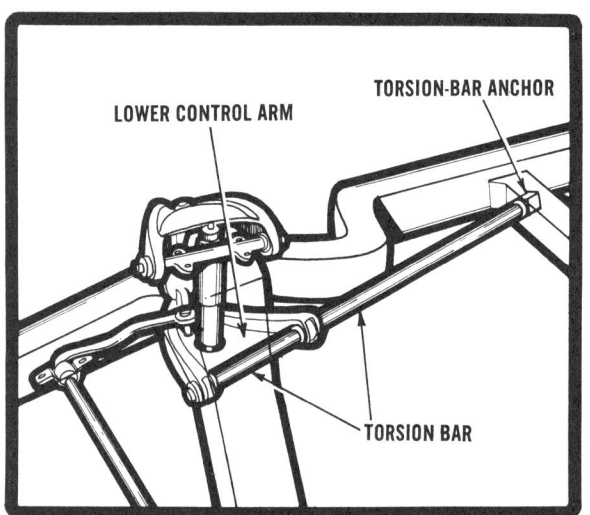

Chrysler Corporation cars and some imported models use torsion bars instead of springs in the front suspension. The torsion bars are actually two rods of spring steel. One end of the bar is fixed solidly to a part of the frame behind the wheel. The other end is attached to the lower control arm. As the arm rises and falls with wheel movement, the bar twists and absorbs most of the road shocks before they can reach the body. Like a spring rebounding after being compressed, the bar untwists when the pressure is released.

Wheel alignment

Wheel alignment is the angular settings of the front wheels in relation to the steering and suspension parts. By measuring with special equipment five alignment angles designed into each car model at the factory, the alignment technician can tell if the angles meet the manufacturer's recommended specifications engineered for maximum steering control and tire life.

Three angles can be adjusted:

Caster—the fore-and-aft tilt of the wheels which affects directional steering control.

Camber—how far the wheels tilt in or out at the top. Excessive tilt causes the wheel to pull toward the direction in which it's leaning, like laying an ice cream cone on its side and giving it a push.

Toe-in—the front wheels must be set slightly pigeon-toed at the front to offset their tendency to flex outward with the car in motion.

All three angles affect tire wear.

The two other measurable angles, steering axis inclination and toe-out, have no adjustment. If they do not meet specifications, it means some part of the suspension or steering linkage is bent or excessively loose.

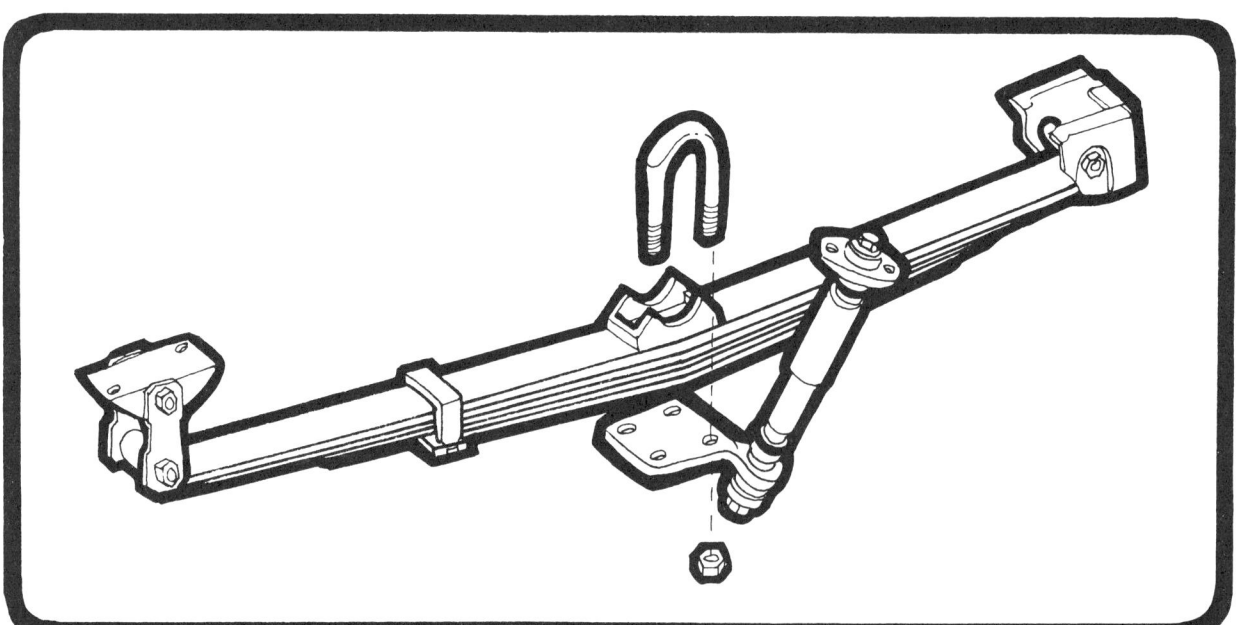

Many cars still use leaf springs as part of the rear suspension system. Leaf springs are the most primitive form of suspension but still find many applications on modern cars.

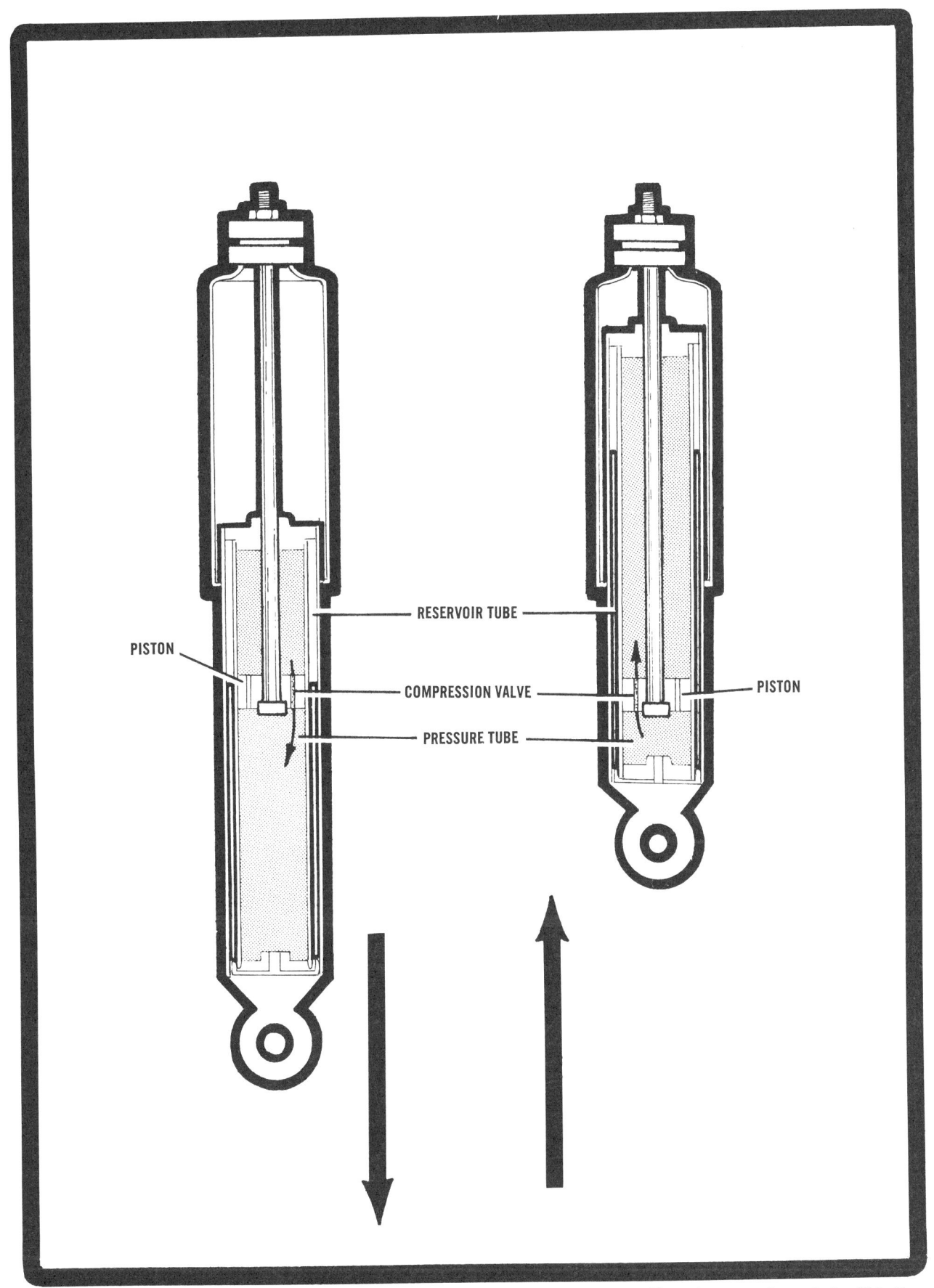

Shock absorbers damp any sudden road impact by squeezing oil through various orifices (compression valve) within the cylinder. When a wheel hits a road irregularity and travels upward forcing the shock absorber piston upward, this is called the jounce cycle. When the wheel travels downward, taking the piston with it, this is called the rebound cycle.

THE BRAKING SYSTEM

When you step on the brake pedal, you activate a sophisticated system designed by the manufacturer to stop your car in the shortest possible distance. The factors involved are the condition of the brakes, the condition of the tires and your own reaction time.

There are two types of brakes—drum brakes and disc brakes.

Drum brakes

When you push down on the brake pedal, you apply pressure to a master cylinder containing fluid. A high pressure is created in fluid lines leading to smaller cylinders at each wheel. The fluid pressure forces the brake shoes against brake drums. Friction between shoes and drums slows or stops the wheels.

As soon as you take your foot off the pedal, pressure eases and springs pull the brake shoes away from the drums so the wheels can turn freely again.

Disc brakes

Many cars are equipped with drum brakes on rear wheels and disc brakes on front wheels. Some have discs at all four wheels. The disc is attached to the wheel and turns with it. Straddling the disc is a U-shaped device called the caliper.

Just as in the drum brake, the compressing fluid is forced through the system when you push down on the brake pedal. The pressure forces friction pads inside the caliper against the disc and your car slows down or stops.

Dual braking system

For maximum safety, modern cars use a dual braking system, with a separate system for the front and rear wheels. If the fluid escapes from one system, the car still has brakes on two wheels. A light on the instrument panel warns you when the system is not working.

The dual system works like the single system, except that it has two master cylinders.

Power brakes

On cars equipped with power brakes, a special vacuum booster between the pedal and the master cylinder reduces the effort required to apply the brakes. Power brakes do not slow or stop the car faster than non-power brakes. They only require less foot pressure, which makes for easier driving.

Parking brakes

The parking brakes are operated by a small foot pedal or handle. When you step on the pedal or pull the handle, you pull on steel cables attached to the rear brake shoes. The parking brakes are held in position by a finger-like device that fits into one of a series of notches in the handle shaft or foot pedal lever.

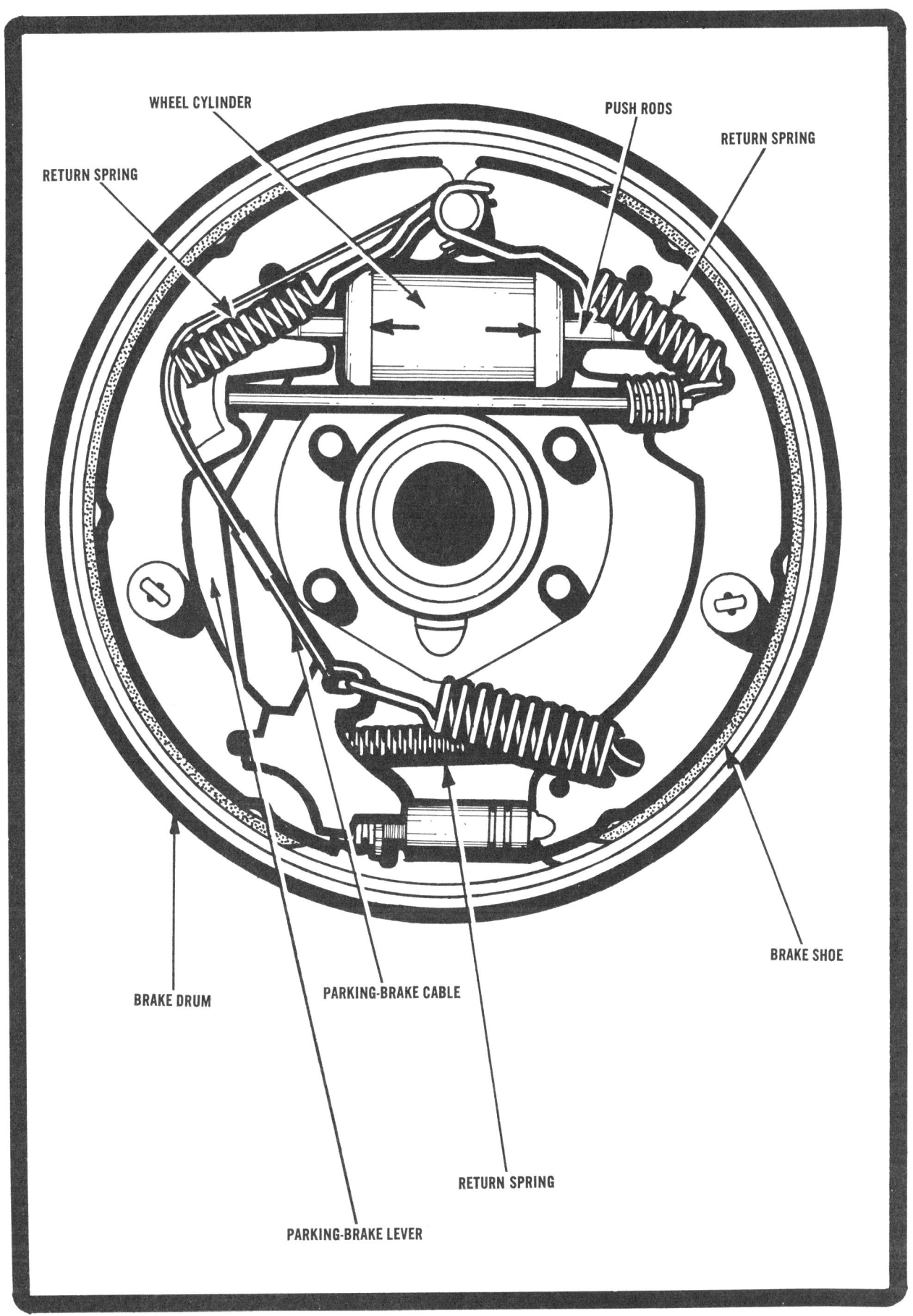

Typical drum brake components.

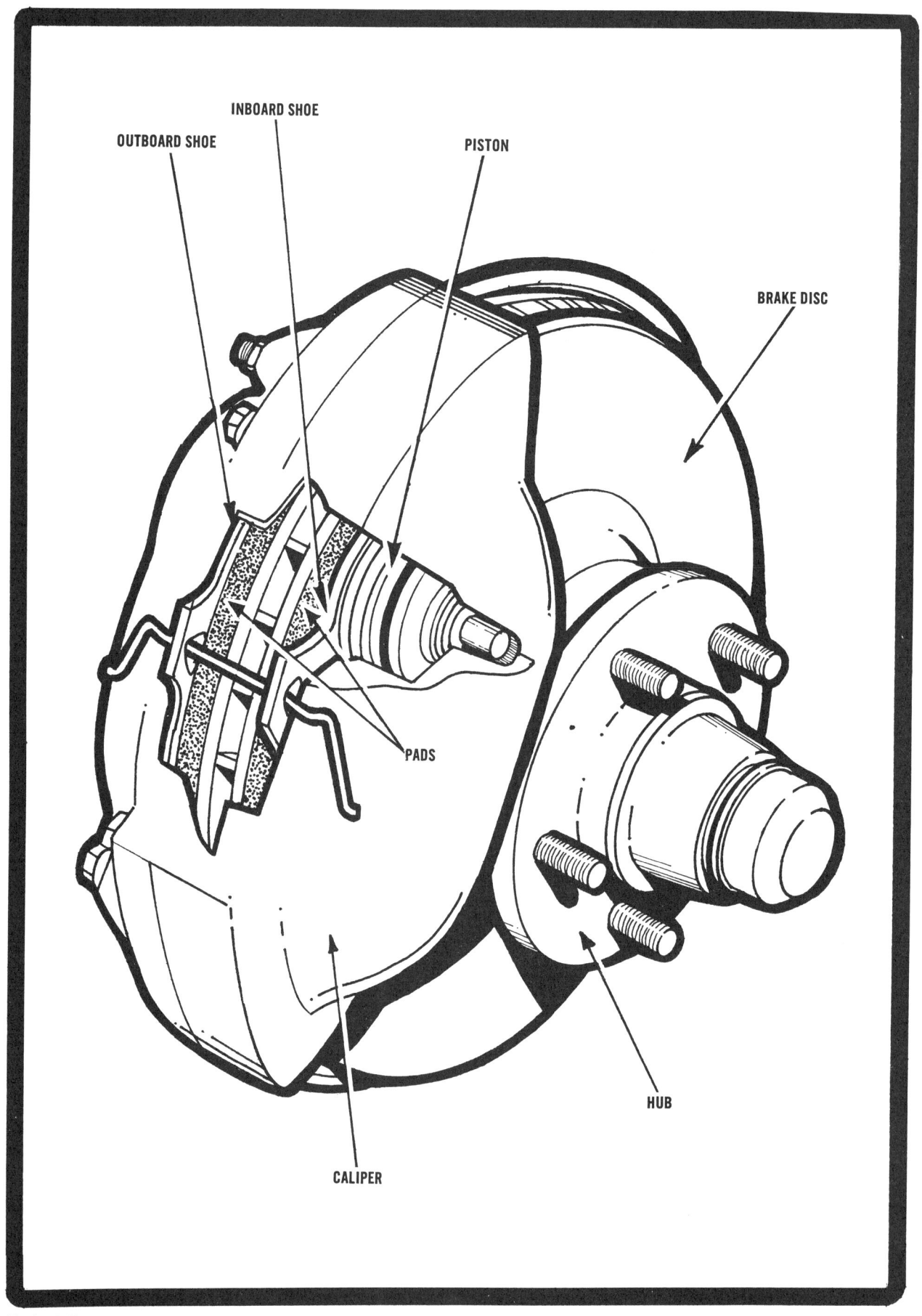

Typical disc brake components.

Setting Up Shop

Before you can work on your own car, you need at least three things: tools and equipment, parts, and a place to work. The fourth vital ingredient is information—available in this book and in specific workshop manuals on your car.

Before you even consider specifics, think about what you want to do, why you want to do it, and how much—time, money, and energy—you want to put into working on your own car. Of course, the more you put into being a home mechanic, the more you get out of it. But before you set yourself up in a full-fledged machine shop, ask yourself if that is what you really want to do.

First, what *do* you want to do to your car? It makes sense to start off doing the simplest maintenance jobs that your service station has been doing—possibly quite badly—and then work up to big ticket items. No matter how advanced you become, there will always be some jobs you will not want to tackle or that are beyond your skills and equipment. For instance, given a compressed air system and tire mounting machines, a service station or professional tire shop can do this job in a minute or so, charge you a couple of bucks and make a big profit. Doing it yourself however, with hand tools, rubber-faced hammers, and sweat takes much longer, and simply is not worth it for most home mechanics.

If you are mechanically inclined and could never keep your fingers out of the machinery *and* a car enthusiast who is just getting started, then you will probably want to do a lot of do-it-yourself repairs. Perhaps you will make a lifetime hobby of it or even turn pro. On the other hand, if you do not really love machinery or get a big kick out of making it work right, there are still a lot of easy car repair jobs you can handle that will save you pots of money over the years. Think about it. Deciding what you really want to do determines where and how you will set up shop, what tools you will buy, the kinds of parts you will purchase, and how much time and effort you will put into learning about your car and developing the skills needed to work on it at the level you want.

One other general consideration of importance to all beginning or advanced home mechanics is safety. Obviously, there is no satisfaction or cash saving in adjusting your own brakes if you drop the car on your head, burn down the house, or cause a wreck by doing the job wrong in the process.

A PLACE TO WORK

Drive through the back streets of any large city or small town and, chances are, you will see some big auto repair and/or modification jobs in progress right there on the street. If that is the only place available to you for work, then that is where you will have to work. It is not the ideal choice, but most home mechanics have done repair jobs this way.

For most of us, a driveway, apartment parking area, private garage, or stall in a parking garage will become our home mechanic's service bay. With a little bit of luck, you will also have a workbench in a basement or some other place where assemblies can be rebuilt, tools stored, and jobs done at a reasonable temperature with proper light and power for an electric drill or other power tools.

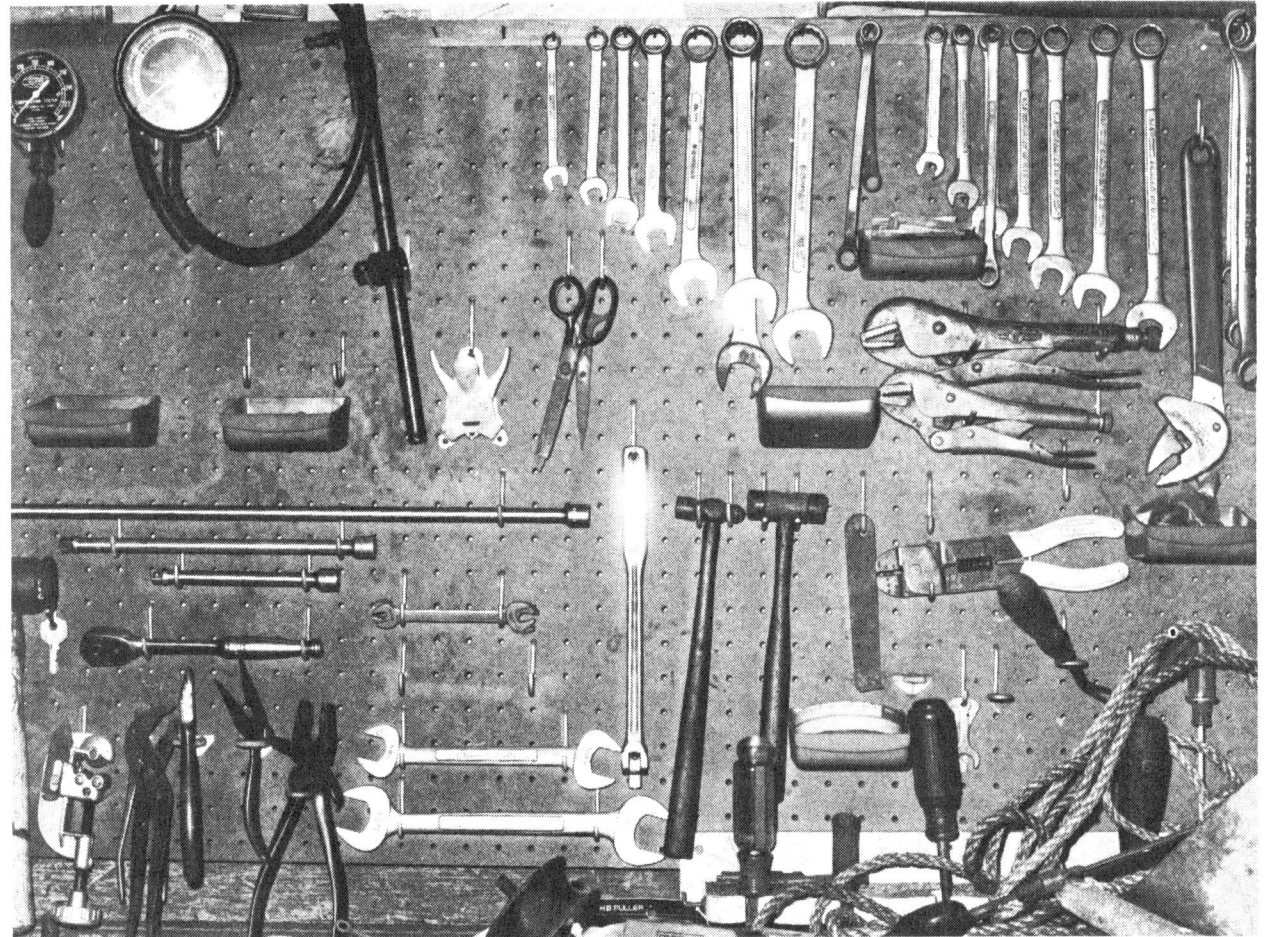

A pegboard is a versatile way to display and store tools where you can find them easily.

The place available to you for car work will determine the kind of jobs you can handle. A quick oil change in the driveway makes sense, but you would not want to do an in-chassis engine rebuild in a snowstorm if you can avoid it.

Do-it-yourself commercial auto repair shops have sprung up in many parts of the country recently. These operations provide a service bay complete with hoist, tools, manuals, parts—sometimes at discount prices—and a professional mechanic to help you get unstuck should problems develop. The cost is typically $3.50 per hour for the use of the space and equipment.

Such shops can be of special value to rank beginners and advanced home mechanics. The beginner can get the help he or she needs while learning how to do the job right. The money saving may be minor compared with having the job done professionally, but the capability developed is worthwhile. Also, you will get a chance to work with various brands of tools and equipment, so when the time comes to buy your own, you will have a better idea of what you want. The advanced home mechanic may be able to work fast enough to profit from such an arrangement and from the special tools available to him there.

However, for the intermediate home mechanic who has his own tools, the price of the working stall adds up fast and work progresses relatively slowly. So, for him, most routine maintenance jobs like oil changing and minor tuneups can better be done at home.

The floor you will be working on is the first consideration when setting up a home workshop. A smooth, reinforced concrete slab that is both flat and level is the ideal. If you are lucky enough to have access to such an area, cherish it and keep it clean. Then you will be able to roll your creeper easily when working under the car, jack the car up safely and put it solidly on stands, find dropped parts, and even see better because the light surface reflects natural and artificial light.

The next best and more common working surface is blacktop driveway. It is not usually as level or smooth as concrete. A jack or jack stand may dig into it—especially in hot weather—and oil or fuel spills can soften it. Still, it is a better work surface than gravel, packed earth or grass because it is much cleaner and does not swallow up small parts or even small tools.

One trick when working over gravel, earth, or grass is to put down a plastic ground cloth of the type sold by building supply stores or camping outfitters. Then dropped nuts will not disappear into the gravel or hide forever in the grass. You can move around on it more easily yourself even without a creeper.

Ideally, your workbench or workshop should be in the same heated, electrified garage where you park the car while working on it. Actually, this is often quite possible to arrange. But if you have to work outdoors or the place where you leave the car is not secure enough to keep tools and parts, then a separate shop in your basement or a locking area in the basement of your apartment house is the next best thing.

The basic workbench may be as simple as an old door resting on a couple of sturdy sawhorses or an old, but not good, sideboard picked up at a flea market. Look around, figure the space available for it, and use your imagination. The workbench top should be solid but the surface does not have to be smooth or particularly good. Since it will eventually become oil stained, if possible, have a separate bench for woodworking and auto repairs if you do both. Otherwise, dirt from the car work will damage your woodworking projects.

A working stall or garage, workbench, and workshop are all necessities for the advanced home mechanic, but you can get started with a lot less. Of course, if the space is available to you and money is no object, you can set up as fancy and professional a shop as you like. Some home automotive shops are just as impressive as some of the fancy woodworking or metal machining shops enthusiasts have set up in their basements.

RAISING THE CAR

Once you have gotten a place to work on your car and a workshop of sorts—even if it is only an open tool box at the edge of your driveway—the next thing you need is a way to raise the car off the ground so you can get under it safely. The important word in the last sentence is S-A-F-E-L-Y. Dropping a car with you under it can be—and has been—fatal.

Bumper jack

The bumper jack that comes with your car is just about adequate for picking up one corner or end while you gingerly and quickly remove one wheel and replace it with another. It will also serve, if you are just starting out as a home mechanic, to raise the car enough to put safety stands under it. DO NOT get under the vehicle until you have made certain it is resting solidly on the stands. A word about picking the right safety stands in a minute.

Garage jacks for home mechanics run the price gamut from about $5 to several hundred dollars. If you can find a garage sale—that is, a real, professional garage that is going out of business—you may be able to buy a professional jack and or stands at a price you can afford. If not, you have a number of choices of equipment made for home mechanics.

Scissors jack

The scissors jack is the cheapest adequate jack for home mechanics. The price is about $10. It is a mechanical jack consisting of a diamond-shaped frame with a horizontal jack screw through it. Turning a long crank handle collapses the diamond and raises the jack. It is easier to use and a lot safer than a bumper jack. But always remember that no jack is solid enough to hold a car while you are under it.

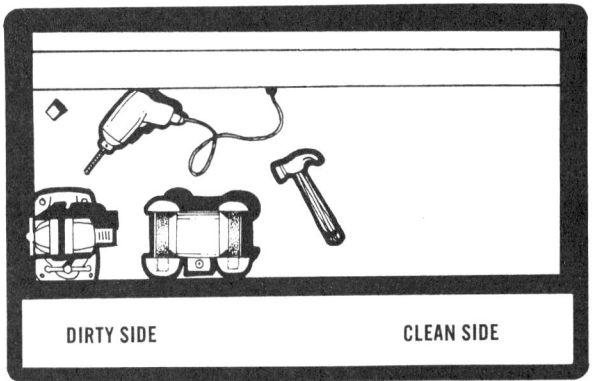

This workbench plan has clear working area at one end and grinding and cutting area with vise at the other.

A bumper jack, even when used on large flat area, is too unstable to be safe for anything other than tire changing.

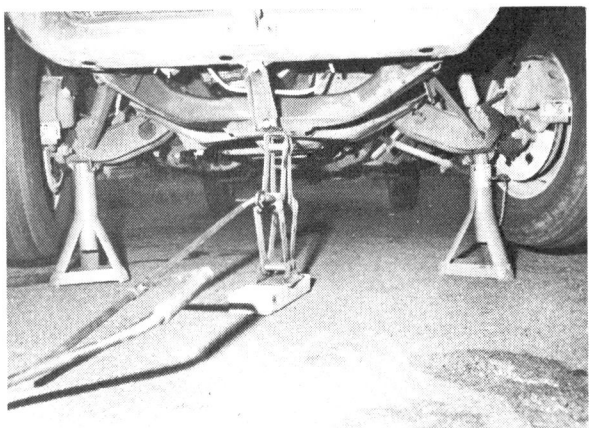

A scissors jack is the cheapest way for you to raise your car. Low-cost safety stands support car when you have to get under to work on it.

Hydraulic jack

Small hydraulic jacks with prices starting at about $10 look more attractive than they really are for home mechanics. These use hydraulic fluid to raise a ram when you operate a pump. The smaller sizes work slowly, tip easily, and—like any hydraulic jack—the seals can leak. This could let the car down. Everything that has been said here and elsewhere about not getting under a jacked up car without safety stands goes double for hydraulic jacks.

Trolley jack

Within the last several years, a number of small trolley jacks that look like miniature garage jacks have come on the market at prices ranging from $50 to about $150. One of these—probably in the $75 price range—is your best bet. A jack like this will make all your jacking chores much easier, safer, and faster.

Jack stands

Jack stands come next. These can be the simple pin-type stands consisting of two concentric pieces of pipe. One is split to form feet and the other has a lift pad on top. A steel pin goes through horizontal holes to adjust the height of the stand by pinning the two pipes together at the required height. These are the cheapest and hardest to use. The price ranges upwards from about $4 each.

Professional jack stands made of heavy, forged steel with a ratchet locking arrangement, cost a lot more but are quicker, more solid, and easier to use. It would be best to pick them up used if possible. New ones are nice to have but prices range sharply upwards from $10 apiece.

Ramps

The other way you can get a car up to change the oil or work underneath is on ramps. A good set of pressed steel ramps sells for $18 to $40, and is worth every penny. If, however, like most do-it-yourselfers, your object is to save money rather than spend it, you can build a pair of very serviceable wooden ramps for free.

The secret of free wooden ramps is the cargo skid. These are heavy wooden frames used by truckers to ship various cargoes from the factory to the wholesale or retail store. A visit to a truck terminal or department store should net you a couple of free cargo skids for the favor of taking them away. If you have to buy new lumber, making wooden ramps will cost more than buying better ones made of metal.

To make your ramps, start by taking the skid apart and removing all the nails. This will give you a collection of boards and two 8- or 9-inch by 3-inch planks about 4 feet long. Lay out a diagonal cut leaving 10- or 12-inch full width at each end to become the side pieces of two ramps using the large planks. Cut the boards to fit the width of your ramps and nail them on the ends and upper surfaces. The whole job only takes a couple of hours if you can get the use of a circular saw to make the diagonal cuts and to trim the boards.

Ratchet jack stands used by professional mechanics cost more but are sturdier and quicker to adjust.

Two hydraulic jacks, one with a trolley like a small professional garage jack, is the ultimate for the home mechanic.

This trolley scissors jack is handy. You can judge if the convenience is worth the extra cost.

One idea that will make your ramps easier to handle once you have built them is to space the boards just far enough apart so you can reach through with your hand to pick them up.

While you are in the woodworking business, make yourself some wheel chocks. These should be about 4 inches high by the width of your tires by about 8 inches long. You will need at least four and more than that will turn out to be useful. One goes on each side of each wheel remaining on the ground when you pick up your car.

A few short lengths of 2x8 lumber and 4x4 balks come in handy as jack pads and many other uses when you are working on your car.

PARTS CLEANING

Whenever you work on a car, you will always have greasy, dirty parts to be cleaned.

When you first start out, you will need a lot of rags or paper towels. One way to get good disposable wipes for free is to save used paper towels. A basket or paper bag in the kitchen will quickly collect as many as you can use. Even though they've been used for hand drying and are thrown in the bag wrinkled and damp, they dry into just what you need for drying an oil drain plug or wiping out a valve cover.

Once you progress beyond the point where a few second hand towels will cover your cleaning needs, you have a couple of parts cleaning choices. You can cut the side out of a 10-quart square can like the ones bulk oil comes in, fold over the edges so you do not cut yourself, and then use either kerosene or diesel fuel and an old paint brush—or a new parts washing brush at about a buck—for your basic parts cleaning.

Never use gasoline as a parts washing liquid. Yes, it does a fine job. But a number of guys have been severely—sometimes fatally—burned when a spark set off the fumes. Even if you work outdoors, there is no way you can safely work with a liquid as volatile and flammable as gasoline. Besides, the lead in the fuel is not very good for your hands.

An even better parts cleaning system is to go the professional route. For about $15, you can get a 5-gallon pail of parts cleaning solution complete with a perforated basket to immerse small parts or hold one end of big ones while you wash them down with the brush. These solutions are emulsifiers that turn grease to soap when you hose down the cleaned parts with water. They are non-flammable and do a fine cleaning job. Rubber gloves are a good idea when you use them because the phenolics used are hard on the hands.

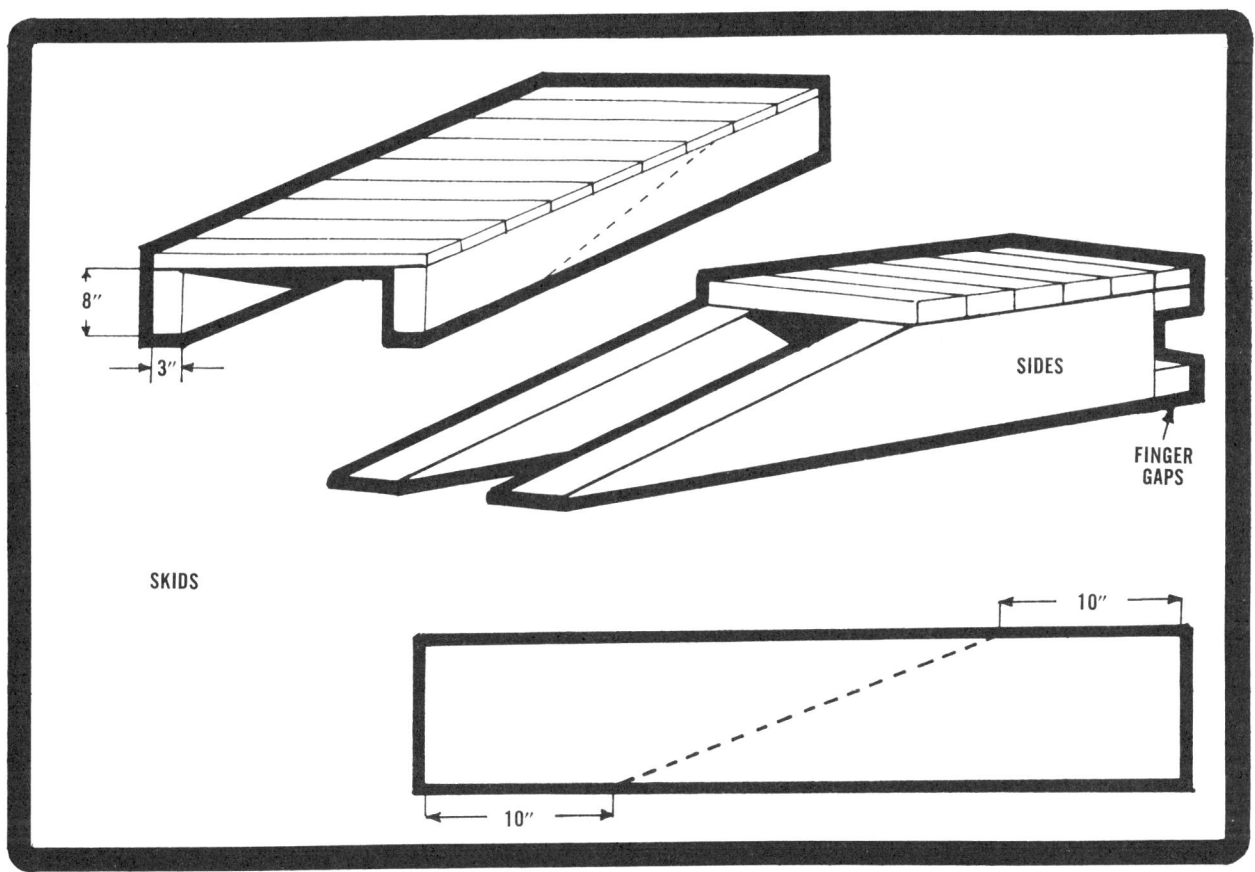

This pattern for cutting ramp sides from cargo skid shows how simple it is to make your own ramps.

A solution of one of the strong detergents used for cleaning kitchen floors, in an old plastic dishpan, is another good way for a home mechanic to clean parts safely and effectively. While we are on the subject of the kitchen, once you have done a thorough job of cleaning some mechanical parts, you can improve on your work by running them through the dishwasher when nobody is looking. But make sure they are free of grease and solvent residues before you do.

How clean should mechanical parts be before you put them back together? About as clean as fresh-washed tableware and dishes. Many early parts failures in major work done by home mechanics are caused by dirt installed with the component when it was assembled by working on a dirty bench in a dusty area. This has even been known to happen in jobs done by professional auto mechanics.

One thing you can do to make your job easier is by keeping your engine really clean. There are spray cans of engine degreasers available from almost all auto parts sources that will do this job effectively. They all work well. You simply spray them on the engine after covering the distributor cap and carburetor, then hose them off. If you are working in your own driveway, put down a generous layer of old newspapers to catch the dirt. This way, you will not have a black spot on the gravel for the next couple of years.

Another place to clean your engine is one of the numerous do-it-yourself car washes which have drains capable of handling the residue.

Cleaning up

To take care of the oil you are bound to spill on that concrete floor you looked so hard to find, use a cat box litter which is sold in any grocery store under a number of brand names. It will soak up the spill so you do not slip in it, prevent staining the floor, and can be swept up easily.

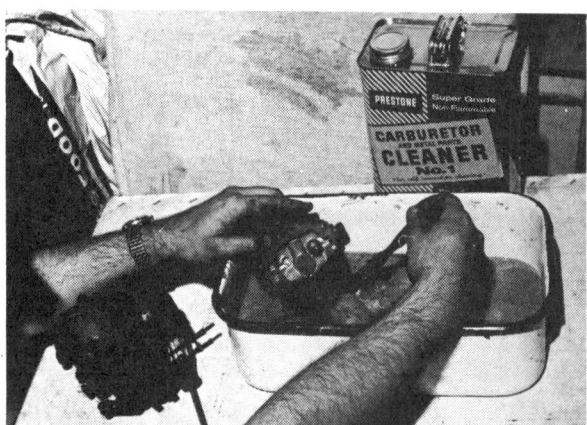

Parts cleaning in an old pan using commercial solvent costs little but works well.

MISCELLANEOUS SHOP EQUIPMENT

Work clothing

Work clothing comes next on your list. No matter how neat you are, car work is often dirty work. The black grease you will be getting on your clothes can defy the efforts of the most powerful washing machine. So, get yourself some coveralls or other heavy denim work clothes and keep them for car work. In the short, as well as the long run, you will save quite a bit of money by not ruining your other work clothes that you use when doing yard work or other dirty jobs around the house or apartment.

While you are out getting clothes, get a pair of comfortable work boots—preferably with reinforced steel toes. If you have ever dropped a hammer or a heavy auto part on your foot, you will agree that the modest investment is well worth it in avoiding smashed or bruised toes.

Lighting

You will also need good lighting. If possible, set up shop in a well-ventilated area where you also have electricity. Then try to pick up some used fluorescent light fixtures or, if not possible, buy a couple of new ones. A double-tube 4-foot light over the bench will make a big difference in the quality of any work you do.

For working directly on the car, you will need either a standard drop light or one of the newer fluorescent tube drop lights. The fluorescent costs quite a bit more than the couple of bucks you will spend on a cheap drop light ($20 plus is par), but it is both easier and safer to work with. For one thing, it does not pose the same shock hazard since it works with a transformer that cuts the 117-volt house current down to 12 volts. And, for another, it is a lot cooler so you are less apt to burn yourself on it.

Fire extinguisher

Fire is a distinct possibility whenever you work on an automobile with gasoline that can spill when you change a fuel filter or do other carburetor or fuel system work. Therefore, get a good CO_2 or Purple K fire extinguisher intended to deal with oil or electrical fires. Make sure it is charged and keep it handy. With an extinguisher at hand, a small fire can be snuffed out before it causes real damage or danger.

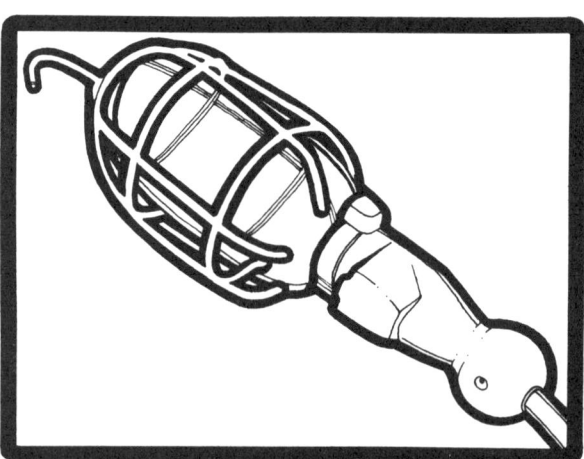

The latest type drop light eliminates side auxiliary plug-in to reduce shock hazard. Cage protects bulb.

Many professional shops use special squirt-pump dispensers and waterless hand cleaner. The initial cost for one of these setups is about $10. If you do a lot of car work, one is well worth the cost. Or, you can buy small cans of the cleaner for a lot less and it works just as well when you scoop it out of the can with your fingers. Use paper towels to wipe off the excess cleaner/grease mixture. Follow up with ordinary soap and water using a hand or fingernail brush.

The special soaps or soap powders you can buy do a respectable job of hand cleaning, but they are a bit rougher on the skin than the waterless cleaners.

There are also various grease emulsifiers that you can apply to your hands and work in under the nails before starting a job. Then, when you are ready to clean up, you simply wash your hands and off comes the grease and the emulsifier under it. The emulsifiers help, but do not work miracles.

While you will have to consider all these aspects of home auto repair if you get deeply involved, fortunately most of them can be handled as they come up. This way, you will not have to make a major cash outlay all at once to set up a complete home auto repair shop.

TOOLS AND EQUIPMENT

Whole encyclopedias have been written about the tools of various trades, car repair included. Here we will cover hand tools, power tools, bench tools, bench power tools, special tools, mechanical gauges, electrical test equipment, and scopes.

Some items are things you must have to do a certain repair on your car. Others help you to work faster but are not strictly necessary—though they do make it possible to do better work. And then there are the tools and equipment that would be nice but which you can do very well without.

Before we get into specifics, consider what you are doing as a home mechanic that is different from what a pro is doing. You are trading your time and effort to avoid the high cash outlay required for most minor and some major auto maintenance and repair jobs. The pro is making a living by working on cars. He is trading his time for your money. He works 50 weeks a year. Speed on the job, whether he has to beat a flat rate schedule or just get the work out, is his stock in trade. Thus, if there is a special tool that will save him 10 minutes doing a job and that job comes up roughly once a week, that tool saves him 500 minutes a year—about 8½ hours. Assuming he earns $5 per hour, those 8½ hours are worth more than $40 to him. If the tool costs $10, he cannot afford *not* to buy it.

You, on the other hand, will be doing the job once a year or perhaps only once every other year. If there is a way to get the job done—and done right—without that special tool, you owe it to yourself to do it without the tool. Otherwise, you become a tool collector rather than a money-saving home mechanic. Part of the satisfaction of home auto work is in knowing that you beat the system.

Another consideration, before we get into the specifics of tool buying and using, is what these tools will be bought to do. If you are working on your car because you love it, then the tools you use are as important to you as sporting equipment. Then, since their quality will determine—at least in part—the pleasure you get from using them, you should at least consider buying the best. The pro cannot afford anything less because he will be using them all day, every day, and better tools mean faster work and so more profit.

If, on the other hand, you are working on your car purely to save money and avoid the trouble of getting service for it at the mechanic's convenience rather than your own, then you want the least expensive tool that will do the job you require effectively.

The problem is to know how good is good enough for your purposes. As a rule of thumb, you will find that the very cheapest tool is almost always so inadequate that buying it is a waste of money. The very best is so super-adequate for your purposes that buying it is also a waste of money. So your best bet is the moderately priced tool that falls in the middle.

Let us get down to discussing specific tools.

WRENCHES

A wrench is the first tool you think of when you consider automotive tools. Ever since the first car was bolted together some time in the last century, bolts have been holding cars and most of their parts together. To turn a bolt, you use a wrench. Since the bolts that hold your car together are hidden in various inaccessible places, it takes a great variety of wrenches to turn all of them. Luckily, if you have a car that is relatively easy to service, you will not have to turn many of the tougher-to-reach bolts.

Open-end wrench

The simplest wrench is the open-end. It has one or two C-shaped ends with flat sides that fit over a hex-head bolt. By pulling on the handle of the wrench, you can turn the bolt.

Take a close look at what happens when you apply force to the handle of the wrench to turn a tight bolt. The flats of the open-end wrench bear on two corners of the bolt. This tends to round off those corners. It also tends to try to spread the parallel sides of the wrench opening. If the bolt is a tight one, you may round it off so much you cannot get it out at all. The better the wrench, the more closely it will fit the bolt and stronger steel will keep it from spreading as much. Thus, a good open-end wrench really works better than a cheaper one. It is often also lighter as well.

The very least expensive open-end wrenches are made from stamped sheet steel. They bend easily. They round off nuts and bolts. Do not buy them.

Useful open-end wrenches are made from steel forgings shaped to fit your hand as well as a specific size hex head nut or bolt. Some pretty good ones are left just as they were forged with the exception of the openings that are machined to size. These are the least expensive and will serve you well. For very little extra, you can buy chrome-plated wrenches. These look a lot better, wil not rust, and are easier to wipe clean. They are also a lot nicer to use. Most home mechanics and many professionals use them.

Slightly better finish and tougher steels drive the price up fast, making the best wrenches several times as costly as the ordinary ones. Handle some and look at them before deciding what will do the job to your satisfaction.

In the last five years, a new open-end wrench design has become increasingly accepted. Instead of straight sides on the opening, the sides curve and form knobs that press against the side of the hex nut or bolt rather than the corner. These wrenches fit more loosely so they are easier to get on the fastener and they turn rounded-off bolts better than straight wrenches. They are also much less apt to round off a bolt in the first place.

Most wrenches come in sets. Or you can buy them individually. It will usually pay to buy a standard set of open-end wrenches. Sooner or later, you will come across fasteners of most common sizes. Besides, each wrench in a set costs less than when bought separately.

When you use an open-end wrench, pull the handle towards you whenever possible rather than pushing it away. Should the wrench slip, you are much less apt to scrape your knuckles when pulling on the wrench. You can also exert more force to move a tight nut or bolt.

Box wrench

The next most common type of wrench is a box wrench. Like the open-end, it is made from a steel bar but the opening forms a ring rather than a letter C. The inside of the ring will be shaped in the form of a hexagon or 12-sided figure to fit over a hexagonal nut or bolt.

The box or ring will not spread the way the jaws of an open-end wrench will and the sides grip all six corners of the nut. So, with a box wrench, you can apply a lot more torque to a tight nut or bolt without the risk of slipping off it or rounding off the corners. The disadvantage is that you have to lift the box opening off the nut every time you reposition the wrench for another swing. This is slower than slipping an open end over the nut.

Some newer box wrenches have fluted openings. These flutes do the same job as the knobs on the jaws of the new style open-end wrenches by gripping the hex a little in from the corners to avoid rounding off.

Six-point openings let you twist harder but the more common 12-pointers fit on the fastener in more positions—an advantage when working in tight quarters. For larger nuts, 12-point box wrenches work fine. For really tiny ones, 6-point wrenches sometimes work better.

Combination wrench

Combination wrenches are just that, a combination of box-and open-end wrenches on opposite ends of the same bar. These enable you to start a tight fas-

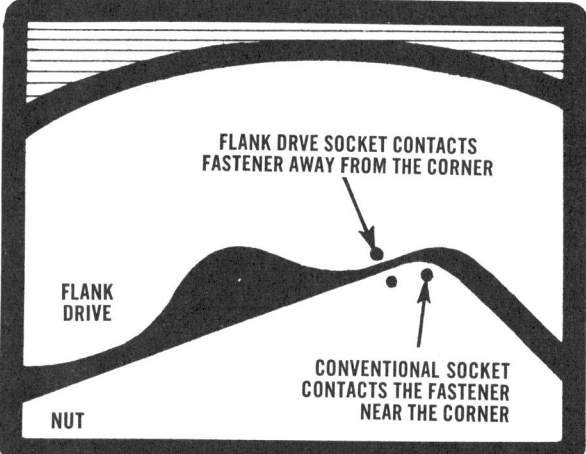

Stress patterns show how latest curved opening sockets and open-end wrenches avoid rounding off corners of nuts.

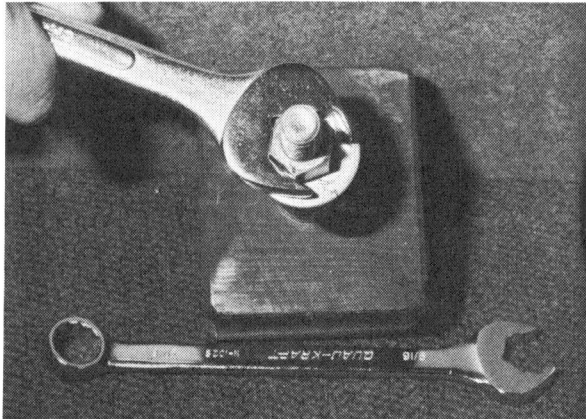

An open-end wrench with curved opening ratchets and turns nut hex in from corners to avoid rounding them off.

Pull, do not push, on wrench handle to avoid possible slips that could injure your hand when you apply heavy pressure.

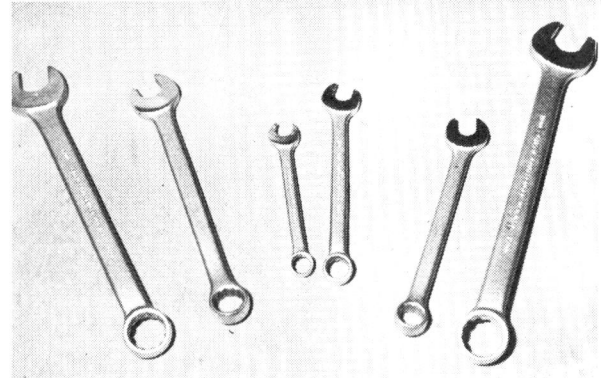

Open-end wrenches combined with box wrenches offer you the greatest versatility after socket wrenches.

tener with the box-end and then undo it more easily with the open-end once it is started but before it is loose enough to turn with your fingers.

If you are just starting out, a set of combination wrenches of reasonable quality will be more useful than a set that is all open-end or all box-end. It will cost a little more than either of these, but it will do more jobs for you and do them better. One set of combination wrenches will cost less than a set of box wrenches and a set of open-ends.

Flare-nut wrench

A flare-nut wrench is a sort of cross between the box wrench and an open-ender. It offers some of the best features of each type and was designed specifically for tightening brass nuts connecting metal tubing used in fuel, hydraulic, and other fluid lines.

Flare-nut wrenches are specialized tools of particular value to the professional mechanic who will use them often. You may not use them enough to justify their relatively high cost. If you use it carefully, the right size open-end wrench usually does the job.

Wrench openings include a standard open-end, a new style open-end, and a box opening with 12 points and hex opening flare nut wrench.

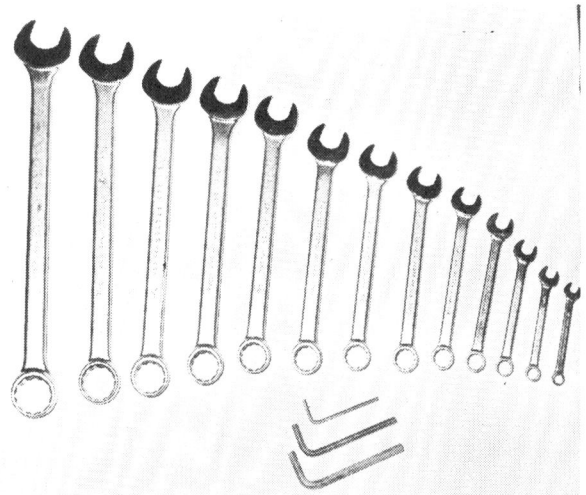

Buying a complete set of combination box and open-end wrenches costs less than buying each wrench separately. Allen wrenches shaped like letter L fit in socketed bolts.

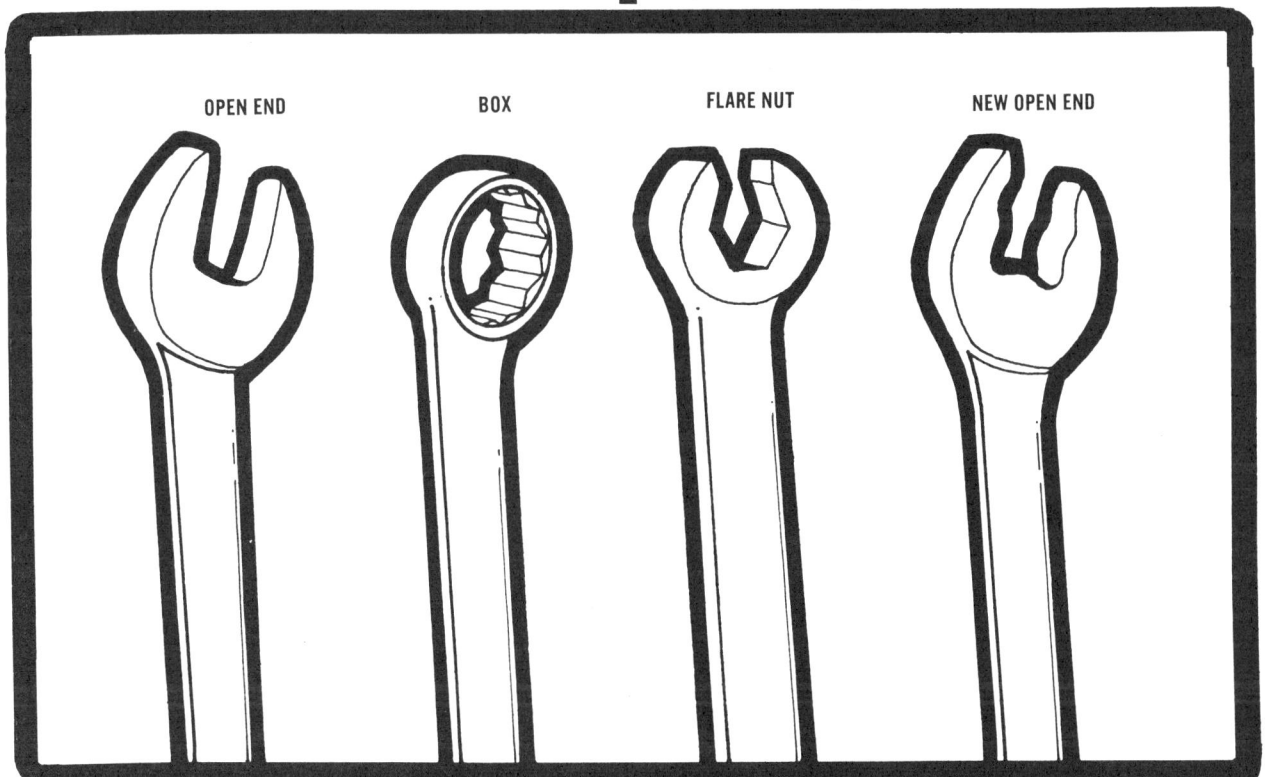

Adjustable wrenches

These descendants of the now nearly forgotten monkey wrench are often necessary when you cannot carry a complete set of fixed-opening wrenches with you. Or for turning nuts and bolts of odd sizes which you encounter so rarely it does not seem worth getting a special wrench to fit them. Many mechanics view all adjustable wrenches with scorn, but they can be valuable tools, especially in the beginning when your tool collection has not had time to grow big enough to cover all your needs.

When using an adjustable wrench, set it to fit the fastener tightly, adjusting it after fitting the wrench to the hex. Pull on the handle on the same side as the stronger fixed jaw to loosen a tight bolt.

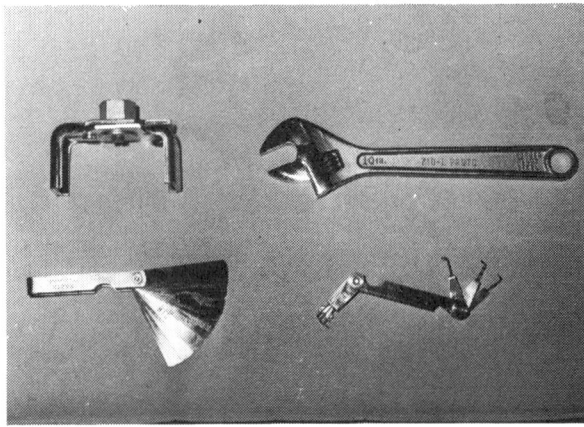

An adjustable open-end wrench, upper right, is shown with spark plug feeler, lower right, plain feeler gauge, lower left, and one type of spin-on oil filter wrench, top left.

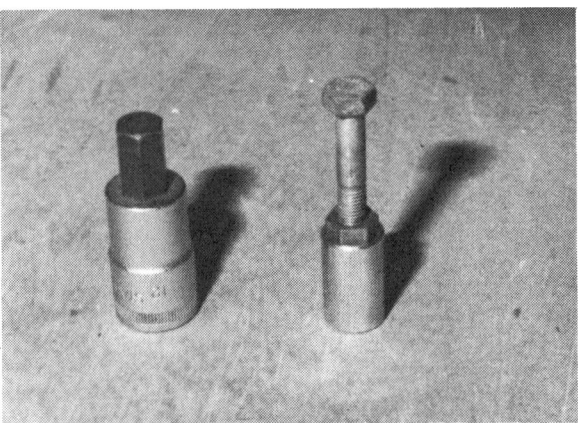

Allen socket works with socket sets but has male hex rather than female. A homemade version of this tool is achieved by locking two nuts on a bolt.

Adjustable wrenches are weaker than those with fixed openings and they are usually used by people who have relatively little mechanical experience. This combination often leads to damaged tools, so check an adjustable wrench carefully before you use it. Make sure the jaws are parallel when you look at the end and the side of the wrench. Check that they are not wobbly, and that there are no cracks, particularly in the narrow web area where the movable jaw fits into the body of the tool. The adjustment screw should turn smoothly throughout the full range of opening sizes.

Some of the latest adjustable wrenches have a locking feature which clamps the jaws a bit tighter on the bolt you are turning and locks them there. These are expensive, but they are the best type of adjustable open-end wrench for the amateur mechanic since they are less apt to round off nuts and bolt heads.

Allen wrench

An Allen wrench is required for more automotive work every year, particularly on German cars. This is an L-shaped hexagonal bar that fits in a hole in the end of the fastener. The internal hex is stronger than an external one and these wrenches can be used with more force in tighter places than other types. Most American Allen wrenches come as L-shaped bars with hexagonal cross sections of different sizes. They are cheap and will often do the job. Many European car applications call for special Allen sockets rather than the American-style keys to turn them.

Socket wrench

The socket wrench and handle set, after combination box and open-end wrenches, is usually the second type to be acquired by most home mechanics. Since it is one of the most versatile wrenches, perhaps it should be the first.

A socket wrench is simply a steel cylinder shaped to fit over a bolt and turn it when it is twisted by a ratcheting handle. The square end of the handle fits into a square hole in the socket. There are a great variety of extensions and handles that snap into sockets to turn them.

You should get ⅜-inch square drive sockets and extensions as these will be adequate for most automotive work. Professional mechanics often prefer the more rugged ½-inch square drive size, but these are heavier as well as stronger than ⅜-inch and

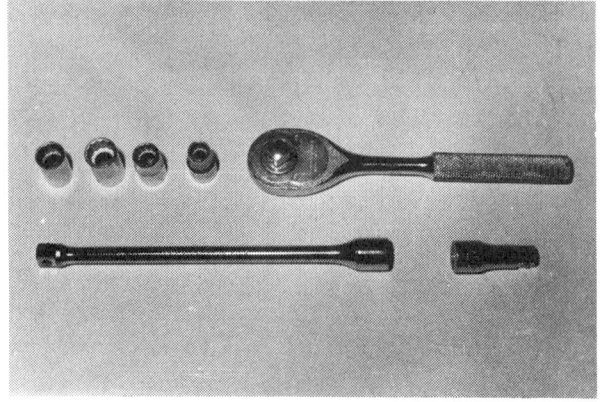

A simple socket set consists of sockets, upper left, ratchet handle, top right, and two extensions, bottom.

therefore more tiring to use if you are not accustomed to working with them. Handle a set of each size before you buy, and then pick the ones you like the feel of best. You will not go wrong working with either ½- or ⅜-inch sockets and handles.

Whatever size you prefer for your personal use, chances are you will end up with some tools in the next size up or down. Adaptors you can plug into your sockets will enable you to use your handles and extensions with different size sockets.

For more delicate work, you can get ¼-inch square drive sockets and handles. These are cute, but you can usually use small ⅜-inch sockets for most of this work.

The same goes for the big brute ¾-inch and 1-inch square drive sockets used for removing wheel lugs on trucks and for other big nuts or bolts. If there is a specific bolt on your car that requires such a socket, you will have to get one to turn it. The rear wheel hub nut on rear-engine VWs is an example. Get a breaker bar to turn it and pass up the much more expensive ratchet handle.

Socket openings take the same form as those in box wrenches. They come in 4-, 6-, 8-, and 12-point styles for square and hex-head fasteners. Some of the best of the modern sockets have flutes machined or swaged into the angles between the flats so they will not round off the corners of the hex, just like the newer and better box wrench openings. These are worth getting in preference to straight-cut sockets but only if they do not cost much more and you do not have the others already.

Sockets come in standard depths for most nuts and deep sockets are made for removing spark plugs and nuts that have a lot of bolt sticking out from them. Standard sockets will do almost everything you need done with the exception of spark plug work. For this, get a 13/16-inch spark plug socket. It fits most standard plugs in both metric and inch standard engines with a few exceptions on late-model cars. Check what size plugs your car has and then get the right socket to handle them.

Buy your sockets by the set. They come in neat metal trays to keep them in order and to prevent loss when not in use. A small set usually costs less than $10 in either metric or inch sizes.

Good quality sockets are available from almost all auto parts and supply sources. Prices vary greatly between top quality professional tools which are sold through distributors, and the super cheap tools with hex rather than square drive holes. Take the time to examine an example of each of these, and you will see the difference immediately. The top quality socket is much smaller and lighter than the cheaper version designed to fit the same size bolt. It is smoothly contoured, beautifully finished and chrome plated. The bottom-line socket will have much thicker walls to keep it from breaking the first time it is used. The reason for this disparity is the quality of the steel used to produce each socket. Soft, low-carbon steel in the cheaper socket must be thicker even though it is less strong than the chrome vanadium of the top-line socket.

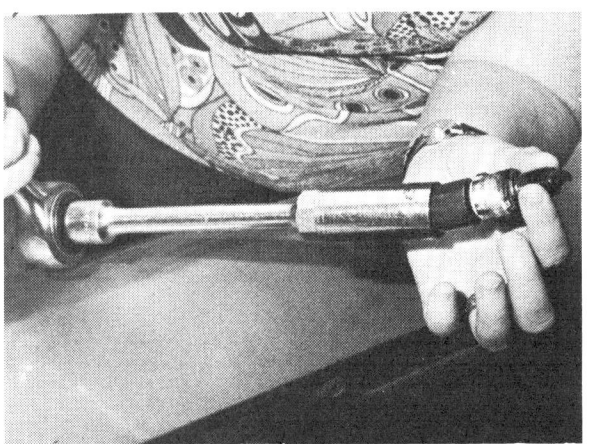

A spark plug socket is deep enough to fit over the plug and has a rubber insert to hold the plug once it is out of the engine.

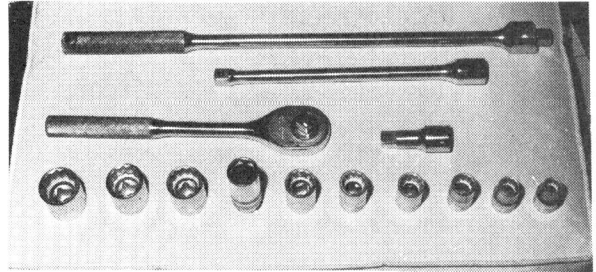

A fancy socket set includes more sockets and a breaker bar, top, which is used to free tight nuts or bolts.

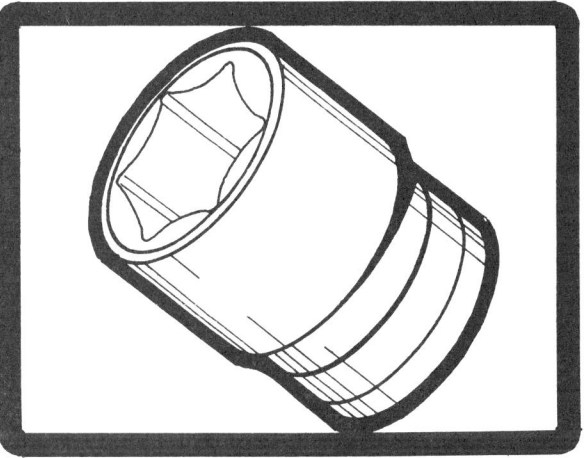

Fluted sockets work similarly to box wrenches to avoid stressing nut corners and rounding them off.

To a professional mechanic who works with his wrenches all day, the lighter weight counts for a lot more than it does to you who only use yours occasionally and then for less time. But, you do care because the thinner walls of the good sockets help them fit in tight places where thicker ones will not.

As with all your other tool purchases, the middle price level brings a big increment in quality over the lowest possible price and yet the sockets cost little more than half as much as the most expensive you can get.

And, what are the most expensive tools? Those made of solid stainless steel. They are beautiful—but completely out of sight for most professionals, let alone amateur, mechanics.

Having decided on your sockets, give a bit more thought to the ratchets and handles you will use to turn them. Again, quality varies greatly and directly with price but in this case, price is really less of an object because you will require only one ratchet handle to turn your many sockets. Since you hold the handle in your hands, you should select it carefully. If there is something you do not like about it, you will be irked every time you use it.

Handles take many forms and prices range from less than $5 to nearly $30 for ¼- and ¾-inch straight ratchet designs. You will be looking at the ⅜- and ½-inch ratchets for openers. These range from about $8 to $12.50. If you are on a tight budget, the ⅜-inch size is cheaper as well as lighter and does well for most uses.

Your first ratchet handle will probably be a straight handle with a ratchet that can be set for ON or OFF to tighten or loosen nuts and bolts. The hand grip should feel comfortable to you, the general finish should be smooth, and the length relatively short. Given a choice of two handle lengths, pick the shorter one for your ratchet.

You also get a choice of the number of teeth in the ratchet. The finest teeth enable you to work in tighter spaces because it takes less handle swing-arc to reach the next tooth to get a new bite. Bigger teeth—fewer clicks per turn—are more rugged but may not give you a small enough swing. Since your wrenches will not be used all day, every day, the convenience factor of finer teeth usually outweighs the strength advantage of bigger ones. But only if you do not abuse your ratchet by using it to break loose really tight bolts.

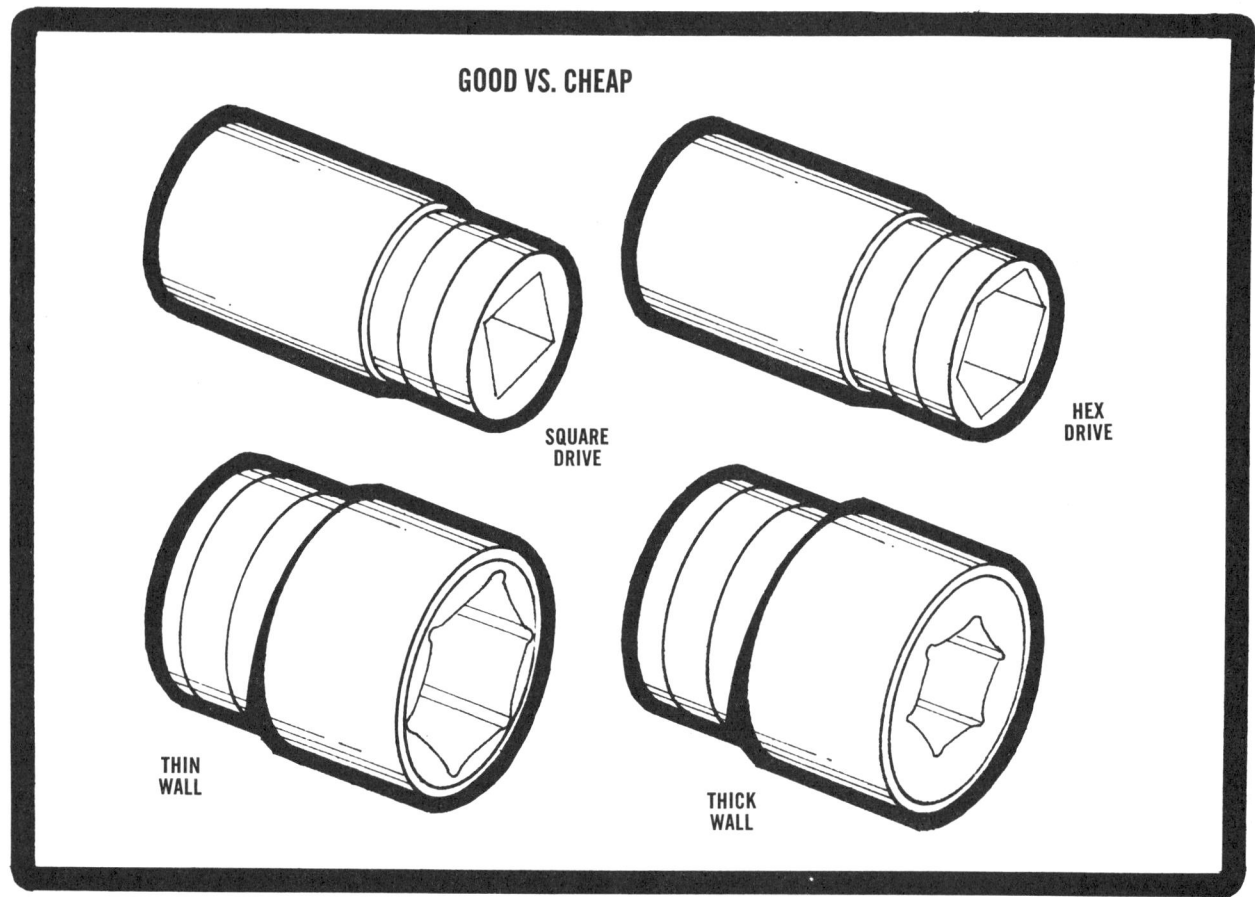

Socket quality is inversely related to weight with thinner walled finely finished tools having more strength than heavier hex-drive types made of softer metal.

Flexible ratchet heads have appeared in the last few years and offer a real advantage, especially to the home mechanic. These have a wrist-action hinge between the ratcheting head and the handle. It means you can swing the handle over or under an obstacle. Reading about it is not impressive, but working with one of these handles after having used a straight handle for years can be a revelation. Some of these ratchets have special kinks in the handle for still greater convenience in removing spark plugs.

On many jobs, the straight wrench works better than the articulated one. But when you have to bend the handle to do the job at all, there is no choice other than the flexible-head design. Therefore, your first ratchet handle should be jointed. Then, if you do a lot of work in tight places, a real shortie straight handle ratchet might be your next addition.

After, or perhaps even before, you get a ratchet handle, you should buy a breaker bar. This, or a slide-bar handle, turn sockets like a ratchet without the ratchet feature. While not so convenient, use it to break loose tight fasteners and avoid the wear and strain on your ratchet. Breaker bar handles are longer than standard ratchet handles which makes it a bit easier to turn a tight bolt. The same strictures about not increasing leverage with a pipe or hammering on the handle applies to ratchets—especially—and breaker bars as it does to box or open-end wrenches.

Ratchets sometimes come with a locking button designed to retain the socket or extension and to pop it off when you need to change. These can be more trouble than simply pulling off the socket over its spring-loaded ball retainer. Try handles using both systems and then pick the one that works best for you.

Extensions are simple steel rods with a square drive socket on one end and a drive-square on the other. They come in various lengths. Get them all, including at least one long one. A typical set of extensions includes 3-, 6-, 10-, and 20-inchers.

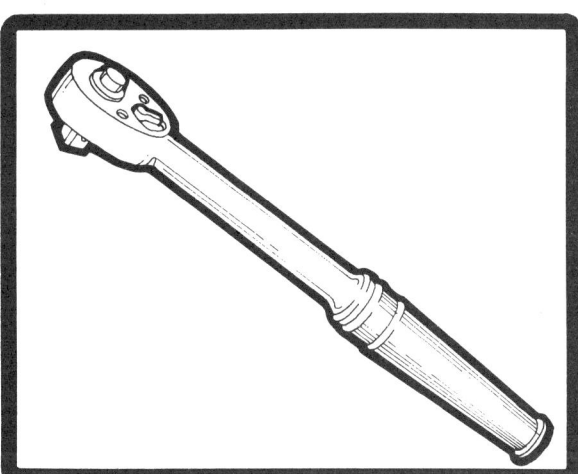

Ratchets are available with short handles for tightening nuts in hard to get at places.

Here is a place to save money by buying the middle quality level. As with sockets, the very top line extensions are a bit smoother and prettier but there are other tools you can get for the price differential that you need more.

Universal joints are supposed to make it easier to reach a buried bolt. However, they tend to flop around a lot and rarely have they been absolutely necessary. If you have a job for one, get it. Or if it comes as part of a set, fine.

Adaptors let you use ⅜-square-drive handles and extensions to turn ¼- or ½-inch sockets. If you have both ⅜- and ½-inch sockets, by all means get an adaptor rather than a complete set of handles and extensions. Adaptors go both ways. So if you have ⅜-inch sockets and a ½-inch drive torque wrench, get both.

Crow foot wrenches are simply socket heads that look and work like open ends but plug into your ratchet or extensions. If you need one to turn a specific bolt on your car, get it. Otherwise, pass.

Speeder handles look like an old fashioned brace but with a square drive end rather than a chuck to hold a wood boring bit. Use them to spin loosened nuts or bolts on or off. Again, the rule about getting one that you really like applies because it is a tool you will use often. They are especially useful for cranking on wheel lugs or nuts where there are a number of fasteners to turn that are easy to reach.

Specialty socket wrench tools abound. They include sockets with built-in universal joints, stud removers, crow foot wrenches, and screwdrive bits, both Allen and straight. Other accessories for your socket wrench collection could include deep sockets and super-deep sockets, and magnetic inserts to keep from dropping a nut out of a socket once you have removed it. Most of these are frills—nice if you can afford them and will use them enough to justify their cost, but not really necessary.

Other ratcheting wrenches include ratcheting box wrenches which are a little bulkier than straight box wrenches so their drive heads can ratchet inside the end of each wrench. They are not terribly expensive. But they are primarily tools to speed the work of the pro rather than meet the needs of the home mechanic for low-cost mechanical job capability.

Socket wrenches come singly or in sets. And the sets vary from complete thousand-dollar outfits containing all the tools a pro would ever need, plus some that even he might never use, to a tray of eight or ten commonly used ⅜-inch drive sockets on sale for less than $10. If you like the handles, probably a starter ⅜-inch square drive set consisting of eight sockets—⅜-, 7/16-, ½-, 9/16-, ⅝-, 11/16-, and ¾-inch 12-pointers plus a 13/16-inch deep socket for spark plugs—three extensions—3-, 6-, and 10-inch—reversible ratchet handle, 10-inch breaker bar, 7-inch slide bar, speeder, U-joint, and tool box would be a good deal. These sell for under $50 and contain good quality tools. They can be had for still less when on sale.

Still, this set contains the duplication of a slide bar and breaker bar handles plus a U-joint which you may or may not want. Its box is handy, but will be too small to hold all the tools you will be getting. So that, too, may become superfluous. In the long run, it is often a better deal to build up your own set to meet your needs.

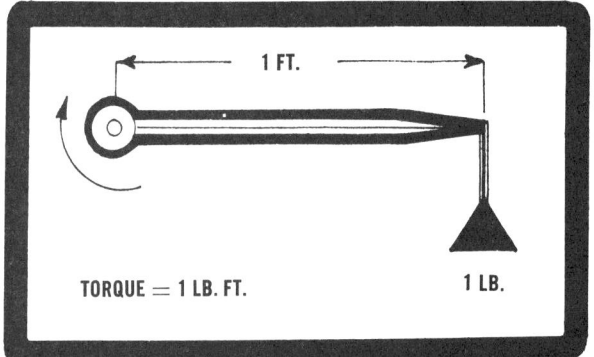

The torque diagram shows how 1 pound on a lever 1 foot long applies 1 lb. ft. of torque or twist at center axis.

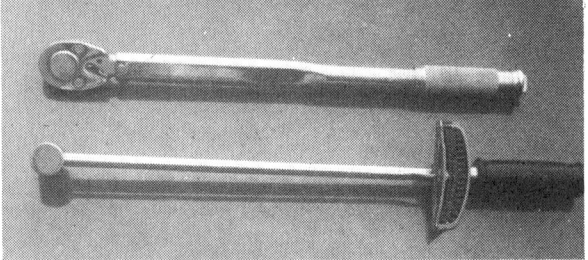

Torque wrenches include the expensive micrometer type, top, and the deflecting beam design, below.

Use a torque wrench on manifold bolts, head bolts, plugs, wheel bearings, etc. as specified in workshop manuals.

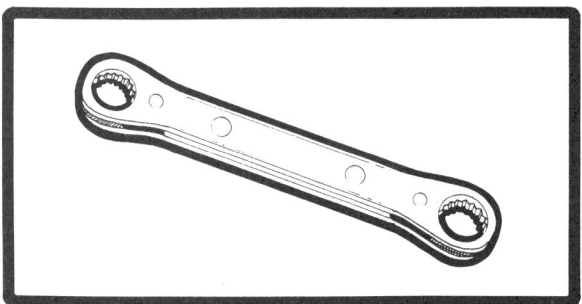

The ratcheting box wrench does not have the strength of the fixed design but it is a timesaver.

Torque wrenches

A torque wrench measures the torque—twisting force—you use to tighten a nut or bolt. While you may develop a pretty accurate feel with years of practice, there is no substitute for a torque wrench on a number of jobs you will be doing as you get more deeply involved in working on your car. They are necessary for replacing cylinder heads, covers on transmissions, connecting rod and main bearing caps, intake and exhaust manifold nuts, and desirable for spark plugs and even wheel lug nuts.

The reason you care about bolt tightening torque is that uneven tightness can warp expensive castings like cylinder heads and cause their gaskets to leak. Excessive torque can twist or stretch bolts right off, shear studs, and strip threads. Insufficient torque can cause elusive leaks of oil, water, vacuum, combustion gases, fuel, and hydraulic fluids in the various automotive systems.

Torque is measured in pounds-feet (lbs. ft.)—often incorrectly called foot-pounds, which is a measure of energy. In the automobile repair field, almost everyone says foot pounds. It is the more accepted usage. So in this chaper we will use the term foot pounds, even though we know it is technically incorrect. One foot pound (ft. lb.) is a weight of 1 pound at the end of a lever 1 foot long. It does not have to be moving the lever to exert that much torque or twist at the supporting end of the lever. For smaller fasteners and screws, torque is also measured in inch pounds (in. lbs.). One in. lb. is the amount of torque applied by a 1-pound weight on a 1-inch lever.

Torque wrenches come both plain and fancy. The fancier types are easier and quicker to use but do not offer you any increment in accuracy worth their cost. The plain deflecting beam wrench is the one for you at $10 to $20. The torque range you need to cover is 0-150 ft. lbs. Most of these have ½-inch drive squares that plug right into your sockets and extensions. If you standardize on ⅜-inch square drive, get a ½-to-⅜-inch adaptor. And, if you want to treat yourself, a ½-inch square drive ratchet that turns your torque wrench into a ratchet handle. Remember, though, just because you have an extra long ratchet handle in the form of your torque wrench, do not use it for a breaker bar. Your torque wrench is a precision measuring instrument and you would not want to spoil its accuracy by bending it.

Just so you know what they are, fancier torque wrenches which cost two or three times as much as the simple type come with dial gauges to read the torque figure or as self-limiting micrometer adjustment types that click and will not exceed preset torque figures. These are faster and you can not overtorque by carelessness. But they are often less precise than the much cheaper deflecting beam wrench.

Torquing accurately takes a certain amount of skill and care. First, make sure the threads of the fastener are clean, free of nicks or burrs, and not gummed up with heavy grease or old paint. Oil them lightly or apply a spray of anti-seize compound. Using a speeder, run down the nuts until they almost arrive but do not tighten them. If thread damage makes the nut hard to turn, measure the amount of torque required and add this to the spec from your manual.

(Example: The cylinder heads on a 1972 351 Ford V8 call for 95 to 105 ft. lbs. torque. If it takes 10 ft. lbs. to turn the nut before it touches the cylinder head, tighten it to 105 to 115 ft. lbs.)

Now you are ready to start torquing. The same manual that told you how tight to torque also shows bolt tightening sequences. Following the diagram, apply a smooth, steady force on the wrench holding its pivoting handle so it bears on its pivot until you read 10 ft. lbs. less than the spec. Do this to all the bolts in the sequence. Then go around again applying the final 10 ft. lbs. With new fasteners, it's good practice to torque them correctly and then release each nut about one turn and re-torque for final accuracy. This smooths the threads and seats and makes the final job more precise.

When you need to re-torque a cylinder head, do not simply apply the wrench. It takes about 10 extra ft. lbs. to break loose the nut or bolt—sometimes much more—which could overtighten it. Using a breaker bar, first loosen the fastener about a turn and then re-torque in the correct sequence.

Adaptors on torque wrenches that change the effective length of the wrench must be allowed for in the readings. The instructions that come with your wrench will cover this.

Specialized wrenches

Ignition wrenches come as both open-end and box wrenches. They are merely very small wrenches for turning the very small nuts used in mechanical distributors and, mostly on older cars, for securing the primary wires to the coil. An extensive set costs between $5 and $10, so the cost is not prohibitive.

When considering specialized wrenches like these it's a good idea to hold off buying them until you have a specific job for them to do.

A ratcheting open-end wrench is another specialized tool. This wrench looks like an ordinary open-end wrench with one long and one short jaw. The short jaw grips the side of the nut away from the direction you turn it and then slips over the nut when you swing the wrench for a new bite. This makes for faster nut-turning. But a set of ratcheting open-ends costs as much as a set of the much more useful standard open-end wrenches.

A tappet wrench is simply an open-end wrench with a longer than standard handle and a much thin-

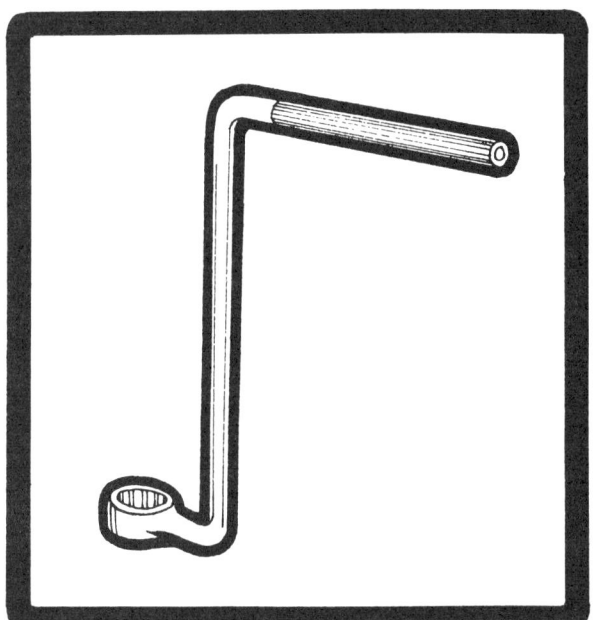

Special wrenches are bent to fit around obstructions and save time.

Offset angles for open-end wrenches come in 15° steps between a straight and a right angle.

ner cross-section. It is used for adjusting the valve tappets on L-head engines which have two hardened steel nuts locked together to set the valve clearance. Since working space is limited and engine heat makes these nuts extremely tight, tappet wrenches are made of the toughest steels to stand the strain and are therefore expensive. Usually, you use two of the same size at one time. If you need a pair to adjust the valves on your engine, ordinary wrenches simply will not do the job. If you do not need them, do not buy them.

Wrench offset is a consideration when buying any box, open-end or combination wrenches. The head of each wrench may be offset, or angled, to make it easier to reach the nuts and bolts you will be working on. A 15° or 30° offset is the most common angle for open-end wrenches. But most tool companies make wrenches that go from straight (0°) to right angle (90°) openings in 15° increments. You might need one of these to turn a specific bolt on your car that can be reached in no other way. But if you do not have such a bolt, you do not need a wrench for it.

Some box or open-end wrenches have handles bent like pretzels to reach specific nuts on specific cars. Starter bolts and distributor locking bolts that are buried in the machinery may require one of these special wrenches. However, in most cases, you can reach the bolt and turn it—though not conveniently—with standard tools. These are pro tools that save enough time to justify their cost. But since you can usually get the job done somehow without them, they are not really necessary.

While wrenches are not normally abused quite as badly as screwdrivers, these simple tools are used dangerously and incorrectly amazingly often. It is poor practice to hit a wrench with a hammer to start a stubborn bolt. However, if nothing else will work, use a soft-faced hammer with a plastic, rubber, or copper striking surface. It is also bad practice to slip a piece of pipe over a wrench to apply added force through longer leverage. Each wrench is designed with a handle length calculated to apply the correct torque to the size fastener it fits. So, using excessive force may well round off the hex head, stretch or break the bolt or stud, or damage the wrench. If and when it slips, you could get hurt.

Good wrench handling practice calls for pulling rather than pushing on the handle, as we have mentioned, both for greater force and less risk of hurting yourself. If working space only allows you to push on a wrench, use a box wrench rather than an open-end if possible and push with an open hand rather than one clasped around the tool. This way you are less apt to scrape your knuckles.

Clean, dry wrenches working on a clean dry engine are a lot less apt to slip than greasy wrenches turning bolts mired in muck. In the interests of keeping the dirt out of the components you are disassembling, doing faster and better work, saving your knuckles, and avoiding unnecessary trouble, clean off the area you are working on as much as possible before starting the job. Then keep a lot of wipes handy to clean your tools and dry your hands as you go along.

Fixed opening wrenches come in three size standards—metric, U.S., and Whitworth. If you own an older British car or motorcycle, it will have a number of Whitworth fasteners, and you will need a set of Whitworth wrenches to turn them. Most cars built in England after the early 1950s have Unified System bolts which take standard U.S.-style wrenches and threads compatible with U.S. National Fine (USNF) or U.S. National Coarse (USNC) threads of the same basic sizes.

Metric and U.S. sizes will probably be more important to you. Chances are, you will have to buy both, though perhaps not at the outset. If you have an American car—with a couple of notable exceptions—it will have standard U.S. SAE (Society of Automotive Engineers) fasteners. These are measured in inches across the flats of the hexagonal head on the fastener. Thus a 9/16-inch open-end wrench will be about .005-inch larger than 9/16-inch between the sides of its opening to fit a 9/16-inch hex-head. Get U.S. standard wrenches to work on such cars. These wrenches also work on most of the British cars imported into this country in recent years.

The metric system is coming. By about the mid-1980s it will be here for everything and by then you will need metric wrenches to work on any car from any country. Now, you need them for European and Japanese autos plus the engine on the Ford Pinto and just about everything on the Chevrolet Chevette. GM is designing all new components to the metric system, so more and more metric tools will be required to work on them. The other car makers will not be far behind.

The way to tell what measurement system is used on your car is to consult its owner's or workshop manual. Then buy the system you require for that car now, and put off getting wrenches of other sizes until you need them.

SCREWDRIVERS

Screwdrivers are, without a doubt, the most abused tools you have. Good ones should be kept for work on screws. Few of us do that. Therefore, you need some of the best you can afford and a couple of cheap ones you can be careless with. These can also be ground to fit special screws if you have to turn a couple of odd sizes on your car.

Standard screwdrivers for slotted screws come in a variety of sizes. You need at least three—small, medium, and large. An extra large screwdriver with a long shank can be endlessly useful for lining up parts and dealing with big screws. Short or knobby screwdrivers help work in tight places such as under the dash.

Most cars also use Phillips screws. These have cross slots in their heads and come in four sizes: #0, #1, #2, and #3. You can probably get by with a size #2 in the beginning, but will probably need the others eventually.

Reed and Prince tips look a lot like Phillips tips but are much more sharply pointed and do not interchange. Like other specialized tools, either you need them or you don't. Buy as required.

The same goes for clutch or butterfly screwdrivers. If you have the fasteners and need to turn them, get the right tool. Many newer cars use these screws.

Fancy screwdrivers include offset or ratchet head models, special starters for different types of screws that hold the screw while you start it in its threads, magnetic screwdrivers with interchangeable tips of different sizes, test light screwdrivers with built-in electrical system test lamps, and flashlight screwdrivers which shine a light on screws in dark corners.

All of these have their uses but they are tools to acquire as you require them—unless your ambition is to become a tool collector. There is nothing wrong with tool collecting, but first ask yourself if you can afford it—in storage space as well as money.

PLIERS

High quality is most noticeable and valuable in pliers—even more than in screwdrivers. The stresses developed can be great and cheap pliers simply cannot stand up to them. Cheap pliers are awkward. They slip, spread their jaws, do not work smoothly, break, and are both dangerous and unpleasant to use. It is far better to get fewer good ones than to have lots of poor pliers. And good pliers are never cheap. Any pair of pliers that costs less than $2 new is suspect and the ones you will use for years will cost several times that amount.

Pliers include, left to right, locking, common, wire hose clamp, wire stripping, needle nose, water pump, and brake.

You need at least three pair for general use: regular slip-joint steel pliers about six to eight inches long, long nose pliers about six inches long, and diagonal wire cutting pliers also about six inches long. Next on your list should come a set of linesman's pliers about eight inches or bigger, and then mechanic's pliers with a number of openings up to two inches and handles about 10 inches long. The better quality of this type have arc-shaped grooves to control the size of adjustments rather than indentations along a slot. They are strong enough to justify their added cost and weight, though the others will do for starters and cost about half as much.

Those are the basic pliers you need to start out. Eventually you may want to add specialized pliers to handle special jobs. There are pointed tip pliers for spreading or closing circlips, and oddly hooked pliers for installing or removing brake springs. You can do the job without them, but it is much easier with them. Some pliers are specially grooved to squeeze spring-type hose clamps. They are a nice addition if you use these clamps, but it is probably wiser to spend the money on stainless steel worm drive clamps rather than pliers.

Cutting pliers of various kinds include oversize diagonal cutters, compound leverage cutting pliers, insulation strippers, and many kinds of metal shears or snips.

Locking jaw pliers take many forms. These should be included in your tool collection early in the game. A typical toolbox will have 8-, 6-, and 4-inch long locking pliers. You will find them endlessly useful for holding parts together while inserting fasteners, holding bolts when you can not keep a wrench from falling off the opposite end from the one you are trying to turn, unscrewing studs, and many other jobs. They come with slightly curved and straight jaws. Either style is useful but you probably do not need both. Get the big one first and then add the others as you need them or find them.

Locking jaw pliers are also made with specially shaped jaws for welders to hold workpieces together. You do not need these unless you are interested in welding.

HAMMERS

The basic hammer for auto mechanics is the ball peen with one flat striking surface and one rounded end for setting rivets. Get a good one with an 8-, 12- or 16-oz. head. The best ones have drop forged, heat treated heads and hickory handles. Expect to pay from about $6 to $10 for a good 12-oz. ball peen. You can get cheaper ones, but the handles often break or heads fly off. The metal in the head can chip, throwing off dangerous chunks of steel. The basic rule when working with a machinist's hammer is never to hit a hardened surface with it. This means another hammer head, hardened steel rod, anvil, or auto part. That is what causes chipping or splitting.

Mostly, your hammer will be used with cold chisels, drifts, or to shape unhardened metal parts. A cold chisel is a steel bar with a hardened cutting edge for shearing steel. They come in various sizes. A set can prove useful. You can use them for cutting off rusted-

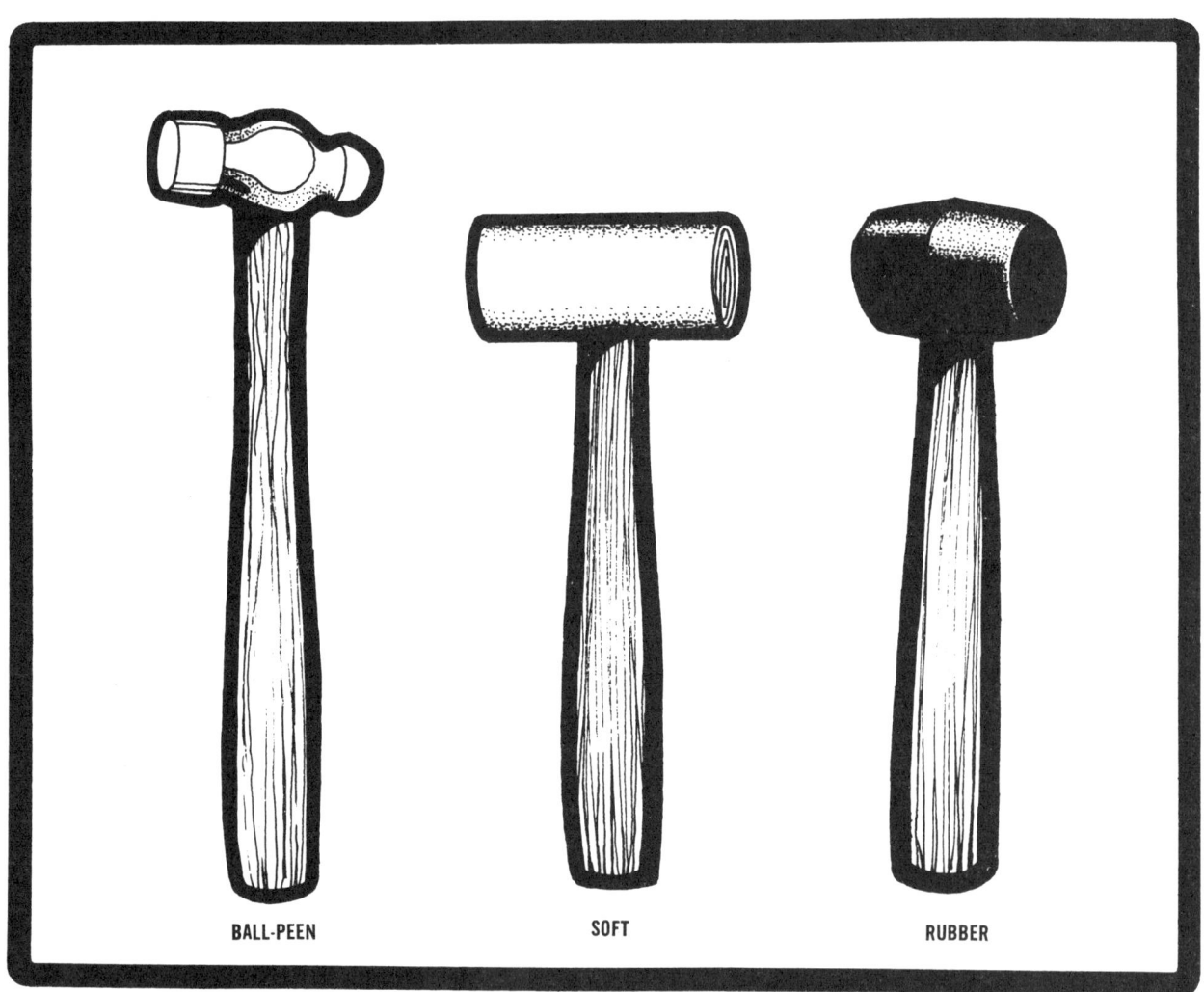

BALL-PEEN　　　　　SOFT　　　　　RUBBER

The most commonly used hammers are the ball peen and the soft face. A rubber mallet can be used where parts must not be marred.

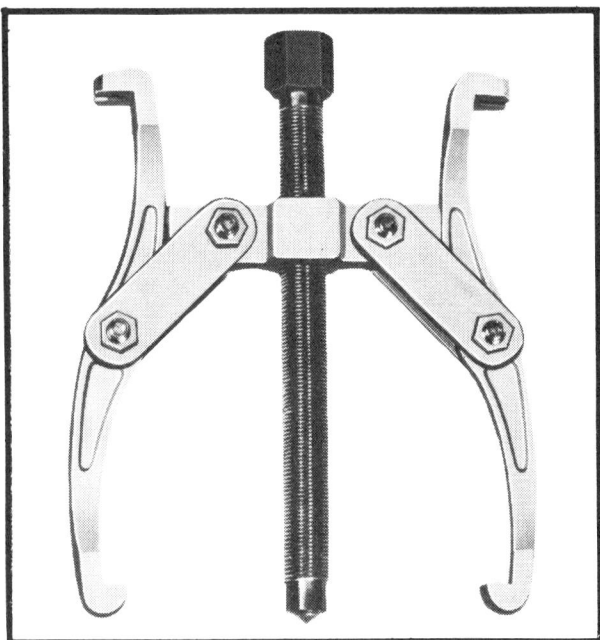

Pullers are expensive but can prevent damaging much more expensive parts.

on bolt heads, removing exhaust system parts, and similar jobs where there is no chance of saving the fastener and it must be removed.

A drift is a round steel punch with a flat tip used for driving pins into or out of assemblies. If it has a point on the end, it is a center punch used for marking metal before drilling a hole in it so the drill bit will not walk around the hole but will start off right. Drifts or large size center punches can be useful for lining up sheet metal parts when bolting them together.

There are several other hammers you will find useful. The one most often used is a copper faced hammer originally intended for undoing the winged nuts that secured wire wheels before they were made illegal in 1967. It can be used on machined parts without damaging them. It is particularly useful for removing brake drums without a puller and other similarly difficult jobs.

A plastic tip mallet works better where less force is needed or for tapping a carburetor body to jar dirt loose from the float valve.

A rubber mallet is needed for replacing snap-on hubcaps and similar jobs where you do not want to bend or mar relatively light metal. This is one instance where the cheaper version does just about as well as the more expensive tool.

It is good practice to wear safety glasses when using a hammer on metal to prevent getting a steel chip in your eye.

SPECIALIZED HAND TOOLS

There are a number of tool companies which make specialized automotive hand tools. The assortment is almost endless and the degree of specialization impressive. Some of these are absolutely necessary to do a job or remove a part and they are often relatively inexpensive. Most of them are timesavers for professional mechanics.

Here are a few assorted examples.

The work you do will determine the special tools you need. Most big mail order catalogs and tool maker's catalogs give details on current prices and tools available.

Puller

Pullers are a whole specialized tool story in themselves. They come in all sizes for separating stuck or press-fitted parts. Small ones for lifting battery post clamps can cost as little as 59¢ and large ones for removing flywheels can cost between $50 and $100.

Wheel pullers are usually used to remove rear brake drums on live-axle vehicles. They can be had as cheaply as $10. Fancier versions go up quickly in price.

Press

If you need a bearing pressed onto an axle, it is a job that is done off the car. You can take the axle into a machine shop, buy the bearing and have them press it on for you. The cost is low and you still get to save money without buying a press by doing most of the bolts-off, bolts-on work yourself.

Valve spring compressor

A valve spring compressor is useful if you plan to strip the valves out of a cylinder head yourself. Since the cost is about $7, it may make sense to get one if you are doing a valve job. However, you can get by very well without one.

Other specialized tools

More and more tools are being designed specifically for you, the home mechanic. These are often low cost ways of doing high cost jobs. The tool may be as simple as a thread chasing nut—simply a hardened steel nut that can be used in place of a much more expensive die for cleaning screw threads. A small set of such nuts costs about $3 compared with dies at $3 each. Sure, it takes longer to do the job, but it gets it done.

Other specialized hand tools are specifically designed to replace the power tools of the pro. One of these is the hand impact wrench. This is a hand-held driver for high strength sockets that can be set either to tighten or loosen.

One of the jobs you can start with is lubrication. This can call for a bunch of specialized tools right at the beginning, but fortunately they are relatively inexpensive. You will need a wrench to turn the drain plug in your car's oil pan. This may be a standard hex which a box, socket, or open-end wrench can turn. Or it may be an indented square. Special drain plug wrenches are available for from $3 to about $6. Sometimes you can use a ½-inch square drive extension without a socket for this job. But more often, you need the special tool. Some imports have oversize Allen bolts for drain plugs. Fiats take a 12-mm Allen. If you can not find one, you may be able to make it by carefully grinding down the ½-inch hex-drive key that comes with low quality socket sets for about a buck and a half. Metric Allen wrenches in large sizes are also available to go on standard ½- and ⅜-inch square-drive socket turners.

For a drain pan, you can buy a cheap plastic dishpan or make one out of a 10-qt square oil can. This has the advantage of being shallower. You might not have to jack up the car, but be sure to fold over the cut edges so you do not cut yourself when fishing for the oil drain plug which often falls in with the drained oil.

To change the oil filter you need a wrench to unscrew a stuck spin filter. These are priced under $3. Most consist of a metal band with a handle that grips the filter to turn it. You can get by using a cold chisel and a hammer on the exposed edge of a spin-on. Professional mechanics cringe when told of this method, but it works easily.

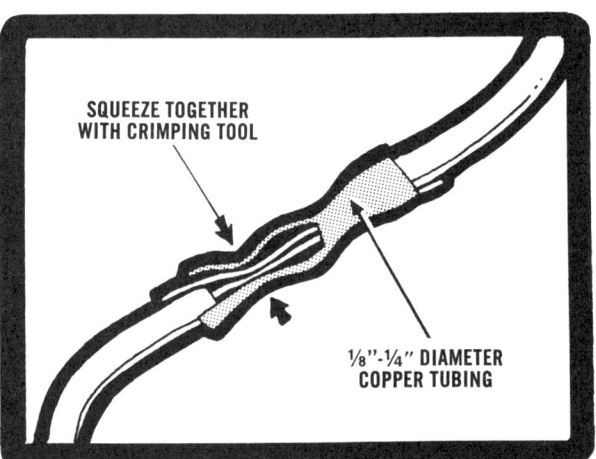

Crimper fastens solderless connectors to make wire splices by crimping terminals over wires for fast electrical repairs.

For general lubing you will need an oil can. Get one with a pump lever as these are the most convenient around a car. Also get a pump-action sprayer to dispense penetrating oil. If you object to aerosols, a spritz pump on a plastic bottle does the job almost as well without freon emissions and at lower cost.

For chassis greasing, you need a hand operated grease gun and lots of secondhand paper towels. The gun should take grease cartridges because they are much easier to handle than bulk grease and have a long lever to develop the pressure required to force grease into fittings. If your car does not have them, you will also need fittings. Lube points are making a comeback on 1976 cars, so you will be seeing more of them.

WIRING TOOLS

Sooner or later, you will be making some repairs to the electrical system of your car. This calls for simple circuit testing—see the Electrical Instruments section later in this chapter—and working with wires. You will need wire cutters—covered under Pliers—an insulation stripper, and a means of splicing various sizes of electric wiring.

One very good wire stripper is the one that comes as a part of a solderless connector plier. But there are other simpler and fancier strippers. Most have sharp edges like wire cutters and round nicks of different sizes so the blades cut the insulation without cutting the wire. These work well. A yank on the wire after cutting the insulation pops off the end to be stripped. Some have built-in end-poppers. These are great if you have a lot of wire to strip. You can also use a pocket knife to strip wires. Wire strippers come at 69¢ and up. The combination crimper-stripper sells for under $5. The wire stripper with the built-in end-popper runs about $7 and up.

Once the wire is cut to length and stripped, you will splice or attach it to something. Solderless terminals do this neatly but expensively. These are copper—often cadmium plated—sleeves that fit over the wire and are crimped in place with a special crimper that looks like a blunt-jawed pair of pliers. Terminals come with or without insulation sleeves and cost under 10¢ each. They also come in a great variety of push connectors, rings, forks, and other designs for snapping, screwing, or clamping to electrical accessories.

For straight wire splicing, you can twist the wires together and solder them. It is a little slower than working with a solderless connector, but the joint is permanent and is less apt to become corroded in the future.

Once the wires are joined, you have to seal and insulate the splice. Black plastic electrical tape is the standby and it works well. You can also get heat-shrinkable plastic tubing that does an even better job.

Use a hacksaw for cutting bolts, nuts, sheet metal, tubing, and exhaust pipes.

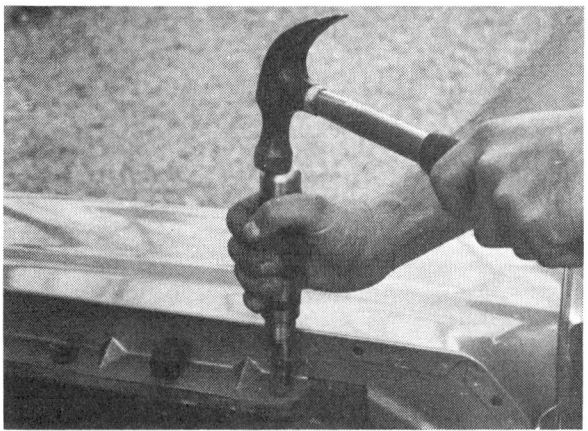

Hand impact wrench can jar difficult bolts loose. It works with special sockets.

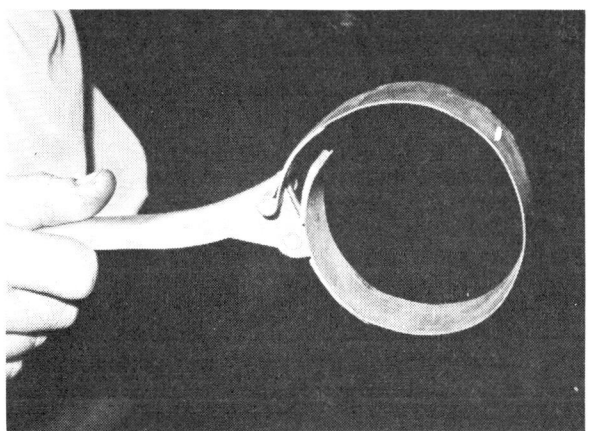

An oil filter wrench removes spin-on filter and is relatively cheap. Tighten filter only hand tight.

METAL CUTTING TOOLS

Much of home auto repair work consists of unbolting a defective part and replacing it with a new or rebuilt part. But, sooner or later, you are going to come up against a repair that calls for cutting metal. The cold chisels already described do this, but the most useful metal cutters are hacksaws and files. You probably will not be fitting precision parts such as engine bearings by cutting metal. But you almost certainly will be cutting off an exhaust pipe, removing a rusted-on shock absorber nut, or attempting to make screw threads usable after they have been damaged.

Hacksaw

The hacksaw is simply a U-shaped frame with a handle. The blade is stretched across the open side of the U and tightened with a wing nut. Install the blade so it cuts as you push the saw away from you.

Hacksaw blades are a subject in themselves, but you need only a general-purpose metal cutting blade. Since you will not use it often, save money by buying an expensive blade instead of a low price one. The best blades have hardened teeth that last much longer and they are also a lot less apt to break. In addition, a high quality blade makes any metal cutting chore a lot easier, cuts faster for less work, and makes a smoother cut.

For cutting thin sheet metal you need a fine blade and for heavier and/or softer metal you want fewer teeth for a coarser cut. Tell the clerk where you are shopping what you want to cut and he will help select the correct number of tpi—teeth per in.—to cut it smoothly and efficiently. Then buy the most expensive blade he has of that type.

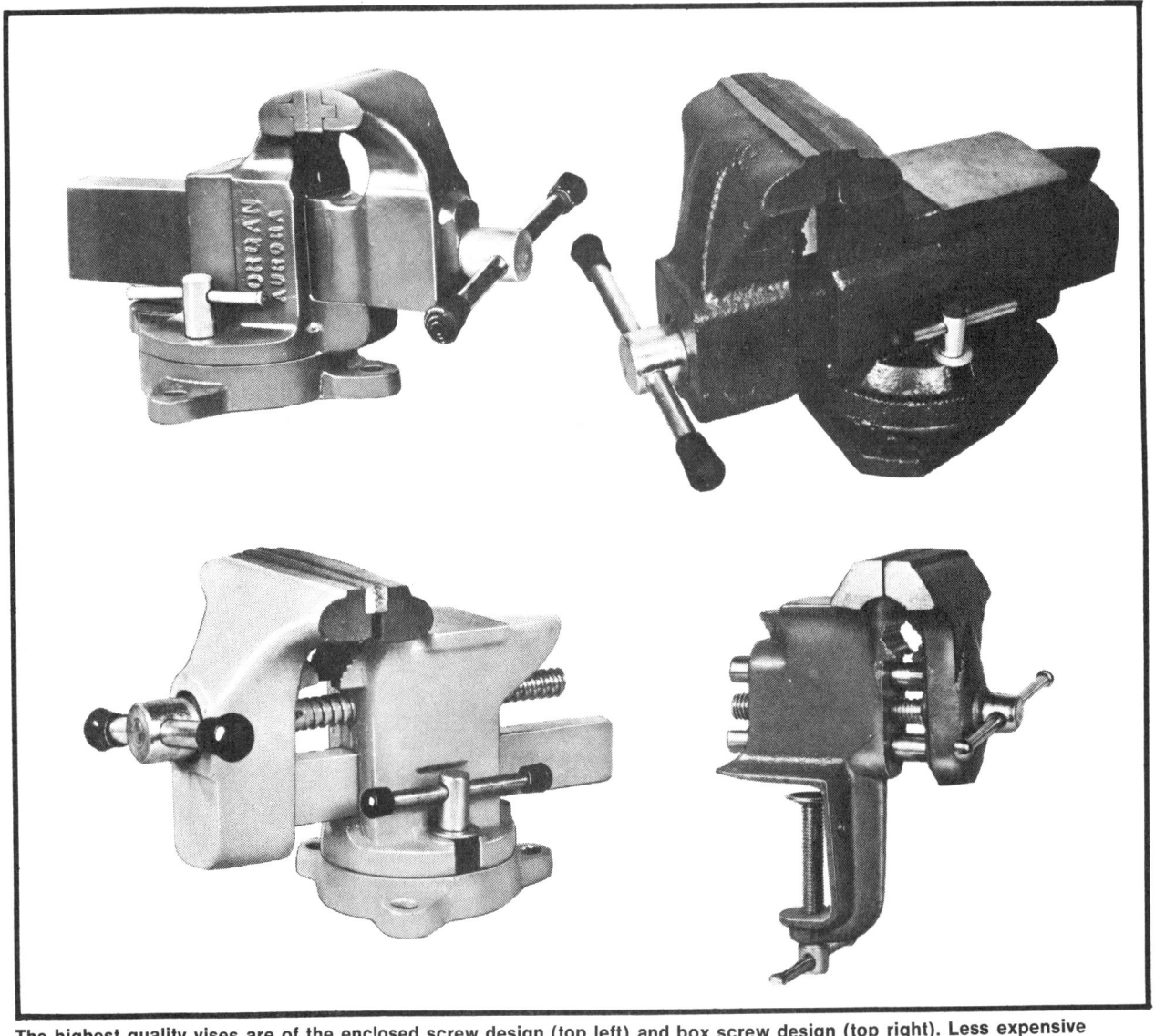
The highest quality vises are of the enclosed screw design (top left) and box screw design (top right). Less expensive vises have exposed screws (bottom) but may have other features such as auxiliary pipe jaws.

Files

You will need only a couple of files. Start out with an ignition point file. This is small, finely cut, and designed to file ignition points—but you will not be using it for that. You can use it to sharpen spark plugs by filing the electrodes before regapping them. And, occasionally, for smoothing a sharp edge on a piece of metal or repairing a screw.

Special retreading files have teeth designed to match screw threads so you can use them to clean up threads on a bolt. These come in different sizes for different threads and can be of special value if you are working on an older car where replacements for some parts are hard to get.

A nut splitter is another metal cutting tool but probably one you can live without. It fits over a rusted-on nut and has a screw jack you can tighten with a wrench to force a chisel blade into the nut. This will crack it—making it possible to remove it without damaging the bolt or stud. Then you can replace the ruined nut with a new one. You can do the same job with a hacksaw or cold chisel by applying a little more time and effort.

Tools for exhaust work

If you work on exhaust systems, aside from a good penetrating oil, a few inexpensive special tools will help a lot. In most exhaust system work, the hard part of the job is getting off the old parts. The easy way to do this is by cutting nuts or bolts and by splitting the pipes where they refuse to separate. A muffler cutter, a specially shaped cold chisel with an angled shank makes this easier. These cost $3 and up. They are worth the price. Chain cutters are great for chopping out corroded sections of pipe. But they cost about $15 to do a job that doesn't take a lot longer with a cold chisel. Expanders are handy for stretching pipes so they will fit over each other as they were designed to. At $15 and up, one can save a pipe that would cost more than that to replace.

The other metal-cutting tool you may need is a tubing cutter for chopping off lengths of fuel pipe or brake tubing. It is a clamp with a jack screw that clamps a cutting wheel on the tube to make a smooth, square cut. The price is about $4.

BODY REPAIR TOOLS

Somehow, fewer home mechanics get involved with body repairs than other types of auto repair. Since auto body repair is mostly hand work and time and care count for a lot, you can often do the job as well as a pro because you can afford to take the time you cannot afford to pay him to take. A fairly complete set of body tools costs about $75. But to be able to use them effectively you must be a skilled auto body repairman.

POWER HAND TOOLS

There are three basic power tools for home mechanics. But high cost keeps most of us down to a portable electric drill. The other two—a saber saw and a power wrench, while useful, probably cost more than they will be worth to you. The saw might be a good investment because you can also use it for general home repairs. But the wrench—at about $75 for an electric model is beyond the scope of most.

Two drills will come under consideration—a ¼-inch and a ⅜-inch. The ¼-inch drill runs faster—usually 2250 rpm—but the greater power and capacity of the slower-turning ⅜-inch drill make it worth the few dollars extra that it costs. A reversing model with variable speeds is worth its price to you because it can also be used as a nut runner or power screwdriver once the fasteners are loose. Such a drill does not have the torque to break a nut loose and should never be used for that job. Price: $20 to $50.

Attachments make the hand-held power drill the most versatile for home craftsmen. Besides boring

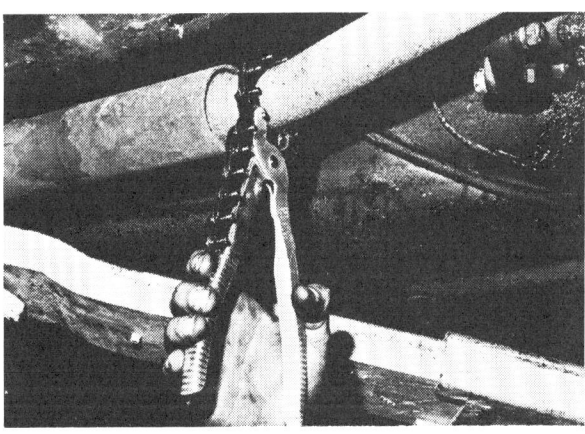

A chain cutter is a specialized exhaust system tool that cuts only round pipes.

holes and buffing wax, your drill wire brushes carbon and does many body-shop jobs.

CAUTION: Do not wash and wax your car and then use you electric drill to buff the wax while standing in the puddles of water left from washing the car. Several hundred people a year are fatally injured in this way.

The most useful attachment you can get for your electric drill is a drill stand. This is a simple sheet metal frame to hold your drill horizontally on your workbench. Snap or clamp the drill into the stand. Insert a small grinding wheel in the chuck and put on your safety glasses. Working slowly and carefully, you can do most of the metal grinding jobs—like cold chisel sharpening—that a bigger and better grinder could do, but at a cost of a couple of dollars for the stand and another couple for the wheel. This is only a fraction of the cost of a grinder.

BENCH TOOLS

Using the fender of your car for a workbench and locking pliers for a vise may be the way you start. But a workbench and fixed tools on it will have to come if you get serious about working on your car. Benches have been discussed. Bench tools for auto repairs come in two types—power and hand operated.

Vise

The most important bench tool is a vise. As with many other tools, you do not need the very best vise you can buy. But you do need a good one that is big enough. Obviously, there is no way most of us are going to get a $120 machinist's vise unless we can get it used from an equipment sale when a service station or garage closes down. For $15 to $25 you can get a light duty machinist's vise with a built-in anvil that will serve most of your needs.

Things to look for when selecting it are size and weight. The bigger and heavier the better, within reason—say 12- to 40-lbs. for a vise with 3½- to 5-inch jaws. Do not look askance at the 3½-inch jaw-width vises. They will hold a starter while you work on it. And that is a typical job you may be doing.

Look for a vise with a box frame to guide the moving jaw and cover the jack screw that closes it. Keeping filings off the threads and out of the nut make it much easier to turn the handle and adds greatly to the life and usefulness of the vise.

The first thing to do when you get it home—before mounting it solidly on your workbench with bolts that go right through—is to take it completely apart. Apply a good grade of molybdenum disulphide grease to the jackscrew and nut. Then put it back together and mount it. This preventive maintenance should keep your vise happy for years without further attention beyond wiping it clean.

Others

Other bench tools are power tools. We have already mentioned the possibilities of a drill stand. If you work up a step beyond that, the most versatile and useful bench tool is a power grinder. Set it up with one general purpose wheel and a wire wheel on the other end. You will find it endlessly useful.

Sources for bench grinders are the same as other power tools. While the $20 light duty jobs may give you the bare capability you require, you could probably do as well with a drill stand at less cost. The next move up is at least a 5- or 6-inch wheel. The 7-inch size is pretty standard. But at this size you are looking at about a $70 tool. As with electric drills, look for anti-friction bearings and at least medium duty service ratings. Easy-to-remove end covers help when you want to change a wheel. Built-in lights are useful but add considerably to cost. A water tray for cooling hot workpieces is useful and many models have one. But the important thing is to get one with good eye protection, fully enclosed wheels, and solid tool rests. A well-worn but better quality tool from a garage sale is probably a better deal than a light duty model brand new.

Grinding is dirty work. So mount your grinder either on a pedestal if you can find one cheap—a new one goes for about $30—or at one end of your workbench well away from the area where you may be working on mechanical parts that could suffer from grit in the works.

ODDS, ENDS, AND TOOL BOXES

One of the jobs that you may contemplate in the future is to make a major component swap. Most of the work required in changing an engine, for example, is simple bolting and unbolting to remove the parts in the way. Once you disconnect the engine you can lift it out of the chassis. The factory or professionally rebuilt engine—on which you have traded in your tired or broken mill—is an equally simple bolt-in replacement. The savings can be considerable on such a job. But there is a lot of work involved. Aside from the standard hand tools, you will need a hoist and a sky hook to do this job.

Hoist

The hoist is easy. You need good rope and chain hoists capable of picking up an engine and a support for it. Imports with small engines may require lifting 300 to 500 lbs. Large American car engines with transmission attached go as high as 1000 to 1500 lbs. The bigger jobs may require a professional shop because of the weight. But smaller engines can be supported by the rafters in a house or garage if proper supports are added to spread the load.

Rope hoists with nylon cord cost the least. One with a 2000-pound rating goes for as little as $5. But a more competent nylon rope cable puller-hoist with hand lever and ratchet drum mechanism costs three to four times as much. Get into wire cables and you are up to about $25. As capacities rise, price goes up steeply. A ¾-ton geared cable hoist with a crank instead of a lever starts at about $40. Professional chain hoists for ½-ton and 1-ton lifts cost from $55 to $80 and up.

Since safety is involved—dropping an engine can be extremely dangerous to both you and your car—you want one with ample reserve capacity. But since you will not be using it often you do not want to have a fortune tied up in it either. A nylon or wire cable hoist with at least ¾-ton capacity at about $25 makes sense. Or if you need more capacity and have a hook to hang it on, you might rent a bigger chain hoist for $5 or $10 to handle a specific job.

Creeper

Everyone has seen a professional mechanic roll under a raised auto on a creeper. It does make his job easier and speeds his work, but it probably will not help you nearly as much. He is working on a good concrete floor and your floor may not be so smooth. He has the car safely raised on stands or a service lift so there is extra working clearance. There just is not room under most cars for you and a creeper unless the car is raised. Cheap versions cost $10 and good ones can cost twice that. Unless you really need one for moving an engine or transmission once it is out of the car, a creeper may be a luxury you can do without. The decision is yours.

Creeper seat

A creeper seat is something you will find very useful. It is simply four casters on a metal tray with a raised seat over it. Tools and parts go in the tray and you can sit on the seat while working on brakes or other repair jobs which seem to require stooping or kneeling unless the car is raised on a hoist. A creeper seat can prevent an aching back.

Where to keep your tools

Once you start collecting car repair tools, you will need a place to keep them. In the beginning, a simple tool box or maybe even a .50 caliber surplus ammo box will hold everything. But you will soon outgrow it. If you have a more or less permanent shop in a secure area, a pegboard is the answer. You can arrange your wrenches, sockets, handles, hammers, pliers, screwdrivers, and any other tools on it in such a way that each one has a place. You will be able to find tools quickly and not spend half of your working time looking in the bottom of a dark box for a missing tool.

Another answer is the relatively inexpensive steel shelving which is strong enough to hold smaller tool boxes, parts, and other equipment.

Then there are the big, fancy mechanic's tool chests. These are about the best and most secure way to keep your tools, but also the most expensive. For a really large tool collection, you may need $300 or more worth of tool chests. Considering the value of the tools, this investment makes sense. But the cost may well be prohibitive.

More realistically, you can get a 2-drawer tool box with a top compartment for less than $20. This should hold most of the stuff that will not go on the peg board. It is reasonably transportable and you should be able to find the tool you want.

You have probably seen the ads for wet or dry shop vacuum cleaners. If money is no object, it might be worth getting. However, a $1.19 fiber bristle push broom seems to work quite well.

Non-automotive tools you may find useful are putty knives for gasket scraping, razor scrapers for removing stickers from windshields, and a Pop riveter. Pop rivets work in blind holes for relatively light sheet metal fastening jobs. Drive rivets handle heavier jobs without a special tool required for setting them.

GAUGES

Gauges come in two basic types—mechanical and electrical or electronic. You will need both. Time was when a set of feelers or even a thin dime—a real silver dime at that—would do for setting point gaps, but now you need a dwell meter as well.

Mechanical test equipment

You still need feeler gauges for much automotive work. These are inexpensive flat strips of steel graduated in thickness which you slide between two parts to check the clearance between them. A complete set sells for under $3. Even though you will use relatively few leaves on the gauge set, they are so cheap that it pays to have the complete set.

Flat feelers come in straight thicknesses and in go-no-go sets. A straight gauge has each blade of a given thickness—say .012-inch throughout its length. A go-no-go set has the tip of each leaf ground to the nominal size of the blade but the body of the blade behind the tip is about .001-inch thicker. Using these blades you insert the feeler in the gap—clearance measured between the rocker arm and the valve stem, for instance—and then try to insert the thicker part of the blade. If it goes in, you readjust the clearance until only the thinner section fits.

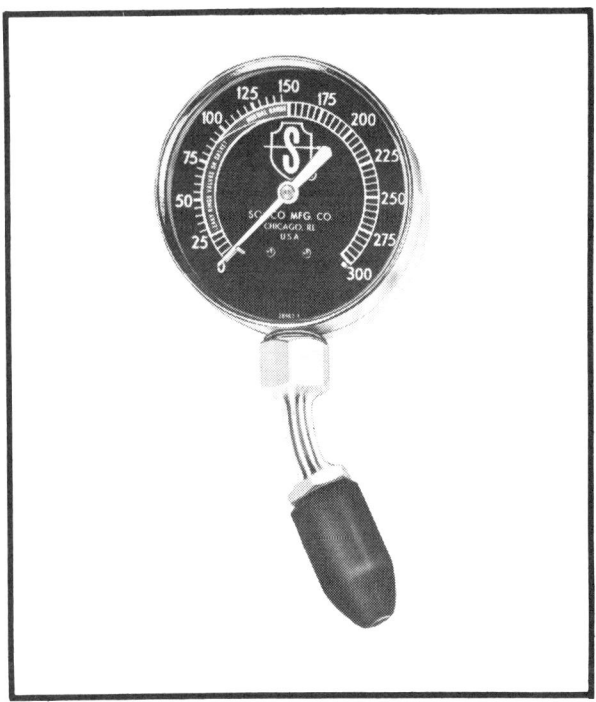

A compression gauge with rubber seal is held in spark plug hole by hand pressure while readings are taken.

A compression gauge with a screw-in connector is the only way to make a compression check if the plug opening in the cylinder head is hard to get at or covered by other engine components. Flexible hose snakes around obstacles.

For less experienced mechanics, go-no-go gauges can be useful but you can do the same thing with a straight set of feelers by using the 3-finger system. In this system, you set the gap using the specified feeler and then check it with the size larger and the size smaller blade from the same feeler gauge set. The smaller blade should slip in freely with no drag and the larger size should be so tight you almost cannot push it into the gap.

You cannot use a flat feeler gauge to gap spark plugs because the electrodes tend to become dished in a way that would give you an inaccurate reading. You need a wire feeler gauge set for plug gaps. These are inexpensive too—most sets cost from 50¢ to one dollar. They come as sets of wires and small flat blades—one of the most useful configurations—as L-shaped wires in a metal frame, and as U-shaped loops on a flat metal disc. Some of the latter type used to be made with a small magnifying glass in the center—a useful addition—but these have not been around in years.

One more detail in selecting a spark plug gauge: Get one that measures gaps all the way from .020- to .100-inch. Some new cars with electronic ignition systems specify gaps the old gauges cannot measure with their .040-inch blades. However, in a pinch you can use two blades together, .035- and .040- to check a .075-inch gap, for instance.

Brass or plastic feeler blades are needed to check clearances on many of the new electronic ignition systems because steel feelers would stick to the magnetic pickup and give you a false reading. Get one if you need it, but reserve it for ignition work only because the soft blade wears with use and then gives inaccurate readings. This also holds for steel feelers that have gotten rusty or are very old.

Thread gauges look a little like a set of feeler gauges, but have serrated edges which match various screw thread pitches. These can be useful if you must replace a bolt. They are cheap enough at about one dollar a set for you to pick one up.

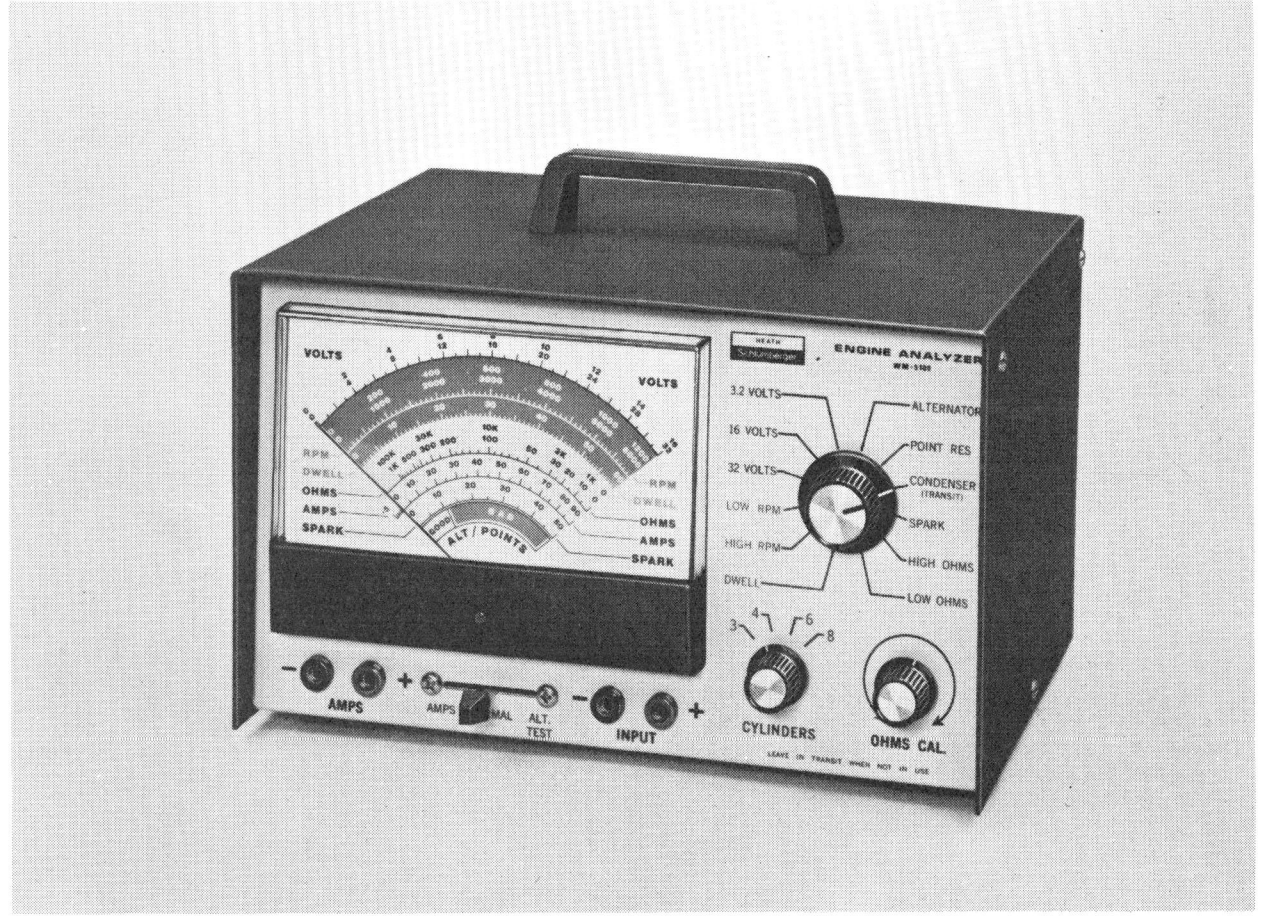

An engine analyzer is really an automotive electrical multi-tester that measures volts, ohms, rpm, dwell and other functions. You can get along quite well with a more simple combination tach-dwell meter.

Plastigage is used to check engine bearing clearances. It comes as wire-like plastic extrusions of different sizes which you clamp between the bearing shell and the crankshaft journal after cleaning off all the oil. Then unbolt the bearing cap and compare the flattened plastic strip with a chart on the paper envelope the Plastigage sticks come in to read the clearance. Plastigage is cheap, accurate, and is available at auto parts jobbers and machine shops.

Micrometers and vernier or dial gauge calipers will be needed by machinists doing major engine rebuilding. But they are rarely required by home auto mechanics even if they do an occasional engine job. A micrometer looks like a small C-clamp and gives readings in thousandths of an inch. The vernier caliper is a bit less accurate but measures inside or outside diameters or gaps up to about five inches for most sizes and hole depths. A good one is accurate to about .001-inch but costs $20 or more. Dial calipers cost twice that and are for machinists rather than for you. There are only a few occasions when you would have use for a micrometer. Measuring wear on a disc brake rotor is one.

Compression gauges come plain and fancy. But most home mechanics can use the simplest type—if it fits their cars. A compression gauge has a dial that reads from 0 to 300 psi (pounds per square inch). You insert it in a spark plug hole and crank the engine to check the compression developed in each cylinder. This test is a vital part of engine tuneup, because without proper compression none of your careful work can pay off in better mileage and performance.

The simplest compression testers have a short, angled spout with a rubber cone on the end which you press into the spark plug hole and hold in place with your hand while a helper cranks the engine with the starter. If you cannot reach your spark plug holes—as is the case on many V-8 engines and some others—you need a fancier gauge with a flexible hose that screws into the plug opening. These cost about $15. Compression testers come with complete instructions.

Looking a lot like a compression gauge, a vacuum gauge measures intake manifold vacuum with the engine running. Some models also measure fuel pump output pressure. These cost from $6 to about $10 and, like compression testers, come with complete instructions. Properly used, vacuum gauge readings can tell you a lot about your engine's health and efficiency.

While on the subject of pressure gauges, tire gauges should come under consideration. There are two types—the pencil type that sticks out a calibrated rod to indicate pressure and the dial type that reads like a compression gauge. Pencil gauges cost from 79¢ up to a couple of dollars and dial gauges start at about a dollar and go up to more than $10. Both types can be accurate. But the dial gauge is easier to read. Get one with a range of 5 to 35 psi because that is the range you need for passenger car tires. Also, the markings are further apart than in the more common 5-to-55-lb. models.

Tire tread depth gauges cost only a dollar or two and give you a reading on, obviously, tire tread depth. They are really a frill since you can use a Lincoln-head penny to tell if your tires are legal. Stick it

A vacuum gauge checks valves, manifold leaks, and carb setting on vacuum side and fuel pump output on pressure side. It is a handy, multi-use gauge.

into the shallowest groove and if Lincoln's head is covered by the tread, you've got at least 1/16-inch of tread. If the top of his head clears the rubber, you need a new tire.

Belt tension gauges are considered necessary by professional mechanics. But you can do quite well without one. The cheapest ones sell for less than $10 but most cost twice that or more. Drive belts cost less than this and you can make a pretty accurate guess on tension simply by deflecting the belt with your thumb.

Hydrometers wind up the mechanical test equipment section. You need two—one to test your antifreeze concentration, the other for the battery. Both testers come in two types. One uses a glass float in a glass syringe to measure the specific gravity of the liquid under test. The other has four or five tiny plastic balls in a similar but much smaller syringe. Each ball is made of material of a different specific gravity and you test the fluid by the number of balls which float or sink. Simple hydrometers cost about $1.50 and less.

Coolant testers with simple floats or plastic balls cost as little as a dollar. Fancy models with thermometers built in to allow for coolant expansion when hot cost more than $10. The plastic balls expand or contract at the same rate as the coolant to give accurate readings.

Whatever the type, an antifreeze tester measures the ethylene glycol concentration in the coolant to tell you whether or not your car is safe from freezing at low temperatures. It will not tell you the anti-corrosion protection left in your coolant.

Radiator pressure testers are another tool that might be found in the advanced novice mechanic's workshop, but are not absolutely necessary. All you need to know is whether or not the system is pressurizing. If it is, you can feel how hard the top hose is when the engine is hot by pinching it with your fingers. You can make a further check by releasing the radiator pressure cap part way while the engine is warm. if there is pressure, you will hear it hiss.

Headlight aimers bridge the gap between mechanical and electrical testers. Most of them are strictly mechanical. If your state has an inspection that requires headlight aiming, one might pay for itself. But at about $20, it is easier to adjust lights at night against a white wall.

Using a headlight aimer is quicker and easier than working with dabs of tape and a yardstick on a white wall, but costs more. Forget aimers until your basic shop is complete.

Electrical test equipment

A whole book could be written about electrical testers and how to use them. There are lots of different types. Fortunately, you need not be concerned with all of them. Up until recently, they were not necessary. But more sophisticated autos make them necessary. And ever-stiffer smog control requirements make even the once-exotic exhaust gas analyzers worthy of consideration. Sure, you may end up with more than $100 in equipment. But a good smog-control tuneup could cost that much all by itself. The kinds of car tuning you do will determine the testers you need.

If you limit your ambitions to basic tuneup—replacing spark plugs, points, condenser, setting ignition timing, replacing filters (oil, air, and fuel), and cleaning and tightening electrical connections, then you can get by with a lot less equipment than you would need for serious troubleshooting or major engine modifications.

The basic preventive maintenance tuneup calls for the compression and vacuum gauges already discussed plus a power timing light and a combination tachometer and dwell meter, usually called a tach-dwell meter. Total cash outlay is about $60.

The tach-dwell meter is used for setting ignition point gap on cars that still have points (most cars made in the past two years in the U.S.A. have electronic ignition systems that are pointless), and for adjusting carburetor idling speed. If your car has no points, you can still measure the dwell. But all you can do to correct it is replace an expensive electronic black box. Timing on most electronic ignition systems should stay put for the life of the engine. Thus, even if you need a tach-dwell meter to work on your present car, your next one may make it obsolete.

Dwell is simply the percent of time the points are closed measured in degrees of distributor cam rotation. Timing is the point where the spark plug of the No. 1 cylinder fires measured in degrees of crankshaft rotation. While the dwell should remain fairly constant at different engine speeds, timing is greatly affected by engine speed and must be checked at indicated engine rpm—usually idling.

133

Tach-dwell meters sell for as little as $10 or $12 and for as much as a couple of hundred when incorporated into fancy multi-meter test systems. They also come with a built-in timing light for about $35 and up. To use a tach-dwell meter, you must set the instrument for the number of cylinders in your engine (some only read for Sixes or V-8s, in which case you must double the readings in your head for Threes or Fours) and connect two alligator clips to the engine wiring—the hot lead to the primary circuit (small) wire from the coil to the distributor and the other to ground.

Many tach-dwell meters also make a number of other useful electrical tests. One of these can be valuable enough to justify its extra cost. The added tests you care about are a high rpm scale, 0-6000 rpm in addition to the low scale 0-1200 rpm required to set idling speed, voltage readings in 0-3.2 and 0-16 (if you work on trucks with 24-volt systems, a 0-32-volt scale is needed), point resistance to check ignition point resistance and save unneeded replacements, amperage for checking generator or alternator output, and ohms to check electrical resistance and spot open circuits like burned out bulbs. A substitute condenser is rarely needed.

Tach-dwell and multiple-test meters come as small as hand-held meters that can be hard to read or as substantial instruments you rest on a workbench or fender. The larger ones are easier to use.

Cost varies depending on quality plus number of features. For a complete multi-tester, expect to pay at least $30 and up to $50 or $60 for ready-to-go instruments. If you do electronic kit building, you can save a bit of money by assembling your own instrument from Heath, Knight, or one of the other mail-order electronic kit companies.

Timing lights come with neon or stroboscopic tubes. You want a strobe (or power timing light as it is sometimes called) because the much brighter light makes it much easier to see the timing marks. Since you must work near the whirling fan blades while using an electronic device that is connected to a high voltage spark plug wire, the strobe helps you stay far enough away to keep out of trouble. That makes it worth its $17 to $40 price tag compared with about $3 or $4 for the dull, orange neon light.

At a price a bit lower than the battery powered timing light, you can get one that plugs into a 120-volt wall socket. These add to the shock hazard and must work where there is a power source. Since the savings between one of these and one of the lower priced lights that use power from your car's battery is only a couple of dollars, we recommend the battery powered light.

Timing lights have plastic or metal housings shaped something like a pistol. The plastic housings are safer, cheaper, and a bit less apt to break if dropped than the metal ones.

To use a power timing light, connect its power clips to the car battery posts and T-adaptor between the No. 1 spark plug and its lead. Some timing lights have the adaptor built into the input lead. Others use a separate adaptor and have an alligator clip you attach to it. The built-in type is handier if you work on a car with a conventional ignition wiring harness.

In addition to electrical engine test instruments like these, you might also consider a battery charger. Small trickle chargers start at about $10 and prices range upwards to well over $100 for pro models. For less than $20, you can get a 4-amp model with automatic shutoff that will be completely adequate for your needs. As with other electrical gear, battery chargers come with instructions. Hookup is simple.

Following are two electronic test instruments you need to know about but probably do not need to own. These are the oscilloscope and the exhaust gas analyzer.

The oscilloscope looks like a small television screen which produces trace patterns that show what is happening to the voltage passing through your car's ignition system. In theory, you can take one look at the pattern and tell immediately what is wrong. In

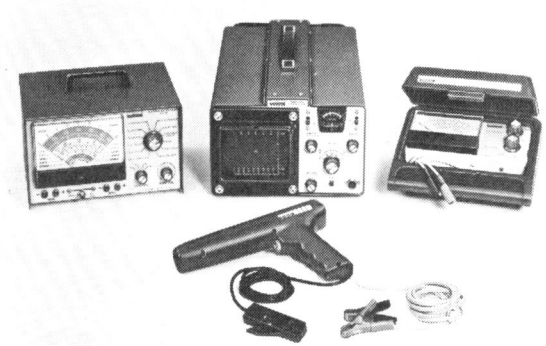

An oscilloscope, top center, speeds ignition system troubleshooting, but is quite costly.

Electrical testers check, from left to right, primary ignition output; volts; and engine rpm and point dwell angle.

practice, it takes a pretty well trained eye to spot troubles quickly. What is more, there are very few things you can spot on a scope that you cannot also identify by examining the parts or using a much cheaper electrical multi-tester.

And oscilloscopes—even the ones intended for enthusiastic home mechanics—do not come cheap. A kit to build a simple oscilloscope used to be available for about $100 several years ago. But the current model with a 12-inch screen for pros combines a lot more functions and costs nearly four times that.

More necessary than the oscilloscope is the exhaust gas analyzer. While you need it to check emissions on modern smog-controlled cars, good, professional infrared instruments can cost several thousand dollars. Cheaper ones that go for something between $100 and $200 are not quite so far out of reach. But there are many other tools you need more. And, there is a very good chance that new laws requiring still more stringent smog control on future cars will make any instrument you buy obsolete.

PARTS BUYING

SOURCES

Local service station or new car dealer

Car parts and the tools we have discussed come from a number of sources. Many parts can be purchased at your local service station—at a high, retail price. This also holds true for a new car dealer, with the addition that there are some parts for your car—proprietary parts—that you cannot get anywhere else. These are parts like cylinder heads, fenders, and others that are not needed in enough quantity for anyone to set up in competition with the car maker to supply them. Or they may require such expensive tooling no one can afford to produce them at a profit.

Go to a dealer if it is handy, if his prices for most things are not seriously out of line—check with other local sources—and, of course, if you need something not available elsewhere. When a car is new, you may want to get factory (OEM—Original Equipment Manufacturer) parts to be certain you keep your warranty in force even if the repair is not something that can be done under warranty.

Auto parts jobber

The auto parts jobber and machine shop supplies most of the parts bought by local service stations and the smaller professional repair shops. He has two prices for everything—a mechanic's price and a retail price. Since perhaps 30% of his business is now cash-over-the-counter from do-it-yourself mechanics, he will most likely grant you the mechanic's price once you become known to him. If you do a fair bit of business through the shop you may be able to set up an account with the store and pay for everything monthly.

Parts jobbers are a good source of parts and tools because you are dealing with professional auto parts countermen who are accustomed to dealing with professional mechanics. They know a lot more about their business—and yours—than a clerk in an auto department or a discount store does. And unless they are too rushed, they will usually help you get good quality parts to do the job.

The prices, with the discount, will be about average. They run a bit higher than those charged by department stores, discount houses, and mail order auto specialty houses, but they are lower than prices at new car dealers and service stations.

In addition to parts, most of the best jobber shops also run machine shops. They can completely rebuild an engine, turn a brake drum, rebuild a cylinder head, boil out a cylinder block, turn down a crankshaft, fit bearings, assemble press-fitted parts—in short they handle all the jobs the smaller shops farm out. By farming out your work to them directly, you save the commission on the deal which would be collected by the garage or service shop as part of their repair fee.

If there is some specialized machine work you require, the jobber shop knows where to get it done. Often, they will do it on commission for you. This will cost a percentage, but can save you hours of searching out a shop that can dynamically balance a crankshaft for you, cc your cylinder head, or magnaflux a suspect front suspension part.

Speed or custom shops

Speed shops or custom car shops can be a good source of special parts or specialized machine shop services. On some things their prices will be on a par with, or cheaper than, your local jobbers. They specialize in hot rod work and if that is your major interest, they are the place to go with your business.

Specialty stores

Auto specialty stores are another source of parts and tools. Their prices are generally lower. But quality will also be lower. They are better for dress-up or trim items than for hard parts like wheel bearings or ignition points.

Discount or department stores

Auto departments in department or discount stores offer about the lowest prices for most parts and tools you will find anywhere. The quality of branded, known merchandise is okay and, especially when bought on sale, you can get many things at true bargain prices. The best things to buy here are sealed cans of antifreeze, motor oil by the case—but watch out for brand names that look familiar but are a little different from the known brand—fast-moving parts that require frequent replacement such as oil filters, air filters, and ignition parts. Brand name spark plugs can also be an excellent deal.

Local auto departments of the big mail order houses offer the lure of one-stop auto supply shopping and usually have good quality parts at prices very little higher than the super discounters. Sears, J. C. Penney and Montgomery Ward are the really big names in this field. These are good places to look for tools on sale. You may be able to get a $15 wrench set for $9.95 when an equivalent quality tool set would cost $20 at the parts jobber.

Mail order

Mail order opens the shelves of some of the largest auto parts suppliers to you at very reasonable prices. The biggest name in this field is J. C. Whitney & Co. Even considering that you must pay postage on top of the catalog prices, you can do very well on both hard parts and fast moving items at a mail order house. The only drawback to dealing with one is the wait while your order is being filled. Most of them are very prompt. Between one and three weeks for delivery to your door is par for the course with most orders arriving in under two weeks. If you know ahead of time what equipment or parts you need for a specific automotive job, mail order is a good way to go. The catalogs often list parts you will not find on a jobber's shelves or even in a mail order store's local auto department.

New or rebuilt?

At all of these parts stores, you have a choice of new or rebuilt parts for most items. Some items like fuel pumps, alternators, clutch pressure plates, starters, and voltage regulators are usually better if bought new rather than rebuilt. A lot depends on the quality of the rebuilding shop, though. Some remanufacturers, as they like to call themselves, produce parts that are definitely better than new. Check both the price and the guarantee that comes with the parts. The higher the price and the better the guarantee, then probably the higher the quality of the component. Super low prices on rebuilt parts usually point to poorer quality workmanship that will show up in shorter life and more early failures than the higher priced remanufactured items. If you are fixing up a car to sell it, these may be just what you want. But otherwise, it is better to purchase the better quality items.

Wrecking yards

Auto wrecking yards can be a superior source for a number of the parts you will be needing—particularly if yours is an older model car. Most of the better yards are tied in with others across the country by teletype. So there is an excellent chance they can get something for you that would be hard to come by through other sources.

In mechanical parts, wreckers are a good source for engines, transmissions, complete rear axle assemblies, wheels, tires, batteries, starters, and generators or alternators. Most of these parts will come with a guarantee stating that you can exchange them for another if they do not work. Engines will be guaranteed not to have cracked blocks or burn oil, for example.

If your car is far from new, it may make little economic sense to put a new or rebuilt engine in it. But an engine from a low-mileage wreck could extend the usefulness of the car for another couple of years at half the cost of a rebuilt. In other words, if your car has a life expectancy, when repaired, of another 25,000 miles, do you really want to give it a 50,000-mile engine?

Body parts, especially doors, fenders, hoods, deck lids, seats, trim, light fixtures, steering wheels, and other non-moving parts are better than new ones when bought used. Better than new ones? If you buy a new door, you get just that, the door, in prime and completely without any other parts. You have to remove the latches, hinges, chrome trim, window mechanism, inside trim panel, weatherstripping, etc. from your bent or rusted out door and install them on the new one. Then you have to paint it to match your car. A used door can be checked for dents, rust, etc. and, with a little bit of luck, you may be able to find one already painted the right color to match your car. The price will be about half to two-thirds that of a new door. And putting it in your car will be a lot less work than building up a shell and installing that.

Parts that are usually not worth getting from wrecking yards are voltage regulators, windshield wiper motors, carburetors and similar parts that may have been weather-damaged from outside storage and, which will cost negligibly less than rebuilt parts.

As a general rule of thumb, used parts should cost about half as much as new ones.

Replacement glass, particularly windshields, is probably the worst deal at a wrecking yard. The price is hardly less than new glass because of the labor required to remove it. Glass is scarce in the wrecking yard because so much is broken before the cars even arrive. Rear axles are a good deal. The demand for them is low because they rarely break. Yet the supply is good because they often survive in serviceable condition when the rest of the car does not.

Now, you are in business. You know how to set up to do any auto repair or maintenance job you might care to tackle, where to do it, where to get the tools and parts required, and finally how to do it in a businesslike and safe manner.

Every auto job you undertake will teach you something about your car and yourself. And as you become more experienced, you will learn how to do your own maintenance, do it as well or better than the pros can do it for you, and at far less cost.

Basic Engine Tuneup

If your car is not running right, if it just does not have that old zip when you floor the gas pedal, if it just does not feel right anymore, chances are, your engine needs a tuneup.

An engine tuneup is a series of procedures that restore engine performance, reduce exhaust emissions, increase fuel mileage and prolong the useful life of the engine.

Since an engine tuneup is actually one form of preventive maintenance and is one of the most important elements of proper vehicle service, it should be performed at regular intervals rather than after a failure occurs. Every 10,000 miles is a good rule-of-thumb schedule for periodic engine tuneups if you are an average driver. If your car is used less frequently, say, 4000-5000 miles a year, then you must use a different schedule for tuneups—a time schedule rather than a mileage schedule. In this case, a tuneup once a year will keep your car running at peak efficiency. If your car puts on extremely high mileage, like 40,000 or 50,000 miles a year, obviously, your tuneup schedule should be, say, every 15,000 miles.

Different driving conditions will call for different servicing schedules also. For instance, lots of driving in dusty conditions will call for more frequent periodic service, as will lots of stop-and-go driving. Long distance trips and highway miles are easier on a car and will require less frequent tuneups. The point is, periodic engine tuneup is a necessary part of keeping a car running right and a tuneup could save you a long walk home or an expensive tow job.

If one of the following warning signs is present, your engine probably needs a tuneup right now:
1. Engine performance is noticeably sluggish.
2. Engine consistently stalls.
3. Engine is hard to start.
4. Engine misfires or stumbles.
5. Engine hesitation or surge is noticeable, especially in high gear at highway speeds.

What is a tuneup?

An engine tuneup consists of a specific series of operations. There are definite limitations as to what a tuneup can and cannot do for an engine's performance. But, if carried out regularly on an engine in otherwise good repair, it guarantees optimum performance and gas mileage.

It is usually possible to get an engine running smoothly by making a few simple cleanings and adjustments. But do not expect trouble-free operation and maximum economy unless an engine tuneup is complete and thorough.

Before you begin

Before beginning any tuneup and before using the instructions in this book, it is recommended that you completely read through the procedures and study the diagrams. Read them through twice if you can. These readings will give you an overall view of what the operations will consist of and what you can expect next as you proceed from step to step.

QUICK TUNEUP TIP

Before beginning an engine tuneup, have on hand all the tools and equipment you will need. There is nothing more frustrating than having to stop a job right in the middle because you do not have something you need to complete the job.

TOOLS AND EQUIPMENT YOU NEED

Before beginning, you should have the following tools and equipment on hand:
1. Work light if you are working in a dimly lit area.
2. Screwdriver set, 4-inch for tight, cramped areas, 8-inch for general adjustments, and slim 12-inch for use in keeping carburetor throttles fully opened when necessary.
3. Pliers.
4. Spark plug socket, ratchet and extension. Set should preferably use ⅜-inch drive and extensions should be 1-inch, 3-inch and 6-inch sizes.
5. Compression testing gauge.
6. Remote starter switch for use in cranking engine if you have no assistant to help you.
7. Feeler (thickness) gauges—flat type for ignition point gap settings, round type for spark plug gap.
8. Allen wrench set for adjusting points on some cars.
9. Distributor wrench or appropriate socket with long extension and swivel joint to loosen distributor from block when making timing adjustments.
10. Ignition wrench set to remove and install condenser-to-points lead and distributor-to-coil lead.
11. Torque wrench to tighten spark plugs.
12. Tachometer and dwell meter to properly set dwell and engine idle.
13. Timing light to properly time engine.
14. Vacuum gauge to check the engine vacuum.

Also, be sure to read the section on parts and equipment before beginning. Have the right tools, equipment and parts on hand before you begin. There is nothing more frustrating than to begin a job and then find out you do not have everything you need.

There is a list of safety precautions, both for you and your vehicle, which must be observed to assure that your engine tuneup will be completed successfully and safely.

Lastly, if you desire even more complete or advanced information on any of the operations discussed in this book, consult the Motor Auto Repair Manual or other Motor books which pertain to the subject you are particularly interested in.

Safety precautions

Before proceeding with the tuneup operations, be sure to observe the following precautions, both for your own safety and that of your vehicle:
1. Park vehicle on level ground.
2. Place the shift lever in the Park position on automatic transmission equipped vehicles, or in Neutral for manual shift vehicles.
3. Apply the parking brake.
4. Check for proper brake operation including the parking brake.
5. Chock the front wheels with pieces of wood, cinder blocks or something similar as a further precaution against unwanted vehicle movement.
6. Check level of coolant in radiator. If your car has a clear plastic overflow tank, check the level in the tank.

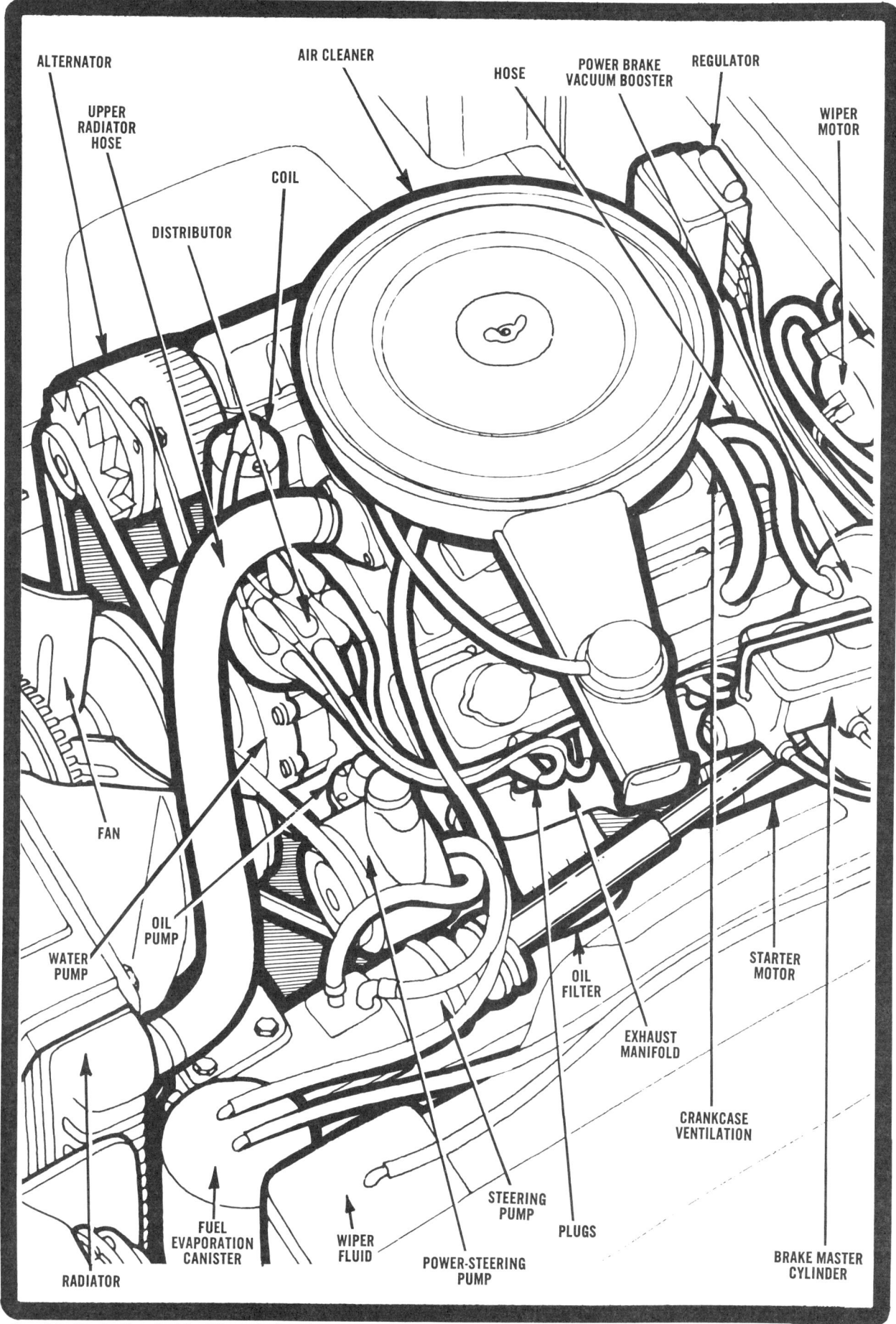

Use this illustration to identify underhood components.

> **QUICK TUNEUP TIP**
> Before beginning the job, read through all the instructions at least once and preferably twice to get an overview of what you will be doing and in what order you will be doing it.

CAUTION: If the engine is hot, do not take off the radiator cap without first relieving the pressure in the radiator. If you do not know how to relieve the pressure, wait until the engine is cool enough to touch it with your hand. Then remove the cap to check coolant level. Removing the cap on a hot radiator will result in hot coolant erupting from the radiator and possibly burning you.

7. Warm up engine to its normal operating temperature, then shut it off.
8. Check all the vehicle instruments and warning lights to assure that the engine is operating normally with no malfunctions. Warning lights should all light up when the ignition key is in the On position. Then they should all go out (except the parking brake warning light if you vehicle has one) when the vehicle is cranked and started. If any warning light does not go on with the key in the On position, the circuit is malfunctioning and should be repaired. The following gauges or warning lights should be checked:
    (a) gasoline gauge.
    (b) temperature gauge—registers engine coolant temperature, or,
    temperature indicator warning light—registers engine overheat condition.
    (c) oil gauge—registers engine oil pressure, or oil indicator warning light—registers unacceptably low oil pressure.
    (d) ammeter—registers battery charging or discharging, or charge indicator warning light—registers if charging system is not operating.
9. Put seat and fender covers in position to keep from scratching paint and soiling seats. An old blanket is ideal if you do not have regular fender covers. Do not use anything that will scratch paint or tear upholstery.
10. Check engine oil level and add oil if necessary.
11. If vehicle is equipped with an automatic transmission, start engine and check the transmission fluid level. This is done with the dipstick which is usually found right near the firewall of the engine compartment.

Parts and equipment you will need

To complete a thorough engine tuneup and to be able to follow the instructions in this book, you will need to have on hand certain parts which will be replaced, plus certain tools and equipment to do the job efficiently and correctly.

The parts you will need are:
1. Spark plugs, the number depending on how many cylinders your engine has (or new spark plug gaskets if old plugs will be reused).
2. Ignition breaker point assembly.
3. Condenser.
4. Fuel filter.
5. Air filter.
6. Positive crankcase ventilation (PCV) valve.
7. PCV filter (if used).
8. Distributor cap and rotor (as necessary).
9. Ignition wires (as necessary).
10. Fuel vapor canister or canister filter (as required).

Be sure to get the right parts for your particular engine. If you are not sure of the specific engine in your vehicle, consult your owner's manual, manufacturer's information plate or decal located somewhere under your hood or on the firewall. Or ask a mechanic friend or a neighbor who knows something about cars. Your neighborhood auto parts supply store will have someone working there who can tell you what you need.

It would be ideal to have all these tools before you begin. However, you may not want to invest the money in tools and equipment right now. If that is the case, chances are you may already have some of these items. You may be able to borrow other items and make do with what you can accumulate without actually going out and buying everything. It should be noted, however, that all the tools and equipment above are necessary if you are to do a thorough first class job.

What you will be doing

Before getting into any of the specific operations, it will be helpful for you to know all the steps involved in a complete basic engine tuneup. The following list is just that—a list. You will notice that there are no explanatory steps here because each step will be explained in detail a little further on in the book. So this list is just for your general orientation before you begin.

With that in mind, you should know that a basic engine tuneup consists of the following steps performed in the following order. It is important to follow the correct order to do a thorough job.

Job 1. Check the engine vacuum.
Job 2. Remove the spark plugs.
Job 3. Perform a compression test.
Job 4. Service the spark plugs.
Job 5. Service the distributor cap.
Job 6. Service the distributor rotor.
Job 7. Service the advance mechanism.
Job 8. Check the ignition wires.
Job 9. Service the ignition breaker points and condenser.
Job 10. Service the battery and battery cables.
Job 11. Replace the fuel filter.
Job 12. Replace the PCV valve and crankcase ventilation filter.
Job 13. Service or replace the air filter.
Job 14: Service or replace the manifold heat control valve.
Job 15. Service the carburetor, choke and linkages.
Job 16. Instrument checkout.
Job 17. Road test the vehicle.

> **QUICK TUNEUP TIP**
> To do a thorough tuneup on your car's engine, you must complete all 17 steps of the procedure. Taking short cuts will result in an incomplete job and probably poor engine performance.

JOB 1. CHECK THE ENGINE VACUUM

Engine vacuum check can be more easily accomplished than a compression test, and will usually tell more about the overall condition of the engine. For example, a compression test will not indicate that the carburetor needs adjustment or the the ignition timing is late. However, if a vacuum reading indicates that the compression is low, there is a burned valve or that the head gasket is defective, a compression test will further substantiate these facts.

TAKING THE VACUUM READING

1. Start the engine and allow it to idle until it reaches its normal operating temperature.
2. Turn the engine off.
3. Remove the air cleaner housing and air filter. If you disconnect any vacuum hoses from the air cleaner housing, make sure that you plug them up. This can be done by inserting a suitable size nail, screw or punch into the open end of the hose.

Sometimes it is easier to disconnect these hoses from the carburetor or intake manifold. In such cases, obtain a length of hose (3-4 inches) and of the same inside diameter and plug one end of the hose in the same manner as above and connect the other end of the hose to the carburetor or intake manifold fitting.

INTERPRETING THE READINGS

Normal reading, Fig. 1, Section A

A steady reading of 18-20 inches Hg. is considered normal. However, on late model cars, the vacuum readings can be as low as 12 inches Hg. due to the late ignition timing. When the throttle is jabbed wide open and then released, the needle will drop to below 5 inches Hg., then jump back to about 25 inches Hg. and eventually return to its original reading.

Low and steady reading, Fig. 1, Sections B and C

Low and steady readings usually indicate a loss of power in all the cylinders caused by late ignition timing, defective ignition system, late valve timing, or a loss of compression due to leaking piston rings. The gauge behavior will be much like that of a normal engine, except that the readings will be much lower —about 4-5 inches Hg. Thus, the reading will be around 14-15 inches Hg. while the engine is idling. When the throttle is jabbed wide open and then released, the needle will drop to about zero, then bounce back to about 22 inches Hg. and eventually to its original reading.

Very low and steady reading, Fig. 1, Section D

A very low and steady reading of about 4-8 inches Hg., indicates a leaking carburetor gasket or leaking intake manifold gasket.

Fluctuation between a high and low reading, Fig. 1, Section E

A fluctuation between a high and a low reading usually indicates a blown cylinder head gasket between two adjacent cylinders. A compression test of the engine will substantiate this fact.

1. Obtain a vacuum source to connect the vacuum gauge hose to. The idea here is to obtain a vacuum source which is downstream of the carburetor. Do not use a vacuum source from the carburetor as these sources are ported and usually will not indicate full manifold vacuum. The vacuum applied to the automatic transmission modulator or power brake unit is full manifold vacuum. So you can connect the vacuum gauge to either one of these sources using a T-fitting. Or you can disconnect either one of these units and connect the vacuum gauge hose directly to the source. If the car is not equipped with an automatic transmission or power brakes, you will find a pipe plug screwed into the manifold. Remove this plug using a suitable tool, (usually 7/16-inch, 1/2-inch or 9/16-inch box wrench or socket or a 3/8-inch Allen wrench will be necessary), and install the correct size fitting supplied with vacuum gauge.

> **QUICK TUNEUP TIP**
> If the vacuum reading indicates that there are serious internal engine problems, do not proceed with the tuneup. Instead, take your car to a professional mechanic for advice.

2. Connect the vacuum gauge hose to the fitting, whether it be the one already on the engine or the one you installed.
3. Start the engine and allow it to idle until it reaches its normal operating temperature.
4. Check the low idle speed using a tachometer. The low idle speed should be set to manufacturers specifications. If not, adjust as necessary. Refer to the procedures described further on on how to use a tachometer. Adjust the low idle speed.
5. Take the vacuum reading. Make sure that you allow for the lower readings obtained at higher altitudes. For every 1000 feet, the readings will be 1 inch Hg. less.

Rapid fluctuation as the engine speed is increased, Fig. 1, Section F

A rapid fluctuation of the needle as the engine speed is increased indicates a loss of power in one or more cylinders, caused by a leaking intake manifold gasket, a leaking cylinder head gasket, burned valves, weak valve springs or defective ignition system.

Rapid fluctuation at idle, Fig. 1, Section H

A rapid fluctuation of the needle at idle usually indicates that the valve guides are worn.

Regular fluctuation, Fig. 1, Section H

A regular fluctuation of the needle at idle usually indicates burned or leaking valves.

Intermittent fluctuation, Fig. 1, Section H

An intermittent fluctuation of the needle at idle of about 4-5 inches Hg. usually indicates a defective ignition system or sticking valves.

Slow fluctuation, Fig. 1, Section G

A slow fluctuation of the needle at idle of about 4-5 inches Hg. usually indicates improper idle mixture adjustment of the carburetor, restricted crankcase ventilation (PCV system), or a leak in the carburetor or intake manifold gaskets.

Slow fluctuation over 2 inches Hg., Fig. 1, Section J

A slow fluctuation of the needle over a range of about 2 inches Hg. usually indicates that the spark plug gaps are too close.

Gradual drop of the reading at 2000 rpm, Fig. 1, Section K

A graduate drop of the reading when the engine speed is held at 2000 rpm usually indicates a restriction in the exhaust system.

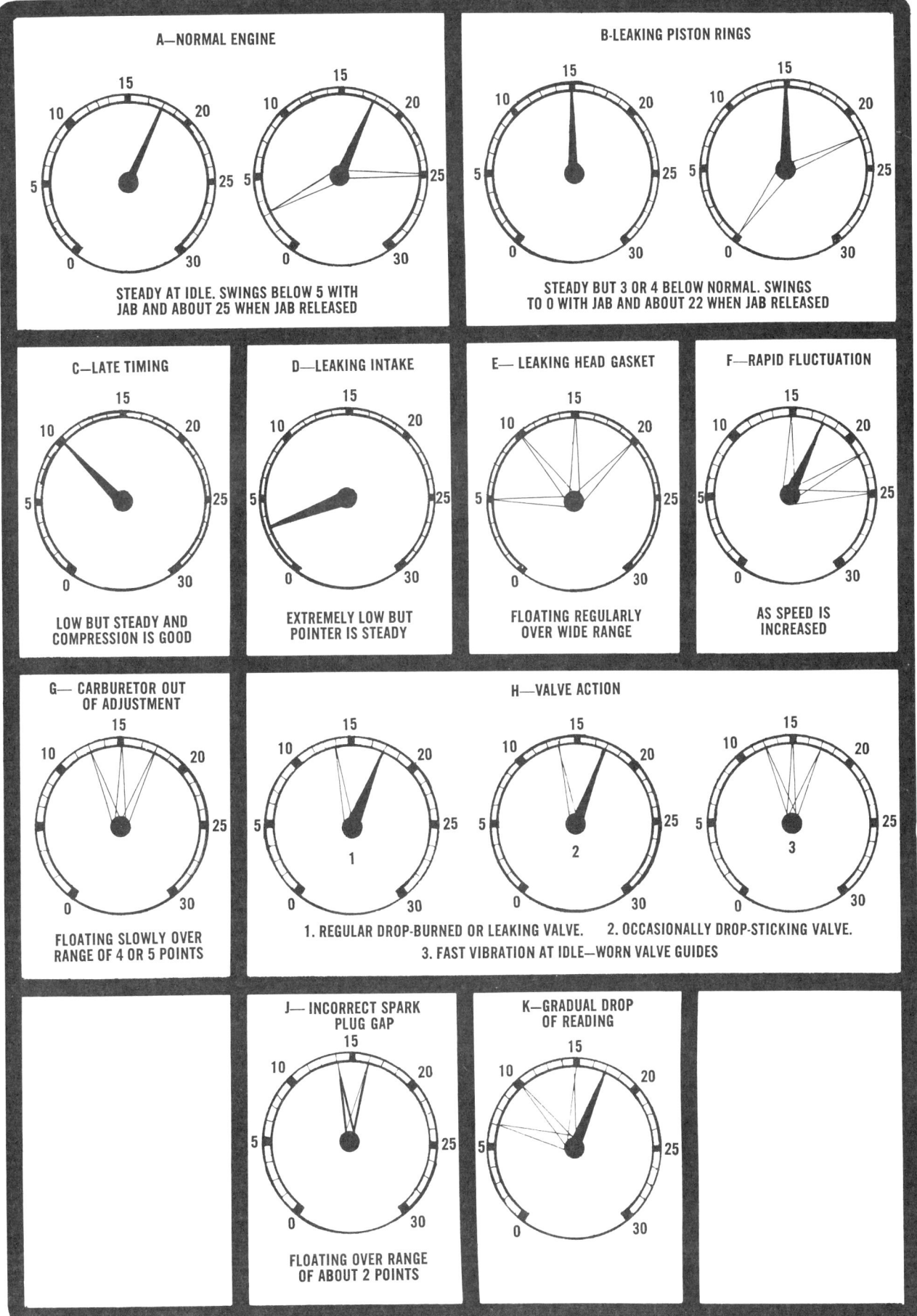

Fig. 1. Engine manifold readings.

QUICK TUNEUP TIP
Be careful not to let accumulated dirt fall into the spark plug hole as you remove the plug from the cylinder head.

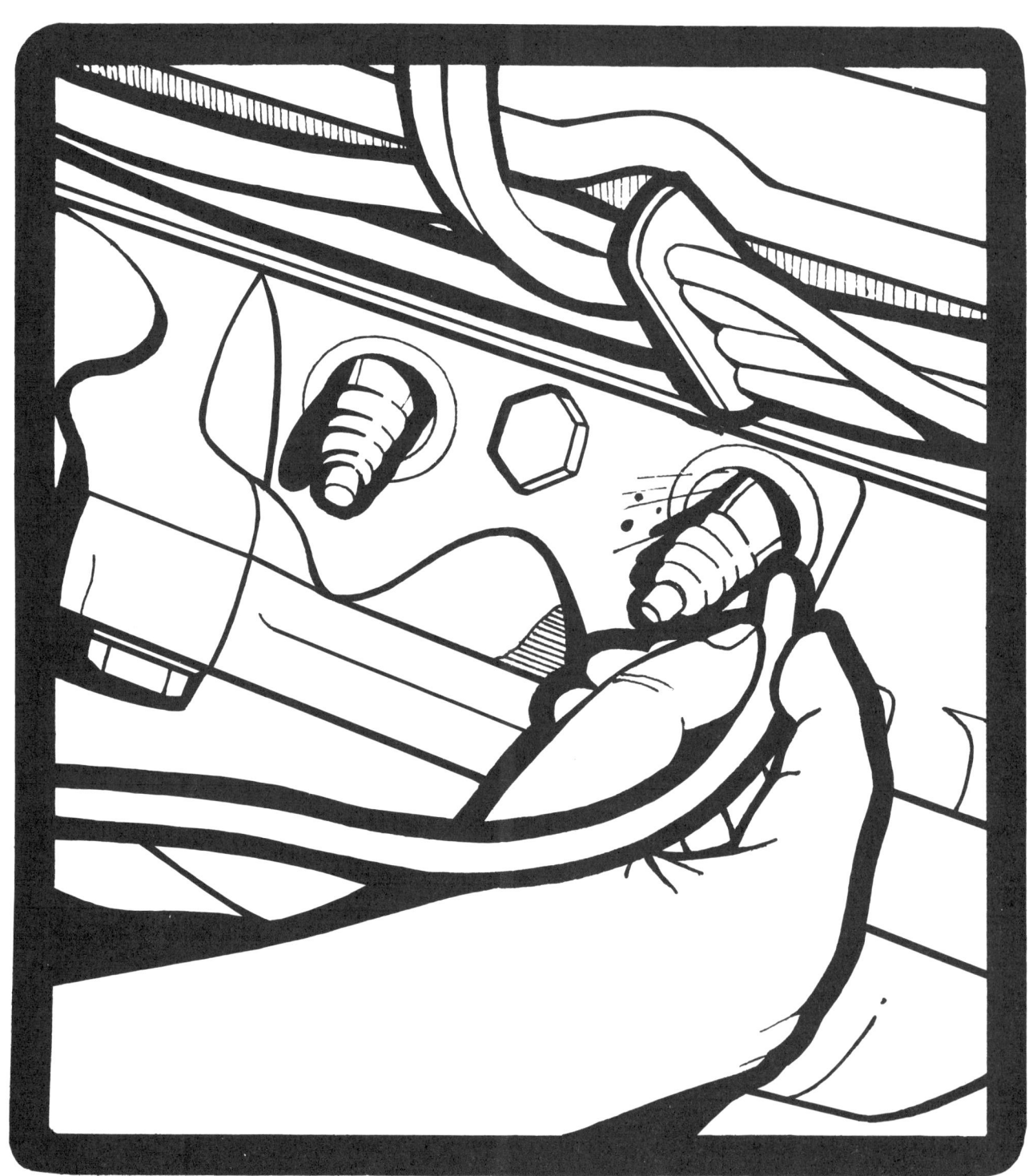

Fig. 2. Before loosening the plug, blow away accumulated dirt.

> **QUICK TUNEUP TIP**
>
> Be sure to mark the ignition wires before pulling them off the spark plugs. This will make it much easier to replace them after the new plugs are installed.

JOB 2. REMOVE THE OLD SPARK PLUGS

Procedure

1. Mark all ignition wires since they must be replaced in the same sequence. This can be accomplished in several ways.
   (a) Marking tags and attaching them to the ignition wires, according to the engine firing order, front to rear on inline engines, or D1 through D4 on driver's side and P1 through P4 on the passenger side on V8 engines.
   (b) Use a white magic marker or nail polish to mark each ignition wire with a white spot. One spot for the first wire, two spots for the second and so on.
2. Remove the spark plug wires from the spark plugs by twisting the boot approximately ¼-turn, and freeing it from spark plug.
3. Put wire off by the boot only. Pulling on wires may cause internal breakage.
4. Before loosening plug, blow out loose dirt adjacent to spark plug. If a compressed air supply is not available, you can accomplish this by blowing through a soda straw or a rubber hose, Fig. 2.
5. Install the proper size spark plug socket (13/16-inch or ⅝-inch) to a spark plug. Attach ratchet wrench to socket and turn counterclockwise. Loosen all spark plugs approximately one turn, breaking loose any accumulated carbon adjacent to the spark plugs.
6. Attach the ignition wires back onto the spark plugs in proper sequence.
7. Start engine and accelerate to approximately 1200 rpm (just a little above idle speed). The slight compression leakage around each plug will blow out the loosened carbon.
8. Remove the ignition wires from the spark plugs once again.
9. Remove all spark plugs. Keep the plugs separate and identified so that reference may be made to the specific cylinder each was removed from.

Spark plug removal is sometimes difficult due to the plug's location on the engine. Various engine accessories may be in the way of direct access. Sometimes the simplest of tools is the most helpful. Experience is required to determine the application and correct use of combinations of extensions, ratchets and wrenches. Special tools such as a spark plug socket with a hex at the drive end or a flexible head ratchet make the most difficult job easy.

Keep plugs in order

Since the condition of each spark plug tells a story about the cylinder it was removed from, keep the plugs in some order so that they can be related back to their respective cylinders. A simple way of doing this is to fabricate a spark plug holder from a block of wood. The holder shown in Fig. 3 allows arrangement of removed plugs for any engine in such a way that they can be readily identified with the cylinders they were removed from. Placing the plugs in the holder with the connector end down allows plug inspection without removal from the holder.

QUICK TUNEUP TIP
Your spark plugs can give you a lot of information as to the condition of each cylinder. Be sure you can tell which cylinder a plug came from.

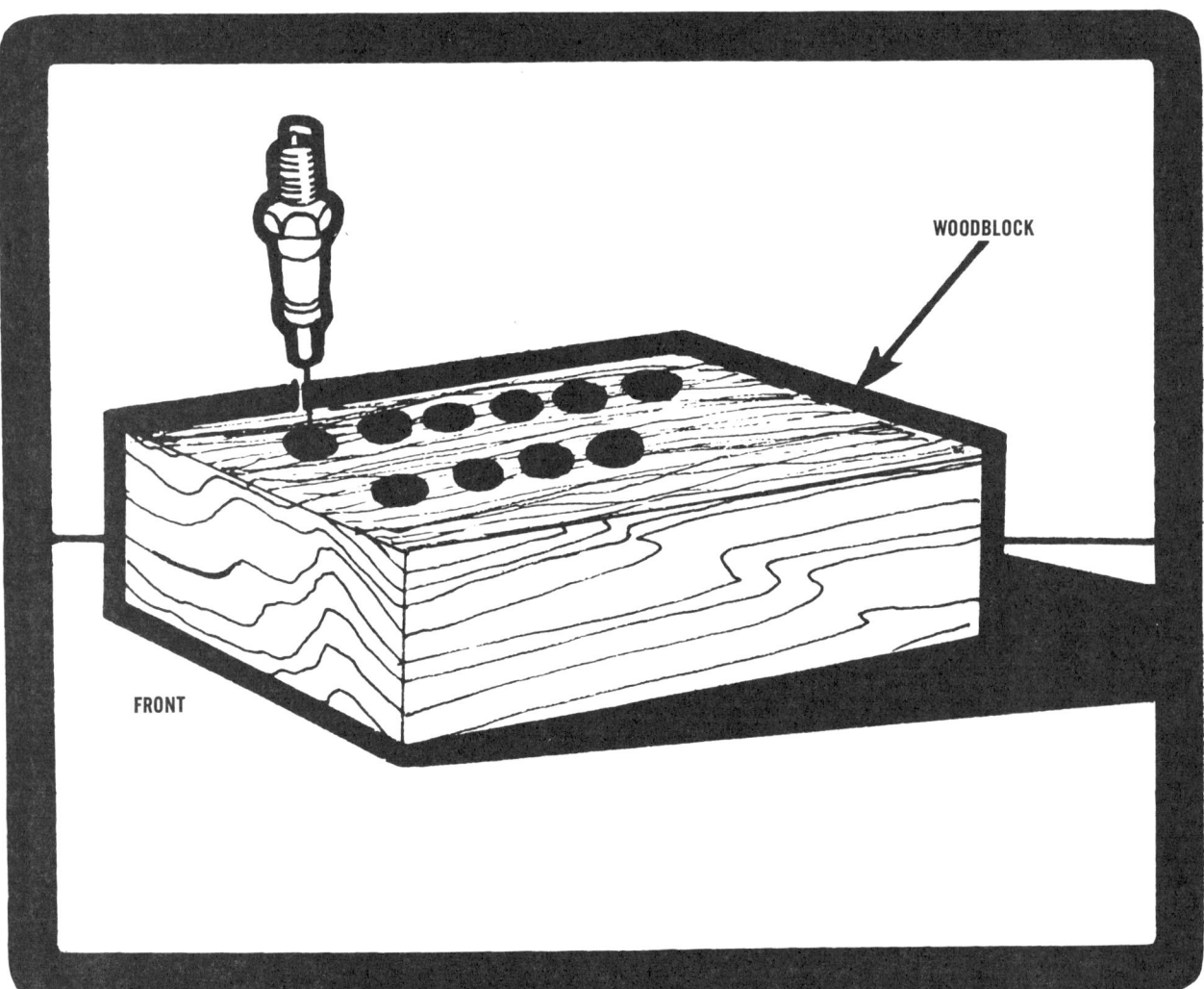

Fig. 3. Typical fabricated spark plug holder.

QUICK TUNEUP TIP

A compression test will give you an even more accurate picture of your engine's overall condition than can a vacuum test.

If compression is bad on a cylinder, have the necessary repairs made before wasting money on a tuneup.

JOB 3. PERFORM A COMPRESSION TEST

A compression test is important because it gives you a general idea of the mechanical condition of your engine. An engine with low or uneven compression indicates that there is something mechanically wrong internally. Such an engine cannot be successfully tuned to give peak performance. Therefore, it is essential that improper compression be corrected before proceeding to any of the other operations of the tuneup.

A compression test can help tell you the condition of the piston rings, valves and head gaskets. By comparing test compression readings with design specifications, you can tell whether a specific cylinder is properly functioning and providing its share of the engine's overall power output. Abnormal engine conditions will result in compression leakage during each of the four strokes of the cycle and will reduce engine efficiency.

To achieve accurate results, the following conditions must be observed:

1. Readings should be taken with the engine at normal operating temperature.
2. Readings should be taken only with the carburetor throttle fully opened to assure that a full charge of air is reaching the cylinder. If you have an assistant, this can be accomplished merely by having your assistant floor the gas pedal. If no helper is available, the throttle can be opened at the carburetor by pulling back the throttle cable or linkage and inserting a long, slim screwdriver to hold open the throttle valve butterflies.
3. All spark plugs must be removed to prevent excessive engine drag during cranking.
4. Crank the engine the same number of revolutions for each cylinder while taking readings. This is the only way to establish an accurate basis of comparison between all cylinders.
5. Readings should be noted after the first engine revolution and then again after the last revolution to fully determine the cylinder's condition.
6. The *thick* cable leading from the center of the distributor to the ignition coil must be disconnected at the distributor and grounded to the engine block. This cable is called the *secondary* distributor lead.

If you are using a remote control starter switch to crank the engine while taking a reading:

1. Disconnect the *primary distributor* lead (the *thin* electrical wire connecting the distributor to the ignition coil) from its negative post on the coil.
2. Turn the ignition switch to the On position. Failure to do this will result in a damaged grounding circuit on the ignition switch.

To hook up the remote control starter switch:

1. Attach either of the two cables to the starter solenoid terminal marked S. The solenoid is mounted either on top of the starter motor or mounted separately on the wheelwell panel or firewall.
2. Attach the other cable of the starter switch to the positive (+) terminal of the battery.

Of course, you can use an assistant inside the car to crank the engine using the regular ignition key switch.

There are two types of compression gauges in general use. One is the more common push-in type. The other is the screw-in type. In cost cases, the simpler push-in type allows the job to be done easily. For difficult to reach spark plug port locations, a screw-in universal compression gauge should be used. This type has a flexible hose and threaded adaptor which threads into the hard-to-reach spark plug port. The screw-in type gauge allows you to take a reading without having to physically hold the gauge in place as with the push-in type.

Taking the compression reading

1. Insert the compression gauge into the spark plug port, Fig. 4.
2. Now crank the engine at least eight full revolutions. You can count the revolutions by noting the rise and fall of the sound of the engine.
3. Have a paper and pencil handy to note the readings while cranking the engine. Remember to note the reading after the first revolution and after the last revolution.
4. Repeat for each cylinder, making sure you crank the engine the same number of times for each cylinder.

Normally, the compression readings should show about 75 psi after the first engine revolution and the minimum specified pressure by the eighth revolution. Cylinder variation between the highest and the lowest cylinder readings must not exceed manufacturer's specifications. Here are two examples of readings for American cars.

Example 1:

Lowest cylinder reading must be within 80% of the highest for American Motors, Chrysler Corporation and General Motors engines.
Normal Compression

Cylinder	1	2	3	4	5	6	7	8
Pressure (psi)	179	171	166	173	160	164	178	157

The highest cylinder pressure on the above engine is 179 psi. Cylinder number 8 has lowest pressure reading, but is within 80% of cylinder number 1 (80% of 179 is 143). Thus the compression pressures on this particular engine are considered normal.

Example 2:

Lowest cylinder reading must be within 75% of highest reading on Ford Motor Company engines.
Abnormal Compression

Cylinder	1	2	3	4	5	6
Pressure (psi)	139	145	104	152	131	143

The highest cylinder pressure on the above engine is 152 psi. Cylinder number 3 has the lowest pressure reading, but is not within 75% of cylinder number 4 (75% of 152 is 114). Thus the compression pressure on this particular engine is considered abnormal. This condition, accompanied by low speed missing, indicates an improperly seated valve or a worn or broken piston ring.

If your engine is exhibiting low compression readings (anything below 100 psi is too low) or uneven compression readings, do not go any further in the tuneup procedure. Internal engine repair work is probably necessary and there is no point in proceeding with a tuneup until the abnormal condition is repaired.

If your engine indicates marginal compression, continue the tuneup procedure to restore engine performance as well as can be expected. But the condition causing the marginal compression should be rectified as soon as possible.

If your engine indicates normal or excessive compression, continue the tuneup procedure.

Excessive compression readings

Compression pressure readings of comparatively new engines, say, any engine with 10,000 miles or less, may be considerably higher than what is considered either normal or minimum for that engine. This is perfectly normal since pistons, piston rings and other parts have just broken in and are forming an extremely tight seal in the cylinder with little or no leakage or compression.

If the engine is older and compression readings reveal higher than normal readings, the excessive compression pressures are most likely caused by carbon deposits in the combustion chambers.

Various combustion chamber cleaners containing a combination of solvents, penetrating agents and lubricating oil can be used to remove deposits from the carburetor intake manifold, valves and combustion chambers. They should be used according to label instructions. It is important that the engine be hot for maximum effectiveness of these cleaners.

The compression pressure test, then, is not an all-conclusive test. But under normal circumstances, it can be used effectively in determining basic engine condition and whether your labor in performing a thorough tuneup will be worthwhile.

QUICK TUNEUP TIP

When using a compression gauge, be sure you are getting a tight seal between the gauge and the spark plug port. Otherwise, your readings will not be accurate.

Low or uneven compression readings

If the compression readings are low or uneven in one or more cylinders, add several squirts of engine oil through spark plug openings of the affected cylinders. Recheck the compression of the affected cylinders. If the compression improves, the piston rings are probably worn. If the compression does not improve much, the valves are probably sticking, seating poorly or are burned. If the compression is low on two adjacent cylinders and the addition of oil improves the compression reading, the cylinder head gasket between these cylinders is probably damaged.

Fig. 4. Insert compression gauge in spark plug hole.

> **QUICK TUNEUP TIP**
>
> After the old spark plugs are removed, check the brand and model number to make sure they were the right ones for your engine. Before installing new plugs, be sure they are the correct heat range for your engine.

JOB 4. SPARK PLUG SERVICE

Plug inspection

When servicing spark plugs, first inspect them thoroughly. Inspection should include the appearance and condition of both ends of the insulator, the electrodes, seat gasket and the shell of the plug.

Frequently, the same type of spark plug used in two different engines of the same make and model of automobile will show wide variation in appearance. Such differences are caused by different engine conditions—its piston rings, carburetor setting, kind of fuel used, and the conditions under which the engine is operated. That is, sustained high speeds, heavy loads, continual low speed stop-and-go driving, light loads, etc. Thus you can determine how suitable the spark plug is for the type of operation to which your vehicle is subjected.

A more detailed discussion of spark plug heat ranges and choice of plugs for various conditions will follow a little later in this book.

Examining plug gaskets

The first important check after removing the spark plugs is to examine the spark plug gaskets. The gasket performs two important functions.
1. It dissipates heat from the insulator tip.
2. It maintains a gastight seal between the plug and its seat in the cylinder head to avoid loss of compression.

If a spark plug gasket is not tightly seated, leaking combustion gases will cause overheating of the plug. This shortens the life of the plug due to excessive wear of the overheated electrodes and, in addition, may lead to preignition.

If the gasket is flattened too much, the spark plug shell may be distorted or cracked. Or the plug gap may be changed by the excessive torque.

Fig. 5 shows a spark plug gasket before installation in an engine, a gasket properly tightened, one insufficiently tightened and one excessively tightened. Frequently a plug gasket will look excessively flattened after being installed to the proper torque. The amount of flattening is determined somewhat by variations in the steel, and by the heat treating and copper plating used in the manufacture of the gasket. If in doubt, section or cut the flattened gasket in half. The upper and lower sections of the gasket should be separated by a very small gap. This indicates proper installation. If a spark plug gasket is not tightly seated, leaking combustion gases will cause overheating of the spark plug. This shortens the life of the plug due to excessive wear of the overheated electrodes and in addition, may cause preignition.

When a properly installed spark plug is removed, the areas of contact of the gasket with the plug and with the seat in the cylinder head will show up as clean, bright, unbroken surfaces. If the plug installation was faulty, discolored or corroded gasket surfaces will indicate leakage. The leakage could be caused by insufficient torque or uneven plug seats due to damage or the accumulation of dirt on either of the contact surfaces.

Use a new spark plug gasket every time you install a new or cleaned spark plug to insure proper spark plug performance and long life.

Examining the spark plug

When examining a spark plug, there are five important conditions to look for:

1. **Worn.** Electrodes worn from long service. Requires cleaning or replacement.
2. **Dirty.** Oil or fuel additive fouling. Coatings and deposits on insulator and electrodes. Requires cleaning or replacement.
3. **Wide gap.** Resulting from normal or rapid wear. Requires regapping or replacement.
4. **Broken or shorted insulator.** Breakage of the upper end by mechanical damage, or cracked lower insulator tip due to excessively high operating heat of the spark plug. Requires replacement.
5. **Damaged shell.** Threads stretched or broken. Shell cracked due to mishandling or excessive tightening. Requires replacement.

Worn spark plugs

Under normal operating conditions, spark plugs wear out due to the destructive action of intense heat, sulphur and lead compounds in the fuel and from the bombardment of the electric spark on the electrodes.

It is reasonable to expect about 12,000 miles of useful life from a spark plug which has been cleaned and regapped at regular intervals. But operating conditions are an important factor and the life expectancy of the plug will vary with the type of engine use.

Plugs which have been in operation for a reasonable period of normal service, or plugs with insulators worn down from excessive sand-blast cleaning, or with electrodes deeply pitted or worn too thin for proper regapping, are no longer effective in producing the kind of performance required. They should be replaced with new plugs. Worn plugs cause loss of power, loss of speed, hard starting, general sluggish performance and, of course, increase undesirable exhaust emissions.

Spark plugs with brown to grayish tan deposits and slight electrode wear indicate normal spark plug wear, correct spark plug heat range and mixed periods of high and low speed driving. Spark plugs having this appearance may be cleaned, regapped and re-installed.

> **QUICK TUNEUP TIP**
> After removing the old plugs, examine the gasket as well as the electrode. The gasket can tell you whether the plug was installed correctly or not.

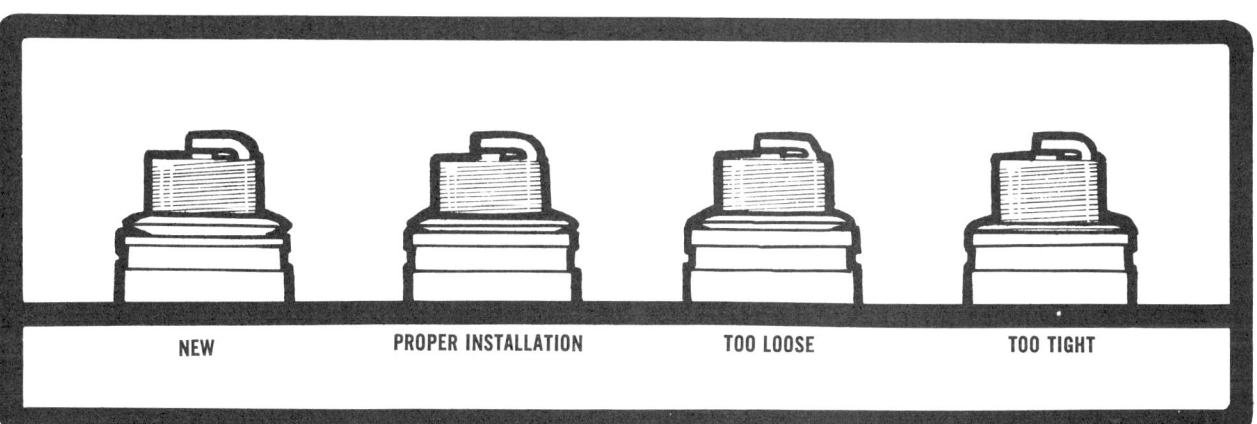

Fig. 5. Spark plug gasket inspection.

Dirty spark plugs

One of the most frequent causes of spark plug misfiring is dirt on the top of the insulator. When combined with moisture, the dirt shunts the high tension current across the insulator top to shell and away from the firing end. These dirt accumulations, which usually contain oily substances, should be cleaned with a suitable solvent.

Wet, black deposits on the firing end of the plug indicate an oil-pumping condition due to worn valve guides, valve stem seals, piston rings, pistons, cylinders or sticky valves. In most cases, plugs in this condition can be used after proper cleaning and re-gapping.

ASH DEPOSITS

Hard, baked-on black carbon deposits result from using too cold a plug in an oil-burning engine. To correct, overhaul the engine and/or use a hotter heat range spark plug.

Soft, fluffy, dry, black carbon deposits indicate excess fuel in the combustion chamber. This can result from the breaking-in period or when the engine is operated at low speeds, or from too rich a fuel mixture, excessive idling, a stuck manifold heat riser or an improperly operating automatic choke. Using too cold a plug will also allow excessive carbon buildup. If the fouling continues, a change to a plug type one or two steps hotter may also be necessary.

Red, brown, yellow and white colored coatings on the insulator are by-products of combustion and come from the fuel and lubricating oil. Under severe operating conditions, these deposits may cause intermittent missing, especially at high speeds and on hard pulls.

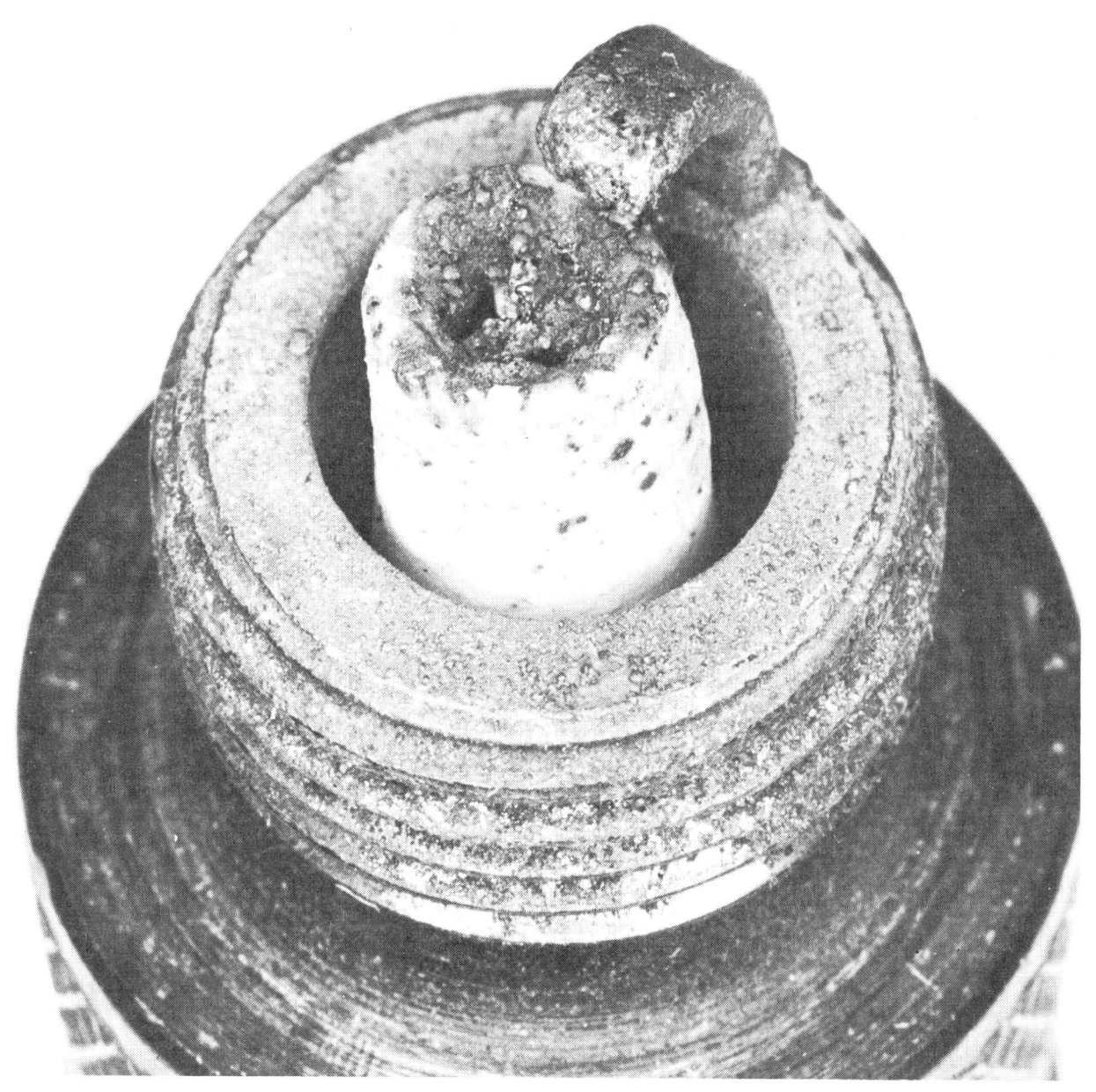

PRE-IGNITION

Most powdery deposits have no adverse effect on the operation of the plug. However, with an abnormal increase in combustion chamber temperature these deposits melt and form a shiny glaze coating which acts as an electrical conductor and shorts out the plug.

Deposits that are packed between the insulator and the shell of the plug cannot be completely removed, and the spark plug should be replaced. We recommend replacement even if the insulator is not too heavily coated.

INSULATOR GLAZING

Wide gaps

After several thousand miles of service, due to the combined action of intense heat, pressure and corrosive gases within the combustion chamber and the spark discharges, the spark plug gap widens and must be regapped. If the electrodes have worn so thin that regapping would only add a few hundred miles of satisfactory performance, the plug should be replaced.

Appreciable gap wear at low mileage usually indicates that the engine is operating under excess loads or that the wrong type of plug (too hot) is being used. Before changing to a cooler plug, the heat range should be checked. If the plug showing rapid electrode wear is the type recommended, the seat gasket should be checked. If the gasket appearance is satisfactory, use spark plugs at least one step colder.

Cracked (or shorted) insulator

The spark plug is designed to conduct electrical energy of several thousand volts to the spark gap in the combustion chamber. This electrical energy will always take the path of least resistance, and several conditions can divert it away from the spark plug.

SPLASHED DEPOSITS

A shorted upper insulator, causing flashover, is caused by a dirty or oily upper insulator or by excessive gap width caused by improper setting when the plug was installed, or by undue gap wear.

Sparking through the insulator to the shell results from a visible or invisible fracture in the insulator caused by careless removal or installation of the spark plug. Frequently this fracture is not visible as it is located at the upper gasket shoulder inside the shell crimp. When testing these plugs in a compression box tester, sparks may be seen around the shell

NORMAL

at this point and, in some cases, also across the electrode gap. As compression is stepped up, increasing the resistance across the gap, the spark will occur only through the fracture, as this is then the path of least resistance from the center wire to shell. There is no remedy except replacement with a new plug.

A cracked lower insulator is generally easily seen, especially after the spark plug has been cleaned. One cause for this is carelessness in regapping, either bending the center wire to adjust the gap—which should never be done—or allowing the gapping tool to exert pressure against the tip of the center electrode or insulator when bending the side electrode to adjust the gap. The only remedy is a new spark plug.

CARBON DEPOSITS

Fracture or breakage of the lower insulator may also occasionally occur if the engine has been operated for sustained periods with heavy detonation or preignition. This type of failure is referred to as heat shock failure. Over-advanced ignition timing and low grade fuel are usually responsible for heat shock failures. Rapid increase in tip temperature under severe operating conditions causes the heat shock, and fracture results. The only real cure here is to correct

OVERHEATED

the operation, although a colder plug may help. The type being used should also be checked against that specified by the manufacturer, as a plug that is hotter than recommended might result in fracture of the lower insulator under severe operating conditions. If the type recommended is being used, a cooler type should be used if the engine is to operate continually under this severe condition.

Damaged shell

This condition occurs very infrequently and is always due to mishandling, especially excessive tightening during installation. It generally takes the form of a crack in the vee of the thread next to the gasket

Restoring plug performance

If there is low mileage on the spark plugs, say, no more than about 5000, proper cleaning and regapping will usually restore engine performance. However, spark plugs are relatively inexpensive compared to the overall improvement they make in an engine's performance, that it hardly seems worth the time and effort to clean and regap old plugs. Besides,

OIL DEPOSITS

new spark plugs are the only way to get really optimum engine efficiency. If there are 10,000 or more miles on the plugs it is almost a necessity to replace the plugs to restore peak engine performance.

Spart plugs are frequently blamed for faulty engine operation or other conditions which they are not causing. Replacement of old spark plugs with new ones may temporarily improve poor engine performance because of the lower demand new plugs make on the ignition system. But new plugs cannot permanently cure poor engine performance caused by:
1. Damaged secondary wiring.
2. Worn distributor cap or rotor.
3. Worn rings, valves or cylinders.
4. Weak ignition coil.
5. Worn ignition contact points.
6. Faulty carburetion or other engine malfunctions.

The heat range system

The heat range of a spark plug is determined primarily by the length of the lower insulator. The longer this is, the hotter the plug will operate; the shorter it is, the cooler the plug will operate, Fig. 6.

Normal or average driving is assumed to be a mixture of idling, slow speed and high speed operation, with some of each making up the daily total. Occasional or intermittent high speed driving is essential to good spark plug performance as it provides increased and sustained combustion heat that burns away any excess deposits of carbon or oxide that may have accumulated from frequent idling or slow speed driving.

To give good performance, spark plugs must operate within a certain temperature range (neither too hot nor too cool). If the spark plug remains too cool, oil, soot, carbon and lead compounds are deposited on the insulator, causing fouling and missing. If the plug runs too hot, the electrodes wear rapidly, and under extreme conditions, premature ignition (preignition) of the fuel mixture may result.

Frequently the wrong type of spark plug, one with an improper heat range for the engine, is installed when replacing spark plugs originally fitted by the engine manufacturer. Such misapplication may lead to poor performance.

The heat range system makes it possible to select the type of spark plug that will operate within the correct temperature range for each specific engine.

Where abnormal operating conditions cause chronic carbin or oil fouling of the plugs, the use of a type one number higher (a hotter type) than recommended will generally remedy the trouble. By the same formula, where chronic preignition or rapid electrode wear is experienced, a type with one number lower (a cooler type) will generally be found satisfactory.

Spark plug reach and thread

Spark plugs are manufactured in several different thread sizes and reaches. Reach is the distance from the gasket seat to the end of the shell. All spark plugs have a number on the insulator, Fig. 7, which designates the plug thread size as well as the relative position in the heat range system.

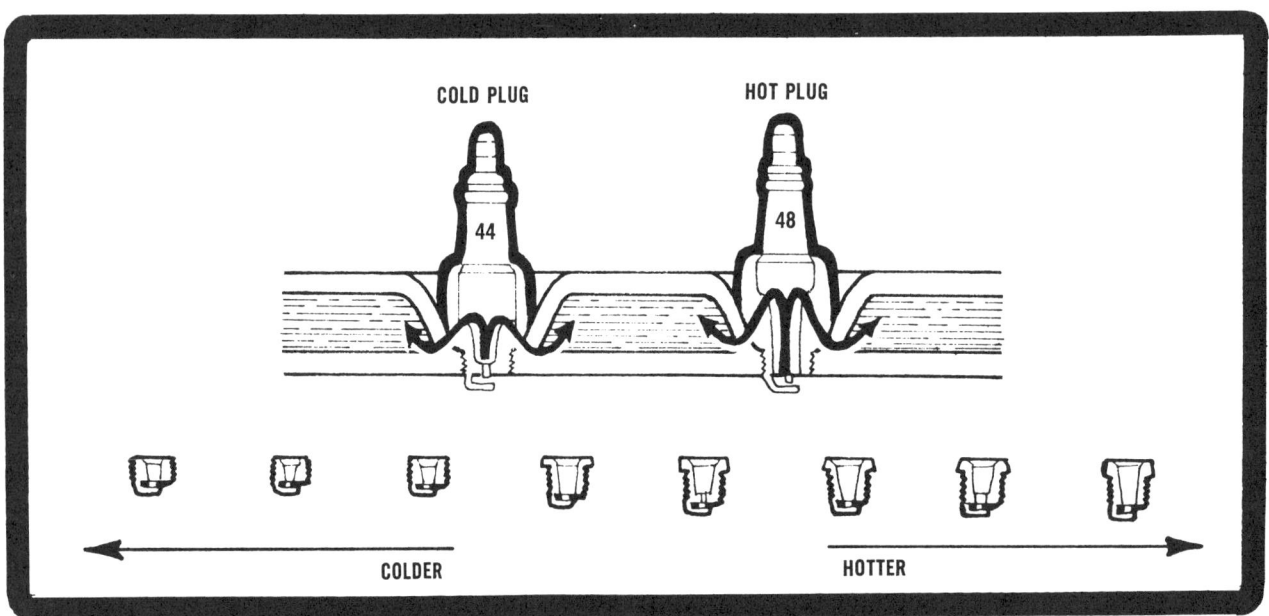

Fig. 6. Spark plug heat range system.

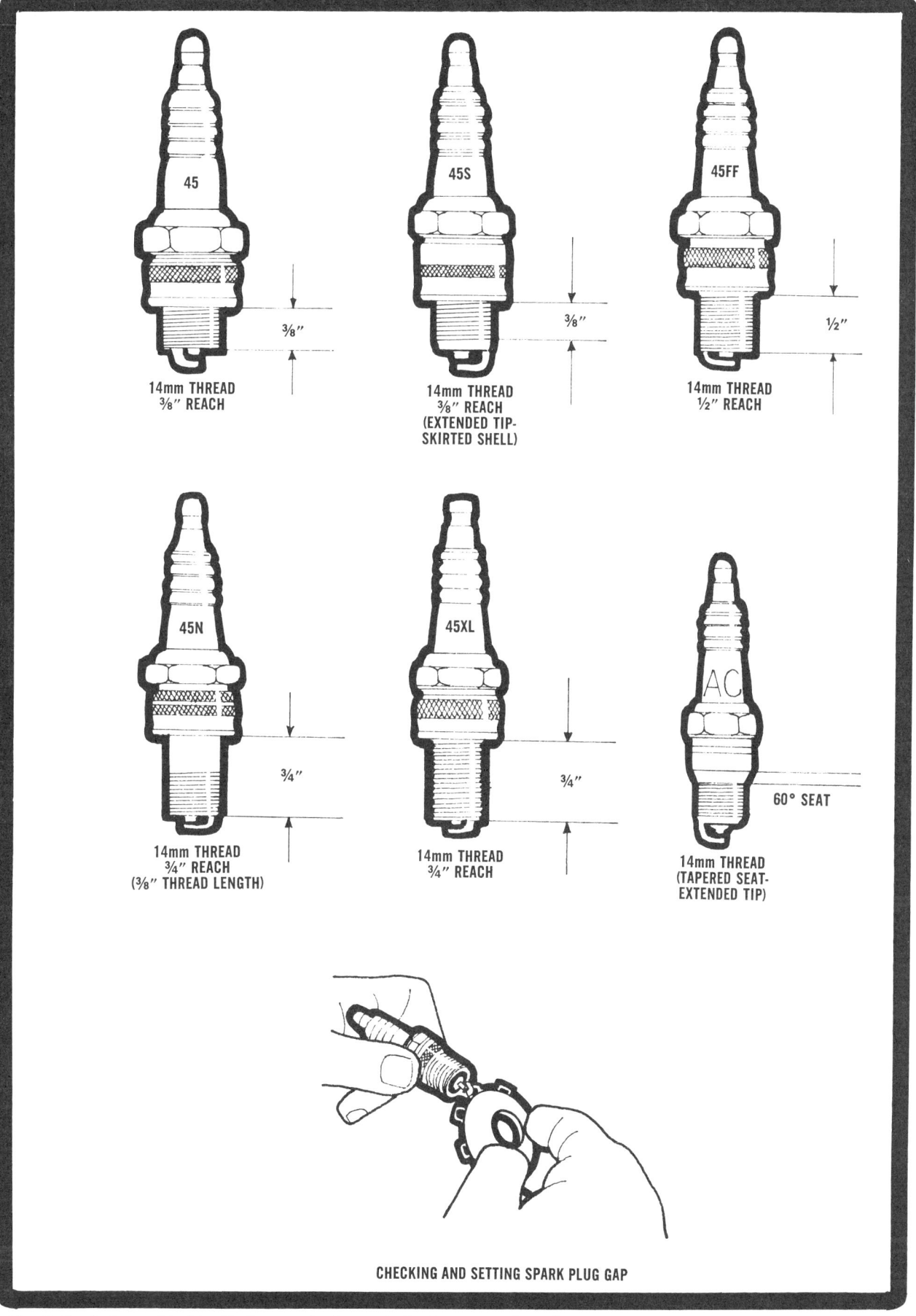

Fig. 7. Symbols used to identify the spark plug as to heat range and reach.

The spark plug should be regapped to the exact specification given by the auto manufacturer. Always use a round wire type gauge. The gap gauge shown in Fig. 8 provides an exact method of gap measurement. A flat feeler gauge cannot accurately measure the true gap width, Fig. 9.

In regapping, adjust only the side (ground) electrode. Never bend the center electrode as side pressure on it may crack or break the insulator tip. Do not use gapping pliers.

Replace plugs with cracked or broken insulators, or with electrodes badly burned, pitted or worn so thin that the short period of additional good performance they might render would not justify their reinstallation. If the majority of the plugs in an engine are worn out, replacement of the entire set is recommended.

Before installing a new plug, always adjust the gap setting (bending the side wire only) to the exact limits established by the engine manufacturer.

INSTALL SPARK PLUGS

All spark plugs except the tapered seat type use seat gaskets which are of the folded-over type. They are of special design and are made of cold rolled steel, copper plated and chromic-acid dipped. Recommended gaskets retain proper sealing characteristics and require lower torque pressures for installation. Always install a new spark plug seat gasket with each new or cleaned plug. Also be sure the cylinder head threads and plug seats are clean and free from any dirt or scale deposits which might interfere with the proper seating of the plug and gasket. Dirty or carboned cylinder head threads should be cleaned with a greased threadchaser of the proper size. Tapered seat spark plugs do not use a gasket.

When using any spark plug that is different from the original equipment specification, be very certain that the new plug has the same reach or length of thread as the original equipment plug.

If the new plug threads are too long, the exposed threads inside the combustion chamber will become corroded and carbon covered, which may damage the threads in the cylinder head when the plug is removed. If a plug with short threads is used, the exposed cylinder head threads will become carboned up or partially burned away, which would prevent proper plug installation of a plug with the correct reach. Extended reach spark plugs when used in

Fig. 8. Never use a flat thickness gauge to gap spark plugs, as they give inaccurate readings.

some engines may interfere with the pistons. This of course would cause extensive internal damage.

Screw the plug by hand all the way down until it seats on the gasket fingertight. If a torque wrench is used, the torque values for spark plugs with seat gaskets should be 20-25 ft. lbs. when new gaskets are used, and the spark plug and engine threads are thoroughly clean. The torque for tapered seat spark plugs is 15 ft. lbs. for 14 mm spark plugs and 15-20 for 18 mm spark plugs.

Since spark plug torquing is frequently difficult because of accessibility, the following rule of thumb will produce plug installations that are neither too tight nor too loose. Tighten the spark plug finger tight and then turn it with a spark plug wrench ½ to ¾ turn, for all except tapered seat spark plugs and ⅙ turn for tapered seat spark plugs.

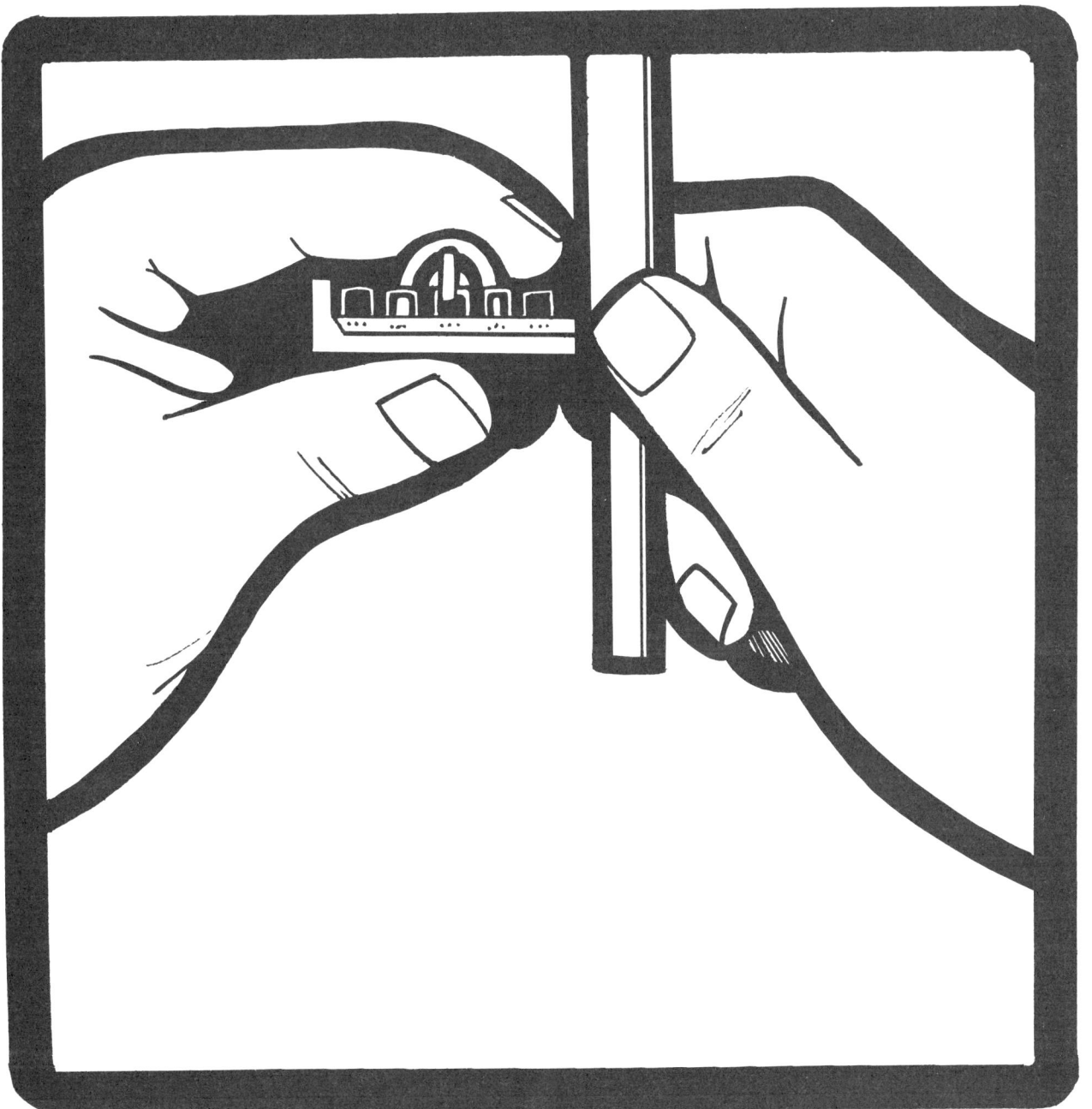

Fig. 9. Always use a round wire gauge to gap the spark plugs.

> **QUICK TUNEUP TIP**
>
> In servicing the distributor, it is easy to forget to check the cap itself for cracks. A cracked distributor cap will result in poor engine performance.

JOB 5. SERVICE THE DISTRIBUTOR CAP

Remove spark plug wires and coil secondary wire, one at a time, and check cap and coil tower for corroded sockets. Clean dirty or corroded sockets with a cap cleaning brush (Fig. 10). Remove distributor cap, clean cap and inspect for cracks, carbon tracks and burned or corroded terminals. Corroded inserts should be scraped clean to maintain a low resistance path for current flow. Replace cap where necessary.

NOTE: When replacing cap, hold new cap next to cap being replaced and replace one wire at a time starting with No. 1, Fig. 10.

JOB 6. SERVICE THE ROTOR

Clean the rotor and inspect for damage or deterioration. Corrosion may be cleaned from the rotor tip, but excessive burning will require rotor replacement.

Tension of the rotor to cap spring must be sufficient to insure good contact with the carbon button in the center of the distributor cap, Fig. 10.

JOB 7. SERVICE THE ADVANCE MECHANISM

Check the distributor centrifugal advance mechanism by turning the rotor in a clockwise direction as far as possible, then releasing the rotor to see if the springs return it to its retarded position. If the rotor does not return readily, the distributor must be disassembled and the cause of the trouble corrected.

Check to see that the vacuum spark control operates freely by turning the breaker plate, or distributor body on inline 6-cylinder models, counterclockwise to see if the spring returns it to the retarded position. Any stiffness in the operation of the vacuum spark control will affect the ignition timing. Correct any interference or binding condition noted.

On *Ford* and *Chrysler* cars, the advance weights are not readily visible. So have a professional mechanic perform this check.

ERODED TOWER

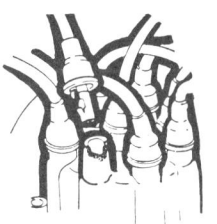

INSPECTION OF DISTRIBUTOR CAP TOWERS

CARBON PATH

CLEANING AND INSPECTION OF OUTSIDE OF DISTRIBUTOR CAP

CARBON PATH

CLEANING AND INSPECTION OF INSIDE OF DISTRIBUTOR CAP

CRACKED

REPLACING DISTRIBUTOR CAP

BURNED OR ERODED INSERT TERMINALS

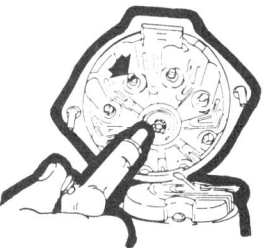

BLOWING OUT INSIDE OF DISTRIBUTOR CAP AND INSPECTION OF INSERT TERMINALS

ROTAR TIP CORRODED  INSUFFICIENT ROTAR CONTACT SPRING TENSION

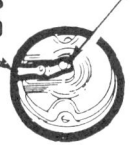

ROTAR INSPECTION

CLEANING IGNITION COIL

CLEANING TOWER INSERT

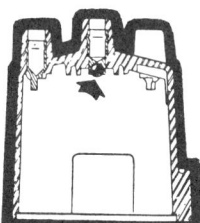

INSPECTION OF CARBON ROTAR BUTTON

Fig. 10. Cleaning and inspecting the distributor cap, rotor and coil.

QUICK TUNEUP TIP

Any cracks, breaks or deterioration in ignition wires can result in poor spark travel and arcing. You will notice an engine miss or rough running if your ignition wires need replacing.

JOB 8. CHECKING THE IGNITION WIRES

1. Inspect the wires for damage such as cuts, pinches, cracks, worn insulation or damaged boots. Bend each wire and check for small cracks.

2. Check, also, for rubber deterioration. The rubber will feel spongy or brittle if the wire is deteriorated.
3. Wires which are physically damaged should be replaced.

JOB 9. SERVICE THE IGNITION BREAKER POINTS AND CONDENSER

NOTE: Some 1974 and all later cars are equipped with electronic ignition systems which require no contact points or condenser. The General Motors electronic ignition systems can be easily identified by the massive distributor cap and the absence of an external ignition coil. All other electronic ignition systems can be identified by removing the distributor cap. In place of the conventional contact points and condenser, there will be a reluctor in place of the cam and a pick-up coil in place of the contact points.

Examine distributor points and clean or replace if necessary. Contact points with an overall gray color and only slight roughness or pitting need not be replaced.

Under normal operating conditions, distributor contact points will provide many thousands of miles of service. Points which have undergone several thousand miles of operation will have a rough surface but this should not be interpreted as meaning that the points are worn out.

Dirty points should be cleaned with a clean point file. Use only a few strokes of a clean, fine-cut contact file. The file should not be used on other metals and should not be allowed to become greasy or dirty. Never use emery cloth or sandpaper to clean contact

QUICK TUNEUP TIP

Ignition points that are installed incorrectly or misadjusted can shut your engine down completely so that it will not run at all. So pay extra attention when installing ignition points.

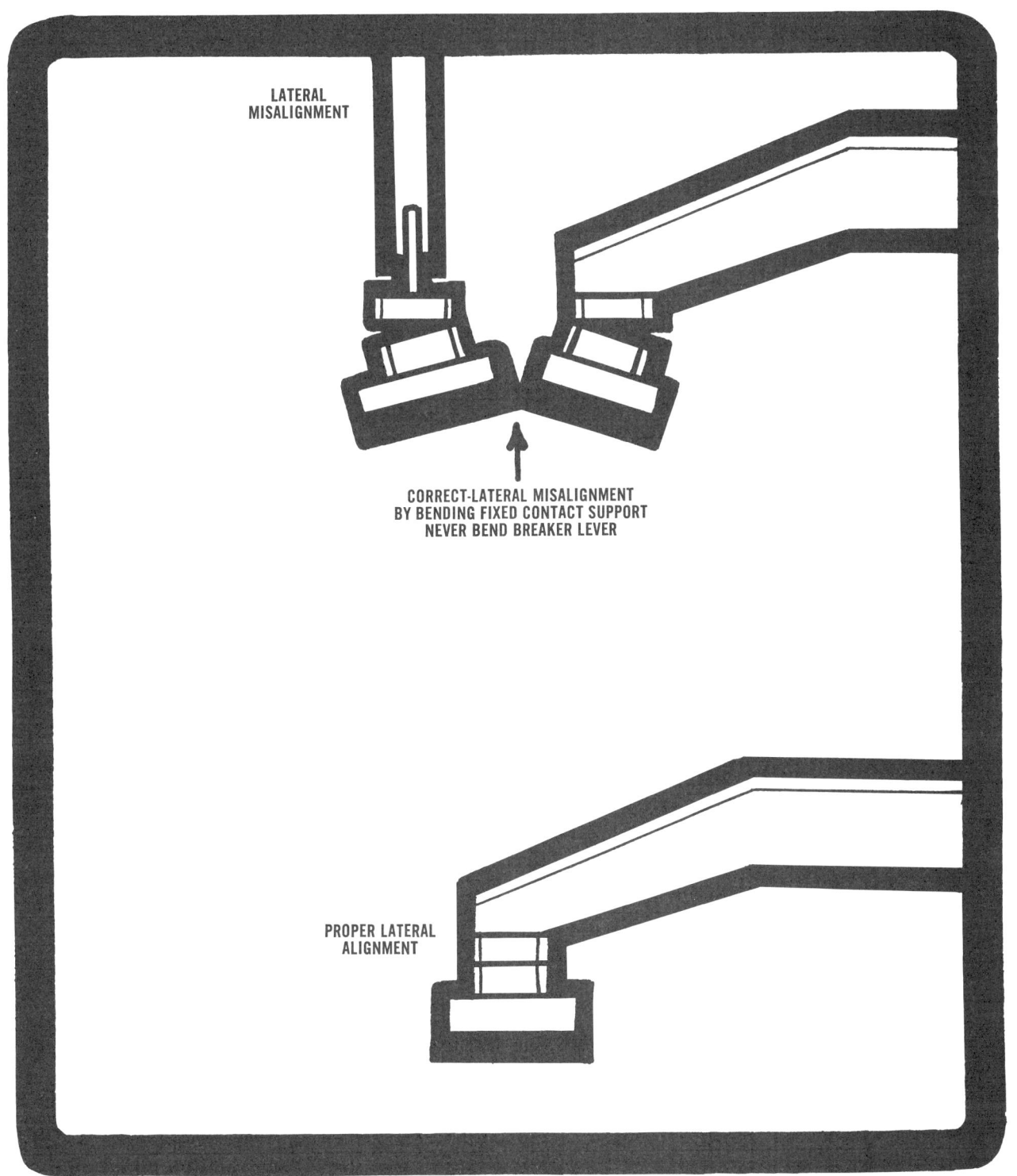

Fig. 11. Correct and incorrect point alignment.

QUICK TUNEUP TIP

Ignition points that are burning out or failing prematurely indicate other ignition maladies. If you are experiencing ignition point problems, look elsewhere for the cause.

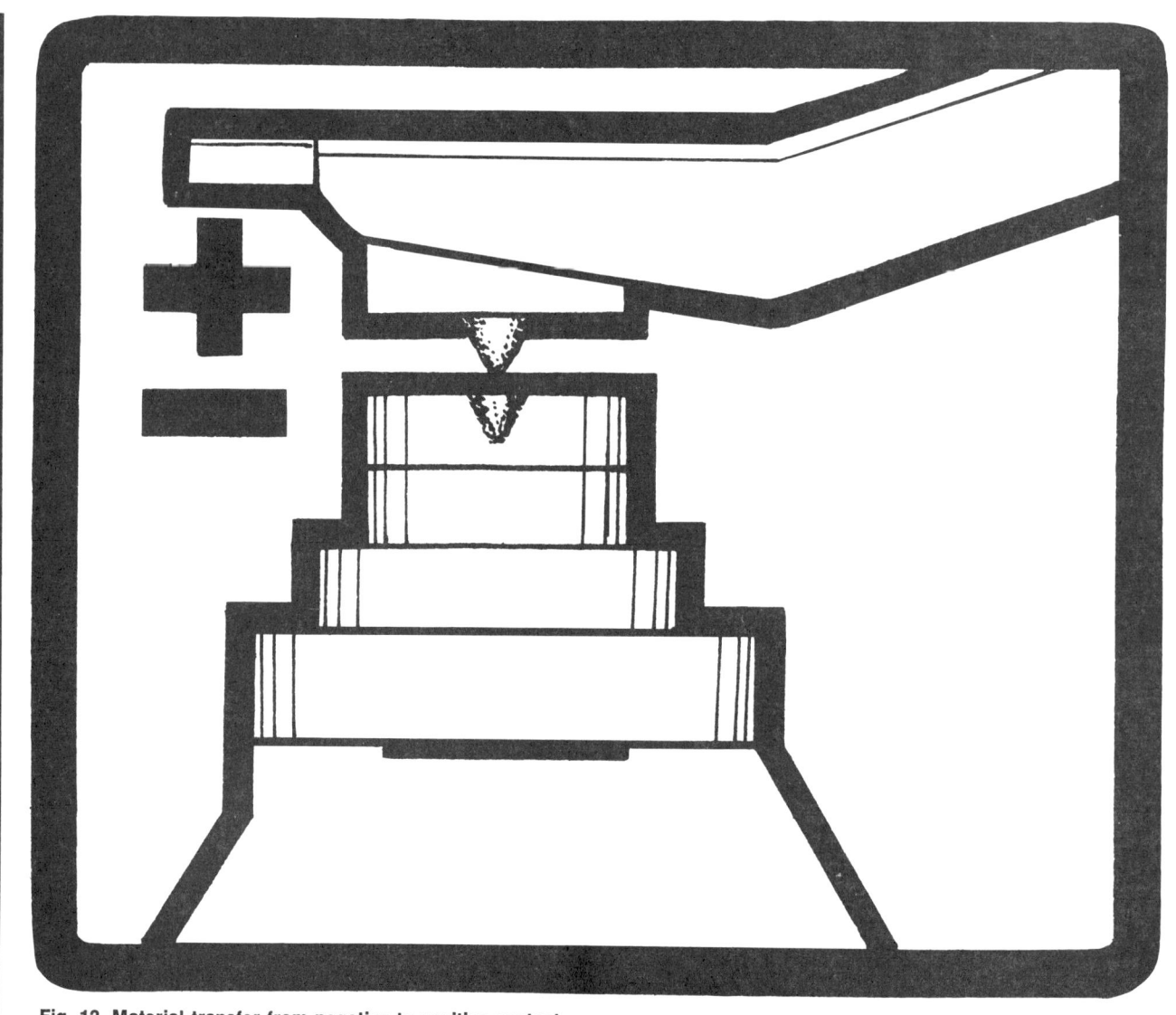

Fig. 12. Material transfer from negative to positive contact.

points since particles will embed and cause arcing and rapid burning of points. Contact points after considerable use will not appear bright and smooth, but this is not necessarily an indication that they are not functioning satisfactrorily. Do not attempt to remove all roughness nor dress the point surfaces down smooth. Merely remove scale or dirt. Replace points that are burned or badly pitted.

NOTE: When relatively new points are found to be burned or badly pittted, the ignition system and engine must be checked to determine the cause of trouble so it can be eliminated. Unless the condition causing point burning or pitting is corrected, new points will provide no better service than the old points.

Contact point burning will result from high voltage, the presence of oil or other foreign material, a defective condenser and improper point adjustment. High primary voltage causes an excessively high current flow through the contact points, burning them rapidly. High voltage can result from an improperly adjusted or inoperative voltage regulator.

Oil or crankcase vapors which work up into the distributor and deposit on the point surfaces will cause them to burn rapidly. This is easy to detect since the oil produces a smudgy line under the contact points. A clogged PCV system will permit crankcase pressure to force oil or vapors up into the distributor.

High resistance in the condenser circuit will prevent normal condenser action, causing the contact points to burn rapidly. Such resistance can be caused by a loose condenser mounting or lead connection, or by poor connections inside the condenser. These cannot be corrected.

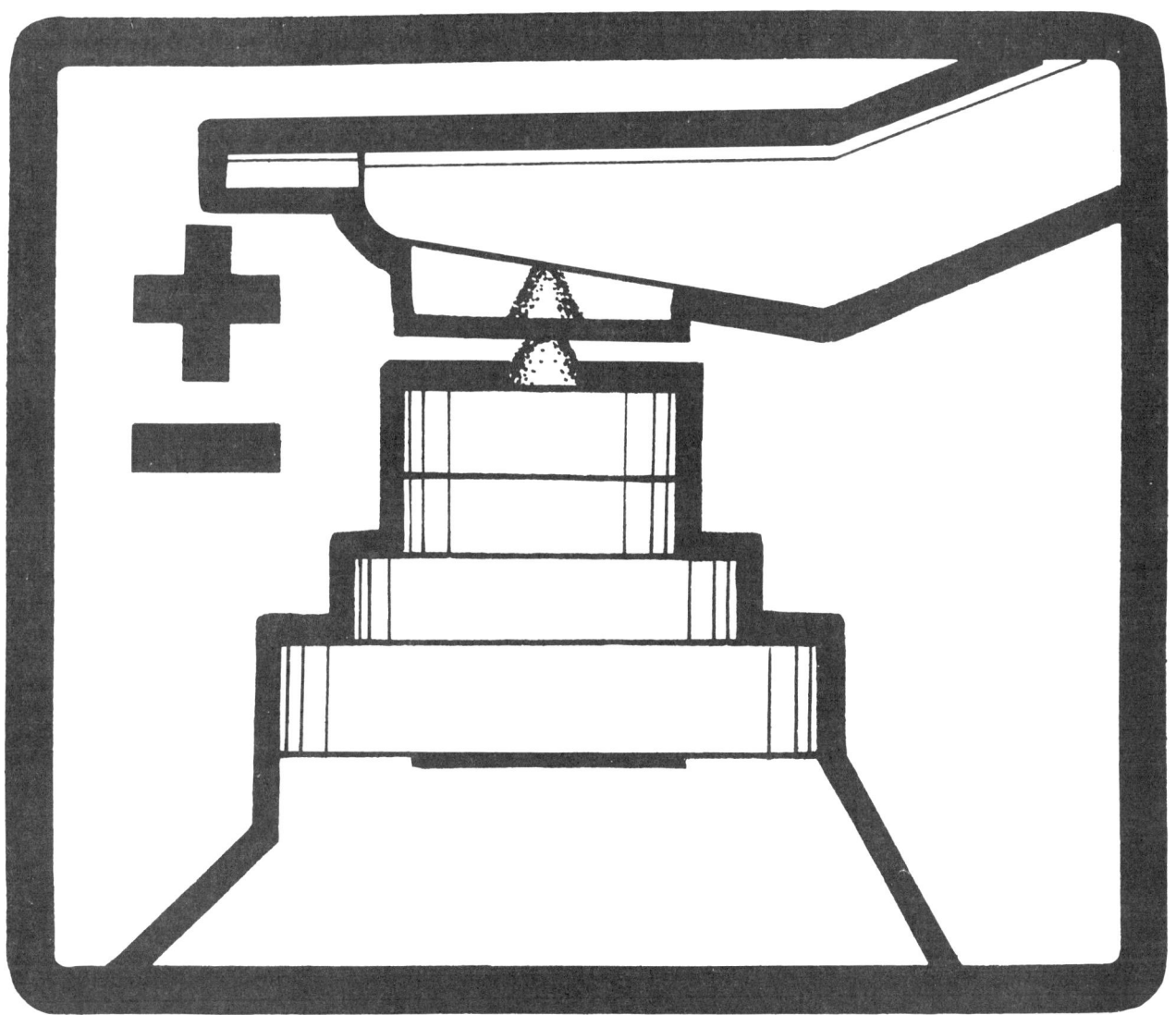

Fig. 13. Material transfer from positive to negative contact.

QUICK TUNEUP TIP

Ignition points that are in otherwise good condition can be reused if the point surfaces are lightly filed smooth. But the cost is so low for new points that it usually does not pay to fool around with the old ones.

BREAKER POINTS AND CONDENSER REPLACEMENT

1. Remove the distributor cap. The distributor cap is retained either by two latches, Fig. 15, two retaining screws, Fig. 16, or two bale clips, Fig. 17. To remove the first type depress the latches using a flat screwdriver, Fig. 15, then turn the latches one half turn in either direction and lift the cap off the distributor. To remove the second type, just back off the retaining screws using

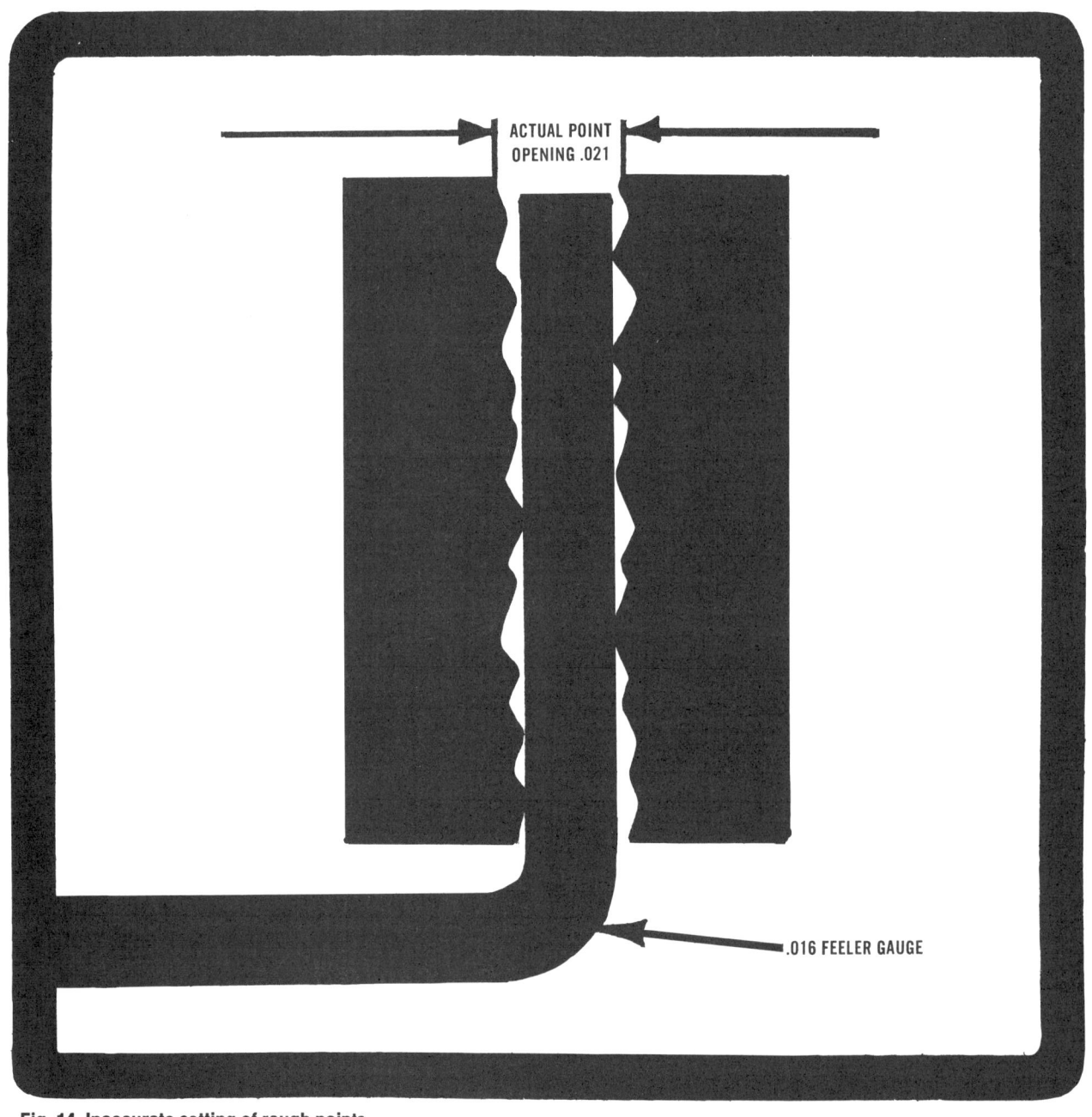

Fig. 14. Inaccurate setting of rough points.

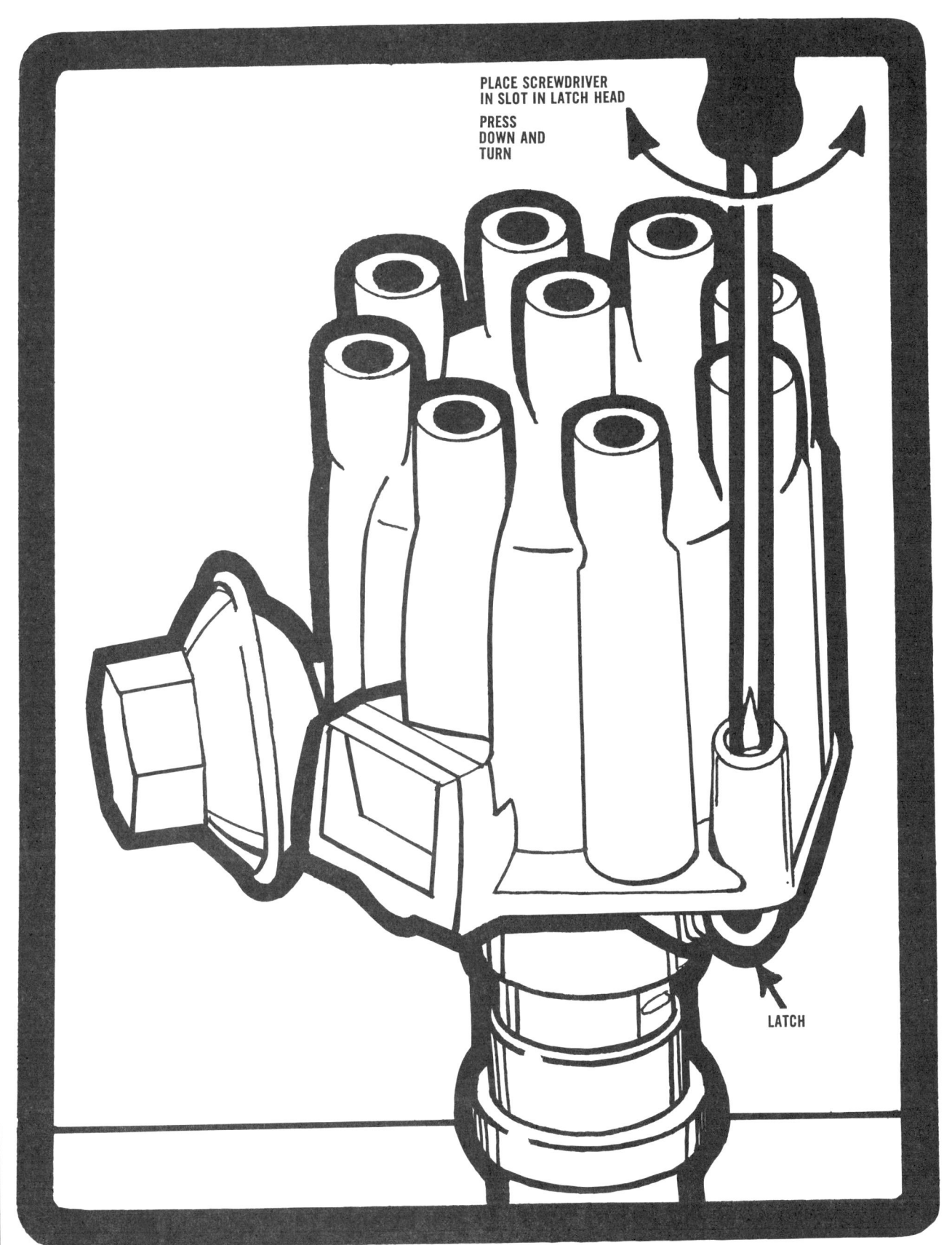

Fig. 15. Engaging or disengaging the latches on a Delco Remy V8 distributor cap.

a flat screwdriver, Fig. 16, and lift the cap off the distributor. To remove the third type, insert a flat screwdriver between the bale clip and distributor

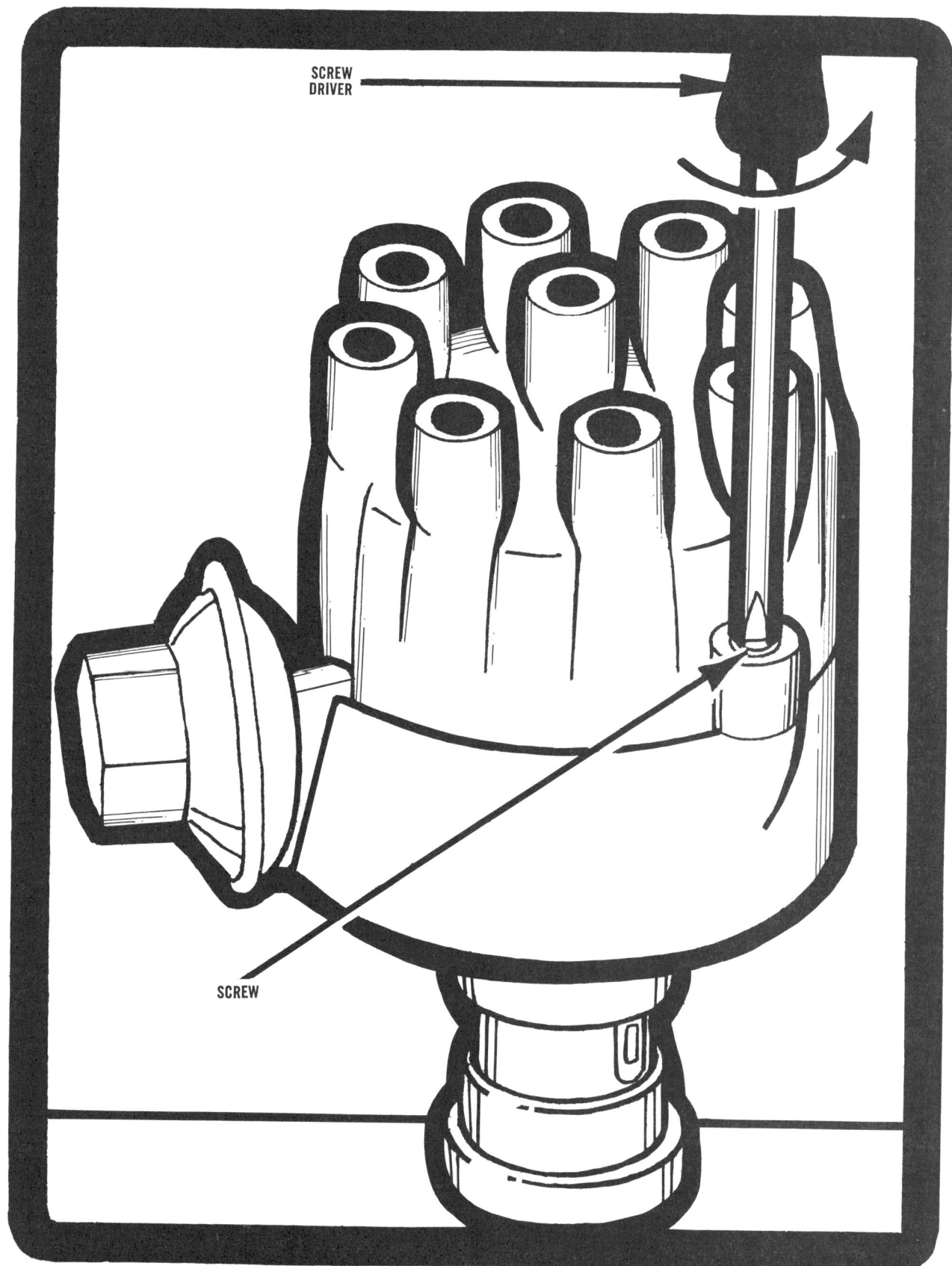

Fig. 16. Loosening or tightening the retaining screws on a typical General Motors distributor cap.

cap, Fig. 17, and pry the clips to disengage them from the cap and lift the cap off the distributor.

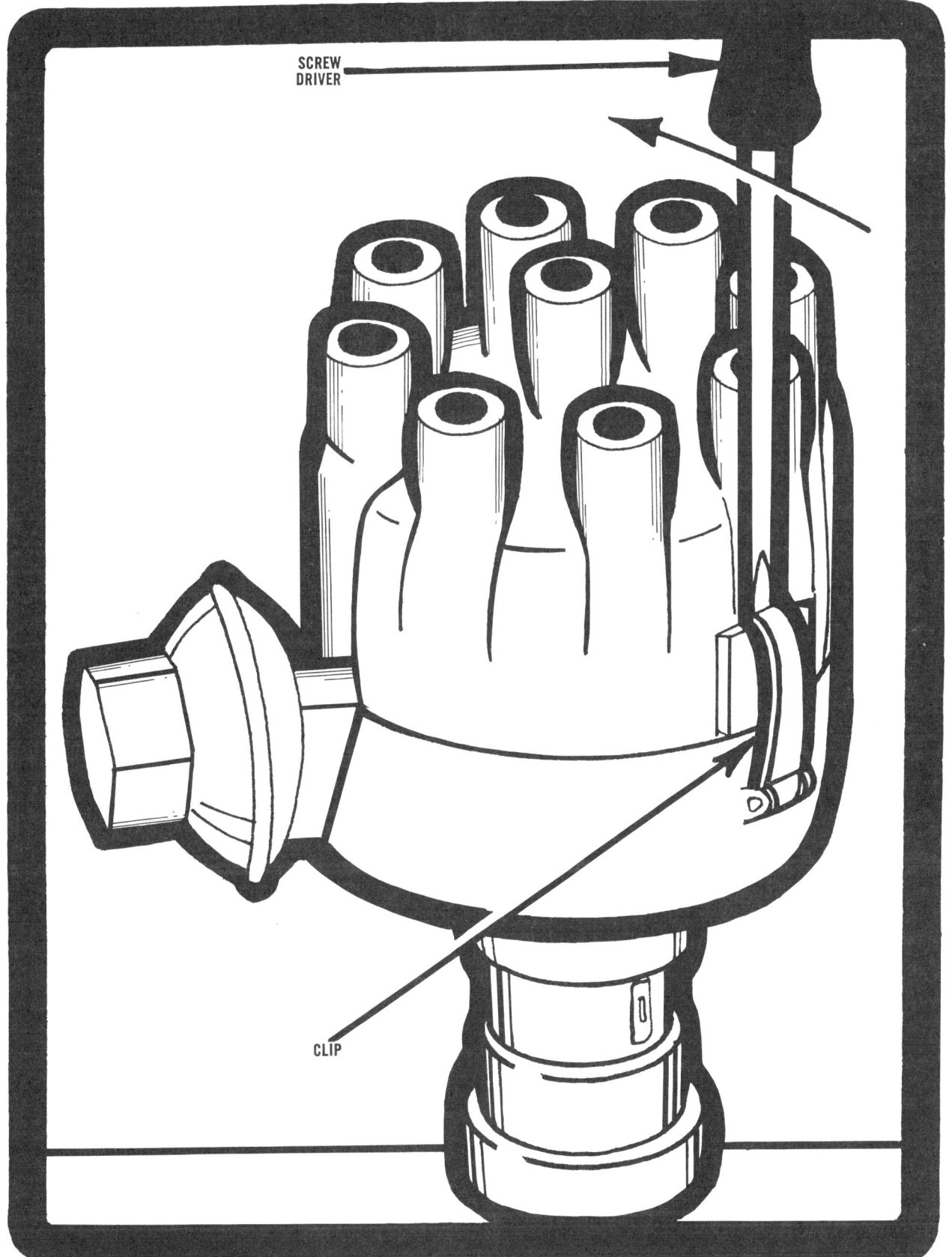

Fig. 17. Disengaging bale clips to remove the distributor cap. Typical of Chrysler Corp. and Ford Motor Co.

QUICK TUNEUP TIP

When removing the rotor on a GM Delco Remy distributor, be careful not to drop the two retaining screws into an inaccessible place under the hood.

2. Remove the rotor. If the rotor has two retaining screws, remove them using a flat screwdriver, Fig. 18, and lift the rotor off the weight base. Notice the square and round locating tabs underneath the rotor, Fig. 19. These tabs must be correctly positioned on the weight base when the rotor is reinstalled. If the rotor does not have any retaining screws, place two fingers underneath

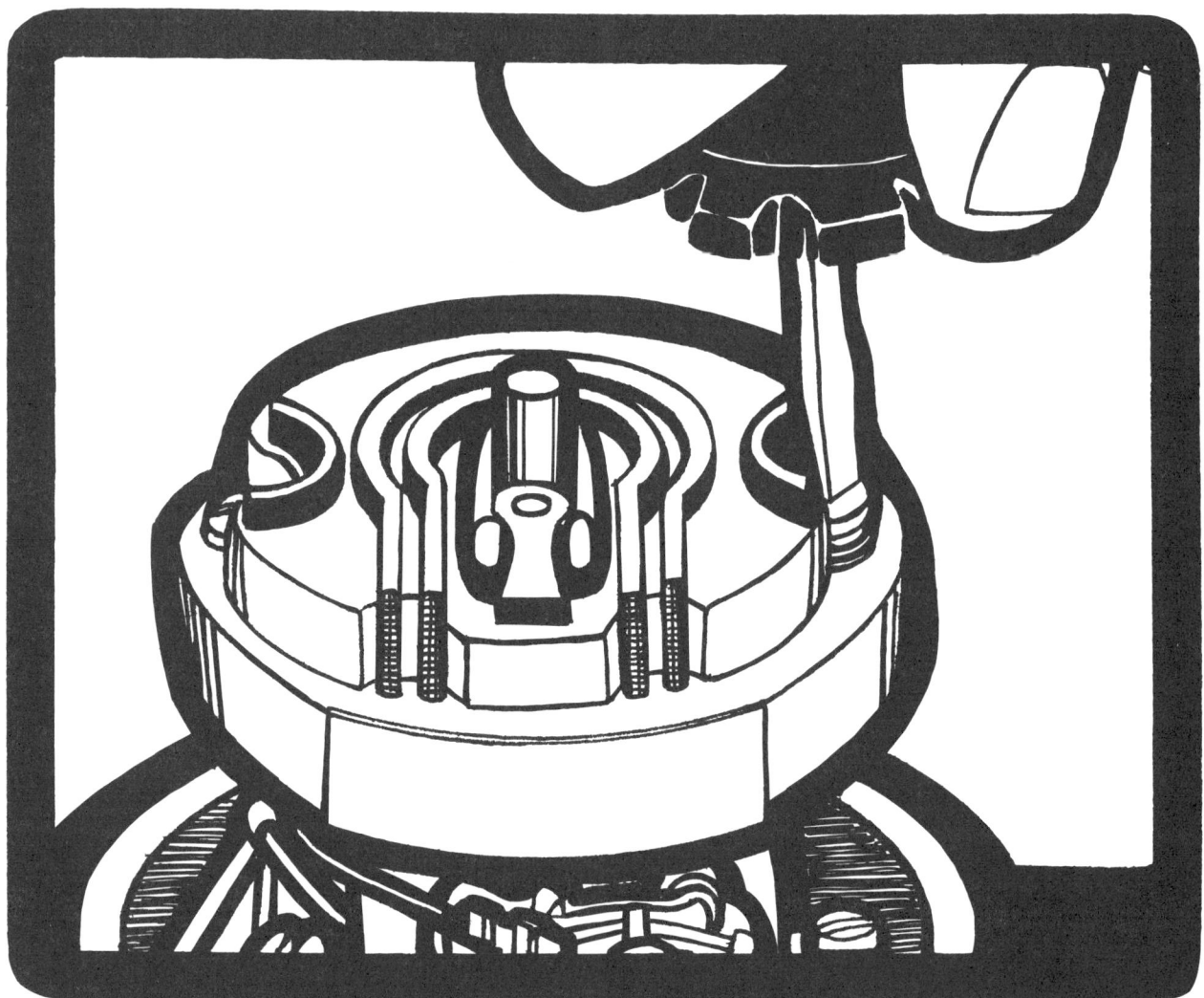

Fig. 18. Removing or installing the rotor retaining screws on a Delco Remy V8 distributor.

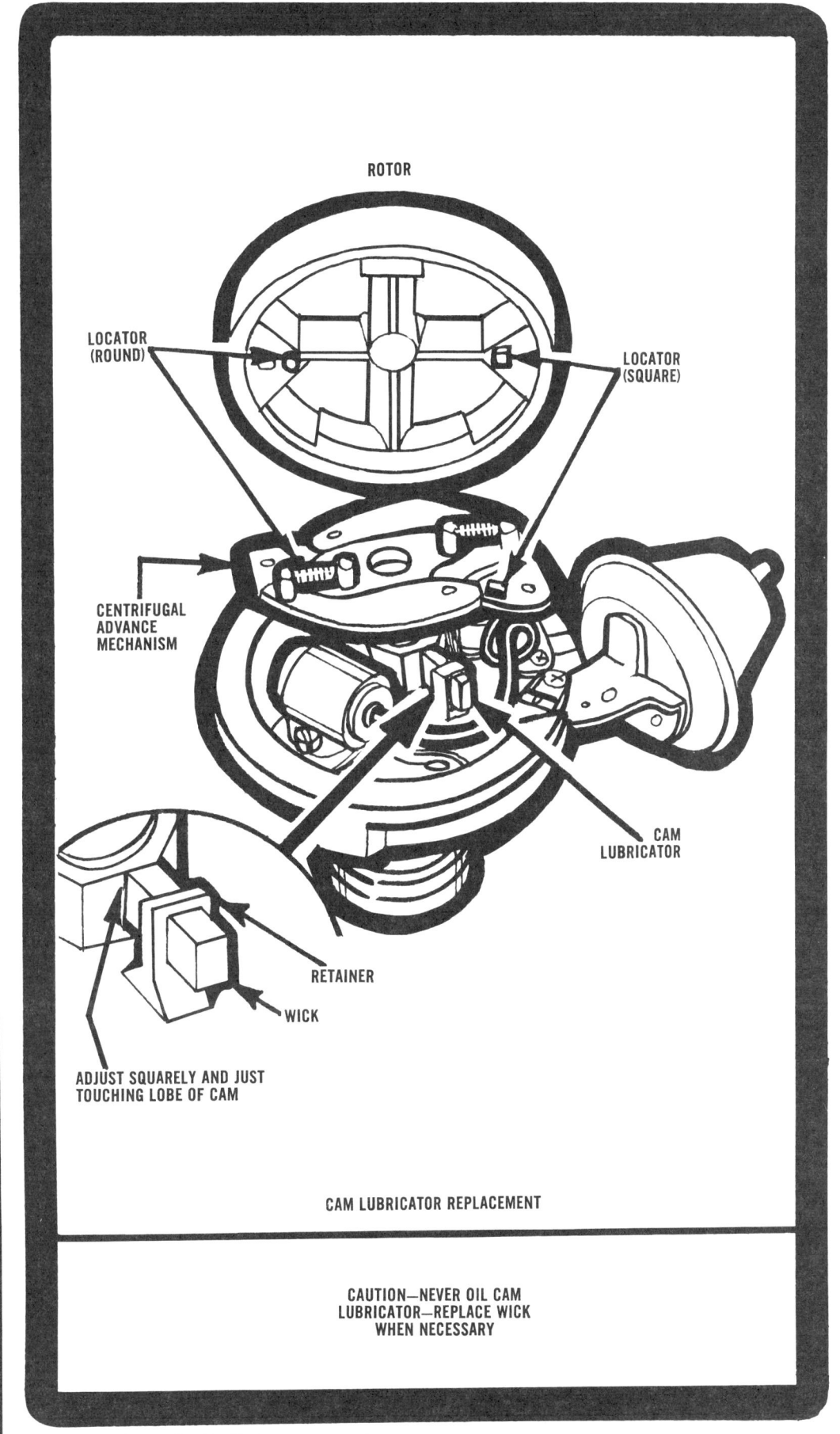

Fig. 19. Delco Remy V8 distributor components.

QUICK TUNEUP TIP

After removing the rotor from the distributor, check it for corrosion on the rotor tip. If there is any evidence of rust, replace the rotor.

the rotor, Fig. 20 or grasp the rotor, Fig. 21, and pull rotor off the distributor shaft. Notice the locating tab inside the rotor and the slot on the distributor shaft. The tab and slot must be correctly aligned when the rotor is reinstalled.

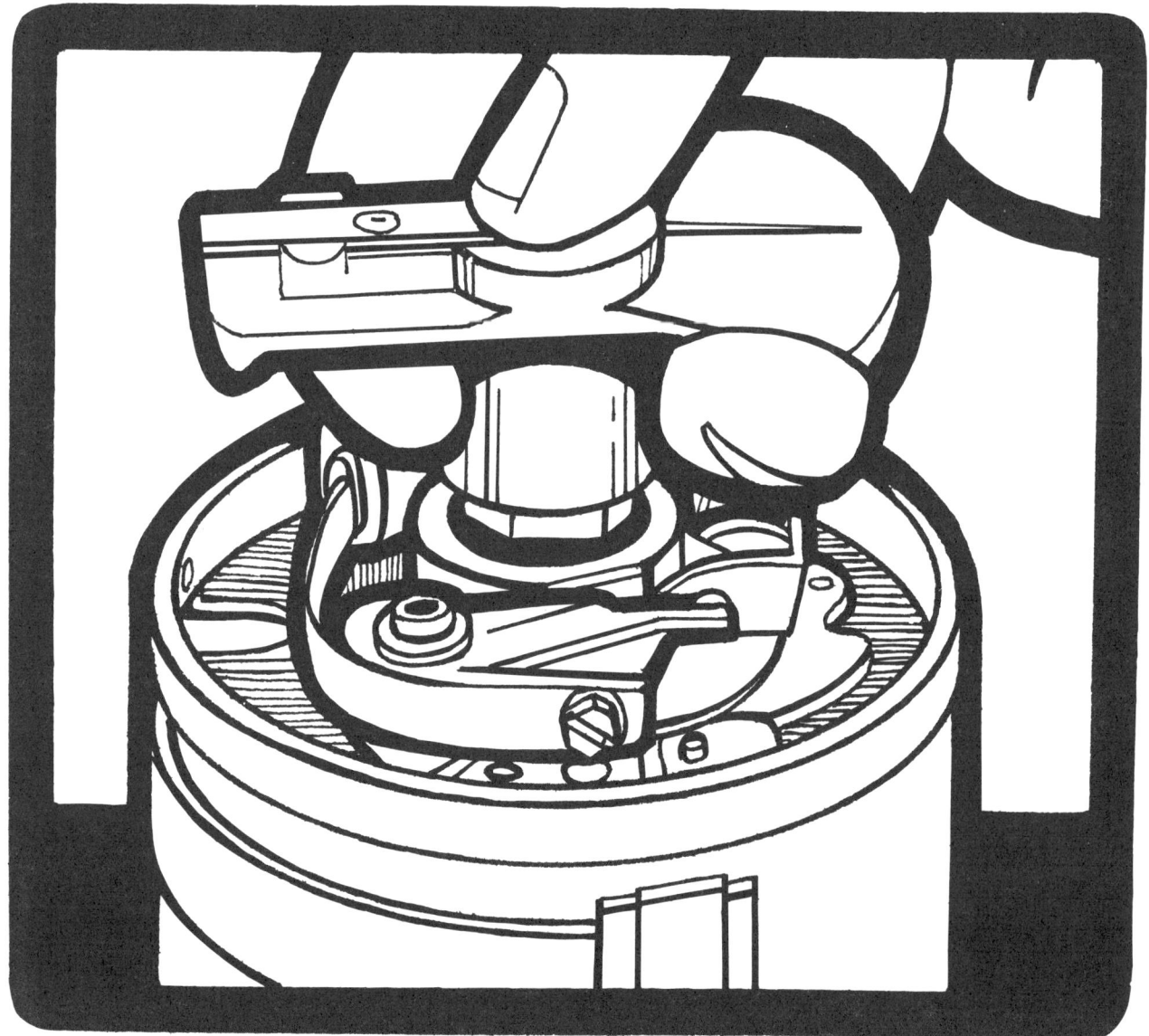

Fig. 20. Removing a typical Chrysler or Ford rotor.

QUICK TUNEUP TIP

The tension of the rotor to the distributor cap spring must be sufficient to insure good contact with the carbon button in the center of the distributor cap. If you find insufficient tension, replace the rotor or the distributor cap or both.

Fig. 21. Removing a typical General Motors 6-cylinder rotor.

3. Disconnect the condenser and coil leads from the points. The leads are retained to the points by a screw, a nut or quick disconnect, Fig. 27. If the leads are retained by a screw, loosen the screw using a flat screwdriver and disconnect the leads, Fig. 23. If they are retainend by a nut, Fig. 24, loosen the nut using a suitable size wrench (usually 5/16 inch) and disconnect the leads. If the leads are retained by a quick connect, just slip the leads up from behind the clip, Fig. 22.

NOTE: Some General Motors vehicles are equipped with Uni-Set breaker points (one piece breaker points and condenser). When replacing these points, just loosen the contact points retaining screws and slide the points and condenser out. In the event that the Uni-Set points are not available, you can install the two piece point and condenser. However you must install a radio

QUICK TUNEUP TIP
Dirty ignition points should be cleaned with a clean point file. Use only a few strokes of a fine-cut contact file. Never use emery cloth or sandpaper to clean ignition points.

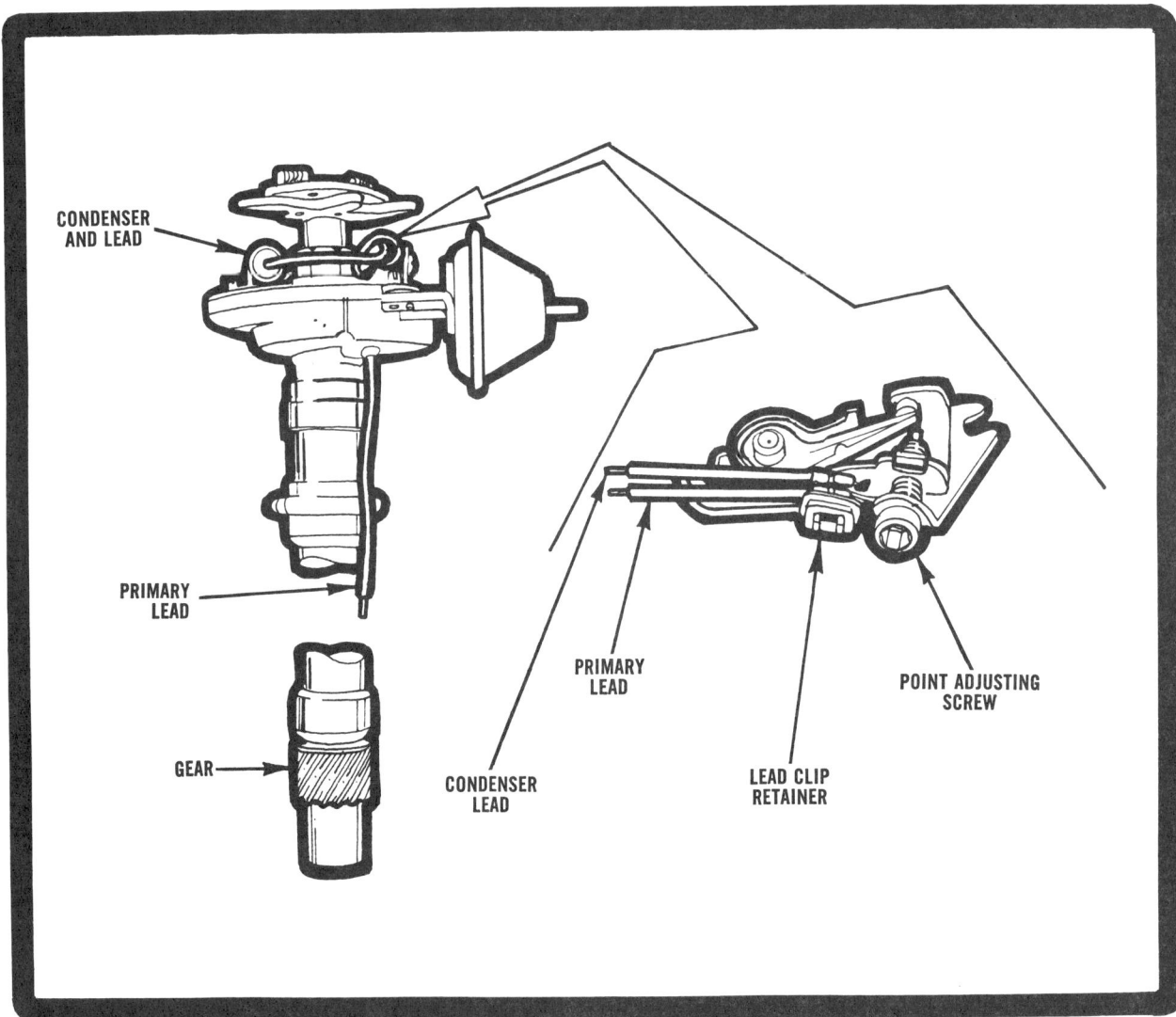

Fig. 22. Condenser and coil lead clip type retainer.

QUICK TUNEUP TIP

High series resistance in the condenser circuit will prevent normal condenser action, causing the ignition points to burn rapidly. Such resistance can be caused by a loose condenser mounting or lead connection, or by poor connections inside the condenser. Replace the condenser.

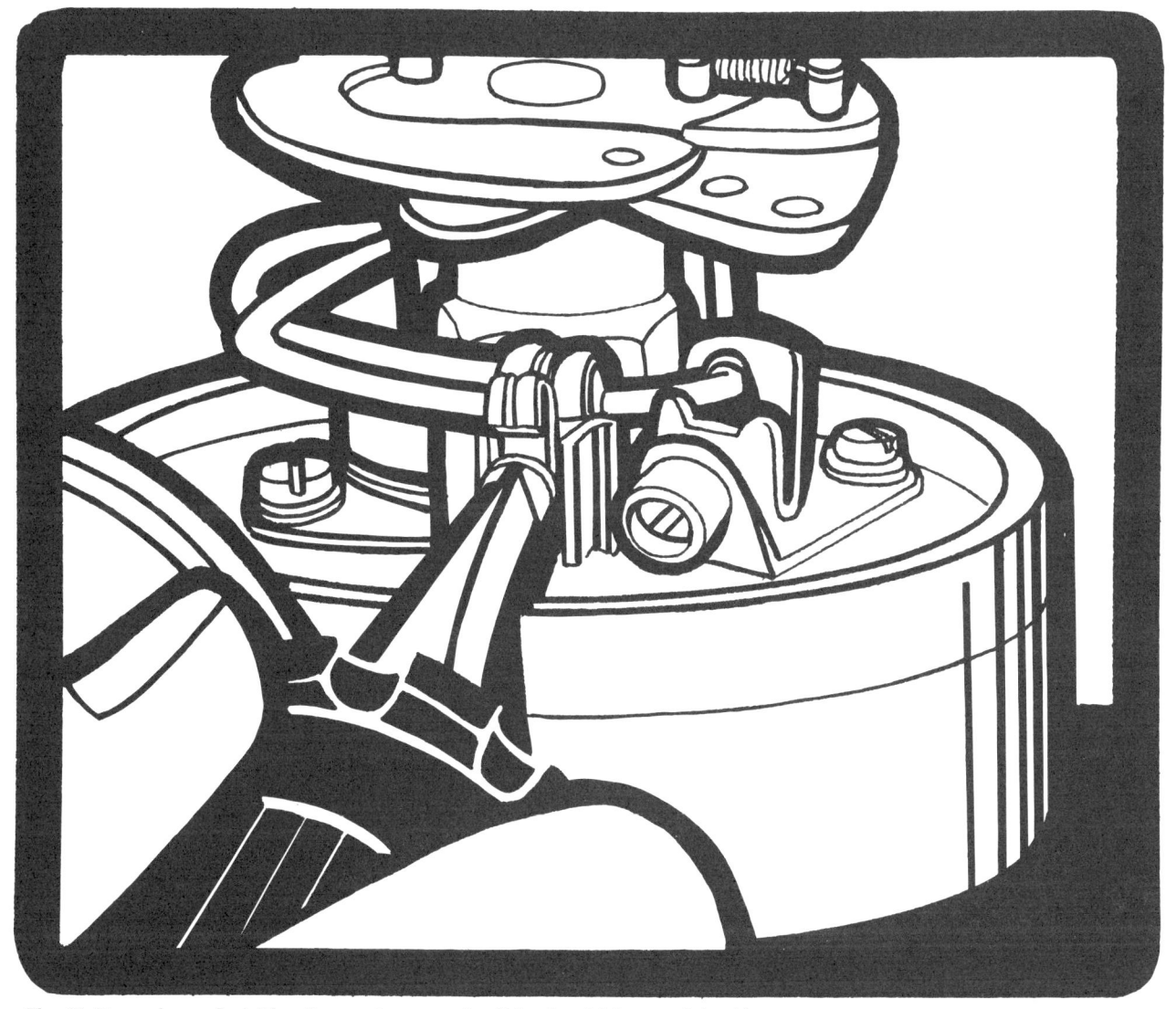

Fig. 23. Removing or installing the condenser and coil leads which are retained by a screw.

QUICK TUNEUP TIP

If you are not installing new ignition points, the old points should be cleaned before they are adjusted with a feeler gauge. Using a feeler gauge on rough or unclean points will result in inaccurate adjustment.

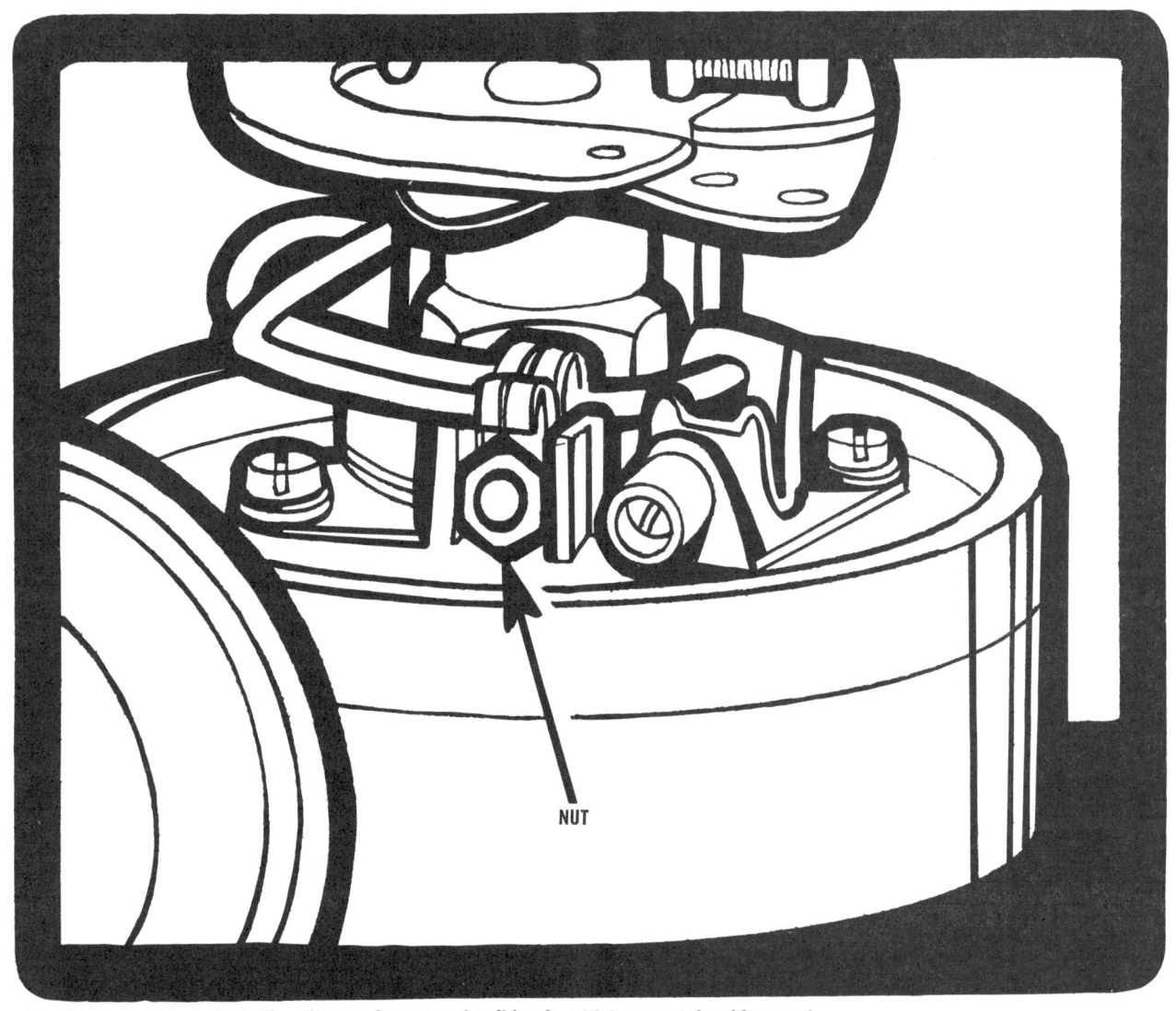

Fig. 24. Removing or installing the condenser and coil leads which are retained by a nut.

QUICK TUNEUP TIP

Because of the importance of point opening for good low speed engine performance and cam dwell angle for high speed engine performance, the cam angle should be checked after adjusting and aligning the points.

shield over the points to prevent radio interference. A conversion kit from the manufacturer is available to install this shield, a wick and breaker plate which is drilled and tapped to accept the condenser retaining screw. If the old breaker plate is drilled for the condenser and radio shield, this conversion kit is not required, although you still must install the radio shield.

4. Remove the points. On external adjustment Delco Remy points, using a flat screwdriver, loosen the two retaining screws, Fig. 25, just enough to slide the points off the breaker plate, all other points will be retained by either one or two screws. To remove these points, remove the

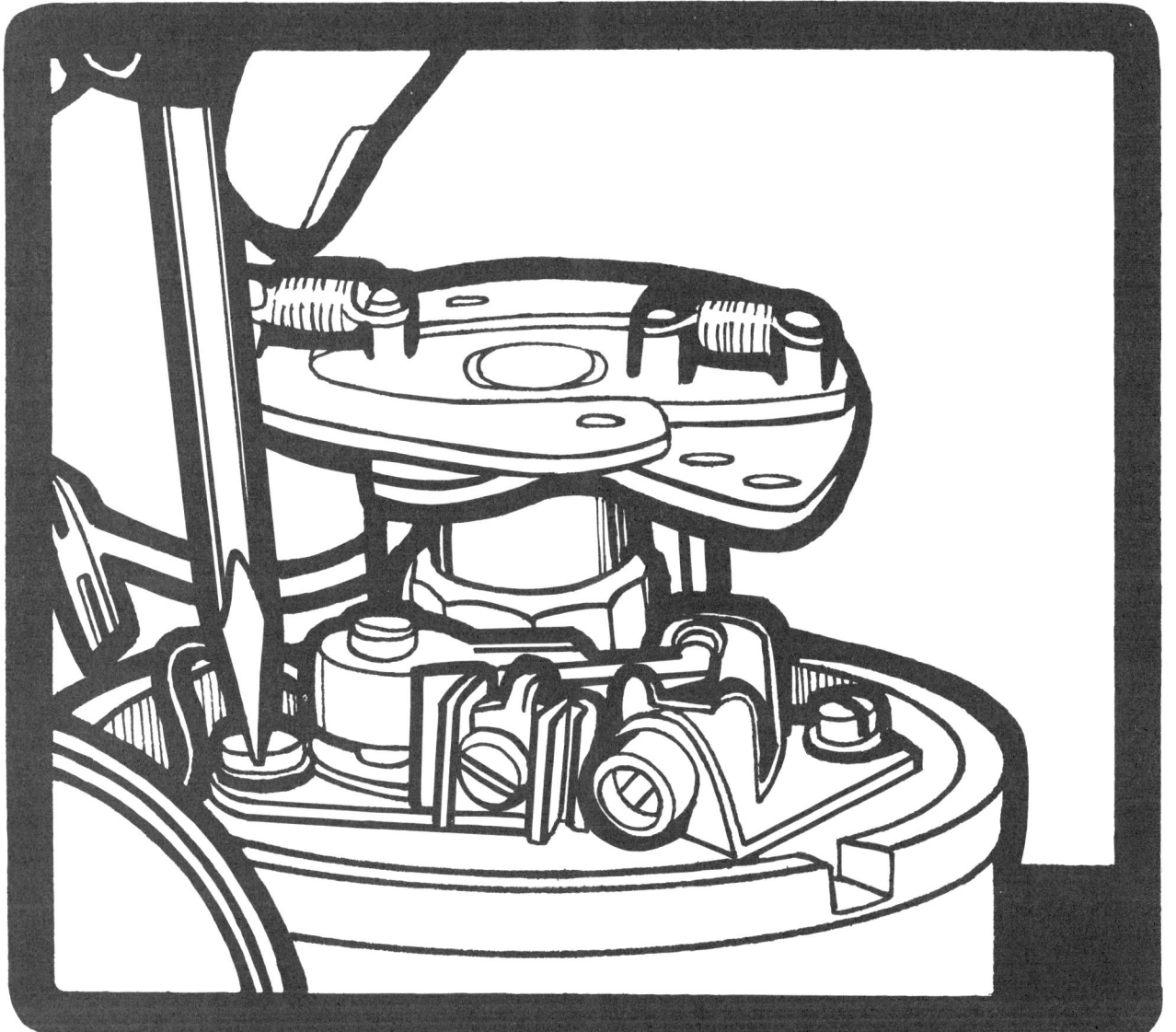

Fig. 25. To remove the points on GM Delco Remy external adjustment distributors, loosen the retaining screws and slide the points out. To install points, just slide the points back in and tighten the retaining screws.

QUICK TUNEUP TIP

Oil and crankcase vapors which work up into the distributor and deposit themselves on the point surfaces will cause them to burn rapidly. This is easy to detect. The oil produces a smudgy line under the contact points. A clogged PCV system will permit crankcase pressure to force oil or vapors up into the distributor.

retaining screw(s), Fig. 26, and lift the points off the breaker plate. Some points use an eccentric screw to adjust the points. This screw does not have to be removed. You will notice this by the eccentric action of the head when it is being turned.

NOTE: Be careful not to drop any screws into any distributor, as the distributor may have to be removed to retrieve the screw.

5. Remove the condenser. If the condenser slides into the retaining bracket, just loosen the retaining clamp screw, Fig. 27, using a flat screwdriver and slide the condenser out of the bracket. If the condenser and bracket are one piece, remove the bracket retaining screw, Fig. 28, and remove the condenser and bracket as an assembly. Again, be careful not to drop any screws into the distributor.

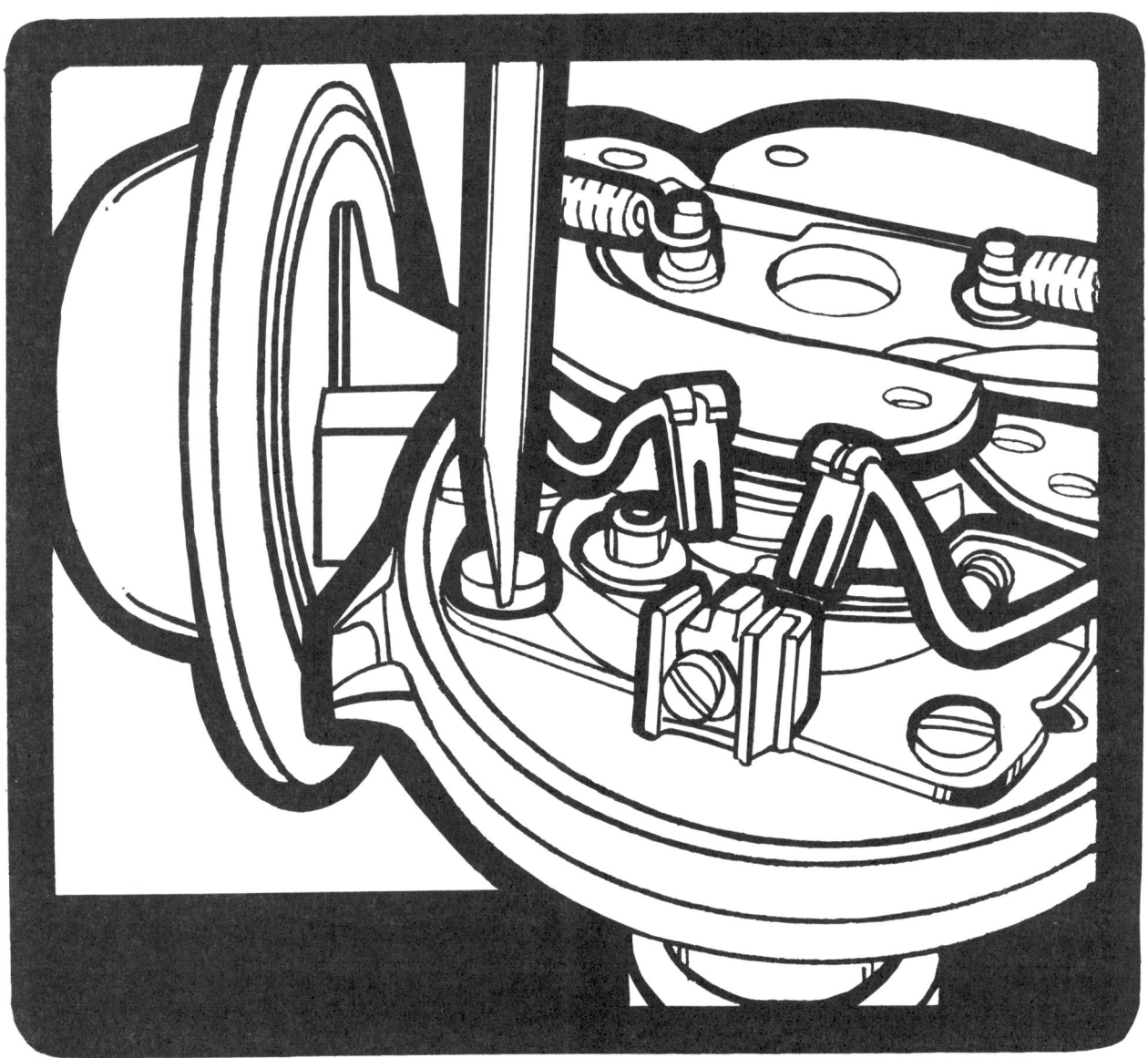

Fig. 26. Removing or installing the contact point retaining screws.

QUICK TUNEUP TIP

Proper alignment of ignition points is important to long point life. If the full faces of the points do not touch each other, the ability of the points to dissipate heat is greatly reduced. This causes excessive point burning and premature failure.

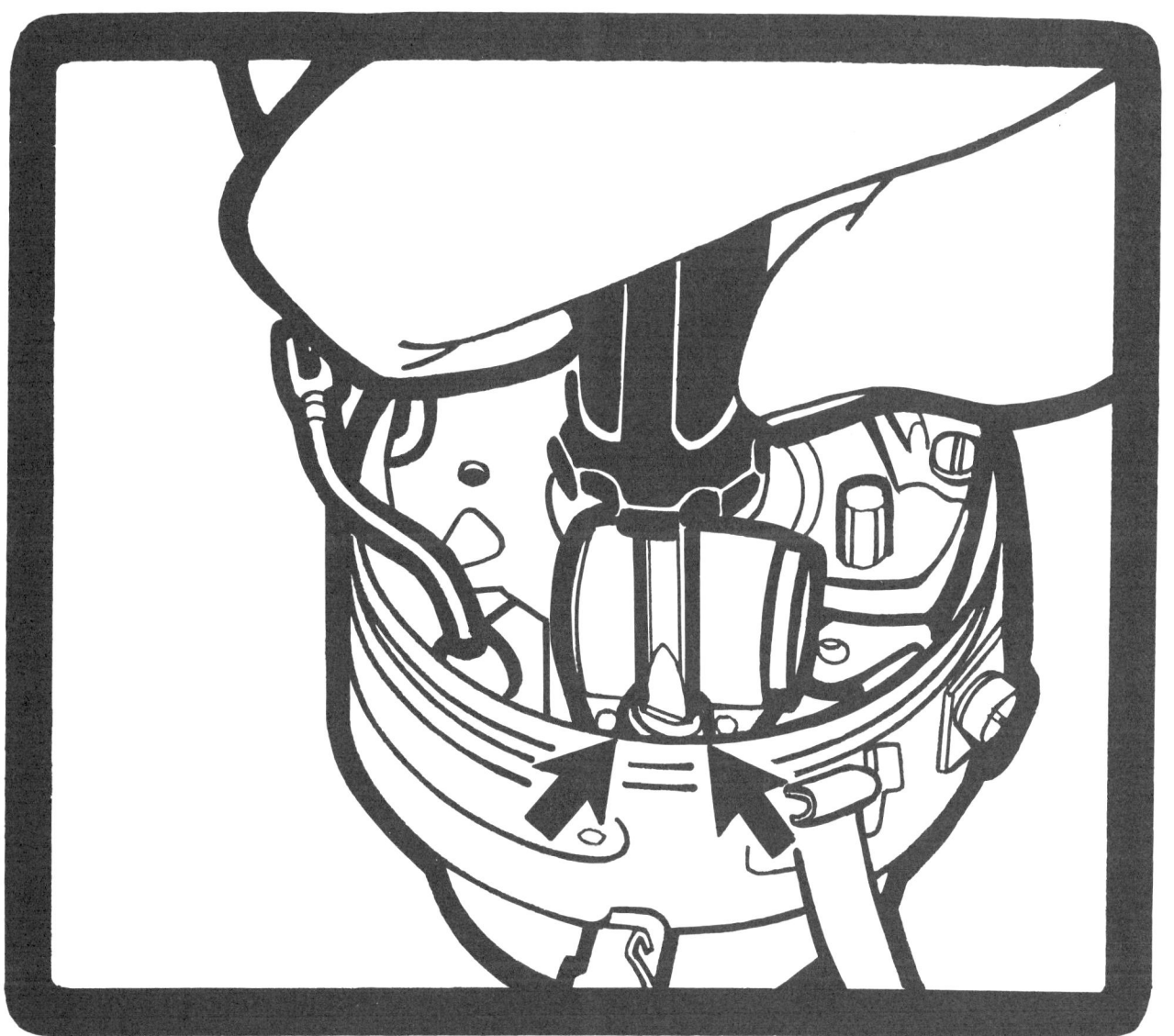

Fig. 27. Removing or installing the condenser. Separate condenser and bracket type.

6. Using a clean cloth, wipe off the breaker plate and cam.
7. Install the condenser. If you removed the condenser by sliding it out of its retaining clamp, slide the new condenser into the clamp and tighten the retaining screw, Fig. 27. If you removed the condenser and clamp as one unit, install the new condenser and clamp onto the breaker plate, aligning the holes in the bracket and the tangs in the breaker plate and install and tighten the retaining screw, Fig. 28. Make sure that you use the same screws which were originally removed. If you install screws which are too long, they may interfere with the operation of the advance mechanism and possibly cause damage to the distributor.
8. Install the points. On external adjustment Delco Remy points, slide the points onto the breaker plate and under the retaining screw heads and tighten the retaining screws, Fig. 25. On all other points, place them on the breaker plate and install

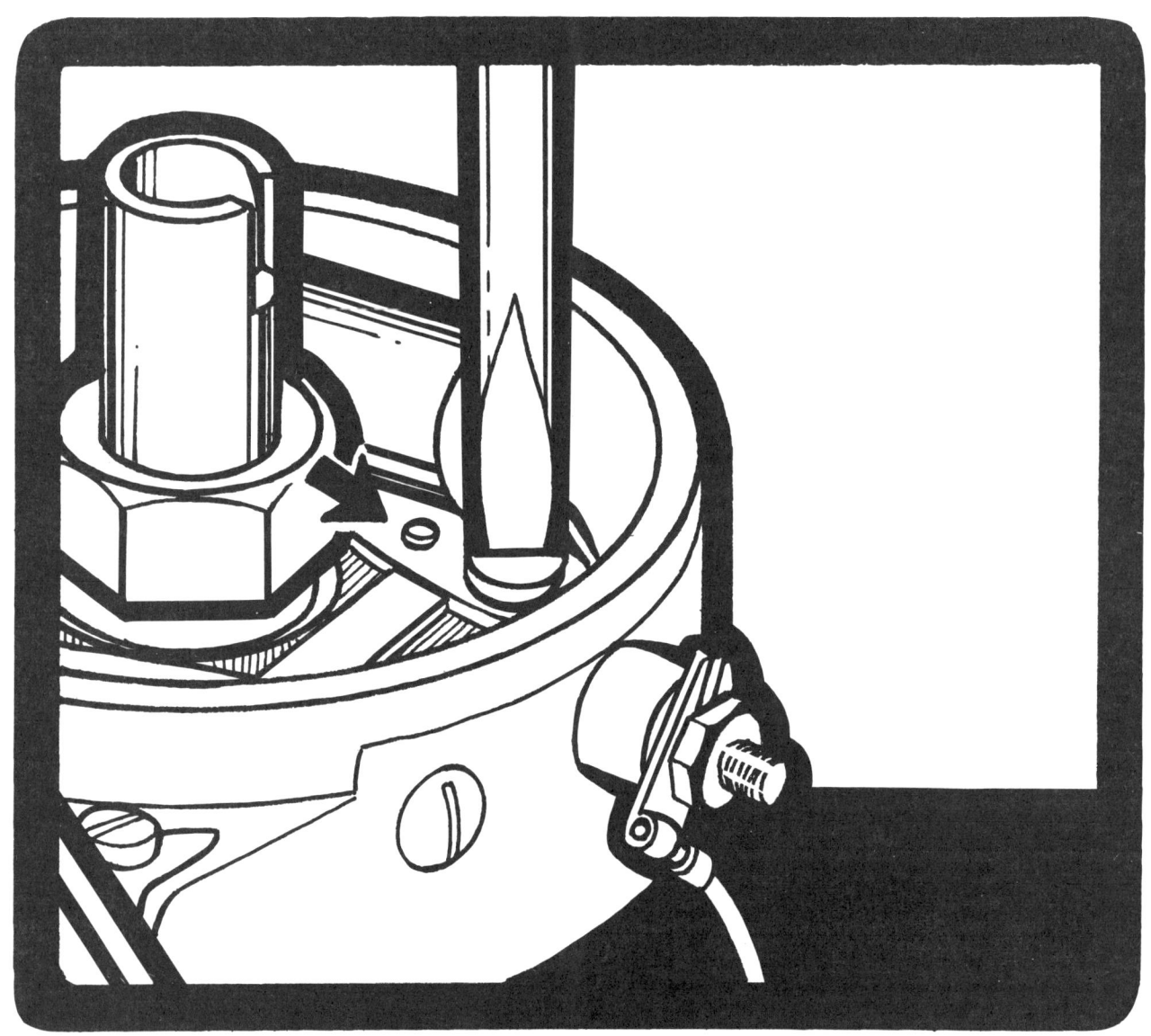

Fig. 28. Removing or installing the condenser. One piece condenser and bracket.

QUICK TUNEUP TIP

Some Ford distributors have a ground wire which is also retained by one of the screws holding the points. When you tighten this screw, hold the connector stationary. This will prevent it from turning with the screw and grounding out against the breaker point spring.

and tighten the retaining screws, Fig. 26. Some points have a pivot post which must be properly inserted in the hole in the breaker plate, or have a hole through which a pivot post secured to the breaker plate must be inserted, Fig. 27. Some

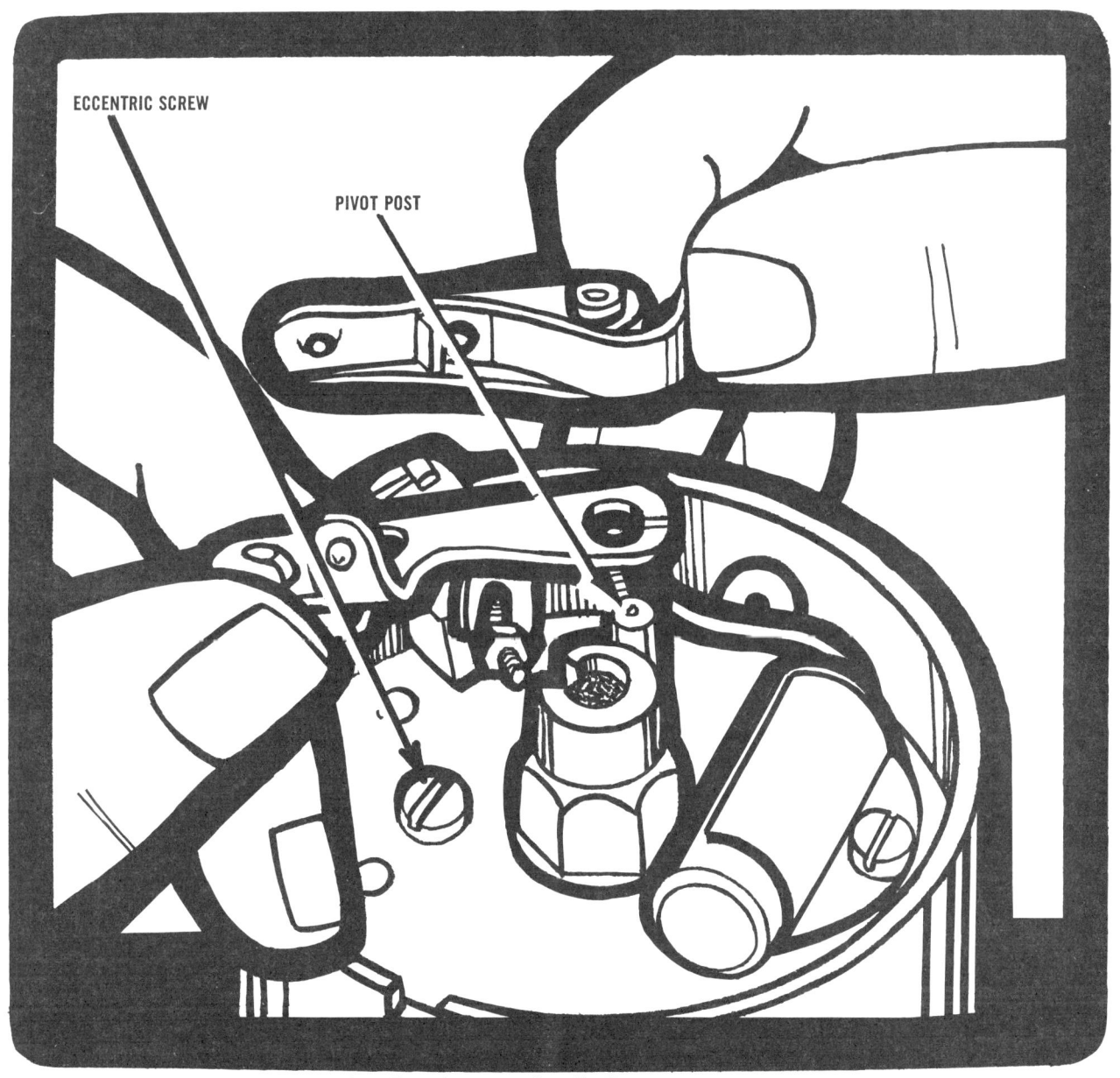

Fig. 29. Pivot post mounted contact points. Note the eccentric adjusting screw.

QUICK TUNEUP TIP

GM Delco Remy distributors have a different arrangement for the ignition points than do either Ford or Chrysler distributors. Be sure you have been following the procedures and illustrations for your type of distributor.

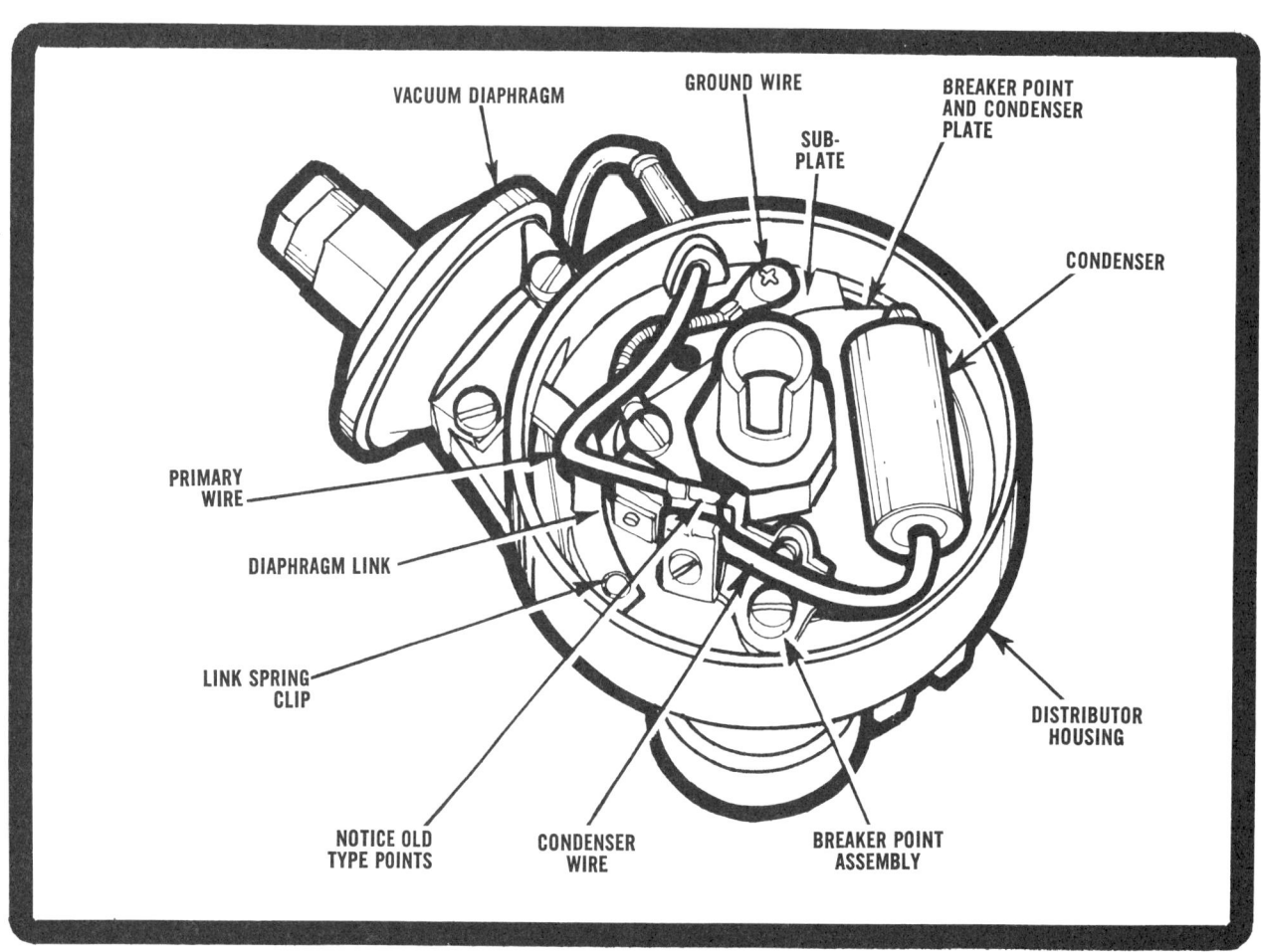

Fig. 30. Typical Ford Motor Co. distributor. Notice the ground lead which must be correctly positioned to avoid grounding out the points.

QUICK TUNEUP TIP

When reconnecting the condenser and coil leads to the points, be sure the procedure is followed exactly. An incorrect hookup could ground out the lead and prevent the engine from starting.

vehicles, such as Fords, have a ground wire, Fig. 30, which is also retained by one of the screws which retains the points. When you tighten this screw, hold the connector stationary, to prevent it from turning with the screw and grounding out against the breaker points spring. Again, remember to use only the screws which were originally removed. If the screws require replacement, use screws of the same size and length as those removed.

9. Reconnect the condenser and coil leads to the points. If the points do not have a quick disconnect terminal, the leads must be inserted between the breaker points spring and the plastic insulator, Figs. 22 and 31. To do this, push the spring toward the cam using a screwdriver, then insert the leads betwen the plastic insulator and the metal base of the points, as this will ground out the leads and prevent the engine from starting. To connect the leads on points with a terminal screw or nut, just slide the leads, Fig. 31, behind the screw, Fig. 23, or nut, Fig. 24, and tighten the screw or nut using a flat screwdriver or suitable size wrench (usually 5/16 inch).

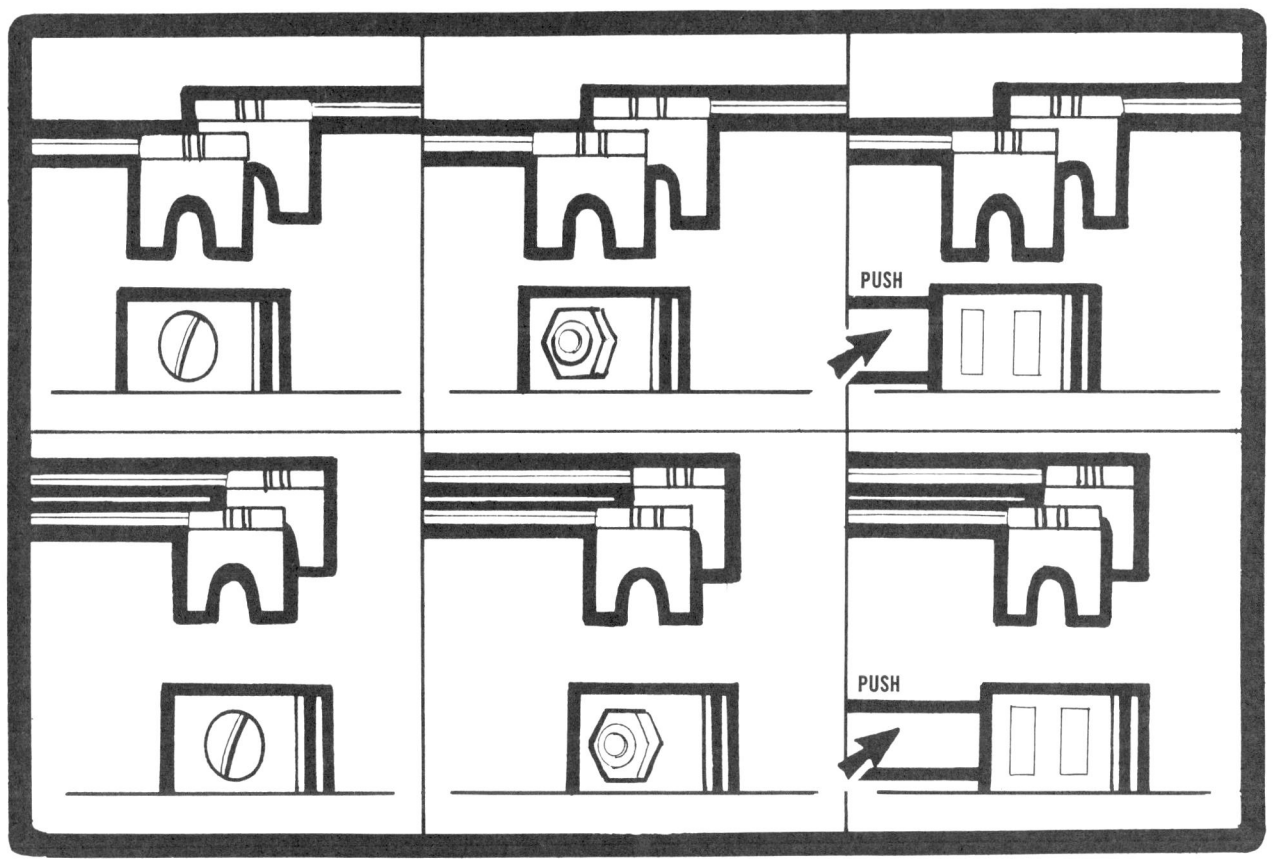

Fig. 31. Condenser and coil lead arrangement.

10. Adjust the point gap. For this procedure you may need an assistant to crank the engine, either by hand or by turning the ignition key. If you have the engine cranked over by the ignition key, be very careful to keep your hands and clothing away from the fan, belts and pulleys. Also, keep away from the secondary ignition wires to prevent an electrical shock. Turn the engine until the breaker point rubbing block is aligned with one of the highest points on the cam, Fig. 32. If the ignition key is used to turn the engine, make sure that it is off before proceeding further:

(a) External adjustment Delco Remy points can be adjusted in any one of the three methods. The first method is to have the engine running and adjust the points by turning the adjusting screw with an Allen wrench, Fig. 33. The second method is to have the engine running and turn the adjusting screw clockwise with an Allen wrench until the engine

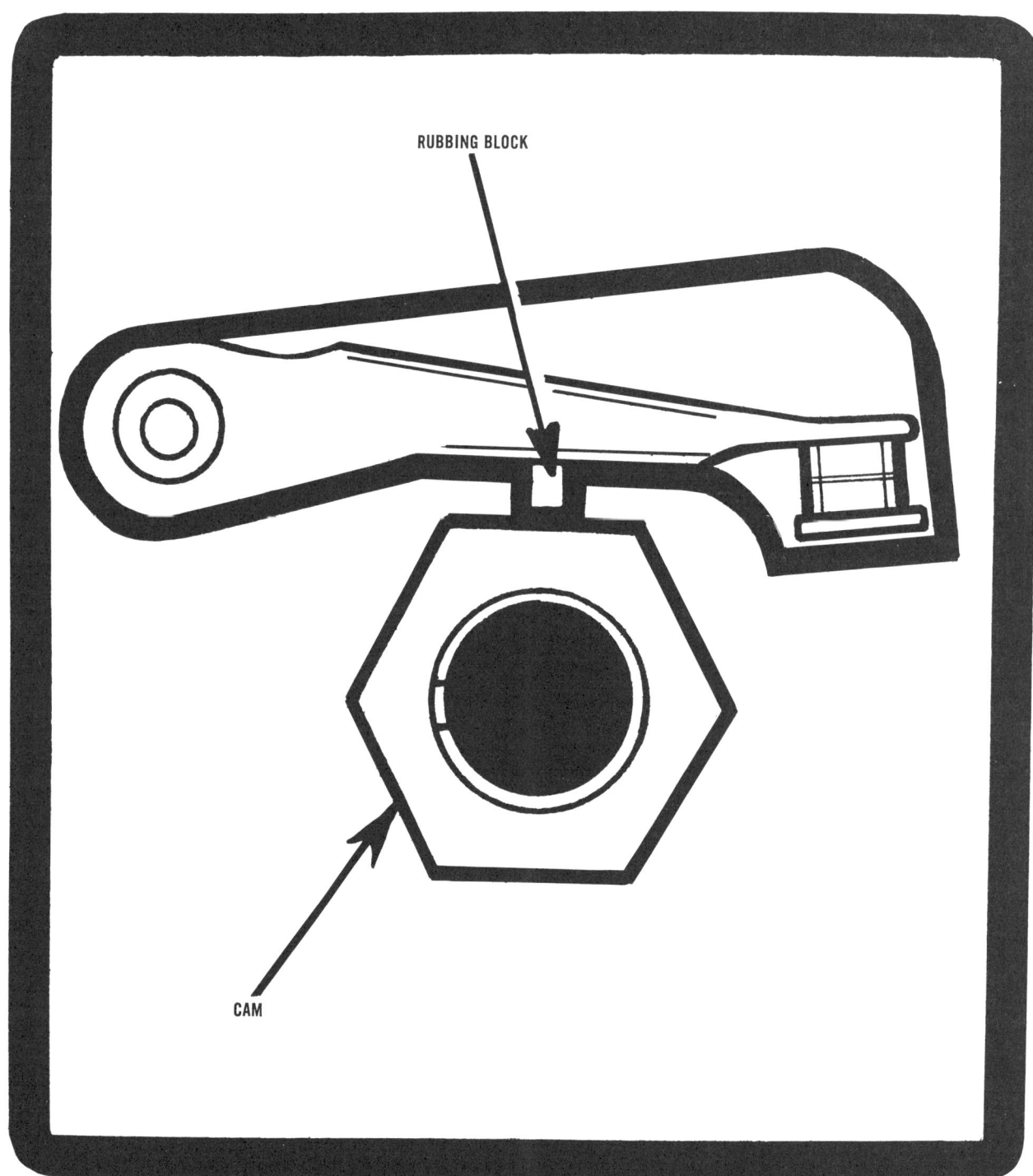

Fig. 32. Align the rubbing block on the points with one of the highest points on the cam.

misses, then back off the adjusting screw with an Allen wrench, Fig. 33, one complete turn, and turn back in again ½ turn. The third method is to insert a thickness gauge between the contacts, then turn the adjusting screw with the suitable size Allen wrench, in or out until a slight drag is felt on the thickness gauge when it is removed.

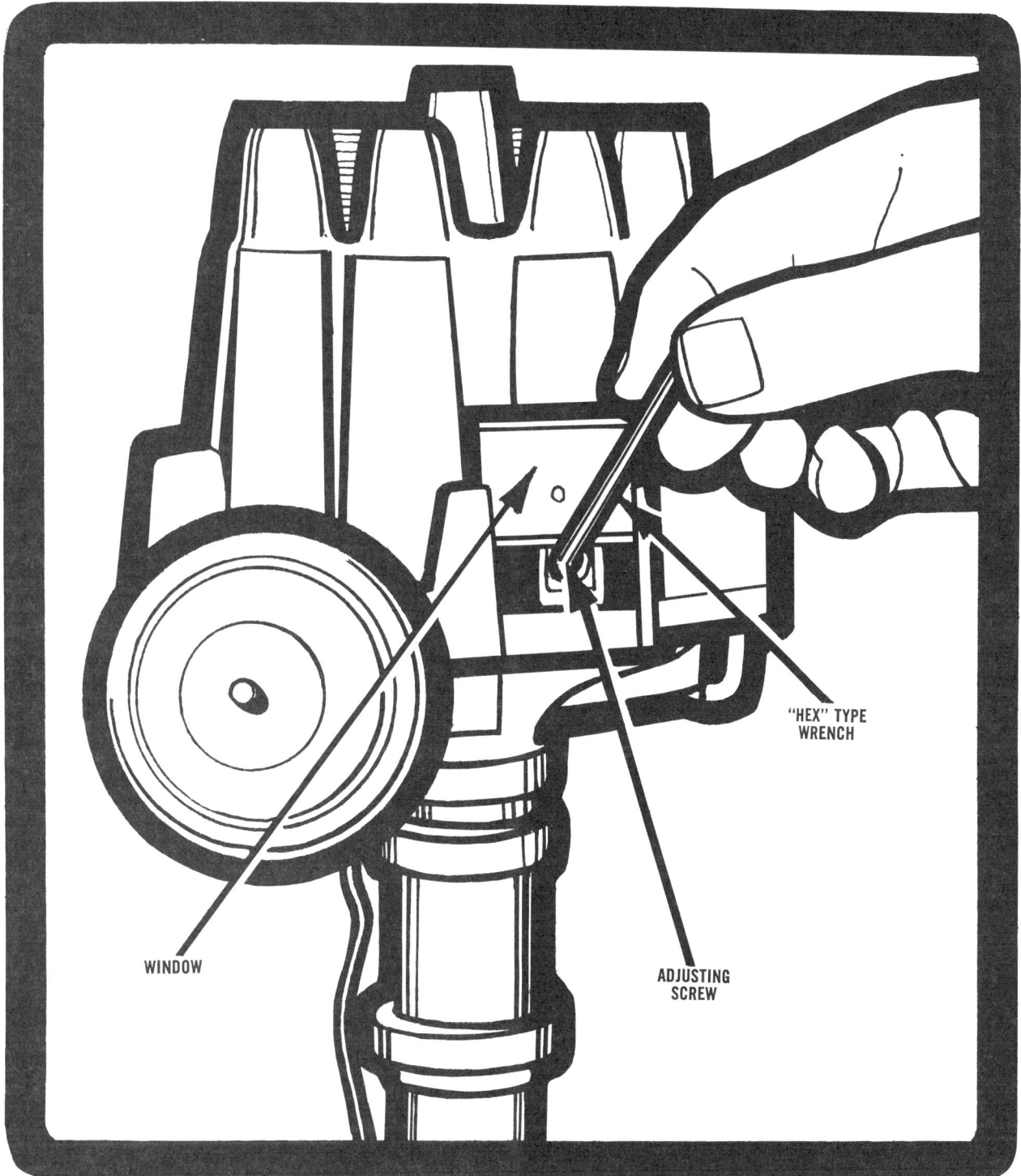

Fig. 33. Setting external adjustment Delco Remy points.

QUICK TUNEUP TIP

New ignition points must be set to a slightly larger opening as the rubbing block will wear down slightly while seating to the cam.

(b) On points with a slot at the base of the breaker points and a slot in the breaker plate, Fig. 34, adjust as follows: Make sure that the points retaining screws are just snug enough so that the points can be moved back and forth using a screwdriver placed in the slots. Insert a thickness gauge of the correct size between the contacts, then insert a flat screwdriver into the slot in the breaker plate and the slot at the base of the points. Turn the screwdriver as required to open or close the points until a slight drag is felt on the thickness gauge when it is removed. Tighten the retaining screws and recheck the adjustment.

(c) On points with an eccentric adjusting screw, Fig. 29, proceed as follows: Make sure that the retaining screw is snug enough so that the points can be moved back and forth when the eccentric adjusting screw is turned. Insert the correct size thickness gauge between the contacts, then using a flat screwdriver, turn the eccentric adjusting screw as required to open or close the points, until a slight drag is felt on the thickness gauge when it is removed. Tighten the retaining screw and recheck the adjustment.

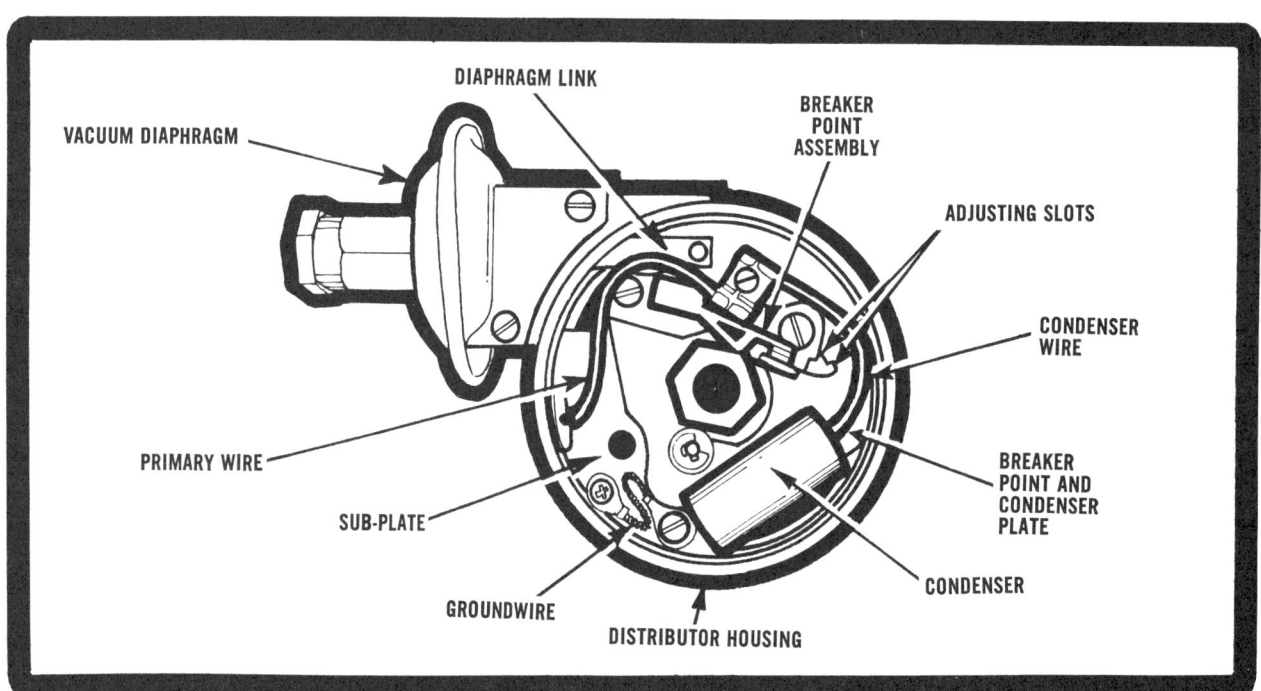

Fig. 34. Illustration shows location of adjusting slots in the breaker plate and at the base of the points.

QUICK TUNEUP TIP

Degrees of dwell and point gap are not necessarily the same. It is possible to have a correct gap but an incorrect dwell. This is why bending the breaker arm is not recommended.

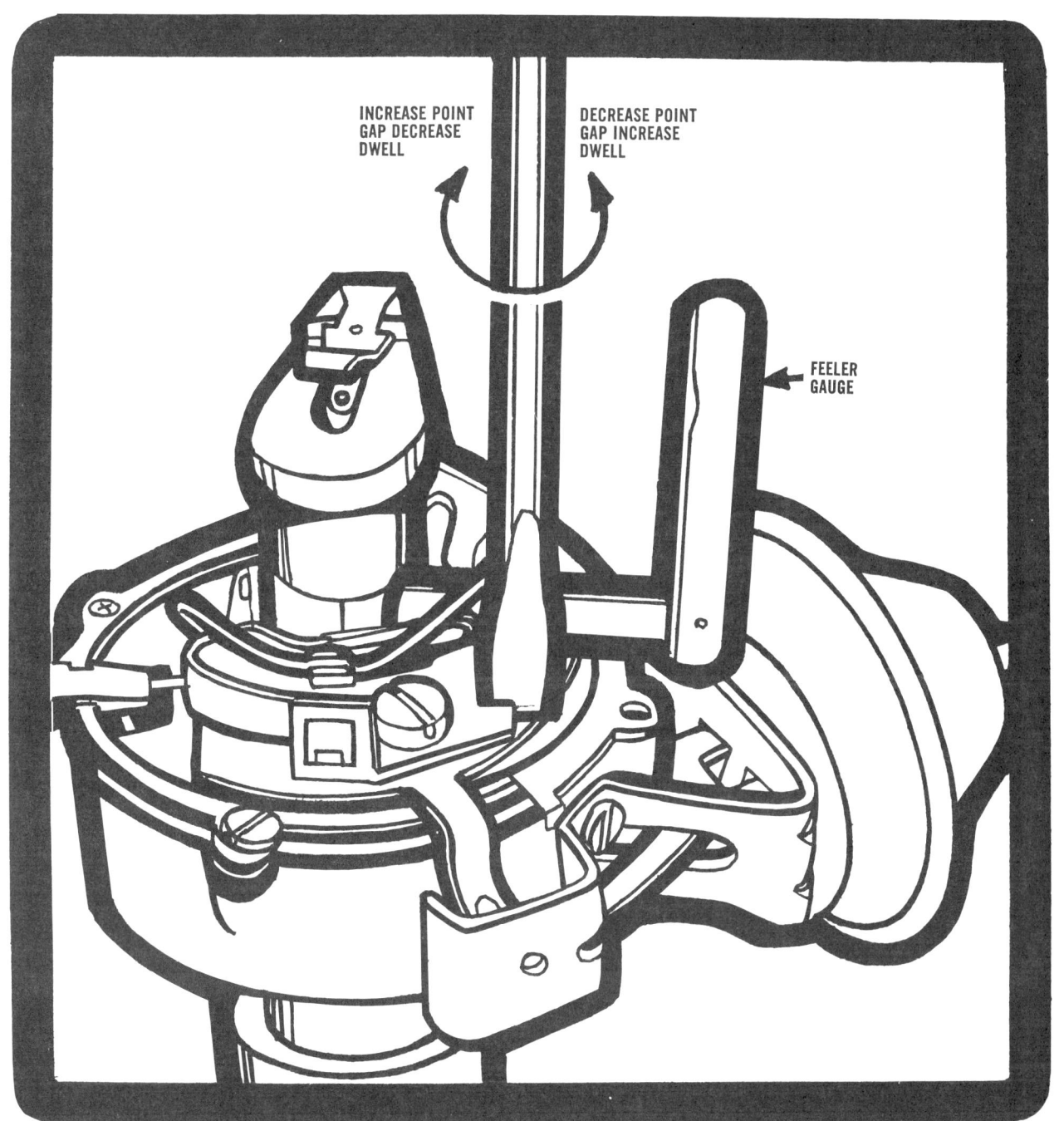

Fig. 35. Setting the point gap using a thickness feeler gauge and flat screwdriver.

QUICK TUNEUP TIP

Where it is difficult to get both a correct gap and correct dwell, use the correct dwell setting. After adjusting the alignment, readjust the point gap.

Point alignment

Proper alignment of contact points is important to point life (see Fig. 11). If the full faces of the points do not touch each other, the ability of the points to dissipate the heat resulting from the primary current is reduced, causing excessive point burning.

Point pitting

Contact point pitting results from an unbalanced condition in the ignition system which causes transfer of tungsten from one point to the other, with the result that a tip builds up on one point while a pit forms on the other. The direction in which the tungsten transfers can be used as a basis for analysis and correction of this condition. If the material transfers from the negative to the positive point (Fig. 12), increase the condenser capacity. If the material transfers from the positive to the negative point (Fig. 13), reduce the condenser capacity.

While most condensers are of the same capacity range, say, .18 to .23 mfd, any box of condensers will have high and low representatives within the specification range. When a condition is noted on a car that requires tailoring of the condenser, measure the condenser from the car on a tester and select an appropriate measured condenser. If there has been very little material transfer, leave the original condenser in the car. Replacing it with a new, unmeasured condenser may actually give a poorer operating set of points than before the tuneup. An easy rule for tailoring condensers is the minus minus minus rule. If the minus or negative point is minus material, the condenser is minus capacity or should be increased in capacity. The rule, of course, works just as well as a plus plus plus rule.

Grounded Point		Insulated Point
Pit	Increase Capacity	Hill
Hill	Decrease Capacity	Pit

Adjust distributor contact point gap according to specifications found in Tuneup Specification tables, using a feeler gauge or dial indicator. The breaker arm rubbing block should be on the cam lobe during adjustment.

NOTE: Contact points should be cleared before adjusting with a feeler gauge if they have been in service.

Using a feeler gauge on rough or uncleaned points is not recommended since accurate gauging cannot be done on such points. The gauge measures between high spots on the points instead of the true point opening (Fig. 14).

New points must be set to a slightly larger opening as the rubbing block will wear down slightly while seating to the cam.

11. Apply a small dab of cam lubricant onto the cam. This lubricant is usually supplied with the new points in a small plastic capsule.
12. Install the rotor. If the rotor was retained by two screws, place it over the weight base. Make sure that the square and round locating tabs underneath the rotor are installed on the corresponding square and round holes in the weight base, Fig. 19. Install and tighten the retaining screws, Fig. 18. If the rotor was lifted off the distributor shaft, align the locating tab inside the open end of the rotor with the slot on the distributor shaft and slide the rotor onto the shaft. Make sure that the rotor is firmly seated on the shaft.
13. Install the distributor cap onto the distributor. Make sure that the locating tab on the cap is properly aligned with the locating slot in the distributor housing. If the distributor cap was retained by two latches, depress the latches using a flat screwdriver, and turn the latches in either direction, until they engage the notch underneath the distributor housing, Fig. 15. If the distributor cap was retained by two screws, tighten the screws using a flat screwdriver, Fig. 16. If the distributor cap was retained by two bale clips, position the clips onto the cap, press the clips until they engage the cap, Fig. 36.

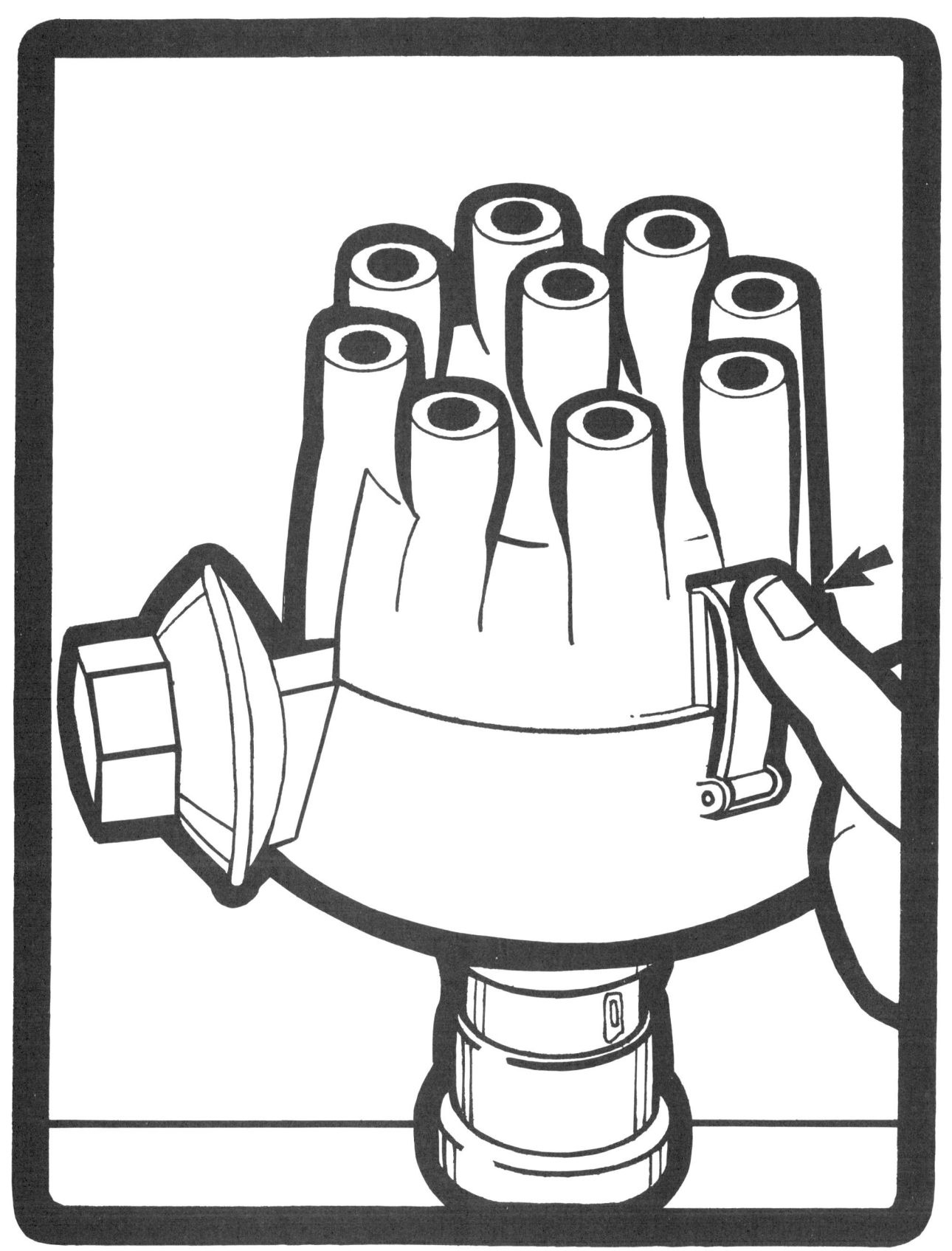

Fig. 36. Engaging the bale clips onto the distributor cap.

JOB 10. SERVICE THE BATTERY AND BATTERY CABLES

Inspect the battery and battery cables and perform necessary service on these components.

Inspect for signs of corrosion on the battery, cables and surrounding area, loose or broken carriers, cracked or bulged cases, dirt and acid, electrolyte leakage and low electrolyte level. Fill cells to proper level with distilled water or water passed through a demineralizer to eliminate the possibility of harmful impurities being added to the electrolyte.

The top of the battery should be clean and the battery hold-down bolt properly tightened. Particular care should be taken to see that the top of the battery is kept clean of acid film and dirt because of the possibility of current flow between the terminals, as this will slowly discharge the battery. For best results in cleaning batteries, wash first with a dilute ammonia or soda solution to neutralize any acid present and then flush off with clean water. Care must be taken to keep the vent plugs tight so that the neutralizing solution does not enter the cell. After cleaning, apply a coat of petrolatum to the battery hold-down bolts and cable clamps. The hold-down bolt should be kept tight enough to prevent the battery from shaking around in its carrier, but it should not be tightened to the point where the battery case will be placed under severe strain.

To insure good contact, the battery cables should be tight on the battery posts. If the battery posts or cable terminals are corroded, the cables should be removed and cleaned with a soda solution and a wire brush as described further on.

If the battery has remained undercharged, check for a loose alternator belt, defective alternator, high resistance in the charging circuit, oxidized regulator contact points, or a low voltage setting.

If the battery has been using too much water, the voltage regulator setting should be checked, as it may be too high.

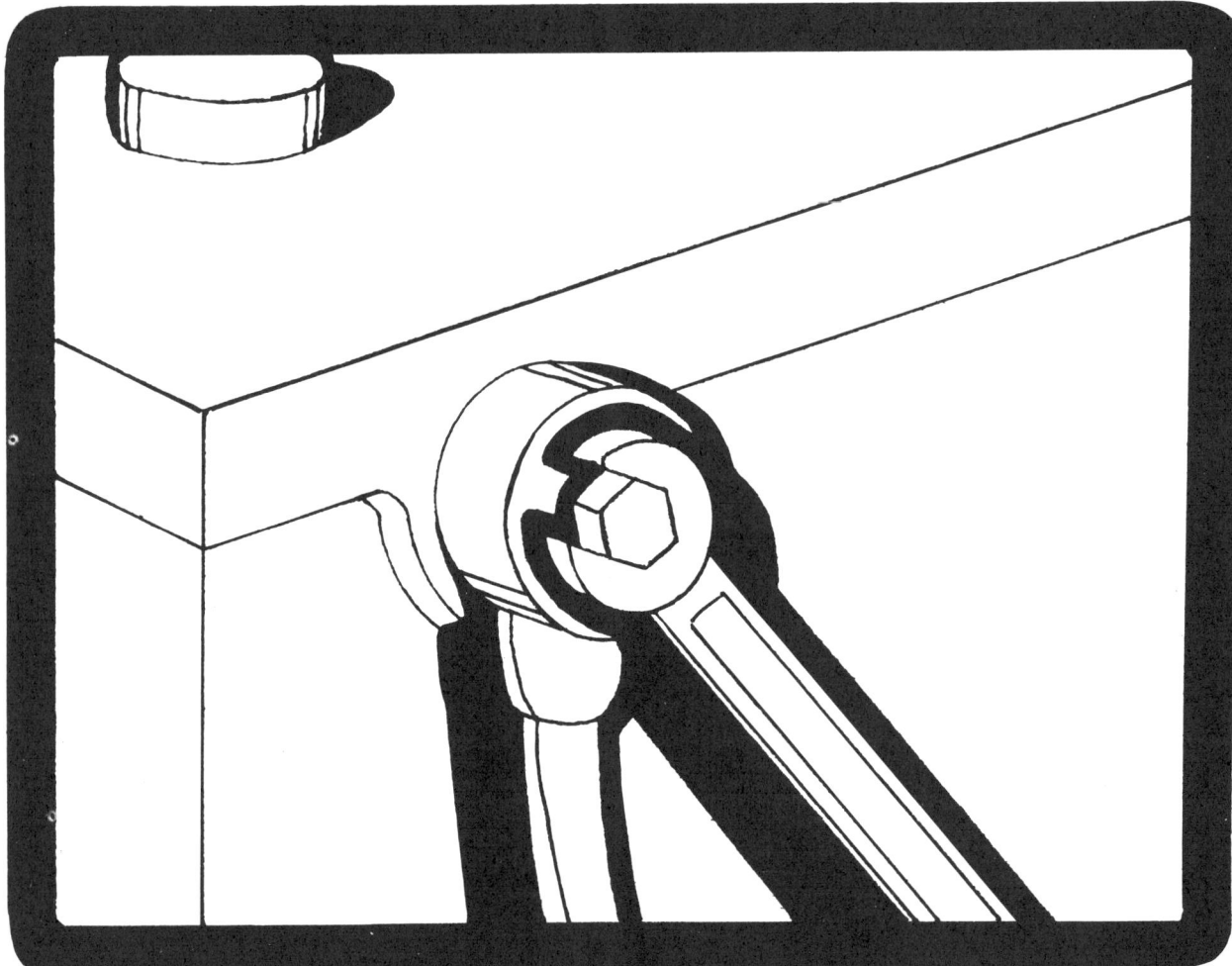

Fig. 37. Loosening side terminal battery cable.

QUICK TUNEUP TIP

Keep the top of your battery clean of acid film and dirt. Foreign matter may be a conductor of current flow between the terminals which can slowly discharge the battery.

BATTERY CABLE REMOVAL

1. On side terminal batteries, loosen the retaining bolts using a ⅜-inch wrench and disconnect the cable from the battery, Fig. 37.
2. On all other type batteries, loosen the cable retaining bolt using a ½-inch or 9/16-inch box wrench, Fig. 38 and lift the cable off the battery posts. Some cables can be removed by squeezing the tabs on the cable terminal using a pair of pliers, Fig. 39, and lifting the cable off the battery posts.

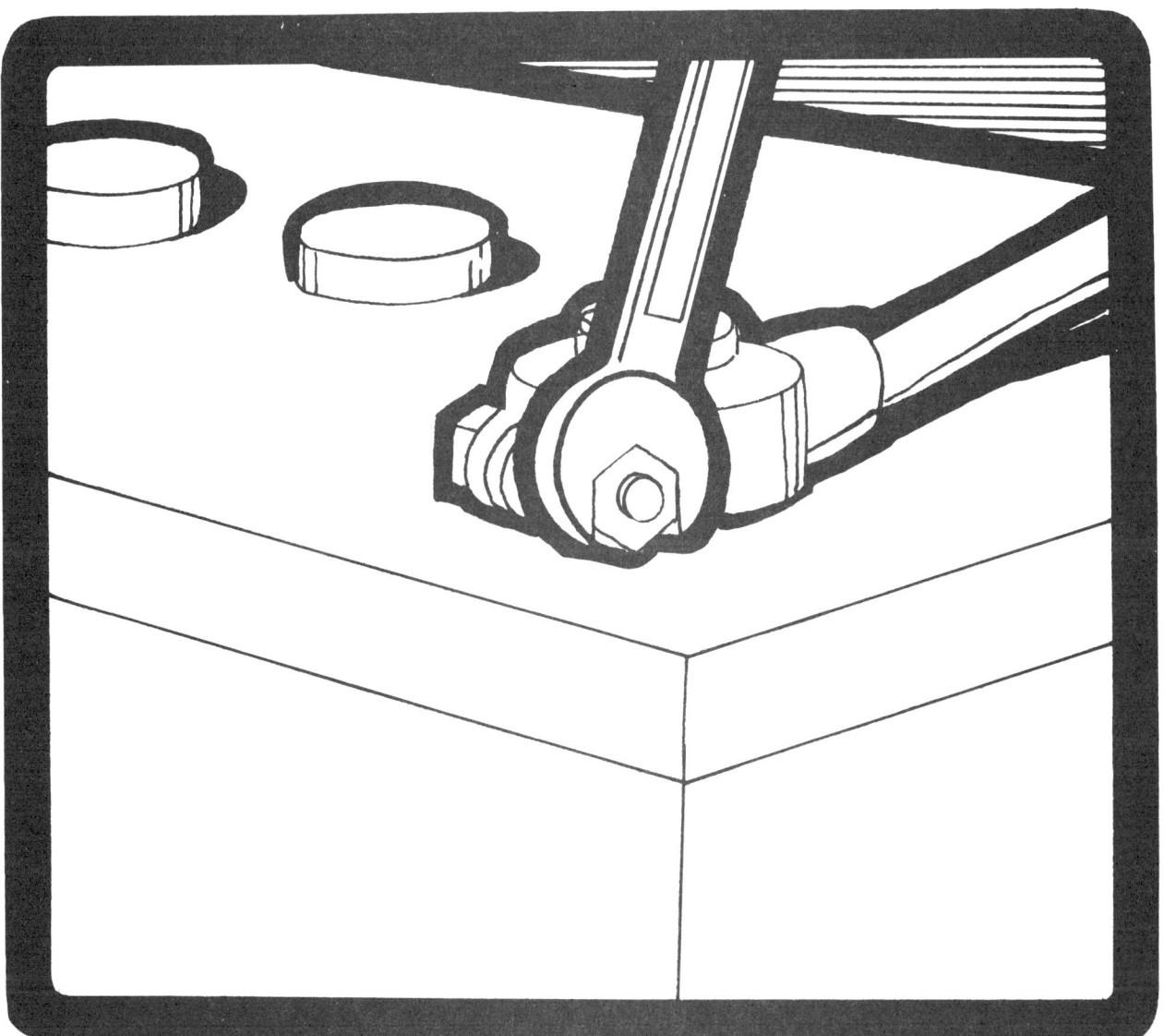

Fig. 38. Loosening top mounted battery cable terminals, which are retained with a bolt and nut.

QUICK TUNEUP TIP

The most efficient method of cleaning a battery surface is to first wash with a dilute ammonia or baking soda solution to neutralize any battery acid that may be present. Then flush off with clean water.

3. If the battery terminals are difficult to remove, use a terminal puller, Fig. 40. Place the legs of the puller underneath the terminal and tighten the puller screw until the terminal is removed.

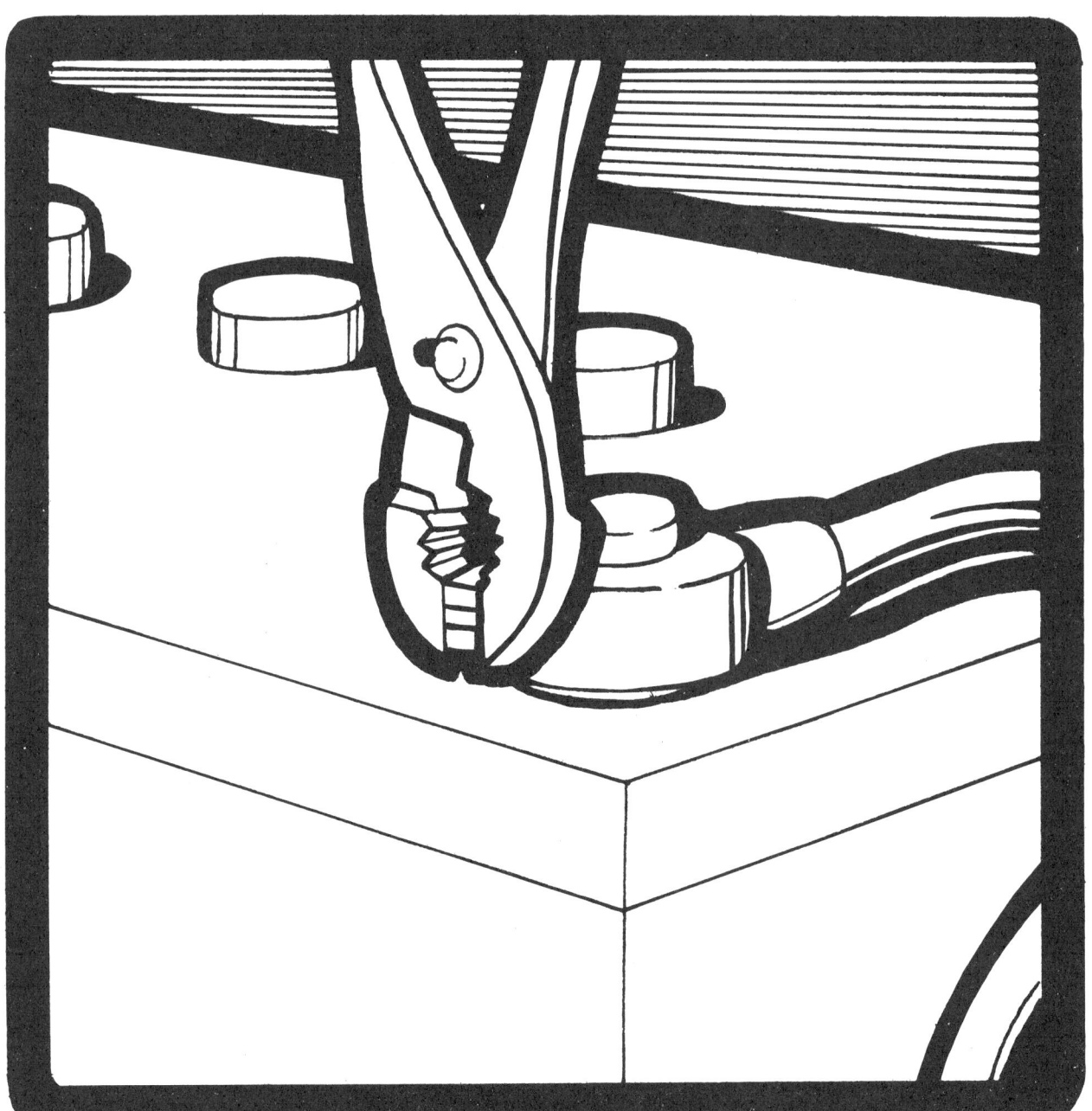

Fig. 39. Spreading top mounted battery terminals.

> **QUICK TUNEUP TIP**
> If the battery has been using a lot of water, look for an incorrect setting for the voltage regulator. Most likely, the regulator setting is too high.

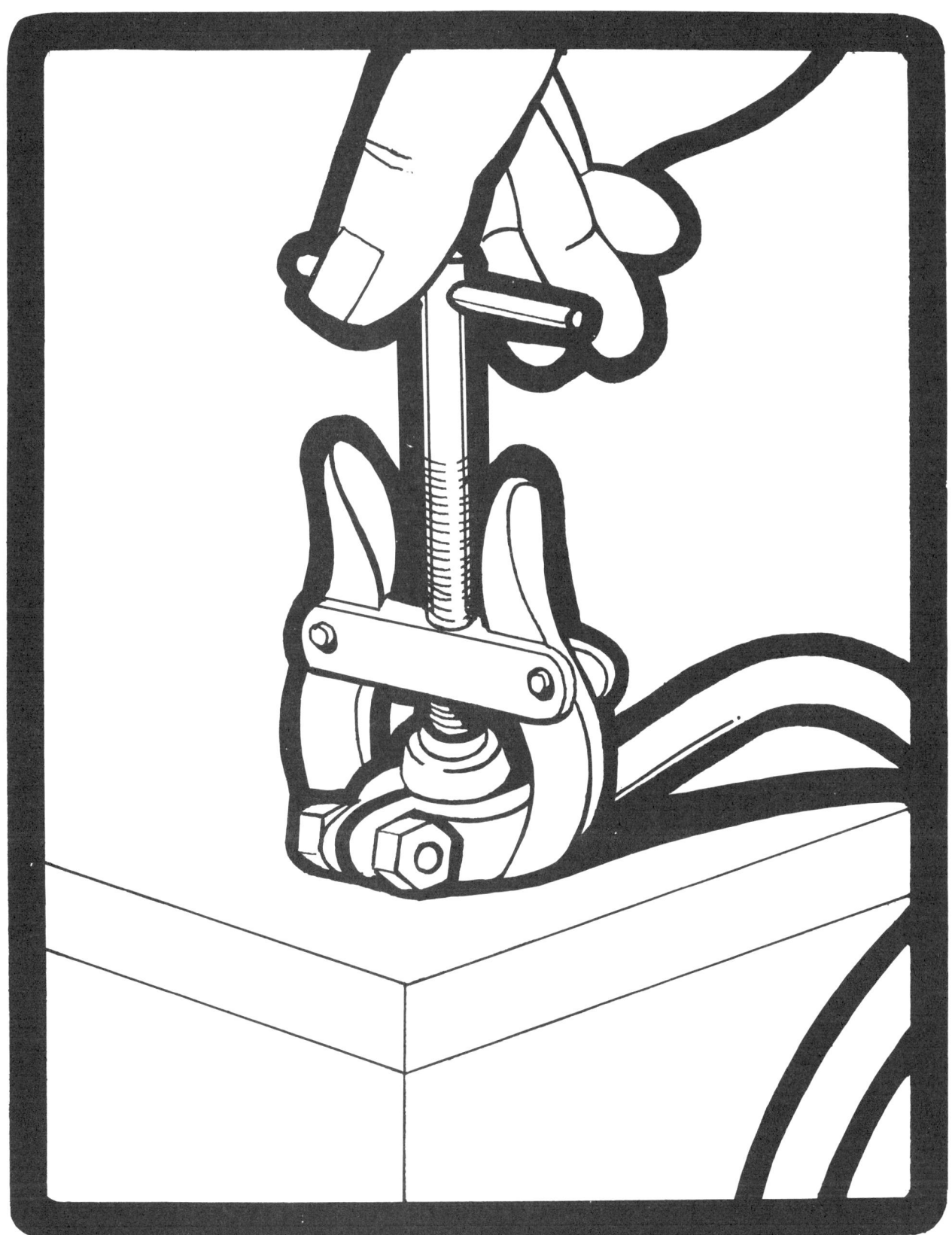

Fig. 40. Removing cable terminal with a battery-cable puller.

QUICK TUNEUP TIP

To insure good contact, you must be positive that the battery cables are tight on the battery post. If the posts or cable terminals are corroded, clean and wire brush them before installation.

4. Clean the cable terminals and battery posts using a terminal and post wire brush, Fig. 41.
5. Clean the battery top using a solution of soda and water. Make sure that the battery is thoroughly cleaned and dried. Make sure that you cover the battery caps to avoid entry of the soda and water solution into the battery.
6. Before installing the cables, apply a coat of petroleum jelly to the inside of the terminal and on the battery post to avoid corrosion.
7. To install the cables on a side terminal battery, place the cables onto the battery and tighten the retaining screws using a ⅜-inch wrench.
8. To install the cables on all other types of batteries, place the cables on the battery post and force them all the way down. If the cable is not completely bottomed, place a suitable size socket over the terminal, Fig. 42, and gently tap the socket using a hammer until the terminal is properly positioned.
9. Tighten the terminal bolts using a ½-inch or 9/16-inch box wrench.
10. Coat the outside of the terminals with petroleum jelly to prevent corrosion.

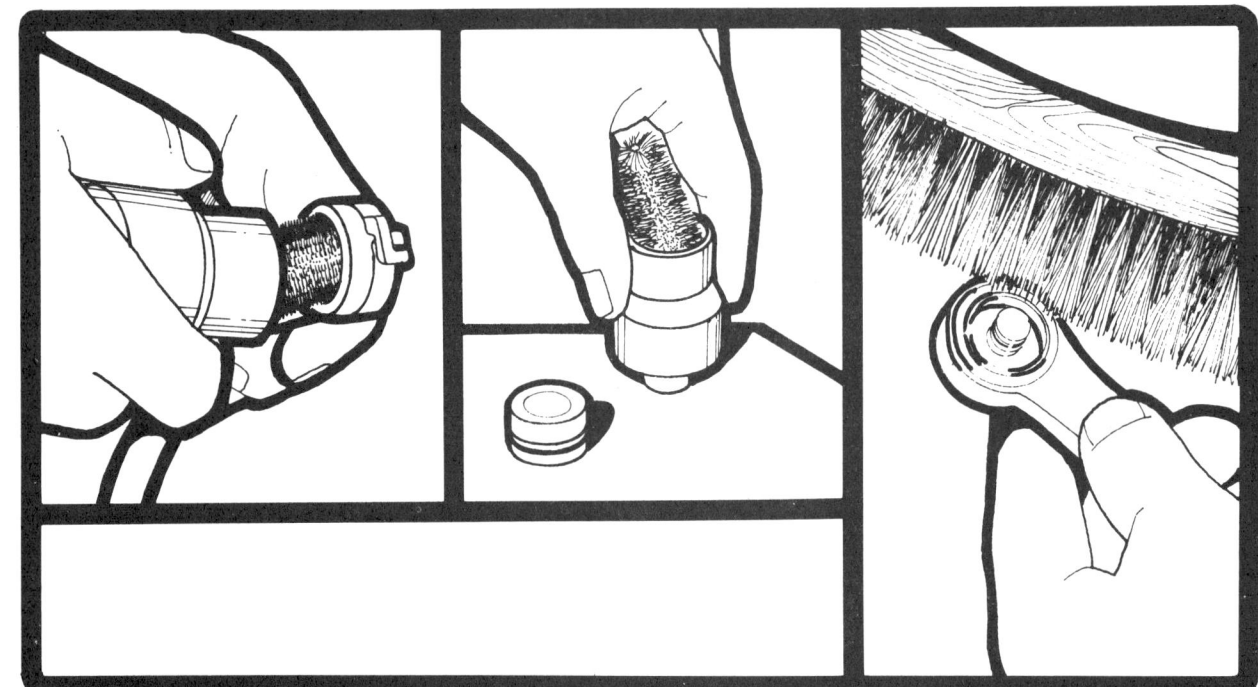

Fig. 41. Cleaning the battery posts and cable terminals.

QUICK TUNEUP TIP
When cleaning your battery's surface, take care to keep the vent plugs tight. This will keep the neutralizing cleaning solution from entering the battery cell.

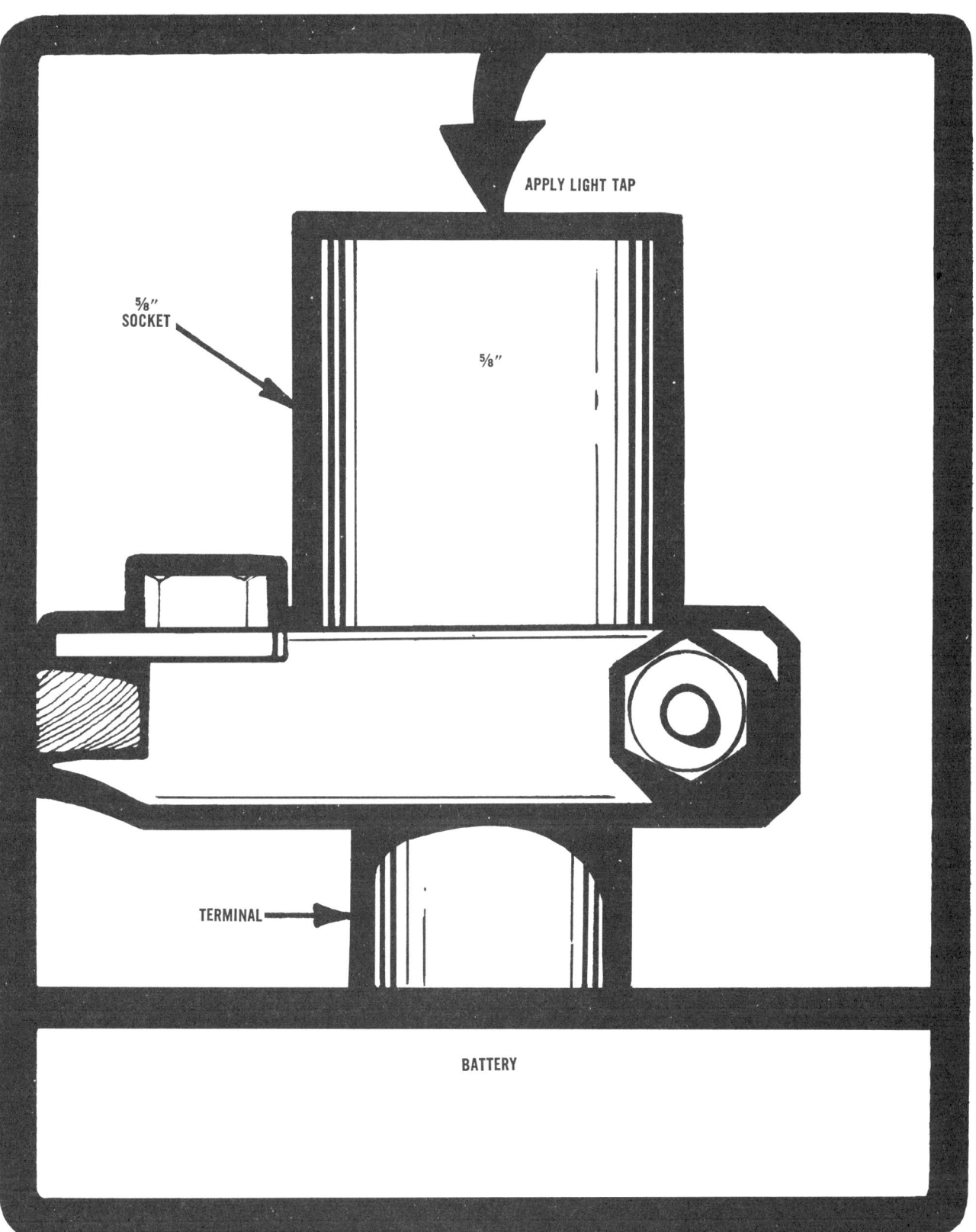

Fig. 42. Installing cable terminal.

QUICK TUNEUP TIP

When testing a battery with a hydrometer, if the electrolyte level is too low to check, first add water to the proper level. Then give the battery a high rate charge for at least 15 minutes to insure that the added water is thoroughly mixed with the electrolyte. A hydrometer test may now be made.

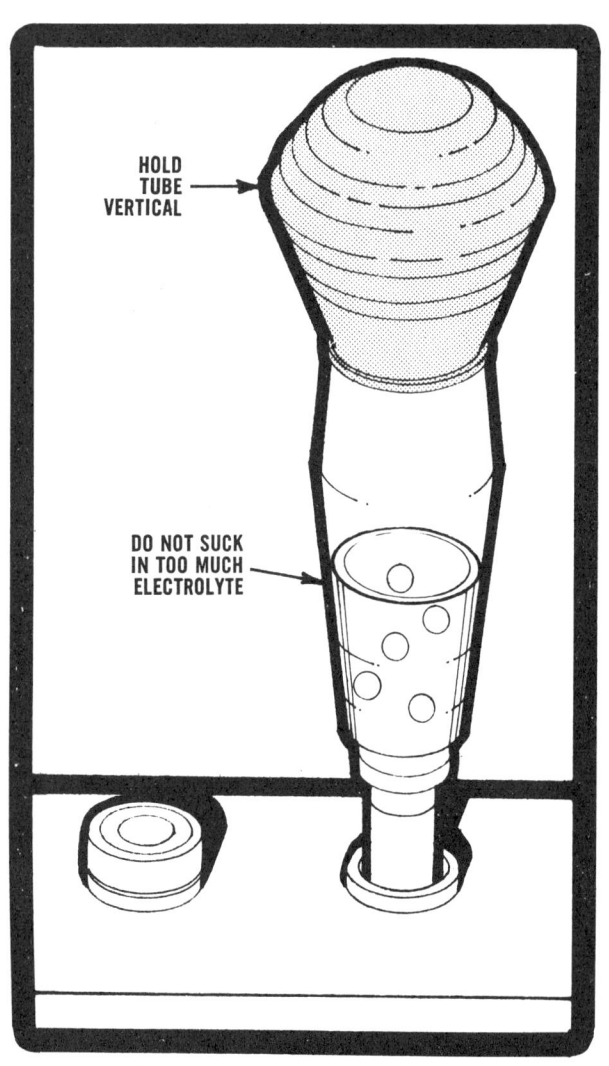

Fig. 43. Hydrometer comparison test.

Hydrometer test

If the battery has not been performing well, perform the specific gravity cell comparison test by taking and recording the hydrometer reading of each cell (Fig. 43). Interpret the results as follows:

If specific gravity readings show a difference between the highest and lowest cell of .050 (50 points) or more, the battery is defective and should be replaced. If specific gravity readings show a difference between the highest and lowest cell of less than .050 (50 points), the battery is good and should be left in service.

Posts, cable clamps and the top should be cleaned, water should be added and the battery recharged if required.

NOTE: If the electrolyte level is too low to check by means of the hydrometer, add water to the proper level. After the addition of water, the specific gravity check cannot be made until the battery is charged at a rate high enough to cause vigorous gassing for a period of fifteen minutes or more. This insures that added water is thoroughly mixed with the electrolyte before a specific gravity reading is taken.

JOB 11. REPLACE THE FUEL FILTER

Internal type

The internal type fuel filter which is made of sintered bronze or pleated paper is located in the float bowl of the carburetor at the fuel inlet, Fig. 44. This is on most vehicles equipped with Rochester carburetors or some Holley carburetors and in the fuel pump on Cadillac models, Fig. 45. To replace these filters, proceed as follows:

1. Using a line wrench, Fig. 46, on the fuel inlet fitting (usually ½-inch or 9/16-inch) and an open end wrench (usually 1-inch) on the inlet fitting nut, Fig. 46, remove the fuel inlet fitting. First, place a rag around the fuel inlet fitting, then loosen the fitting about one turn and allow the fuel pressure to bleed down.
2. Using a suitable size wrench (usually 1-inch) remove the fuel inlet fitting nut and fuel filter. Notice the direction in which the filter is pointing and the arrangement of the spring and washer. If the spring was removed, be sure that you install it first and then the filter.

Fig. 44. Removing or installing fuel filter located at the fuel inlet fitting.

QUICK TUNEUP TIP

A clogged fuel filter may result in symptoms similar to those of a defective carburetor. If your car is acting as if it has a bad carburetor, be sure to first check the fuel filter for signs of clogging.

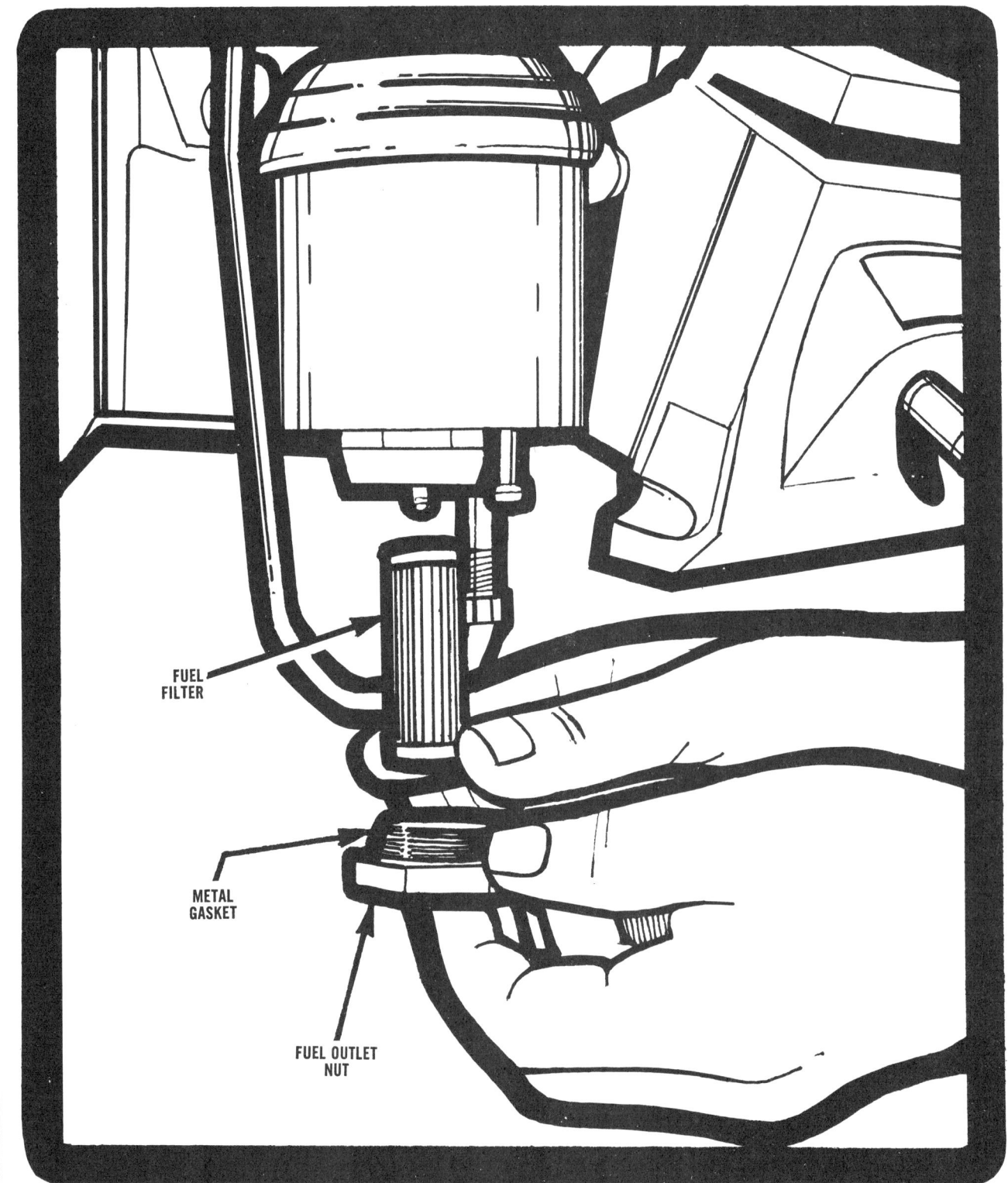

Fig. 45. Removing or installing fuel filter mounted in the fuel pump.

3. Install the fuel filter. If you are installing a pleated paper type filter, make sure that the opening on the end of the filter is facing toward the fuel line and away from the carburetor. If you are installing a sintered bronze type, make sure that the end with the larger opening is facing toward the fuel line and away from the carburetor.
4. Place the washer on the inside of the fitting nut and screw the fitting nut into the carburetor. Tighten the fitting nut securely using a suitable size wrench (usually 1-inch). Do not overtighten, as the threads can be easily stripped.
5. Screw the fuel inlet fitting into the fitting nut. Tighten the fitting securely using a suitable size line wrench (usually ½-inch or 9/16-inch).
6. Start the engine and check for leaks at the fittings. If leaks are evident at the fitting nut, loosen the fuel inlet fittings as in step 1 and tighten the fitting nut an additional ⅛-turn and tighten the fuel inlet fitting.

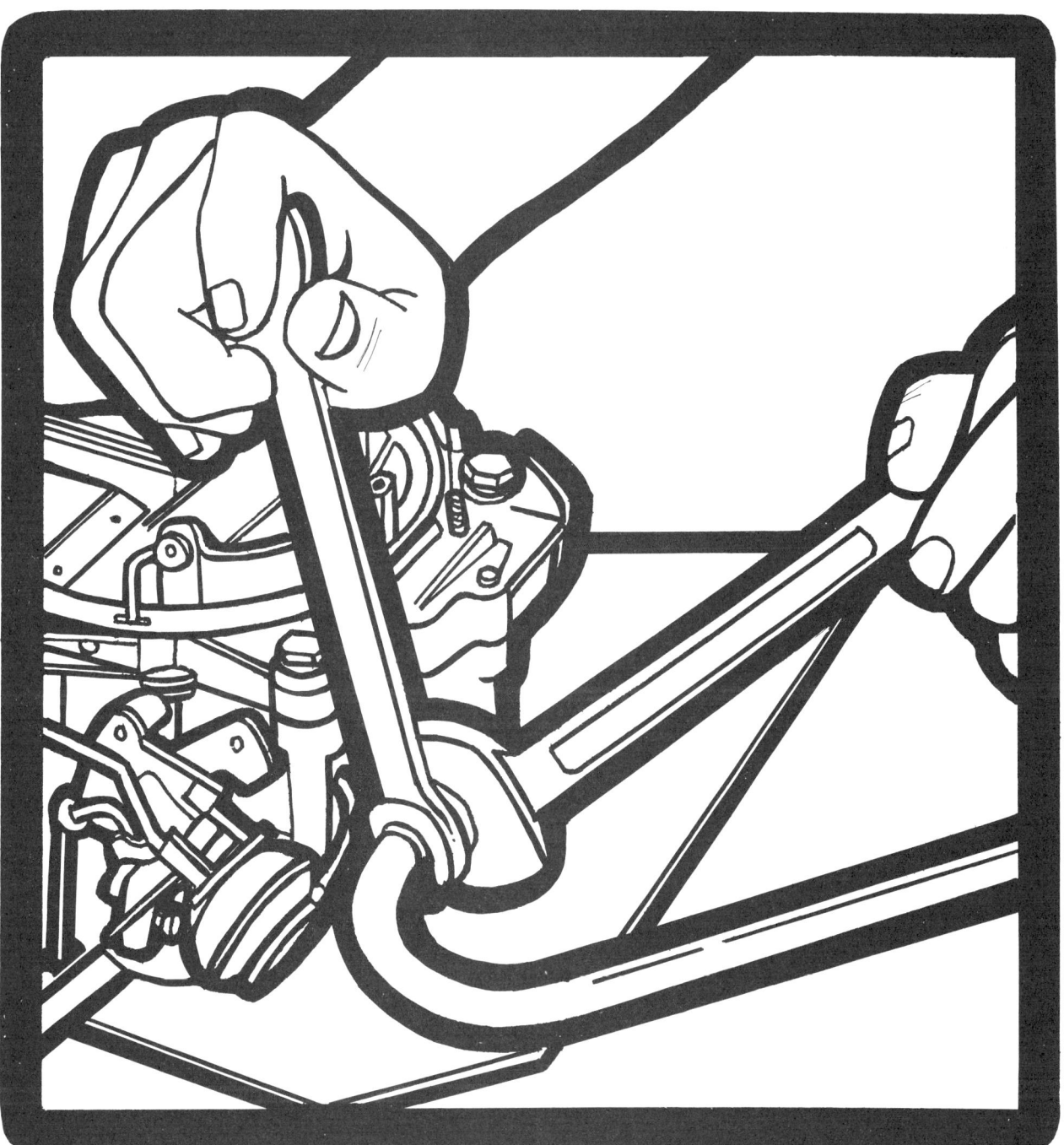

Fig. 46. Disconnecting the fuel inlet fitting from the carburetor.

External type

There are two types of external filters. The first as used on Chrysler vehicles is in-line, located between the carburetor and fuel filter, Fig. 47. The second as used on most Ford vehicles has one end screwed into the carburetor float bowl and the other end is attached to the fuel line. To replace these filters, proceed as follows:

1. There are two types of clamps used to secure the filter onto the fuel line. A flat metal type and a round wire type. To remove the flat metal type, cut it with a pair of side cutters. To remove the round wire type, use a pair of pliers then squeeze the ends together and slide the clamp over the rubber hose and onto the fuel line.
2. Remove the fuel filter by twisting the hose off one end of the fuel line and then the other. On Ford vehicles, disconnect one end of the hose off the fuel filter and unscrew the other end of the fuel filter off the carburetor.

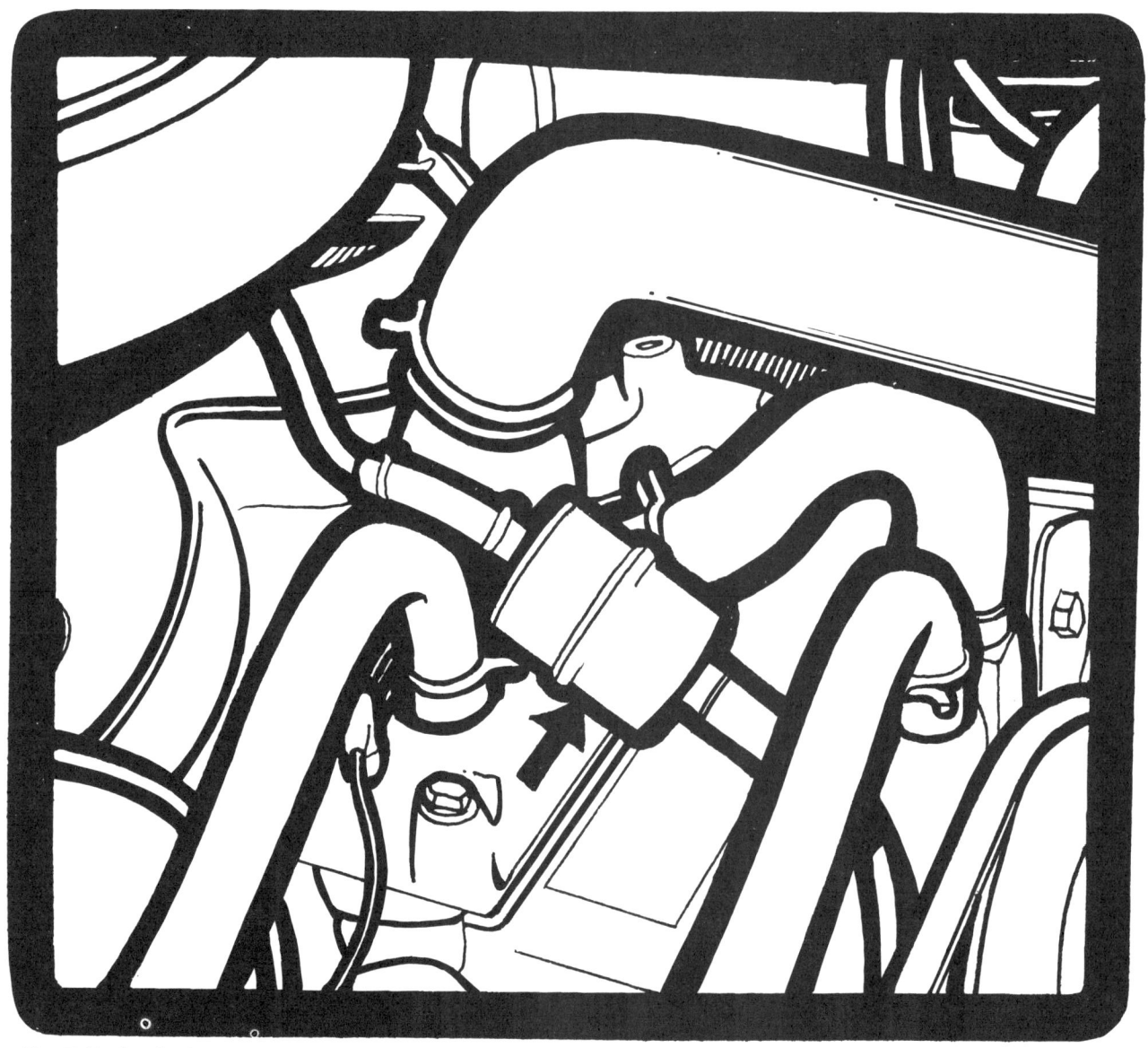

Fig. 47. Typical in-line fuel filter installation.

QUICK TUNEUP TIP

After installing a new fuel filter, start the engine and check for fuel leaks. Needless to say, leaking gasoline can be extremely dangerous.

3. Remove the old wire type clamps off the fuel lines.
4. Install the hoses supplied with the fuel filter onto the new filter and install the clamps to retain the hoses. Spread the clamps with a pair of pliers and slide the clamps over the hoses until the clamps are over the fuel filter fittings, Fig. 48.
5. Install the fuel filter. Position one clamp onto each end of the fuel line. The fuel filter is marked with an arrow, make sure that this arrow is pointing towards the carburetor and away from the fuel pump. Slip one end of the fuel filter hose over the fuel line and then the other. Using a pair of pliers, squeeze the ends of the clamp together and slide the clamp over the rubber hose. Repeat this on the other clamp.
6. On Ford models, screw the threaded end of the fuel filter into the carburetor and connect the rubber hose to the filter using the same procedure as in step 5.
7. Start the engine and check for fuel leaks. If leaks are evident, slide the clamps off the rubber hoses, push the fuel lines further into the hoses and reinstall the clamps.

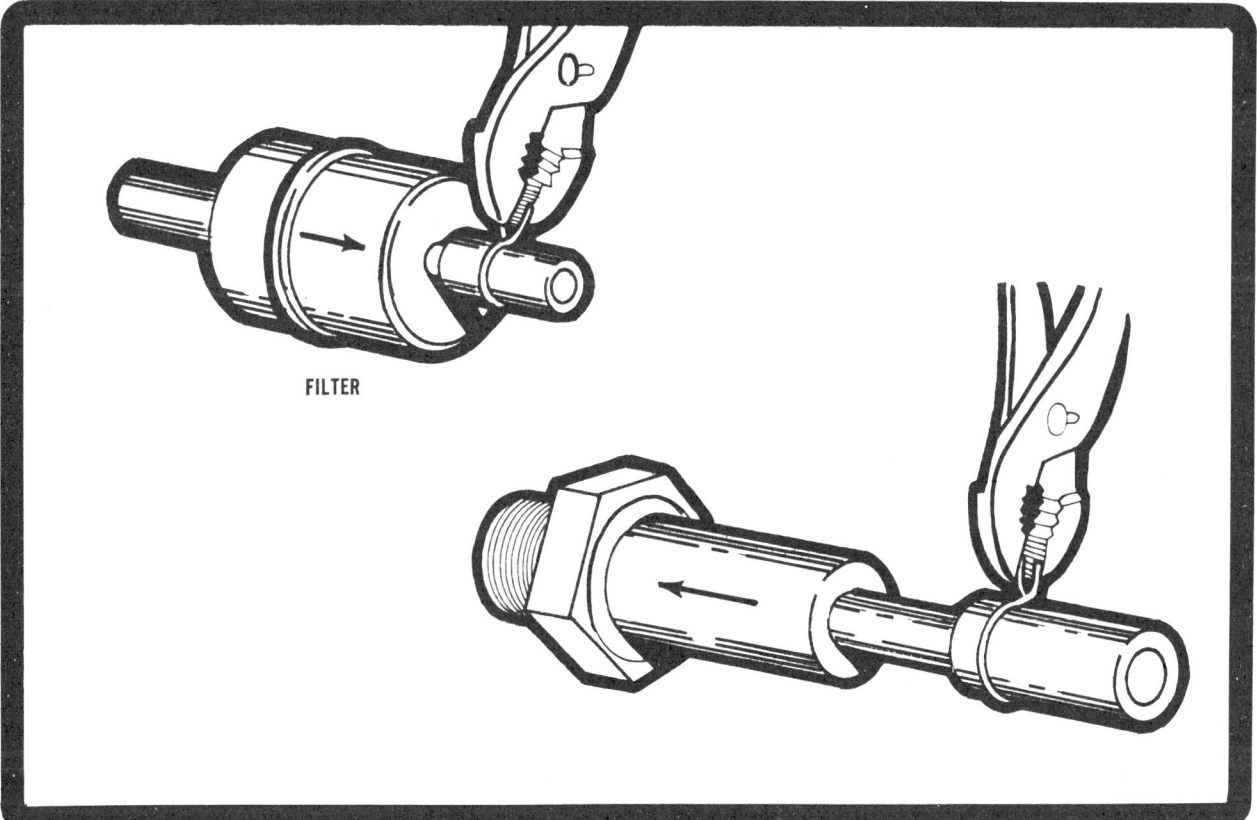

Fig. 48. Positioning the clamps onto the fuel filter hoses.

JOB 12. REPLACE THE PCV VALVE AND CRANKCASE VENTILATION FILTER

PCV VALVE SERVICE

The PCV valve is located in the valve cover on most engines, Fig. 49. A hose, usually ⅜-inch inside diameter, is attached to the PCV valve and is routed to the base of the carburetor. The crankcase ventilation filter is located in the air cleaner housing on General Motors vehicles, Fig. 50. On all other vehicles, the crankcase ventilation filter is on the valve cover, Fig. 51. To replace the PCV valve, proceed as follows:

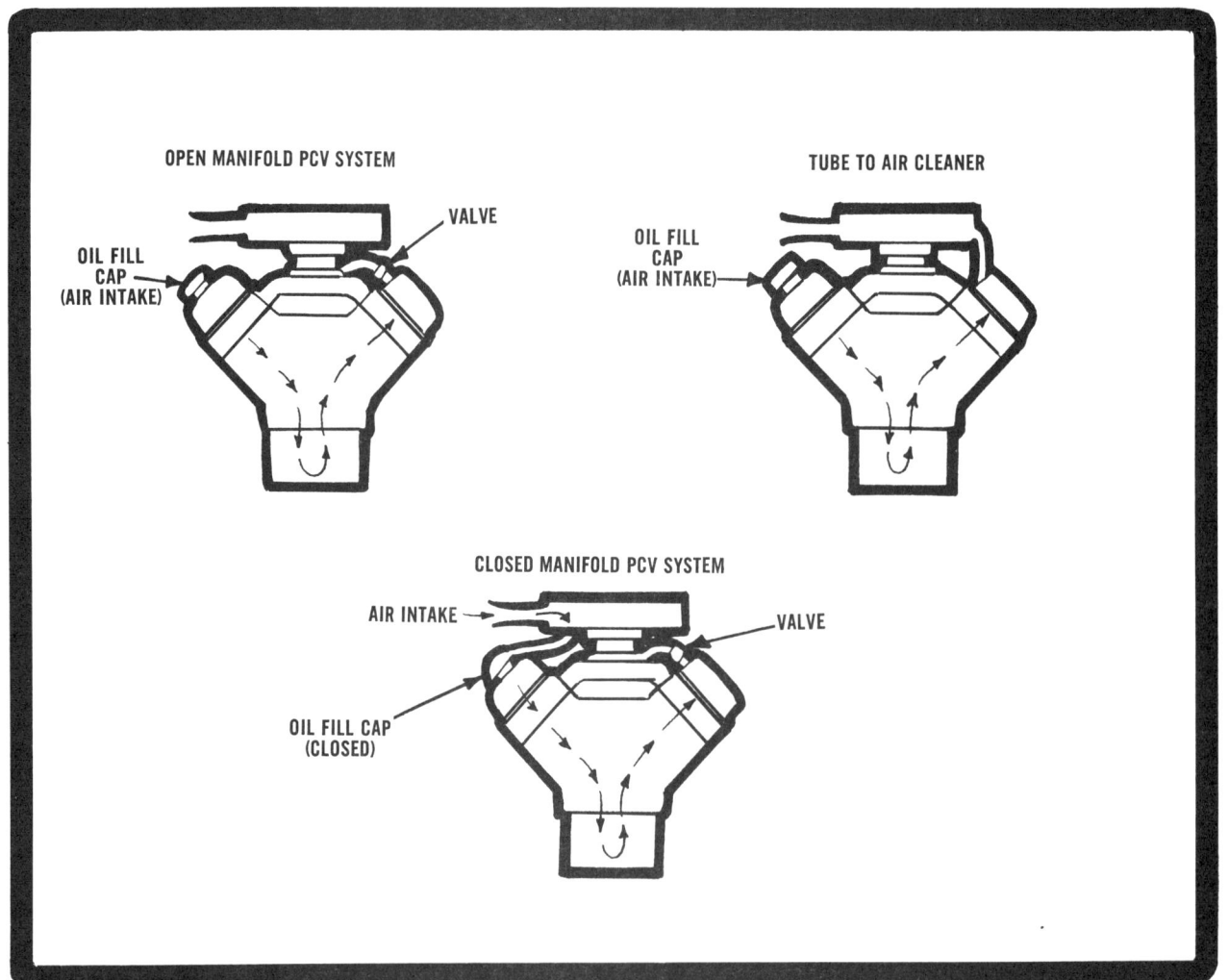

Fig. 49. Typical PCV valve installation.

QUICK TUNEUP TIP

Clogged crankcase ventilation filter can seriously impair engine performance. It is one of the most overlooked items in an engine tuneup. The symptoms of a clogged filter are often wrongly diagnosed as other major engine problems.

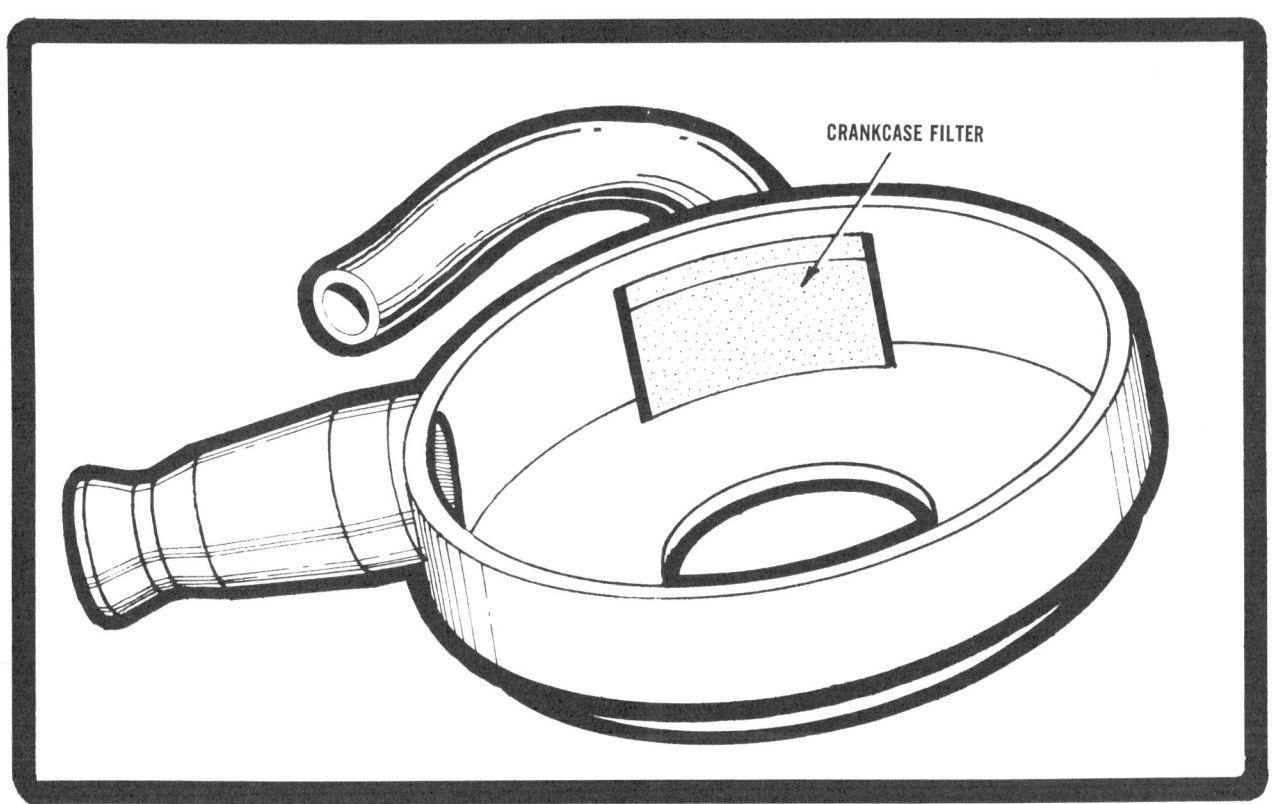

Fig. 50. Crankcase ventilation filter on General Motors vehicles.

QUICK TUNEUP TIP

It is not always necessary to replace a PCV valve. After removing the valve, shake it. If it rattles, it is working properly and can be reused. If it does not make a sound, it is clogged and needs replacement.

CRANKCASE VENTILATION FILTER REPLACEMENT

General Motors cars
1. Remove the wing nut from the air cleaner housing.
2. Remove the air cleaner housing top.
3. Disconnect the hose from the filter by pulling it off.
4. Slide the retaining clip off the filter by pushing it with a flat screwdriver, Fig. 50.
5. Remove the filter from the air cleaner housing.
6. Install the filter into the air cleaner housing.
7. Slide the new retaining clip onto the filter so that it engages the grooves in the filter.
8. Slide the hose onto the filter.
9. Install the air cleaner housing top and tighten the wing nut securely.

All other cars
1. Disconnect any hose or hoses from the filter. If there are any clamps retaining the hoses, squeeze the ends of the clamps together and slide the clamps over the hose.
2. Remove the filter from the valve cover by turning it counterclockwise one-half turn.
3. Install the new filter onto the valve cover, by aligning the tangs on the filter with the slots in the valve cover and turning the filter clockwise one-half turn.
4. Reconnect the hose or hoses onto the filter.
5. If any clamps were used to retain the hoses, squeeze the ends of the clamps together and slide the clamps onto their original positions.

1. Pull the PCV valve from the valve cover.
2. If there are any clamps retaining the hose, use a pair of pliers and squeeze the ends of the clamp together and slide the clamp over the hose.
3. Pull the PCV valve out of the hose.
4. Slide the smaller end of the new PCV valve into the hose.
5. If any clamps are used, squeeze the ends of the clamp together using a pair of pliers and slide the clamp onto its original location.
6. Install the PCV valve into the valve cover.

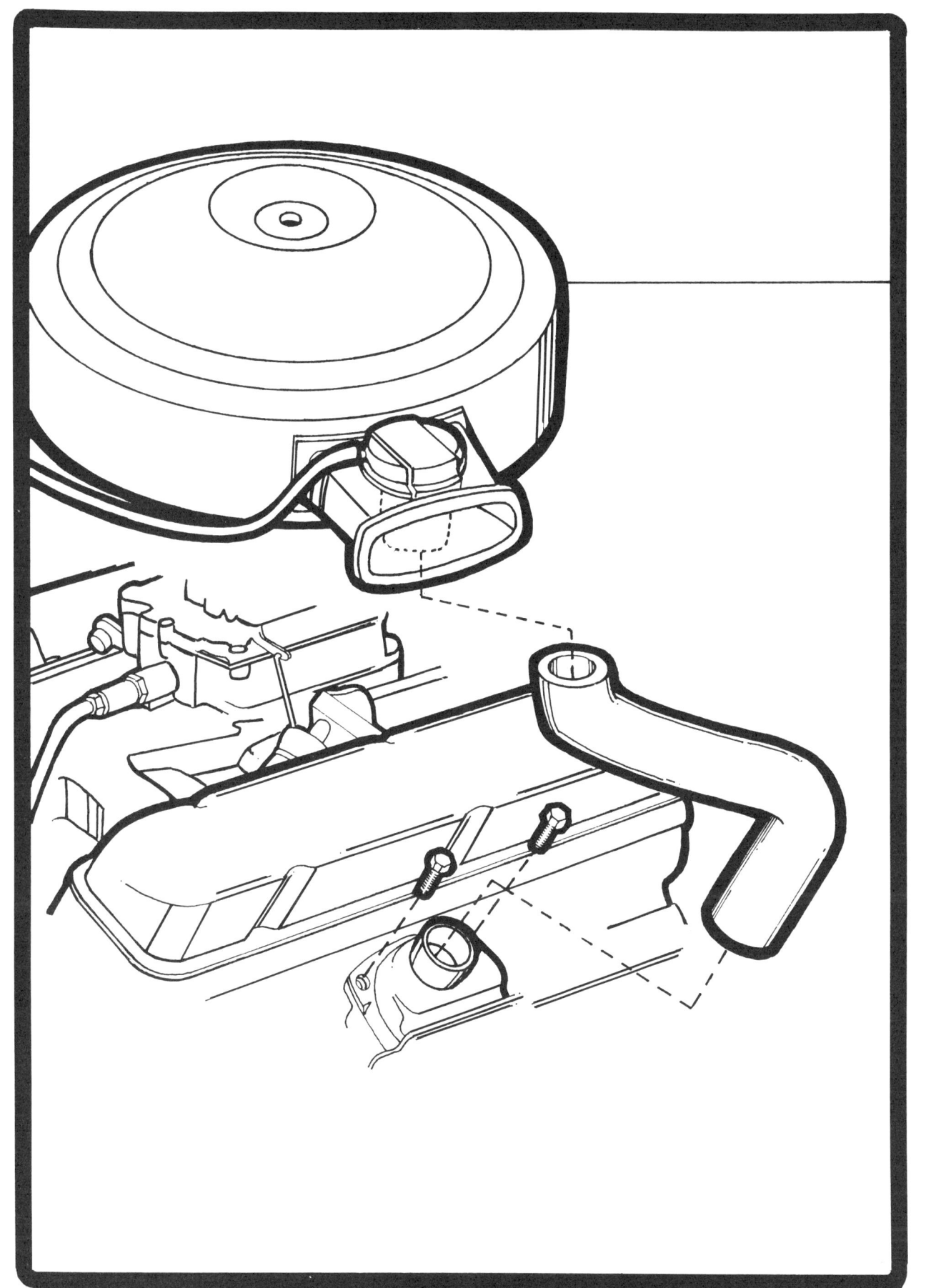
Fig. 51. Typical crankcase ventilation filter installation on all vehicles except General Motors.

JOB 13. SERVICE OR REPLACE THE AIR FILTER

This section will explain how to service the filtering element of the air cleaner. It should be stressed here that a clogged air filter element will greatly affect exhaust emissions as well as power, performance and gasoline economy.

There are basically three different types of air cleaners. They are, Fig. 52:
1. Oil wetted paper element.
2. Polyurethane element.
3. Combination oil wetted paper and polyurethane elements.

Each of these types of air cleaner elements is serviced differently. Service procedures for each type are outlined below.

Cleaning
1. Remove the wing nut from the top of the air cleaner housing.
2. Remove the air cleaner housing cover or the housing itself, as necessary.

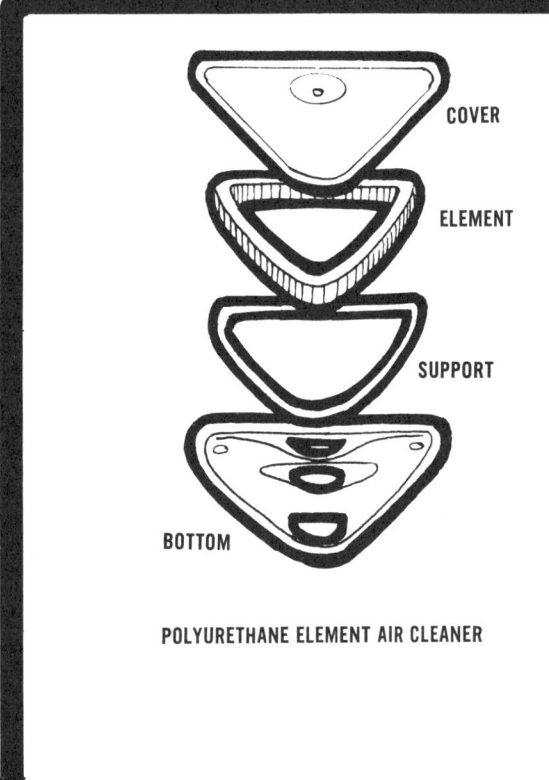
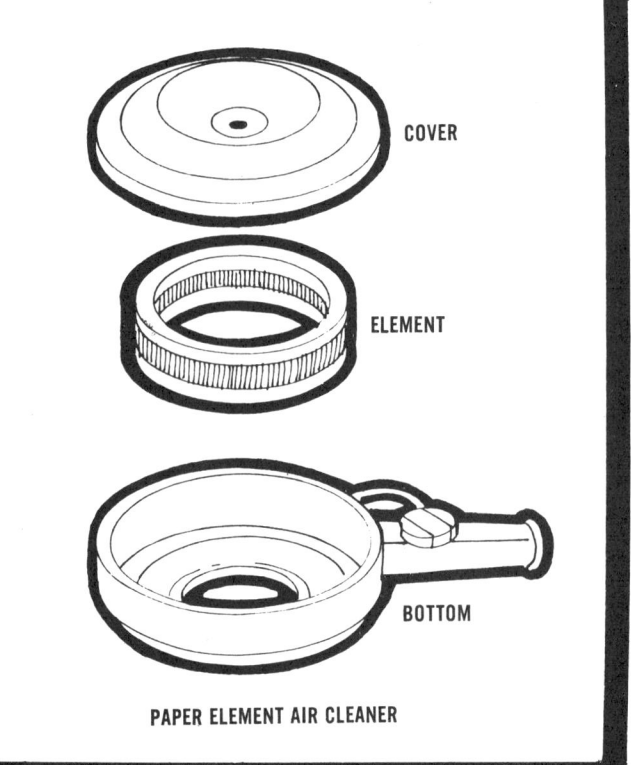

Fig. 52. Two basic types of air filters.

3. Remove air cleaner element.
4. Inspect top and bottom seals for deformation or cracking. These surfaces must be smooth and uniform.
5. Inspect element for punctures or splits by looking through the element towards a light bulb, Fig. 53.

Fig. 53. Inspecting the air cleaner element using an inspection light.

6. Tap element on smooth flat surface to dislodge dirt particles, being careful not to damage elements, Fig. 54.
7. Internal portions of the air cleaner cover and bottom should be cleaned. If washed with solvent, surfaces should be dried thoroughly.

   NOTE: Do not submerge bottom section of thermostatic air cleaners in solvent.
8. On units incorporating an antibackfire screen, clean the screen in kerosene or another suitable solvent.

At approximately 24,000-mile intervals, replace the element. It should also be mentioned here that the PCV breather filter, on units so equipped, should be replaced at this time.

Polyurethane element

The polyurethane element should be inspected, cleaned and reoiled approximately every 12,000 miles or more often depending upon the severity of operating conditions. To properly service the element, perform the following:

1. Remove cover wing nut, cover and filter element.
2. Visibly check the element for tears or rips and replace if necessary.
3. Clean all accumulated dirt and grime from the

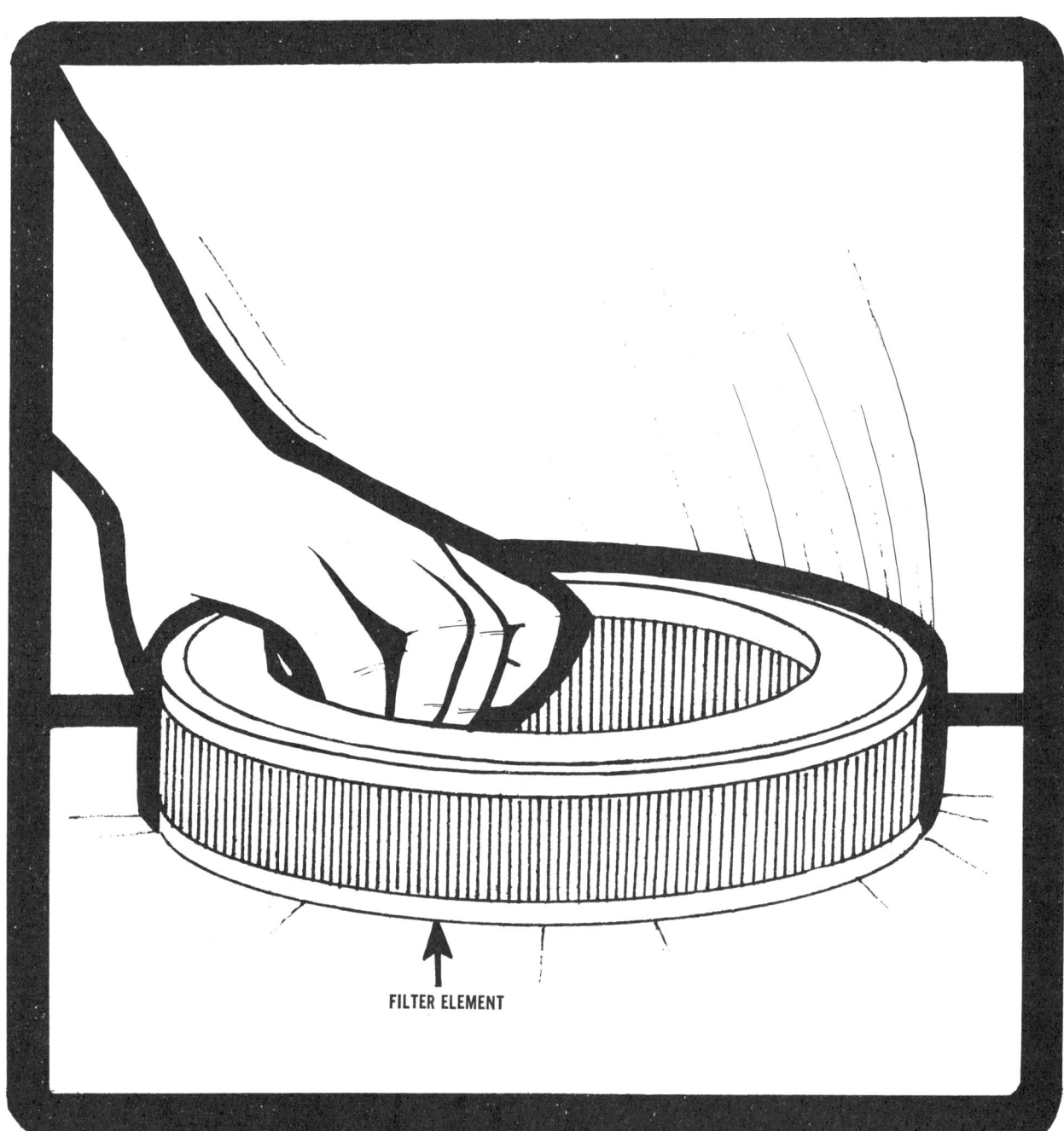

Fig. 54. Dislodging any dirt particles from the air cleaner element.

air cleaner bottom and cover. Discard the air-horn-to-air-cleaner gasket.
4. Remove the support screen from the element and wash the element in kerosene or mineral spirits, then squeeze out excess solvent (Fig. 55).

   NOTE: Never use a hot degreaser or any solvent containing acetone or a similar compound.

5. Dip element into light engine oil and squeeze out excess oil.

   NOTE: Never shake, swing or wring the element to remove excess oil or solvent as this may tear the polyurethane material. Instead, squeeze the excess from the element.

6. Install element on screen support.
7. Using a new gasket, replace air cleaner body over carburetor air horn.
8. Place the element in the air cleaner. Care must be taken that the lower lip of the element is properly placed in the assembly and that the filter material is not folded or creased in any manner that would cause an imperfect seal. Take the same precautions when replacing the cover so that the upper lip of the element is in proper position.
9. On units so equipped, remove and clean the flame arrestor with kerosene or another suitable solvent.
10. Replace the cover and wing nut.

Fig. 55. Cleaning polyurethane element.

> **QUICK TUNEUP TIP**
>
> When removing the air filter holddown wing nut, take care not to strip the threads on the threaded mounting post. If the post is stripped, the nut will not hold down the air filter tightly and the engine will not be running at maximum efficiency.

JOB 14. SERVICE OR REPLACE THE MANIFOLD HEAT CONTROL VALVE

Check the manifold heat control valve (Fig. 56) for freedom of operation. To free up the valve, tap the control valve shaft back and forth with a small hammer and rotate the counterweight back and forth until the valve is free. To prevent recurrence of the problem, apply a good quality manifold heat control solvent to both ends of shaft.

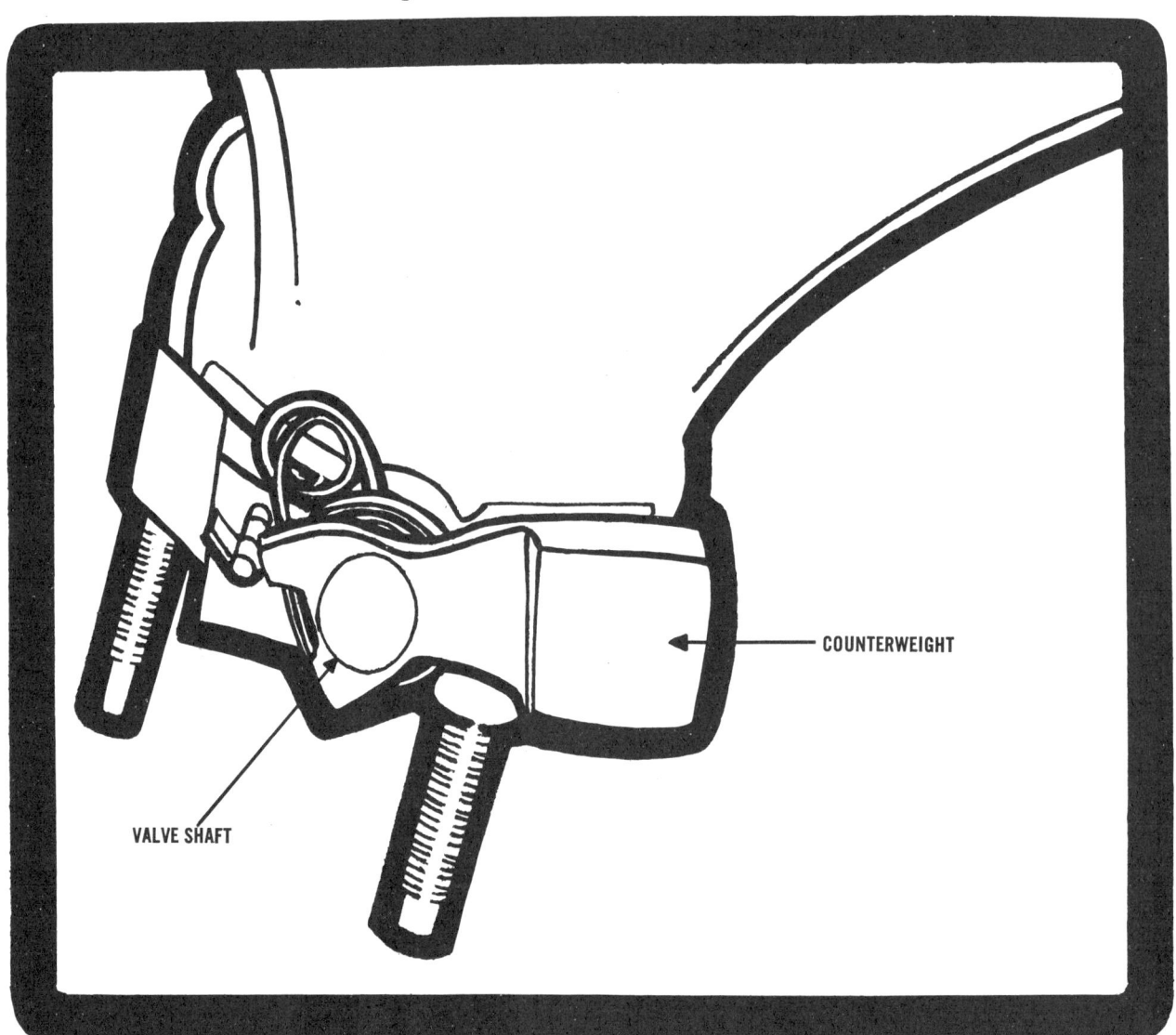

Fig. 56. Typical heat riser valve.

> **QUICK TUNEUP TIP**
>
> A quick way to free up a manifold heat control valve is to tap the valve shaft back and forth with a small hammer. Then rotate the counterweight back and forth until the valve is free.

JOB 15. SERVICE THE CARBURETOR, CHOKE AND LINKAGES

Outlined below are basic carburetor checks that should be included in every tuneup. They are quick visual inspections of external components (linkage, choke, idle vent, unloader and vacuum break) that can greatly affect proper vehicle operation, especially during starting. Adjustment of the fast idle, slow idle and idle fuel mixture are not covered here, but will be covered under *Instrument Checkouts*.

CLEANING THE CARBURETOR

CAUTION: 1975 and 1976 vehicles are equipped with catalytic converters in the exhaust system. No carburetor cleaner is to be used internally on these vehicles. Such cleaners will render the catalytic converter inoperative.

Clean the exterior of the carburetor and inside the barrels using a spray type carburetor cleaner. Spray the barrels while the engine is running and hold the throttle slightly open to prevent the engine from stalling. Spray the exterior of the carburetor and linkages and allow the cleaner to soak for a few minutes. Spray again to wash off the deposits. Wipe the carburetor off using a clean cloth.

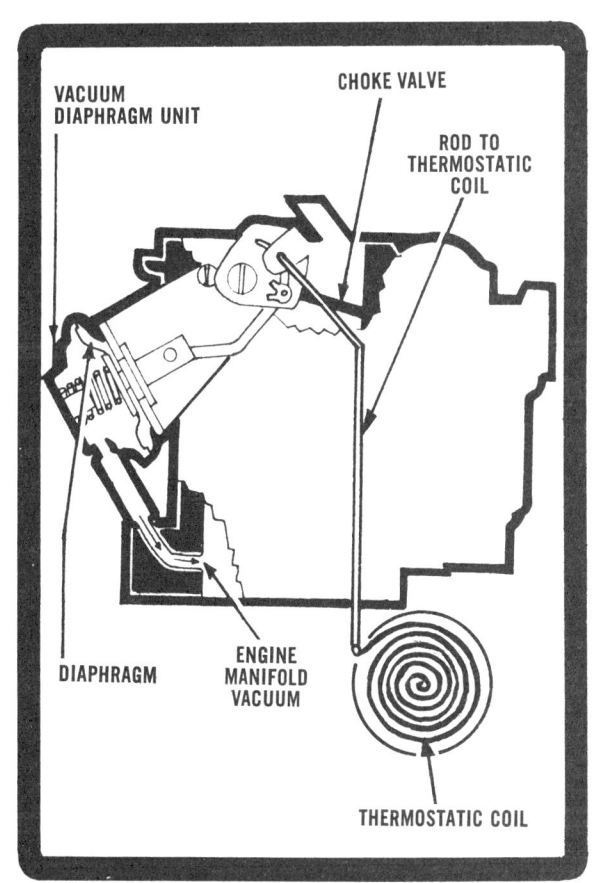

Fig. 57. Adjusting well type choke.

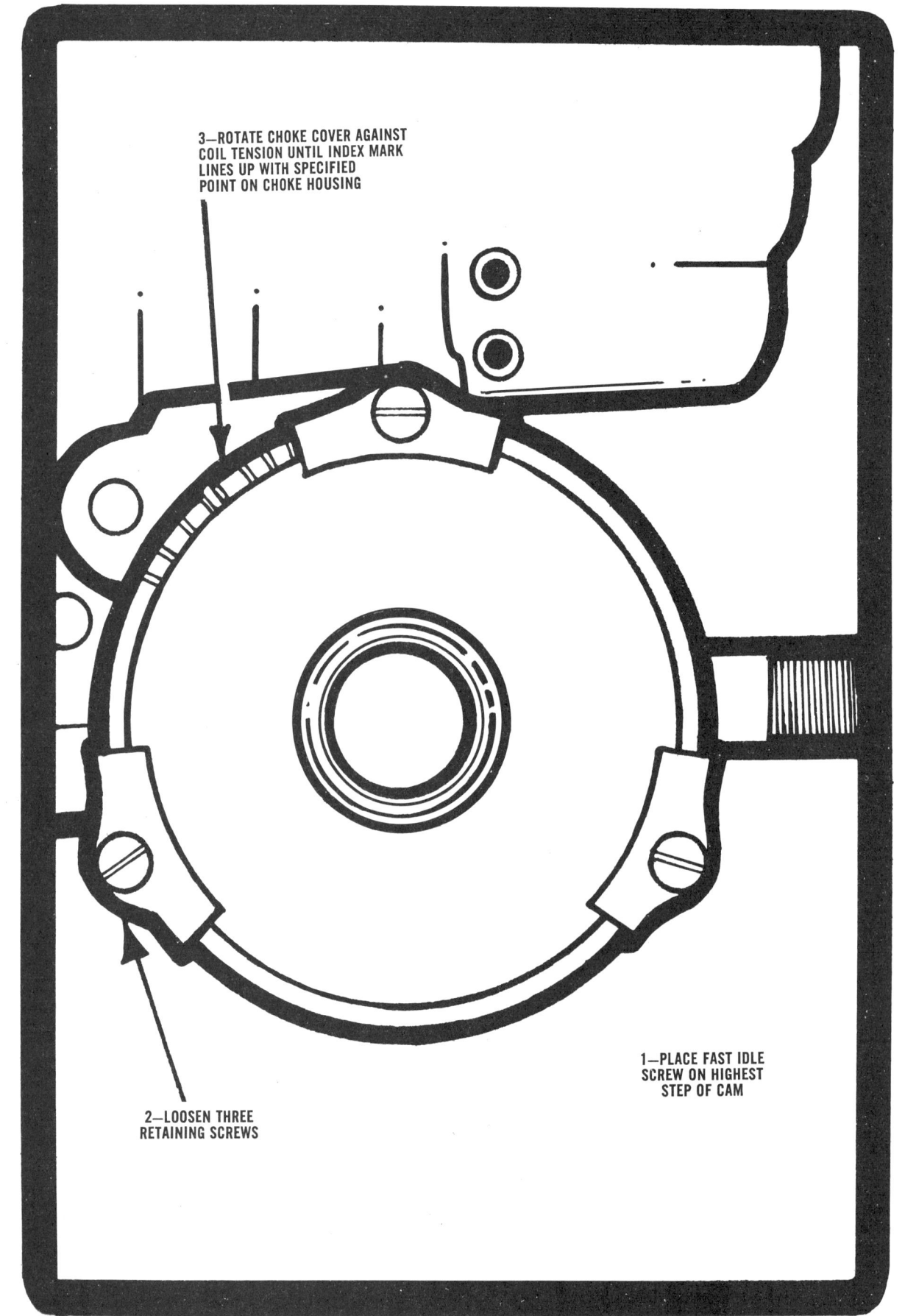

Fig. 58. Adjusting carburetor mounted type choke.

QUICK TUNEUP TIP

Proper choke operation is extremely important for proper engine performance. The choke helps your engine start when it is cold. But if it sticks open, it can make the engine run roughly and sluggishly.

LINKAGE

Carburetor linkage should be checked for looseness, bends, binds, kinks (cable linkage), etc. The linkage should be manually opened and closed to determine if WOT (wide open throttle) can be obtained and if the linkage and the spring will allow the throttle lever to freely return to idle position.

WELL TYPE CHOKE ADJUSTMENT

Proper choke operation greatly affects vehicle operation and exhaust emission content. The choke should be checked as follows:

With automatic choke

1. Remove air cleaner and check to see that choke valve and rod move freely.
2. Check choke adjustment as follows:
   Hold choke valve closed and push rod downward to contact stop. The top of rod should be even with bottom of hole in choke lever.
3. If necessary, adjust rod length by bending rod at offset bend, Fig. 56. Bend must be such that rod enters choke lever hole freely and squarely.
4. Connect rod at choke lever and install air cleaner.

Carburetor mounted type choke, Fig. 57

Loosen the three retaining screws using a flat screwdriver, then rotate the choke cover against the spring tension until the index mark on the choke cover is aligned with the index mark on the choke housing, Fig. 57. Refer to manufacturers' specifications.

With manual choke

1. Remove air cleaner.
2. Push hand choke knob in to within 1/8 inch of instrument panel.
3. Loosen choke cable clamp at carburetor bracket and adjust cable through the clip until the choke valve is wide open.
4. Tighten cable clamp at carburetor bracket and check operation of choke valve to ensure full closed and wide open positions.
5. Install air cleaner.

QUICK TUNEUP TIP

To properly tune your engine, it is not necessary to have a garage full of elaborate electronic test equipment. However, you should have a tachometer, dwell meter and timing light.

JOB 16. INSTRUMENT CHECKOUT

So far we have only discussed the adjustment and replacement procedures performed with the engine off. Now that the necessary parts have been replaced and related adjustments made, the engine must be started and the job finalized by accurately setting the carburetor and distributor to achieve a smooth running and top performing engine. With the engine running, the primary and secondary resistances, the starter motor circuitry, the ignition and charging circuitry and other related systems and components must be checked out.

This finalizing stage of the tuneup is what separates a mediocre job from a quality tuneup. In order to do a quality job, elaborate equipment is not needed, though more than simply a timing light and feeler gauge are required. In order to properly finalize a quality tuneup, the following equipment is needed:
1. Tachometer.
2. Dwell meter.
3. Timing light.

This equipment is not complicated. It comes in various forms and combinations depending upon the particular manufacturer. The following presentation will treat each of these devices as a separate piece of equipment. Before using any of the above, the particular manufacturer's instructions on its use should be read carefully. The equipment should also be periodically checked for accuracy against known good equipment and all meters should be properly zeroed.

It should also be mentioned here that more sophisticated equipment is available.

Warm up engine

Before proceeding into finalizing the tuneup, the engine must be warmed up to normal operating temperature. Set the parking brake and place the transmission in Neutral, then start the engine and run it until normal operating temperature is reached. This should be approximately 10-15 minutes with a cold engine.

This warmup will insure that proper lubricant viscosity is provided at each component and that each component is at operating temperature and size.

DWELL CHECK WITH DWELL METER

Once the engine is normalized, the next step is to set the point dwell. Although the points are set with a feeler gauge when initially installed, it is necessary to verify this adjustment with a dwell meter. The dwell meter measurement is the duration of time the points are closed. Check the point gap with the dwell meter and make the necessary adjustment as follows:

1. Attach dwell meter leads as shown in Fig. 59.
2. With engine at idle, observe reading. It should be as given in the Tuneup Specifications chart in the Specifications chapter.
3. If the reading is not within specifications, adjust the points to specification.

With the dwell meter still attached, check for dwell variation as follows:

Slowly accelerate engine to 1500 rpm and note dwell reading. Return engine to idle, and note dwell reading. Dwell reading at no time should vary more than 3 degrees. If dwell reading varies more than 3 degrees, check for worn distributor shaft, bushings or breaker plate or loose breaker plate.

QUICK TUNEUP TIP

Your final adjustments will not be accurate unless your engine is fully warmed up to normal operating temperature. The warmup insures that proper lubricant viscosity is provided at each component and that each component is at normal operating size.

IDLE, IDLE FUEL MIXTURE AND TIMING ADJUSTMENT

These three adjustments—idle, idle fuel mixture, and timing—are the most important adjustments made on a vehicle equipped with exhaust emission control equipment. Each adjustment must be made in a definite sequence due to the interdependency of one upon another. These adjustments must be made precisely without variation from factory recommendations. When these adjustments are made correctly (with all other related components within specifications) the exhaust emission level of the particular vehicle will be brought down to a minimum. But just as important, proper vehicle operation and feel will be established. The emission systems used on new vehicles have been developed as systems. Like any other system, they are dependent upon each component functioning as it was designed to for the system. In order for each component to function correctly as part of the system, it must be within specifications. If one component is out of specifications, the operation of the other components will be affected. Consequently, do not try to deviate from the recommended procedures or specifications. A slight deviation of one component will affect the operation of another, and then another, and so on.

Proper adjustment of the idle, idle fuel mixture and timing is deemed so important that the manufacturer has installed a decal in the engine compartment of every vehicle equipped with exhaust emission devices giving exact instructions and specifications for these adjustments, Fig. 60.

As you go through this adjustment procedure, you will note that the setting of the idle fuel mixture is quite exact. The vacuum gauge is no longer used for this adjustment because it lacks sensitivity. A tachometer is used to achieve the proper adjustment because of its ability to sense slight amounts of

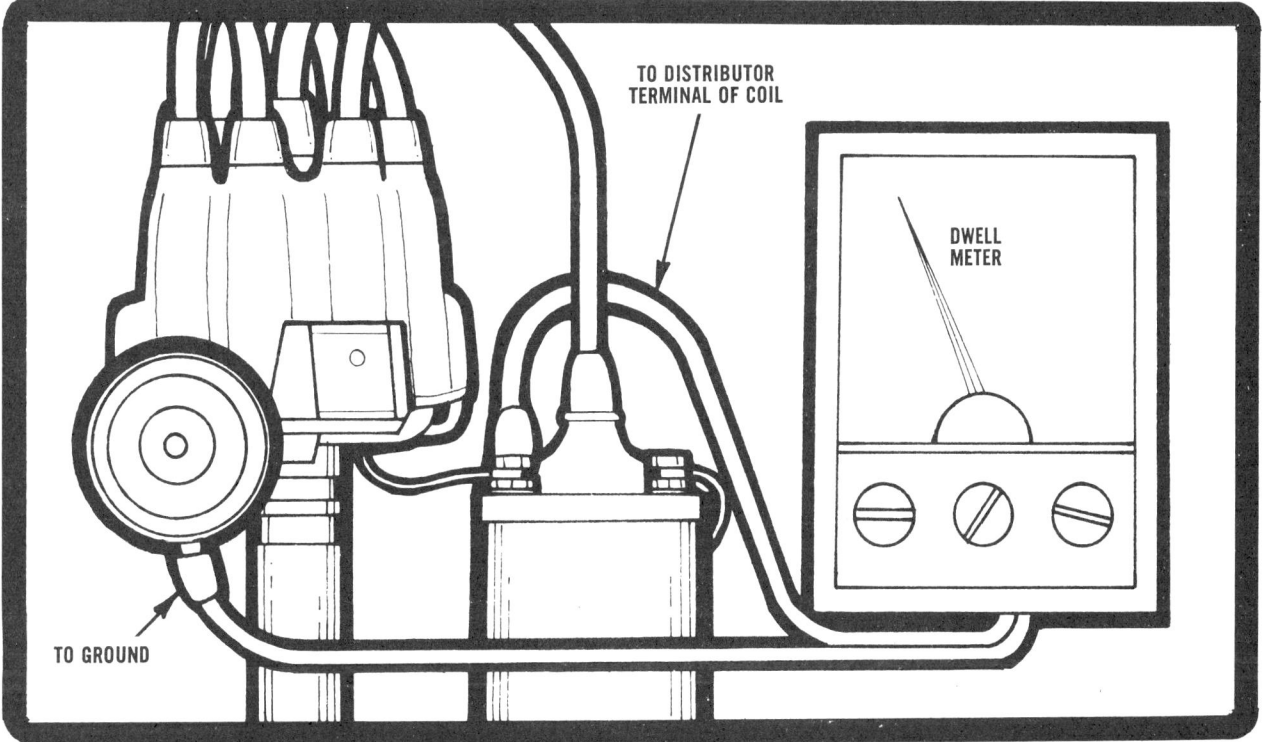

Fig. 59. Checking the engine dwell.

VEHICLE EMISSION CONTROL INFORMATION

ENGINE FAMILY	302 CATALYST EGR AIR (2CMF)		
ENGINE DISPLACEMENT CID	302 CID		
SPARK PLUG	ARF 42 GAP .042 .046		
DISTRIBUTOR BREAKERLESS			
CHOKE HOUSING	MAN TRANS		
NOTCH SETTING	AUTO TRANS	3 RICH	
TRANSMISSION	AUTO NEUTRAL	AUTO DRIVE	MANUAL NEUTRAL
IGNITION TIMING	8°BTDC		
TIMING RPM	500		
CURB IDLE RPM A/C		700	
CURB IDLE RPM NO A/C		700	
IDLE MIXTURE ARTIFICIAL ENRICHMENT			
RPM GAIN		15 80	
RPM RESET		15 70	
THIS VEHICLE REQUIRES MAINTENANCE SCHEDULE "B"			

MAKE ALL ADJUSTMENTS WITH ENGINE AT NORMAL OPERATING TEMPERATURES, A/C AND HEADLIGHTS OFF.

CURB IDLE ADJUST WITH THROTTLE SOLENOID POSITIONER ENERGIZED, THERMACTOR AIR ON, ALL VACUUM HOSES CONNECTED AND AIR CLEANER IN POSITION WHENEVER CURB IDLE IS RESET. CHECK AND ADJUST THE DECEL VALVE ACCORDING TO THE SERVICE MANUAL.

IDLE MIXTURE PRESET AT THE FACTORY. DO NOT REMOVE THE LIMITER CAP(S). CONSULT THE SERVICE MANUAL FOR DESCRIPTION OF ARTIFICIAL ENRICHMENT METHOD OF IDLE MIXTURE ADJUSTMENT TO BE USED ONLY DURING TUNE UPS AND MAJOR CARBURETOR REPAIRS. IDLE MIXTURE MUST BE MEASURED WITH THERMACTOR AIR OFF.

INITIAL TIMING ADJUST WITH HOSES DISCONNECTED AND PLUGGED AT THE DISTRIBUTOR.

REFERENCE TO A/C, THROTTLE SOLENOID, THERMACTOR AIR AND DECEL VALVE APPLICABLE ONLY IF THE ENGINE IS SO EQUIPPED. CONSULT SERVICE PUBLICATIONS FOR FURTHER INSTRUCTIONS ON TIMING AND IDLE SET.

THIS VEHICLE CONFORMS TO U.S.E.P.A. REGULATIONS APPLICABLE TO 1975 MODEL YEAR NEW MOTOR VEHICLES. THIS VEHICLE ALSO CONFORMS TO THE STATE OF CALIFORNIA CERTIFICATION STANDARDS APPLICABLE TO 1975 MODEL YEAR NEW MOTOR VEHICLES

FORD MOTOR COMPANY   929   D5DE 9C385 TA

CALIFORNIA

VEHICLE EMISSION CONTROL INFORMATION

ENGINE FAMILY	302 "A" CATALYST EGR AIR (1CEF)		
ENGINE DISPLACEMENT CID	302 CID		
SPARK PLUG	ARF 42 GAP .042 .046		
DISTRIBUTOR BREAKERLESS			
CHOKE HOUSING	MAN/TRANS	INDEX	
NOTCH SETTING	AUTO/TRANS	3 RICH	
TRANSMISSION	AUTO NEUTRAL	AUTO DRIVE	MANUAL NEUTRAL
IGNITION TIMING			6°BTDC
TIMING RPM			550
CURB IDLE RPM A/C			900
CURB IDLE RPM NO A/C			900
IDLE MIXTURE ARTIFICIAL ENRICHMENT			
RPM GAIN			10 100
RPM RESET			10 60
THIS VEHICLE REQUIRES MAINTENANCE SCHEDULE "A"			

MAKE ALL ADJUSTMENTS WITH ENGINE AT NORMAL OPERATING TEMPERATURES, A/C AND HEADLIGHTS OFF.

CURB IDLE ADJUST WITH THROTTLE SOLENOID POSITIONER ENERGIZED, THERMACTOR AIR ON, ALL VACUUM HOSES CONNECTED AND AIR CLEANER IN POSITION. WHENEVER CURB IDLE IS RESET, CHECK AND ADJUST THE DECEL VALVE ACCORDING TO THE SERVICE MANUAL.

IDLE MIXTURE PRESET AT THE FACTORY. DO NOT REMOVE THE LIMITER CAP(S). CONSULT THE SERVICE MANUAL FOR DESCRIPTION OF ARTIFICIAL ENRICHMENT METHOD OF IDLE MIXTURE ADJUSTMENT TO BE USED ONLY DURING TUNE UPS AND MAJOR CARBURETOR REPAIRS. IDLE MIXTURE MUST BE MEASURED WITH THERMACTOR AIR OFF.

INITIAL TIMING ADJUST WITH HOSES DISCONNECTED AND PLUGGED AT THE DISTRIBUTOR.

REFERENCE TO A/C, THROTTLE SOLENOID, THERMACTOR AIR AND DECEL VALVE APPLICABLE ONLY IF THE ENGINE IS SO EQUIPPED. CONSULT SERVICE PUBLICATIONS FOR FURTHER INSTRUCTIONS ON TIMING AND IDLE SET.

THIS VEHICLE CONFORMS TO U.S.E.P.A. REGULATIONS APPLICABLE TO 1975 MODEL YEAR NEW MOTOR VEHICLES D5TE 9C485 AEA

FORD MOTOR COMPANY   948

49 STATES AND CANADA

Fig. 60. Typical engine compartment decal.

rpm variation. You may feel this is unnecessary. One would naturally think that if the idle mixture is made as lean as possible exhaust emissions will be reduced. This is true up to a point. However, if the idle mixture is made too lean, the emission content may increase above acceptable limits.

The amount of carbon monoxide exceeds acceptable limits when idle speeds are set too rich. Conversely, the amount of hydrocarbons exceeds acceptable limits if the idle mixture is set too lean.

Consequently, the idle fuel mixture must be set somewhere between these two limits. The procedure outlined below (also on every decal) will fix this adjustment somewhere between these two extremes. This adjustment will also fix the settings so as to achieve the smoothest possible idle without sacrificing emission levels, economy or performance. If a smooth idle cannot be achieved following this procedure, there are other malfunctions in the system.

The most frequent reasons found for rough idle are a plugged PCV system or a vacuum leak at the carburetor, intake manifold, head gasket, or at other vacuum take-off points.

1. With the engine at operating temperature and tachometer installed, set idle mixture screws until a maximum rpm is achieved. Next, adjust idle speed screw (or idle stop solenoid screw) to obtain the manufacturer's specified idle rpm.

   NOTE: Operation of the idle solenoid will be explained in detail later on in this section.
2. Check engine timing as described further on and adjust as necessary.
3. Adjust mixture screw in to obtain a 20 rpm drop (lean roll), Fig. 61.

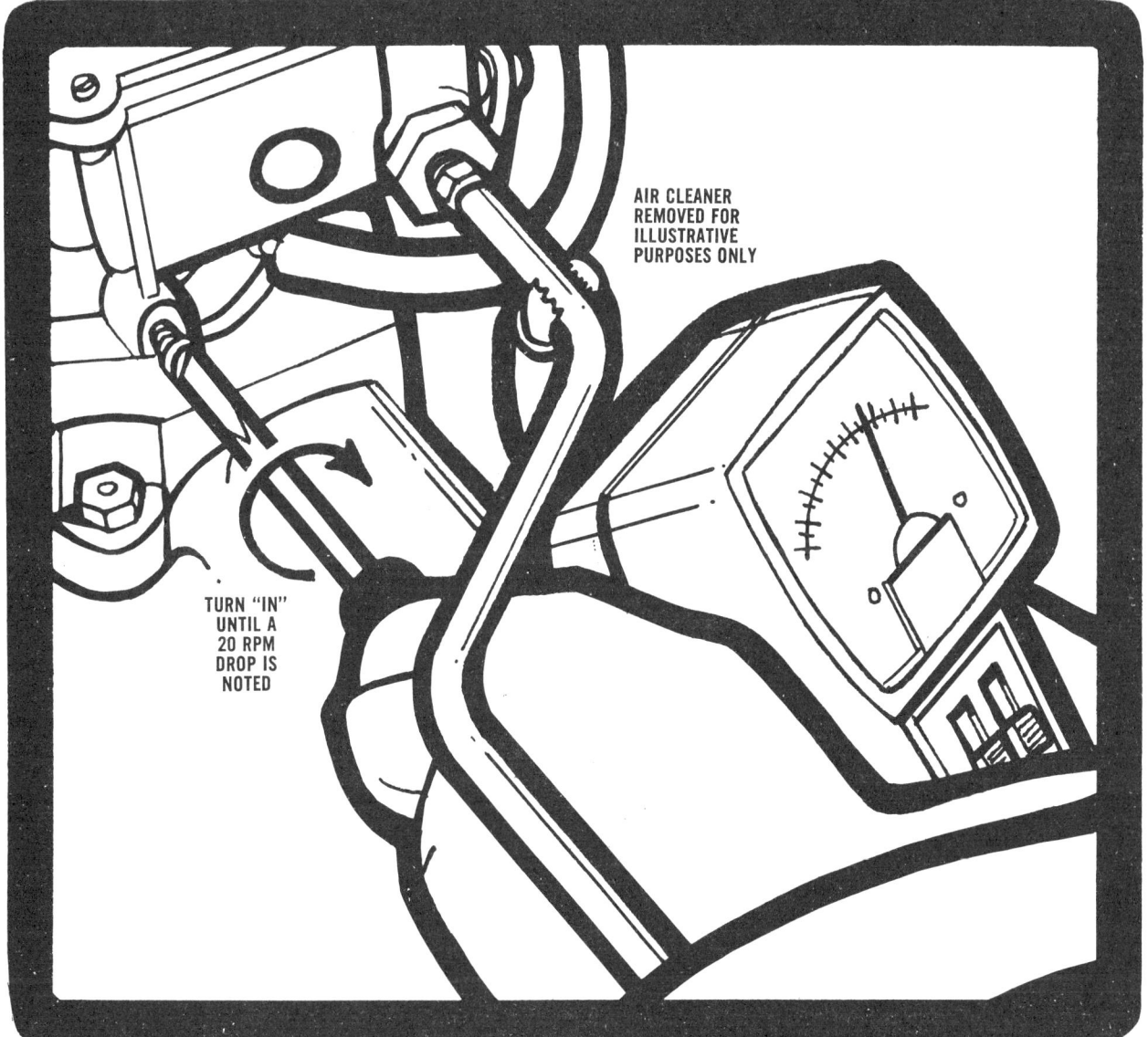

Fig. 61. Turning the idle mixture screw in until a 20 rpm drop (lean roll) is obtained.

4. Adjust mixture screw out ¼-turn, Fig. 62.
5. Repeat steps 3 and 4 for second mixture screw (if so equipped).
6. Readjust idle speed screw (or solenoid screw) if necessary to obtain specified idle rpm.
7. On units incorporating an antidieseling solenoid, electrically disconnect the solenoid and adjust the carburetor idle speed screw to obtain the specified rpm, Fig. 63.

NOTE: It should be stressed here that the above procedure has continually referred to the specifications given on the decal affixed within the engine compartment of every vehicle equipped with exhaust emission control devices.

ADJUSTING THE ANTIDIESELING SOLENOID

1. Start the engine and adjust the slow idle speed using the slow idle speed screw. Refer to manufacturer's specifications.
2. Energize the idle solenoid by turning the ignition key to RUN position. Then back out the plunger screw two turns from the fully bottomed position and slide the solenoid into the bracket so that the plunger just contacts the carburetor lever. Tighten the bracket retaining screw to secure the solenoid.
3. Back out the carburetor low idle speed screw approximately one turn. Final adjusting of the low idle speed must be performed as outlined on the engine decal to establish the specified low speed idle, Fig. 63.
4. Proceed with the carburetor adjustment as outlined on the engine decal, Fig. 60.

FAST IDLE SPEED ADJUSTMENT

1. Adjust the low idle speed as described previously.
2. Connect a tachometer onto the engine.
3. Manually set the fast idle lever on the highest step of the cam.
4. Bend the fast idle lever or turn the fast idle adjusting screw as required to obtain the specified rpm as outlined on the engine decal.

CHECKING AND ADJUSTING THE TIMING

1. Locate the timing marks, Fig. 64. Every engine has two timing marks. One is a stationary pointer or tab which is marked off in degrees and is usually attached to the timing case cover. The other mark is on the damper or pulley. This mark is not stationary, but appears to be so because of the stroboscopic effect of the timing light. To locate the timing marks, first wipe off all grease and dirt from the stationary pointer or tab and from the damper or pulley. Disconnect the secondary lead from the coil to prevent the engine from starting, then crank the engine on the damper or pulley until the marks are visible. Reconnect the secondary lead to the cable after locating the timing marks.

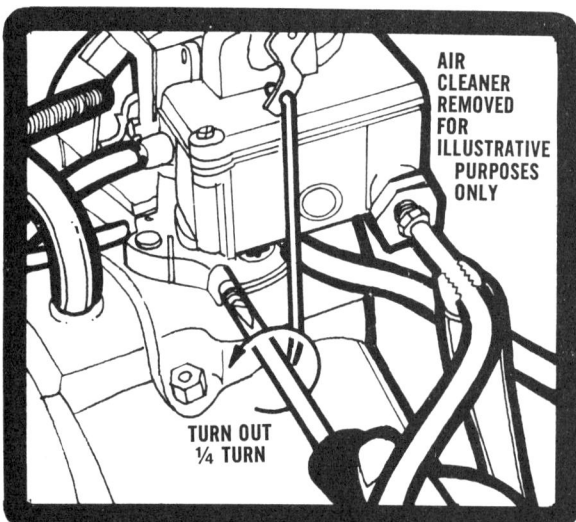

Fig. 62. Backing the idle mixture screw out ¼ turn.

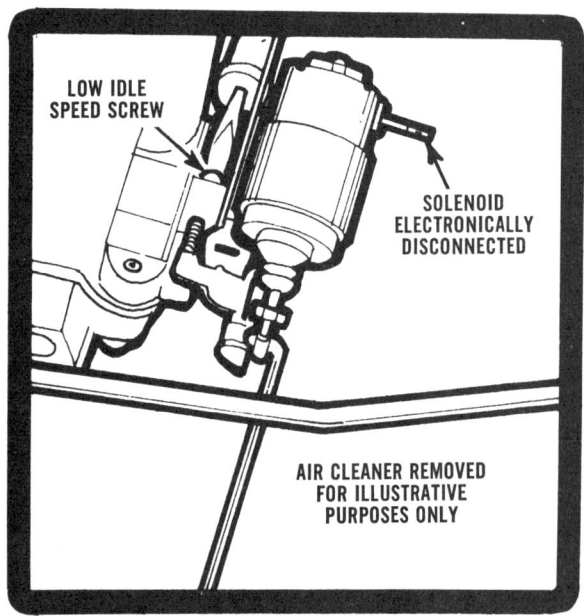

Fig. 63. Idle stop solenoid adjustment.

QUICK TUNEUP TIP

Setting the initial ignition timing is one of the most critical adjustments you will make in tuning an engine. Too much timing and the engine will knock and ping. **Not enough, and you will get poor performance and gas mileage. Make sure the setting is right on the money.**

2. Place a mark on the stationary pointer or tab and on the damper or pulley using white paint or nail polish. If these are not available, use white chalk. Refer to the manufacturer's specifications for the exact markings.
3. Locate the number 1 spark plug. On all 4- and 6-cylinder engines, this spark plug is the first one at the front of the engine closest to the radiator. On all V8 engines except those on Cadillac and Ford Motor Co. vehicles, this is the first one at the front of the engine, closest to the radiator and on the driver's side of the vehicle. On Cadillac and Ford Motor Co. vehicles, this is the first one at the front of the engine, closest to the radiator and on the passenger side of the vehicle.
4. Connect the timing light, Fig. 65. If you are using a neon type timing light, disconnect the number 1 spark plug and connect one lead of the timing light to the spark plug and connect the other lead to the spark plug cable. If you are using a D.C. powered timing light, connect the thick single lead to the number 1 spark plug using the appropriate adaptors, Fig. 64, then connect the red lead to the positive terminal of the battery and the black lead to the negative terminal of the battery. If you are using an A.C. powered timing light, connect the thick single lead to the number 1 spark plug using the appropriate adaptors and plug the other leads to a 110-120 volt A.C. power source.
5. Disconnect the vacuum advance line from the vacuum advance mechanism and plug the open end of the hose using a suitable size screw, nail or punch.

Fig. 64. Checking the ignition timing with a timing light. Note the timing mark locations which are typical of all vehicles.

6. Connect a dwell-tachometer to the engine. Connect the red lead to the terminal on the coil which leads to the ignition distributor. Connect the black lead to a suitable ground. Start the engine and make sure that the ignition dwell and the idle speed are correctly set. Refer to the manufacturer's specifications for pertinent information required for setting the timing.
7. With the engine running, point the timing light, Fig. 64, at the timing marks and squeeze the trigger button. The timing light will make the timing marks appear stationary. If the timing is correctly set, the two timing marks will align with each other according to manufacturer's specifications. If the timing is incorrectly set, the timing marks will not align with each other.

CAUTION: Do not touch the fan with the timing light and make sure that you keep your hands and clothing away from the fan, belts and pulleys. In cases where it is impossible to see the timing marks because of the engine components, such as A/C pump, power steering pump etc., it may be safer and easier to remove the fan belt and pump belts as necessary so that you can get the timing light closer to the timing marks. If you remove the belt, make sure to check the timing in as little time as possible to avoid overheating the engine.

8. If the timing needs adjusting, loosen the distributor hold-down bolt using a suitable wrench (½-inch or 9/16-inch), just enough so that there is a slight drag on the distributor when it is turned. On some engines, such as V8's, you will need a special distributor wrench (½-inch or 9/16-inch), Fig. 66, to loosen the distributor hold-down bolt. In the absence of such a wrench, try using a socket (½-inch or 9/16-inch), a swivel joint, proper length extension and ratchet.
9. With the distributor loose, point the timing light, Fig. 64, at the timing marks. Squeeze the trigger button and turn the distributor as necessary to align the timing marks according to the manufacturer's specifications. If the idle speed increases as the distributor is turned, make sure to readjust it to specifications and recheck the timing marks.

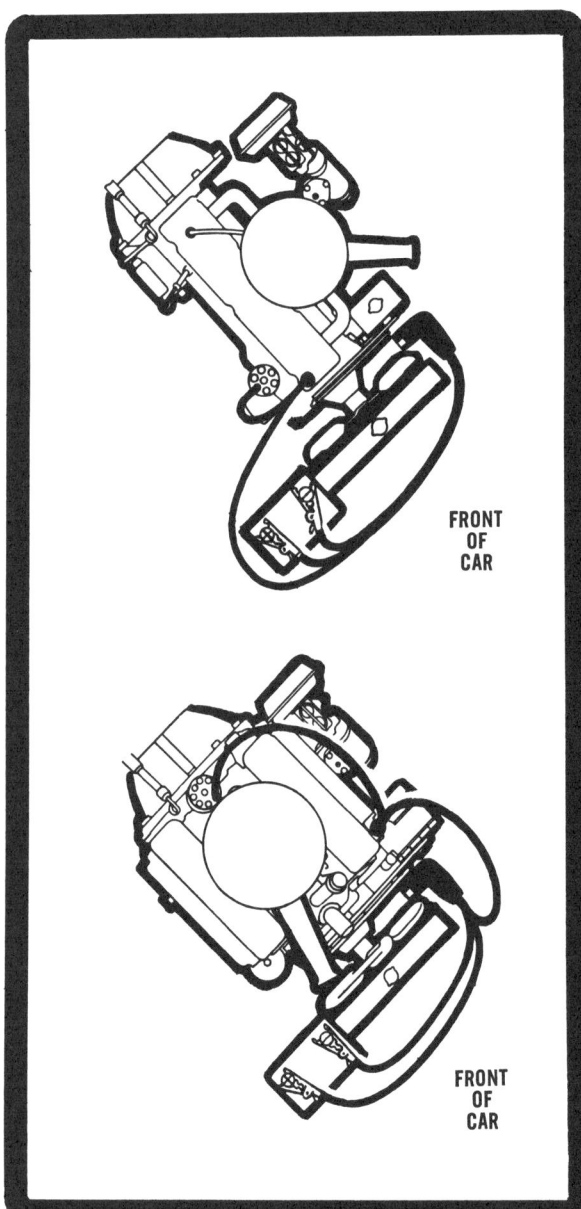

Fig. 65. Connecting the timing light to the number 1 spark plug.

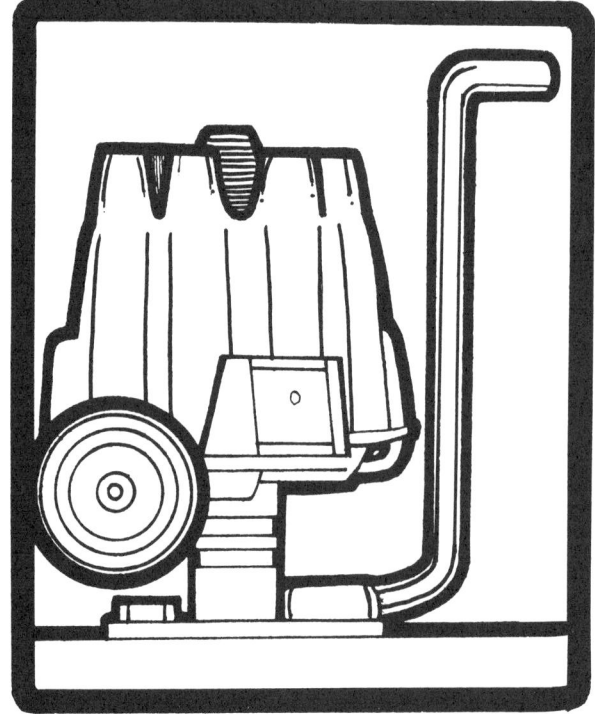

Fig. 66. Loosening distributor hold-down bolt using special distributor wrench.

10. After properly adjusting the timing, retighten the hold-down bolts using the same tools that were used to loosen it. Recheck the timing as described previously to make sure that the distributor did not move when the hold-down bolt was tightened.
11. Check the advance mechanism. Point the timing light, Fig. 64, at timing marks and accelerate the engine while observing the timing marks. The timing mark on the pulley or damper should move in the advance direction and past the timing pointer or tab. If little or no movement is noted, the distributor's advance mechanism should be checked by a qualified mechanic.
12. Turn the engine off.
13. Unplug the vacuum advance line and reconnect it to the vacuum advance unit.
14. Disconnect the timing light and reconnect the spark plug wire to the spark plug.
15. Readjust the engine idle to manufacturer's specifications as previously described.
16. Disconnect the dwell-tachometer.

CHECKING COIL POLARITY

Most coils are marked positive (+) and negative (−) at the coil primary terminals. If the leads are reversed on the coil, the engine performance may be affected. If the coil polarity is not marked, it can be checked by using the following procedure. Disconnect any one of the spark plug wires. Then slide the rubber boot over the wire to expose the terminal and reconnect the wire. Start the engine, then disconnect the exposed wire from the spark plug and hold the point of a lead pencil as shown in Fig. 67. If the spark flares between the spark plug and the pencil, the polarity is correct. If the spark flares between the cable and the pencil, the polarity is incorrect and the leads should be reversed on the coil.

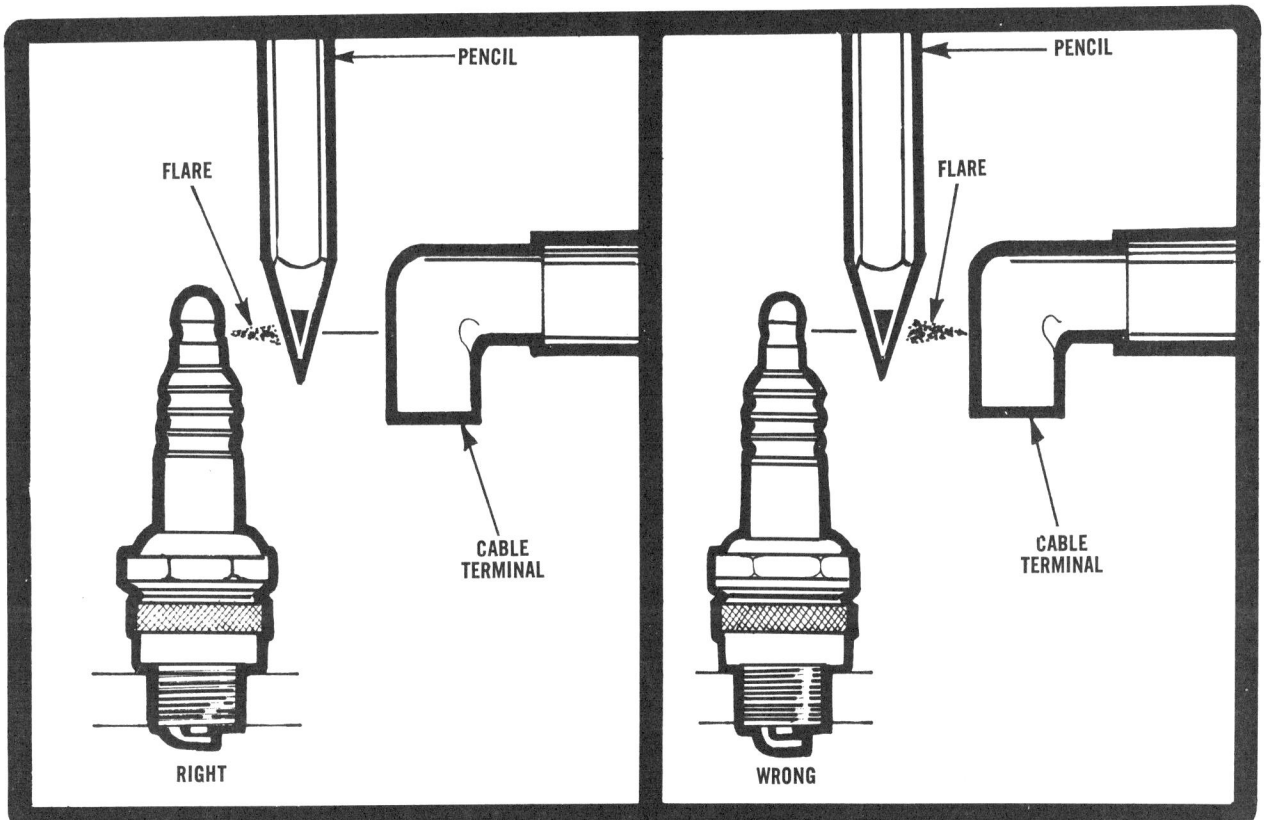

Fig. 67. Checking the coil polarity.

JOB 17. ROAD TEST THE VEHICLE

It only stands to reason that the very last step of a quality tuneup is to road test the vehicle. Although each system has been thoroughly tested, it is only after a satisfactory road test that the job can be considered completed. No matter how elaborate or sensitive the equipment, you cannot duplicate every operating condition a vehicle will be subjected to on the road. This is why a road test should be run, covering as many different kinds of operating conditions as possible.

TROUBLESHOOTING FLOW CHART

ENGINE

Symptom	Probable Cause	Remedy
A. Engine misses at all speeds.	1. Leaking intake manifold gasket.	1. Torque intake manifold bolts to manufacturer's specifications. If leak still exists, remove intake manifold and install a new gasket. On vehicles with an air pump emission control system, make sure that antibackfire valve is not stuck in the open position.
	2. Late ignition timing or valve timing.	2. Check ignition timing and adjust as necessary to manufacturer's specifications. Check valve timing with a vacuum gauge. If reading is below 18 inches Hg., the valve timing is probably late. To correct this problem, the engine must be disassembled as necessary to gain access to the timing chain and/or gears and camshaft. The timing chain and/or gears or camshaft must be replaced as necessary to correct the cause of late valve timing.
	3. Low compression due to leakage past piston rings.	3. Perform compression test. If it is determined that the cause of this problem is worn piston rings, the engine must be disassembled as necessary to gain access to the piston rings and the piston rings replaced as necessary.
	4. Partial or complete loss of power in one or more cylinders due to leaking head or intake manifold gasket, leaking valve(s) or defective valve springs.	4. Perform vacuum test. If needle fluctuates steadily as engine speed is increased, one or more of the problems is indicated. To check for leaking head gasket or valves, perform a compression test. If the head gasket or valves are at fault, disassemble the engine as necessary and replace the affected part(s) as necessary. To check for leaking intake manifold gasket, squirt engine oil around parting surfaces of intake manifold and cylinder head(s). If engine idle speed is affected as the oil is squirted, correct problem as described previously in step 1. To check for weak valve springs, remove springs and have them checked on a spring scale. If tension is not within manufacturer's specifications, replace the affected springs.
	5. Loss of power in one or more cylinders due to defect(s) in ignition system.	5. Check point dwell and ignition timing and reset as necessary. If malfunction still exists, proceed as follows: Inspect condition of points, condenser, distributor cap, rotor, spark plugs, wires and ignition coil. Replace all parts which are defective or questionable with new ones.
	6. Fuel mixture too lean or too rich.	6. Check carburetor float level and float drop and adjust as necessary to manufacturer's specifications. If malfunction still exists, overhaul or replace carburetor.
	7. Excessive back pressure in exhaust system.	7. Perform vacuum test. A slow drop of the needle while engine is idling indicates a restriction in the exhaust system. To correct this problem, remove the exhaust system and check for obstructions or kinks and bends in the pipes and mufflers. Also check exhaust manifolds for obstructions.
	8. Defective fuel pump.	8. Check fuel pump pressure. If pressure is not within manufacturer's specifications, replace fuel pump.

ENGINE / continued

Symptom	Probable Cause	Remedy
B. Engine misses at low or idle speeds.	9. Valve adjustment set too tight.	9. Reset valve adjustment to manufacturer's specifications.
	10. Worn camshaft lobes, bent push rods or worn valve lifters.	10. Check valve lift using a dial indicator. If valve lift is not within manufacturer's specifications, disassemble engine as necessary and check push rods, valve lifters and camshaft and replace any affected parts.
	11. Loss of power in one or more cylinders due to defect in ignition system.	11. Check point dwell and ignition timing and reset as necessary to manufacturer's specifications. If problem still exists, proceed as follows: Inspect condition of points, condenser, distributor cap, rotor, spark plugs, wires and ignition coil. Replace all parts which are defective or questionable with new ones.
	12. Leaking intake manifold system.	12. Squirt engine oil around parting surfaces of intake manifold and cylinder head(s). If engine idle speed is affected as the oil is squirted, torque intake manifold bolts to specifications and recheck for leaks. If leak still exists, replace the intake manifold gasket. On vehicles with air pump emission control system, make sure that antibackfire valve is not stuck in the open position.
	13. Dirty air cleaner.	13. Replace air cleaner.
	14. Leaky valves.	14. Perform compression test. If test indicates that valves are leaking, disassemble engine as necessary and have a valve job performed.
	15. Fuel mixture too lean or too rich.	15. Check carburetor float level and float drop and adjust as necessary to manufacturer's specifications. If malfunction still exists, overhaul or replace carburetor.
	16. Defective fuel pump.	16. Check fuel pump pressure. If pressure is not within manufacturer's specifications, replace fuel pump.
C. Poor high speed performance or lack of power. (Note that the altitude at which the vehicle is operated will have an effect on engine performance. A vehicle that operates normally at low altitudes, will not necessarily perform satisfactorily at high altitudes and vice versa).	17. Incorrect ignition timing.	17. Reset ignition timing to manufacturer's specifications.
	18. Advance mechanism not operating properly.	18. Check operation of centrifugal and vacuum mechanisms using a timing light. If either is malfunctioning, replace as necessary.
	19. Defect(s) in ignition system.	19. Inspect condition of points, condenser, distributor cap, rotor, spark plugs, wires and ignition coil. Replace all parts which are defective or seem questionable.
	20. Fuel mixture too lean or too rich.	20. Check carburetor float level and float drop and adjust as necessary to manufacturer's specifications. If malfunction still exists, overhaul or replace carburetor.
	21. Defective fuel pump.	21. Check fuel pump pressure. If pressure is not within manufacturer's specifications, replace the fuel pump.
	22. Dirty air cleaner.	22. Replace air cleaner.
	23. Excessive back pressure in exhaust system.	23. Perform vacuum test. A slow drop of the needle indicates a restriction in the exhaust system. To correct this problem, remove the exhaust system and check for restrictions or kinks or bends in the muffler and pipes. Also check exhaust manifold for obstructions.
	24. Positive crankcase ventilation system clogged.	24. Replace PCV valve and clean out or replace hoses as necessary.

ENGINE /continued

Symptom	Probable Cause	Remedy
	25. Worn lifters, camshaft lobes or bent push rods.	25. Check valve lift using a dial indicator. If valve lift is not within manufacturer's specifications, disassemble engine as necessary and check push rods, valve lifters and camshaft and replace any affected parts.
	26. Manifold heat control valve stuck in closed position.	26. Free up valve using solvent.
	27. Sticking valves or low compression.	27. Perform compression test. If test indicates valves are leaking, disassemble engine as necessary and perform valve job.
D. Valve noise.	28. Defective lifter(s) or valve clearance incorrectly adjusted.	28. Replace lifter(s) or adjust valve clearance to manufacturer's specifications.
	29. Weak or broken valve springs or excessively worn valve guides.	29. Replace valve springs if broken or weak. If valve guides are excessively worn, ream valve guides to next oversize and install corresponding oversize valves.
	30. Oil level too low or too high.	30. Add or drain oil as necessary to bring oil level to specifications.
E. Detonation (ping or spark knock).	31. Overheated engine.	31. Determine cause of overheating and correct as necessary.
	32. Octane rating of fuel too low for engine.	32. Change to a fuel of higher octane rating.
	33. Timing advanced excessively.	33. Reset timing to manufacturer's specifications.
	34. Excess carbon deposits in combustion chamber.	34. Add combustion chamber conditioner to engine. If problem still exists, remove cylinder head(s) and clean out the deposits.
F. External engine oil leakage.	35. Improperly seated or broken gaskets at timing chain cover, fuel pump, oil filter, oil pan or valve covers.	35. Torque the bolts retaining the affected parts to specifications. If leak still exists, replace the affected gasket.
	36. Worn timing chain cover oil seal or rear main seal.	36. Disassemble engine as necessary and replace the affected seal.
	37. Leaking distributor housing seal or gasket.	37. Replace gasket or seal.
	38. Leaking intake manifold seal or gasket.	38. Replace gasket or seal.
	39. Oil pan plug cocked or loose.	39. Torque plug to specifications, or replace with new self-tapping plug, if oil pan threads are stripped.
G. Internal engine oil leakage (Indicated by blue smoke emitting from the tailpipe).	40. Worn or damaged valve stem oil seals.	40. If blue smoke emits from the tailpipe when the engine is first started, the valve stem oil seals are probably defective. To correct this problem, replace the valve stem oil seals.
	41. Valve guides and/or valve stems excessively worn.	41. Ream valve guides to next oversize and install the corresponding oversize valves.
	42. Plugged drain back holes in cylinder head.	42. Clear out drain back holes.
	43. Oil being sucked in past the intake manifold gasket.	43. Torque intake manifold bolts to manufacturer's specifications. If leak still exists, replace intake manifold gasket.
	44. Punctured automatic transmission modulator diaphragm.	44. Replace modulator.
	45. Worn piston rings.	45. Replace piston rings.
	46. Excessively worn connecting rod bearings.	46. Replace connecting rod bearings.
	47. Too low engine oil viscosity.	47. Drain and add the correct type and amount of oil.

TROUBLESHOOTING FLOW CHART

IGNITION SYSTEM

Symptom	Probable Cause	Remedy
A. Engine will not crank.	1. Defective ignition switch.	1. Connect a jumper wire between the battery and the starter connections. If the solenoid clicks, the ignition switch is defective. Replace the switch to cure the problem.
	2. Loose or broken battery connections.	2. Clean cable terminals and tighten connections. Replace cables which are damaged.
	3. Defective neutral safety switch on vehicles with automatic transmissions.	3. Replace defective neutral safety switch.
	4. If starter clicks, but engine will not crank.	4. Check for defective connections or defective starter motor. Repair or replace as necessary.
B. Engine cranks but will not start.	5. Burned or pitted contact points.	5. Replace contact points and condenser.
	6. Corroded distributor cap towers or eroded terminals.	6. Replace distributor cap.
	7. Moisture in distributor cap or on spark plug wires.	7. Remove cap and dry out. Wipe spark plug cables dry.
	8. Excessive distributor condenser resistance, output capacity or leakage.	8. Check with condenser tester. Make sure that all the connections are tight. Replace condenser if not within manufacturer's specifications.
	9. Defective coil.	9. Pull center wire from the distributor cap and hold about 3/8-inch from a good ground. Crank the engine. If there is no spark or if the spark is weak, the coil is defective. Before replacing the coil check all the wiring of the primary circuit and correct as necessary.
	10. Improper primary resistance.	10. Momentarily bypass the ballast resistor with a jumper wire while cranking the engine. If the engine starts, replace the ballast resistor.
	11. Insufficient fuel supply at the carburetor.	11. Look into the carburetor and open the throttle. If fuel squirts into the carburetor throat, the fuel system is not at fault. If no fuel is evident, check the fuel pump pressure. If the fuel pump is OK, the trouble is in the carburetor.
	12. Extremely low compression.	12. Determine cause of low compression by performing a compression test and correct as necessary.

IGNITION SYSTEM / continued

Symptom	Probable Cause	Remedy
C. Hard starting at all times.	13. Weak spark.	13. Check condition of breaker points and all of the primary circuit wiring. Correct as necessary.
	14. Grounded or open ignition coil circuits.	14. Connect a 110-volt test lamp across the primary terminals of the coil. If the lamp does not light, the primary circuit is open. Connect the test lamp between the high tension terminal and the primary terminals. If no sparks are evident at the probes, there is an open in the secondary circuit. Touch one probe to the coil casing and the other probe to the primary and high tension terminals. If sparks are evident at the test probes, the coil windings are grounded.
	15. Spark plugs need adjustment or are fouled.	15. Clean and readjust the spark plug gaps.
	16. Defective spark plug cables.	16. Replace cables which are frayed or cracked.
	17. Low charge or defective battery.	17. Recharge or replace battery as necessary.
	18. Defective starter or solenoid.	18. Repair or replace starter or solenoid as necessary.
	19. Insufficient fuel supply.	19. Check for fuel delivery by looking down the carburetor throat and operating the throttle lever. If no fuel sprays into the carburetor throat, check the fuel pump pressure. If the fuel pump is OK, the trouble is in the carburetor.
D. Hard starting when cold.	20. One or more components not operating satisfactorily.	20. Take the vehicle to a qualified mechanic to have it checked out.
	21. Low battery charge or defective battery.	21. Recharge or replace the battery as necessary.
	22. Binding choke linkage.	22. Free up the choke linkage using a suitable choke cleaner.
	23. Oil viscosity too high.	23. Drain the oil and add the proper type and amount of oil.
E. Hard starting when hot.	24. Insufficient spark intensity between spark and ground.	24. If the spark cannot jump a ⅜-inch gap, check the ignition system for defects and correct as necessary.
	25. Choke stuck in closed position.	25. Free up choke using a suitable choke cleaner. Adjust as necessary according to manufacturer's specifications.
	26. Defective starter motor or starter motor circuit.	26. Check starter and circuit and repair or replace as necessary.
	27. Engine overheating.	27. Check cooling system, and correct as necessary. If coolant temperature gauge or light did not indicate an overheating condition, check the circuits.
F. Engine stalls.	28. Spark plugs fouled or incorrectly gapped.	28. Clean and regap spark plugs.
	29. Voltage drop across the ballast resistor does not meet specifications.	29. Check ballast resistor resistance and replace as necessary.
	30. Breaker points dirty or corroded.	30. Clean or replace breaker points as necessary.

IGNITION SYSTEM / continued

Symptom	Probable Cause	Remedy
G. Engine runs but misses steadily at all speeds.	31. One or more defective spark plugs.	31. Connect a tachometer and check the rpm drop as each spark plug cable is disconnected. No rpm drop when a particular spark is disconnected indicates that that spark plug is defective. **CAUTION:** Do not perform the above test on vehicles equipped with catalytic converters.
	32. Defective spark plug cables.	32. Check the resistance of each cable. Replace cables which do not meet the manufacturer's specifications.
	33. Defective distributor cap.	33. Inspect distributor cap for cracks, burned or eroded terminals, corrosion in the sockets or carbon tracking. Replace or repair as necessary.
H. Engine runs but misses intermittently at all speeds.	34. Dirty or corroded breaker points.	34. Clean or replace contact points as necessary.
	35. Excessive condenser resistance, output capacity or leakage.	35. Check with condenser tester. Make sure that all the connections are tight. Replace condenser as required.
	36. Defective coil.	36. Check with coil tester and replace if defective.
	37. Worn insulation, broken strands and loose or corroded terminals in the primary winding.	37. Check voltage drop across the primary resistance wire or ballast resistor with a voltmeter. Replace defective units if not within manufacturer's specifications.
I. Engine runs but misses at idle.	38. Incorrect contact point setting.	38. Readjust gap and check with dwell meter.
	39. Worn distributor shaft bushing or cam.	39. Replace the bushing or cam as necessary.
	40. Faulty coil or condenser.	40. Check coil and condenser with tester and replace as necessary.
J. Engine runs but misses at high speeds.	41. Spark plugs fouled or incorrectly gapped.	41. Clean and regap spark plugs as necessary.
K. Poor high speed performance.	42. Ignition timing too late.	42. Reset timing to specifications.
	43. Defective contact points.	43. Replace contact points and condenser.
	44. Spark plugs fouled, incorrectly gapped or of the incorrect heat range for the specific engine.	44. Clean and regap spark plugs. If spark plugs are of the incorrect heat range, reinstall the correct spark plugs for the specific engine.
	45. Defective coil or condenser.	45. Test coil and condenser and replace as necessary.
L. Excessive fuel consumption.	46. Contact points dirty or incorrectly adjusted.	46. Clean or replace as necessary and regap points to manufacturer's specifications.
	47. Ignition timing incorrectly adjusted.	47. Readjust ignition timing to manufacturer's specifications.
	48. Distributor advance mechanism malfunctioning.	48. Check advance mechanism on tester and repair or replace as necessary.
M. Poor acceleration.	49. Ignition timing set too late.	49. Readjust ignition timing to manufacturer's specifications.
	50. Plugs fouled or incorrectly gapped.	50. Clean and regap spark plugs to manufacturer's specifications.
	51. Dirty contact points.	51. Clean contact points as necessary and regap to manufacturer's specifications.
N. Engine knock or excessive pinging.	52. Timing incorrectly set.	52. Readjust timing to manufacturer's specifications.
	53. Spark plug heat range incorrect for specific application.	53. Install spark plugs of the correct heat range for the specific engine.

TROUBLESHOOTING FLOW CHART
FUEL SYSTEM

Symptom	Probable Cause	Remedy
A. Hard starting under all conditions.	1. Insufficient fuel in carburetor.	1. Check fuel pump output by disconnecting line from carburetor and checking for fuel delivery when the engine is cranked. If there is no fuel delivery, check all the lines for obstructions. If all the fuel lines check out OK, replace the fuel pump.
B. Hard starting when cold.	2. Choke closes when the engine is hot.	2. Inspect for binding choke linkages and correct as necessary.
	3. Persistent vapor lock.	3. Wrap the fuel line between the fuel pump and carburetor with asbestos to minimize the heat transfer from the engine to the line.
	4. Carburetor flooding.	4. Check fuel pump for excessive pressure with a pressure gauge. If fuel pressure is excessive, replace the fuel pump. If fuel pump checks out OK, check the float level, needle and seat in the carburetor. Correct or replace as necessary.
C. Engine stalls.	5. Idle speed set too low.	5. Reset idle speed to manufacturer's specifications.
	6. Idle fuel mixture too lean.	6. Reset idle mixture to manufacturer's specifications.
	7. Faulty choke operation.	7. Correct as necessary.
	8. Incorrect carburetor float setting.	8. Adjust carburetor float setting to manufacturer's specifications.
	9. Dirt or water in the fuel tank, fuel lines, pump, filter or carburetor.	9. Clean out the fuel system.
	10. Clogged or restricted PCV valve.	10. Clean or replace the PCV valve as necessary.
	11. Dashpot (if used) incorrectly adjusted.	11. Check adjustment according to the manufacturer's specifications. Adjust as necessary.
	12. Carburetor linkage needs adjustment.	12. Clean carburetor linkage. Adjust as necessary.
	13. Carburetor accelerating pump stroke incorrectly set.	13. Check accelerating pump adjustment. Adjust as necessary according to manufacturer's specifications.
D. Engine misses erratically at all speeds.	14. Dirt or water in the fuel system. 15. Clogged fuel filter. 16. Carburetor float level set too high.	14. Clean out the fuel system. 15. Replace the fuel filter. 16. Readjust carburetor float level according to manufacturer's specifications.
E. Engine misses at idle only.	17. Idle mixture improperly adjusted.	17. Readjust idle mixture according to manufacturer's specifications.
	18. Restrictions in the idle fuel system of the carburetor.	18. Remove, disassemble and clean out the carburetor.
F. Engine misses at high speed only.	19. Erratic fuel pump pressures.	19. Check fuel pump pressure and replace fuel pump if not within manufacturer's specifications.
	20. Carburetor power valve or passages clogged or damaged.	20. Disassemble carburetor and clean or replace components as necessary.
	21. Restrictions in the fuel system.	21. Clean or correct as necessary.
G. Poor acceleration.	22. Throttle linkage incorrectly adjusted.	22. Readjust throttle linkages as necessary.
	23. Carburetor accelerating pump incorrectly adjusted.	23. Readjust carburetor accelerating pump to manufacturer's specifications.
	24. Incorrect carburetor float setting.	24. Readjust carburetor float setting according to manufacturer's specifications.
	25. Leaking power valve, gasket or accelerating pump.	25. Repair or replace components as necessary.

Periodic Maintenance

Why periodic maintenance?

If you visit your dentist *before* you get a toothache, you will save yourself a lot of pain, inconvenience and expense. The same principle applies to your car. Regular inspection and routine maintenance can prevent major—and expensive—repairs.

Periodic maintenance is the practice of performing certain preventive service jobs on a car on a regularly scheduled basis. Maintenance is defined as the upkeep of equipment.

There are several very good reasons for engaging in the practice of periodic maintenance. But none is as important as this.

According to the Motor and Equipment Manufacturers Association, more than 60% of the cars in the country are running inefficiently. In addition to wasting gasoline and causing their owners to lose valuable time and money because of breakdowns, inefficient automobiles are causing deaths and injuries on the highway.

More than one out of eight accidents involves a vehicle that is not in adequate working order. These accidents cause 5000 deaths and 200,000 serious injuries annually.

There are certain other benefits you reap by adhering to a periodic maintenance schedule:

1. Periodic maintenance allows you to uncover and immediately correct deficiencies in mechanical performance while these deficiencies are still minor in nature. You are able to correct them before they cause a major breakdown and a more expensive repair.
2. Periodic maintenance allows you to uncover and immediately correct deficiencies in safety-oriented equipment before they become serious and cause an accident.
3. Periodic maintenance allows you to prepare your car to meet the ravages of extreme weather conditions.
4. Periodic maintenance is generally required to keep a car's warranty in effect.

Watch time and mileage

The engineers who designed your car spent many hours in the laboratories and on the proving grounds to find out how long each major part would work before it needed lubrication, adjustment or replacement. The service recommendations in your owner's manual and in this chapter are based on those tests.

Remember that time is just as important as mileage. Some materials, such as rubber, deteriorate from exposure to the elements even when the car is not in use.

If most of your driving is local, the engine never really warms up. So water vapor and unburned fuel do not get hot enough to boil away and escape through the crankcase ventilation system. Instead, they just dilute the engine oil. That is why car makers recommend that oil should be changed every four to six months when the car is driven less than 1000 miles per month.

Most joints in the steering and suspension system are sealed and require lubrication at infrequent intervals. However, there are exceptions, even in late-model cars. Some parts may need lubrication as often as every 4000 miles. Check the recommendations in your owner's manual or later on in this chapter.

Service is required

How and where you drive also influences service requirements. Most automobile manufacturers specify more frequent changes of transmission fluid and adjustment of the transmission when the car is used to tow a trailer. If you drive in dusty territory, the air cleaner should be serviced at shorter intervals than those specified for normal service.

Most joints in the steering and suspension system are sealed and require lubrication at infrequent intervals. However, there are exceptions, even in late-model cars. Some parts may need lubrication as often as every 4000 miles. Check the recommendations in your owner's manual and in the charts in this chapter.

Service is seasonal too

Before the development of lubricants and coolants suitable for year-around use, it was necessary to change to a winter-grade oil and add antifreeze when the weather turned cold. Now, in most sections of the country, you can use a multi-grade oil, such as 10W-30, at all times. The 10W-30 designation means the oil flows as freely at low temperature as a 10W (winter-grade) oil, and yet holds its body at high temperature just as well as a 30 (summer-grade) oil. If you encounter extremely high or low temperatures, seasonal changes may be necessary.

The same coolant should be used throughout the year and should be changed once a year. Fall is the best time of year to change the coolant to be sure you have maximum protection against freezing.

Normally, no seasonal changes of transmission or rear axle lubricants are necessary. However, some manufacturers recommend the use of winter lubricants in manual transmissions for easier shifting in cold weather.

CHECKLISTS FOR PERIODIC MAINTENANCE

Periodic maintenance involves many different tasks. The purpose of this chapter is to place periodic maintenance into perspective and outline the following:
1. What should be done on a day-to-day basis.
2. What should be done on a weekly basis.
3. What should be done on a monthly basis to check safety-oriented equipment.
4. What should be done seasonally—pre-winter and pre-summer.
5. Where to check for fluid leakage.
6. What can be done to assure safety and mechanical efficiency during a trip.

The balance of this chapter consists of three sections. The first is a series of lists of checks that you should use as a guide to what services your car needs at particular intervals. Once you are into the regular routine of periodic maintenance, these checkouts will have become second nature and you will not have to use these lists any further. But until you are into that routine, you will find the lists useful and informative.

The second part of the chapter consists of the manufacturer's recommended maintenance schedules for all four major U.S. automakers. The tables cover all models from 1969 to 1976. Generally, these recommended service intervals must be met or exceeded to keep a vehicle's warranty in effect. So these maintenance schedules are very important if you have a late model car still under warranty.

If your car is no longer under warranty, the manufacturer's recommended service intervals are a good guide if you want to do a minimum of periodic maintenance on your car. Frankly, our own recommendations are more extensive than the manufacturer's.

The third part of this chapter covers information you should have before starting any long trip with your car. Because vacation time is usually a hectic one with everyone anxious to get to the vacation spot, the means of transportation to the vacation—the car—is often neglected. Which is the reason why there are so many breakdowns on vacation trips. You will also find very useful information in case of a road emergency—a situation that hopefully will be avoided by the wise use of the information in this chapter.

Replace light bulbs that have burned out to be sure you are seen by other motorists.

Regular preventive maintenance can insure that your car will be delivering maximum performance and gas mileage.

CHECKS YOU SHOULD MAKE EVERY DAY

These are the most basic checks and only take a few minutes a day. You can check all of them almost by simply walking around the car. On a few, you will need a helper. If there is no helper available, you can use a wall or garage door reflection to check some of the lights.

1. Headlights, low beam.
2. Headlights, high beam.
3. Parking lights.
4. Sidemarker lights, right side front and rear.
5. Sidemarker lights, left side front and rear.
6. Taillights.
7. Stoplights.
8. License plate light.
9. Turn signals, left side front and rear.
10. Turn signals, right side front and rear.
11. Hazard flasher warning lights, front and rear.
12. Horn.
13. Windshield wiper action.
14. Windshield washer function.
15. Inside rearview mirror cleanliness and position.
16. Outside rearview mirror(s) cleanliness and position.
17. Front windshield cleanliness.
18. Rear windshield cleanliness.
19. Side window cleanliness.
20. All tires (including the spare) in case any has lost air and is going flat.

CHECKS YOU SHOULD MAKE EVERY WEEK

On these checks, you are getting into two basic maintenance areas—levels of vital fluids in your car and subjective on-the-road feelings from your car. Your car is constantly sending messages to you through feel, through sound, through the way it handles. You should be cognizant of these messages. And be alert to any unusual sounds, feels, vibrations, etc. while your car is moving down the road.

WITH THE CAR STATIONARY

1. Engine oil level.
2. Battery fluid level.
3. Radiator coolant level.
4. Windshield washer reservoir fluid level.
5. Brake master cylinder fluid level.
6. Power steering reservoir fluid level.
7. Automatic transmission fluid level.
8. Tire air pressure.
9. Tires for cuts, embedded stones, and unusual wear pattern.
10. Windshields and windows for small chips or cracks.
11. Exterior paint, for minor nicks and scratches that should be touched up before they become extensive.
12. Seat belts for cuts and wear.

ON THE ROAD

1. Brake performance.
2. Automatic transmission performance.
3. Manual transmission and clutch performance.
4. Steering.
5. Engine performance.
6. Instrument operation.
7. Any rattles?

Eliminating leaks, particularly from faulty brakes, is an important safety measure.

Keep the windshield washer fluid reservoir filled so you do not run out of fluid on a rainy or snowy night.

MONTHLY SAFETY INSPECTION

It is imperative that certain safety components of your car be checked regularly to insure that they are functioning and functioning correctly. These extremely important components are part of the overall safety package of your vehicle. Malfunctions of any of these components can cause much worse than a breakdown. They could cause a serious accident.

BRAKES

1. Test brake pedal action.
2. Check master cylinder fluid level.
3. Examine brake lines.
4. Test parking brake.

STEERING

1. Test steering action.
2. Check power steering reservoir fluid level.

LIGHTS AND HORN

1. Check function of all lights and horn.
2. Check headlight alignment.
3. Check turn signal operation.
4. Check hazard warning flasher light operation.

SHOCK ABSORBERS

1. Check for leakage.
2. Check for wear.

SEAT BELTS

1. Check hardware for firm latching.
2. Check belts for cuts and wear.

TIRES

1. Check inflation.
2. Check wear pattern.
3. Look for cuts.
4. Remove embedded stones.

EXHAUST SYSTEM

1. Check for leaking exhaust system components.
2. Test for actual or potential failure.

VISIBILITY

1. Check all glass for chips and cracks.
2. Check windows for operation.
3. Check mirrors for looseness.
4. Check windshield washer operation and fluid level.
5. Check windshield wiper operation.
6. Check windshield wiper blades for integrity.
7. Check defroster action.

DOOR LOCKS AND LATCHES

1. Check door lock and latch performance.
2. Check hood latch.
3. Check trunk latch.

Install new windshield wiper blades as needed to be sure that your vision will not be impaired in inclement weather.

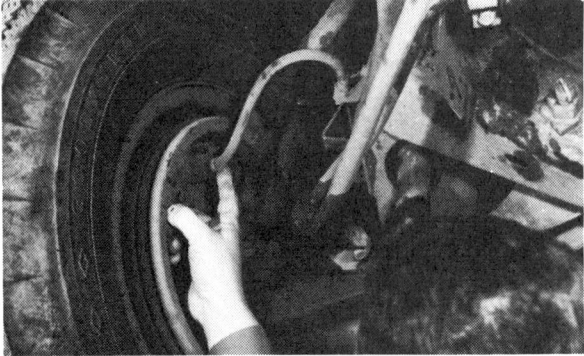

Brake lines must be inspected, too, as they are also an important part of dependable braking.

Keep the brake fluid reservoir full, so you do not find yourself without brakes when coming down a steep hill.

Tires should be checked frequently for cuts and bulges that can lead to a blowout when you are going at high speed. Embedded stones should be removed before they damage the tire.

SEASONAL MAINTENANCE

Some services need be performed only once or twice a year, under normal driving conditions which cover 10,000-12,000 miles. They are often referred to as seasonal checks, and most of them are looked after because of certain climatic conditions that exist in certain areas of the country. For instance, you wouldn't worry about a pre-winter checkup if you live in southern California. If you live in Minnesota, you will pay plenty of attention to it.

Many motorists use the seasonal changes as a reminder to perform more extensive safety checks. Please remember that these are only guidelines. If, for instance, your car begins to show symptoms of needing a tuneup in the middle of December, you should not wait until spring to have the tuneup done.

PRE-WINTER SERVICES

Cooling system
1. Drain and flush system.
2. Inspect hoses and connections.
3. Add fresh coolant.
4. Check the strength of the coolant to make sure it meets the temperature needs of your area.
5. Test the radiator pressure cap.
6. Make sure the thermostat functions properly.
7. See that drive belts are in good condition and properly adjusted.

Battery
1. Inspect, test and replace if necessary.
2. Clean the cable terminals and the battery itself.
3. Make sure cables are in good condition.

Ignition system
1. Are spark plugs in sound condition.
2. Are the distributor points and condenser OK.
3. Check to see that the distributor cap and rotor are not damaged.
4. Check also the ignition coil, and primary and secondary wiring.
5. Is a complete tuneup needed?
6. Set ignition timing (and carburetor slow idle speed) to manufacturer specification.

Fuel system service
1. Set the other carburetor settings properly—fast idle speed and idle mixture.
2. Check the condition of the carburetor air cleaner filter element. Replace if dirty.
3. Set the automatic choke to manufacturer specification for cold weather operation.

Lubrication
1. Change the oil and oil filter if an oil change is due or if the grade of oil in the engine is not suitable for the winter temperature in your area.
2. Lubricate the chassis.
3. Lubricate body points.

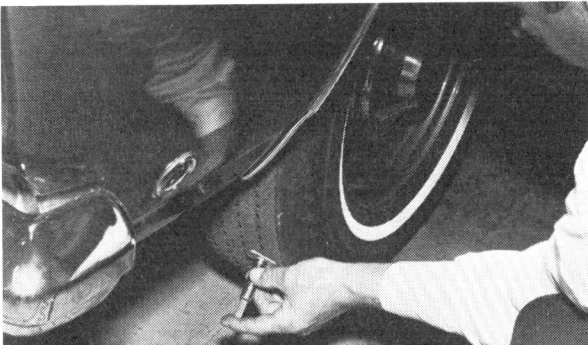

Use a tread depth gauge to tell you if your tires still have at least 1/16-inch tread—the minimum legal and safe limit.

Seat belts need checking, too. A worn belt or loose mounting bolts can lead to seat belt failure if you are in a crash.

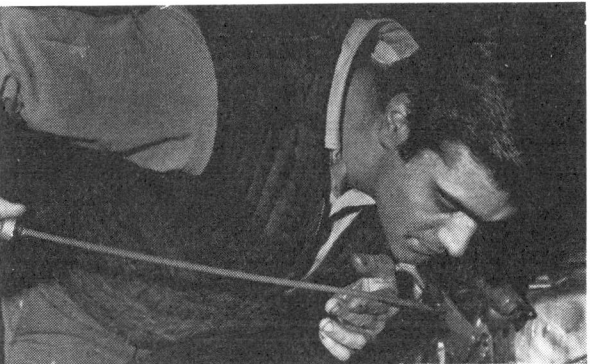

Check the oil level at frequent intervals. Oil level below the safe limit can lead to serious engine damage.

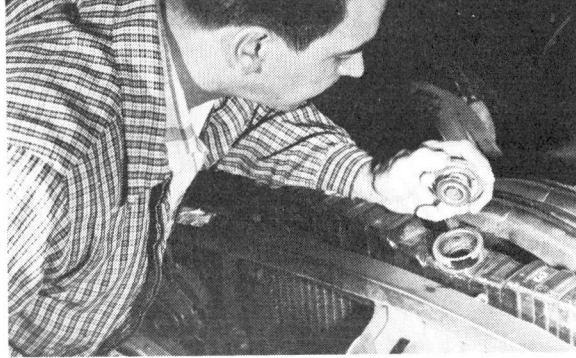

Coolant must be kept at the proper level to keep your engine running at the correct temperature.

Tires
1. Mount snow tires after inspecting them for adequate tread, general condition and pressure.
2. Check front tires for tread, general condition and pressure.
3. Balance wheels on which snow tires have been mounted.
4. If snow tires are unnecessary in your area, rotate your regular tires.

Brakes
1. Check fluid level in the master cylinder. Top off, if necesary.
2. Check system for leaks.
3. Inspect linings for excessive wear.
4. Are brakes adequately adjusted?

Suspension and steering
1. Check steering linkage for tightness.
2. Check power steering reservoir fluid level. Top off, if necessary.
3. Check power steering pump drive belt for wear and adjustment.
4. Check shock absorbers for leakage and wear.
5. Does the front end need realignment?

Visual equipment
1. Check windshield wiper blades for good condition and proper adjustment.
2. Check windshield wipers for proper function.
3. Check windshield washer system for proper function.
4. Check fluid in windshield reservoir. Top off, if necessary.
5. Check front windshield defroster for proper operation.
6. If your car is so equipped, check the rear windshield defroster for proper operation.
7. Check lights and all warning signals for proper function.
8. Check front and rear windshields, all side windows, and all mirrors for condition. There should be no cracks or chips.

Other important inspections
1. Check the exhaust system condition. No leaks should be detectable and all parts should be firmly suspended by hangers and clamps.
2. Check the automatic transmission fluid level and have transmission bands adjusted if necessary.
3. Check the heater for proper operation.

PRE-SUMMER SERVICES

Cooling system
1. Check the system for leaks.
2. Drain and flush the radiator.
3. Test the radiator pressure cap.
4. Check drive belts for wear and proper tension.
5. Check thermostat operation.
6. Check all hoses and clamps for condition, and make sure clamps are tight.
7. Refill system with fresh antifreeze, if needed, or with used antifreeze if less than two years old.
8. Add rust inhibitor-water pump lubricant.

Exhaust system
1. Check muffler and pipes for rusted-through spots.
2. Check clamps for tightness.
3. Lubricate manifold heat control valve.

Brakes
1. Check brake linings for wear.
2. Check fluid level in the master cylinder. Replenish, if necessary.
3. Check system for leaks.
4. Are brakes properly adjusted?

Lubrication
1. Change oil and oil filter if oil change is due or if the grade of oil in the engine is not suitable for the summertime temperature in your area.
2. Lubricate the chassis.
3. Lubricate body points.
4. Check the PCV valve. If not functioning properly, replace.

Battery
1. Inspect, test and replace if necessary.
2. Clean the cable terminals and the battery itself.
3. Make sure cables are in good condition.

Ignition system
1. Inspect spark plugs for condition.
2. Inspect distributor points and condenser for condition.
3. Check to see that the distributor cap and rotor are sound.
4. Check the ignition coil, and primary and secondary wiring.
5. Set ignition timing and carburetor idle speed to manufacturer's specification.

Tires
1. Remove snow tires.
2. Inspect all tires for adequate tread and general condition. Discard questionable tires.
3. Rotate tires.
4. Balance wheel tire assemblies.
5. Inflate tires to recommended pressure.

Suspension and steering
1. Check steering linkage for looseness.
2. Check power steering fluid level. Top off, if necessary.
3. Check power steering pump drive belt for wear and adjustment.
4. Check shock absorbers for leakage and wear.
5. Check front end alignment.

Visual equipment
1. Check windshield wiper blades for condition and proper adjustment.
2. Check windshield wipers for proper function.
3. Check windshield washer system for proper function.
4. Check fluid in the windshield washer reservoir. Top off, if necesary.
5. Check lights and all warning signals for proper function.

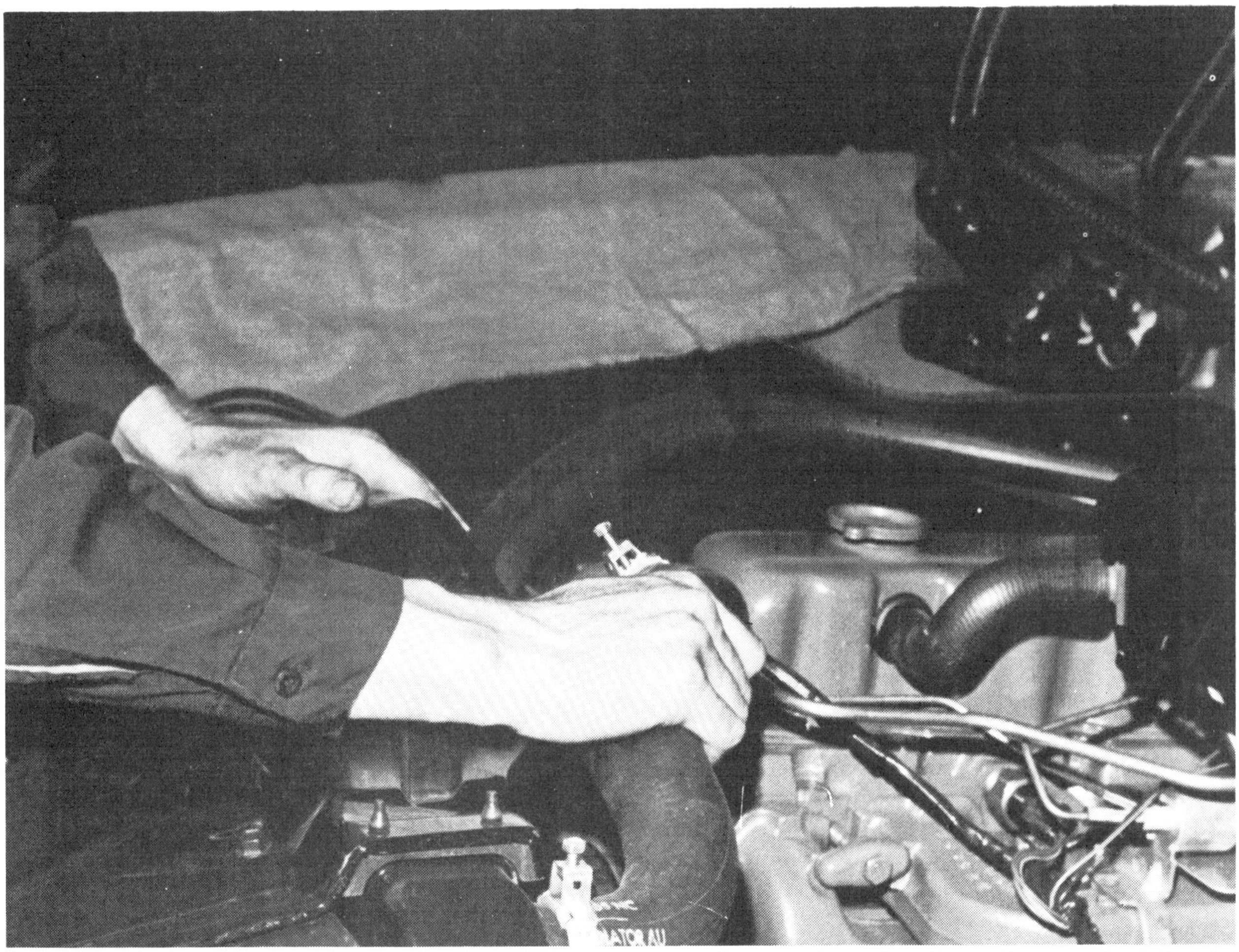

Check cooling system hoses for cracks and leaks, which can cause disastrous loss of coolant and an overheated engine.

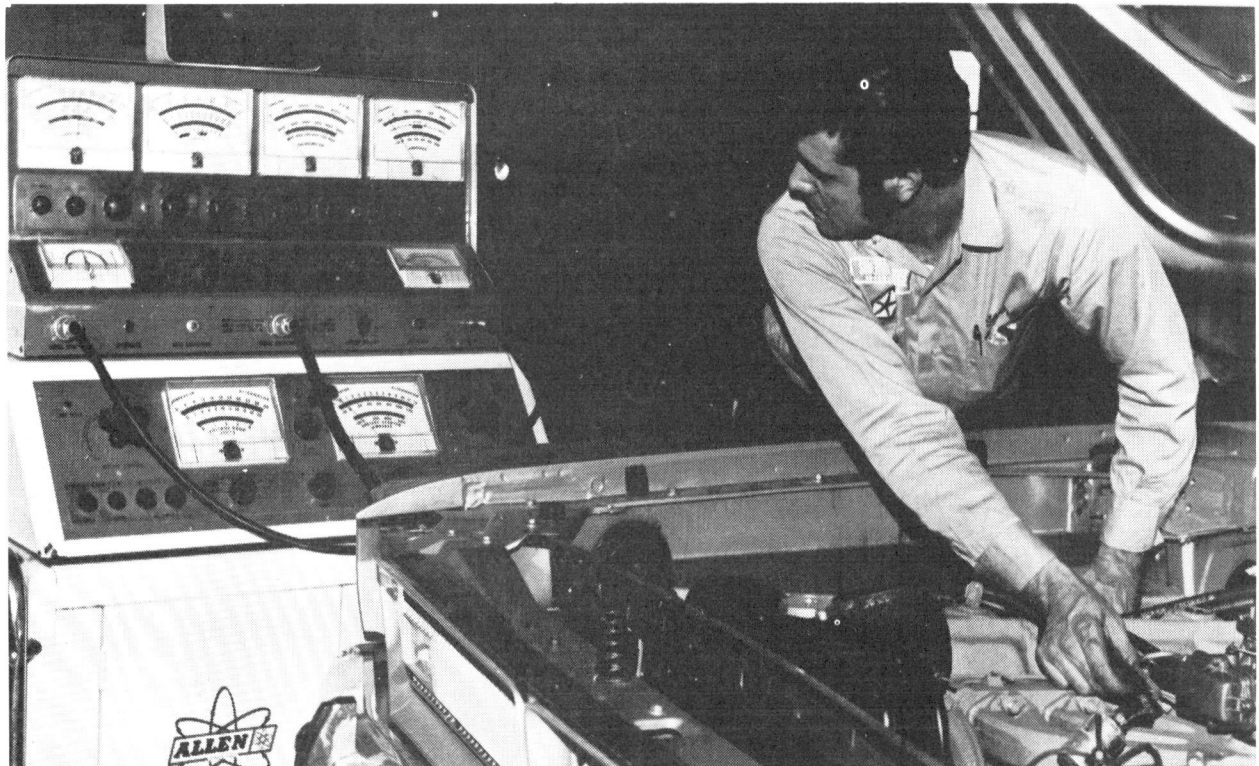

An engine tuned to specifications runs better and gives improved fuel economy.

CHECKING FOR LEAKAGE

Fluid leakage at any point is a definite sign of pending trouble. Some leaks are warnings of safety hazards to come. Others are merely signs of pending equipment failure. In any case make it a point to periodically check the following for indications of fluid leakage:

THE ENGINE

Signs of engine oil at the following locations indicate loose bolts or a bad gasket at that location. If the leak is not checked, you will be wasting a lot oil. Loss of oil could lead to complete or partial engine failure.
1. Front oil seal.
2. Timing gear cover.
3. Fuel pump mounting.
4. Oil filter seat.
5. Oil pan.
6. Rear oil seal.
7. Valve covers.

BRAKES

Indications of brake fluid loss should be immediate cause of investigation. Loss of brake fluid is a definite safety hazard. Check for brake fluid loss at the following areas:
1. Master cylinder. If the master cylinder loses so much fluid so it needs a constant refilling when you check it, there is a leak.
2. Brake fluid on the sidewall of a tire indicates that fluid is leaking from the brake cylinder in that wheel.
3. Check brake lines and connections for signs of leakage.
4. Check brake line-to-master cylinder connections for signs of leakage.

COOLING SYSTEM

1. With the engine cold, check the coolant level in the radiator. If there is a substantial drop from one check to the next, check for a cooling system leak.
2. Inspect radiator and heater hoses and hose connections for signs of leakage.
3. Examine the radiator closely for whitish deposits that indicate leaking fluid.
4. Examine thermostat housing, radiator drain plug, engine drain plug(s), heater hoses and heater for signs of leaking coolant.

POWER STEERING SYSTEM

Warm up engine. Shut it off. Check fluid level in the power steering reservoir. If the level is low, add fluid and check the system for leaks as follows:
1. Start engine and turn steering wheel from one stop to the other a couple of times.
2. Shut off engine.
3. Look for leaks at power steering hose connections, power steering gear and power steering pump.

SHOCK ABSORBERS

Inspect shock absorbers, especially at seal covers, for shock absorber fluid, which has a brown tint to it. A slight trace of dampness is OK. If the leak is heavy, replace the shock.

Replace the fuel filter cartridge as recommended in your owner's manual. A clogged filter can lead to engine malfunction and you may find yourself stuck.

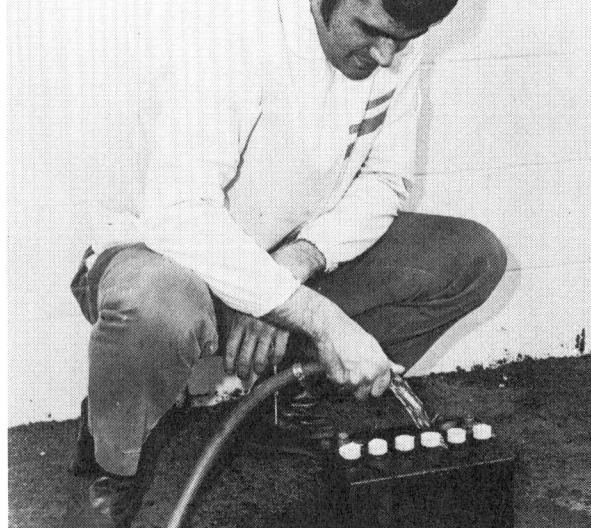

Keep your battery clean. Dirt, acid film and corrosion around the battery posts can lead to early failure.

BEFORE YOU TAKE A TRIP

If you follow a regular maintenance schedule, your car should be ready for either short or long hauls at any time. However, for longer trips it is a good idea to make a few special checks.

GENERAL INFORMATION

Wheels that are unbalanced or out of line often go unnoticed when you are just driving around town, but they can cause severe vibration at high speed or create uneven tire wear in just a few hundred miles of turnpike travel. You'll save time and grief by having them checked.

Fan belts and other drive belts should be inspected and replaced if there is any doubt about their condition. The same precaution applies to radiator hoses.

Be sure you have the necessary tools for changing tires or making minor repairs. For safety's sake, carry the basic emergency equipment recommended by auto experts—a flashlight, screwdriver, pliers, tire gauge, jack, extra fan belt, flares or reflectors, and a first aid kit.

Front wheels should be aligned regularly. Correct alignment allows the wheels to run true, which makes for a safer, more stable vehicle. Correct alignment will also give you longer and more even tire wear.

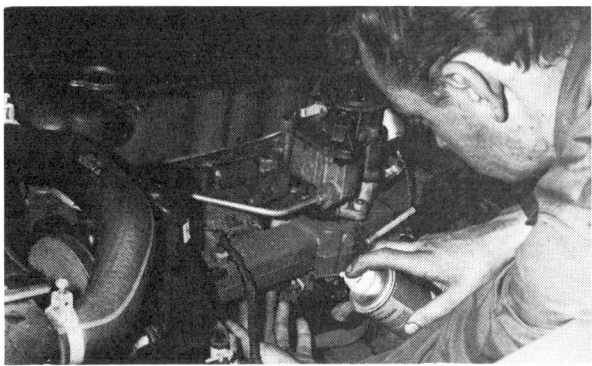

The manifold heat valve should be lubricated regularly to prevent it from sticking. Generally, the valve sticks in the heat position, making the intake manifold too hot. Economy and power suffer as a result.

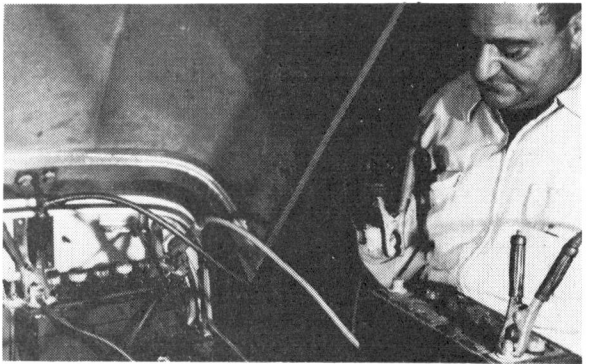

When using jumper cables, be sure the hookup is correct (positive to positive and negative to negative). An incorrect hookup can permanently damage the ignition system and the battery.

TRIP CHECKLIST

The following checklist of things to do before taking off on a trip will assure that the trip will be a safe one, hopefully without any breakdowns to mar the occasion.
1. Check oil level. Note the condition of the oil and have it changed if dirty or if a change is due.
2. Check the coolant level in the radiator and inspect radiator hoses.
3. Check the automatic transmission fluid level.
4. Check the level of the power steering fluid in the power steering reservoir.
5. Check the brake fluid level in the master cylinder and look for signs of fluid leakage.
6. Check all tire pressures including the spare, with tires cold. Inflate the tires four pounds extra if you are going to carry a full carload or if you will be driving at high speed. Check the depth of tire tread and see that tires are not damaged. Work embedded stones out of the tread.
7. Clean headlights and windshield.
8. Fill the windshield washer reservoir with fluid.
9. Check windshield wiper blades and replace if they are worn or brittle.
10. Inspect fan belts for fraying and looseness. Replace, if damaged. Adjust to proper tightness.
11. Check battery electrolyte level, and the battery's state of charge.
12. Check the operation of turn signals, hazard warning flasher lights, stoplights, taillights, and backup lights.
13. Set up and store your on-the-road emergency tool kit.
14. Fill the gas tank.
15. Have an enjoyable, safe trip.

AN ON-THE-ROAD EMERGENCY KIT

It is recommended that you carry the following items with you to be able to handle on-the-road emergencies:
1. Copy of the Motor Troubleshooter guide.
2. Flares.
3. Good lug wrench and jack.
4. Jumper cables.
5. Screwdrivers, pliers and wrenches.
6. Strong tow rope or chain.
7. Old blankets.
8. Folding camp shovel.
9. Fire extinguisher.
10. Rags or strong paper towels.
11. A cream hand cleaner.
12. Windshield de-icer spray (in winter only).
13. Windshield scraper-brush (in winter only).
14. Small snow shovel (in winter only).
15. Bag of sand (in winter only).
16. Extra warm coats and blankets (in winter only).
17. First aid kit.
18. Pencils and notebook.
19. Spare coins for meters and phone calls.
20. Flashlight.
21. Road maps.
22. Extra electrical fuses.
23. Pocket tire pressure gauge.
24. Extra fan belt, two spark plugs, set of ignition points.
25. This book.

MANUFACTURER'S RECOMMENDED SERVICE SCHEDULES

AMERICAN MOTORS

1968-69 MODELS

Services to be done	Mileage (odometer reading)													
	4,000	8,000	12,000	16,000	20,000	24,000	28,000	32,000	36,000	40,000	44,000	48,000	52,000	56,000
Change engine oil and install new oil filter *every four (4) months or at indicated mileage, whichever occurs first*	▼	▼	▼	▼	▼	▼	▼	▼	▼	▼	▼	▼	▼	▼
Clean V8 engine oil filler cap	▼	▼	▼	▼	▼	▼	▼	▼	▼	▼	▼	▼	▼	▼

1968-69 MODELS/continued

Services to be done	Mileage (odometer reading)													
	4,000	8,000	12,000	16,000	20,000	24,000	28,000	32,000	36,000	40,000	44,000	48,000	52,000	56,000
Clean 6-cyl. engine PCV wire-gauze filter			◆	★	◆	★◆		◆	★	◆		★◆		
Replace PCV valve				▼		▼			▼			▼		
Clean carburetor air cleaner element	◆	★◆	◆	★◆	◆			◆	★◆	◆	★◆		◆	★◆
Replace carburetor air cleaner element						▼						▼		
Replace fuel filter			★●			▼			★●			▼		
Inspect and correct fluid levels	▼	▼	▼	▼	▼	▼	▼	▼	▼	▼	▼	▼	▼	▼
Inspect and correct drive belts		▼		▼		▼		▼		▼		▼		▼
Inspect and correct operation of exhaust manifold heat valve	◆	★◆	◆	★◆	◆	★◆	◆	★◆	◆	★◆	◆	★◆	◆	★
Adjust automatic transmission rear band	▼													
Tune automatic transmission	◆	★●	★●◆●	★●	★●	▼	★●	★●◆●	★●	★●	▼	★●	★●	
Verify manual transmission clutch adjustment			◆	★		◆		★	◆			★◆		
Inspect and lubricate chassis			◆●		★	◆		★	◆			★◆		
Replace engine coolant and tuneup cooling system	1968 models—every 24 months													
	1969 models—after first 24 months and every 12 months thereafter													
Inspect and adjust choke; adjust carburetor idle speed and mixture			▼			▼			▼			▼		
Check ignition timing			▼			▼			▼			▼		
Rotate distributor cam lubricator			▼						▼					
Replace distributor cam lubricator						▼						▼		
Inspect ignition points, coil, and spark plug wires; replace if required			▼			▼			▼			▼		
Inspect spark plugs, clean and re-gap (or replace) if required			▼			▼			▼			▼		
Inspect "Air-Guard" hose connections (V8 engine with manual transmission)			▼			▼			▼			▼		
Perform factory recommended road test to evaluate performance and handling	▼	▼	▼	▼	▼	▼	▼	▼	▼	▼	▼	▼	▼	▼
Verify tire pressure to specification	▼	▼	▼	▼	▼	▼	▼	▼	▼	▼	▼	▼	▼	▼
Inspect brake lining condition and parts			◆	★		◆		★	◆			★◆		
Align front suspension			▼		▼		▼		▼		▼		▼	▼
Balance tires			▼		▼		▼		▼		▼		▼	▼
Rotate tires			▼		▼		▼		▼		▼		▼	▼
Perform body lubrication			▼		▼		▼		▼		▼		▼	▼

▼—All models
★—1968 models only
◆—1969 models only
●—Recommended if service has been under severe operating conditions

1970-72 MODELS

Services to be done	Mileage (odometer reading)											
	6,000	12,000	18,000	24,000	30,000	36,000	42,000	48,000	54,000	60,000	66,000	72,000
Change engine oil and install new oil filter *every six (6) months* or at indicated mileage, whichever occurs first—more often under severe operating conditions	▼	▼	▼	▼	▼	▼	▼	▼	▼	▼	▼	▼
Replace engine coolant and tuneup cooling system	1970-71 models: after first 24 months and every 12 months thereafter											
	1972 models: before start of third winter season and then every fall											
Engine oil filler cap (filter type)—clean	▼	▼	▼	▼	▼	▼	▼	▼	▼	▼	▼	▼
Fluid levels (including battery)—inspect and correct	▼	▼	▼	▼	▼	▼	▼	▼	▼	▼	▼	▼
Heat valve (exhaust manifold)—inspect and lubricate	▼	▼	▼	▼	▼	▼	▼	▼	▼	▼	▼	▼
Drive belts (condition and tension)—inspect and correct	▼	▼	▼	▼								
Carburetor air cleaner element—clean	★◆■	★◆■	★◆	■	★◆	★◆■	★◆	■	★◆	★◆■	★◆	■
Carburetor air cleaner element—replace			★◆●	■	★◆	■	★◆●	■	★◆	■	★◆●	■

1970-72 MODELS

Services to be done	Mileage (odometer reading)											
	6,000	12,000	18,000	24,000	30,000	36,000	42,000	48,000	54,000	60,000	66,000	72,000
PCV valve—replace; PCV filter (6 cylinder)—clean		★ ◆	■	★ ◆	■	★ ◆	■	★ ◆	■	★ ◆	■	★ ◆
Fuel filter element—replace		▼		▼		▼		▼		▼		▼
Manual transmission—verify clutch adjustment	★ ◆	★ ◆	■	★ ◆		★ ◆ ■		★ ◆	■	★ ◆		★ ◆ ■
Automatic transmission—adjust rear band	★ ◆											
Automatic transmission—complete tuneup	★ ◆ ●	★ ◆ ●		★ ◆ ●	★ ◆ ■	★ ◆ ●		★ ◆ ● ■	★ ◆ ●	★ ◆ ●		★ ◆ ● ■
Complete chassis lubrication			★ ◆ ●	■	★ ◆	★ ◆ ● ■		★ ◆ ●	■	★ ◆		★ ◆ ● ■
Complete emissions control precision tuneup		★ ◆	■	★ ◆	■	★ ◆	■	★ ◆	■	★ ◆	■	★ ◆
Brakes (lining condition and parts)—inspect		★ ◆	■	★ ◆		★ ◆		★ ◆	■	★ ◆		★ ◆
Complete body lubrication	■	★ ◆ ■	■	★ ◆ ■	■	★ ◆ ■	■	★ ◆ ■	■	★ ◆ ■	■	★ ◆ ■
Front suspension—align		★ ◆	■	★ ◆		★ ◆ ■		★ ◆	■	★ ◆		★ ◆ ■
Tires—verify inflation, check condition, rotate, balance	▼	▼	▼	▼	▼	▼	▼	▼	▼	▼	▼	▼
Factory recommended road test (performance and handling)	▼	▼	▼	▼	▼	▼	▼	▼	▼	▼	▼	▼

▼—All models
★—1970 models only
◆—1971 models only
■—1972 models only
●—Recommended if service has been under severe operating conditions

1973-76 MODELS

Services to be done	Mileage (odometer reading)															
	5,000	10,000	15,000	20,000	25,000	30,000	35,000	40,000	45,000	50,000	55,000	60,000	65,000	70,000	75,000	80,000
Change engine oil and install new oil filter every five (5) months or at indicated mileage, whichever occurs first—more often under severe operating conditions	▼	▼	▼	▼	▼	▼	▼	▼	▼	▼	▼	▼	▼	▼	▼	▼
Replace engine coolant and tuneup cooling system	1973: Before start of third winter season and then every fall thereafter — 1974-76: At 25,000 miles or 25 months, whichever occurs first and then at the start of every winter season															
"Twin-Grip" rear axle—change lubricant						▼						▼				
Automatic transmission tuneup*	1973: Every 25,000 miles or 2 years, whichever occurs first — 1974: Every 25,000 miles or 25 months, whichever occurs first — 1975-76: Every 30,000 miles or 30 months, whichever occurs first															
Fluids (including battery)—inspect and correct level	▼	▼	▼	▼	▼	▼	▼	▼	▼	▼	▼	▼	▼	▼	▼	▼
Complete body lubrication and brake inspection			▼			▼			▼			▼			▼	
Front suspension—inspect/correct camber, caster and toe			▼			▼			▼			▼			▼	
Manual transmission clutch—inspect/correct adjustment			▼			▼			▼			▼			▼	
Fuel filter element—replace			▼			▼			▼			▼			▼	
Carburetor air cleaner element—replace			★		◆	★ ■ ◄		★	◆			★ ■ ◄			★	
Complete chassis lubrication					★	■ ◄				★ ◆		■ ◄			★ ◆	
Heat valve (exhaust manifold)—inspect and lubricate	★ ◆	★ ◆		★ ◆	★ ◆	■ ◄	★ ◆	★ ◆		★ ◆	★ ◆	■ ◄	★ ◆	★ ◆		★ ◆
Drive belts—inspect condition and tension	★ ◆	★ ◆	◄	★ ◆	★ ◆	■ ◄	★ ◆	★ ◆	◄	★ ◆	★ ◆	■ ◄	★ ◆	★ ◆	◄	★ ◆
EGR valve service	1973-74 only: Service at 10,000 mile intervals if leaded fuel is used — Service at 25,000 mile intervals if lead-free fuel is used															

1973-76 MODELS/continued

Services to be done	Mileage (odometer reading)																
	5,000	10,000	15,000	20,000	25,000	30,000	35,000	40,000	45,000	50,000	55,000	60,000	65,000	70,000	75,000	80,000
Complete precision emission control tuneup			★			★ ◆ ■			★ ◆			★ ◆ ■ ◀			★ ◆	

▼—All models
★—1973 models only
◆—1974 models only
■—1975 models only
◀—1976 models only
*Recommended if service has been under severe operating conditions

NOTES TO AMERICAN MOTORS MAINTENANCE GUIDES:
Complete chassis lubrication includes inspection and lubrication of—
1. Front suspension ball joints.
2. Front wheel bearings.
3. Clutch levers and linkage.
4. Turning radius stop plate and bracket.

Complete body lubrication and brake inspection includes—
1. Inspection and correction, as needed, of brake linings and other parts.
2. Hood latch and hinges.
3. Door latches, lock cylinders and door hinges.
4. Trunk lid (or tailgate) hinges and latches.
5. Front seat racks.
6. Ash tray slides.
7. Glove box door latch and hinge.
8. Courtesy light switch buttons.
9. Apply silicone lubricant to all door, window and trunk (or tailgate) rubber weather seals.

Complete precision emission control tuneup includes—
1. Air-Guard system hoses—inspect and correct as required.
2. Carburetor air cleaner element—replace.
3. Choke linkage—inspect for free movement.
4. Coil and spark plug wires—inspect and replace as required.
5. Distributor advance mechanisms—check and correct as required.
6. Distributor cap and rotor—inspect and replace as required.
7. Drive belts—inspect condition and tighten or correct as required.
8. Engine oil filler cap (filter type)—clean and soak in oil.
9. Fuel filter element—replace.
10. Fuel system cap, tank, lines and connections—inspect for integrity and correct as required.
11. Fuel vapor inlet filter at charcoal canister—replace.
12. Heat valve (exhaust manifold)—inspect and lubricate.
13. Idle speed (curb and fast) and mixture—check and reset as required.
14. Ignition timing—check and set as required.
15. PCV filter (6-cylinder)—clean.
16. PCV hoses—inspect and replace as required.
17. PCV valve—replace.
18. Spark plugs—replace.
19. TAC system hoses—inspect and correct as required.
20. Transmission controlled spark system—inspect and correct as required.
21. Vacuum fittings, hoses and connections—inspect and correct as required.

CHRYSLER

1968-74 MODELS

Services to be done	Maintenance Interval								
	Monthly	Every 3 months or 4,000 miles, whichever occurs first	Every 6 months or 8,000 miles, whichever occurs first	Every 6 months	Every 12 months	Every 12 months or 12,000 miles, whichever occurs first	Every 18,000 miles	Every 24 months or 24,000 miles, whichever occurs first	Every 36 months or 36,000 miles, whichever occurs first
Battery—check fluid level	X								
Cooling system—check fluid level	X								
Engine crankcase oil—replace		X							
Power steering fluid—check level		X							
Carburetor air filter—inspect and/or clean		X							
Engine oil filter—replace			X						
Tire rotation			X						
Carburetor choke shaft—inspect, clean, and apply solvent				X					
Manifold heat control valve—inspect and apply solvent				X					
Transmission—check fluid level				X					
Rear axle—check fluid level				X					
Steering gear (manual)—check fluid level				X					
Steering linkage—inspect				X					
Suspension ball joints—inspect				X					
Universal joints—inspect				X					
Brake master cylinder—check fluid level				X					
Brake hoses—inspect				X					
Headlights—aim				X					
Hood latch and safety catch—inspect, clean and lubricate				X					
Carburetor air filter—replace					X				
Cooling system—check and service as required					X				

1968-74 MODELS/continued

Services to be done	Monthly	Every 3 months or 4,000 miles, whichever occurs first	Every 6 months or 8,000 miles, whichever occurs first	Every 6 months	Every 12 months	Every 12 months or 12,000 miles, whichever occurs first	Every 18,000 miles	Every 24 months or 24,000 miles, whichever occurs first	Every 36 months or 36,000 miles, whichever occurs first
Crankcase ventilation system—inspect						X			
Crankcase inlet air cleaner—clean and lubricate						X			
Throttle linkage—lubricate						X			
Brakes—inspect						X			
Exhaust gas recirculation system ('73 and '74 models)—inspect and service as required						X			
Front wheel bearings—lubricate						X			
Fuel vapor storage canister ('71 and later models)—replace filter						X			
Spark plugs—replace							X		
Carburetor air filter (paper)—replace								X	
Crankcase ventilator valve—replace								X	
Distributor (non-electronic ignition only)—service and lubricate								X	
Fuel filter—replace								X	
Brake pedal linkage bushings—lubricate								X	
Front suspension ball joints									X
Steering tie rod ends									X
Clutch torque shaft bearings									X

The following to be lubricated when necessary:
  Body mechanisms
  Clutch release bearing sleeve, fork fingers and pivot
  Column-mounted gearshift linkage
  Floor-mounted gearshift controls
  Parking brake mechanism
  Speedometer cable									

1975-76 MODELS

Services to be done	Every 6 months	Every 6 months or 5,000 miles, whichever occurs first	Every 12 months or 10,000 miles, whichever occurs first	Every 10,000 miles	Every 12 months or 15,000 miles, whichever occurs first	Every 15,000 miles	Every 24 months or 30,000 miles, whichever occurs first	Every 25,000 miles	Every 30,000 miles	Every 36 months or 35,000 miles, whichever occurs first
Carburetor choke shaft—apply solvent	X									
Fast idle cam and pivot pin—apply solvent	X									
Exhaust system—check for leaks, missing or damaged part	X									
Brake master cylinder—check fluid level	X									
Transmission and rear axle—check fluid level	X									
Brake and power steering hoses—check for deterioration or leaks	X									
Air conditioner—check belts, sight glass and operation of controls	X									
Ball joints, steering linkage, and universal joints—inspect seals	X									
Hood lock, release mechanism and safety catch—lubricate	X									
Engine oil—change		X								
Power steering—check fluid level		X								
Drive belts—check condition and tension		X								
Upper and lower control arm bushings—inspect		X								
Cooling system—check and service as required			X							
Engine oil filter—replace	X (first time only)		X							
Tires—rotate				X						
Brake linings—inspect				X						
Cooling system—drain, flush and refill					X		X (first time only)			
EGR system—check operation and service as required						X				

1975-76 MODELS/continued

Services to be done	Every 6 months	Every 6 months or 5,000 miles, whichever occurs first	Every 12 months or 10,000 miles, whichever occurs first	Every 10,000 miles	Every 12 months or 15,000 miles, whichever occurs first	Every 15,000 miles	Every 24 months or 30,000 miles, whichever occurs first	Every 25,000 miles	Every 30,000 miles	Every 36 months or 35,000 miles, whichever occurs first
Idle speed and air/fuel mixture—check and adjust						X				
PCV valve—check operation						X				
Tappet adjustment (6 cyl. engine)						X				
Underhood rubber and plastic components (emission hoses)—inspect						X				
Vapor storage canister filter element—replace						X				
Front wheel bearings—inspect								X		
Automatic transmission (severe usage only)—change fluid and filter, adjust bands								X		
Automatic choke—check and adjust									X	
Carburetor air filter—replace									X	
Crankcase inlet air cleaner—clean									X	
Fuel filter—replace									X	
Ignition cables, distributor cap and rotor—check									X	
PCV valve—replace									X	
Manifold heat control valve—apply solvent									X	
Spark plugs—inspect*									X	
Ball joints and tie rod ends—lubricate										X

*Long-life spark plugs are expected to perform satisfactorily for at least 50,000 miles.

FORD
1968-74 MODELS

Services to be done		Service Interval (Number of months or thousands of miles, whichever occurs first)								
		6	12	18	24	30	36	42	48	54
Engine oil—change①		X	X	X	X	X	X	X	X	X
Oil filter—replace①		X			X		X		X	
Oil filler breather cap—clean			X		X		X		X	
Exhaust control valve—lubricate and free		X	X	X	X	X	X	X	X	X
Fuel system filter—replace		X								
Carburetor air cleaner element②	Check		X				X			
	Replace				X				X	
Idle fuel mixture—adjust	4 cyl.		X	X	X		X		X	
	6 and 8 cyl.	X			X					
Fast idle speed—adjust	4 cyl.		X	X	X		X		X	
	6 and 8 cyl.	X			X					
Curb idle speed and TSP off speed—adjust	4 cyl.		X	X	X		X		X	
	6 and 8 cyl.	X			X					
Carburetor throttle, choke and delay valve—check	4 cyl.		X	X	X		X			
	6 and 8 cyl.	X			X					
Carburetor air valve—check		X			X					
Deceleration valve—check		X	X		X		X		X	
Crankcase emissions filter in air cleaner—replace②					X				X	
Engine valve clearance (2000 cc and 2800 cc)—adjust				X	X		X		X	
Intake manifold bolts—torque	4 cyl. and V6	X		X		X		X		X
	6 and 8 cyl.		X							
Exhaust manifold bolts (4 cyl.)—torque		X								
Fuel vapor emissions system—inspect					X				X	
PCV valve—replace					X				X	
PCV system	Check		X				X			
	Clean				X				X	
Initial ignition timing—adjust	4 cyl. and V6	X	X		X		X		X	
	6 and 8 cyl.—conventional	X			X				X	
	6 and 8 cyl.—breakerless			X			X			

1968-74 MODELS/continued

Services to be done		6	12	18	24	30	36	42	48	54
Distributor points—4 cyl. and V6	Inspect	X								
	Replace		X		X		X		X	
Distributor points, 6 and 8 cyl.—replace					X				X	
Distributor cap and rotor—inspect	4 cyl.		X		X		X		X	
	6 and 8 cyl.—conventional				X				X	
	6 and 8 cyl.—breakerless			X			X			
Spark plug wires—inspect	Conventional ignition①		X		X		X		X	
	Breakerless ignition①③			X			X			
Spark plugs—replace	Conventional ignition①④		X		X		X		X	
	Breakerless ignition①③④				X		X			
Spark control systems and delay valve—check					X		X		X	
Air cleaner temperature control and delay valve—check					X		X		X	
Thermactor system—check							X		X	
Mounting bolts on all belt-driven accessories (4 cyl.)—torque					X		X		X	
Evaporative emissions canister—inspect	4 cyl.				X		X		X	
	6 and 8 cyl.						X		X	
EGR system and delay valve—check⑤					X		X		X	
Drive belt tension—check		X								
Drive belt condition—inspect					X		X		X	
Coolant condition and protection—check⑥					X		X		X	
Cooling system hoses and clamps—inspect							X		X	
Automatic transmission—check fluid level		X			X		X		X	X
Brake master cylinder—check fluid level		X	X	X	X	X	X	X	X	X
Steering linkage—check for looseness and damaged seals					X		X		X	
Front suspension ball joints—lubricate							X			
Steering linkage (Ford, Mercury)—lubricate							X			
Power steering valve ball stud (Maverick, Comet)—lubricate							X			
Front suspension inner arm shaft bushings (Maverick, Comet)—lubricate							X			
Rear axle fluid—check level		X			X		X		X	X
Automatic transmissions bands—adjust⑦			X							
Brake linings, hoses, lines—inspect						X			X	
Front wheel bearings—clean, repack						X			X	
Manual transmission—check fluid level		X			X		X		X	X
Clutch linkage and pedal free play—adjust		X	X	X	X	X	X	X	X	X

NOTES:

①—Normal oil change is every 6,000 miles or four months, whichever occurs first. Normal oil filter change is at first 6,000 miles or four months and at alternate oil change periods thereafter. If operating under severe service conditions, change oil every two months or 3,000 miles and oil filter every four months or 6,000 miles. Under severe service conditions check spark plug wires and clean and regap spark plugs every four months or 6,000 miles, whichever comes first. Severe service include:
  1. Extended periods of idling or low-speed operation.
  2. Towing trailers over 2,000 pounds gross loaded weight.
  3. Driving short distances (less than 10 miles) while outside temperature remains below 10° F for 60 days or more.
  4. Excessive dust conditions.

②—More often if operated in severe dust conditions.
③—Perform at each 12,000 miles or 12 months on engines using leaded fuel.
④—If spark plugs are not replaced at 12,000 miles or 18,000 mile intervals, replace the complete plug set at time of plug malfunction.
⑤—Clean the exhaust passages in the EGR valve, carburetor, spacer and intake manifold.
⑥—If the coolant looks dirty or rusty, clean the cooling system and refill it with the correct solution of cooling system fluid and water. Drain and flush cooling system and replace coolant every 36,000 miles or 36 months.
⑦—Each 12,000 miles for severe service conditions.

1975-76 MODELS

Services to be done		5	6	10	12	15	18	20	24	25	30	35	36	40	42	45	48	50
Engine oil—change①②		AB	C	AB	C	AB	C	AB	C	AB	ABC	AB	C	AB	C	AB	C	AB
Oil filter—replace①②		AB	C			AB	C			AB	C	AB			C	AB		
Intake manifold bolts/nuts—torque			C ⑭			B	C	A			C ⑭				C ⑭			
Exhaust control valve—lubricate, check③			C		C	B	A	C			BC		C	A	C	B	C	
Fuel system filter—replace			C			B	A											
Carburetor air cleaner element④	Check				C	B							C		B			
	Replace						A	C			B			A			C	
Emissions filter in air cleaner④	Check				C	B							C		B			
	Replace						A	C			B			A			C	

1975-76 MODELS/continued

Services to be done		5	6	10	12	15	18	20	24	25	30	35	36	40	42	45	48	50
Idle fuel mixture—adjust	All except 4 cyl.		C			B		A	C		B			A		B	C	
	4 cyl.		C		C	B		A	C		B		C	A		B		
Fast idle speed—adjust	All except 4 cyl.	AB	C			B		A	C		B			A		B		
	4 cyl.	AB	C		C	B		A	C		B		C	A		B	C	
Curb idle speed—adjust		AB				B		A			B			A		B		
Curb idle speed and TSP off speed—adjust	All except 4 cyl.		C						C									
	4 cyl.		C		C				C				C			C		
Throttle solenoid off speed—adjust		AB																
Air cleaner temp. control and delay valve—check ⑤						B		A	C		B			A		B	C	
Throttle and choke linkage and delay valve or air valve—check	All except 4 cyl.		C ⑤			B		A	C ⑤		B			A		B		
	4 cyl.		C ⑤		C ⑤	B		A	C ⑤		B		C ⑤	A		B		
Fuel deceleration valve—check ⑤		AB ⑭	C		C	B ⑭		A ⑭	C		B ⑭		C	A ⑭		B ⑭	C	
Engine valve clearance (2800)—adjust					C	B		A	C		B		C	A		B	C	
Fuel vapor emissions system—inspect								A	C		B			A			C	
PCV valve—replace								A	C		B			A			C	
PCV system ⑤	Check				C	B		A						C	A	B		
	Clean							A	C		B						C	
Initial ignition timing—adjust						B	C	A			B			C	A	B		
Ignition system—check ⑥						B		A			B				A	B		
Distributor cap and rotor—inspect ⑦						B	C	A			B			C	A	B		
Spark plugs—replace ① ⑧						B	C	A			B			C	A	B		
Spark plug wires—check ⑨						B	C	A			B			C	A	B		
Crankcase breather cap (if so equipped)—check ⑮					C				C					C			C	
Spark control system and delay valve—check ⑤					C	B		A	C		B			C	A	B	C	
Thermactor system—check ⑤						B		A	C		B			A		B	C	
Evaporative emissions canister—inspect ⑤ ⑩	All except 4 cyl.							A	C		B			A			C	
	4 cyl.				C			A	C		B			C	A		C	
EGR system and delay valve—check ⑤ ⑪					C				C					C			C	
Drive belt tension—check			C			B		A										
Drive belt condition—check					C				C		B			C	A	B	C	
Belt-driven accessories (4 cyl.)—check ⑫					C	B		A	C		B			C	A	B	C	
Coolant condition and protection—check ⑬					C	B		A	C							B	C	
Coolant—replace										B	C	A						
Cooling system hoses and clamps—check									C			B	AB				C	
Exhaust system heat shield—inspect ⑯		AB				AB			AB					AB				
Transmission fluid level—check		AB	C			AB	C		ABC						C	AB		
Rear axle fluid level—check		AB	C			AB	C		ABC						C	AB		
Brake master cylinder fluid level—check		AB	C		C	AB	C		C		ABC			C	C	AB	C	
Clutch linkage and free play—inspect		AB	C		C	AB	C		C		ABC			C	C	AB	C	
Steering linkage (looseness and seals)—inspect					C	AB			C		AB			C		AB	C	
Automatic transmission band—adjust ⑰	Normal svc.					C	AB											
	Severe svc.	AB			C	AB			C		AB			C		AB	C	
Brake linings, hoses, front wheel bearing lubrication—inspect									C	AB					C			AB
Front suspension and steering linkage—lubricate											AB							
Front suspension ball joints—lubricate											C							
Automatic transmission (continuous service only)—replace fluid											AB							
Exhaust system—inspect ⑱						C			C		AB			C			C	

NOTES:

Three maintenance schedules, identified by the letters A, B and C, are specified in the chart. The schedule applying to the particular vehicle is identified on a decal on the glove box door which displays either an A, B or C.

① —For A and B rated cars—when operating the vehicle under severe service conditions, change engine oil every 2½ months or 2,500 miles. Change oil filter the first oil change and every 5 months or 5,000 miles thereafter. Check, clean and regap spark plugs every 5,000 miles.

For C rated cars—when operating the vehicle under severe service conditions, change oil every 2 months or 3,000 miles and the oil filter every 4 months or 6,000 miles. Clean and regap spark plugs every 4 months or 6,000 miles.

Severe service conditions include:
- Extended periods of idling or low-speed operation.
- Driving short distances (less than 10 miles) while outside temperature remains below 10° F for 60 days or more.
- Excessive dust conditions.

② —For C rated cars—normal oil change is at every 6,000 miles or 4 months, whichever occurs first. Normal oil filter change is at first 6,000 miles or 4 months and at alternative oil change periods thereafter.

③ —Lubricate and free up at each oil change (C rated cars only).

④ —Replace more often if operated in severe dust conditions.

⑤ —Adjust, repair or replace as required.

⑥ —For A rated cars—check with scope (recheck after any maintenance or repair).

⑦ —Clean or replace as indicated by scope check.

⑧ —If not replaced at 12,000 or 18,000 mile intervals, replace complete set at time of plug malfunction.

⑨ —Repair or replace wires as indicated by scope check and verified by continuity check.

1975-76 MODELS/continued

⑩—Replace canister if contaminated by water, oil, etc.
⑪—Check exhaust passages in EGR valve, carburetor spacer, and intake manifold.
⑫—Check and torque to specifications.
⑬—If coolant is dirty or rusty in appearance, the system should be drained, cleaned and refilled with the prescribed solution of cooling system fluid and water.
⑭—Four-cylinder and V-6 only.
⑮—More often if operated in severe dust conditions.
⑯—Remove accumulated debris or replace shield as required. Perform each 5,000 miles for severe service usage over unpaved roadways or off-road applications.
⑰—Severe service operation (see note 1 for definition of "severe service.")
⑱—Perform each 6,000 miles for severe service usage over unpaved roadways or off-road applications.

GENERAL MOTORS

1968-74 MODELS

Services to be done	Maintenance Interval		
	Every 4 months or 6,000 miles, whichever occurs first	Every 12 months or 12,000 miles, whichever occurs first	Every 24 months or 24,000 miles, whichever occurs first
Change engine oil (modify interval to every two (2) months or 3,000 miles if car is driven under severe operating conditions)	X		
Engine oil filter—replace	Replace at first oil change and every second oil change thereafter		
Fluid levels, all—check and add if necessary	X		
Crankcase ventilation filter—clean*	X		
Linkages (transmission, throttle, manual shift, clutch, cruise control)—lubricate		X	
Body hinges, hood stops, latches and rubber parts—lubricate	X		
Tire pressures—check when cold	X		
Tires, except spare—rotate	At 6,000 mile intervals		
Drive belts—check and adjust	X		
Steering linkage—lubricate and check for lash and wear, check seals for damage	Inspect at this interval	X	
Air conditioner—service system		At 12 month intervals	
Carburetor—replace fuel inlet filter		X	
Spark plugs—clean and gap or replace		X	
Distributor points—adjust or replace; set timing		X	
Carburetor—adjust idle speeds and mixture		X	
PCV system—replace valve; clean hoses		X	
Battery—clean terminals and cables		X	
Cooling system—pressure test, wash radiator cap and add coolant if necessary		X	
Air cleaner element—replace*			X
Automatic transmission—change fluid and clean or change strainer		X (Under heavy duty conditions or extreme stop-go driving)	X (Under normal conditions)
Engine coolant—service system and install new coolant		At 24 month intervals	
Brake system warning light—check operation		X	
Ball joints—lubricate and check for lash and wear and inspect seals for damage	X (Beginning with '71 models)	X ('68, '69, '70 models)	
Front wheel bearings (rear wheel bearings on front wheel drive vehicles)—repack	When brake service requires drum or disc removal		
Speedometer cable—lubricate			X
Brake lines and hoses—inspect	X		
Exhaust system—inspect	X		
Power steering belt, fluid level, pipes and hoses	X		
Canister filter—replace (beginning with '71 models)		X	
Headlight aim—check		X	
Anti-spin differential—change		X (One time only—at first 12,000 mi. or 12 months)	

1968-74 MODELS/continued

Services to be done	Every 4 months or 6,000 miles, whichever occurs first	Every 12 months or 12,000 miles, whichever occurs first	Every 24 months or 24,000 miles, whichever occurs first
Chassis—lubricate		X (1973-74 models)	
Final drive axle boots and output shaft seal—check condition			X
Manifold heat valve—check operation		X	
EGR valve—check operation		X (1973-74 models)	
CEC valve and hoses (6 cyl. only)—check operation		X	
Idle stop solenoid—check operation		X	
A.I.R. system (6 cyl. only)—check operation and condition			X (1973-74 models)
TVS—check switch and hoses		X (1973-74 models)	
Engine compression—check			X
Spark plug wires—inspect and clean		X (First at 24,000 miles or 24 months)	

*May require more frequent service under dusty operating conditions.

1975-76 MODELS

Services to be done	Every 6 months or 7,500 miles, whichever occurs first	Every 12 months or 15,000 miles, whichever occurs first	Every 18 months or 22,500 miles, whichever occurs first	Every 12 months	Every 30,000 miles	Every 60,000 miles
Chassis—lubricate	X					
Fluid levels—check	X					
Engine oil—change	X					
Engine oil filter, V8's and in-line 6's—replace		X (First one at 6 months or 7,500 miles)				
Engine oil filter, V6—replace	X					
Tires—rotate	Bias-belted every 7,500 miles. Steel-belted radials at first 7,500 miles; then every 15,000 miles					
Differential (or final drive, front-drive cars)—change lubricant		X (Every 15,000 miles if car pulls trailer)				
Air conditioning system—check charge and hose condition				X		
Cooling system—wash radiator cap and filler neck, pressure test system, inspect and tighten hoses, clean radiator core		X				
Cooling system—drain, flush and refill with new coolant					X	
Front wheel bearings (rear bearings in front drive vehicles)—clean and repack					X	
Final drive axle boots and output shaft seal—check condition					X	
Automatic transmission—change fluid and service filter					X ('75 models)	X ('76 models)
Manual steering gear—check seals					X	
Clutch cross shaft—lubricate					X	
Tires and wheels—check condition	X					
Exhaust system—check condition	X					
Drive belts—check condition and adjustment	X ('75 models)	X ('76 models)				
Front and rear suspension and steering system—check condition	X					
Brakes and power steering—check all lines and hoses	X					

1975-76 MODELS/continued

Services to be done	Maintenance Intervals					
	Every 6 months or 7,500 miles, whichever occurs first	Every 12 months or 15,000 miles, whichever occurs first	Every 18 months or 22,500 miles, whichever occurs first	Every 12 months	Every 30,000 miles	Every 60,000 miles
Drum brakes and parking brake—check condition of linings; adjust parking brake		X				
Throttle linkage—check operation and condition		X				
Underbody—flush and check condition		X				
Bumpers—check condition		X				
Thermostatically controlled air cleaner—check operation	X (First service)		X			
Carburetor choke—check operation	X (First service)		X			
Engine idle speed adjustment	X (First service)		X			
EFE valve—check operation	X (First service)		X			
Carburetor—torque attaching bolts or nuts to manifold	X (First service)		X			
Vacuum advance system and hoses—check operation	X (First service—'76 models)	X ('75 models)	X ('76 models)			
Carburetor fuel inlet filter—replace		X				
PCV system—check operation		X				
PCV system—replace filter and valve					X	
Idle stop solenoid or dashpot—check operation			X			
Spark plug and ignition coil wires—inspect and clean			X			
Spark plugs—replace			X (Every 22,500 miles)			
Engine timing adjustment and distributor check			X (Every 22,500 miles)			
ECS system—check and replace filter					X (Or 24 months whichever is first)	
Fuel cap, tank and lines—check condition					X (Or 24 months whichever is first)	
Air cleaner element—replace					X	

MANUFACTURER'S NEW CAR WARRANTIES, 1969-1976

AMERICAN MOTORS

1969
ALL MODELS

American Motors Corporation*, as manufacturer, (hereinafter referred to as "American") warrants to the original retail purchaser this new 1969 model car, including equipment and accessories thereon supplied by American, delivered to the original retail purchaser by an authorized American Motors Dealer, to be free from defects in material and workmanship under normal use and service during the time and mileage limits and subject to all the other provisions, conditions and limitations set forth below.

1-Year/12,000-mile portion of warranty

This portion of the warranty applies to the entire car (except as limited herein) for 1 year from the date of delivery of the vehicle to the original retail purchaser, or until it has been driven 12,000 miles, whichever first occurs. If the car has been used prior to delivery to the original retail purchaser, the time and mileage limitations shall begin on the date such prior use commenced.

5-Year/50,000-mile portion of warranty

This portion of the warranty applies (except as limited herein) to the car's power train components, specifically: Group 1, consisting of engine block, head, internal engine parts, water pump and intake manifold; Group 2, consisting of transmission case and internal parts, transmission vacuum control and torque converter; Group 3, consisting of drive shaft, universal joints, rear axle housing and internal parts. American warrants these components to be free from defects in material and workmanship under normal use and service for 5 years from the date of delivery to the original retail purchaser or until the car has been driven 50,000 miles, whichever first occurs. If the car has been used prior to delivery to the original retail purchaser, the time and mileage limitations shall begin on the date such prior use commenced. The 5-year/50,000-mile portion of the warranty does not apply to systems related to those power train components listed above and accessory units, such as, but not limited to, ignition, fuel and cooling systems, engine and transmission controls and linkage, including manual gear shift lever and clutch assembly, and any part of the wheel hubs, drums and brake systems.

Exclusions

This warranty shall not apply to:
1. Tires (which are covered by the tire manufacturer's warranty);
2. Normal maintenance services, such as, but not limited to, engine or automatic transmission tuneup, fuel system cleaning, valve carbon removal, brake and clutch adjustments, wheel alignment and balancing and similar mechanical or body adjustments;
3. Replacement of service items, such as, but not limited to, spark plugs, ignition points, condensers, filters, clutch and brake linings, automatic transmission bands and clutch plates, light bulbs, wiper blades, belts and hoses;
4. Deterioration of soft trim, decorative bright metal trim, painted parts, other appearance items and rubber or rubber-like parts, due to wear or exposure;
5. Any car that has been repaired or altered in any manner so as to affect adversely its performance or reliability, nor to any car which has been modified for high performance characteristics;
6. Repairs or service necessary as a result of using parts not sold or approved by American;
7. Any car which has been subject to misuse, negligence or accident, so as, in the judgment of American, to adversely affect the performance or reliability of the car or any part thereof;
8. Any car operated outside of the United States or Canada;
9. Any car on which the odometer reading has been altered so that the exact mileage cannot be determined;
10. Any component not having received the required maintenance specified in the Mechanical Maintenance Schedule for 1969 Cars contained in the 1969 American Motors Owner's Manual.

American Motors Corporation's obligation

American's obligation under the warranty is limited to repairing or replacing without charge, except as otherwise provided, at an authorized American Motors Dealer's place of business, any part of this 1969 car that proves to be defective within the applicable provisions of the warranty. To obtain warranty service, the owner must present a valid American Motors Owner Identification Card to the servicing American Motors Dealer.

No other warranty

THIS WARRANTY IS IN LIEU OF ALL OTHER WARRANTIES, EXPRESS, IMPLIED OR IMPLIED IN LAW, OF AMERICAN OR OTHERS, INCLUDING, BUT NOT LIMITED TO, IMPLIED WARRANTIES OF MERCHANTABILITY OR FITNESS FOR A PARTICULAR PURPOSE, LOSS OF USE OF CAR, LOSS OF WAGES, INCONVENIENCE OR OTHER ITEMS WHICH WOULD BE CONSIDERED CONSEQUENTIAL DAMAGES AND ALL OTHER OBLIGATIONS OR LIABILITY ON THE PART OF AMERICAN OR OTHERS, AND AMERICAN NEITHER ASSUMES NOR AUTHORIZES ANY OTHER PERSON TO ASSUME FOR IT OR FOR OTHERS ANY OTHER OBLIGATION OR LIABILITY.

Transfer of warranty

The second retail purchaser may obtain the benefit of any unexpired portion of this warranty, as limited below, provided:
1. Application for the transfer of the unexpired portion of the warranty is submitted through an authorized American Motors Dealer within 30 days or 1000 miles, whichever first occurs, following the date of purchase of the car by the second retail purchaser;
2. A fee of $25.00 is paid to the dealer;
3. The dealer advises American that inspection indicates the car has received the required maintenance specified in the Mechanical Maintenance Schedule for 1969 Cars contained in the 1969 American Motors Owner's Manual.

Under this warranty, on each repair visit the second retail purchaser must pay the first $25.00 on repairs made to each major power train group, specifically set forth as Groups 1, 2 and 3 above, after the expiration of the 1-year/12,000-mile coverage and prior to the expiration of the 5-year/50,000-mile coverage.

*For cars sold in Canada, American Motors (Canada) Limited.

1970—HORNET, GREMLIN
1971—ALL MODELS

American Motors Corporation* (hereinafter referred to as "American"), as manufacturer, warrants to the owner that it will repair or replace any part of each new 1970 Hornet or Gremlin, including equipment and accessories thereon supplied by American, delivered to the original retail purchaser by an authorized American Motors Dealer, which proves to be defective in material or workmanship under normal use and service. This warranty shall apply for 1 year from the date of delivery of the vehicle to the original retail purchaser, or until it has been driven that number of miles which is equal to the difference between 12,000 miles and the mileage indicated upon the odometer of the vehicle on the date that the vehicle is first delivered to the original retail purchaser, whichever first occurs, subject to all other provisions, conditions and limitations set forth herein. If the car has been used prior to delivery to the original retail purchaser, the time limitation shall begin on the date such prior use commenced.

Exclusions

This warranty shall not apply to:
1. Tires (which are covered by the tire manufacturer's warranty);
2. Normal maintenance services, such as, but not limited to, engine or automatic transmission tuneup, fuel system cleaning, valve carbon removal, brake and clutch adjustments, wheel alignment and balancing and similar mechanical or body adjustments;
3. Replacement of service items, such as, but not limited to, spark plugs, ignition points, condensers, filters, clutch and brake linings, automatic transmission bands and clutch plates, light bulbs, wiper blades, belts and hoses;
4. Deterioration of soft trim, decorative bright metal trim, painted parts, other appearance items and rubber or rubber-like parts, due to wear or exposure;
5. Any car that has been repaired or altered in any manner so as to affect adversely its performance or reliability, or to any car which has been modified for high performance characteristics;
6. Repairs or service necessary as a result of using parts not sold or approved by American;
7. Any car which has been subject to misuse, negligence or accident, so as, in the judgment of American, to affect adversely the performance or reliability of the car or any part thereof;
8. Any car on which the odometer reading has been altered or on which the odometer has not been properly maintained or repaired so that it does not reflect the actual mileage;

9. Any component not having received the required maintenance specified in the Mechanical Maintenance Schedule for 1970 Cars contained in the 1970 American Motors Owner's Manual;
10. Any car operated outside the United States or Canada.

American Motors Corporation's obligation

American's obligation under the warranty is limited to repairing or replacing without charge at an authorized American Motors Dealer's place of business, any part of this 1970 car that proves to be defective within the applicable provisions of the warranty. To obtain warranty service, the owner must present a valid American Motors Owner Identification Card to the servicing American Motors Dealer.

No other warranty

THIS WARRANTY IS IN LIEU OF ALL OTHER WARRANTIES, EXPRESS, IMPLIED OR IMPLIED IN LAW, OF AMERICAN OR OTHERS, INCLUDING, BUT NOT LIMITED TO, IMPLIED WARRANTIES OF MERCHANTABILITY OR FITNESS FOR A PARTICULAR PURPOSE. AMERICAN DOES NOT ASSUME ANY RESPONSIBILITY FOR LOSS OF USE OF CAR, LOSS OF WAGES, INCONVENIENCE OR OTHER ITEMS WHICH WOULD BE CONSIDERED CONSEQUENTIAL DAMAGES. AMERICAN NEITHER ASSUMES NOR AUTHORIZES ANY OTHER PERSON TO ASSUME FOR IT OR FOR OTHERS ANY OTHER OBLIGATION OR LIABILITY.
*For cars sold in Canada, American Motors (Canada) Limited.

Warranty coverage for subsequent owners

Each owner after the first owner of a 1970 new Hornet or Gremlin is eligible for any unused warranty coverage.

If a previously issued Owner Identification Card (required to obtain warranty service) is not available, a replacement—with the subsequent owner's name on it—may be purchased through your local American Motors Dealer.

1970
AMBASSADOR, REBEL, JAVELIN, AMX

American Motors Corporation* (hereinafter referred to as "American"), as manufacturer, warrants to the original retail purchaser that it will repair or replace any part of each new 1970 Ambassador, Rebel, Javelin or AMX, including equipment and accessories thereon supplied by American, delivered to the original retail purchaser by an authorized American Motors Dealer, to be free from defects in material or workmanship, under normal use and service.

1-Year/12,000-mile portion of warranty

This portion of the warranty applies to the entire car (except as limited herein) for 1 year from the date of delivery of the vehicle to the original retail purchaser, or until it has been driven that number of miles which is equal to the difference between 12,000 miles and the mileage indicated upon the odometer of the vehicle on the date that the vehicle is first delivered to the original retail purchaser, whichever first occurs, subject to all other provisions, conditions and limitations set forth herein. If the car has been used prior to delivery to the original retail purchaser, the time limitation shall begin on the date such prior use commenced.

5-Year/50,000-mile portion of warranty

This portion of the warranty applies (except as limited herein) to the car's power train components, specifically: Group 1, consisting of engine block, head, internal engine parts, water pump and intake manifold; Group 2, consisting of transmission case and internal parts, transmission vacuum control and torque converter; Group 3, consisting of drive shaft, universal joints, rear axle housing and internal parts. American warrants that it will repair or replace any of the previously named power train components which prove to be defective in material or workmanship under normal use and service for 5 years from the date of delivery to the original retail purchaser or until the car has been driven that number of miles which is equal to the difference between 50,000 miles and the mileage indicated upon the odometer of the vehicle on the date the vehicle is first delivered to the original retail purchaser, whichever first occurs, subject to all other provisions, conditions and limitations set forth herein. If the car has been used prior to delivery to the original retail purchaser, the time limitation shall begin on the date such prior use commenced. The 5-year/50,000-mile portion of the warranty does not apply to systems related to those power train components listed above and accessory units, such as, but not limited to, ignition, fuel and cooling systems, engine and transmission controls and linkage, including manual gear shift lever and clutch assembly, and any part of the wheel hubs, drums and brake systems.

Exclusions

This warranty shall not apply to:
1. Tires (which are covered by the tire manufacturer's warranty);
2. Normal maintenance services, such as, but not limited to, engine or automatic transmission tuneup, fuel system cleaning, valve carbon removal, brake and clutch adjustments, wheel alignment and balancing and similar mechanical or body adjustments;
3. Replacement of service items, such as, but not limited to, spark plugs, ignition points, condensers, filters, clutch and brake linings, automatic transmission bands and clutch plates, light bulbs, wiper blades, and hoses;
4. Deterioration of soft trim, decorative bright metal trim, painted parts, other appearance items and rubber or rubber-like parts, due to wear or exposure;
5. Any car that has been repaired or altered in any manner so as to adversely affect its performance or reliability, nor to any car which has been modified for high performance characteristics;
6. Repairs or service necessary as a result of using parts not sold or approved by American;
7. Any car which has been subject to misuse, negligence or accident, so as, in the judgment of American, to affect adversely the performance or reliability of the car or any part thereof;
8. Any car on which the odometer reading has been altered or on which the odometer has not been properly maintained or repaired so that it does not reflect the actual mileage;
9. Any component not having received the required maintenance specified in the Mechanical Maintenance Schedule for 1970 Cars contained in the 1970 American Motors Owner's Manual;
10. Any car operated outside of the United States or Canada.

American Motors Corporation's obligation

American's obligation under the warranty is limited to repairing or replacing without charge, except as otherwise provided, at an authorized American Motors Dealer's place of business, any part of this 1970 car that proves to be defective within the applicable provisions of the warranty. To obtain warranty service, the owner must present a valid American Motors Owner Identification Card to the servicing American Motors Dealer.

No other warranty

THIS WARRANTY IS IN LIEU OF ALL OTHER WARRANTIES, EXPRESS, IMPLIED OR IMPLIED IN LAW, OF AMERICAN OR OTHERS, INCLUDING, BUT NOT LIMITED TO, IMPLIED WARRANTIES OF MERCHANTABILITY OR FITNESS FOR A PARTICULAR PURPOSE. AMERICAN DOES NOT ASSUME ANY RESPONSIBILITY FOR LOSS OF USE OF CAR, LOSS OF WAGES, INCONVENIENCE OR OTHER ITEMS WHICH WOULD BE CONSIDERED CONSEQUENTIAL DAMAGES. AMERICAN NEITHER ASSUMES NOR AUTHORIZES ANY OTHER PERSON TO ASSUME FOR IT OR FOR OTHERS ANY OTHER OBLIGATION OR LIABILITY.

Transfer of warranty

The second retail purchaser may obtain the benefit of any unexpired portion of this warranty provided:
1. Application for the transfer of the unexpired portion of the warranty is submitted through an authorized American Motors Dealer within 30 days or 1000 miles, whichever first occurs, following the date of purchase of the car by the second retail purchaser;
2. A fee of $25.00 is paid to the dealer;
3. The dealer advises American that inspection indicates the car has received the required maintenance specified in the Mechanical Maintenance Schedule for 1970 Cars contained in the 1970 American Motors Owner's Manual.

Under this warranty, on each repair visit the second retail purchaser must pay the first $25.00 on repairs made to each major power train group, specifically set forth as Groups 1, 2 and 3 above, after the expiration of the 1-year/12,000-mile coverage and prior to the expiration of the 5-year/50,000-mile coverage.
*For cars sold in Canada, American Motors (Canada) Limited.

1972-1975
ALL MODELS

When you buy a new 1972 car from an American Motors dealer, American Motors Corporation* guarantees to you that, except for tires, it will pay for the repair or replacement of any part it supplies that is defective in material or workmanship.

This guarantee is good for 12 months from the date the car is first used or 12,000 miles, whichever comes first. All we require is that the car be properly maintained and cared for under normal use and service in the 50 United States or Canada and that guaranteed repairs or replacements be made by an American Motors dealer.

This guarantee is in lieu of all other guarantees or warranties, express, implied or implied in law, of American Motors Corporation or others, including implied warranties of merchantability or fitness for a particular purpose.
*In Canada: American Motors (Canada) Ltd.

1976
ALL MODELS

Full 12-month/12,000-mile warranty

When you buy a new 1976 AMC car from an American Motors dealer, American Motors Corporation* guarantees to you that, except for tires, it will pay for the repair or replacement of any part it supplies that is defective in material or workmanship. This guarantee is good for 12 months from the date the car is first used or 12,000 miles, whichever comes first. All we require is that the car be properly maintained and cared for under normal use and service in the fifty United States or Canada and that guaranteed repairs or replacements be made by an American Motors dealer.

This guarantee excludes consequential damages.
*In Canada: American Motors (Canada) Ltd.

CHRYSLER CORPORATION

1969
(EXCLUDING THOSE EQUIPPED WITH 426 CU. IN. ENGINES)

Chrysler Corporation warrants this vehicle to the first registered owner only against defects in material and workmanship in normal use as follows: (1) the entire vehicle (except tires)* for 12 months or 12,000 miles of operation after the vehicle is first placed in service, whichever occurs first, from the date of sale or delivery thereto; and (2) the engine block, head and all internal engine parts, water pump, intake manifold, transmission case and all internal transmission parts, torque converter (if so equipped), drive shaft, universal joints, rear axle and differential, and rear wheel bearings for 5 years or 50,000 miles of operation after the vehicle is first placed in service, whichever occurs first, from the date of such sale or delivery. Any part of this vehicle found defective under the conditions of this warranty will be repaired or replaced, at Chrysler's option, without charge at an authorized Imperial, Chrysler, Plymouth, or Dodge dealership.

Chrysler Corporation assumes no responsibility for:
- Routine maintenance such as oil changes, tune ups, front end alignment, wheel balancing, replacement of spark plugs, oil filters, etc.;
- Repairs necessitated by accident, abuse, negligence, or use of parts not approved by Chrysler;
- Normal deterioration of hoses, belts, upholstery, soft trim, or appearance items, due to wear or exposure;
- Loss of use of the vehicle, loss of time, inconvenience, or other consequential damages.

Required maintenance services

As a condition to this warranty coverage, the following Required Maintenance Service must be performed:
1) Change engine oil every 90 days or 4000 miles, whichever occurs first;
2) Replace the engine oil filter every second oil change;
3) Clean the carburetor air filter every six months and replace every two years;
4) Check the operation of the crankcase ventilator valve and clean the oil filter cap every six months and replace the ventilator valve every year.

Annual validation of required maintenance services and mileage

As an express condition of the 5 year/50,000 Mile Warranty Coverage under this warranty, the owner must submit a validation form to Chrysler Motors Corporation annually. Each year, on the anniversary date of sale or delivery of the vehicle to the first registered owner, the owner must: 1) furnish an authorized Chrysler, Plymouth, Imperial or Dodge dealer evidence that all Required Maintenance Services were performed at the proper intervals; 2) have the dealer certify on a validation form supplied by Chrysler Motors Corporation (a) the dealer's receipt of evidence of such maintenance and (b) the vehicle's then current mileage; and 3) mail such completed validation form to Chrysler Motors Corporation at the address indicated on the form.

This warranty will not apply to any vehicle on which the odometer has been altered so that the vehicle's actual mileage cannot be determined.

This warranty is the only warranty applicable to the vehicle and is expressly in lieu of any warranties or conditions otherwise implied by law, including but not limited to implied warranties of merchantability or fitness for a particular purpose. The remedies under this warranty shall be the only remedies available to the owner of the vehicle or any other person, and neither Chrysler Corporation, Chrysler Motors Corporation, nor the authorized selling dealer assumes any other obligation or responsibility with respect to the condition of the vehicle, and neither assumes nor authorizes anyone to assume for any of them, any additional liability.

This warranty applies only to vehicles manufactured and operated in the United States, Canada, Puerto Rico and the Virgin Islands. Vehicles operated elsewhere shall be entitled to service only on the basis of the warranty applicable to the country in which operated.

*Tires are warranted separately by the tire manufacturer.

1970
(EXCEPT THOSE EQUIPPED WITH 426 CU. IN. "HEMI" OR 440 CU. IN. "SIX-PACK" ENGINES).

Chrysler Corporation warrants this vehicle to the first registered owner as follows:
- For 12 months or 12,000 miles, whichever occurs first—the entire vehicle, except tires;
- For 5 years or 50,000 miles, whichever occurs first—the engine block, head and all internal parts, water pump, intake manifold, transmission case and all internal transmission parts, torque converter, drive shaft, universal joints, rear axle and differential.

Any part of this vehicle manufactured or supplied by Chrysler Corporation (except tires) found defective in material or workmanship will be repaired or replaced by an authorized Chrysler Motors Corporation dealer at his place of business without charge for parts or labor.

Warranty repairs should be obtained from your Selling Dealer unless he has ceased to do business as an authorized Chrysler Motors Corporation dealer, or you are travelling or have moved to a different locality and cannot return to your Selling Dealer.

This warranty commences on the date of sale to the first registered owner or the date the vehicle is first placed in service, whichever occurs first.

This warranty will not apply to any vehicle on which the odometer mileage has been altered. Nor will it apply to: (1) normal deterioration due to wear or exposure; (2) normal maintenance services and the parts used in connection with such services; (3) repairs required as a result of accident, abuse, negligence, racing, or failure to perform the maintenance services specified in this warranty folder; (4) vehicles manufactured and/or operated outside the United States, Canada, Puerto Rico or the Virgin Islands.

THIS WARRANTY IS IN LIEU OF ANY OTHER WARRANTIES OR CONDITIONS, INCLUDING MERCHANTABILITY OR FITNESS FOR A PARTICULAR PURPOSE. THE REMEDIES UNDER THIS WARRANTY ARE EXCLUSIVE AND NEITHER CHRYSLER CORPORATION NOR CHRYSLER MOTORS CORPORATION ASSUMES NOR AUTHORIZES ANYONE TO ASSUME FOR THEM ANY OTHER OBLIGATION.

CARS EQUIPPED WITH HIGH PERFORMANCE 426 CU. IN. "HEMI" OR 440 CU. IN. "SIX PACK" ENGINES

Chrysler Corporation's warranty on cars equipped with these high performance engines is the same as the warranty on other passenger cars and subject to the same terms and conditions, as set forth above, except that this warranty applies to the entire vehicle (except tires) for 12 months or 12,000 miles, whichever occurs first, ONLY. The 5 year or 50,000 mile coverage on the power train and other components DOES NOT APPLY to cars equipped with these high performance engines.

CARS EQUIPPED WITH MAXIMUM PERFORMANCE 426 CU. IN. "HEMI" ENGINES

Chrysler Corporation's Passenger Car Warranty does not apply to cars equipped with maximum performance 426 cu. in. "hemi" engines designed and intended for use in supervised acceleration trials, circuit racing, and other competitive "speed" events. Cars equipped with these "maximum performance" engines ARE SOLD "AS IS" WITHOUT ANY WARRANTY EITHER EXPRESS OR IMPLIED INCLUDING MERCHANTABILITY OR FITNESS FOR A PARTICULAR PURPOSE.

1971-1973
ALL MODELS

Chrysler Corporation warrants this vehicle for 12 months or 12,000 miles, whichever occurs first, according to the following terms:

This warranty commences on the date of original retail sale or original use whichever occurs first.

Any part of this vehicle manufactured by Chrysler Corporation (except tires) found defective in material or workmanship will be repaired or replaced, at Chrysler's option, by the Selling Dealer at his place of business without charge for parts or labor.

If the Selling Dealer has ceased to do business as an authorized Chrysler Motors Corporation dealer, or the owner is traveling or has moved to a different locality and cannot return to the Selling Dealer, the owner may obtain warranty repairs at any other authorized Chrysler Motors Corporation dealership.

This warranty will not apply to:
- Any vehicle on which the odometer mileage is altered;
- Normal maintenance services (as outlined in the Operator's Manual supplied with this vehicle) and the parts used in connection with such services;

- Repairs necessitated by accident, abuse, negligence or racing;
- Loss of use of the vehicle, loss of time, inconvenience or other consequential damages.

THIS WARRANTY IS IN LIEU OF ANY OTHER WARRANTIES OR CONDITIONS, INCLUDING MERCHANTABILITY OR FITNESS FOR A PARTICULAR PURPOSE. THE REMEDIES UNDER THIS WARRANTY ARE EXCLUSIVE AND NEITHER CHRYSLER CORPORATION NOR CHRYSLER MOTORS CORPORATION ASSUMES NOR AUTHORIZES ANYONE TO ASSUME FOR THEM ANY OTHER OBLIGATION.

1974
ALL MODELS

WARRANTY PERIOD: Chrysler Corporation warrants this vehicle for 12 months or 12,000 miles, whichever occurs first, according to the following terms:

WHAT IS COVERED BY THE WARRANTY: Any part of this vehicle manufactured or supplied by Chrysler Corporation (except tires) found defective in material or workmanship.

WHO IS ELIGIBLE: All owners of this vehicle during the warranty period are covered by this warranty.

WARRANTY START DATE: The warranty starts on the date of sale to the original retail purchaser or on the date this vehicle is originally placed in service, whichever occurs first.

OBTAINING WARRANTY SERVICE: Warranty service will be provided by the Selling Dealer at his place of business. The Selling Dealer will repair or replace, at Chrysler's option, the defective part without charge for parts or labor.

In the event the owner cannot return to the Selling Dealer (the Selling Dealer has ceased to do business as an authorized dealer or the owner is travelling, has moved or is living in a different locality and cannot return to the Selling Dealer), the owner may obtain warranty service at any authorized Chrysler Motors Corporation dealership.

WHAT IS NOT COVERED BY THE WARRANTY: This warranty will not apply to:
- Any vehicle on which the odometer mileage is altered;
- Normal maintenance services (as outlined in the Operator's Manual supplied with this vehicle) and the parts used in connection with such services;
- Repairs necessitated by accident, abuse, negligence or racing;
- Loss of use of the vehicle, loss of time, inconvenience or other consequential damages.

THIS WARRANTY IS IN LIEU OF ANY OTHER WARRANTIES OR CONDITIONS, INCLUDING MERCHANTABILITY OR FITNESS FOR A PARTICULAR PURPOSE. THE REMEDIES UNDER THIS WARRANTY ARE EXCLUSIVE AND NEITHER CHRYSLER CORPORATION NOR CHRYSLER MOTORS CORPORATION ASSUMES NOR AUTHORIZES ANYONE TO ASSUME FOR THEM ANY OTHER OBLIGATION.

1975-1976
ALL MODELS

FOR THE FIRST 12 MONTHS OF USE, ANY CHRYSLER MOTORS CORPORATION DEALER WILL FIX, WITHOUT CHARGE FOR PARTS OR LABOR, ANY PART OF THIS CAR WE SUPPLY (EXCEPT TIRES) WHICH PROVES DEFECTIVE IN NORMAL USE, REGARDLESS OF MILEAGE.

This warranty applies to all cars operated in the 50 United States and Canada except those placed in police or taxi service and is extended to all owners during the warranty period.

This is the only warranty made by Chrysler Corporation applicable to this vehicle.

Cars placed in police or taxi service

The warranty period on such cars is the first 12 months of use or 12,000 miles, whichever occurs first. In all other respects, the above warranty remains the same.

Special policies & programs

*90-day adjustment period

The first 90 days after this vehicle is placed in use, regardless of mileage, will be considered the "break-in" period. To assure your satisfaction with your new car, any adjustment(s) required during this period will be performed by any Chrysler Motors Corporation dealer without charge for parts or labor unless the adjustment is required as a result of improper care, accident, fire, abuse, or negligence.

After the first 90 days of use, adjustments are considered owner-maintenance responsibility unless required in connection with the repair or replacement of a part we supplied which proves defective during the warranty period.

*Replacement of selected wear items

Some parts of this vehicle such as wiper blades, fuses, bulbs, hoses and belts while not defective may simply wear out in normal use during the first 12 months. The owner is expected to take care of these items as part of normal maintenance.

We recognize, however, that the replacement of the following items should they wear out is expensive. Furthermore, we recognize that because of the expense involved, the owner might have some reservation as to whether the item wore out as a result of normal use or because of a defect. Therefore, to eliminate this concern on the part of the owner, the following is our policy:

During the first 12 months of normal use, regardless of mileage, should any of the following parts wear out, they will be replaced by any Chrysler Motors Corporation dealer without charge for parts or labor:
- Brake drums, linings, discs, pads
- Clutch disc or pressure plate
- Muffler, tailpipe, shock absorbers
- Headlamp sealed beam units

*Free loaner—overnight warranty repairs (participating dealers)

Participating dealers will supply a loaner for overnight use (local use only) "free-of-charge" if warranty repairs cannot be completed from morning until evening of the same working day. The loaner, whenever possible and where scheduling permits, will be a 1975 Model car. Loaners, generally, will not be made available for weekend use.

To be eligible for a loaner, the owner MUST make an appointment in advance for both the warranty repair(s) and the loaner.

In the event an owner cannot return the loaner when repairs are completed, the dealer will charge the owner his standard "service rental fee" for the "extra" days the owner retains the loaner.

All owners are urged to return loaners when scheduled, so that other owners awaiting loaners will not be inconvenienced.

The terms and conditions relating to the use and operation of the loaner vehicle shall be governed by the terms and conditions of the loan or rental agreement between the participating dealer and the owner.

• Tires

Factory-installed tires are covered separately by the tire manufacturer's "Tire Adjustment Policy" and not by Chrysler.

Although the specific terms of these policies will differ, generally, tire manufacturers will cover their tires for the life of the original tread against defects in material and workmanship and failures caused by normal road hazards such as fabric breaks, cuts, bruises and snags. The tire adjustment policies do not cover damage or failure caused by punctures, running flat, fire, wrecks, chain cuts, irregular wear, abuse, etc. Generally, tire adjustment policies provide that any tire determined to be defective or damaged within the terms of the Tire Adjustment Policy will be repaired or replaced at the tire manufacturer's option. If replacement is made, the owner must pay the tire manufacturer's current adjustment base price, plus transportation charges and taxes for such tire less a pro rata allowance based on the amount of the original tread remaining on the tire replaced. In some instances, the owner may also be required to pay a service charge.

Tire adjustments may be obtained from the tire manufacturer's authorized service stations, or a Chrysler Motors Corporation dealer providing such service. If necessary, a Chrysler Motors Corporation dealer will assist an owner in requesting an adjustment.

Tire manufacturer's "Tire Adjustment Policies" specifically provide that they do not cover consequential damages.

*Batteries (excluding Mopar long life batteries)

Factory-installed Mopar batteries which prove defective will be replaced on the following basis: During the first 12 months of service, regardless of mileage, a defective battery will be replaced by any Chrysler Motors Corporation dealer without charge for parts or labor.

Thereafter, and for up to the first 36 months of service, a defective battery will be replaced on a pro rata adjustment basis. The pro rata adjustment provides the owner credit towards the purchase of a new †Mopar battery of equal or greater capacity. For each unused month of service (up to 36), the owner will receive a credit of 1/36 of the current suggested retail price of the new battery.

Note:

A battery which is merely discharged is not considered defective.
†In Canada—Chryco
*Not applicable to cars placed in police or taxi service.

FORD MOTOR COMPANY

1969
ALL MODELS

Ford* warrants to the first retail purchaser only of a 1969 North American Ford-built passenger car or standard two-wheel drive light truck that the Selling Dealer, at his place of business, and using new Ford parts or Ford Authorized Remanufactured parts, will repair or replace, free of charge including related labor, any of the following parts that are found to be defective in factory materials or workmanship in normal use and service in the United States, Canada, or Puerto Rico within a period of:

12 months from the date of original retail delivery or 12,000 miles of operation, whichever occurs first, with respect to all parts (except tires and tubes);

5 years from the date of original retail delivery or 50,000 miles of operation, whichever occurs first, with respect to the engine block and head, internal engine parts, water pump, intake manifold, transmission case, internal transmission parts, torque converter, drive shaft, universal joints, rear axle, and differential.

If, on delivery to the first retail purchaser, the vehicle has been in Ford or dealer service (such as a demonstrator) the time and mileage limitations shall begin with the date the vehicle was first placed in such service.

In the event the Selling Dealer has ceased to do business, or the purchaser is travelling or has moved to a different locality, replacements or repairs may be made by any authorized dealer of Ford. A vehicle normally operated in another country will be provided with warranty coverage authorized for that country.

Conditions

1. *Ownercard.* Ford will furnish the purchaser with an Ownercard which must be presented to obtain warranty service.
2. *Usage.* The warranty does not cover damage from accident, fire, or other casualty, misuse or racing, or deterioration of paint, bright metal, or soft trim from normal use or exposure.
3. *Odometer.* This warranty will not apply to any vehicle on which the odometer has been altered so that the actual mileage of the vehicle cannot be determined.
4. *Required Maintenance.* This warranty will not apply to the repair or replacement of any part caused by failure to perform the required maintenance services set forth in this 1969 Warranty Facts Booklet. These maintenance services are required because of normal wear and use and their cost is not covered by the warranty.
5. *Owner Responsibility.* During the warranty periods, it may become necessary for the owner to:

• Replace spark plugs, ignition points and condenser, wiper blades, brake and clutch linings or pads, hoses, moulded rubber or rubber-like items, and filters;

• Adjust carburetor, ignition, transmission bands, belts or brake or clutch systems;

• Clean fuel, coolant, and brake systems, remove sludge or carbon deposits;

• Add oil, coolant, fluids and lubricants;

• Align headlights and front wheels, and balance wheels.

Typically, these replacements and services are required because of normal wear and use, and are the owner's responsibility. Their costs will not be covered by the warranty, unless the original part is found to be defective in factory material or workmanship.

Ford assumes no responsibility for loss of use of the vehicle, loss of time, inconvenience or other consequential expense. This warranty is expressly IN LIEU OF any other express or implied warranty, condition or guarantee on the vehicle or any part thereof, including any implied WARRANTY OF MERCHANTABILITY OR FITNESS, and of any other obligation on the part of Ford or the Selling Dealer.

*"Ford" is Ford Motor Company for a vehicle purchased by the owner in the United States. "Ford" is Ford Motor Company of Canada, Limited, for a vehicle purchased in Canada.

Availability of unexpired warranty to second retail purchaser

If the vehicle is acquired by a second retail purchaser at any time prior to the expiration of five years from date of delivery to the original retail purchaser and before the vehicle has been driven 50,000 miles, the second retail purchaser may purchase from Ford the unexpired portion of the New Vehicle Warranty, provided:

1. Application is made to an authorized dealer of Ford within 30 days or 1,000 miles, whichever first occurs, after acquisition of the vehicle by the second retail purchaser;
2. A fee of $25.00 is paid to the dealer; and
3. The dealer advises Ford that inspection indicates the vehicle has received required maintenance as specified in this 1969 Warranty Facts Booklet.

The second retail purchaser will pay the first $25.00 on each repair visit for repairs made to power train components after the expiration of the 12 months/12,000 miles coverage and prior to the expiration of the 5 years/50,000 miles coverage.

1970
(EXCEPT MAVERICKS AND CORTINAS)

Ford and its Selling Dealer warrant, with respect to each 1970 model passenger car (except Maverick and Cortina) or light truck† built by Ford, that the Selling Dealer will repair or replace, at his place of business, any part (except tires and tubes which are warranted separately by their manufacturers) that is found to be defective in factory materials or workmanship in normal use in the United States, Canada, Puerto Rico or the U.S. Virgin Islands within 12 months from the date of original retail delivery or original use by Ford or any of its dealers, whichever is earlier.

Under this warranty, repairs or replacements will be made free of charge for both parts and labor, and the Dealer will use Ford parts or Ford Authorized Remanufactured parts.

In addition, during the first 90 days of the warranty period (Break-In Period), the Dealer will provide the following adjustments and services, if needed, without charge unless the need for them is clearly the result of accident, fire or other casualty, misuse or racing:

• Wheel Balancing
• Wheel Alignment
• Headlight Alignment
• Adjustments to: Carburetor, Distributor, Valves, Belts, Transmission, Clutch, and Brake System
• Cleaning of: Fuel, Cooling, and Brake Systems
• Addition of: Engine Coolants, Power Steering, Brake, and Air Conditioning Fluids
• Tightening of: Nuts, Bolts, and Fittings

After the 90-day Break-In Period, such adjustments and services will be considered normal maintenance resulting from use; the owner will be charged unless the need for them is clearly the result of a defect in factory materials or workmanship.

This warranty does not cover: *damage* from accidents, fire or other casualty, misuse or racing; *failures* caused by modifications of any part of the vehicle; *normal replacement* of service parts such as spark plugs, ignition points and condenser, filters or wiper blades; *addition* of oil or other lubricants; *periodic maintenance* services listed in the Owners Manual.

If the owner is traveling or has moved a long distance from the Selling Dealer or needs emergency repairs, or if the Selling Dealer is no longer in business, any authorized Ford or Lincoln-Mercury dealer will perform necessary repairs, replacements, adjustments and services hereunder.

Ford and the Selling Dealer assume no responsibility hereunder for loss of use of the vehicle, loss of time, inconvenience, commercial loss or consequential damage. Except for responsibility for personal injuries shown to have resulted from a defect, this warranty is expressly IN LIEU OF any other express or implied warranty, condition or guarantee with respect to the vehicle or any part thereof, including any implied WARRANTY OF MERCHANTABILITY OR FITNESS.

†Bronco, Ranchero, Econoline, F100, F250, F350, P350, P400.

1971
(EXCEPT CAPRI, COMET, MAVERICK AND PINTO)

Coverage provided

Ford* and the Selling Dealer jointly warrant with respect to each 1971 model passenger car (except Capri, Comet, Maverick and Pinto) or light truck† built by Ford that, for a period of 12 months or 12,000 miles, whichever occurs first, the Selling Dealer will repair or replace any part that is found to be defective in factory materials or workmanship (except tires which are warranted separately by their manufacturers).

The 12-month or 12,000-mile, whichever occurs first, warranty period will begin on the date of original retail delivery or the date of original use by Ford or any of its dealers, whichever is earlier.

Under the warranty, repairs or replacements will be made free of charge for both parts and labor using Ford parts or Ford Authorized Remanufactured Parts. The repairs or replacements will be performed by the Selling Dealer following delivery of the vehicle to his place of business in the United States or Canada. If the owner is traveling or has moved a long distance from the Selling Dealer or needs emergency repairs, any authorized Ford of Lincoln-Mercury dealer will perform the repairs.

This warranty will apply to a vehicle purchased by a member of the United States Armed Forces through an authorized Post Exchange or Navy Ship's Stores Facility.

†Bronco Pickup, Club Wagon Bus, Ranchero, Econoline, F100, F250, F350, P350, P400.

Special break-in period adjustments and services

During the first 90 days of the warranty period, the following adjustments and services, if required, will be provided without charge unless the need for them is clearly the result of accident, fire or other casualty, misuse, negligence, racing, failure of parts not supplied by Ford, or modifications to the vehicle:
- Wheel Balancing • Wheel Alignment • Headlight Alignment
- Adjustments to: Carburetor, Distributor, Valves, Belts, Transmission, Clutch and Brake System
- Cleaning of: Fuel, Cooling and Brake Systems
- Addition of: Engine Coolants, Power Steering, Brake, Air Conditioning, Transmission and Axle Fluids
- Tightening of: Nuts, Bolts and Fittings

After the 90-day Break-In Period, such adjustments and services will be considered normal maintenance resulting from use; the owner will be charged unless the need for them is clearly the result of a defect in factory materials or workmanship.

What is not covered by the warranty

The vehicle owner should provide maintenance service for the vehicle in accordance with schedules contained in the applicable Owner's, Operator's or Car Care and Operation Manual. Some maintenance services may require parts replacements during the warranty period due to normal wear and usage; the replacement of such parts as spark plugs, ignition points and condenser, filters, wiper blades, emission control valve, brake and clutch linings, engine belts and hoses, and the addition of oil will be at the owner's expense. However, parts replacements and oil additions required because of a defect rather than normal wear and usage will be made without charge under the warranty.

Damage from accidents, fire or other casualty, misuse, negligence, or racing, and failures caused by parts not supplied by Ford or modification of any part of the vehicle are not covered by the warranty.

This warranty will not apply to any vehicle on which the odometer has been altered so that the actual mileage of the vehicle cannot be determined.

This warranty does not apply to a vehicle purchased in the United States or Canada which is registered in or normally operated in another country. In this circumstance, the vehicle may be eligible for coverage under the warranty authorized for the country of operation.

Neither Ford nor any of its dealers assume any responsibility under this warranty for any loss of use of the vehicle, loss of time, inconvenience, commercial loss or consequential damages.

Disclaimer of implied warranties

Except for responsibility for personal injuries shown to have resulted from a defect, THIS WARRANTY IS EXPRESSLY IN LIEU OF any other express or implied warranty, condition or guarantee agreement or representation by any person with respect to the vehicle or any part thereof, including ANY IMPLIED WARRANTY OF MERCHANTABILITY OR FITNESS.

If you have a warranty problem

The dealer from whom you purchased your vehicle has the primary responsibility for performing warranty repairs. His Service Department has the qualified technicians and up-to-date equipment required to provide complete warranty service for your vehicle. Moreover, he values you as a customer for all of his products and services.

In the event that you should encounter a warranty service problem, we suggest that you contact the Owner or the General Manager of the Selling Dealership. If he cannot resolve the problem, we suggest that you contact the Service Manager or the Customer Relations Manager at the appropriate Ford or Lincoln-Mercury District Office. The address and telephone number of the District Office servicing your area are shown in the applicable Owner's, Operator's or Car Care and Operation Manual.

1972 ALL MODELS

Basic warranty

Ford and the Selling Dealer jointly warrant with respect to each 1972 model passenger car or light truck*, sold by Ford that for a period of 12 months or 12,000 miles, whichever occurs first, the Selling Dealer will repair or replace any part that is found to be defective in factory materials or workmanship (except tires which are separately warranted by their manufacturers). The 12-month or 12,000-mile warranty period will begin on the date of original retail delivery or the date of original use by Ford or any of its dealers, whichever is earlier.

Under the warranty, repairs or replacements will be made free of charge for both parts and labor using Ford Service Parts or Ford Authorized Remanufactured Parts. The repairs or replacements will be performed by the Selling Dealer following delivery of the vehicle to his place of business in the United States or Canada. If the owner is traveling or has moved a long distance from the Selling Dealer or needs emergency repairs, any authorized Ford or Lincoln-Mercury dealer will perform the repairs.

This warranty will apply to a vehicle purchased by a member of the United States Armed Forces through an authorized Post Exchange or Navy Ship's Stores Facility.

Battery warranty

In addition to coverage by the basic warranty, if the battery installed in the vehicle at time of delivery is found to be defective after the first 12 months or 12,000 miles but within 36 months from the earliest date of original retail delivery or first use, it can be exchanged for a new Motorcraft or Autolite battery of equal or greater capacity on a pro rata basis at any Ford or Lincoln-Mercury dealer or Motorcraft or Autolite battery dealer. For each month remaining in the 36-month period the pro rata credit will be 1/36 of the current suggested retail price of the battery being replaced.

This pro rata warranty period applies only to vehicles used for normal service. For batteries installed in Police cars or Taxicabs, the Dealer can advise of the adjustment period applicable to the battery in the particular vehicle.

Special break-in adjustments and services (except Capri, Comet, Maverick and Pinto)

During the first 90 days of the basic warranty period (except for Capri, Comet, Maverick and Pinto), the following adjustments and services, if required, will be provided without charge unless the need for them is clearly the result of accident, fire or other casualty, misuse, negligence, racing, failure of parts not supplied by Ford or modifications to the vehicle:
- Wheel Balancing • Wheel Alignment • Headlight Alignment
- Adjustments to: Carburetor, Distributor, Valves, Belts, Transmission, Clutch and Brake System
- Cleaning of: Fuel, Cooling and Brake Systems
- Addition of Engine Coolants, Power Steering, Brake, Air Conditioning, Transmission and Axle Fluids
- Tightening of: Nuts, Bolts and Fittings.

After the 90-day Break-In Period, such adjustments and services will be considered normal maintenance resulting from use; the owner will be charged unless the need for them is clearly the result of a defect in factory materials or workmanship.

What is not covered by these warranties

It is important that the owner have the maintenance services listed in the applicable Owner's Manual and Emissions Systems Warranty and Maintenance Schedules Booklet (placed in the vehicle at the time of manufacture) performed at the time or mileage intervals indicated; failure to do so may constitute misuse. The labor, parts and lubricants costs of all maintenance services are not covered by the warranties and will be charged to the owner. These maintenance services include the replacement of parts such as spark plugs, ignition points and condenser, filters, wiper blades, emission control valve, spark control components, brake and clutch linings, engine belts and hoses, and the addition of oil due to normal wear and use. However, parts replacements and oil additions required because of a defect rather than normal wear or usage will be made without charge under the warranties.

Neither Ford nor any of its dealers assume any responsibility under these warranties for any loss of use of the vehicle, loss of time, inconvenience, commercial loss or consequential damages. Damage from accidents, fire or other casualty, misuse, overloading, negligence, or racing, and failures caused by parts not supplied by Ford or by modification of any part of the vehicle are not covered by the warranties.

These warranties will not apply to any vehicle on which the odometer has been altered so that the actual mileage of the vehicle cannot be determined. These warranties will not apply to any vehicle purchased in the United States or Canada which is registered in or normally operated in another country. In this circumstance, the vehice may be eligible for coverage under the warranty authorized for the country of operation.

If you have a warranty problem

The dealer from whom you purchased your vehicle has the primary responsibility for performing warranty repairs. His Service Department has the qualified technicians and up-to-date equipment required to provide complete warranty service for your vehicle. Moreover, he values you as a customer for all of his products and services.

In the event that you should encounter a warranty service problem, we suggest that you contact the Owner or the General Manager of the Selling Dealership. If he cannot resolve the problem, we suggest that you contact the Owner Relations Manager at the District Office of the Ford Customer Service Division. The address and telephone number of the District Office servicing your area are shown in the applicable Owner's Manual.

Disclaimer of implied warranties

Except for responsibility for personal injuries shown to have resulted from a defect, THIS WARRANTY IS, to the extent allowed by law, EXPRESSLY IN LIEU OF any other express or implied warranty, condition or guarantee agreement or representation by any person with respect to the vehicle or any part thereof, including ANY IMPLIED WARRANTY OF MERCHANTABILITY OR FITNESS and the repairs, replacements, adjustments and services provided for in these warranties constitute the owner's exclusive remedy.

*Bronco Pickup, Club Wagon Bus, Ranchero, Econoline, F100, F250, F350, P350, M400 and P400.

1973
(EXCEPT CAPRI, COMET, COURIER, MAVERICK AND PINTO)

Ford and the Selling Dealer jointly warrant with respect to each 1973 model pasenger car or light truck* (except Capri, Comet, Courier, Maverick and Pinto) sold by Ford that for a period of 12 months or 12,000 miles, whichever occurs first, the Selling Dealer will repair or replace free of charge any part except tires that is found to be defective in factory materials or workmanship under normal use in the United States or Canada. The 12-month or 12,000-mile warranty period will begin on the date of original retail delivery or date of original use, whichever is earlier.

All Ford and the Selling Dealer require is that you properly operate, maintain and care for your vehicle. Warranty repairs using Ford Service Parts or Ford Authorized Remanufactured Parts will be made by your Selling Dealer at his place of business. If you are traveling, have moved a long distance from your Selling Dealer, or need emergency repairs, any authorized Ford or Lincoln-Mercury Dealer will perform the warranty repairs for you.

During the first 90 days of the warranty period (except for Capri, Comet, Courier, Maverick and Pinto) the following adjustments and services, if required in normal use, will be provided free of charge: wheel balancing; wheel alignment; headlight alignment; adjustments to carburetor, distributor, valves, belts, transmission, clutch, and brake system; cleaning of fuel, cooling, and brake systems; addition of fluids, except fuel, engine oil and washer fluids; and tightening of: nuts, bolts, and fittings. After the 90-day break-in period, such adjustments and services will be considered normal maintenance resulting from use.

To the extent allowed by law, THIS WARRANTY IS IN PLACE OF all other warranties, express or implied, including ANY IMPLIED WARRANTY OF MERCHANTABILITY OR FITNESS. Loss of use of the vehicle, loss of time, inconvenience, commercial loss or consequential damages are not covered by this warranty.

*Bronco Pickup, Club Wagon Bus, Ranchero, Econoline, F100, F250, F350, P350, M400, P400.

1974
(EXCEPT CAPRI, COMET, COURIER, MAVERICK, MUSTANG II AND PINTO)

Ford and the Selling Dealer jointly warrant for each 1974 model passenger car or lightt truck (P400 or lower series) sold by Ford that for the earliest of 12 months or 12,000 miles from either first use or retail delivery, the Selling Dealer will repair or replace free of charge any part except tires that is found to be defective in factory materials or workmanship under normal use in the United States or Canada.

All Ford and the Selling Dealer require is that you properly operate, maintain and care for your vehicle, and that you return for warranty service to your Selling Dealer's place of business or to any authorized Ford or Lincoln-Mercury dealer if you are traveling, have moved a long distance or need emergency repairs. Warranty repairs will be made with Ford Authorized Service or Remanufactured Parts.

To the extent allowed by law, THIS WARRANTY IS IN PLACE OF all other warranties, express or implied, including ANY IMPLIED WARRANTY OF MERCHANTABILITY OR FITNESS. Under this warranty, repair or replacement of parts is the only remedy.

1975
(P400 OR LOWER SERIES)

Ford and the Selling Dealer jointly warrant for 1975 model cars and light trucks sold by Ford that the Selling Dealer will repair or replace free any parts, except tires, found under normal use in the U.S. or Canada to be defective in factory materials or workmanship within the earliest of 12 months or 12,000 miles from either first use or retail delivery.

All we require is that you properly operate and maintain your vehicle, and that you return for warranty service to your Selling Dealer or any Ford or Lincoln-Mercury Dealer if you are traveling, have moved a long distance or need emergency repairs. Warranty repairs will be made with Ford Authorized Service or Remanufactured Parts.

To the extent allowed by law, THIS WARRANTY IS IN PLACE OF all other warranties, express or implied, including ANY IMPLIED WARRANTY OF MERCHANTABILITY OR FITNESS. Under this warranty, repair or replacement of parts is the only remedy.

1976
LIMITED WARRANTY
(P400 OR LOWER SERIES)

Ford and the Selling Dealer jointly warrant for 1976 model cars and light trucks sold by Ford that the Selling Dealer will repair or replace free any parts, except tires, found under normal use in the U.S. or Canada to be defective in factory materials or workmanship within the earliest of 12 months or 12,000 miles from either first use or retail delivery.

All we require is that you properly operate and maintain your vehicle, and that you return for warranty service to your Selling Dealer or any Ford or Lincoln-Mercury Dealer if you are traveling, have moved a long distance or need emergency repairs. Warranty repairs will be made with Ford Authorized Service or Remanufactured Parts.

THERE IS NO OTHER EXPRESS WARRANTY ON THIS VEHICLE.

ANY IMPLIED WARRANTY OF MERCHANTABILITY OR FITNESS IS LIMITED TO THE 12 MONTH/12,000 MILE DURATION OF THIS WRITTEN WARRANTY.

NEITHER FORD NOR ANY OF ITS DEALERS SHALL HAVE ANY RESPONSIBILITY FOR LOSS OF USE OF THE VEHICLE, LOSS OF TIME, INCONVENIENCE, COMMERCIAL LOSS OR CONSEQUENTIAL DAMAGES.

Additional (beyond 12 months/12,000 miles) limited (36 month) warranty on batteries

After the first 12 months or 12,000 miles but within 36 months from the earliest date of original retail delivery or first use, if the original battery is found to be defective, it can be exchanged for a new Motorcraft battery of equal or greater capacity on a pro rata basis at any Ford or Lincoln-Mercury Dealership or Motorcraft battery Dealership. For each month remaining in the 36-month period the pro rata credit will be 1/36 of the current suggested retail price of the battery being replaced.

This pro rata warranty period applies only to vehicles used for normal service. For batteries installed in police cars or taxicabs, the Dealer can advise of the adjustment period applicable to the battery in the particular vehicle.

Tire adjustment reference

Tires are subject to separate service adjustments, during the life of the original tread, offered by the manufacturer, not by Ford or the Selling Dealership. If you have a tire problem, take your vehicle to a representative of the tire manufacturer. Your Selling Dealer will help you discuss tire problems with the tire manufacturer's representative if you need assistance.

The policies of the various tire manufacturers generally provide that if during the life of the original tread a defect in factory material or workmanship is found in a tire installed on the vehicle when it was delivered, credit will be given toward the purchase of a new tire at the tire manufacturer's Adjustment Base Price. The credit is based on the amount of original tread left on the tire. The owner will be charged for taxes, and in some cases, transportation and/or service charges may be made. Damages resulting from a defective tire are not covered.

GENERAL MOTORS

1969
ALL MODELS

General Motors Corporation, the manufacturer, warrants to the original retail purchaser each new 1969 model passenger car and chassis (herein referred to as "Vehicle") including all equipment and accessories thereon (except tires) supplied or manufactured by General Motors, to be free from defects in material and workmanship under normal use and service during the time and mileage limits and subject to the limitations and exclusions hereinafter set forth.

Limitations

Time and mileage

This Warranty applies to the entire Vehicle (except tires) for 12 months after the date of delivery to the original retail purchaser or until the Vehicle has been driven for 12,000 miles, whichever first occurs.

Upon the expiration of the 12 months/12,000 miles Warranty coverage this Varranty continues to apply to the Vehicle's power train components (specifically, (1) cylinder block, head, all internal engine parts, water pump and intake manifold; (2) transmission case and all internal transmission parts including torque converter; (3) propeller shaft and universal joints; (4) rear axle, differential and axle shafts) until the expiration of five years from the date of delivery to the original retail purchaser or until it has been driven for 50,000 miles, whichever first occurs.

If, at the time of delivery to the original retail purchaser, the Vehicle has been in factory or dealer service (as a demonstrator, for example) the time and mileage limitations shall be caculated from the date the Vehicle was first placed in such factory or dealer service.

Manufacturer's obligation

General Motor's obligation under this Warranty is limited to repairing or replacing, at its option, any part or parts which are returned to an authorized General Motors dealer at such dealer's place of business and which examination shall disclose to General Motor's reasonable satisfaction to have been defective in material or workmanship. Such repair or replacement shall be performed by any authorized General Motors dealer at such dealer's place of business without charge.

Exclusions

This warranty shall not apply to:
1. Any Vehicle on which the odometer mileage has been altered and the Vehicle's actual mileage cannot be readily determined;
2. Any Vehicle for which the owner does not possess a General Motors Protect-O-Plate issued in owner's name for such Vehicle;
3. Normal maintenance services (such as engine tuneup, fuel system cleaning, carbon or sludge removal, brake and clutch adjustments and wheel alignment and balancing);
4. The replacement of service items (such as spark plugs, ignition points, positive crankcase ventilator valves, filters and brake and clutch linings) made in connection with normal maintenance services;
5. Normal deterioration of soft trim and external appearance items due to wear and exposure;
6. The repair or replacement of any part the failure of which is caused by lack of performance of required maintenance as specified by General Motors in the 1969 New Vehicle Warranty and Owner Protection Plan folder;
7. Any part of any Vehicle which has been subject to misuse, negligence, alteration or accident, or which shall have been repaired outside of an authorized General Motors dealer's place of business so as in any way, in the reasonable judgment of General Motors, to affect adversely its performance and reliability; or
8. Any Vehicle registered and normally operated outside the United States or Canada (the warranty applicable to such Vehicle shall be that authorized by General Motors in the country where such Vehicle is registered and normally operated).

Sole warranty

This Warranty is the only warranty applicable to the vehicle and is expressly in lieu of all other warranties, expressed or impied, including any implied warranty of Mechantability or Fitness For A Particular Purpose.

Availability of unexpired warranty time and mileage coverage to the second retail purchaser

If the Vehicle is acquired by a second retail purchaser at any time prior to the expiration of five years from the date of delivery to the original retail purchaser and before the Vehicle has been driven 50,000 miles, the second retail purchaser may obtain a Protect-O-Plate on the Vehicle entitling him to the benefits of the unexpired portion of the Warranty coverage to the original retail purchaser, subject to the provisions, limitations and exclusions of such Warranty, provided:
1. Application for the Protect-O-Plate is made to an authorized General Motors dealer within 30 days or 1,000 miles Vehicle usage, whichever first occurs, following the date of purchase of the Vehicle by the second retail purchaser;
2. A fee of $25 is paid to the dealer; and
3. The dealer advises General Motors that inspection indicates the Vehicle has received required maintenance as specified by General Motors in the 1969 New Vehicle Warranty and Owner Protection Plan folder.

It is a condition to General Motor's obligation to the second retail purchaser who holds a General Motors Protect-O-Plate in his name that such second retail purchaser pay the first $25.00 on each repair or replacement made with respect to each power train component under the Warranty after the period between the expiration of the 12 months/12,000 miles coverage and prior to expiration of the 5 years/50,000 miles coverage.

1970
ALL MODELS

General Motors Corporation warrants to the original retail purchaser that it will repair or replace, at its option, any parts of each new 1970 General Motors passenger car vehicle and chassis (referred to as "Vehicle"), including all equipment and accessories thereon (except tires) manufactured or supplied by General Motors, which are returned to an authorized General Motors dealer at his place of business and which examination discloses to General Motor's reasonable satisfaction to be defective in material or workmanship under normal use and service. Such repairs and replacements shall be performed by such dealer without charge.

This Warranty is subject to the following provisions:

Limitations

12 Month—12,000 Mile Coverage

This Warranty applies to the entire Vehicle (except tires) for 12 months from the date of delivery to the original retail purchaser or until the Vehicle has been driven for 12,000 miles, whichever first occurs.

5 Year—50,000 Mile Coverage

Upon expiration of the 12 month/12,000 mile Warranty coverage, this Warranty continues to apply to the Vehicle's power train components until the expiration of five years from the date of delivery to the original retail purchaser or until it has been driven for 50,000 miles, whichever first occurs. Vehicle's power train components are:

- cylinder block, head, all internal engine parts, water pump and intake manifold;
- transmission case and all internal transmission parts including torque converter;
- propeller shaft and universal joints; and
- drive axle, differential and axle shafts.

If, at the time of delivery to the original retail purchaser, the Vehicle has been in factory or dealer service (as a demonstrator, for example) the time and mileage limitations shall be calculated from the date the Vehicle was first placed in such factory or dealer service.

Exclusions

This Warranty shall not apply to:
1. Normal maintenance services (such as, engine tuneup, fuel system cleaning, carbon or sludge removal, brake and clutch adjustments and wheel alignment and balancing);
2. The replacement of service items (such as, spark plugs, ignition points, positive crankcase ventilator valves, filters and brake and clutch linings) made in connection with normal maintenance services;
3. Normal deterioration of soft trim and external appearance items due to wear and exposure;
4. The repair or replacement of any part, the failure of which is caused by lack of performance of required maintenance as specified by General Motors in the "1970 New Vehicle Warranty and Owner Protection Plan" folder attached;
5. Any part of a Vehicle which has been subject to misuse, negligence, alteration or accident so as in any way, in the reasonable judgment of General Motors, to affect adversely its performance and reliability;
6. Any Vehicle on which the odometer mileage has been altered and the Vehicle's actual mileage cannot be readily determined;
7. Any Vehicle for which the owner does not possess a General Motors Protect-O-Plate issued in owner's name; or
8. Any Vehicle registered and normally operated outside the United States or Canada (the warranty applicable to such Vehicle shall be that authorized by General Motors in the country where such Vehicle is registered and normally operated).

Sole warranty

This Warranty is the only Warranty, expressed or implied, applicable to the Vehicle. General Motors neither assumes nor authorizes any other person to assume for it any other obligation or liability in connection with the Vehicle.

Availability of unexpired warranty coverage to the second retail purchaser

The second retail purchaser only may obtain a Protect-O-Plate on the Vehicle entitling him to the benefits of any unexpired portion of the warranty coverage available to the original retail purchaser, subject to the conditions of the warranty, provided:

1. Application for the Protect-O-Plate is made to an authorized General Motors dealer within 30 days or 1,000 miles, whichever first occurs, following the date of purchase;
2. A fee of $25.00 is paid to the authorized General Motors dealer; and
3. The authorized General Motors dealer advises General Motors that inspection indicates the Vehicle has received required maintenance as specified by General Motors in the 1970 New Vehicle Warranty and owner Protection Plan folder.

It is a condition to General Motors's obligation to the second retail purchaser, who holds a General Motors Protect-O-Plate in his name, that he pay the first $25.00 on each repair or replacement made with respect to each power train component under the warranty after expiration of the 12 month/12,000 mile coverage.

1971-1972
ALL MODELS

What is warranted and for how long

General Motors Corporation warrants to the owner of each 1971 or 1972 model General Motors passenger car (except Nova and Vega 2300) that for a period of 12 months or 12,000 miles, whichever first occurs, it will repair, or at its option replace, any defective or malfunctioning part of the car—except tires which are warranted separately by the tire manufacturer.

The 12 month/12,000 mile warranty period shall begin on the date the car is delivered to the first retail purchaser or, if the car is first placed in service as a demonstrator or company car prior to sale at retail, on the date the car is first placed in such service.

This warranty covers only malfunctions resulting from defects in material or workmanship.

What is not covered by the warranty

This warranty does not cover:
1. Malfunctions resulting from misuse, negligence, alteration, accident, or lack of performance of required maintenance services;
2. The replacement of maintenance items (such as spark plugs, ignition points, positive crankcase ventilator valve, filters, brake and clutch linings) made in connection with normal maintenance services;
3. Loss of time, inconvenience, loss of use of the car or other consequential damages;
4. Any car on which the odometer mileage has been altered and the car's actual mileage cannot be readily determined; or
5. Any car registered and normally operated outside the United States or Canada. The warranty for these cars shall be that authorized for the country in which the car is registered and normally operated.

General Motor's obligations

1. Repairs qualifying under this warranty will be performed by any authorized General Motors dealer within a reasonable time following delivery of the car to the dealer's place of business.
2. General Motors will pay the authorized General Motors dealer for the repair or replacement under the warranty of any part of the car found to be defective, or the cause of a malfunction.
3. During the first 90 days of the warranty period, any authorized General Motors dealer will make the following service adjustments, if needed, at no charge to the owner:
- Wheel alignment and balancing
- Adjustments to the carburetor, distributor points or timing, drive belts, transmission, clutch and brake system
- Cleaning of fuel, cooling or brake systems
- Tightening of bolts, fasteners and fittings

Owner's obligations

1. After the first 90 days of the warranty period, the service adjustments specified in item 3 of "General Motor's Obligations" are considered to be items of normal maintenance resulting from use and are to be paid for by the owner.
2. The car must be delivered to an authorized General Motors dealer's place of business during regular business hours for performance of the service adjustments as specified in item 3 of "General Motor's Obligations", or for the performance of warranty repairs. The dealer must be furnished with the Protect-O-Plate for preparation of the work order to be signed by the owner.
3. The owner is responsible for the following required maintenance services which may be performed by any repair outlet regularly performing such services:

Engine oil

Maintain at proper level. Change every 4 months or 6,000 miles, whichever first occurs, or every 2 months or 3,000 miles, whichever first occurs, depending upon type of car service. See Owner's Manual for details as to change frequency, oil quality and viscosity.

Engine oil filter

Replace at first oil change and every second oil change thereafter.

Chassis lubrication

Lubricate suspension every 4 months or 6,000 miles, whichever first occurs. Maintain all oil and fluid levels.

This is the only express warranty applicable to 1971 model General Motors passenger cars and General Motors neither assumes nor authorizes anyone to assume for it any other obligation or liability in connection with such cars.

What to do if there is a question regarding warranty

The satisfaction and good will of owners of General Motors products are of primary concern to General Motors dealers. In the event a warranty matter is not handled to your satisfaction, the following steps are suggested:
1. Discuss the problem with your General Motors dealership management.
2. Contact the Division Zone Office closest to you as listed in the General Motor's Owner's Manual.
3. Contact the Owner Relations Manager.

1973-1974
ALL MODELS

What is warranted and for how long

General Motors Corporation warrants to the owner of each model General Motors passenger car (except Nova and Vega) that for a period of 12 months or 12,000 miles, whichever first occurs, it will repair any defective or malfunctioning part of the car—except tires which are warranted separately by the tire manufacturer. This warranty covers only repairs made necessary due to defects in material and workmanship, and needed service adjustments during the first 90 days of the warranty period.

The 12 month 12,000 mile warranty period shall begin on the date the car is delivered to the first retail purchaser or, if the car is first placed in service as a demonstrator or company car prior to sale at retail, on the date the car is first placed into such service.

What is not covered by the warranty

This warranty does not cover:
1. Conditions resulting from misuse, negligence, alteration, accident, or lack of performance of required maintenance services;
2. The replacement of maintenance items (such as spark plugs, ignition points, positive crankcase ventilation valve, filters, brake and clutch linings) made in connection with normal maintenance services;
3. Loss of time, inconvenience, loss of use of the car or other consequential damages;
4. Any car on which the odometer mileage has been altered and the car's mileage cannot be readily determined; or
5. Any car registered and normally operated outside the United States or Canada. The warranty for these cars shall be that authorized for the country in which the car is registered and normally operated.

General Motor's obligations

1. Repairs qualifying under this warranty will be performed by any authorized General Motors dealer within a reasonable time following delivery of the car to the dealer's place of business.
2. During the first 90 days of the warranty period, any authorized General Motors dealer will make any needed service adjustments.
3. General Motors will pay the authorized General Motors dealer for any repairs or 90-day service adjustments under the warranty.

Owner's obligations

1. After the first 90 days of the warranty period, needed service adjustments referred to in item 2 of "General Motor's Obligations" are considered to be items of normal maintenance resulting from use and are to be paid for by the owner.
2. The car must be delivered to an authorized General Motors dealer's place of business during regular business hours for performance of warranty repairs, or service adjustments.
3. The owner is responsible for maintenance services which may be performed at the owner's option by any repair outlet regularly performing such services.

This is the only express warranty applicable to 1973 and 1974 model General Motors passenger cars and General Motors neither assumes nor authorizes any one to assume for it any other obligation or liability in connection with such cars.

What to do if there is a question regarding warranty

The satisfaction and goodwill of owners of General Motors products are of primary concern to General Motors dealers. In the event a warranty matter is not handled to your satisfaction, the following steps are suggested:
1. Discuss the problem with your General Motors dealership management.
2. Contact the Division Zone Office closest to you as listed in the Division Owner's Manual.
3. Contact the Customer Services Manager.

1975 ALL MODELS EXC. CARS EQUIPPED WITH 140 CUBIC INCH 4-CYLINDER ENGINE

What is covered

General Motors Corporation, warrants to owners of 1975 passenger cars which are registered and normally operated in the United States or Canada:
- The General Motors dealer of the owner's choice will make any repairs on any part of the car, except tires, made necessary because of defects in material or workmanship for 12 months or 12,000 miles of use, whichever first occurs, from the date the car is delivered to the first retail purchaser or first placed in service as a demonstrator or company car, whichever is earlier, and will make any needed service adjustments during the first 90 days of use.
- Warranty repairs and needed service adjustments will be performed without charge to the owner by the General Motors dealer, at its place of business within a reasonable time after delivery of the car to the dealer.

What is not covered

- Repairs and service adjustments required because of misuse, negligence, alteration, accident, or lack of reasonable and proper maintenance are not covered, nor are the replacement of maintenance items (such as spark plugs, positive crankcase ventilation valves, filters, brake and clutch linings) made in connection with normal maintenance services.
- Loss of time, inconvenience, loss of use of the car or other matters not specifically included are not covered.
- Any car registered and normally operated outside the United States or Canada. The warranty for these cars shall be that authorized for the country in which the car is registered and normally operated.

General Motors Corporation does not authorize any person to create for it any other obligation or liability in connection with these cars.

1976 LIMITED WARRANTY ALL MODELS EXC. CARS EQUIPPED WITH 140 CUBIC INCH 4-CYLINDER ENGINE

What is covered

General Motors Corporation warrants to owners of 1976 passenger cars which are registered and normally operated in the United States or Canada:
- The General Motors dealer of the owner's choice will make any repairs on any part of the car, except tires, made necessary because of defects in material or workmanship for 12 months or 12,000 miles of use, whichever first occurs, from the date the car is delivered to the first retail purchaser or first placed in service as a demonstrator or company car, whichever is earlier, and will make any needed service adjustments during the first 90 days of use.
- Warranty repairs and needed service adjustments will be performed without charge to the owner by the General Motors dealer, at its place of business within a reasonable time after delivery of the car to the dealer.

What is not covered

- Repairs and service adjustments required because of misuse, negligence, alteration, accident, or lack of reasonable and proper maintenance are not covered, nor are the replacement of maintenance items (such as spark plugs, positive crankcase ventilation valves, filters, and brake linings) made in connection with normal maintenance services.
- Loss of time, inconvenience, loss of use of the car or other matters not specifically included are not covered.
- Any car registered and normally operated outside the United States or Canada. The warranty for these cars shall be that authorized for the country in which the car is registered and normally operated.

General Motors does not authorize any person to create for it any other obligation or liability in connection with these cars. ANY IMPLIED WARRANTY APPLICABLE TO THIS CAR IS LIMITED IN DURATION TO THE DURATION OF THIS WRITTEN WARRANTY. GENERAL MOTORS SHALL NOT BE LIABLE FOR CONSEQUENTIAL COMMERCIAL DAMAGES RESULTING FROM BREACH OF THIS WRITTEN WARRANTY OR ANY IMPLIED WARRANTY.

1975½–1976 CHEVROLET VEGA AND MONZA, AND PONTIAC ASTRE WITH 140 CUBIC INCH 4-CYLINDER ENGINE

Limited warranty

General Motors Corporation, guarantees to the owner of the 1976 vehicle identified on the cover and equipped with a 140 Cubic Inch 4 Cylinder Engine that any authorized Chevrolet or Pontiac dealer will make repairs without charge to the owner on those engine parts listed below made necessary because of defects in material or workmanship. Repairs will be made within a reasonable time after delivery of the Vehicle to a Chevrolet or Pontiac dealer at its place of business. This guarantee shall remain in effect until the Vehicle has accumulated 5 years or 60,000 miles of use, whichever first occurs, from the date of delivery to the first retail purchaser or date first placed in service as a demonstrator or company car, whichever is earlier.

Engine parts covered

This guarantee applies to the cylinder block, cylinder heads, all internal engine parts, intake and exhaust manifolds and water pump.

Effect on new vehicle warranty

This guarantee in no way limits the terms of the New Vehicle Warranty.

Exclusions

This guarantee does not cover:
1. Repairs required because of misuse, negligence, alteration, accident, lack of reasonable and proper maintenance, or replacement of maintenance items (such as spark plugs, positive crankcase ventilation valves, filters) made in connection with normal maintenance services.
2. Loss of time, inconvenience, loss of use of the vehicle or other matters not specifically included.
3. Any repairs if the Vehicle is registered and normally operated outside the United States or Canada or if the Vehicle's odometer is altered so that actual mileage cannot be determined.

General Motors does not authorize any person to create for it any other obligation or liability in connection with the 140 Cubic Inch 4 Cylinder Engine parts covered by this guarantee. ANY IMPLIED WARRANTY APPLICABLE TO THESE ENGINE PARTS IS LIMITED IN DURATION TO THE DURATION OF THIS WRITTEN GUARANTEE. GENERAL MOTORS SHALL NOT BE LIABLE FOR BREACH OF THIS GUARANTEE OR ANY IMPLIED WARRANTY.

Cooling System Maintenance

The modern engine and heat

Today's engines, straitjacketed by emission controls and obligated to power air conditioning and other convenience accessories, develop a tremendous amount of heat for the cooling system to dissipate. There have been many improvements in cooling system components in the last several years, but all they have done is enable the system to keep pace with the greater demands being made upon it. Therefore, the cooling system should be given major service once a year and a quick feel-and-look inspection whenever you do work under the hood.

Understanding the cooling system

Cooling system service and troubleshooting begin with an understanding of fluid under pressure, for the modern system typically is operating at 12 to 18 pounds per square inch (psi). The pressurization is needed to raise the boiling point of the fluid (about three degrees for each psi). The pressure is provided by a valve in the radiator cap, which keeps the lid on until the specified pressure is built up. If the fluid is heated so that excessive pressure is developed, it pushes up on the radiator cap valve, overcoming a calibrated spring, permitting the pressure to bleed off by allowing fluid to escape. In older cars, the fluid simply poured out of an overflow tube onto the ground until system pressure dropped to the specified level and the valve could close. In most (but not all) modern

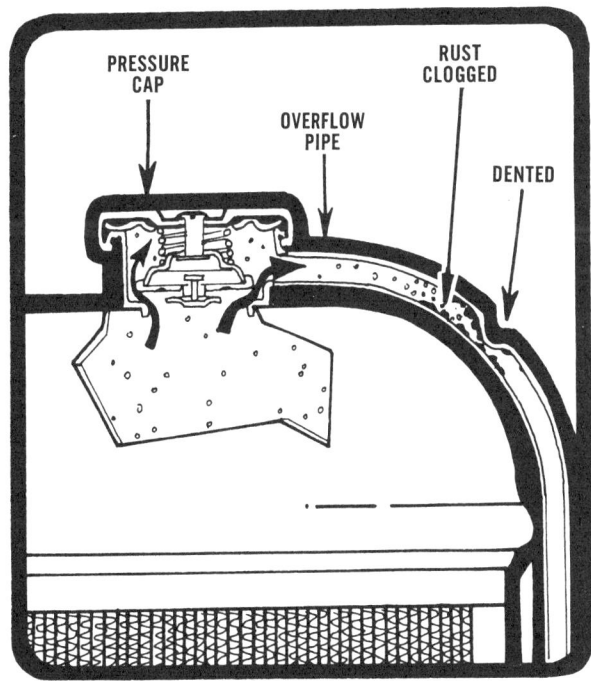

Fig. 1. When coolant expands, it pushes up on radiator cap valve, permitting coolant to flow through the overflow tube. In standard cooling systems, the tube emptied onto the ground and the coolant was lost.

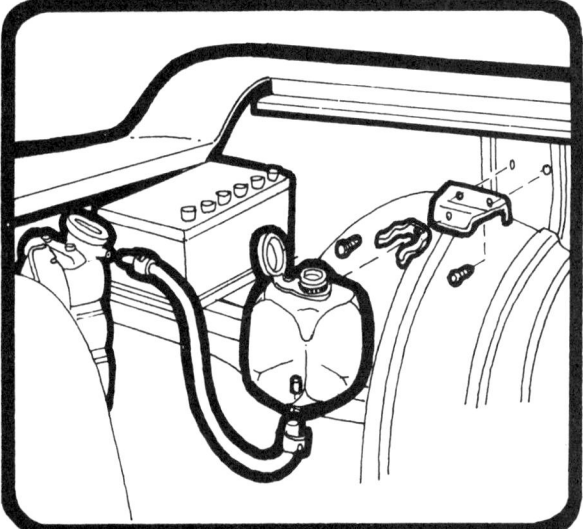

Fig. 2. With coolant recovery system, overflow tube connects to a reservoir, and coolant is saved. When engine cools down, a vacuum is created in the cooling system as the coolant contracts. The vacuum draws open a valve in radiator cap and sucks coolant from reservoir to refill radiator.

cars, the fluid flows into an overflow reservoir, from which it can be drawn back into the system when the fluid cools and contracts, which lowers pressure. This eliminates much of the periodic topping up of the radiator. See Figs. 1 and 2.

Why not simply increase the spring pressure of the cap valve still further, which would increase the boiling point and further reduce overflow of coolant? There are two answers: 1) engine temperatures already are at a practical peak, and if raised much more, would affect engine performance and the durability of some underhood components; 2) the radiator, hoses, hose connections and some of the gasket-sealed joints in the cooling system cannot stand significantly greater pressure without blowing apart. As things stand, just minor deterioration of some of the sealing points in the system can result in substantial leakage because of the high pressures.

There is one other measure that can be taken to raise the boiling point of the fluid, and it is included in the car manufacturers' calculations of cooling system performance—use of antifreeze in the system all year around. The right type of antifreeze not only prevents winter freeze-ups, but raises the boiling point of the water, the exact increase depending on the concentration. With a 50-50 mixture of antifreeze and water, the boiling point is 226°F, compared with 212° for plain water. In a 14 psi system, it is 263° compared with 248° for water. When a car is crawling along in heavy traffic on an 80- or 90° day, it is not uncommon for temperature of the water-and-antifreeze mixture, called the coolant, to exceed 250°.

Operating the system at this higher temperature without boilover adds another dimension to cooling system performance—superior rate of heat transfer from the radiator to the outside air. Add this feature to the fact that quality antifreeze has a balanced blend of rust and corrosion inhibitors, and you can understand why antifreeze now is a summer as well as a winter coolant.

The reference to the right type of antifreeze is important. The car manufacturers specify a permanent type, which means an antifreeze of ethylene glycol (a petroleum derivative) plus a good concentration of effective rust and corrosion inhibitors. The major brands are formulated to meet car manufacturers' specifications, so they will function properly for one to two years. Off-brands often contain cheaper, less effective inhibitors, and in some cases are diluted with water so they contain much less than the normal 91-94% of ethylene glycol.

When name-brand permanent antifreeze was about $1.50 a gallon, it was so inexpensive few people would even look for anything cheaper. Now that prices are much higher, you should be very careful to avoid the off-brands. You should also be wary of methanol antifreeze, which is a form of alcohol that was used as an antifreeze many years ago when cooling systems were not pressurized. Its boiling point is only 180°, so clearly, it will not last very long in a modern cooling system. To maintain the antifreezing protection with methanol, you would have to repeatedly top up the system. Some off-branders, looking for price leaders, are selling methanol antifreeze through consumer outlets once more.

NOTE: The term permanent does not mean that the antifreeze can be used forever, only that it will not boil off or lose its antifreeze characteristics. However, after a period of time the rust and corrosion inhibitors are worn out. Although you can buy small containers of compatible inhibitors to add to the old antifreeze, you should not do so, for even with a well-inhibited antifreeze, some rust and other particles will accumulate in the system and they should be flushed out. If they are not, they can clog cooling system passages. In addition, rust that adheres to the walls of the cooling system pasages can impede the transfer of heat from the cylinders and engine parts, shortening their life.

Quantity of antifreeze

For good winter protection against freeze-up and summer protection against overheating, a 50-50 mixture of water and quality antifreeze is recommended by the car manufacturers, with a 70-30 antifreeze and water mixture recognized as ideal.

The 50-50 mix will protect to minus 34° on freeze and add 14° to boilover protection. A 70-30 solution will protect to minus 84° and add 26° to the boiling point. Adding still more antifreeze to the mixture increases the boiling point, but the freeze protection drops. A 100% antifreeze solution boils at 330°, but freezes at only minus 9°. This is undesirable from both ends, for minus 9° is inadequate in most northern areas and the 330° boiling point is much too high for the engine. See Fig. 3.

Even the extremes provided by the 70-30 mix may sound excessive, but they really are not. All cooling

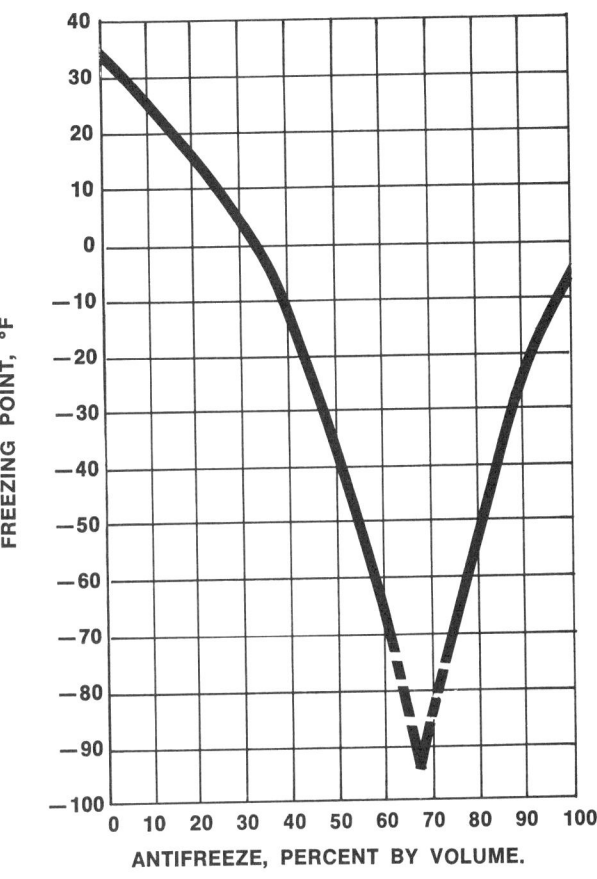
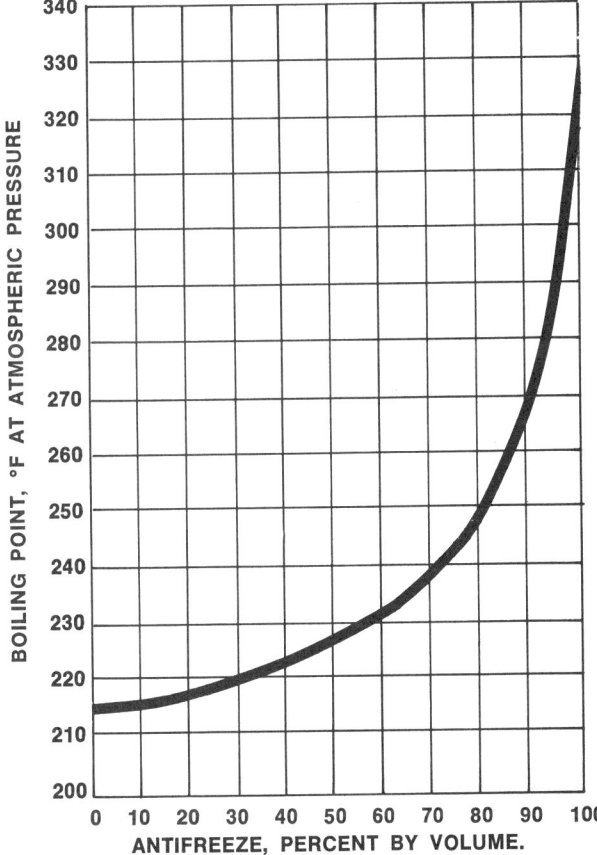

Fig. 3. Freezing and boiling points of coolant with various percentages of antifreeze in the system.

systems leak a certain amount of coolant. When you top up at a service station, you normally add only water, diluting the mixture. Therefore, the reserve protection is desirable.

For example, even a healthy cooling system without an overflow reservoir can leak a total of five quarts a year. If total capacity is 13 quarts, and you have nine quarts of antifreeze at the beginning, after a year of topping up with water the protection level is about 42%, which covers the car down to only minus 17° and reduces the added boilover protection from 26° to only 11°.

With the 50-50 mix (6½ quarts of antifreeze), the percentage drops to 30, at which the freezing point of the coolant is only plus 4° and the extra boiling protection is only plus 7°.

COOLING SYSTEM COMPONENTS

Refer to Fig. 4 to locate the cooling system components discussed below.

Type of radiator

There are two basic types of radiators in use today—the downflow and the crossflow. See Fig. 5. The downflow is the older design, and it can be identified by the top and bottom location of the tanks (inlet at top, outlet at bottom). The coolant absorbs heat in the engine, passes through the thermostat housing and a radiator hose at the top into the inlet tank, which also has the neck for the radiator pressure cap. It flows down through finned tubes, giving up its heat to the air passing through and enters the outlet tank. The water pump on the engine draws the cooled fluid from the outlet tank (via the lower radiator hose) back into the engine.

The crossflow, a design that exposes a lot of cooling surface to the airflow in a modern low-slung car, has the tanks on the sides of the radiator, as shown in Fig. 5, and the radiator cap neck is at the top of the outlet tank. The upper radiator hose, as in the downflow design, is also the inlet hose, and it is located at the top of the inlet tank. The lower hose is also the outlet hose, and it is located at the bottom of the outlet tank.

If the car has an automatic transmission with a transmission oil cooler built into the outlet tank of the radiator, the cooler line connections will be horizontally located in the bottom of a downflow, vertically located in the side of a crossflow.

Radiator drain

Most radiators have a drain cock (a sort of faucet) to facilitate draining out the coolant. It is always threaded into the bottom of the outlet tank, so regardless of type of radiator, it should be easy to find. You may, however, have to slip underneath the car to see it, Fig. 6.

Some radiators only have a drain plug, which must be removed with a socket wrench and ratchet. As explained in the service section of this chapter, it can be replaced with a drain cock.

There is no drain plug or cock on the 1972 Chevrolet Vega, and most 1973 Oldsmobile Omegas, Chevrolet (all models) and Pontiac (all models). The drain plug was reinstalled in production on all these cars late in the 1973 model year as a result of objections from the automotive service industry.

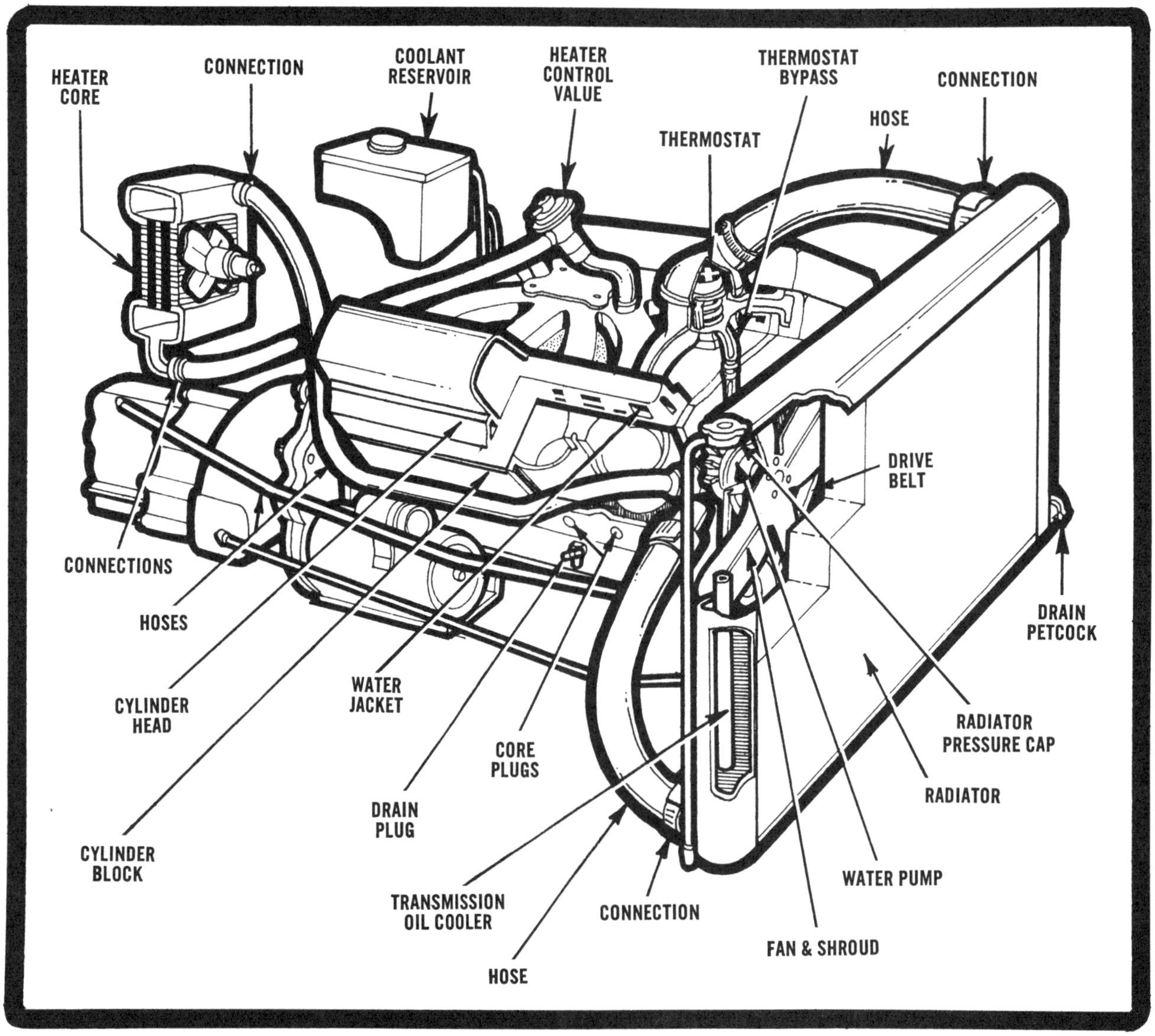

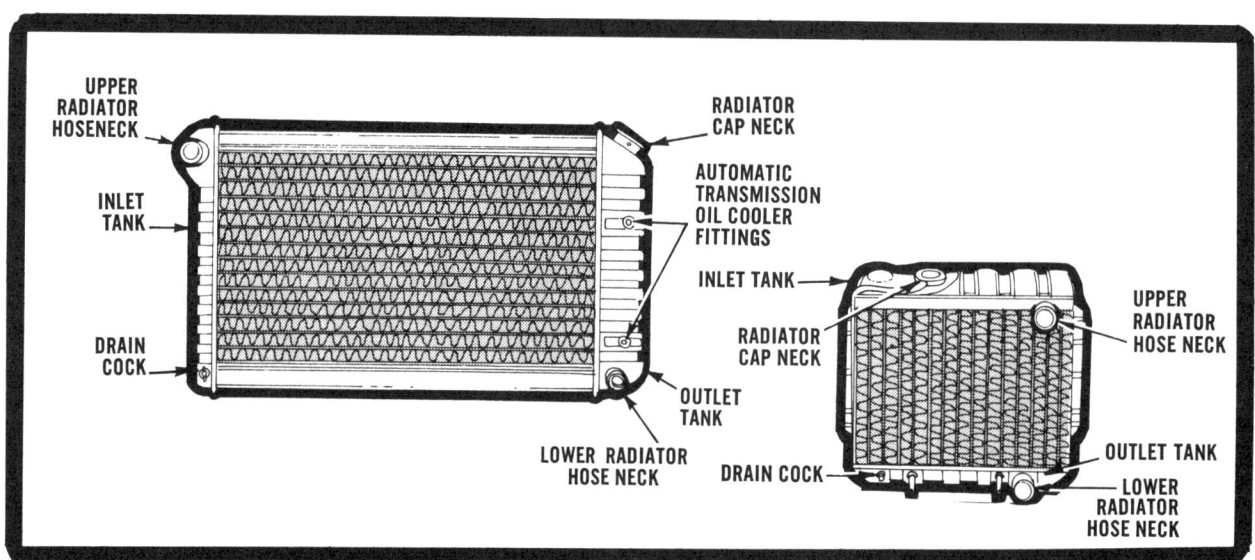

Fig. 4. Layout of typical liquid cooling system.

Fig. 5. A look at a crossflow and a downflow radiator. Notice that on the crossflow shown, the radiator cap neck is on the outlet tank. On the downflow it is on the inlet tank.

Fig. 6. Closeup look at the drain cock, a type of faucet.

Engine block drain

Opening the radiator drain plug or cock only permits coolant in the radiator to drain out. Anywhere from 40% to 75% of the coolant remains in the engine block, and to drain this out, you may remove plugs threaded into the side of the engine block. There is one plug on a 6-cylinder or in-line 4-cylinder, and two plugs on a V-type engine. The plugs are on the side of the block (one on each side of a V-type), approximately in the center. A few 6-cylinders may even have a drain cock instead of the plug.

The drain plugs invariably become rust-frozen in place, and virtually impossible to remove safely, so the best procedure is to leave them there. It is so rare for anyone to remove block drain plugs that they were eliminated on Buicks in 1974.

This clearly presents a problem to the owner who wants to install a 50-50 or 70-30 antifreeze mixture. The subject is covered under the headings Flushing The Cooling System and Installing Antifreeze later in this chapter.

Heater hoses

The heater has two hoses, an inlet and an outlet. To determine which is which, look at the engine compartment (and refer to Fig. 4), and find two rubber hoses of ⅝- or ¾-inch inner diameter (about 1-inch outer diameter). On most cars, Pacer and Chevette the notable exceptions, you will not be able to see the heater, but the heater hoses will go through the firewall.

In the engine compartment they are connected to the engine. The inlet is connected to the side or top center of the engine. The outlet goes to the water pump at the front. The inlet hose also may be identified by the presence of the heater control valve, which normally is mounted on the engine (and the inlet hose is connected to it) or it is spliced into the hose somewhere along its route to the firewall.

Bypass hose

The water pump circulates coolant through the engine. When the engine is cold the thermostat is closed, and the coolant follows a circuit that bypasses the thermostat. In a few engines there is a bypass passage built in, but in most cases the coolant flows through a bypass hose, connected to the water pump or built as a projection from the lower radiator hose, and attached to the cylinder head or thermostat housing.

Thermostat housing

Replacing a thermostat is a standard service job, described later in this chapter. To find the thermostat, just follow the upper radiator hose to the engine. The hose neck on the engine is part of a housing that encloses the thermostat.

COOLING SYSTEM MAINTENANCE

Removing radiator cap

Removing the radiator cap may seem so obvious as to be unworthy of discussion. However, improper technique has caused serious burns and other injury to both professional and novice mechanics.

There are three types of radiator caps and the technique for each is different. If you want a common denominator, the safety rule is to remove the radiator cap only when the system is cool. This, however, is impractical in many service and troubleshooting operations, and inconvenient in some emergency service situations.

The danger in removing the cap from a hot or overheated system is that the sudden release of pressure results in hot coolant spewing out.

WARNING: Removing a radiator cap on a hot system is extremely dangerous. Use the utmost caution.

All pressure radiator caps make provisions for the safe release of pressure. If the cap has a lever or push-button in the top, lifting the lever or pushing the button will depressurize the system. See Fig. 7. You will hear the whoosh and when it stops, you can safely remove the cap.

If there is no lever, there is a safety stop. Twist the cap counterclockwise carefully without applying any downward pressure on the top, and the cap will butt up against a stop. At this point, pressure will open the valve in the cap and as with the other designs, you will hear the whoosh of the pressure release. After the pressure is off, push down on the top of the cap with your palm and use your fingers to twist off the cap.

Some caps will be more difficult to twist than others. If the cooling system has an overflow reservoir, there are two rubber gaskets in the cap to insure a tight seal. To discourage cap removal with an overflow reservoir, the cap is often round (no ears to hold), and with this design a piece of corrugated rubber may be helpful (see Fig. 8). On Chrysler Corporation cars since 1975, the cap is designed for easy removal. It is a 2-piece design, and the top twists while the valve assembly inside remains stationary, eliminating the need to turn a part that has a tendency to stick.

Use of flushing chemicals

Before you make any decisions about flushing, you should see how dirty the coolant is. Remove the radiator cap and draw out some of the coolant with a syringe. Empty the syringe into a clear glass and inspect. If you see dirt and rust particles, oil and grease, a chemical cleaner should be poured into the system.

With just a light accumulation of foreign matter in the coolant, use a fast flush, the type that circulates and does its job as you drive for 50 to 100 miles. It dissolves oil and grease and loosens a small amount of rust. If the coolant is very dirty (rust-colored), use a 2-step chemical flush, which will dissolve a lot of rust and corrosive scale in the water jacket.

WARNING: The 2-step flush procedure is quite time-consuming and the chemical itself is highly caustic. It may remove rust particles that are sealing pinholes in the radiator or heater, resulting in coolant leaks. Therefore, it should be used only when necessary. However, the time and risk it entails should not discourage you from using it if the coolant is really rusty. If rust sealed a hole, a subsequent use of a container of cooling system sealer will also do the job.

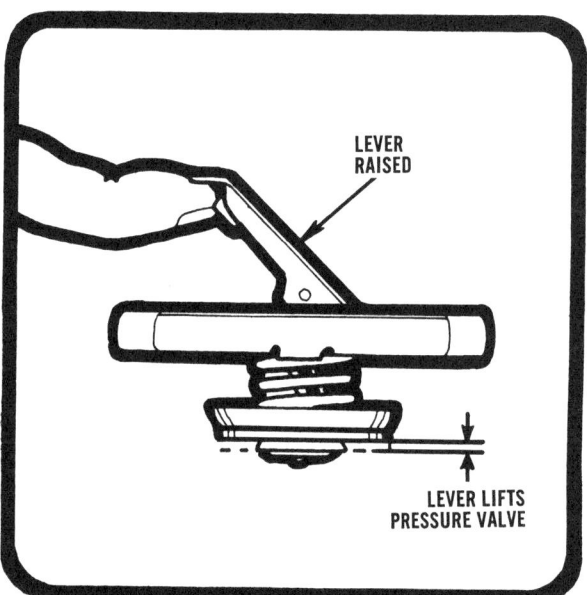

Fig. 7. Radiator cap with lever to release pressure.

The fast cleaner can be poured in before flushing the system, although the best procedure is to flush first. The 2-step caustic type should be poured in only after a reverse pressure flushing, as described later in this chapter. Then allow the engine to idle for half an hour with the heater set in HIGH position. Repeat the reverse pressure flush, add the acid neutralizer, run the engine at idle for another half hour, and follow with a third reverse pressure flush.

NOTE: Watch the engine carefully (and the temperature gauge or warning light) during the time it is idling, to be sure it doesn't overheat. To minimize this possibility, the engine should be allowed to cool overnight before pouring in the acid cleaner, and permitted to cool for a couple of hours before pouring in the neutralizer. If you run the engine at fast idle—1500 to 2000 rpm—it should not overheat.

Measuring radiator capacity

Because so few radiators have sufficient capacity to permit installing enough antifreeze for a 50-50 mixture, and none has the capacity for a 70% antifreeze concentration, you may wish to measure the radiator capacity before you select the method of flushing. If the radiator capacity is inadequate for a 50-50 mix, or if you wish to install a 70% antifreeze concentration, you must open the engine block drain(s), install a flushing tee (see Flushing Method 2 or use one of the makeshift options discussed in Installing Antifreeze.) Removing the engine block drain plugs is not recommended.

Begin by checking the capacity of your car's cooling system (see Specifications section). Select a pail or pan with a capacity equal to somewhat over 50% of system capacity and place it under the radiator drain plug or cock. Remove the radiator cap, top up radiator with water, and open the drain cock or remove the plug.

NOTE: 1972 Chevrolet Vega, 1973 Chevrolet, Pontiac, Oldsmobile Omega without drain plug or cock: Disconnect lower radiator hose from radiator as explained in Service section of this chapter.

Let the radiator drain completely and measure the amount, perhaps by pouring the coolant into quart or gallon containers. If the coolant drained is less than 50% of system capacity, use Flushing Method 2, or refer to Installing Antifreeze to consider the other options.

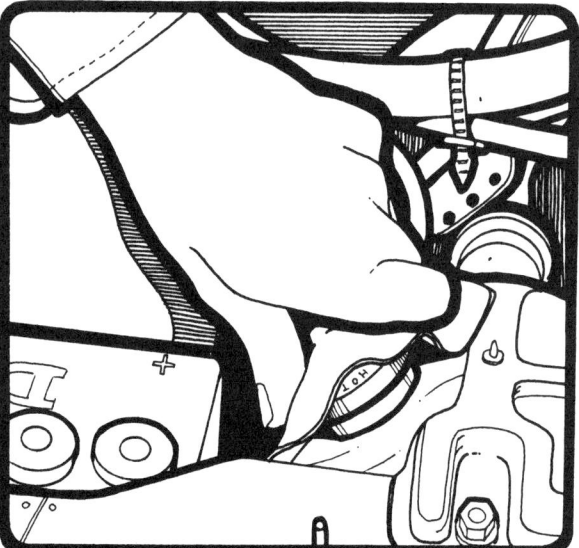

Fig. 8. Twisting off radiator cap without ears using a piece of corrugated rubber.

FLUSHING THE COOLING SYSTEM

Although there are many flushing techniques, some require professional equipment, such as a pressure gun, flushing machine or the use of a lift. The flushing procedures in this chapter are designed for the amateur mechanic with a garden hose. None requires removal of the engine block drain plugs, therefore the job can be done without a jack or lift. All these methods leave the cooling system filled with water. Installing antifreeze is covered in the section immediately following.

Flushing method No. 1: Simple flush

If you are willing to service your cooling system once a year without fail, and can begin with a new car, the simple flush should be adequate for a number of years.

1. Remove radiator cap and open drain cock, remove plug or disconnect lower radiator hose if necessary to drain radiator, Fig. 9.
2. After radiator is empty, close drain cock, reinstall plug or reconnect hose. Top up radiator with fresh water, reinstall radiator cap, turn heater control to HIGH and start engine. Place hand on radiator inlet tank to determine when thermostat opens. You will feel the inlet tank get hot when thermostat permits water to flow through to the radiator. Five minutes after thermostat opens, stop the engine, Fig. 10.
3. Again remove radiator cap, open drain cock, remove drain plug or disconnect lower hose if necessary and allow radiator to drain completely, Fig. 11. Repeat 2.

The complete flushing procedure should be repeated as often as needed until the coolant draining from the radiator is clean. Tests have shown that if the radiator is flushed with this method three times, an average of 88% of loose rust and old coolant is removed. If the job is done four times, about 94% is removed, five times, approximately 97%.

Flushing method No. 2: Flushing tee

The use of a flushing tee is a relatively new procedure, but it is fast becoming the most popular for both novice and professional mechanics. The flushing tee (Fig. 12) is a T-shaped piece of plastic tubing with a sealing cap. It is spliced into the heater inlet hose, using a razor blade to cut the hose, and attached to the hose with clamps, using a screwdriver. The tee is available as a single part for under a dollar, or in a complete kit, which includes a double-female adaptor to permit attaching a garden hose to the tee, hose clamps, and a coolant deflector (covered later).

The professional connects a special flushing machine to the tee, but you simply attach a garden hose

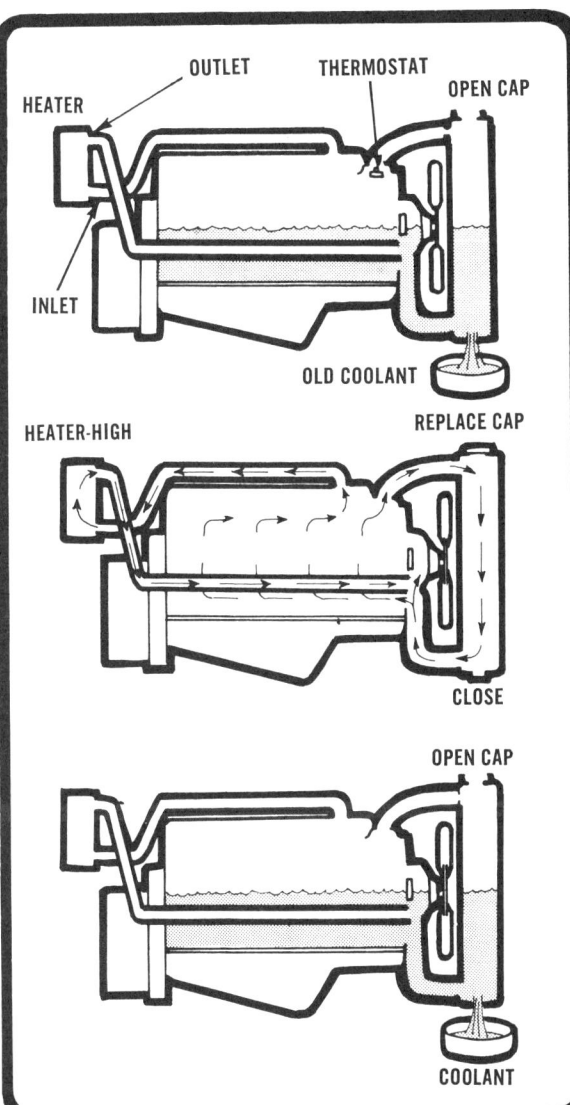

Fig. 9. First step of simple flush is to drain radiator.

Fig. 10. Second step of simple flush is to top up system with water, run engine with heater on until five minutes after thermostat opens.

Fig. 11. Third step of simple flush is to drain the radiator once more, which permits more of the contaminants to be removed. After five drains, 97% of foreign matter is removed from cooling system.

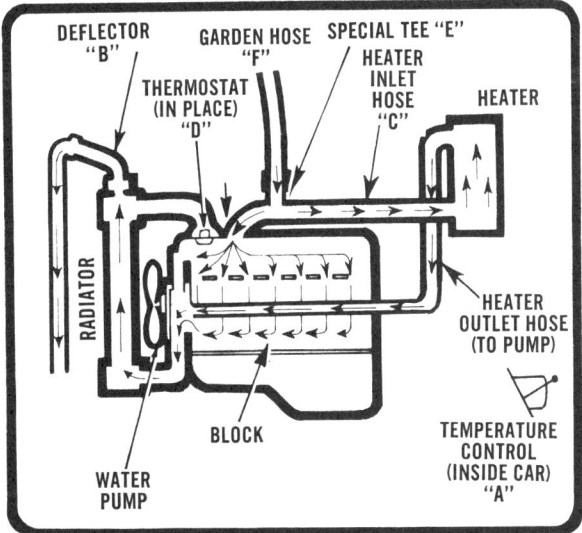

Fig. 12. Flushing tee is piece of plastic spliced into heater hose, and connected to garden hose with double-female adaptor. Diagram shows how heater flows to clean out system.

271

and turn on the water. It courses through the engine and the radiator in a direction counter to normal circulation. This form of reverse flushing loosens a fair amount of rust deposits. See Fig. 13.

The water deflector in the kit fits into the radiator cap neck, so that when water comes flowing up and out of the radiator, it does not splash.

NOTE: The deflector cannot be used with the cross-flow radiator. Instead, leave the radiator cap in place and disconnect the upper radiator hose from the thermostat housing. Bend and twist the hose (loosen the clamp on the radiator neck) so that the hose rests on the fan shroud or radiator and is not aimed at the fan.

To flush out the system with a tee installed, follow this procedure:

1. Remove cap from tee, thread on double-female adaptor and connect garden hose, Fig. 13.
2. On downflow radiators, remove radiator cap and install deflector in cap neck, so that deflector outlet is aimed forward. On cross-flow radiators, disconnect upper hose from radiator and reposition as explained earlier.
3. Start engine and run at idle speed.
4. Turn heater control to HIGH position. Turn on garden hose.
5. When water is flowing out of deflector or upper hose runs clean for two minutes, turn off garden hose, stop engine, remove adaptor from tee and reinstall cap securely.

Flushing method No. 2A

The tee permits reverse flushing of the engine and radiator, but not of the heater. Heater passages are narrower than those in the radiator, so they can clog more easily. If you wish to reverse-flush the heater, install a second tee in the heater outlet hose, then proceed as follows:

1. Disconnect heater inlet hose from tee or heater control valve, whichever is closest to point where hose goes through firewall to heater core. Or if heater core is in engine compartment, merely disconnect hose from heater core inlet neck if desired.
2. Aim disconnected end of hose so it will not splash water on engine.
3. Connect garden hose to tee in outlet hose, using double-female adaptor.
4. Pinch off heater outlet hose between tee and water pump, using vise pliers.
5. Turn on garden hose and water will flow through heater in opposite to normal direction. When the water has been running clean for two minutes, turn it off.
6. Disconnect double-female adaptor, reinstall tee cap, remove vise pliers and reconnect heater inlet hose.

Flushing method No. 3: Moderate reverse flush

If radiator capacity permits, you can reverse flush the entire cooling system (radiator, engine block and heater core) with the following procedure, which requires a large round cork or rubber stopper.

Fig. 13. A look at the flushing tee actually connected to garden hose with double-female adaptor. Pinching off inlet hose with vise pliers was done to minimize spillage of hot coolant, but is not absolutely necessary.

1. Remove the radiator cap, open drain cock, remove drain plug or disconnect lower radiator hose if necessary to drain radiator completely, Fig. 14.
2. Disconnect heater outlet hose from water pump and plug hose neck with cork or rubber stopper. Force end of garden hose tightly into disconnected end of heater hose, Fig. 15.
3. Reinstall radiator cap. Disconnect upper radiator hose from thermostat housing and reposition it as necessary (slackening hose clamp on radiator neck if required) to direct it away from fan. If possible, attach a long piece of hose to the end of the upper radiator hose to facilitate this, Fig. 16.
4. Run engine at idle, set heater control to HIGH and turn on water to garden hose, Fig. 17.
5. When water gushing out of upper radiator hose runs clean for two minutes, stop engine, turn off garden hose, and drain radiator, Fig. 18.
6. Remove cork or rubber stopper from heater inlet hose neck, reconnect heater and upper radiator hoses and close radiator drain cock, reinstall drain plug or reconnect lower radiator hose, Fig. 19.

Fig. 14. First step of moderate reverse flush is to drain the radiator.

Fig. 15. Second step of moderate reverse flush is to disconnect heater outlet hose to water pump, force garden hose into hose end, and plug hose neck on water pump with stopper.

Fig. 16. Next, reinstall radiator cap, close drain cock, attach extension hose to upper radiator hose.

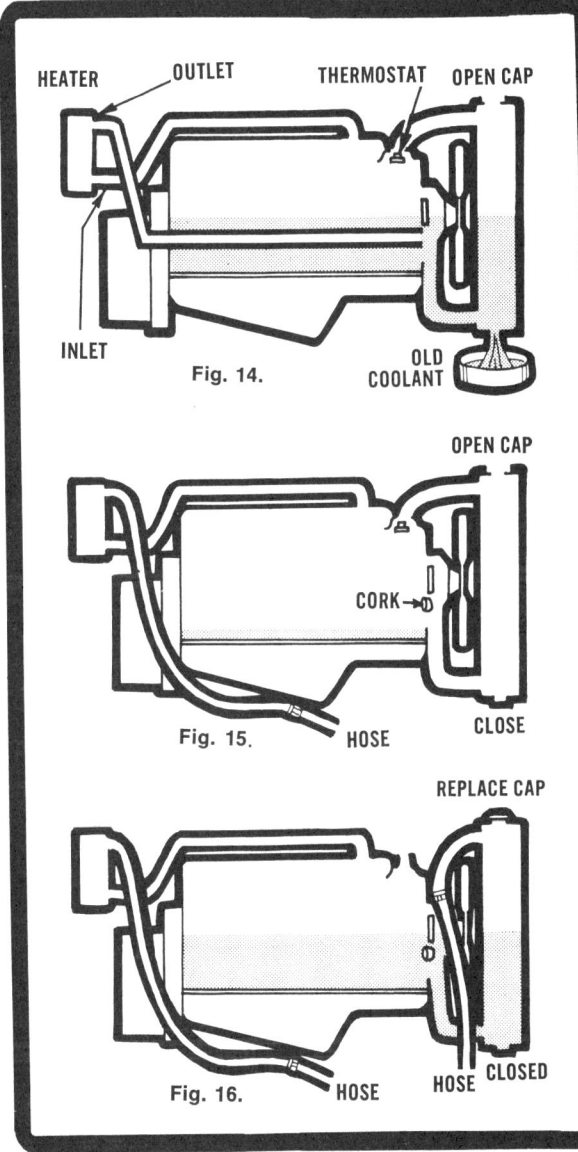

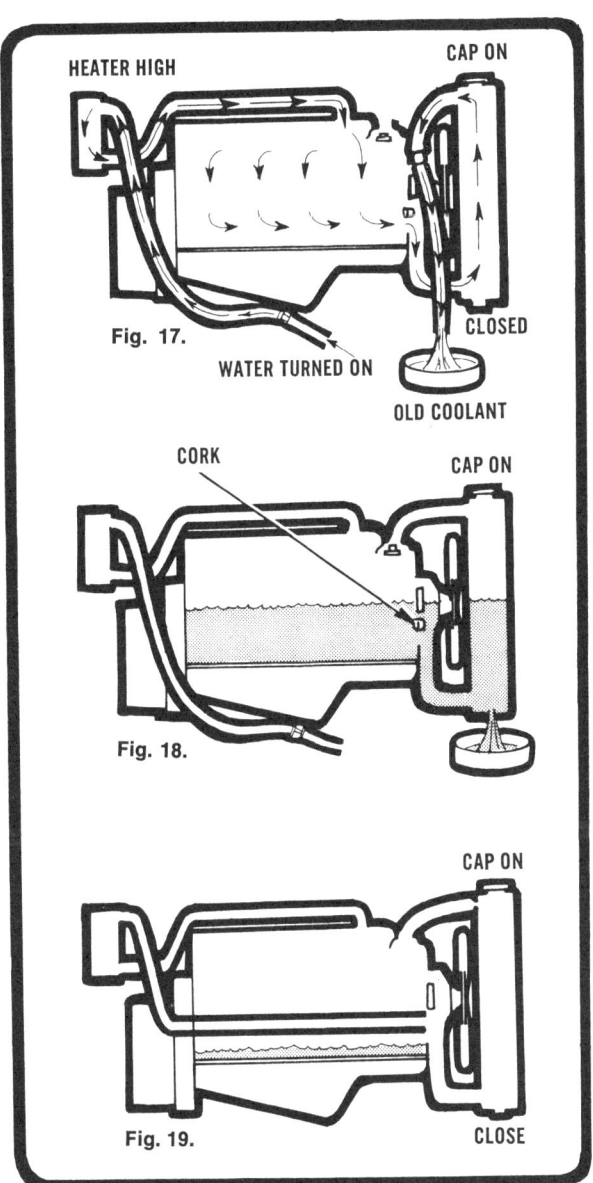

Fig. 17. Turn on water to garden hose and it will course through heater, engine block, up radiator and out upper radiator hose.

Fig. 18. Drain radiator to prepare for addition of antifreeze.

Fig. 19. Remove garden hose and stopper, and reconnect heater hose to water pump.

INSTALLING ANTIFREEZE

If your measurements of radiator capacity indicated that you cannot install the desired percentage of antifreeze merely by draining the water from the radiator and filling it only with antifreeze, you have the following choices:

1. If you installed the flushing tee, remove the cap from it. Pour antifreeze into the radiator and when it is full, start the engine and immediately turn the heater control to HIGH. Water will flow out of the tee, permitting you to add more antifreeze to the system as the level in the radiator drops. You will lose very little antifreeze and once you have the desired amount in the system, you can quickly cap the tee.

   NOTE: You must keep pouring in the antifreeze as the water flows out through the tee, or the engine could overheat. This is particularly important on the Chevrolet Vega aluminum 4-cylinder engine, which can be destroyed very quickly if the cooling system is four quarts or more low on coolant.

2. You can disconnect the heater inlet hose from the engine and attach another hose of the same size to the engine hose neck. Aim this new hose away from the engine to avoid splashing. Start the engine. If the heater control valve is on the engine, the hose you have connected is actually to the heater valve, so simultaneously turn the heater control to HIGH. Water will flow out of the hose, permitting you to install the desired amount of antifreeze into the radiator. Clearly, the need to disconnect a hose and refit the heater hose can result in more lost antifreeze than with the tee arrangement. Perhaps with a helper you can speed up the reconnection and minimize the loss. As with Method 1, keep the radiator topped up as the water pours out from the hose to prevent the possibility of engine damage.

3. If the difference between radiator capacity and the amount of antifreeze you wish to install is very small, and the car has an overflow reservoir, just pour straight antifreeze into the reservoir. In normal driving, the antifreeze will mix with the water in the cooling system.

These methods do involve some lack of precision, and in the cases of 1 and 2, some loss of antifreeze. In any case, an extra pint of antifreeze should be added to cover the situation.

If ambient temperatures are below freezing, you should immediately drive the car for 15 to 30 minutes with the heater control in the HIGH position to insure a satisfactory mix of the water and antifreeze.

COOLING SYSTEM INSPECTION

Whenever you are doing underhood service, you should make a quick inspection of the cooling system.

Antifreeze protection

Although a cooling system may start out with an adequate concentration of antifreeze after a flush and fill, the protection level soon drops. The leakage from a healthy system can be quite substantial over thousands of miles, and the normal topping up with water dilutes the antifreeze further, perhaps making the concentration inadequate. To check, you need an antifreeze hydrometer, a tool that measures the specific gravity of the coolant compared with plain water, and provides an indication of anti-freezeup protection. The hydrometer is a syringe-like device with a float inside. To use, you draw a sample of coolant from the radiator fill neck and watch the float, which reaches a level in the hydrometer. The float has temperature markings and whatever mark is at the level of the coolant is the temperature at which the antifreeze and water mixture will freeze, Fig. 20. A 50-50 antifreeze and water mixture freezes at minus 34°F, so if the hydrometer indicates a freezing point of minus 34°, you know the antifreeze percentage is 50.

NOTE: Even the best of hydrometers is not particularly accurate, and the worst can be off by 20°. A professional quality hydrometer, which has a thermometer built in, so you can correct the specific gravity reading for the temperature of the coolant, is the best choice, and even it may be off 5°. There is a device called a refractometer, with accuracy to one degree, but it is expensive and more than you really need.

If the antifreeze protection has dropped to minus 20° or higher, top up with straight antifreeze the next time you need a quart of coolant.

HOSES AND CLAMPS

Squeeze and look at all coolant hoses (two radiator, two heater, one bypass on most cars, and on Pinto, Bobcat, Mustang II and Vega with the 2-barrel carburetor, two hoses to the automatic choke housing). If they feel hard and brittle, or if they swell when the engine is warmed up, they should be replaced. Also check the hose clamp connections carefully, and if you think the clamp may have cut into the hose, loosen it and move it aside. See Fig. 21. Tighten all clamps that have an adjusting screw, if necesary.

RADIATOR CAP AND NECK

Remove the cap and look at the pressure valve gasket. If it is indented and the cooling system has been losing coolant, the cap is suspect, and it should be checked on a pressure tester, as described in the Troubleshooting section.

If the system has an overflow reservoir, the cap has a second gasket in the inside perimeter, Fig. 22. If it shows any clearcut signs of deterioration, the cap should be replaced.

Wipe the entire cap neck, including the inside surface against which the pressure valve gasket seats, to remove dirt and rust that could prevent the gasket from seating properly, Fig. 23.

RADIATOR EXTERIOR

An accumulation of bugs, leaves, road film, etc. should be cleaned from the radiator fins, using a brush, household detergent and a water hose (on cars with air conditioning, the finned condenser sits in front of the radiator, and its surface is the one that becomes restricted by bugs, leaves and film). Anything that can block the flow of air through the radiator can contribute to overheating.

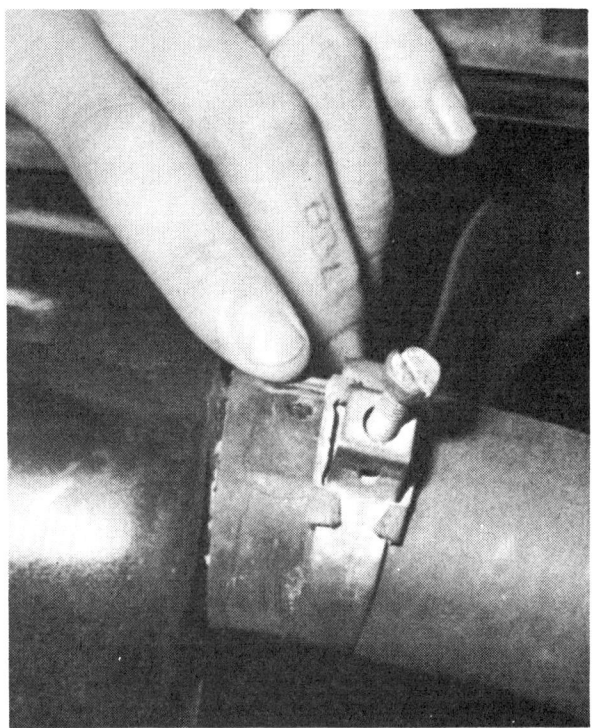

Fig. 21. Moving hose clamp aside to check area under clamp for cracks or cuts.

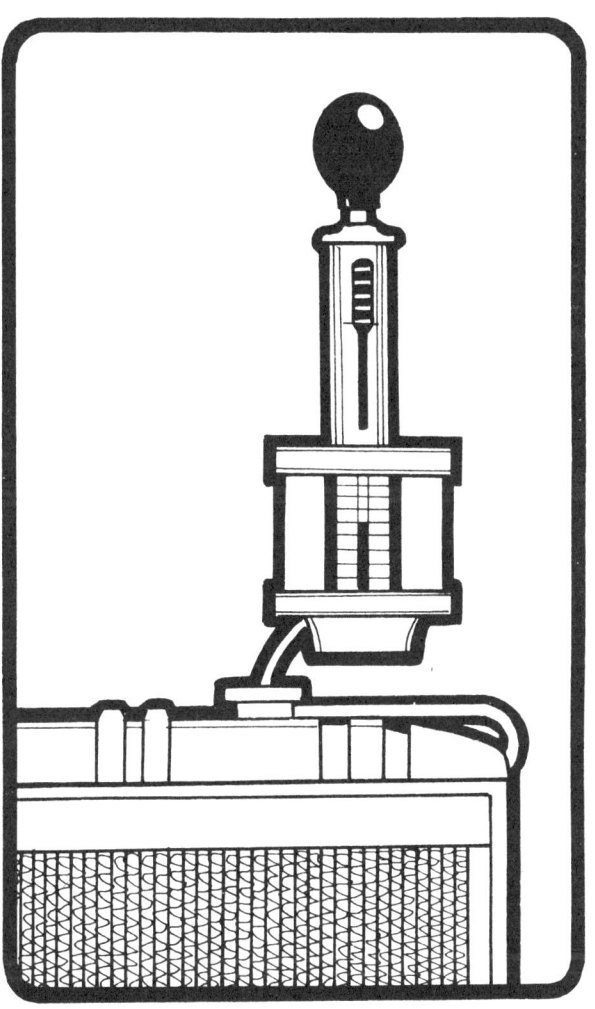

Fig. 20. Antifreeze hydrometer permits fair estimate of protection level.

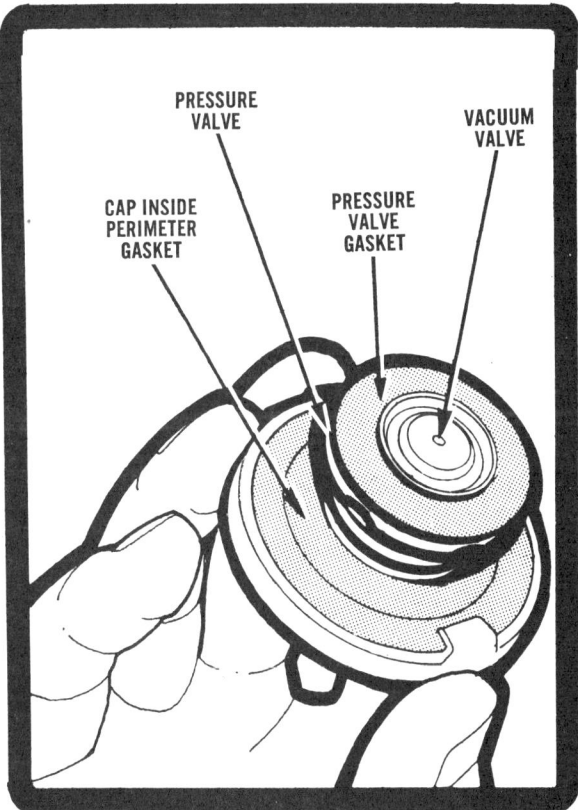

Fig. 22. A look at the radiator cap used in a coolant overflow system. Like all pressure caps it has the pressure valve and gasket, the vacuum valve (that opens when the coolant cools) plus an additional part, an air-sealing gasket in the cap's inside perimeter. This insures that when the vacuum valve opens, only coolant in the overflow reservoir, not air, will be sucked into radiator.

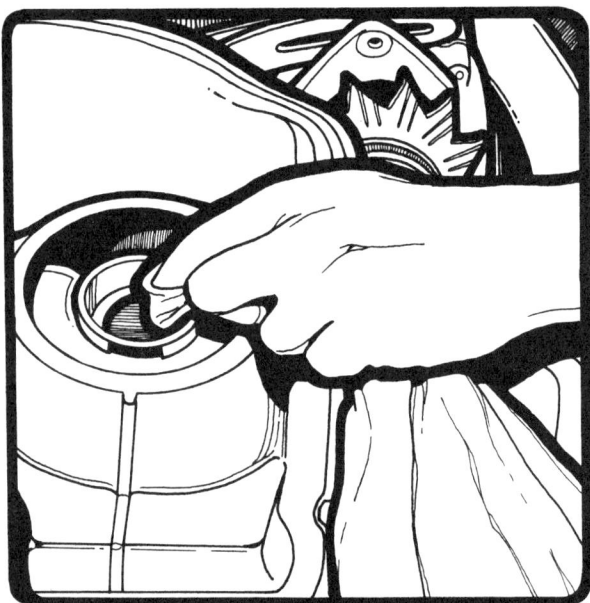

Fig. 23. Cleaning of radiator fill neck. Do not forget to wipe inside surface.

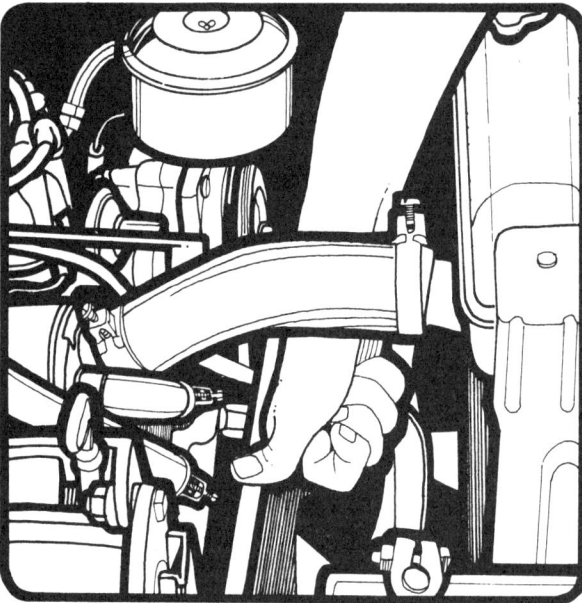

Fig. 24. Pressing down on belt midway between pulleys to make a rough check of belt tension. Under thumb pressure, belt should deflect ½-inch.

DRIVE BELT AND PULLEYS

The fan belt should be inspected for grease or oil soaking, and it should be twisted over and checked for cracks or splitting. If any of these conditions exist, the belt should be replaced, as described in the Service section. Also press down on the fan belt at a point midway between generator and fan pulleys (see Fig. 24). If the belt deflects more than half an inch under thumb pressure, it should be readjusted, also as described in the Service section.

With the engine running at idle, stand at the left or right side of the engine compartment and look at the fan pulley. If it seems to be wobbling, it is either loose or cocked. Loose pulley bolts may be tightened, but a cocked pulley must be replaced.

TROUBLESHOOTING THE COOLING SYSTEM

It might seem that the only basic problem you will have to troubleshoot is overheating. It is admittedly the most common, but there is another—overcooling. This means that the engine does not reach full operating temperature. The problem normally is noticed only in cold weather, when the low coolant temperature causes poor heater and defroster performance.

OVERCOOLING

Overcooling is a serious cold weather problem, for if the engine does not reach correct operating temperature (180° to 205°), engine parts do not operate at their designed-in clearances. The engine runs less efficiently and uses more gasoline. **Important:** Overcooling, which is caused by a defective thermostat (opens too much) or if the thermostat is left out, can occur in cold weather even on a car prone to overheating in hot weather.

1. Look at the temperature gauge if your car is so equipped. If the needle is below 180° (or the dial midpoint) after the car has been driven for seven to 10 miles, proceed to the next step.
2. If car has downflow radiator, put inlet tank thermometer into the coolant (see Fig. 25). The thermometer is more accurate than a dashboard gauge and its use is better than relying on the gauge reading alone.
3. If the temperature in the inlet tank is low, double-check by turning on the heater. Poor heater performance (air that is not very hot) can be caused by clogged passages in the heater core, but in collaboration with low thermometer readings can confirm overcooling. Do not confuse lack of heat with blower problems. If the heater is not working, even very hot air will not be circulated adequately to warm the passenger compartment. The blower motor, however, is easy to hear, so you should not have difficulty determining if it is working.

4. If you can confirm an overcooling problem, replace the thermostat as explained in the Service section.

OVERHEATING

Engine overheating is always associated with loss of coolant. However, in some respects like the chicken and the egg, it is not always clear which came first. It is possible for overheating to occur first, resulting in boiling of the coolant and its loss through the overflow tube as the pressure valve in the radiator cap opens. Or some coolant may leak out of the system, with the result that the remaining coolant is unable to get rid of the heat as fast as the engine develops it.

The first step in troubleshooting, therefore, is to find out what the basic problem is, loss of coolant or overheating. On a late-model car with a clear plastic overflow reservoir, this first step is simply a matter of looking at the reservoir. If the reservoir level rises noticeably just before the engine overheats, the problem is overheating, not loss of coolant.

NOTE: Follow test procedure given in this section.

Overflow kit

If your car does not have an overflow reservoir, it is easy enough to retrofit one. Many kits priced at under $15 are available. A quality kit should include the following:

1. A clear plastic reservoir with quart markings to indicate fluid level. If there is no room in the engine compartment for a rigid reservoir, you will have to purchase a kit with a flexible one, in which case the fluid level markings (if there are any) will not be meaningful.
2. A replacement radiator cap, with an air sealing gasket in the cap's inside perimeter.
3. A sight glass tube which can be spliced into the upper radiator hose (Fig. 26) so you can check coolant level and flow at a glance. Of course, this sight glass (made of plastic) adds to the cost of the kit, and few manufacturers include it, but it is a worthwhile feature to look for, although not absolutely essential.

Fig. 25. Inserting radiator thermometer in inlet tank to measure coolant temperature. This can be done on downflow radiators only. The crossflows have the fill neck on the outlet tank.

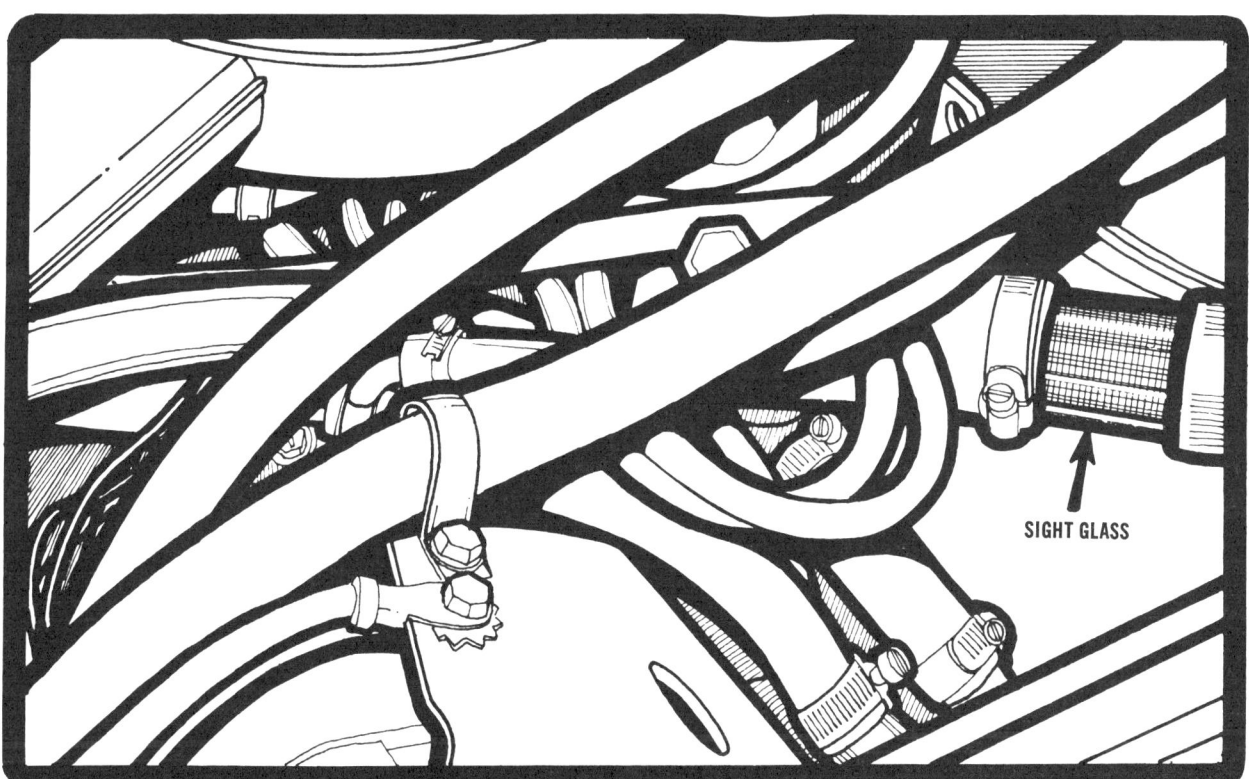

Fig. 26. Sight glass that is spliced into upper radiator hose is a desirable feature in a retrofit coolant recovery kit. However, it is not always available.

Catchpot

If your car does not have an overflow reservoir and you do not wish to install one, you can improvise something of at least 1-gallon capacity to serve as a coolant catchpot during troubleshooting. A plastic gallon container from milk or household cleaning agent will do. With wire and tape, attach the bottle under the hood, making sure it is level. Disconnect the radiator overflow hose from its mounting clips and direct it into the bottle, as shown in Fig. 27.

Test procedure

1. Make sure coolant level in radiator is at specified level and coolant temperature is well below boiling (120°F or less).
2. Drive car until overheating occurs, staying in your immediate neighborhood so you can get to your driveway without difficulty. If you are using the catchpot setup, drive on smooth roads to minimize spillage.
3. At the first sign of overheating, stop the engine and lift the hood. If the overflow reservoir level has risen markedly or if the catchpot is full, the problem is overheating causing coolant loss, not vice versa.

Causes of overheating resulting in overflow

Defective pressure cap on radiator

If the valve is weak or is not seating properly in filler neck, proper pressure will not be built up in system. The coolant will force the weak valve open (or will leak past the valve's rubber seal if that is defective) and flow into the reservoir, or onto the ground on cars without a reservoir or catchpot.

The only sure way to test the pressure cap valve is with a pressure tester—an air pump with a pressure gauge. The pump permits the operator to apply air pressure equal to the rating of the cap (12 to 18 psi) and watch the gauge to see if the pressure leaks out. The pressure tester also can be used to check for leaks in the cooling system itself (at hose connections, water pump, head gasket, etc.) by fitting it to the cap neck and applying air pressure.

A pressure tester is priced at $30 to $50, but if you do not wish to make the investment, you can bring your car to a service station for testing. Although most stations charge for pressure testing the system, they usually test only the pressure cap free, with the expectation that if you need a cap, you would buy it there. If you want your own pressure tester, be sure to buy the standard type with a hand operated pump, Fig. 28, not the type that requires an independent source of air pressure.

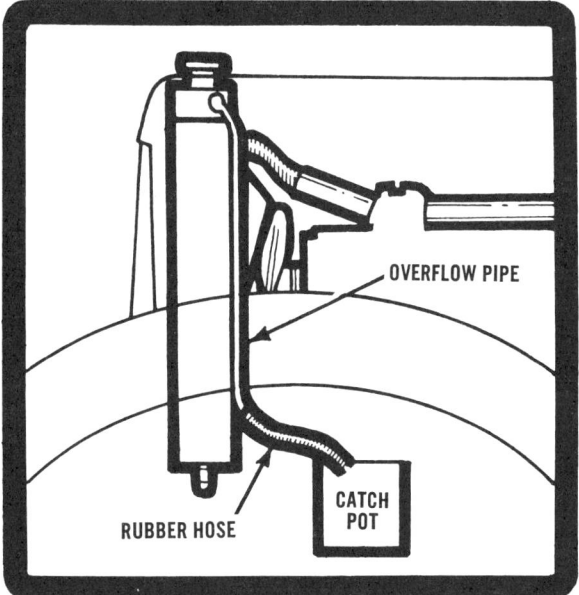

Fig. 27. Catchpot arrangement to check for coolant overflow loss on cars without reservoir.

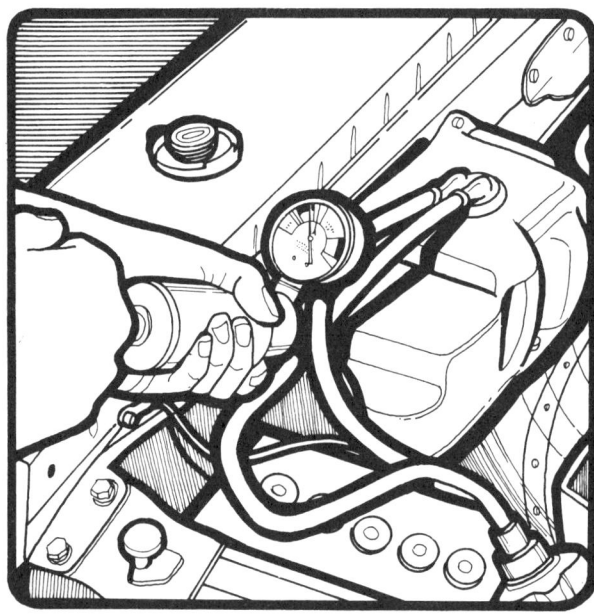

Fig. 28. Pressure tester with hand pump is best.

Defective thermostat

If the thermostat fails to open, coolant cannot flow into the radiator inlet tank. Normally, thermostats fail by opening too much or too quickly, causing overcooling in cold weather, or they stick closed almost completely, causing very rapid overheating. If the overheating occurs within a couple of miles of driving, the thermostat is suspect.

NOTE: The overheating may be so rapid within the engine that the engine may stall before there is significant overflow into the reservoir or catchpot.

If the thermostat was replaced very recently, it is possible that the wrong unit was fitted, or that it was installed incorrectly. The shape of some thermostat housings is such that the thermostat can be installed the wrong way, or that an unsuitable thermostat will fit. If the cooling system had performed properly for some time with the thermostat in the car, however, you can assume that the thermostat is the correct part but possibly defective.

To test a thermostat, you must know how it opens, and different designs open differently. A simple way to find out is to look carefully at the thermostat, place it in a pot of boiling water, then remove it. Put it under cold running water and watch it carefully. You should see some part gradually moving (which will be the valve) toward the closed position.

Place the thermostat in a pan of water once more, this time hanging it with wire so it does not touch the pan but is covered with water, which should be cool. Place the pan on a stove, turn on the burner and watch carefully. The valve movement is very gradual and it may not be easy to catch the initial opening. Hold a radiator thermometer in the water. See Fig. 29.

When you see the valve has clearly moved, read the thermometer. It will probably read about 150° if the thermostat is good. From your experiment with the boiling water, you should know what the full opening looks like, and this time check the temperature at which that occurs. The specified temperature should be stamped somewhere on the thermostat, but in any case, it should not be fully open before 175° or later than 205°.

Defective fan belt

If the fan belt is too loose, or has deteriorated, it will not transfer power from the crankshaft pulley to properly drive the water pump and, on most cars, the fan. As a result, both coolant circulation through the system and air flow through the radiator will be reduced, and the engine will overheat.

In addition to the visual inspection and quick thumb-pressure check of the belt described under Cooling System Inspection, you should precisely check the belt with a tension gauge, as shown in Fig. 30, and compare the reading with specifications. If specifications are not readily available, use these numbers as a general guideline for troubleshooting. If the belt is ⅜- to ½-inch wide and tension is above 50 lbs., belt looseness is probably not a cause of overheating. Typical fan belt specifications are 70 lbs. and

Fig. 29. Testing thermometer in pot of boiling water with radiator thermometer.

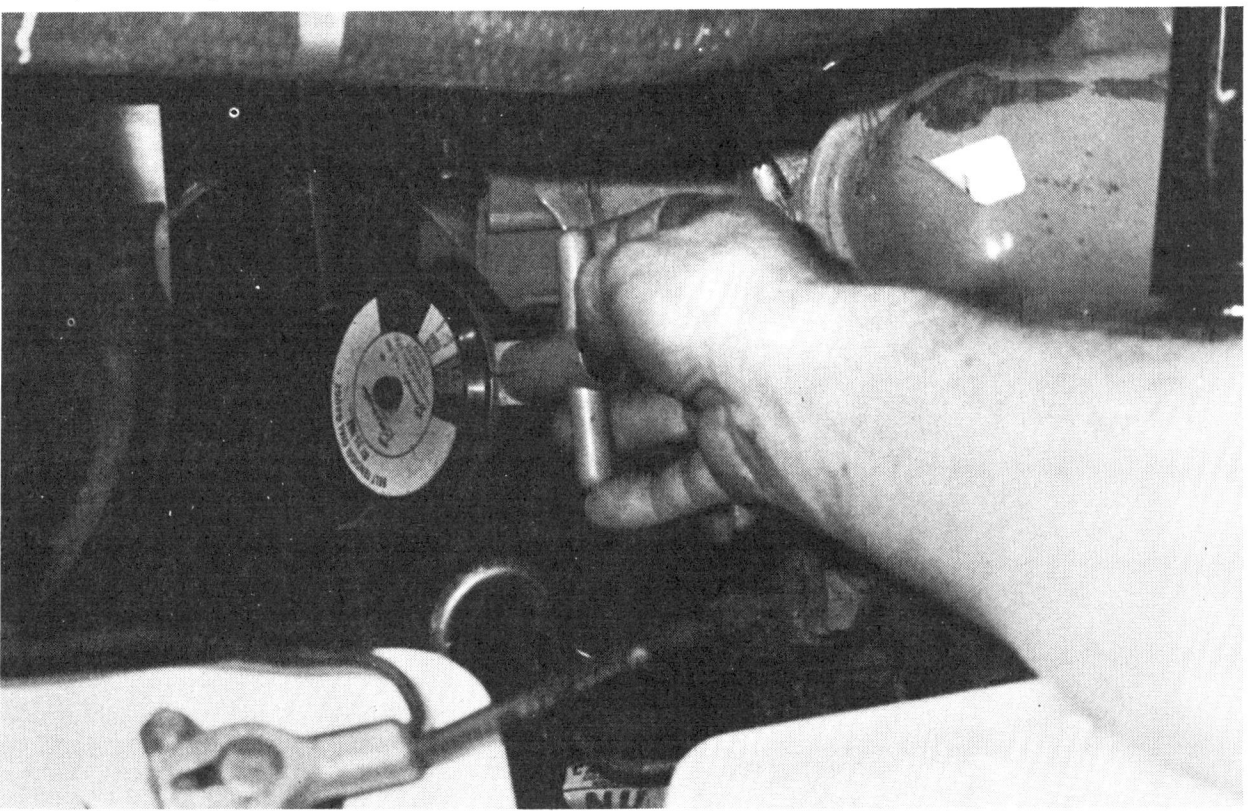

Fig. 30. Checking belt tightness with a tension gauge, which hooks onto a section of belt as shown.

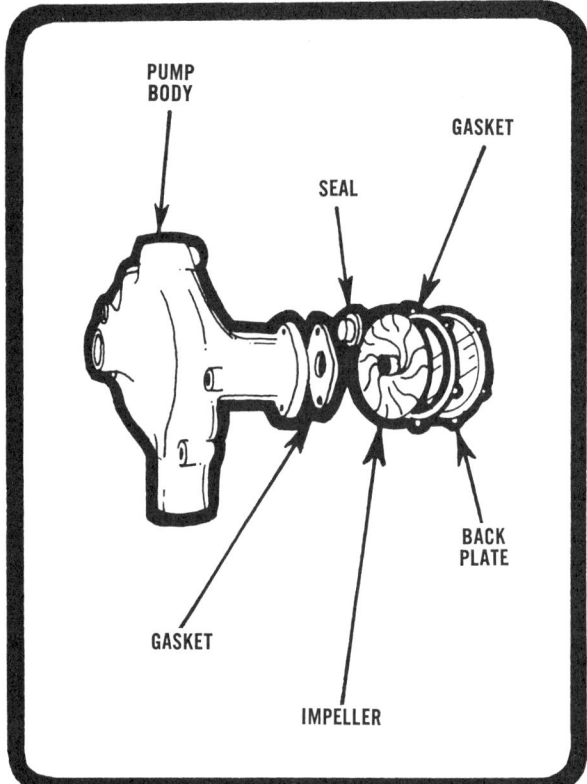

Fig. 31. Exploded view of water pump. Defective seal or gasket is most common cause of leaks.

Fig. 32. Cutaway section of radiator shows how tubes are virtually plugged by solder bloom over their tops.

up, but with 50 the belt should not slip so badly as to be a major cause of overheating.

Water pump failure

The best way to test a water pump is to temporarily remove the temperature sensor from the engine and thread a pressure gauge into its hole to the water jacket. In the absence of a pressure gauge, start the engine when cold and let it idle as you squeeze the upper radiator hose. You should be able to squeeze the hose rather easily until the thermostat opens in a few minutes, at which time the pump should immediately build up pressure in the hose. Another quick check, if you have installed a flushing tee, is to turn the heater control to HIGH, remove the tee cap and start the engine. If the pump is working, coolant should immediately gush out of the tee. Refit the cap immediately to minimize coolant loss.

Water pumps are normally very reliable. If they fail the usual problems are:

1. Failure of the pump bearing. You will hear a growling noise from the pump and the pump pulley may wobble.
2. Fracture of the pump shaft. Pump pulley may wobble or fan may move forward toward the radiator, perhaps even into the radiator, ruining it.
3. Leakage past gasket or bearing seal. A clearcut coolant leak problem. See Fig. 31.
4. Internal wear on engines with high mileage (housing erodes). The only positive check you can make is to remove the pump and inspect it.

Fan malfunction

Three different types of fans are used on late-model American cars: fixed-type, fluid clutch and flexible plastic.

The fixed-blade fan, bolted to the water pump pulley, is the most reliable but because it runs even when unneeded, it costs performance and gas mileage. The only dangers the fixed fan faces are a cocked pulley, loose or deteriorated belt, defective water pump and through mishandling during service, the possible need for removal.

The same is true for the flexible plastic fan, whose blades flex to reduce power required to turn the fan during highway cruising.

The fluid clutch fan, which comes on only when needed, has a thermostatic control. This type is the most complex, although the most fuel-efficient. To check it out:

1. Try to spin fan by hand when engine is cold. It should spin reasonably freely.
2. Start engine and look at the fan. It should be virtually stationary.
3. When the engine is at full operating temperature, fan should suddenly engage and begin to spin almost as if it were firmly bolted to the belt pulley. You will hear a roar as the fan engages.

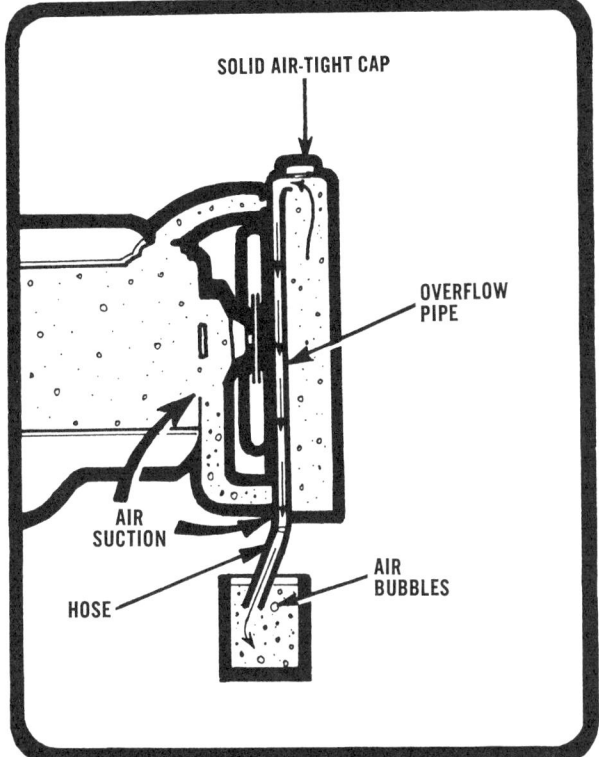

Fig. 33. Bubbling in overflow reservoir or catchpot is sign of foaming coolant or violent coolant circulation.

Clogged radiator

With today's antifreezes, a radiator seldom becomes clogged with rust and other particles. However, this can occur if maintenance has been poor. A more common occurrence is for the radiator to be effectively plugged by excessive corrosion at the inlet side of the tubes. In this case, the corrosion-sensitive solder joints for the tubes virtually bloom with corrosive deposits and restrict the tubes. Thus, although the tubes themselves are clear, very little coolant can flow through them. See Fig. 32.

To test for a clogged radiator, warm up the engine and run your fingers over the finned surface. It should be hot at the inlet side and become gradually cooler as you reach the outlet side. On a downflow radiator, run your hand across from top to bottom. On a cross-flow, start at the inlet side and run your hand up and down, working across to the outlet side. If you feel cold spots, you have a radiator plugging problem.

If the plugging occurs in cold weather and freezing of coolant is possible, let the cooling system thaw out. Do not attempt to warm it up by running the engine, or damage can result.

If acid-cleaning does not help and the plugging is caused by solder bloom or rust clogging, have the radiator removed by a professional mechanic or radiator shop for disassembly and cleaning.

Collapsing or rotted hose

If the lower radiator hose collapses because of defective support spring inside or from internal decay, the coolant flow to the pump is restricted, and water circulation is impeded. A quick check is to feel the hose, and if it is spongy, remove it for inspection.

Poor air flow through radiator

The coolant transfers heat to the air. If the fins at the front of the radiator (or the condenser on air conditioned cars) are clogged, the air flow is restricted. On air conditioned cars the air flow through condenser and radiator affects the performance of both cooling and air conditioning systems.

Foaming coolant

If the coolant is filled with air bubbles, its volume is increased but its ability to transfer heat is decreased. In the typical situation, the increased coolant volume forces the pressure valve in the radiator cap open and coolant flows out into the overflow tube.

Foaming has the following primary causes:
1. An antifreeze without sufficient anti-foam additives (an off-brand) or one in which the antifreeze has been used so long that the additives are depleted.
2. A defective water pump seal or poor lower hose connection at the pump. Either of these conditions may not result in noticeable coolant loss, but they can permit air to be drawn into the system.
3. Deteriorated cap perimeter seal on overflow reservoir systems which allows air to be drawn past it into system, instead of coolant from the reservoir.
4. Exhaust gas leakage through the cylinder head gaskets.

The overflow reservoir or the use of the catchpot described earlier will indicate the problem. With the radiator topped up and the engine warm, but not yet overheating, observe the reservoir or catchpot while a helper holds the gas pedal down about half-way. If you see bubbling, there is foaming, Fig. 33.

Begin the detailed testing by checking the tightness of the lower radiator hose connections and the water pump mounting bolts. If you have a pressure tester, check the system by pressure testing at the radiator fill neck, a procedure that can confirm a leak.

If tightening the hose clamp connections and water pump bolts eliminates the bubbling, the problem apparently has been solved. If not, proceed to the next test, for exhaust gas leakage:

1. Engine must be cold. Remove the water pump-fan belt.
2. Drain a gallon of coolant from the radiator, then remove the upper radiator hose and the thermostat, as described in the Service section of this chapter.
3. Pour water in the radiator until the level builds up in the thermostat housing, and stop when it just starts to overflow the housing. Put your hand over the radiator cap neck to minimize spillage.

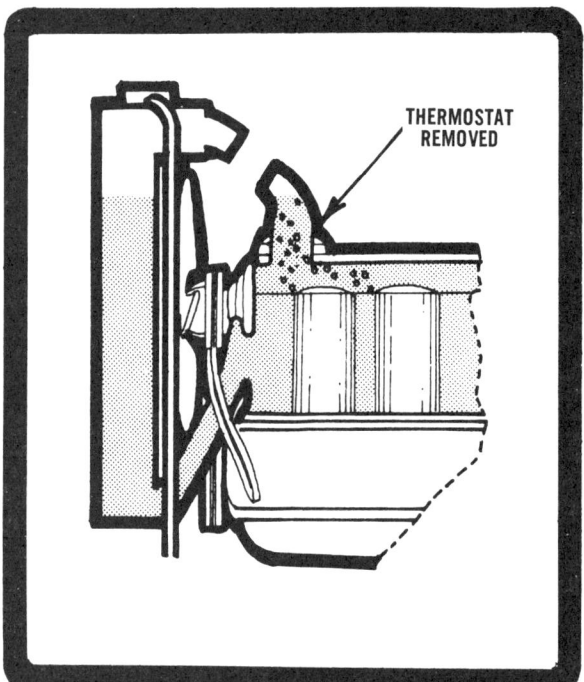

Fig. 34. Test of exhaust gas leakage into cooling system.

4. Have a helper start the engine and floor the gas pedal six to eight times, as you watch the thermostat housing hose neck. If you see bubbles or a sudden rise of liquid as the gas pedal is floored or as the engine drops back to idle speed, you have evidence of exhaust gas leakage, Fig. 34.

You must make this test very quickly, for once the coolant (not under pressure) starts to boil, you'll see steam bubbles and these can fool you.

The test procedure will pick up major exhaust gas leaks. The possibility of small exhaust leaks contributing to an overheating problem can be checked by repeating the test (after the engine has completely cooled), but with the rear wheels jacked up, front wheels chocked, as follows:

1. Start engine and put transmission in a forward gear. (Drive or second).
2. Accelerate engine gradually and apply the brakes intermittently. If you see bubbling almost immediately, that is exhaust gas leakage.

Bubbles that show up on this second test probably can be corrected by simply tightening the cylinder head gasket nuts or bolts to specifications, using a torque wrench. Major leaks disclosed in the first test should be followed up by removing the cylinder heads and replacing the gaskets, a job you may wish to leave to a professional mechanic.

Violent coolant circulation

What may appear to be foaming may actually be violent coolant circulation, caused by a loose or broken baffle in the radiator inlet tank. The coolant circulation becomes turbulent and mixes with the little air in the top tank. The only way to isolate this problem from foaming is by pressure testing and checking for exhaust leakage. If these tests do not show up other problems, try topping up the radiator (to minimize the amount of air) and repeat the inspection for bubbles in the overflow reservoir or catchpot. A reduction in bubbling with the topped-up radiator indicates the possibility of a loose or broken baffle, and at this point you should let a radiator shop check it out.

Afterboil and other operating conditions

If an engine is turned off immediately after operating under heavy loads (open-throttle driving) or is shut after being allowed to idle for long periods in hot weather, hot spots in the cooling system can cause the coolant to afterboil, because the water pump is no longer providing circulation. These hots spots may exist even in a relatively clean cooling system, because of individual engine design factors, although they are more common in one that has been neglected.

The boiling coolant can push open a slightly weak pressure valve in the radiator cap and coolant is lost to the overflow. In a car with an overflow reservoir, the vacuum that results from the coolant loss should be filled by coolant from the reservoir, as the vacuum valve in the radiator cap opens. If the gasket in the cap's inner perimeter is deteriorated, however, the system does not refill with coolant, but with air, drawn past the defective gasket. This is easy to spot, for the overflow reservoir level remains high even after engine cooldown. Even without a recovery reservoir, afterboil is obvious if you look. The overflow hose or tube gushes out a pool of coolant onto the ground shortly after the engine is shut down.

Although some afterboil can be considered the normal result of severe operating conditions, it is good practice to have the radiator cap pressure tested, to determine if it is contributing to the problem.

OTHER OPERATING CONDITIONS THAT CAN CAUSE ENGINE OVERHEATING

No engine is immune to overheating. If you sit in a traffic jam, even the healthiest cooling system can overheat. For exhample, on a hot day, a late-model car traveling at 30 mph up a 7° hill will operate with a coolant temperature of about 256°. With a 15 psi cap and a 50-50 water and antifreeze mixture, the boiling point of the coolant is only 266°. If the antifreeze level is a bit less, and if the cap is only a 12-psi model, there goes the 10° margin. If there's corrosion in the system to retard heat transfer, or if the car is pulling a trailer, the engine almost surely will overheat. In short, the modern cooling system has very little margin of safety.

If you're going up a steep hill, turn off the air conditioning to take a load off the engine and reduce coolant temperature 10° to 20°. If necessary, turn on the heater all the way to HIGH, which will lower coolant temperature another 5°. In heavy traffic, take the transmission out of gear and lightly hold the gas pedal down to raise engine speed to fast idle. This will increase fan speed to a more efficient level.

Engine tuning and brakes

If the engine is out of tune, it develops less power and strains harder to do its job. On today's emission controlled cars in particular, this can easily cause overheating. Dragging brakes are another possibility, because the engine is strained to overcome their effect. The drum brakes with their self-adjusting mechanism, for example, are very prone to dragging. A simple check is to jack up the car, turn the wheels, listen for scraping and feel for drag. With rear wheels, do not confuse the fact that the rear axles must turn the gears in the differential, with brake drag.

Loss of coolant

Many overheating problems are caused by loss of coolant, and although most of them are obvious, some are not, particularly those that are internal. Even external leaks may require careful inspection to trace.

External leakage

Carefully inspect radiator, engine block, hose connections and hoses themselves. If you have a pressure tester, fit it to the radiator cap neck to confirm (by loss of pressure) leaks from sources that may not be obvious.

If there is leakage into the passenger compartment, the heater core is the likely suspect, and servicing it is a job for a professional. Other less-than-common sources of leaks are:

1. Water pump. When leaks occur, Fig. 31, they are usually at the gasket joint with the engine block, at the seal and from a cracked pump casting (usually the result of frozen coolant). Do not confuse pump leakage with the light seepage from the vent hole in the pump, which is normal, Fig. 35.
2. Core plugs. In the process of casting an engine block, holes from the exterior to the water jacket remain. These are capped with core plugs, circular discs that are driven into the holes (see Fig. 36). Engine vibration can loosen these discs and permit coolant to leak out. Installing a replacement core plug is not a difficult job for a weekend mechanic if a leaking core plug is accessible. Refer to the Service section later in this chapter.
3. Cracked cylinder head or engine block. If the engine cylinder head or block is cracked, coolant can leak out. This condition, usually the result of water freezing solid in the engine, normally also ruins other parts of the engine and is an obvious thing when it occurs.
4. Radiator drain cock. If the radiator drain cock loosens, or if the valve inside the cock deteriorates, it can leak. First, attempt to tighten by turning the drain cock handle. If that fails, replace the drain cock. If the problem is a loose drain cock, remove the assembly, coat the threads with plumber's water sealer and reinstall, tightening securely.
5. Thermostat housing. The thermostat housing is a hot spot and it can warp, particularly during overheating. In this situation, even a new housing gasket may not seal the leak. To correct, refer to the Service section later in this chapter.

In most cases of external leaks, dye in the antifreeze will assist you in locating the sources.

Fig. 35. Vent hole in water pump may allow some coolant to seep out but this is normal.

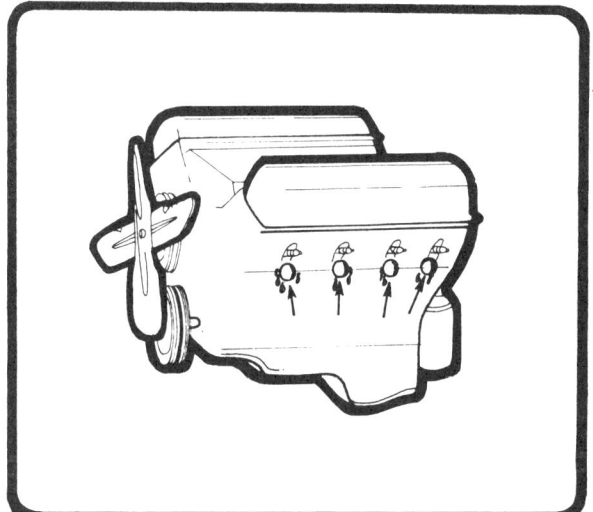

Fig. 36. If core plugs leak, they must be replaced.

Internal leakage

Coolant leakage into the engine or transmission is a serious problem, frequently requiring complete rebuilding or replacement of the engine or transmission. The leakage usually occurs both ways. That is, coolant leaks into the engine or the transmission oil cooler (which is built into the radiator) and the oil leaks into the cooling system. The cooling system can be cleaned of oil, using a flushing agent, but the engine or transmission cannot.

Antifreeze causes sticking of piston rings and water causes rusting on cylinder bores and bearing surfaces. Antifreeze also ruins clutch plates, bands and seals in the automatic transmission.

When antifreeze leaks into the engine oil, there is a fair chance the engine can be saved if you catch the problem early enough. Drain the oil and flush the engine with an engine purge (a light solvent oil). The engine may not be in perfect shape, but it could run acceptably for tens of thousands of miles.

Unfortunately, once coolant leaks into a transmission oil cooler, the transmission's life remaining is probably going to be short. The first symptoms are harsh shifting, and transmission performance is down-hill from there on.

Spotting the leakage

The leakage of coolant into engine oil may be spotted when you check the dipstick. Dye from the antifreeze, water drops, or a milky mixture of coolant and oil may appear on the dipstick. When the leakage is past the head gasket, it also is normally accompanied by exhaust gas leakage, for which you can test as described earlier.

When coolant leaks into the transmission oil cooler, some transmission oil also leaks out into the cooling system. It shows up as a strawberry-colored oil film in an overflow reservoir, or as an oily residue at the end of the coolant overflow tube.

NOTE: On many 1973-75 cars built by General Motors, the automatic transmission oil cooler leak is the result of defective solder joints on the cooler, and repair of the transmission is paid for by GM, despite the fact that the car is well past the warranty period. Check with your dealer.

COOLING SYSTEM REPAIRS

The most common replacement and repair jobs you can accomplish on a cooling system are described in this section.

The only special tools necessary, aside from the pressure tester and thermometer used in diagnosis, are a belt tension gauge and, on cars with spring clamps, hose clamp pliers.

RADIATOR OR COOLANT BYPASS HOSE REPLACEMENT

The two radiator hoses and the coolant bypass hose are held at each end by a clamp, one of the designs shown in Fig. 37. All types but the spring design can be loosened with a screwdriver (see Fig. 38). If the clamp is old and corroded and stuck to the hose, loosening the screw may not be enough on some designs, in which case you'll have to pry the clamp a bit.

If the hose is stuck, shove in a screwdriver and try to pry it loose (see Fig. 39). If the working angle is poor for the screwdriver, or if the hose is really stuck, cut the hose off the neck with a single-edge razor blade.

CAUTION: Be very careful when prying under the hose. Radiator fittings are extremely fragile and might bend or break if too much force is exerted.

If the hose is held by spring clamps, Fig. 40, you will be in for a struggle unless you have spring clamp pliers. There are many types of pliers designed for these clamps, including ordinary slip-joint pliers with recesses cut into the jaws to grip each end of the clamp. To release the clamp you must squeeze the ends together, and if you try to use ordinary pliers, the ends surely will slip off. The spring clamp tends

Fig. 37. Some of the hose clamps in use. The large one is a double-wire design with adjusting screw. Inside it at top left is a cheap band type. At top right is a spring-clamp design. At the bottom is a worm-drive, the easiest and best, but the most expensive.

Fig. 38. This is another type of band clamp, and like the others, it is loosened by turning a screwdriver.

Fig. 39. Unfortunately, just loosening adjusting screw does not always free up clamp. But a little prying action between hose and clamp frees it up.

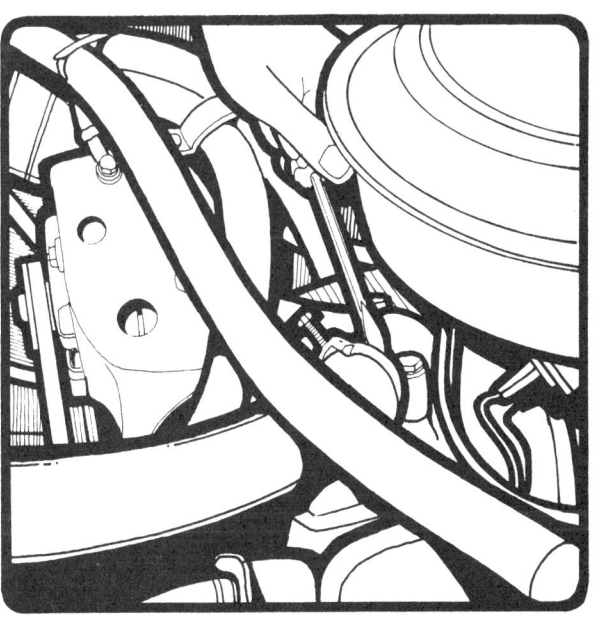

Fig. 40. This bypass hose came with spring clamps. So if you are going to use them, special pliers are a must. Hose shown is a silicone rubber premium design. A good purchase (although expensive), because bypass hose life is short in today's hot engine compartments.

to dig into the hose and cause slightly faster hose deterioration at the contact point than a band clamp. The best procedure is to discard the spring type and install a worm-drive band clamp, but if you insist on re-using the one you have, at least invest in a pair of special pliers. If you are planning to discard the spring-type, you may be able to skip the purchase of special pliers if you can push a screwdriver underneath the clamp and force it off the hose neck. Or you may be able to cut away the old hose all around the clamp and then pull the clamp off with ordinary pliers.

Selecting a hose

The replacement hose you install should be carefully selected. If you buy it from a discount center and have to find the part number from a catalog all by yourself, make sure you read the listings carefully, because many different hoses are used on a single car in the same model year. Even if you buy from a professional parts jobber, check to see that the replacement hose is a close match for the original, particularly if the original is a molded type. If you try to bend the wrong hose to fit, you may kink it and restrict coolant circulation.

NOTE: Many lower radiator hoses have a spring inside to prevent the hose from collapsing under certain conditions. If the original hose has a spring, so should the replacement.

Installation

1. With old hose removed, wire brush the hose necks to remove foreign material, Fig. 41.
2. To ease installation, coat hose neck with a soap solution. This is important particularly if you install a silicone rubber coolant bypass hose (a premium-priced heat resistant, guaranteed-for-life-of-car design), which is not easy to slide on a neck, or reposition.
3. Slide the hose in position so that it is completely on the neck at each end, to avoid possibility of kinking and to provide room for proper positioning of the clamp. Except for the worm-drive clamp, which can be opened completely, the clamp must be loosely placed over the hose prior to fitting its end on the neck.
4. Locate the hose clamp at the midpoint of the hose section on the neck and tighten.

REPLACING AND ADJUSTING A FAN BELT

Replacing a fan belt (the belt that goes around the fan-water pump pulley and alternator pulley on most cars) is not a difficult job. However, on a car with power steering and air conditioning, it may prove to be tedious. The reason is that the belts that drive these accessories, plus perhaps a belt for the anti-pollution air pump used on many cars, probably will have to be removed first. Even if the old belt has snapped, it may be necessary to remove other belts in order to be able to install the replacement belt.

To remove a belt you must find out what method is used to tension it. The most commonly used tensioning systems are:

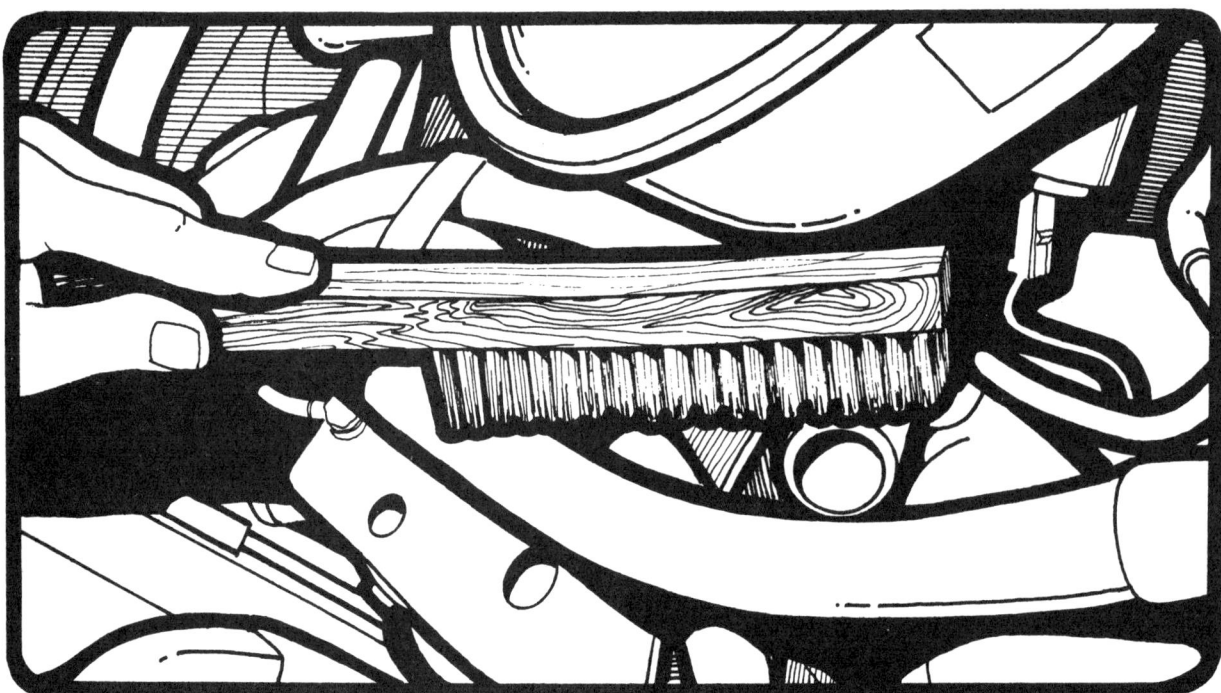

Fig. 41. Wire brush hose neck before installing new hose.

1. The component is mounted on a bracket with bolts (two or more) passing through straight elongated holes. Tension on the belt is adjusted by loosening nuts and moving the component in or out (with the bolts sliding through the elongated holes). To remove the belt completely, the component is pushed in as far as it will go, which releases tension on the belt, permitting you to take it off the pulley. As shown in Fig. 42, a Ford power steering pump has the elongated holes, plus a stud and nut adjuster. Turning the nut moves the pulley in or out, and when tension is correct, the nuts on the bolts in the elongated holes are tightened to complete the job.

Fig. 42. Bolts and nuts in elongated holes, and stud and nut adjuster are used on this Ford power steering pump.

2. The component is held by two bolts, one of which serves as a pivot. The other passes through a bracket with a long, curved adjusting hole, as shown in Fig. 43. The pivot bolt, or its nut, is loosened first, then the bolt through the adjusting hole. The component can swing in an arc that is the same as the long hole in the adjusting bracket. In this design, the belt is tightened by pushing the component away from the engine, using a pry bar of some type. This is the most common method used, and is invariably found on American cars. The adjusting bracket is at the alternator.
3. An idler pulley is used. This is a pulley that powers no component but simply positions the belt properly. The idler pulley can be moved in or out, or perhaps off to an angle, to change belt tension. The typical idler pulley is held in place by a bolt or stud, and nut. Once it is loosened, the pulley can be repositioned. On Ford products there is a square hole in the pulley bracket to permit inserting a ½-inch drive breaker bar for leverage. On Dodge Colt, the pulley shaft has a shaped section that accepts an open-end wrench for leverage, Fig. 44.

NOTE: On Chrysler Corp. 6-cylinder engines the power steering bracket has a ½-inch square hole, accessible from the rear of the pump, to adjust tension. Use a ratchet or breaker bar and a long ½-inch drive extension. On American Motors V-8 engines, the ½-inch square hole is used on most alternator brackets to facilitate fan belt adjustments.

CAUTION: Before removing a belt, observe carefully around which pulleys the belt wraps. If the belt fails to loosen sufficiently after pushing the adjusting components in or turning the adjuster all the way, you may have to twist the belt off the pulley.

The replacement belt

The replacement belt should be checked for width and length. The width is very critical, for a belt that is just a bit too wide or too narrow will not fit properly in the pulley grooves, and as a result will not transfer power smoothly. The new belt will have a circumference slightly smaller than the old belt, if the old belt has stretched. It may be necessary to use a screwdriver to pry the new belt over the pulley edge into the pulley groove.

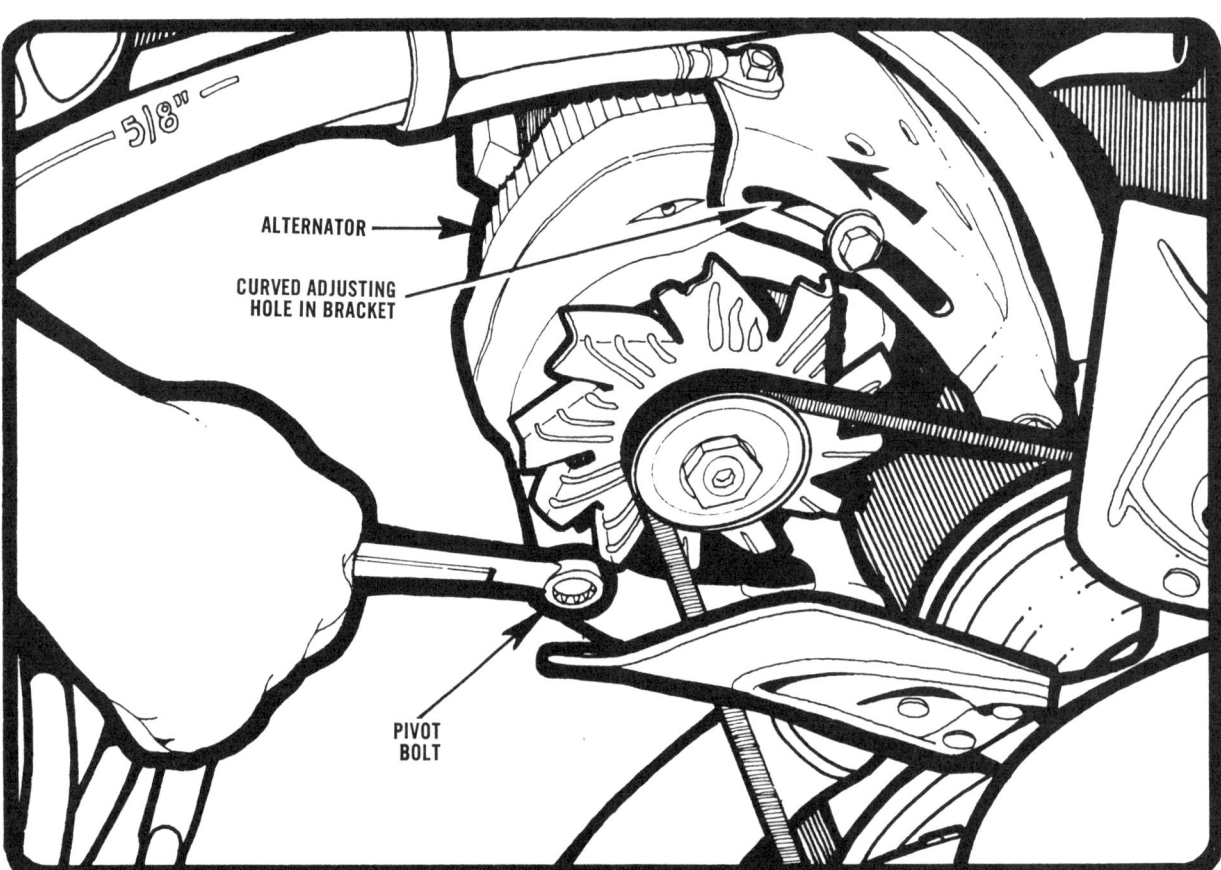

Fig. 43. Standard adjuster is curved adjusting hole in bracket, and pivot bolt.

Fig. 44. Idler pulley setup. Wrench tilting to left has loosened pulley nut. Wrench tilting to right is on pulley shaft's shaped section. When it turns pulley shaft, the pulley is repositioned to increase or decrease belt tension by means of an eccentric.

Use of pry bar

Be extremely careful in positioning a pry bar if there is no special provision for leverage. When tensioning a power steering pump belt, for example, there may be a thick metal boss or ear against which the pry bar can lean. Never lean a bar against the pump reservoir.

When tightening an alternator belt, have a helper hold the alternator out if possible, unless there is a provision for the pry bar. If you must use a bar, do not lean against alternator fins unless you have a special bracket, available at many auto parts stores, that holds the alternator for belt tightening, and accepts a breaker bar to ease the job.

A design feature that may be found in greater use is a hole in the alternator bracket, which permits leaning a bar against a safe part of the alternator. It is used on the Chevette, as shown in Fig. 45.

The belt should be tightened with the tension gauge in place, hooked onto the belt. Good practice is to loosen the bolts that hold the component belt tensioned, just enough to move the component. This way, very little bolt tightening is necessary to secure the adjustment.

HEATER HOSES

Replacing a heater hose is the same as changing a radiator or bypass hose, with one important difference. It is often so difficult to get to the heater that disconnecting the hose from that end is impractical.

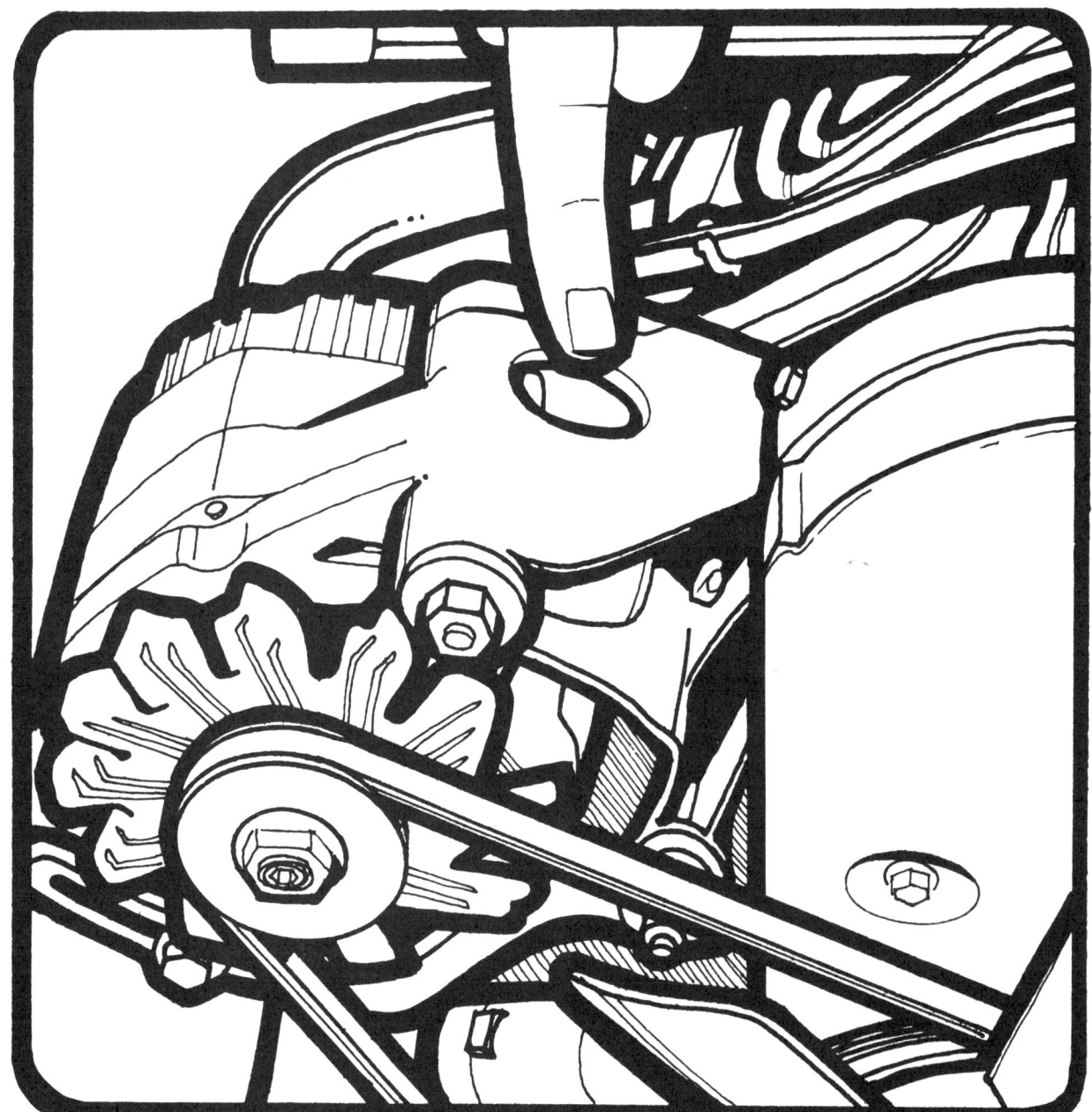

Fig. 45. Chevette has hole for pry bar to adjust belt tension.

Normally it is also unnecessary, for the typical heater hose hardens and deteriorates only in the area of its connection to the engine.

Therefore, a simple procedure is to disconnect the hose only at the engine, cut off only the deteriorated section and join a new section to the old (and to the engine), using a radiator flushing tee as a connector between the two sections of hose. As with radiator hoses, discard spring clamps or cheap band clamps and use a worm-drive clamp for both the tee connections and the connection to the engine and water pump.

NOTE: On cars with coolant hoses to the automatic choke, which are connected into the heater hoses with plastic tees somewhat similar to flushing tees, you may be able to simply replace the heater hose section up to the tee, or reposition the tee when installing a new section of heater hose.

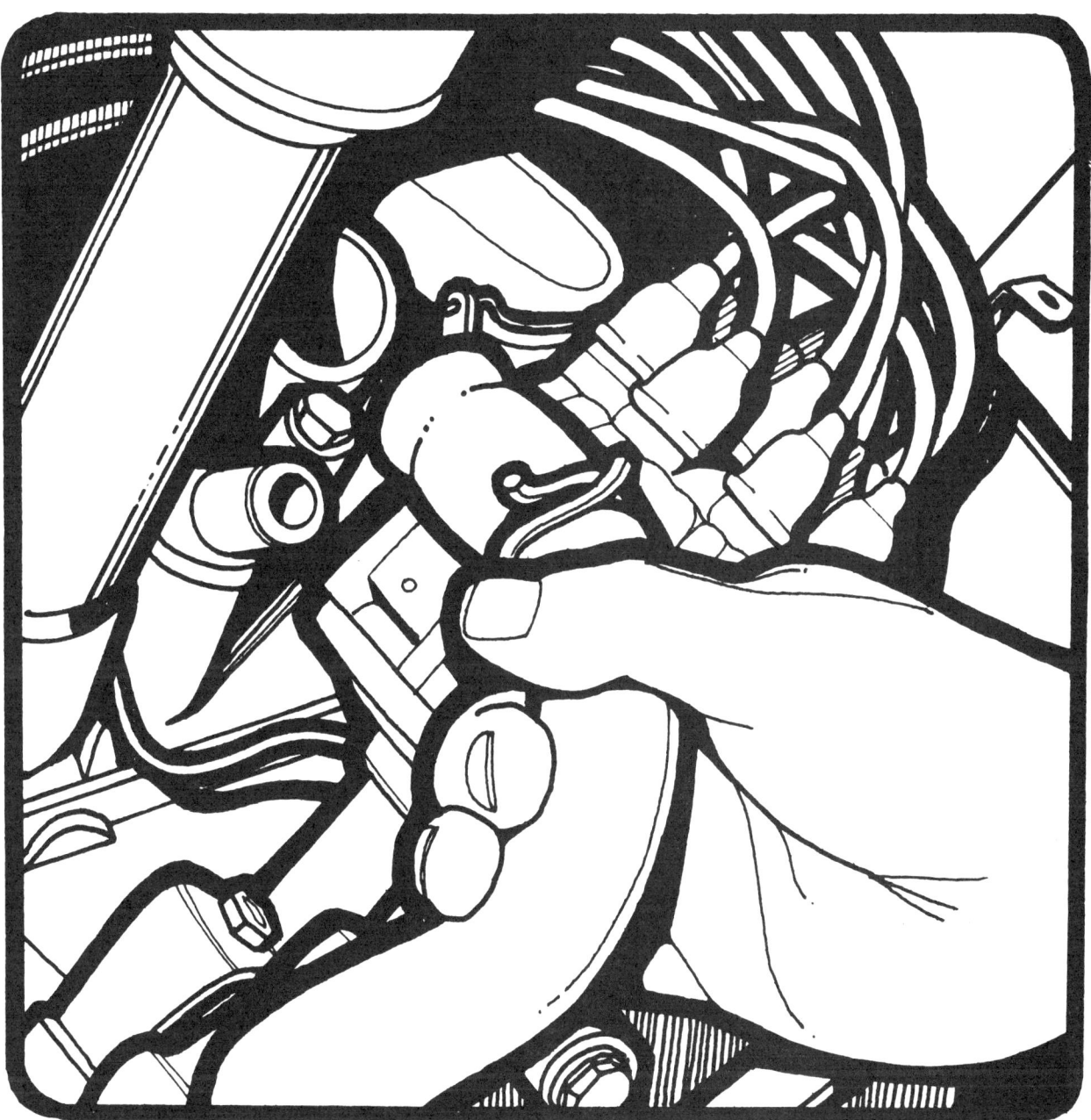

Fig. 46. Coolant bypass hose was attached to thermostat housing, and it had to be removed. Notice that it has a spring-type clamp.

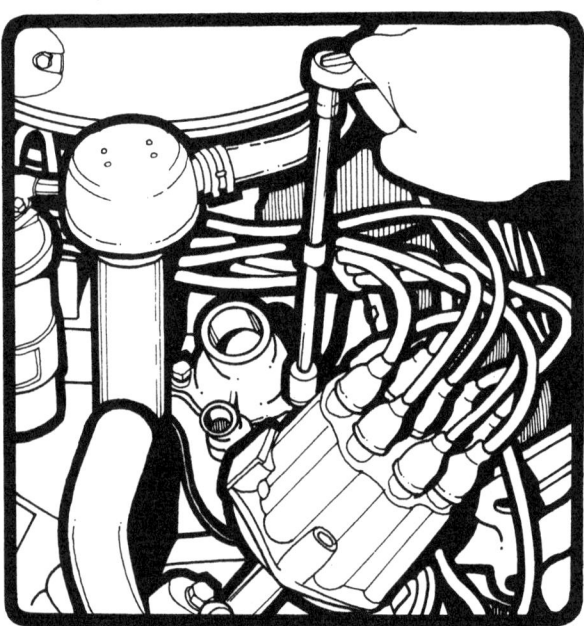

Fig. 47. Ratchet extensions and socket make removal of thermostat housing bolts easy.

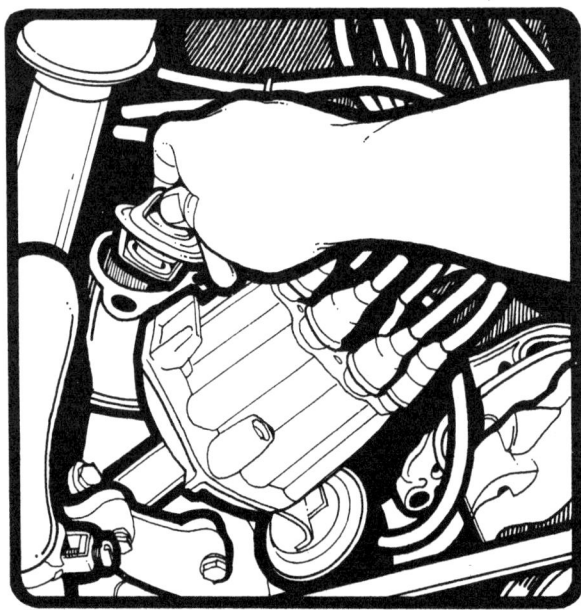

Fig. 48. After noting how the old thermostat looks when installed, remove it and put the new one in the same way.

Automatic choke hoses

Ford Pinto and Mustang II, Mercury Bobcat and Chevrolet Vega, 2-barrel carburetors only

The 2-barrel carburetor's automatic choke on Ford Pinto and Mustang II, Mercury Bobcat and Chevrolet Vega receives the heat to unwind the thermostatic coil from hot engine coolant pumped through hoses into and out of the choke housing. The coolant hoses are connected to the heater hoses by plastic tees, somewhat similar to flushing tees, spliced into the heater hoses.

The choke hoses, like others, are retained by band or spring clamps, and the hose replacement procedure is the same as for other types.

THERMOSTAT REPLACEMENT

All except Ford Pinto and Mustang II, and Mercury Bobcat, 2000 cc, 4-cylinder engines.

The thermostat housing is a cup-like part that covers or holds the thermostat on the engine and has a neck for the upper radiator hose. To replace the thermostat under it, follow this procedure:

1. Drain radiator, disconnect upper radiator hose.
2. If coolant bypass hose is attached to thermostat housing, also disconnect it, Fig. 46.
3. Remove bolts or nuts holding thermostat housing to engine, Fig. 47.
4. Lift housing from engine. If housing sticks, use putty knife in gasket joint to free it.
5. Scrape old gasket from housing and engine with putty knife. Do not use screwdriver.
6. After noting manner of installation, lift out thermostat, Fig. 48.
7. Place straight edge or machinist's ruler across gasket surface of thermostat housing and see if .005-inch feeler gauge will slip under at any point. Position ruler or straight edge at various points on housing gasket surface and repeat check with feeler gauge. If .005-inch feeler slips underneath, surface is badly warped, Fig. 49.
8. Level warped surface with fine flat file as shown in Fig. 50. Housing should be retained in vise, and level. Check work with ruler and feeler gauge.

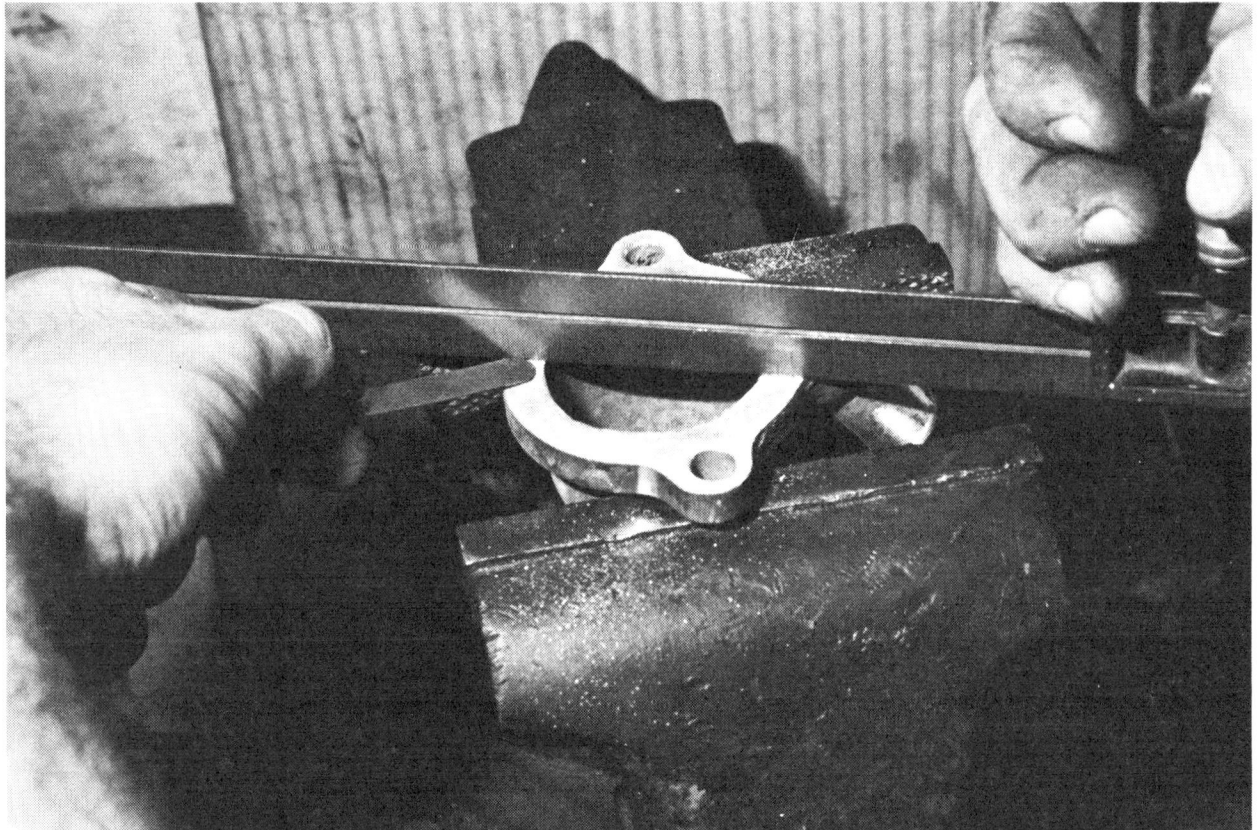

Fig. 49. Place straight edge across thermostat housing gasket surface and try to slip feeler gauge strip underneath.

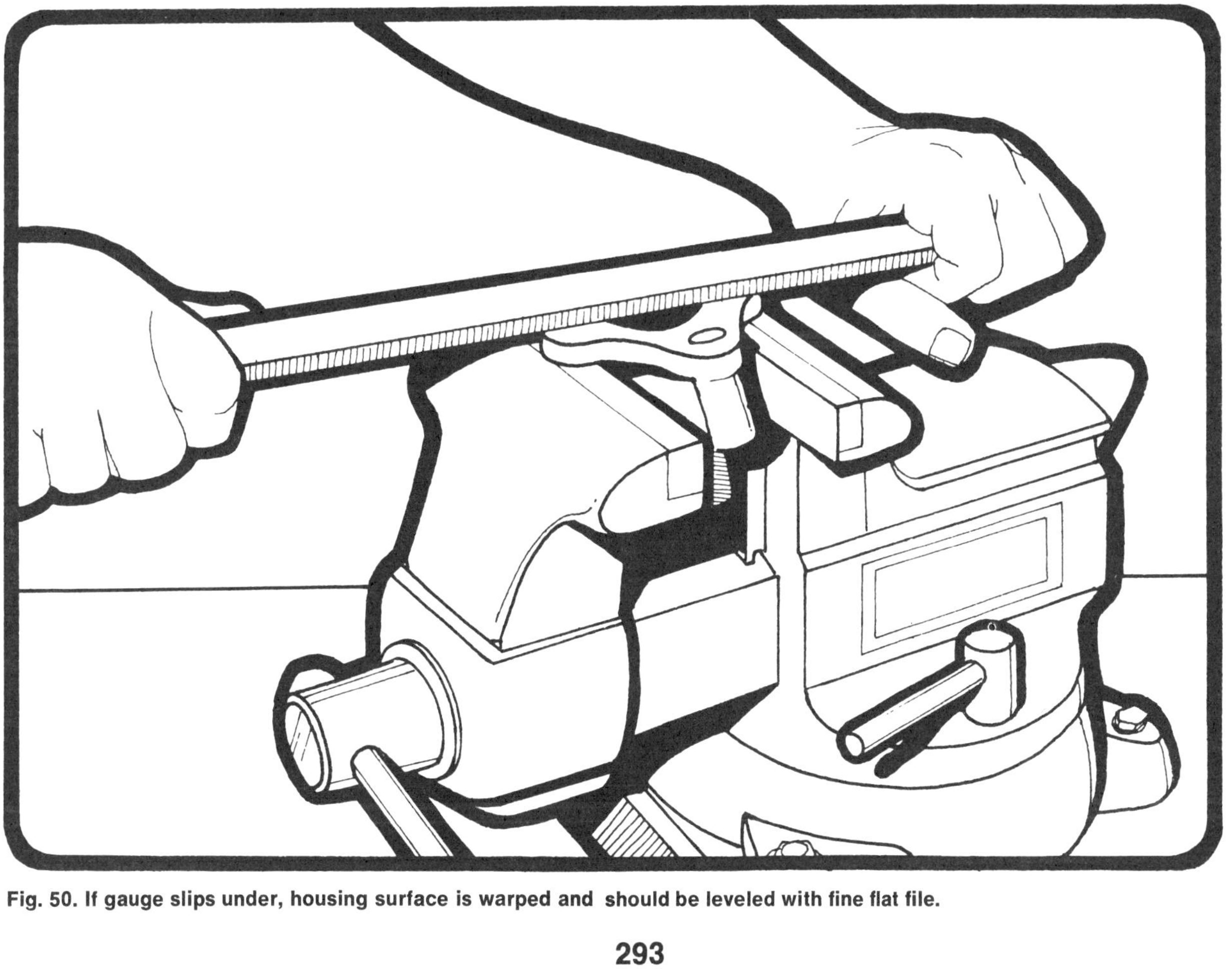

Fig. 50. If gauge slips under, housing surface is warped and should be leveled with fine flat file.

9. Apply thin film of non-hardening sealer to thermostat housing. Put new gasket in place, Fig. 51.
10. Install new thermostat, reinstall housing and bolts or nuts, then reconnect coolant hose or hoses.
11. Run engine, checking for leaks. If housing leaks, stop engine, remove housing, recheck for warpage, and put a second gasket over the first if warpage is within .005-inch.

NOTE: All car manufacturers now approve silicone rubber sealer in place of a gasket. This sealer, sold in flexible tubes, is applied in a thin (1/8-inch wide) bead around the housing (in addition, bead should encircle each bolt or stud hole). Put a thin film of engine oil on the engine's mating surface before installing the housing, so the sealer will not adhere.

Pinto, Mustang II and Bobcat with 2000 cc, 4-cylinder engine.
1. Follow steps 1 through 4 for standard thermostat replacement.
2. Thermostat remains in housing. Remove retaining clip with needle-nose pliers and screwdriver, then take out thermostat and sealing ring. See Fig. 52.
3. Follow steps 5 through 10 for standard thermostat replacement.
4. Install new thermostat and sealing ring. Retaining clip may be re-used.
5. Follow step 11 for standard thermostat replacement.

RADIATOR REMOVAL

Radiator service is a job for the specialist who has the equipment and experience necessary to disassemble and repair the part.

Fig. 51. Apply coating of non-hardening sealer to housing surface before positioning gasket.

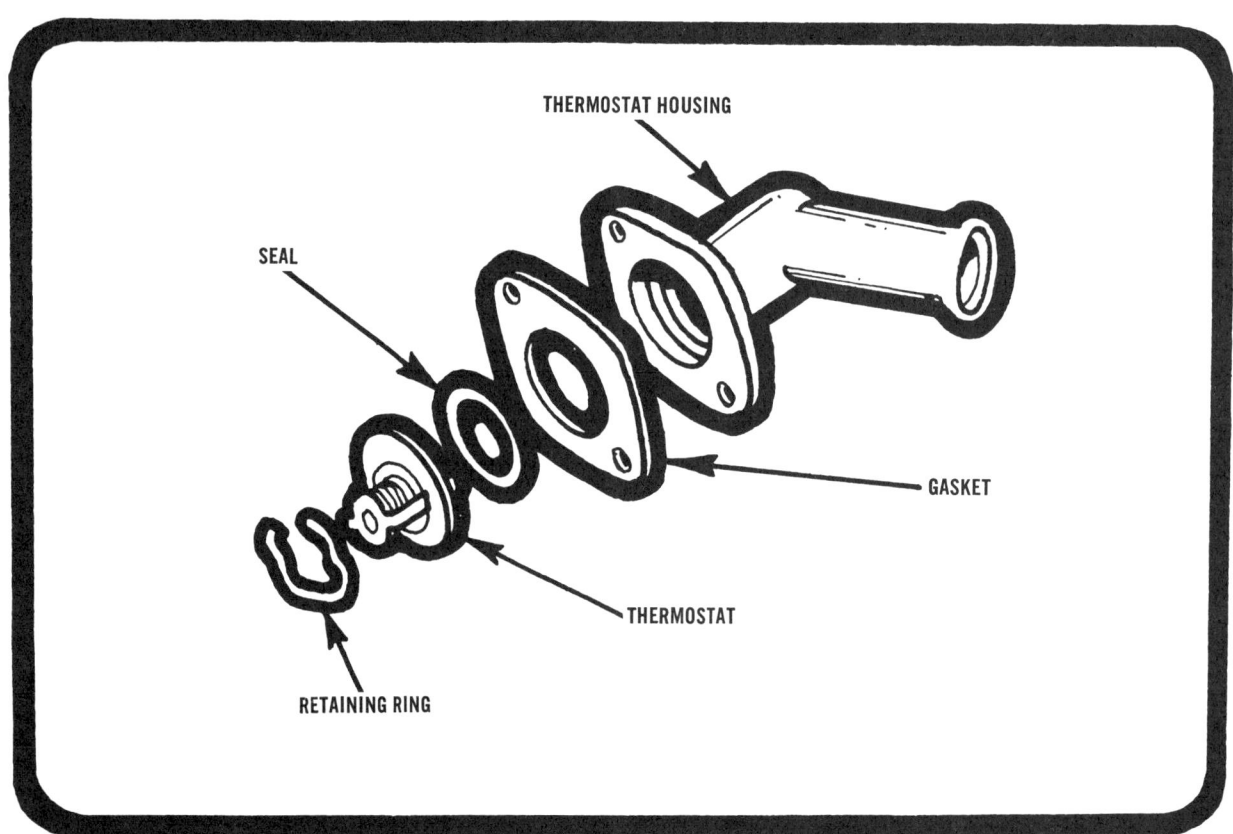

Fig. 52. On Ford Pinto, Mustang II and Mercury Bobcat models with 2000cc 4-cylinder engine, the thermostat is retained in its housing by a retaining ring or clip. Note the position of the thermostat seal.

TROUBLESHOOTING FLOW CHART
COOLING SYSTEMS

Symptom	Probable Cause	Remedy
A. Overheating due to cooling system malfunction.	1. Low water level.	1. Fill to proper level. See note 1 below. Check system for leakage.
	2. Clogged radiator passages.	2. Clean with proper solution, reverse flushing or by boiling out with chemicals. See note 2 below.
	3. Thermostat stuck in closed position.	3. Replace thermostat if testing shows defect.
	4. Thermostat installed upside down.	4. Install correctly with sensing unit to block.
	5. Fan, water pump, drive belt slipping.	5. Adjust or replace belt as necessary.
	6. Frozen coolant.	6. Thaw system. Then drain and replace with proper solution. See note 3 below.
	7. Defective radiator pressure cap or cap seat.	7. Replace cap if defective or not correct.
	8. Clogged or kinked inlet or outlet water hoses.	8. Replace defective hose.
	9. Overflow tube blocked.	9. Open tube passage or replace.
	10. Defective temperature gauge.	10. Check with test gauge.
	11. Defective water pump.	11. Replace pump.
	12. Radiator fins clogged with foreign matter.	12. Clear fins of dirt and obstructions.
	13. Defective cylinder head gasket.	13. Replace head gasket.
	14. Fan too far from radiator.	14. Move closer with shims between pulley and fan. See note 4 below.
	15. Fan with insufficient blade area or pitch.	15. Replace with large fan or one with more blades. Correct pitch by bending evenly.
	16. Defective water distribution tube (on some inline engines).	16. Replace tube.
B. Overheating due to engine malfunction.	17. Improper ignition timing.	17. Adjust timing to space.
	18. Manifold heat control valve jammed open.	18. Free valve.
	19. Blown head gasket.	19. Replace head gasket.
	20. Incorrect valve timing.	20. Time valves properly.
	21. Exhaust system blocked.	21. Clear exhaust system.
C. Overheating due to other factors.	22. Slipping clutch.	22. Adjust or replace clutch.
	23. Dragging brakes.	23. Adjust or free brakes.
	24. Vehicle driven too long in lower gear.	24. Check driving habits or driving conditions.
	25. Surrounding temperatures too high.	25. Correct with larger radiator, or a fan with more blades. Or increase idle speed.
D. Water loss through overflow.	26. Water level too high.	26. Allow settling as needed.
	27. Weak pressure valve in radiator cap.	27. Pressure-test cap and replace if necessary.
	28. Defective thermostat.	28. Replace thermostat.
	29. Loose or defective fan belt.	29. Adjust or replace belt.
	30. Water pump failure.	30. Replace water pump.
	31. Slipping fan clutch.	31. Replace fan clutch.
	32. Clogged radiator.	32. Flush with 2-step acid cleaner. If this does not work, remove radiator and have it professionally serviced.
	33. Collapsing or rotted radiator hose.	33. Replace hose.
	34. Poor air flow through radiator.	34. Clean foreign matter from front of radiator or AC condenser.
	35. Foaming coolant.	35. a. Worn out or low-quality antifreeze should be replaced. b. Sources of air leaks into system should be found and corrected. c. Exhaust gas leakage source should be corrected.
	36. Violent coolant circulation.	36. Have loose or broken baffle in radiator repaired.
	37. Severe operating conditions.	37. Install overflow reservoir kit on cars not so equipped. Turn AC off, heater on.
	38. Engine out of tune.	38. Tune engine.
	39. Brakes dragging.	39. Check brake self-adjusters and repair as necessary.

COOLING SYSTEMS/continued

Symptom	Probable Cause	Remedy
E. Overheating due to external leaks.	40. Check for leaks at hose connections, radiator, water pump, core plugs, thermostat housing, cylinder head. 41. Water pump leaks through vent holes, corroded tubes. 42. Loose or rusted-through core hole (freeze-out) plug. 43. Defective gasket—cylinder head, thermostat housing, water pump, etc. 44. Heater core leaks. 45. Leaks through engine accessory bolts or studs that pass into water jacket. 46. Loose or stripped threads on oil cooler fittings to radiator (auto. trans.). 47. Thermostat replaced cocked on seat.	40. When source of leak is found, replace part or tighten connection or mounting bolts as necessary. 41. Pressure test for leaks. Replace pump if required. 42. Replace plug. 43. Replace gasket. Torque evenly to specified pressure. 44. Repair or replace core. 45. Remove bolts or studs. Replace after proper sealing. See note 6 below. 46. Tighten, reseal or replace fittings or radiator as required. 47. Replace thermostat properly.
F. Overheating due to internal leaks.	48. Leaking transmission oil cooler. 49. Loose cylinder head gasket. 50. Cracked engine block. 51. Cracked cylinder head or engine block bore. 52. Oil cooler cracked inside radiator.	48. Replace cooler, flush out cooling system and replace hoses; have transmission rebuilt. 49. Tighten or replace head gasket. 50. Replace block. 51. Replace head or engine. Or weld with required technique. 52. Repair or replace radiator.
G. Engine runs too cold.	53. Defective or missing thermostat. 54. Coolant passes around thermostat. See 10 above.	53. Install proper thermostats. 54. Correct as necessary. See note 7 below.
H. Fan belt fails to hold its adjustment.	55. Stretching of poor quality belt. 56. Failure to install double belt drives as matched pair. 57. Adjustment unit mounting not secure. 58. Weak adjustment bracket bends. 59. Adjustment lockscrew yields. 60. Belt improperly installed. 61. Incorect belt used. Adjustment set at limit. 62. Pulleys out of line with each other. See 5, 39, 40-45 above.	55. Replace with better belt. 56. Renew both belts in a 2-belt drive. 57. Tighten generator, alternator or idler pulley support. 58. Stiffen bracket or replace. 59. Secure with new bolt, flat washers, lock washer and lockout. 60. Belt should not touch center groove of pulley. 61. Replace with correct belt. 62. Align pulleys by shims or by adjustment of belt-driven accessories.
I. Poor heater performance.	63. Defective thermostat. 64. Restricted hose. 65. No thermostat. 66. Clogged heater core. 67. Defective control valve.	63. Replace thermostat. 64. Flush hose or reposition to eliminate kink. 65. Install thermostat. 66. Reverse flush heater core; if this does not help, have core professionally replaced. 67. Replace control valve.

Note 1. Doublecheck all fittings after engine is hot. Allow work-out of air bubbles and time for thermostat to open. At this time, more coolant will be necessary. Thermostat will not usually open unless it is immersed in coolant.

Note 2. Reverse flushing means forcing preferable hot water or water plus flushing solution through radiator and/or the engine block in reverse direction to normal flow. Disconnect radiator hoses and remove the thermostat.

Note 3. Use caution with antifreeze protection gauge. Testing a mixture of several different antifreezes is not accurate. Allow a safe reserve of at least ten degrees.

Note 4. Where possible, provide a minimum of one inch clearance between the fan and closest radiator projection. The motor may slide forward a little on a quick stop, or downhill.

Note 5. A rust mark, antifreeze stain or repeated wet spot around hose connections, gasket lines or the radiator seams or core often indicates leaks. Other tools are not necessary.

Note 6. All studs or bolts entering water chambers should be treated with a good sealer and well secured.

Note 7. Some vehicles have extra height in their thermostat housings. It is important to replace the lockwire or flat locking ring that holds the thermostat up against its housing. Also make sure that the heavy rubberlike seal is in place to prevent coolant bypassing the thermostat to the radiator.

Exhaust System Maintenance

The importance of a sound exhaust system

Your car's exhaust system has two functions. One, to carry away the poisonous, lethal gases from the passenger compartment. Two, to muffle the sound of the engine to a socially acceptable level. If a leak develops anywhere in the system, fumes could drift upward through holes and crevices in the car's underbody and into the passenger compartment. This can make you or others in the car ill. If you must continue on your trip before the leaking exhaust system can be repaired, open all windows as you drive.

Unfortunately, a damaged exhaust system does not always emit a signal. Although in cases where the muffler springs a leak, a roar may be heard. More often than not, however, an exhaust system fails in one of the other components, such as the exhaust pipe or tailpipe. The escaping carbon monoxide issues no warning, and the first indication of danger could be illness.

We hope the foregoing emphasizes the importance of conducting a thorough exhaust system inspection periodically. Since the inspection is simple to do and takes only a few moments, performing it once every six months or so would be a smart safeguard. The purpose is to spot an exhaust system in its about-to-fail state so it can be replaced before danger develops.

A muffler with wall damage such as this can allow dangerous gases to seep into the passenger compartment.

HOW TO INSPECT AN EXHAUST SYSTEM

The exhaust system begins at the exhaust manifold. From the engine compartment or from beneath the car (wherever you are best able to see), examine the joint formed by the exhaust pipe connecting to the exhaust manifold. The presence of white powdery deposits on the connection signifies that the exhaust manifold-exhaust pipe flange gasket is leaking or that bolts are loose.

Start the engine and look at the exhaust manifold-exhaust pipe joint. Listen. If you see exhaust puffing through the joint and/or hear a popping sound, the gasket is bad or bolts are loose. Turn off the engine.

From beneath the car, visually examine every part of the exhaust system for cracks, holes, extreme rusting and general damage. Working back from the exhaust manifold, check the exhaust pipe—perhaps two separate pipes—a front, nearest the exhaust manifold, and a rear muffler, tailpipe, clamps and hangers.

Many cars also have resonators, which are merely second mufflers. A resonator is smaller than the main muffler and may be positioned to the front or to the rear of the main muffler, in the exhaust pipe or in the tailpipe, respectively. The resonator's job is to help the muffler reduce engine noise. The resonator, if one is present, should be examined along with the rest of the exhaust system.

Most cars have a single exhaust system. But some with 8-cylinder engines have two systems. A car with

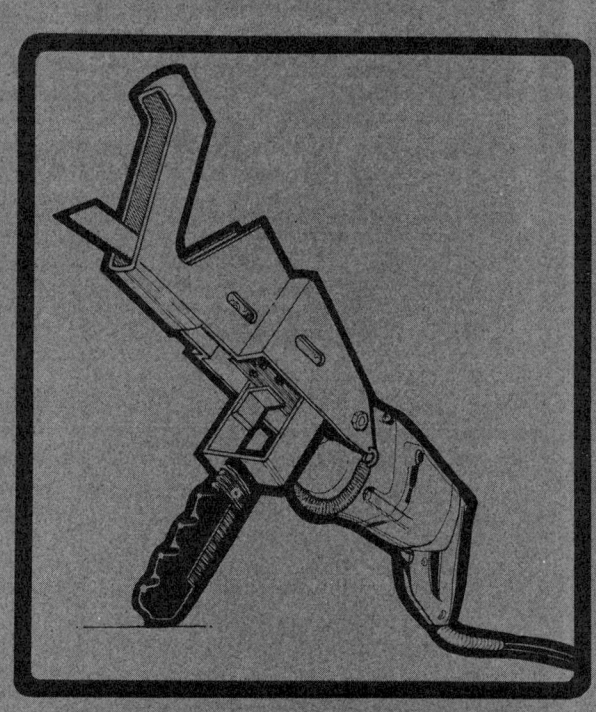

Power saws are made especially to allow quick and easy removal of exhaust systems. However, power tools are expensive. A hacksaw will do the same job slower, and for a much smaller investment.

TOOLS AND EQUIPMENT YOU NEED FOR EXHAUST SYSTEM SERVICE

1. **Penetrating oil to free frozen nuts.**
2. **A sharp metal chisel and hammer to knock frozen nuts free if penetrating oil will not work.**
3. **Socket and ratchet wrench. Open-end wrenches.**
4. **A tool to quickly saw away the complete exhaust system if parts are not salvageable. You can buy an electrically powered tool or you can use an ordinary hacksaw.**

    CAUTION: Do not use a torch to free frozen nuts or to cut away useless parts. In the hands of a nonprofessional, a torch used beneath a vehicle near fuel lines and fuel tank can be very dangerous.

5. **Exhaust system joint sealer.**
6. **Torque wrenches calibrated in foot pounds and inch pounds (optional).**

The joint between pipes is normally clamped together.

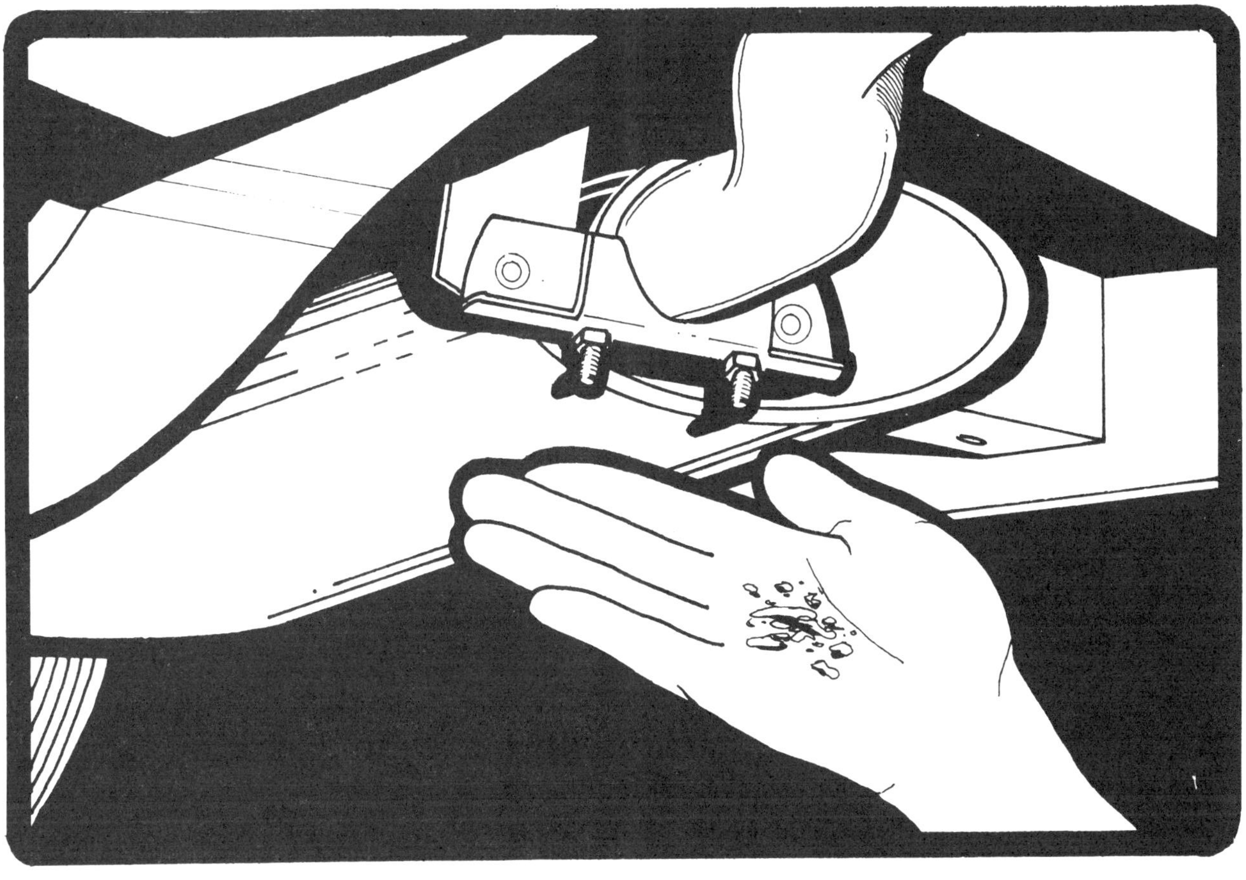

Exhaust system parts that shed rust are parts that have already failed or are in the process of failing.

a dual system has one of the systems servicing the cylinders of the left bank of the engine and one of the systems servicing the cylinders of the right bank of the engine. Both systems, although separate, are virtually the same in makeup and layout. Both should be examined during an exhaust system examination.

Beginning with 1975 and continuing with 1976 models, most cars incorporate a part called a catalytic converter in the exhaust system. This device is designed to combat air pollution. It is a component of the exhaust system and should be checked visually for damage during an exhaust system examination.

You can determine if your car has a catalytic converter, if you do not already know, by looking at the exhaust pipe between engine and muffler. The catalytic converter is shaped differently than muffler or resonator. If the car has both a catalytic converter and a resonator, the resonator will be positioned in the tailpipe.

Continue your exhaust system examination by tapping each part (*except* a catalytic converter) with a wrench. A sound part will emit a ringing noise. One which has failed or is about to fail will produce a dull thud.

Look to see that hanger assemblies are not broken. This would cause an otherwise sound pipe or muffler to bang against another part of the car and become damaged.

The final test is to start the engine and visually examine the entire exhaust system. If the system has a previously undetected hole you will probably see exhaust puffing from it.

Muffler and resonators are usually held to the vehicle by means of hanger assemblies. A hanger can break loose, resulting in irreparable damage to the part it is holding. So when inspecting an exhaust system make sure hangers are not damaged and are held firmly.

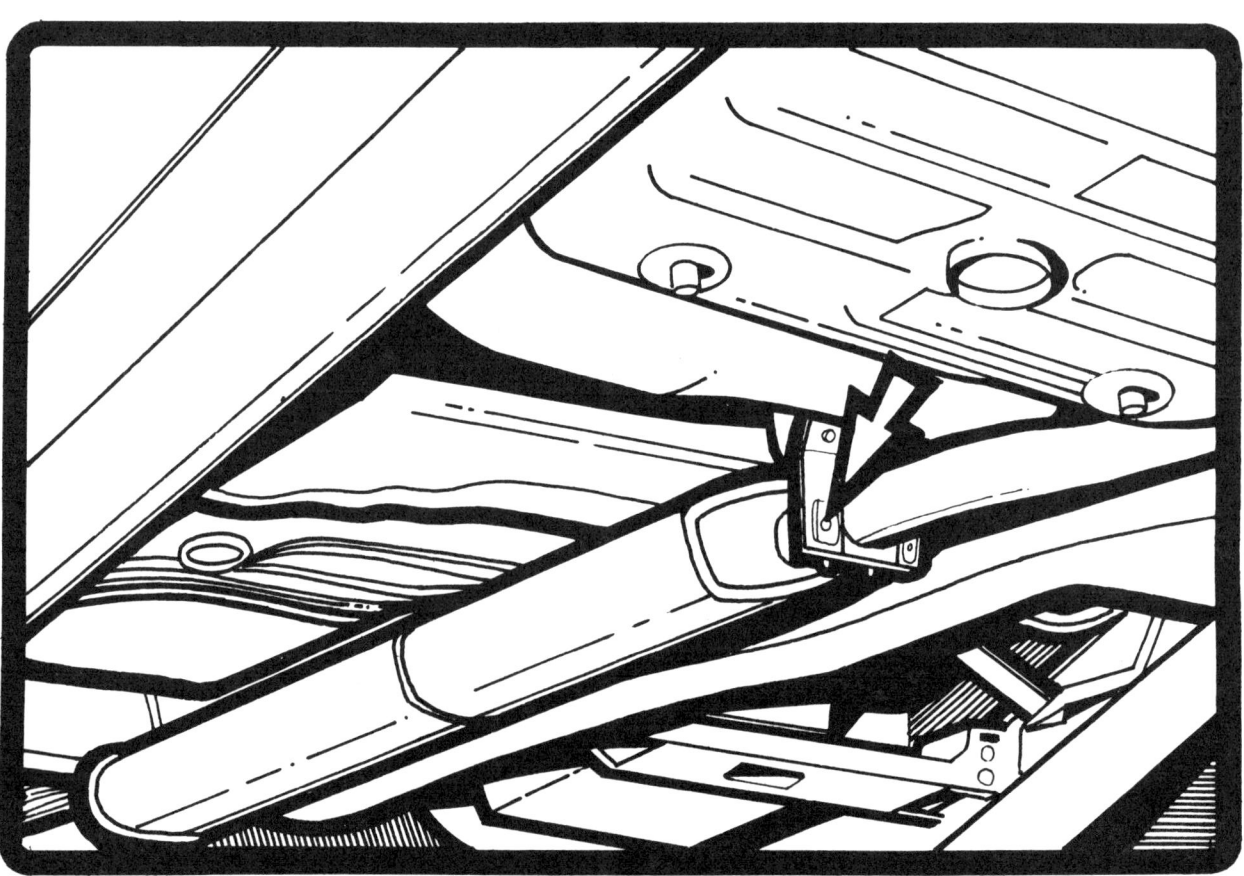

Use new clamps whenever installing new or reusable exhaust system parts. Joints should be coated with sealer before installing a clamp.

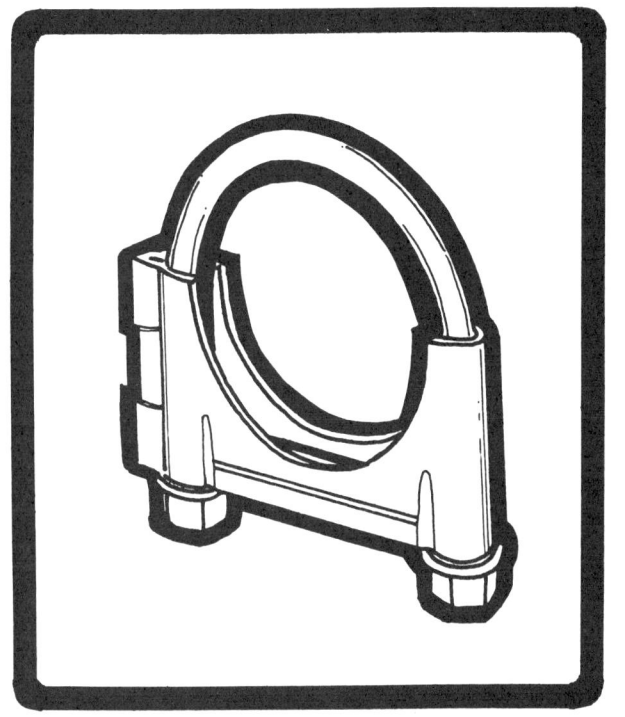

This is the counterweight of the heat control valve. Try to move the counterweight. If it moves, the valve is operating freely.

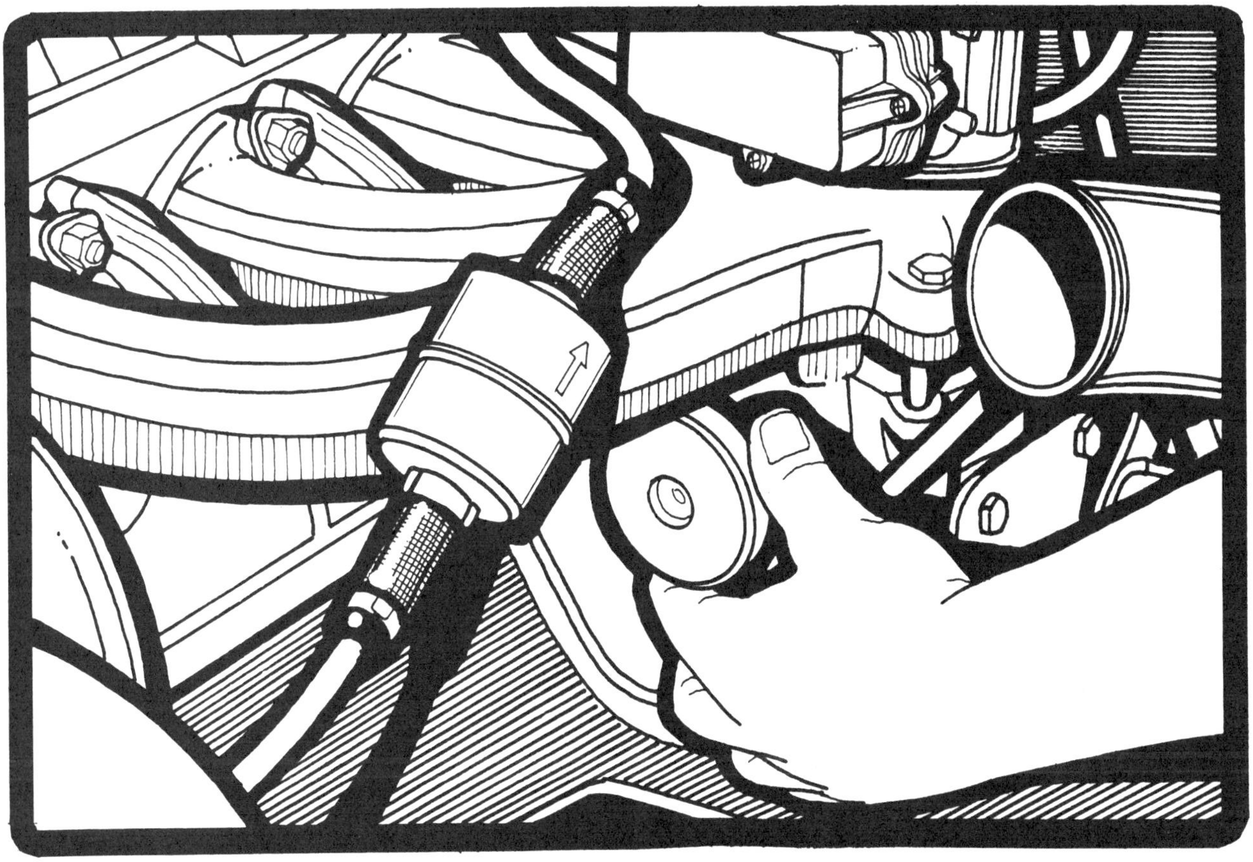

REPLACING EXHAUST SYSTEMS

This section contains instructions which apply to every car. For specific instructions regarding individuals models, see car sections further on in this chapter.

GENERAL PROCEDURES

1. To make the task easier, the car should be raised and firm supports (jack stands) placed at four places on the frame. Be sure to observe all safety precautions when working underneath your car. The car should be lowered onto the supports so the vehicle is resting on the frame. In some instances, this is necessary to provide you with ample clearance to remove and replace exhaust system parts.

    You may be able to do the job with the car on the ground while you are flat on your back, preferably on a creeper. However, the task will be infinitely more difficult. If you are able to borrow a lift for the time it will take you to replace the exhaust system, it would be advantageous.

2. Before working on your exhaust system, make sure all parts are cold. If the engine has been running, allow it to cool down for a minimum of three hours.
3. The most difficult part of the job is frequently loosening frozen fasteners. Drown the stubborn nut or bolt with an ample amount of penetrating oil, and allow the oil to work for five to 10 minutes. If it is just not possible to release the fastener after this, cut it away with your chisel.
4. If you release one end of an exhaust or tailpipe and must work on the other end, support it so that the pipe does not bend. A length of soft wire wrapped around the pipe and tied to an adjacent rail or crossmember makes an adequate support.
5. When parts are reassembled, there will be a number of common joints, such as between the tailpipe and muffler and between the exhaust pipe and muffler. Before clamping these parts together, coat the joint with a sufficient amount of exhaust system joint sealer. The sealer prevents leaks—not the clamp.

If you have access to drive-on ramps, this is probably the safest way to raise your car for exhaust system work.

After using a bumper jack to temporarily raise the front of the car, place sturdy safety jack stands under the A-frames as shown.

At the rear of the car, the safety jack stands should be placed directly under the rear axle assembly toward the outer end of the axle tubes.

6. If the exhaust pipe is removed from the exhaust manifold, determine if there is a gasket. If there is (not all joints are equipped with a gasket), discard the gasket and replace it with a new one. Once the joint is disassembled, the gasket loses effectiveness.
7. If you have torque wrenches, use them to tighten fasteners where torque specifications are given. However, if a torque wrench is not available, you can get by without one if you use caution.

Tighten fasteners securely. But do not tighten them to a point where pipes will be crushed. Fasteners should be tightened enough to prevent parts from moving and banging against the underbody or an adjacent area.

NOTE: If any exhaust system part is damaged, you must replace it! You cannot repair a damaged exhaust system!

AMERICAN MOTORS CORPORATION

IMPORTANT: Instructions outline complete dismantling of exhaust systems from front (engine end) to rear. If less than complete overhaul is needed, consult that portion of the instructions necessary to replace the damaged part(s).

All models with 6-cylinder engines without catalytic converter

NOTE: Models *with* 6-cylinder engines and catalytic converter are the 1975 and 1976 Matador with 258 cu.-in. engine and manual transmission, and all 1975 and 1976 6-cylinder models built for sale in California. The following instructions do *not* apply to these models.

If you have a power tool that drives sockets, such as an impact wrench, use it to remove exhaust system nuts and bolts. However, using a power tool to tighten exhaust system fasteners is tricky. You may crush pipes by overtightening a nut. Here, it is best to use hand tools.

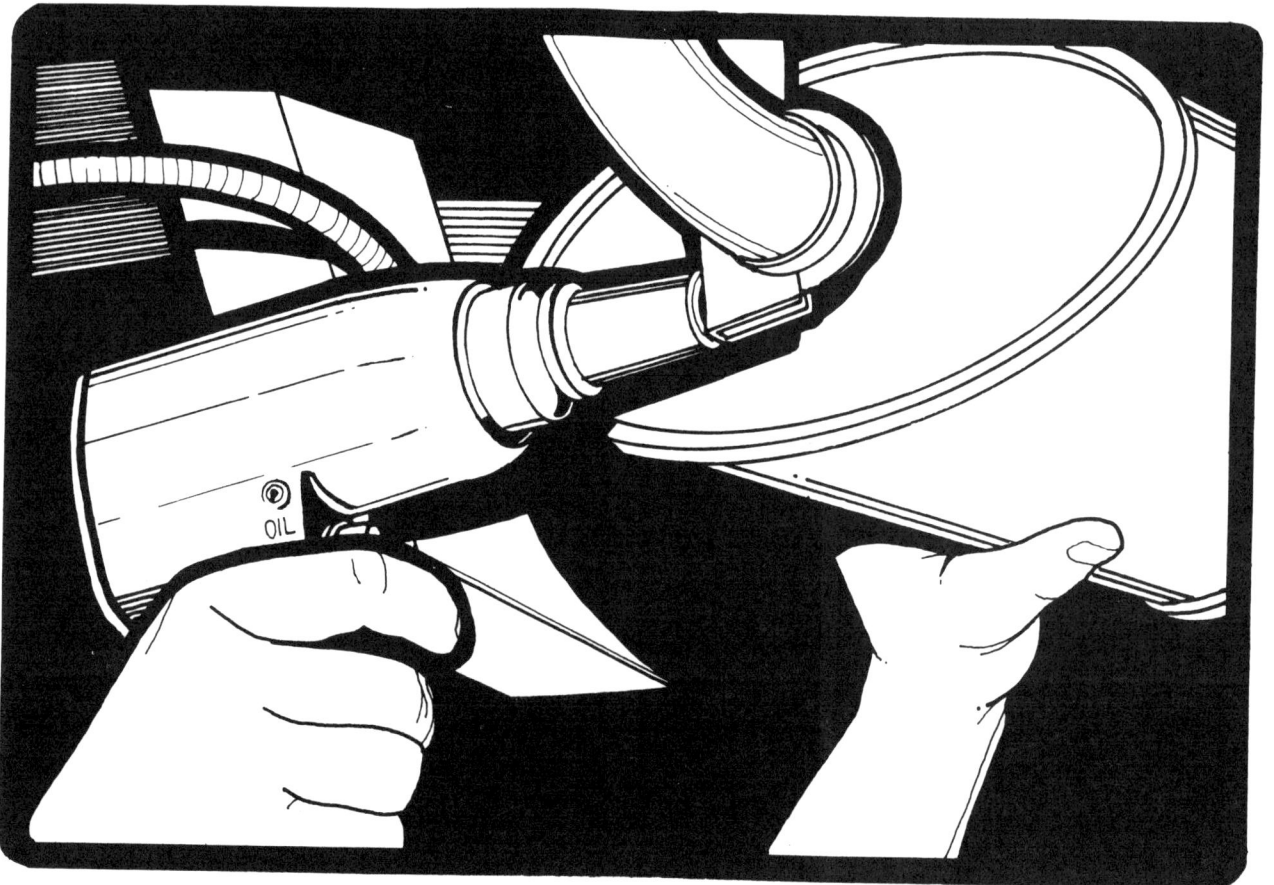

1. Be sure all parts are cold. If the engine has been running, allow it to cool down for three hours.
2. Salvage parts in usable condition.
3. Raise the vehicle extremely carefully and get beneath the vehicle.
4. Unbolt the two bolts holding the front exhaust pipe flange to the exhaust manifold.
5. Disconnect the front exhaust pipe from the one-piece rear exhaust pipe-muffler assembly by removing the clamp at the front-to-rear exhaust pipe joint.
6. Remove the front exhaust pipe by removing the front pipe's clamp screw. The clamp is located at approximately the pipe's midsection. Spread the clamp. Slide the pipe out.
7. Disconnect the tailpipe from the muffler by removing the tailpipe-to-muffler clamp.
8. Remove the tailpipe from the car by loosening the rear tailpipe clamp and spreading the clamp.
9. Drop the rear exhaust pipe-muffler assembly by disconnecting the assembly from its hanger assembly.

NOTE: If the parts are not in usable condition, you do not have to take pains to disconnect them one from another. Cut them loose in the easiest manner possible.

10. Examine all brackets, hangers and clamps. Remove and discard those which are badly corroded, damaged or deteriorated.

Install new and/or reusable exhaust system components in the following manner:

1. Install bracket and hangers if they have been removed.
2. Set the front exhaust pipe clamp in position to receive the front exhaust pipe.
3. Set the front exhaust pipe into its clamp. Engage the clamp bolt and tighten just enough to hold the pipe, but also permit the pipe to be maneuvered.

NOTE: If reusing the front exhaust pipe clamp, it can be reshaped by crimping it closed with a pair of pliers.

4. Make sure the front exhaust pipe-to-exhaust manifold seal is in straight position. Attach the front exhaust pipe to exhaust manifold.
5. Tighten the two front exhaust pipe-to-exhaust manifold flange bolts.
6. Slide the rear exhaust pipe-muffler assembly firmly onto the front exhaust pipe.
7. Attach the muffler to its hanger assembly.
8. Position the rear exhaust pipe to front exhaust pipe clamp around the joint. Tighten the nut.
9. Slide the tailpipe securely into the rear of the muffler, positioning the tailpipe into its clamp at the rear. Engage the clamp bolt.

NOTE: If reusing the tailpipe clamp in the rear, the clamp may be reshaped by crimping it closed with a pair of pliers.

10. Position the tailpipe to muffler clamp around the joint and tighten the nut.
11. Go back over the entire system. Make sure that each hanger and clamp bolt or nut is securely tightened. Be sure the exhaust system is aligned so there is no stress on parts and that no part can bang against any area of the car.
12. Lower the car to the ground.

American Motors 6-cylinder engine exhaust system.

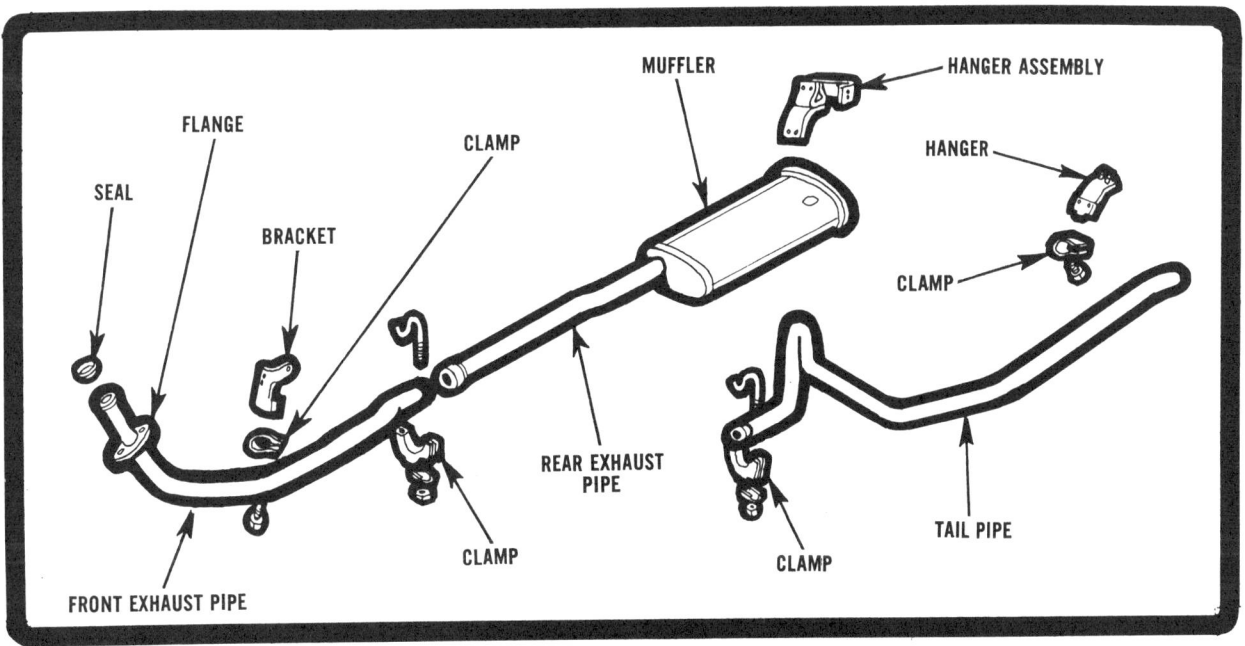

All models with 8-cylinder engines and single exhaust systems

Salvage parts in usable condition and/or remove exhaust system components as follows:

1. Be sure all parts are cold. If the engine has been running, allow it to cool for three hours.
2. Raise the car observing all safety precautions. Get beneath the vehicle.
3. Remove the two bolts holding the front exhaust pipe flange to the exhaust manifold serving the cylinders on the left bank of the engine.
4. Remove the two bolts holding the front exhaust pipe flange to the exhaust manifold serving the cylinders on the right bank of the engine.
5. Disconnect the front exhaust pipe from the rear exhaust pipe by removing the clamp at the front-to-rear exhaust pipe joint.
6. Remove the front exhaust pipe by removing the clamp holding the pipe at its midsection.
7. Disconnect the rear exhaust pipe from the muffler by removing the clamp at the muffler-rear exhaust pipe joint.
8. Disconnect the tailpipe from the muffler by removing the tailpipe-to-muffler clamp.
9. Drop the tailpipe by removing the clamp holding the pipe at its rear.
10. Drop the muffler by disconnecting the part from its hanger assembly.

    NOTE: If the parts are not in usable condition, you do not have to take pains to disconnect them one from another. Cut them loose in the easiest manner possible.

11. Examine all brackets, hangers and clamps. Remove and discard those which are badly corroded, damaged or deteriorated.

Install new and/or reusable exhaust system components in the following manner:

1. Beneath the car, install bracket and hangers if they have been removed.
2. Set the front exhaust pipe clamp in position to receive the front exhaust pipe.
3. Set the front exhaust pipe into its clamp. Engage the clamp bolt. Tighten enough to hold the pipe, but also permit the pipe to be maneuvered.
4. Make sure the front exhaust pipe-to-exhaust manifold seal at the exhaust manifold serving the left bank of cylinders is in straight position. Attach the front exhaust pipe to the left side exhaust manifold.
5. Make sure the front exhaust pipe-to-exhaust manifold seal at the exhaust manifold serving the right bank of cylinders is in straight position. Attach the front exhaust pipe to the right side exhaust manifold.
6. Tighten the front exhaust pipe-to-exhaust manifold flange bolts on both the left and right sides.
7. Slide the rear exhaust pipe firmly on to the front exhaust pipe. Attach and tighten the clamp at the joint formed by the two pipes.
8. Slide the muffler onto the rear exhaust pipe.
9. Attach the muffler to its hanger assembly.
10. Attach and tighten the clamp at the joint formed by the rear exhaust pipe and muffler.
11. Slide the tailpipe securely into the rear of the muffler. Position the tailpipe into its clamp at the rear. Engage the clamp bolt.
12. Position the tailpipe-to-muffler clamp around the joint and tighten the nut.
13. Go back over the entire system. Make sure that each hanger and clamp bolt or nut is securely tightened. Be sure the exhaust system is aligned so there is no stress on parts.
14. Lower the car to the ground.

Models with 8-cylinder engines and dual exhaust systems

A dual exhaust system is really two individual exhaust systems. Each of which is arranged exactly as a single exhaust system for each bank of cylinders. Each exhaust system in a car possessing dual-exhaust serves one side of the engine. Therefore, treat each part of a dual exhaust system as a single system. Consult instructions already presented under the heading, *All Models with 8-Cylinder Engines and Single Exhaust Systems.*

Chrysler Corporation 6-cylinder engine exhaust system used in Dart and Valiant.

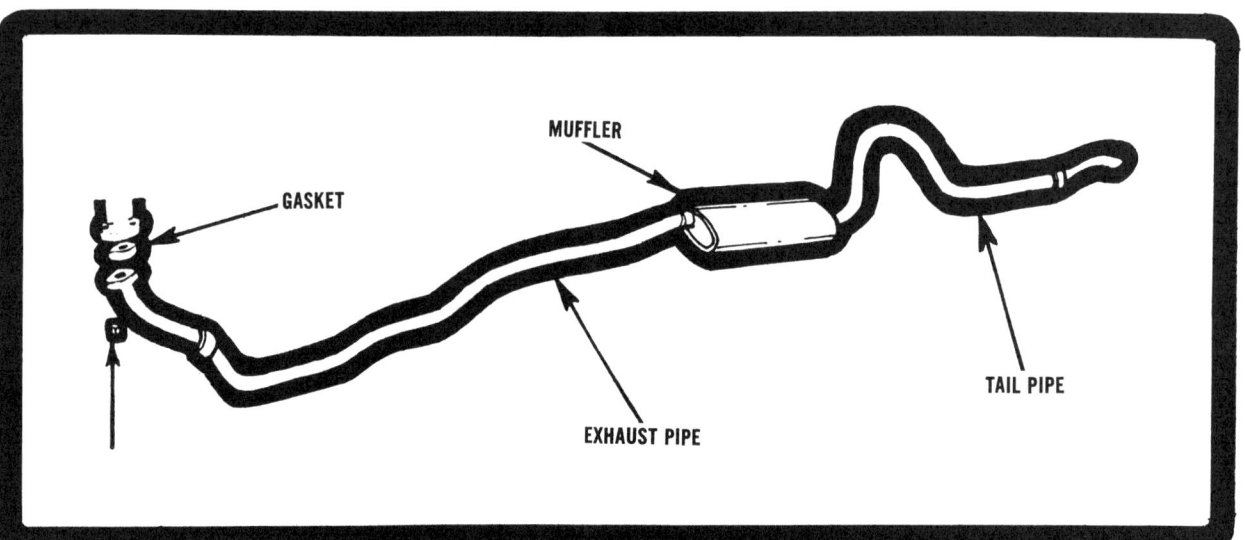

CHRYSLER CORPORATION

IMPORTANT: Instructions outline complete dismantling of exhaust systems from front to rear with the expectation of salvaging parts for reuse. If a part is not in reusable condition, it may be cut off in any manner that is easiest as long as an adjacent part, which can be reused, is not destroyed in the process.

CAUTION: Before working on the exhaust system of your car, make sure all parts are cold. If the engine has been running, allow it to cool down for three hours.

Valiant and Dart models with 6-cylinder engines

1. Raise the car observing all safety precautions. Get beneath the car.
2. Remove the two nuts holding the exhaust pipe flange to the exhaust manifold.
3. Discard the gasket between the exhaust pipe flange and exhaust manifold.
4. Remove the two U-bolt nuts at the U-bolt holding the front of the exhaust pipe at its neck.
5. Support the long exhaust pipe so it will not drop to the ground and be damaged. Continue to disconnect the muffler-exhaust pipe assembly, which is a one piece unit.
6. Examine the exhaust pipe U-bolt hanger assembly. Remove and replace the hanger assembly if damaged or deteriorated. Torque bolt and washer to 50 ft. lbs.
7. Remove the U-bolt holding the muffler and tailpipe together.
8. Slide the muffler forward so it disengages from the tailpipe. Lower the muffler-exhaust pipe assembly to the ground.
9. Examine the muffler-tailpipe U-bolt hanger assembly. Remove and replace if damaged or deteriorated. Torque the bolt, washer and nut to 200
10. Remove the bolt holding the tailpipe support to the car's frame rail. Lower the tailpipe to the ground.

    NOTE: Some models have a resonator as an integral part of the tailpipe. That is, resonator and tailpipe form a one-piece unit. Thus if one or the other is damaged, the entire unit must be replaced
11. Examine the tailpipe support. If damaged or deteriorated, remove and replace.
12. Install the exhaust pipe and muffler assembly first by attaching the exhaust pipe to its U-bolt. Engage U-bolt nuts loosely.

    CAUTION: Support the muffler as you work at the exhaust pipe to keep it from falling and being damaged.
13. Install a new gasket between the exhaust pipe flange and exhaust manifold. Engage the two connecting nuts loosely.
14. Install the small pipe extension at the rear of the muffler through the hole in the U-bolt hanger assembly.
15. Attach the small pipe extension at the rear of the muffler and tailpipe securely together.
16. Secure the tailpipe to the tailpipe support. Engage the bolt loosely.
17. Install the U-bolt at the muffler-tailpipe joint. Engage the two U-bolts nuts loosely.
18. Make sure the entire exhaust system is properly aligned so there is no stress on any part.
19. Torque fasteners securely or to specification as follows:
    (a) Exhaust pipe-to-exhaust manifold nuts: 35 lbs. ft.
    (b) Exhaust pipe U-bolt nuts: 95 lbs. in.
    (c) Muffler-to-tailpipe U-bolt nuts: 150 lbs. in.
    (d) Tailpipe support bolt: 200 lbs. in.
20. Lower the car to the ground.

Valiant and Dart models with 8-cylinder engines, single exhaust

1. Raise the car observing all safety precautions. Get beneath the car.
2. Remove the two nuts holding the exhaust crossover pipe to the exhaust manifold serving the left bank of cylinders. Discard the gasket.
3. Remove the two nuts holding the exhaust crossover pipe to the exhaust manifold serving the right bank of cylinders. Discard the gasket.
4. At the muffler, remove the U-bolt and saddle holding the exhaust pipe and muffler at their common joint. Separate the two parts. The exhaust pipe and muffler are not an integral assembly. They are separate units.
5. At the exhaust pipe's midsection, remove the two clamp screws attaching the clamp to the bracket held to the car's frame. This releases the exhaust pipe.

6. Lower the exhaust pipe to the ground.
7. At the rear of the muffler, remove the U-bolt holding muffler and tailpipe together.
8. Slide the muffler forward, away from the tailpipe. Lower the muffler to the ground.
9. Examine the muffler-tailpipe U-bolt hanger assembly. Remove and replace if damaged or deteriorated. Torque the bolt, washer and nut to 200 lbs. in.
10. Remove the bolt holding the tailpipe support to the car's frame rail. Lower the tailpipe to the ground.

   NOTE: Some models have a resonator as an integral part of the tailpipe. That is, resonator and tailpipe form a one-piece unit. Thus, if one or the other is damaged, the entire unit must be replaced.

11. Position the exhaust pipe. Attach the pipe at its midsection with the clamp. Engage the two clamp bolts loosely.
12. Install a new gasket to the left side exhaust crossover pipe flange. Attach the flange loosely to the left side exhaust manifold. Do the same on the right side.
13. Slide muffler and exhaust pipe together. Attach the U-bolt and saddle around the common joint. Attach U-bolt nuts and washers loosely.
14. Engage tailpipe to muffler with the U-bolt. Attach nuts and washers loosely.
15. Attach the rear of the tailpipe to the car frame rail by means of the tailpipe support. Engage the bolt loosely.
16. Make sure the exhaust system is properly aligned so there is no stress on any part.
17. Torque fasteners securely or to specification, as follows:
    (a) Exhaust pipe-to-exhaust manifold nuts: 24 lbs. ft.
    (b) Exhaust pipe-muffler U-bolt nuts: 150 lbs. in.
    (c) Exhaust pipe midsection clamp bolts: 200 lbs. in.
    (d) Muffler-tailpipe U-bolt nuts: 150 lbs. in.
    (e) Tailpipe support bolt: 180 lbs. in.
18. Lower the car to the ground.

Valiant and Dart models with 8-cylinder engines, dual exhaust

NOTE: A dual-exhaust system is really two identical (or almost identical), but individual systems in the same car. Each system is generally arranged to serve one cylinder bank of a larger size 8-cylinder engine. The discussion below describes how to replace one of these exhaust systems. Obviously, the procedure is the same for both systems.

1. Raise the car observing all safety precautions. Get beneath the car.
2. Remove the two nuts holding the exhaust pipe to the exhaust manifold. Discard the gasket.
3. Support the exhaust pipe to keep it from falling and being damaged as you continue your work in the rear.
4. Detach the nuts at the rear of the muffler holding the U-bolt connecting the muffler and tailpipe.
5. Examine the muffler-tailpipe U-bolt hanger assembly. Remove and replace if damaged or deteriorated. Torque the bolt, washer and nut to 200 in. lbs.
6. Remove the fasteners retaining the muffler to its hanger. Lower the muffler-exhaust pipe to the ground.

Chrysler Corporation 8-cylinder engine dual exhaust system.

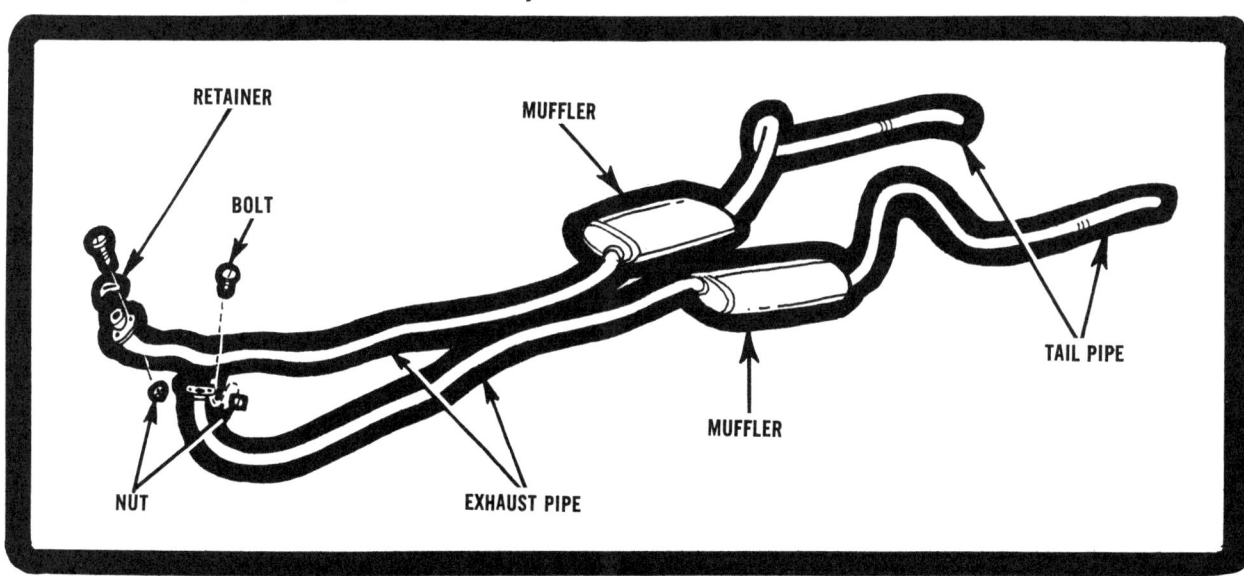

7. Loosen the rear of the tailpipe at the tailpipe support. Lower the tailpipe to the ground.
   NOTE: Some models have a resonator as an integral part of the tailpipe. If tailpipe or resonator is damaged, the entire unit must be replaced.
8. Place the muffler-exhaust pipe assembly into position. Support the end of the exhaust pipe with a prop or suitable stand to prevent damage as you work on the muffler end.
9. Attach the muffler hanger to the muffler. Engage the nut and washer loosely.
10. Install a new gasket to the exhaust pipe flange. Attach the flange loosely to the exhaust manifold.
11. Insert the small pipe extension at the rear of the muffler through the hole in the U-bolt hanger assembly.
12. Secure the tailpipe to the tailpipe support. Engage the bolt loosely.
13. Securely attach the small pipe extension at the rear of the muffler to the tailpipe.
14. Install the U-bolt at the muffler-tailpipe joint. Engage the two U-bolt nuts loosely.
15. Make sure the entire exhaust system is properly aligned so there is no stress on any part.
16. Torque fasteners securely or to specification, as follows:
    (a) Exhaust pipe-to-exhaust manifold nuts: 24 lbs. ft.
    (b) Muffler-to-muffler hanger: 24 lbs. in.
    (c) Muffler-to-tailpipe U-bolt nuts: 150 lbs. in.
    (d) Tailpipe support bolt: 50 lbs. in.
17. Lower the car to the ground.

Fury, Satellite, Coronet, Charger and Challenger models with 6-cylinder engines

1. Raise the car observing all safety precautions. Get beneath the car.
2. Unbolt the front exhaust pipe from the rear exhaust pipe.
3. Disconnect the front exhaust pipe flange from the exhaust manifold.
4. Lower the front exhaust pipe to the ground.
5. Notice that the front of the rear exhaust pipe is attached by a clamp to a bracket. Remove this clamp. Support the pipe so it will not fall to the ground and become damaged. Continue your work at the muffler end.
6. At the front of the muffler, disengage the saddle clamp holding the rear exhaust pipe to the muffler.

Typical Chrysler Corporation muffler clamp arrangement.

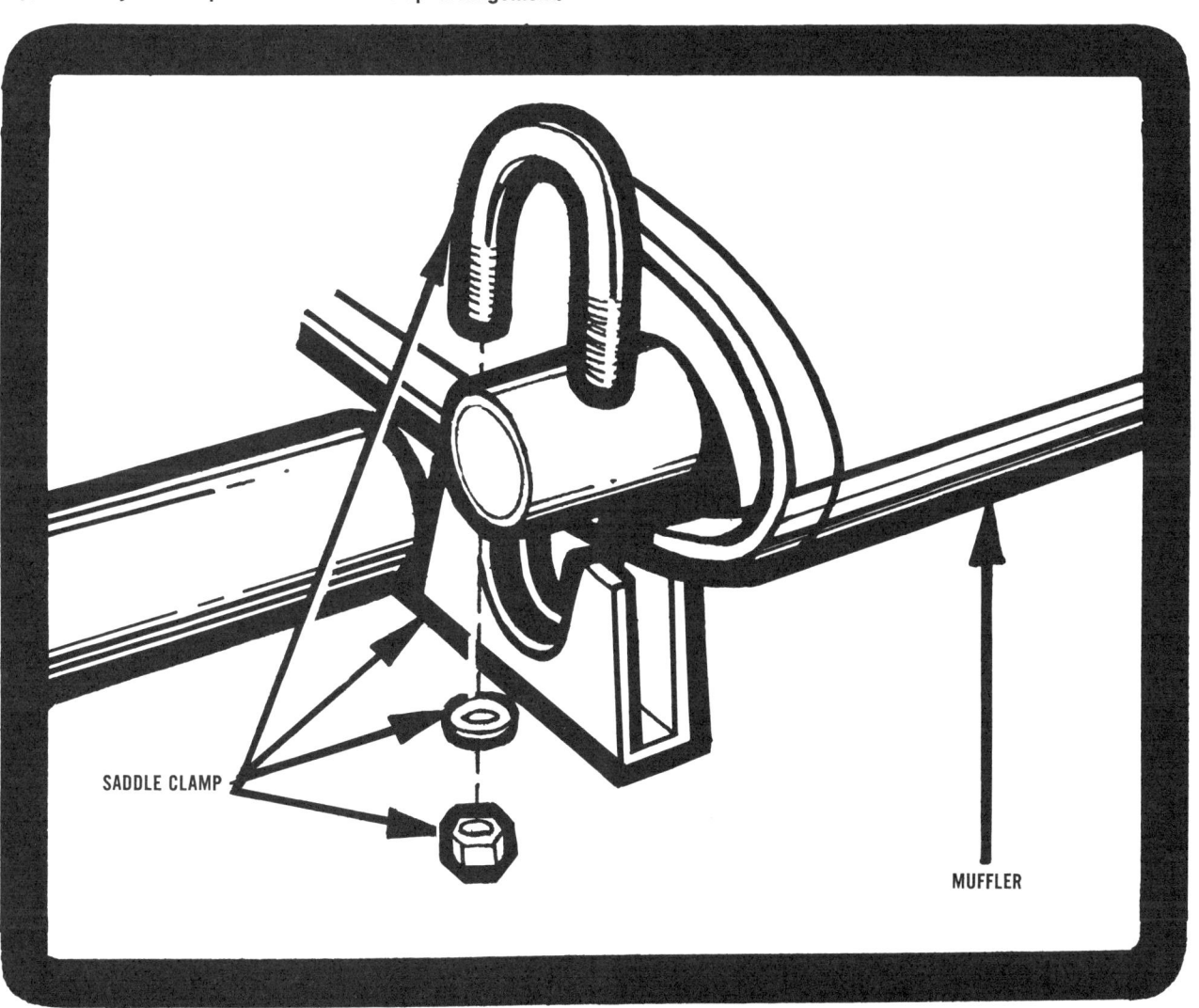

7. Pull the rear exhaust pipe forward, disengaging it from the muffler. Lower the pipe to the ground.
8. At the rear of the muffler, disengage the bolts securing the muffler and tailpipe together at the common hanger assembly.
9. Pull the muffler and tailpipe apart. Lower the muffler to the ground.
10. Examine the common muffler-tailpipe hanger. If damaged or deteriorated, replace. Torque the attaching bolt to 200 lbs. in.
11. At the rear of the tailpipe, unbolt the tailpipe support. This will release the tailpipe from its hanger.
12. Lower the tailpipe to the ground.
13. Examine the tailpipe hanger. If damaged or deteriorated, replace. Torque the bolt to 200 lbs. in.
14. Begin reassembly by securing the rear exhaust pipe in its bracket. Attach the clamp and engage the bolts loosely. Support the rear of the exhaust pipe (muffler end) so the pipe remains straight and undamaged as you continue working.
15. Place the front exhaust pipe into position and attach it to the rear exhaust pipe. Bolt the two together loosely.
16. Using a new gasket, attach the front exhaust pipe flange to the exhaust manifold. Engage bolts loosely.
17. Insert the small pipe extension in the rear of the muffler into its hanger assembly. Connect the front muffler assembly to the rear exhaust pipe.
18. Place the saddle clamp around the rear exhaust pipe-muffler joint. Engage bolts loosely.
19. Connect the tailpipe to the muffler and clamp the joint together at the hanger assembly. Engage bolts loosely.
20. Connect the tailpipe support strap to the tailpipe support hanger. Attach the bolt loosely.
21. Make sure the exhaust system is properly aligned so there is no stress on any part.
22. Torque fasteners securely or to specification, as follows:
    (a) Front exhaust pipe to exhaust manifold nuts: 35 lbs. ft.
    (b) Front exhaust pipe to rear exhaust pipe bolts: securely.
    CAUTION: Do not crush pipes.
    (c) Rear exhaust pipe to muffler clamp nuts: 150 lbs. in.
    (d) Muffler to tailpipe clamp nuts: 150 lbs. in.
    (e) Tailpipe strap support bolt: securely.
23. Lower the car to the ground.

Typical Chrysler Corporation exhaust pipe connection arrangement.

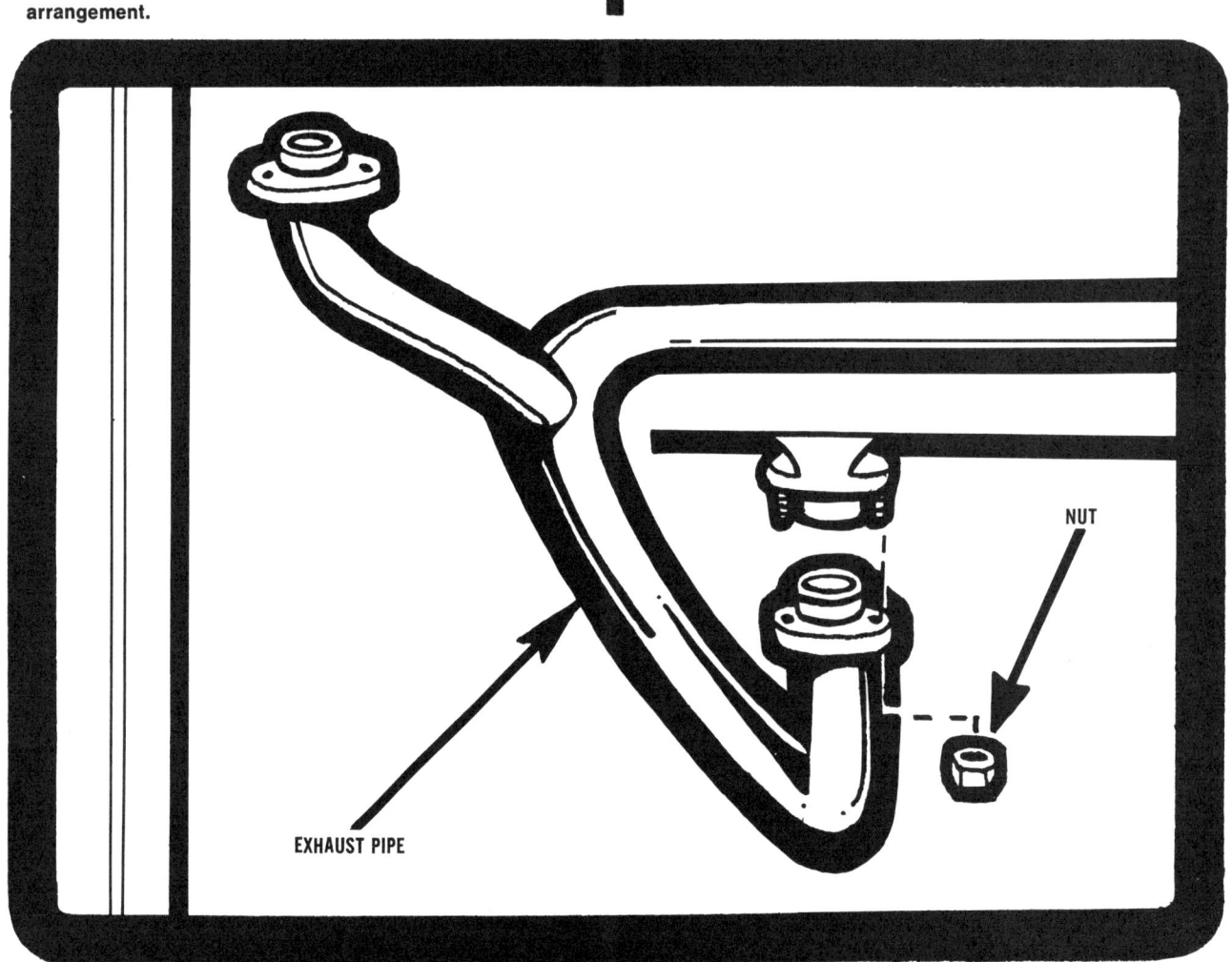

Fury, Satellite, Coronet, Charger and Challenger models with 8-cylinder engines, single exhaust

The procedure for replacing exhaust systems in these cars is identical to the procedure in the same models with 6-cylinder engines (see above). There is only one difference.

The front exhaust pipe is a crossover type, possessing two branches. One branch is connected to the exhaust manifold serving the left bank of cylinders. The other branch is connected to the exhaust manifold serving the right bank of cylinders.

Fury, Satellite, Coronet, Charger and Challenger models with 8-cylinder engines, dual exhaust

NOTE: A dual exhaust system is two identical (or almost identical), but individual systems in the same car. Each system is usually arranged to serve one bank of cylinders of a larger size 8-cylinder engine. The discussion below describes how to replace one of the two exhaust systems. Obviously, the procedure is the same for both systems.

1. Raise the car observing all safety precautions. Get beneath the car.
2. Remove the clamp securing the front exhaust pipe to the rear exhaust pipe. It is located just to the rear of the front exhaust pipe neck.
3. Unbolt the flange securing the front exhaust pipe to the exhaust manifold. Discard the gasket.
4. Pull the front exhaust pipe loose. Remove it from the car.
5. At the muffler, unbolt the saddle clamp holding the rear exhaust pipe to the muffler.
6. You will find the pipe clamped to a bracket near the middle of the rear exhaust pipe. Release the clamp bolt.
7. Pull the rear exhaust pipe loose. Remove it from the car.
8. Remove the clamp at the rear of the muffler holding it to the tailpipe.
9. Detach the bolt securing the muffler support strap to the frame rail.
10. Disconnect the muffler and tailpipe. Remove the muffler.
11. Examine the common muffler-tailpipe hanger. If damaged or deteriorated, replace. Torque the attaching bolt to 200 lbs. in.
12. Unbolt the tailpipe support strap. Remove the tailpipe.

Typical Chrysler Corporation tailpipe and resonator arrangement.

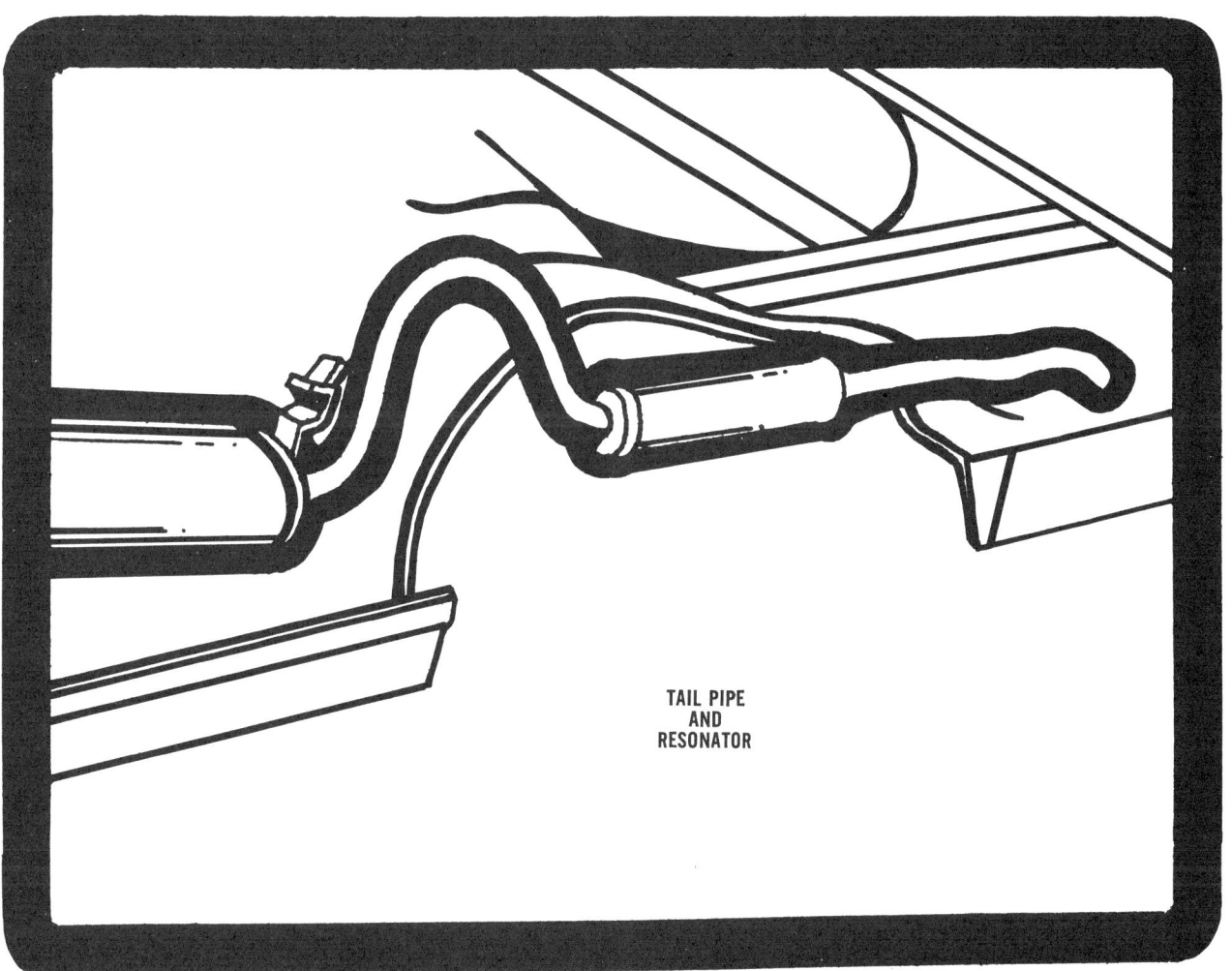

TAIL PIPE AND RESONATOR

13. Examine the tailpipe hanger. If damaged or deteriorated, replace. Torque the bolt to 200
    NOTE: Some models have a resonator as an integral part of the tailpipe. Resonator and tailpipe form a one-piece unit. If one or the other is damaged, the engine unit must be replaced.
14. Position the exhaust pipe and clamp it to the bracket. Engage bolts loosely.
15. Support the other end of the long rear exhaust pipe to prevent damage to the pipe as you continue your work.
16. Connect the front exhaust pipe and the rear exhaust pipe. Clamping them together loosely.
17. Using a new gasket, attach the front exhaust pipe flange to the exhaust manifold. Engage bolts loosely.
18. At the muffler end of the rear exhaust pipe, connect pipe and muffler. Loosely bolt the muffler support strap to the frame rail.
19. Attach the saddle clamp to the joint formed by the muffler and rear exhaust pipe. Engage clamp fasteners loosely.
20. Connect the tailpipe and muffler at the support bracket. Attach the support clamp loosely.
21. Attach the tailpipe support strap to its bracket. Engage the bolt loosely.
22. See that the exhaust system is properly aligned so there is no stress on any part.
23. Torque fasteners securely or to specification, as follows:
    (a) Front exhaust pipe to exhaust manifold nuts: 24 lbs. ft.
    (b) Front exhaust pipe to rear exhaust pipe clamp nuts: securely.
    CAUTION: Do not crush pipes.
    (c) Rear exhaust pipe midsection clamp bolts: 95 lbs. in.
    (d) Rear exhaust pipe to muffler saddle clamp nuts: securely.
    CAUTION: Do not crush pipes.
    (e) Front exhaust pipe to muffler clamp assembly nuts: 150 lbs. in.
    (f) Muffler support strap bolt: 200 lbs. in.
    (g) Tailpipe support strap bolt: securely.
24. Lower the car to the ground.

Typical Chrysler Corporation tailpipe support arrangement.

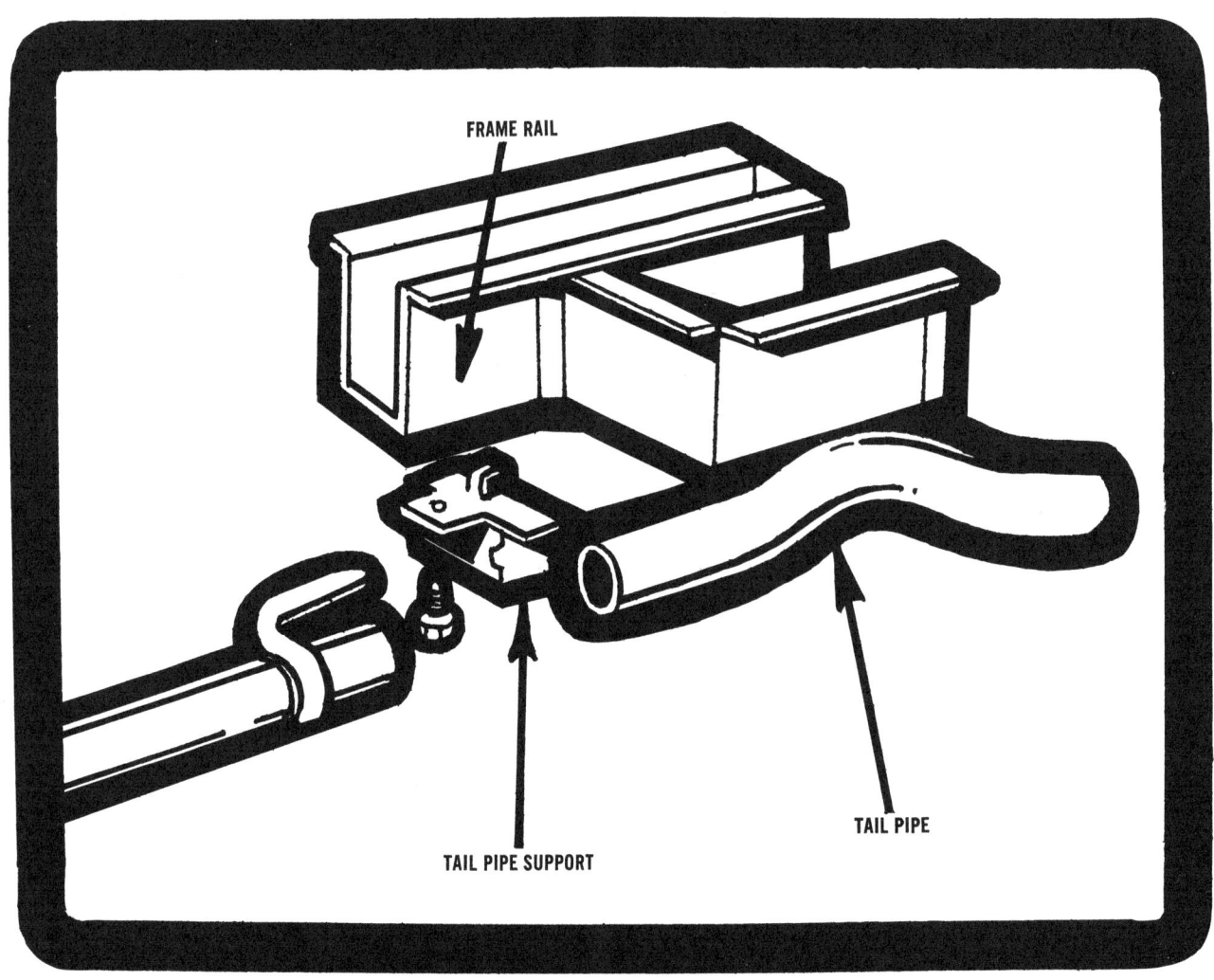

Gran Fury, Monaco, Polara, Chrysler and Imperial models, single or dual exhaust

NOTE: Single and dual exhaust systems of these models are virtually the same. The primary difference is that in a car with a dual exhaust system there are two identical systems—one serving each bank of cylinders. The only exception is that the model with a single exhaust system uses one front exhaust pipe of the crossover type. That is, it is a single pipe having two branches—one going to the left exhaust manifold and the other to the right exhaust manifold. In a car with a dual exhaust system, there are two front exhaust pipes, each serving its own system.

1. Raise the car observing all safety precautions. Get beneath the car.
2. Remove the clamp holding the front and rear exhaust pipes together.
3. In a car with a single exhaust system, remove both left and right front exhaust pipe flanges from the left and right exhaust manifolds, respectively. In a car with a dual exhaust system, remove the front exhaust pipe flange from the exhaust manifold on the side of the car you are working on.
4. Pull front and rear exhaust pipes apart. Remove the front exhaust pipe.
5. At the rear of the muffler, remove the support clamp securing it to the tailpipe.
6. At the rear of the tailpipe, remove the support clamp bolt holding the tailpipe support to the bracket assembly.
7. Detach the tailpipe from the muffler and remove the tailpipe from the car.
8. At the rear exhaust pipe's midsection, you will find a support bracket assembly. Remove the U-bolt holding the pipe to the assembly.
9. Remove the one-piece rear exhaust pipe and muffler assembly from the car.
10. To reassemble the system, position the rear exhaust pipe into its midsection support bracket. Engage the small pipe extension at the rear of the muffler into the hanger assembly. Engage the rear exhaust pipe support bracket clamp nuts loosely.
11. Connect the front exhaust pipe to the rear exhaust pipe. Engage clamp bolts loosely.
12. Connect the front exhaust pipe flange to the exhaust manifold. Engage nuts loosely. Use a new gasket. If the car has a single exhaust, be sure to attach both sides of the front exhaust pipe to its respective exhaust manifold.
13. Couple the tailpipe to the muffler at their common hanger support. Engage bolts loosely.

Typical Chrysler Corporation exhaust pipe support arrangement.

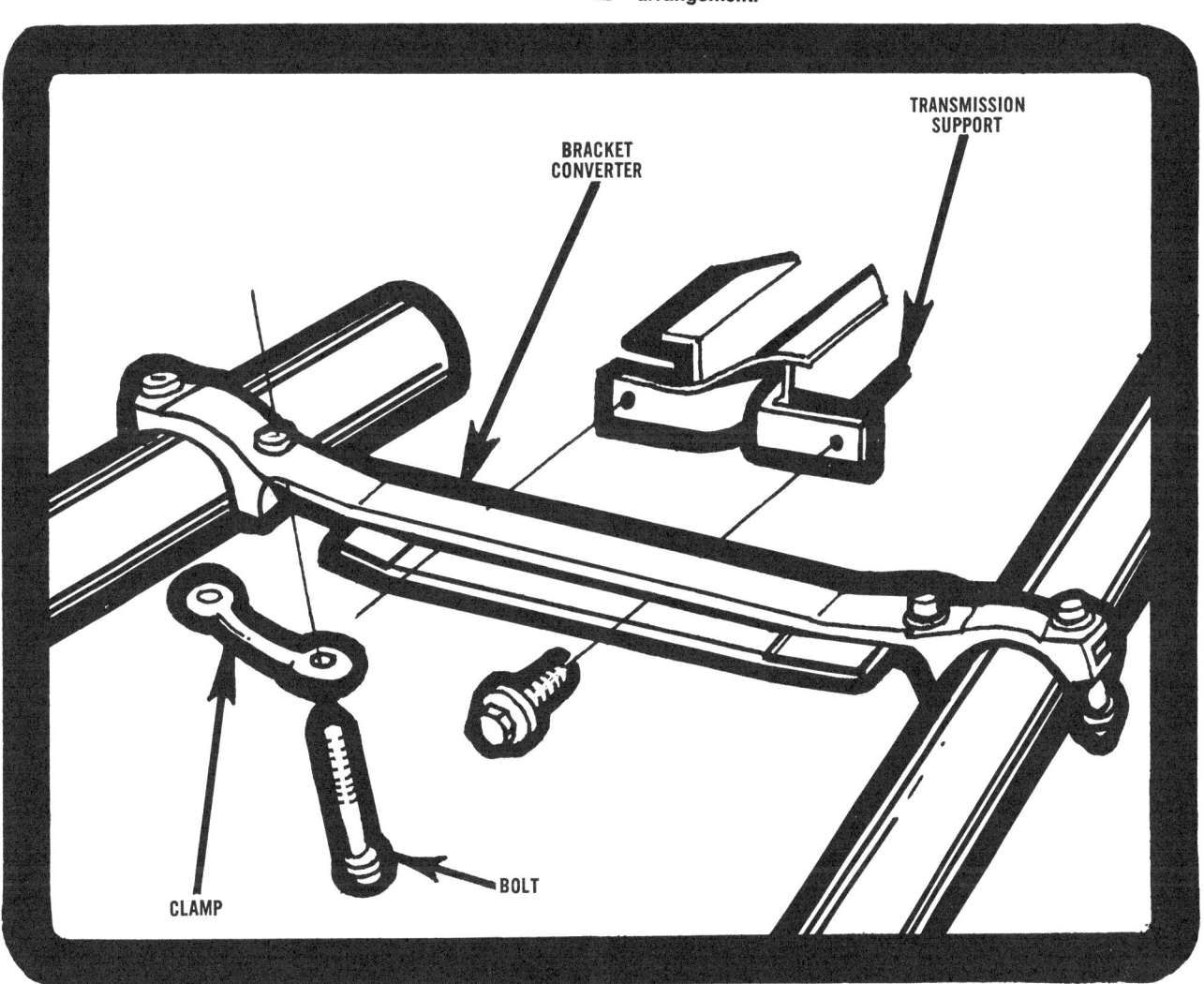

14. Attach the tailpipe rear support to its bracket. Engage the bolt loosely.
15. See that the exhaust system is properly aligned so there is no stress on any part.
16. Torque fasteners securely or to specification, as follows:
    (a) Front exhaust pipe to exhaust manifold nuts: 24 lbs. ft.
    (b) Front exhaust pipe to rear exhaust pipe clamp bolts: securely.
    CAUTION: Do not crush pipes.
    (c) Exhaust pipe midsection support clamp bolts: 95 lbs. in.
    (d) Muffler and tailpipe support assembly nuts: securely.
    CAUTION: Do not crush pipes.
    (e) Tailpipe support strap bolt: 95 lbs. in.
17. Lower the car to the ground.

Typical Chrysler Corporation clamp and support arrangement.

FORD MOTOR COMPANY

IMPORTANT: Instructions outline complete dismantling of exhaust systems from front to rear with the expectation of salvaging parts for reuse. If a part is not in reusable condition, it may be cut off in any manner that is easiest as long as an adjacent part, which can be reused, is not destroyed in the process.

CAUTION: Before working on the exhaust system, make sure all parts are cold. If the engine has been running, allow it to cool for three hours.

All models with 4-cylinder engines (Pinto, Mustang II, and Bobcat)

1. Raise the car observing all safety precautions. Get beneath the car.
2. Remove fasteners from the hanger which attaches the exhaust pipe in about its midsection to the pipe bracket.
3. Support the pipe to keep it from falling and being damaged as you continue your work in other areas.
4. Remove the nuts attaching the exhaust pipe to the resonator inlet pipe.
5. Remove the nuts attaching the exhaust pipe flange to the exhaust manifold.

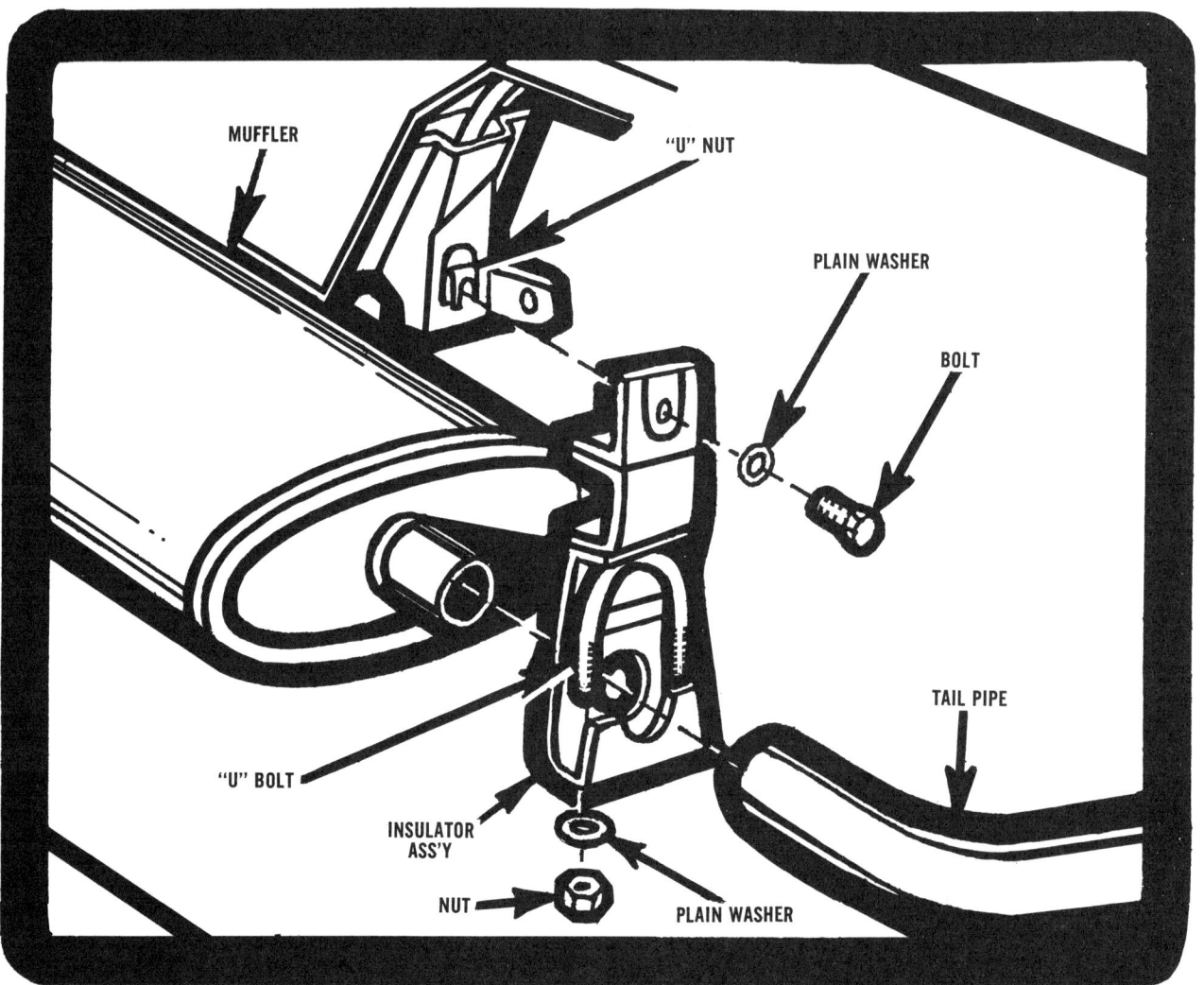

6. Release the exhaust pipe and remove it from the vehicle.
7. Turn your attention to the resonator inlet pipe, resonator, resonator-to-muffler pipe, muffler and tailpipe.

   NOTE: The resonator inlet pipe, resonator-to-muffler pipe, muffler and tailpipe are all welded together in a single unit if the exhaust system is the car's original one.

8. Support the assembly by attaching a piece of soft wire around the resonator inlet pipe and tying it to a suitable member.
9. At the front of the muffler, loosen and remove the hanger bolts securing the assembly to the vehicle's underbody.
10. At the rear of the muffler, loosen and remove the bolts holding the muffler (and the rest of the assembly) to the hanger bracket.
11. Release the one-piece assembly and lower it to the ground.
12. Begin reassembly.

    NOTE: Instead of the two pieces which come with the original exhaust system for these models, replacement exhaust parts are normally furnished in four separate pieces that are assembled together with clamps. The four pieces are: (1) exhaust pipe, (2) resonator and resonator inlet pipe assembly, (3) resonator-to-muffler pipe, (4) muffler-tailpipe assembly.

13. Loosely attach the exhaust pipe to the hanger at about its midsection.
14. Connect the exhaust pipe flange to the exhaust manifold. Attach the nuts loosely.
15. Support the resonator inlet pipe to keep the resonator assembly from being damaged as you connect the resonator inlet pipe to the rear of the exhaust pipe. Seal and attach the clamp securely.

    CAUTION: Do not crush pipes by overtightening the clamp.

16. Suspend the resonator-to-muffler pipe from the hanger assembly. Attach bolts loosely.
17. Attach the resonator-to-muffler pipe to the rear of the resonator with a clamp.

    CAUTION: Do not crush pipes by overtightening the clamp.

18. Secure the muffler-tailpipe assembly. Attach the rear of the muffler to the hanger assembly. Attach the bolts loosely.
19. Attach the resonator-to-muffler pipe to the front of the muffler with a clamp.

    CAUTION: Do not crush pipes by overtightening the clamp.

20. See that the exhaust system is properly aligned so there is no stress on any part.
21. Tighten fasteners securely or to specification as follows:
    (a) Exhaust pipe-to-exhaust manifold nuts: 25-35 lbs. ft.
    (b) Exhaust pipe midsection bracket nuts: 17-28 lbs. ft.
    (c) Resonator-to-muffler pipe support bracket nuts: 108 lbs. in.
    (d) Muffler hanger assembly bolts: 108 lbs. in.
22. Lower the car to the ground.

All models with 6-cylinder engines

1. Raise the car observing all safety precautions. Get beneath the car.
2. Remove fasteners from the hanger which attaches the exhaust pipe at about its midsection to the pipe bracket.

Typical Ford Motor Company 4-cylinder engine single exhaust system.

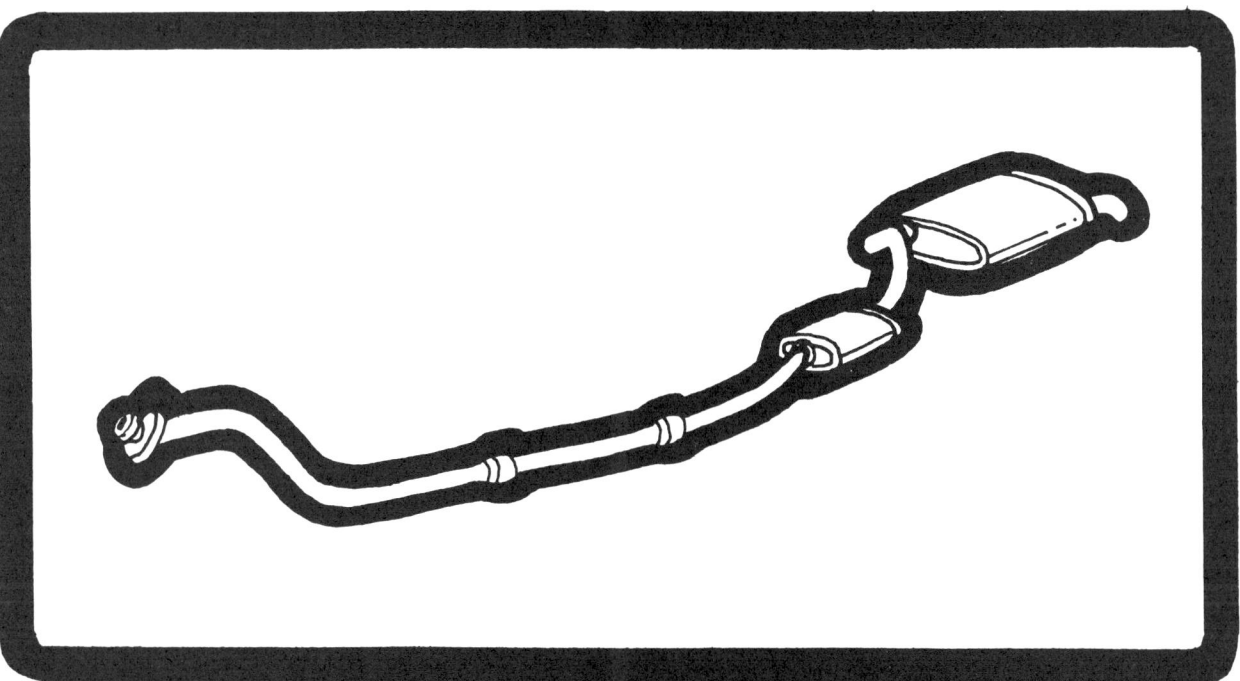

3. Support the pipe to keep it from falling and being damaged as you continue your work in other areas.
4. Remove the nuts attaching the exhaust pipe to the resonator inlet pipe.
5. Remove the nuts attaching the exhaust pipe flange to the exhaust manifold.
6. Release the exhaust pipe. Remove it from the vehicle.
7. Turn your attention to the resonator inlet pipe, resonator, resonator-to-muffler pipe, muffler and tailpipe.

   NOTE: The resonator inlet pipe, resonator, resonator-to-muffler pipe, muffler and tailpipe are all welded together in a single unit if the exhaust system is the car's original one.
8. Support the assembly by attaching a piece of soft wire around the resonator inlet pipe and tying it to a suitable member.
9. At the rear of the resonator, loosen and remove the two bolts holding the resonator to its hanger assembly.
10. At the rear of the muffler, loosen and remove the two bolts holding the muffler-tailpipe to its hanger assembly.
11. Release the one piece assembly. Lower it to the ground.
12. Begin reassembly.

    NOTE: Instead of the two pieces which come with the original exhaust system, replacement exhaust parts are normally furnished in four separate pieces that are assembled together with clamps. The four pieces are: (1) exhaust pipe, (2) resonator and resonator inlet pipe assembly, (3) resonator-to-muffler pipe, (4) muffler-tailpipe assembly.
13. Loosely attach the exhaust pipe at about its midsection to the hanger.
14. Connect the exhaust pipe flange to the exhaust manifold. Attach the nuts loosely.
15. Support the resonator inlet pipe to keep the resonator assembly from being damaged as you connect the resonator inlet pipe to the rear of the exhaust pipe. Seal and attach the clamp loosely.
16. Attach the resonator to its hanger. Secure bolts loosely.
17. Connect the front of the resonator-to-muffler pipe to the rear of the resonator. Secure the joint with a clamp.
18. Attach the muffler-tailpipe assembly to its hanger. Secure bolts loosely.
19. Connect the rear of the resonator-to-muffler pipe to the front of the muffler. Secure the joint with a clamp.
20. See that the exhaust system is properly aligned so there is no stress at any point.
21. Tighten fasteners securely or to specification as follows:
    (a) Exhaust pipe-to-exhaust manifold nuts: 25-35 lbs. ft.
    (b) Exhaust pipe midsection bracket nuts: 8-14 lbs. ft.
    (c) Exhaust pipe-to-resonator inlet pipe flange: 20-30 lbs. ft.
    (d) Resonator-to-resonator hanger bolts: 10-20 lbs. ft.
    (e) Muffler-to-muffler hanger bolts: 8-14 lbs. ft.

    CAUTION: In securing clamps, tighten them sufficiently to hold pipes steady. But do not overtighten and crush pipes.
22. Lower the car to the ground.

Typical Ford Motor Company 8-cylinder single exhaust system.

11. Attach the exhaust pipe branches to the left and right side exhaust manifolds. Secure nuts loosely.
12. Work the replacement tailpipe over the rear crossmember. Allow it to rest on the crossmember.
13. Connect the front of the muffler to the rear of the exhaust pipe. Attach the muffler to its hanger assembly. Engage bolts loosely.
14. Install the clamp around the muffler-exhaust pipe joint.
15. Connect the rear of the muffler to the front of the tailpipe.
16. Install the clamp around the muffler-tailpipe joint.
17. Attach the rear of the tailpipe to its hanger.
18. See that the exhaust system is properly aligned so there is no stress at any point.
19. Tighten fasteners securely or to specification as follows:

    (a) Exhaust pipe branches-to-exhaust manifolds: 25-35 lbs. ft.
    (b) Exhaust pipe-to-muffler clamp: 25-35 lbs. ft.
    (c) Muffler-to-muffler hanger bolts: 8-14 lbs. ft.
    (d) Tailpipe-to-muffler clamp: 25-35 lbs. ft.
    (e) Tailpipe support strap bolts: 8-14 lbs. ft.
20. Lower the car to the ground.

Continental Mark III and Mark IV, and Thunderbird

NOTE: The original equipment exhaust system in these models contains the same parts—crossover exhaust pipe, and a single assembly consisting of the muffler, muffler-to-resonator pipe, and resonator and tailpipe.

1. Raise the car observing all safety precautions. Get beneath the car.
2. Support the exhaust pipe with a piece of soft wire so it does not fall and become damaged when disconnected.
3. Disconnect the branches of the crossover exhaust pipe at the left and right side exhaust manifolds.
4. Disconnect the rear of the exhaust pipe from the front of the muffler.
5. Release the exhaust pipe. Lower it to the ground.
6. Support the rear of the muffler-to-resonator pipe with a piece of soft wire so the assembly will not fall and become damaged when disconnected.
7. Remove the bolts holding the resonator to its hanger.
8. Remove the bolts holding the muffler to its hanger.
9. To remove the assembly from the car, work the unit forward and up and over the crossmember.
10. Begin reassembly by supporting the exhaust pipe to prevent damage.
11. Attach the branches of the exhaust pipe to the left and right exhaust manifolds. Secure bolts loosely.
12. Work the tailpipe-resonator assembly into position. Allow the pipe to rest on the crossmember as you attach the resonator to its hanger. Engage bolts loosely.
13. Connect the front of the muffler with the rear of the exhaust pipe. Clamp loosely.
14. Attach the rear of the muffler to its hanger assembly. Engage bolts loosely.
15. Connect the rear of the muffler with the front of the tailpipe and clamp loosely.
16. See that the exhaust system is properly aligned so there is no stress at any point.

Models with 8-cylinder engines, single exhaust Granada, Monarch, Comet, Maverick

The arrangement of the exhaust systems in these cars is the same as the exhaust system in models with 6-cylinder engines. Therefore, the replacement instructions outlined above apply. The only difference is that a crossover type exhaust pipe is used. One branch of which goes to the exhaust manifold on the left side of the engine. The other branch goes to the exhaust manifold on the right side of the engine.

All other models except Lincoln, Continental Mark III and Mark IV, and Thunderbird

1. Raise the car observing all safety precautions. Get beneath the car.
2. Loosen the clamp. Disconnect the exhaust pipe from the muffler.
3. Support the exhaust pipe to keep it from falling and being damaged as you continue working at the exhaust manifold end.
4. Disconect the exhaust pipe branches from the exhaust manifolds on the left and right sides of the engine.
5. Release the exhaust pipe and lower it to the ground.
6. At the rear of the tailpipe, loosen the tailpipe strap from the hanger.
7. At the rear of the muffler, loosen and release the muffler from the hanger.

    NOTE: The original exhaust system has the muffler and tailpipe as an assembly.
8. Move the tailpipe up and over so it clears the rear crossmember as you move the muffler and tailpipe assembly toward the front of the car to remove it from the vehicle.
9. Begin reassembly.

    NOTE: Replacement muffler and tailpipes are usually provided as two separate pieces rather than as one assembly.
10. Support the exhaust pipe so you can attach it to the exhaust manifolds without fear of damage.

17. Tighten fasteners securely or to specification as follows:
    (a) Exhaust pipe branches-to-exhaust manifolds: 25-35 lbs. ft.
    (b) Exhaust pipe-to-muffler clamp: 25-35 lbs. ft.
    (c) Tailpipe-to-muffler clamp: securely.
    (d) Muffler-to-hanger assembly bolts: 8-14 lbs. ft.
    (e) Resonator-to-hanger assembly bolts: 8-14 lbs. ft.
18. Lower the car to the ground.

Models with 8-cylinder engines, dual exhaust

The exhaust systems in cars having dual exhausts are identical in arrangement to the exhaust system in models having a single exhaust (see *models with 8-cylinder engines, single exhaust*) except that there are two individual systems. Each is treated as the single exhaust system described above for the particular vehicle.

GENERAL MOTORS

IMPORTANT: Instructions outline complete dismantling of exhaust systems from front to rear with the expectation of salvaging parts for reuse. If a part is not in reusable condition, it may be cut off in any manner that is easiest as long as an adjacent part, which can be reused, is not destroyed in the process.

CAUTION: Before working on the exhaust system, make sure all parts are cold. If the engine has been running, allow it to cool down for three hours.

General Motors recommends that exhaust system components have a clearance of at least ¾-inch from the floor pan. This will avoid possible overheating of the floor pan and possible damage to passenger compartment carpets.

6. Remove the muffler from the muffler hanger by removing the bolt.
7. Lower muffler and tailpipe to the ground.
8. Examine tailpipe and muffler hangers for damage and deterioration. Replace if necessary.
9. Begin reassembly by supporting the exhaust pipe on the muffler hanger so the pipe will not fall as you work.
10. Attach the exhaust pipe loosely to the exhaust manifold with the securing nuts.
11. Connect the exhaust pipe to muffler. Attach the muffler loosely to the muffler hanger.
12. Clamp muffler and exhaust pipe together loosely.
13. Connect tailpipe and muffler. Attach the tailpipe loosely to the tailpipe hanger.
14. Clamp muffler and exhaust pipe together loosely.
15. See that the exhaust system is properly aligned so there is no stress on any part.
16. Tighten fasteners securely or to specification as follows:
    (a) Exhaust pipe-to-exhaust manifold nuts: 15 lbs. ft.
    (b) Exhaust pipe-to-muffler clamp: 9 lbs. ft.
    (c) Muffler-to-muffler hanger: 25 lbs. ft.
    (d) Tailpipe-to-muffler clamp: 9 lbs. ft.
    (e) Tailpipe-to-tailpipe hanger: 25 lbs. ft.
17. Lower the car to the ground.

Models with 6-cylinder engines

NOTE: In some models, a resonator is an integral part of the tailpipe. In these models, if tailpipe or resonator is damaged, the entire assembly should be replaced. In other models, resonator and tailpipe are held together by a clamp so that the damaged component alone can be replaced. Still other models have tailpipes but not resonators. An examination of the tailpipe will quickly tell you the arrangement in your GM car.

1. Raise the car observing all safety precautions. Get beneath the vehicle.

Models with 4-cylinder engines

NOTE: The original exhaust systems in 4-cylinder engine models consist of an exhaust pipe and a welded together muffler-tailpipe assembly. Replacement parts usually consist of an exhaust pipe, an individual muffler, and an individual tailpipe. Individual parts are secured by clamps.

1. Raise the car observing all safety precautions. Get beneath the car.
2. Remove the exhaust pipe at the exhaust manifold by loosening nuts.
3. Remove the nuts holding the exhaust pipe clamp to the muffler.
4. Lower the exhaust pipe to the ground.
5. Remove the tailpipe from the tailpipe hanger by loosening the bolt.

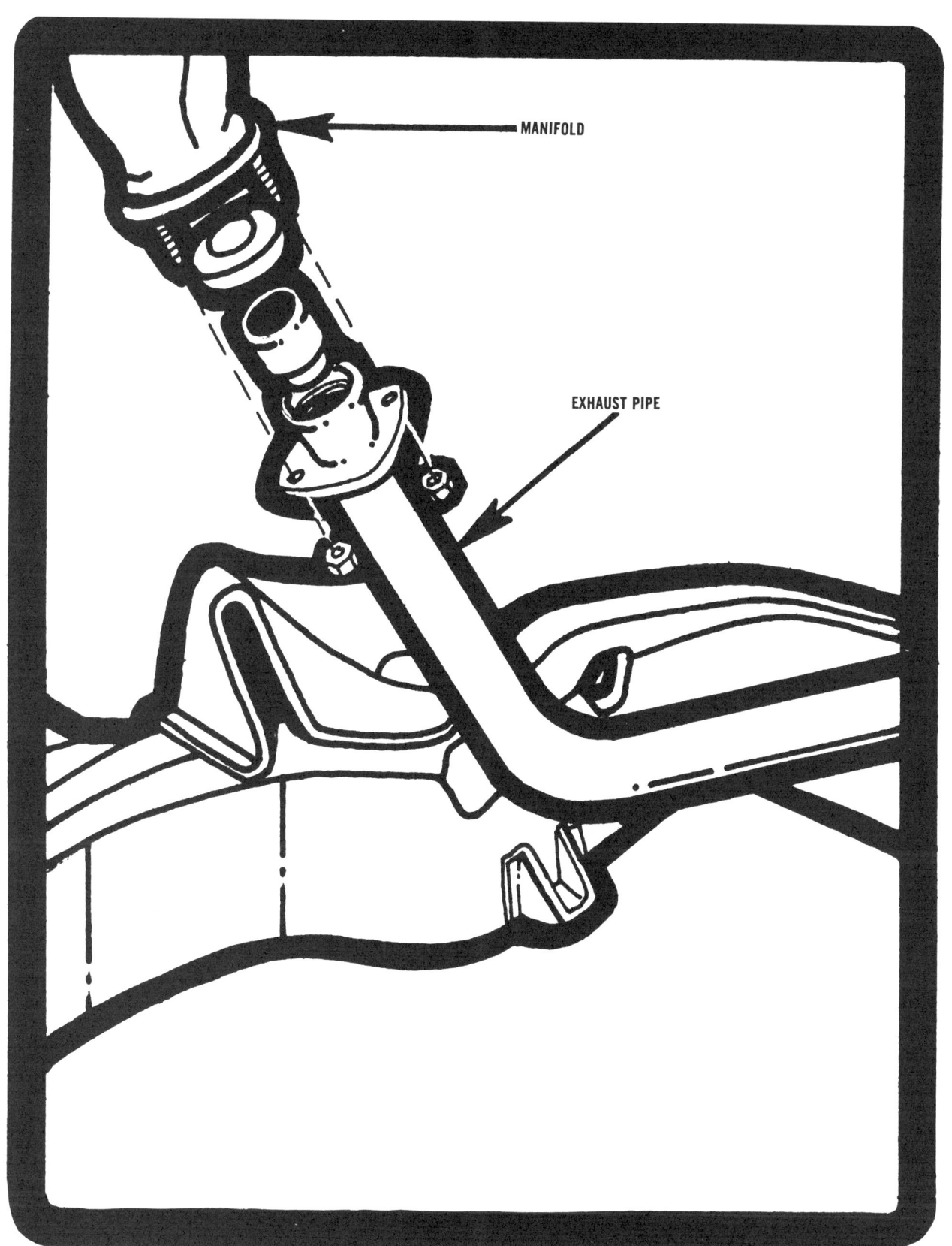
On many GM models, the seal between the exhaust pipe and exhaust manifold is a positive ball joint type. A gasket is used on other models.

2. Unbolt the exhaust pipe from the exhaust manifold.
3. Support the exhaust pipe to keep it from falling as you continue work at the muffler.
4. Detach the exhaust pipe to muffler clamp. Separate the pipe and muffler.
5. Lower the exhaust pipe to the ground.
6. Detach the tailpipe-to-muffler clamp or resonator-to-muffler pipe clamp at the muffler. Separate pipe and muffler.
7. Support the pipe to keep it from falling as you continue working.
8. Remove the muffler from its hanger assembly by loosening the bolt. Lower the muffler to the ground.
9. If the vehicle has a detachable resonator, loosen the tailpipe-to-resonator clamp at the rear of the resonator.
10. Lower the resonator and the muffler-to-resonator pipe assembly to the ground.
11. Detach the tailpipe from its hanger strap. Lower the tailpipe to the ground.
12. Examine the muffler and tailpipe hangers for damage and deterioration. Replace if necessary.
13. Begin replacement by positioning the exhaust pipe and supporting it to keep it from being damaged.
14. Attach the exhaust pipe to the exhaust manifold. Engage bolts loosely.
15. Connect the exhaust pipe to the muffler. Secure the muffler to its hanger assembly. Engage bolts loosely.
16. Place the clamp around the exhaust pipe-muffler joint and engage nuts loosely.

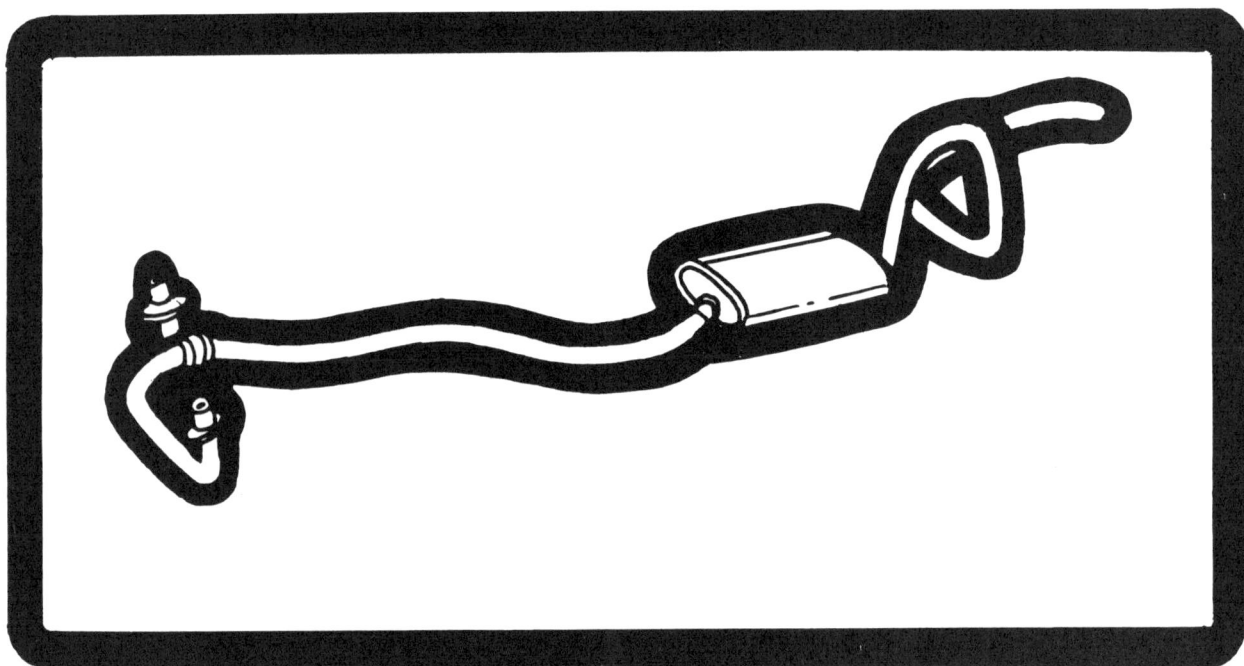

Typical General Motors 8-cylinder engine single exhaust system without resonator. Found mostly on sedans.

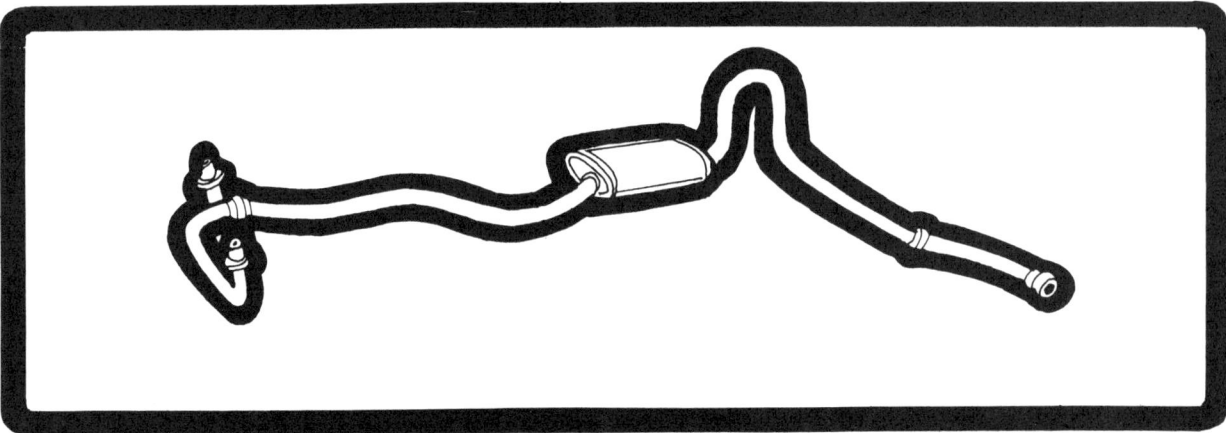

Typical General Motors 8-cylinder engine single exhaust system without resonator as used on station wagon models. Note the extended tailpipe.

17. If the system is equipped with a resonator, position the resonator and resonator-to-muffler pipe assembly. Support the pipe to keep it from being damaged.
18. Connect the resonator-to-muffler pipe to the muffler. Clamp the joint. Engage nuts loosely.
19. Connect the tailpipe to the resonator and clamp the joint. Engage nuts loosely.
20. Attach the tailpipe to its hanger. Engage the bolt loosely.
21. If the system does not have a resonator, connect tailpipe to the muffler. Clamp loosely. Attach the tailpipe to its hanger. Engage the bolt loosely.
22. See that the exhaust system is properly aligned so there is no stress on any part.
23. Tighten fasteners securely or to specification as follows:
    (a) Exhaust pipe-to-exhaust manifold nuts: 18 ft. lbs.
    (b) Exhaust pipe-to-muffler clamp: 15 ft. lbs.
    (c) Tailpipe-to-resonator-to-muffler pipe clamp: 15 ft. lbs.
    (d) Muffler hanger bolt: 10 ft. lbs.
    (e) Tailpipe-to-resonator clamp: 15 ft. lbs.
    (f) Tailpipe hanger bolt: 10 ft. lbs.
24. Lower the car to the ground.

Models with 8-cylinder engines

General Motors cars having 8-cylinder engines employ either a single or a dual exhaust system. The arrangement of the two systems is the same except for these differences:

1. The dual exhaust system is really two identical single exhaust systems. Each has an exhaust pipe, muffler and tailpipe. One system serves the cylinders on the engine's left side. The other system serves the cylinders on the engine's right side.

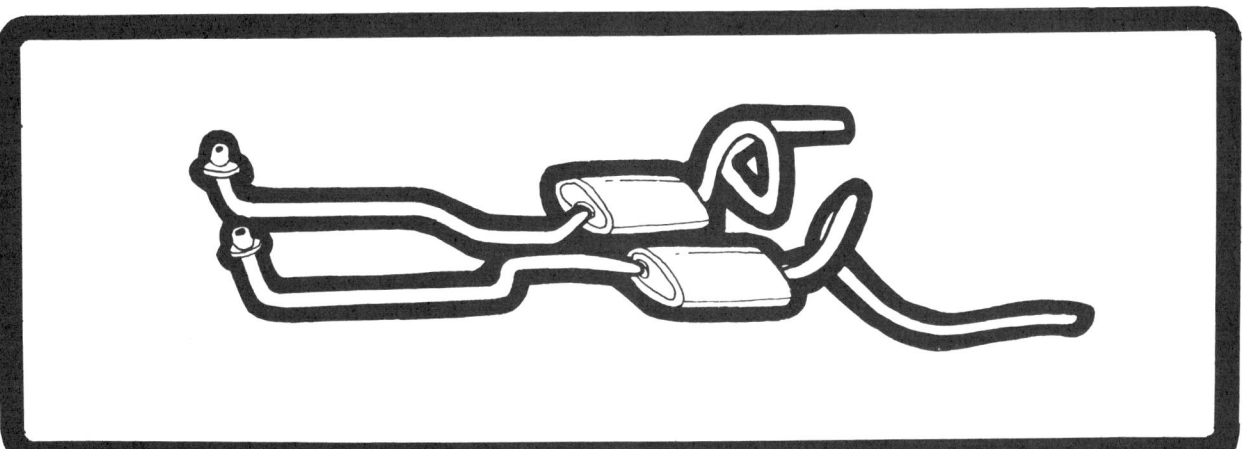

General Motors 8-cylinder engine with dual exhaust and no resonators.

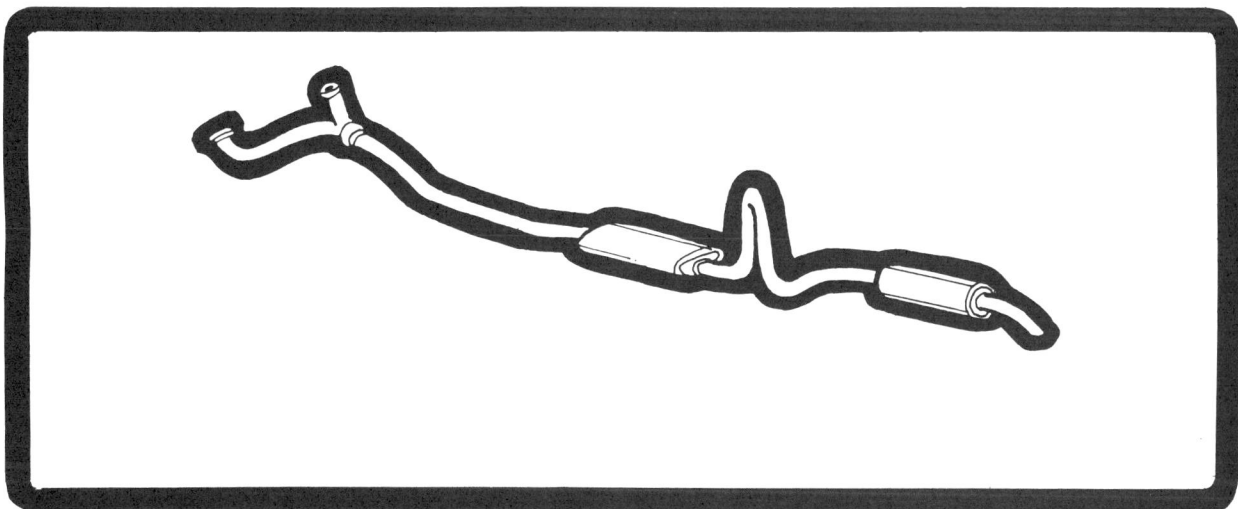

General Motors 8-cylinder engine with single exhaust and resonator.

321

2. Other than the way in which the exhaust pipes connect to the exhaust manifold, the two individual systems of a dual exhaust system and the single system of a single exhaust system are virtually identical.
3. The exhaust pipe of the single exhaust system has two branches. One connecting to the exhaust manifold on the engine's right side, and the other connecting to the exhaust manifold on the engine's left side.

IMPORTANT: The exact procedure is used to replace an exhaust system (whether single or dual) in a GM car with an 8-cylinder engine as is used to replace the exhaust system in a GM car with a 6-cylinder engine with the following differences:

1. If the car has a single exhaust system, disconnect the left branch of the exhaust pipe from the left exhaust manifold and the right branch of the exhaust pipe from the right exhaust manifold.
2. If the car has a dual exhaust system, disconnect the exhaust pipe from either the left or right side exhaust manifold, depending upon which of the two systems you are replacing.

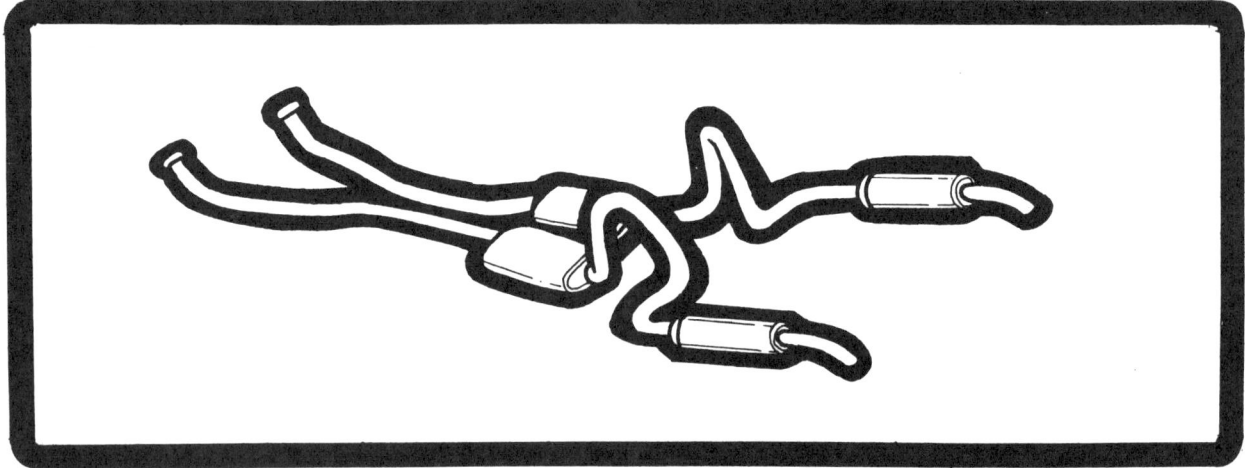

General Motors 8-cylinder engine with dual exhaust and resonators.

SERVICING CATALYTIC CONVERTERS

The major domestic automobile manufacturers have turned to the catalytic converter in 1975 in order to comply with HC and CO federal emissions standards. The 1975 acceptable standards of hydrocarbons (HC) and carbon monoxide (CO) emissions have been cut by 50% from their respective 1974 levels. California has been subjected to a 65% cut in these increasingly stringent standards.

HC and CO result from unburned or partially burned molecules of gasoline and motor oil. There were two possible methods available to automakers by which the federal standards for 1975 could be met. One solution could have been modifications upstream in the combustion chambers and the other was by downstream devices designed to function after the combustion process was completed. Catalytic converters were designed to suit the latter situation.

For 1975, General Motors has incorporated catalytic converters throughout their model line. Chrysler and FoMoCo have elected to meet federal standards by way of a combined application of converters on 75% of their domestic products along with a more balanced utilization of pre-1975 emissions controls.

Description

The purpose of the catalyst is twofold. First, it is able to make a chemical reaction proceed at a quicker rate, and second, although it enters into the chemical reaction, it emerges unchanged. It is able to repeat the same process over and over. Emission control catalysts are being produced either in the form of pellets or as a unitized monolithic structure. Contained in a muffler-like chamber added to the exhaust system, a suitable catalyst will change HC and CO pollutants into harmless water vapor and carbon dioxide.

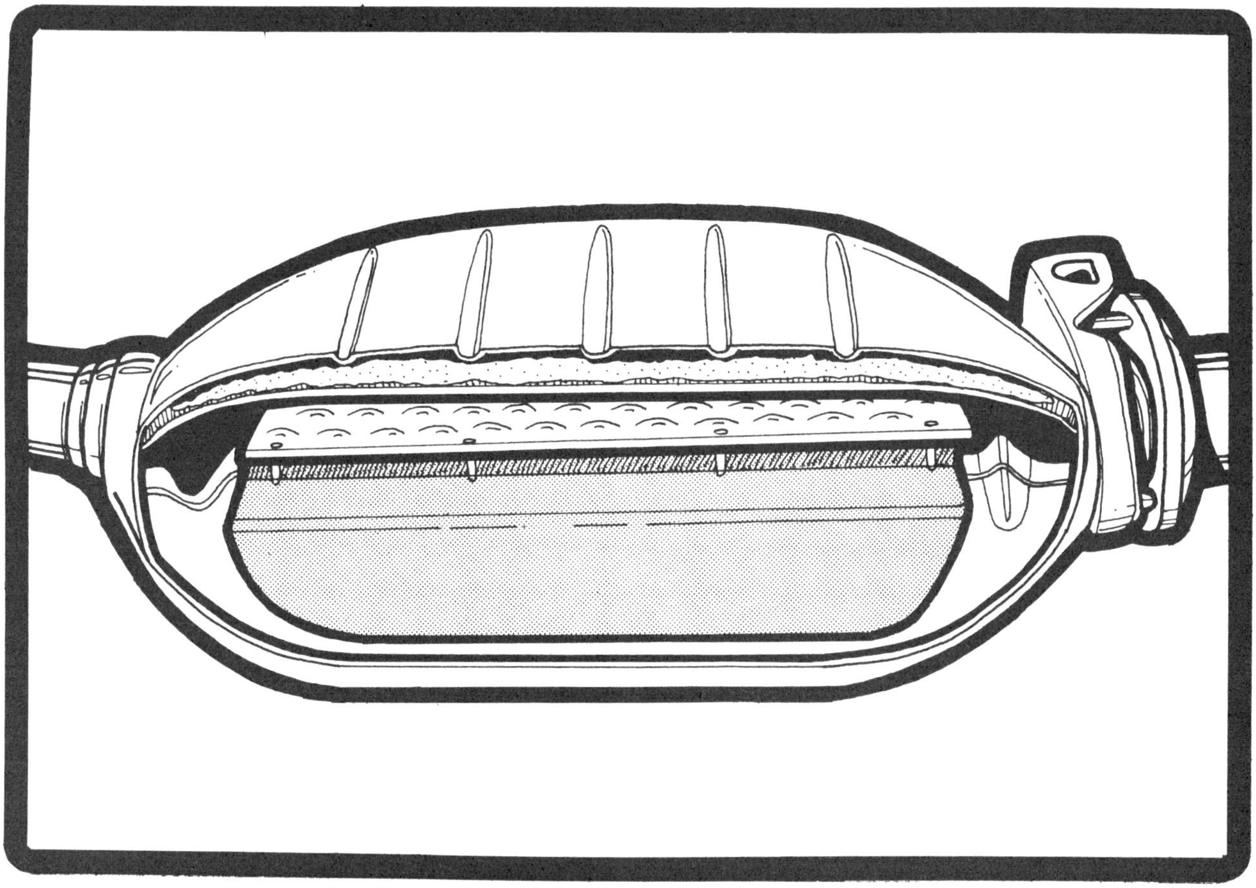

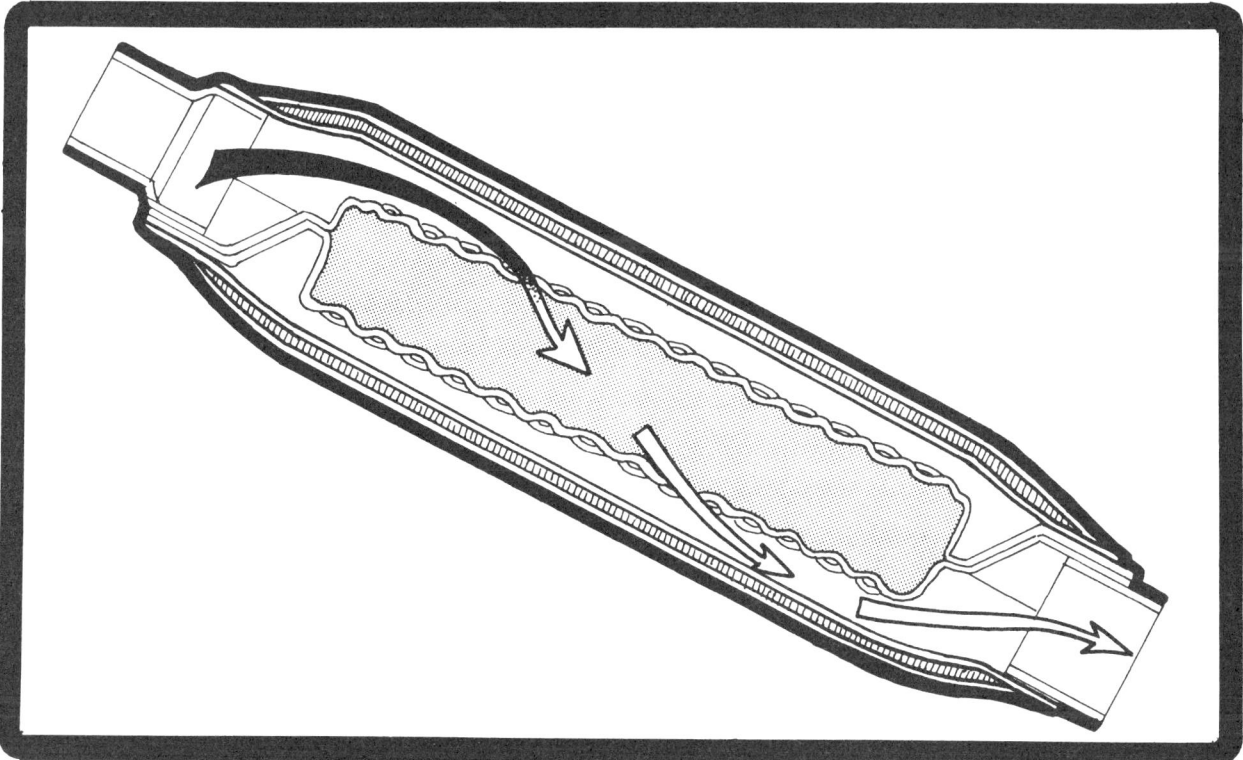

Cutaway of GM catalytic converter. Catalyst material is coated onto pellets which exhaust gases pass through.

As exhaust gases pass through the converter, hydrocarbons and carbon monoxide are converted to water vapor and carbon dioxide.

The catalyst itself consists of a relatively porous substrate of an inert material—alumina—in pellet or monolith form on which small amounts of catalytically active material are deposited. Few chemical elements have the type of chemical activity required of a proper catalytic agent. Two of the popular elements in use are noble metals—platinum and palladium. Resulting production catalysts have a relatively large surface area exposed to the exhaust stream.

Noble metal catalysts require the use of lead-free gasoline. Leaded fuel will coat the catalytic surface, rendering it ineffective.

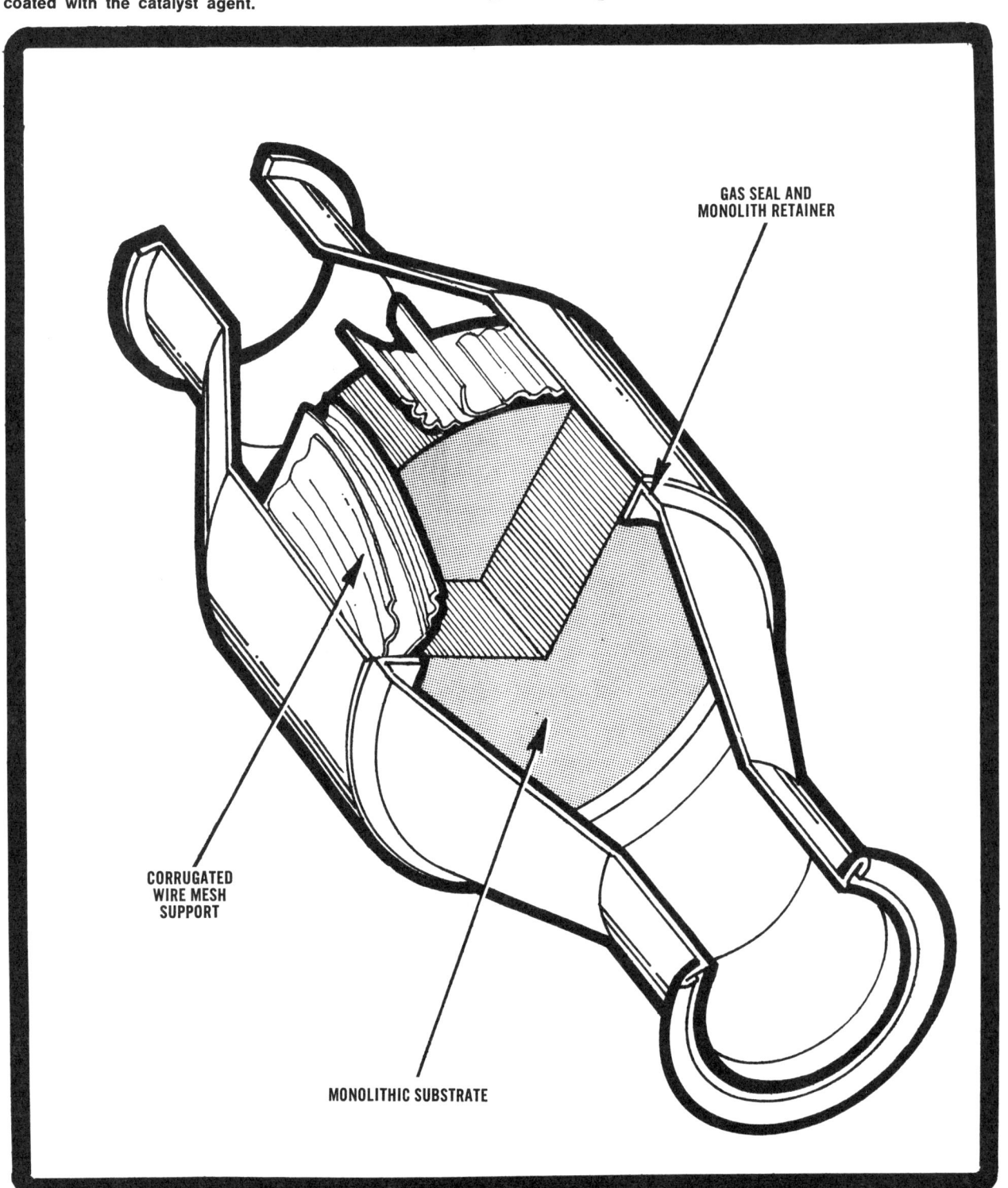

Ford Motor Company catalytic converter cutaway. This converter uses a monolith which is coated with the catalyst agent.

- GAS SEAL AND MONOLITH RETAINER
- CORRUGATED WIRE MESH SUPPORT
- MONOLITHIC SUBSTRATE

Cutaway of Chrysler Corporation catalytic converter. Again, monolith is coated with catalyst agent.

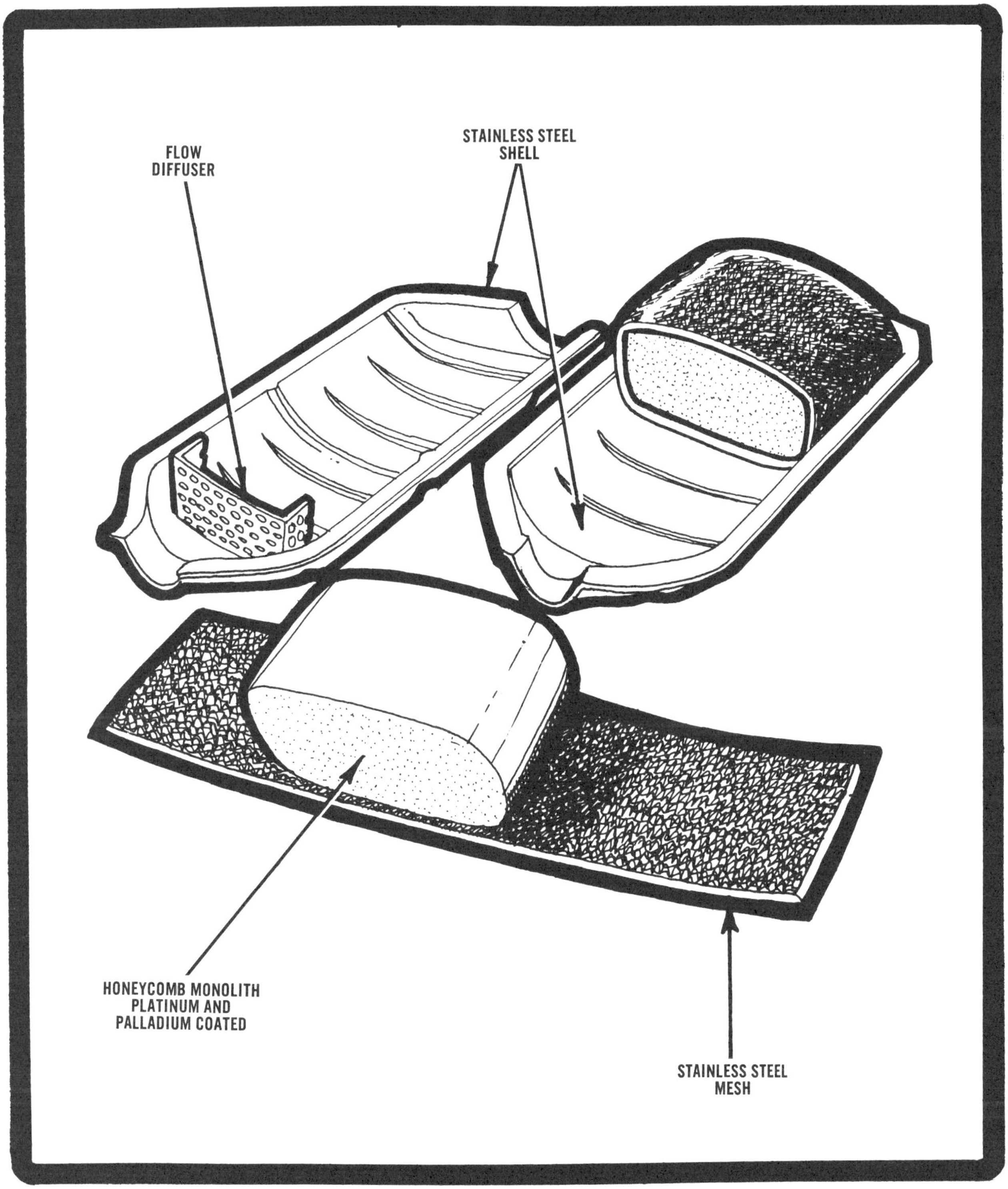

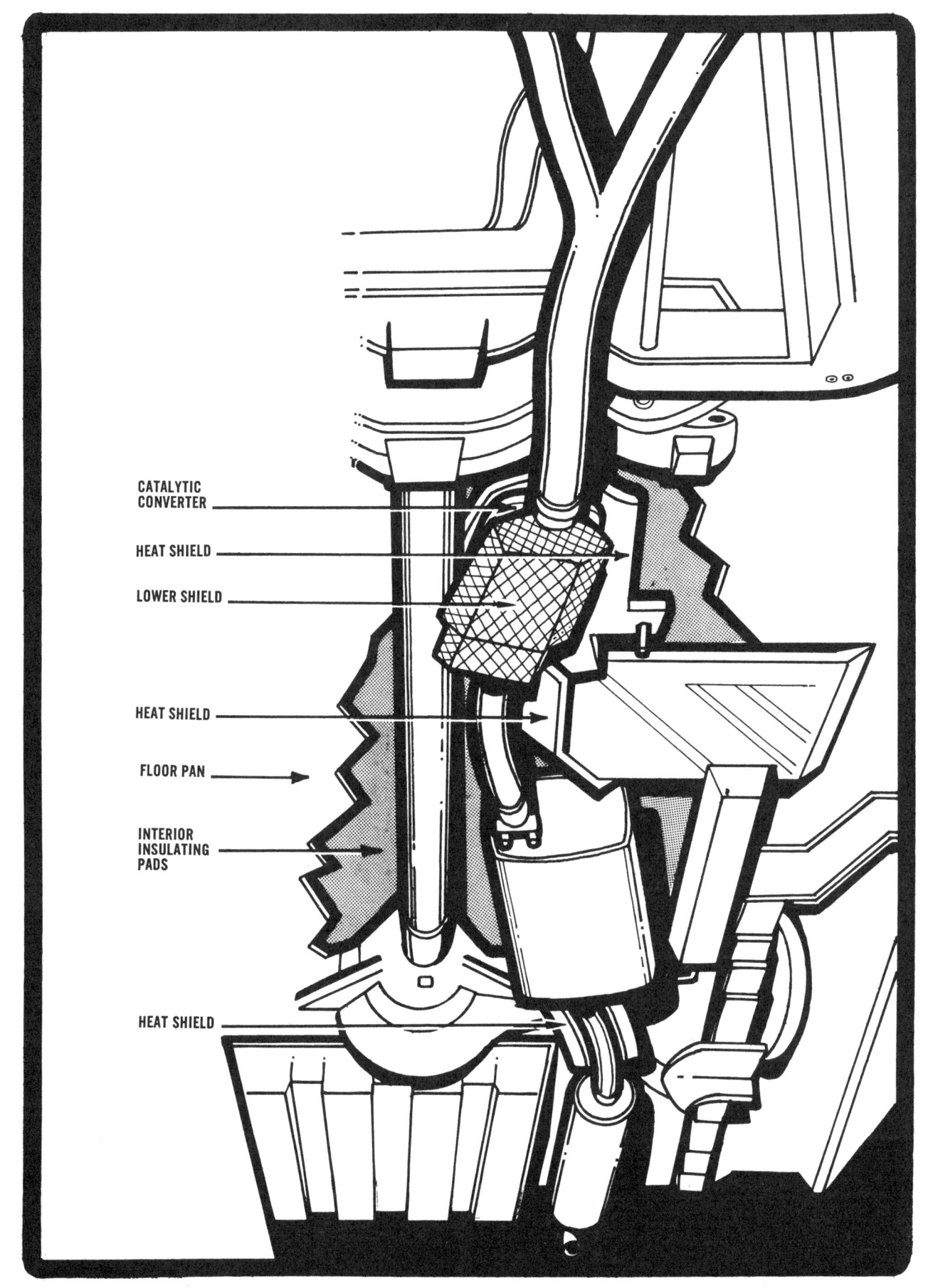

Illustration shows the heat shields which are installed on every Chrysler Corporation car using a catalytic converter.

To prevent inadvertent use of leaded fuels, 1975 model cars have a smaller diameter fuel tank filler neck opening. Federal regulations require most gasoline stations to provide unleaded fuels through pump nozzles of coordinated design. All major gasoline stations offer lead-free gas for 1975 models. The use of leaded gas in an emergency situation will not have any lasting effects on the converter. But there will be a temporary rise in emission levels. Catalyst durability is warranted by the manufacturer for 50,000 miles.

The catalyst must be hot to do its job. Normal operating range is 900° to 1500° F, with peak temperatures in the 1800° range. Because of the close proximity of these high temperatures to the passenger compartment, insulation of the pellets or the monolith is critical. Substantial heat shielding is necessary to prevent abnormal heating of the car's interior. Grass shields are incorporated in order to shield the converter from undergrowth. Systems are also incorporated which protect the converter from backfire and from sub-freezing temperatures.

Catalytic converters are installed in the exhaust system upstream from the muffler as close as possible to the exhaust manifold.

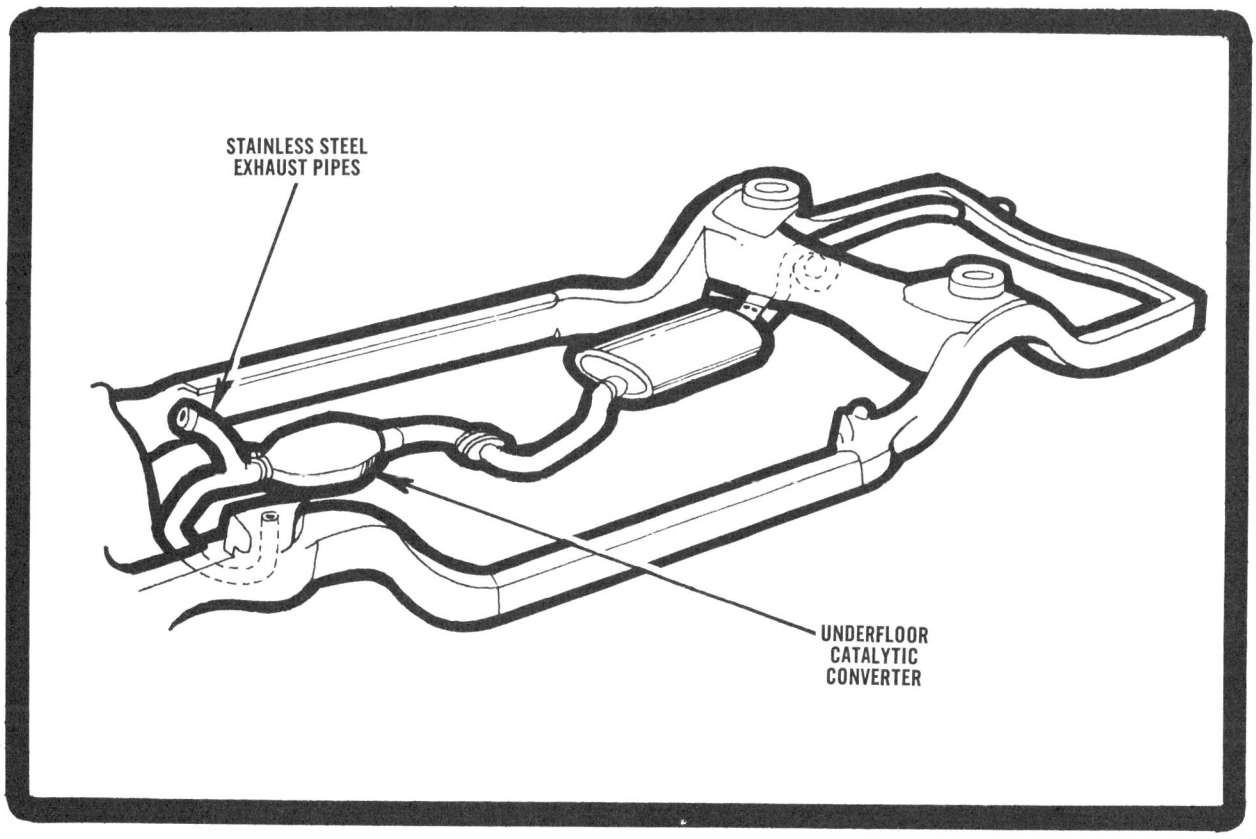

TROUBLESHOOTING FLOW CHART

EXHAUST SYSTEM

Symptom	Probable Cause	Remedy
A. Leaking exhaust.	1. Leaks at pipe joints.	1. Reseal joints with exhaust system sealer. Tighten clamp bolts securely. If leaks persist, replace pipes.
	2. Rusted out pipes.	2. Replace.
	3. Damaged gasket at exhaust pipe-exhaust manifold joint.	3. Replace.
	4. Rusted out muffler.	4. Replace.
B. Exhaust noise.	5. Blown out muffler or exhaust pipe.	5. Replace damaged part.
	6. Leak at exhaust pipe-exhaust manifold connection.	6. Replace damaged gasket and/or tighten loose bolts.
	7. Exhaust manifold cracked.	7. Replace.
	8. Leak between exhaust manifold and cylinder head.	8. Tighten manifold to cylinder head stud nuts or bolts to specification.
C. Engine hard to warm up or will not return to normal idle.	9. Heat control valve is frozen.	9. Most cars have this valve which can be serviced by finding the valve's counterweight beneath the exhaust manifold. If there is no counterweight, there is no valve. Free the valve by applying liberal quantities of manifold heat control valve solvent to the counterweight. If the valve does not free itself, replace the valve.

Servicing

The catalytic converters that are used in Chrysler and Ford vehicles are not serviceable. After determining that the catalyst has lost its effectiveness, the complete catalytic converter asembly must be replaced. This operation is similar to replacing a muffler.

The converters used on General Motors and American Motors vehicles are serviceable. A special tool is used to remove a large drain plug after a vacuum is created within the converter. A special vibrator will help to drain the unit of pellets. Once emptied, the container can be refilled with recommended replacement catalyst pellets in a similar vacuum-assisted manner.

Illustration shows how exhaust gases pass through catalyst before exiting through the rest of the exhaust system.

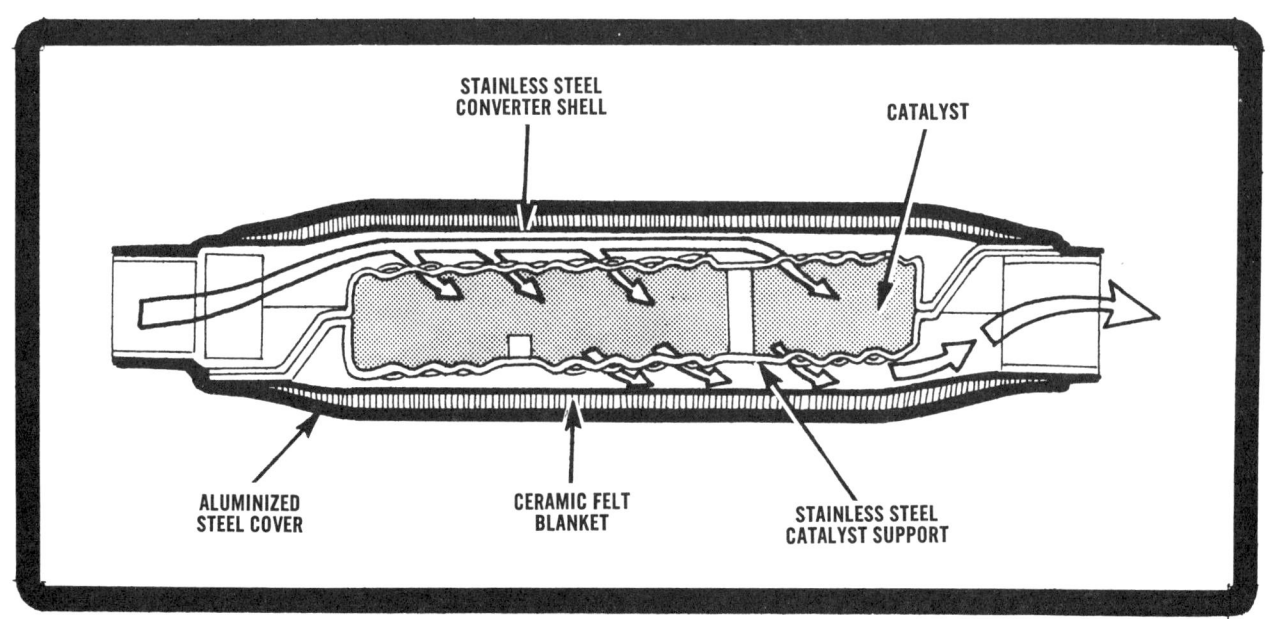

Lubrication Guide

There are many things you can do to increase your car's longevity and maintain its performance. But proper lubrication on schedule is the most important of them. You may think of lubrication as just an engine oil change every now and then. There is much more to it. It involves selecting the right kinds of lubricants and filters, and knowing where, when and how to use them. If you did nothing else on your car but lubricate it properly, you would reduce your repair costs significantly.

WHAT AND WHEN TO LUBRICATE

The parts of the car that may require periodic lubrication are: drivetrain (engine, transmission, driveshaft and rear axle), front suspension; steering, parking brake, clutch and transmission linkages; front wheel bearings, distributor cam and body hinges.

At one time, cars required lubrication of most of these components every 1000 miles or even less. Today, the typical lubrication intervals are much greater, ranging from 4000 miles or three months for an oil change up to 36,000 miles for chassis lubrication, and a few previously lubricated parts have lubed-for-life designs.

The lengthening of lubrication intervals does not mean that lubrication is less important, only that the improvements in lubricants have increased their useful life.

Whatever the interval recommended by the car manufacturer (as explained in your owner's manual), it is important to understand that the recommendations are based on so-called "normal operating conditions." The car makers' ideas of normal are a fairyland, in which temperatures are always above freezing but never very hot, traffic is always light, the roads are very good, and the motorist always makes a trip long enough to permit the engine to warm up fully. The average motorist encounters winter cold and summer heat, rain, snow and traffic jams, and may use the car for frequent short trips to the supermarket, train or bus station. He may even pull a trailer on a summer vacation trip. As for smooth roads, forget it.

The latter setup is what car makers consider to be severe operating conditions, and for which they often specify (in fine print) that more frequent service is necessary. If actual recommendations are made, they often are for service to be performed at intervals about half as long as for normal conditions.

Another factor to remember: as your car ages, it needs more frequent service. The engine that might be tolerant of an oil and filter change at 6000-mile intervals when it is young, may need it at 4000-mile intervals after 50,000 to 60,000 miles, because engine wear permits greater leakage of exhaust gases and other combustion products into the crankcase, diluting the oil. The ball joint seals that held in the grease very well when the car was new also age, and so chassis lubrication at shorter intervals is advisable.

It would take laboratory testing on the individual car to determine the ideal service intervals at every stage of a car's life. As a general rule, however, once a car is four years or older, the following intervals represent a good maintenance approach. Please note that the mileage figures are based on 1000 miles per month of driving. If you drive less, the service should be performed on a time basis equivalent. That is, 12,000 miles or 12 months, whichever comes first, 7500 miles or seven to eight months, whichever comes first, etc.

ENGINE OIL AND FILTER: change every 4000 miles. If car has been run exclusively on lead-free gas, every 6000 miles. Note: Volkswagen Beetle has no oil filter. Engine oil, therefore, should be changed every 2500 miles.

CHASSIS LUBRICATION: every 6000 miles. Also lubricate moving parts without fittings.

TRANSMISSION OIL AND FILTER: change oil and replace filter (or clean strainer) every 24,000 miles, every 12,000 if the car occasionally pulls a trailer, every 6000 if it normally pulls a trailer. Note: oil change intervals also apply to manual transmissions. But there is no filter to replace.

FRONT WHEEL BEARINGS: lube and adjust every 12,000 miles. Also lubricate body hinges.

REAR AXLE OIL: change every 36,000 miles, every 24,000 if the car occasionally pulls a trailer, every 12,000 if the car normally pulls a trailer.

ENGINE OIL MAINTENANCE

Engine oil never wears out as such. However, it loses its ability to lubricate properly because it becomes contaminated with airborne dirt, metal particles from engine wear, and byproducts of the combustion process that leak past even healthy piston rings into the crankcase.

Some of the combustion byproducts combine with oil to form the tar-like deposit called sludge. The lead in ordinary gasoline is one of the contributors to sludge, so the car that runs on lead-free gasoline produces less sludge. Because this results in less contamination of the engine oil, the drain intervals on cars using lead-free gas can be extended somewhat.

CHOOSING THE RIGHT OIL

Buying engine oil, whether for oil changes or just topping up when the dipstick reads a quart low, is not a straightforward proposition. There are many brands, grades and quality levels from which to choose.

The oil industry has a trade association, the American Petroleum Institute, but although API and the car manufacturers provide test procedures and standards, there is no industry policing of what an oil refiner puts in his car or on the label. A refiner could recommend an inadequate product for use in a late-model car.

The reputable refiners do not do this. Your best guarantee is the refiner's reputation. In addition to the brands marketed by major oil companies, primarily through their service stations, there are many smaller refiners of high-quality products, such as Castrol, Kendall, MacMillan, Quaker State, Pennzoil, Wolf's Head and Valvoline. There also are oils marketed by reputable department store chains under their own name, and if a chain has a large automotive department, you can trust the oil. Additionally, there are independent regional refiners with good reputations.

You should avoid discount price off-brands, even if their names sound very close to those of the name brands, even if they are sold in large stores.

Quality levels

Just because an oil carries a well-known brand name, however, does not mean it is suitable for your car. The biggest refiners, including the international oil companies, market less expensive oils for certain light duty uses. Price competition being what it is, these oils often make their way into outlets selling to the public.

The oil can should have service classification letters printed somewhere on the container. Here is what the letters are and what they mean.

For Service SE. This is the highest classification for passenger cars and the oil is recommended by the refiner for all cars built since 1972, and some 1971 cars that were particularly demanding on oil (and as a result the car maker specified SE). An SE oil also passes all requirements for lower grade oils, so the can may contain all the lower markings in addition to the SE. Compared with the lower grades, it has greater protection against oil oxidation (a contaminating effect), corrosion and high temperature deposits (an important factor on emission-controlled engines, which run much hotter than those without controls).

For Service SD. This is the second highest classification, and it refers to an oil designed for 1968-70 and many 1971 models. An SD oil also passes all requirements for lower grades, so the can may contain all the lower markings in addition to the SD. Compared with the lower grades, it provides more protection against high and low temperature engine deposits, wear, rust and corrosion.

For Service SC. Previously called MS, it is the oil that was introduced for 1964-67 cars, and it was the first of the really high quality oils. An SC oil also passes all requirements for lower grades, so the can may contain all the lower markings in addition to the SC. Oils designed for this service contain additives for some control of high and low temperature deposits, rust and corrosion, and have some anti-wear (high-oiliness) additives.

For Service SB. Previously called ML-MM, this a minimum quality oil, the kind you may see in 2- to 5-gallon containers. It has additives to retard bearing corrosion, oil oxidation and scuffing of parts. This type of oil was introduced in the 1930s and really was adequate only for cars built through the 1950s.

For Service SA. This is the lowest classification, and it carries no performance standards. There is no automobile for which it is suitable.

Just because several oils have the same service classification, this does not mean they are exactly the same. There are performance requirements for each classification (except SA). But reputable refiners exceed the minimums by a comfortable margin, and the greater the margin, the better the protection your engine gets and the longer is the useful life of the oil.

Viscosity

The thickness of an oil (actually how easily it flows) is called its viscosity. It is also referred to as its weight. The standard procedure, set up by the Society of Automotive Engineers, is to number oils according to thickness. The higher the number, the thicker or heavier the oil. All numbers are preceded by the letters SAE (for the society that sponsors the standards). If a number is followed by the letter W, the thickness was measured at 0°F. If no letter follows, it was made at 210°F.

Oil normally thins out as it is heated. But it is possible, by use of additives or because of natural qualities in some oils, to retard the thinning out. Therefore, an oil with a viscosity of 10 at 0°F (therefore, a 10W oil) might also be able to pass the thickness test for a 30, 40, or even 50 or 60 weight oil at 210°F. An oil with this characteristic is called a multi-viscosity oil and may carry a designation of 10W-30, 10W-40, etc.

This is a highly desirable characteristic. If the oil is relatively thin at low temperature, if will flow easily and provide good lubrication when the engine is first started. It also will be easier to pump, and therefore will reduce or eliminate starting and cold-running difficulties caused by an oil that is too thick to pump readily.

By remaining relatively thick as the engine warms up, the oil can continue to provide good lubrication when an ordinary 10 weight oil might be too thin.

There is only one disadvantage to the use of additives to provide these multi-viscosity characteristics. As the oil accumulates mileage, these additives are used up, and the oil loses some of this ability to provide the wide viscosity range performance. It is possible to restore this by pouring in a can of oil thickener, a product that is widely advertised under hundreds of brand names, after a few thousand miles. The typical oil thickener, however, jumps the viscosity by 20, and the 10W-40 can become something closer to a 30W-60, which might be entirely to much thickness for easy starting and good lubrication at low temperatures. It comes down to this. Without a lab test, you do not know what you have in the crankcase. So it is better to simply change to new oil rather than add an additive.

Single viscosity oils—5W, 10W, 20, 30, 40, 50, etc.—also are widely available. Typically, they do not change with mileage as quickly as multi-viscosity oils. In the summer, as SAE 30, 40 or 50 would not impede starting if ambient temperatures in your area are consistently above freezing. In winter, you probably could get by nicely with a 20 weight oil if the temperatures are not consistently around the zero mark or less. Although most refiners put their best into the multi-viscosity oil, many also make high quality (SE) single viscosity lubes too.

Picking an oil viscosity

Multi-viscosity oils cost more than single viscosity. But they can be used year round. Therefore you can standardize on one oil in most cases and buy it by the case—the cheapest way. Because the viscosity range (called the index) drops with mileage, a 10W-40 or greater range is a good starting point. If you change your oil very frequently, a 10W-30 is fine.

In very cold climates, that is, rarely above 60°F and consistently below zero in winter, a 5W-30 or 5W-40 is the best choice.

Where the temperature variations are too great for one oil, buy two grades. If, however, you garage the car, you probably can get by with the 10W-40 year round. Keeping the car indoors, even if the garage is unheated, will normally preclude starting difficulties caused by overly thick oil. Another possibility: if the temperatures are low during winter and the car is left outdoors, a coolant heater (an electric heater that plugs into a household outlet and keeps the coolant warm) can be installed. This not only will ease winter starting, but will enable you to turn on the car's passenger compartment heater immediately.

Top-up oil

If you occasionally have to buy a quart of oil for top-up at a service station, you need not add the same multi-viscosity oil. A single grade oil is less expensive, and although it does not have as much additive content as the multi-viscosity type, it also does not have to perform as long. The typical engine burns a quart of oil every 1500 to 2500 miles. So if you change every 4000, the quart of top-up oil only has to work for 1500 to 2500 more miles. If you tend to run the maximum possible mileage between oil changes, buy the multi-viscosity type. In any case, if your engine uses an SE oil, do not buy anything less.

Pennsylvania oils

Many oils from Pennsylvania are heavily promoted as superior for your car. There is some truth to the advertising claims. A Pennsylvania oil has a greater natural viscosity index. That is, it thins out less than other oils as it is heated. However, there are many additives that can be put into oil to increase the viscosity index. All quality oils, including Pennsylvania, use these additives and have a viscosity index higher than a Pennsylvania without additives. Additives in oil wear out and after a few thousand miles, the Pennsylvania oil may start to outperform other oils. Your car's operating conditions and oil drain intervals determine if this later-mileage advantage is significant. Most of America's cars run with non-Pennsylvania oil, so the issue is clearly not a critical one.

Reclaimed oils

Used crankcase oil that has been cleaned of foreign material is available at a bargain price. But it's no bargain for a late model car. The oil has none of the protective additives an oil needs, and its viscosity is anything but predictable.

Synthetic oils

There are some partly or wholly non-petroleum oils, called synthetics, currently on the market, including a few produced for automotive use. There is evidence that the best of them can last for a long time (30,000 miles) and provide a small increase in gas mileage (up to 0.5 mile per gallon). The better performance occurs because the quality of lubrication does not deteriorate as quickly with mileage as a conventional oil. However, supplies are small and at $3 to $5 a quart, compared with 50¢ to 70¢ per quart of petroleum based oil (when purchased in a case of 24 quarts), the synthetic oil probably does not pay, particularly if you change the oil yourself. There is an additional complicating factor with synthetic oil. The oil filter must be changed at 10,000 to 15,000 miles. When this is done, about a quart of that expensive oil is lost.

CAUTION: If you decide to buy a synthetic oil for the convenience of a long drain interval, be sure you are buying from a reputable refiner.

CHECKING OIL LEVEL

The engine oil should be kept at the FULL mark on the dipstick, although it is safe to wait until the level is at the ADD mark to pour in a quart. An engine should *not* be run a quart low, and old wive's tales that the engine runs best that way are wrong. If the engine ran best with a quart less oil, the car maker would mark the dipstick differently, put in a quart less oil and save millions of dollars a year.

The level should be checked only after the engine has been shut off for at least a few minutes. This allows oil in various parts of the engine enough time to

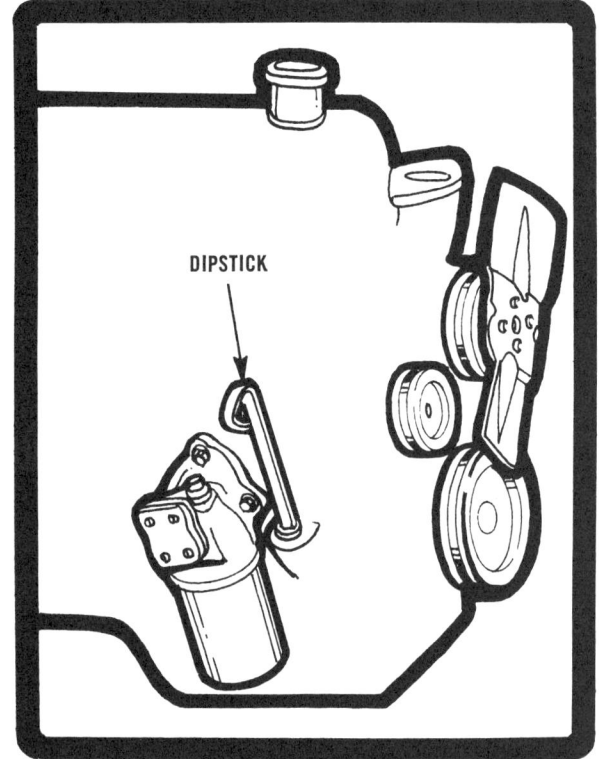

Fig. 1. Checking engine oil level.

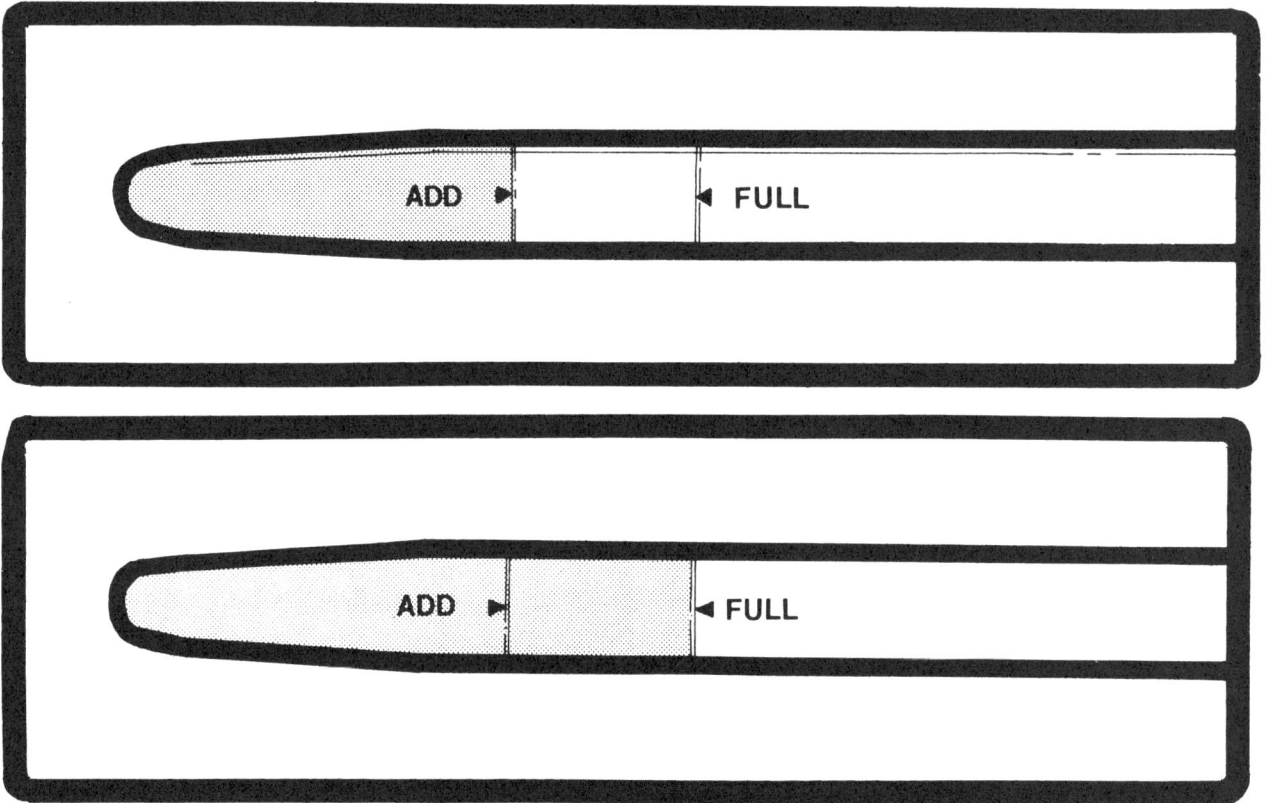

drain down to the crankcase. A true reading will be obtained. The car should be on reasonably level ground.

To check the oil, Fig. 1:

1. Locate the dipstick on the engine. It is usually on one side or the other, but sometimes near the front of the engine. The dipstick is a long metal rod the end of which is curled into a circle so you can insert a finger into the circle and pull it out of its tube.
2. Use a rag to wipe off all the oil on the dipstick.
3. Look at the end of the dipstick. You should be able to see markings such as ADD and FULL.
4. Insert the dipstick back into the tube. Make sure you push in the dipstick as far as it will go.
5. Now pull the dipstick straight out. Try not to rub the sides of the tube with the dipstick as you are pulling out.
6. Read the oil level by inspecting the end of the dipstick. If the oil level is at the ADD mark, you need a quart of oil. If it is on the FULL mark, your level is OK.

In some extreme instances, where the car has been run very low on oil, you may not get a reading at all. In this case, put in a quart and take another reading. Continue to check the dipstick and add until the oil level is at the FULL mark.

DRAINING THE OIL

The engine oil should be drained when it is hot. At this time it is a bit thinner, therefore flows more freely and carries more contaminants out with it. The oil should be drained into a pan of at least six quarts capacity.

1. Begin by locating the oil drain plug. If you have never seen someone do the job before, start by locating the engine. Then look underneath at the bottom of the engine, where you will see a sheet-metal pan hanging down from the engine block. This is the crankcase oil pan, the engine's oil reservoir. At a low point somewhere on the pan, you will see what appears to be the head of a bolt threaded into the pan, Fig. 2. The bottom location of the "bolt" and its seeming "in the middle of nowhere" position will confirm that it is the oil drain plug.

Most oil drain plugs are hex-head. So you can use a box, open end or socket wrench to remove it, Fig. 3. The socket and ratchet is the beginner's best choice because you just set the ratchet in the unthread position and when you get underneath you will not have to wonder which way to turn to loosen the plug. If you have an open end or box wrench and become disoriented underneath, remember that when lying on your back, the shank of the wrench should move from your left leg to your right one.

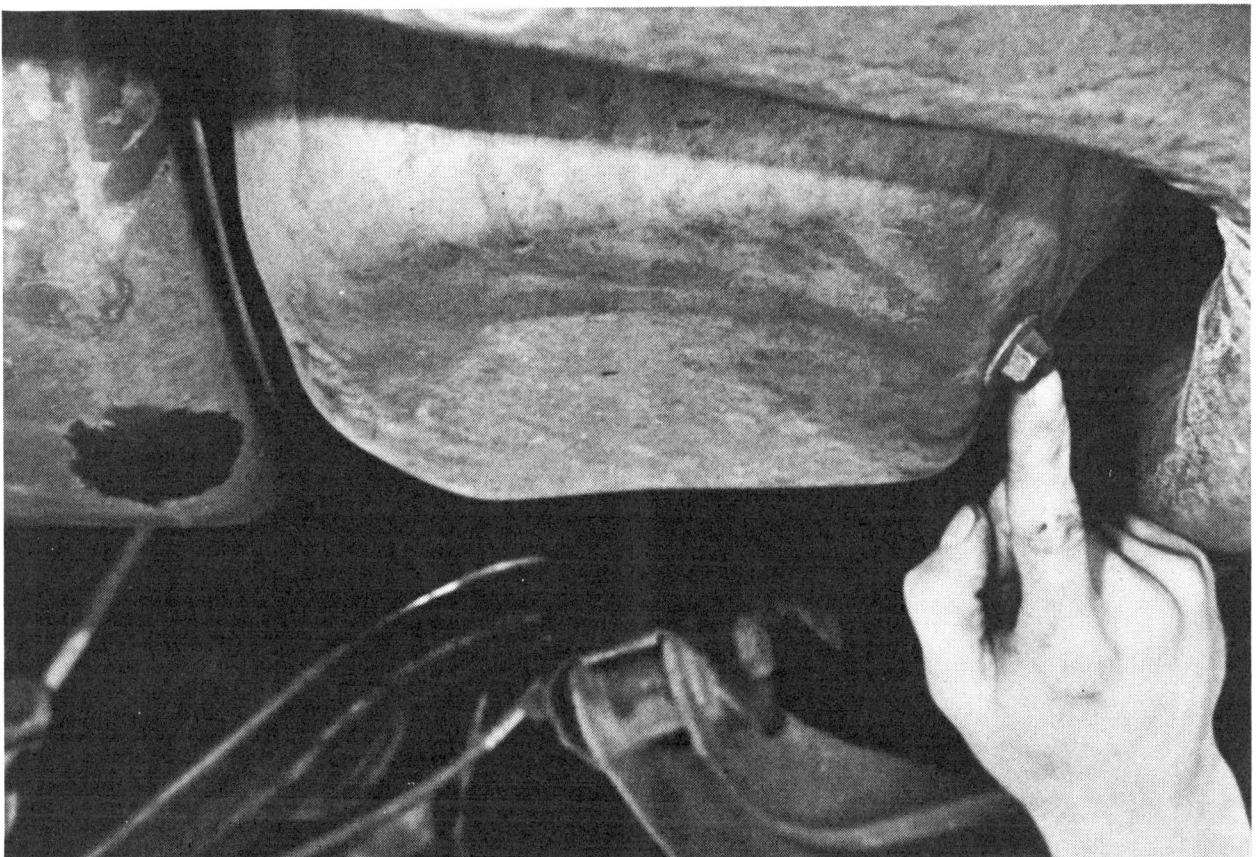

Fig. 2. Locating the engine oil drain plug.

2. If the plug is very tight, whack the free end of the wrench with a hammer to shock it loose.
3. Once the plug breaks loose, stop turning.
4. Move out of the way and slip the drain pan underneath. Then continue to loosen the plug until it can be turned with the fingers.
5. Remove the wrench and continue to loosen the plug with your fingers but hold it in. When the plug is completely unthreaded (but held in the hole by your hand), pull it away very quickly. If you do not, dirty oil will pour out of the hole and run down your arm.
6. Allow several minutes for the oil to drain out.
7. Then carefully rethread the plug back in by hand.

NOTE: If the plug had a washer, be sure to re-use it. Do not apply force to turn the plug. It should thread back in easily. If it does not, you have not caught the threads right and if you apply force with a wrench you will cross the threads, ruining them. Once the plug is finger tight, put the wrench back on again and tighten the plug some more. Do not apply a great deal of muscle or you may strip out the threads, which also will ruin them.

You can tell if you have overtightened and stripped the threads by the fact that the plug will change from a feeling of tight to one of vaguely loose, and no reasonable amount of additional tightening will make the plug tight again.

In this case, do not leave the plug in or the oil will leak out. Remove the plug and install a synthetic rubber oil drain plug, which does not require threads to seal. The rubber plug is sold in an inexpensive kit in many auto parts stores.

If you are going to change the oil filter, this should be done next. Otherwise, be sure to refill the engine with oil. Then start the engine and check the drain plug for leaks. Do not be alarmed if the oil light comes on when the engine is started. It may take a minute or so for oil pressure to be restored through the system and the light to go off.

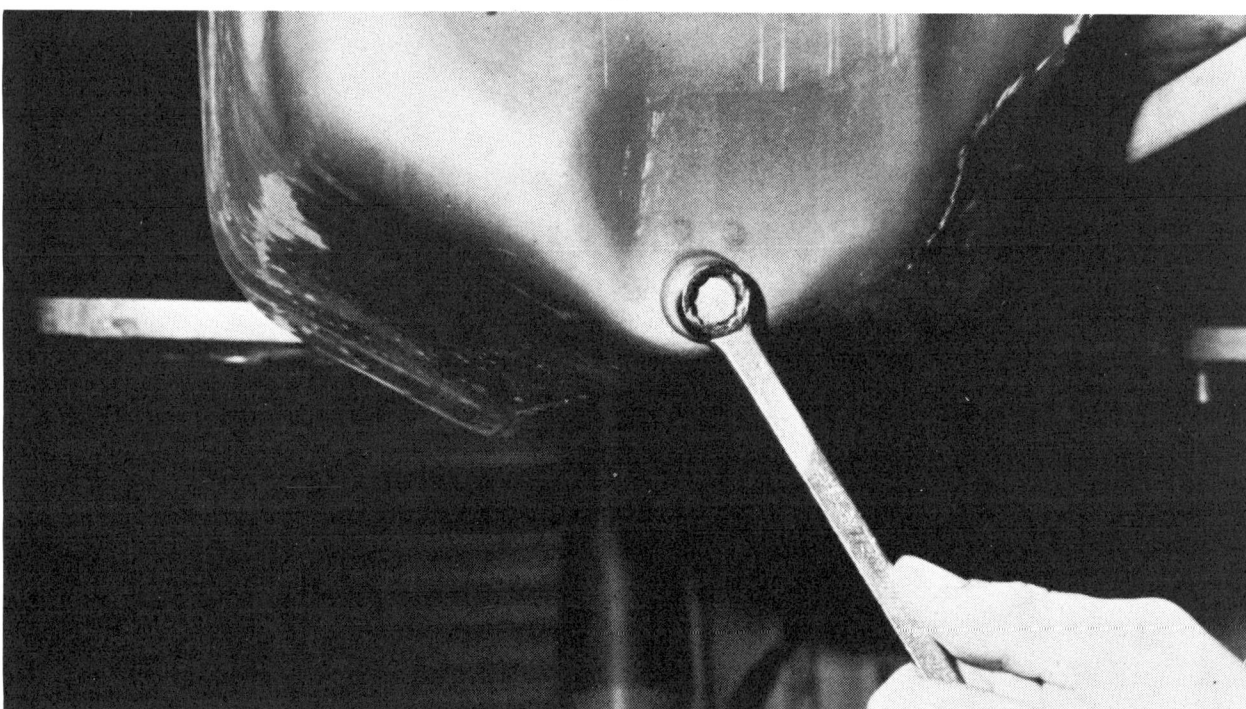

Fig. 3. If drain plug is typical, it has a hex head and can be loosened with box wrench (as shown) or open-end, in addition to ratchet and socket.

CHOOSING AN OIL FILTER

When you buy an oil filter, as with engine oil, you are making a blind purchase, for two reasons: 1) You cannot see inside very well. 2) Even if you cut the filter apart for a good look, you probably would not be able to tell what quality filter you had. The reputation of the manufacturer or marketer is your only guide. If the filter is a private brand sold in a discount chain, you should be wary. For as is the case with engine oil, small automotive departments have limited expertise and often make decisions based primarily on price. Even if the filter is actually made by one of the leading manufacturers, it need not be the top quality model.

Here are key differences between a top filter and an off-brand, so even though you cannot tell the difference, you can justify in your mind the extra cost of a name brand:

1. If the filter is pleated paper, as most are, the paper in a topline filter is a much more expensive grade. It will stop finer dirt particles with greater consistency.
2. The pressure relief valve will work according to car maker's specifications. The relief valve is the part that opens when the filter is clogged or when the oil is too thick to flow through the filter (as in cold weather). The valve prevents the engine parts from starving for oil. With off-brand filters, the valve may open at much lower pressure. In this case, oil that should be going through the filter is permitted to bypass it, despite the fact that the filter isn't clogged. Or the relief valve may be too strong, and the engine will starve for oil. See Fig. 4.
3. The filtering element's end seals may be weak, in which case dirty oil can leak past them, by-passing the filter element completely. High quality filters are end-sealed with a hard setting plastic. Cheap filters use glued cardboard.

Double filters

Some manufacturers feature double filters, sort of a filter in a filter. One of the filters is coarse, the other fine. The theory is that if you extend oil and filter change intervals, and the fine filter clogs, the coarse filter still will be able to provide some protection. The theory is fine but the practice is questionable. What happens is that much of the oil flows through the coarse filter and some harmful dirt that would have been caught by a fine filter can get through. A single filter of high quality is your best buy and best protection, and it usually costs less than the double filter.

Fig. 4. Pen points to spring-loaded relief valve in a pleated paper filter that has been cut apart. Valve spring must meet car manufacturer's precise specifications for the filter to operate properly.

Non-paper filters

Not all oil filters are made of the popular pleated paper (which really is a heat-cured, resin-impregnated cellulose). Some are packed wood shavings and cotton fibers, others are wound cotton, still others are pleated felt. The paper filter, when made as a topline by a leading manufacturer, is the most consistent performer. There is a new entry which is selling a filter with a disc of oil additive inside. The additive disc is supposed to replenish the additives in engine oil as they are used up in service. The product is too new for an evaluation at this time.

Toilet paper

The toilet paper filter, actually an adaptor that permits you to use a roll of toilet paper as a filter, should be avoided, despite some extravagant claims for it. The adaptor converts the engine's full-flow filtering system, in which all the oil passes through the filter before going to engine parts, into a partial flow, in which only a fraction of the oil goes through the roll of toilet paper. This adaptor, therefore, constitutes a violation of most car maker's warranties. It cannot be justified on a cost basis because of the relatively high price of the adaptor. And despite its fans, there is evidence it can be harmful.

CHANGING THE OIL FILTER

When you buy a new oil filter for you car, open the box, see what it looks like, and you will be able to find the old one on your engine. The typical oil filter is on the side of the engine (left or right), somewhere threaded onto the engine block. On some cars you will have to look underneath to see it, but it will be there somewhere.

The modern oil filter is a spin-on canister .This means that you just unthread the old canister, throw it away and thread the new one on. The job requires an oil filter wrench, and there are many designs, Figs. 5 through 8.

The strap type is the most popular, but you must be sure to get one that will fit your car's filter. Some strap wrenches are too small for certain filters. Others are too large and will not tighten properly around the canister. If you have a set of chain-type vise pliers, you have a universal filter wrench, Fig. 9. But it is not as easy to use as a wrench made for the purpose.

The replacement of an oil filter is customarily done with an oil change, for these reasons:

1. An oil filter that is doing its job is supposed to clog up, and that occurs in almost the same amount of time it takes for the oil to require draining. The typical filter probably has some remaining life, but how much is problematical.
2. Up to a quart of oil is trapped in the filter. So if you want to start out with a full charge of clean oil, you also must replace the filter.
3. The job usually requires working from underneath, and with an oil drain pan. When you're doing an oil change, the car already is jacked up and the oil drain pan is underneath.

CAUTION: Be sure to observe all safety precautions and use proper safety stands when working under you car.

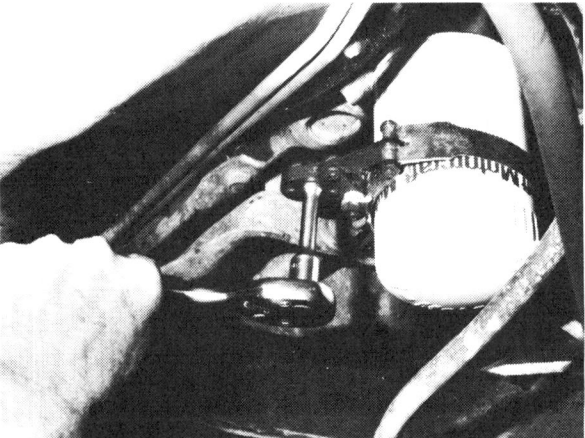

Fig. 5. Filter is being loosened with a strap-type filter wrench that is used with ratchet and extension as shown. This design fits into close quarters very well.

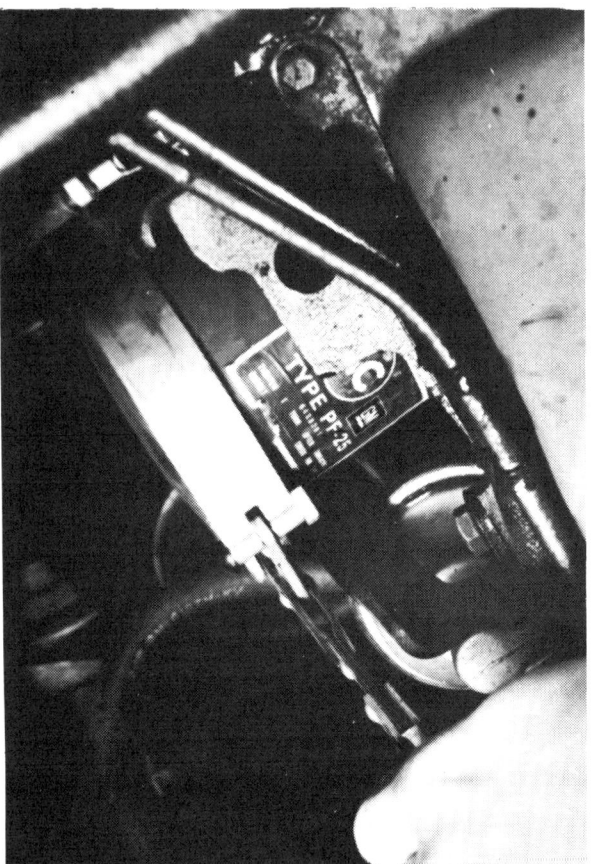

Fig. 6. Strap-type filter wrench shown in this photograph has a built-in handle, so it requires proper positioning to allow room to swing handle.

Fig. 7. This filter wrench tightens coil-leaf spring around filter canister, so it handles many sizes very well. Open-end, box or ratchet wrench is used with it.

Fig. 8. This type of wrench is like a pair of pliers.

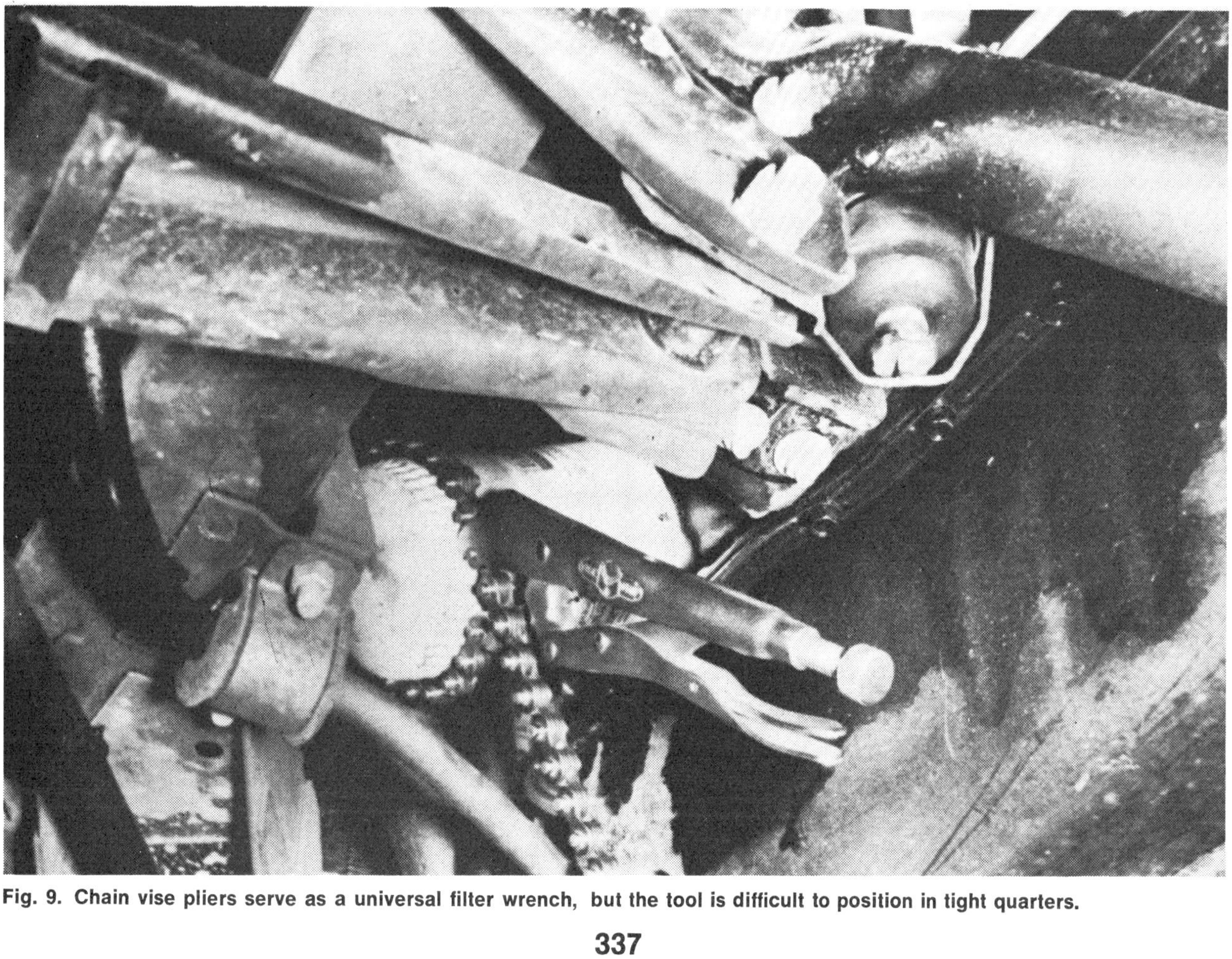

Fig. 9. Chain vise pliers serve as a universal filter wrench, but the tool is difficult to position in tight quarters.

Procedure

The replacement procedure for all spin-on oil filters is as follows:

1. Position the wrench around the filter canister. If the strap-type with a built-in handle is used, be sure that the handle is located so that when it is moved and the strap is tightened, there still is room to swing the handle a couple of inches more in the counterclockwise direction, so the filter can be loosened.
2. Turn the wrench counterclockwise to loosen the filter. If the filter is extremely tight and will not budge, and you have the strap wrench or chain vise pliers, move the band or chain closer to the engine side of the filter. The closer the strap is to the engine, the easier it will be to loosen. **Note:** if the filter still will not loosen, remove the wrench, drive a large chisel through the canister near the base and shock the filter loose with hammer blows on the chisel. The filter will be destroyed and will leak so keep a pan and rag handy. But it was headed for the garbage bag anyway.
3. Once the filter is loose, remove the wrench and complete the removal by hand. A drain pan should be placed underneath the filter, for some oil will leak out of the engine and filter.
4. Clean any dirt particles from the filter's gasket surface on the engine. Also clean the male threads onto which the filter spins.
5. Coat the rubber gasket of the new filter with a film of clean engine oil. Also oil the filter's female threads.
6. Thread the filter onto the engine and hand tighten only, Fig. 10. If there is any oil on the filter canister or your hands, you may not be able to adequately tighten the filter. So clean off before tightening. You may tighten as much as you can by hand. Just make sure you do not apply so much muscle that you crush the filter canister. Do not use the filter wrench to tighten the filter.
7. Check engine oil level, adding oil to bring it up to the FULL mark. Start the engine and check for leaks.

Fig. 10. After lubing male and female threads, and filter rubber gasket with engine oil, start filter back by hand, then hand tighten only.

CHASSIS LUBRICATION

In the mid-1960s, it seemed that the chassis lubrication job was going to be eliminated. Intervals of more than 30,000 miles were common and in a few cases, lifetime lubrication was achieved. The pressure on the car makers to make their cars safer, however, brought the return of the grease job. The last holdout, Cadillac, installed grease fittings with the start of 1975 production.

FINDING THE FITTINGS

The first time you do a grease job you will spend much of the time looking for the fittings. Fig. 17, a chart, tells you how many fittings the car has and in what basic area they are located. But you will have to do the actual finding. Fig. 18 shows the typical front end locations on General Motors cars, Fig. 19 on Ford products, to give you the idea.

As you find a fitting, wipe it off with a clean rag. This will help you spot it later and also prevent you from injecting dirt with the grease.

INJECTING THE GREASE

The injection tip of the grease gun should be a catch fit on the fitting nipple. That is, once in place it will not slip off. Slight, straight-on pressure is all that is necessary for the gun tip to engage the fitting. Once that is done, pump the handle. On older cars (mid-1960s and before), it was a matter of watching the rubber grease seal on whatever the fitting was threaded. When the old grease came out, you stopped pumping. Today's tighter seals may require somewhat more careful injection to prevent them from being damaged. Here are current recommendations:

AMERICAN MOTORS AND FORD: Pump slowly until the rubber boot can be felt or seen to swell slightly.

CHRYSLER CORP. AND GENERAL MOTORS: Pump slowly until grease starts to flow from bleed holes at the base of the seals, or until the seals start to swell.

FITTING FAILS TO TAKE GREASE

If the fitting fails to take grease, the lubricant will ooze out between fitting and the tip of the gun. Do not just keep pumping, hoping some grease is getting in, or you will have a mess. It is normal for a bit of grease to seep out. But if the fitting is obviously not taking grease, it should be replaced. It is possible you could free up a frozen fitting by pushing in on the spring-loaded ball in the nipple, but the likelihood of restoring the fitting to normal function is almost non-existent.

Fig. 17. Use this chart to determine how many grease fittings your car has and generally where to find them.

CAR	BALL JOINTS	STEERING LINKAGE	UNIVERSAL JOINT	CLUTCH CROSS SHAFT
All Ford products	4	4	0	0
All Chrysler products	4	5	0	0
All American Motors	4	2	0	0
Buick	4	7	1(a)	0
Oldsmobile exc. Toronado	4	7	1(a)	1(b)(d)
Olds Toronado	4	4	0	0
Pontiac	4	7	1(a)	1(b)(d)
1975-on Cadillac exc. Eldorado	4	7	1(a)	0
1975-on Cadillac Eldorado	4	5	0	0
Chevrolet	4	7	1(a)	1(c)(d)
Volkswagen	2	2	0	0

Notes:

a: Flush fitting on rear (constant velocity) universal joint on full-size models except wagons.

b: Fitting or plug, used on all compacts and subcompacts, some intermediates. Replace plug with fitting.

c: Plug. Replace with fitting.

d: At 30,000 mile intervals, sooner only to eliminate binding in linkage.

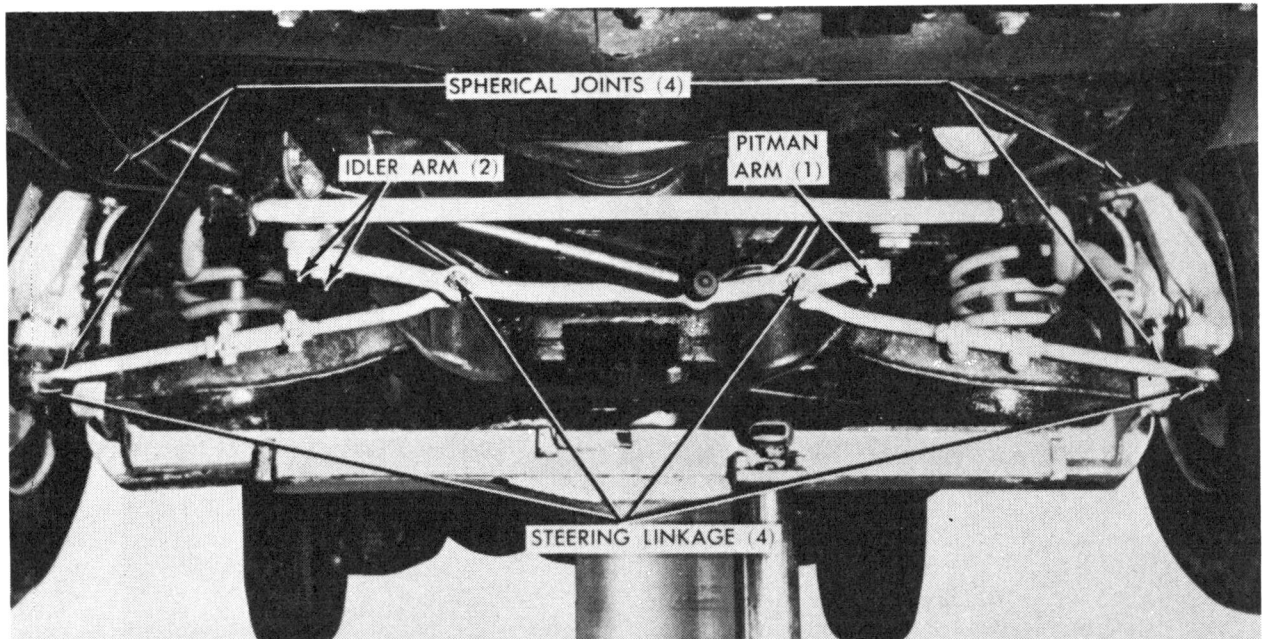

Fig. 18. Typical General Motors front end, with locations of grease fittings indicated by arrows.

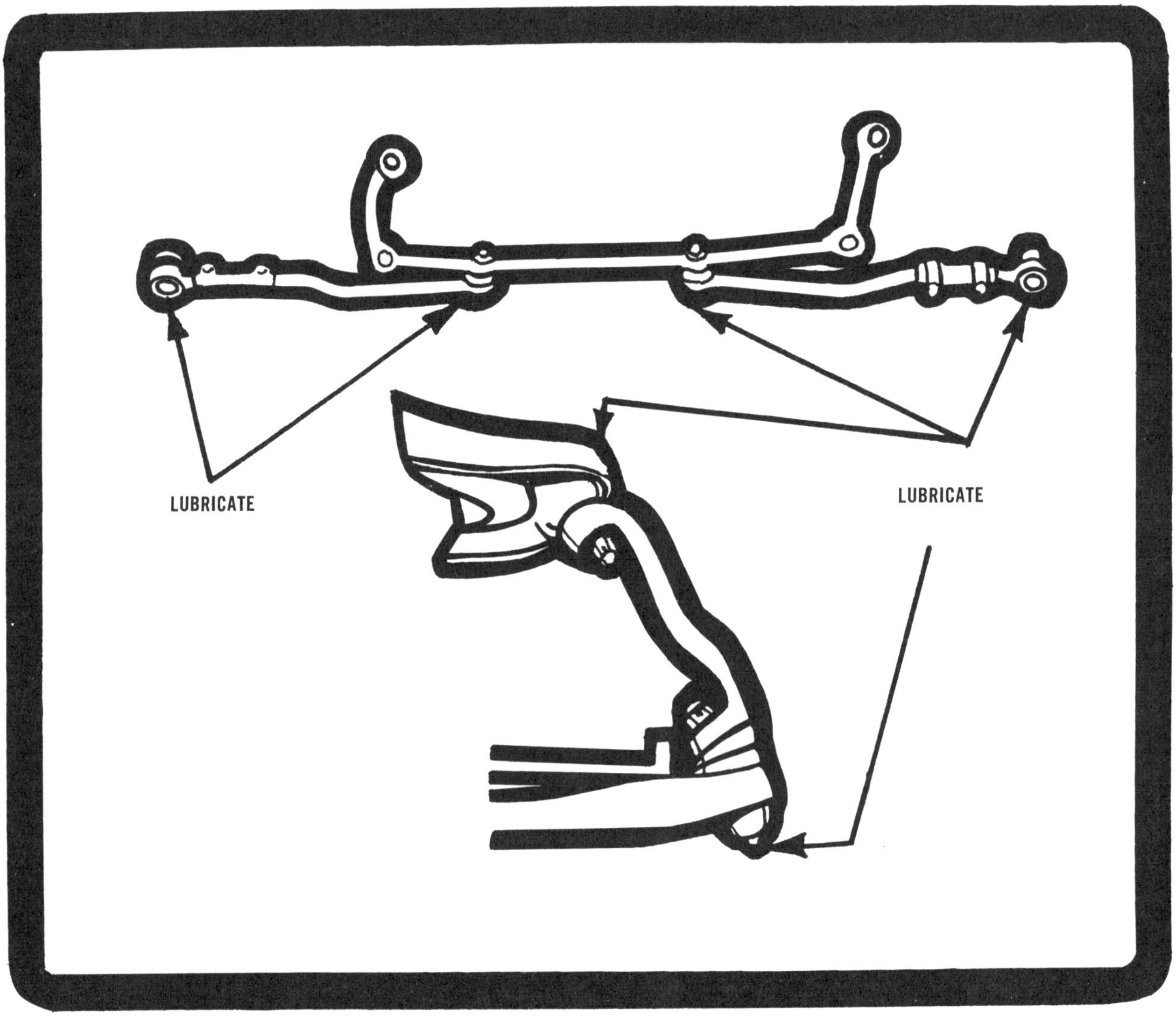

Fig. 19. Typical Ford product front end, showing locations of grease fittings on ball joints and steering linkage.

TOOLS AND EQUIPMENT FOR LUBE SERVICE

CHASSIS LUBRICATION

To lubricate the chassis of your car, you need the following:

• A squeeze-handle type cartridge grease gun, Fig. 11. This is the tool that injects grease through the fitting into the part to be lubricated. Most grease guns come with steel injection tubes and unfortunately, most fittings are in locations that cannot be reached with the solid steel tube. Therefore, be sure to obtain a flexible line, Fig. 12. A squeeze-handle gun and the flexible line should be rated at 4500 pounds per square inch or more to properly inject.

You could buy an air-operated grease gun with a bulk grease canister. But you would need an air compressor to operate it. Or you could obtain a bulk grease canister with a squeeze handle gun. But it is much more expensive than the cartridge type and is an unnecessary space-taker in your garage. The typical cartridge is very inexpensive and contains enough grease for three to four jobs.

• The grease. There are several grades of chassis grease available in cartridges. But what is sold in your area will determine your purchase. If it is possible to obtain a moly grease (a grease with a 3-10% concentration of a lubricating compound called molybdenum disulphide), this should be your choice. It will provide the most effective

Fig. 11. Squeeze-handle type cartridge grease gun with steel injection tube. Grease is being applied to a lower ball joint fitting.

long term lubrication. If you can, obtain a grease cartridge carrying the brand name of a leading refiner.

NOTE: Moly grease is required for all cars with long chassis lubrication intervals (25,000 and up). If you use a standard grease, a 6000-mile interval is maximum.

NOTE: If temperatures in your area are consistently below freezing during any season, the grease used should be labeled water resistant.

• Grease fittings. Not all cars have grease fittings, Fig. 13. If your car is a Ford or American Motors product, or pre-'75 Cadillac, it may have plugs instead, Fig. 14. There are special grease guns that can inject without a fitting, but as a novice mechanic, your best bet is to use the standard gun, remove the plugs and install grease fittings. The fittings are so inexpensive that the practical approach is to buy one for each plug, install the fittings as a permanent item and discard the plugs. This will make the next grease job a lot faster than if you try to move one fitting from plug hole to plug hole.

NOTE: On many Ford products the plugs are located in areas where the clearances are too tight for use of a conventional grease fitting, Fig. 15. In this case, obtain right angle grease fittings, Fig. 16, which still are a close fit but can be tightened into a position that permits the use of a standard grease gun.

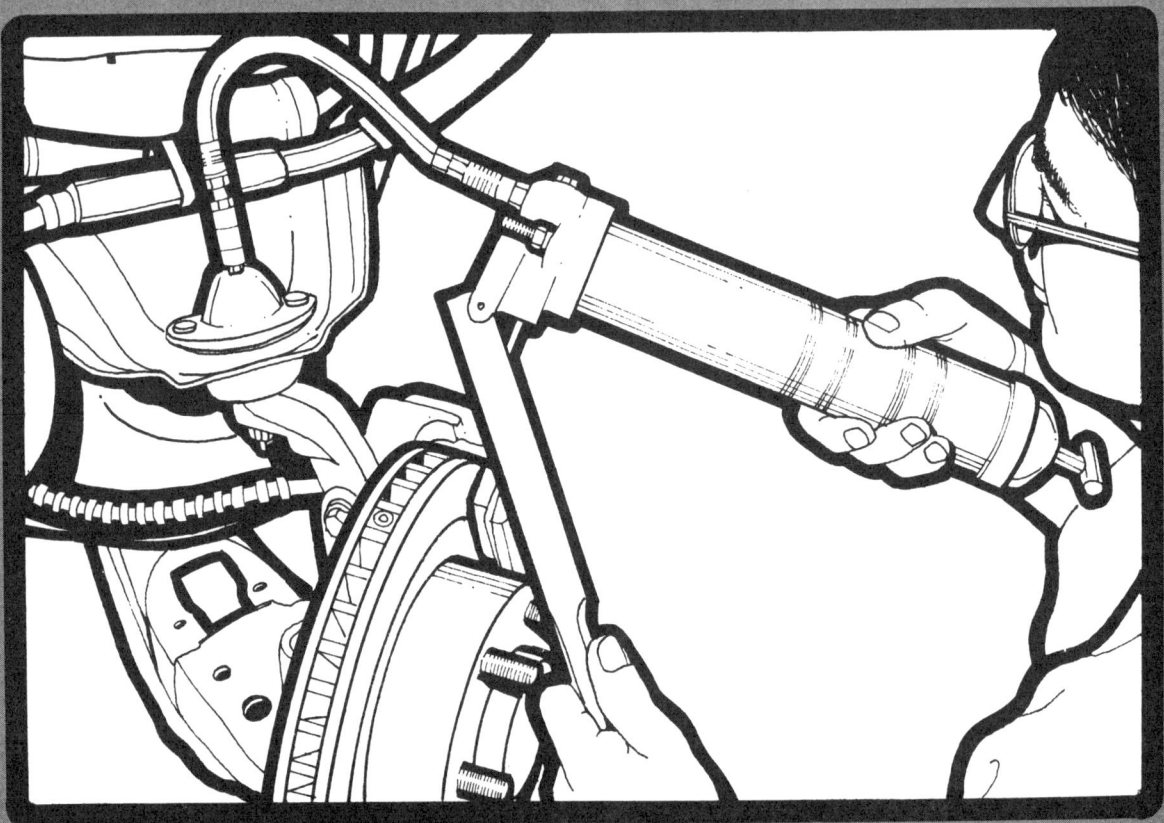

Fig. 12. Flexible injection tube is required for most fittings, even when most of car body is cut away, as in this photograph.

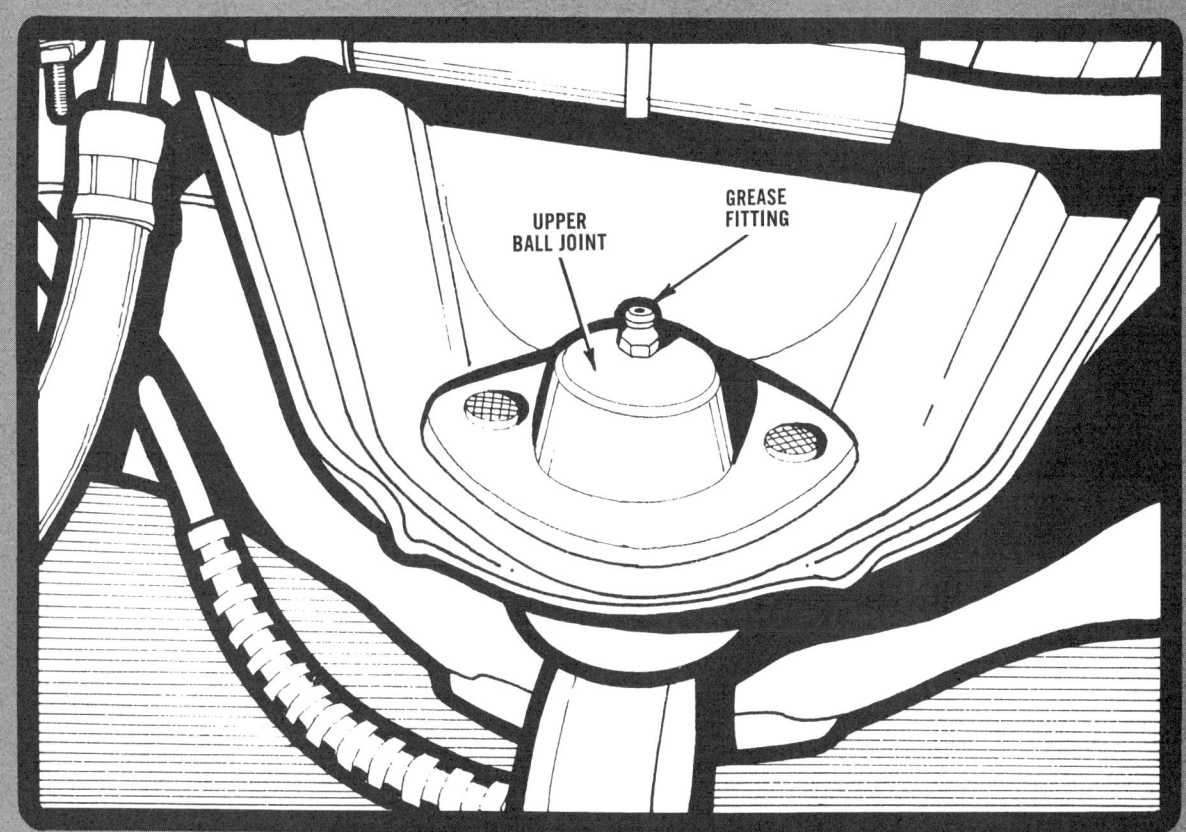

Fig. 13. This is an upper ball joint with a grease fitting. Specially shaped nipple end catches tip of injection tube of grease gun.

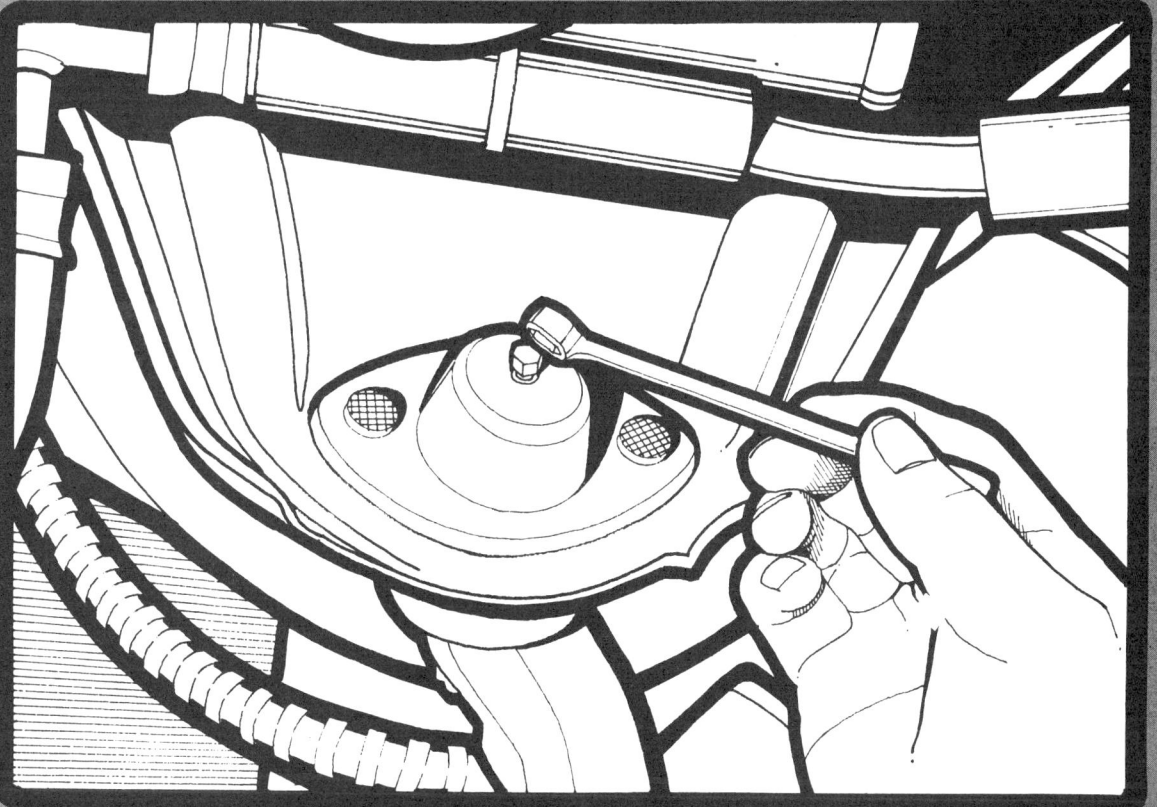

Fig. 14. If plug is used instead of fitting, remove plug with wrench and install fitting.

Fig. 15. This part of Ford steering linkage is too close to crossmember for a standard fitting and grease gun, so remove lug with wrench as shown.

Fig. 16. Then install a right angle grease fitting, which is being tightened with wrench so the nipple is aimed straight down, permitting you to get a grease gun on it.

UNIVERSAL JOINTS

All universal joints on late model cars are lubed-for-life with the exception of the constant-velocity U-joint on most full-size General Motors cars. The constant-velocity joint is the rear one, and it has a grease fitting that is flush with the surface into which it is threaded. Therefore, a conventional grease gun tip cannot be used. Obtain a special pencil-point shaped tip (available from large automotive parts jobbers), which threads into a standard grease gun tube. Apply chassis grease to the fitting until you see seepage from the U-joint itself. This should be done as part of every chassis lubrication, Fig. 20.

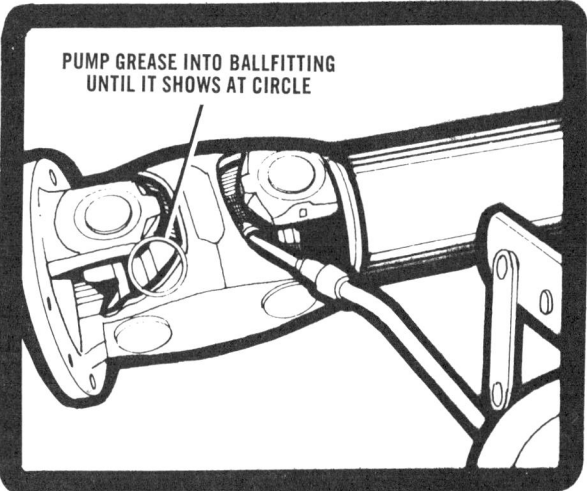

Fig. 20. Using tapered-tip tube adaptor to grease constant velocity universal joint on General Motors full-size cars.

JOINTS WITHOUT FITTINGS OR PLUGS

In addition to the joints that have fittings or plugs, service the following with a smear of chassis grease:

American Motors
- Pivot points of the shift linkage on manual or automatic transmission.
- Steering stop plate.
- Clutch release idler lever (disassemble and pack with grease).

Chrysler Corp.
- Pivot points of the shift linkage at the transmission (manual or automatic).
- Clutch linkage pivot points, Fig. 21.
- Gearshift control mechanism. It is at the bottom of the steering column on column-shift cars. On floor-mounted shift cars, remove bezel that holds the rubber boot to the floor and pull the boot up on the lever to expose the shift mechanism. Use a grease gun or putty knife to pack all sliding and pivoting surfaces, Figs. 22 and 23.
- Parking brake linkage pivot points. See Figs. 24, 25 and 26.

Ford Motor Co.
- Steering stop pad surfaces, Fig. 27.
- Parking brake cable guides, levers and linkage.
- Clutch linkage (lever and rod connections), Figs. 28 and 29.
- Manual or automatic transmission linkage, Figs. 30, 31 and 32.
- Kickdown linkage pivot points (from gas pedal linkage to automatic transmission).

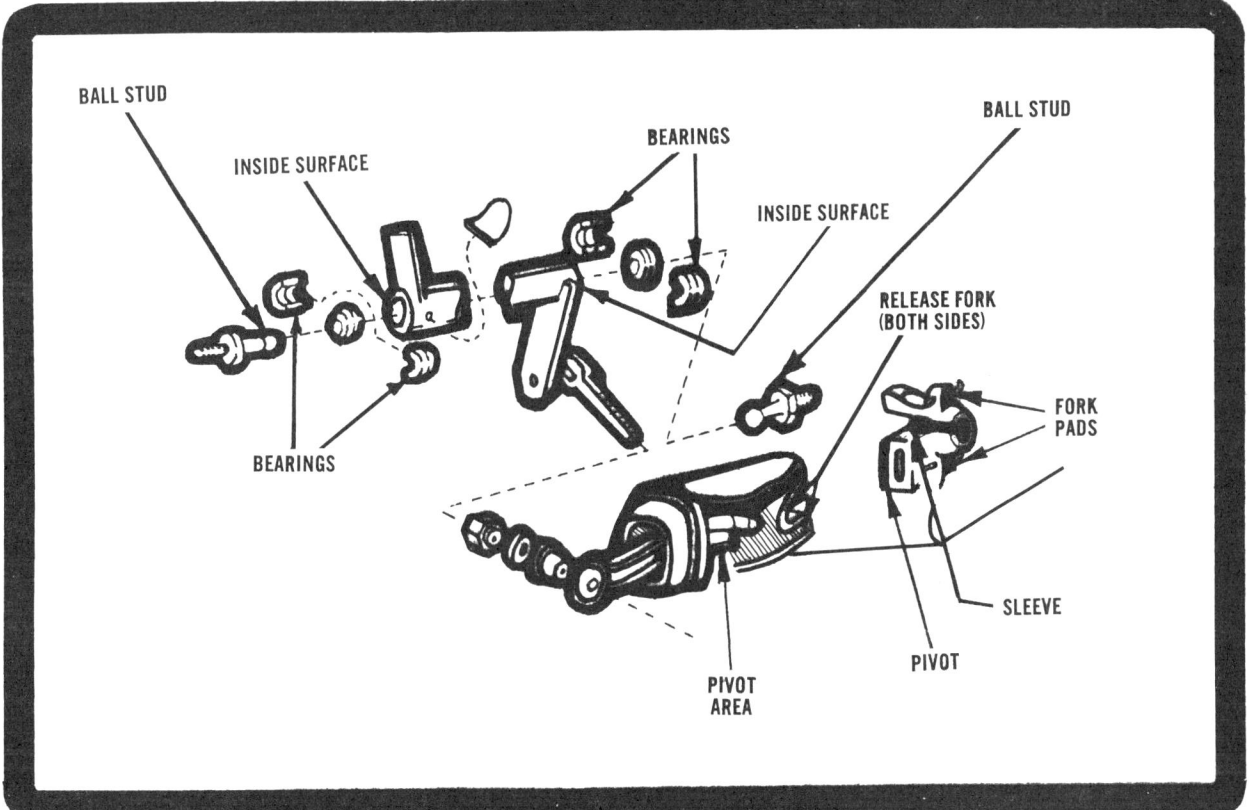

Fig. 21. Arrows point to areas to be greased on typical Chrysler product clutch linkage.

General Motors

- If clutch cross shaft has a lube plug, remove it and install a fitting (a few pumps on grease gun at 30,000-mile intervals). If, as is also common, there is no plug, dab grease on clutch fork joint and cross shaft.

- Manual or automatic shift linkage lever contacting faces and pivot points. **Note:** Do not lube control cable on console floor shift for automatic transmission.

- Parking brake cable guides and joints of all operating links and levers.

Fig. 22. Arrows point to areas on front of floor-mounted shift linkage, that should be greased.

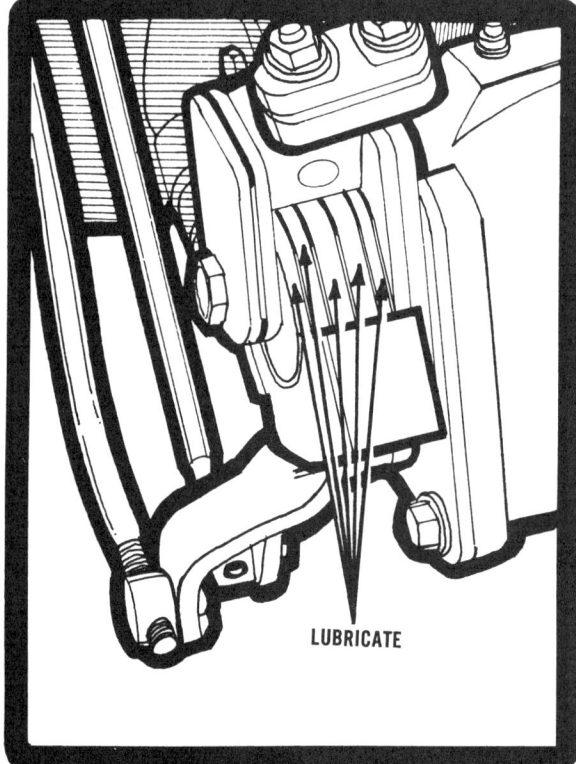

Fig. 23. Arrows point to areas on rear of floor-mounted shift linkage, that should be greased.

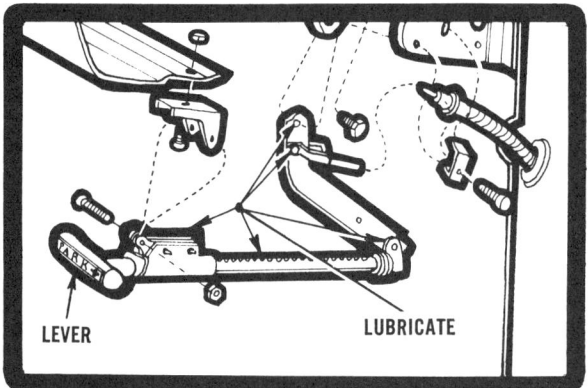

Fig. 24. Arrows point to areas on hand-operated parking brake linkage, that should be greased.

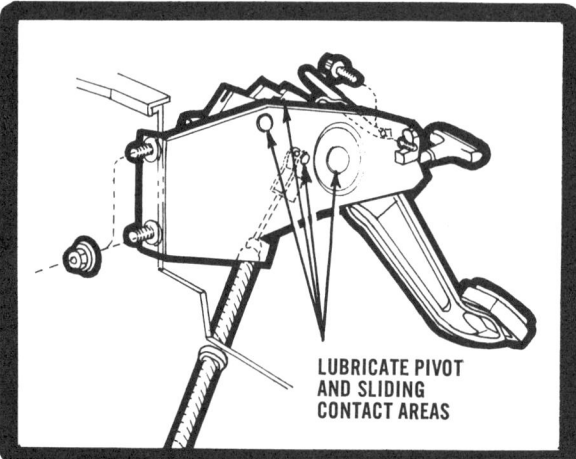

Fig. 25. Arrows point to areas on Chrysler intermediates' foot-operated parking brake, that should be greased.

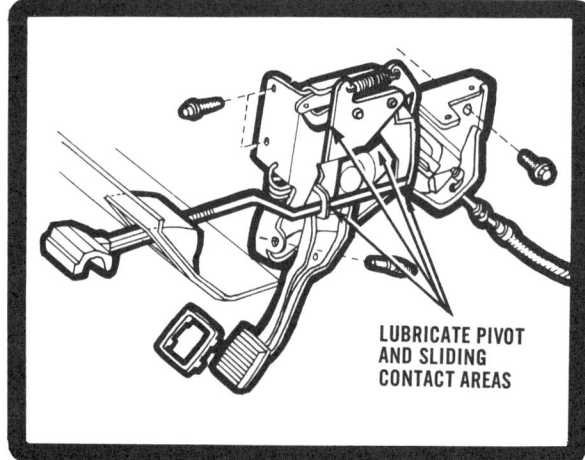

Fig. 26. Arrows show where to grease linkage of foot-operated parking brake on full-size cars.

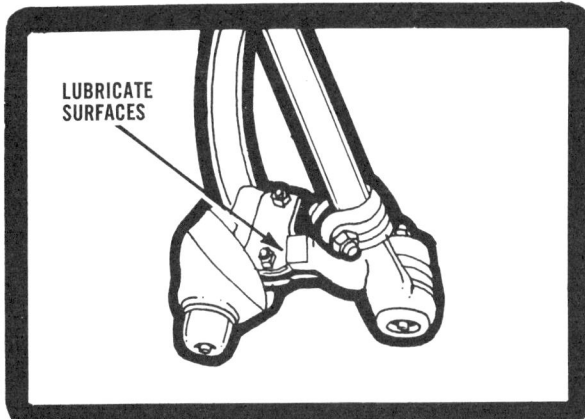

Fig. 27. Steering stop pad surfaces on Ford products. Arrows show where to apply grease.

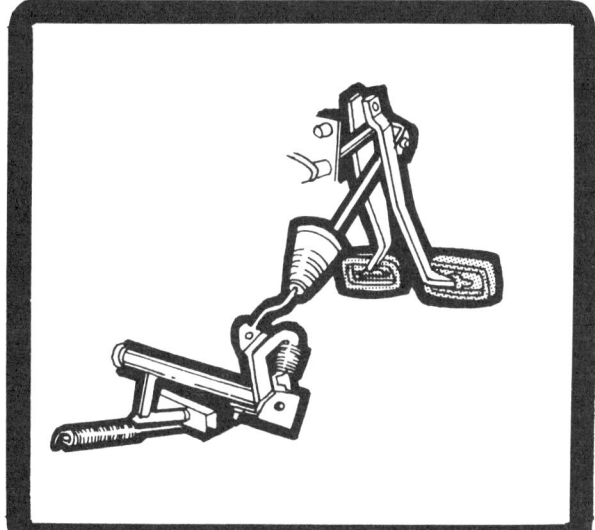

Fig. 28. Typical clutch linkage on Ford products except Pinto, Mustang II and Bobcat.

Fig. 29. Pinto, Mustang II and Bobcat clutch linkage.

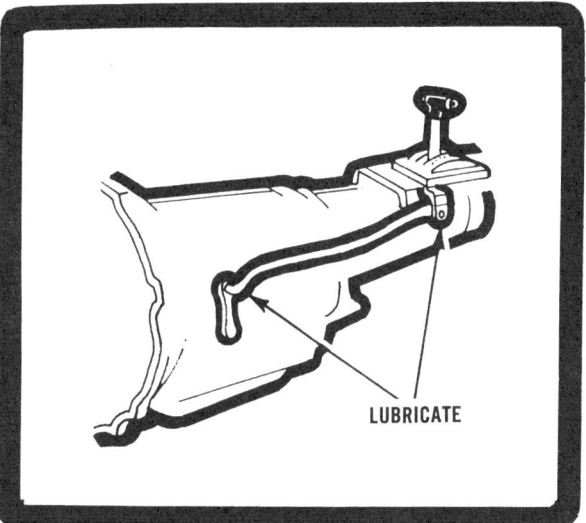

Fig. 30. Automatic transmission linkage lube points, floor shift on Pinto, Mustang II and Bobcat.

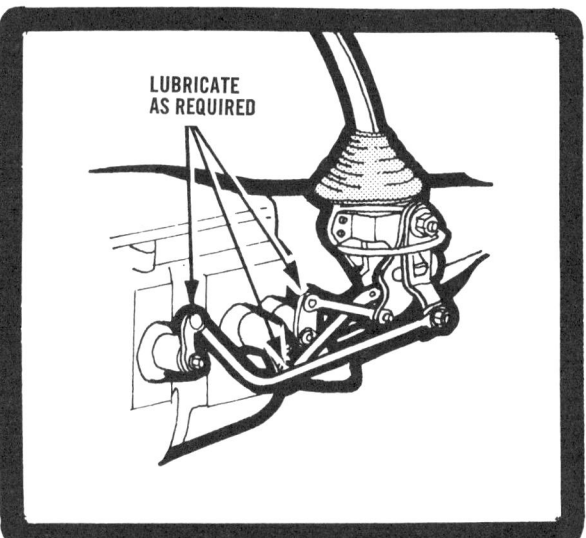

Fig. 31. Manual transmission linkage lube points, Ford products except subcompacts, floor shift.

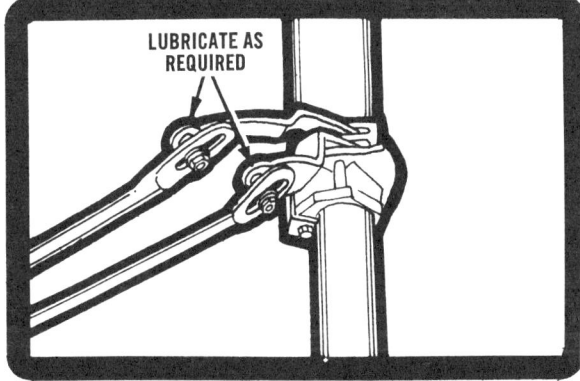

Fig. 32. Automatic transmission linkage lube points, Ford column shift.

AUTOMATIC TRANSMISSION FLUID MAINTENANCE

In an automatic transmission, the oil not only lubricates but operates the shift valves and applies the bands and clutches. The fluid level must be maintained at the proper mark on the dipstick. If the level is even a pint low (out of a total capacity of eight or more quarts), the automatic transmission may malfunction.

CHECKING OIL LEVEL

Transmission oil level should be checked and adjusted when the fluid is warm (a few miles of driving is sufficient) and the car is on a reasonably level surface with the engine idling. Then proceed as follows:
1. With your foot on the service brake (and the parking brake on if possible), move the shift lever into each position (P-R-N-D-L on most cars) and then back again, stopping in Neutral on Chrysler Corp. cars or American Motors cars with Torque Command, in Park on all other domestic cars.
2. Remove the automatic transmission dipstick, wipe clean and reinstall. Making sure that it is firmly seated. On many cars the stick may have to be twisted to seat properly. The automatic transmission dipstick is usually located behind the engine very close to the firewall.
3. Pull the stick and read the oil level. If it is at the ADD mark, insert a hose of suitable thickness or special automatic transmission funnel into the dipstick tube.
4. Wedge a funnel into the open end of the hose or funnel and pour half the contents of a quart can (one pint) into the funnel and allow it to empty into the dipstick tube.
5. Wipe the dipstick clean. Remove the hose. Reinstall the stick and withdraw to recheck the level. If necessary, add additional fluid to bring the level up to the FULL mark. But be careful not to overfill. If an extra pint of oil is added to the transmission, it may be enough to cause oil foaming, which will result in erratic shifting.

Choosing fluid

There are three automatic transmission fluids commonly sold in retail stores:
- Dexron (or Dexron II): the fluid recommended for all GM, Chrysler, American Motors and many imported cars.
- Type F: the fluid specified for all Ford products.
- Type A: the fluid that was used through the mid-1960s, not suitable for present cars. Even the latest version (introduced in the early 1960s), called Type A suffix A, should not be used on a late model car.

Do not use Dexron in a Ford product or Type F in other than a Ford built car, even to merely add a pint. The fluids have different frictional characteristics and the wrong fluid will affect the shifting of the transmission. As with engine oils, the refiner's reputation is your best guide to brands.

BUYING A TRANSMISSION OIL FILTER

Most automatic transmissions have a replaceable oil filter in the oil pan. Chrysler products and American Motors cars with Torque Command have a dacron-and-felt disc filter. General Motors Turbo Hydra-Matic has a sealed canister pleated paper type. The replacements generally available duplicate original equipment and include a new gasket for the oil pan (and for the Turbo Hydra-Matic, a replacement O-ring seal on the filter neck). As with engine oil filters, stick with a name brand.

Ford products and some American Motors cars have only a cleanable strainer. If it has not been cleaned in some time it may be so coated with varnish formed during high temperature operation, that replacement is the only practical answer. A replacement strainer will probably be available most readily at the car dealer's parts department, although some large independent parts jobbers also stock the item. If the strainer appears to be cleanable, soak in an automotive solvent, agitating periodically until it is clean. Allow it to air dry before installation.

NOTE: Some solvents require neutralization with water. Check the directions on the solvent container.

CHANGING TRANSMISSION OIL AND FILTER

The automatic transmission drain plug was eliminated from the oil pan on American cars in the 1960s. Therefore, it is necessary to drop the transmission oil pan to change the oil. Only a few quarts of oil are drained when the pan is removed, perhaps a third of the total capacity. But the fresh oil that can be added is sufficient to restore the performance of the fluid.

To change transmission oil, jack up the car high enough so you can slip underneath, and use the following procedure:

1. Locate the transmission oil pan. It is a flat bottom sheetmetal pan a foot or two to the rear of the engine (to the side of the engine on front-wheel-drive cars), bolted to the transmission. The transmission is the component into which the driveshaft is fitted (except on front-wheel-drive cars). Put a large flat drain pan of one to 1½ gallon capacity under the transmission oil pan.

2. Remove all screws holding the pan to the bottom of the transmission, Fig. 33, except those at the front, which should only be loosened. This will permit tilting the pan slightly down at the rear, so the oil drains out only at that location. Support the pan with one hand, so the weight of the oil does not cock it if the pan happens to be free. **Note:** If the pan sticks, free it up with a putty knife at the joint.

Fig. 33. Removing transmission oil pan retaining screws.

3. When most of the oil has drained out, remove the front screws and lower the pan, Fig. 34.
4. Replace the oil strainer or filter assembly, Fig. 35. You have a new filter to install, so identifying the old one and noting the way in which it is retained should pose no problem. **Note:** On GM Turbo Hydra-Matic transmissions, the filter has a long neck with an O-ring. Make sure the old O-ring comes out with the filter and position the new one at the bulge on the neck for installation.

Fig. 34. Lowering transmission oil pan after most of oil has drained out.

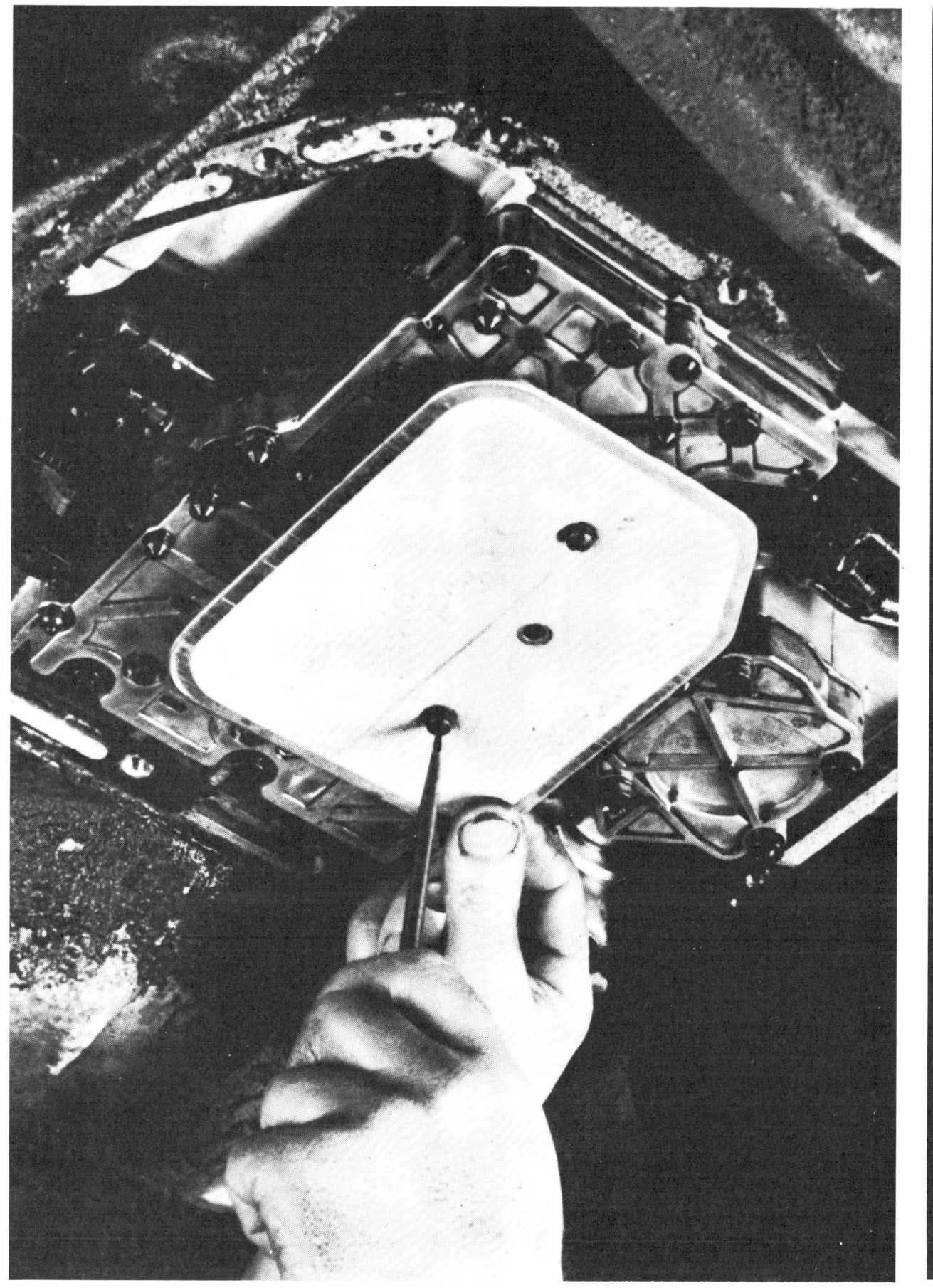

Fig. 35. Installing transmission oil filter on Chrysler products.

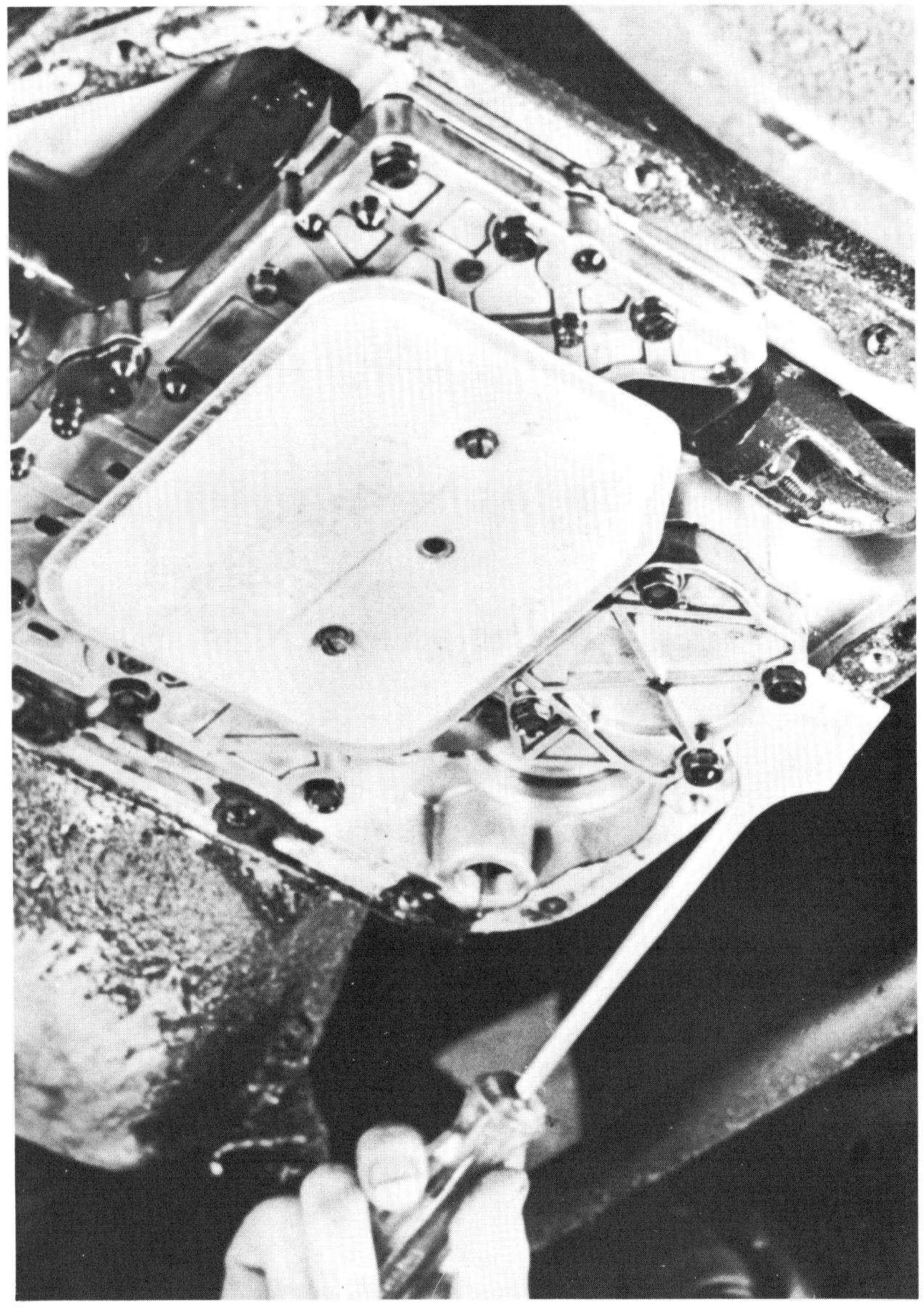

Fig. 36. Scraping gasket residue from transmission surface.

5. Scrape off the old gasket with a putty knife and clean gasket residue from grooves in the pan with a screwdriver. Also scrape gasket residue from the transmission's gasket surface, Fig. 36.
6. Invert the oil pan and place it on a flat surface with a flashlight (turned on) underneath. If you can see light leakage, the pan is cocked and should be straightened or replaced. To straighten, brace the cocked section on a flat surface and gently flatten with a hammer.
7. Clean the interior and exterior of the pan. Coat the pan's gasket surface with a film of non-hardening sealer. Then place the gasket on it, Fig. 37.
8. Install the drain pan, threading in all bolts finger tight.
9. Tighten all bolts evenly with a wrench, working in a criss-cross fashion. To insure even tightening, use a torque wrench and work to specifications, typically 10 lbs. ft. on most transmissions.

Fig. 37. After a thin film of non-hardening sealer has been spread on oil pan's gasket surface, install the gasket as shown.

WHEEL BEARINGS

When the front wheels seem to wobble and lose directional stability, one common cause is damaged or improperly adjusted front wheel bearings. To extend the life of these important parts they should be periodically inspected, lubricated and readjusted. The job is commonly done as part of a brake job.

Because a complete brake job is best left to a professional mechanic, most likely he will also repack and adjust your wheel bearings at the same time. Repacking wheel bearings is a relatively simple job that almost any novice mechanic can successfully complete. However, the hard part is the bearing adjustment. The tapered roller bearing used on today's cars must be adjusted very precisely, in most cases using a torque wrench on the bearing nut. The procedure and torque specifications vary from make to make.

For these reasons, we recommend that you leave both repacking and adjustment of wheel bearings to a professional mechanic.

MANUAL TRANSMISSION LUBRICATION MAINTENANCE

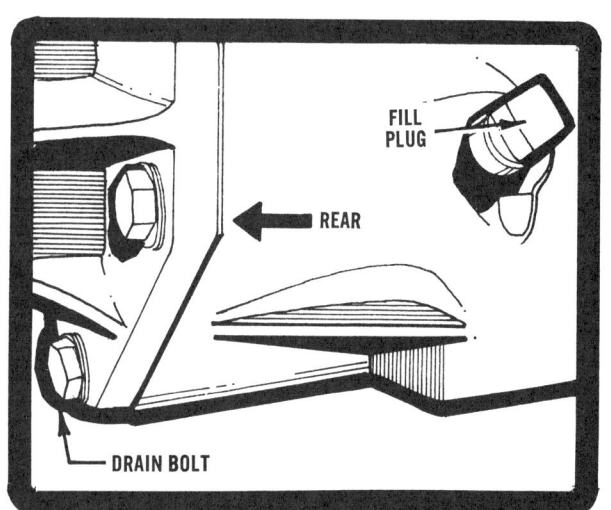

Fig. 38. Lowest extension housing bolt can be used as an oil drain plug on many cars, for once bolt is removed, transmission oil drains out.

All manual transmissions have an oil fill plug on one side of the gearbox. But only Chrysler products have true drain plugs in the bottom of the gearbox. However, on some American Motors cars, Oldsmobile, some Ford intermediates (Torino, Montego lines) and Chevrolet except Chevelle and Monte Carlo, there is an equivalent. The bottom bolt of the bolts that hold the extension housing to the transmission, will if removed, permit the oil to drain out. The extension housing (see Fig. 38) is the rear section bolted to the transmission at its front and splined into the driveshaft at its back.

If there is no drain plug or bolt, you must siphon the old oil out of the fill plug hole with a siphon gun, available in auto parts jobbers.

CHECKING OIL LEVEL

1. Locate fill plug, which has either a male or female square head, (Fig. 39). Some of the plug's threads are normally exposed, so you can tell the plug is not a bolt. Look on either side of the transmission, at about the midpoint in height.

2. Remove plug. Oil should just dribble out of the bottom of the hole. **NOTE:** If female square plug is used, ratchet square or extension rod end will fit in to turn plug, Fig. 41.

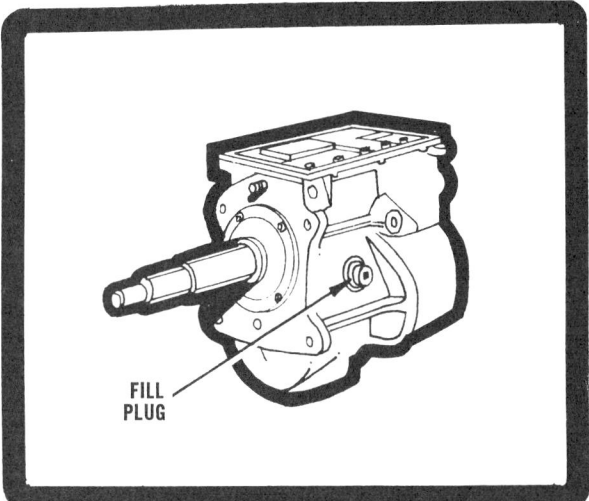

Fig. 39. Transmission with female square head fill plug.

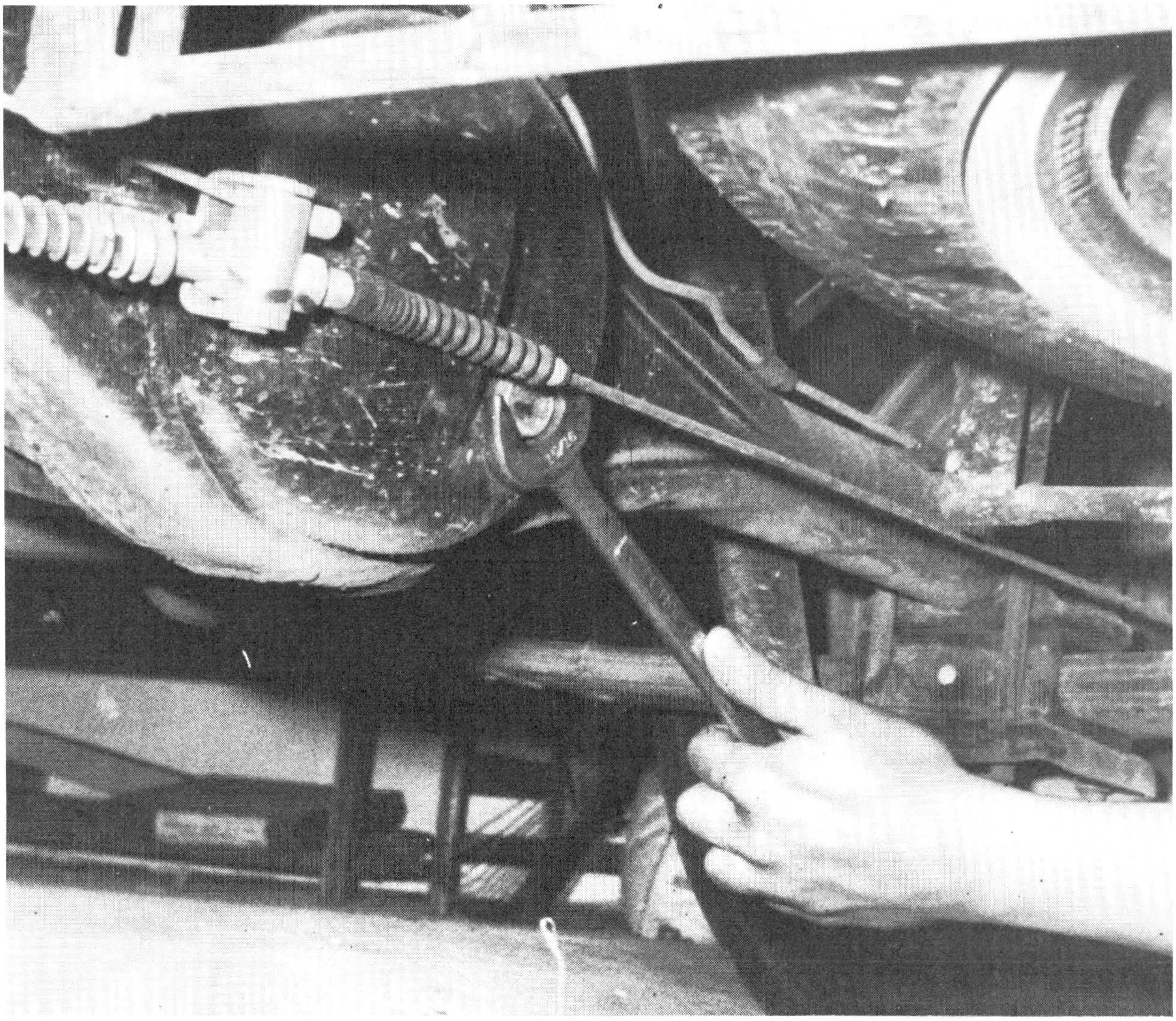

Fig. 40. Removing hex head fill plug with open-end wrench. Box wrench or ratchet-socket setup also could be used.

DRAINING OIL

Remove drain plug if there is one. If siphon gun is used, not as much oil will be removed, but enough so that a refill will revive the overall oil supply.

Which oil to use

A hypoid gear oil 80 or 90 viscosity, should be used in all manual transmissions year round. The oil should meet the American Petroleum Institute specification GL-4 as a minimum and preferably GL-5.

NOTE: Chrysler Corp. also permits the use of 140 viscosity hypoid gear oil in its manual transmissions if they are noisy and temperatures are above freezing, or Dextron automatic transmittion fluid in consistently below-zero temperatures.

REFILLING TRANSMISSION

Simply fill the transmission through the oil fill plug until the proper level is reached. When oil begins to dribble back out, proper level is reached.

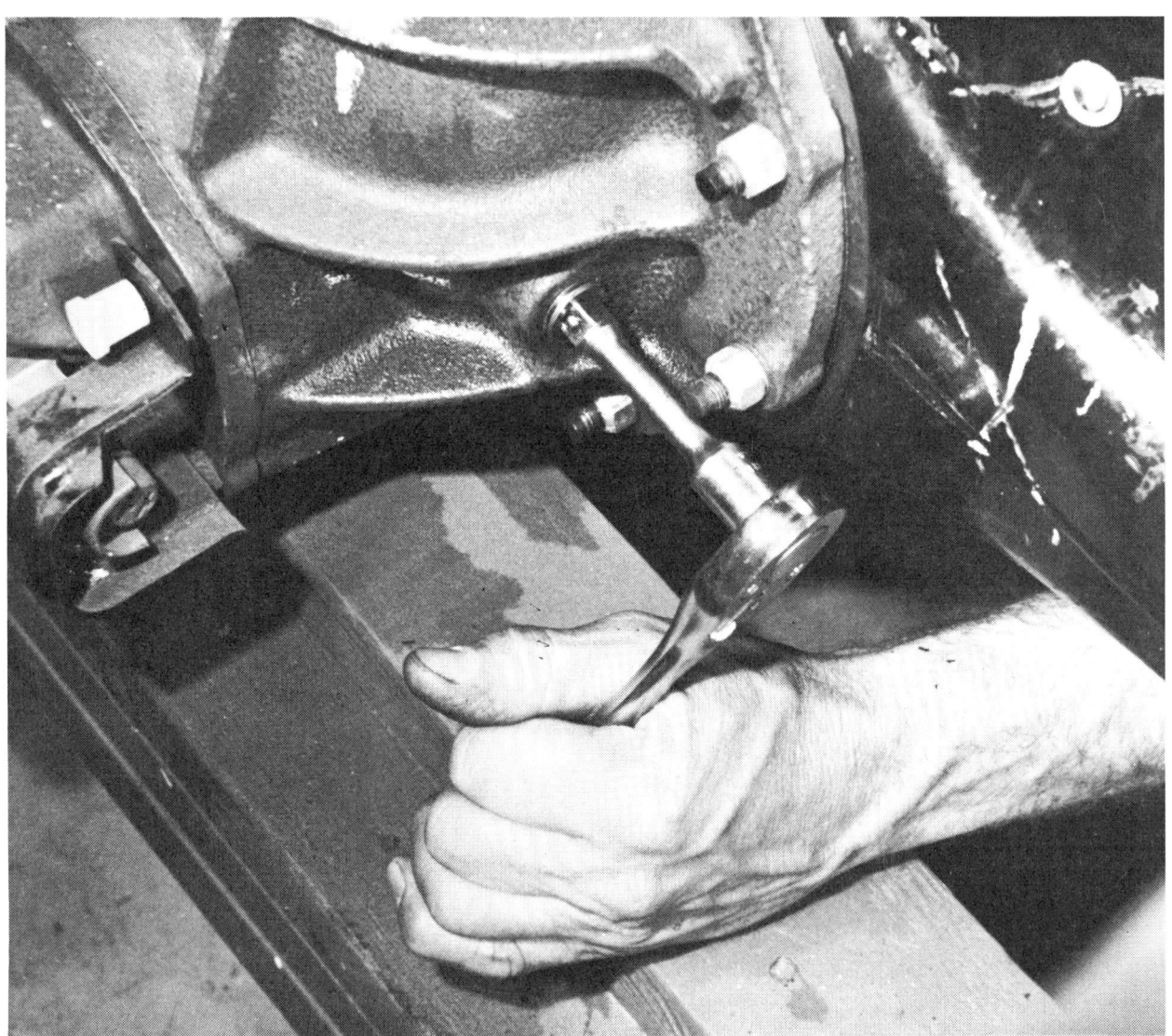

Fig. 41. If female square head plug is used, ratchet or extension square fits in to turn plug.

REAR AXLE LUBRICATION MAINTENANCE

The rear axle has a fill plug somewhere near the midpoint of the differential housing (that big bulge on rear axle), either on the front or rear. The plug has either a square male or female head. Older cars may have a drain plug at the bottom of the housing. But late-model cars do not. Use a siphon gun inserted in the fill plug hole to extract old oil.

CHECKING OIL LEVEL

1. Locate fill plug, which has either a male or female square head.
   NOTE: Car must be reasonably level.
2. Remove plug, Fig. 40. **Note:** If female square head is used, ratchet square or extension fits in to turn plug (Fig. 41). If the specification below calls for for a level lower than the bottom of the fill plug hole, insert finger down into hole and estimate depth to oil level.

American Motors
Level with bottom of fill plug hole.

Chrysler Corp.
- 7¼-inch axle (rear cover has nine bolts): ⅝-inch below bottom of fill plug hole.
- 8¼-inch axle (rear cover has 10 bolts). ⅛-inch below bottom of fill plug hole.
- 8¾-inch axle (rear cover is welded to housing): level with bottom of fill plug hole.
- 9¼-inch axle (rear cover has 12 bolts): ⅜-inch below bottom of fill plug hole.

Ford Motor Co.
All *Thunderbirds and Lincoln Continentals:* Loosen plug and back out slowly. If seepage occurs around threads, level is correct and plug should be turned back in to prevent loss. If oil has been removed, you can top up past level of drain plug hole by jacking up appropriate end of car a bit more (front if fill plug hole is at front of housing, rear if hole is at rear of housing). An additional four ounces should be sufficient.

All *subcompacts (Mustang II, Pinto, Bobcat):* ¼-inch below bottom of fill plug hole.

All *compacts, intermediates and full-size* cars except above: level with bottom of fill plug hole.

General Motors
NOTE: On *Cadillac Eldorado and Oldsmobile Toronado,* the final drive, which is bolted to the transmission case at the left front of the engine, is the equivalent of the rear axle on conventional rear-drive cars. The fill plug on these cars is on the left side of the final drive.

Chevrolet and Pontiac: level with bottom of fill plug hole.

Buick and Oldsmobile: level to within ⅜-inch below bottom of fill plug hole except below:

Oldsmobile Toronado: if there is an oil level line stamped next to fill plug, oil level should be at that line.

Buick Apollo Wagon: level to within ¾-inch below bottom of fill plug hole.

Cadillac (including Eldorado): level to within ½-inch of bottom of fill plug hole.

SELECTING OIL

On conventional axles, use an 80 or 90 viscosity hypoid gear oil that meets API specification GL-5. With limited slip differentials, obtain a special lubricant from the car dealer. If special oil is not available, do not remove old lubricant, but merely top up with GL-5 oil. Filling the limited slip differential housing with this oil, however, could produce a chattering noise.

PREVENTING THOSE SQUEAKS AND RATTLES

In addition to keeping the vital systems of your car in good running condition, preventive lubrication service can also cure many of those elusive squeaks and rattles your car develops with age. Some of the more obscure areas that should occasionally be lubed with a squirt of engine oil are windshield wiper arm pivots, door hinges, hood hinges, and door push buttons (not the locks).

Other minor items which need occasional lube service are:

- door strikers (a stick lubricant)
- window channels (aerosol silicone lube)
- door lock and speedometer cable (graphite lubricant)
- hood latch (grease)
- spring shackles and shock absorber bushings (brake fluid)
- fender skirts (silicone lube)
- pedal linkages (aerosol silicone lube)

A few typical causes of knocks, squeaks and rattles are:

- friction of loose, dry parts rubbing together
- excessive wear in a shaft and its bearing or bushing
- loose part, like muffler tail pipe
- misaligned shafts, causing excessive wear
- gears, pulleys, etc., that run out-of-true

POWER STEERING RESERVOIR MAINTENANCE

All cars with power steering have a dipstick built into the power steering pump reservoir cap, Fig. 42. To check level, remove dipstick, wipe clean, reinstall and remove. If level is below FULL mark, top up with power steering fluid available from a car dealer or service station. Do not use automatic transmission fluid in the power steering system except in an emergency.

MANUAL STEERING GEARBOX MAINTENANCE

The manual steering gearbox on late model cars is lubed-for-life and no changes or topping up is necessary. If there are indications of leaking seals, the leak should be repaired and the gearbox filled with a manual steering gear lubricant by a professional mechanic. If the special lubricant is not available, a high-quality 90 viscosity hypoid gear oil can be used. Do not pump in chassis grease. If necessary to top up the gearbox after repair, the following guidelines should be used:

American Motors
Remove cover plate bolt from hole marked LUBE. Oil level should be within ½- or ¾-inch below bottom of hole.

Chrysler Corp.
Oil level should be high enough to cover worm gear inside.

Ford Motor Co.
All models except those with rack-and-pinion steering (subcompacts): Oil should be level with bottom of filler plug hole.

General Motors
Remove bolt in center of gearbox top cover and adjust oil level to bottom of bolt hole.

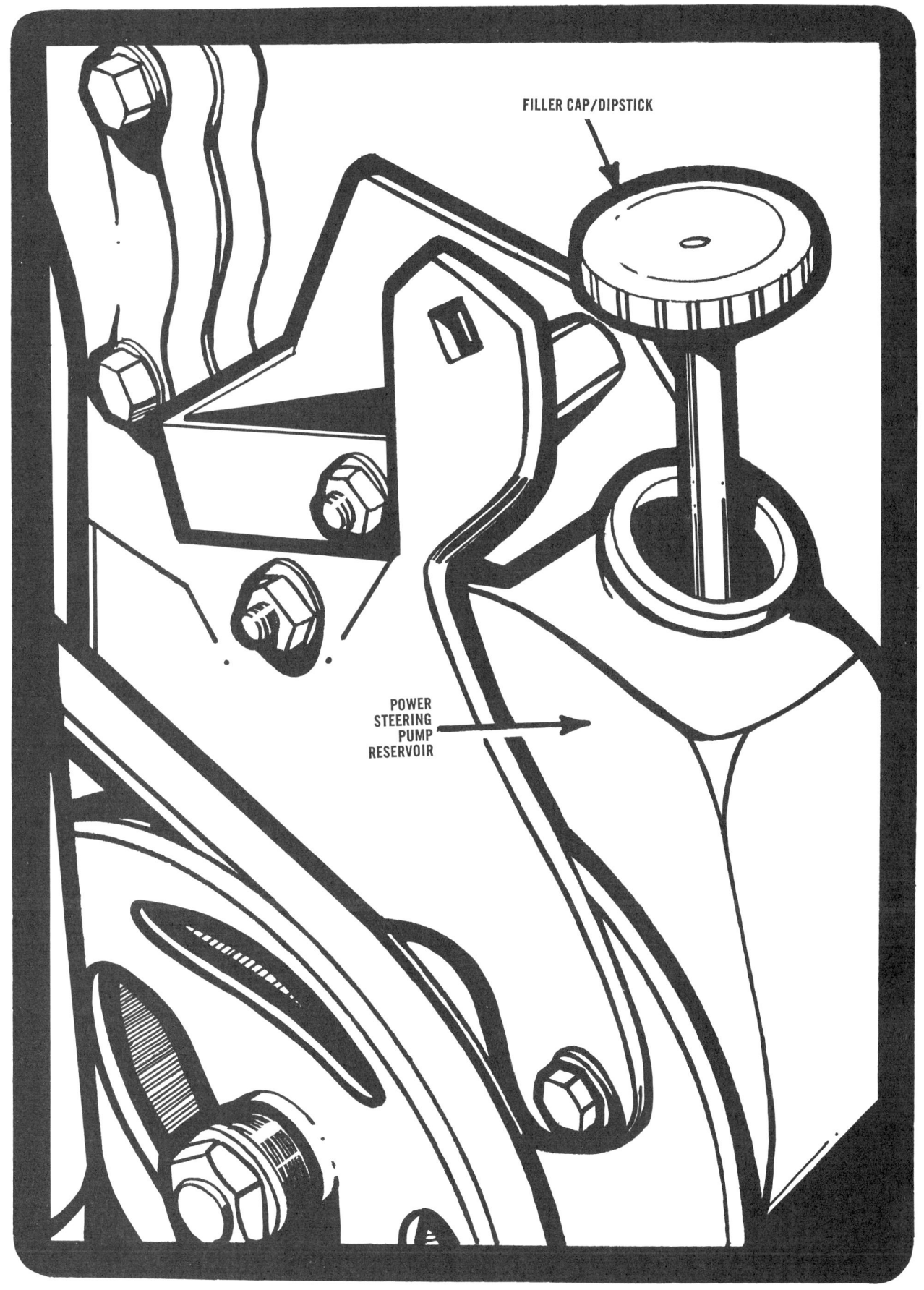

Fig. 42. Dipstick is built into oil reservoir cap on typical power steering pump.

BODY PARTS LUBRICATION

Hood, door and trunk lid hinges, and door pushbuttons should be lubed annually, using a penetrating oil or a silicone lubricant. The hood release mechanism's moving parts should be lubed with wheel bearing grease. After applying the lube, repeatedly actuate the part (open and close the door, lid or hood, or push the button) to work the lubricant in. **NOTE:** Door locks should be serviced only with a graphite or silicone lubricant. See Figs. 43 and 44.

Fig. 43. Penetrating oil applied to hood hinge pivots.

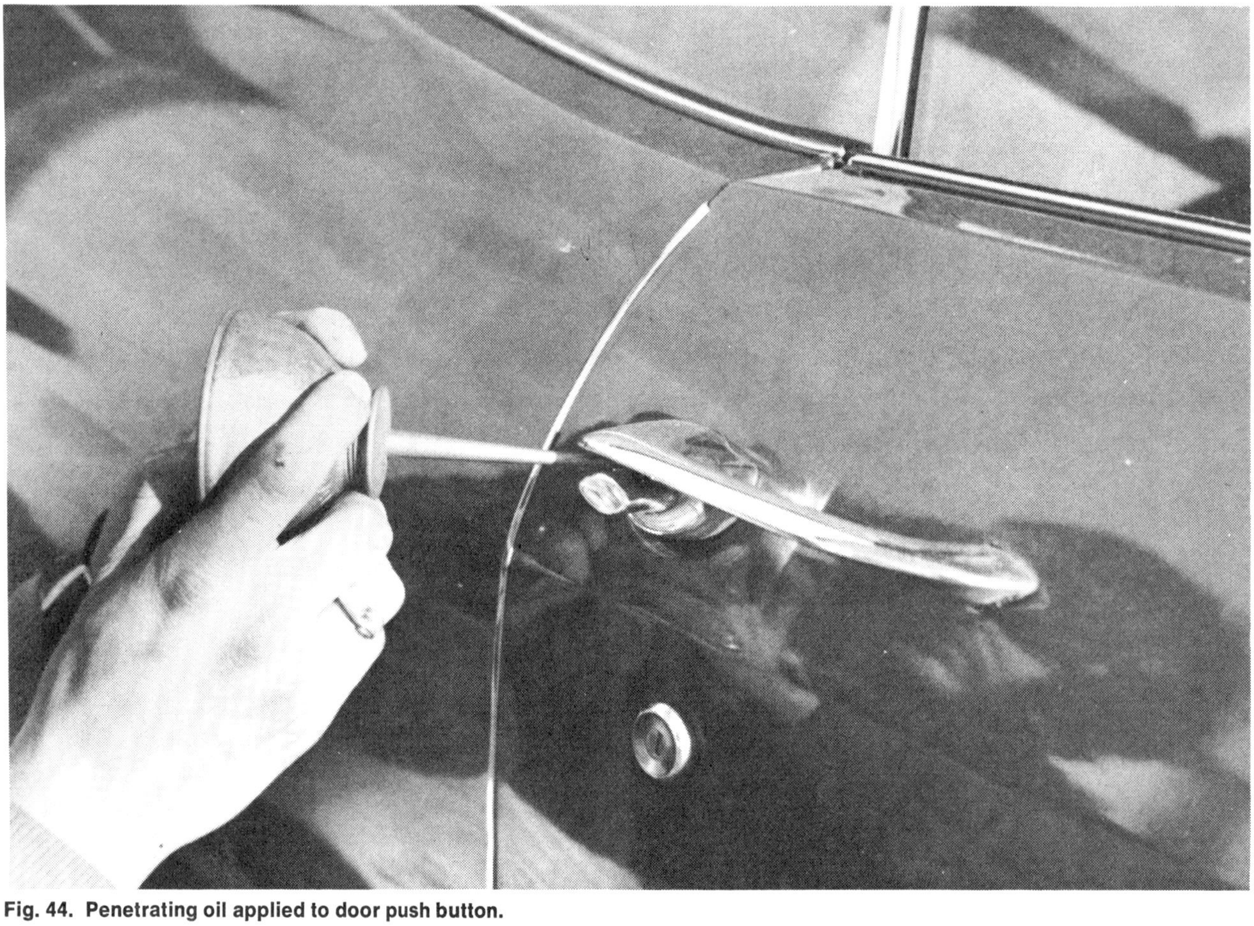

Fig. 44. Penetrating oil applied to door push button.

Tires

A few years ago, buying a new automobile was a lot easier than it is today. There simply were not that many really different cars to choose from. Tire buying was easier too. About all you needed to know was the size.

Today, it is a different story. The selection of automobiles available, whether American or imported, has become almost infinite. And this has also made tire buying a bit more complicated. You still have to know the size, but there are other considerations too.

Now you hear more about tire construction, body cord materials, belt materials, tread designs, policies and adjustment programs, as well as performance characteristics. The fact is, there *is* a wider choice of tires today—there has to be to accommodate a more sophisticated automotive industry.

In the last few years, there have been many new concepts introduced in the tire field—new tire constructions, profiles and materials.

Today, tires with new designations—78-series, 70-series and 60-series; belted bias and radial—dominate the market. Also, new cord materials such as polyester, fiberglass and steel have been introduced, in addition to rayon and nylon.

In order for you to select tires intelligently, you should be familiar with current tire size designations, materials and principal construction fundamentals.

CONSTRUCTION FUNDAMENTALS

A normal tire has four parts—the tread, the sidewall, the bead which holds the tire securely to the metal wheel rim, and fabric plies. The tire's strength is determined by the character of these plies. They vary in number and in the material they are made of. The fabric plies also give the tire its stability and resistance to bruises, fatigue and heat. Without these plies, a rubber tire would be little more than a soft rubber balloon. The fabric plies give the tire its skeletal structure. The latest developments have been in the areas of tread width and ply construction.

Bias-ply construction

A few years ago, this was the most common type of construction found in tires. Almost every car wore bias-ply tires. Bias-ply tires are still used frequently mainly because of their low cost. But as tire fabricating has become more technologically advanced, other construction methods have become more popular because of their inherently better characteristics.

In bias-ply construction, the fabric cords or plies are molded to the carcass of the tire in a crisscrossed pattern much like a herringbone tweed. The angle these cords make with each other determines certain characteristics of the tire—high speed stability, ride harshness and handling. Generally speaking, the lower the cord angle, the higher the degree of high speed stability. Also, the lower the cord angle, the more harsh a tire will ride. Usually, cord angles are about 35° from the centerline of the tire, giving strength to both sidewall and tread. Alternate plies extend in opposite directions.

These layers of cord or plies can be made of one of several materials—rayon, nylon and polyester. Bias-ply tires come in either 2-ply, 4-ply, 6-ply or 8-ply. Most 2-ply tires now use very strong, heavy plies and have the equivalent strength of four normal plies. These tires are designated as 2-ply/4-ply rating. The same can hold true for a 4-ply tire. It may carry an 8-ply rating.

This conventional construction provides flexibility and 2-directional strength in both tread and sidewall areas. It is a very serviceable construction and one that has been a standard in the tire-making industry for many, many years.

Bias-belted construction

The belted bias tire has gained wide acceptance as an original equipment and replacement tire. It offers the car owner high mileage and great resistance to road hazards, plus excellent traction.

Basically, the belted bias is an extension of the bias-ply tire which, as we said before, is constructed with two or four plies of a strong inner fabric to which

Your automobile's tires are often called upon to take abuse that you may not have taken into account. So when choosing new tires, be sure they are up to the demands you may impose upon them.

THE TIRE OF THE FUTURE?

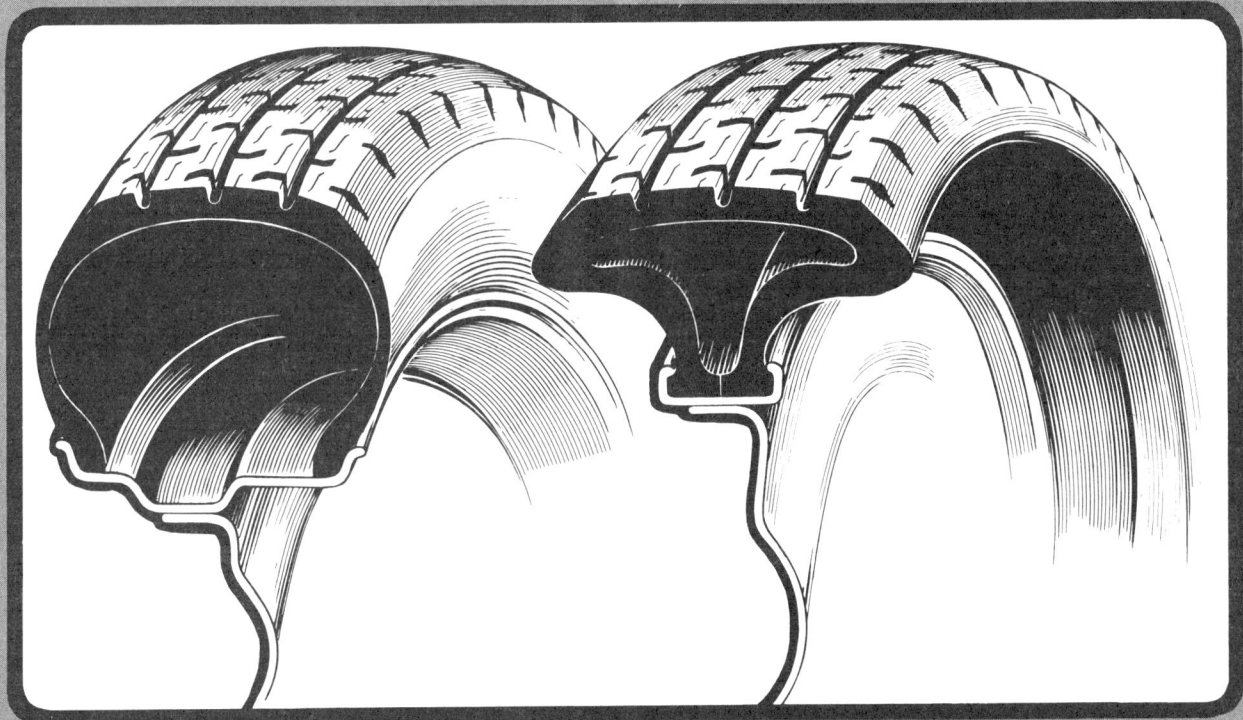

All tire companies are continually researching different construction methods, construction materials and sizes. One company, Pirelli Tire Corporation, recently introduced an experimental tire which it considers the logical successor to today's radial. When fitted to its special wheel, Pirelli's tire of the 1980s (right) will be only 50% as high as it is wide, or about one-third lower compared to a tire of today (left). Born of a completely revolutionary tire operating principle—compression not tension—invented by Pirelli, the tire has a radical triangular shaped section, thicker all-rubber sidewalls and greater tread area extending across the width of the tire. Pirelli engineers are calling it the safest tire ever. The company claims the design can be used for all vehicles including cars, trucks, motorcycles and off-road vehicles.

TIRE BUYING MADE SIMPLE

It is not simple, of course. But here are some rules of thumb that you can use as a reminder when selecting new tires.

First, never choose a smaller size than those which came with the car. Tires should always be replaced with the same size designation, or approved options, as recommended by the automobile or tire manufacturer. Interchangeability of different types and profiles of tires is not always possible due to differences in load ratings, tire dimensions, fender clearances and rim sizes, particularly with older cars.

Tires of different size designations, constructions and stages of wear may affect vehicle handling and stability. For best all-around car handling performance, tires of the same type or construction should be used on all four wheel positions unless designed for special service to improve performance, for example, winter-type tires.

However, while not recommended, it may be permissible to mix your present tires with other size designations or constructions provided they are used in pairs on the same axle.

IMPORTANT: Check the owner's manual or tire instructions affixed to vehicle for automobile manufacturer's recommendations before you replace or mix tires.

When radial tires are used with bias or belted-bias constructions on the same vehicle, the radials must always be placed on the rear axle.

If selecting only a pair of replacement tires in the same size and construction as on the car, they should be put on the rear wheels for better traction, handling and extra protection against flats. A single new tire should be paired on the rear axle with the tire having the most tread depth of the other three.

A break-in period is also recommended for all new or previously unused tires—the tires on a new car, the spare put on after a flat and all replacements. Limiting speed to 60 mph for the first 50 miles of driving enables the many complex elements in a tire to adjust gradually to each other and function as an integral unit.

the rubber sidewalls and tread are bonded. The belted bias tire begins in the same way, with inner plies like a conventional tire. Then, before the tread is applied, the belts which encircle the circumference of the tire are added.

A tire with belted bias construction keeps its tread firmly on the road, thus greatly reducing tread squirm, a major cause of tire wear. The belts make the tire much more resistant to punctures, cuts and bruises.

A belted bias tire can be made of several combinations of materials. It is the construction principle, the combination of body plies and belts, more than the materials, which give the tire its many advantages.

Plies and belts of various combinations of rayon, nylon, polyester, fiberglass and steel are used with belted bias construction.

The belted bias tire, though more expensive than the conventional tire, provides greater value for the motorist. For an investment of approximately 25% more, he can expect to gain up to 40% more mileage compared with a regular bias tire.

Radial-ply construction

The radial tire provides the best combination of wear, handling and overall performance of any type of tire.

A radial tire has a body made of cords which run straight up and over in hoop fashion from rim-edge to rim-edge.

To provide puncture resistance, long life and tread stability, two or more very stable and strong belts are run around the tire's circumference under the tread. The belts encircle the tire to add support to the body and to help hold the tread grooves open for effective traction. The belts also enable the elements of the tread pattern to resist the normal tendency to squeeze closed during road contact, effectively prolonging tread life.

This combination results in a tire with extremely flexible sidewalls and a strong stable tread area in contact with the road surface. The tire deflects more than bias or belted tires and therefore has a soft or underinflated look.

Radial tires are produced with various combinations of rayon, polyester, steel cord or other new fibers in plies and belts.

Because the manufacturing process for a radial tire is more complicated, it naturally costs more than other tire types. The difference in initial purchase price will be compensated for through the greater tread wear. Tread mileage for radial tires is frequently guaranteed for 40,000 miles.

Because the radial has a quicker steering response, radials should not be mixed with other types of tires. More about this later.

This drawing illustrates the differences between bias-ply, radial-ply and bias-belted tires. In a conventional bias-ply tire (left) the cords cross the tire at an angle. In a radial-ply tire (center) the cords run straight across, and an additional layered belt of fabric is placed between the plies and the tread. The bias-belted tire (right) combines these concepts, with the cords crossing at an angle and a belt between the plies and tread.

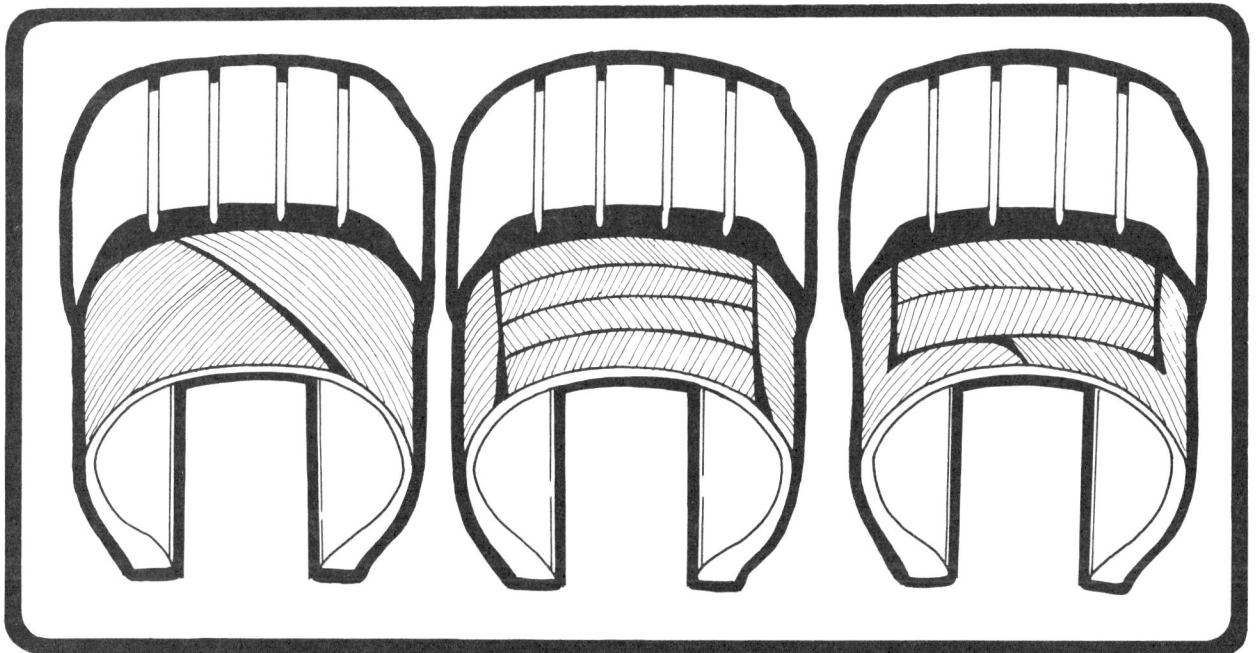

Firestone has developed a new type of tire (lower photo) which can be driven without damage some 50 miles after going flat. The new Steel Radial 500 ACT (Advanced Concept Tire) is constructed in a way that should a flat occur the tire will settle firmly onto the wheel rim. It will not wobble, as does a conventional tire (upper photo) when air pressure is lost. The driver therefore is able to maintain complete control of the car.

TIRE SIZES

The profile ratio of a tire is the relation of the tire's cross-section height (from tread to bead) compared to its cross-section width (from sidewall to sidewall). A 70-series tire, for example, has a profile ratio of 70, i.e., the height of the tire is 70% of the width.

For many years, a profile ratio of approximately 83 was considered standard or conventional for most bias-ply passenger car tires. With the advent of bias-belted and radial-ply constructions, lower profile tires with ratios of 78, 70 and even 60 have become popular. Today, most new cars are equipped with 70 or 78-series tires.

Both tire construction and profile ratio can have a pronounced influence on the handling and performance characteristics of an automobile. In selecting new tires, therefore, it is advisable to first check the car manufacturer's specifications in the car owner's manual. As an added aid, the Tire Application Guide for Passenger Cars on the following page provides suggestions for preferred combinations of tire profiles and constructions.

Prior to 1967, common tire size designations were all numbers, such as 7.75-14 or 9.50-15. In numerical designations, the first number, e.g. 7.75, refers to the approximate cross-section width of an inflated tire in inches and the second number, 14, is the rim diameter.

Tires with all-number size designations have an 83 profile ratio and are all but obsolete except on low-line economy tires made by secondline tire companies.

With the advent of wider profile ratios in 1967, a new series of size designations using letters and numbers went into effect. Tires from 78-series through 50-series use the letters A through N to identify size, with A being the smallest tire and N the largest. The letter is followed by a number to indicate the tire's approximate section height to width ratio, followed by the rim diameter. For instance, on an F78-14 tire, the number 78 means that the tire is 78% as high as it is wide. The number 14 indicates that it fits a 14-inch rim. Radial tires are available in several size designations. One uses a combination of metric and inch designations. In the case of a 195 R 14 size, for example, the numbers 195 refer to the approximate cross-section width in millimeters. R means radial and 14 is the rim diameter in inches. Radials of the 78, 70, 60 and 50-series use the same size designations as their bias or belted bias-ply equivalents with the addition of the letter R.

Even this letter designation system is not universally accepted however. Some companies are using a metric system to designate a 70-series tire. So you might see a tire marked 185 70-13. This is a 70-series tire that is equivalent to the old 185 metric size.

Elsewhere in this chapter, you will find a chart that lists all currently available tire sizes and their interchangeability with other tires using different size designations.

OTHER TIRE MARKINGS

You might see a tire marked GR70VR-15. This tire fits on a 15-inch rim and it is a 70-series radial, size G. But what is the V in there for? This is a speed designation. There are three letters used to indicate at what maximum speed a tire is safe. A tire marked S is good for up to 113 mph. A tire marked H is good

A typical radial tire has an open tread pattern for good water dissipation on wet roads.

to 130 and a tire marked V is safe to 165 mph. These designations are given after a tire is operated at that speed for 24 hours under a full load.

You can learn a lot about a tire by reading the sidewalls. Here are some examples of how to read a sidewall and what the various designations mean:

Example A

F78-14 (Replaces 7.75-14). This indicates a current size marking for a popular-size 78-series tire, together with its equivalent bias tire size designation.

Load Range B. The letter B indicates a 4-ply rating. As letters progress in the alphabet, load range increases. For example, D would be the same as a former 8-ply rating.

Max. load 1500 lbs. @ 32 psi maximum pressure. This indicates the tire's load limits and maximum cold inflation. For normal operation, follow pressure recommendations in owner's manual or on instruction sticker in car.

Radial tires are available in all aspect ratios. A 50-series radial (above) has an extremely wide tread and is used mostly in high performance applications.

The tire on the left appears to need air. But it does not. It is a radial tire and built that way. In a radial tire the cord material runs radially from rim to rim, which gives the tire a bulging appearance. The conventional bias-belted construction tire on the right, also with the proper air pressure, has a straighter sidewall configuration. Owners of radial tires must follow the air pressure recommendation in their car's operating manual rather than add air until the tire looks "right."

Load Range. The load range system is now being used in tire marking with letters (e.g., Load Range B,C,D, etc.) to identify tires with their particular load and inflation limits and service requirements. While the old ply rating system has been phased out, both designations may be used on tire sidewalls and are shown in the tables.

For example, Load Range B tires may be marked 4-ply rating/2-ply, or 4-ply, Load Range C tires, 6-ply rating/4-ply, or 6-ply, and Load Range D tires, 8-ply rating/4-ply, 8-ply rating/6-ply or 8-ply.

Ply Rating. Older tires marked 4-ply rating/2-ply have the same load carrying capacity as a current or most recent 4-ply tire of the same size at the same inflation. Tires marked 8-ply rating/4-ply have the same load carrying capacity as 8-ply rating tires of the same size at the same inflation, regardless of the actual number of plies. These criteria apply even though no industry-wide definition of ply rating exists.

4 plies under tread (2 xxxx Cord + 2 xxxx Cord), Sidewall 2 plies xxxx Cord). This indicates tire ply composition which depends upon materials used.

DOT xxxx xx xxx. The letters DOT certify compliance with Department of Transportation tire safety standards. Adjacent to this symbol is a tire identification number, the first two characters of which identify the tire manufacturer. The remaining characters identify size, type and date of manufacture. When buying new tires, be sure seller records your name, address and tire identification numbers as required by federal law.

Tubeless. The tire must be marked either tubeless or tube-type. If a radial tire, the word radial must also be carried.

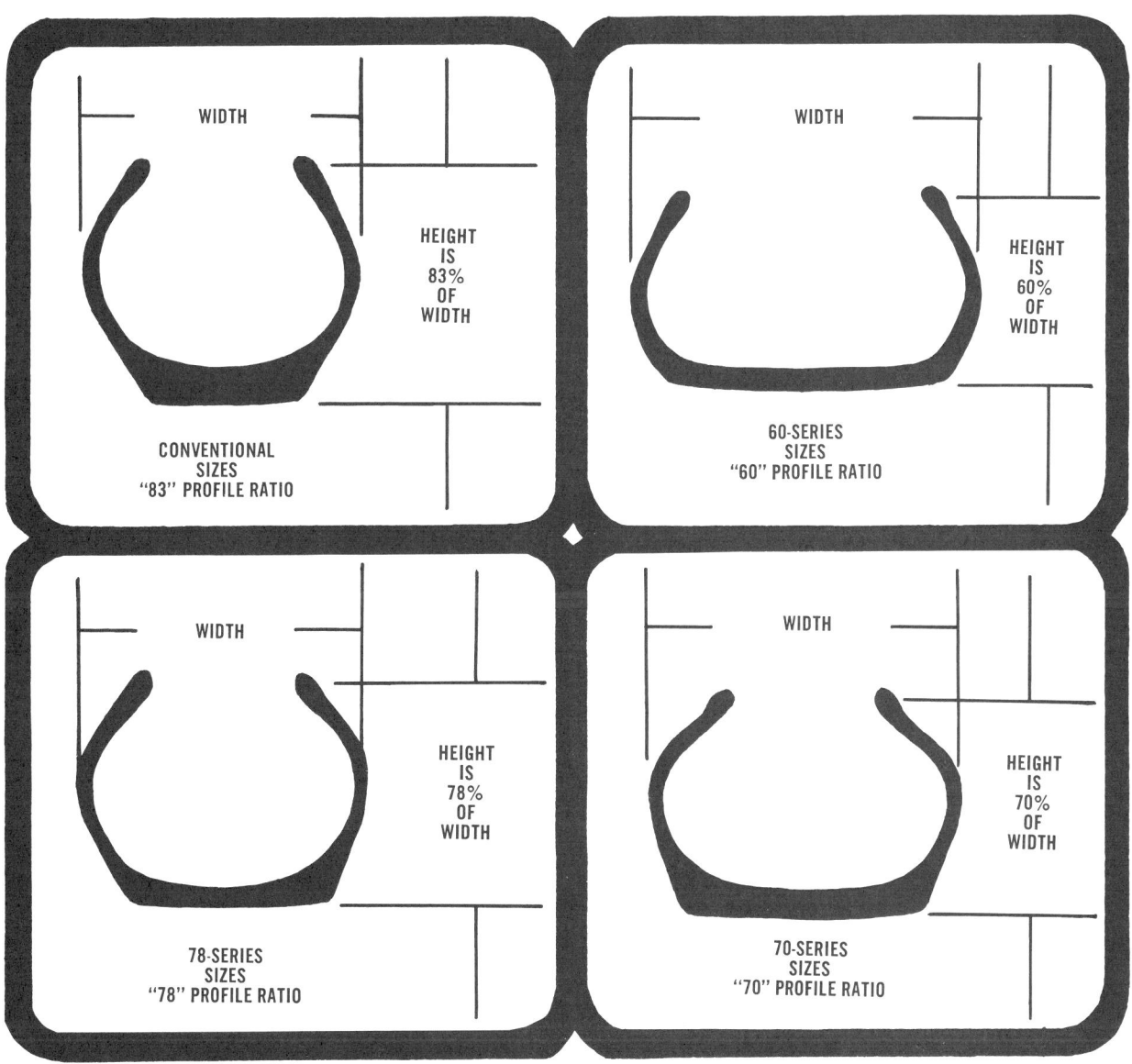

A comparison of the height-to-width profile ratios of the four most common tire sizes.

Example A

Example B

Example B
Tubeless GR70-15. The G refers to the size and load-carrying capacity. This tire can carry a maximum of 1620 pounds per tire when inflated to maximum air pressure of 32 psi. Four of these tires have a total capacity of 6480 pounds. The load on each tire of this size, including the weight of the car, its passengers and cargo, should never exceed the 1620 pound limit. The R indicates that it is a radial tire. The 70 shows that the height of a cross section of this tire is 70% of its width. The 15 shows that it is meant for a 15-inch diameter wheel. Radial again shows the type of construction.

Load Range B. This Load Range code is another indication of the tire's load and inflation capability. Load Range B is the most common. Higher load range tires are also available and required on some vehicles.

DOT. This stands for the Department of Transportation. It certifies that the tire complies with the federal government tire safety standards.

Tread. 4 Plies-2 Plies Polyester and 2 Plies Steel Cord/Sidwall-2 Plies Polyester. Every tire has similar markings to reveal the material and the number of plies in the body and in the belt, if it is a belted tire. This tire has a total of four plies in the tread area, including two plies and two additional belt plies.

TIRE MATERIALS

A couple of years ago, nylon was the accepted material for producing top quality tires, having supplanted rayon as the best tire cord material. Today, it is not as clear cut. Nylon is still used extensively. But polyester is also very big in the tire field and rayon is making a strong comeback. Each has its place in the marketing mix as a tire cord material. Rayon was used for years and years before the nylon revolution in the early '60s. Rayon is a good cord material for tires that are subjected to normal, standard duty use. That is, low to moderate speed use in urban areas on paved roads. Rayon will deliver good performance under these conditions but just does not have the inherent strength needed to cope with high speed, long mileage runs for extended periods or abusive use on rough, unpaved or semi-paved roads. However, rayon is the least expensive of all the cord materials and rayon tires will generally be less expensive than comparable nylon or polyester tires.

Lately, rayon has made a comeback as a cord material because some companies have developed a special kind of rayon with much greater tensile strength. Tire cord make of high tensile rayon is less expensive than nylon cord tires and almost as strong and tough—but not quite. Rayon has also been used recently as a belting material in both bias-belted and radial-ply tires.

Some companies have recently introduced rayon cord tires with rayon belts under the tread and also rayon cord tires with fiberglass belts. Both types are a vast improvement over rayon non-belted tires and good buys for the customer who wants added strength and stability of a belted tire but does not want to pay premium tire prices.

Nylon is still the strongest, toughest tire cord material made. It is stronger, pound for pound, than steel. It is also elastic and able to take a terrific

Steel belts under the tread give the best penetration protection against road hazards.

amount of abuse without coming apart—an ideal material for tire cord. Almost all high performance and high speed tires are still made of nylon cord. Nylon has only one disadvantage. When a nylon tire equipped car is parked for any length of time, the nylon cord material cools and takes a "set." It actually flattens out at the point where the tire is laying on the ground. When the car is again driven, the flat spot in the tire remains until the nylon heats and expands. Under normal conditions, this takes only a block or two even in very cold weather. However, many people object to the thump caused by this slight flat spot on a cold nylon tire.

Polyester is relatively new to the tire business, having been formulated only in 1962. Polyester cord tires were not marketed in earnest until around 1968. Then, when all the American car manufacturers announced that their 1970 models would all be equipped with polyester cord tires as standard equipment, polyester became a tire cord material as great in importance as nylon and rayon.

Actually, polyester cord combines the best qualities of nylon and rayon but without the disadvantages. It is almost a perfect compromise cord material in that it is almost as good as the other materials in many areas and is better in some. For example, a polyester cord tire runs as smooth as a rayon tire but is much tougher. It is almost as tough as a nylon tire but rides much smoother and does not flat spot even after standing for weeks.

Fiberglass as a reinforcing material for rubber has also been a relatively new development. Pontiac Motor Division of General Motors Corp. used a fiberglass-reinforced rubber belt to drive the overhead camshaft in a new engine introduced in 1964. Since then, fiberglass has been used more extensively by the rubber companies in various forms. In 1966, layers of fiberglass were laid under the tread of a conventional bias-ply tire and the fiberglass belted bias-ply tire was born.

A few years ago, when bias-belted tires were standard equipment on about 98% of all new cars, fiberglass was the fastest growing material in terms of tire usage. Today, with more and more companies going to steel belted radials as standard equipment, fiberglass usage has dropped off somewhat. It is still very big on the aftermarket in the replacement tire field and you will be seeing some new cars with fiberglass belted bias-belted tires as original equipment.

Recently, some companies have introduced all fiberglass radial tires with fiberglass used for the cord and belting material. These tires are said to be as strong as steel belted radials. But because fiberglass is a less expensive material than steel, the cost of fiberglass radials is less than steel belted radials.

The most advertised tire today is the steel belted radial. The advantages are obvious—steel is much, much tougher than either rayon or fiberglass as a belt material. The disadvantages are a slightly rougher ride because the steel belt does not give or expand under impact as does a rayon or fiberglass belt.

The other disadvantage, of course, is cost. Steel belted radials are a premium tire and they command a premium price.

But taking your own driving style, load requirements and automobile into account, you might not need the best possible tire.

WHEN DO YOU NEED NEW TIRES?

The first consideration is a matter of time. Most people average about 10,000 miles a year. You should have a pretty good idea of whether you are above or below this average. How many people drive the car? Is it used as part of your business? And driving habits are important. Is the car driven hard? Then there is the mechanical condition of the car. Do you take pretty good care of it? Is the front end likely to be in good alignment at any given time?

Only you can know these things. And overriding all of them, inspection is a must. You must look at your tires. Assuming you haven't had some tire trouble with one or more of them recently, the only way you can tell when your tires need replacing is to inspect them.

We recommend looking at your tires closely at least once a month. Certainly you should never go more than 5000 miles without checking them over.

If a tire is smooth, obviously it has gone too far. Get a new one. If the tire is worn unevenly, it indicates a mechanical malfunction somewhere. The tire probably should be replaced and the condition that ruined it should be fixed. Uneven wear can indicate several things wrong—misalignment, which is the most common reason for fast wear, worn shock absorbers, a worn, loose front end, an out-of-balance condition, or a combination of all these. Grabbing brakes can be a problem, too, but this is not often a leading cause of uneven wear. Check the Troubleshooting section in this chapter for more information on how to read tread patterns.

Assuming the wear is even but evident, there are two other ways you can tell if you have the tread necessary for safe driving. One is tread wear bars.

Every tire produced since 1969, when the Department of Transportation came into being, is built with these treadwear indicators. They are molded right into the tire and they look the same regardless of which company made the tire. A treadwear bar appears as a smooth bar running across the tread area. It shows up when the tread is worn down to 2/32s of an inch of tread depth. Two thirty-seconds. That is 1/16 inch. It is the minimum tread depth accepted by many states. The government describes such a tire as bald. In other words, when the tread-wear bar shows up, the tire is no longer capable of delivering the traction you need for safety. A new tire has a non-skid tread depth of about 11/32-inch or a little less than a half-inch.

You might ask why they do not make treads deeper. The answer is heat. The number one enemy of long tire wear is heat, and a thicker tread runs hotter. The hotter the tire runs, the quicker the tread wears away.

Of course, if you never drove more than 25 miles an hour, tire manufacturers could probably make a tire with inch-thick tread that would run 75,000 miles. But, of course, our highways and lifestyle demand that we drive faster than 25 mph.

The other way to tell if your tires are worn past the safe tread depth is the old Lincoln-head penny trick. Put a Lincoln-head penny into a groove in your tread, with the top of Lincoln's head pointing toward the tire. If you can see all of the head, it is time to change. The tread is less than 1/16-inch in depth. It is past the point where it will give you safe traction and the protection you need from puncturing objects.

HOW TO BUY NEW TIRES

Once you have determined that you need new tires, how do you know which ones to buy? How do you know which tires are right for you? What is the right size, material, construction type for your car?

You can largely determine the answers to these questions by asking yourself five other questions.

How fast do you drive? You know the answer to this. And when you are shopping for tires, it is no time to be less than candid about speed. Incidentally, speed and mileage do not go together. The man who drives consistently at 35 mph will get more than twice the mileage of the guy who zips along most of the time at 65 or better. So, how fast you drive is important. *Where you drive* is, too. If you spend a lot of time on rough roads, it is a factor in tire selection. If you drive on high-speed expressways or freeways a lot, this too, is important.

Another question is *how often is your car loaded with people and luggage* or camping gear? Another, *how long do you intend to keep your car?* Are you going to run it another 10,000 miles or less? Or are you going to rack an additional 30,000 or 40,000 miles before you trade it in? Lastly, and this is probably the most important, *what kind of driver are you?* Are you an easy driver who favors gradual starts and stops? Are you average? Or do you push it most of the time?

Those are the questions. Your answers will pretty well enable you to narrow down the selection of a tire that will do the best job for you. If you plan to trade the car before too long, you certainly would be in error to buy a tire that is built to go 40,000 miles. Obviously.

Some tires are suited for life in the suburbs. Others are best for the superhighway. Light tires on a vehicle that carries heavy loads is a mistake. Buying the wrong tire is wasteful, and can be downright dangerous. The trick is to get the tire you need.

To gauge what you might expect in tire wear and performance, consider the tires that came on your car as original equipment. These are comparable to the so-called firstline tires made by the five major tire producers. While there are no industry-wide standards pertaining to quality levels, firstline generally means of a quality on a level with the tires shipped to Detroit for use on new automobiles as original equipment. Secondline means something less in quality level and, in our opinion, thirdline is not really worth considering. All of the major manufacturers offer premium level tires, which are more costly than first or 100-level tires. These make up the top of the line. If they can provide you with something other than tire wear—such as prestige or knowing you own the best—then you may well give this some thought. However, assuming you were satisfied with the performance of your O.E. tires, and if you want a tire that will last for many miles of safe driving, you probably should buy a 100-level or firstline tire. For longer wear, you should go premium. For a station wagon that frequently carries heavy loads, you may want heavy duty 6- or 8-ply rated tires. You can probably get by with a secondline tire on a second car that is used for shopping and short commuting. If you do not expect to keep your car long, then thirdline tires are a possibility. These are also acceptable if you use a car just to go a few miles a day to the train or bus station.

AVOIDING TIRE INJURIES

Proper air pressure and careful driving will prevent most injuries. However, when a chuckhole, curb or other object is struck with sufficient force, a tire can be injured without any visible evidence of damage, even when correctly inflated, eventually resulting in failure.

Impact of tire hitting curb or chuckhole can cause a non-repairable injury.

Driving even a short distance on a seriously underinflated or flat tire will result in damage inside the tire which cannot be repaired.

Many different types of snow tires are available for different needs. However, if you have radial tires on the front of your car, you must also use radial snow tires. Top left, steel studs offer good traction even on glare ice. Above, steel belts offer the greatest road hazard protection. Left, special tread patterns are available for traction in mud as well as snow.

Retreads fall into the same category, although you should know the reputation of the retreader intimately before investing in these. Good retreads are good. But the converse is true, too, bad ones are *really* bad.

For long, sustained, high speed runs on the open road, the radial has no equal. It runs cooler. It handles well. It is quiet. And the long mileage is an added bonus. In tests, engineers have found that most radials deliver from 40 to 100% more mileage than other tires. Of course, they cost more initially too. But their lower rolling resistance helps you get slightly better gas mileage. One drawback: if your car is not engineered for radials and a slightly harsher ride at lower speeds bothers you, then you better check into other types.

Price is a fairly good indicator of new tire quality, but only if you know the dealer with whom you are dealing. Otherwise you may find yourself looking at two tires that look alike, while one is $18 and the other twice that much. The cheaper tire may have a lower grade of fabric and a narrower, shallower tread that will wear rapidly on the road. The costlier tire may be a better bargain, especially if you can get the salesman to modify the cost of mounting and balancing the tire. Your best bet: know the dealer.

Whatever you buy, the mileage you will get depends to a great extent on how you treat them. For the first 50 miles or so, stay under 50 miles an hour, to allow the tire bodies a chance to flex and break in. Generally avoid quick starts and stops and excessive speeds, not to mention fast cornering. Make sure that your front end alignment is correct and the shock absorbers are in good condition. Have the alignment checked at least every 10,000 miles. If you have more than 15,000 miles on your shocks, it would not hurt to have them checked over for wear and effectiveness.

Above all, keep your tires properly inflated. Check inflation regularly while the tires are cool. One more thing. Slow down. Not just around town, but slow down generally. You may get a lot more than extra mileage out of it.

Snow tires

When radial tires became popular several years ago, many experts were saying that a radial's traction was so much better than bias-ply or bias-belted tires that snow tires were no longer necessary.

While it is true that the traction of most radial tires is much better than tires made with other construction methods, even the best radial will not give you the traction of a real snow tire in snow. A radial may give you perhaps 40% of the traction of a snow tire. But is 40% traction enough?

Obviously, if you live in an area where little snow falls, the answer could be yes. On the other hand, if you live in a more northern region where snow falls frequently and heavily, you will probably want to have all the traction you can get.

In extreme cases, even plain snow tires may not be enough. You may have to use studded snow tires or even tire chains with snow tires to get you through the winter.

Which solution is best will depend on the winter driving conditions of your particular section of the country.

A welded-type chain might be best for occasional emergency use—like a trip to a ski resort. But for infrequent use around the city, two or three strap-on chains would be more convenient since they can be installed easily without jacking up the car.

In most northern states, snow tires are a necessity —but they will not help you on glare ice. However, studded tires with either ceramic or tungsten studs buried in the tread will perform on packed snow or ice almost as well as chains. Before buying studded tires, check if they are legal to use in your state. Some states have a cutoff date when they can and cannot be used.

The best buying times for snow tires or chains are either during the fall sales or during an off season or clearance sale.

Today, snow tires are made in all three types of construction—bias-ply, bias-belted and radial-ply—so that you can properly match your front tires with the right type of snow tire.

It is essential for safe handling that you match the type of tire construction at all four wheels of your car. If you have radial front tires, you must use radial snow tires too, or your car will exhibit rather strange handling characteristics which could prove unstable in an emergency situation.

In addition to construction, snow tires are also made in various profile ratios, again to match the type of tire you have on the front of your car.

The ideal situation is to have the same construction type and profile ratio tires at all four corners of your car. This is the safest way to go. If this is not possible, it is still OK to differ in profile ratios providing the construction type is the same.

For example, it is still OK to have, say, 70-series radials on the front and 60-series radial snow tires on the rear. Or, 78-series bias-belted on the front and 70-series radial snows on the rear. Or even 60s on the front and 78s on the rear, providing they are all the same construction.

Do not put radials on the front and bias-belted on the rear, or any other similar combination.

TIRES AND INCLEMENT WEATHER

Stopping on a wet road can take up to 4 times the normal distance on a dry road, up to 10 times on glare ice.

REDUCE SPEED TO AVOID SKIDS!

Test traction on different road surfaces and in bad weather by occasional light braking.

Keep tires properly inflated. To avoid swerve on braking, front tire pressures must be equal.

Do not tailgate.

Slow down on slippery roads. When braking, pump to avoid locking wheels which can cause skid.

IF A SKID STARTS

Take foot off gas, keep off the brakes, steer in direction of skid. When car is straightened out, pump brakes gently to slow down.

WINTER NOTE: Since cold weather reduces the tire pressure approximately one pound per square inch for every 10° drop in temperature, tire inflation should be checked more frequently during winter months to be sure pressures are at levels recommended by your car owner's manual.

OIL FILM

Light rain or drizzle, especially after a dry spell, produces a thin greasy film on the road surface which is almost as slippery as ice. Be on your guard against other skid hazards, including wet leaves and mud and sand, dirt or gravel on dry roads.

RAIN

Water on the pavement reduces traction, and as the water accumulates on the road surface, tires begin to hydroplane or surfboard as speed increases, particularly over 40 mph. This can lead to loss of traction and control of the vehicle.

SNOW, SLUSH AND ICE

Under winter conditions road surfaces are obviously slippery—twice as hazardous in the freezing range, around 32°, as at 0°. Snow tires or studded tires are recommended. Studded tires double the traction of regular tires on glare ice.

Here are some tire saving tips that will assure you of getting all the mileage that was built into a set of tires.

- Check air pressure regularly when tires are cold—before starting out. Maintain car owner's manual specified inflation.

- When traveling overloaded or prior to a long trip, inflate your tires accordingly. This usually means increasing the air pressure. See owner's manual.

- Drive with anticipation. Avoid jamming on brakes at traffic lights and intersections. Eliminate jackrabbit starts. Corner at posted speeds. Drive around chuckholes and curbs.

- Check your tires before, during and after a long trip.

- Do not bleed your tires during a long trip because of increased pressure.

- Inspect tires frequently for irregular wear patterns that could signify bad shocks, misalignment, out-of-balance tires. Keep in mind that most tires are worn out due to defective front-end steering parts. Regular car care inspections can help you receive all the mileage that has been built into your tires.

- Check valve stem and dust cap if tire seems to be losing air consistently.

- Be sure your spare tire is properly inflated at all times and ready to roll if and when necessary.

- Rotate your tires every 6000 to 8000 miles. An excellent time also to have them inspected for any puncturing objects, stones wedged between the ribs, etc.

- When your tires are worn down to the wear bar indicators it means you have only 2/32 of an inch of tread remaining on your tires. Time to buy a replacement.

- Consolidate your shopping trips around town to make maximum use of your car when it is out. Make one trip serve for several trips to the grocery, library, drug store, cleaners, etc.

Wet roads require different driving techniques. Driving on wet roads with bald tires is the surest way we know of to become involved in an accident.

TIRE MAINTENANCE

Tires should be inspected regularly for excessive or abnormal tread wear, fabric breaks, cut or other damage.

A bulge or bump in the sidewall or tread is reason for discarding a tire. A bulge indicates that the tread or sidewall has separated from the tire body. The tire is a candidate for an imminent blowout.

Tire treads should be inspected regularly. Bumps, bulges or knots indicate possible separation of tread or sidewall from the tire body. The tire should be removed from the wheel and examined by an expert. In all likelihood, you will have to replace the tire.

Look also for small stones or other foreign bodies wedged in the tread. These can be removed by prying them out carefully with a screwdriver. This will help prevent flats or costly tire damage which can lead to failure. This preventive maintenance is normally done at the service station when tires are rotated, the oil changed or the car lubricated. But there is no substitute for periodic personal inspection for greater assurance.

Surveys show that while tires are involved in less than 1% of all highway accidents, in more than half of these cases the tires are bald or worn to the cords. Bald tires have also been found to be up to 44 times more likely to have flats as new tires. The risk of

skidding, which is 5 to 10 times more likely with average tread depth on wet roads as on dry roads, is doubled with bald tires.

Inflation pressure

Proper inflation is the key to maximum performance from any tire. Too little air or too much air in a tire will cause rapid and uneven wear.

Underinflation brings excessive wear to the outer edges of the tire and also causes the tire to generate excessive heat—one of the greatest causes of tire wear and failure.

Overinflation causes faster wear in the center groove area and in addition makes the tire more susceptible to breaks due to hitting objects or holes in the road.

A few minutes once a month to check air pressure can result in dollars saved through extra mileage. The spare should also be checked at the same time.

The proper air pressure for your tires is listed in the owner's manual for your car.

Tires should always be checked when they are cool because pressure will build up after the tires have been run. Never reduce built-up pressure when the tires are hot.

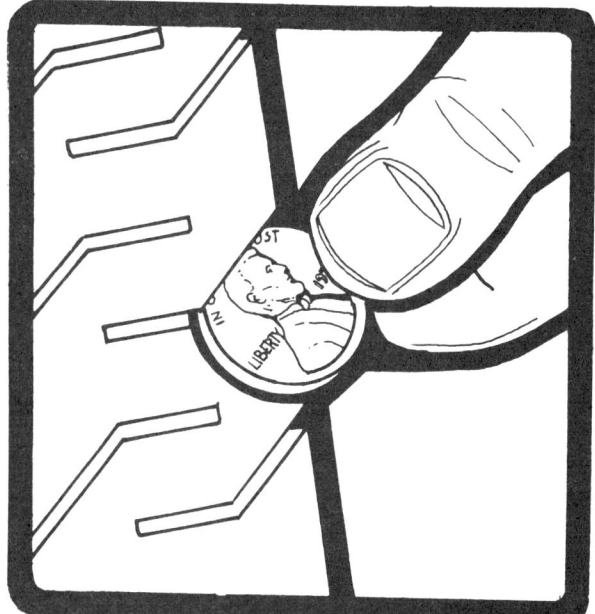

Measure the depth of your tire tread by using the top edge of a penny. If the top of Lincoln's head shows, the tread is worn below 1/16-inch and the tire should be replaced.

Look for tread or sidewall cuts, cracks or snags deep enough to expose the tire ply cords. When any part of the cord or fabric is exposed, replace the tire.

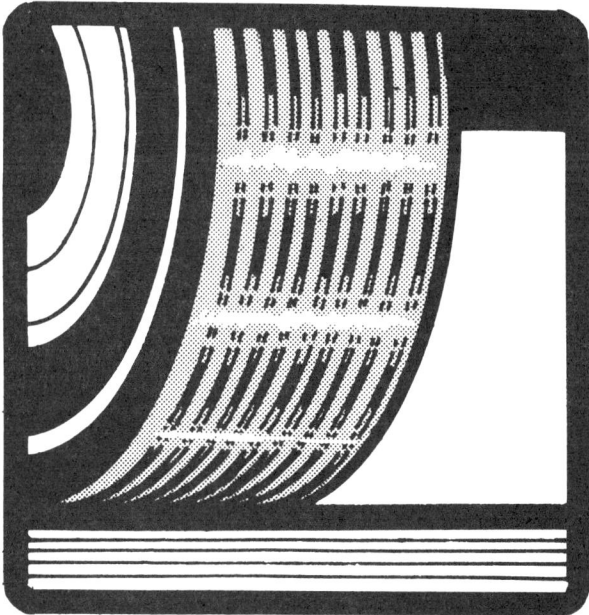

Tires built since 1968 have tread wear bars built into the tread. When these smooth bands appear in two or more adjacent grooves, the tread is worn below 1/16-inch depth. The tire should be replaced.

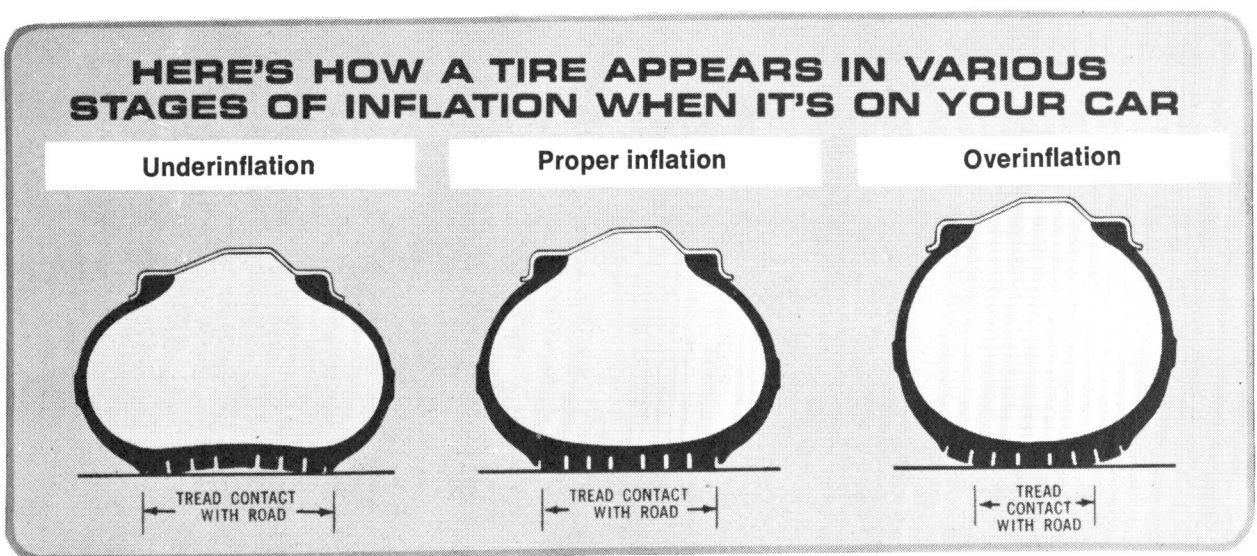

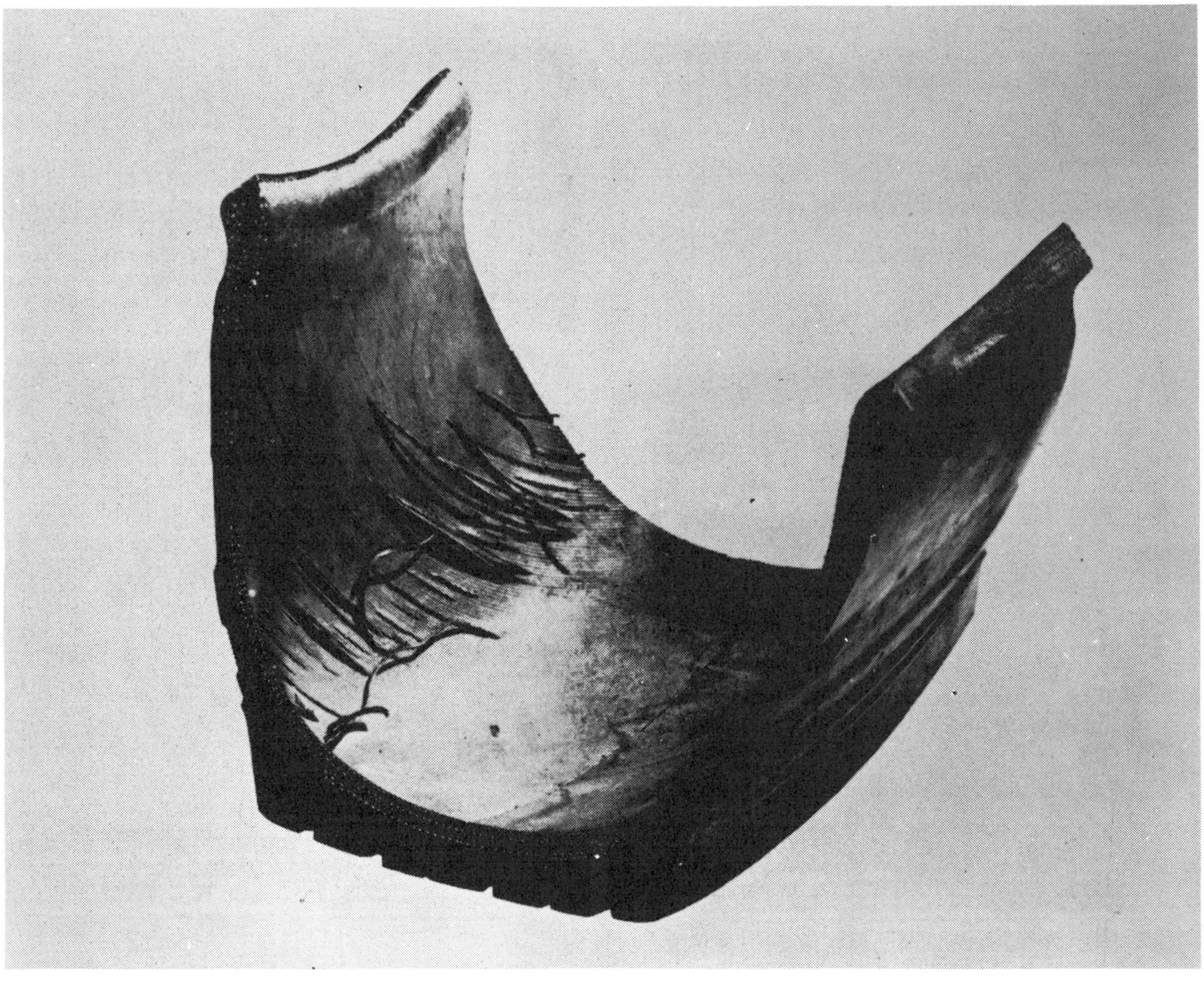

Permanent tire damage such as this occurs when a tire is driven for even a short distance in either a severely underinflated or flat condition. This type of damage is permanent.

However, there are certain times when it may be advisable to go to a higher pressure. For example, four additional pounds of pressure should be added if you plan to travel long distances at turnpike speeds, when pulling a trailer or carrying a heavy load.

However, under no condition should the level exceed the maximum cold pressure specified on the tire's sidewall normally listed as 32 pounds for an average passenger car tire.

Other checks

Neglect of the car's front end suspension system—shock absorbers, springs, wheel alignment—can wreak havoc with tires, as can the lack of proper balancing of a tire-wheel combination.

The result of any of these conditions will be non-uniform wear, including cupping or flat spots.

Improper tire wear can occur on any car, no matter how new. Therefore, every car owner should begin the habit of frequent visual inspection of the car's tires.

In addition to these checks, be constantly on the alert for the indications that your tires need replacements. These indications were discussed previously under When Do You Need New Tires?

Briefly, look for:
1. Tread or sidewall cuts, cracks or snags deep enough to expose tire ply cords, or when any part of cord or fabric is exposed, replace tires.
2. Tread worn to level of wear bars built into all new tires since 1969. When these smooth bands appear in two or more adjacent grooves, replace tires.
3. Tread worn below 1/16-inch depth in two or more adjacent grooves or where ply cords show. Measure depth with top edge of a penny. If top of Lincoln's head shows, replace tires.
4. Bumps, bulges or knots indicating possible separation of tread or sidewall from tire body. Tire should be removed from the wheel and examined by an expert. Replace tires.

Tire valves should be in good condition and equipped with valve caps or valve extensions to keep out dirt and moisture. When replacing tires, it is a good idea to replace valves, too.

Rims or wheels should also be in sound condition and missing or defective bolts, nuts and lugs replaced.

Any tire marked *Unsafe for highway use, Not for highway use,* or *For racing purposes only,* should not be used on public roads.

Tire valves

About every other tire change, you should change the valve. Snap-in replacement valves for tubeless tires are carried by tire dealers and are lubricated so that you can pop them into the wheel's valve opening. The replacement should match the original in length and in TR number (molded into the valve base).

Whitewalls

Some whitewalls come from the factory with a colored protective coating on the white portion. That coating should be removed before you use the tires, since it is not as flexible as the rubber and tends to crack, causing the sidewalls to deteriorate. In no case should a whitewall be driven more than 50 miles without removing the coating.

To get it off, wet the tire surface thoroughly with warm water, let it soak for a minute, and then wash off the coating with a soft-bristle brush or a sponge. The coating can also be removed in a jet-spray car wash by close jetting. Never use gasoline or other petroleum solvents or a wire brush.

Road dirt that collects on whitewalls should be removed only with soap or a non-abrasive cleaner and, when necessary, a soft-bristle brush. Oil-based cleaning fluids, gasoline and kerosene deteriorate the rubber and may discolor whitewalls.

If a tire suffers a sidewall cut, the damage is permanent and the tire should be replaced.

Rotation

There are those who advocate tire rotation. And there are those who claim it is a waste of time and money. Tire companies and automobile manufacturers are advocates. Manufacturers of front-end alignment and wheel-balancing equipment, in general, argue against rotation, contending that alignment and wheel balancing should be performed frequently instead, to prevent mechanical failures that cause rapid tread wear.

One cannot argue with the fact that front end alignment and wheel balancing are very important procedures if you wish to remedy a problem that is causing unnecessary tire wear. However, there is too much technical evidence available to allow one to dismiss the value of rotation.

The purpose of rotation is to equalize normal tire wear. There is such a thing as normal wear. Nothing lasts indefinitely. By equalizing this wear evenly over the entire tread surface, you extend tire life.

Front tires experience normal wear primarily on their outer shoulders, as a result of cornering maneuvers. Rear tires experience normal wear primarily in the center because of the power thrust from the rear axle. This is assuming a typical rear-end-driven automobile rather than a front-wheel-drive vehicle.

Rotation equalizes this wear so that no one section wears away faster than an adjacent area. According to one tire company, rotating tires every 5000 miles provides you with 20% more mileage from each tire.

Even among the advocates of tire rotation, there is some disagreement on how it should be done. Some say that the spare tire should be included in the rotation plan, thereby equaling wear on all five tires. Others claim that a more economical plan is to keep the spare in the trunk unused, then buy just three new tires rather than four when replacement time comes around.

Although the jury is still out on this question, most owners usually opt for the plan that includes the spare tire. This is especially true of new car owners who have five new tires to begin with. If you are starting with four new tires, of course, the plan will not work for you. So pick the plan that more closely resembles your real world status.

Radial tires are rotated from front to rear. Bias and bias-belted tires are rotated in crisscross fashion.

If you use snow tires, they should be considered in your overall rotation scheme. That is, plan rotation so it coincides with the time of the year when snow tires have to be mounted. Follow the recommended rotation method illustrated here.

It is wise to provide snow tires with rims of their own, so they do not have to be removed from rims in the spring and put back on rims in the late fall. They can be kept on rims of their own during both storage and use. In this way, you will protect tires from the bead damage which becomes a possibility when you break a tire away from a rim. You can probably buy a couple of used rims for your car from an auto wrecker yard for a few dollars.

A studded snow tire should always be mounted on the same wheel of the car year after year after year. When storing studded snow tires mark each tire in chalk with either an R for Right or an L for Left, depending upon which side of the car the tire was mounted. If studded tires are switched, so that studs rotate in a direction opposite to that in which they rotated previously, studs will twist, loosen, and fly out of their seats in the tread.

When storing tires, lay them flat, off the tread, and keep them away from electricity-producing machinery. Laying the tire flat keeps flat spots from developing over the tread. Electricity-producing machinery creates ozone. Ozone damages rubber.

Wheel balancing

To be quite blunt about it, you cannot balance your wheels yourself. For static or dynamic balancing, expensive machines are required. So leave this job for your local tire store, service station or other facility equipped with the necessary machinery.

However, you should know what is going on when the man is balancing your wheels.

Actually, the term wheel balancing is a misnomer. A wheel by itself may be perfectly balanced. But if its associated tire or brake drum (or disc) is out of balance, the wheel too will be thrown out of balance. In other words, instead of using the term wheel balance, it would be more accurate to speak of wheel-tire-brake drum (or disc) balance. But for the sake of brevity, we will use the more popular term, wheel balance.

As we have mentioned, if a wheel assembly is out of balance, vibration and tire wear could result. For this reason, a wheel and tire should be balanced whenever you mount the tire on the wheel or replace the tire or wheel with a new one. Furthermore, the brake drum or brake disc, tire, and wheel should be balanced as an assembly when you replace the drum or disc.

A replacement brake drum or disc may not be balanced. However, original equipment drums and discs are balanced at the factory when a car is assembled.

There are two types of wheel imbalance—static and dynamic. Consequently, there are two types of wheel-balancing equipment—static and dynamic.

When a wheel assembly is statically out of balance, a heavy spot exists at a single point on the assembly. As the assembly rotates, the heavy spot is forced against the pavement with each revolution of the wheel. This creates a pronounced vertical vibration.

If a wheel assembly is dynamically out of balance, the assembly moves from side to side, causing a horizontal vibration. The wheel oscillates, and the tire scuffs against the pavement, which creates flat spots over the tire.

Static wheel balancing is done by placing a weight equal in mass to the heavy spot on the wheel opposite the spot. In the case of dynamic balancing, a weight equal in mass to that on the outside of the wheel is placed at the same point on the inside of the wheel.

Static imbalance creates vibration mainly at slow speeds, while dynamic imbalance vibration occurs primarily at highway speeds. So, if you normally drive at higher speeds, you should have wheels balanced dynamically. If you drive mainly around town, static balancing is acceptable. However, if you want to be 100% certain that wheel assemblies are balanced perfectly, you should have them balanced both dynamically and statically.

TIRE ROTATION PLANS

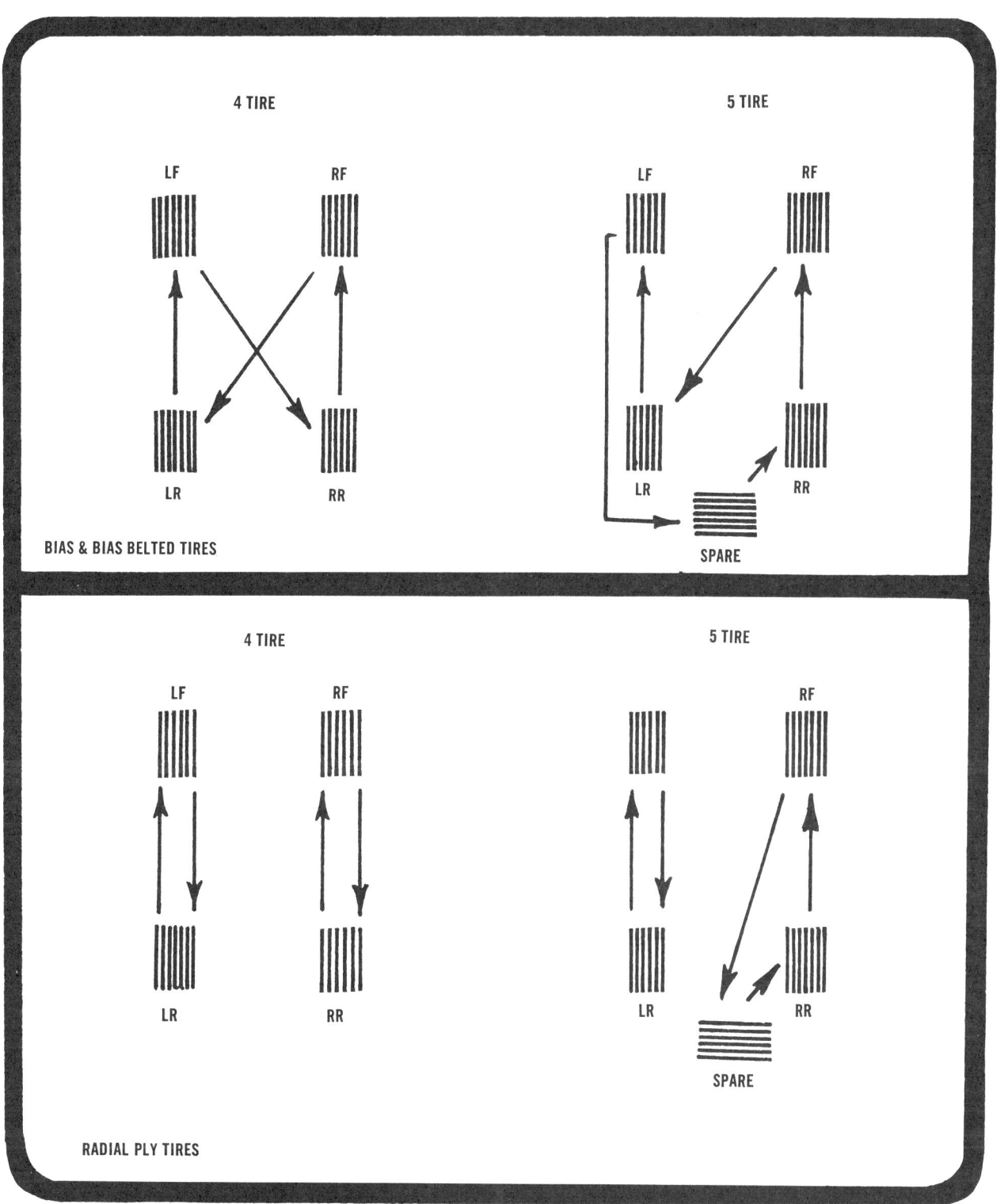

TROUBLESHOOTING ABNORMAL WEAR PATTERNS

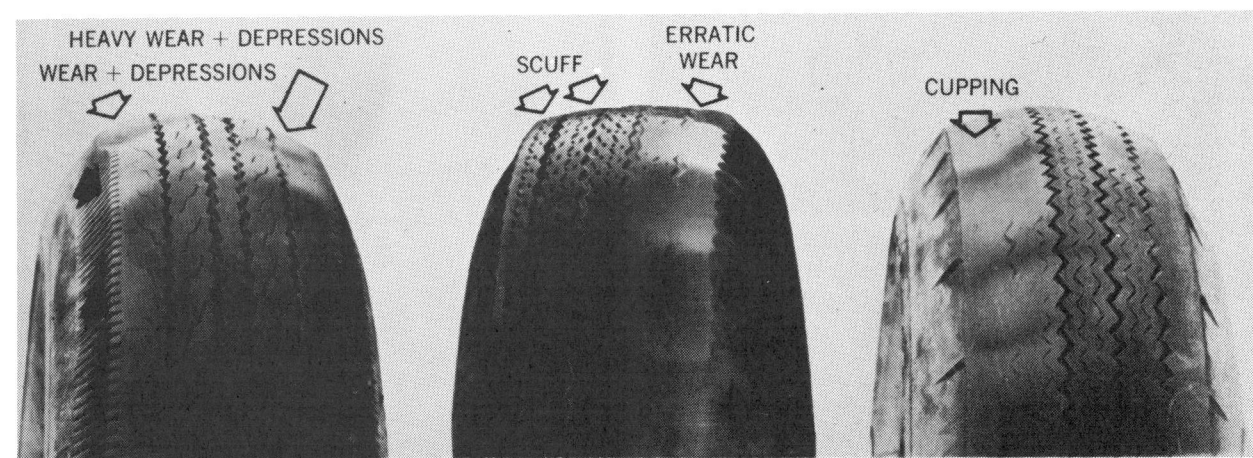

Wear patterns

Tire wear patterns can tell you a lot about your car and the way it is driven. Learn to look at your tires whenever you walk up to your car to use it. This does not mean you have to look at all of them, but notice the ones on the side you approach. If they bulge out more than usual, check their pressures.

If the *center* of the tread shows more wear than the edges, overinflation is the cause. Reduce tire pressure to that specified by the manufacturer for the load and type of driving you do. If the tread is cracking, take the wheel to a shop for an internal inspection.

If the *edges* of the tread show more wear than the center, the cause is underinflation. If serious enough, underinflation may cause hidden fiber damage. The only way to be sure is to have the tire removed from the wheel for an internal inspection. The cure for underinflation wear is proper inflation through regular checks of pressure while cold. You can drive a short distance on a slightly underinflated tire. But if the underinflation is great, pump up the tire or remove it and put on the spare.

If the edges of the tread are worn more than the center and the tire has a *smoothly rounded tread* profile, the driver must take the blame. Fast driving around corners is the cause of the problem.

Tiny *feather edges* on one side of tread blocks are caused by too much or too little toe-in. A slight toe problem (in or out) usually wears rubber from just one tire. A severe toe problem can wear rubber rapidly from both tires or even from all four.

Tread blocks with a *saw-toothed* wear pattern indicate too much or too hard use of brakes. The problem is called heel-and-toe wear. A certain amount of such wear is normal. Rear tires show it less than front tires because they receive a driving force from the engine that wears off the opposite ends of their tread blocks. But only braking forces act on the front wheels of conventional, rear-wheel-drive cars. The remedy is to change driving habits and to equalize abnormal wear by rotation if the problem becomes serious enough to produce tire noises.

Tread with *one side worn off*, on a front wheel, is caused by driving on highly cambered roads or by improper camber setting of that wheel. One-sided front tire wear can also be caused by taking turns too fast.

Uneven or spotty tread wear, which sometimes takes the form of cupping, scalloping, or bald spots around the tire, may be caused by alignment irregularities such as unequal caster or camber, bent suspension parts, out-of-balance wheels, out-of-round brake drums, or brakes that are out of adjustment. Other mechanical problems can also cause such wear. The remedy may be a case for a professional mechanic. Once an uneven wear pattern is set, correcting the cause alone will not improve the pattern. Tire rotation is called for. When placed on a rear wheel, a front tire that has become cupped will partially true its tread.

Noises

A *vibration* or a *whining sound* that is especially noticeable on a smooth road may signal tread abnormalities. Unless it is a wheel tramp that comes once with every revolution of the wheels, it may be tough to tell from differential gear noises.

To tell tire noise from gear or exhaust noise, find a smooth stretch of highway. Drive at various speeds and note the effect of accelerating and decelerating. When it is safe to do so, brake lightly. Axle and exhaust noises change in intensity under these conditions. Tire noises, though, usually stay the same throughout.

If tires seem to be the cause, balance all the wheels, temporarily inflate them to 45 psi, and drive the road again at the same speeds. If the noise is changed or eliminated, deflate one tire at a time to the proper pressure, repeating the road test with each deflation. When the noise returns to what it was, the last tire deflated is probably the offender.

Wheel tramp (also called tire thump) usually occurs between 20 and 40 mph. The bad tire is easy to locate with the tire-at-a-time deflation method. The only cure for a thumper is replacement.

Tire *roughness* from two or more thumping tires, or one tire with more than one thump-spot, most often shows up at speeds between 40 and 70 mph. Tire roughness feels like a low-frequency rumble or vibration. It may be felt in the seat or steering wheel or both. Front tire thumps are most noticeable in the steering wheel, while rear tire thumps usually show up as seat vibrations. To find the troublemaker(s), you may have to replace the tires one at a time with the spare. For this, all tires should be at normal pressure.

An *out-of-balance driveshaft* can feel like thumping tires. To tell one from the other, block up the rear axle, remove the wheels, and accelerate the engine with the transmission in gear. Hold the accelerator pedal at the speed where the vibration was most pronounced. If you feel no vibration, the front or rear tires are the cause. If the vibration is still there, the driveshaft is the likely cause.

Tires that *squeal* easily on turns, or make a loud *hissing* noise as they roll, may also be signaling toe troubles. (The hissing is noise reflected from parked cars that you drive by.) Car handling may or may not be affected.

TIRE REPAIRS

The only repair you should make is to tighten a loose valve core. A loose core lets the tire lose air. When a tire goes flat, inflate the tire and apply soapy water to the valve. Look for bubbles. If they appear, try tightening the valve core.

Speaking of the valve, be sure all valves are equipped with caps. Caps block the entrance of dirt and water into the tire through the valve.

Other than this repair, you should leave the fixing of a flat to a shop that has the necessary tools. Trying to break a bead away from a rim with tire irons, for example, may very likely damage the bead and render an otherwise serviceable tire unusable.

Although you should not make repairs, you should be aware that the only type of repair you should allow someone to make on one of your tires is a permanent repair. A permanent repair is always made from inside the tire out. The tire must come off the rim to have a cold plug and patch, or a chemical and hot vulcanized patch, applied.

Repairs that are made from outside the tire in are temporary at best and will start leaking within a short time.

However, in an emergency, you can temporarily repair leaks in modern tubeless tires if you have a tubeless tire external patching kit. The purpose of such a repair is to keep you on the road, for no more than 100 miles at speeds no higher than 50 mph. But if the hole in the tire is larger than ¼-inch or if the plies are separated around the leak, do not try to repair the tire. Replace it immediately.

To try a repair, you will need a spark plug tire pump, a spark plug wrench and a patch kit.

Procedure

1. First, locate the leak. Ordinarily, you need not remove the wheel to do that. Just listen for the hiss of escaping air. Feel around the tread for escaping air. If necessary, jack up the wheel.
2. Once the leak is found, probe it with a tire patch tool.
3. Feel for metal or glass fragments, and remove any foreign material.
4. Squirt some rubber cement from your patching kit onto the tip of the needle and run it in and out of the puncture.
5. Thread a length of soft rubber plug into the eye of the needle so that half the plug is on each side.
6. Smear rubber cement on one inch of the plug on both sides of the needle.
7. Push the plug into the puncture until one-half inch of the plug is left sticking out.
8. Slowly pull the needle out until the eye is a half-inch out of the hole.
9. If the leak has been stopped, nip off the excess plug on the outside with a knife, razor blade or side cutting pliers.
10. If the plug still leaks, insert a second plug in the cut the same way.

By the time you get the car off the jack, the tire should be ready for driving. At the first opportunity, have a shop remove the tire from the rim, inspect it for internal damage, and make a lasting repair if the tire is salvageable.

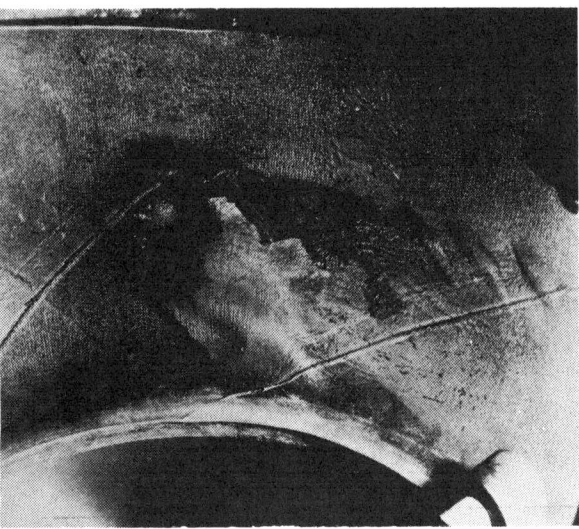

Top, flats should be repaired by using a permanent repair method such as the plug and patch combination. Other approved inside repair methods include chemical and hot vulcanized patches and head-type plugs. Above, sidewall damage such as this is not repairable. Discard the tire.

CHANGING A FLAT TIRE

Flat tires occur less frequently than they used to, but every motorist eventually gets stuck with one. Removing the flat and putting on the spare is simple when an orderly series of steps is followed. To make the changing both easier and safer, carry two wooden chocks, a rubber mallet, a small can of light oil, and warning flares or reflectors.

Caution: Be sure the car is on level ground before you change a tire.

Every automobile comes from the factory equipped with a jack to be used in changing flats. However, if you plan to work beneath the car, you must support it more solidly with jack stands or wheel ramps.

1. To change a front tire, place a manual transmission in gear, an automatic transmission in park. Engage the parking brake. Chock the front and back of the rear wheel that is diagonally opposite the one you are changing. To change a rear tire, chock both front wheels.
2. Remove the tire iron, jack and spare tire from the trunk.
3. Using the tapered end of the tire iron, pry off the wheel cover.
4. With the lug wrench end of the tire iron, loosen each lug nut two turns. The lugs may be tight. Hold the tire iron as shown for greater leverage.

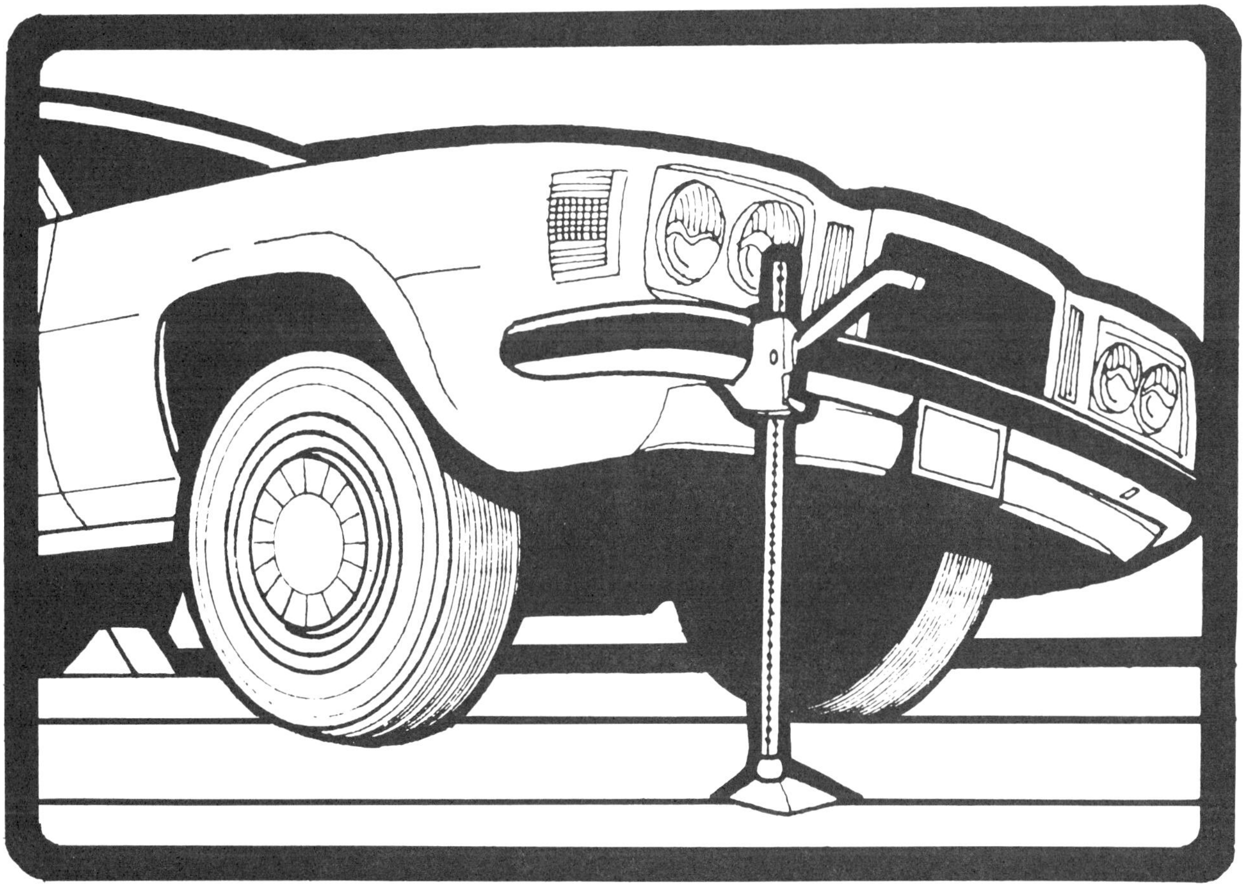

Using the bumper jack that came with your car, raise the corner of the car with the flat. Be sure to raise the car high enough to get the flat tire completely off the ground.

5. Set up the jack and raise the car until the wheel you are replacing is two to three inches off the ground.

Remove the wheel cover with the tapered end of a tire iron or a large screwdriver.

6. Remove the lug nuts and put them in the upturned wheel cover.
7. Pull off the wheel and squirt several drops of light oil onto the studs to prevent rusting.
8. Mount the spare tire on the studs and screw in the lug nuts by hand. Tighten with the tire iron until the wheel turns.
9. Using the jack, lower the car until the tire touches the ground.
10. Finish the tightening of the lug nuts in the criss-cross sequence shown. Turn them as tight as you can.
11. Slip the wheel cover into position and tap around its rim with a rubber mallet until it is firmly seated.
12. Disengage the jack and pull out the chocks. Place all the equipment and the flat tire in the trunk before you leave.

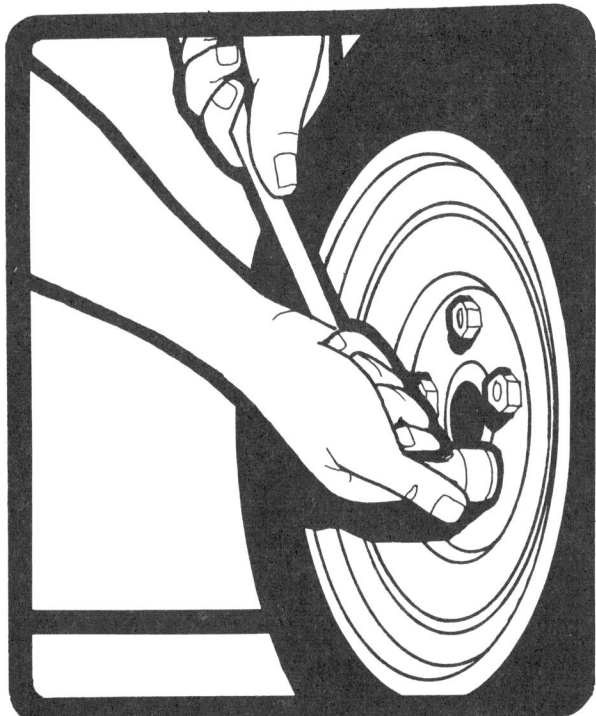

Remove the lug nuts by gripping the tire iron as shown for best leverage.

Keep the loose lug nuts inside the wheel cover to prevent their loss while you are busy changing tires.

KEEP TIRES PROPERLY INFLATED FOR THE LOAD

The load which a tire will safely carry depends on its size, its load range (or ply rating) and its inflation pressure. Proper inflation is the most important rule in tire safety and tire mileage.

Regardless of brand, all tires of the same size and load range (or ply rating) are rated to carry the same load at any given inflation pressure. Proper inflation for various loads may be found in your car owner's manual.

Correct tire inflation decreases rolling resistance thereby increasing gas mileage, providing better traction and braking, easier steering, better cornering and longer, safer tire life. Underinflation will lower load-carrying capacity and can seriously reduce tire life.

SPECIAL TIPS:

Check tire inflation every few weeks and before long trips. Use your own air pressure gauge as service station gauges may be inaccurate.

Do this when tires are cool, before starting out, since pressures can increase up to six pounds per square inch or more when tires are hot from driving. Never bleed hot tires.

Make a mental note of how many pounds per square inch you need and add them when you get to a service station.

For sustained driving at high legal speeds, increase inflation pressure four pounds per square inch over the maximum indicated in car owner's manual or by tire manufacturer.

A little light oil on the studs will allow you to easily remove the lug nuts the next time you get a flat.

TIRE-SAVING DRIVING HABITS

Excessive heat is a tire's worst enemy. Heat results from the flexing of the tire body. Flexing increases rapidly as speed increases. It is aggravated by underinflation or overloading. Running a tire at sustained high speeds under such conditions may raise temperatures above the critical level of about 250° F (water boils at 212° F), reduce its strength and tread life and increase the risk of sudden tire failure.

You can increase tire life by avoiding these practices:
1. Driving at excessive speeds.
2. Fast turns on curves and around corners.
3. Driving over curbs, chuck holes, other obstructions.
4. Jackrabbit starts and panic stops.
5. Driving at excessive speeds on rough washboard roads.
6. Riding on edge of pavement.

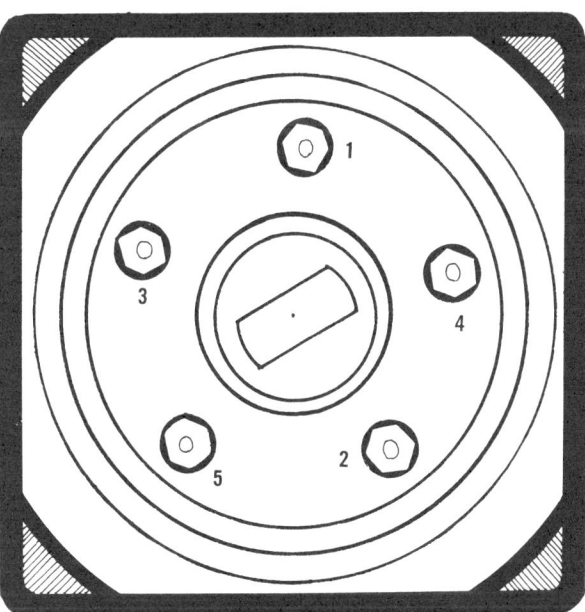

Here is the recommended tightening sequence for lug nuts.

After installing the spare tire, use a rubber mallet to firmly reattach the wheel cover.

TIRE APPLICATION GUIDE FOR PASSENGER CARS

HOW TO USE THE TABLES

Look on the sidewall of your tire to find its size and load range (or ply rating). Locate the tire in the tables. Follow along this line to the right to find the maximum load each of your four tires is rated to carry at the various cold inflation pressures. You can see that for a given tire, the higher the load, the more air pressure is required.

If the load you plan to carry calls for inflation pressures higher than the maximum permitted for your tires, reduce the load, or use the same size tire with a higher load range (ply rating) or use a larger size designation and possibly a different rim, as recommended by the car manufacturer.

NOTES

1. Maximum inflation and load is that shown in the 32 psi column for Load Range B (4-ply rating) tires, 36 psi for Load Range C (6-ply rating) tires, and 40 psi for Load Range D (8-ply rating) tires.

This information is also marked on the sidewalls of all new tires.

2. If you are considering replacing or mixing your present tires (e.g., 7.75-14) with other size designations or types, especially in the wider profiles (78, 70, 60 or 50-series), be sure to check tire or car manufacturers' recommended options for your particular make and model, as interchangeability is not always possible.

TIRES FOR IMPORTED CARS • LOAD LIMITS (LBS. PER TIRE)

Sizes (Bias)	COLD INFLATION PRESSURES—POUNDS PER SQUARE INCH						
	20	22	24	26	28	30	32
"Super Balloon"							
4.80-10	390	430	470	490	510	535	555
5.20-10	440	485	530	555	575	605	625
5.60-12	575	620	670	715	760	795	825
5.20-13	540	590	640	670	710	740	765
5.60-13	620	675	725	770	810	850	880
6.40-14	825	890	960	1000	1050	1090	1130
5.60-15	695	755	815	860	895	935	970
"Low Section"							
5.00-12	465	505	540	565	580	605	625
6.00-12	605	655	705	735	785	815	845
5.50-13	550	595	640	670	710	740	765
6.00-15L	740	800	860	890	930	970	1005

Sizes (Radial)	COLD INFLATION PRESSURES—POUNDS PER SQUARE INCH								
	20	22	24	26	28	30	32	34	36
Metric									
145R13	665	700	735	770	800	835	860	890	920
155R13	730	770	810	845	885	915	950	985	1015
155R15	780	825	865	905	940	980	1015	1050	1085
"70 Series"									
165/70 R 13	750	770	795	815	835	860	880	900	920
175/70 R 13	845	865	890	910	935	955	980	1000	1025
185/70 R 13	940	965	990	1015	1040	1065	1090	1115	1140
195/70 R 13	1045	1070	1100	1125	1155	1180	1210	1240	1265
155/70 R 14	700	720	740	760	780	795	815	835	850
185/70 R 14	990	1015	1045	1070	1100	1130	1155	1180	1210
195/70 R 14	1090	1120	1155	1185	1220	1250	1280	1310	1340
175/70 R 15	940	965	990	1015	1040	1065	1090	1115	1140
185/70 R 15	1040	1070	1100	1130	1155	1180	1210	1235	1265

NOTES: 1. Before obtaining replacement tires for imported cars, consult tire section of automobile manufacturer's owner's manual.
2. Refer to tire sidewall labeling for maximum inflation and load ratings of a particular tire.

"Super Low Section" Sizes (Bias)	COLD INFLATION PRESSURES—POUNDS PER SQUARE INCH						
	20	22	24	26	28	30	32
145-10/5.95-10	475	515	550	580	605	630	650
125-12/5.35-12	420	450	485	510	535	550	570
135-12/5.65-12	465	505	540	570	590	620	640
145-12/5.95-12	550	595	640	665	700	730	755
155-12/6.15-12	605	655	705	735	775	805	835
135-13/5.65-13	520	555	595	625	655	685	710
145-13/5.95-13	585	620	670	705	745	770	800
155-13/6.15-13	640	700	750	780	820	850	880
165-13/6.45-13	715	770	825	865	905	935	970
175-13/6.95-13	795	845	915	955	1005	1045	1085
185-13/7.35-13	870	945	1010	1060	1115	1160	1205
135-14/5.65-14	550	595	640	665	700	730	755
145-14/5.95-14	620	665	715	750	785	815	845
155-14/6.15-14	675	730	780	825	860	895	925
165-14	770	815	880	925	970	1000	1035
175-14	850	915	980	1025	1070	1115	1160
185-14	940	1000	1080	1135	1190	1235	1290
195-14	1025	1105	1180	1235	1290	1345	1400
205-14	1115	1190	1270	1335	1400	1455	1510
215-14	1200	1290	1380	1445	1520	1590	1640
225-14	1280	1380	1465	1540	1620	1700	1750
125-15/5.35-15	495	535	570	600	625	650	675
135-15/5.65-15	575	610	660	690	720	750	775
145-15/5.95-15	650	710	760	790	830	860	890
155-15/6.35-15	730	780	835	875	915	950	985
165-15	805	860	915	970	1015	1060	1105
175-15/7.15-15	880	955	1020	1070	1125	1170	1215
185-15	970	1050	1115	1180	1235	1280	1325
195-15	1060	1135	1215	1280	1335	1390	1445
205-15	1145	1225	1300	1370	1445	1500	1565
215-15	1235	1335	1435	1500	1590	1640	1700
235-15	1435	1545	1660	1735	1825	1895	1965
5.0-15	595	610	660	690	720	750	775
5.5-15	650	710	760	790	830	860	890

TIRE SIZE DESIGNATIONS

LOAD LIMITS (LBS. PER TIRE)

Load Range B (4-ply rating) →
Load Range C (6-ply rating) →
Load Range D (8-ply rating) →

Bias		Bias and Belted Bias				Radial				COLD INFLATION PRESSURES—POUNDS PER SQUARE INCH										
1965-On	Pre-1965	'78 Series'	'70 Series'	'60 Series'	'50 Series'	Metric	'78 Series'	'70 Series'	'60 Series'	'50 Series'	20	22	24	26	28	30	32	34	36	38	40
6.00-13						165 R 13					770	820	860	900	930	970	1010	1040	1080	1110	1140
		A78-13	A70-13	A60-13			AR 78-13	AR 70-13	AR 60-13		810	860	900	940	980	1020	1060	1090	1130	1160	1200
6.50-13		B78-13	B70-13	B60-13	B50-13	175 R 13	BR 78-13	BR 70-13	BR 60-13	BR 50-13	890	930	980	1030	1070	1110	1150	1190	1230	1270	1300
		C78-13	C70-13	C60-13	C50-13		CR 78-13	CR 70-13		CR 50-13	950	1000	1050	1100	1140	1190	1230	1270	1320	1360	1400
7.00-13					D50-13	185 R 13					980 1030 1080 1130 1180 1230 1270 1310 1360 1400 1440 / 980 1030 1080 1130 1180 1230 1270 1310 1350 1400 1440
		D78-13	D70-13	D60-13			DR 78-13	DR 70-13			1010	1070	1120	1170	1220	1270	1320	1360	1410	1450	1490
						195 R 13					1060 1110 1170 1220 1280 1320 1370 1420 1470 1510 1560 / 1070 1130 1190 1240 1300 1350 1400 1440 1490 1540 1580
						155 R 14	ER 78-13		ER 60-13		780	820	860	900	940	970	1010	1040	1080	1110	1140
							AR 78-14		AR60-14		810	860	900	940	980	1020	1060	1090	1130	1160	1200
6.45-14	6.00-14										860 910 960 1000 1040 1080 1120 1160 1200 1240 1270 / 840 900 940 980 1020 1060 1100 1130 1170 1210 1240
		B78-14		B60-14		165 R 14	BR 78-14				890 930 980 1030 1070 1110 1150 1190 1230 1270 1300 / 860 910 960 1000 1040 1080 1120 1170 1200 1240 1280
6.95-14	6.50-14	C78-14	C70-14				CR 78-14	CR 70-14		CR 50-14	950 1000 1050 1100 1140 1190 1230 1270 1310 1350 1390 / 950 1000 1050 1100 1140 1190 1230 1270 1320 1360 1400
						175 R 14					930 990 1030 1080 1130 1170 1210 1250 1290 1330 1370 / 950 1000 1050 1100 1140 1190 1230 1280 1320 1360 1400
		D78-14	D70-14	D60-14			DR 78-14	DR 70-14			1010	1070	1120	1170	1220	1270	1320	1360	1410	1450	1490
7.35-14	7.00-14	E78-14	E70-14	E60-14		185 R 14	ER 78-14	ER 70-14			1040 1100 1160 1210 1260 1310 1350 1400 1450 1490 1540 / 1030 1090 1140 1190 1240 1290 1340 1380 1430 1470 1520 / 1070 1130 1190 1240 1300 1350 1400 1440 1490 1540 1580 / 1040 1100 1160 1210 1260 1310 1360 1410 1450 1500 1540
7.75-14	7.50-14	F78-14	F70-14	F60-14	F50-14	195 R 14	FR 78-14	FR 70-14	FR 60-14		1150 1210 1270 1330 1390 1440 1500 1550 1600 1650 1690 / 1150 1210 1280 1340 1390 1450 1500 1550 1600 1650 1700 / 1160 1220 1280 1340 1400 1450 1500 1550 1610 1650 1700 / 1150 1210 1270 1330 1390 1440 1500 1540 1590 1640 1690
8.25-14	8.00-14	G78-14	G70-14	G60-14	G50-14	205 R 14	GR 78-14	GR 70-14	GR 60-14	GR 50-14	1250 1310 1380 1440 1500 1560 1620 1670 1730 1780 1830 / 1240 1320 1380 1440 1500 1560 1620 1670 1730 1780 1830 / 1250 1310 1380 1440 1500 1560 1620 1680 1730 1780 1830
8.55-14	8.50-14	H78-14	H70-14	H60-14	H50-14	215 R 14	HR 78-14	HR 70-14	HR 60-14		1360 1430 1510 1580 1640 1710 1770 1830 1890 1950 2000 / 1330 1420 1480 1550 1610 1670 1740 1790 1850 1910 1960 / 1360 1440 1510 1580 1650 1710 1770 1830 1890 1950 2010 / 1360 1430 1510 1580 1640 1710 1770 1830 1890 1950 2010
8.85-14	9.00-14	J78-14	J70-14	J60-14		225 R 14	JR 78-14	JR 70-14	JR 60-14		1430 1510 1580 1660 1730 1790 1860 1920 1990 2050 2100 / 1430 1510 1580 1650 1720 1790 1860 1920 1990 2040 2100 / 1430 1510 1580 1660 1730 1790 1860 1920 1980 2040 2100
	9.50-14		L70-14	L60-14				LR 70-14	LR 60-14		1540 1640 1700 1780 1850 1930 2000 2060 2130 2200 2260 / 1520 1600 1680 1750 1830 1900 1970 2040 2100 2170 2230

TIRE SIZE DESIGNATIONS

LOAD LIMITS (LBS. PER TIRE)

Load Range B (4-ply rating) →
Load Range C (6-ply rating) →
Load Range D (8-ply rating) →

Bias		Bias and Belted Bias				Radial				COLD INFLATION PRESSURES—POUNDS PER SQUARE INCH										
1965-On	Pre-1965	'78 Series'	'70 Series'	'60 Series'	'50 Series'	Metric	'78 Series'	'70 Series'	'60 Series'	'50 Series'	20	22	24	26	28	30	32	34	36	38	40
					M50-14						1610	1700	1780	1860	1940	2020	2090	2160	2230	2300	2370
					N50-14						1700	1790	1880	1970	2050	2130	2210	2280	2360	2430	2500
		A78-15	A70-15				AR 78-15				810	860	900	940	980	1020	1060	1090	1130	1160	1200
	6.00-15	B78-15		B60-15			BR 78-15	BR 70-15			890 930 980 1030 1070 1110 1150 1190 1230 1270 1300 / 890 940 990 1030 1080 1120 1160 1200 1230 1270 1300
						165 R 15					870 910 960 1000 1050 1090 1130 1170 1200 1240 1280
6.85-15	6.50-15	C78-15	C70-15	C60-15			CR 78-15	CR 70-15			950 1000 1050 1100 1140 1190 1230 1270 1320 1360 1390 / 950 1000 1050 1100 1140 1190 1230 1270 1320 1360 1400
						175 R 15					980 1040 1080 1130 1170 1230 1270 1310 1360 1400 1440 / 950 1000 1050 1100 1140 1190 1230 1280 1320 1360 1400
		D78-15	D70-15				DR 78-15	DR 70-15			1010	1070	1120	1170	1220	1270	1320	1360	1410	1450	1490
7.35-15		E78-15	E70-15	E60-15	E50-15	185 R 15	ER 78-15	ER 70-15	ER 60-15		1070 1130 1180 1240 1290 1340 1390 1440 1490 1530 1570 / 1070 1130 1190 1240 1300 1350 1400 1440 1490 1540 1580 / 1070 1130 1180 1240 1300 1350 1400 1450 1490 1520 1570
7.75-15	6.70-15	F78-15	F70-15	F60-15		195 R 15	FR 78-15	FR 70-15	FR 60-15		1150 1210 1270 1330 1380 1440 1490 1540 1590 1640 1690 / 1110 1190 1240 1290 1340 1400 1450 1500 1550 1590 1640 / 1160 1220 1280 1340 1400 1450 1500 1550 1610 1650 1700
	7.10-15					205 R 15					1240 1300 1370 1430 1490 1550 1610 1660 1710 1770 1820 / 1190 1270 1320 1380 1440 1500 1550 1600 1660 1710 1760
8.25-15		G78-15	G70-15	G60-15	G50-15		GR 78-15	GR 70-15	GR 60-15	GR 50-15	1250 1310 1380 1440 1500 1560 1620 1680 1730 1780 1830 / 1250 1310 1380 1440 1500 1560 1620 1670 1730 1780 1830
	7.60-15					215 R 15					1340 1410 1480 1550 1620 1680 1740 1800 1860 1910 1970 / 1310 1400 1450 1520 1580 1650 1710 1760 1820 1880 1930
8.55-15		H78-15	H70-15	H60-15	H50-15		HR 78-15	HR 70-15	HR 60-15	HR 50-15	1360 1440 1510 1580 1650 1710 1770 1830 1890 1950 2010 / 1360 1430 1510 1580 1640 1710 1770 1830 1890 1950 2000
8.85-15	8.00-15	J78-15	J70-15	J60-15		225 R 15	JR 78-15	JR 70-15	JR 60-15	JR 50-15	1430 1510 1580 1650 1720 1790 1860 1920 1980 2040 2100 / 1380 1470 1530 1600 1670 1730 1800 1860 1920 1980 2040 / 1430 1500 1580 1650 1720 1790 1860 1920 1980 2040 2100
9.00-15	8.20-15		K70-15					KR 70-15			1460 1540 1620 1690 1760 1830 1900 1970 2030 2090 2150 / 1470 1570 1630 1710 1770 1850 1900 1970 2030 2090 2150 / 1460 1550 1620 1690 1770 1830 1900 1970 2030 2090 2150
9.15-15		L78-15	L70-15	L60-15	L50-15	235 R 15	LR 78-15	LR 70-15	LR 60-15	LR 50-15	1510 1600 1680 1750 1830 1900 1970 2030 2100 2160 2230 / 1520 1600 1680 1750 1830 1900 1970 2040 2100 2170 2230 / 1510 1600 1680 1750 1830 1900 1970 2040 2110 2170 2230
		M78-15					MR 78-15	MR 70-15			1610	1700	1780	1860	1940	2020	2090	2160	2230	2300	2370
7.00-15											1310	1380	1450	1515	1580	1640	1700	1760	1820	1870	1930
		N78-15			N50-15		NR 78-15				1700 1790 1880 1970 2050 2130 2210 2280 2360 2430 2500
8.90-15											1700	1810	1880	1970	2050	2130	2210	2290	2360	2430	2500

TIRE MOUNTING RECOMMENDATIONS

READ ACROSS FOR FRONT TIRE RECOMMENDATION / READ DOWN FOR REAR TIRE RECOMMENDATION

Construction → ↓	SERIES ▼ (PROFILE) →	Bias on Front				Belted Bias on Front			Radial on Front			
		CONVENTIONAL (83 SERIES)	78 SERIES	70 SERIES	60/50 SERIES	78 SERIES	70 SERIES	60/50 SERIES	METRIC	78 SERIES	70 SERIES	60/50 SERIES
Bias on Rear	Conventional (83 series)	Preferred	Acceptable	NO	NO	Acceptable	NO	NO	NO	NO	NO	NO
	78 Series	Acceptable	Preferred	Acceptable	NO	Acceptable	NO	NO	NO	NO	NO	NO
	70 Series	Acceptable	Acceptable	Preferred	NO	Acceptable	Acceptable	NO	NO	NO	NO	NO
	60/50 Series	Acceptable	Acceptable	Acceptable	Preferred	Acceptable	Acceptable	Acceptable	NO	NO	NO	NO
Belted Bias on Rear	78 Series	Acceptable	Acceptable	Acceptable	NO	Preferred	Acceptable	NO	NO	NO	NO	NO
	70 Series	Acceptable	Acceptable	Acceptable	NO	Acceptable	Preferred	NO	NO	NO	NO	NO
	60/50 Series	Acceptable	Acceptable	Acceptable	Acceptable	Acceptable	Acceptable	Preferred	NO	NO	NO	NO
Radial on Rear	Metric	Acceptable	Acceptable	Acceptable	NO	Acceptable	Acceptable	NO	Preferred	Acceptable	Acceptable	NO
	78 Series	Acceptable	Acceptable	Acceptable	NO	Acceptable	Acceptable	NO	Acceptable	Preferred	Acceptable	NO
	70 Series	Acceptable	Acceptable	Acceptable	NO	Acceptable	Acceptable	NO	Acceptable	Acceptable	Preferred	NO
	60/50 Series	Acceptable	Acceptable	Acceptable	Acceptable	Acceptable	Acceptable	Acceptable	Acceptable	Acceptable	Acceptable	Preferred

Preferred — Preferred applications. For best all-around car handling performance, tires of the same size and construction should be used on all wheel positions.

Acceptable — Acceptable, but not preferred applications. Consult your car owner's manual and do not apply if vehicle manufacturer recommends against this application.

NO — NOT RECOMMENDED

IMPORTANT: ALWAYS CHECK THE VEHICLE MANUFACTURER'S RECOMMENDATIONS BEFORE REPLACING TIRES WITH DIFFERENT SIZES AND/OR CONSTRUCTIONS.

General Instructions

1. This chart is intended for use as a guide for tire applications on conventional passenger vehicles. Tires of different basic construction—bias, belted bias and radial—may vary in series (profiles), dimensions and ride characteristics. These differences may seriously affect vehicle handling characteristics.

2. Adherence to recommended inflation pressures is important for proper vehicle and tire performance. Follow the recommendations of the vehicle or tire manufacturer.

3. SIZES—Never mix different tire sizes on the same axle.

4. CONSTRUCTION—Never mix different constructions (bias, belted bias or radial) on the same axle.

5. STATION WAGONS AND ALL VEHICLES USED IN TRAILER TOWING SERVICE—It is recommended that tires on all wheel positions of these vehicles be of the same size and construction (bias, belted bias or radial). These vehicles may require a Load Range C or D tire.

6. WORN TIRES—It is preferred that tires having approximately the same amount of tread depth remaining be placed on the same axle.

Shock Absorbers and Handling

WHY SHOCK ABSORBERS ARE NEEDED

The term shock absorber is actually a misnomer. A shock absorber does not absorb road shocks at all. Your car's springs actually perform that function. However, if a spring were left unimpeded, it would continue to oscillate up and down after hitting a bump. And because your car's springs support the chassis of your car, and the car's body is attached to the chassis, the whole car would bob up and down until internal friction in the spring itself caused the spring to stop oscillating. It might be many minutes later before the oscillations ceased.

Of course, on the road, your wheels are constantly hitting road imperfections and hazards. So the springs would be in constant oscillation. And so would the chassis and body of your car.

Obviously, this would not only be uncomfortable for you and your passengers, it would also be unsafe. A car moving down the road bobbing up and down uncontrollably is obviously an unsafe vehicle. Such an unstable car would be extremely difficult to control and would not be very maneuverable.

With this condition to work with, early automobile designers recognized the need to damp out these oscillations and control spring movement to a degree that would permit safe, controllable motion. That is, enough motion to absorb road shock but not too much so that the vehicle was unstable.

Because today's modern shock absorber actually does this job—it damps out oscillations—you may also hear a shock absorber referred to as a damper. But the more common term is shock absorber. Or just shock for short.

It stands to reason, then, that any indication of instability as you drive your car should be sufficient cause to make you want to test your car's shock absorbers. Indications of instability would be wheel shimmy, a feeling of road shocks, the car bobbing up and down for a long period after hitting a road shock, or a general feeling of uncontrollability in the vehicle's handling. Also, any clunking sounds from beneath the vehicle when the car hits a bump or makes a turn should make you suspicious of weak, worn shock absorbers.

SHOCK FAILURE— THE HIDDEN HAZARD

Shock absorber failure is insidious. Shocks do not go bad all at once. Unlike a tire that goes flat, leaving no doubt that failure has occurred, shock absorbers lose their ability to maintain vehicle stability over a period of time. Deterioration is gradual.

Because failure occurs slowly as a car is driven mile after mile, drivers are seldom aware of the differences in handling characteristics that weakened shock absorbers produce. Therefore, since a danger-

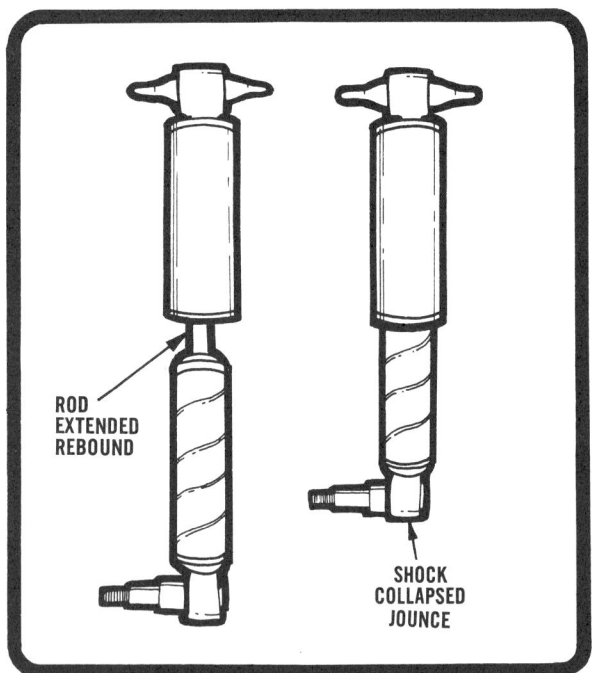

A shock absorber extends and retracts according to suspension movement of the car.

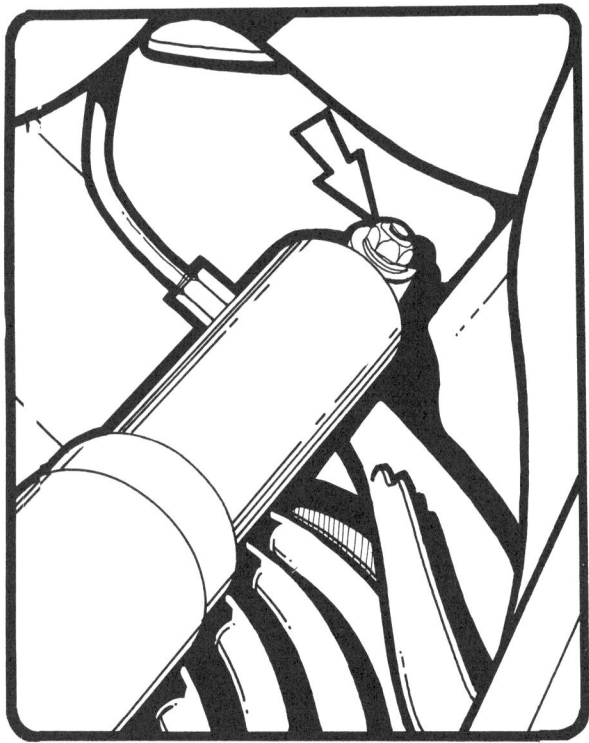

Arrow indicates typical upper mounting bolt location of a rear shock absorber.

ous situation can develop and exist without you being aware of it, it is strongly suggested that you take a few minutes every six months to test the shock absorbers in your car.

The testing procedure we recommend is outlined later in this chapter. But first it is necessary to understand how shock absorbers work and what can go wrong with them.

HOW SHOCK ABSORBERS WORK

A shock absorber can be described as a telescopic, double-acting, hydraulic component.

The term telescopic refers to the fact that a shock absorber assembly consists of two cylinders. One, the upper assembly, overrides the other, the lower assembly, in the same way that one tube of a telescope rides over the other tube.

The term double-acting refers to a shock absorber's ability to damp out movement in two directions.

1. On compression, when wheels and the rest of the car are pushed together. In this position, the two cylinders of shock absorbers are pushed together. This is also called the jounce cycle.
2. On rebound, when the wheels and the rest of the car return to normal riding position. In this position, the two cylinders are extended from compression to their pressure off position.

The upper cylinder of a shock absorber contains no component other than a long piston rod. It serves primarily as a nest into which the lower cylinder homes and as a dust cover. The long piston rod extends down through the upper cylinder into the lower cylinder and culminates in a piston assembly.

The main shock absorbing component inside the lower cylinder, though, is a measured amount of hydraulic fluid. It is hydraulic fluid which does the actual job of controlling movement.

All shock absorbers work the same way. They are firmly attached to an upper and lower support. The upper support is a stationary source, such as the wheel housing, so that the upper cylinder will not move. The lower support is a component of the car's suspension system which is also attached to a spring, such as the lower control arm. Thus, any impact received by the spring will be damped by the shock.

As wheels hit bumps, the lower cylinder section of a shock absorber moves with the wheel and is telescoped into the upper cylinder section. As the two cylinders compress together, the piston plunges into the thick hydraulic fluid, forcing the fluid through various small orifices. The fluid slows and controls the movements.

Following impact, shock absorbers extend themselves. The lower cylinder slides from the upper cylinder. The piston retracts and fluid that was displaced returns to the lower cylinder from storage.

HOW SHOCKS AFFECT HANDLING

These sequence photos illustrate how good shocks and poor shocks can affect vehicle stability. The left sequence, top to bottom, shows how a car with good shock absorbers reacts to hitting a railroad crossing at approximately 30 mph. Notice how the car does not pitch wildly and recovers quickly. The right sequence, top to bottom, shows the same car at the same speed at the same railroad crossing—but with worn shock absorbers. Notice how the car pitches almost uncontrollably and how it has still not recovered stability in the last photo. Obviously, a car equipped with good shock absorbers is easier to control and a safer vehicle.

HOW AND WHY SHOCK ABSORBERS FAIL

There is no way to predict the life expectancy of shock absorbers. Also, do not be misled into believing that so-called heavy duty shocks will outlast standard duty units. The terms heavy duty and standard duty do not refer to the length of service shocks provide, but rather to the type of service they are intended to perform. Of course, standard duty shock absorbers used under heavy duty conditions will fail much sooner than if they were used for what they are intended. We will discuss heavy duty and standard duty in more detail below.

Shock absorber life expectancy depends primarily on the roads over which a car is driven. Shocks can provide safe, adequate service for as long as 50,000 miles, or they can fail in as little as 5000 miles.

Shock absorbers that are mounted on a car which is operated only on smooth and level interstate highways and turnpikes will perform for many, many thousands of miles. Conversely, if the same car were driven over back country, washboard-type roads, shocks would fail in a comparatively brief period of time. Obviously, a shock absorber which must work harder on bad roads will deteriorate sooner.

Allow us to stress one very important point in connection with this. Shock absorber manufacturers generally advise car owners to replace shock absorbers at 20,000 to 30,000 miles. This advice is intended for people who do not inspect shocks periodically. Also, it assumes operation over more or less good highway. The fact of the matter is that shock absorbers may fail long before 20,000 miles is reached, or they may last long after 30,000 miles.

IMPORTANT: The only way to guard against premature replacement, assure yourself of adequate performance, and protect yourself against the hazards imposed by driving with weak shocks is to inspect units every six months.

Shock absorbers fail in three ways:
1. The seal cover which is supposed to keep hydraulic fluid inside the lower cylinder deteriorates and hydraulic fluid is lost.
2. Parts that mount the shock absorber firmly at the top and bottom cylinders (more often at the bottom), wear excessively and loosen. This causes the shock to wobble. A shock absorber that has side-play cannot provide strong damping action. Furthermore, a loose shock absorber causes control instability.
3. Internal parts, such as the piston and various springs, wear excessively. This helps upset adequate shock damping capability. Of the three types of damage, this is the one which takes longest to occur.

Shock absorbers should be checked periodically for leakage, especially in the area of the piston shank and seal. In this illustration, the pencil is pointing to the area where most leaks start.

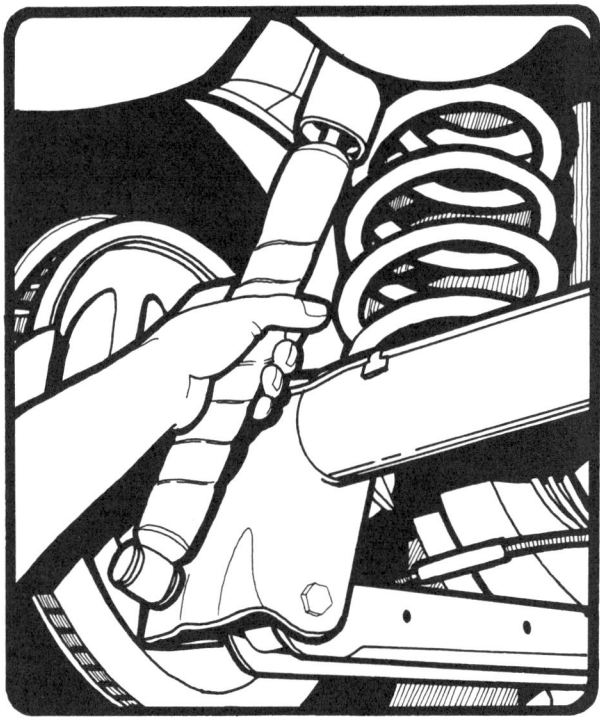

You can easily test a shock absorber for looseness by firmly grabbing hold of the body of the shock and yanking it back and forth. You will feel any looseness.

Testing shocks for wear is easy. Simply bounce one corner of your car up and down. If the car continues to bounce more than twice before settling level, the shock is worn and should be relaced.

IMPORTANT: A shock absorber cannot be repaired. Other than for a loosened mounting bolt, which may be tightened, when any of the conditions we have just described occur, the shock absorber must be replaced.

HOW TO TEST SHOCK ABSORBERS

You do not need tools to test shock absorbers. Here is how to proceed:

1. Park the car on level pavement. Turn off the engine.
2. If the vehicle is equipped with automatic transmission, set the transmission selector quadrant in P (Park). If the vehicle is equipped with manual transmission, set the transmission stick in gear—that is, in any position except Neutral.
3. Set the parking brake firmly.
4. Stand at any corner of the car.
5. Place your hands on the bumper or fender and press down with as much force as you can muster. When the corner reaches its maximum downward point, let up.
6. Proceed in this manner until the car is rocking up and down.
7. When things are really rocking, and on a downstroke when the corner has been pushed to its maximum point, quickly remove your hands from the bumper or fender. Keep your eyes on what happens.
8. If the car's body comes up one time and settles level, the shock absorber in the particular corner is probably in adequate condition. If the car's body bounces up and down and up again—that is, if it keeps jouncing instead of settling level and in a smooth manner—the shock absorber in that corner of the car is weak.
9. Perform this test at each of the vehicle's other three corners.

Weak front shock absorbers may also be revealed by testing the car on the road. Select a road with a smooth pavement and do the test during a period of the day or night when traffic is not a factor.

Drive the car at a speed of 10 miles per hour. When you are cruising at this speed, tap your brake pedal lightly. Do not slam the brakes.

Note if the front end of the car dips and the rear end rises. If dip and rise are experienced, front shocks probably are to blame.

You should proceed with one other test before definitely concluding that shock absorbers which have passed tests so far are in adequate condition.

This test is as follows:

1. With the car parked on level pavement and the engine turned off, set the parking brake firmly. Place an automatic transmission in D or a manual transmission in gear.

2. Spread a large cloth, such as an old bedspread, beneath the car. This can be either in front or rear. You will use this to lie on. Or use a creeper to get under the car.

   By way of advice, if you are going to perform work on your car which involves getting beneath the vehicle, such as lubrication as well as shock absorber inspection, you should investigate the advisability of purchasing a mechanic's creeper.
3. Get beneath the car at one corner and examine the shock absorber's lower cylinder. If there is hydraulic fluid on the cylinder case, the shock absorber is definitely shot and should be replaced.

   Caution: An oily film on a shock absorber does not mean that the part has gone bad. Fluid should be heavy. If hydraulic fluid is leaking from a shock absorber, there is little doubt. You will know it.
4. If possible, grasp the shock absorber and shake it back and forth. We say if possible because of the fact that some shock absorbers are mounted inside coil springs or the control arm and cannot be grasped.

   If the shock absorber can be grasped, see if it demonstrates any amount of wobble. If so, take an open- or box-end wrench from your tool kit. Using all your strength, tighten the shock absorber fastener.

   Test the unit for wobble once again. If movement prevails, the bushing through which the bolt fits is worn. The shock absorber should be removed from the car and replaced.
5. Test each of the other three shock absorbers in the same way.

CHOOSING NEW SHOCKS

Once you have determined that you need new shock absorbers, the next task is to choose the right type of replacement shock. This might sound easy on the surface. But the fact is, there are many different *types* (not brands) of shocks to choose from.

Go into an auto parts supply house and you will see standard, heavy duty, radial tuned, racing and competition, overload, air and spring shock absorbers. To help you make an intelligent choice, let us look more closely at some of the more common types of shock absorbers.

Standard duty shocks

Most original equipment shock absorbers can be defined as standard duty. Standard duty shocks usually have a 1-inch diameter body and provide adequate service for most vehicles that are used normally and do not see strenuous service. They are best for cars that are driven mostly on smooth roads and for cars that do not carry full loads of cargo and/or passengers.

Standard duty shocks do not have the capacity to control violent or abnormal vehicle movement such as over rough roads or with full loads. On normal cars in normal use, they provide a soft ride. That is, they do not damp out a great deal of movement but allow the car to move to a certain extent to spread out the movement over a longer period of time.

Standard duty shocks, left, usually have a 1-inch diameter body and provide adequate service for normal use. A heavy duty shock, right, usually has either a 1½-inch or a 1⅜-inch diameter body.

Heavy duty shocks

Heavy duty shocks provide much more damping action than standard duty shocks. They will make your car ride firmer with less rocking and up and down movement. Heavy duty shocks will help your vehicle to be more controllable if you carry heavy loads. Your car will feel more responsive and more stable with heavy duty shocks. However, do not install them if you do not like a firmer ride.

Heavy duty shocks come in two grades. The best heavy duty units usually have a 1½-inch or 1⅜-inch valve body, so the added capacity gives the shock more control capacity. They are also the most expensive.

Not as good are heavy duty shocks which have the same 1-inch valve body as a standard duty shock, but get their added control by having internal valving modifications which cause the hydraulic fluid to flow slower, thereby inducing more damping action as the piston moves through it.

Overload shocks

Shock absorbers ordinarily do not support anything. They do not support the car body or suspension components or any part of the car. Therefore, when a heavy load is placed in a vehicle, the vehicle's springs do all the supporting. This sometimes causes the rear of the car to sag lower than the front if a load is placed in the trunk. And in extreme conditions where the passenger compartment is also full, the whole car can sag lower than the original design height.

This sagging can be very dangerous. If the rear end sags, your headlight aim will be off and you may be blinding oncoming drivers—a very dangerous condition. Because the rear or all of the car is lower to the ground, the chance of striking a foreign object is much greater. This could cause damage to the car or worse—cause you to lose control of the car. Lastly, a car whose suspension travel is taken up by a load cannot be very stable because the suspension components are not working effectively.

Overload shocks are heavy duty shock absorbers with auxiliary springs wound around the body of the shock absorber. The shock acts in the normal manner. But the auxiliary coil spring helps support heavy loads and reduces the tendency for the car to sag.

Overload shocks can be effective in maintaining a level vehicle even with a heavy load. They are available for most vehicles for both the front and rear of the car. The only disadvantages are that when the vehicle is unladen, the auxiliary springs tend to make the ride a little more harsh and the vehicle sit higher than a stock vehicle without the overload shocks.

An overload shock is merely a heavy duty shock absorber with an auxiliary spring attached.

Air shocks

A third type of shock absorber is the air shock, which is used in the rear of a car only for supporting very heavy loads, such as a trailer. Air shocks are installed the same way as ordinary rear shock absorbers or overload shocks. But they have the addition of an air line which connects each shock absorber to a common tee where lines join together and converge into a single air line. The air line culminates at an air valve which projects through an easy-to-reach access area, such as the trunk floor, rear panel, or rear bumper.

Air is added to or bled from air shocks, depending upon the load being imposed on the vehicle, by means of the air valve. Adding air or bleeding air is done in the same way as you would add or bleed air from a tire.

When you know you are going to haul a heavy load, you would pull into a service station and use the air hose to inflate air shocks to the rating suggested by the air shock manufacturer for the weight of the load. When no support is needed, air is bled from the shocks by pushing in on the air valve core. However, most manufacturers of air shocks recommend that a minimum of 20 psi of air pressure be maintained in air shocks at all times. Air pressure is determined with an ordinary tire air pressure gauge.

In effect then, you have air doing the same job as the auxiliary spring on the overload shock. However, you do not have the disadvantages when the vehicle is unladen.

CAUTION: If you plan to have air shocks installed in your car for the first time, make sure that air lines are positioned away from parts that get hot, such as exhaust system parts. Lines are generally made of plastic which can be damaged by heat. Also, keep the air valve covered with a tire valve cap to prevent dirt from entering the system.

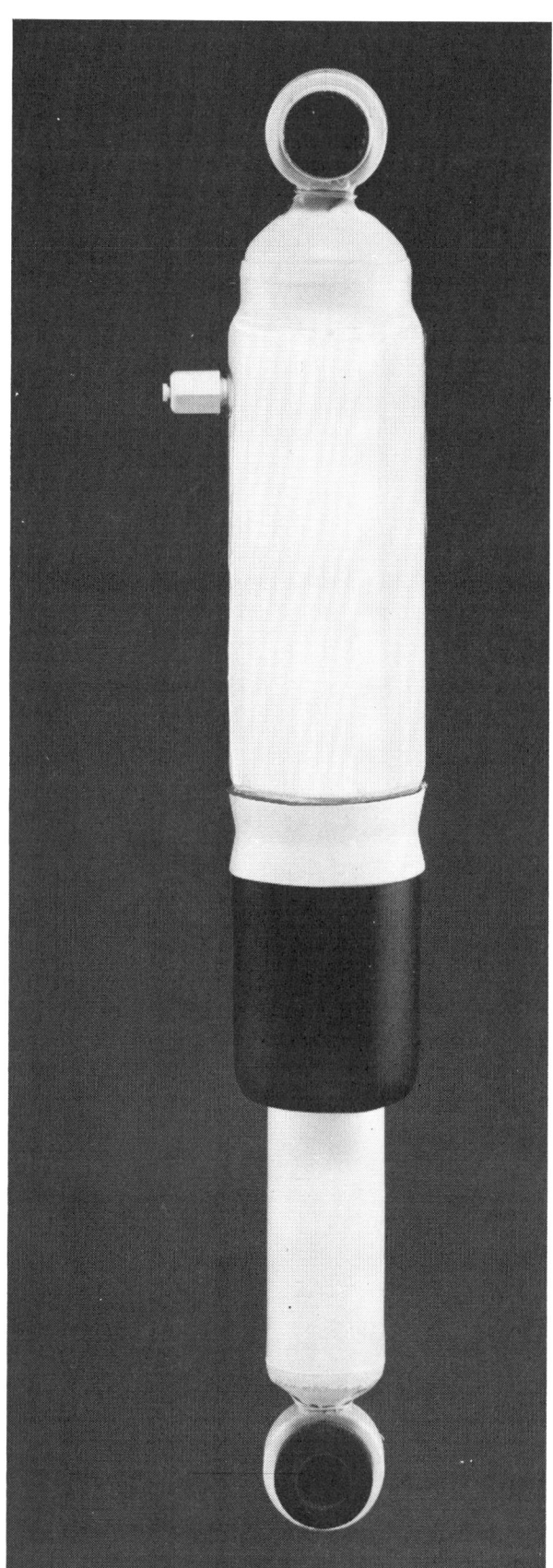

An air shock is a conventional heavy duty shock absorber which has an air chamber attached to the shock body.

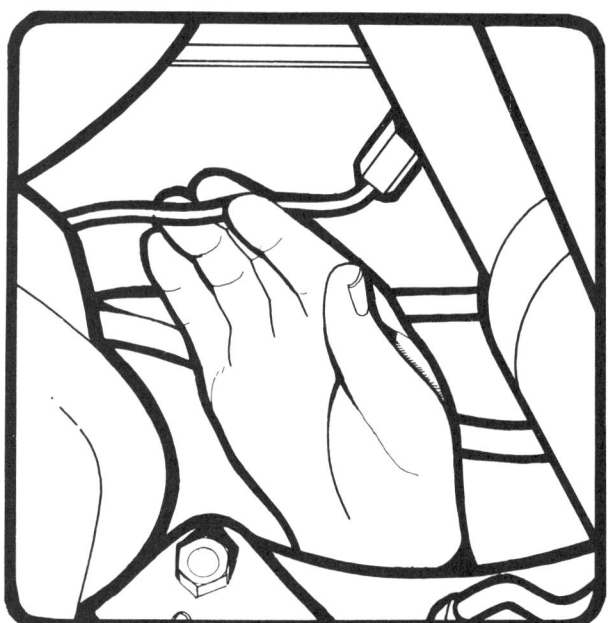

An air line allows compressed air to be added or subtracted from the air chamber of the shock, thus varying its load carrying capacity and the vehicle's height.

Air shocks require just a bit more work to replace than conventional shock absorbers. Air has to be bled and the air lines disconnected at each shock with a wrench. The procedure you follow is the same as we will describe in this chapter.

Automatic load levelers

The automatic load leveler system is an optional piece of equipment now offered by car manufacturers for their more expensive models. Some of the highest priced luxury cars, including Eldorado, Seville, Imperial and Lincoln, have automatic load leveling systems added as standard equipment.

The automatic load leveler system consists of two air shock absorbers in the rear of the car that are served by an air compressor. As a load is imposed on the car, the compressor, which is operated by the engine, automatically feeds air through a pressure-regulating valve to the shock absorbers. When the load is relieved, the shock absorbers automatically purge themselves of air.

CAUTION: You should not attempt to replace or otherwise service an automatic load leveler system. The setup is complicated and requires special training and tools. However, you can replace the *front* shock absorbers of a car equipped with automatic load levelers.

Competition and racing shocks

These shock absorbers are just what their name implies. In most cases, they are designed to give maximum control at a sacrifice in ride comfort. They are generally not suitable for street use and should not be considered for installation unless you actually plan to engage in some sort of racing activity. In such cases, seek advice on various types and usage from someone who is engaged in the same type of racing you are planning to enter.

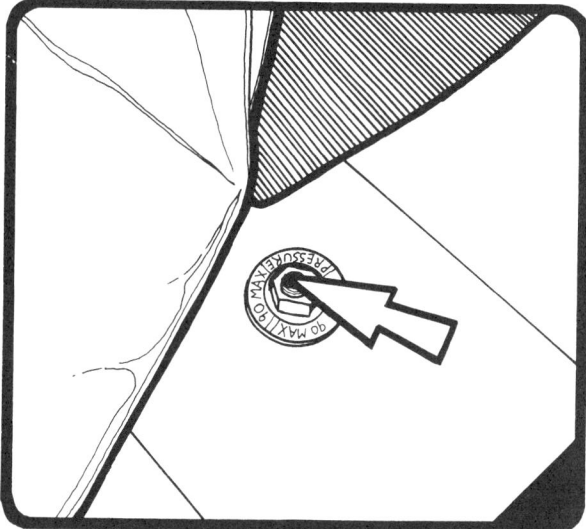

Both air shocks have air added or bled through a single air valve. This one is in the car's trunk.

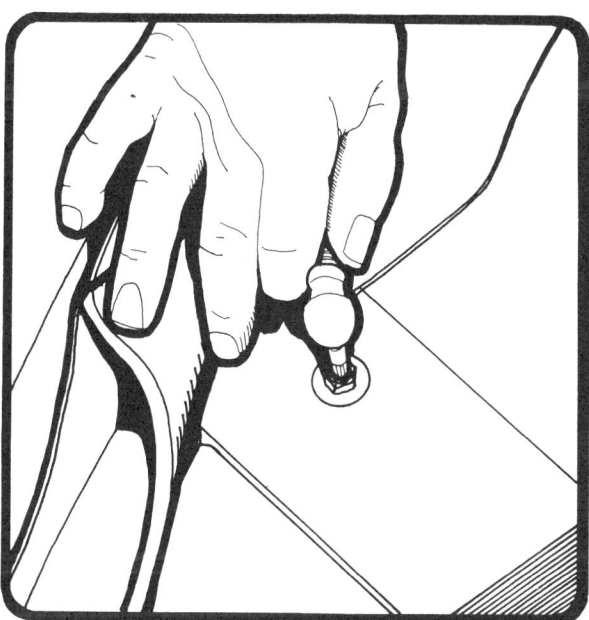

Air can be added to air shocks in the same way that air is added to your car's tires.

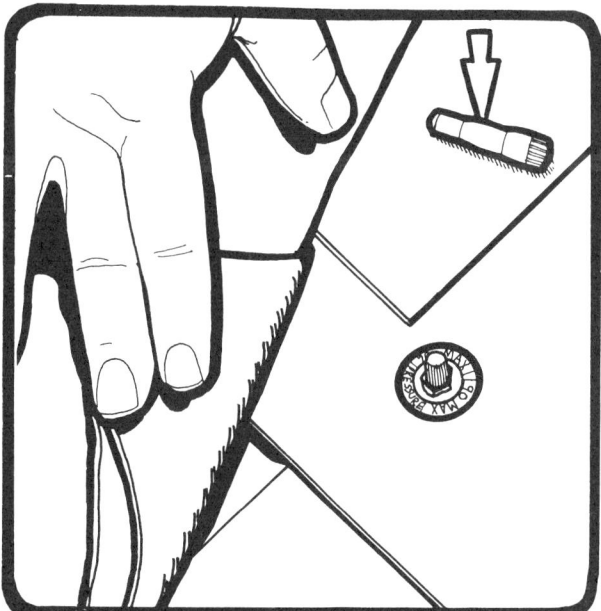

An air shock valve should be protected from dirt with a valve cap, just as you protect a tire's air valve with a cap. The arrow points to a valve extension which can be screwed to the valve for added convenience in filling the air chamber.

SHOCK ABSORBER REPLACEMENT

One or two

There is one more important point that should be mentioned. A controversy exists concerning whether shock absorbers should be replaced individually or whether shock absorbers on the same axle (front or rear) should be replaced as a pair although one may still be in relatively sound condition.

No definite stand can be taken here. Those who advocate replacing shock absorbers in pairs contend that failing to do so may cause the car to sway during operation. Those who claim that shocks should be replaced as individual units as each fails argue that replacing them in pairs may result in needless expense.

The facts are these:

• Failure of one shock absorber does not necessarily mean failure of the other. It is true, however, that when a shock on one side of the axle goes bad, chances are that the shock on the other side of the axle has weakened considerably and will soon fail, if it has not already.

• Although failure to replace one shock and not the other may cause sway, the condition does not occur as a rule. Besides, if sway does occur, you can then replace the other shock to rectify the situation.

The decision is yours.

SHOULD YOU DO IT YOURSELF?

There are few tasks you can do on a car yourself which are easier than replacing shock absorbers. But there may be a question as to whether doing the replacement yourself actually pays. From a tool standpoint you will need ordinary open- or box-end wrenches. However, using sockets makes it much easier to break stubborn fasteners loose.

Wrenches, of course, have to fit the fasteners of your particular shock absorbers. Exact size is easily determined by simply trying one size after another until the right size is determined.

In addition to wrenches, you will need a support to prop the rear axle. Supporting the rear axle is necessary to relieve tension on rear shocks and make removal easier. This is true in the rear only.

Ideally, though, working conditions are made much easier if the whole car can be raised. The best way of doing this is to lift the car by means of a frame contact or 2-post lift of the type available at service stations and garages. If you have a friend in the business who will let you use his lift during a slack period, you are fortunate.

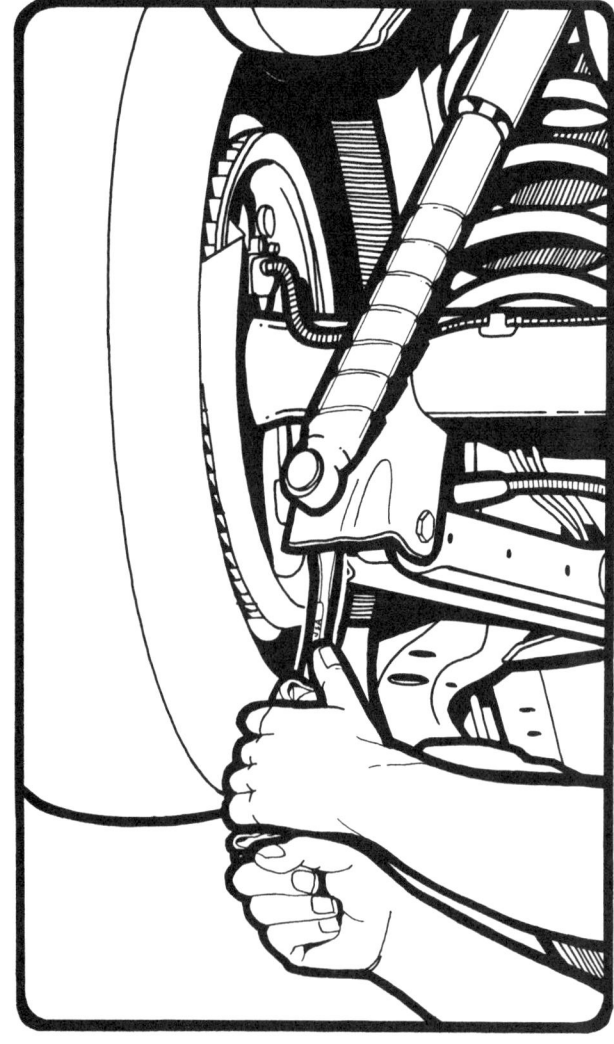

When tightening shock absorber bolts, use the correct size wrench to avoid rounding the head. The nut or bolt head should fit the wrench exactly.

If you can get the car on a lift, you can use a professional model floor jack stand to relieve tension on the rear shock absorbers. If a lift is not available, you can keep the car on the ground to remove front shocks.

To support the rear axle, the ideal tool is a heavy duty hydraulic service jack of the type used in professional shops and service stations. This is the type that has an arm on which the axle rests and is operated by means of a long handle. Unfortunately, the tool costs over $100.

The second best way to take the strain off the rear shocks is with a heavy duty hydraulic hand jack. These jacks range in price from about $15 to $30 and in holding capacity from 1½ to 20 tons. The holding capacity you need depends on the weight of your car. But give yourself a safety margin and purchase a jack having a capacity in excess of the weight of the car. For example, if your car weighs 2500 pounds, buy a jack having a 3-ton capacity.

Another alternative is to purchase two heavy duty jack stands to use in conjunction with your bumper jack. Jack up the car using the bumper jack. Place the jack stands on each end of the rear axle as near to the shock absorbers as you can get them, and lower the car so weight is evenly distributed on the jack stands. Jack stands cost about $5 each.

Caution: Never get beneath a car which is supported by a bumper jack only. It is not safe.

Once you have tools, doing shock absorber replacement yourself can save you almost $50 each time out. A few telephone calls will convince you of this.

You will find that the cost of having a professional service shop install four heavy duty shock absorbers on a late model vehicle is about $80—$15 each for the shocks and $20 for labor.

The cost when you do the job yourself is about $32. This represents a savings of $48. For $32 you will be getting the best quality heavy duty shock absorber from a leading national chain store.

Doing shock absorber replacement yourself has an additional benefit. Most professional garages will not guarantee new shock absorbers for a period of time which exceeds the guarantee issued by the shock absorber manufacturer. But many national department stores (Sears is one) guarantee their highest quality shock absorbers for as long as you own the car. If a shock goes bad, you can get a replacement free of charge by returning the faulty unit.

This section begins with general instructions, which are followed by directions for specific models. It deals with the replacement of non-automatic level control shock absorbers.

TOOLS AND EQUIPMENT YOU NEED

1. Penetrating oil to free frozen mounting retainers. Penetrating oil is available in either spray or squirt-type cans.
2. Open- and box-end wrenches.
3. Sockets and ratchet wrench.
4. Socket extension.
5. Ratchet wrench extension.
6. Torque wrench.

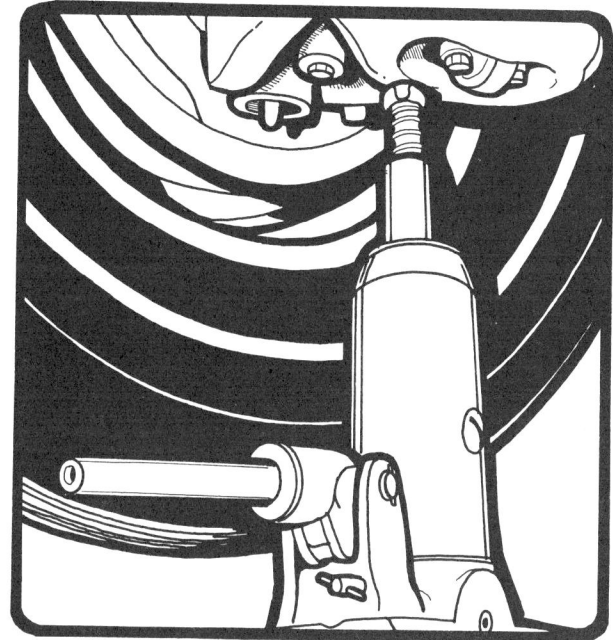

Before replacing shocks, suitable support should be placed under the suspension component that will relieve pressure on the shock absorber.

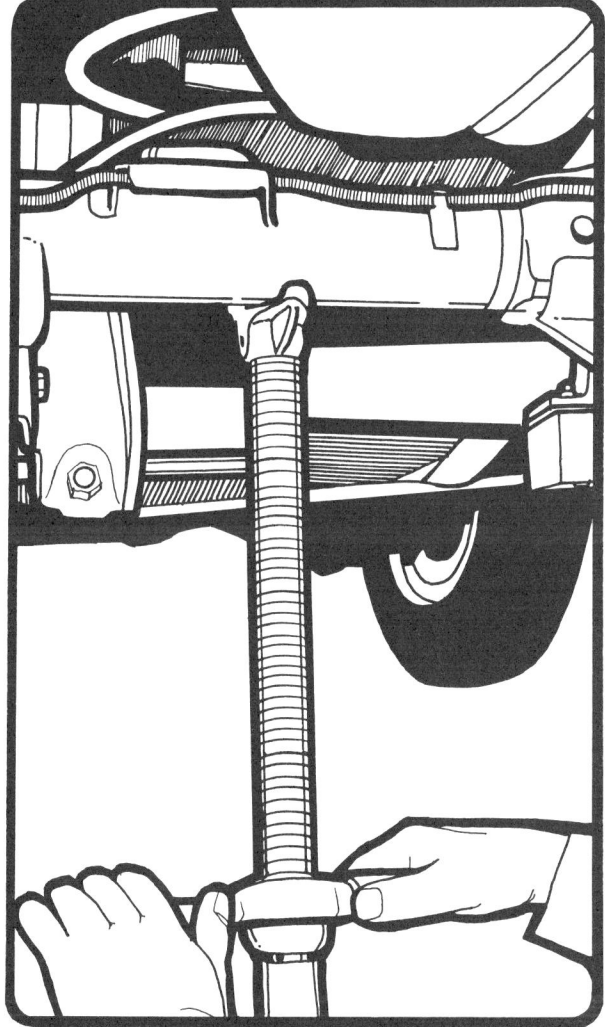

A hydraulic hand jack or safety jack stands can be used to support the suspension member. Be sure the jack or jack stand is positioned securely.

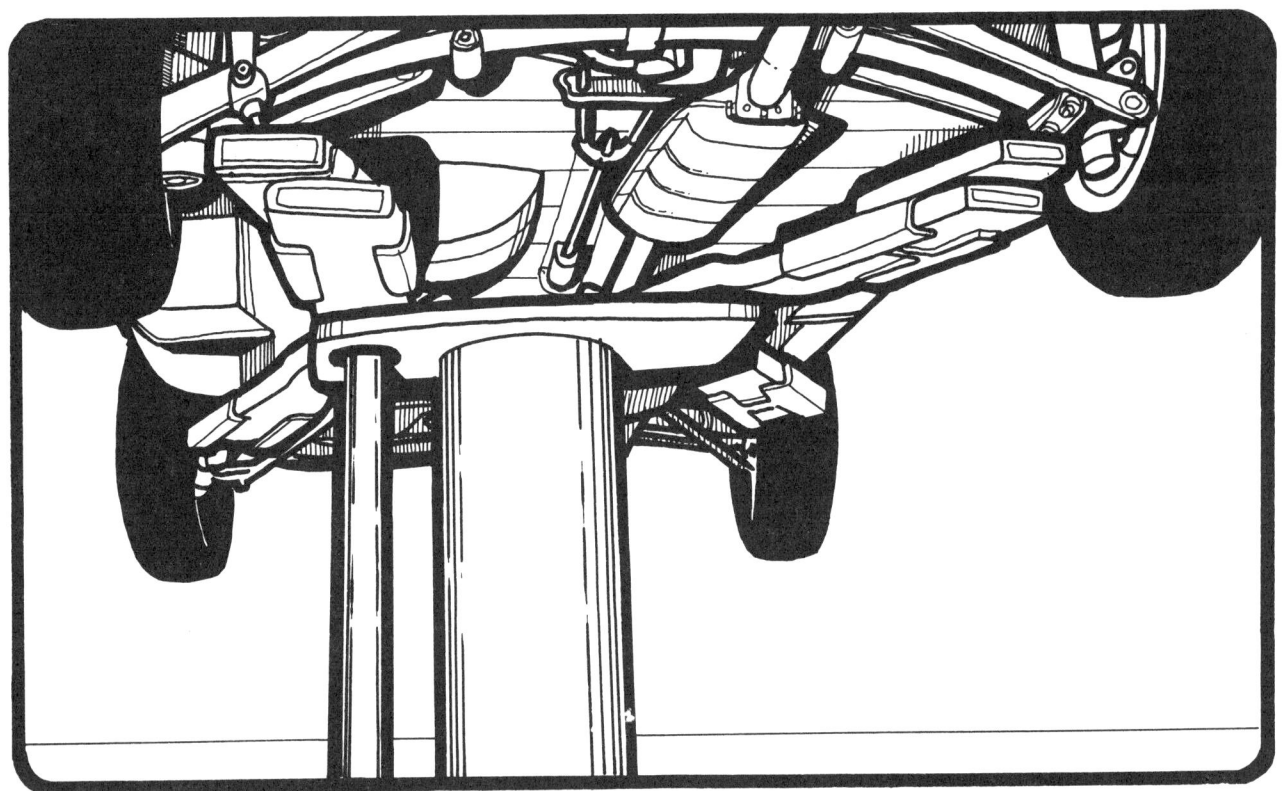

If possible, use a lift at a local gas station or repair shop. This is the most convenient and safest way to replace shock absorbers or to do any other work under a car.

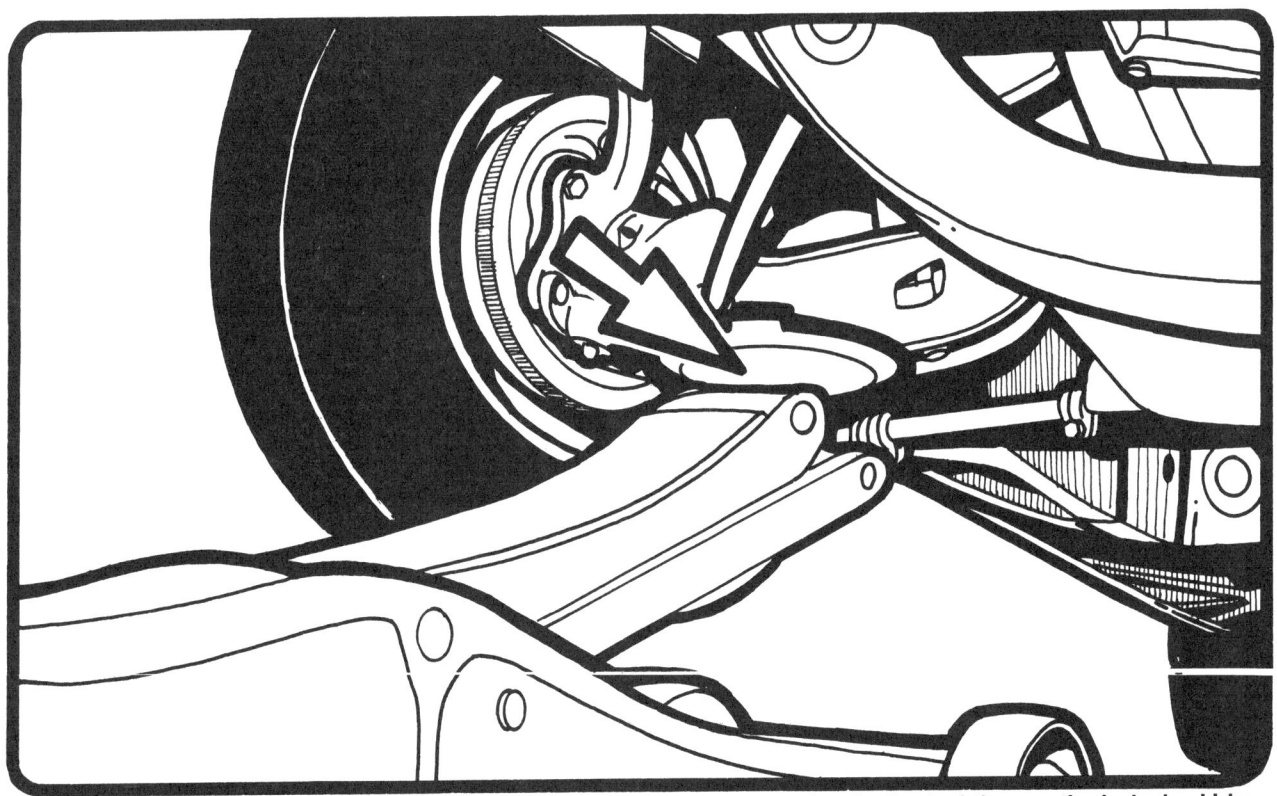

If you use a garage-type hydraulic jack, be sure it is positioned properly. To raise the front of the car, the jack should be under an A-frame as shown.

REPLACING FRONT SHOCK ABSORBERS

General
1. Set the parking brake firmly. Place an automatic transmission in Park, set a manual transmission in gear. Chock the rear wheels.
2. Jack up the front of the car so tires clear the ground. Use a hydraulic jack if possible or support the vehicle with jack stands.
3. If top mounting retainers have to be reached from beneath the car, the procedure may prove easier if you remove the tire and wheel assembly.
4. If mounting retainers are frozen, spray or squirt penetrating oil over the entire surface of the retainer assembly until oil begins dripping from the mounting. Allow oil to penetrate for a minimum of five minutes.

AT THIS POINT, GO DIRECTLY TO THE SPECIFIC PROCEDURES FOR YOUR MAKE AND MODEL

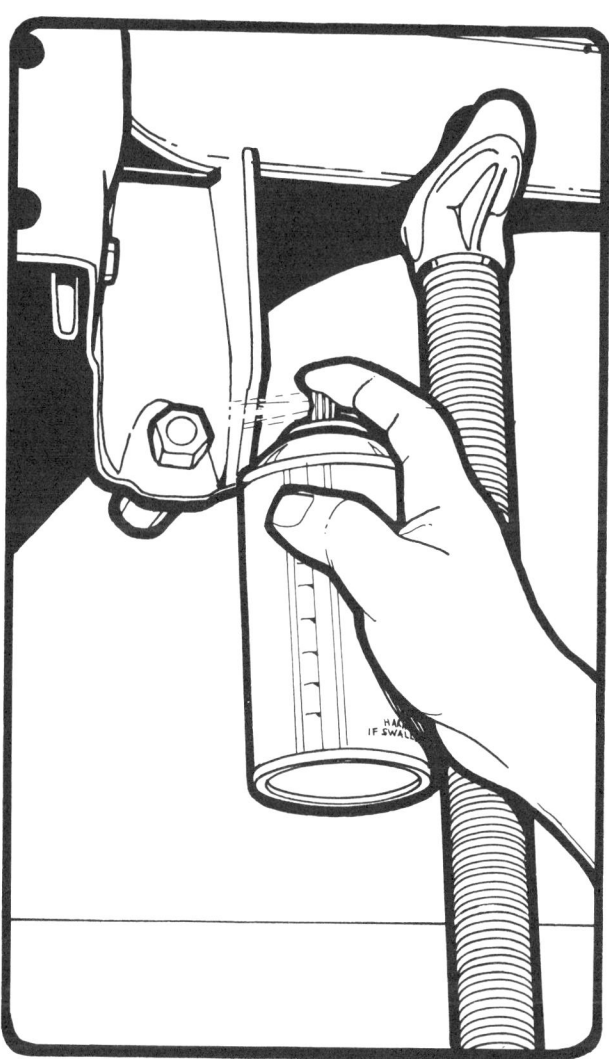

Use penetrating oil to free stubborn bolts.

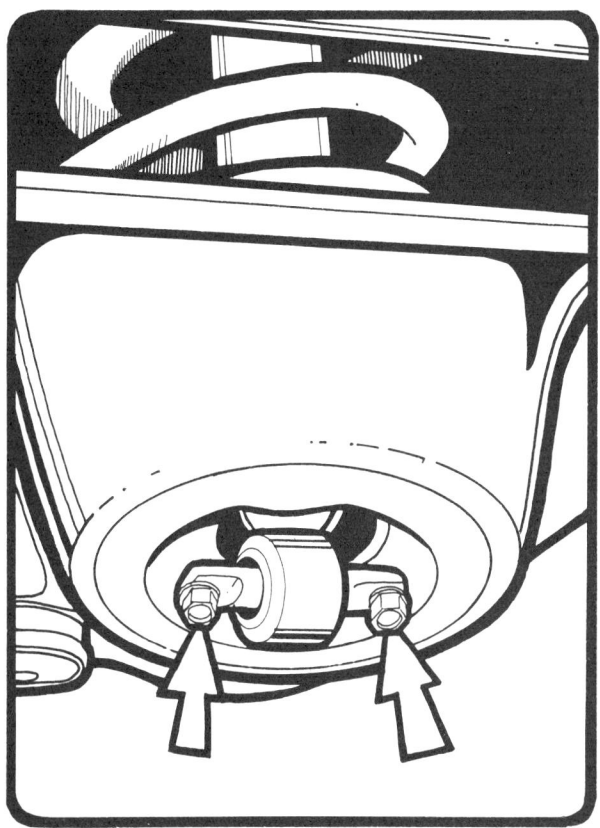

Most front shock absorbers are attached to the lower control arm by bolts as shown. To remove the shock, remove both the bottom and top bolts. Then lower the shock through the control arm.

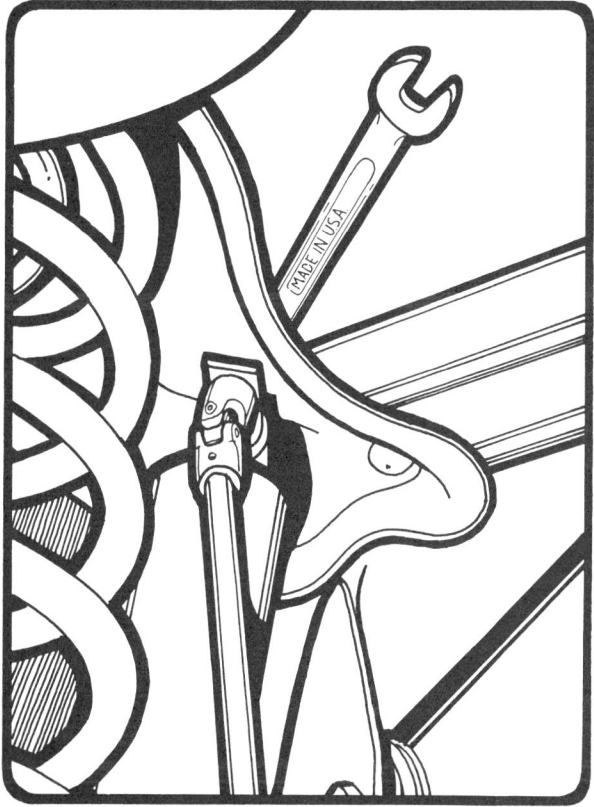

Use an open-end wrench and a socket extension to remove the top mounting bolts.

REPLACING REAR SHOCK ABSORBERS

General

1. Set the parking brake firmly. Place an automatic transmission in Park, place a manual transmission in gear. Chock the front wheels.
rear axle as near to shock absorbers as possible
2. Raise the car so the frame is supported.
3. Place hydraulic jacks or jack stands under the and lift the rear axle so it is supported.

   CAUTION: Failure to support the rear axle and frame may cause serious injury and/or damage.
4. Use penetrating oil if shock absorber retainers are frozen.

IMPORTANT: Before installing front or rear shock absorbers, mount each unit upright in a vise on your workbench. Push and pull the shock through its full travel several times to purge any trapped air in the cylinder. Hold shocks in an upright position until they are installed.

AT THIS POINT, GO DIRECTLY TO THE SPECIFIC PROCEDURES FOR YOUR MAKE AND MODEL

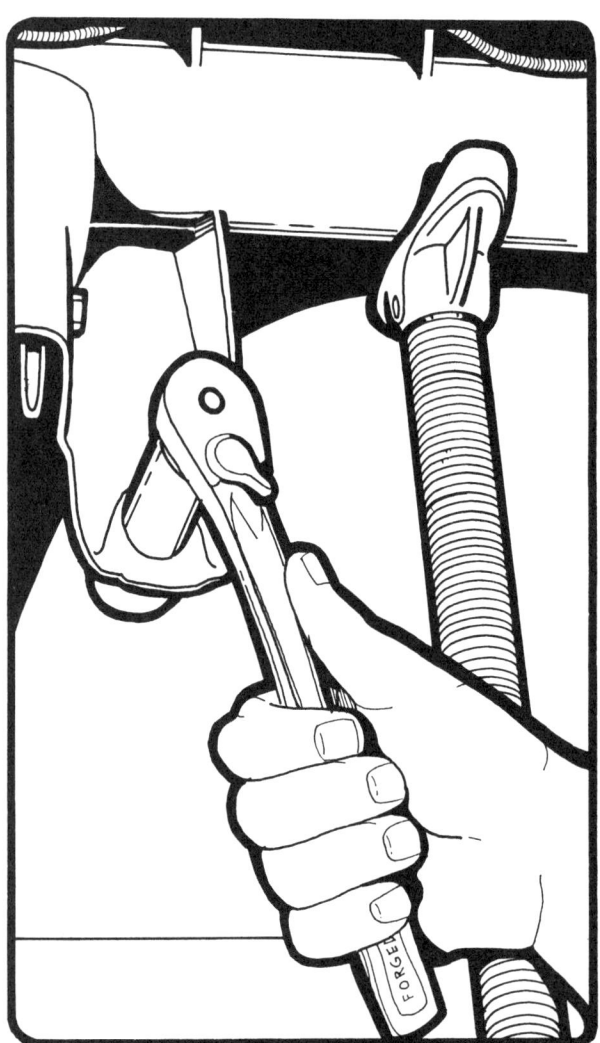

The lower mounting bolt on most rear shocks is connected to a shock mounting plate. To remove the shock, simply unfasten the bolt.

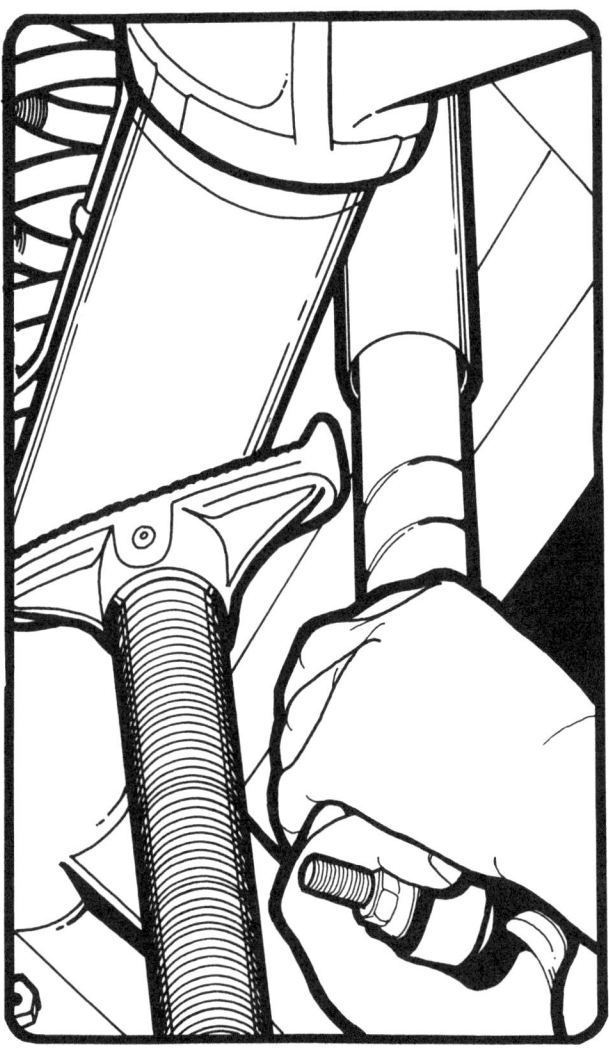

With fasteners removed, the shock is drawn from position.

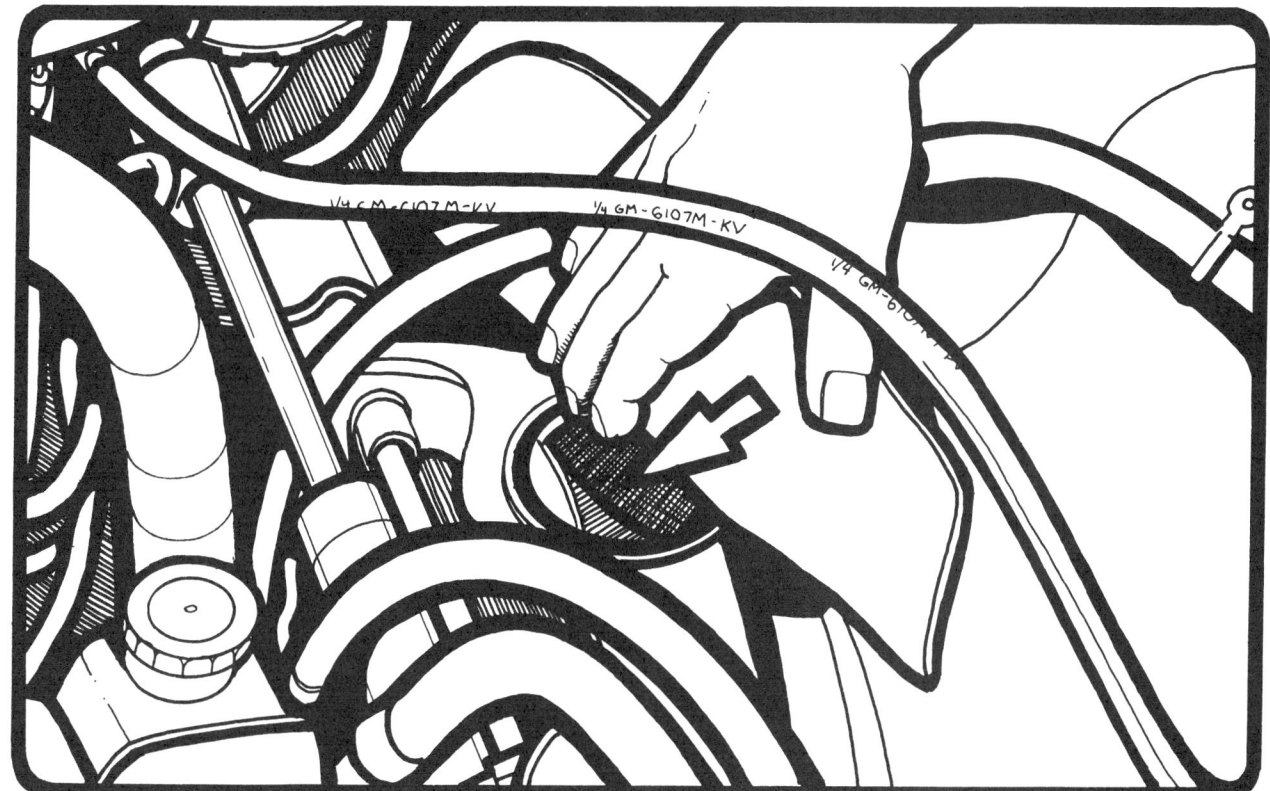

If the top mounting bolts of the front shocks are not easily located from below, look for them through access holes (arrow) near an inner fender panel in the engine compartment. At the rear of some cars, access to the top mounting bolts is gained through the floor of the trunk.

AMERICAN MOTORS

Replacing front shock absorbers
1968-69, all models

1. Lift the engine compartment hood.
2. Disconnect the single top mounting nut, washer and grommet on the shock absorber stem, which is projecting through the wheelhouse.
3. Beneath the car, disconnect the single bottom mounting nut, washer and grommet holding the shock to the lower control arm.
4. Reach up and compress the shock absorber.
5. Draw the shock absorber from its position in the lower control arm.
6. Work the new shock absorber into position inside the lower control arm.
7. Reach up and extend the shock absorber so it reaches its mounting position in the wheelhouse and in the lower control arm.
8. Attach the shock absorber to the lower control arm, tightening the nut to 20 lbs. ft.
9. Attach the shock absorber to the top of the wheelhouse, tightening the nut to 20 lbs. ft.

Replacing front shock absorbers
1970-76, all models

1. Remove the two nuts, washers and grommets holding the bottom shock absorber mounting bracket to the lower spring seat.
2. Lift the engine compartment hood.

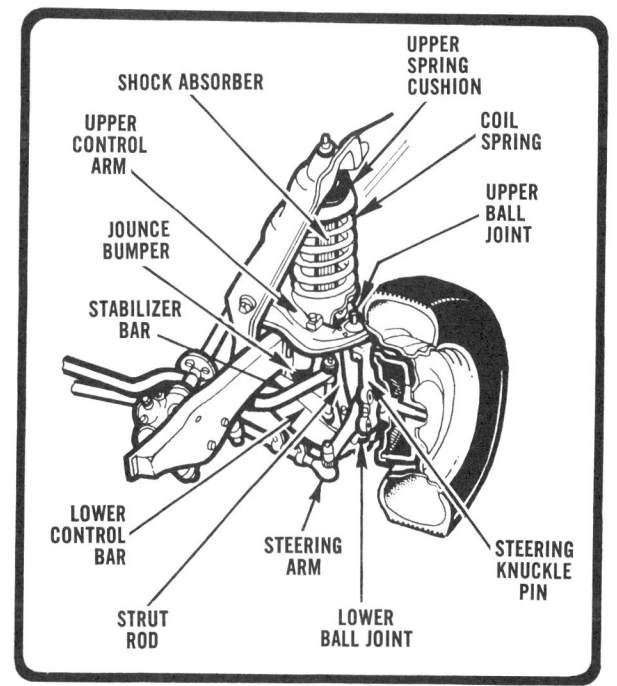

Typical American Motors front suspension.

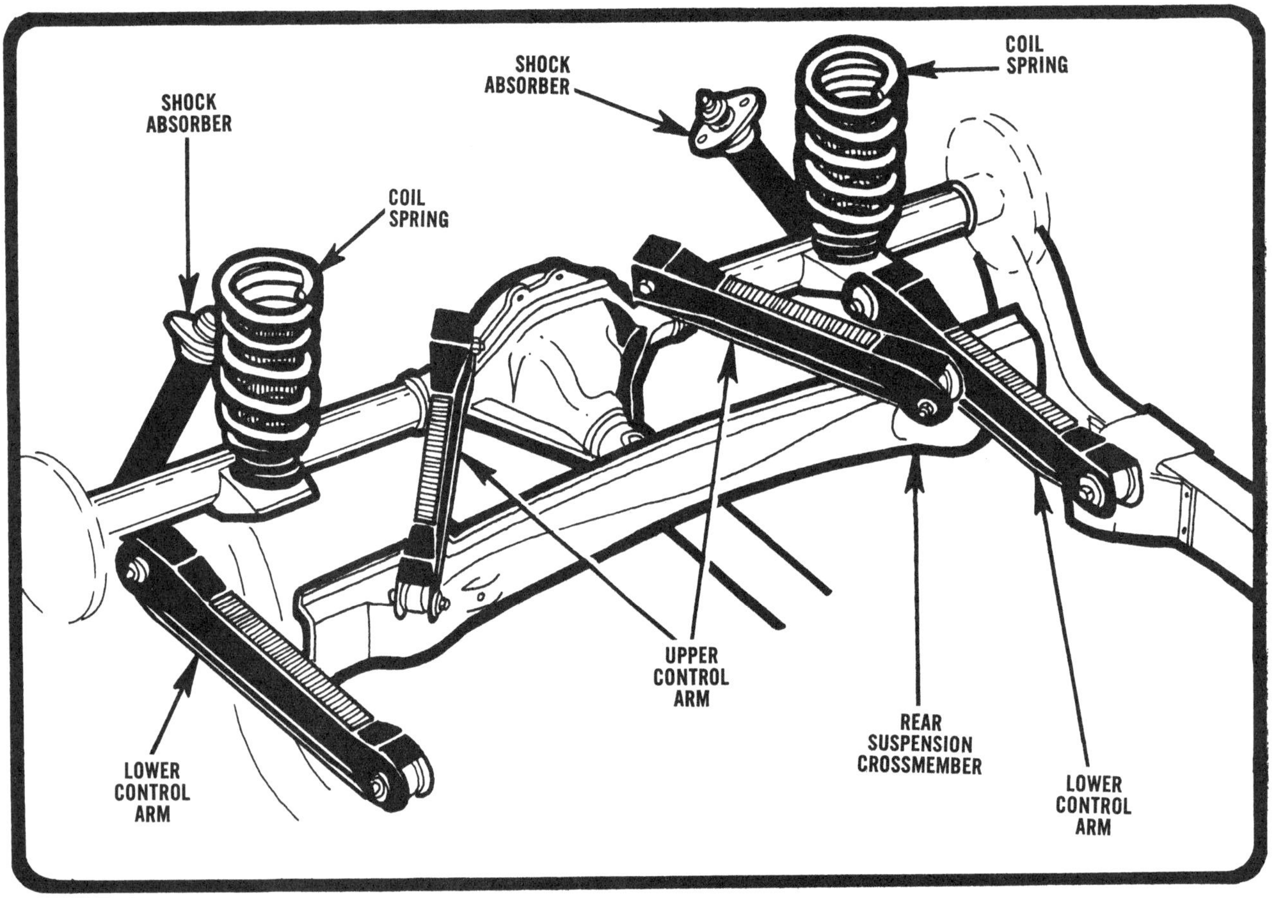

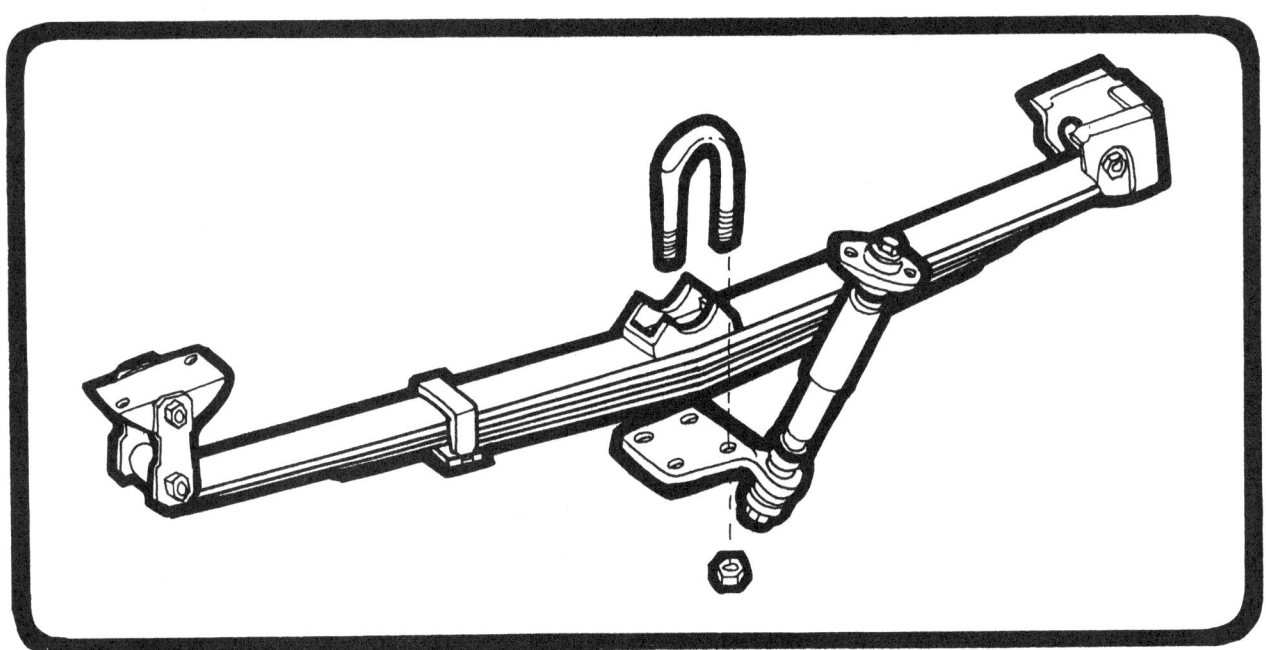

Typical American Motors rear suspension on models with coil springs.

Typical American Motors rear shock absorber installation on models with leaf springs.

3. Observe that the top mounting of the shock absorber protrudes through an upper mounting bracket on the wheelhouse. Remove the retaining nut and bolt from this bracket.
4. Lift the bracket.
5. The shock absorber, still attached to the bracket, will come out through the top of the wheelhouse.
5. Remove the grommets from the two lower mounting studs.
6. Remove the shock absorber upper retaining nut, grommet and washer to separate the shock absorber from the upper mounting bracket. Discard the shock absorber and all hardware. Retain the upper mounting bracket.
7. Insert the stem of the new shock absorber through the hole in the upper mounting bracket. Attach the grommet, washer and retaining nut. Tighten the retaining nut to 8 lbs. ft.
8. Extend the shock absorber to its full rebound position.
9. Place the two grommets onto the lower mounting studs.
10. Lower the shock absorber down through the wheelhouse in the engine compartment so it extends through the coil spring.
11. Beneath the car, maneuver the lower mounting so the attaching studs fall into the holes in the lower spring seat.
12. Install the two grommets, washers and nuts on the lower mounting studs.
13. Tighten the lower shock absorber mounting nuts to 15 lbs. ft.
14. In the engine compartment, install the retaining nut and bolt to the upper mounting bracket.
15. Tighten the upper mounting bracket retaining nut and bolt to 20 lbs. ft.

Replacing rear shock absorbers
1968-76, all models

1. Raise the car and support the rear axle.
2. Remove the lower mounting nut, washer, and grommet.
3. Remove the two bolts which hold the upper shock absorber bracket to the car. Draw the shock absorber and bracket from the car.
4. Remove the upper mounting nut and grommet holding the upper bracket to the shock absorber. Discard the shock absorber and hardware. Retain the bracket.
5. Place a new retainer and grommet on the new shock absorber's stem.
6. Place the upper mounting bracket in position on the stem. Install the grommet, retainer and nut, and tighten the nut to 8 lbs. ft.
7. Position the shock absorber so the upper mounting bracket lines up with its mounting holes in the vehicle.
8. Compress the shock.
9. Install bolts through the upper mounting bracket holes and tighten them to 15 lbs. ft.
10. In cars with leaf springs (Hornet, Gremlin, Rambler), slide a new retainer and grommet onto the lower mounting stem.
11. Extend the shock absorber so the lower mounting stem extends through the hole in the spring plate.
12. Install grommet, retainer and nut, and tighten the lower mounting nut to 8 lbs. ft.
13. In cars with coil springs (Matador, Ambassador), extend the shock absorber after the upper mounting bracket has been attached so the lower cylinder lines up with the axle tube.
14. Attach bolts and retainers, and tighten the lower mounting bolts to 8 lbs. ft.

BUICK

Replacing front shock absorbers
1968-76, all models

1. Lift the engine compartment hood and locate the shock absorber upper mounting nut access holes in the wheelhousings.
2. Open the covers to the access holes.
3. Using a short extension on a ratchet, remove the shock absorber upper mounting nut, retainer, and grommet.
4. Get beneath the car and remove the two mounting bolts from each shock absorber.

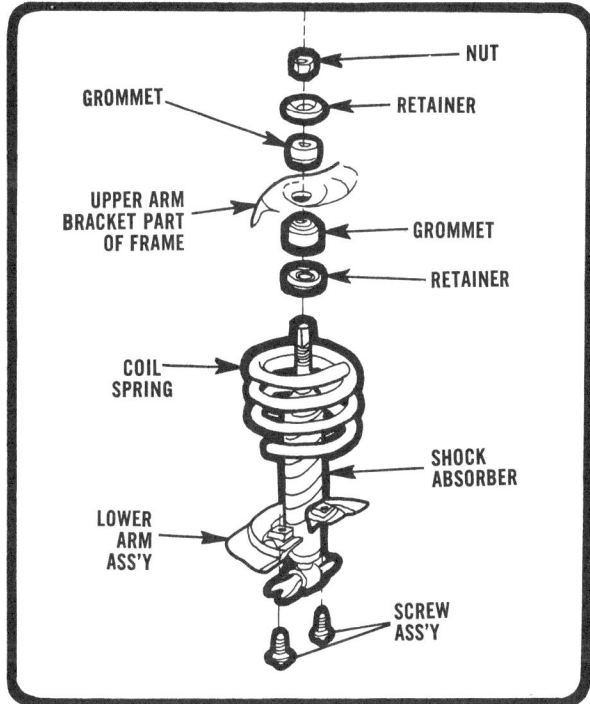

Typical General Motors front shock absorber installation.

5. Lower the shock absorber through the lower control arm.
6. Extend the new shock absorber to its full length.
7. Place a grommet retainer and grommet, in that order, on the upper shock absorber stem.
8. Maneuver the shock up through the lower control arm and coil spring until the upper stem extends through the hole in the wheelhouse.
9. Extend the two mounting bolts through the two lower mounting holes. Screw them into their respective nuts on the lower control arm.
10. Torque the lower mounting bolts to 20 lbs. ft.
11. In the engine compartment, place the grommet, positioner and nut on the shock absorber stem, and torque the nut to 8 lbs. ft.

Replacing rear shock absorbers
1968-76, all models

1. Jack up the car and support the rear axle.
2. Remove the rear tire and wheel assemblies.
3. Disconnect the single bolt, lockwasher, and nut from the shock absorber's lower end.
4. Out from under the car and working through the wheelhousing, reach in behind the brake drum and disconnect the two bolts, washers, and nuts from the shock absorber's upper mounting.
5. Position the new shock absorber so the holes in the unit's mounting plate align with the holes in the car's frame bracket.
6. Attach upper mounting hardware fingertight.
7. Align the lower shock bushing with the hole in the bracket that is welded to the rear axle tube.
8. Insert the bolt through the bushing. Place a washer on the threaded end of the bolt.
9. Slide the bolt through the hole in the bracket.
10. Insert a lockwasher and run the nut up fingertight.
11. Tighten the upper mounting nut to 20 lbs. ft. The shock's stud must not be allowed to rotate as bolts are being tightened. Hold it with a box- or open-end wrench.
12. Remove supports and lower the car to the ground. Car weight must be on the rear wheels when tightening the lower mountings.
13. Tighten the lower nut to 65 lbs. ft. The shock absorber stud must not be allowed to rotate. Hold it with a box- or open-end wrench.

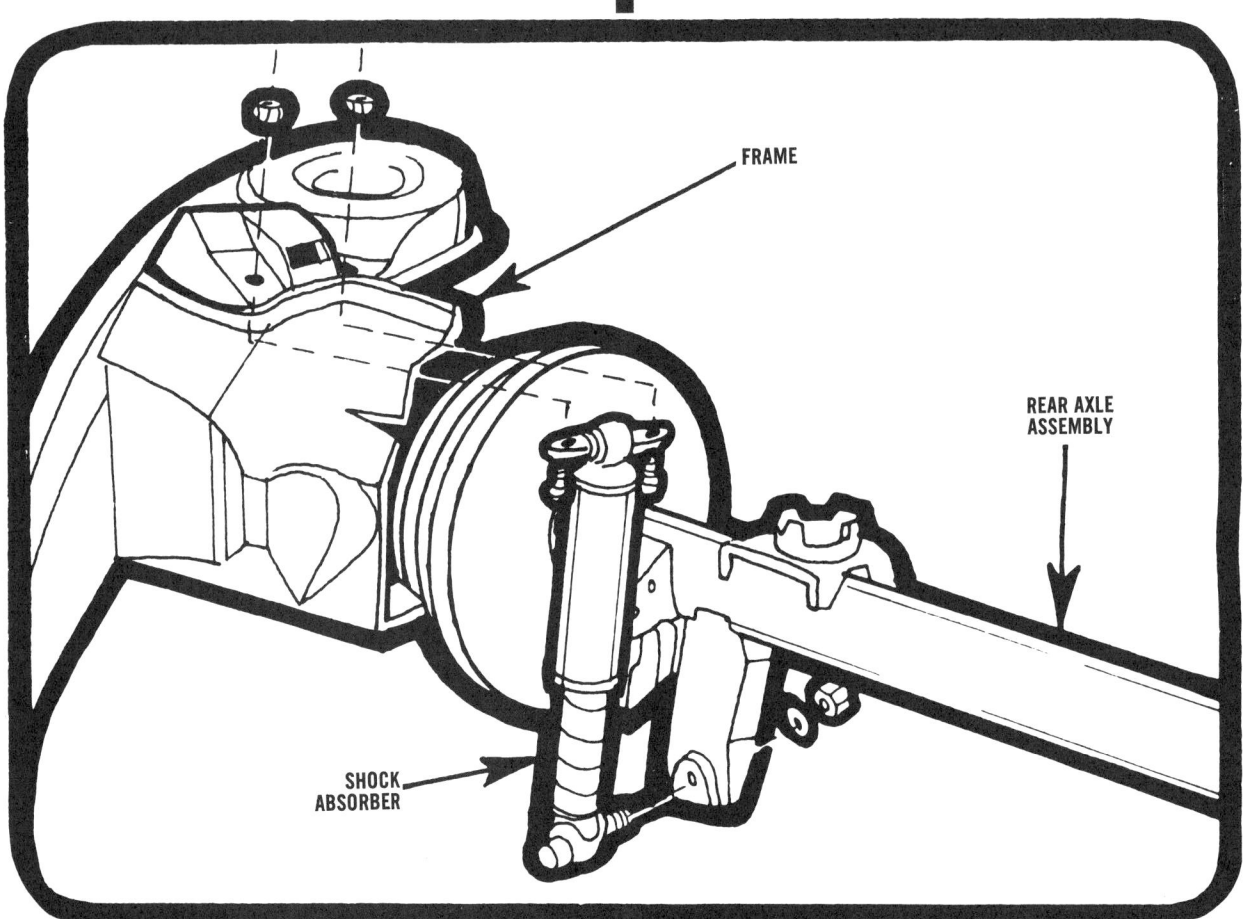

Typical General Motors rear shock absorber installation on models with coil springs.

CADILLAC

Replacing front shock absorbers
1968-76, all models except Eldorado

1. Raise the hood to the engine compartment.
2. Find access holes to the shock absorber's top mountings in the wheelhousings. Remove covers.
3. Grasp the shock absorber upper stem with a wrench to keep the stem from turning. The stem is squared at the top to permit this.
4. With another wrench, remove the upper retaining nut and retainer at the frame spring tower.
5. Beneath the car, remove the bolt, nut and lockwasher which hold the lower end of the shock absorber to the lower suspension arm.
6. Remove the shock absorber through the bottom of the lower suspension arm.
7. Install a retainer in the new shock absorber's upper stem.
8. Extend the shock absorber fully.
9. Insert the shock absorber up into the coil spring, guiding the upper stem through the grommet in the wheelhouse.
10. Place the lower end of the shock into position in the lower suspension arm. Install the bolt, lockwasher and nut.
11. Tighten the bolt of the shock's lower mounting to 55 lbs. ft.
12. Install the retainer and nut to the shock absorber's upper stem.
13. Holding the stem with a wrench so it will not turn, tighten the upper nut to 75 lbs. ft.

Replacing rear shock absorbers
1968-76, all models except Eldorado and Seville

CAUTION: Rear shock absorbers lie near brake lines. Be very careful not to strike brake lines with tools during shock absorber replacement. Lines may be damaged.

1. Raise the car and support the rear axle.
2. Take a 12-point, ½-inch box-end wrench and bend it to a 45° angle 1-inch back from the center of the box-end diameter.
3. With this wrench, grasp the shock absorber mounting nuts at the rear frame kickup.
4. Remove the two upper retaining bolts and nuts.
5. Unbolt the shock at its lower mounting, holding the stem next to the grommet so the stem does not turn. Remove the retaining nut.
6. Remove the shock absorber from its mounts.
7. Work the upper mounting of the new shock absorber onto the frame kickup.
8. Install the upper retaining nuts and bolts. Using the homemade wrench described above to grasp the upper mounting nuts, tighten the bolts to 12 lbs. ft.
9. Guide the shock's lower stud into its mounting bracket.
10. Install the retaining nut.
11. Tighten the retaining nut to 50 lbs. ft.
12. Remove supports and lower the car to the ground.

Replacing front shock absorbers
1968-76 Eldorado

1. Keep the car on the ground.
2. Reach up and disconnect the shock absorber at its upper mount.
3. Disconnect the shock absorber at its lower mount.
4. Compress the shock absorber from the top down.
5. Work the lower mount free from the mounting bolts. If necessary, insert a screwdriver under the mount's inner sleeve to detach the bolt.
6. Guide the shock down and toward the rear of the car to get it free, moving it past front wheel drive components.
7. Compress the new shock absorber and guide it up through the opening in the upper control arm.
8. Position the unit on the lower attaching stud. Use a screwdriver inserted inside the mount inner sleeve, if necessary, to get the stud through the bushing.
9. Pull the shock to extension from the top, extending it into the frame attaching bracket. Have someone press down on the fender to compress the suspension, which will facilitate installation.
10. Line up the shock upper mounting holes in shock and frame attaching bracket.
11. Install the upper attaching bolt and nut. Tighten the nut to 75 lbs. ft.
12. Install the lockwasher and lower attaching nut. Tighten the nut to 75 lbs. ft.

Replacing rear shock absorbers
1968-76 Eldorado and Seville

You are advised to leave testing and installation of rear shock absorbers to a qualified Cadillac service technician. Shock absorbers in the rear ends of the Eldorado are not standard units. 1968-70 models employed two shocks per rear wheel—one vertical shock and one horizontal shock. Models since 1971 and Seville employ automatic level control.

CHEVROLET

Replacing front shock absorbers
1968-76, all models except Chevette and Vega

1. Raise the car following the safety instructions in the first part of this chapter.
2. From below, grasp the shock absorber's upper stem with an open-end wrench to keep the stem from turning. The stem is squared to permit this.
3. Remove the upper stem retaining nut.
4. Remove the two bolts holding the shock's lower pivot to the lower control arm.
5. Pull the shock from the car through the hole in the lower control arm.
6. Place a new retainer and rubber grommet on the upper stem of the new shock absorber.
7. Extend the shock fully.
8. From below, guide the shock up through the lower control arm and coil spring, so the upper stem passes through the mounting hole in the upper control arm frame.
9. Install the upper grommet, retainer and nut over the shock absorber's upper stem.
10. Hold the upper stem with an open-end wrench to keep it from turning.
11. Tighten the upper retaining nut to 90 lbs. in. for all models except the Chevrolet, which should be tightened to 150 lbs. in.
12. Install the retainers which attach the shock's lower pivot to the lower control arm.
13. Tighten the lower mounting retainer to 20 lbs. ft. for all models except Corvette, which is tightened to 150 lbs. in.
14. Lower the car to the floor.

Replacing front shock absorbers
Chevrolet Chevette and Vega, and
Pontiac Astre, all models

1. In the engine compartment, find the shock absorber upper stem extending from the wheelhousing.
2. Hold the stem tightly and remove nut, retainer and grommet.
3. Raise the car.
4. Unscrew the two bolts from the lower end of the shock absorber, remove the old shock from the car and discard.
5. Place a new retainer and grommet on the upper stem of the new shock absorber.
6. Extend the shock and install the upper stem through the spring tower.
7. Install lower bolts and tighten to 20 lbs. ft.
8. Lower the car to the floor.
9. Install a new upper grommet retainer and nut to the shock absorber stem.
10. Hold the stem firmly to keep it from turning and tighten the nut to 120 lbs. in.

Replacing rear shock absorbers
1968-76 Chevrolet, Monte Carlo, and Chevelle

1. Jack up the car and support the rear axle.
2. Reach up and disconnect the upper shock absorber mounting by removing the two retaining bolts. If the car is a station wagon, reach in between the tire and frame and place a wrench on the nuts located between the body and frame. Then reach up with an extension and detach the upper mounting bolts as you turn bolts and nuts in opposing directions.
3. Disconnect the shock absorber from its lower attaching bracket by grasping both the stud and nut with wrenches and turning in opposing directions.
4. Remove the old shock absorber.
5. Work the new shock absorber into position and install the two upper mounting bolts fingertight.
6. Position the lower attaching stud in the axle bracket and attach the lockwasher and nut fingertight.
7. Tighten the upper attaching bolts to 12 lbs. ft.
8. Hold the lower attaching stud with a wrench and tighten the nut to 65 lbs. ft.
9. Remove supports and lower the car to the ground.

Replacing rear shock absorbers
1968-76 Nova

1. Jack up the car and support the rear axle.
2. Remove the lower mounting bolt from the shock absorber eye.
3. Withdraw the two bolts from the shock absorber upper mounting bracket.
4. Remove the shock absorber.
5. Extend the new shock absorber and position it in place. Install the two upper attaching bolts fingertight.
6. Insert the shock absorber eye into the lower mounting bracket and install the bolt and nut.
   Caution: The lower mounting bolt must be to the rear.
7. Tighten the lower mounting bracket nut to 45 lbs. ft.
8. Tighten the two upper mounting bolts to 18 lbs. ft.
9. Remove supports and lower the car to the ground.

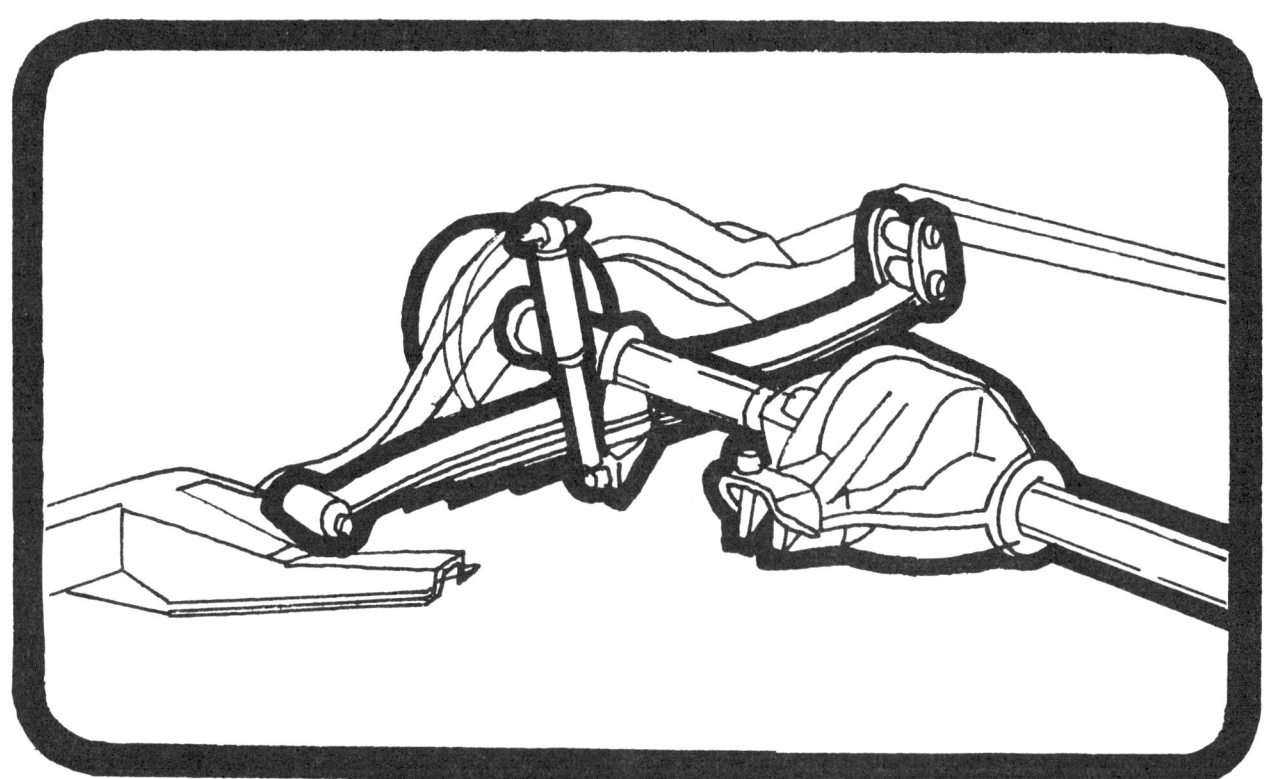

Typical General Motors rear shock absorber installation on models with leaf springs.

Replacing rear shock absorbers
1968-76 Camaro
1. Jack up the car and support the rear axle.
2. Remove the shock absorber's lower nut, retainer and grommet, so the unit can be loosened from its position on the bracket welded to the leaf spring.
3. Reach up and remove the two upper attaching bolts from the bracket attached to the frame.
4. Insert a new retainer and grommet on the new shock absorber's lower stem.
5. Extend the shock absorber so the holes in the unit's mounting bracket, which is inserted through the upper eye, align themselves with the holes in the upper mounting bracket on the frame.
6. Screw on the upper retaining bolts fingertight.
7. Place the lower stem into the mounting hole in the bracket that is welded to the spring.
8. Insert the lower grommet, retainer, and nut.
9. Tighten the upper mounting bolts to 18 lbs. ft.
10. Tighten the lower mounting bolts to 8 lbs. ft.
11. Remove supports and lower the car to the ground.

Replacing rear shock absorbers
Chevrolet Chevette, Vega and Pontiac Astre
1. Raise the car and support the rear axle.
2. Reach up and unscrew the two upper attaching bolts.
3. Remove the attaching bolt from the shock's lower end.
4. Remove the shock from the car and discard.
5. Extend the shock and position its lower end in the lower bracket and its upper end so the two holes in its eye-bracket line up with the two holes in the upper mounting bracket.
6. Install upper retaining bolts and tighten them to 18 lbs. ft.
7. Install the lower shock retaining bolt and nut and tighten to 42 lbs. ft.
8. Remove supports and lower the car to the ground.

Replacing rear shock absorbers
1968-76 Corvette
1. Raise the car and support the rear axle.
2. Hold the upper mounting stud with a wrench while disconnecting the upper mounting bolt. When it is loose, slip the bolt out of the frame bracket.
3. Remove the shock absorber's lower mounting nut and lockwasher.
4. Slide the shock upper eye out of the frame bracket and pull the lower eye and grommets off the strut rod mounting shaft.
5. Install the new shock absorber by sliding the upper mounting eye into the frame mounting bracket. Install bolt, lockwasher and nut fingertight.
6. Place a grommet on the strut rod mounting shaft.
7. Install the shock's lower eye on the strut rod mounting shaft.
8. Install the inboard grommet, washer and nut on the strut rod mounting shaft.
   Caution: Install the washer with the curve pointing inward, away from the grommet.
9. Tighten the upper mounting bolt and nut to 50 lbs. ft.
10. Tighten the lower mounting nut to 35 lbs .ft.
11. Remove supports and lower the car to the ground.

CHRYSLER CORPORATION

Replacing front shock absorbers
1968-76, all models

1. Raise the car.
2. Remove the wheel and tire assemblies.
3. Reach in under the fender and loosen the upper shock absorber nut and retainer, leaving the upper stem of the shock free.
4. This applies to Valiant, Dart, Fury, Coronet, Barracuda, Challenger, Cordoba and Charger. Remove the shock's lower attachment bolt from the side of the lower control arm by grasping both bolt and nut with wrenches and exerting opposing force on the tools. This leaves the eye of the shock absorber free.
5. This applies to Gran Fury, Monaco, Chrysler, Imperial, Aspen and Volare. Remove the nut, retainer and bushing from the bottom of the lower control arm. This leaves the lower stem of the shock absorber free.
6. Push upward on the shock, compressing it. Then, pull the unit from the car by releasing it from its top mounting bushing.
7. If the rubber bushing in the upper mounting bracket looks worn, dried out or cracked, pry the inner sleeve from inside the bushing with a screwdriver or knife. Then cut out the bushing.

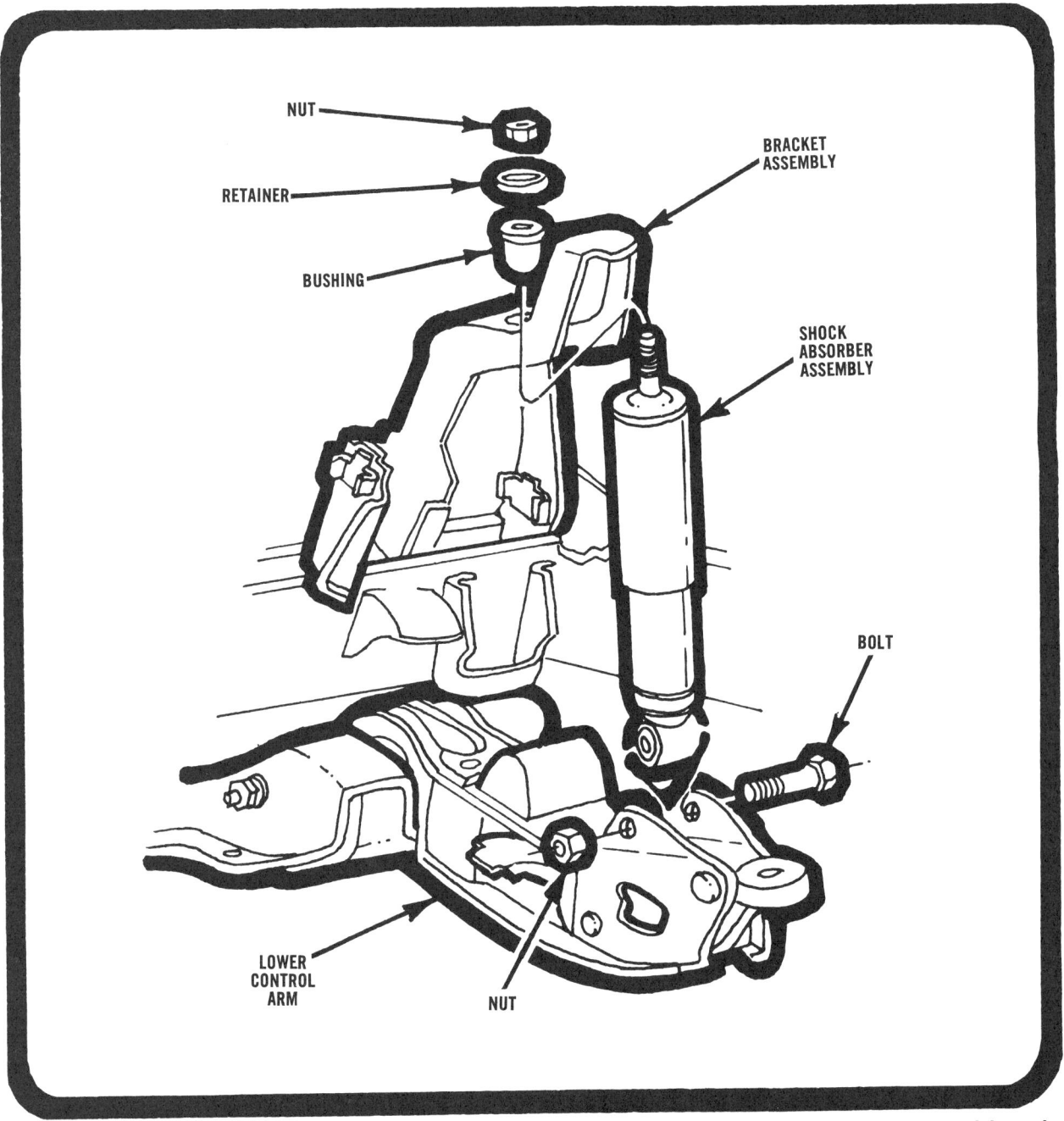

Typical Chrysler Corp. front shock absorber installation for Dart, Valiant, Fury, Coronet, Barracuda, Challenger, Cordoba and Charger.

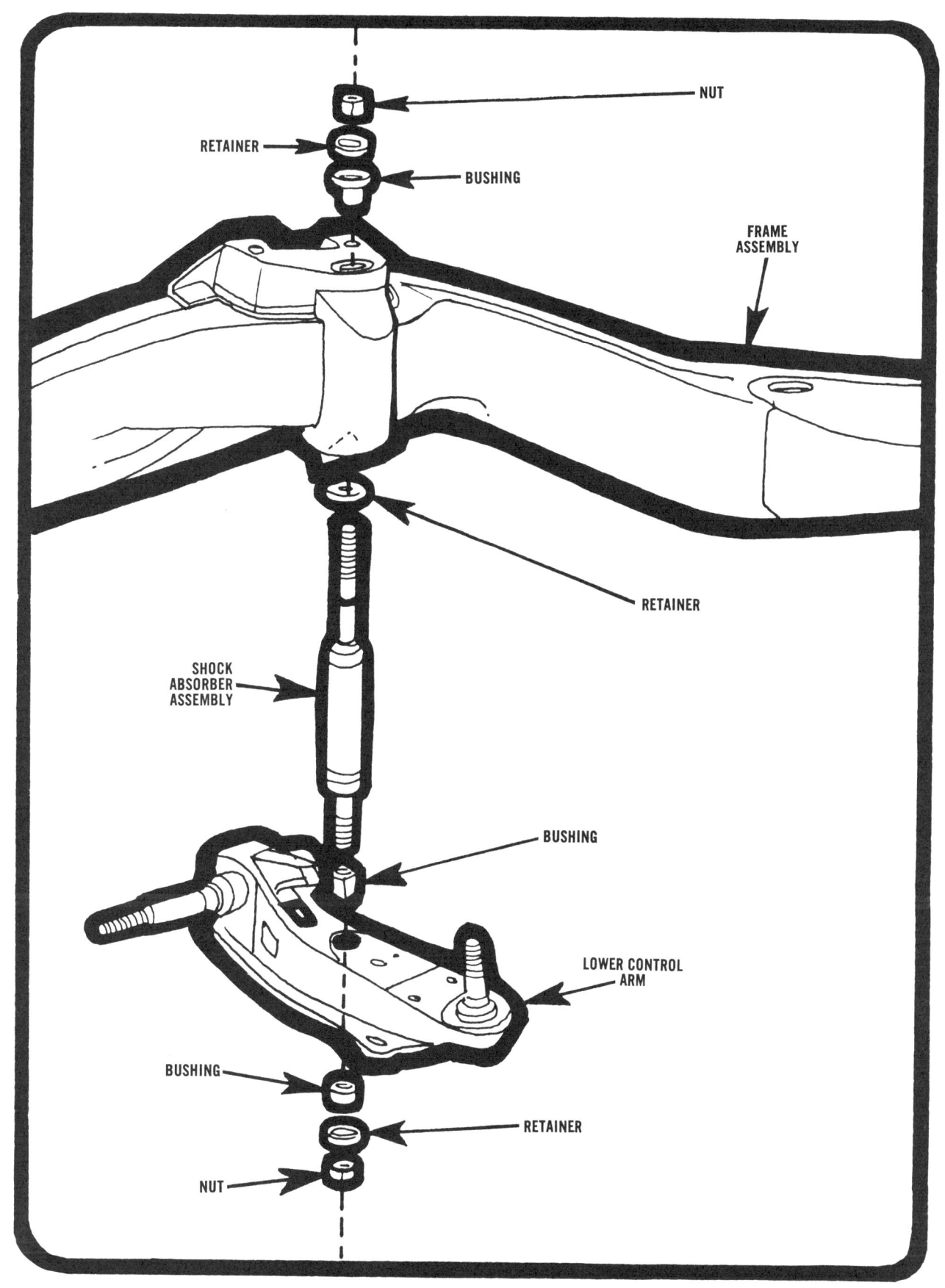

Typical Chrysler Corp. front shock absorber installation for Gran Fury, Monaco, Chrysler, Imperial, Aspen and Volare.

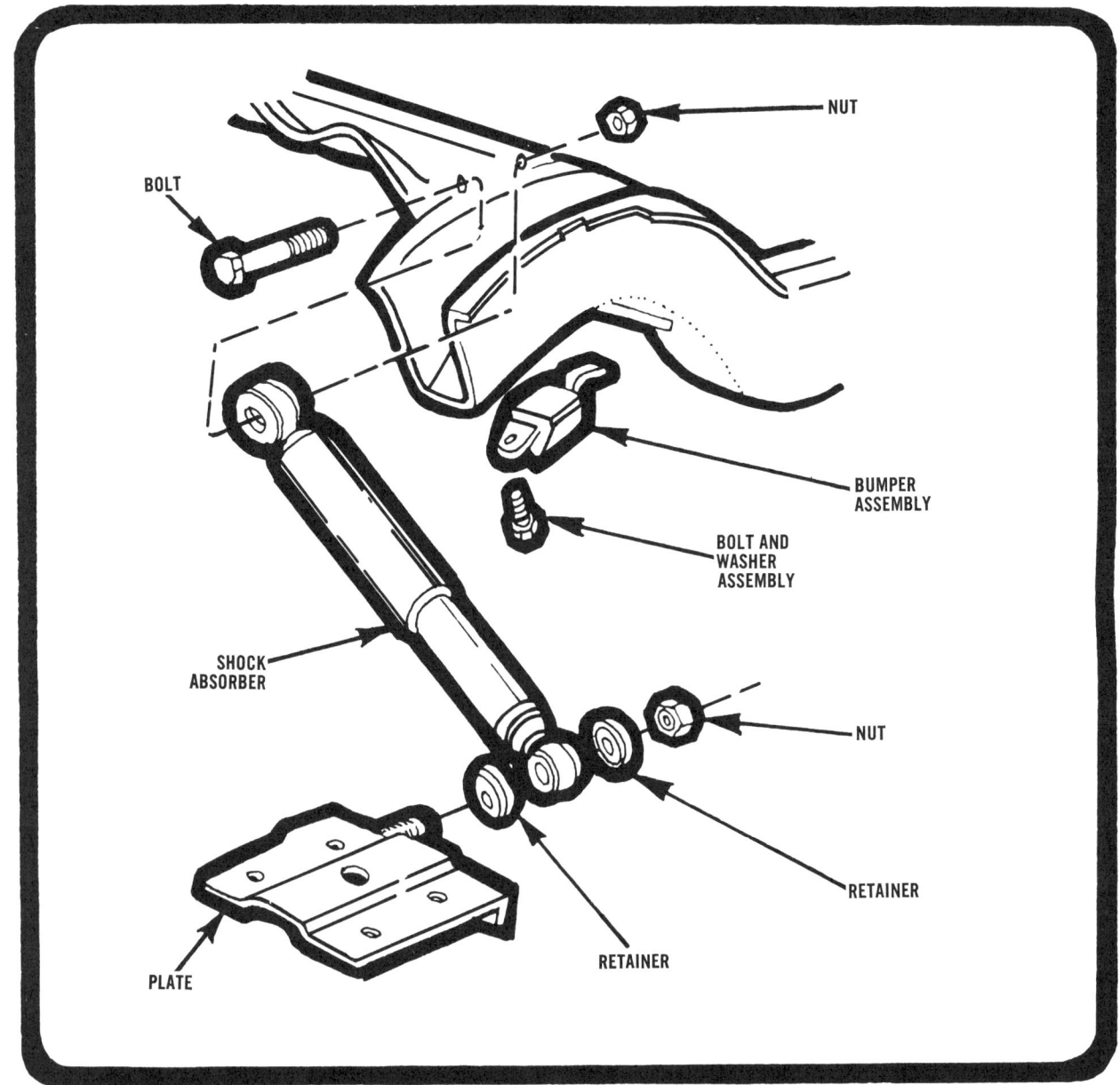

Typical Chrysler Corp. rear shock absorber installation for all models except Dart and Valiant.

8. Remove the inner sleeve from a new bushing. Soak the bushing in warm water to make it pliable and work the bushing into the upper mounting bracket hole with a twisting motion. Then, tap it in place with a hammer.
9. Carefully tap the inner steel sleeve into the bushing hole.
10. Compress the new shock absorber.
11. Insert the shock's upper stem into the upper mounting bushing.
12. Install the upper retainer and upper nut. The retainer's concave side must be in contact with the rubber bushing.
13. Lower the car to the ground and tighten the shock's upper nut to 25 lbs. ft.
14. In the case of Gran Fury, Monaco, Chrysler, Imperial, Aspen and Volare, install the bushing way up on the lower stem of the shock absorber.
15. Extend the shock so the lower stem protrudes through the hole in the lower control arm, and attach bushing, retainer and nut.
16. Tighten the nut to 50 lbs. ft. (The car must be on the ground).
17. In the case of Valiant, Dart, Fury, Coronet, Cordoba, Charger, Barracuda and Challenger, extend the shock and align the unit's lower eye with the holes in the lower control arm.
18. Insert the bolt and attach the nut.
19. Tighten the nut to 35 lbs. ft. (The car must be on the ground).

Replacing rear shock absorbers 1968-76, all models

1. Jack up the car and support the rear axle.
2. Remove the nut and retainer which hold the shock absorber's lower mounting to the spring plate mounting stud.
3. Slide the lower end of the shock from the mounting stud.
4. Remove the retainer which may remain on the stud.

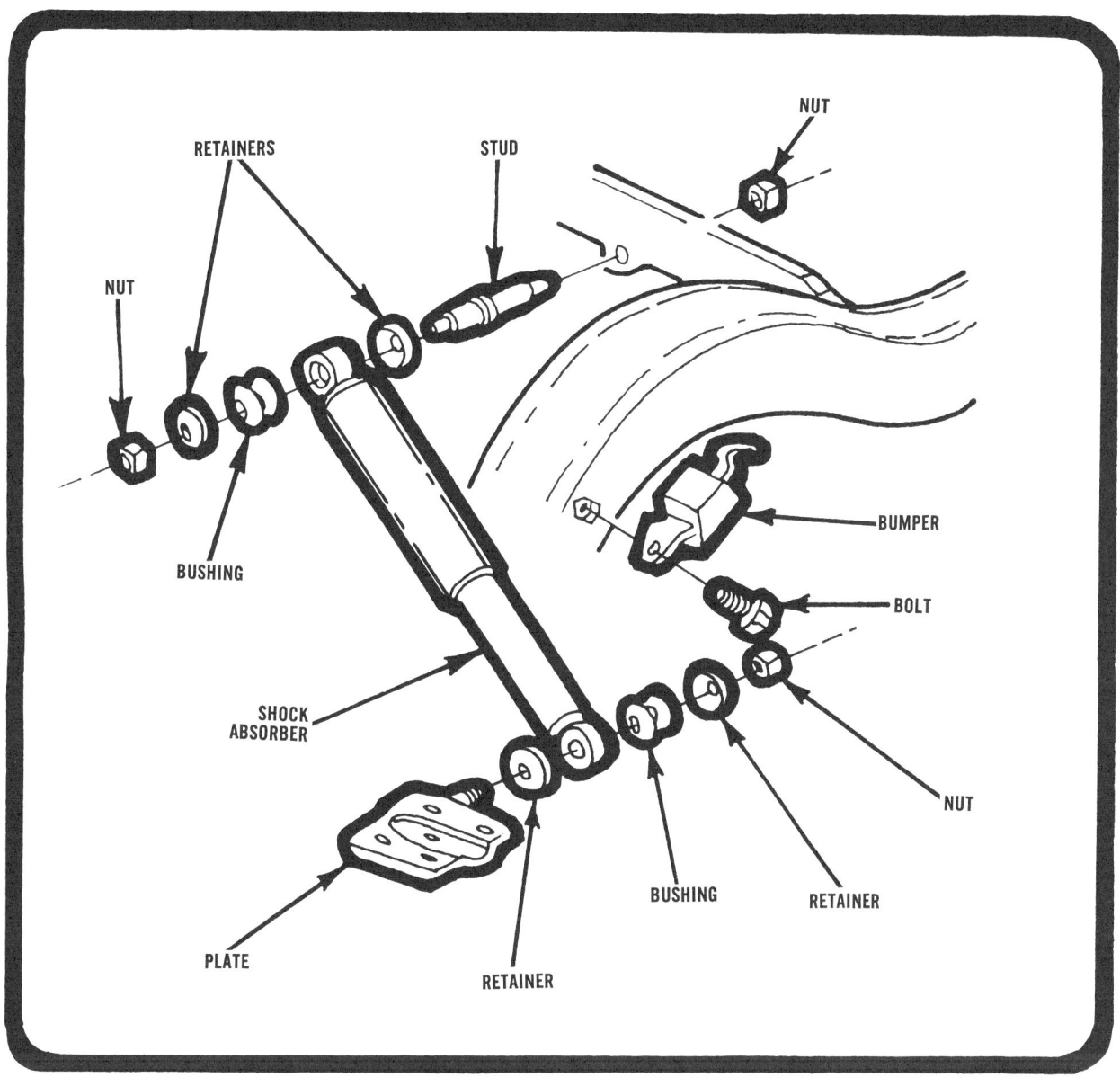

Typical Chrysler Corp. rear shock absorber installation for Dart and Valiant.

5. In the case of Dart and Valiant, loosen and remove the nut retainer from the upper shock absorber mounting stud. Slide the shock off the stud and remove the retainer.
6. In the case of all other models, remove the upper mounting bolt and nut from the frame crossmember and remove the shock absorber. The mounting nut in the Barracuda and Challenger is reached from inside the luggage compartment.
7. In the case of Dart and Valiant, slip a new retainer on the shock absorber mounting stud.
8. Slip the shock's upper mounting onto the mounting stud, followed by another retainer and nut. Tighten the nut fingertight.
9. In the case of all other models, align the shock absorber upper eye with the mounting hole in the frame crossmember and slip on the bolt. Attach the nut and tighten fingertight.
10. Slip a new retainer on the stud of the lower shock absorber mounting plate.
11. Extend the shock and slip the lower eye on to the stud.
12. Insert retainer and nut. Tighten the nut fingertight.
13. Remove supports and lower the car to the ground so the full weight of the vehicle is on the wheels.
14. In Dart and Valiant, tighten the upper nut to 50 lbs. ft.
15. In all other models, tighten the upper nut to 70 lbs. ft.
16. In all models, tighten the lower nut to 50 lbs. ft.

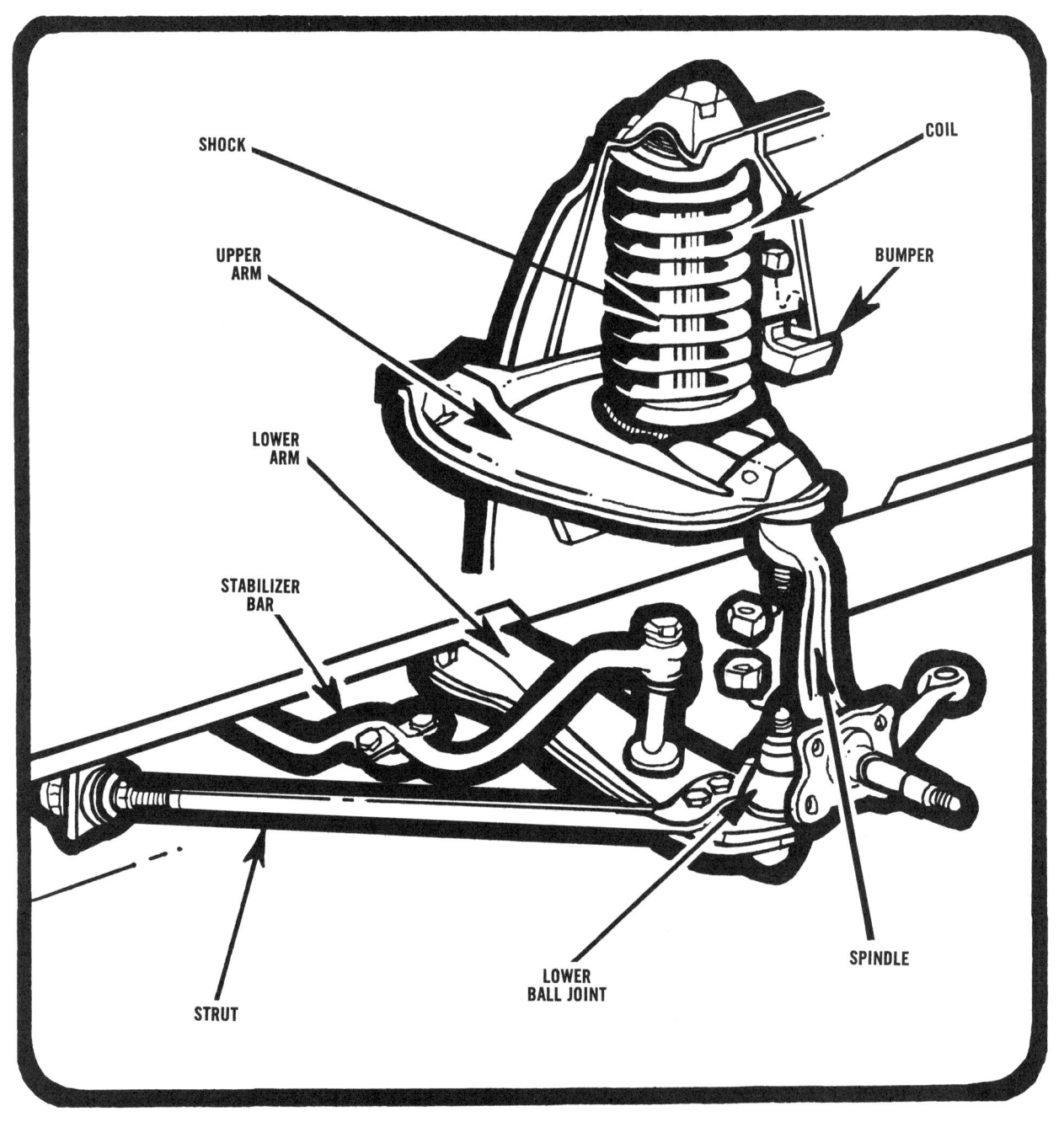

Typical Ford Motor Co. front shock absorber installation for models with the spring located on the upper control arm.

FORD MOTOR COMPANY

Replacing front shock absorbers

Note: The following discussion applies to models having coil springs positioned on the lower control arm—all full-size 1968-76 Ford and Mercury models—Thunderbird, Lincoln, Mark III, Mark IV, Pinto, Mustang, Bobcat, and Elite, 1972-76 Torino, 1972-76 Montego, and 1974-76 Cougar.

1. Reach up and remove the upper mounting nut, washer and bushing.
2. Compress the shock and remove the washer and bushing from the upper stem.
3. Raise the car.
4. Remove the shock absorber from its lower mounting on the lower control arm by disconnecting the two thread-cutting bolts attaching the shock bracket which extend through the eye of the shock to the control arm.
5. Let the shock slide down through and out the coil spring and the opening in the lower control arm.
6. Place a new bushing and washer on the new shock absorber's upper stem.
7. Extend the new shock.
8. Work the shock up through the control arm and coil spring. Engage the shock's upper stem in the mounting hole in the upper mounting seat.
9. Install the two thread-cutting bolts through the holes in the shock's lower bracket and into the holes in the lower control arm.
10. Tighten the two lower bolts to 70-80 lbs. ft.
11. Lower the car to the ground, so the weight is on the wheels.
12. Reach up and place a new bushing and washer on the shock's top stem and install a new nut.
13. Tighten the upper mounting nut to 22-30 lbs. ft.

Note: The following discussion applies to all models having coil springs positioned on the upper control arms—Maverick, Comet, Granada, Monarch, Falcon, Fairlane, 1968-73 Cougar, 1968-71 Montego, and 1968-71 Torino.

1. Lift the engine compartment hood.
2. Remove the shock absorber's upper mounting bracket-to-spring tower attaching nut.
3. Raise the car.
4. Locate the two nuts holding the two shock absorber retaining bolts to the upper control arm.
5. Remove the two nuts, their washers and insulators.
6. Beneath the hood again, lift the shock absorber and bracket (attached to one another) from the spring tower and from the car.
7. Disconnect the shock absorber from the bracket. Discard the shock. Retain the bracket.
8. Place a new shock absorber and the bracket together, tightening the shock-to-bracket bolts to 10-16 lbs. ft.
9. Install insulators on the shock's lower attaching studs.
10. Maneuver the shock absorber down through the spring tower. See to it that the shock's lower mounting studs fall into the holes in the pivot plate.
11. Screw the two nuts on to the shock's lower studs, tightening them to 8-12 lbs. ft.
12. Install the three shock absorber upper mounting bracket-to-spring tower attaching nuts. Tighten the nuts to 32-48 lbs. ft.
13. Lower the vehicle.

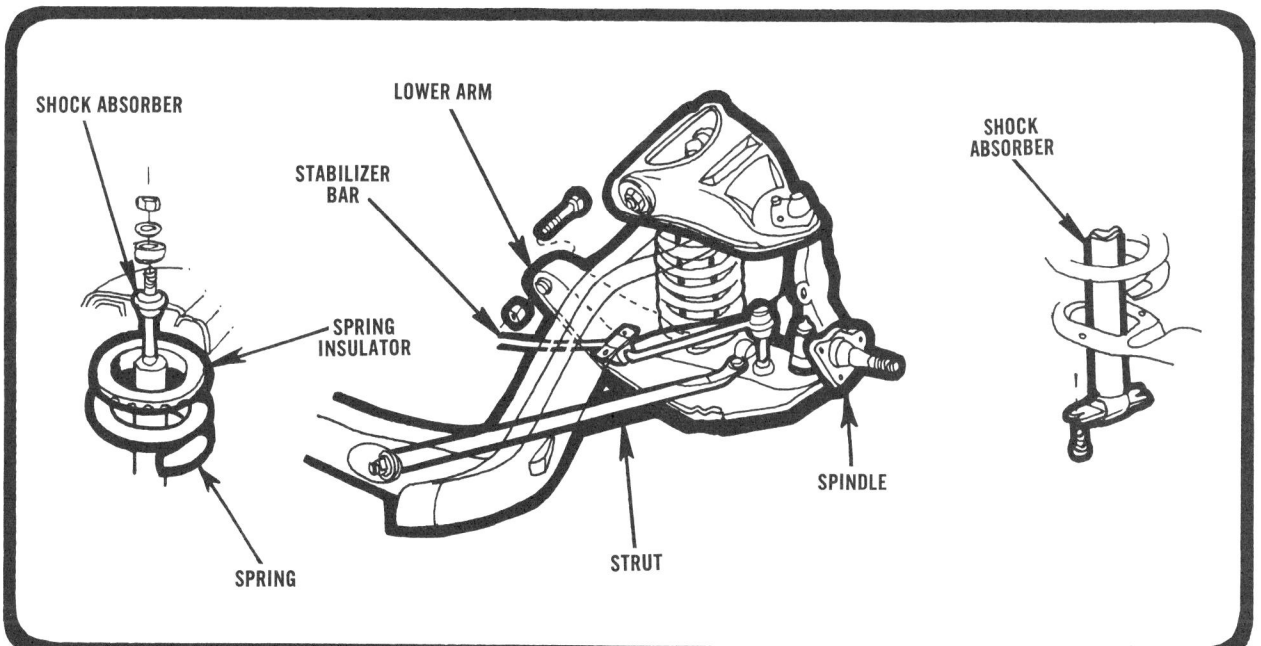

Typical Ford Motor Co. front shock absorber installation for models with spring located on the lower control arm.

Replacing rear shock absorbers

Note: This discussion applies to all models having leaf springs—1968-76 Maverick, Comet, Granada, Monarch, Falcon, Fairlane, Mustang, Pinto, and Bobcat, 1968-73 Cougar, 1968-71 Montego, and 1968-71 Torino.

All models except Mustang, Pinto and Bobcat

1. Jack up the car and support the rear axle.
2. Remove the nut, washer and grommet from the lower shock absorber stem where the stem intercepts the plate welded to the spring.
3. Compress the shock and remove the grommet and washer from the lower stem.
4. Remove the nut from the shock's upper mounting bolt.

NOTE: The upper mounting nut for all models except 1971-73 Comet, Maverick, and convertibles is reached from inside the luggage compartment. The upper mounting nut for 1971-73 Comet and Maverick is reached from below. The upper mounting nut for convertibles is reached by removing the rear seat and opening the access covers.

5. Remove the shock absorber from the car.
6. Insert the stud in the upper eye of a new shock absorber through the hole in the mounting bracket and attach the nut fingertight.
7. Compress the shock and place washer and bushing on the unit's lower stem.
8. Work the shock into the lower end of the plate which is welded to the spring.

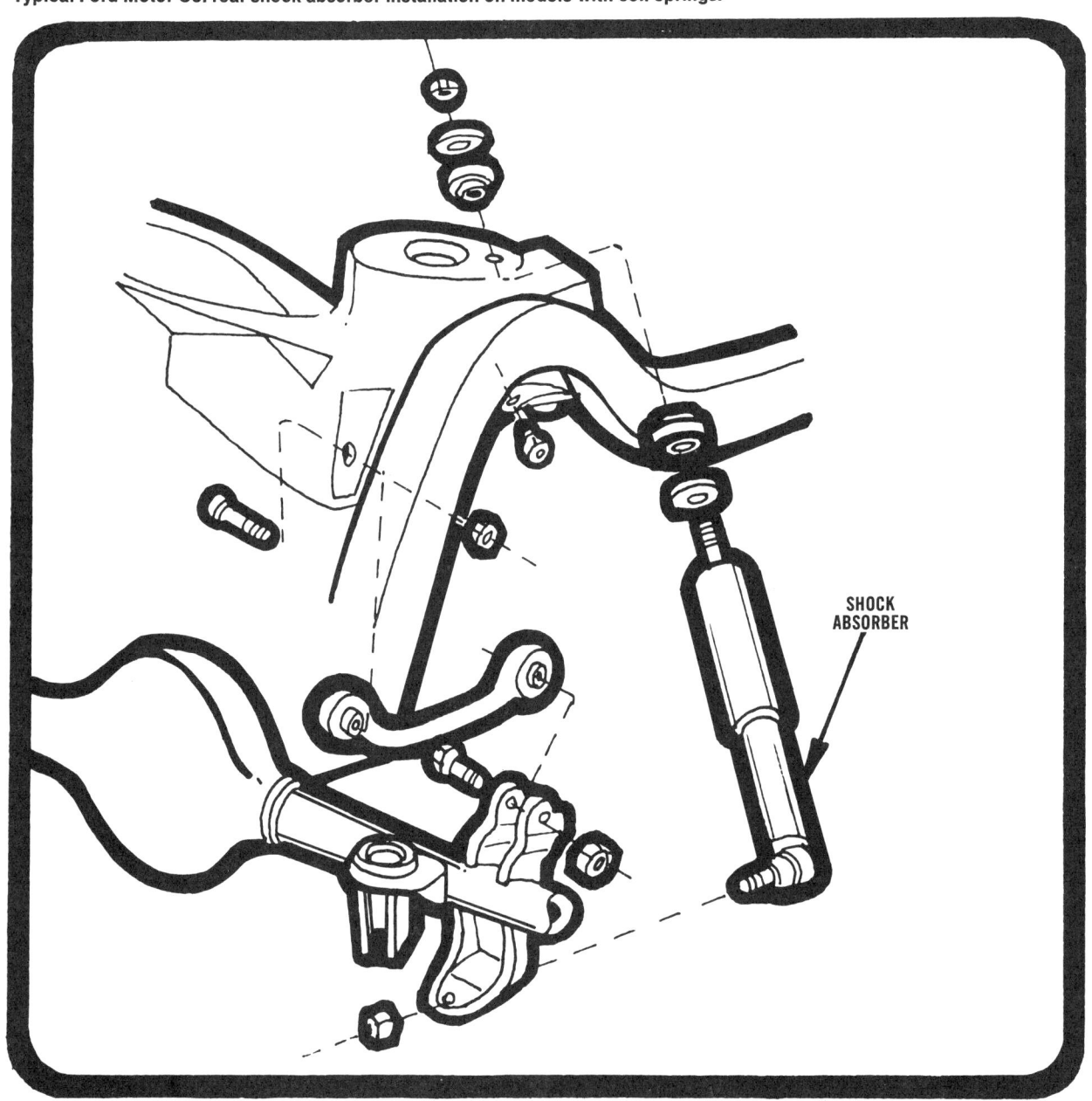

Typical Ford Motor Co. rear shock absorber installation on models with coil springs.

9. Attach the grommet, washer and nut to the lower stem. Tighten the nut to 14-26 lbs. ft.
10. Tighten the shock's upper mounting nut to 45-65 lbs. ft.
11. Remove supports and lower the car.

Mustang, Pinto and Bobcat sedans

1. Jack up the car and support the rear axle.
2. Disconnect the bolt and nut from the shock absorber's lower end at the point where the shock connects to the spring plate.
3. Reach up and remove the three bolts holding the shock's mounting bracket to the vehicle's underbody.
4. Compress the shock and remove the unit from the car.
5. Unscrew the shock from the mounting bracket. Discard the shock. Retain the bracket.
6. Insert washer and bushing on the shock absorber's upper stem and connect the stem through the mounting bracket. Secure with bushing, washer and nut, tightening the nut to 14-26 lbs. ft.
7. Beneath the car again, attach the mounting bracket to the underbody of the vehicle with the three attaching bolts. Tighten the attaching bolts to 10-14 lbs. ft.
8. Install the lower end of the shock absorber to the spring plate with bushing, washer, bolt, and nut.
9. Tighten the lower mounting bolt of Mustang to 30-50 lbs. ft. Tighten the lower mounting bolt of Pinto and Bobcat to 14-20 lbs. ft.
10. Remove supports and lower the car to the ground.

Pinto and Bobcat station wagons

1. Jack up the car and support the rear axle.
2. Remove the nut, washer and bushing from the shock absorber's lower stem.
3. Compress the shock so the lower stem is pulled from its seat in the spring plate. Remove the washer and bushing from the stem.
4. Reach up and detach the two nuts holding the shocks upper end to the studs on the body member.
5. Remove the shock absorber from the car.
6. Place a washer and bushing on the new shock absorber's lower stem.
7. Install the new shock so the holes in the shock's upper mounting brace, which extends through the eye, intercepts the studs protruding from the body crossmember.
8. Attach the two upper attaching nuts and tighten them to 14-26 lbs. ft.
9. Push the shock's lower stem through the spring plate.
10. Install bushing, washer and nut, and tighten the nut to 14-26 lbs. ft.
11. Remove supports and lower the vehicle to the ground.

Note: The following applies to models having rear coil springs—1968-76 full-size Ford and Mercury models, Thunderbird, Lincoln, Mark III, Mark IV and Elite, 1974-76 Cougar, 1972-76 Montego, and 1972-76 Torino.

1. Raise the car and support the rear axle.
2. Reach up near the wheelhousing to the upper side of the spring's upper seat and remove the nut, washer and insulator from the shock absorber's upper stem.

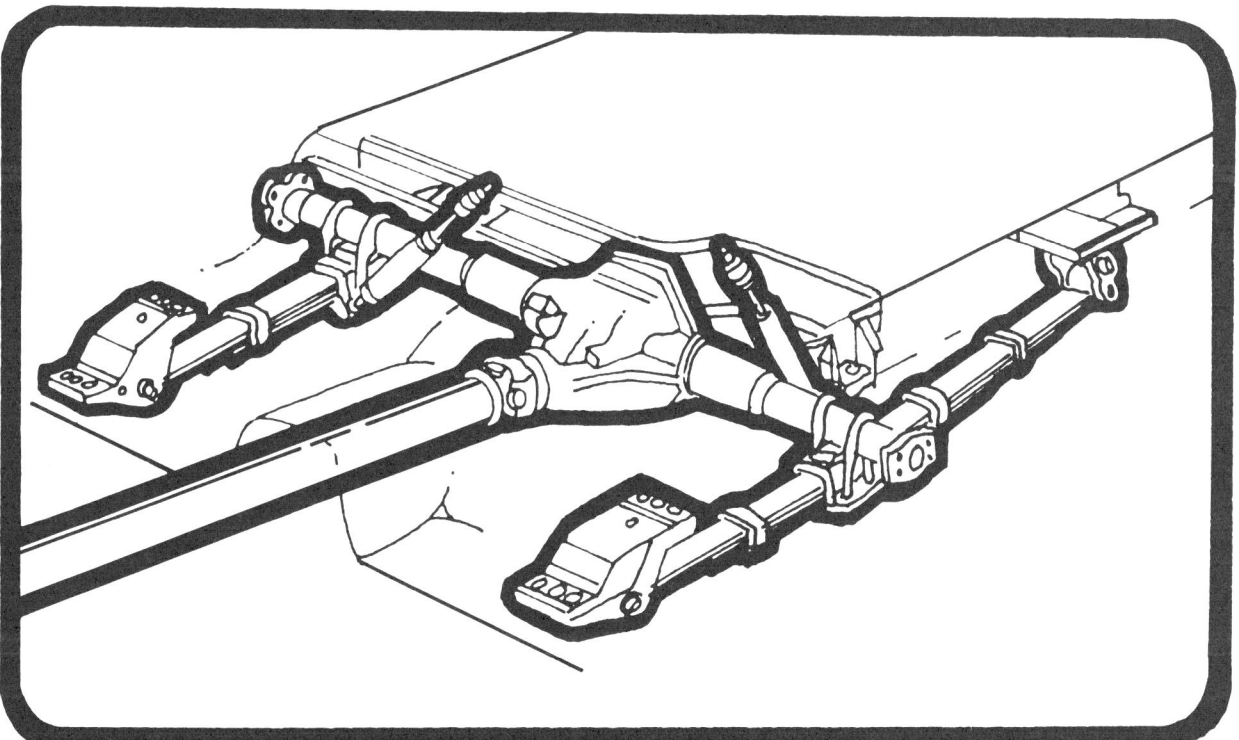

Typical Ford Motor Co. rear shock absorber installation on models with leaf springs.

3. Compress the shock from the top down, so the upper stem clears the hole in the spring seat.
4. Remove the shock's inner insulator and washer from the upper stem.
5. Down at the shock's lower mounting, simply remove the attaching nut from the shock's lower stud.
6. Knock the lower stud from the shock mounting bracket on the axle housing. Discard the shock.
7. Place an inner washer and inner insulator on a new shock absorber's upper stem.
8. Maneuver the new shock so the upper stem engages the hole in the spring seat (upper).
9. Hold the shock steady and install the outer insulator, washer and nut to the upper stem. Tighten the nut to 20-26 lbs. ft.
10. Extend the shock and place its lower mounting bolt through the hole in the mounting bracket on the axle housing.
11. Install the nut, tightening it to 65-85 lbs. ft.

OLDSMOBILE AND PONTIAC

Replacing front shock absorbers
1968-76, all models except Toronado and Astre

1. Lift the engine compartment hood and locate the shock absorber upper mounting nut access holes in the wheelhousings.
2. Open the covers to the access holes.
3. Using a short extension on a ratchet, remove the shock absorber upper mounting nut, retainer, and grommet.
4. Get beneath the car and remove the two mounting bolts from each shock absorber.
5. Lower the shock absorber through the lower control arm.
6. Discard the old shock.
7. Extend a new shock absorber to its full length.
8. Place a retainer and grommet on the upper shock absorber stem.
9. Move the shock up through the lower control arm and coil spring until the upper stem engages the hole in the wheelhousing.
10. Screw the two mounting bolts into the two lower mounting holes and engage them with their respective nuts. This attaches the shock's lower end to the lower control arm.
11. Tighten the lower mounting bolts to 20 lbs. ft.
12. Back in the compartment now, place the grommet, retainer and nut on the shock absorber stem. Tighten the nut to 10 lbs. ft.

1968-76 Toronado

1. Raise the car.
2. Reach up and grasp the upper attaching nut with a wrench and the upper attaching bolt with a socket.
3. Remove the upper attaching bolt and nut.
4. Do the same to the lower attaching bolt and nut.
5. Carefully maneuver the old shock absorber from the car and discard.
6. Extend the new shock absorber and work it up into position so the upper eye engages the holes in the mounting bracket.
7. Insert a bolt and secure it fingertight with its nut.
8. Do the same at the shock's lower mounting.
9. Tighten both upper and lower mounting nuts to 90 lbs. ft.

1975-76 Astre
See Chevette and Vega in Chevrolet section

Replacing rear shock absorbers
1968-76, all models except
Omega, Firebird, Ventura, and Safari wagons

1. Jack up the car and support the rear axle.
2. Remove the rear tire and wheel assemblies.
3. Disconnect the lockwasher and nut from the shock absorber's stud.
4. Working through the wheelhousing, reach in behind the brake drum and disconnect the two bolts, washers, and nuts from the shock's upper mounting.

   Note: If you do not want to go through the trouble of removing tire and wheel assemblies, reach up with one hand holding an open-end wrench and grasp the shock's upper retaining nut. With the other hand, reach up with an extension and socket and grasp the bolt. Remove fasteners.

5. Position the new shock absorber so the holes in the shock's mounting bracket align with the holes in the car's frame.
6. Attach upper mounting hardware fingertight.
7. Set the shock's lower end so holes line up with holes in the mounting bracket.
8. Insert hardware so the shock's lower end is secured.
9. Tighten upper mounting nuts to 20 lbs. ft. and lower mounting nut to 65 lbs. ft. With Toronado, tighten upper mountings to 25 lbs. ft. and the lower nut to 75 lbs. ft.
10. Remove supports and lower the car to the ground.

Replacing rear shock absorbers
Omega, Firebird, Ventura and Safari wagons
1. Raise the car and support the rear axle.
2. Remove the shock's single lower mounting bolt from the shock absorber eye, loosening the shock from its lower anchor plate.
3. Reach up and withdraw the two bolts holding the shock to the upper mounting bracket.
4. Remove the old shock absorber from the car and discard.
5. Extend the new shock absorber and maneuver it into position.
6. Loosely install the two shock absorber upper attaching bolts.
7. Square the shock absorber's eye with the mounting holes in the lower anchor plate and install bolt and nut. The nut must be to the rear.
8. Tighten the lower mounting nut of Omega and Ventura to 45 lbs. ft., of Firebird to 10 lbs. ft., and of Safari wagons to 65 lbs. ft.
9. Reach up and tighten the upper bolt to 20 lbs. ft.
10. Remove supports and lower the car.

SELECTING SHOCK ABSORBERS

- *GENERAL CONDITION*
The car's suspension system is in good condition. The car is used for equal amounts of around town and highway driving or primarily in the city. There are no heavy loads imposed on the vehicle.

SHOCK ABSORBER TO USE
Standard or heavy duty.

- *GENERAL CONDITION*
The car's suspension system is in good condition. The car is used primarily for highway and expressway driving or over bad roads. There are no heavy loads imposed on the vehicle.

SHOCK ABSORBER TO USE
Heavy duty.

- *GENERAL CONDITION*
The car is nose-heavy and has a decided understeer. This is characterized by the tendency of the front end to slide to the outside of a turn. The condition is normally caused by inadequate front spring pre-load.

SHOCK ABSORBER TO USE
Front overload.

- *GENERAL CONDITION*
The car is tail-heavy, with the tail dragging when you go up an incline, such as a driveway. The car may also oversteer and wander. There is inadequate rear suspension support, brought about by weak rear springs. The suspension has a tendency to bottom out.

SHOCK ABSORBER TO USE
Rear overload.

- *GENERAL CONDITION*
The vehicle is used to carry heavy loads and/or tow a trailer. The rear end cannot support the load properly. The suspension has a tendency to bottom out.

SHOCK ABSORBER TO USE
Depending upon the weight of the load, either rear overload or air shocks.

TROUBLESHOOTING FLOW CHART

FRONT ENDS

Symptom	Probable Cause	Remedy
A. Noise from front end.	1. Loose or worn front wheel bearings. 2. Worn shock absorbers. 3. Loose steering gear. 4. Worn control arm bushings. 5. Worn strut bushings.	1. Adjust, if possible, or replace. 2. Replace. 3. Tighten or replace worn parts. 4. Replace worn parts. 5. Replace worn parts.
B. Too much steering play.	6. Loose or worn front wheel bearings. 7. Loose or worn steering shaft coupling. 8. Loose steering gear. 9. Worn tie rod ends. 10. Worn idler arm. 11. Incorrect steering gear adjustment.	6. Adjust, if possible, or replace. 7. Tighten or replace worn parts. 8. Tighten or replace worn parts. 9. Replace. 10. Replace. 11. Adjust to specifications.
C. Front wheel shimmy.	12. Loose or worn front wheel bearings. 13. Wheels or tires out of balance. 14. Tires out of round or uneven tire wear. 15. Worn tie rod ends. 16. Worn strut bushings. 17. Incorrect front wheel alignment (particularly caster). 18. Worn shock absorbers.	12. Adjust, if possible, or replace. 13. Balance wheels and tires. 14. Replace worn tires. Determine cause of uneven wear and correct (front end alignment usually). 15. Replace. 16. Replace. 17. Align front end. 18. Replace.
D. Instability (wander).	19. Low or uneven tire pressure. 20. Loose wheel bearings. 21. Broken or weak rear spring. 22. Bad shock absorber. 23. Worn idler arm. 24. Improper steering gear adjustment. 25. Loose or worn strut bushings. 26. Incorrect front wheel alignment.	19. Inflate tires properly. 20. Adjust. 21. Replace. 22. Replace. 23. Replace. 24. Adjust to specification. 25. Replace. 26. Align front end.
E. Hard steering.	27. Low or uneven tire pressure. 28. Loose, worn or glazed drive belt. 29. Low power steering fluid level. 30. Inoperative power steering system. 31. Ball joints require lubrication. 32. Steering gear low on lubricant. 33. Steering gear not adjusted properly. 34. Incorrect front wheel alignment.	27. Inflate tires properly. 28. Adjust or replace. 29. Add fluid. 30. Find faulty component and correct. 31. Lubricate. 32. Add lubricant. 33. Adjust steering gear to specification. 34. Align front end.
F. Car pulls to one side when not braking.	35. Low or uneven tire pressure. 36. Broken or weak rear spring. 37. Power steering control valve not adjusted properly. 38. Worn strut bushings. 39. Incorrect front wheel alignment (particularly camber).	35. Inflate tires properly. 36. Replace. 37. Adjust to specification. 38. Replace worn parts. 39. Align front end.

Brake Service

PLEASE READ THIS BEFORE PROCEEDING INTO THIS CHAPTER

This is probably the most complex chapter in this book. While we have every reason to believe that all the repair procedures given here are within the realm of the novice mechanic, we suggest that you look over the chapter before beginning any brake service work. If you feel the procedures are too complex for you to handle, do not attempt them. Instead, have all your brake service work done by a professional mechanic.

Brake service is nothing to fool around with. Your brakes are extremely critical to safe vehicle operation. So do not take chances if you feel unsure of your own mechanical ability.

CAUTIONS FOR THE NOVICE MECHANIC

Before plunging ahead with your own brake system repairs and maintenance, there are a few sobering thoughts to think about. And you should think about them seriously.

Your car's brakes are its prime safety system. Every time you step on the brake pedal, you are calling upon your car's braking system to perform a function that may determine whether or not you are involved in a road accident. In some cases, your life may depend on the correct functioning of your car's braking system.

In other words, it is not a system for you to be tampering with if you do not know what you are doing. If you want to try out your mechanical prowess, pick some other system of your car to begin with. For instance, if you try your own maintenance and repairs on your cooling system, probably the worst that could happen would be that you might get stuck somewhere and have to take a long walk for help.

With your car's brake system, if you foul up a job, you might find yourself with no brakes in an emergency situation. And we need not mention what might befall you in such a situation.

What *can* you do

This is not to say that there are not some jobs related to the braking system that cannot be successfully completed by a novice mechanic. We fully cover these jobs in this chapter. To be more specific, you will find step-by-step procedures for replacing disc brake pads, step-by-step procedures for adjusting drum brakes and parking brakes, plus maintenance information. You will not find any information on how to reline drum brakes or anything that concerns the hydraulic system of your brakes.

In the opinion of the editors of this book, there are many places where a novice can go wrong once he begins to reline drum brakes or disconnect parts of the brake's hydraulic system. And just one slight mistake in following a procedure can result in a possible tragedy.

Prolonging brake life

More than anything, your driving habits will determine the life expectancy of your vehicle's brakes. When driving down hills, change to a lower gear and let the engine braking effect do some of the work of slowing down the vehicle. While driving, do not ride the brakes. Not only will this cause premature wear, it will also cause the brakes to overheat and fade. And unless you have to make panic stops, do not jam on the brakes.

ROUTINE MAINTENANCE

Periodically, check the level of the brake fluid in the master cylinder. A reasonable interval is every time you change your engine oil.

Checking the fluid level is easy. Locate the master cylinder under the hood by using the illustration here to see what it looks like. Then, simply unlatch the cylinder, remove the top and look at the fluid level.

If the fluid level is low (more than ¼-inch below the top edge of the reservoir), add only the approved type heavy duty brake fluid. Also, check for leaks around the hoses, lines and at the wheels. If brake fluid has contaminated the brake linings, they will have to be replaced. If this is the case, it is good practice to replace the brake linings on the opposite wheel to maintain balanced braking action. Note that on vehicles equipped with disc brakes, a slightly lower than normal brake fluid level does not necessarily have to mean that there is a leak in the system. The design of disc brake systems is such that as the disc brake linings wear, the brake fluid takes up the displaced area behind the piston, as the piston moves outward to compensate for wear. However, do not let this be a determining factor whenever a low fluid level condition is encountered.

At least once a year, more often if you do a lot of driving, or drive constantly in heavy stop-and-go city traffic, remove, or have your mechanic remove the brake drums and inspect the linings. If the brake linings are permitted to wear excessively, the metal rivets which are used to secure some of the lining to the shoe, or the steel locking of the brake shoe itself may grind grooves in the drum's braking surface. In such cases, the drum will have to be resurfaced or if beyond specified tolerances, replaced.

While you have the wheel off to inspect linings and pads, also inspect all hydraulic brake lines at the same time. Look for leaks, cracked lines, lines that have been rubbed thin by rubbing against a suspension part or any other sign of wear or deterioration.
CAUTION: Do not attempt to disconnect any hydraulic lines yourself, Take your car to a professional mechanic to replace any hydraulic lines. He is qualified to do the job safely and correctly.

GENERAL ADJUSTMENTS

All modern vehicles are equipped with automatic brake adjusters on drum brakes, which maintain proper brake adjustment and proper pedal height. For these adjusters to function properly, most vehicles have to be driven in reverse several times and the brake firmly applied. Be sure to perform this procedure in a safe area and away from traffic. If this fails to bring the pedal up to an acceptable height, remove the brake drums and inspect the adjusters. They might be jammed or rusted.

The design of disc brakes is such that they do not require periodic adjustment. As the linings slowly wear out and the brake pedal is applied, the piston in the caliper slowly moves out toward the rotor to compensate for brake pad wear. The area displaced directly behind the piston is slowly occupied by the brake fluid. For this reason, disc brakes require a greater amount of brake fluid.

The need for parking brake adjustment is usually indicated when the parking brake foot pedal or handle has to be moved a greater distance then specified to firmly apply the brake.

As the linings eventually wear out and have to be replaced, it is wise to remember that the rest of the brake system components have been in service just as long as the linings. At this time, it is very important to check the master cylinder, wheel cylinders, drums, shoe retaining springs and shoe retracting springs. If these parts are not checked at this time, more than likely they will not be checked until the following overhaul, or until the brakes finally fail—in which case it will be too late.

Also, when the brakes are relined, have your mechanic clean, inspect and repack the wheel bearings with approved lubricant. He should also adjust the wheel bearings to manufacturer's specifications to prevent wheel wobble and unbalanced braking action. And just to be on the safe side, new seals should be installed to prevent the wheel bearing grease from contaminating the new brake shoes.

Procedures such as checking the master cylinder, wheel cylinders, and internal components of drum brakes are best left to a professional mechanic as is the repacking of wheel bearings. The actual repacking is a relatively simple procedure. However, adjusting wheel bearings is a job best left to a qualified mechanic. But if the mechanic is already inspecting your drums, it is a simple matter for him to repack the bearings at the same time.

INSPECTION

Brake lines and linings

Remove one of the front wheels and inspect the brake disc, caliper and linings. Use the procedures for your make and model later on in this chapter.

Do not get any oil or grease on the linings. If the pads are worn to within 0.30-inch of the surface of the steel shoe, replace both sets of shoe and lining pad assemblies. It is recommended that both front wheel sets be replaced whenever a respective shoe and pad is worn or damaged. Inspect and, if necessary, replace rear brake linings also.

If the caliper is cracked or fluid leakage through the casting is evident, it must be replaced as a unit.

Shoe and pad wear

If visual inspection does not adequately determine the condition of the pad, a physical check will be necessary.

To check the amount of pad wear, remove a wheel from the car, the caliper from the steering knuckle, and the shoe and pad assemblies. Use the procedures for your make and model later on in this chapter. Three thickness measurements should be taken with a micrometer across the middle section of the shoe and lining—one reading at each side and one reading in the center.

When a shoe and pad assembly has worn to a thickness of 3/16-inch, it should be replaced. If pads do not require replacement, reinstall them in their original inner and outer locations.

Brake roughness

The most common cause of brake chatter on disc brakes is a variation in thickness of the disc. If roughness or vibration is encountered during highway operation or if pedal pumping is experienced at low speeds, the disc may have excessive thickness variation. To check for this condition, measure the disc at 12 points with a micrometer at a radius approximately one inch from edge of disc. If thickness measurements vary by more than .0005-inch, the disc should be replaced with a new one.

Excessive lateral runout of the brake disc may cause a knocking back of the pistons, possibly creating increased pedal travel and vibration when brakes are applied.

Before having the runout checked, wheel bearings should be adjusted. The readjustment is very important and will be required at the completion of the test to prevent bearing failure. Wheel bearing adjustments and lateral runout checks are both jobs for a professional mechanic.

DISC BRAKE SERVICE

Brake disc

Servicing of disc brakes is extremely critical due to the close tolerances required in machining the brake disc to insure proper brake operation. In manufacturing brake discs, tolerance of the rubbing surfaces for flatness is .001-inch and usually for parallelism .0005-inch.

The maintenance of these close controls of the shape of the rubbing surfaces is necessary to prevent brake roughness. In addition, the surface finish must be non-directional and maintained at a micro-inch finish. This close control of the rubbing surface finish is necessary to avoid pulls and erratic performance and promote long lining life and equal lining wear of both left and right brakes.

In light of the foregoing remarks, refinishing of the rubbing surfaces should not be attempted unless precision equipment, capable of measuring in micro-inches (millionths of an inch), is available. Obviously, a job for a professional mechanic.

GENERAL PRECAUTIONS

1. Grease or any other foreign material must be kept off the caliper, surfaces of the disc, and external surfaces of the hub during service procedures. Clean metal parts with a soft wire brush. Handling the brake disc and caliper should be done in a way to avoid deformation of the disc and nicking or scratching of the brake pads.
2. If inspection reveals that any rubber piston seals are worn or damaged, they should be replaced immediately by a professional mechanic.
3. During removal and installation of a wheel assembly, exercise care so as not to interfere with or damage the caliper splash shield, the bleeder screw or the transfer tube.
4. Front wheel bearings should be adjusted to specifications by a professional mechanic.
5. Be sure the vehicle is centered on a hoist before servicing any of the front end components to avoid bending or damaging the disc splash shield on full right or left wheel turns.
6. Before the vehicle is moved after any brake service work, be sure to obtain a firm brake pedal.
7. The assembly bolts of the 2-piece caliper housings should not be disturbed.

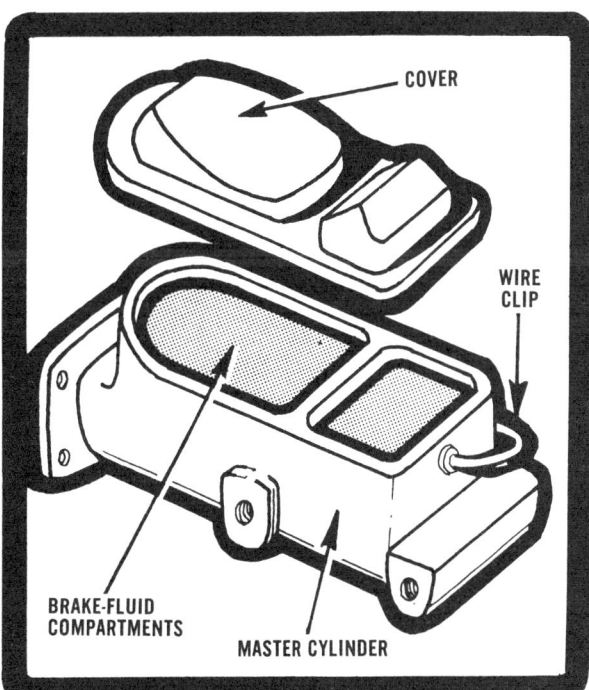

Before beginning any brake work, siphon off about ⅔ of the brake fluid from the master cylinder. This will prevent excess fluid from slopping all over the engine compartment.

HOW TO SAFELY RAISE YOUR CAR

To work on the front of the car, position safety jack stands under the suspension control arm. Be sure the jack stands are securely in position before beginning work.

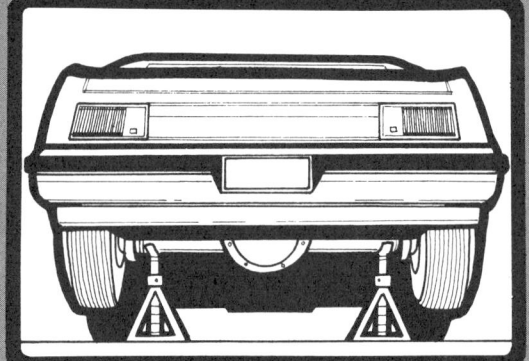

To work on the rear of the car, position the safety jack stands securely under the rear axle assembly. Be sure the jack stands are securely in position before beginning work.

As an alternative to safety jack stands, you can use steel ramps to safely raise the car. The disadvantage here is that both ends of the car cannot be raised at the same time.

PROCEDURES FOR ALL MODELS

NOTE: Before beginning any brake work, remove two thirds of the brake fluid from the master cylinder, to prevent overflow.

1. Chock the wheels which are not being worked on. Use a block of wood or stone placed directly against the tire.
2. Place vehicle in gear (first gear for manual transmission vehicles and Park for automatic transmission vehicles).
3. Raise the vehicle using a suitable jack. Make sure to properly position the jack underneath the vehicle.
    CAUTION: The jack supplied with the vehicle is intended for tire changing purposes only, and should not be used to raise the vehicle. It is unstable and usually cannot raise the vehicle sufficiently so that the jack stands can be placed underneath the vehicle.
4. Properly position a jack stand underneath each frame rail, and carefully lower the vehicle.
    CAUTION: Be careful when positioning jack stands. Some vehicles have unibody construction and do not have frame rails. In such cases the jack stands will have to be placed underneath the differential (rear axle assembly) or underneath the crossmember. Refer to the owner's manual for specific applications. Jack stands when improperly positioned, can damage metal tubing, rubber hoses or electrical wiring, which usually runs along the frame rails. Also, do not place jack stands in such a manner that when the vehicle is lowered, the vehicle will be suspended by the steering components, such as the idler arm, drag link, tie rod ends, etc. This can bend the steering components and cause the front end to become misaligned.
5. Using the tapered end of the jack handle or a large flat bladed screwdriver, pry off the wheel covers. The wheel covers make a convenient tray for keeping all the small parts of the individual wheel assemblies together.
6. Using the jack handle or a socket of the correct size, remove the wheel and tire assembly retaining nuts.
    NOTE: Some vehicles use lefthand threaded studs and nuts, and will require that the nuts be turned clockwise for removal. These studs can usually be indentified by an L stamped on the exposed end of the stud.
7. Remove the tire and wheel assembly.

AT THIS POINT, GO DIRECTLY TO STEP 8 OF THE SPECIFIC PROCEDURES FOR THE DISC BRAKE SYSTEM ON YOUR CAR. YOU CAN DETERMINE WHAT SYSTEM YOUR CAR HAS BY REFERRING TO THE DISC BRAKE APPLICATION CHART IN THIS CHAPTER.

BENDIX OPPOSED PISTONS

Brake pad removal

1969-70 American Motors and 1969 Buick

8. **On 1969 Buick models:**
    (a) Remove the upper and loosen the lower caliper mounting bolt. Then rotate the upper end of the caliper rearward.
    (b) Remove two thirds of the total brake fluid capacity from the master cylinder to prevent overflow of the brake fluid.
    (c) Push pistons in until they are bottomed in the caliper bore.
9. **On 1969-70 American Motors:**
    (a) Loosen the caliper mounting bolts. Then hold lower edge of the caliper and remove lower bolt. Shake the caliper until all shims fall out and keep these in a paper cup marked "Lower."
    (b) Press in on the upper edge of the caliper to hold the shims on their upper mounting bolt. Remove the bolt and mark these shims as "Upper."
    NOTE: Original shim thickness must be replaced in same locations when caliper is reinstalled.
    (c) Support the caliper assembly to the frame rail or suspension using a length of wire hooked around the caliper and attached to a suitable anchor point.
10. Using a pair of screwdrivers between the shoe and pistons, press the pistons until they are bottomed in their cylinders and remove the pad assembly from the calipers.

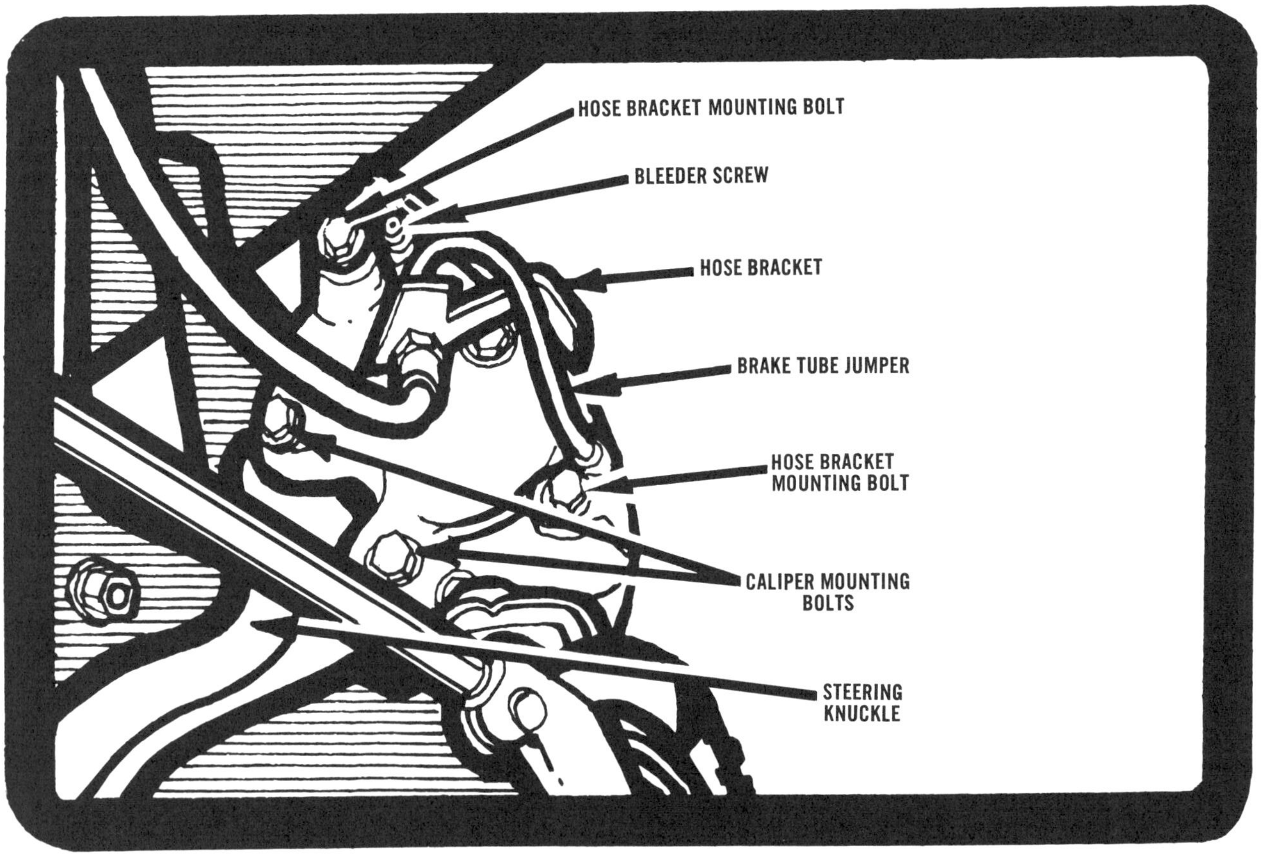

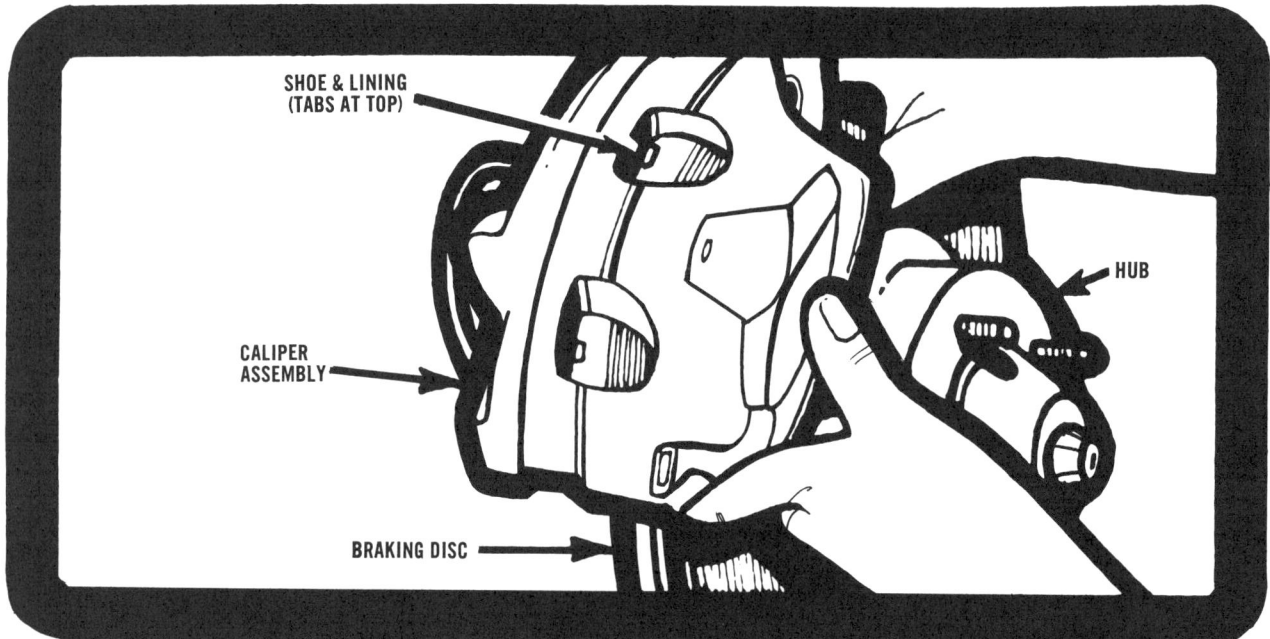

Fig.1. Installed caliper assembly.

Fig. 2. Removing or installing caliper.

1969 Belvedere and Coronet
8. Remove the caliper-to-steering knuckle bolts. Fig. 1.
9. Remove the caliper from disc by sliding it up and away from disc, Fig. 2.
10. Remove brake pad assemblies one at a time through the bottom opening, Fig. 3.

Brake pad installation

All models
1. Referring to Fig. 3, slide the pad assembly into place on the caliper, one at a time, with the curved portion (with tabs) entering first and the metal shoe against the open ends of pistons. Using your fingers, spread the pads apart until the pistons are seated in their bores.
2. Slide the caliper into place over the disc and align the mounting holes. As the caliper is being installed, be sure that the pad slides easily along the brake disc.
3. Install the caliper mounting bolts and torque to 85 ft. lbs. for American Motors, Belvedere and Coronet and to 70 ft. lbs. for Buick models.

NOTE: On American Motors cars, the original shim thickness must be installed in the same location between the caliper mounting lugs and bracket.

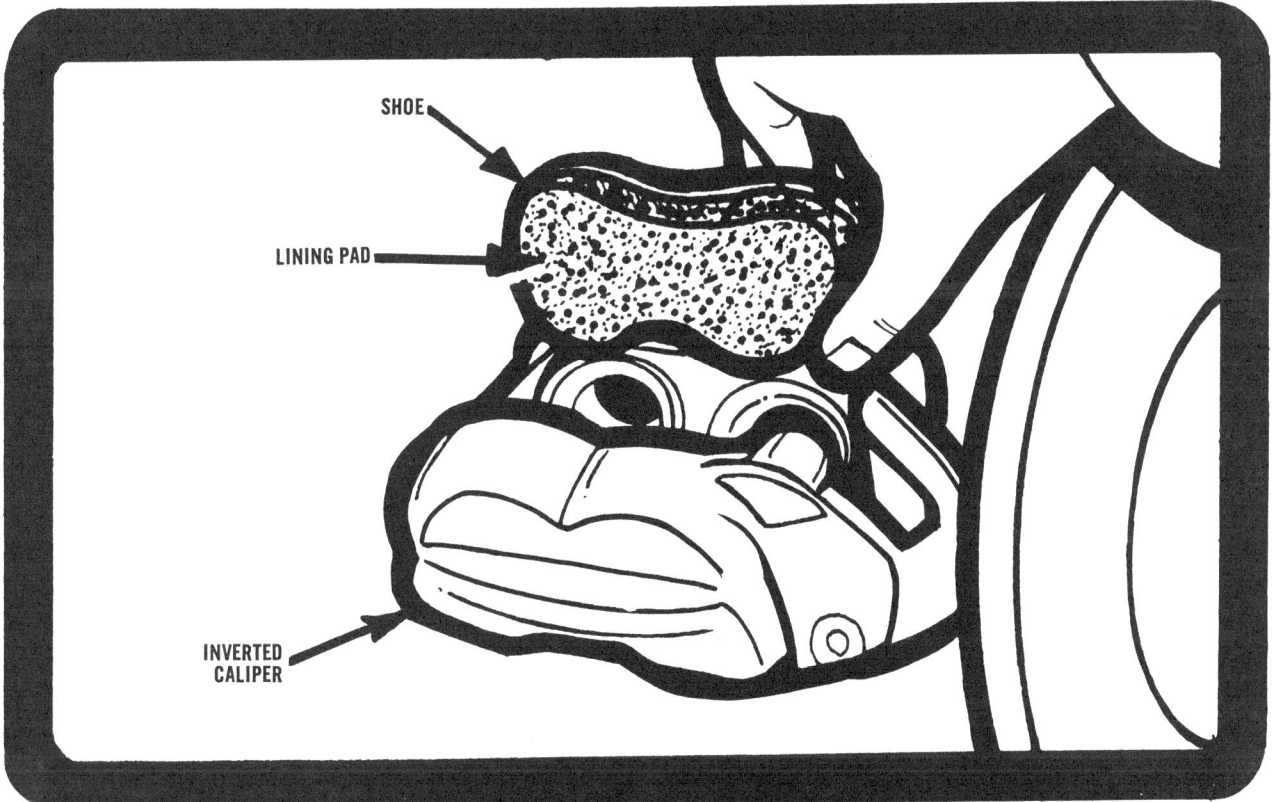

Fig. 3. Removing or installing brake shoe and pad.

4. Assure that disc rotates freely and with minimum drag.
5. Replace the tire and wheel assembly.
6. Install the tire and wheel assembly retaining nuts. Then using the jack handle or correct size socket, tighten the retaining nuts.
7. Install the wheel covers. Use a rubber mallet and tap around the outer edge of the cover to fully seat it against the wheel.
8. Raise the vehicle using a suitable jack. Make sure to properly position the jack underneath the vehicle.
9. Remove the jack stands from underneath the vehicle and carefully lower the vehicle.

CAUTION: Road test the vehicle and make several heavy stops from 40 mph to wear off any foreign material on the brakes and to seat the pads. The vehicle may pull to one side if this is not done.

DELCO-MORAINE OPPOSED PISTONS

Brake pad replacement

8. Remove the cotter pin from the inboard end of the retaining pin. On 1969-70 models with heavy duty brakes, two retaining pins must be removed, one from each end of the caliper.

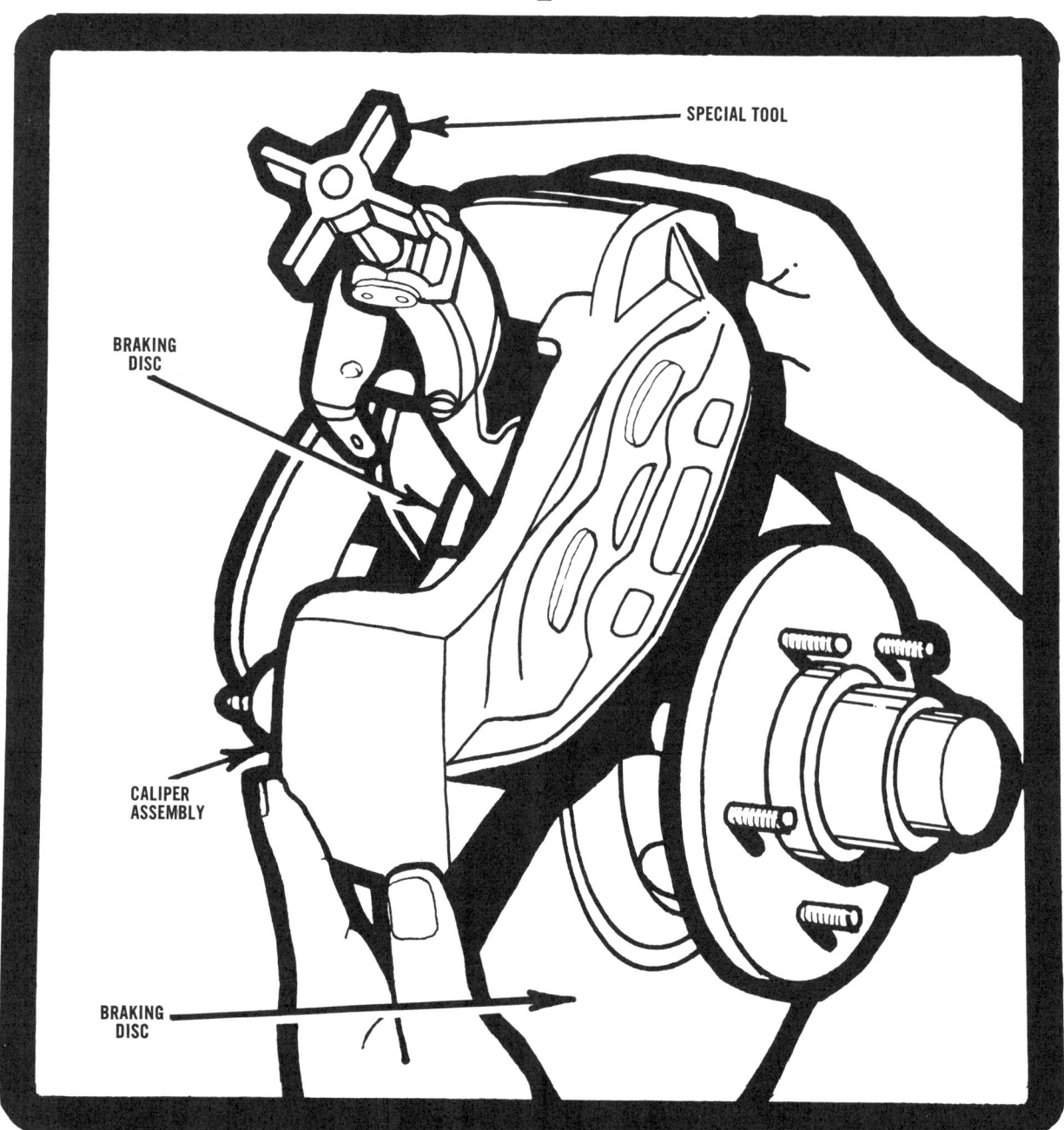

Fig. 4. Use a compressing tool to compress brake pads and piston.

TOOLS REQUIRED FOR BRAKE SERVICE

- THE FOLLOWING TOOLS ARE REQUIRED TO SERVICE DISC BRAKES:

Flat screwdrivers, 6- and 12-inch.
Slip joint pliers.
Vise grip pliers.
Socket wrenches, 3/8-, 7/16-, 1/2-, 9/16-, 5/8-, 11/16- and 3/4-inch.
Ratchet handle.
Combination wrenches, 3/8-, 7/16-, 1/2-, 9/16-, 5/8-, 11/16- and 3/4-inch.
Allen wrenches, 3/8- and 7/16-inch.
Torque wrench, 150 lbs. ft. capacity.
Torque wrench, 50 lbs. in. capacity.
Brake adjusting tool.
Ball peen hammer.
C-clamps, 4- and 6-inch.
Drift and punch.
Jack stands.
Suitable jack, preferably a 1½-ton.
Lug wrench.
Soft copper wire.
Assortment of cotter pins.
Hand cleaner.

- THE FOLLOWING TOOLS ARE REQUIRED TO ADJUST THE SERVICE BRAKES AND PARKING BRAKES:

Flat screwdrivers, 6- and 12-inch.
Brake adjusting tool.
Combination wrenches, 1/2- and 9/16-inch.
Slip joint pliers.
Vise grip pliers.
Cold chisel, ½-inch wide.
Ball peen hammer.
Jack stands.
Lug wrench.
Suitable jack, preferably 1½-ton hydraulic.

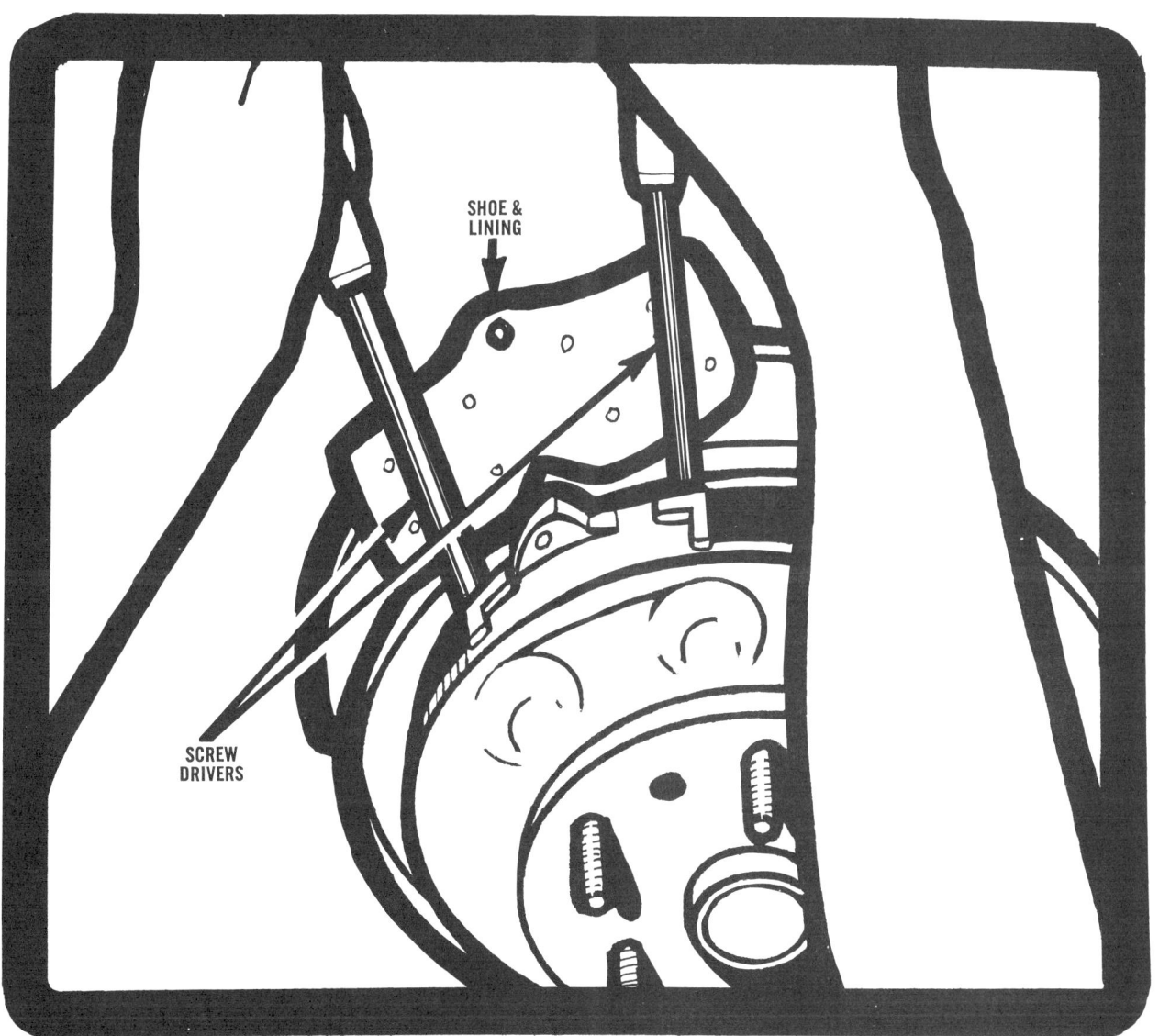

Fig. 4A. Then use screwdrivers to push pistons into caliper to allow brake pad installation.

9. Remove the inboard and the outboard pads by pulling upwards.
10. Install the inboard and outboard pads one at a time. Use two screwdrivers to push pistons back as pads are inserted, Figs. 4 and 4A.
11. Install the retaining pin through outboard caliper half, outboard shoe, inboard shoe and inboard caliper half. Insert a new 3/32 x 5/8 inch plated cotter pin through retaining pin. On 1969-70 models with heavy duty brakes, install the two retaining pins, one at each end of the caliper.
12. Repeat the above procedure at each wheel where the pads are to be replaced.
13. Refill master cylinder to proper level.
14. Replace the tire and wheel assembly.
15. Install the tire and wheel assembly retaining nuts, then using the jack handle or correct size socket, tighten the retaining nuts.
16. Install the wheel covers. Use a rubber mallet and tap around the outer edge of the cover to fully seat it against the wheel.
17. Raise the vehicle using a suitable jack. Make sure to properly position the jack underneath the vehicle.
18. Remove the jack stands from underneath the vehicle and carefully lower the vehicle.

CAUTION: Do not move the vehicle until a firm brake pedal has been obtained.

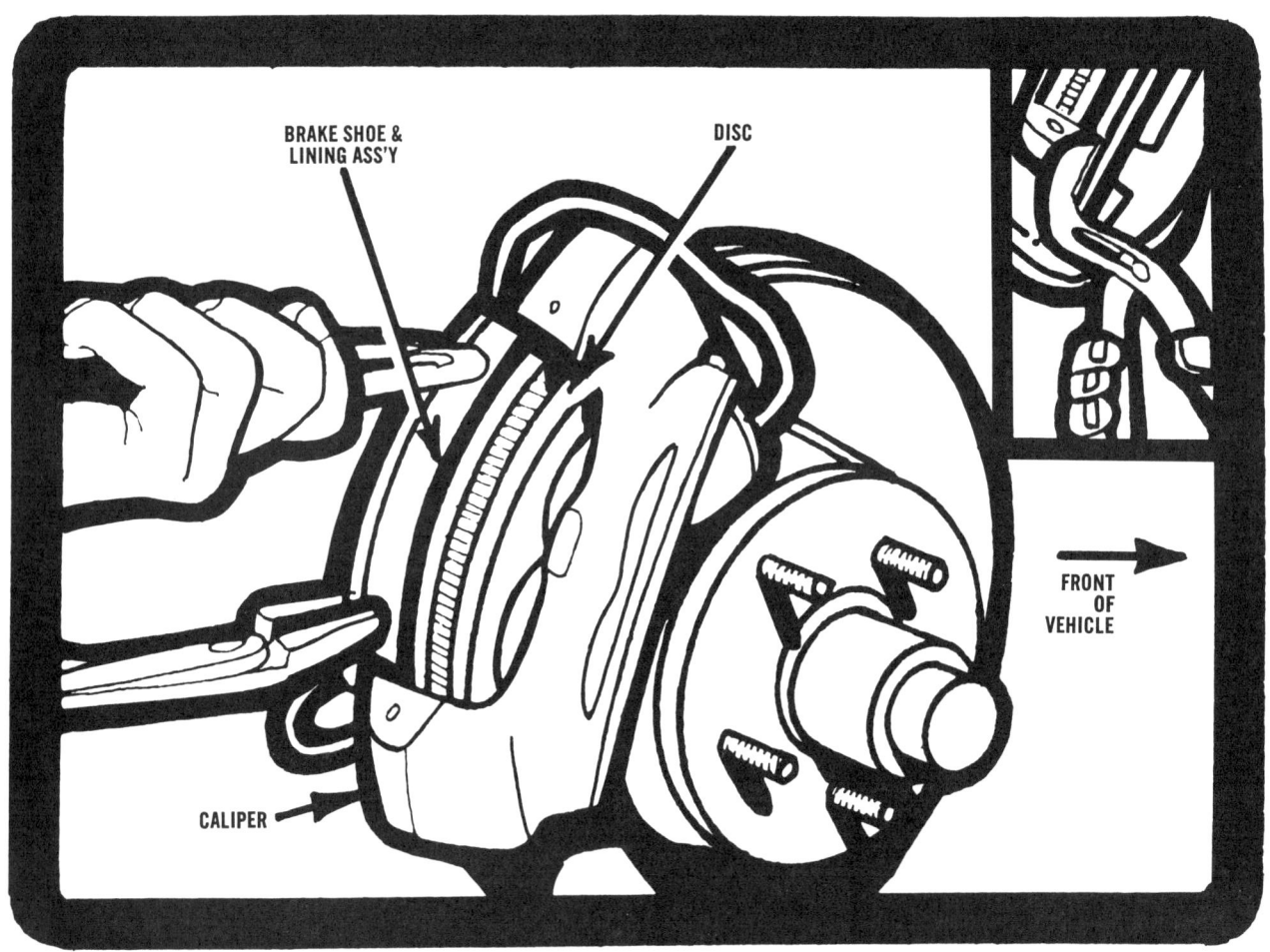

Fig. 5. Removing brake shoe and pad.

KELSEY-HAYES OPPOSED PISTON

Brake pad replacement

8. Remove the pad retainer spring assemblies.
9. Using two pairs of pliers, grasp tabs on outer ends of the pads and remove pads by pulling outward, Fig. 5.

    NOTE: Due to a ridge of rust that may have formed on the disc surface outside of lining contact area, it may be necessary to force the piston back slightly into the caliper bore. This is done by forcing the shoe back with slip-joint pliers placed on corner of the pad and caliper housing as shown, Fig. 5.
10. Push all the pistons back into their bores until bottomed to allow for installation of the new pads. This can be done by placing a flat-sided metal bar against the piston and exerting a steady force until the piston is bottomed.
11. Slide new pads into the caliper with ears of pads resting on bridges of caliper, Fig. 6. Be sure pad is facing toward the disc.

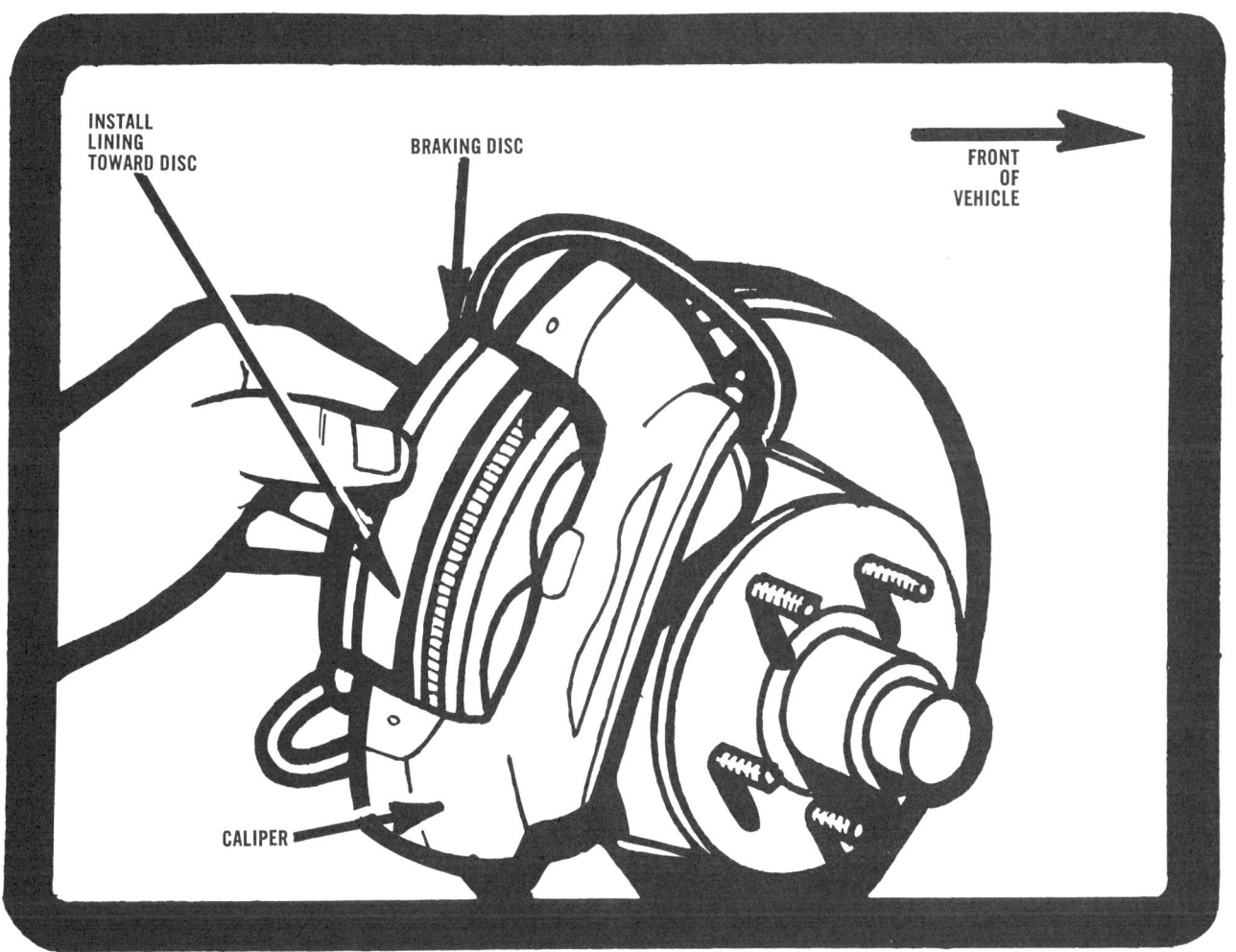

Fig. 6. Installing brake shoe and pad.

DISC BRAKE APPLICATION CHART

Many different disc brake systems are used by auto manufacturers. To find out what disc brake system is on your car, look up the year and make of your car on this chart.

BENDIX OPPOSED PISTONS

American Motors, 1969-70
Buick Full-Size Cars, 1969
Dodge Coronet, 1969
Plymouth Belvedere, 1969

BENDIX SLIDING CALIPER

American Motors, 1975-76

DELCO-MORAINE OPPOSED PISTONS

Camaro 4-Wheel Disc Option, 1969
Corvette, 1969-76

DELCO-MORAINE SINGLE PISTON

Buick Intermediate Cars, 1969-76
Buick Full-Size Cars, 1970-76
Buick Skyhawk, 1975-76
Cadillac, 1969-76
Checker Motors, 1969-76
Chevrolet Line (except Camaro 4-Wheel Disc Option & Corvette), 1969-76
Eldorado, 1969-76
Oldsmobile, 1969-76
Pontiac, 1969-76

FORD CENTER ABUTMENT

Pinto, 1971-73

FORD SLIDING CALIPER

Comet, 1974-76
Cougar, 1974-76
Granada, 1975-76
Ford Full Size, 1973-76
Lincoln Continental, 1973-76
Mark IV, 1972-76
Maverick, 1974-76
Mercury, 1973-76
Monarch, 1975-76
Montego, 1972-76
Mustang II, 1974-76
Pinto, 1974-76
Torino, 1972-76
Thunderbird, 1972-76

FORD 4-WHEEL DISC BRAKE

Granada, 1976
Lincoln, 1975-76
Mark IV, 1975-76
Mercury, 1975-76
Monarch, 1976
Thunderbird, 1975-76

KELSEY-HAYES OPPOSED PISTONS

Dodge Dart, 1969-72
Plymouth Barracuda, 1969
Plymouth Valiant, 1969-72

KELSEY-HAYES FLOATING CALIPER

American Motors, 1971-74
Chrysler, 1969-73
Chrysler Cordoba, 1975-76
Cougar, 1969-73
Charger SE, 1975-76
Coronet, 1975-76
Dodge Challenger & Coronet, 1970-74
Dodge Charger, 1969-74
Dodge Polara & Monaco, 1969-73
Fairlane, 1969-71
Falcon, 1969
Ford Full Size, 1969-72
Imperial, 1970-73
Lincoln Continental, 1970-72
Mark III, 1969-71
Mercury, 1969-72
Montego, 1969-71
Mustang, 1969-73
Plymouth Barracuda, 1970-74
Plymouth Fury, 1969-73 & 1975-76
Plymouth Satellite, 1969-74
Thunderbird, 1970-71
Torino, 1969-71

KELSEY-HAYES SLIDING CALIPER

Chrysler Exc. Cordoba, 1974-76
Dodge Dart, 1973-76
Dodge Monaco, 1974-76
Imperial, Four Wheel Disc Brake, 1974-76
Plymouth Fury, 1974
Plymouth Gran Fury, 1976
Plymouth Valiant, 1973-76

12. Slide remaining pad into caliper, using same procedure as above.
13. Install the pad retainer spring in position on the caliper.
14. Pump the brake pedal several times until a firm pedal has been obtained and pads have been properly seated.
15. Add brake fluid to master cylinder as required.
16. Replace the tire and wheel assembly.
17. Install the tire and wheel assembly retaining nuts. Then using the jack handle or correct size socket, tighten the retaining nuts.
18. Install the wheel covers. Use a rubber mallet and tap around the outer edge of the cover to fully seat it against the wheel.
19. Raise the vehicle using a suitable jack. Make sure to properly position the jack underneath the vehicle.
20. Remove the jack stands from underneath the vehicle and carefully lower the vehicle.

CAUTION: Road test the vehicle and make several heavy stops from 40 mph to wear off any foreign material on the brakes and to seat the units. The vehicle may pull to one side or the other if this is not done. It should not be necessary to bleed the system after replacing linings.

KELSEY-HAYES FLOATING CALIPER

Brake pad replacement

American Motors and Chrysler Corp.

8. Remove two thirds of the total brake fluid capacity from the master cylinder, to prevent overflow of the brake fluid.
9. Remove the caliper guide pins, Fig. 7. On **American Motors and 1969-72 Chrysler Corp.** vehicles, remove the positioners and anti-rattle clips.
10. Slide out outboard and inboard brake pad assemblies from the caliper and adaptor.
11. Remove the inner and outer bushings from the caliper.
12. Install new inner and outer bushings, Fig. 7, then slide the caliper down into position on the adapter and over the rotor. Align the guide pin holes of adaptor with the inboard and outboard brake pads.
13. On **American Motors and 1969-72 Chrysler Corp.** models, install the positioners over the guide pins with the open ends up and facing anti-rattle spring.
14. Press in on the end of the guide pin and thread pin into the adaptor using extreme caution not to cross the threads. Torque guide pins to 30-35 ft. lbs., assuring that the tabs of the positioners are over the machined surfaces of the caliper.

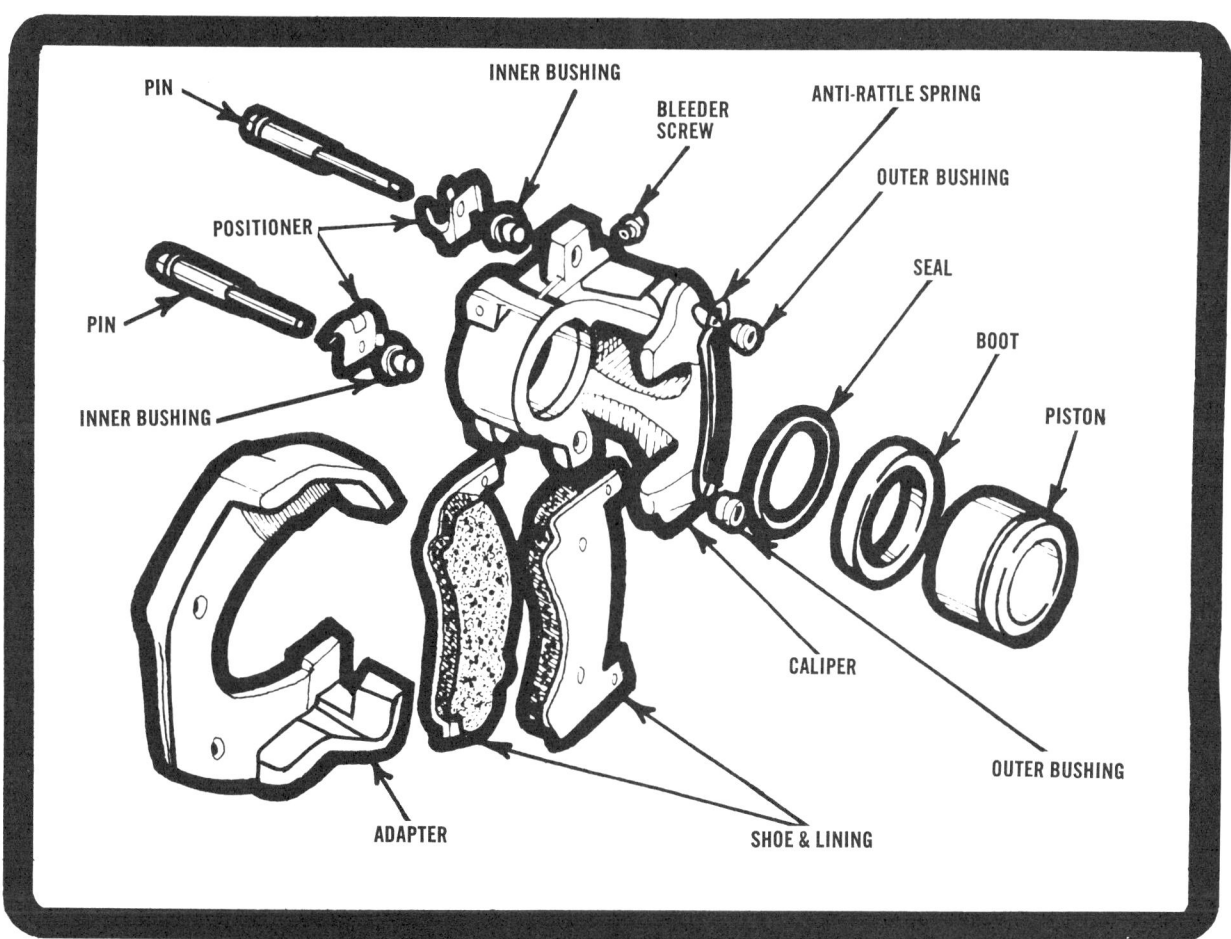

Fig. 7. Exploded view of single piston disc brake assembly. Typical of American Motors and Chrysler Corp.

15. Replace the tire and wheel assembly.
16. Install the tire and wheel assembly retaining nuts. Then using the jack handle or correct size socket, tighten the retaining nuts.
17. Install the wheel covers. Use a rubber mallet and tap around the outer edge of the cover to fully seat it against the wheel.
18. Raise the vehicle using a suitable jack. Make sure to properly position the jack underneath the vehicle.
19. Remove the jack stands from underneath the vehicle and carefully lower the vehicle.

CAUTION: Prior to moving the vehicle, make sure that a firm brake pedal has been obtained.

1969 Fords, all models
8. Remove the caliper as described further on. To aid in the caliper removal, apply a steady inward pressure against the inner pad. Maintain pressure until the piston has bottomed in the caliper bore.
9. Remove the safety wire and the caliper to spindle attaching bolts and lift the caliper from the rotor.
10. Slide the outer two outer pad retaining clips off the retaining pins, Fig. 8. Then remove the retaining pins and remove the pad from the stationary caliper.
11. Slide the inner pad outward until it is free of the hold down springs. Then remove the brake pad.
12. Remove the caliper locating pins and the stabilizer attaching bolts. Then remove and discard the stabilizers.
13. Remove the locating pin insulators from the anchor plate.
14. Install the new caliper locating pin insulators in the anchor plate.

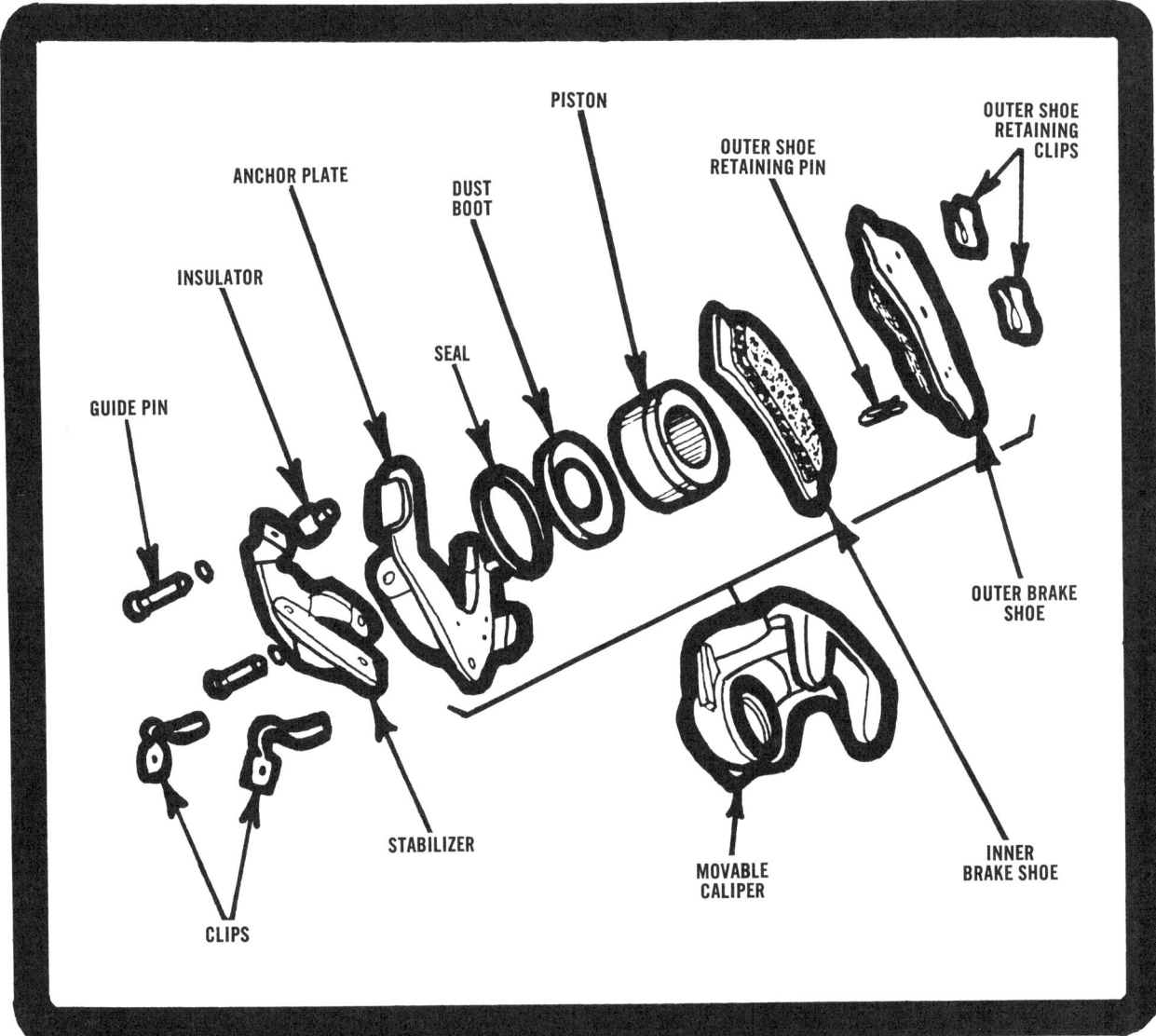

Fig. 8. Exploded view of single piston disc brake assembly. Typical of Ford Motor Co.

15. Position the caliper onto the anchor plate. then install new stabilizers and loosely install the caliper locating pins. Locating pins should be free of oil, grease and dirt.
    NOTE: If the caliper locating pins are rusted or corroded, they should be replaced.
16. Position the outer pad on the caliper and install the two retaining pins and clip.
17. Install the inner brake pad so that the ears of the pad are on top of the anchor plate bosses and under the pad hold down springs.
18. Position the pad assemblies so that the caliper can be positioned over the rotor. Rotate a suitable size hammer handle between the pads to provide proper clearance.
19. Install the caliper over the rotor. Then install the caliper retaining bolts and first torque the upper bolt to 110-140 ft. lbs., then torque the lower bolt to 90-120 ft. lbs. for full size models and 55-75 ft. lbs. for intermediate models. Install safety wire and twist ends at least five turns. Push wire ends against spindle.
20. Have a helper apply moderate pressure on brake pedal. Torque stabilizer retaining screws, using a torque wrench, to 8-11 ft. lbs. and locating pins to 25-35 ft. lbs.
21. Replace the tire and wheel assembly.
22. Install the tire and wheel assembly retaining nuts. Using the jack handle or correct size socket, tighten the retaining nuts.
23. Install the wheel covers. Use a rubber mallet and tap around the outer edge of the cover to fully seat it against the wheel.
24. Raise the vehicle using a suitable jack. Make sure to properly position the jack underneath the vehicle.
25. Remove the jack stands from underneath the vehicle and carefully lower the vehicle.

CAUTION: Before moving vehicle, make certain that a firm brake pedal has been obtained.

1970-72 full size Fords

8. Remove the inner pad hold down clips. Place a small screwdriver under the outer pad retaining clip tang and lift away from the pin groove and slide clip from pad retaining pin. Remove the outer pad retaining clip and remove outer pad.
9. Remove the caliper locating pins and upper stabilizer to anchor plate bolt. Then remove upper stabilizer to avoid the interference with brake hose.
10. Lift the caliper assembly from anchor plate and remove outer pad and retaining pins from caliper assembly.
11. Support the caliper from the suspension with a wire and remove caliper locating pin insulators.
12. Remove the inner pad and inspect the rotor.

1970-73 Fords, intermediate models

8. Remove the caliper by removing the safety wire and the two caliper assembly-to-spindle retaining bolts.
9. Lift caliper assembly from the rotor.
10. Remove the inner brake pad holddown clips and locating pin insulators from the anchor plate and remove the inboard pad.
11. To remove the outer brake pad, place a small screwdriver under the outer pad retaining clip tang and lift away from the pin groove and slide the clip from the brake pad retaining pin. Remove the outer pad retaining clip and remove the outer pad.
12. Install the inner brake pad in the anchor plate and new caliper locating pin insulators.
13. Install the inner brake pad hold down clips and torque retaining screws to 6-10 ft. lbs.
14. Install piston pad retracting tool in caliper with brake pad lances positioned in slots in caliper outer legs and retract piston, Fig. 9. The piston retracting tool can be fabricated from a

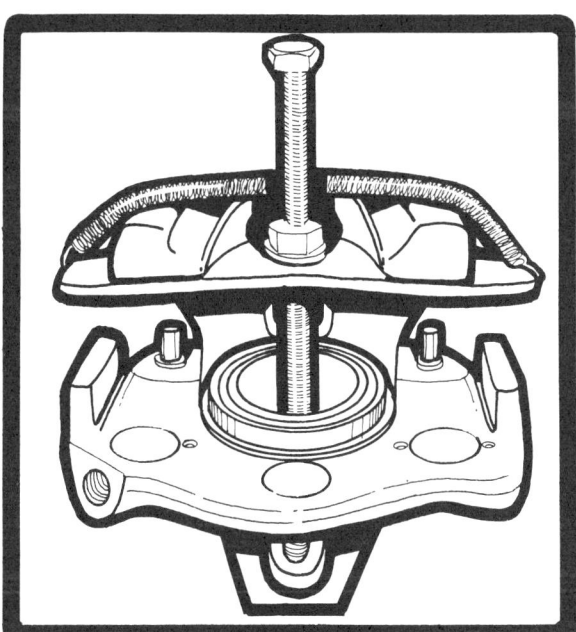

Fig. 9. Using fabricated tool to push piston into caliper.

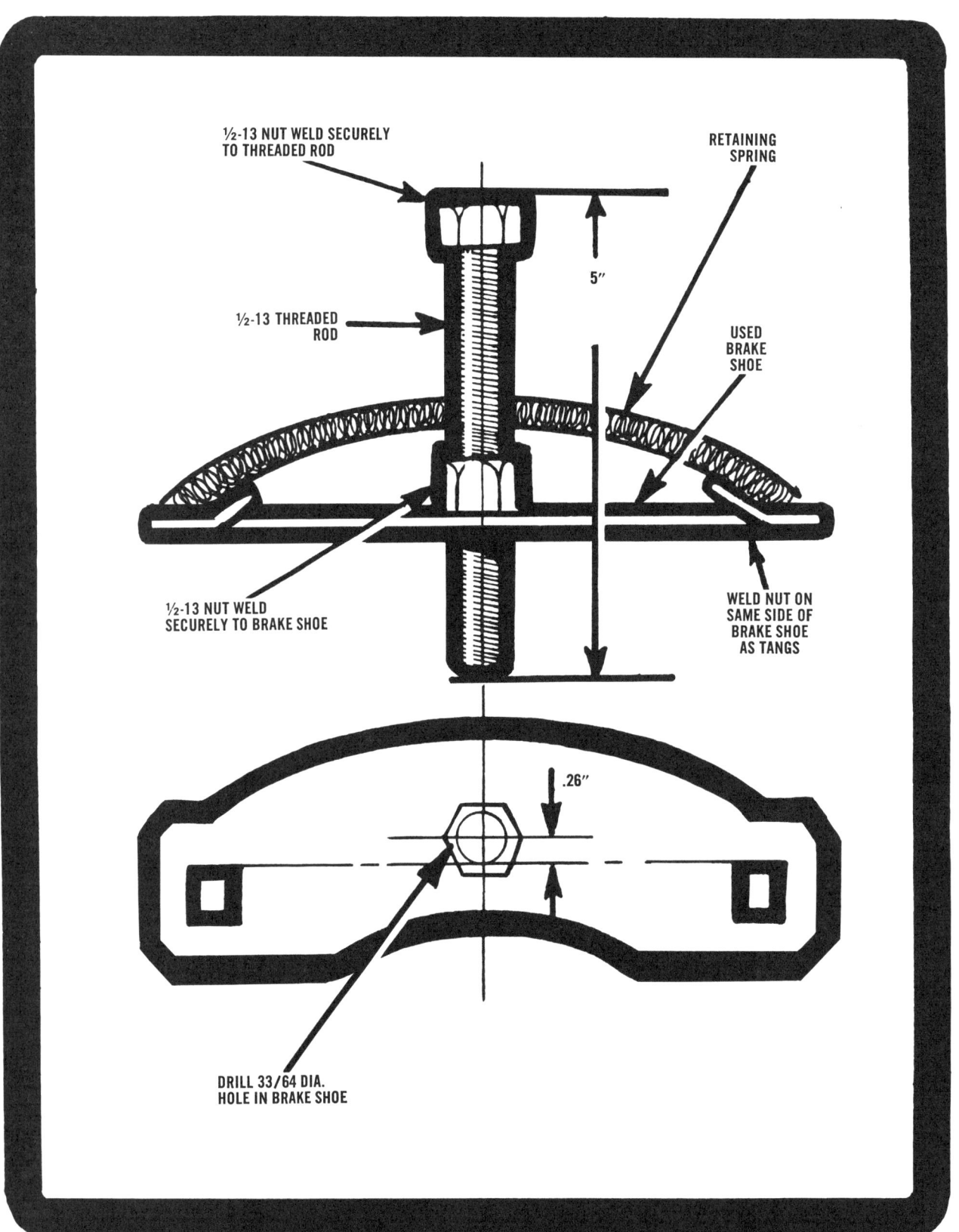

Fig. 10. Piston retracting tool fabrication dimensions.

discarded outer brake pad and threaded rod, Fig. 10. When using piston retracting tool, turn threaded rod one half turn at a time and pause to permit piston to move in seal. As piston nears bottom of travel, reduce time interval to insure bottoming of piston.

15. Install new outer brake pad and lining assembly on the caliper and install retaining pins and clips.
16. Apply the brake pedal several times to seat the brake pads.
17. Replace the tire and wheel assembly.
18. Install the tire and wheel assembly retaining nuts. Using the jack handle or correct size socket, tighten the retaining nuts.
19. Install the wheel covers. Use a rubber mallet and tap around the outer edge of the cover to fully seat it against the wheel.
20. Raise the vehicle using a suitable jack. Make sure to properly position the jack underneath the vehicle.
21. Remove the jack stands from underneath the vehicle.

CAUTION: Prior to moving the vehicle, make sure that a firm brake pedal has been obtained.

DELCO-MORAINE SINGLE PISTON

All exc. Astre, Chevette, Monza, Skyhawk, Starfire and Vega

Brake pad replacement, Fig. 11

8. Using a C-clamp as shown in Fig. 12, push piston back into the caliper bore.
9. Remove the two mounting bolts and lift the caliper from the rotor.
10. Remove the inboard pad, then dislodge the outboard pad and position the caliper on the front suspension so that the brake hose will not support the weight of the caliper.
11. Remove the support spring from the piston.
12. Remove the two sleeves from the inboard ears of the caliper.
13. Remove the four rubber bushings from the grooves in each of the caliper ears.
14. To install, lubricate the new sleeves, rubber bushings, bushing grooves and mounting bolt ends with silicone lubricant.
15. Install the new bushings and sleeves onto the caliper ears.

   NOTE: Position the sleeve so that the end toward the shoe is flush with the machined surface of the ear.

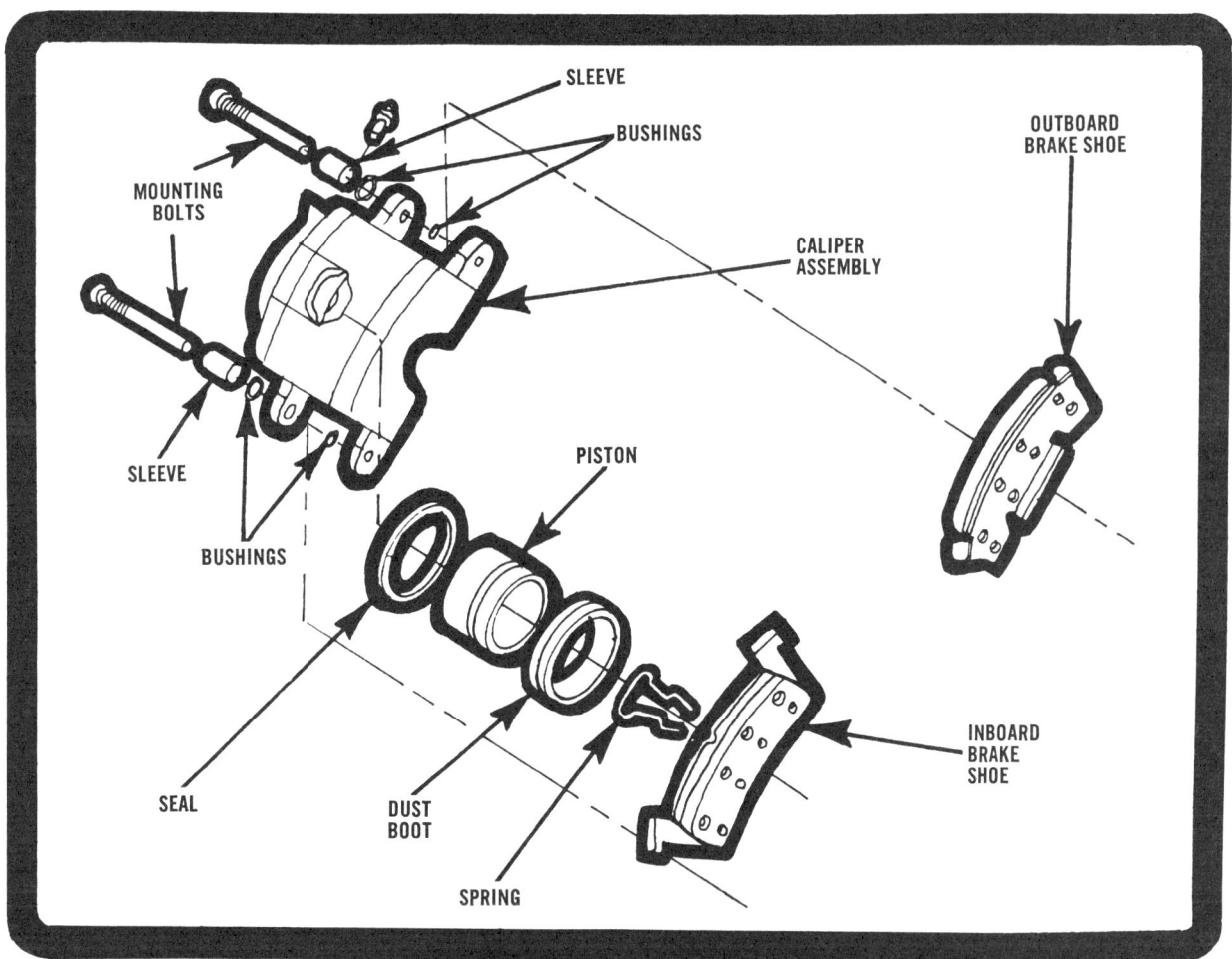

Fig. 11. Exploded view of single piston caliper assembly.

16. Install the pad support spring into the piston cavity in the caliper, Fig. 13.
17. Position the inboard pad in the caliper so that the spring ends centrally contact the shoe edge. Initially, this will place the shoe on an angle. Push upper edge of shoe down until shoe is flat against caliper. When properly seated, spring ends should not extend past shoe more than .100-inch.
18. Position outboard pad in caliper with pad ears over caliper ears and tab at bottom of pad engaged with caliper cutout.

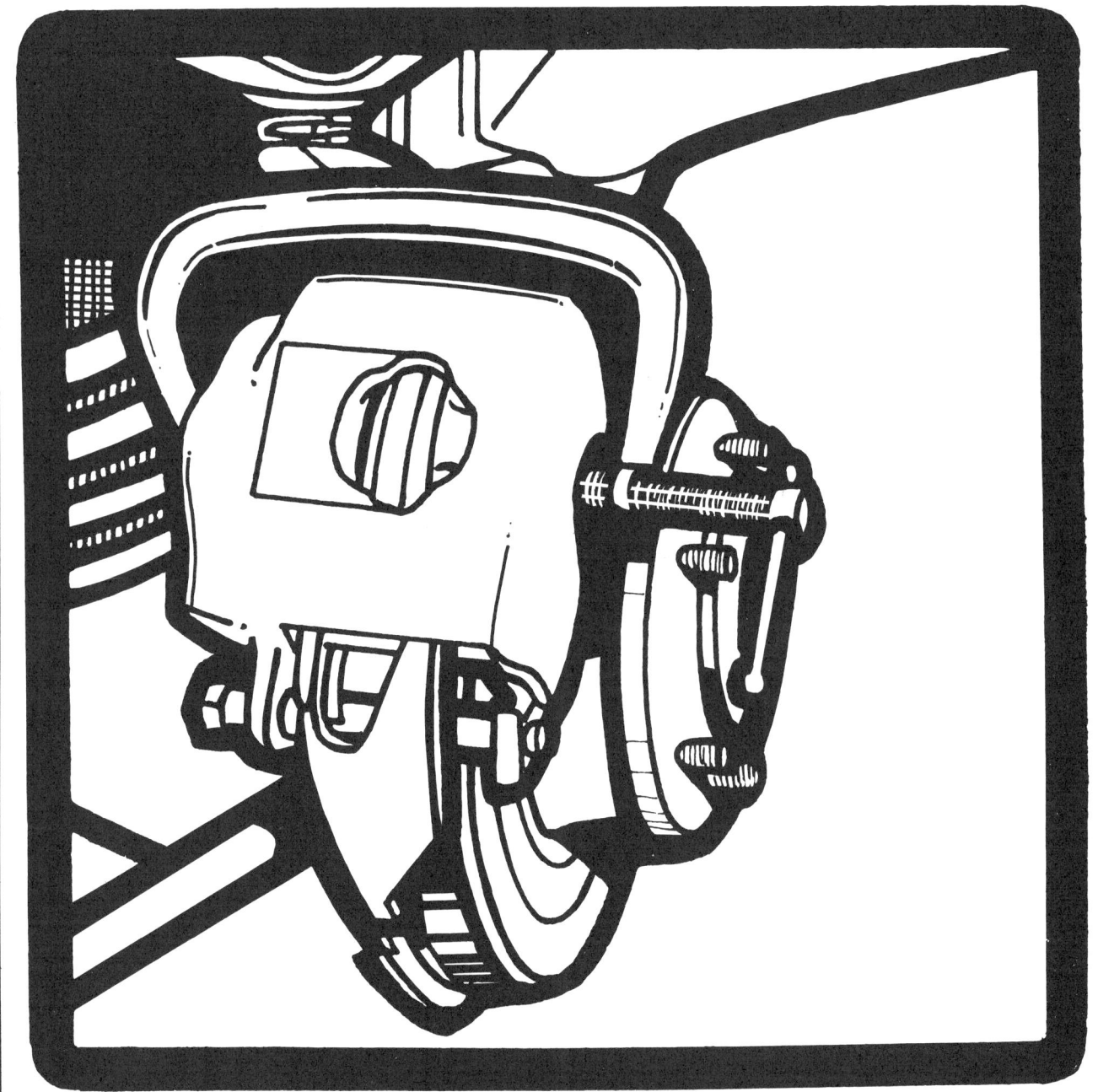

Fig. 12. Using a C-clamp to compress piston and brake pads.

19. With pads installed, lift caliper and rest bottom edge of outboard lining on outer edge of brake disc to be sure there is no clearance between outboard shoe tab and caliper abutment.
20. On 1969-72 models, using a ¼ x 1 x 2½-inch metal bar to bridge caliper cutout, clamp outboard shoe to caliper with a C-clamp. Bend both ears of outboard shoe over caliper until clearance between shoe ear and caliper (measured at both the edge and side of caliper) is .005-inch or less, Fig. 15.
21. Remove C-clamp. Install caliper and torque mounting bolts to 30-40 ft. lbs.
22. On 1973-76 vehicles, clinch upper ears of outboard shoe by positioning pliers with one jaw on top of upper ear and one jaw in notch on bottom shoe opposite ear, Fig. 15. Ears are to be flat against caliper housing with no radial clearance. If clearance exists, repeat clinching procedure.
23. Replace the tire and wheel assembly.
24. Install the tire and wheel assembly retaining nuts. Using the jack handle or correct size socket, tighten the retaining nuts.

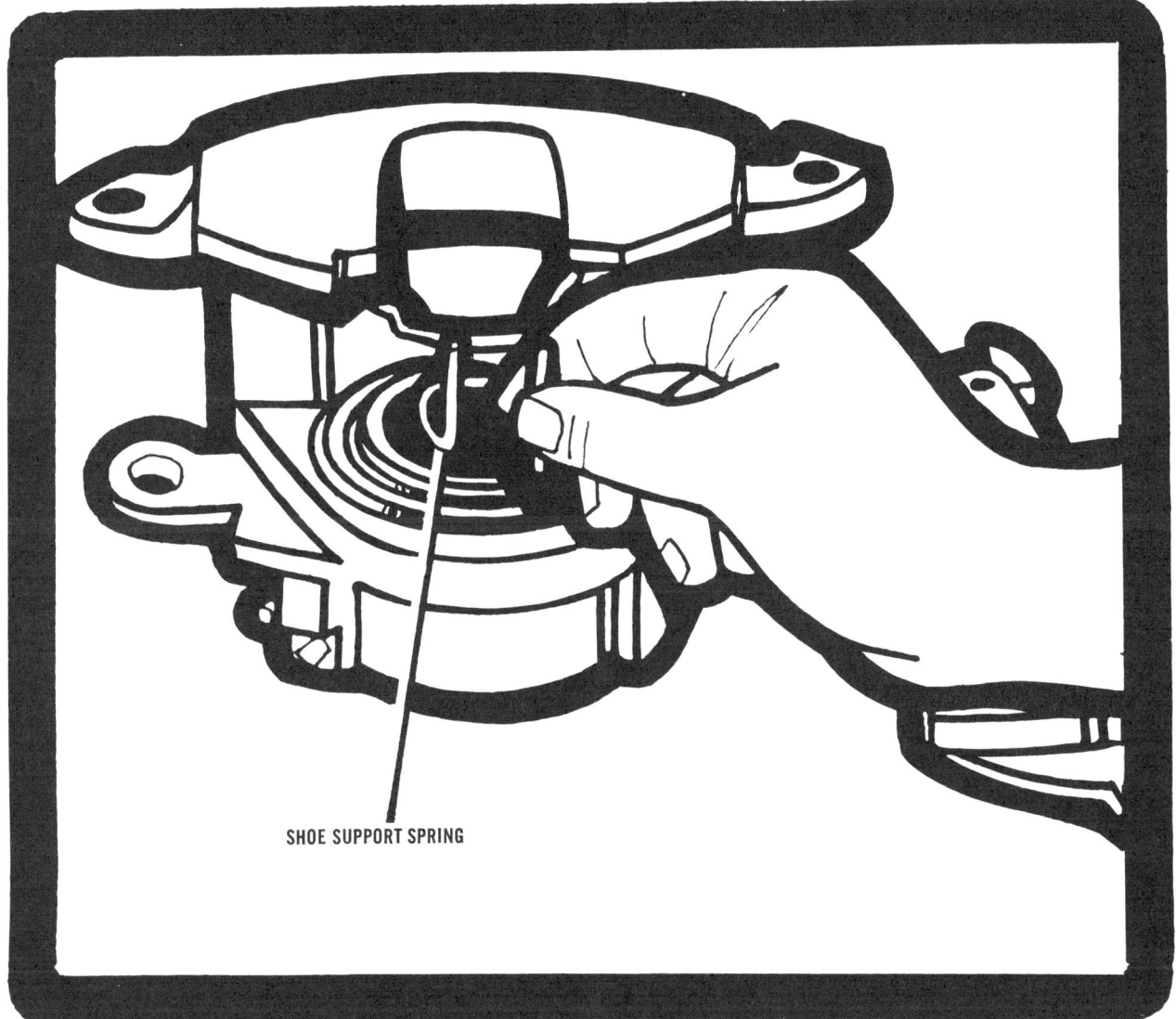

Fig. 13. Support spring installation.

25. Install the wheel covers. Use a rubber mallet and tap around the outer edge of the cover to fully seat it against the wheel.
26. Raise the vehicle using a suitable jack. Make sure to properly position the jack underneath the vehicle.
27. Remove the jack stands from underneath the vehicle and carefully lower the vehicle.

CAUTION: Prior to moving vehicle, make sure that a firm brake pedal has been obtained.

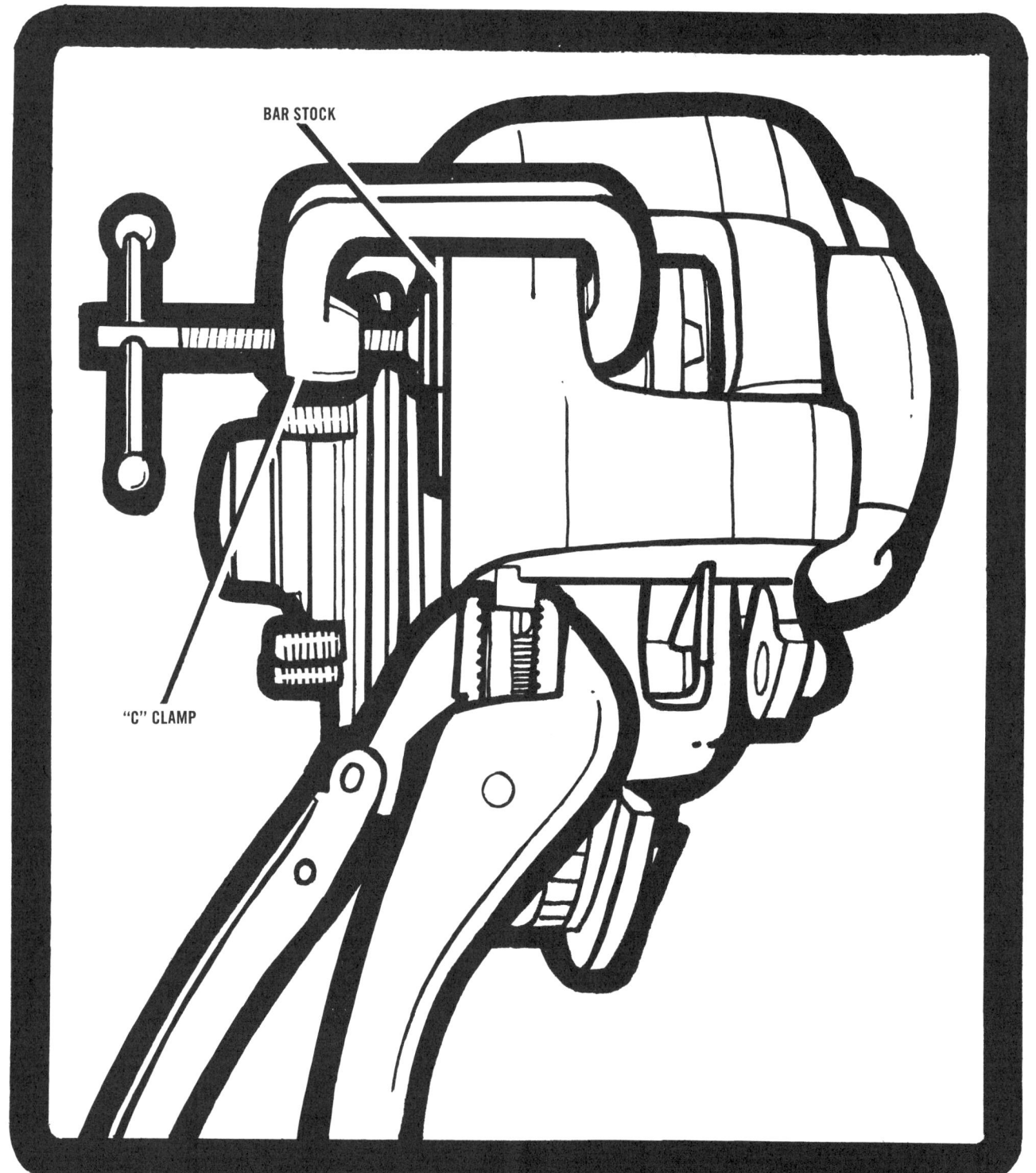

Fig. 14. Fitting shoe and pad onto the caliper, using vicegrip pliers.

444

Astre, Monza, Skyhawk, Starfire and Vega

Brake pad replacement

8. Remove the two mounting pin stamped nuts, Fig. 16 and slide out the mounting pins, Fig. 17.
9. Lift the caliper assembly off the rotor and support the caliper on a suspension component using a length of wire.
10. Slide the inboard and outboard pads past the mounting sleeve openings and remove the mounting sleeves and bushing assemblies.
11. Install the new sleeves with bushings on the caliper grooves, Fig. 18.
    NOTE: The shouldered end of the sleeve must be installed toward the outside.
12. Install inner pad on the caliper and slide the pad ears over the sleeve, Fig. 18. Install the outer pad in the same manner.

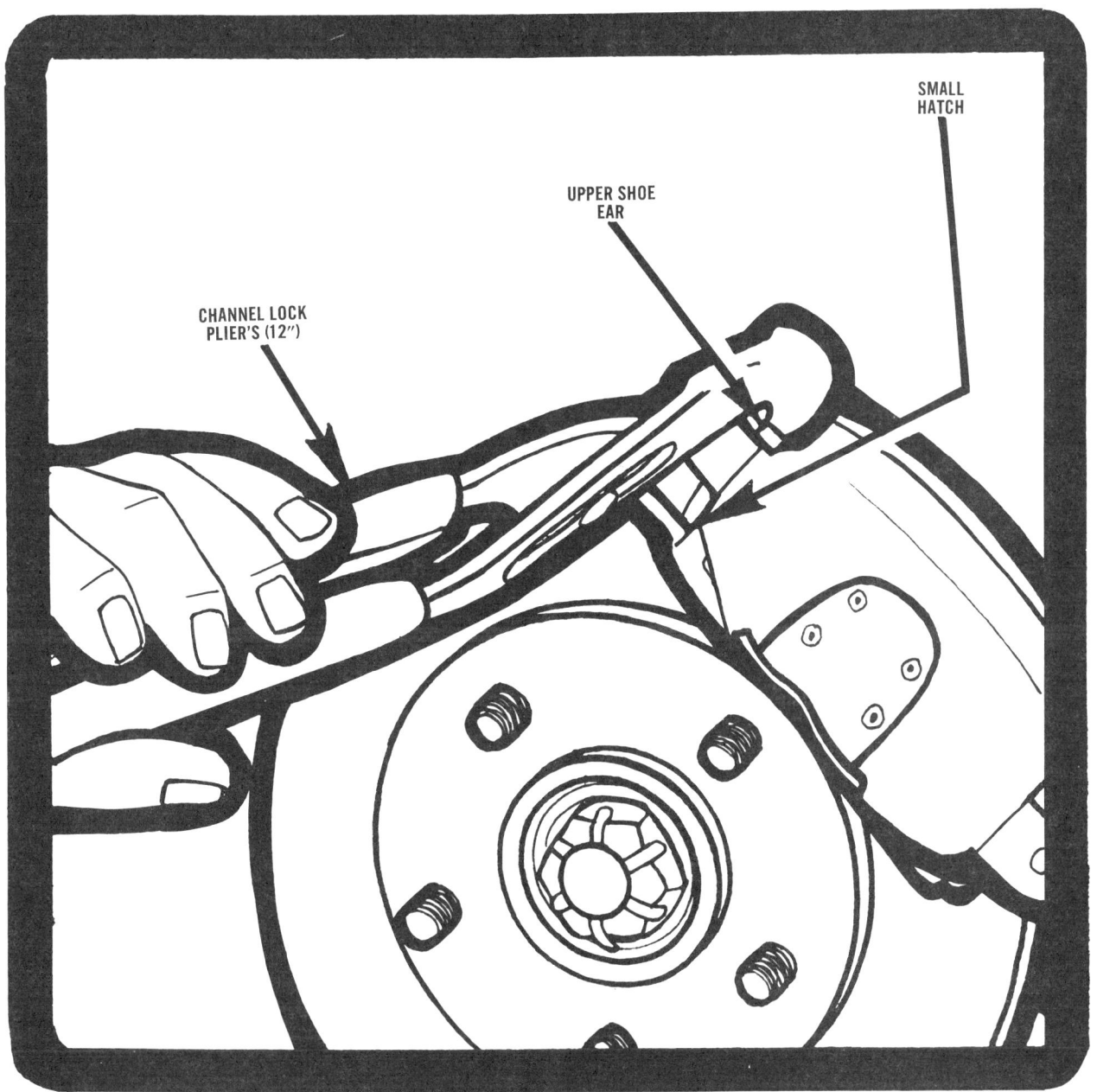

Fig. 15. Clinching loop-eared brake shoe and pad onto the caliper using channel lock pliers.

13. Mount the caliper onto the rotor.
    NOTE: To prevent overflow of the brake fluid capacity, remove two thirds of the brake fluid from the master cylinder.
14. Install mounting pins from the outside in and install the stamped nuts, Fig. 19. Nuts should be pressed on as far as possible using suitable size socket that just seats on the outer edge of the nut.
15. Replace the tire and wheel assembly.
16. Install the tire and wheel assembly retaining nuts. Using the jack handle or suitable size socket, tighten the retaining nuts.
17. Install the wheel covers. Use a rubber mallet and tap around the outer edge of the cover to fully seat the cover against the wheel.
18. Raise the vehicle using a suitable jack. Make sure to properly position the jack underneath the vehicle.
19. Remove the jack stands from underneath the vehicle and carefully lower the vehicle.
20. Add brake fluid to within ¼-inch from the top of the master cylinder.

CAUTION: Prior to moving the vehicle, make sure that a firm brake pedal has been obtained.

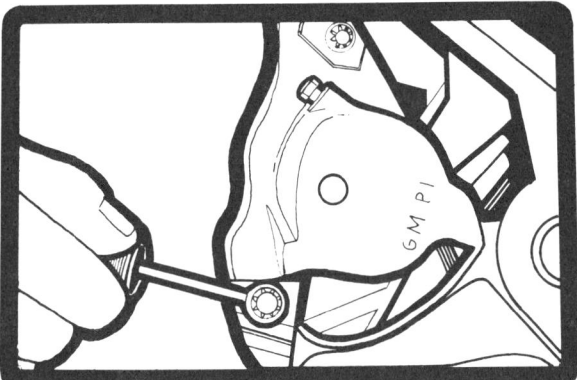

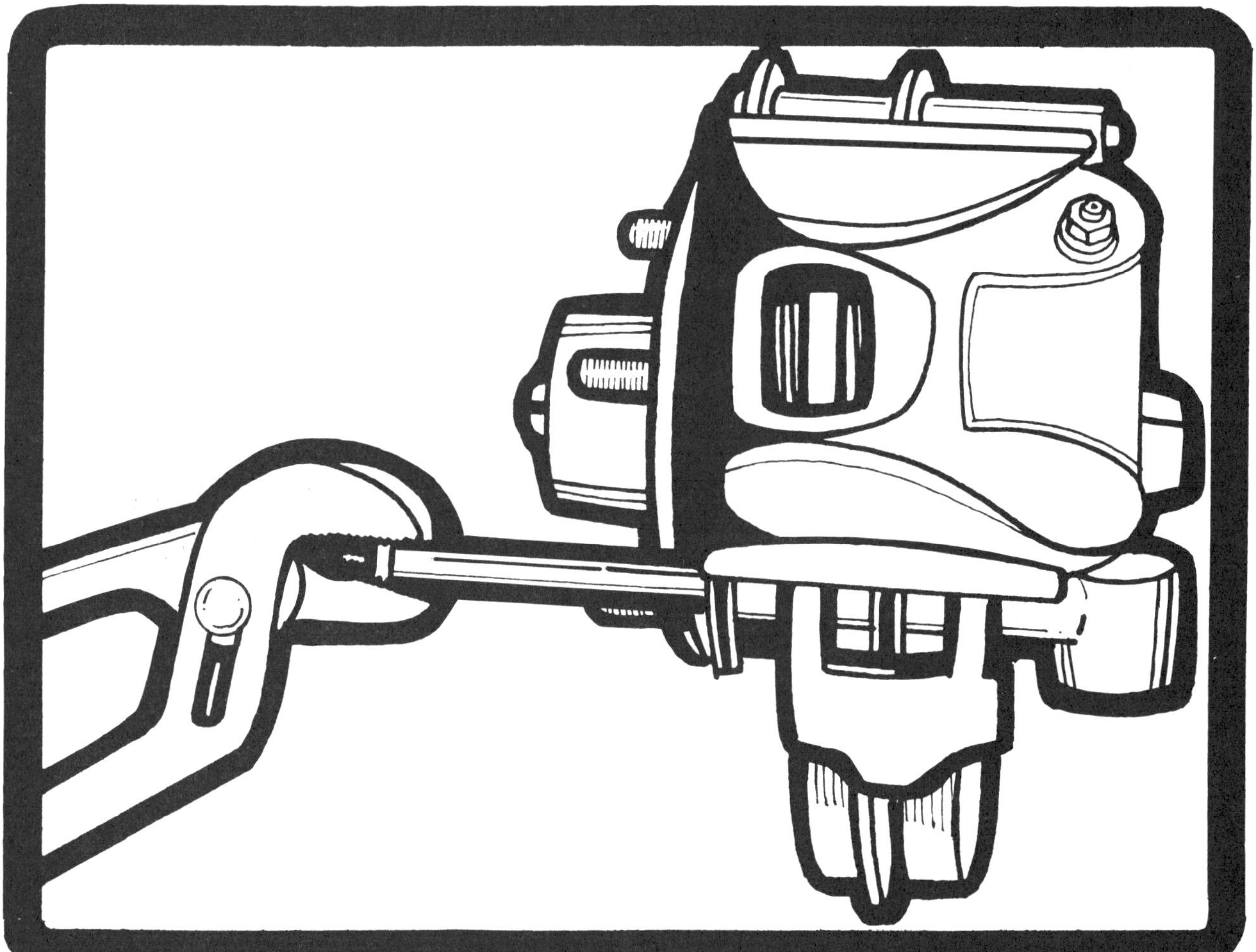

Fig. 16. Removing stamped nuts from mounting pins using a screwdriver.

Fig. 17. Removing mounting pins by pulling out with pliers.

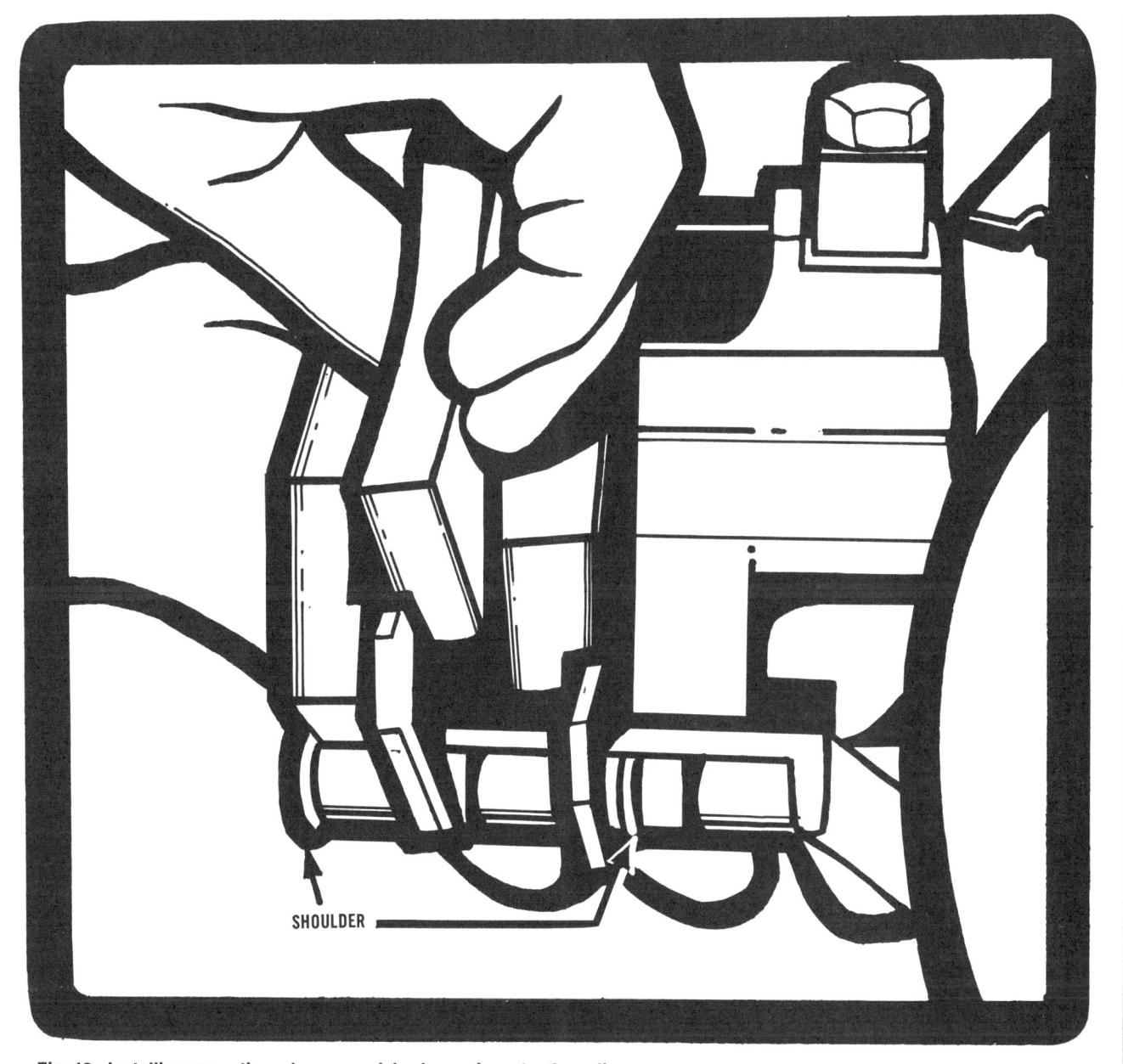

Fig. 18. Installing mounting sleeves and brake pads onto the caliper.

Chevette

Brake pad replacement, Fig. 20

8. Install a 7-inch C-clamp on caliper with solid end of clamp on caliper housing and screw end on metal portion of outboard brake shoe, Fig. 12. Tighten clamp until piston bottoms in caliper bore, then remove clamp.

Fig. 19. Installing the stamped nuts onto the mounting pins using a nut driver.

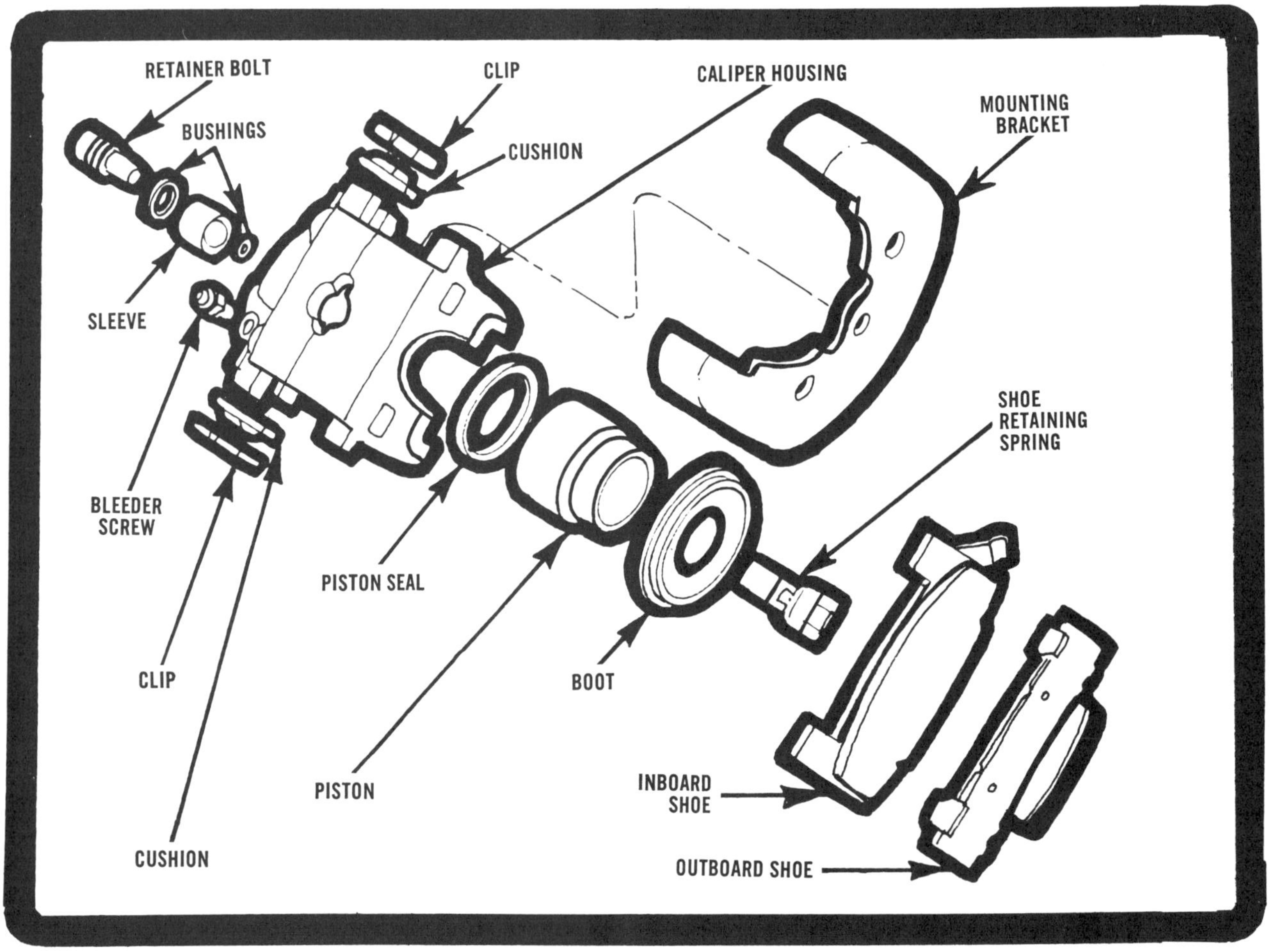

Fig. 20. Exploded view of disc brake caliper assembly.

9. Remove the two steering knuckle-to-mounting-bracket bolts, Fig. 21.

   NOTE: Do not remove the socket head retaining bolts. Support caliper when removing the second bolt to prevent the caliper from falling and rupturing the hydraulic brake hose.
10. Slide the caliper from the rotor. Using a length of wire, tie the caliper to a suspension component to prevent the caliper from falling and rupturing the hydraulic brake hose.
11. Remove the brake pads. If the brake pad retaining spring does not come off with the pads, remove it from the piston.

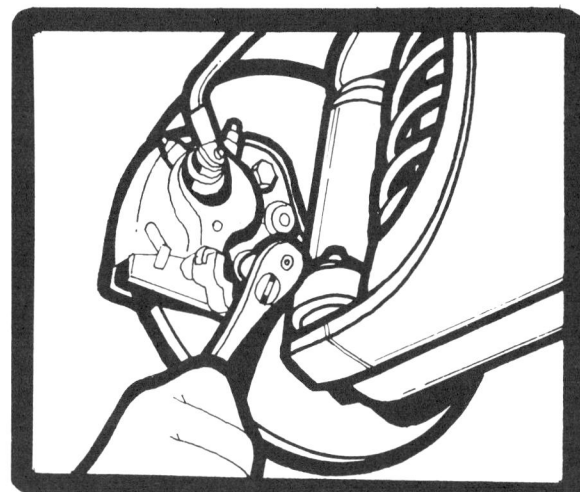

Fig. 21. Removing bracket bolts.

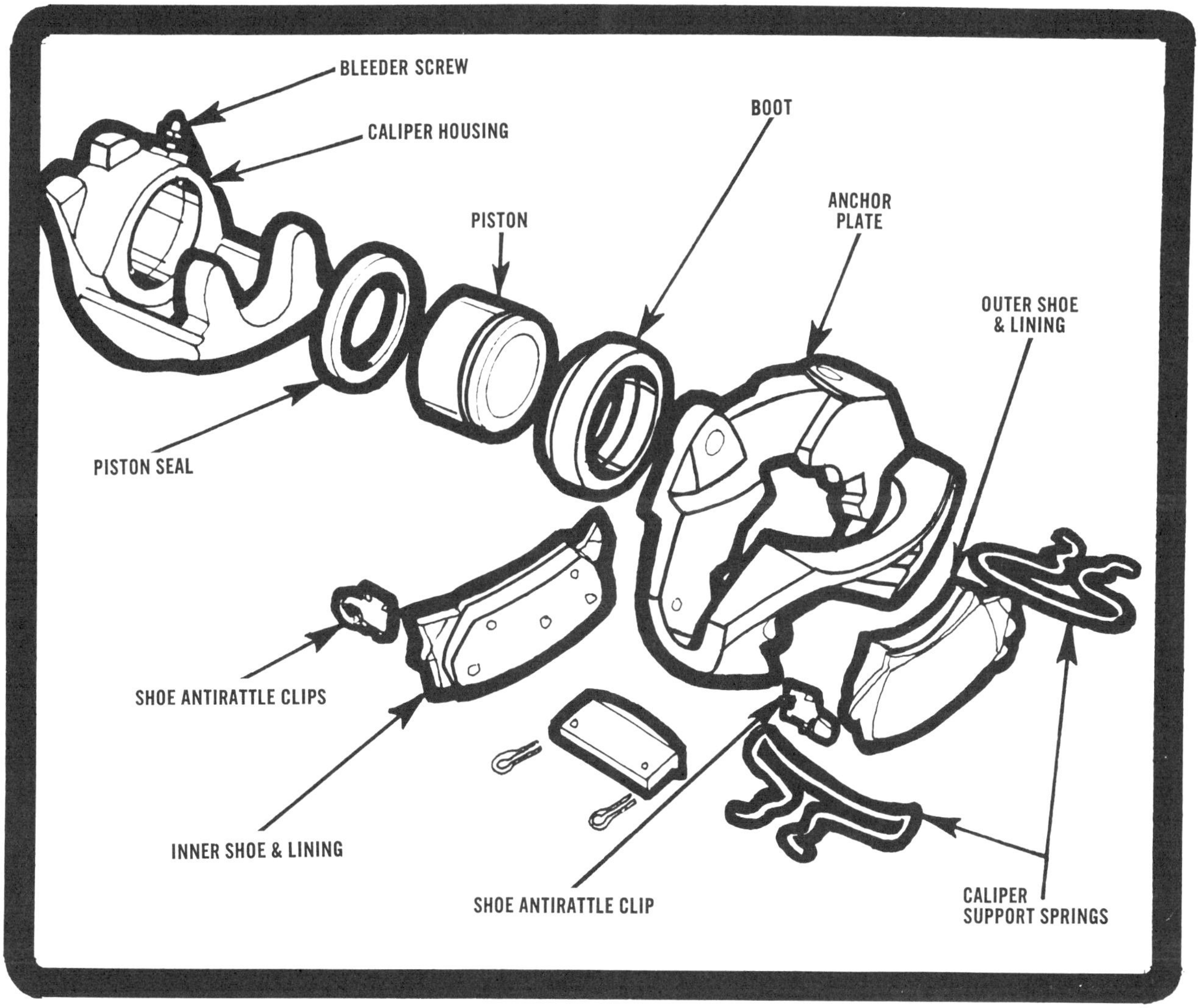

Fig. 22. Exploded view of Ford center abutment type disc brake caliper assembly.

12. To install the pads, position the retaining spring on the inboard pad. Then place single leg in brake pad hole and snap the two outer legs over the notch in brake pad.
13. Position the caliper over the rotor. Align the mounting holes. Then install and torque the mounting bolts to 70 ft. lbs.

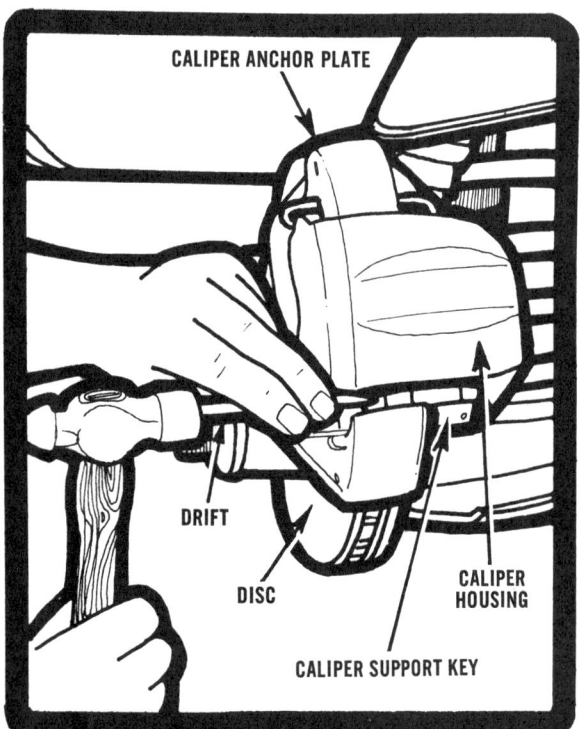

Fig. 23. Removing the caliper support key using a hammer and drift.

14. Using a pair of slip-joint pliers, squeeze outboard pad flanges to caliper. Position jaws of pliers on bottom edge of pad, Fig. 15, and then place other jaw on flange of pad. Squeeze the other brake pad flanges in the same manner. After squeezing, there should be zero to .005-inch (.127 mm) between pads and caliper.
15. Replace the tire and wheel assembly.
16. Install the tire and wheel assembly retaining nuts. Using the jack handle or correct size socket, tighten the retaining nuts. Install the wheel covers. Use a rubber mallet and tap around the outer edge of the cover to fully seat it against the wheel.
17. Raise the vehicle using a suitable jack. Make sure to properly position the jack underneath the vehicle.
18. Remove the jack stands from underneath the vehicle and carefully lower the vehicle.
19. Add brake fluid to within ¼-inch from top of reservoir. Pump brake pedal several times to firmly seat linings against rotor.

CAUTION: Prior to moving vehicle, make sure that a firm brake pedal has been obtained.

FORD CENTER ABUTMENT TYPE

Brake pad replacement, Fig. 22

8. Remove the caliper pins from the caliper support keys.
9. Using a drift and a light hammer, remove the caliper support key, being careful to avoid damaging key or machined surfaces, Fig. 23.
10. Rotate lower end of caliper housing toward the rear and upward and remove caliper from anchor plate. It is not necessary to disconnect hydraulic line for this operation.
11. As the shoe and pad assemblies are now exposed, tilt the upper edge of the pads away from disc and then take out the pads, Fig. 24. Pads are identical and can be interchanged.
12. Take three thickness pad measurements of each shoe and pad.
13. If there is less than .030-inch above the rivet heads, replace the pad on both front wheels.
14. Position the new shoe pad assemblies in anchor plate by tilting the pad and sliding the bottom edge into position.
15. Rotate pads into correct positions, assuring that the pad side is next to the rotor.
16. Place a light coat of high temperature grease on the anchor plate and caliper surfaces that will be contacting each other after the caliper is installed. Do not get grease on brake pads.
17. Place the caliper in the anchor plate, assuring that the top trailing edge of the caliper is properly positioned and the caliper support spring is under the projecting ledge of the caliper.

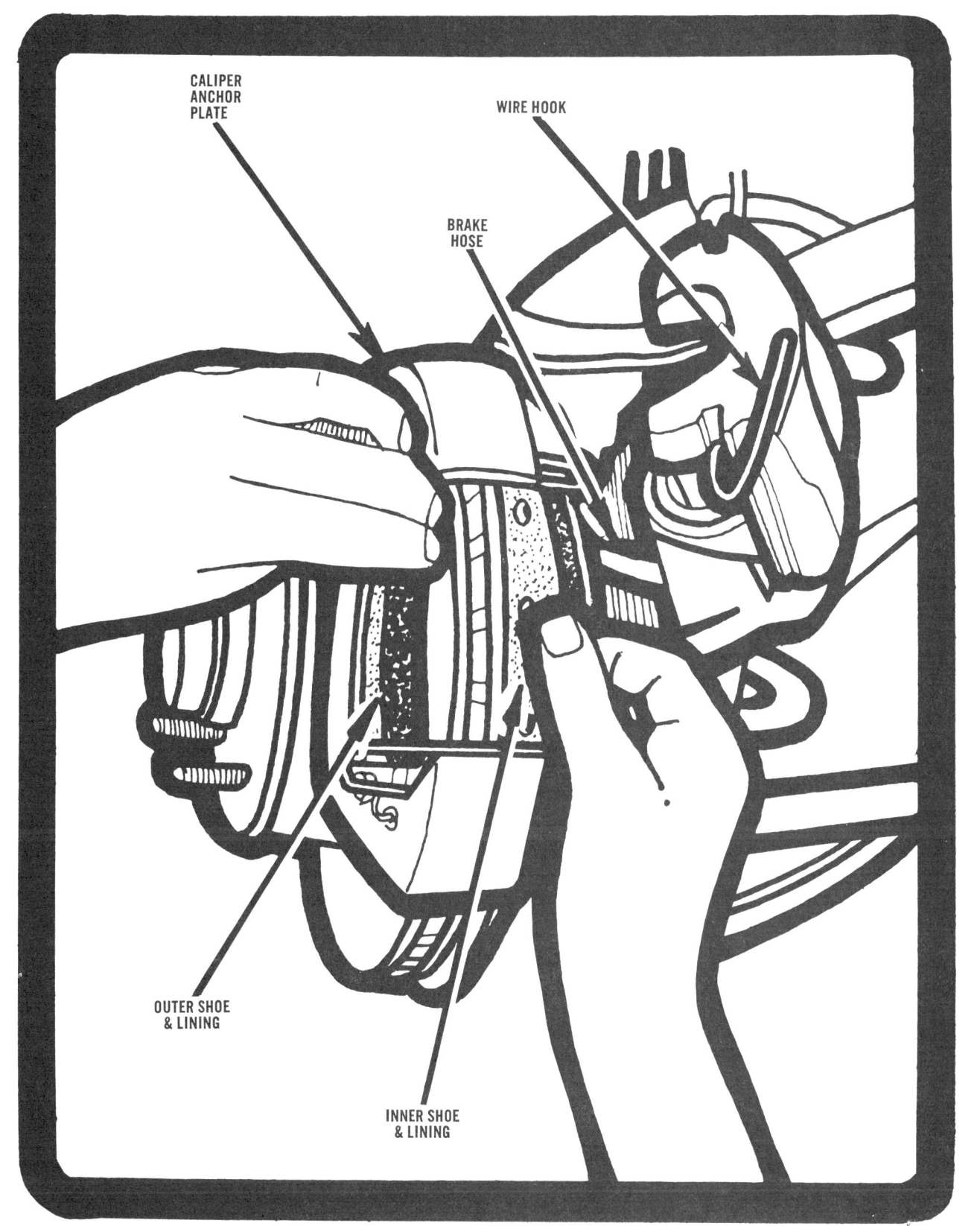

Fig. 24. Removing the shoe and lining assemblies.

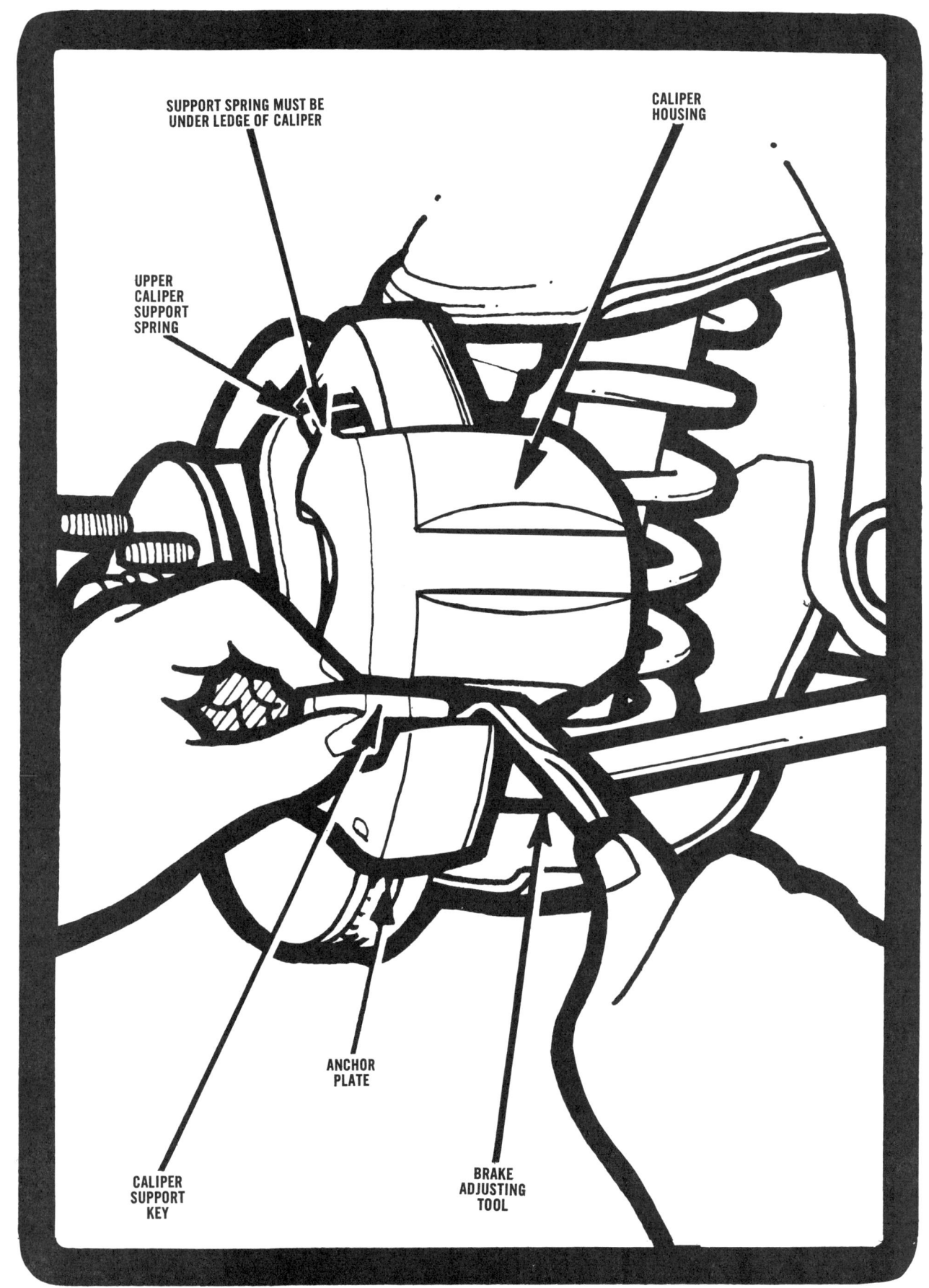

Fig. 25. Positioning the caliper assembly onto the anchor plate.

18. Insert a wide blade screwdriver or brake adjusting tool between the bottom leading edge of the caliper and the adjacent anchor plate surface. Pry downward so that the caliper housing is pressed upward and inward toward the spindle, Fig. 25.
19. Install the caliper support key between the caliper housing and the anchor plate, Fig. 26. Assure that the key is properly positioned and that the caliper support springs are still properly positioned.
20. Center the support key so that the cotter pin holes are on each side of the anchor plate and insert a new cotter pin in each of the holes.
21. Replace the tire and wheel assembly.

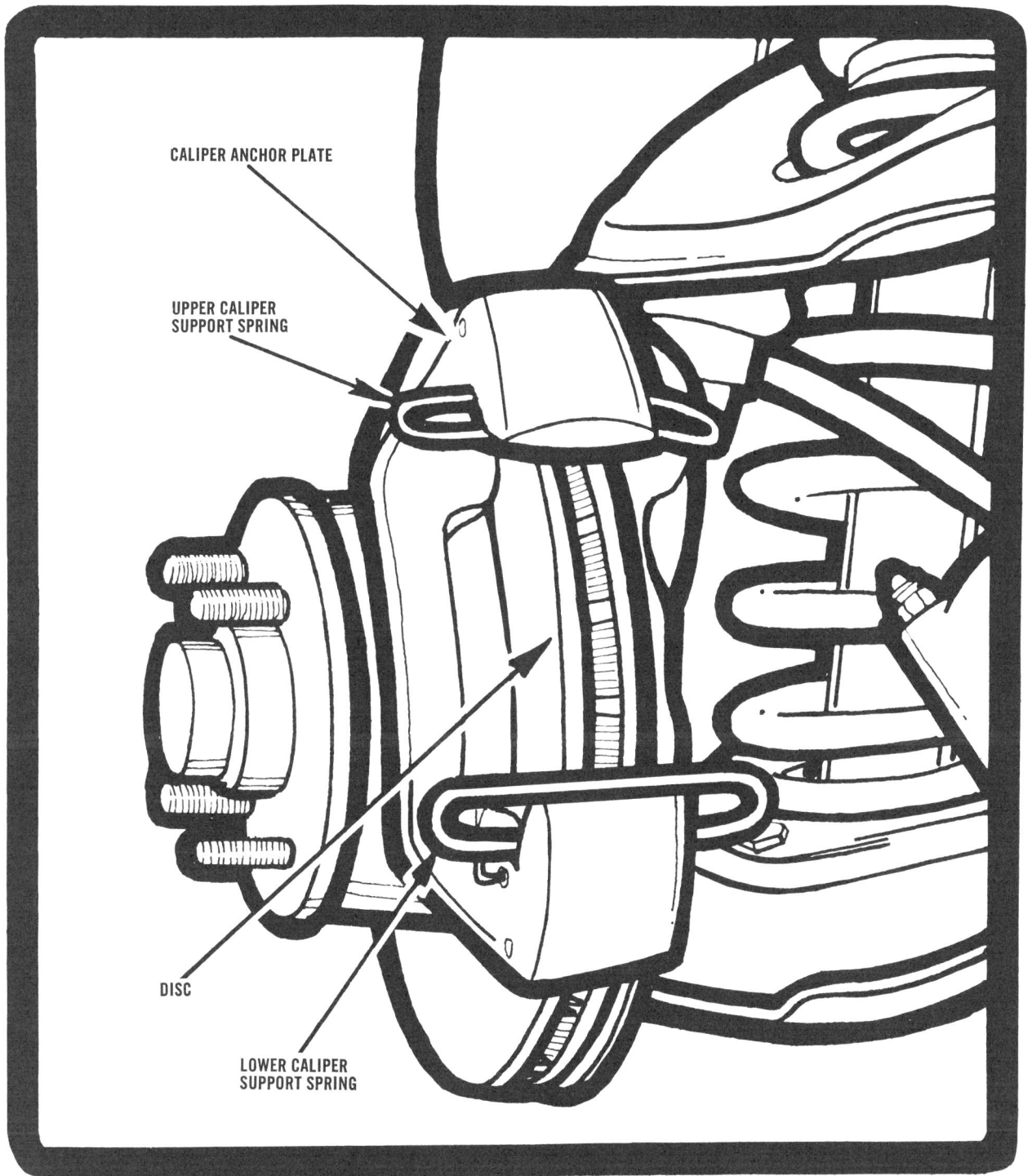

Fig. 26. Caliper support springs properly positioned on the anchor plate.

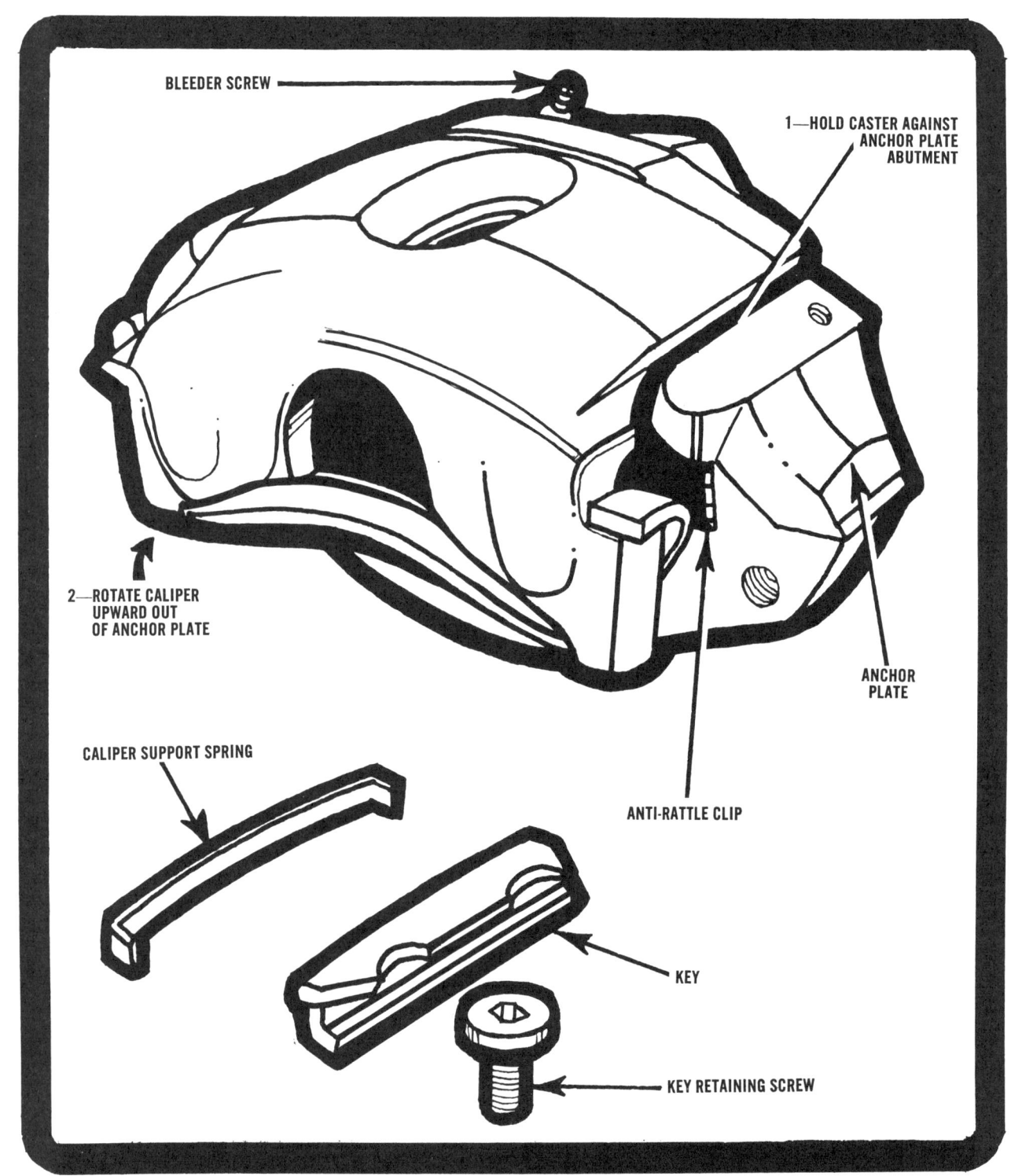

Fig. 27. Removing the caliper assembly.

22. Install the tire and wheel assembly retaining nuts. Using the jack handle or correct size socket, tighten the retaining nuts.
23. Install the wheel covers. Use a rubber mallet and tap around the outer edge of the cover to fully seat it against the wheel.
24. Raise the vehicle using a suitable jack. Make sure to properly position the jack underneath the vehicle.
25. Remove the jack stands from underneath the vehicle and carefully lower the vehicle.

CAUTION: Prior to moving the vehicle, make sure a firm brake pedal has been obtained.

FORD SLIDING CALIPER

Brake pad replacement

8. Remove the retaining screw from the caliper retaining key, Fig. 27.
9. Slide the caliper retaining key and support spring either inward or outward from the anchor plate. Use hammer and drift, if necessary, to remove the key and caliper support spring. Use caution to avoid damaging the key.
10. Lift caliper assembly away from anchor plate by pushing caliper down against anchor plate and rotate upper end upward and out of anchor plate, Fig. 28.
11. Remove the inner pad from the anchor plate. The brake pad anti-rattle clip (inner pad only) may become displaced at this time and if so, reposition it on anchor plate, Fig. 28. Tap lightly on outer pad to free it from caliper.
12. To install new brake pads, use a 4-inch C-clamp and a wooden block 1¾ inches x 1-inch and about ¾-inch thick to seat the piston in the caliper, to provide clearance for the caliper to fit over the new shoes when installed.
13. Make sure that the brake pad anti-rattle spring is in place on the lower end of the inner brake pad with the loop of the clip toward the inside of the anchor plate. Position the inner pad on the anchor plate with the lining facing toward the rotor.

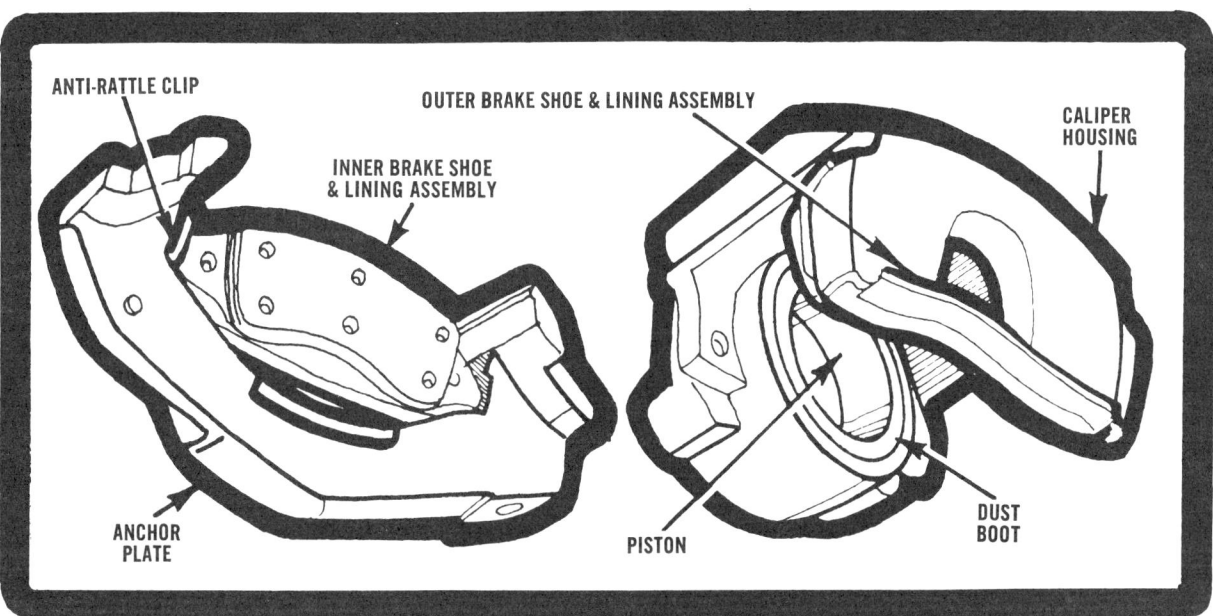

Fig. 28 Caliper and the outer shoe removed from the anchor plate.

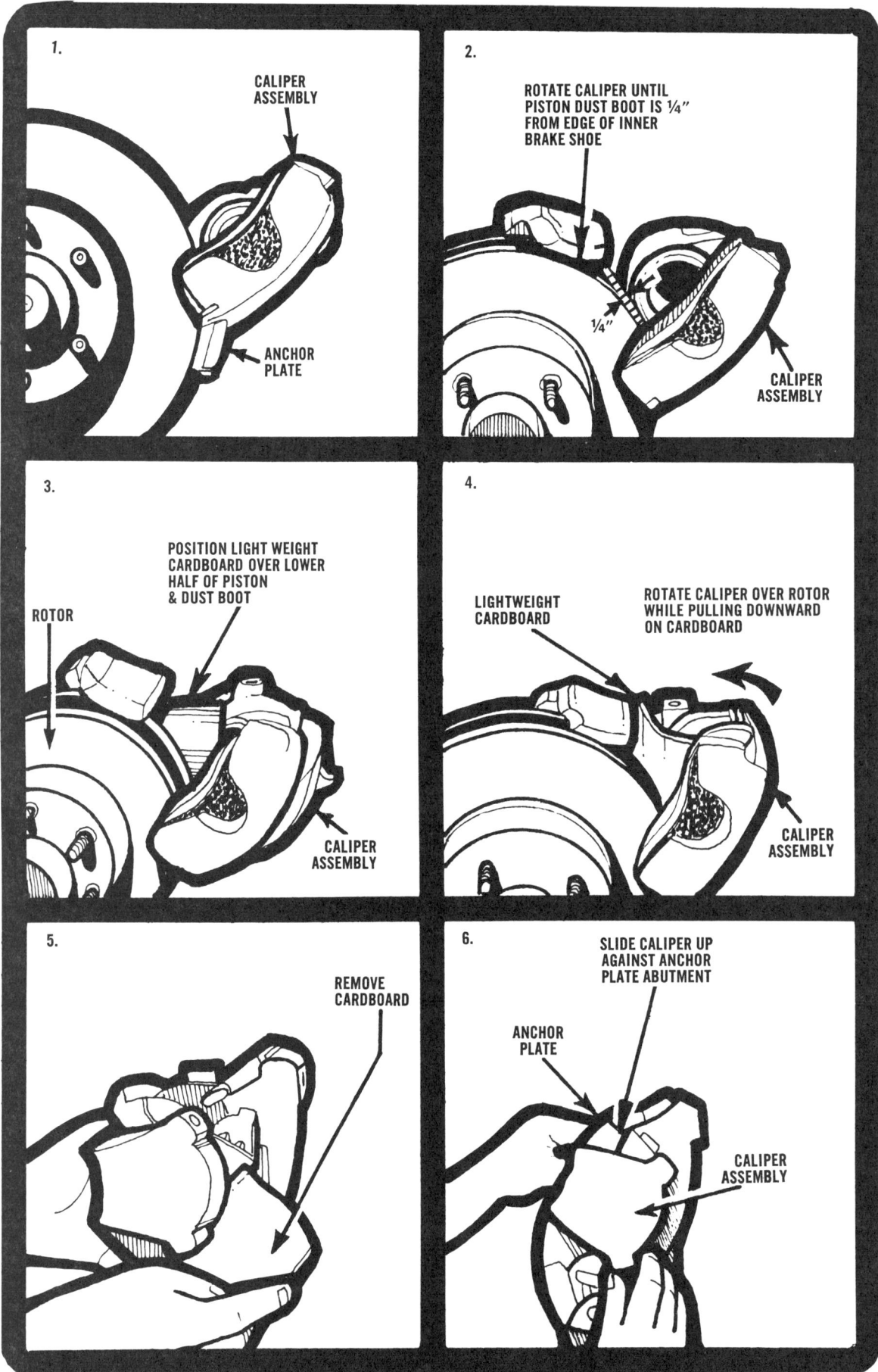

Fig. 29. Caliper assembly installation procedure.

14. Install the outer pad with the lower flange ends against the caliper leg abutments and the pad upper flanges over the shoulders on the caliper legs. The pad upper flanges fit tightly against the shouldered machined surfaces. If the same pads are to be reused, assure that the pads are installed in their original positions as when removed.
15. Remove the C-clamp. The pistons will remain seated in the caliper bore.
16. Position the caliper housing lower V-groove on the anchor plate lower abutment surface.
17. Pivot the caliper housing upward toward the rotor until the outer edge of the piston dust boot is about ¼-inch from the upper edge of the inboard pad, Fig. 29, steps 1 and 2.
18. Position a piece of clean lightweight cardboard between the inboard pad and over the lower half of the piston dust boot, Fig. 29, step 3.

   NOTE: The cardboard is required to prevent pinching the dust boot between the piston and the inboard pad during caliper installation.
19. Rotate the caliper housing toward the rotor until a slight resistance is felt. Then pull the cardboard downward toward the rotor centerline while rotating the caliper over the rotor, Fig. 29, step 4.

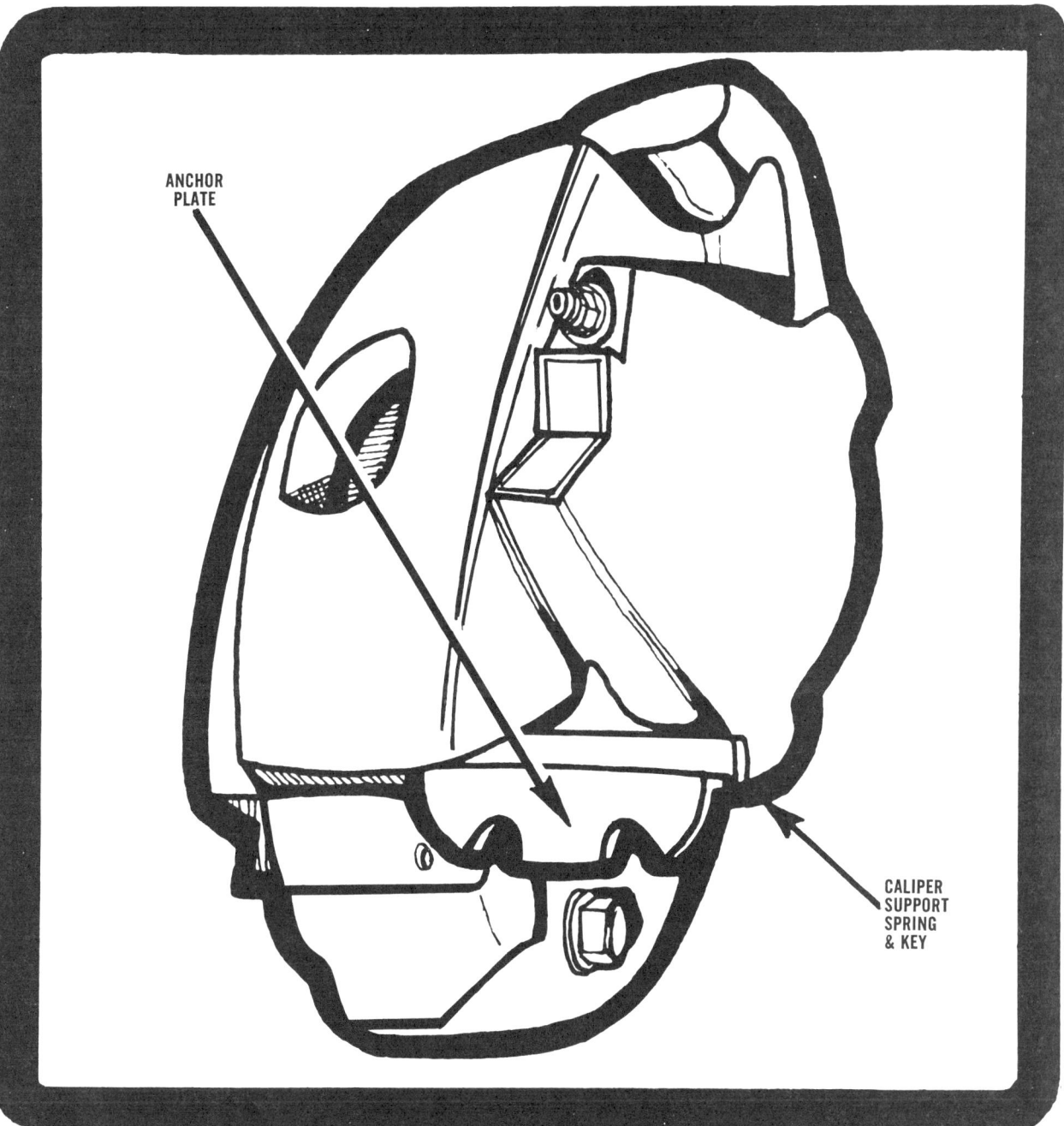

Fig. 30. Installing the caliper support spring and the retaining key.

20. Remove the cardboard and rotate the caliper completely over the rotor, Fig. 29, step 5.
21. Slide the caliper up against the anchor plate upper abutment surface and center the caliper over the upper anchor plate abutment, Fig. 29, step 6.
22. Position the caliper support spring and key in the key slot and slide them into the opening between the lower end of the caliper and the lower anchor plate abutment. Align the key semi-circular slot in the key with the threaded hole in the anchor plate, Fig. 30.
23. Install the key retaining screw and torque to 12-16 ft. lbs.
24. Replace the tire and wheel assembly.
25. Install the tire and wheel assembly retaining nuts, then using the jack handle or correct size socket, tighten the retaining nuts.
26. Install the wheel covers. Use a rubber mallet and tap around the outer edge of the cover to fully seat it against the wheel.
27. Raise the vehicle using a suitable jack. Make sure to properly position the jack underneath the vehicle.
28. Remove the jack stands from underneath the vehicle and carefully lower the vehicle.

CAUTION: Prior to moving the vehicle, make sure that a firm brake pedal has been obtained.

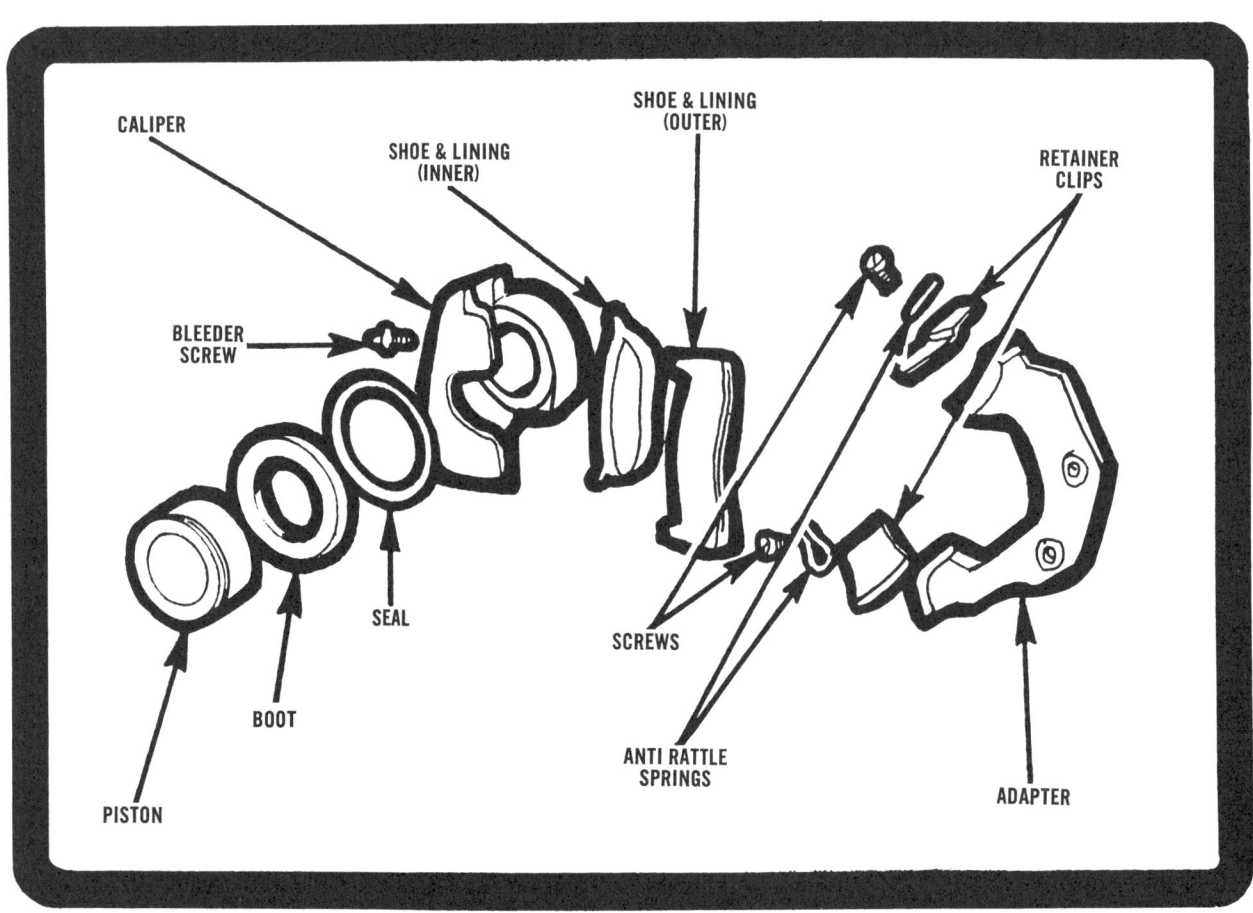

Fig. 31. Kelsey-Hayes sliding caliper type disc brake assembly.

KELSEY-HAYES SLIDING CALIPER

Brake pad replacement, Fig. 31

8. Remove the caliper retaining clips and the anti-rattle springs, Fig. 32.
9. Remove the caliper from the disc by slowly sliding the caliper assembly out and away from the disc.

   NOTE: Using a length of wire, support caliper onto the front suspension to prevent the caliper from falling and rupturing the hydraulic brake hose.

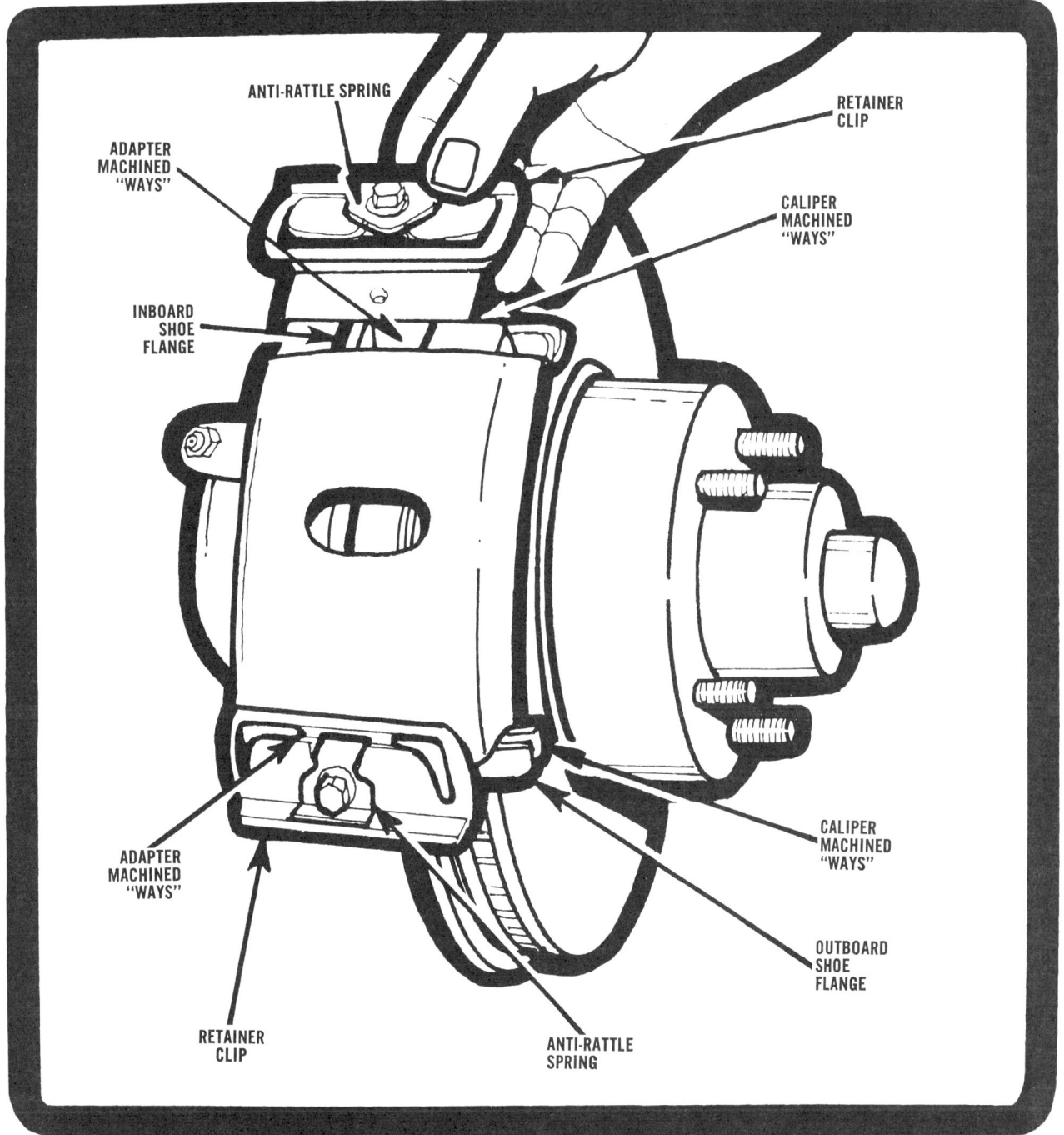

Fig. 32. Removing caliper retaining clips and anti-rattle clips.

10. Remove the outboard pad by prying, using a screwdriver between the pad and the caliper fingers, Fig. 33, since the flanges on the outboard pad retain the caliper firmly.
11. Remove the inboard pad from the adaptor, Fig. 34.

    NOTE: Remove two thirds of the total brake fluid capacity from the master cylinder to prevent overflow of the brake fluid when the pistons are pushed into the caliper bore.
12. With care, push the piston back into caliper bore until it is bottomed.

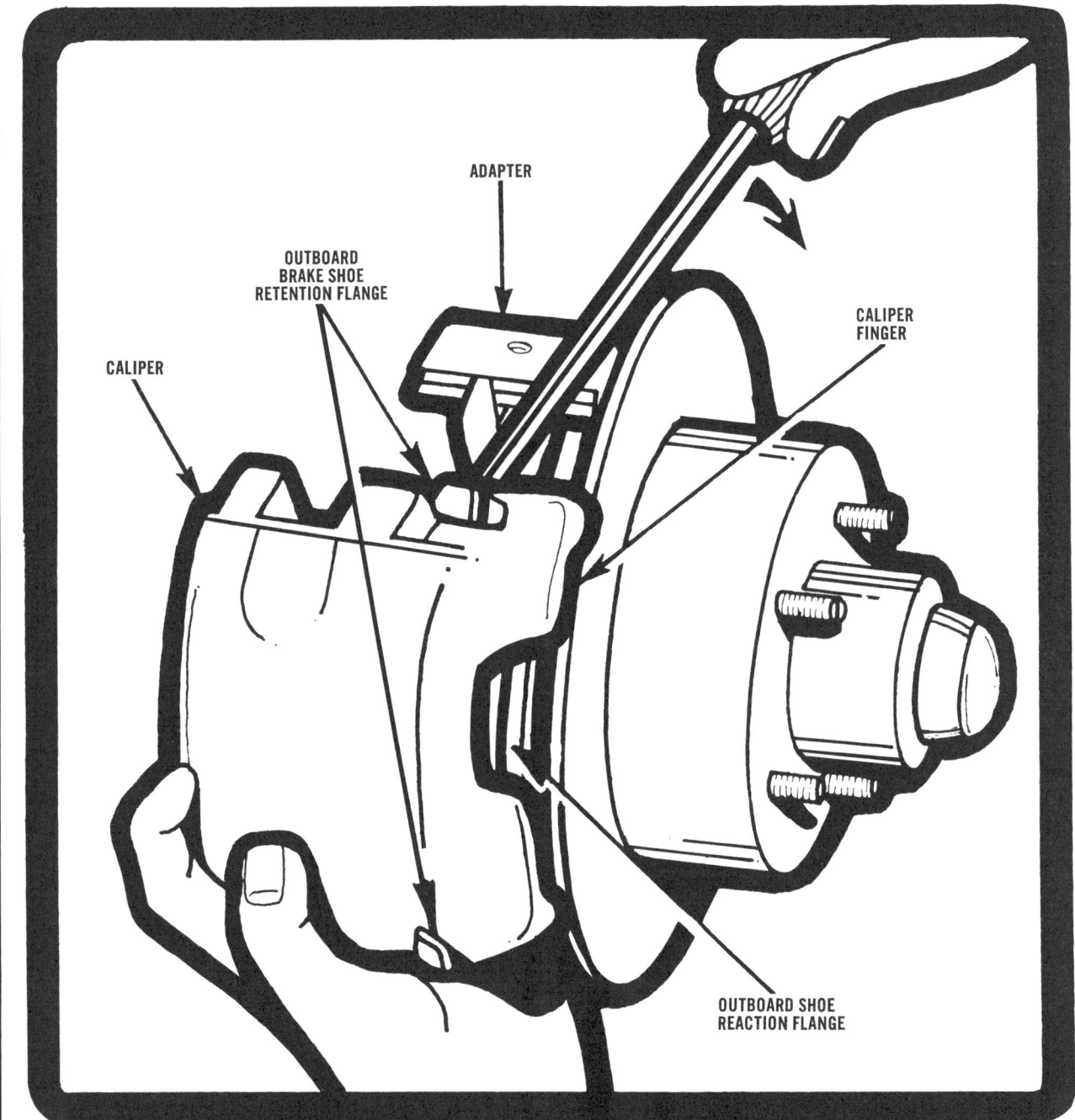

Fig. 33. Removing the outboard shoe.

13. Install new outboard pad into recess of caliper.
    NOTE: No free play should exist between brake pad flanges and the caliper fingers, Fig. 35. If up and down movement of the shoe shows free play, pad must be removed and the flanges bent to provide a slight interference fit, Fig. 36. Reinstall the pad after modification, if pad cannot be finger snapped into place, use light "C" clamp pressure, Fig. 37.
14. Position the inboard pad with flanges inserted in adaptor "ways," Fig. 34.
15. Carefully slide the caliper assembly into the adaptor and over the disc while aligning caliper on the machined "ways" of the adaptor. Fig. 34.
    NOTE: Assure that dust boot is not pulled out from groove when the piston and boot slide over the inboard shoe.

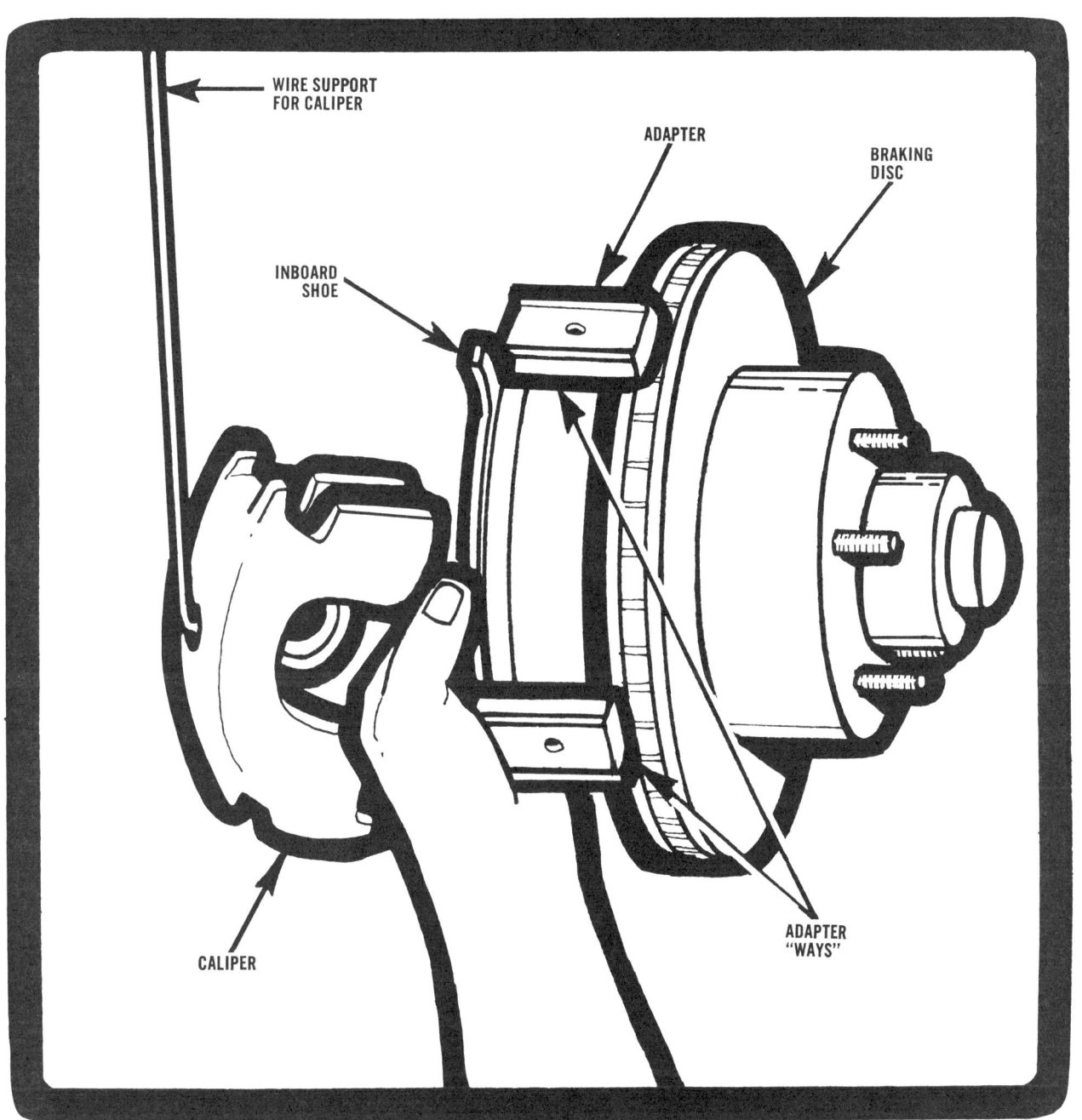

Fig. 34. Removing or installing the inboard pad.

16. Install anti-rattle springs and the retaining clips and torque retaining screws to 180 in.-lbs.
   NOTE: The inboard shoe anti-rattle spring is to be installed on the top of the retainer spring plate, Fig. 32.
17. Replace the tire and wheel assembly.
18. Install the tire and wheel assembly retaining nuts, then using the jack handle or correct size socket, tighten the retaining nuts.
19. Install the wheel covers. Use a rubber mallet and tap around the outer edge of the cover to fully seat it against the wheel.
20. Raise the vehicle using a suitable jack. Make sure to properly position the jack underneath the vehicle.
21. Remove the jack stands from underneath the vehicle and carefully lower the vehicle.

CAUTION: Prior to moving the vehicle, make sure a firm brake pedal has been obtained.

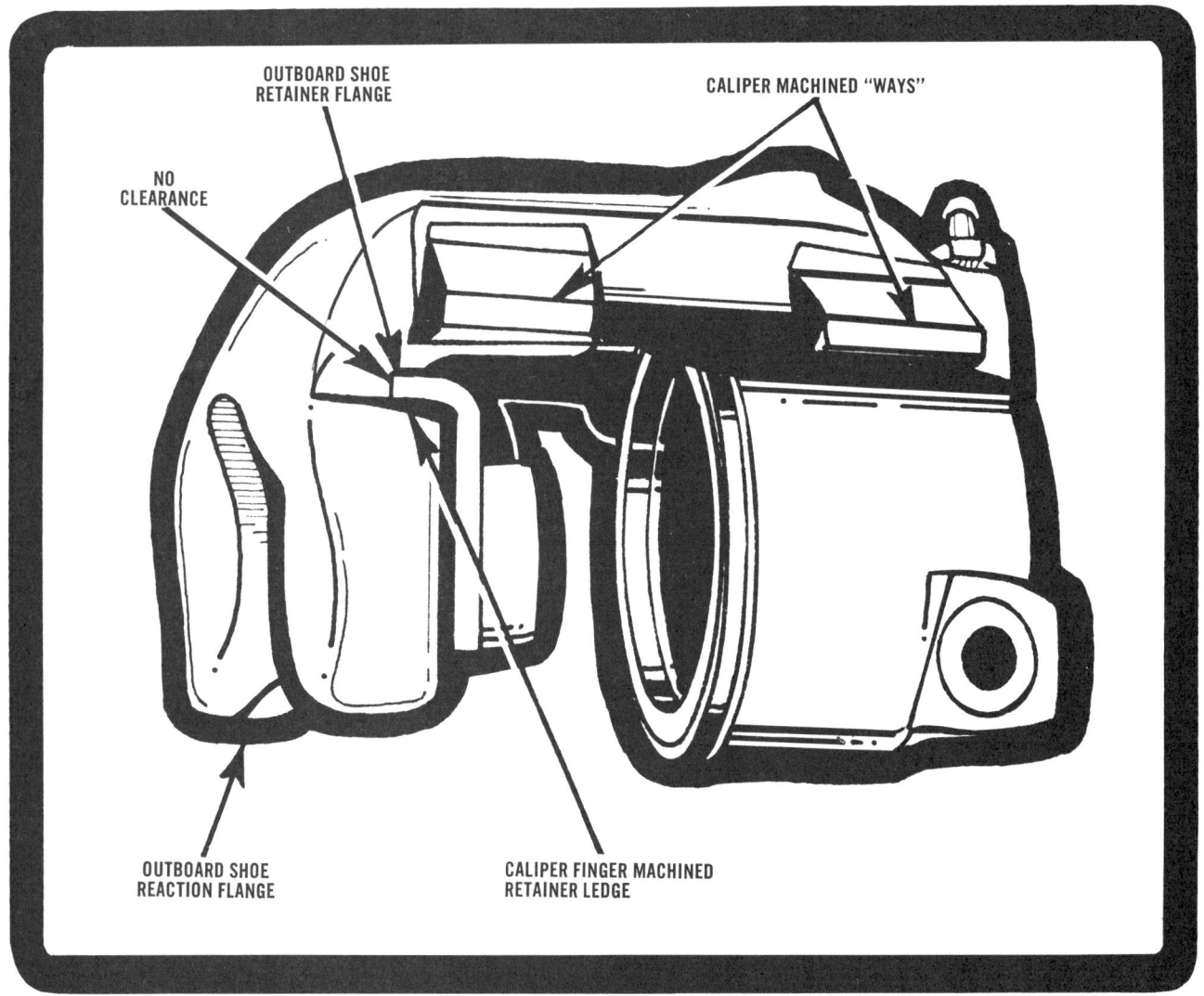

Fig. 35. Installing the outboard shoe onto the caliper finger machined retainer ledge.

FORD REAR WHEEL DISC BRAKES

NOTE: To successfully complete the following procedures, special tools are required, which are available from the vehicle manufacturer or major tool outlets.

Pad and shoe replacement

8. Disconnect the parking cable from the lever, using caution to avoid kinking or cutting the cable or return spring. Then remove the retaining screw from the caliper retaining key, Fig. 38, Step 1.
9. Slide the caliper retaining key and support spring from the anchor plate, Fig. 38, Step 2. If necessary, use a hammer and brass drift using caution to avoid damaging the key on the sliding ways or striking the parking brake lever.

   NOTE: If the caliper cannot be removed due to rust build-up on the outer edge of the rotor, scrape off the loose scale, being careful not to damage the braking surfaces. If the rotor wear or scoring prevents removal of the caliper, it will be necessary to loosen the caliper end retainer ½-turn maximum to allow the piston to be forced back into the caliper bore. To loosen end retainer, remove the parking brake lever and mark or scribe end retainer and caliper housing to assure that end retainer is not loosened more than ½-turn. Force piston back into caliper and move caliper back and forth to center rotor and remove caliper. If the retainer must be loosened more than ½-turn, use caution. The seal between the thrust screw and the housing may be broken and brake fluid will enter the parking brake mechanism chamber. In this case, the end retainer must be removed and the internal parts cleaned and lubricated.

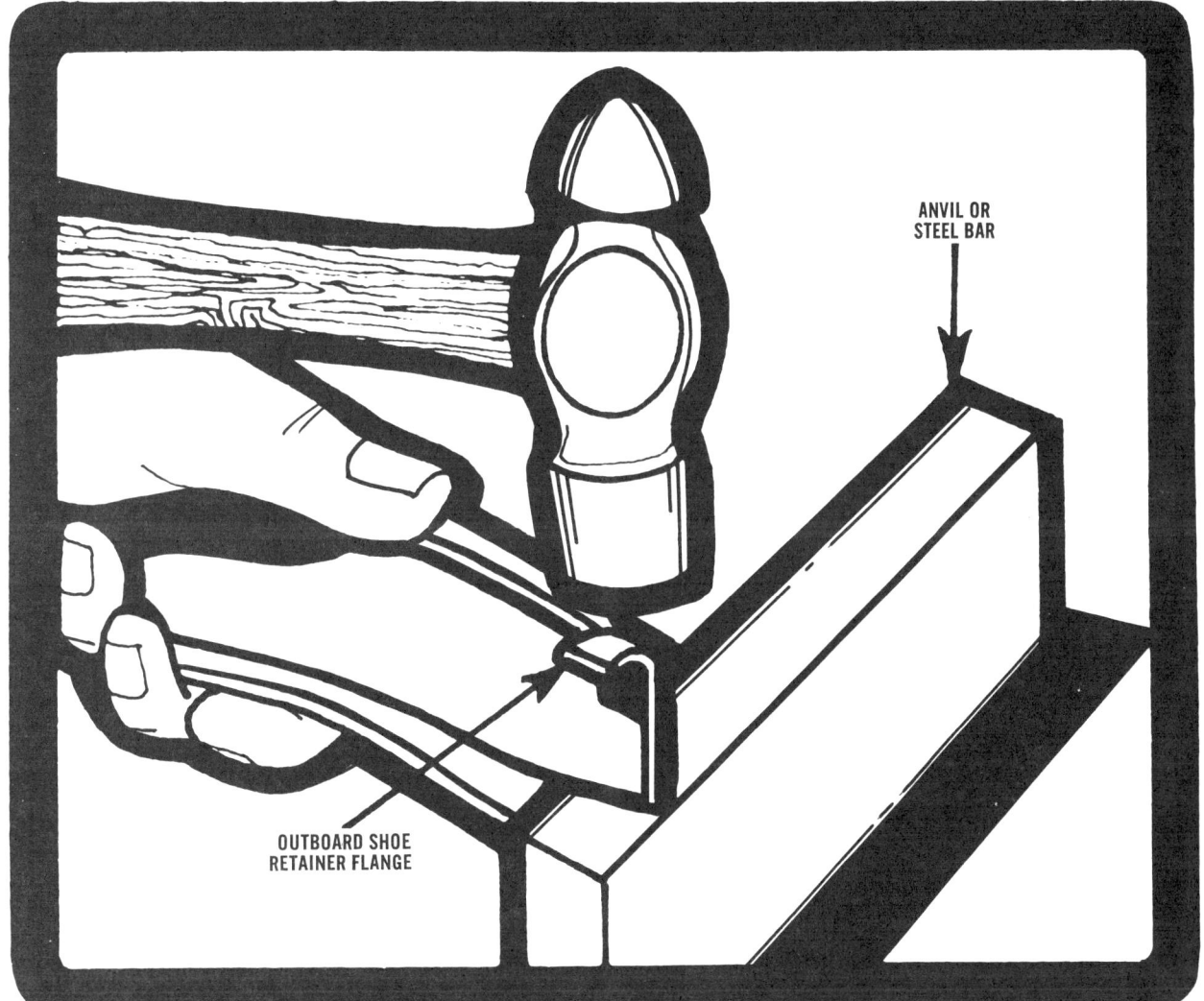

Fig. 36. Bending the outboard shoe retainer flange so that it fits snugly onto the caliper.

10. Remove the inner shoe and pad assembly from the anchor plate. Then tap lightly on outer shoe and pad assembly to free it from the caliper. Mark each pad for identification if they are to be reused.

11. If end retainer has been loosened only ½-turn, reinstall the caliper onto the anchor plate using key. Do not install shoe and lining assembly. Torque the end retainer to 75-95 ft. lbs. and install the parking brake actuating lever on its keyed spline. Lever arm must point down and rearward so that the parking brake cable will pass freely under axle. Torque retainer screw to 16-22 ft. lbs.

    NOTE: The parking brake lever must rotate freely after torquing retainer screw.

12. Remove the caliper from anchor plate. If new shoe and pad assemblies are to be installed, the piston must be bottomed in the caliper bore using tool T57P-2588-B to provide clearance. Remove rotor and install caliper without lining and shoe assemblies in the anchor plate using key only. Install tool and while holding shaft, rotate the tool handle counterclockwise until the tool seats firmly against piston, Fig. 39. Loosen the tool handle about ¼-turn. While holding handle rotate the tool shaft clockwise until piston is fully bottomed in bore (piston will continue to turn even after it is bottomed). Turn tool handle until there is no further inward movement of piston and there

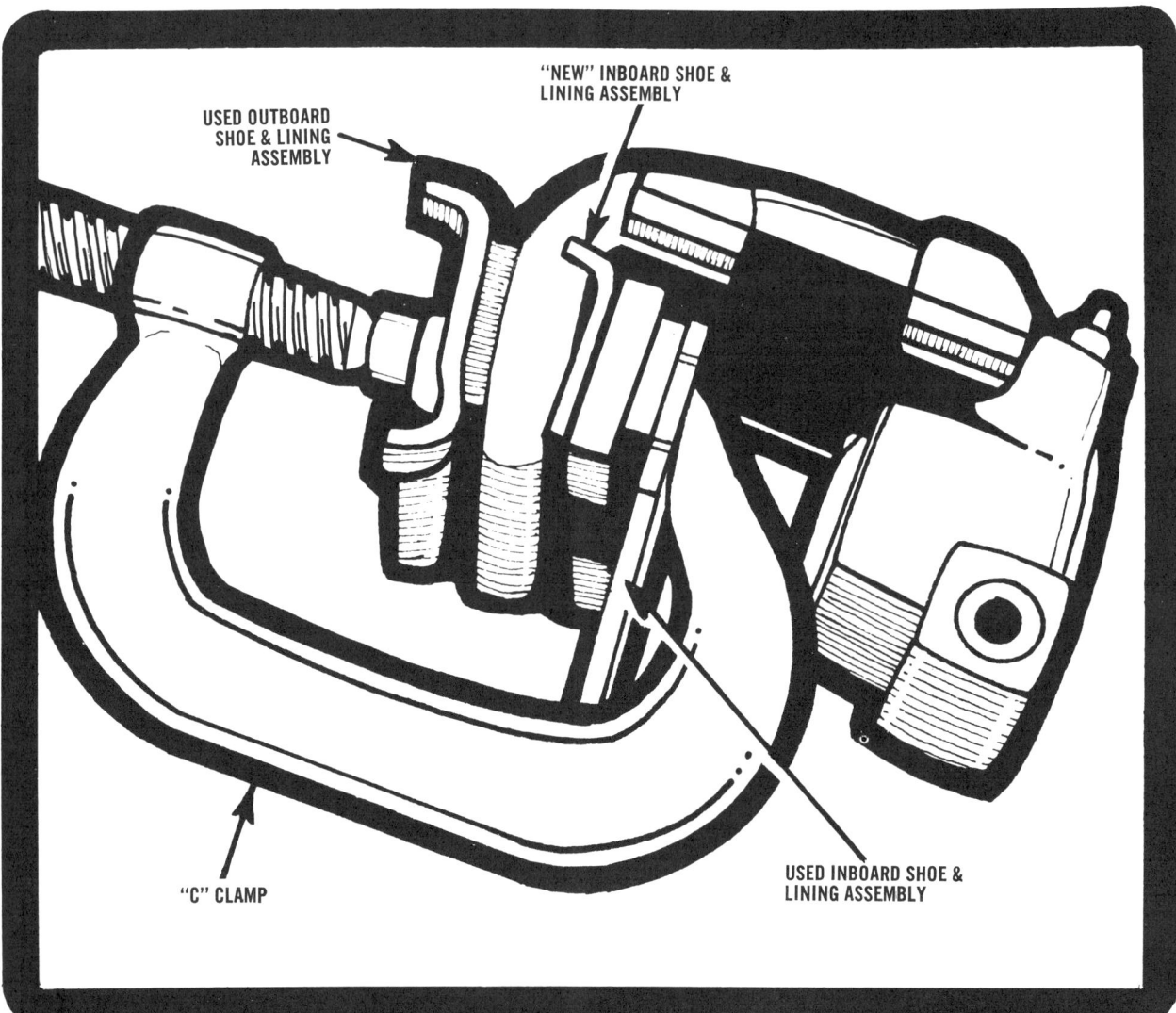

Fig. 37. Installing the outboard shoe onto the caliper using a C-clamp to force the shoe into position.

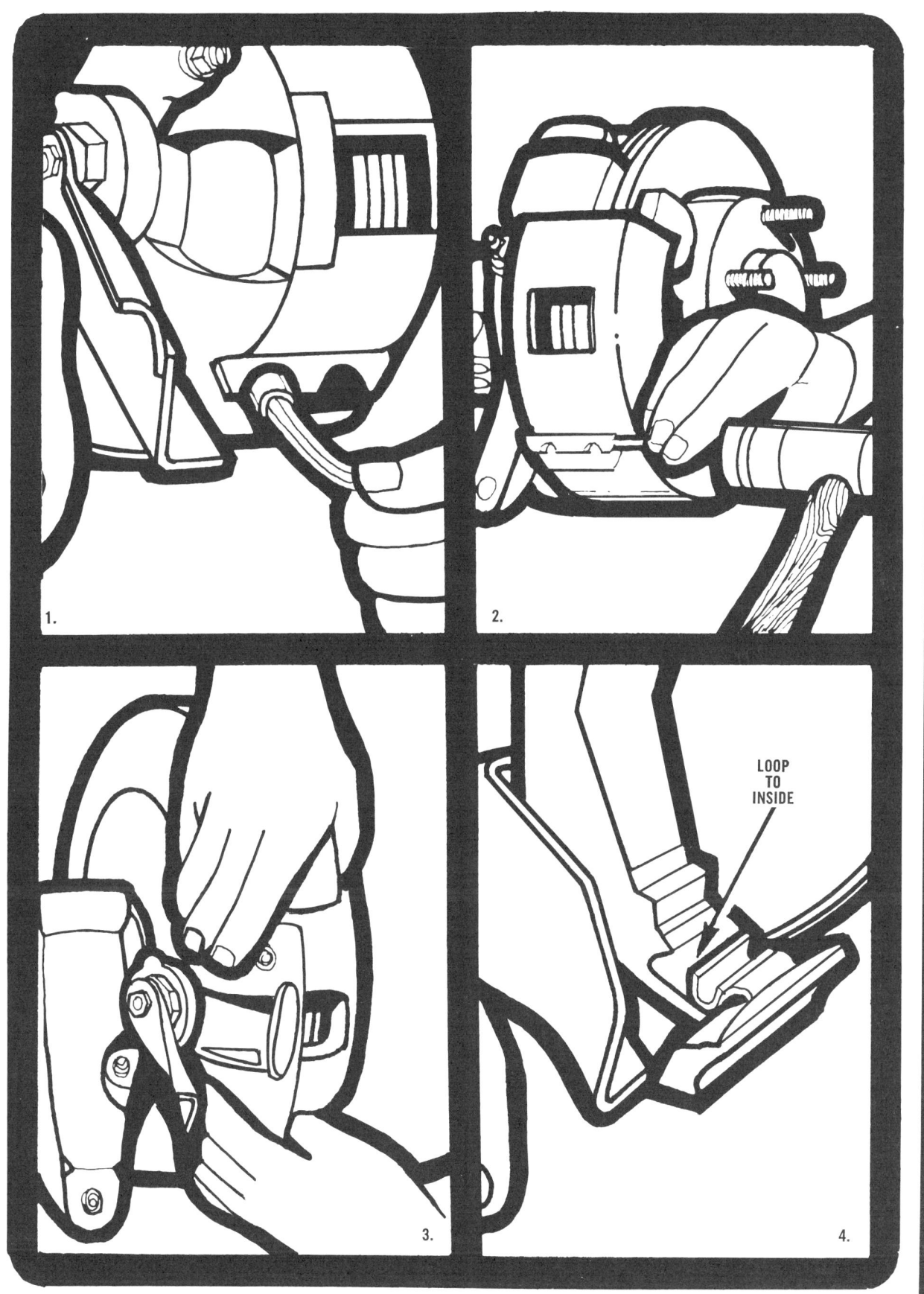

Fig. 38. Rear disc brake caliper removal procedure.

is a firm seating force, then remove the caliper from mounting plate and reinstall rotor.

13. Assure that the brake shoe, anti-rattle clip is in position in lower inner brake shoe support on anchor plate with loop of clip facing toward the inside of anchor plate, Fig. 38, step 4. Position inner brake shoe and pad assembly on anchor plate, Fig. 38, step 3.
14. Install the outer brake shoe and pad with lower flange ends against caliper abutments and brake shoe upper flanges over the shoulders of the caliper legs. The shoe upper flanges fit tightly against machined shoulder surfaces.

    NOTE: If the old brake shoe and pad assemblies are to be re-used, assure that shoes are installed in their original positions as marked for identification during removal.
15. Lubricate the caliper and anchor sliding ways with a suitable molydisulfide grease, using caution to prevent lubricant from getting on braking surfaces, then position caliper housing lower V-groove onto the anchor plate lower abutment surfaces.
16. Rotate the caliper until it is completely over the rotor, using caution not to damage piston dust boot. Then pull the caliper outboard until inner shoe and pad assembly is firmly seated against the rotor. Measure clearance between outer lining and rotor which should be 1/16-inch or less, Fig.

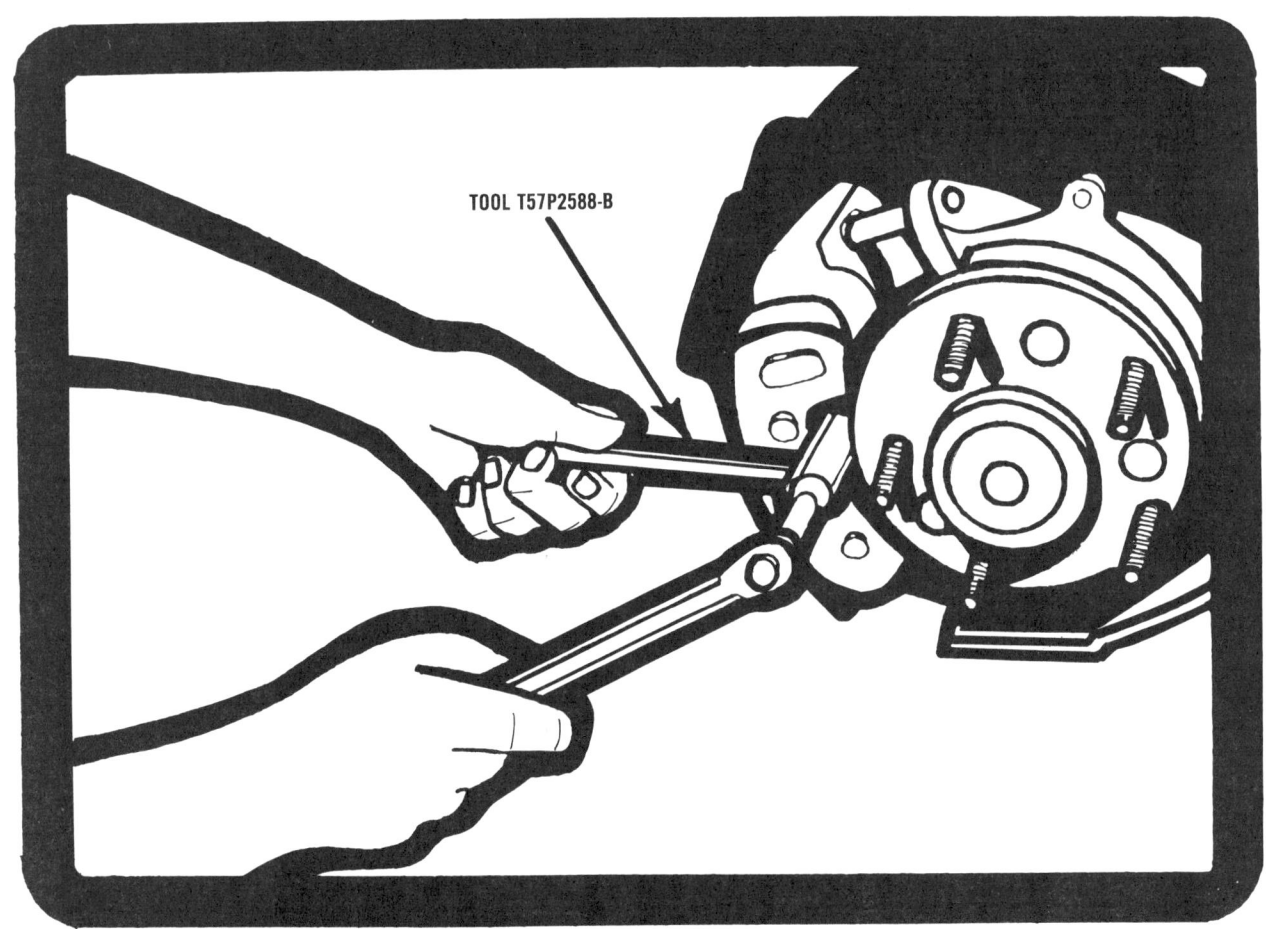

Fig. 39. Pushing piston into caliper housing for brake pad installation.

40. If it is greater, remove the caliper and move piston outward to narrow the gap. Follow procedure in step 12 and note that ¼-turn of the shaft counter-clockwise, moves the piston about 1/16-inch.

CAUTION: A clearance greater than 1/16-turn may allow adjuster to be pulled out of the piston when service brake is applied, causing parking brake to fail to adjust. It will then be necessary to replace piston/adjuster assembly.

17. While holding the caliper against the anchor plate upper abutment surfaces, center the caliper over the lower anchor plate abutment. Then position caliper support spring and key in slot and slide them into the opening between the lower end of the caliper and the lower anchor plate abutment until key semi-circular slot is centered over retaining screw threaded hole in anchor plate.

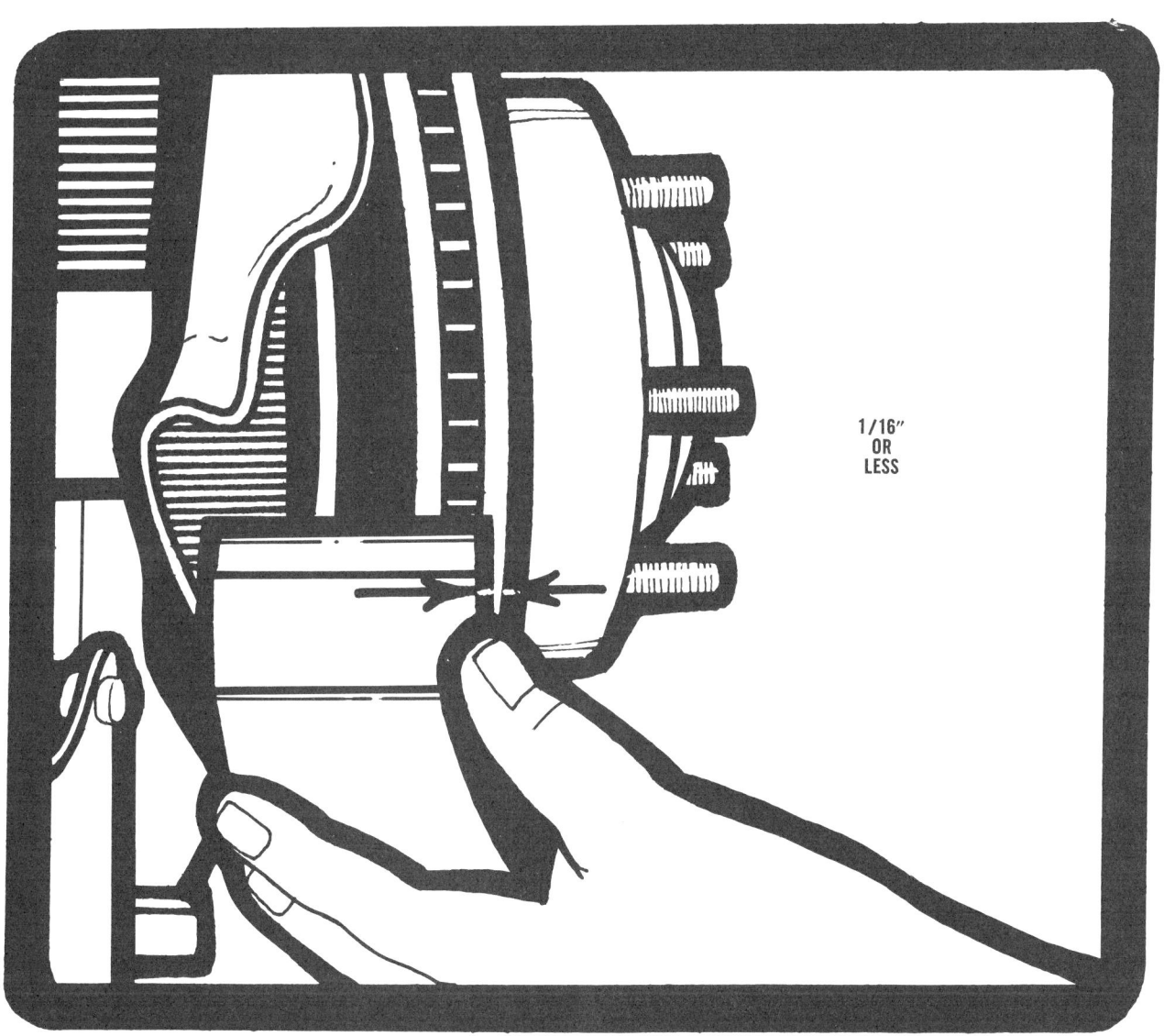

Fig. 40. Checking the brake pad clearance which should be 1/16-inch or less.

18. Install the key retaining screw and torque to 12-16 ft. lbs.
19. Connect the parking brake lever to the lever on the caliper.
20. Replace the tire and wheel assembly.
21. Install the tire and wheel assembly retaining nuts, then using the jack handle or correct size socket, tighten the retaining nuts.
22. Install the wheel covers. Use a rubber mallet and tap around the outer edge of the cover to fully seat it against the wheel.
23. Raise the vehicle using a suitable jack. Make sure to properly position the jack underneath the vehicle.
24. Remove the jack stands from underneath the vehicle and carefully lower the vehicle.

CAUTION: Before moving the vehicle, make certain that a firm brake pedal has been obtained.

BENDIX SLIDING CALIPER

Brake pad replacement, Fig. 41

8. Bottom the piston in the caliper bore by inserting a screwdriver between the inboard pad and piston. Then pry piston back into the caliper bore. The piston can be bottomed in the caliper bore using a C-clamp.
9. Using a ¼-inch Allen wrench, remove the support key retaining screw, Fig. 42. Drive caliper support key and spring from anchor plate with a suitable drift and hammer, Fig. 43.
10. Lift caliper off anchor plate and rotor, Fig. 44. Using a length of wire, support the caliper onto the spring to prevent caliper from falling and rupturing the hydraulic brake hose. Do not allow caliper to hang free.

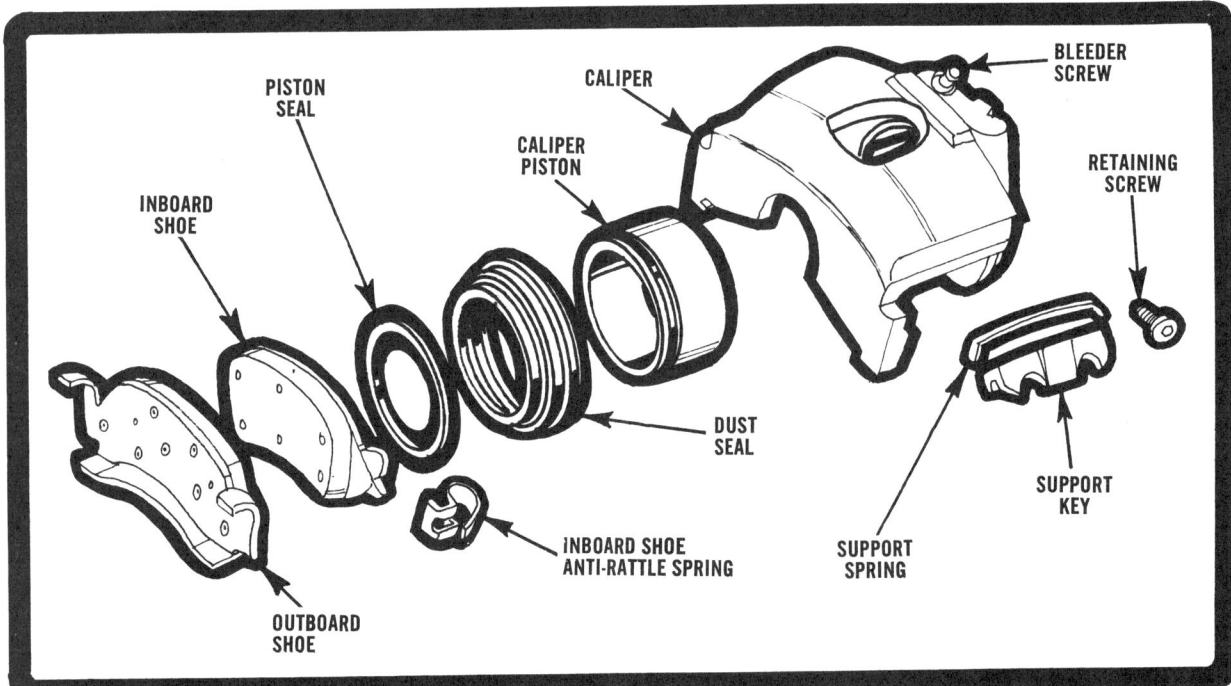

Fig. 41. Exploded view of caliper and brake shoe assemblies.

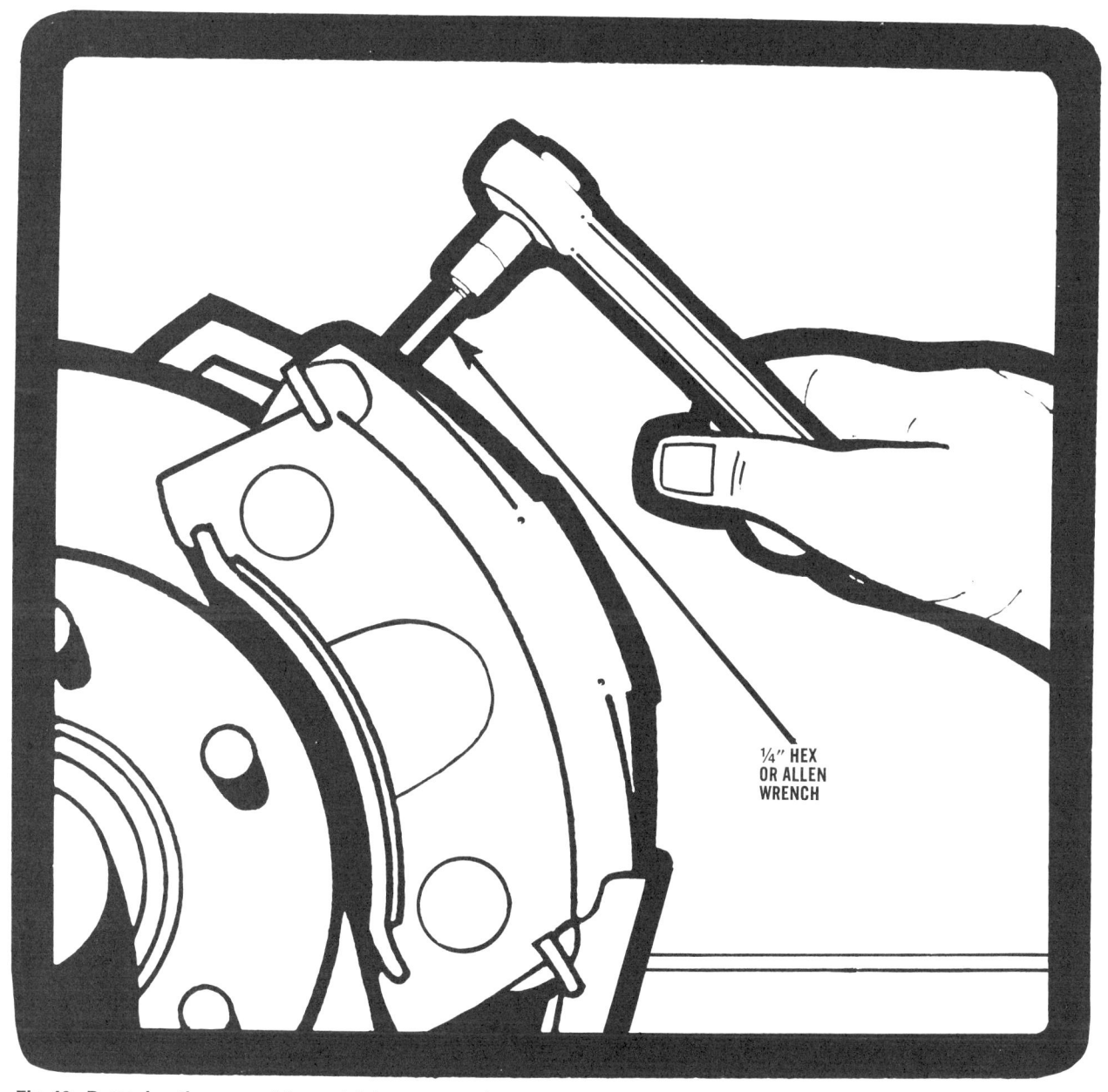

Fig. 42. Removing the support key retaining screw using a ¼-inch allen wrench.

TIPS FOR WORKING ON YOUR CAR'S BRAKES

- Do not begin the job unless you feel you are capable of completing it. Be honest with yourself about your mechanical capabilities.

- Before tackling the job, completely read through the instructions. Be familiar with what you will be doing and in what order.

- Have on hand all the tools you will need before beginning the job.

- Before beginning work, be absolutely positive your car is secure on safety jack stands or drive-on ramps. Do not use your bumper jack for under-car work.

- You are probably not qualified to work on your car's brake hydraulic system. Leave that part of it to a professional mechanic.

- After completing the job, begin your road test cautiously. Once you have established that you have braking power, thoroughly road test the vehicle.

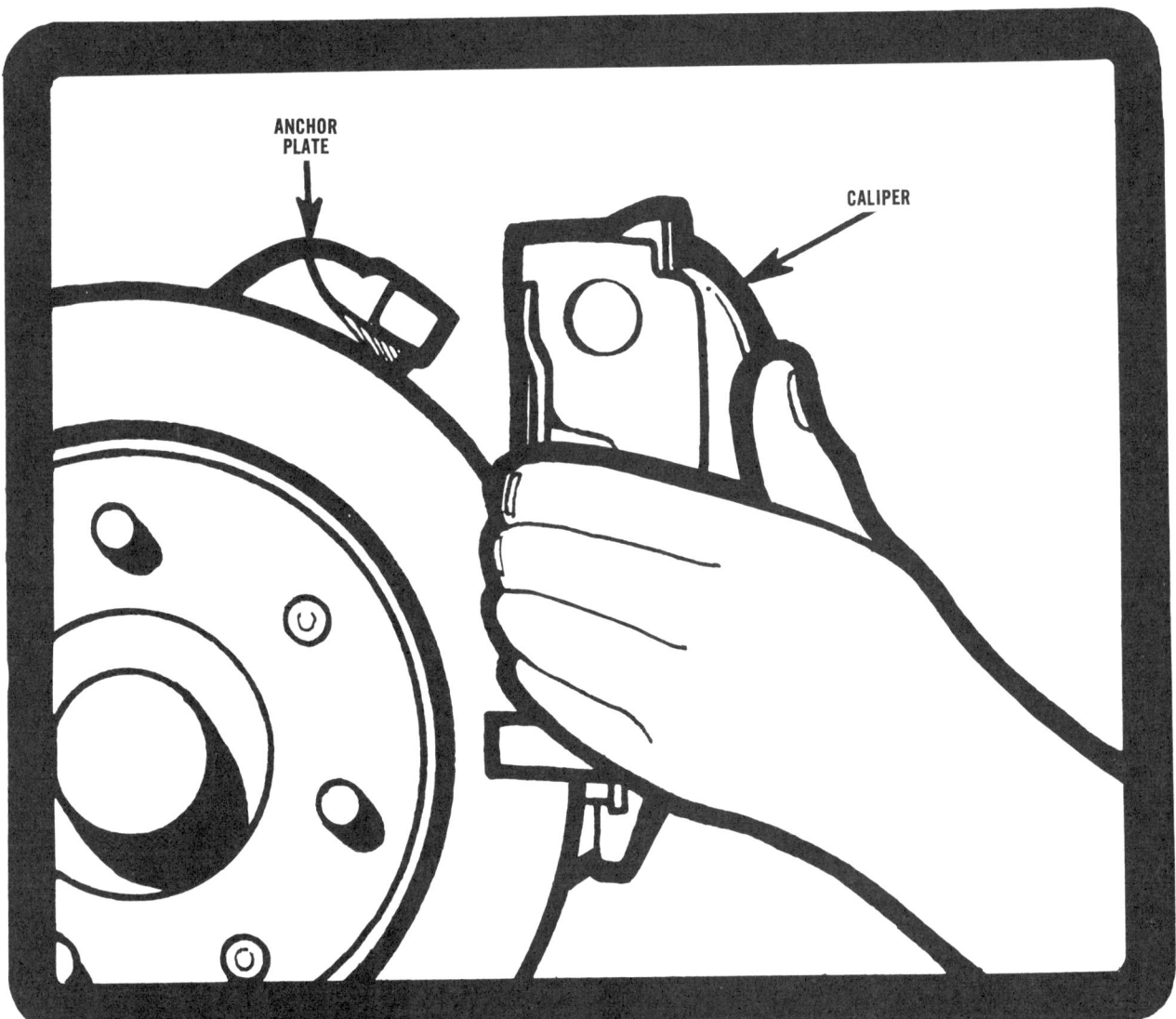

Fig. 43. Removing the support key.

11. Remove the inboard brake pad from the anchor plate, then remove the anti-rattle spring from the brake pad, Fig. 45.
12. Remove the outboard pad from the caliper, Fig. 46. It may be necessary to remove the pad by striking it gently with a hammer.
13. Clean and lubricate the abutment surfaces of the caliper and the anchor plate using molydisulphide grease.

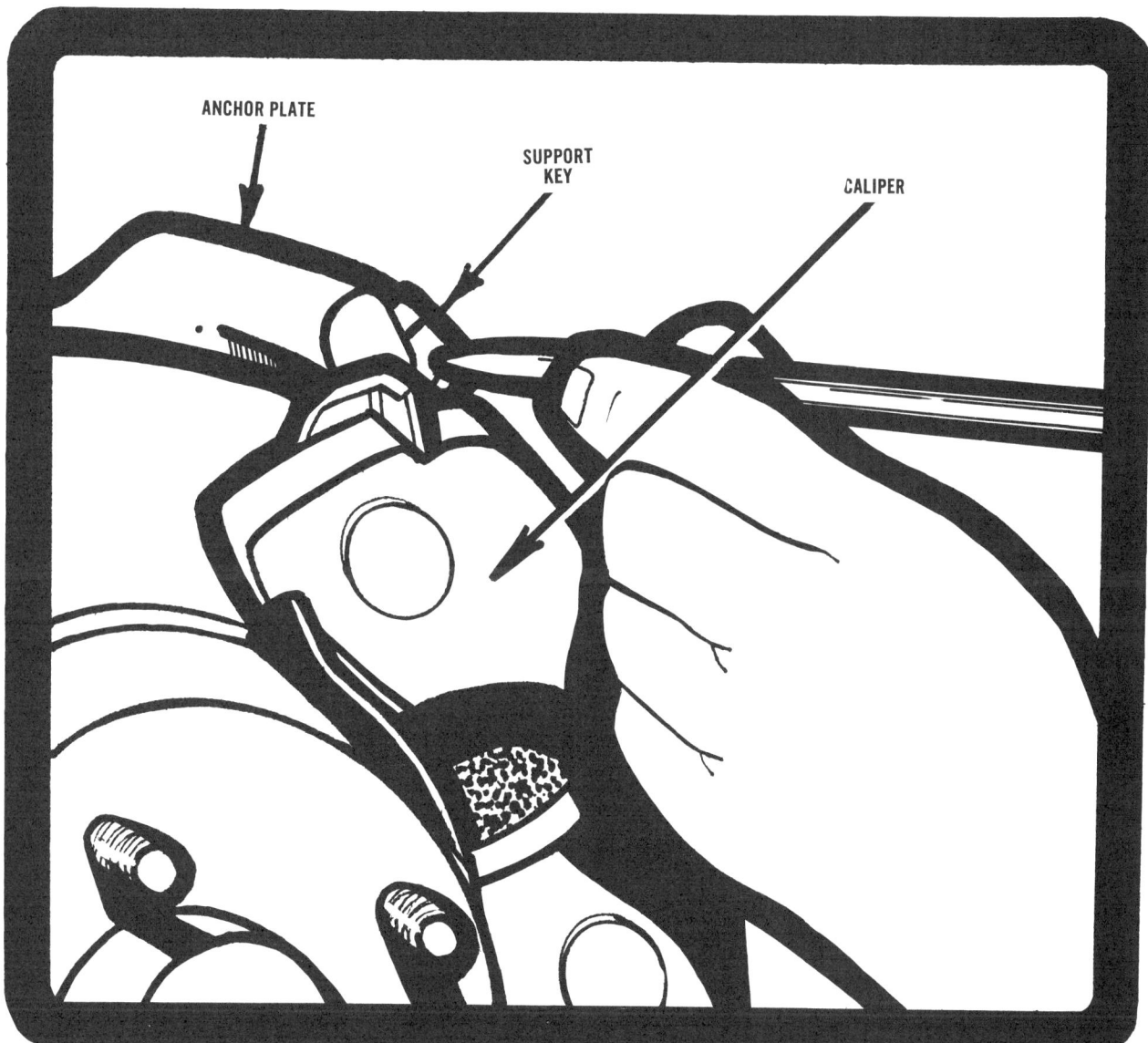

Fig. 44. Removing or installing the caliper assembly.

14. Install the inboard brake pad anti-rattle spring onto the brake pad rear flange, assuring that looped section of the clip is facing away from the rotor, Fig. 47.
15. Install the outboard brake pad into the caliper, Fig. 48, assuring that the brake pad flange is fully seated into the outboard arms of the caliper. It may be necessary to use a hammer to seat the pad.
16. Place the caliper assembly over the rotor and position it into the caliper anchor plate. Make sure that the dust boot is not torn or mispositioned by the inboard brake pad during installation.

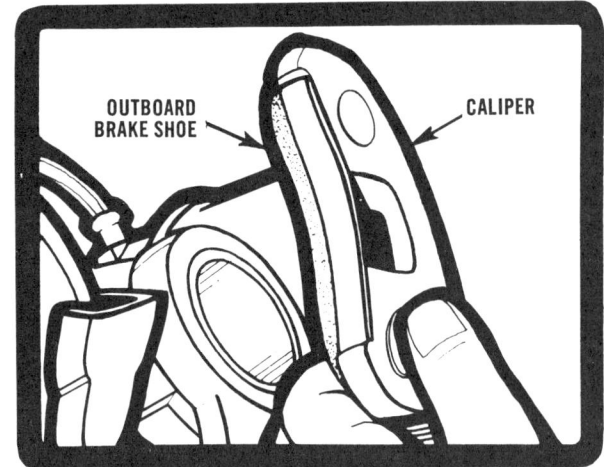

Fig. 46. Removing or installing the outboard brake shoe.

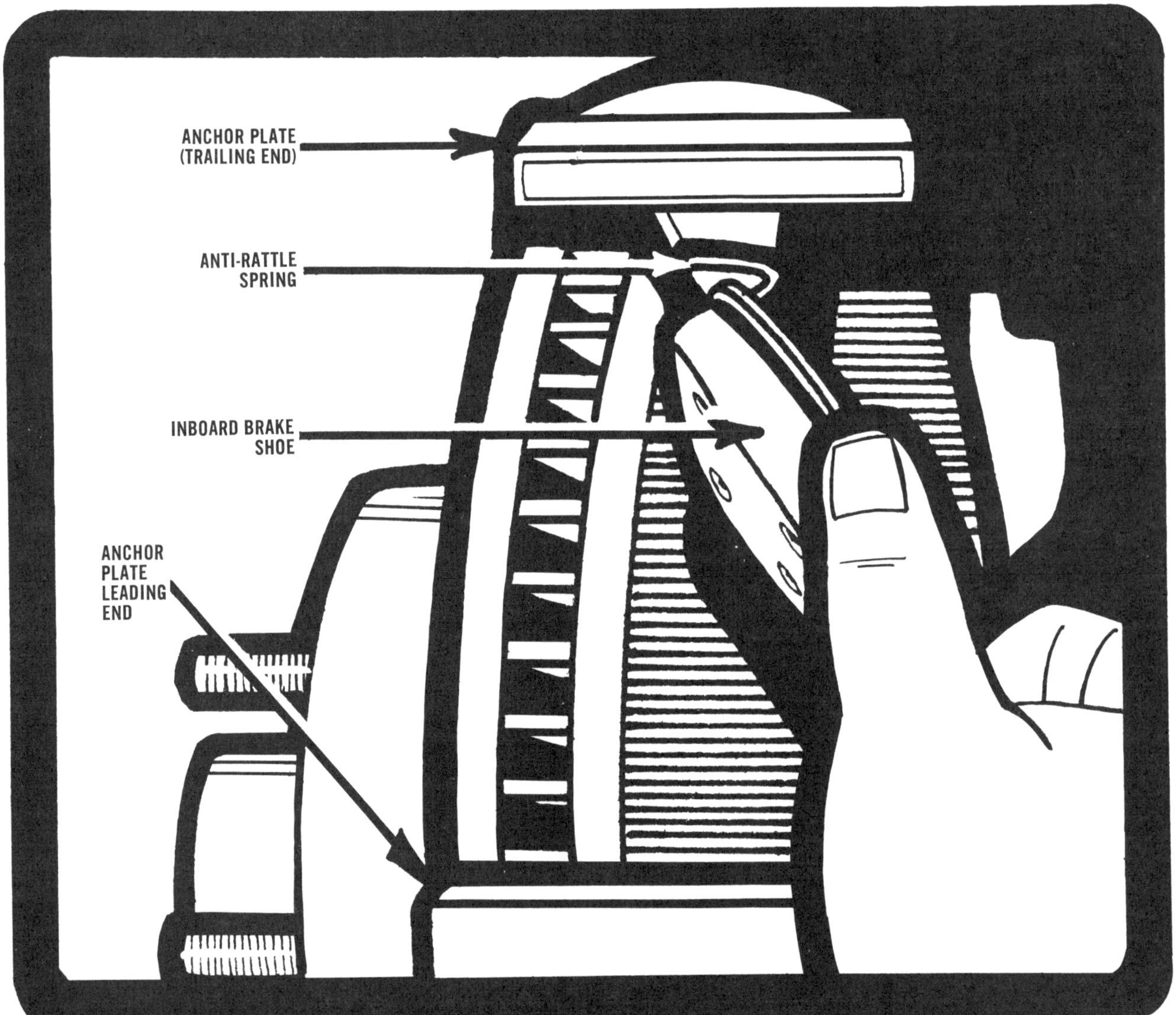

Fig. 45. Removing or installing the inboard brake shoe.

DISC BRAKE ROTOR SPECIFICATIONS

You can use these specifications to measure your disc brake rotor against manufacturer's specifications. If any variation is found, have the rotor checked by a professional mechanic.

CAR	Year	Nominal Thickness	Minimum Thickness	Thickness Variation Parallelism	Run-out (T.I.R.)	Finish (Micro-In.)
AMERICAN MOTORS						
	1969–70	.500	.450	.0005	.005	15–80
	1971–74	1.000	.940	.0005	.005	15–80
	1975	1.190	1.130	.0005	.003	20–60
BUICK (EXC. SKYHAWK)						
Full Size	1969	1.000	.965	.0005	.005	30–50
	1970	1.000	.965	.0005	.004	30–50
	1971–75	1.290	1.230	.0005	.005	30–80
Intermediate	1969–70	1.000	.965	.0005	.004	30–50
	1971–72	1.040	.980	.0005	.004	30–80
	1973–75	1.040	.980	.0005	⑤	30–80
CADILLAC						
Eldorado	1969–73	1.210	1.190	.0005	.008	15–80
	1974–75	—	1.190	.0005	—	—
Seville	1976	1.030	.980	.0005	.005	20–60
All others	1969–70	1.250	1.230	.0007	.002	15–80
	1971–72	1.240	1.220	.0007	.002	15–80
	1973	1.240	1.220	.0007	.005	15–80
	1974–75	—	1.220	.0005	.005	—
CHECKER						
	1969–70	1.240	1.215	.0007	.004	20–60
	1971–75	1.290	1.215	.0007	.005	20–60
CHEVROLET (EXC. MONZA & VEGA)						
Camaro & Chevelle	1969	1.000	.965	.0005	.004	30–50
	1970	1.000	.965	.0005	.002	30–50
	1971–75	1.035	.980	.0005	.005	20–60
Nova	1969	1.000	.965	.0005	.004	30–50
	1970	1.000	.965	.0005	.002	30–50
	1971–75	1.035	.980	.0005	.005	20–60
Chevrolet	1969	1.250	1.215	.0005	.004	30–50
	1970	1.250	1.215	.0005	.002	30–50
	1971–72	1.250	1.230	.0005	.005	20–60
	1973–75	1.285	1.230	.0005	.005	20–60
Corvette	1969–70	1.250	1.215	.0005	.004	30–50
	1971–75	1.250	1.230	.0005	.005	20–60
CHEVROLET VEGA & PONTIAC ASTRE						
	1971–72	.500	.470	.0005	.002	20–60
	1973–75	.500	.455	.0005	.002	20–60
CHRYSLER, DODGE & PLYMOUTH						
Full-Size Exc. Imperial	1969–70	1.250	1.200	.0005	.002	15–80
	1971–72	1.250	1.180	.0005	.002	15–80
	1973–75	1.250	1.180	.0005	.004	15–80
Imperial	1969	.877	—	—	.005	30–60
	1970	1.250	1.200	.0005	.002	15–80
	1971–72	1.250	1.180	.0005	.002	15–80
	1973–75	③	④	.0005	.004	15–80
Intermediate (Exc. Below)	1969	.886	.816	.0005	.005	40
	1970	1.000	.980	.0005	.002	15–80
	1971–72	1.000	.940	.0005	.002	15–80
	1973–75	1.000	.940	.0005	.004	15–80
Dart & Valiant	1969–72	.810	—	.0005	.002	15–80
	1973–75	1.000	.940	.0005	.004	15–80
Challenger & Barracuda	1969	.810	—	.0005	.002	15–80
	1970	1.000	.980	.0005	.002	15–80
	1971–72	1.000	.940	.0005	.002	15–80
	1973–75	1.000	.940	.0005	.004	15–80
FORD MOTOR COMPANY						
Ford & Mercury Full Size	1969	1.185	1.140	.0007	.002	15–80
	1970–72	1.180	1.120	.0007	.003	15–80
	1973–75	1.180⑦	1.120⑧	.0005②	.003⑨	15–80
Ford & Mercury Intermediate	1969	.940	.895	.0007	.002	15–80
	1970–73	.935	.875	.0007	.002	15–80
	1972⑥	1.180	1.120	.0007	.003	15–80
	1973–75①	1.180	1.120	.0005	.003	15–80
Comet & Maverick	1974–75	.870	.810	.0005	.003	15–80
Granada & Monarch	1975	.870⑦	.810⑧	.0005	.003④	15–80
Lincoln	1969	1.245	1.215	.0007	.002	15–80
	1970–72	1.180	1.120	.0007	.003	15–80
	1973–75	1.180	1.120	.0005	.003	15–80
	1974–75	1.180⑦	1.120⑧	.0025	.003⑨	15–80
Mark III, IV & Thunderbird	1969	1.185	1.140	.0007	.002	15–80
	1970–72	1.180	1.120	.0007	.003	15–80
	1973–75	1.180⑦	1.120⑧	.00025⑩	.003⑨	15–80
Mustang II, Pinto & Bobcat	1971–73	.750	.685	.0007	.003	15–80
	1974–75	.870	.810	.0005	.003	15–80
MONZA, SKYHAWK & STARFIRE						
	1975	.500	.455	.0005	.005	20–60
OLDSMOBILE (EXC. STARFIRE)						
Oldsmobile	1969	1.250	1.215	.0005	.004	30–50
	1970	1.250	1.215	.0007	.002	30–50
	1971–72	1.290	1.215	.0005	.002	30–50
	1973–75	1.290	1.215	.0005	.005	30–50
Olds F-85, Cutlass Omega	1969	1.000	.965	.0005	.004	30–50
	1970	1.035	.965	.0005	.004	30–50
	1971–75	1.040	.965	.0005	.004	30–50
Olds Toronado	1969	1.250	1.215	.0005	.004	30–50
	1970	1.250	1.215	.0005	.002	30–50
	1971–75	1.245	1.170	.0005	.002	30–50
PONTIAC (EXC. ASTRE)						
Pontiac Full Size	1969	1.240	1.195	.0007	.004	20–60
	1970–71	1.250	1.215	.0007	.004	20–60
	1972–75	1.285	1.215	.0007	.004	20–60
Pontiac Intermediate Exc. Firebird & Ventura	1969	1.000	.960	.0007	.004	20–60
	1970–71	1.085	.965	.0007	.004	20–60
	1972–75	1.035	.965	.0007	.004	20–60
Pontiac Firebird	1969	1.000	.960	.0007	.004	20–60
	1970	1.040	.965	.0005	.005	30–80
	1971	1.085	.965	.0007	.004	20–60
	1972–75	1.035	.965	.0007	.004	20–60
Ventura II	1971–73	1.035	.980	.0005	.004	20–60
	1974–75	1.035	.965	.0007	.004	20–60

①—Montego, Torino & 1974–75 Cougar.
②—1974–75 Mercury, Front disc. .0004, 1975 rear disc. .0005.
③—Front, 1.250; Rear, 1.000.
④—Front, 1.180; Rear, .940.
⑤—Exc. Apollo .004; Apollo .005.
⑥—Montego & Torino.
⑦—1975 rear disc. .945.
⑧—1975 rear disc. .895.
⑨—1975 rear disc. .004.
⑩—1975 rear disc. .0004

17. Align the anchor with the caliper plate abutment surfaces. Then insert the support key and spring between the abutment surfaces at the trailing end of the caliper and the anchor plate. Using a hammer and brass drift, drive the caliper support key and spring into position. Then install and torque the support key retaining screw to 15 ft. lbs.
18. Add brake fluid to master cylinder to bring level to within ¼-inch from the top. Pump brake pedal several times to seat pads against the rotor.
19. Replace the tire and wheel assembly.

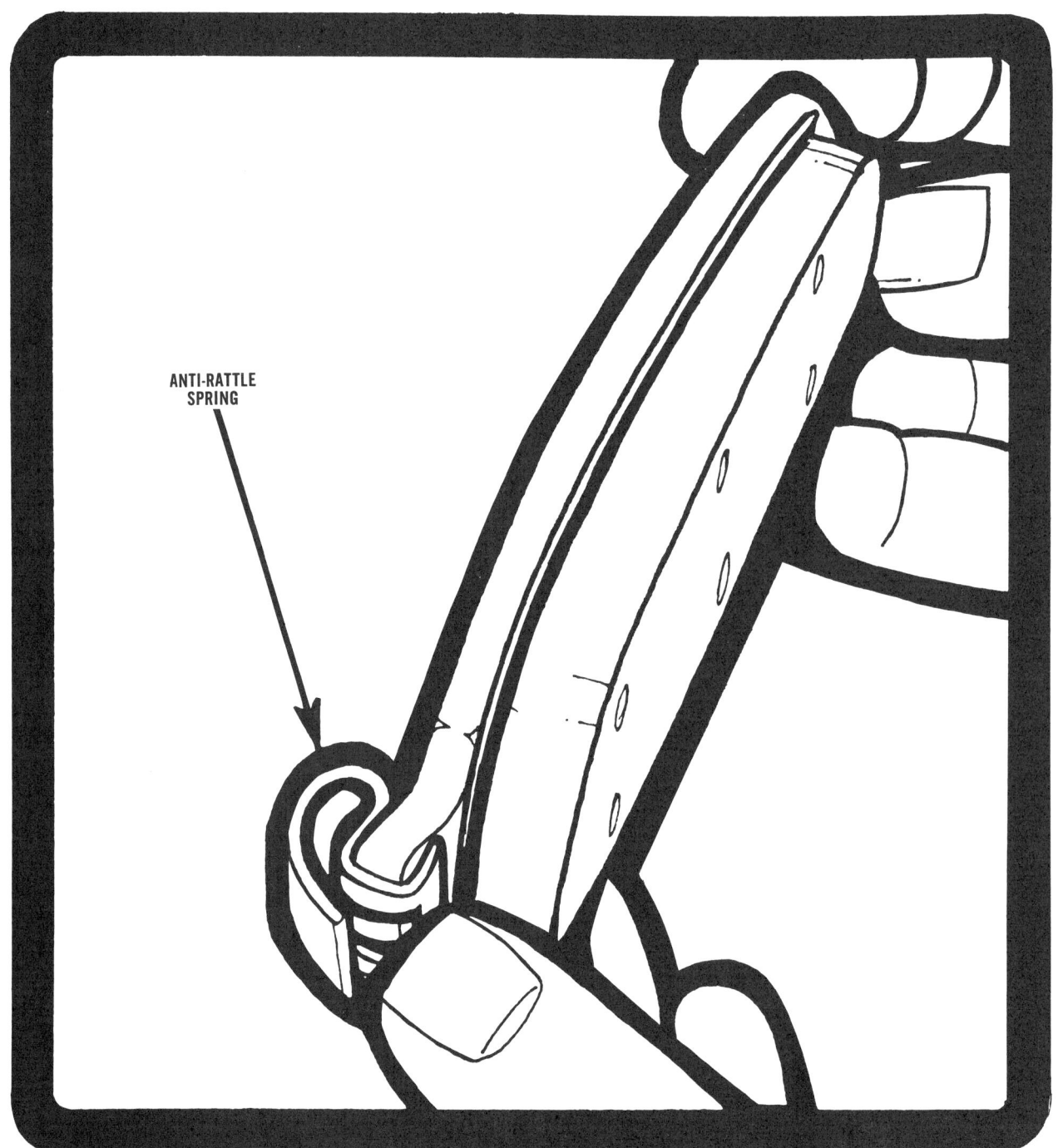

Fig. 47. Installing the inboard brake shoe and anti-rattle spring.

20. Install the tire and wheel assembly retaining nuts, then using the jack handle or correct size socket, tighten the retaining nuts.
21. Install the wheel covers. Use a rubber mallet and tap around the outer edge of the cover to fully seat it against the wheel.
22. Raise the vehicle using a suitable jack. Make sure to properly position the jack underneath the vehicle.
23. Remove the jack stands from underneath the vehicle and carefully lower the vehicle.

CAUTION: Before moving the vehicle, make certain that a firm brake pedal has been obtained.

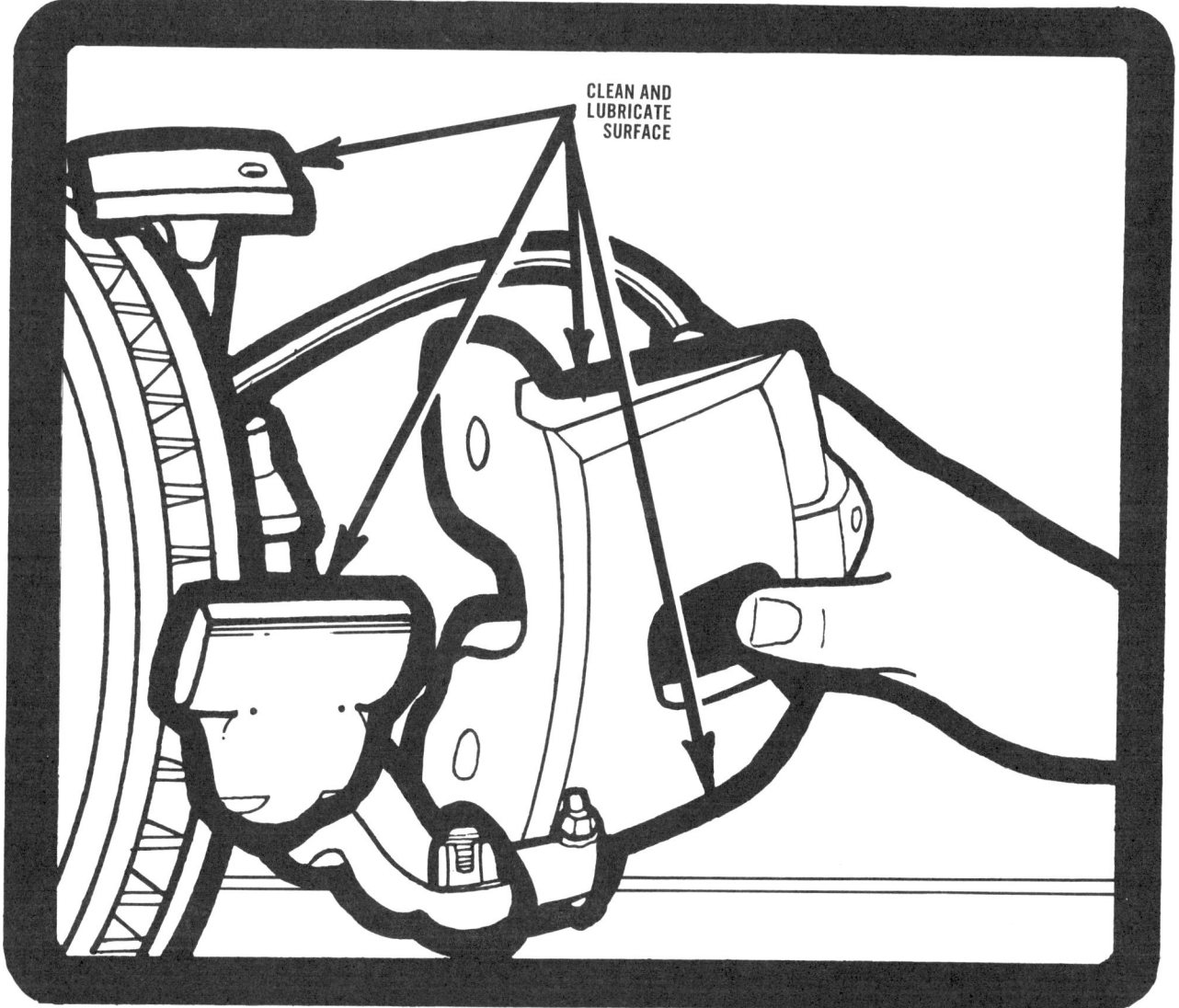

Fig. 48. Caliper and anchor plate abutment surfaces.

DRUM BRAKE ADJUSTMENT SERVICE

GENERAL PROCEDURES FOR ALL MODELS

Before adjusting the service brake and parking brake, the following steps must be carefully followed:
1. Chock the wheels which are not being worked on.
2. If working on the front wheels, place the transmission in first gear for manual transmission vehicles and Park for automatic transmission vehicles.
3. Raise the vehicle using a suitable jack. Make sure you properly position the jack underneath the vehicle.

   CAUTION: The jack supplied with the vehicle is intended for tire changing purposes only and should not be used to raise the vehicle. It is unstable and usually cannot raise the vehicle sufficiently so that jack safety stands can be placed underneath the vehicle.

4. Properly position a jack safety stand underneath each frame rail and carefully lower the vehicle.

   CAUTION: Be careful when positioning jack stands. When improperly positioned, jack stands can damage metal tubing, rubber hoses or electrical wiring which usually runs along the frame rails. Also, do not place jack stands in such a manner that when the vehicle is lowered, the vehicle will be suspended by the steering components, such as the idler arm, drag link, tie rod ends, etc. This can bend the steering components and cause the front end to become misaligned.

NOTE: For vehicles that will require removal of the tire and wheel assembly, proceed as follows:

5. Using the tapered end of the jack handle or a large flat blade screwdriver remove the wheel covers.
6. Using the jack handle or a socket of the correct size, remove the wheel and tire assembly retaining nuts.

   NOTE: Some vehicles use lefthand threaded studs and nuts, and will require that the nuts be turned clockwise for removal. These studs can usually be identified by an L stamped on the exposed end of the stud.

7. Remove the tire and wheel assembly.

AT THIS POINT, GO DIRECTLY TO THE ADJUSTMENT PROCEDURES FOR YOUR SPECIFIC MAKE OF CAR.

AMERICAN MOTORS

Service brakes

These brakes use automatic brake adjusters. To adjust the brakes, drive the vehicle in reverse and make 10-15 hard stops. This will adjust the brakes and bring the brake pedal up to an acceptable height. If the brake pedal fails to reach an acceptable height, the automatic brake adjusters are malfunctioning. Have your mechanic remove the drums and correct the malfunction.

Parking brakes

1. Raise and support the vehicle as described previously.
2. Make sure that service brakes are properly adjusted.
3. On **1969 Rambler** models, pull the parking brake handle to the third notch from the fully released position. On **1969-76 AMC** cars except **1969 Rambler** models, apply the parking brake pedal to the first notch from the fully released position.
4. Tighten the parking brake cable at the equalizer, Fig. 49, to a point where the rear wheels are locked when forward motion of the wheels is attempted by hand rotation.
5. Release the parking brake handle. The rear wheels should rotate freely.

AT THIS POINT, GO DIRECTLY TO THE FINAL PROCEDURES. THEY ARE LOCATED LATER ON IN THIS CHAPTER.

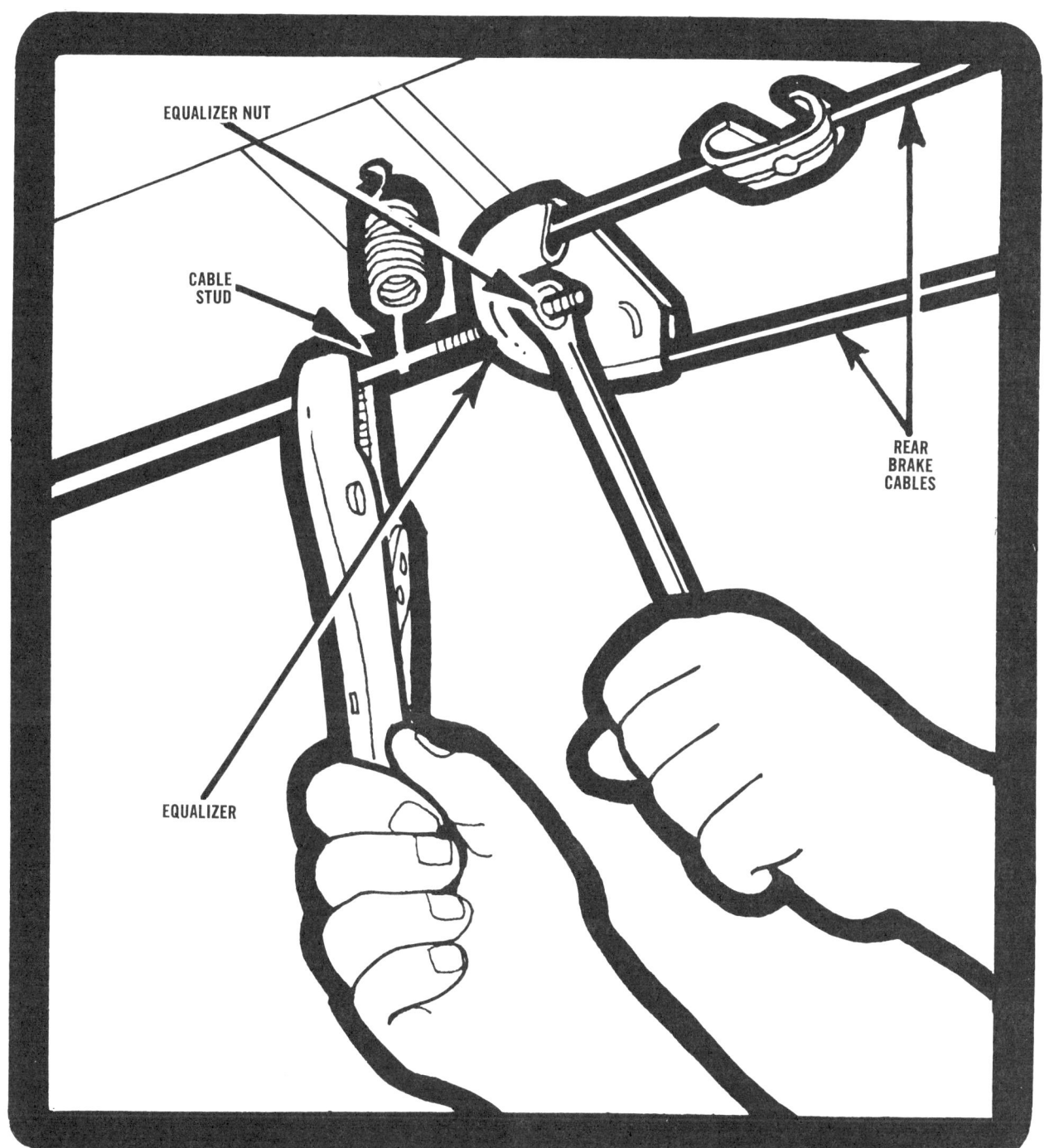

Fig. 49.

CHRYSLER CORP.

Service brakes

1. Raise the vehicle and support it, and remove the tire and wheel assembly as describd previously.
2. Each backing plate has two adjusting hole covers, Fig. 50. Remove the rear cover and turn the adjusting screw upward with a screwdriver or other suitable tool to expand the shoes until a slight drag is felt when the drum is rotated.
3. Remove the drum.
4. While holding the adjusting lever out of engagement with the adjusting screw, back off the adjusting screw about one turn with the fingers.

   NOTE: If finger movement will not turn the screw, free it up. If this is not done, the adjusting lever will not turn the screw during subsequent vehicle operation. Lubricate the screw with oil and coat with wheel bearing grease.
5. Install wheel and drum, and adjusting hole cover. Adjust brakes on remaining wheels in the same manner.
6. If pedal height is not satisfactory, drive the vehicle and make sufficient reverse stops until proper pedal height is obtained.
7. Replace the tire and wheel assembly and lower the vehicle as directed previously.

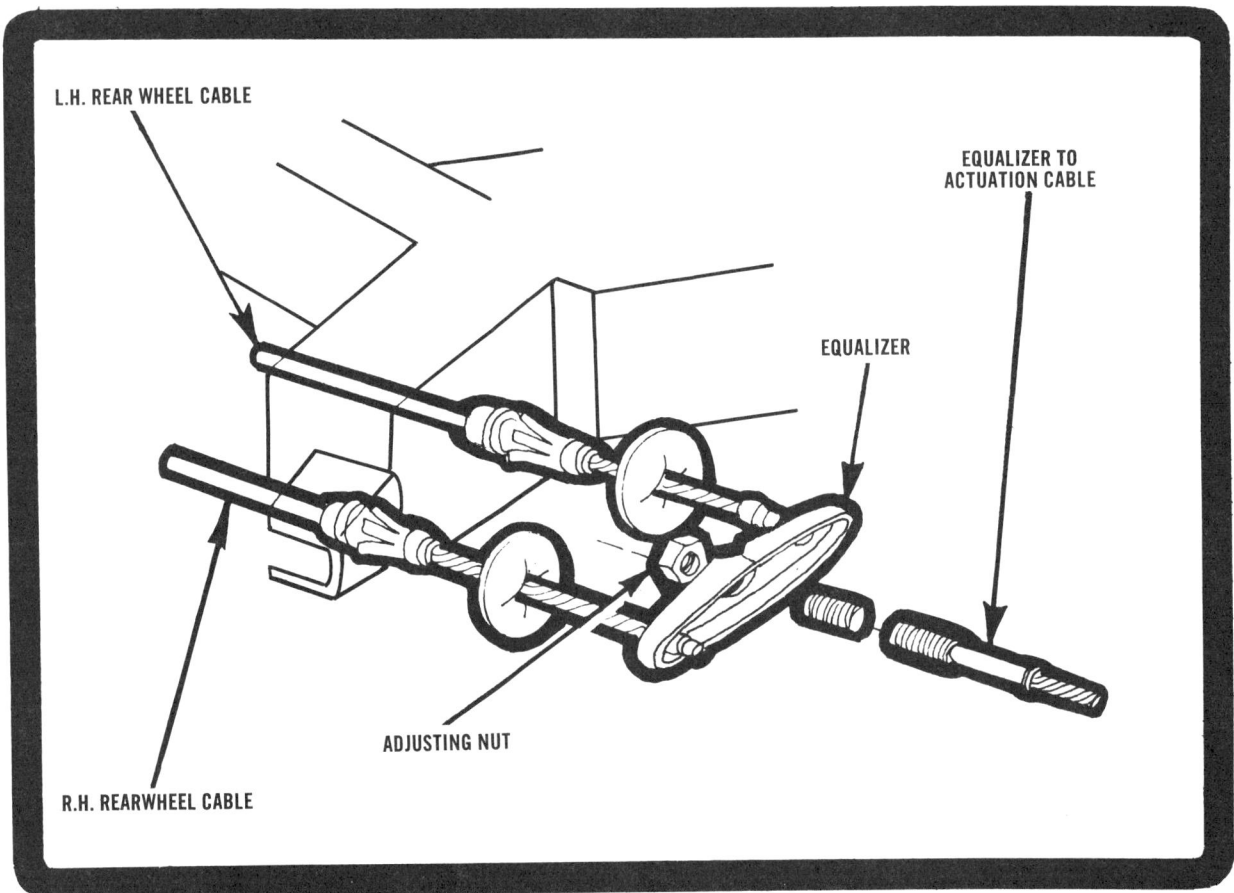

Fig. 50.

Parking brakes

1. Raise and support the vehicle as described previously.
2. Release parking brake lever and loosen cable adjusting nut to be sure cable is slack.
3. With rear wheel brakes properly adjusted, tighten cable adjusting nut, Fig. 49, until a slight drag is felt when the rear wheels are rotated. Then loosen the cable adjusting nut until both rear wheels can be rotated freely.
4. To complete the operation, back off an additional two turns of the cable adjusting nut.
5. Apply and release parking brake several times to be sure rear wheels are not dragging when cable is in released position.

AT THIS POINT, GO DIRECTLY TO THE FINAL PROCEDURES. THEY ARE LOCATED LATER ON IN THIS CHAPTER.

FORD MOTOR COMPANY

Service brakes

1. Raise and support the vehicle and remove the tire and wheel assembly as described previously.
2. Remove the brake adjustment access hole cover from the back of the brake support plate.
3. Using a brake adjusting tool or suitable size flat screwdriver, Fig. 50, rotate the adjusting screw upward to expand the brake shoes, until a slight drag is felt when the drum is rotated.
4. Install the tire and wheel assembly and lower the vehicle.
5. Complete the adjustment by driving the vehicle in reverse and applying the brake pedal several times with a minimum of 50 psi pressure on non-power brakes and a minimum of 25 psi pressure on power brakes. After each stop, drive the vehicle forward.
6. After the brake shoes have been properly adjusted, check the operation of the brakes by making several stops from varying speeds.

Parking brakes
1969 all models
1. Fully release parking brake.
2. Pull brake handle out to third notch from fully released position.
3. Raise and support the vehicle and remove the wheel cover as described previously.
4. Turn locking adjustment nut forward against cable guide on equalizer, Fig. 50, until you feel a heavy drag when turning rear wheels in direction of forward rotation.
5. Release parking brake and make sure brake shoes return to fully released position and no drag is felt when turning rear wheels.

AT THIS POINT, GO DIRECTLY TO THE FINAL PROCEDURES. THEY ARE LOCATED LATER ON IN THIS CHAPTER.

1970-76 all models
1. Raise and support vehicle as described previously.
2. Make sure parking brake is released.
3. Place transmission in neutral.
4. Tighten the adjusting nut against the cable equalizer, Fig. 50, to cause rear brakes to drag.
5. Then loosen the adjusting nut until the rear wheels are fully released. There should be no drag.

AT THIS POINT, GO DIRECTLY TO THE FINAL PROCEDURES. THEY ARE LOCATED LATER ON IN THIS CHAPTER.

GENERAL MOTORS
BUICK EXCEPT SKYHAWK

Service brakes

1. Raise and support vehicle as described previously.
2. Remove adjusting hole cover from backing plate. Turn brake adjusting screw to expand shoes until wheel can just be turned by hand.
3. Use suitable adjusting tool or flat screwdriver, Fig. 50, to hold actuator away from adjuster. Then back off adjuster 30 notches. If shoes still drag, back off one or two additional notches.

   NOTE: Brakes should be free of drag when adjuster has been backed off approximately 12 notches. Heavy drag at this point indicates tight parking brake cables.

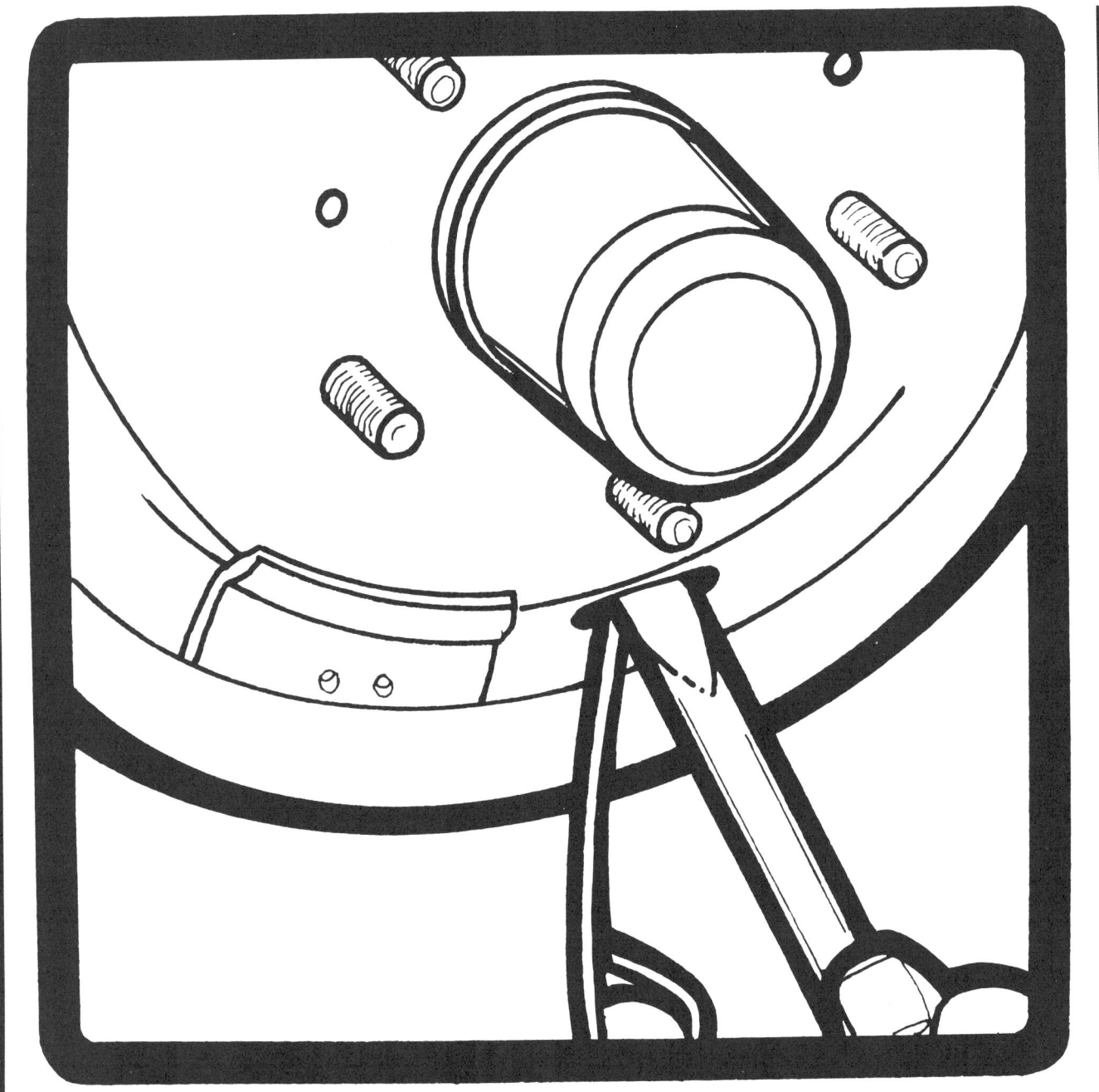

Fig. 51.

4. Install adjusting hole cover and check parking brake adjustment.
5. Adjust the brakes on the remaining wheels in the same manner.
6. After completing final step procedures, if the brake pedal height is not satisfactory, drive the vehicle in reverse and make several hard stops, until the proper brake pedal height is obtained.

Parking brakes

1. Depress parking brake exactly three ratchet clicks on all except Apollo and 1974-76 Estate Wagon, two ratchet clicks on Apollo and six ratchet clicks on the 1974-76 Estate Wagon.
2. Raise and support vehicle as described previously.
3. Loosen jam nut, and tighten adjusting nut, Fig. 49, until rear wheels can just be turned rearward using both hands but are locked when forward motion is attempted.
4. Tighten jam nut and release parking brake. Rear wheels should turn freely in either direction with no brake drag.

AT THIS POINT, GO DIRECTLY TO THE FINAL PROCEDURES. THEY ARE LOCATED LATER ON IN THIS CHAPTER.

CADILLAC

Service brakes

1. Raise and support vehicle and remove the tire and wheel assembly as described previously.
2. Check fluid level in master cylinder and add fluid as necessary to a level ¼-inch below top of reservoir.
3. Check to make certain that parking brake cable and linkage, including levers on rear secondary shoes, are free.
4. Tighten star wheel, Fig. 52, until brake drums can just be rotated forward with a 2-foot bar placed between wheel studs.
5. Disengage adjusting pawl from star wheel with a hooked tool, Fig. 51 and 52, and back off star wheel 40 notches.
6. After completing final step procedures, alternately drive the vehicle in forward, and then in reverse. Moderately apply the brakes in each direction until the brake pedal height is normal and brakes are adjusted satisfactory.

Parking brakes

1. With service brakes properly adjusted, lubricate parking brake linkage at equalizer and cable stud with heat-resistant lubricant. Check for free movement of cables.
2. Depress parking brake pedal about 1¾-inches from full released position.
3. Raise and support the vehicle as described previously.
4. Hold brake cable and stud from turning and tighten equalizer nut, Fig. 49, until a slight drag is felt on either wheel (going forward). After each turn of equalizer nut, check to see if either wheel begins to drag.
5. Release parking brake. No brake drag should be felt at either rear wheel. Operate several times to check adjustment. After adjustment is completed, parking brake pedal should travel 1¾-inches to 2¾-inches.

AT THIS POINT, GO DIRECTLY TO THE FINAL PROCEDURES. THEY ARE LOCATED LATER ON IN THIS CHAPTER.

CHEVROLET EXCEPT CHEVETTE, MONZA and VEGA

Service brakes

1. Raise and support the vehicle and remove the tire and wheel assembly as described previously.
   NOTE: A lanced knock out area is provided in the web of the brake drum for servicing purposes in the event retracting of the brake shoes is required in order to remove the drum.
2. Remove the brake drum. Disengage the actuator from the star wheel and rotate the star wheel by spinning or turning with a screwdriver.
3. Using the brake drum as an adjustment fixture, turn the star wheel until the drum slides over the brake shoes with a slide drag.
4. Turn the star wheel 1¼ turns to retract the brake shoes. This will allow sufficient lining-to-drum clearance so final adjustment may be made.
5. Install the drum.

NOTE: If lanced area in brake drum was knocked out, be sure all metal has been removed from brake compartment. Install new hole cover in drum to prevent contamination of brakes. Make certain that drums are installed in the same position as when removed with the drum locating tang in line with the locating hole in the wheel hub.

6. After completing the final procedures, make final adjustment by driving and stopping in forward and reverse until satisfactory pedal height is obtained.

Parking brakes
1. Raise and support the vehicle as described previously.
2. Apply parking brake two notches from fully released position.
3. Loosen equalizer forward check nut and tighten rear nut until a light to moderate drag is felt when rear wheels are rotated.
4. Tighten check nuts securely.
5. Fully release parking brake and rotate rear wheels; no drag should be present.

AT THIS POINT, GO DIRECTLY TO THE FINAL PROCEDURES. THEY ARE LOCATED LATER ON IN THIS CHAPTER.

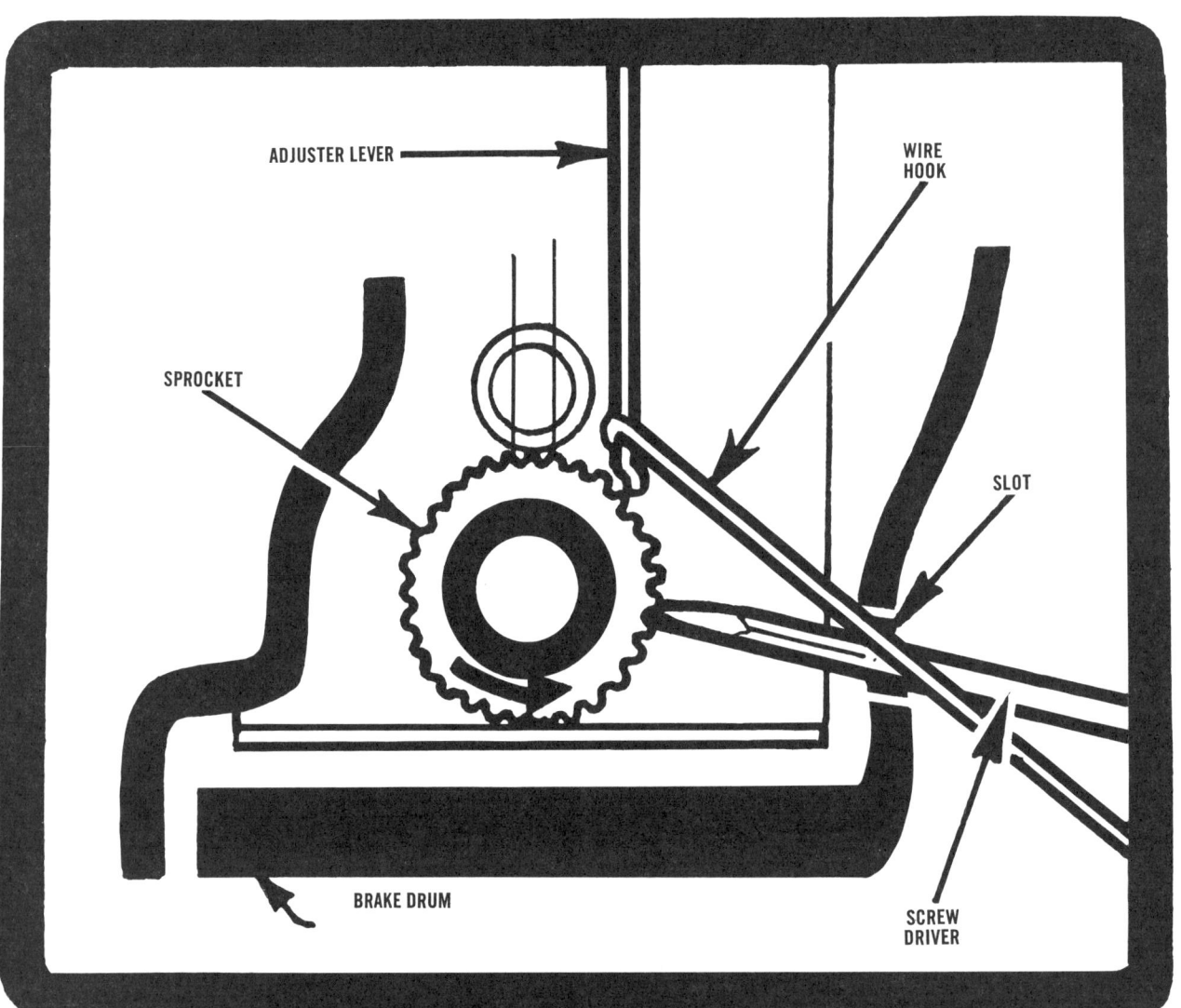

Fig. 52.

OLDSMOBILE EXCEPT STARFIRE

Service brakes
1. Raise and support vehicle and remove tire and wheel assembly as described previously.
2. Remove brake drum.
3. Rotate adjuster, Fig. 50, to expand the brake shoes until brake drum can be installed with just a slight drag.
4. Install brake drum.
5. After completion of the final procedures, make final adjustment by driving the vehicle in reverse. Make several hard stops until the brake pedal height is satisfactory and the brakes are properly adjusted.

Parking brakes
1. Raise and support vehicle as described previously.
2. Fully release the parking brake.
3. Tighten the brake equalizer adjusting nut, Fig. 49, until a heavy resistance is felt while the wheels are being rotated forward.
4. Loosen equalizer adjusting nut 7 full turns.

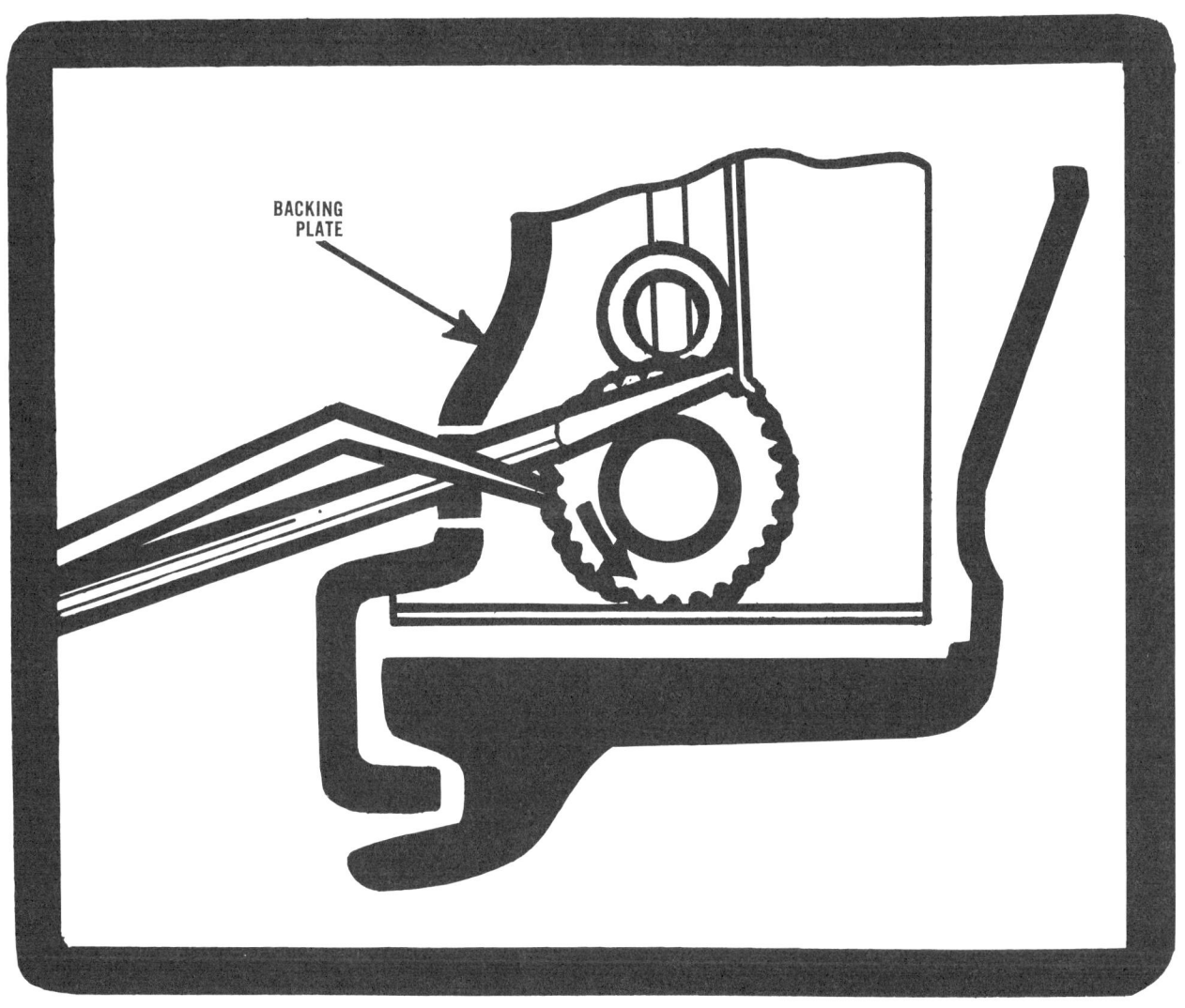

PONTIAC EXCEPT ASTRE

Service brakes
1. Raise and support the vehicle and remove the tire and wheel assembly as described previously.
2. Remove adjusting hole cover from brake backing plate and, from backing plate side, turn adjusting screw upward with a flat screwdriver or adjusting tool, Fig. 50, to expand the shoes until a slight drag is felt when the drum is rotated.
3. Remove brake drum.
4. While holding adjusting lever out of engagement with the adjusting screw, back off the adjusting screw one full turn with the fingers.

Parking brakes
1. Raise and support the vehicle as described previously.
2. Pull parking brake pedal five to seven notches from fully released position.
3. Loosen equalizer rear lock nut. Adjust forward nut, Fig. 49, until a light to moderate drag is felt when rear wheels are rotated.
4. Tighen lock nut. Fully release parking brake and rotate rear wheels to be sure there is no drag.

AT THIS POINT, GO DIRECTLY TO THE FINAL PROCEDURES. THEY ARE LOCATED LATER ON IN THIS CHAPTER.

AT THIS POINT, GO DIRECTLY TO THE FINAL PROCEDURES. THEY ARE LOCATED LATER ON IN THIS CHAPTER.

CHEVETTE, MONZA, SKYHAWK, STARFIRE and VEGA

Service brakes
1. Raise and support vehicle as described previously.
2. Apply parking brake one notch from the fully released position.
3. Loosen equalizer check nut and tighten the adjusting nut until a slight drag is felt when rear wheels are rotated.
4. Tighten check nut securely.
5. Release parking brake and rotate rear wheels. No drag should be present.

AT THIS POINT, GO DIRECTLY TO THE FINAL PROCEDURES.

FINAL PROCEDURES

After the service brakes and parking brakes have been adjusted, proceed as follows:
1. Replace the tire and wheel assembly.
2. Install the tire and wheel assembly retaining nuts. Then using the jack handle or correct size socket, tighten the retaining nuts.
3. Install the wheel covers. Use a rubber mallet and tap around the outer edge of the cover to fully seat the wheel cover against the wheel.
4. Raise the vehicle using a suitable jack. Make sure to properly position the jack underneath the vehicle.
5. Remove the jack stands from underneath the vehicle and carefully lower the vehicle.

CAUTION: Prior to moving the vehicle, make sure that a firm brake pedal has been obtained.

TROUBLESHOOTING FLOW CHART
DISC BRAKES

Symptom	Probable Cause	Remedy
A. Pedal travels excessively.	1. Air or leak in system or insufficient brake fluid in system.	1. Check system for leaks and bleed system. If brake fluid contaminated linings, replace linings in complete axle sets.
	2. Warped or excessively tapered shoe and lining.	2. Replace shoe and linings in complete axle sets.
	3. Excessive rotor runout.	3. Check rotor for excessive runout. Resurface or replace as necessary.
	4. Loose wheel bearings.	4. Readjust wheel bearings to specifications.
	5. Damaged caliper piston seal.	5. Install new piston seal.
	6. Boiling point of brake fluid too low.	6. Drain, flush and add correct type and amount of brake fluid. Bleed brake system.
	7. Brake booster malfunctioning.	7. Replace brake booster.
B. Brake chatter or roughness. Pedal pulsates.	8. Excessive rotor thickness variation.	8. Check rotor for excessive thickness variation. Resurface or replace rotor as necessary.
	9. Excessive rotor lateral runout.	9. Check rotor for excessive lateral rotor runout. Resurface or replace rotor as necessary.
	10. Rear brake drums excessively out of round.	10. Check rear brake drums for out of round. Resurface or replace as necessary.
	11. Loose wheel bearings.	11. Readjust wheel bearings to specifications.
C. Excessive pressure required on pedal to stop vehicle.	12. Contaminated linings.	12. Replace linings in complete axle sets.
	13. Incorrect linings, or linings are of substandard material.	13. Replace linings with approved type.
	14. Frozen or seized piston in caliper.	14. Disassemble caliper and free up piston.
	15. Brake booster malfunctioning.	15. Replace brake booster.
	16. Partial system failure.	16. Check front and rear brake system for failure. Repair as necessary.
	17. Insufficient brake fluid in master cylinder.	17. Fill master cylinder with brake fluid and bleed system. Check for leaks.
	18. Air trapped in hydraulic system.	18. Bleed hydraulic system.
	19. Rear brake not adjusting.	19. Repair automatic adjusters. Adjust rear brakes.
	20. Bent shoe and lining.	20. Replace shoe and lining in axle sets.
D. Vehicle pulls to one side.	21. Contaminated linings.	21. Replace linings.
	22. Unmatched linings installed on vehicle.	22. Install matched set of linings.
	23. Distorted brake shoes.	23. Install new brake shoes.
	24. Frozen or seized piston in caliper.	24. Disassemble caliper and free up piston.
	25. Incorrect tire pressures.	25. Inflate tires to correct pressures.
	26. Front end out of alignment.	26. Align front end to specifications.
	27. Broken front or rear springs.	27. Replace broken springs.
	28. Rear brake pistons sticking.	28. Disassemble rear brakes and free up sticking pistons.
	29. Restricted hoses or lines.	29. Check hoses and lines. Clear out or replace as necessary.
	30. Caliper not properly aligned in relation to rotor.	30. Remove caliper and reinstall. Check alignment.
	31. Unmatched tires on same axle.	31. Tire of the same size and approximately same amount of tread should be installed on the same axle.
	32. Grease or brake fluid on linings or bent shoes.	32. Install new brake shoe and linings in complete axle sets.
	33. Rear brakes malfunctioning.	33. Check for inoperative automatic adjusting mechanism, defective linings, grease or brake fluid on linings, or defective wheel cylinders. Repair or replace as necessary.
	34. Loose suspension parts.	34. Check suspension components. Replace or repair as necessary.
	35. Loose calipers.	35. Torque caliper mounting bolts to specifications.

DISC BRAKES / continued

Symptom	Probable Cause	Remedy
E. Groaning noise when brakes are slowly applied or released or when vehicle is creeping.	36. This noise does not affect operation of brakes and is considered normal.	36. Although no corrective action is necessary for this condition, the noise may be eliminated by slightly increasing or decreasing the amount of effort applied to the brakes.
F. Rattle or brake noise coming from the front wheels when traveling slowly over rough roads.	37. Anti-rattle spring missing or improperly positioned. 38. Excessive clearance between shoe and caliper. 39. Caliper mounting bolts too long. 40. Loose wheel bearings. 41. Splash shield scraping on rotor.	37. Install new anti-rattle spring or properly position it. 38. Install new shoe and lining assemblies. 39. Reinstall caliper mounting bolts of correct size. 40. Readjust wheel bearings to specifications. 41. Adjust shield to provide clearance.
G. Front brakes heat up while driving and fail to release.	42. Driver riding brakes. 43. Improperly adjusted stop light switch. 44. Pedal linkage binding. 45. Residual pressure valve installed in master cylinder. 46. Brake booster malfunctioning.	42. Do not ride brakes while driving. 43. Adjust stop light switch to allow full return of brake pedal. 44. Free up binding pedal linkage. 45. Remove residual pressure valve from master cylinder. 46. Replace brake booster.
H. Leaking wheel cylinder.	47. Damaged or worn caliper piston seal. 48. Scored or corroded caliper piston bore.	47. Disassemble caliper and install new seal. 48. Disassemble and hone caliper.
I. Uneven or grabbing braking action.	49. All probable causes listed under VEHICLE PULLS TO ONE SIDE. 50. Brake booster malfunctioning.	49. All remedies listed under VEHICLE PULLS TO ONE SIDE. 50. Replace brake booster.
J. Brake pedal is depressed with no braking action.	51. Air in hydraulic system or incorrect bleeding procedure used. 52. Brake fluid leakage past primary cup in master cylinder. 53. Leak in hydraulic system. 54. Rear brakes incorrectly adjusted. 55. Bleeder screw open and leaking.	51. Bleed hydraulic system. 52. Recondition or replace master cylinder as required. 53. Check for brake fluid leakage and repair as necessary. If brake fluid leakage contaminated linings, replace linings in complete axle sets. 54. Adjust rear brakes. 55. Close bleeder screw and bleed entire hydraulic system.
K. High pitched squeal without brakes applied.	56. Front linings worn out.	56. Replace front linings in complete axle sets.
L. Dragging brakes. Note that a slight drag is always present in disc brakes after the brakes are applied.	57. Master cylinder pistons not returning correctly. 58. Restricted brake hoses or lines. 59. Incorrect parking brake adjustment. 60. Check valve installed in outlet to front brakes.	57. Check master cylinder for spurt as the pedal is applied. Adjust the pushrod if adjustable and if necessary. Recondition or replace master cylinder. 58. Check for soft hoses and damaged tubes and replace as necessary. 59. Adjust parking brake to specifications. 60. Remove check valve from master cylinder if installed in the outlet to the front brakes.

TROUBLESHOOTING FLOW CHART
DRUM BRAKES

Symptom	Probable cause	Remedy
A. Pedal goes to floor.	1. Low brake fluid level in reservoir. 2. Incorrectly adjusted brakes. 3. Air in hydraulic system. 4. Leaking wheel cylinders. 5. Loose or broken brake lines. 6. Leaking or worn master cylinder. 7. Excessively worn brake shoes.	1. Add brake fluid. Bleed master cylinder. 2. Repair or replace automatic adjuster as required and adjust brakes. 3. Add brake fluid and bleed hydraulic system. 4. Recondition or replace wheel cylinders as required and replace the affected brake shoe assemblies in axle sets. It is recommended that the brake shoe assembly opposite the affected brake shoe be replaced to maintain proper braking action. 5. Tighten or replace brake lines as required. 6. Recondition or replace master cylinder as required. Bleed hydraulic system. 7. Replace brake shoes. Adjust brakes.
B. Spongy brake pedal.	8. Air in hydraulic system. 9. Low boiling point of brake fluid. 10. Excessively worn or cracked brake drums. 11. Broken or worn pedal pivot bushing.	8. Add brake fluid. Bleed master cylinder. 9. Drain, flush and add correct brake fluid. Bleed hydraulic system. 10. Replace faulty brake drums. 11. Replace nylon pivot bushing.
C. Brakes pulling.	12. Incorrect tire pressure. 13. Contaminated brake linings. 14. Front end out of alignment. 15. Incorrect brake adjustment. 16. Unmatched brake lining material. 17. Distorted brake shoes. 18. Restricted hydraulic hoses or lines. 19. Broken rear spring. 20. Unmatched tires on same axle.	12. Inflate tires to correct pressure. 13. Replace affected brake linings. 14. Align front end. 15. Adjust brakes and check brake fluid. 16. Install matched sets of brake linings in complete axle sets. 17. Replace affected brake shoes. 18. Replace plugged brake hoses or lines. 19. Replace broken spring. 20. Install same size tires on same axle.
D. Sqealing brakes.	21. Glazed brake lining. 22. Saturated brake lining. 23. Weak or broken shoe return spring. 24. Weak or broken shoe retaining spring. 25. Unmatched brake lining material. 26. Distorted brake shoes. 27. Bent support plate. 28. Dust in brake drums and brakes. 29. Scored brake drums. 30. Out of round drums.	21. Replace brake linings. 22. Replace affected brake lining. 23. Replace spring. 24. Replace spring. 25. Install matched sets of brake linings in complete axle sets. 26. Replace distorted brake shoes. 27. Replace support plate. 28. Blow out dust in brake drums and brake assembly. 29. Resurface brake drums. 30. Resurface or replace brake drum.
E. Dragging brakes.	31. Inproper brake or parking brake adjustment. 32. Parking brakes engaged. 33. Weak or broken brake shoe return spring. 34. Binding brake pedal. 35. Sticking master cylinder cup. 36. Master cylinder relief port obstructed. 37. Saturated brake linings. 38. Bent or out of round brake drums. 39. Incorrect stop light adjustment.	31. Adjust brakes and add brake fluid. 32. Release parking brake. 33. Replace affected brake return springs. 34. Free up and lubricate brake pedal and linkage. 35. Recondition or replace master cylinder. 36. Blow out relief valve using compressed air. 37. Replace brake linings in complete axle sets. 38. Resurface or replace brake drums. 39. Adjust stop light switch.

DRUM BRAKES / continued

Symptom	Probable cause	Remedy
F. Hard brake pedal.	40. Inoperative brake booster. 41. Incorrect brake lining material. 42. Restricted brake lines or hoses. 43. Frozen brake pedal linkage.	40. Replace brake booster. 41. Install matched set of brake linings, in complete axle sets. 42. Replace or clear out affected brake lines or hoses. 43. Free up and lubricate linkage.
G. Wheel locks.	44. Contaminated brake linings. 45. Loose or damaged brake linings. 46. Wheel cylinder cups sticking. 47. Incorrect wheel bearing adjustment.	44. Replace affected brake linings, in complete axle sets. 45. Replace brake linings in complete axle sets. 46. Recondition or replace wheel cylinders. 47. Clean, repack and adjust wheel bearings.
H. Brakes fade at high speed.	48. Substandard brake linings. 49. Overheated brake drums. 50. Low boiling point of brake fluid. 51. Saturated brake linings.	48. Replace linings, in complete axle sets using approved linings. 49. Inspect for dragging brakes. 50. Drain, flush and add correct brake fluid to system. 51. Replace affected linings in complete axle sets.
I. Surge below 15 mph. Chatter at 30 to 40 mph.	52. Bent or out of round rear brake drums. 53. Bent or out of round front brake drums.	52. Resurface or replace affected drums. 53. Resurface or replace affected drums.
J. Shoe knock.	54. Machine grooves in contact face of brake drums. 55. Weak hold down springs.	54. Sand, resurface or replace brake drums. 55. Replace hold down springs.
K. Brakes do not self-adjust.	56. Adjuster screw frozen in thread. 57. Adjuster screw corroded at thrust washer. 58. Adjuster lever does not engage star wheel. 59. Adjuster installed on wrong wheel.	56. Clean and free up threads. 57. Clean threads and replace thrust washer if necessary. 58. Free up or replace adjuster as necessary. 59. Install adjuster on correct wheel.

Good Vision for Safety

You must see to drive

It may sound simplistic when put in this perspective. But it is still a truism that is inescapable.

You cannot drive a car unless you can see the road ahead.

And other drivers cannot operate their cars safely unless they can see you.

Being able to see the road ahead is a prerequisite for safe vehicle operation. To see the road, your car's various lights and your car's windshield wipers must operate effectively. And of course, other drivers depend on your lights working effectively to locate and place you on the road in relation to their own vehicles.

Bad weather and good vision

In inclement weather, your driving vision is impaired even more than normally. Here is where your windshield wipers become one of the most important safety devices on your car. Lighting, too, is doubly important. In bad weather, lights are frequently used during daylight hours too as a safety device. It does not increase your own vision so much as it makes your vehicle easier for other motorists to see on the road.

Jobs you can do

Most problems in a car's lighting system—which is part of the electrical system, of course—are caused by burned out bulbs, fuses or flasher units. Actual short circuits are much more rare in occurrence. This is a happy state of affairs for you, the novice mechanic, because bulb, fuse, headlamp and flasher replacement jobs are well within your capabilities.

When it comes down to tracing short circuits, aligning headlamps or dimmer switch replacement, we recommend that you leave these jobs for a professional mechanic who has the special tools needed to successfully complete such jobs.

As for the windshield wiper part of this chapter, a novice mechanic will be able to change wiper blades and wiper arm assemblies.

Replacing wiper motors or body panels on concealed wiper systems is beyond the scope of this book and the average novice mechanic.

WINDSHIELD WIPER SERVICE

General check

Your car's windshield wipers are powered by a small electric motor. To protect the windshield and give you maximum vision in rain, sleet or snow, make sure the rubber blades are not cracked, brittle or pulled loose from the blade retainer. Replacement blades are inexpensive and easy to install. The investment is small. The benefit is great—unobstructed vision through a clean windshield.

You can test the wiper units by pulling them about an inch away from the windshield and releasing. They should snap back against the glass. If not, tension may not be sufficient to effectively wipe the glass clean. If the tension cannot be adjusted, you should replace the unit. Merely changing blades will not solve the problem.

Most cars now have windshield washers. To clean a dry windshield while you are driving, first spray the windshield with washer fluid, then turn on the wipers. This protects the glass against scratches. If temperatures drop below freezing in your area, be sure to put protective solvent in the washer container. It is available wherever auto products are sold.

IF WIPER BLADES OR ARMS NEED REPLACEMENT, FOLLOW THE SPECIFIC PROCEDURES HERE FOR YOUR PARTICULAR MAKE AND MODEL.

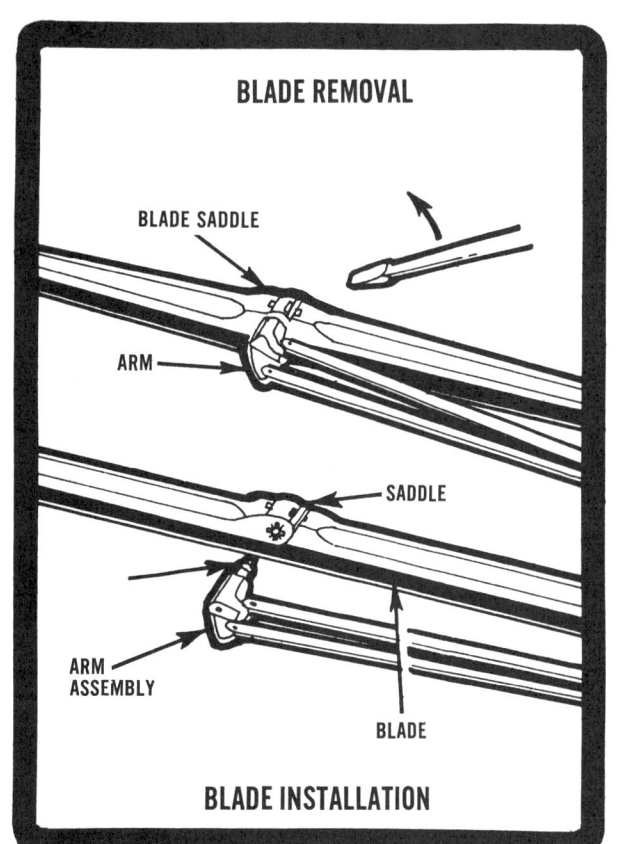

Fig. 1. Pin type blade installation.

AMERICAN MOTORS

Wiper blades

1974-76 Matador X, Fig. 1

1. Insert a suitable tool or small screwdriver into spring release opening of the blade saddle.
2. Depress spring clip and pull blade from the arm.
3. To install, push blade saddle onto the pin so that the spring clip engages the pin. Make sure that blade is securely attached to the arm.

1969-76 except Matador X, Fig. 2

1. Press down on arm to unlatch the top stud.
2. Depress the tab on the saddle and pull the blade from the arm.
3. To install, slide the blade saddle over the end of the wiper arm until locking stud snaps into place. Make sure that the blade is securely attached to the arm.
4. To remove the blade element, squeeze the latch lock and pull the element out, Fig. 3.
5. To install the element, insert element through each of the lever jaws. Make sure that the element is engaged in all of the lever jaws.

TOOLS REQUIRED

- THE FOLLOWING TOOLS ARE REQUIRED TO SERVICE WINDSHIELD WIPERS:

Wiper arm removal tool.
Small flat screwdriver.
12-inch screwdriver.
3/32-inch drill or pin.

- THE FOLLOWING TOOLS ARE REQUIRED TO SERVICE THE ELECTRICAL SYSTEM:

#2 Philips screwdriver.
Flat screwdriver.
Fuse puller.

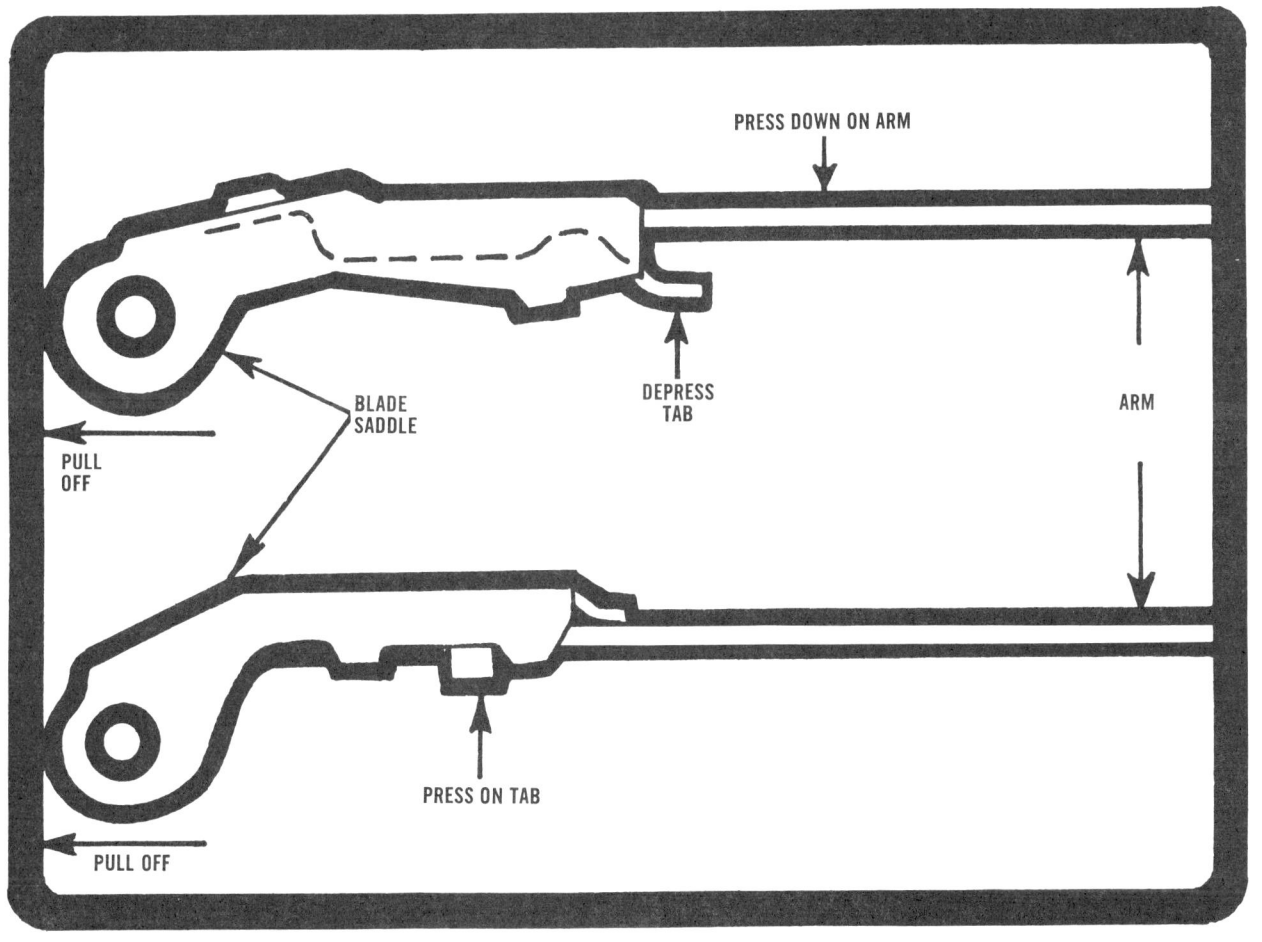

Fig. 2. Trico (top) and Anco (bottom) type blade installation.

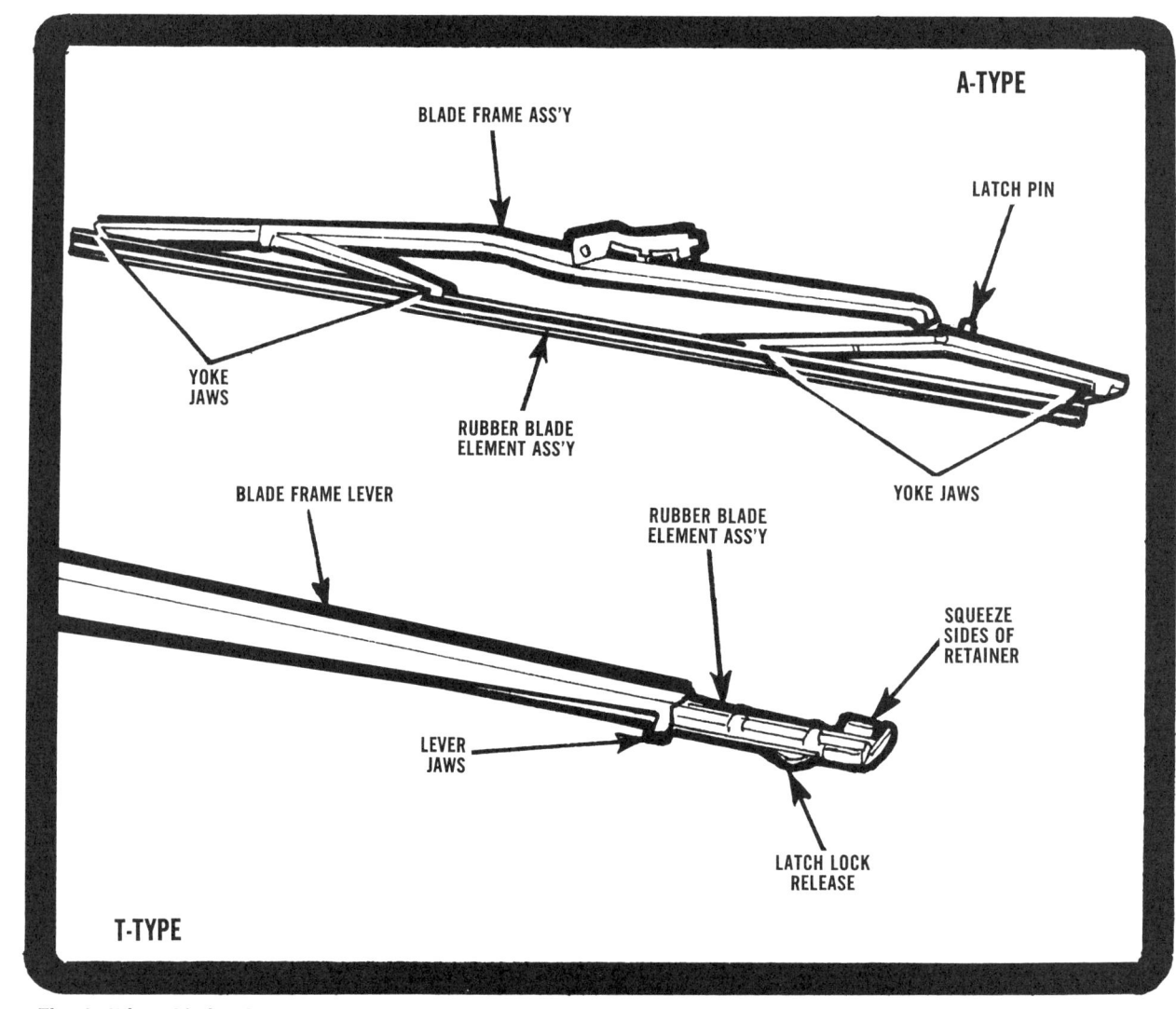

Fig. 3. Wiper blade element installation. Anco (top) and Trico (bottom).

Wiper arms

1974-76 Matador X, Fig. 4
1. Raise arm from windshield and move the slide latch away from the pivot shaft.
2. Disconnect washer hose from connector.
3. Disengage auxiliary arm on driver's side, from pivot pin and remove the wiper arm from the pivot shaft.
4. To install the wiper arm, position the auxiliary arm (driver's side only) over the pivot pin. Then while holding it down, push main arm head over the pivot shaft. Make sure that the pivot shaft is in park position and the blade is positioned against the stop.
5. Hold main arm head on the pivot shaft while raising the blade end of the wiper arm and push the slide latch into the lock under the pivot shaft.
6. Lower the blade onto the windshield. If blade does not touch the windshield, the slide latch is not completely engaged in place.
7. Attach washer hose to connector.

1969-76 All AMC exc. Matador X
1. Lift the arm against the spring tension. Using a screwdriver, slide cap away from serrated shaft.
   NOTE: Arms are stamped L or R to indicate left or right side installation on the vehicle.
2. Operate wiper motor through a few cycles. Then turn it off to position the pivot shafts in park position before installing wiper arms.
3. Install the wiper arms and blades on the pivot shafts with the tips of the blades to the right side of the vehicle.

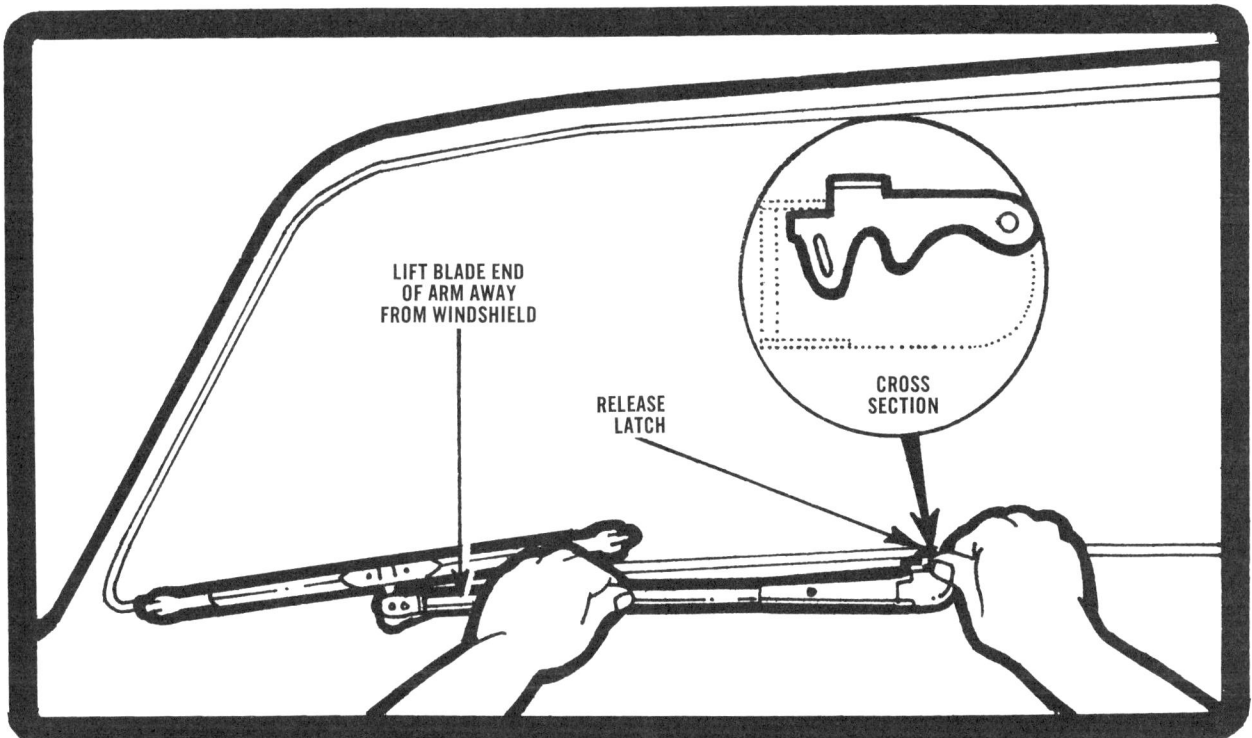

Fig. 4.

GENERAL MOTORS

Wiper blades
All models except Cadillac

1. Two methods are used to retain the wiper blades. The first type uses a press-type release tab. The second uses a coil spring retainer, Fig. 5.

    Press Type Release Tab. Depress the release tab and slide the wiper blade off the wiper arm pin.

    Coil Spring Retainer. Using a screwdriver, insert it on top of the spring and push the spring downward. Slide the blade assembly off the wiper arm.

2. Remove the wiper blade element from the blade assembly. Two methods of retention are used to retain the wiper blade element. The first has a press-type release button. The second has a spring-type retainer clip. To remove the wiper blade element, either push the release button or squeeze the retainer clip and slide the element off the wiper blade. Slide the wiper blade element into the wiper blade.

3. When the wiper element is properly installed, the release button or retaining clip should be at the end of the wiper blade assembly nearest the wiper transmission.

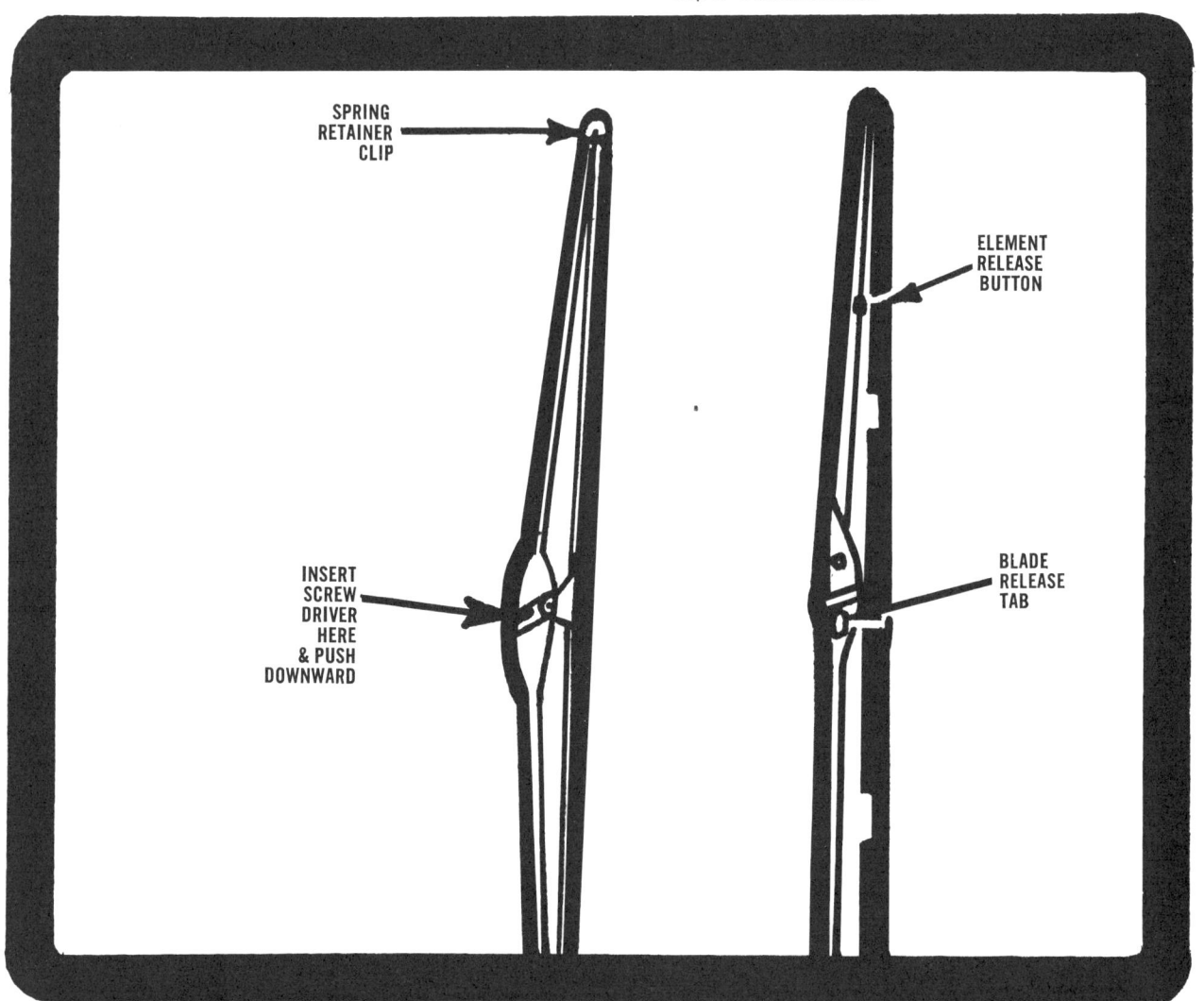

Fig. 5. Wiper blade element and wiper blade retention methods.

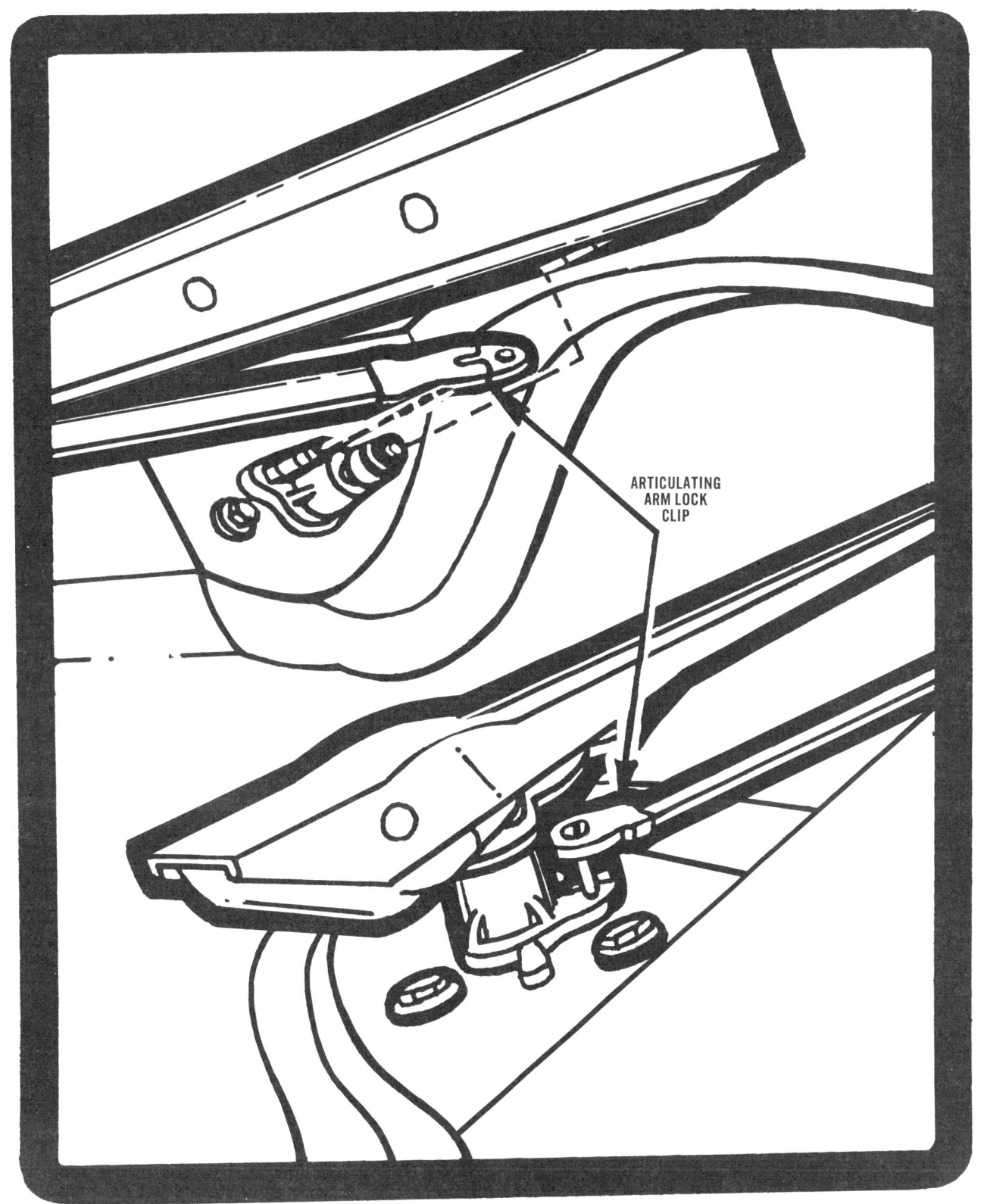

Fig. 6. Articulating lock clip.

Wiper arms

With rectangular motor

1. Position wiper motor in the park position.

   NOTE: The use of a screwdriver or other tool to pry the arm off may distort the arm. Also, paint damage or glass damage may result from the use of improper tools. Special tools are available which will easily and safely remove the wiper arm.
2. Using the appropriate tool, remove arm by prying up to disengage the wiper arm from the serrated shaft.
3. To install arm onto the shaft, rotate the shaft the required distance and direction so that the blades rest in the proper parked position.

With round motor

1. Position the wiper motor in the parked position.
2. Raise hood to obtain access to the wiper arms.
3. On all intermediate models, remove the wiper arm by rocking it off the pivot shaft.
4. On the left arm assembly, slide the articulating arm lock clip, Fig. 6, away from the pivot pin and lift the arm off the pin.
5. On full size models, lift the wiper arm and slide the latch clip, Fig. 7, out from underneath the arm.
6. Remove the arm assembly by rocking it off the pivot pin
7. To install the right arm assembly, align the keyway in the wiper arm with the slot in the pivot shaft and push the arm assembly onto the pivot shaft.
8. To install the left arm assembly, place the articulating arm over the pin and slide the lock clip toward the pin until it locks in place. Install the wiper arm, aligning the keyway in the wiper arm with the slot in the pivot shaft and pushing the arm onto the pivot shaft.

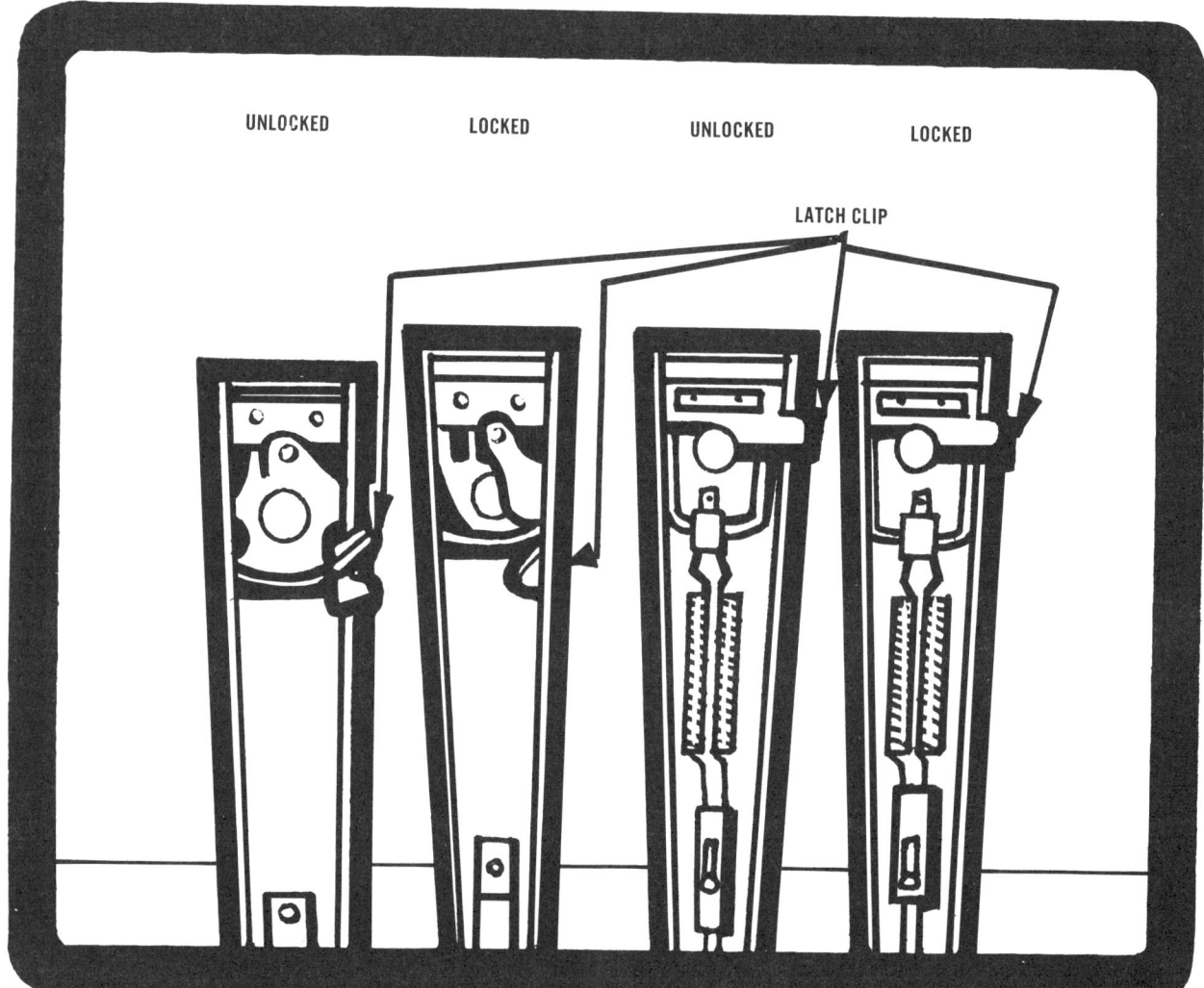

Fig. 7. Wiper arm latch clips.

1969-70 Cadillac
1. Open the hood to obtain access to the wiper arms.
2. Lift the arm off the windshield and insert a 3/32-inch pin or drill into the hole behind the wiper arm, Fig. 8.
3. Remove the wiper arm by rocking it off the pivot shaft. Do not remove the pin or drill.
4. On the left wiper arm assembly, slide the drag link clip toward the end of the arm far enough to disengage the drag link from the pivot pin and remove the wiper arm and drag link.
5. To install the left wiper arm assembly, place the drag link on the pivot pin and secure it by sliding the retainer down toward the pin until it locks in place.
6. Install the wiper arm onto the pivot shaft by rocking the arm into place.
7. Pull outward on the wiper arm and remove the pin or drill from the hole in the wiper arm. Carefully return the wiper arm and blade assembly to the windshield.

1971-76 Cadillac
1. Raise hood to obtain access to the wiper arms.
2. Lift the wiper arm and slide the latch clip, Fig. 7, out from under the wiper arm.
3. Release the wiper arm and remove it from the pivot shaft by rocking it off.
4. On the left arm assembly, slide the articulating arm lock clip away from the pin, Fig. 6, and lift the articulating arm off the pin.
5. To install the left wiper arm, place the articulating arm over the pin and slide the lock clip toward the pin until it locks in place. Install the wiper arm onto the pivot shaft, aligning the keyway in the keyway in the arm with the slot in the pivot shaft.
6. Lift the wiper arm outward and slide the latch clips under the wiper arm. Carefully return the wiper arm and blade assembly to the windshield.

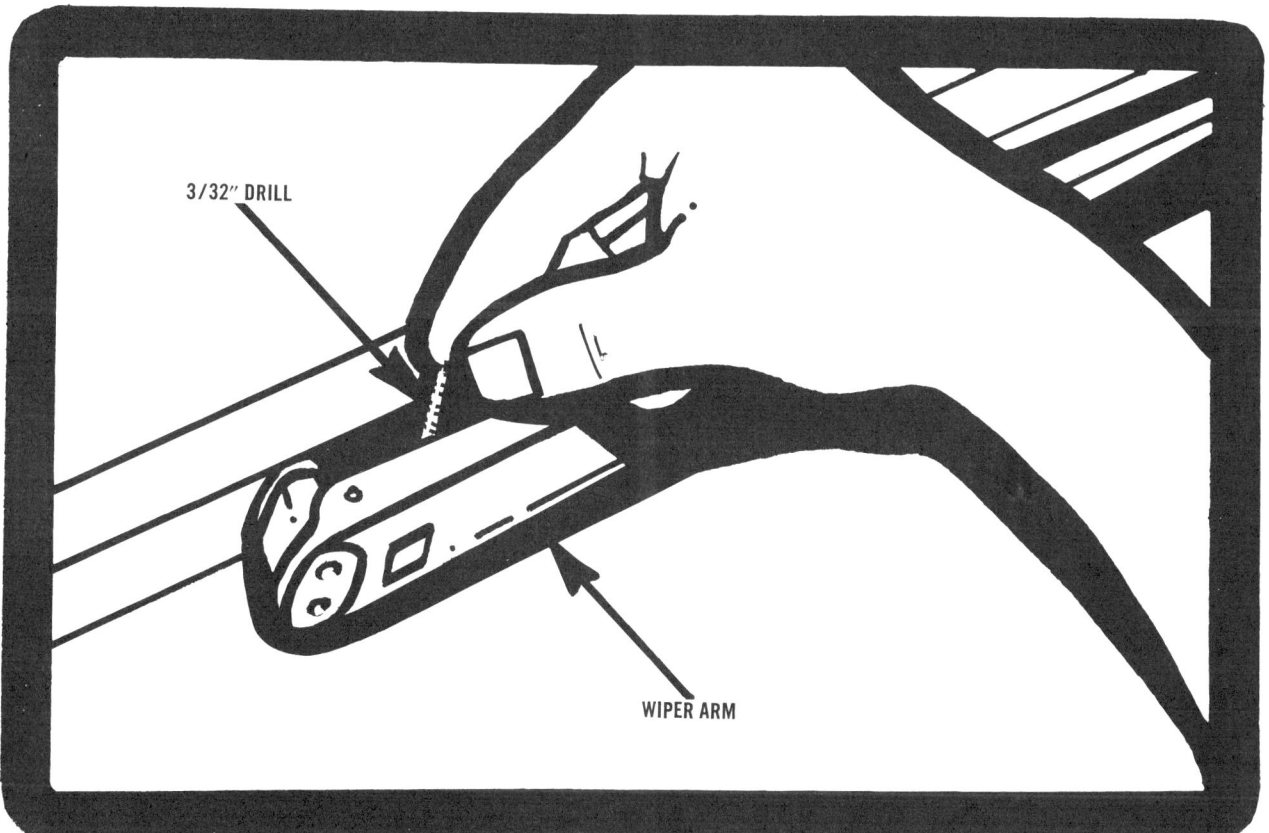

Fig. 8. Installing drill for wiper arm removal on 1969-70 Cadillac.

CHRYSLER CORP.

Wiper blades

1. Turn the wiper switch On and move the wiper blades and arms to a convenient location on the windshield by turning the ignition switch On and Off.
2. Lift the wiper blade and arm off the glass.
3. Depress the release lever on the center bridge and remove the blade from the arm, Fig. 9.
4. Using a screwdriver, depress the release on the end of the bridge. The release will be either a button or lever.
5. Pull the rubber wiping element through the end of the bridge.
6. Install the wiper blade by first starting the end opposite the one with the release latch, into the bridge until the release latch engages the bridge. Make sure that all four bridge claws are engaged and properly positioned on the wiper blade when it is completely installed.
7. Check release latch for positive engagement with the bridge when the blade is completely installed.

Wiper arms

CAUTION: The use of a screwdriver or other tool to pry the arm off may distort the arm in such a manner that the arm will come off the shaft in the future, no matter how carefully the arm is installed. Special tools are available which will easily and safely remove the wiper arm. Also, do not attempt, under any circumstances, to push or bend the spring clip at the base of the arm in an attempt to release the arm. The clip is self-releasing.

1. Place the wiper motor in the park position.
2. On vehicles with *non-concealed wiper arms,* position the special tool on the wiper arm assembly and lift off the wiper arm by gently rocking the tool and arm assembly, Fig. 10.

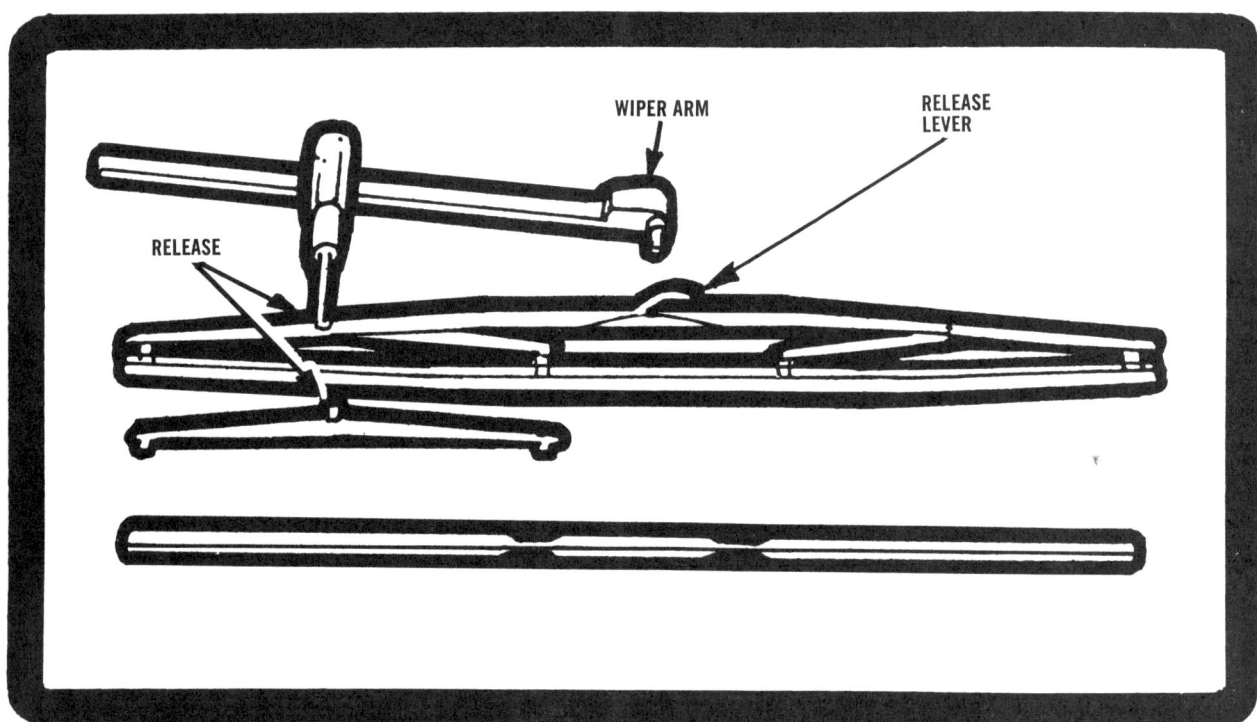

Fig. 15. Side-saddle pin type blade.

Fig. 16. Trico and Anco brand blade element installation.

3. On *1969-70 models with concealed wipers,* lift the hood to gain access. Then insert a .090-inch diameter pin or drill into the hole in the arm assembly, Fig. 11, and pull the wiper arm off the pivot shaft by using a rocking motion.
4. On *1971-76 models with concealed wipers,* lift the hood to gain access. Then lift the arm and pull out the latch and remove the wiper arm from the pivot shaft by using a rocking motion, Fig. 11.
5. To install the wiper arm on vehicles with non-concealed wiper arms, position the tool used to remove the wiper arm in the same manner used to remove it. Then squeeze the tool and wiper arm together and install the wiper arm on the pivot shaft, Fig. 10. Make sure that wiper arm is completely bottomed on the pivot shaft. Also, when installing the wiper arm, make sure to properly position it against the lowest part of the windshield so that the wiper arm and blade will return to park position when the wiper switch is turned off.
6. To install the wiper arm *on 1969-70 models with concealed wiper arms,* insert the .090-inch diameter pin or drill into the hole at the bottom of the wiper arm and install the wiper arm by rocking it onto the pivot shaft, Fig. 11. Raise the arm slightly to release the tension on the pin or drill and remove the pin or drill. With the wiper arm properly installed, the wiper arm should just contact the stops at the bottom of the windshield.
7. To install the wiper arm *on 1971-76 models,* pull the release latch outward, Fig. 12, and install the wiper arm by rocking it onto the pivot shaft. With the wiper arms properly installed, the wiper arm should just contact the stops at the bottom of the windshield.

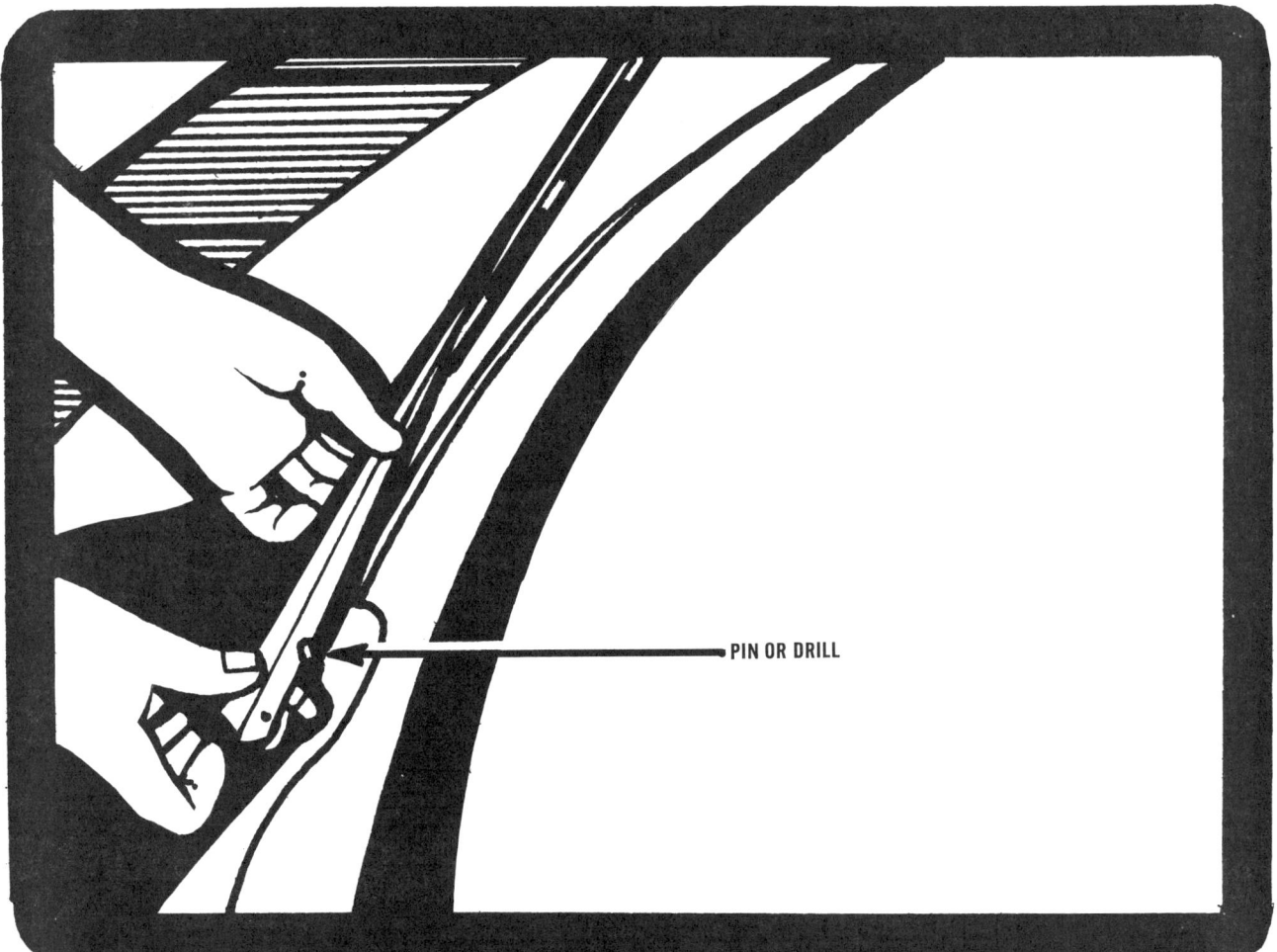

Fig. 11. Concealed wiper arm removal, 1969-70 Chrysler vehicles.

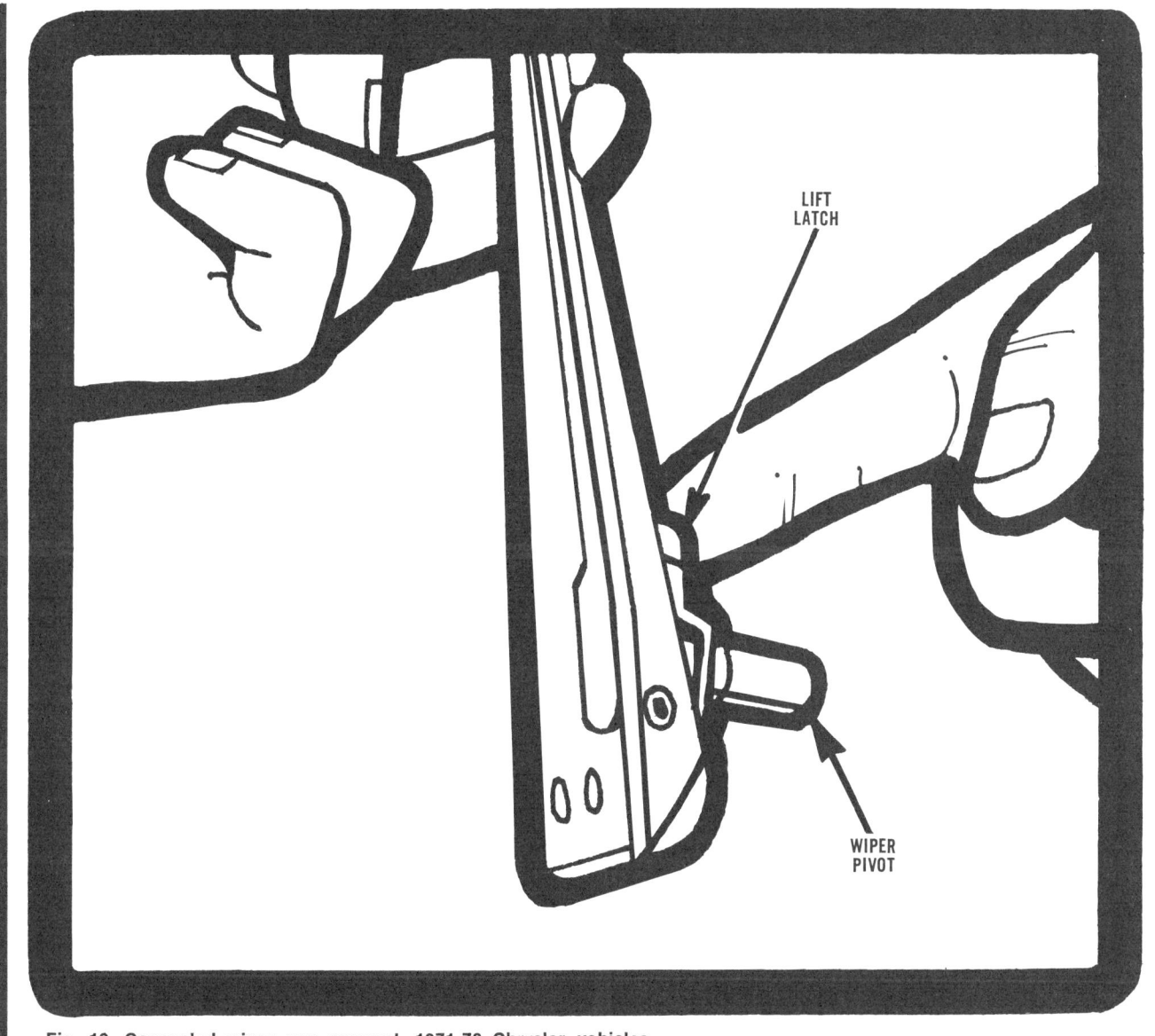

Fig. 12. Concealed wiper arm removal, 1971-76 Chrysler vehicles.

FORD MOTOR CO.

Wiper blades

All Ford and Mercury models

The Trico and Anco blades used come in to two types—either bayonet type or the side-saddle pin type.

To remove a bayonet type Trico blade:
1. Press down on the arm to unlock the top stud.
2. Depress the tab on the saddle, Fig. 13.
3. Pull the blade from the arm.

To remove a bayonet type Anco blade:
1. Press inward on the tab on the saddle, Fig. 14.
2. Pull the blade from the arm.

To install the Trico or Anco type blades, just slip the blade onto the wiper arm and push in until the latch engages the wiper arm. Make sure that the blade is properly engaged to the wiper arm by attempting to pull the blade out.

To remove a side-saddle pin type Trico or Anco blade:
1. Insert an appropriate tool such as a small screwdriver into the spring release opening of the blade saddle, Fig. 15.
2. Depress the spring clip with the tool or screwdriver.
3. Pull the blade off the arm.
4. To install the blade, slip the blade onto the wiper arm and push in until the latch engages the wiper arm. Make sure that the blade is properly engaged to the wiper arm by attempting to pull the blade out.

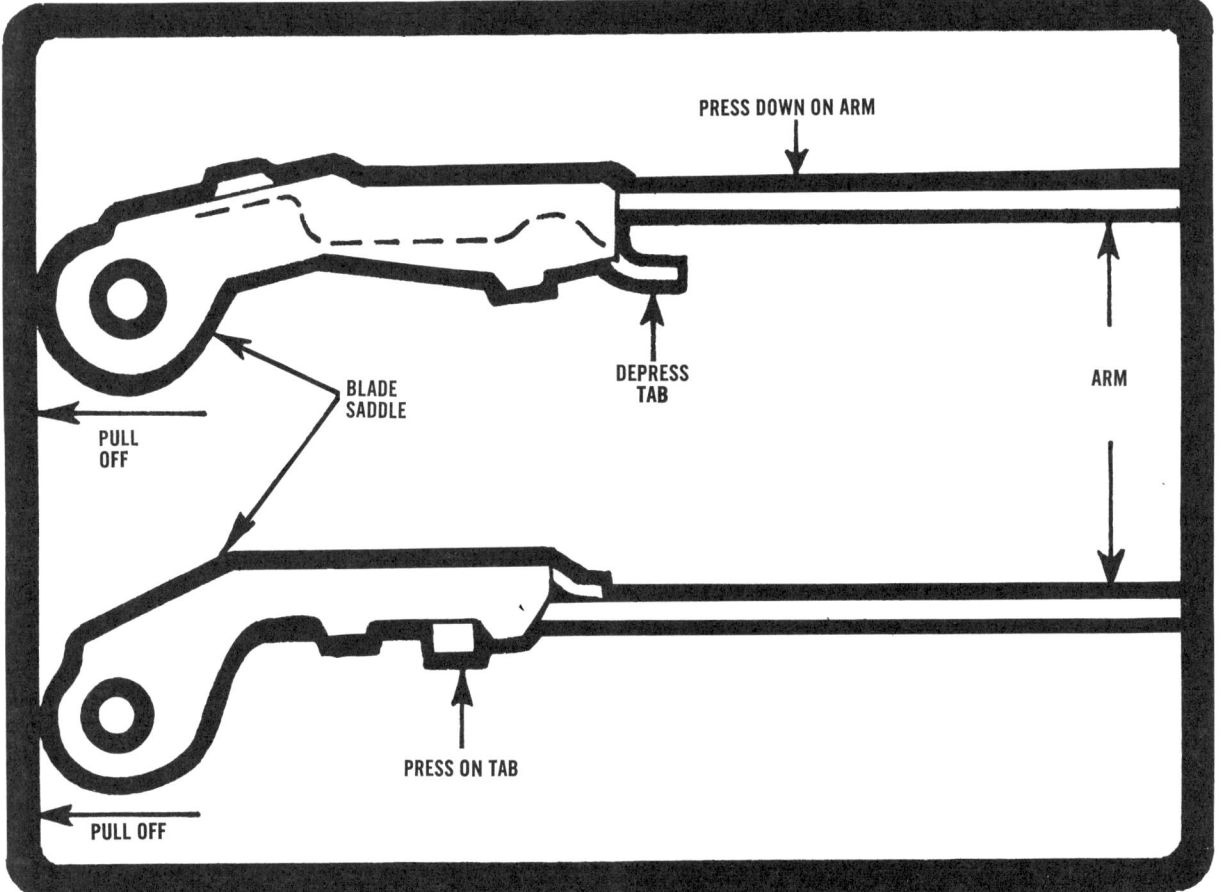

Fig. 9. Wiper blade assembly.

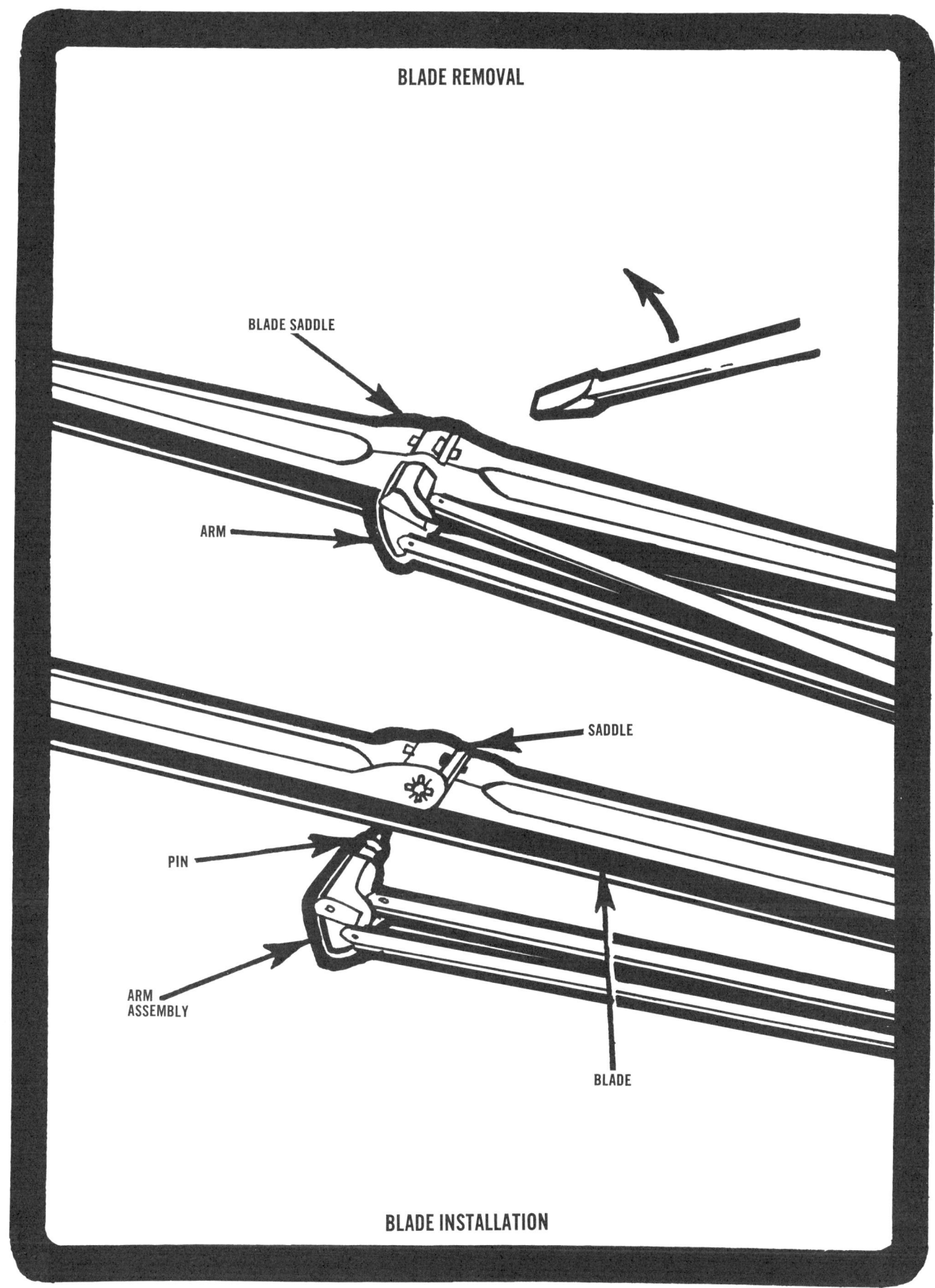

Fig. 10. Non-concealed wiper arm removal.

Wiper blade element

1. To replace the rubber element on a Trico blade, squeeze the latch lock release and pull the element out of the lever jaws, Fig. 16.
2. To remove the rubber element on an Anco type blade, depress the latch pin and slide the element out of the yoke jaws, Fig. 16.
3. To install the element on either type blade, insert the element through the yoke or lever jaws until the latch pin or latch lock engages the rubber element. Make sure that the element is engaged underneath all the claws of the blade.

1969-76 Thunderbird, Ford Full Size and Mercury Full Size; 1969-72 Lincoln Continental exc. 1972 Mark IV; 1970-71 Fairlane, Torino and Montego; 1971-73 Cougar and Mustang

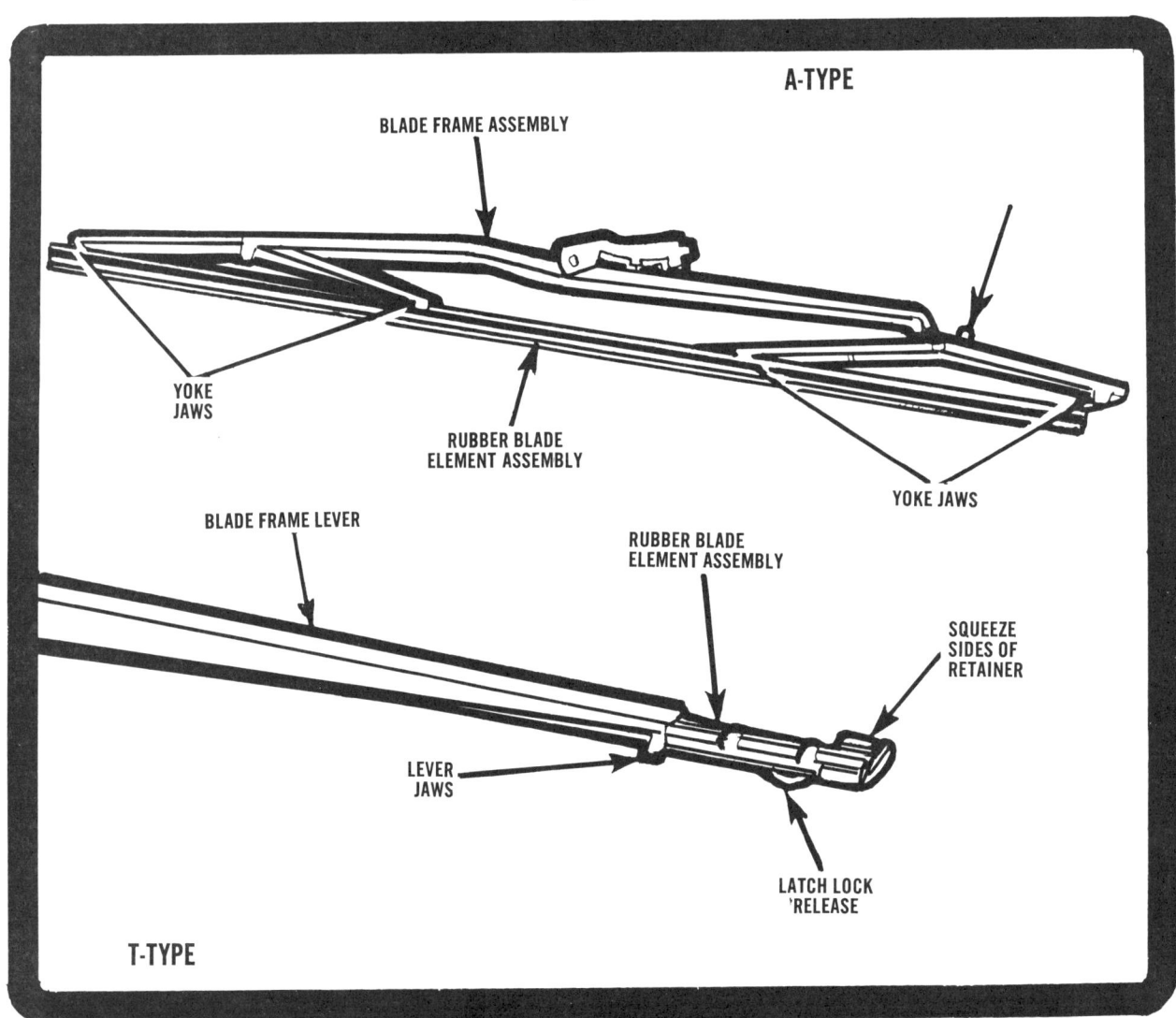

Fig. 13. Trico brand bayonet-type blade.

Wiper arms

1. Swing the arm and blade assembly away from the windshield to release the spring loaded attaching clip in the arm from the pivot shaft.
2. Insert a 3/32-inch pin through the pin hole, Fig. 17, to hold the wiper arm in the release position. Do not remove the pin until after the wiper arm has been reinstalled.
3. Remove the wiper arm by rocking it off the shaft. Do not attempt to pry off the wiper arm using a screwdriver.
4. Before installing wiper arm, make sure that the pivot shaft is in the park position. To install the wiper arm, position it on the pivot shaft and push it into place. Remove the 3/32-inch pin to lock the wiper arm onto the pivot shaft.

1970 Cougar, Falcon, Mustang; 1970-76 Comet, Granada, Maverick and Monarch

NOTE: These models do not have a hole in the wiper arm and blade assembly to install a pin to hold the retaining clip in the released position.

1. Swing the arm and blade assembly from the windshield. This will release the spring loaded retaining clip from the pivot shaft.
2. Remove the wiper arm and blade assembly from the pivot shaft by rocking it off. Do not attempt to pry the arm and blade assembly off using a screwdriver.
3. Before installing the wiper arm and blade assembly, make sure that the pivot shaft is in the park position.
4. To install the wiper arm and blade assembly, hold the wiper arm and blade assembly in the swung out position and push it onto the pivot shaft. The arm will automatically lock onto the pivot shaft.

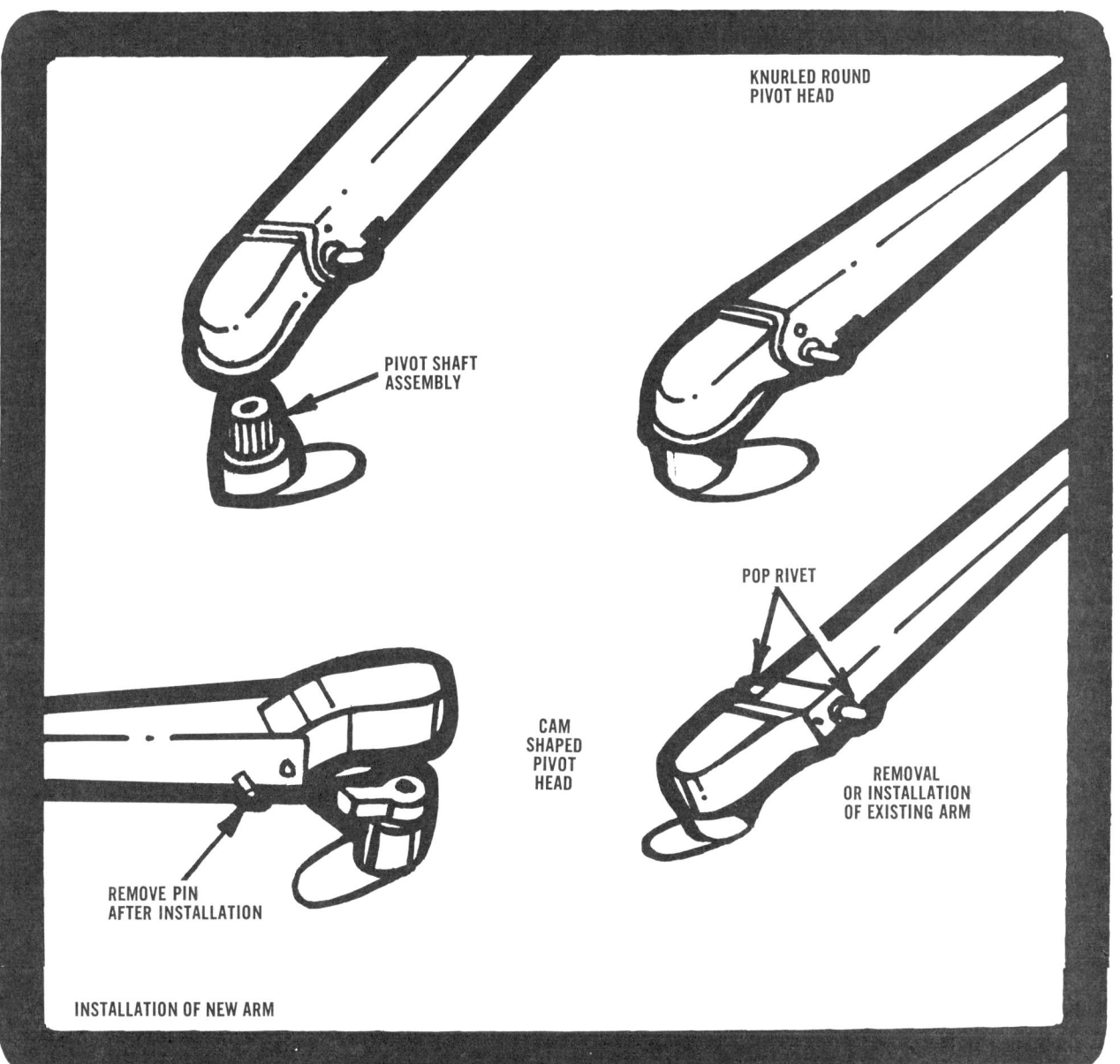

Fig. 14. Anco brand bayonet-type blade.

1972-76 Montego, Torino, Continental Mark IV; 1974-76 Cougar; 1973-76 Lincoln Continental

1. On *1973-76 Lincoln Continental* and *1974-76 Mark IV models,* disconnect the windshield washer hose from the wiper arm.
2. Swing the wiper arm and blade assembly away from the windshield and move the slide latch away from the pivot shaft, Fig. 18. This will unlock the wiper arm from the pivot shaft and hold the wiper arm and blade assembly away from the windshield.
3. Remove the wiper arm and blade assembly by rocking it off the shaft. Do not attempt to pry the wiper arm off the pivot shaft using a screwdriver.
4. Before installing the wiper arm and blade assembly, make sure that the pivot shaft is in the park position.
5. To install the wiper arm and blade assembly, position it on the pivot shaft. Then while holding the arm slightly outward, slide the latch toward the pivot shaft and carefully swing the wiper arm onto the windshield.
6. On *1973-76 Lincoln Continental* and *1974-76 Mark IV* models, reconnect the windshield washer hose to the wiper arm.

Mustang II and Pinto

1. Swing the arm and blade assembly away from the windshield.
2. While holding the assembly in the swung out position, pull the arm off the pivot shaft using the tool shown in Fig. 19.
3. To install the arm and blade assembly, hold the arm and blade assembly in the swung out position and push the arm onto the pivot shaft. Slowly swing the arm onto the windshield.

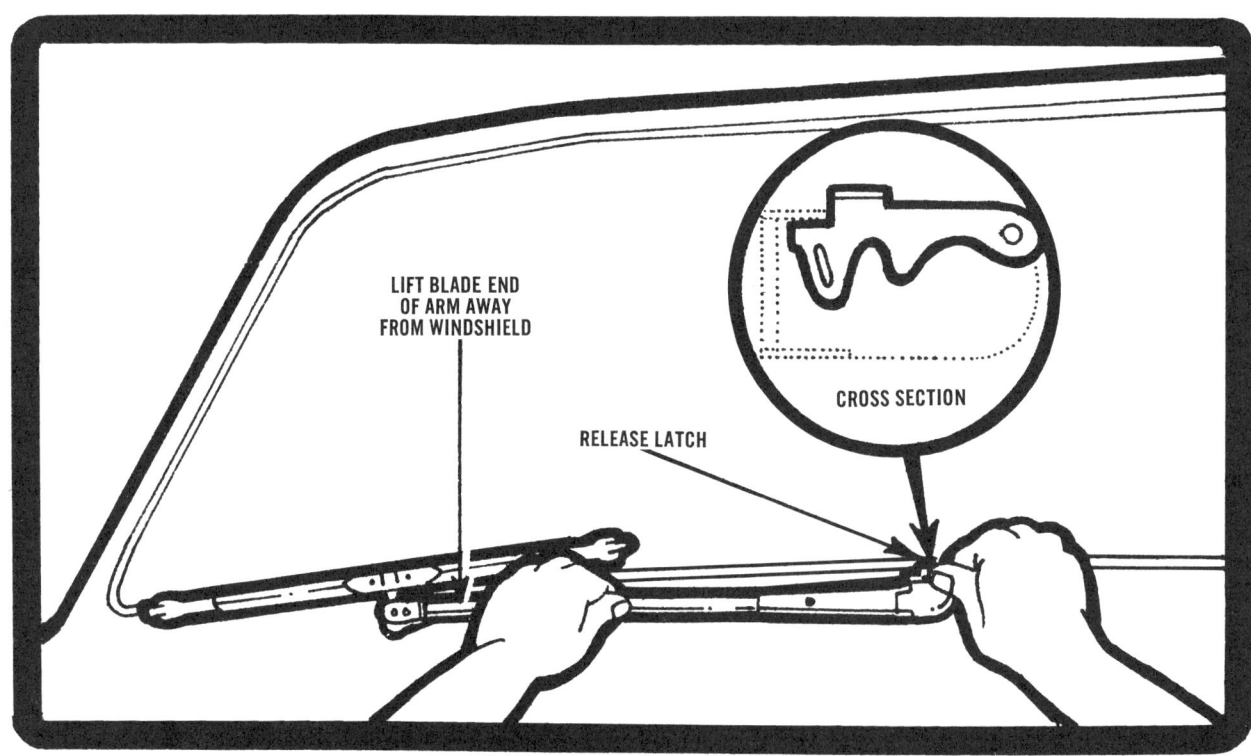

Fig. 17.

LIGHT SYSTEM SERVICE

Your car's lights

All automobiles are equipped with a variety of lights that each perform a specific function. The major lights you'll find on a typical automobile include headlamps (possibly two sets, one for low beams and one for high beams), parking lamps, taillights, brake lights and side markers. In addition, various cars may have auxiliary lighting for interiors, dash gauges, trunk and underhood vision and other sundry locations.

Rear stop lights are always red. So are rear turn signal lights except for those on a few model cars which have amber rear signals. Front turn signal lights are amber. Emergency flasher lights are amber in front and red in the rear. Side marker lights are also amber in front and red in the rear.

Most states require all lights to be fully operative and of the proper color. The reason is so that you and all other drivers can communicate intended changes of direction and other planned maneuvers in plenty of time to avoid accidents.

Once you begin working on your car's lighting, you'll find that the headlamps are of the sealed beam type. That is, you can't remove the bulb alone. You must remove and replace the entire lamp unit including the lens, reflector, etc. It all comes in one piece.

All other lights on a car use a separate bulb. This means that if a bulb burns out, just the bulb need be replaced, not the whole assembly.

Lighting checkout

You can check all lights in less than a minute with a helper outside the car. Turn on the headlights. On dim (low beam), two of the four sealed beam headlights should shine down and to the right. On high beam, the two other headlights flash on and light the road at a greater distance. If your car has only two headlights, both should shine with the dimmer switch in either the low beam or high beam position.

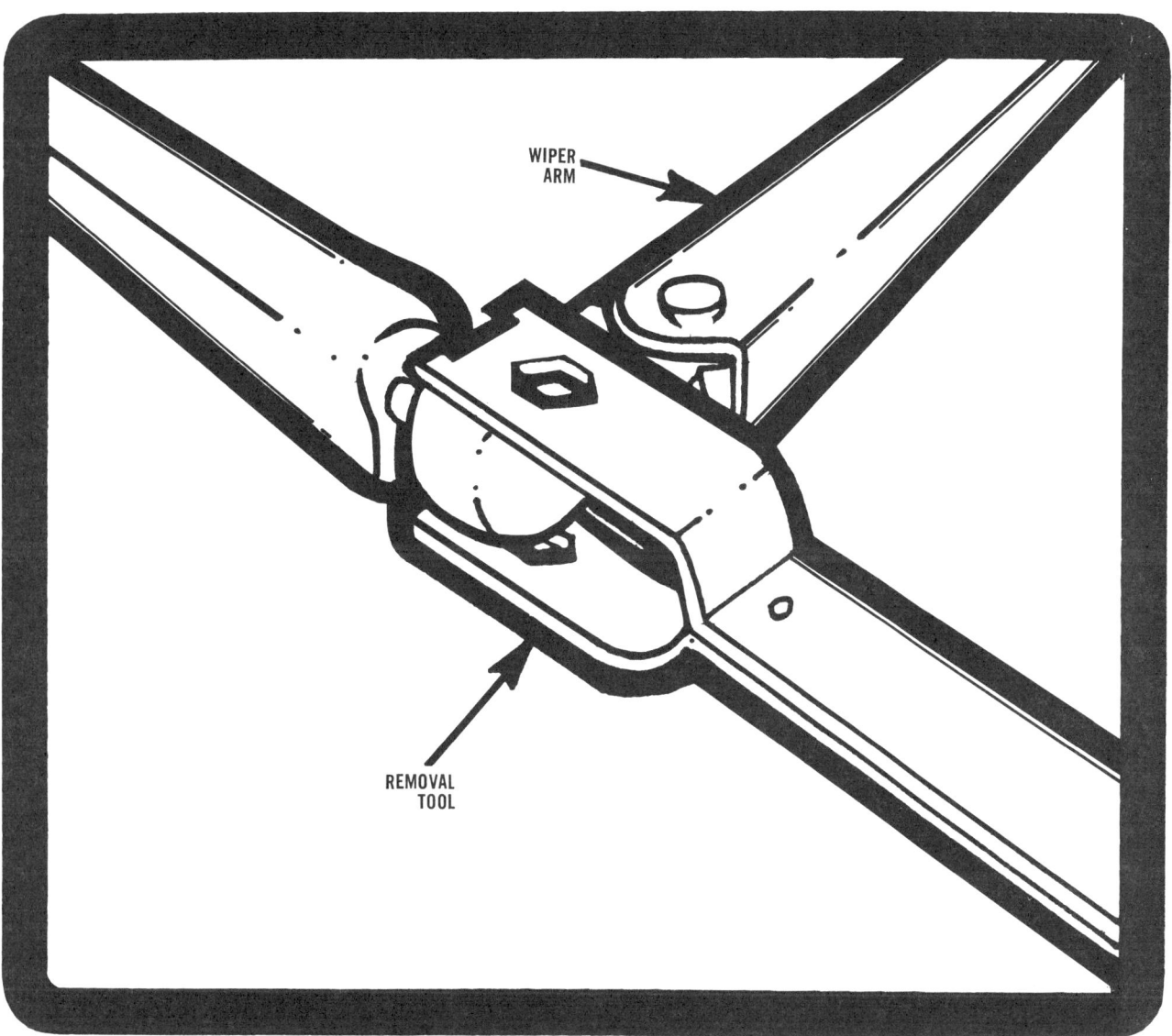

Fig. 18.

Put the turn signal indicator-arm down. The appropriate light on the dashboard should light and click on and off. If it stays on, the indicator bulb, either front or rear on that side, is burned out or the connection is bad. Repeat for the other direction. Flip on the emergency flasher light switch, located on the steering column or dashboard.

Have your helper check the front flashers first. In the rear of the car he can check four sets of lights—the flashers, the driving lights, the stop lights as you push the brake pedal, and the backup lights as you reverse gear.

Headlights drain more electricity from the battery than other lights. So be sure they are turned off when the engine is not running. Start the car before turning on the headlights. Emergency flasher lights should be turned on whenever you stop on the side of the road so other drivers know that your car is stopped. Flashers use very little electrical current and operate with the ignition key turned off.

Headlight aim

Testing headlights for direction and illumination is part of regular safety inspection in 32 states and the District of Columbia. But, required or not, it's equally important that you have your lights tested in a service facility at least once a year.

Make sure headlights are adjusted with the normal load you usually carry in the trunk and in the passenger compartment. Extra weight in the trunk pushes down the rear of the car and raises the headlight beams. Adjusting headlights under this condition, but then driving most of the time with the trunk empty, beams the lights too low. Before making a trip, have the headlights adjusted to the load you will be carrying. This will not be necessary if you have overload or adjustable rear shock absorbers, and can level the car.

HEADLIGHT REPLACEMENT

1. If the vehicle is equipped with concealed headlights, open the doors by turning the headlamps on. Refer to the owners manual on how to keep the doors open while the headlights are off.
2. Remove the headlight trim retaining screws and remove the headlight trim. On some vehicles with concealed headlights, the headlight door has to be removed, Fig. 21.
3. Remove the retainer ring.
    Some retainer rings have three slotted tabs placed 120° apart around the ring. To remove these, loosen the three retaining screws. Then turn the retainer ring counterclockwise until the enlarged portion of the slot comes under the screw heads. Remove the ring.
    Some rings have the tabs, but they are not slotted. In this case, remove the three retaining screws and remove the ring.
    Still another type of retainer ring is held by a hook on one side and a spring on the other. To remove these, just unhook the spring from the retainer ring using a pair of needle nose pliers and disengage the ring from the hook.
    NOTE: When removing retainer ring, be careful. The bulb may slip out.
4. Pull the headlight forward and disconnect the electrical connector, Fig. 22.
5. Connect the wiring connector to the new bulb. On two headlight systems, make sure that a No. 2 lamp is being installed. On four headlight systems, make sure that a No. 2 lamp is being installed on the outboard side and that a No. 1 lamp is being installed on the inboard side.
6. Place the lamp in position. Align the tabs on the lamp with the slots in the adjusting ring.
7. Install the retainer ring. If the retainer ring has three slotted tabs, position the ring with the enlarged portion of the slotted holes over the retaining screw heads, then turn retaining screw clockwise and tighten the screws. If the retainer ring does not have slotted holes in the tabs, position the retainer ring on the adjusting ring and install the retaining screws. If the retainer ring is retained by a spring and hook, use needlenose pliers to engage one side of the retainer ring onto the hook and engage the spring onto the other side of the retainer ring.
8. Check the headlights on both high and low beam to make sure that they are operating properly.
9. Install the headlight trim and retaining screws. If removed, install the headlight door.
10. Have the headlight adjustment checked. It is seldom necessary to have the headlights adjusted after a headlight has been replaced.

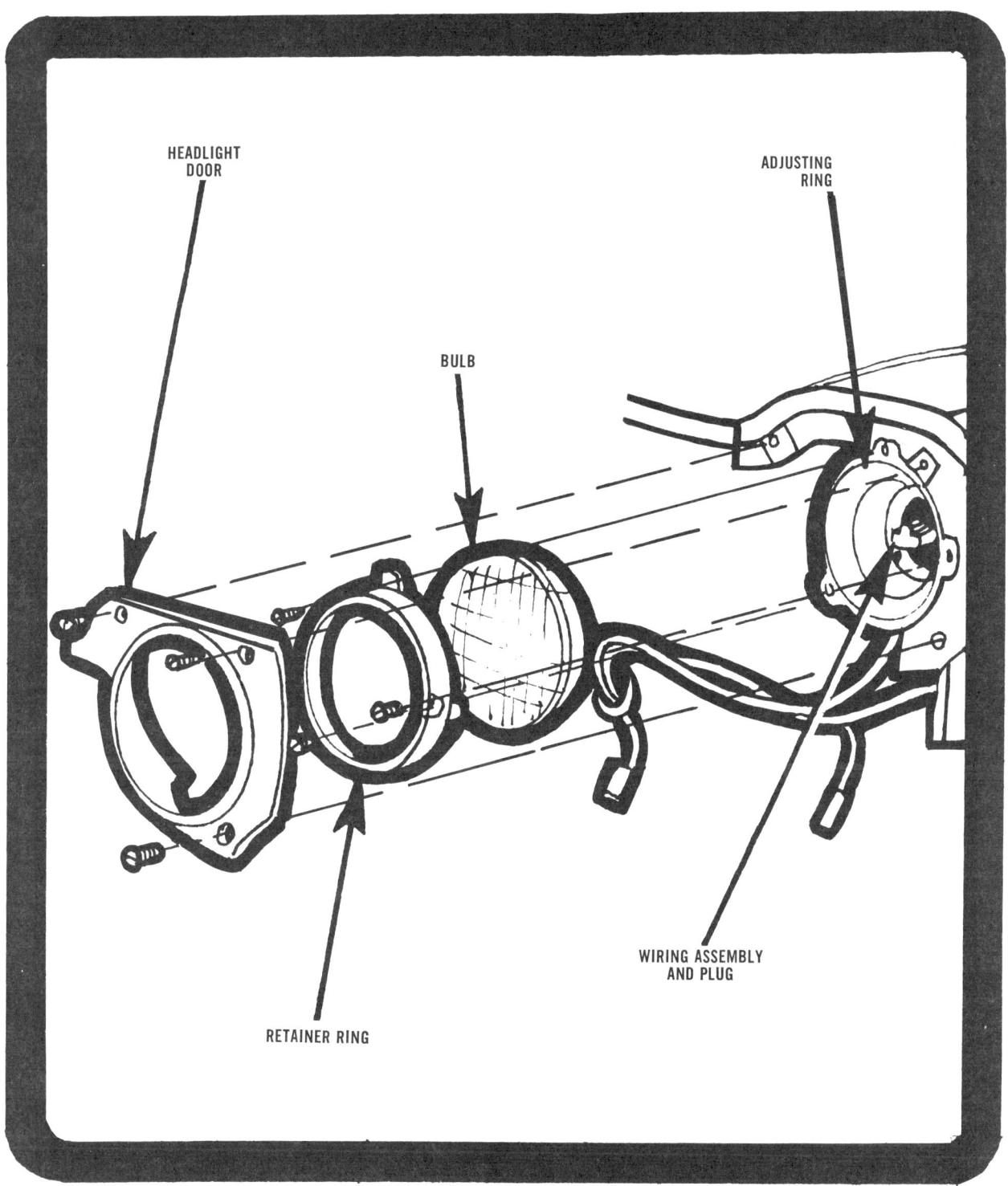

Fig. 21. Typical headlamp installation.

QUICK TIPS FOR ELECTRICAL SERVICE

- If you suspect an electrical problem, first check the fuse box for a blown or defective fuse.
- Remember: You could have a bad fuse without seeing a noticeable separation of the fuse filament.
- To quickly check the condition of a bulb, hold it up to the light and tap it with a finger. If there is any shaking of the filament or loose shreds shaking around inside, replace the bulb.
- Exercise extreme caution when changing fuses. Fuses break easily and the glass particles could cut you.
- Also use extreme caution when inserting a light bulb into its socket. Remember that glass is fragile.
- When inserting a bulb into its socket, make sure there is a good contact between the bulb itself and the contact strip in the socket.
- If the bulb goes on and off when lightly shaken, you are getting a poor contact between the bulb and the socket. Reinsert the bulb and try for a better contact.
- All parking and side marker lights have a sealing rubber gasket behind the lens. When replacing bulbs behind these lenses, take care not to rip this gasket. If you do rip it, replace it with a new one. Otherwise, the whole assembly can fill up with water and short out the bulb.

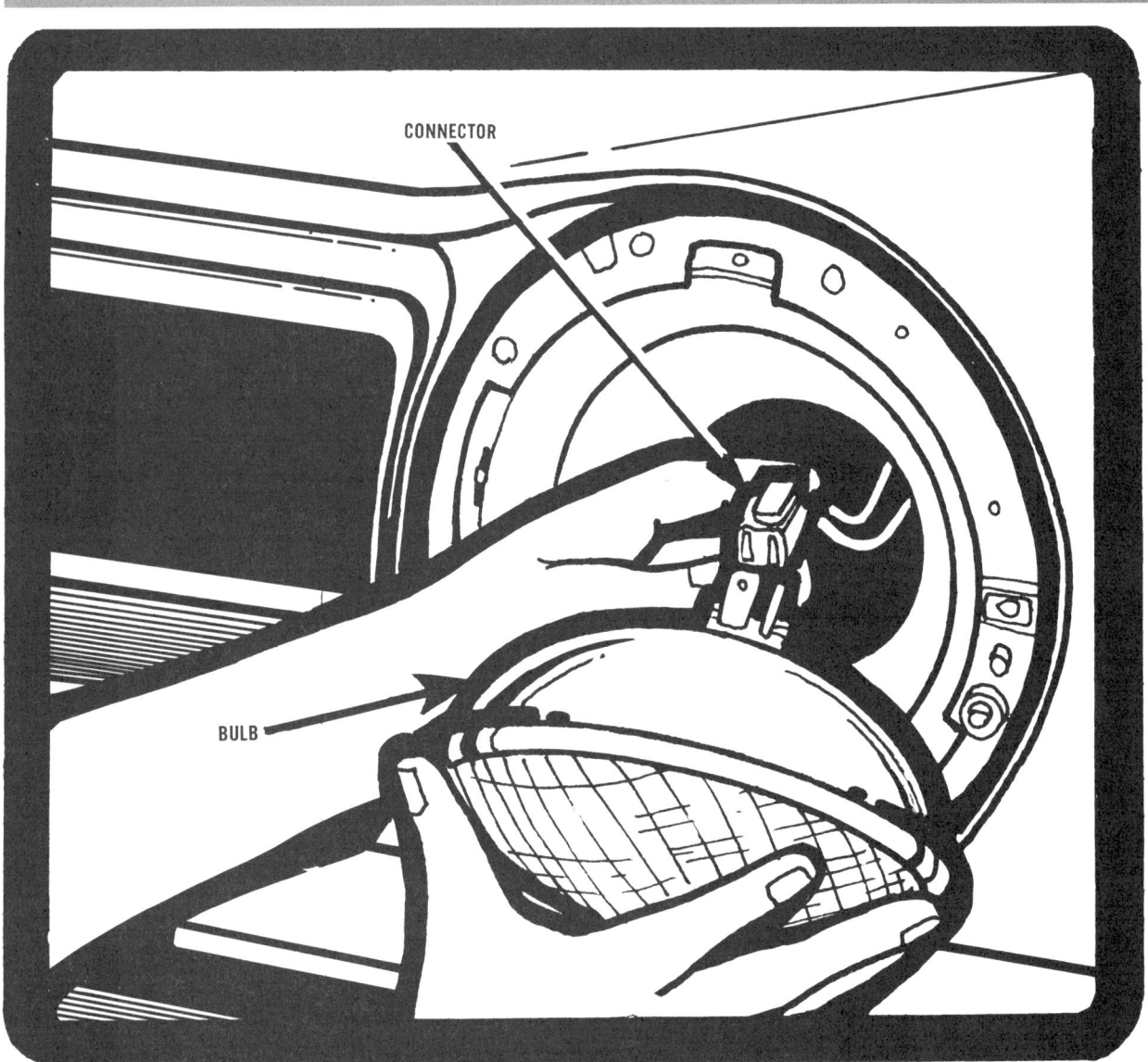

Fig. 22. Disconnecting electrical connector from headlamp.

LIGHT BULB REPLACEMENT

Although the size and appearance of any one specific light bulb may differ, the replacement procedure is usually the same.

CAUTION: When removing a light bulb that has been on, allow it to cool off for about a minute to avoid serious burns.

Dome light replacement, Fig. 20

1. If the dome light does not have screws around it, squeeze the lens and snap the lens out. If the dome light has retaining screws, remove the screws and lens.
2. If the bulb is long and cylindrical shaped and resembles a fuse, insert a screwdriver under the end of the bulb and pry the bulb out of the clips. To install a new bulb, position the bulb on the clips and press it into place.
3. If the bulb is long and cylindrical shaped and the ends are flat, push on the prong toward the bulb and lift the bulb from the prongs.
4. To remove conventional bulbs, depress bulb in socket and rotate counterclockwise and pull bulb from socket. To install the bulb, inspect the pins at the base of the bulb. If the pins are not the same distance from the bottom of the base, the pins must be aligned in the proper slots in the socket. Install bulb into socket and rotate bulb clockwise. If the bulb cannot be rotated, the pins are in the wrong slots. Remove bulb. Then rotate bulb ½-turn and reinstall it.
5. Install the lens.

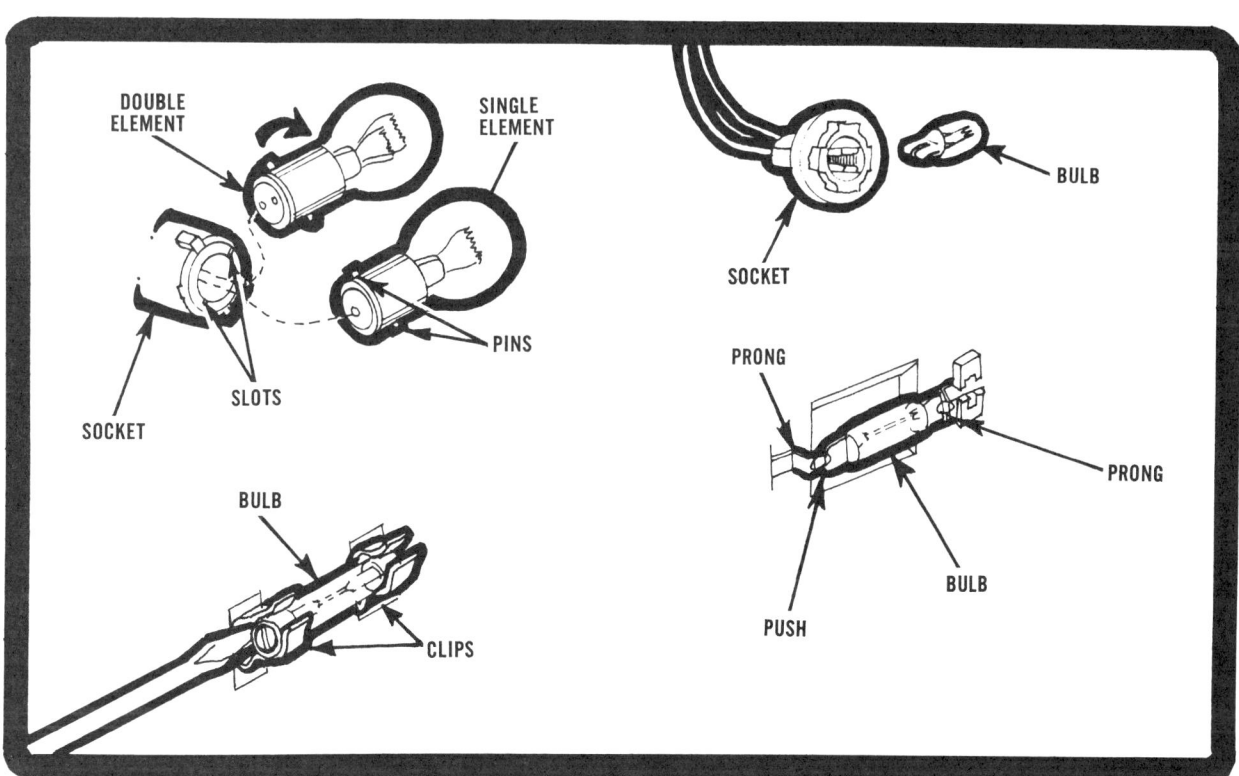

Fig. 23. Typical rear directional, back-up, stop, taillamp and side marker light installation.

Stop lights, turn signal lights, parking and backup lights, Figs. 24 and 24A.

These bulbs are normally installed in the trunk lid, front or rear bumper, front grille or the body of the vehicle. If the lens of the malfunctioning bulb has retaining screws which are visible from the outside of the vehicle, access to the bulb can be obtained by removing the retaining screws and the lens. If no retaining screws are visible from the outside, access to the bulb can be obtained by reaching in through the trunk compartment or engine compartment and removing the socket by either twisting the socket counterclockwise or rocking it, Fig. 20, Fig. 23 and Fig. 24.

1. Determine method of accessibility and remove the bulb from the socket by depressing it, rotating it counterclockwise and pulling it out.
2. Install new bulb. Bulbs with double filaments have the locating pins on base of the bulb staggered to prevent incorrect installation of the bulb. Align the pins on the base of the bulb with the proper slot in the socket. Then insert bulb into the socket and turn it clockwise to lock it in place. If the bulb does not turn, the bulb is incorrectly aligned. Remove the bulb, turn it ½-turn and reinstall it.
3. If the bulb was removed through the trunk compartment or engine compartment, align the tabs on the socket with the slots in the housing and either twist it or rock it into place.
4. If the bulb was removed by first removing the lens, reinstall the lens and retaining screws. Make sure that the gasket is properly positioned.

Side marker lights, Fig. 24

These lights are installed on the side of the fenders and quarter panels. Some vehicles use a wraparound taillight assembly which doubles as the side marker lights. If the side marker lens has retaining screws which are visible from the outside of the vehicle, access to the bulb can be obtained by removing the retaining screws and lens. If not, access can be obtained either through the trunk compartment, engine compartment or behind the fender through the wheel opening.

1. Determine the method of accessibility.
2. Remove the bulb. Two types of bulbs are used. The first type is removed by rotating it counterclockwise and pulling straight out. The second is removed by just pulling it straight out.
3. Install the new bulb. If the bulb was removed by rotating and pulling it out, reinstall it by aligning the pins on the base of the bulb with the slots in the socket. Then insert the bulb into the socket and rotate it clockwise to lock it in place. If the bulb was removed by pulling it, reinstall it by pushing straight in.

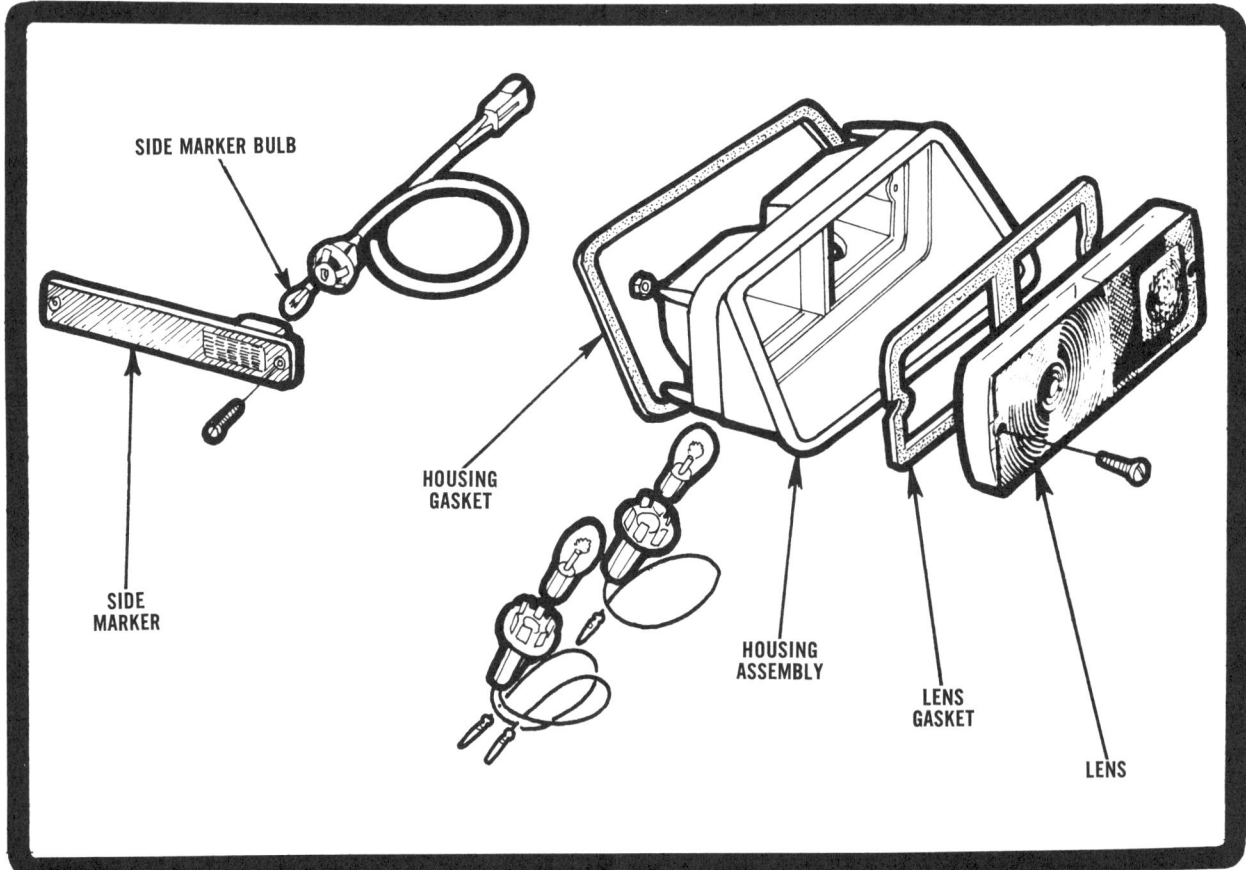

Fig. 24. Typical side marker light installation.

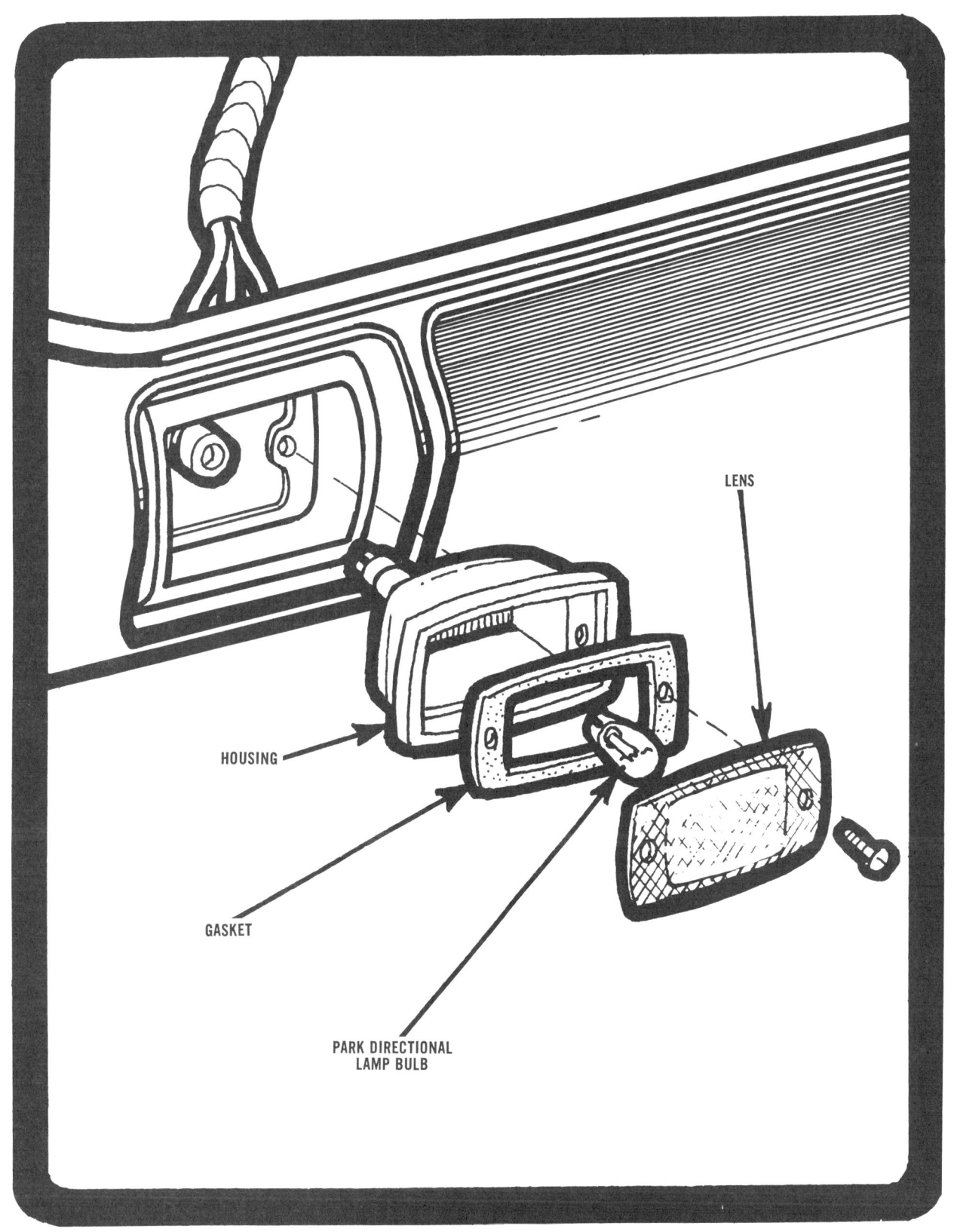

Fig. 24A. Typical front parking and directional light installation.

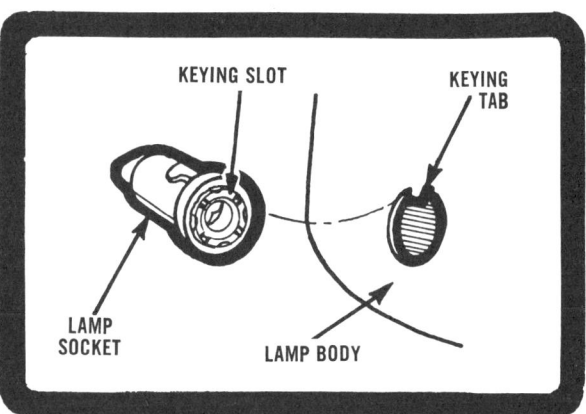

Fig. 25. Light bulb socket. To remove this type, grasp the socket and rock it off.

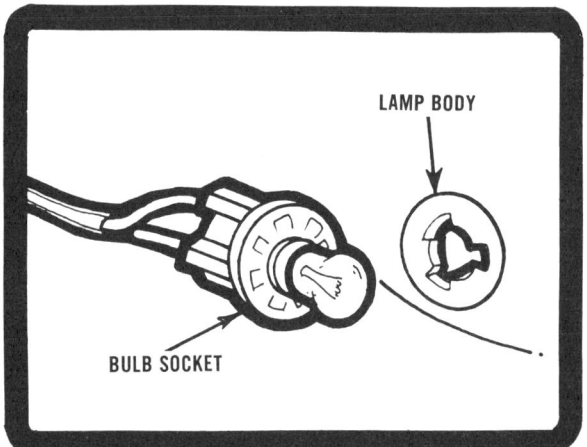

Fig. 26. Light bulb socket. To remove this type, grasp the socket, then rotate it about 1/8 turn and pull it off.

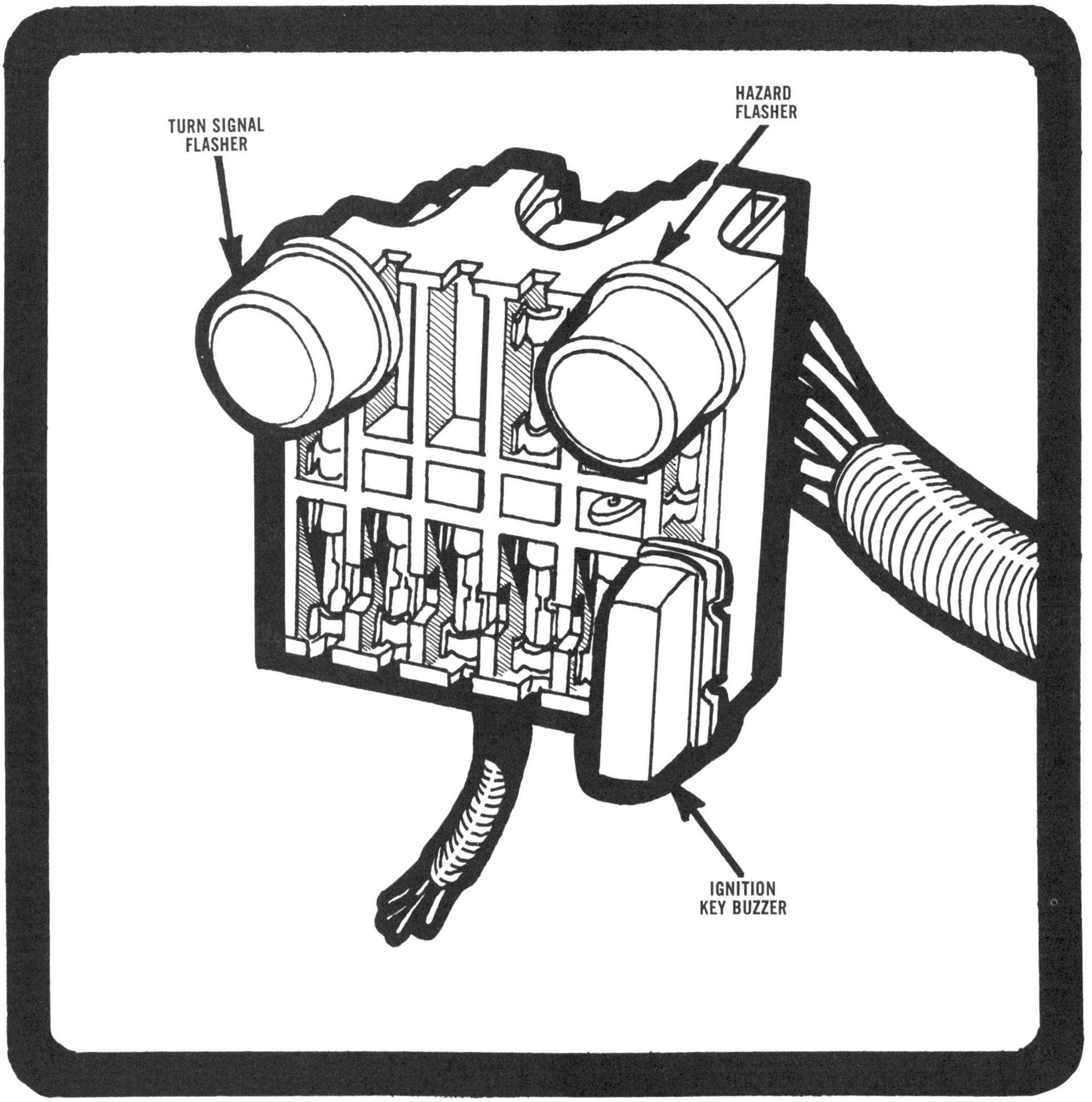

Fig. 27. Typical fuse panel with the turn signal and hazard warning flasher.

4. If the bulb was removed by first removing the lens, reinstall the lens and retaining screws. Make sure that the gasket is properly positioned.
5. If the bulb was removed through the trunk compartment, engine compartment or through the wheel opening, install the bulb and socket, aligning the tabs on the socket with the slots in the housing. Then either twist the socket or rotate it into place.

License plate lights
1. Remove the housing retaining screws.
2. Work the housing out from behind the bumper.
3. Remove the lens retaining screws and remove the lens and gasket.
4. Remove the bulb. Two types of bulbs are used. The first is removed by rotating counterclockwise and pulling straight out. The second by just pulling straight out, Fig. 25 and Fig. 26.
5. Install the new bulb. If the bulb was removed by rotating and pulling out, reinstall it by aligning the pins on the base of the bulb with the slots in the socket. Then insert bulb into socket and twist it clockwise to lock it in place. If the bulb was removed by pulling it out, reinstall it by pushing it straight in.
6. Install the gasket, lens and retaining screws.
7. Work housing back into place and install the retaining screws.

FUSE REPLACEMENT
The fuse panels are usually located attached to the fire wall on the driver's side, underneath the instrument panel or in the glove box, Fig. 27.
1. Make sure that the ignition switch is off.
2. Remove the fuse using a fuse puller, Fig. 28. Check the illustration. If a fuse puller is not available, the fuse can be pried out using half a clothes-pin. Use a firm steady pressure to remove and avoid breaking it.

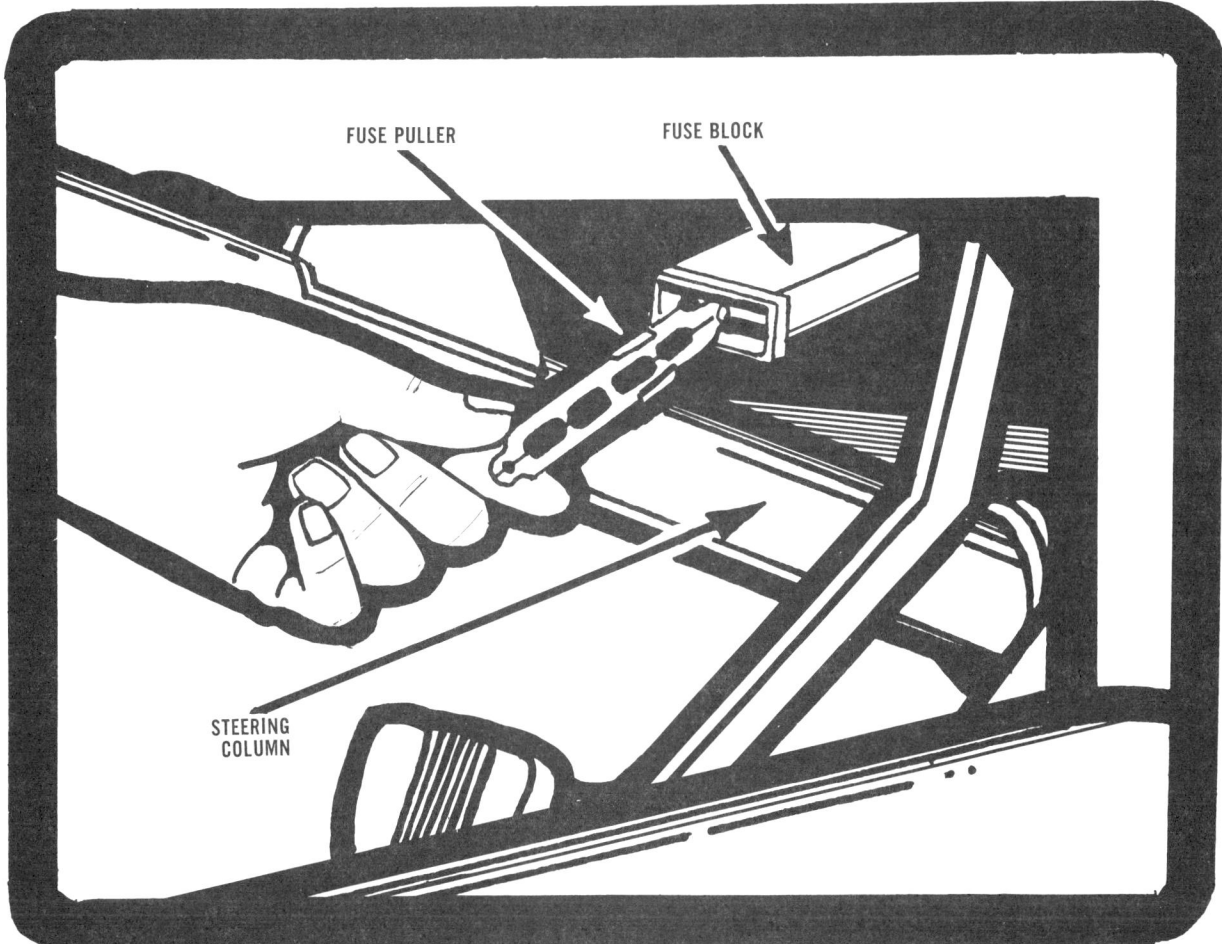

Fig. 28. Pulling fuse from panel using a fuse remover.

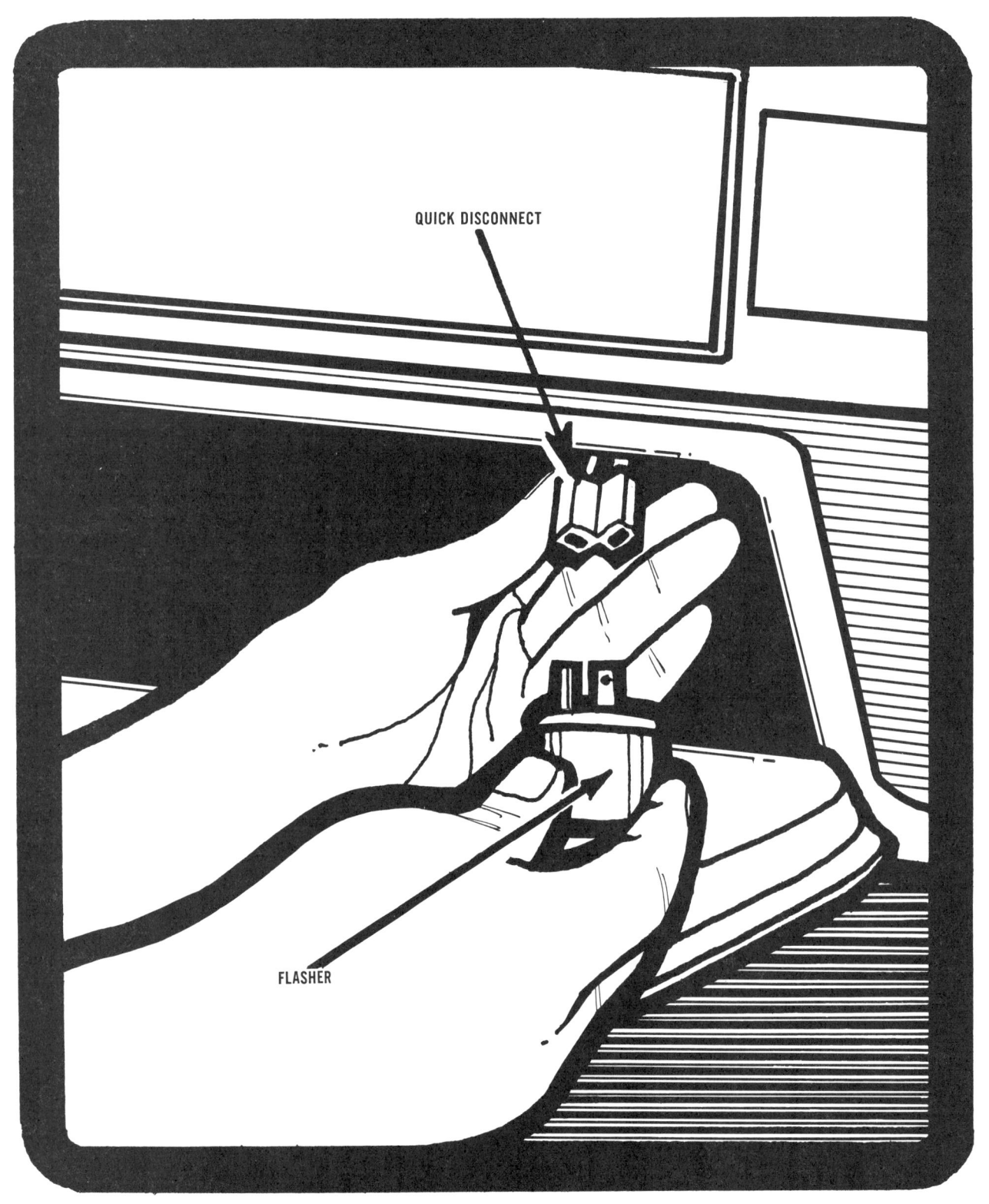

Fig. 29. Tab and slot type flasher.

3. Position the new replacement fuse against the retaining clips. Press both ends of the fuse inward against the clips until the fuse snaps into place.
4. Check operation of the circuit for which the fuse was replaced. If the fuse burns, there is a short in the circuit. Have a qualified mechanic repair the circuit.

TURN SIGNAL AND HAZARD WARNING FLASHER REPLACEMENT

The flashers are mounted in several different ways —plugged into the fuse panel, Fig. 27, tab and slot type, Fig. 29, where the end of the flasher has a slot which engages a tab underneath the instrument panel; retained on a bracket, Fig. 30, or taped to an existing wiring harness.

1. Refer to your owner's manual or the chart here and determine the location of the flasher.
2. Remove the flasher.
   (a) If the flasher is mounted on the fuse panel, pull it straight out.
   (b) If the flasher is of the tab and slot type, disengage the flasher by pulling it off the tab and disconnect the wiring connector.
   (c) If the flasher is retained by a clip, pull the flasher from the clip and disconnect the wiring connector.
   (d) If the flasher is taped onto an existing harness, pull the flasher from the connector and leave the connector attached to the wiring harness.
3. Install the new flasher.
   (a) If the flasher is mounted on the fuse panel, align the prongs on the flasher with the slots in the fuse panel and push the flasher into place.
   (b) If the flasher is of the tab and slot type, connect the flasher onto the wiring connector and engage the slot on the flasher with the tab.
   (c) If the flasher was retained by a clip, connect the flasher onto the wiring connector and snap the flasher into the clip.
   (d) If the flasher is taped onto the wiring harness, just reconnect the flasher onto the connector.

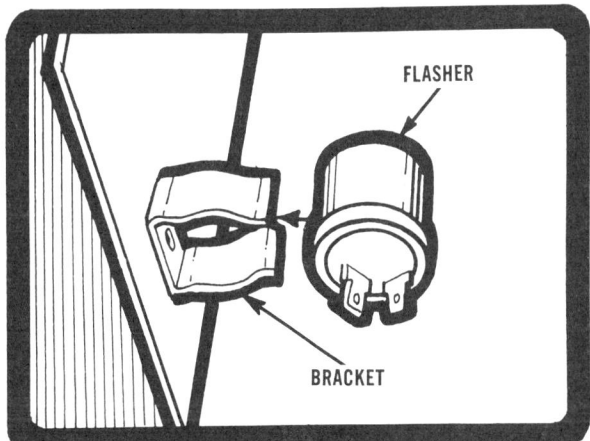

Fig. 30. Bracket-retained type flasher.

FLASHER LOCATIONS

CAR	1969		1970		1971		1972		1973		1974		1975		1976	
	TSF	HWF	TSF	HWF	TSF	HWF	TSF	HWF	TSF	HWF	TSF	HWF	TSF	HWF	TSF	HWF
American Motors	2	3	2⑬	3	2⑮	3	3	3	3	3	3	3	3	4	3	4
Aspen & Volare	—	—	—	—	—	—	—	—	—	—	—	—	—	—	3	4
Astre & Vega	—	—	—	—	5	3	5	3	5	3	5	3	5	3	5	3
Buick, Special & Century	3	3	3	3	3	3	3	3	3	3	3	3	3	3	4	3
Buick Apollo & Skylark	—	—	—	—	—	—	—	—	10	3	10	3	10	3	10	3
Cadillac Exc. Seville	5	5	6	8	⑭	3	⑭	3	⑭	3	⑭	3	⑭	3	⑭	3
Cadillac Seville	—	—	—	—	—	—	—	—	—	—	—	—	—	—	4	3
Camaro	8	3	8	3	8	3	8	3	8	3	8	3	8	3	4	3
Chevelle & Monte Carlo	8	3	1	3	7	3	7	3	4	3	4	3	4	3	4	3
Chevette	—	—	—	—	—	—	—	—	—	—	—	—	—	—	15	3
Chevrolet	8	3	10	3	7	3	7	3	6	3	6	3	6	3	7	3
Chevrolet Nova	8	3	10	3	7	3	7	3	10	3	10	3	10	3	10	3
Chrysler	5	4	5	4	5	4	5	5	5	5	⑰	⑱	5	5	5	3
Comet & Montego	6	5	6	5	5	5	5	5	5	5	5⑲	5⑲	4	3	㉔	3
Cordoba & Charger SE	—	—	—	—	—	—	—	—	—	—	—	—	3	6	15	3⑱
Corvette	⑦	3	⑦	3	⑦	3	⑦	3	⑦	3	⑦	3	⑦	3	⑦	3
Cougar	8	10	8	10	11	6	8	10	8	10	5	5	5	5	3	3
Dart & Challenger	8	5	8	⑧	8	⑧	10	6	8	④	⑰	⑱	4	5	5	5
Dodge	④	①	5	6	①	—	①	5	8	6	⑰	⑱	5㉑	5㉒	㉕	3㉒
Fairlane, Torino & Elite	6	5	6	5	5	5	5	5	5	5	5	5	3	3	3	3
Falcon & Maverick	6	⑨	6	⑨	5	5	5	5	5	5	11	11	11	11	4	3
Firebird, Le Mans & Tempest	3	3	3	3	3	3	3	3	3	3	3	3	3	3	4	3
Ford	6	5	11	3	8	3	8	3	8	3	3	3	3	3	3	3
Ford Pinto & Mercury Bobcat	—	—	—	—	10	10	10	10	10	10	11	11	11	11	11	11
Granada & Monarch	—	—	—	—	—	—	—	—	—	—	—	—	8	4	10	4
Grand Am & Grand Le Mans	—	—	—	—	—	—	—	—	3	3	3	3	3	3	3	5
Imperial	13	13	5	4	5	4	5	5	5	6	⑰	⑱	5	5	—	—
Lincoln	11	11	3⑪	3⑫	6	6	3	3	3	3	7⑳	7⑳	11	3	10⑳	3
Mercury	4	6	11	3	8	3	8	3	8	3	3	3	3	3	3	3
Monza, Skyhawk, Starfire & Sunbird	—	—	—	—	—	—	—	—	—	—	—	—	5	3	14	14
Mustang & Mustang II	1	4	10	8	11	6	8	10	8	10	11	11	7㉓	7㉓	16	16
Oldsmobile	3	3	1	3	4	3	4	3	4	3	4	3	4	3	4	3
Oldsmobile Cutlass	3	3	3	3	4	3	4	3	4	3	4	3	4	3	4	3
Olds. Omega & Pont. Ventura	—	—	—	—	7	3	7	3	10	3	10	3	10	3	10	3
Oldsmobile Toronado	3	3	4	3	4	3	4	3	4	3	4	3	4	3	4	3
Plymouth	⑥	⑤	⑥	6	②	—	②	5	8	6	⑰	⑱	5	5	㉖	3㉗
Pontiac	3	3	3	3	3	3	3	3	3	3	3	3	3	3	3	5
Thunderbird	13	13	⑩	11	11	6	3	3	3	3	3	3	3	3	3	3
Valiant & Barracuda	8	5	8	6	8	6	10	6	8	⑯	⑰	⑱	4	5	5	5

TSF: Turn Signal Flasher. HWF: Hazard Warning Flasher.

① —Location 10 on Coronet & Charger. Location 5 on Polara & Monaco.
② —Location 10 on Belvedere & Satellite. Location 5 on Fury & VIP.
③ —Location 6 on Challenger. Location 5 on Dart.
④ —Location 4 on Coronet & Charger. Location 8 on Polara & Monaco.
⑤ —Location 6 on Belvedere & Satellite. Location 4 on Fury & VIP.
⑥ —Location 4 on Belvedere & Satellite. Location 8 on Fury & VIP.
⑦ —Extreme lower right corner on instrument panel.
⑧ —Location 6 on Challenger. Location 10 on Dart.
⑨ —Location 5 on Falcon. Behind ash tray on Maverick.
⑩ —To right of glove box.
⑪ —Mark III to right of glove box.
⑫ —Mark III to left of glove box.
⑬ —Location 3 on Hornet and Gremlin.
⑭ —On the underside of steering column lower cover.
⑮ —Location 3 on Hornet, Gremlin and Javelin.
⑯ —Location 6 on Barracuda. Location 5 on Valiant.
⑰ —Behind instrument panel, on right side of ash tray.
⑱ —On right side of brake pedal support.
⑲ —Location 11 on Comet.
⑳ —Location 3 on Mark IV.
㉑ —Location 3 on Coronet.
㉒ —On right side of brake pedal support on Coronet models.
㉓ —One flasher used for both systems.
㉔ —Location 4 on Comet. Location 3 on Montego.
㉕ —Location 15 on Coronet. Location 5 on Monaco.
㉖ —Location 15 on Fury. Location 5 on Gran Fury.
㉗ —On right side of brake support on Fury models.

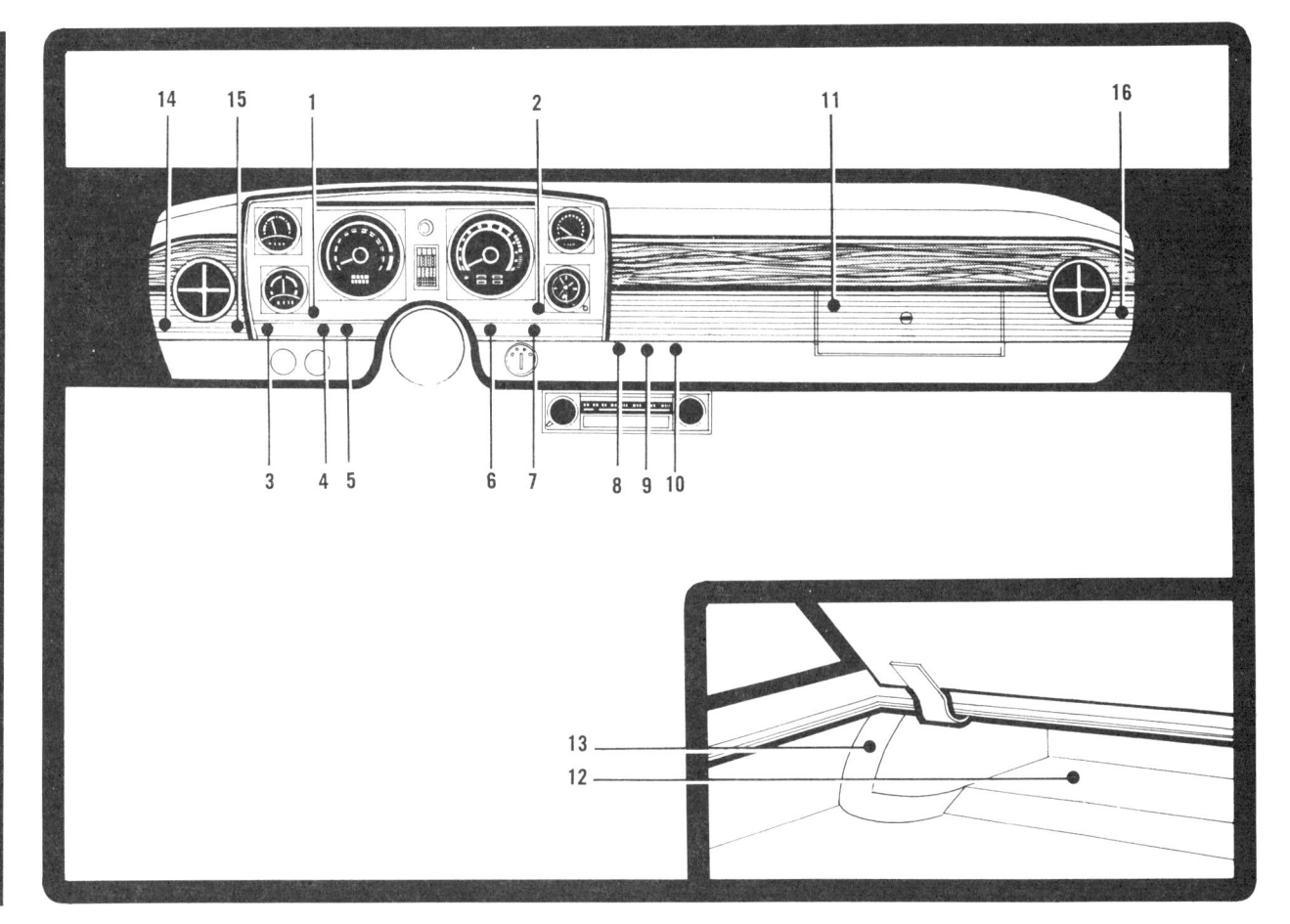

TROUBLESHOOTING FLOW CHART

LIGHTING SYSTEMS

Symptom	Probable Cause	Remedy
A. Lights are very dim.	1. Discharged battery. 2. Loose or dirty connections at battery or ground cable or loose or dirty firewall connector.	1. Recharge or replace battery as necessary. 2. Clean connectors and tighten securely.
B. One light does not work.	3. Burned out bulb. 4. Blown fuse. 5. Faulty wiring or connectors.	3. Replace bulb with correct type replacement. 4. Replace fuse with correct type ampere rating. 5. Check connectors in affected circuit to make sure they are clean and tight. Check wiring for opens or grounds.
C. Turn signal lights flash on one side only.	6. Burned out bulb. 7. Faulty wiring or connectors.	6. Replace bulb with correct type replacement. 7. Check all connectors to make sure that they are tight and clean. Check wiring in affected circuit for opens or grounds.
D. Turn signal lights do not flash on either side.	8. Faulty flasher unit. 9. Blown fuse.	8. Replace flasher unit with correct replacement type. 9. Replace fuse with one of correct ampere rating.
E. Stop lights do not go on.	10. Burned out bulbs. 11. Blown out fuse. 12. Improperly adjusted or defective stoplight switch. 13. Faulty wiring or connectors.	10. Replace bulbs using correct type replacement. 11. Replace fuse using one of correct ampere rating. 12. Adjust or replace switch as required. 13. Check connectors to make sure that they are clean and tight. Check wiring in affected circuit for opens or grounds.
F. Stop lights remain on.	14. Improperly adjusted or defective stoplight. 15. Faulty wiring.	14. Adjust or replace stoplight switch as required. 15. Check wiring in affected circuit for grounds and correct as necessary.
G. Headlights flash on and off.	16. Intermittent headlight switch. 17. Short circuit in wiring. 18. Faulty wiring or connectors.	16. Replace headlight switch. 17. Check wiring in affected circuit for shorts and correct as necessary. 18. Check all connectors to make sure that they are clean and tight. Check wiring for opens or short circuiting.
H. Windshield wipers do not operate.	19. Faulty wiring or connectors. 20. Blown fuse. 21. Faulty wiper switch. 22. Faulty wiper motor. 23. Wiper linkage disconnected or damaged.	19. Check all connectors to make sure that they are clean and tight. Check wiring for opens or short circuiting. 20. Replace fuse with one of correct ampere rating. 21. Replace wiper switch. 22. Replace wiper motor. 23. Reconnect or replace wiper linkage as required.
I. Windshield wipers do not park.	24. Defective windshield wiper park switch.	24. Replace windshield wiper park switch.
J. Windshield washer does not operate.	25. Low fluid level in reservoir. 26. Disconnected or damaged hoses leading to nozzles. 27. Clogged nozzles. 28. Defective washer pump.	25. Add fluid into reservoir as required to bring up level. 26. Reconnect or replace hoses as required. 27. Clear out nozzles or replace. 28. Replace washer pump.

Body and Interior Maintenance

Detailing your car

If you have ever shopped a used car lot you know that, whatever else they neglect, the professionals try to get the vehicles as clean and shiny as possible on the outside and as new looking as possible on the inside. You can be reasonably sure that, for any vehicle with some monetary value left, the pros will shampoo the interior, give it a good vacuuming and polish any chrome or brightwork on the dash and on window and door handles.

Some will go to the extent of putting on seat covers if the upholstery is either ripped or worn. And many will replace the pads on the accelerator and brake pedals. Few will replace weatherstripping unless it is unusually frayed for the supposed age of the car. But most dealers will compound, polish and wax used cars and touch up paint knicks and scratches as well as filling in small dents. They will remove all the rust they can from bumpers and, in general, make the car look as close to new as possible.

It is all part of a process that is about 60% elbow grease and 40% investment in the right tools and materials—a process called detailing the car.

What does this all tell you? First it tells you that a clean car brings more money in resale and therefore is more desirable. But it also tells you that there is a practical limit to how much you should spend to renew and maintain a used car. To the pro, what that limit is depends on which model and how much resale value can be improved. If you are just sharpening a car for the satisfaction that comes in keeping the vehicle new looking as long as possible, you must decide how much time, money and effort will go into achieving that aim.

Here is one tip right away: if you acquire a new car or one professionally detailed, it is easier to institute regular body and interior maintenance than to try to do it after a year or more of neglect.

The basic premise about maintaining body and interior appearance is to make it a routine and keep on top of it. You will find you are spending less time than the man or woman who lets it go for four months, then tries to renew the car in one fell swoop. You will also enjoy your car more if it stays clean.

A car that has been given care and maintenance will not only present a better appearance throughout its useful life, but also return more dollars to you at trade-in time.

EXTERIOR MAINTENANCE

REGULAR WASHING

The first procedure in body maintenance is regular washing. Depending upon where you live and where you drive, the regular washing may be needed once a week or once every three weeks. The latter would mean the car is housed in the country where the air is pure and the owner usually uses it to go to church on Sunday and bingo on Wednesday. For most cars a good washing is needed once a week.

Obviously it is possible to run the car through an automatic car wash to keep it clean. But that costs anywhere from $1.25 to $2.75 a shot and, if you have ever stopped to wipe off the water that did not quite dry under the blower, you know that even the best auto laundry can leave water spots. The worst merely rearrange the surface dirt.

If the exterior is really filthy, it pays to go to the automatic car wash first if you can or even get a hand wash at a service station which has a hand-operated hot water pressure washer. Some people schedule either a hand wash at a service station or a visit to an automatic car wash at least once a month because either method loosens dirt in hard-to-get at places like rocker panels, valence panels, wheels.

But if you have the right equipment you can do almost as good a job with merely a garden hose and a brush attachment plus a wide variety of special car washes. Actually, a mild dish washing detergent is suitable.

Once you have set the approximate time each week you are going to wash the car, you are ready to begin proper washing procedure. You need a hose, preferably the kind that is pressure resistant, a good adjustable spray nozzle, a pail or bucket, two large sponges and a medium bristle cleaning brush plus a large chamois or rag towelling.

Brush attachments come in a variety of designs, one of which also cleans attic windows from ground level. Some have reservoirs for detergent powder, liquid or pellets. These presumably eliminate the need for the pail and sponge routine because the pressure of the water is supposed to carry the requisite amount of car cleaner to the revolving brush head which then can use it to loosen grime. This is a time saver but only if the car comes out as clean as you expect it to be. Otherwise the bucket and sponges do the cleaning job more thoroughly.

Procedure

If you are using a specific car detergent, read the directions and follow them. But the general washing procedure is as follows:

1. With the hose nozzle set to give maximum pressure, wet down the roof and greenhouse of the car. The greenhouse is that part of the automobile, including the windows, above the hood and trunk lid. Always wash or wax a car from the top down because that is the way the water is going to go anyway. Depending upon how big you are and how big the car is, you either do the whole roof or part of a roof at one time.

2. Now take one of the sponges in your pail of car wash suds and, using a circular motion, apply the suds to the roof or part of it. Do not knock yourself out pressing down as hard as you can. If the car is that dirty, you have more than enough suds in the bucket and you must let the detergent suds do some of the work. A good medium pressure is what you want. If the car is dusty, hard pressure will be like sandpapering the vehicle. Dust is often composed of microscopic rock bits as hard as quartz.

When washing a car, always start from top and work down. Hose the car first.

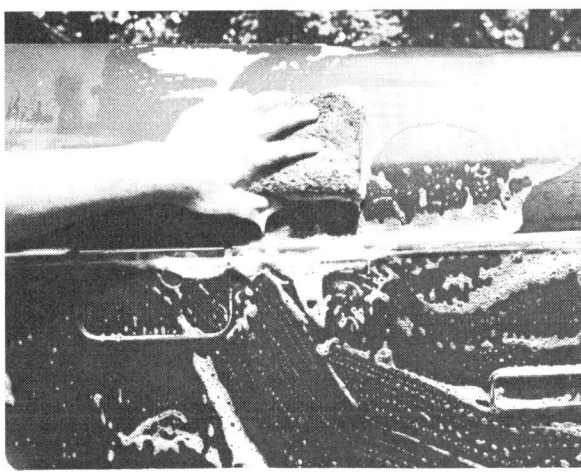

Apply suds liberally to a section of car at a time.

Here are the materials and tools you'll need to maintain your car. It represents an investment under $25.

EQUIPMENT YOU WILL NEED

Exterior:

Wash:	garden hose (preferably with adjustable spray nozzle)
	brush attachment
	car cleaner or mild dishwashing detergent
	2 large sponges
	pail or bucket
	large chamois or other soft rag
Chrome cleaning:	chrome cleaner
	chrome protector
	steel wool
Waxing:	pre-wax cleaner
	polish
	soft rag
Compounding:	compound
	clean, soft rag
Paint touchup:	medium or fine emery cloth
	primer
	masking tape
	paint (spray or small can)
	brush (if not using spray)
Weatherstripping:	rubber dressing
	silicone spray
Vinyl top:	clear vinyl cleaner

Interior:

Vinyl seats:	clear vinyl cleaner
Carpets:	carpet shampoo
	brush
	vacuum (if possible)
Dash instruments:	ammonia solution or window cleaning spray

Be governed also by how sunny it is while you are washing, how generally hot or cold and how much surface you can reach. No matter what the directions on the detergent say, if you are working in full sun, do a little less surface. Otherwise you run the risk of streaking from drying detergent and you will have to do it over. Squeeze out the sponge *before* putting it back into the suds. Some use a second bucket of clear water to rinse it.

3. With the hose set at maximum jet, hose off the surface you have sudsed. Get the suds all off any part of the greenhouse, the part of the car from the glass up.
4. Now take the other sponge in the suds and do another piece of the greenhouse adjoining the cleaned portion and hose that off.
5. Switch sponges and continue until you have the whole roof done as well as window posts. If there are problem spots like bird droppings, dead insects, and leaves that have adhered so long they leave a pattern, you can get a small sponge with a roughened or plasticized side to clean off these areas during the cleaning hosing cycle. Make sure, however, that the rough side cannot scratch either window or paint. Some prefer a small brush, the kind used to apply shoe polish, for this duty but the same warning applies.
6. When you have the roof and greenhouse clean, (it might take several sudsings), wipe it down with your chamois or clean rag toweling. The chamois or some of the synthetic substitutes are far more efficacious in getting all the surface dry because they tend to prevent water spotting and streaking. However, do not worry too much about the windows because you will be doing them over with window cleaner after the wash job.
7. Now proceed to the hood and the top of the front fenders or to the rear deck lid and top of the rear fenders. Remember to direct the hose spray away from the greenhouse as much as possible. Use the same procedure of switching sponges and hosing areas off after you have sponged on the suds. And rub out problem spots. Then chamois, again not worrying about the edge of the areas you are doing.
8. If you did the hood, now do the rear decklid or vice versa. Remember you are working from the top down.

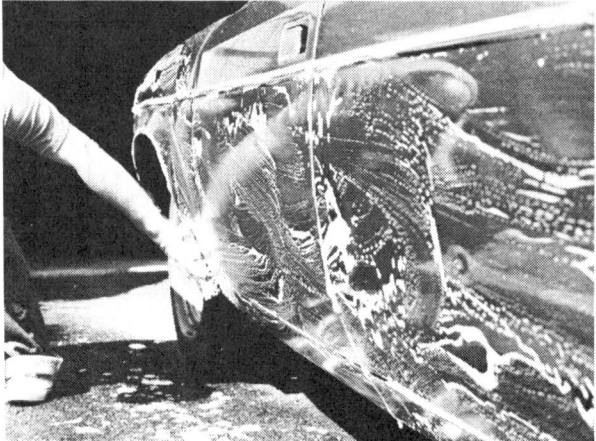

Put an extra dose of suds on the rocker panels and near the wheelwells.

This brush hose attachment rotates for cleaning action and applies suds.

You still must hose off afterward.

Apply window cleaner liberally to inside of window.

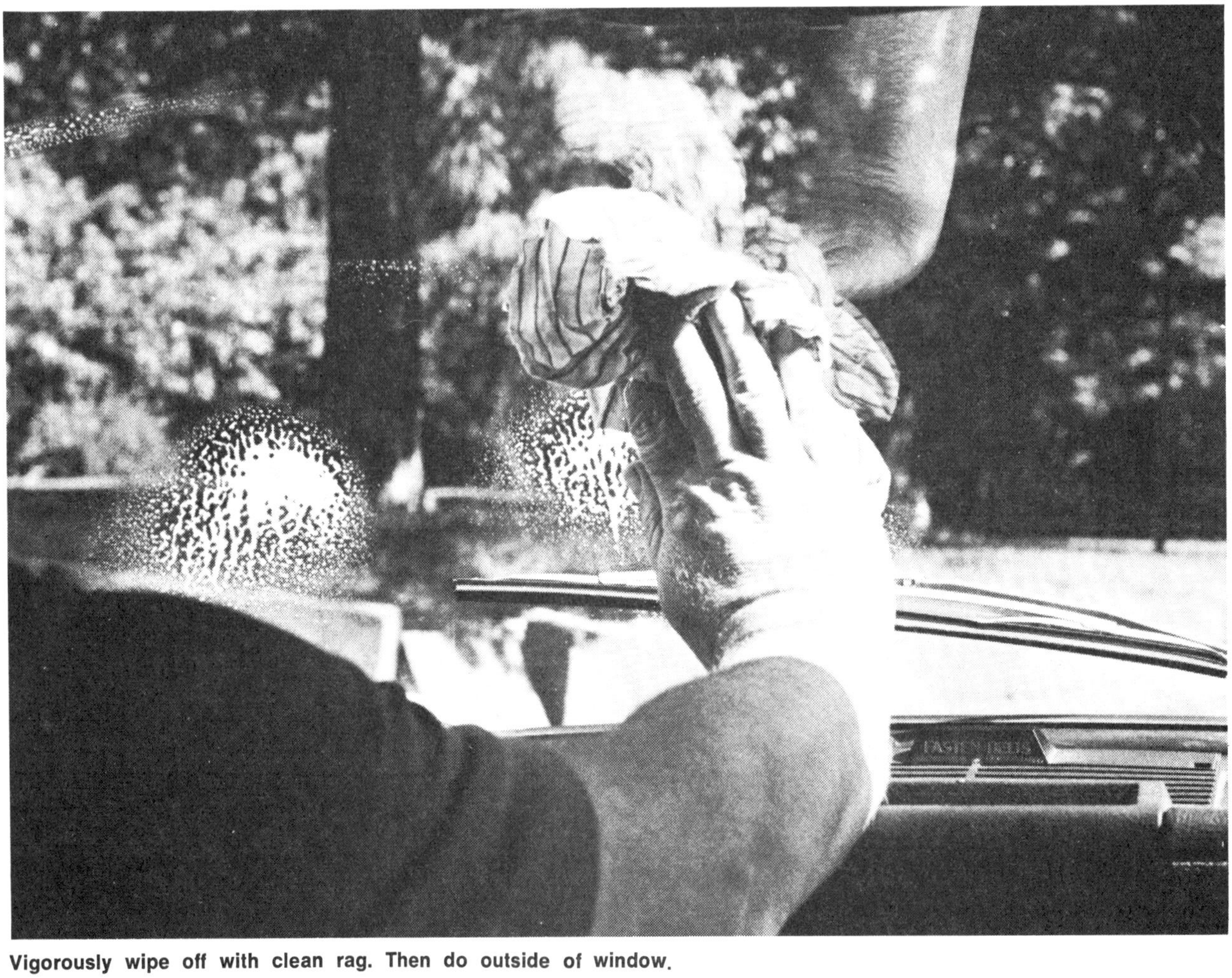

Vigorously wipe off with clean rag. Then do outside of window.

9. The side of the car below the greenhouse should be cleaned working from top to bottom. Forget about the wheels and wheelwell moldings for now although you can hose the wheel covers off. In some areas you are most likely to encounter little black specks or even lumps of road tar on fenders and lower door areas. As with the bird droppings, you must clean this off now. Hopefully these problems will respond to your spot sponge or brush. If they do not, get a special product for the tar in your auto store or try hitting the tar with a household foam cleaner.

   Again it is a case of reading the directions on the product to see if it is harmful to painted surfaces. Just hose the stuff off as you do the suds. Rewash and hose off just to make sure.
10. Wash rocker panels, door jambs, front and rear valence panels and the grille and bumper in that order. Leave the wheels for last.
11. Hose the wheel with maximum jet at close range. Then suds it with a brush remembering to loosen the dirt that accumulates around the wheel rim. Then hose off again. Grease and tar on the wheel is usually much thicker and must be attacked with a specialty or household cleaner. But read the label before you use some detergents on the tire whitewalls. They can have a deleterious effect on the rubber. (Never use any product containing alcohol.) Wipe wheels with rags rather than your chamois, mainly to preserve the chamois from damage.

Clean the windows after you are done washing and drying the car. Any of the many household window cleaners will do. Or else just take another bucket and add ammonia—not too much—to some water.

Newspapers make fine window rags once they are either dipped into the ammonia and water or wet while rubbing off the window foam. Clean the windshield outside and the rear window outside, then the headlight lenses and side view mirrors. When you clean the side windows, roll them down partly after you have wiped the outside. That way you can do the edges which tend to get very dirty.

Now do the insides of the window with the foam, the liquid or the ammonia/water.

Black rubber dressing should be applied to blackwall tires with paint brush. It improves the tire's looks and helps preserve rubber.

Chrome or stainless trim and bumpers need a chrome cleaner to make them sparkle. Follow directions. If you have rust spots or pitting, clean off the rust using a tiny piece of steel wool very judiciously. Then immediately use chrome protector or a good body wax. Severe pitting means the chrome is worn almost off and, unless you want to use silver paint which is very evident, the only true repair is to get the component rechromed.

WHEN WASHING IS NOT ENOUGH

The idea is to get the whole exterior as clean as washing will make it. But that often is not enough. The surface may have been neglected so badly that the paint is dulled. If the car is old enough there may be incipient rust areas on the body. You can spot them if there is a little cluster of what look like bumps under the paint.

All of this indicates the need for special pre-wax cleaners or even compounds. How do you make the decision? Well, for the car that is regularly maintained, a pre-wax cleaner—which usually contains a little compound—is all that you need. If the paint is severely discolored or, as in the case of yellows, whites or pastel colors, still looks dirty even after washing, then you must use compound. You can use compound sparingly instead of chrome cleaner to remove rust on bumpers, etc. But plan on protecting the clean area at once with a coating of wax.

Most chemical companies with an automotive car care line include a pre-wax cleaner, a polish and a compound in their lineup of products. The first two may be in either aerosol cans, liquid or paste form. Compound is always in paste form.

In case you are not familiar with what these types of products do, a polish lays down a coating of wax to protect a paint finish and make it lustrous. A pre-wax cleaner combines wax with a mild abrasive (a minute amount of compound) to actually scrape away mild surface scratches and lay down a wax coating for shine. Compound is simply an abrasive. If rubbed in enough, compound will take off scratched layers of paint and bring the finish down to an underlayer which is not scratched and weathered. Hence, the paint will be shinier than the dull layer just removed.

Use a special brush to get wheels and tires clean.

Rubbed in too much, compound can actually take *all* the paint off a car. Yes, right down to the bare metal.

Compound should be used only if you feel pre-wax cleaners or polishers cannot do the job. The pre-wax cleaner usually has a small amount of compound in it—or at least the same chemicals in a milder form. Thus it may do the job of cleaning out the minute scratches in the paint that have accumulated the dirt. Or it may eliminate weathering on the paint surface.

You must make the judgment. The pre-wax cleaners take a minute amount of paint off the finish and the compounds, white or reddish brown, can take a lot off if you are not careful. If the surface, after washing and drying, is totally dull or if you can see a whole host of minute scratches, you probably need compounding.

COMPOUNDING

As with all cleaning chemicals, the first rule is read the directions on the can and follow them. They will most likely tell you to get a clean soft rag, like a piece of flannel or broadcloth (take off buttons, snaps, etc. before using), dip it in clean water, fold it into a neat small piece and then, take a very small amount of compound on the cloth.

Rub in small circles with only enough pressure to do the job. Rub only until the hand-sized area in question is clean and shiny. The compound is composed of very fine grit which under the microscope turns out to be extremely abrasive diamond-like microns of silica in a chemical paste. If you bear down, it is like a file. So go easy. And work systematically, again from the top down. Rinse and turn the cloth after each compound area is cleaned. Have a good supply of cloth and remember to wet it down.

If you are doing a whole car, consider the use of an attachment to your electric drill which permits polishing. You still apply the compound by hand. But the buffer attachment does the rubbing.

Compounding also can be used on chrome bumpers and most metal work to get off the film of grime that dulls the metal. But *do not* put it on any rubber part of your car—moldings, bumper strips, tires, mud flaps, etc. Like most car cleaners, it contains petroleum and that ages the rubber and leads to cracking.

If your car finish after compounding is still dull or the minute scratches or cracks still dominate the paint so it looks worn, it needs a paint job and there is nothing else you can do. This kind of dullness and minute cracking has been happening more often, usually in areas where air pollution is high or in areas where the ozone content of the air is high (the latter can be in a rural area.) If you live in such an area you are going to have to wax more often to make sure the finish is sealed off from the contaminants.

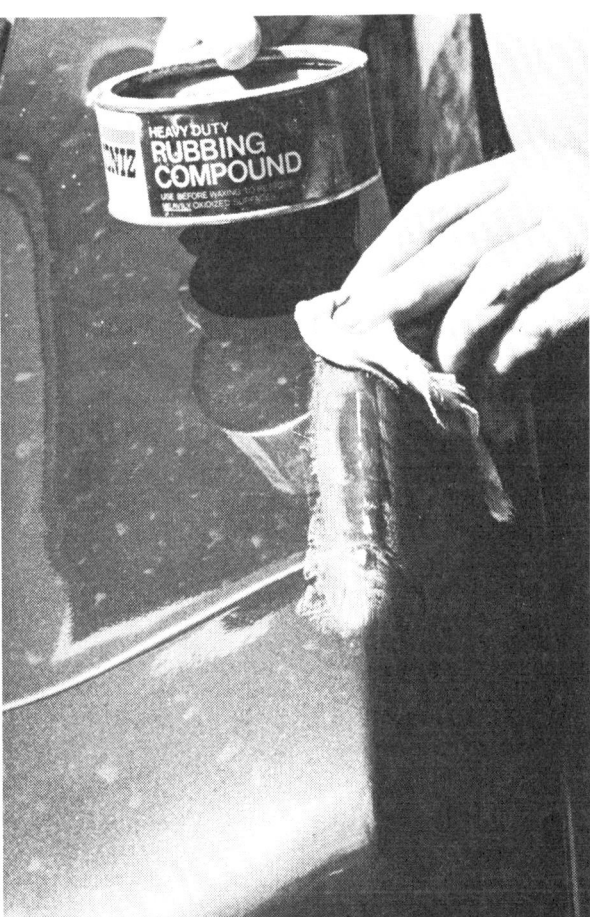

Paint spatter on car finish can be gently rubbed off with regular compound.

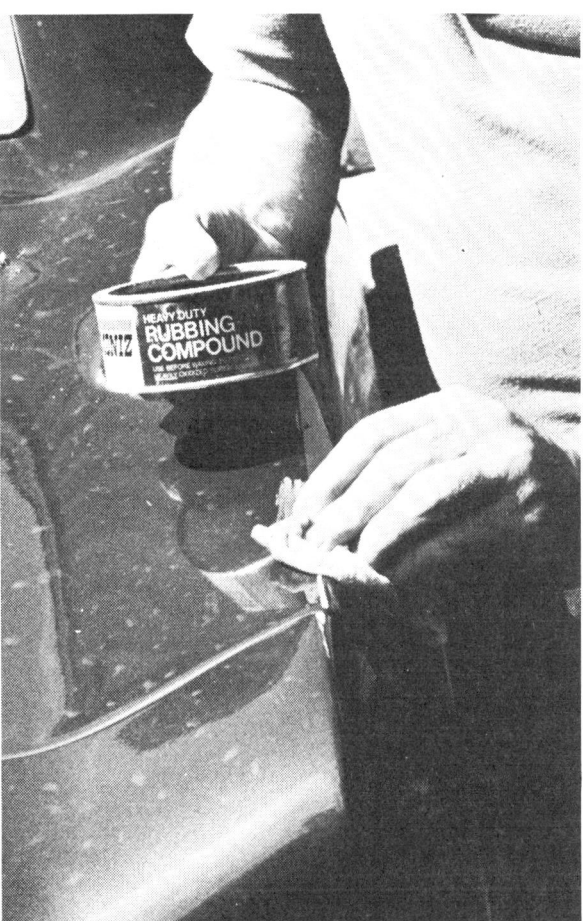

Use damp cloth and turn it frequently when compounding.

WAXING

A well-maintained car does not need a wax job more than once every three weeks even in the most pollution ridden or salt-laden atmosphere. In most areas, a good wax job should last about two months.

Some of the paints used in the past three years are supposed to keep their luster automatically with just soap and water cleaning. We are not going to contradict the car companies. But even such paints tend to stay cleaner with protection. And most of the cars on the road do not have the benefit of the new finishes. The older the car, the less likely it will have such a fiinish.

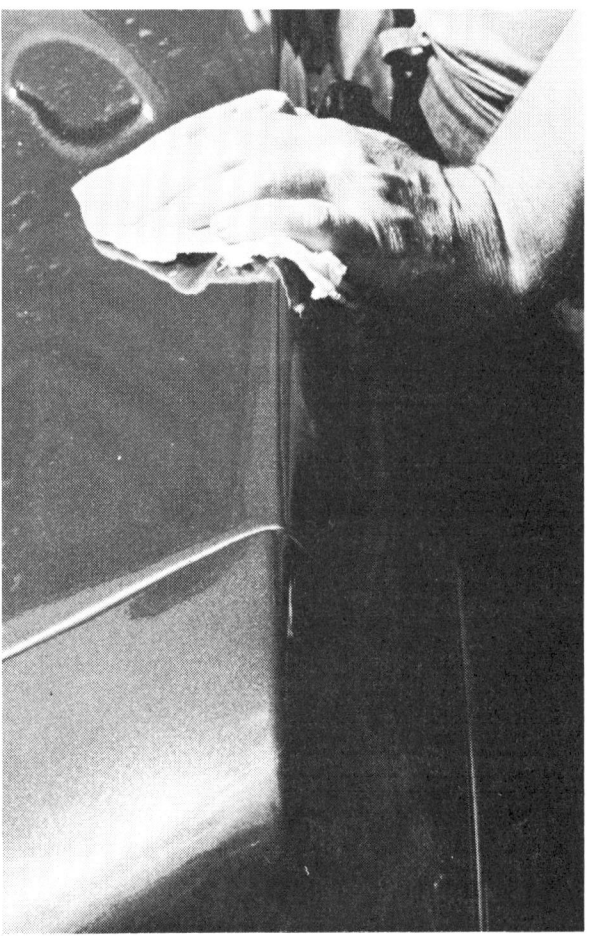

Wipe off with clean cloth. Paint is gone and finish looks like new.

There are literally hundreds of waxes on the market. Some are applied by water just as in the car wash and you allegedly escape the drudgery of applying, buffing and polishing. Others need only be applied and they dry to a luster provided the paint is capable of it and provided it was cleaned thoroughly. A number of companies have softened the wax so it is easy to apply. And there are liquids, impregnated cloths and 2-part systems, all of which promise high luster and protection.

A few contain the same acrylic polymer as some super shining floor waxes. A few have other luster and durability ingredients but all contain carnauba wax. This is the basic ingredient used to make cars shiny for at least the past 40 years. It comes from a tropical palm nut and it is as good today as when Simonizing became a household word—indeed, almost a generic term.

As with other maintenance products, read the directions on the particular brand you are using. Some insist they can be used in the sun. Most prescribe shade. But we think any product is going to work best if you can do your protective waxing inside the garage even though sometimes it gets to be tight quarters.

If you use one of the many conventional paste waxes, pre-softened or not, or one of the liquid creams, here is a general step by step procedure:

1. Thoroughly wash and clean the car. If you try waxing over a car that is less than 100% clean, you are preserving dirt even if there is a cleaning agent in some waxes.
2. If there is no applicator furnished, use clean new non-oily rags which are lint free. Or use one of those household superstrength cleaning cloths if it is not abrasive. Fold it to a hand size rectangle.
3. Apply the wax or wax/polish to the cloth. Do not pour the wax on the finish directly. This is simply wasteful. Use paste waxes sparingly. Again starting from the uppermost painted surface, apply the wax evenly. Most people use circular motions with medium hand pressure.
4. Various products permit you to do various size sections at one time up to the whole car. But a quarter of a roof is a good ballpark goal to begin with. Work to get the paint protection and sheen perfect, rather than to get done as fast as possible. *Follow directions exactly* as to when you should wipe off. Otherwise you will wipe your protection right off. All carnauba wax finishes take time to harden and are actually still hardening 24-72 hours afterward.
5. Turn the cloth to a clean area each time you either scoop out paste wax or pour on some liquid wax. This is precautionary and helps defeat any dust that may have accumulated between waxing and any previous step.
6. To bring the sheen up, wipe lightly with another clean cloth. Or buff with the sheepskin buffing attachment on your power drill.

If you really want the car to look better than most used vehicles, try cleaning and waxing painted areas like the door sills, the areas around the door hinges, door unders and other edges. Remove all unnecessary oil change decals and remember to re-oil or grease door hinges after you have wiped and waxed everything clean.

While working on the door sills, check to make sure the drain holes in the door are unclogged and working. Check the rubber door and window moldings (if any) and see if there are enough door edge nicks to justify:

a) door edge guards—installing them ends nicking, or

b) a major campaign to touch up these and other nicks and minor scratches and dents as well as rust spots, or

c) installing wheelwell molding and rocker panel covers. If rocker panel areas are beat up or have large rust spots and if the edge of the fender around the wheel is not bent out of shape but does show evidence of rust, installing a molding or a cover is really the quick way to solve this problem.

PAINT TOUCHUP

Think about touchup first. If you have a non-metallic enamel or lacquer paint job, you are in much better shape than those owners who have metallic paints as far as getting a matching touchup paint color is concerned. You can match the colors on most U.S. and popular imported cars reasonably well at virtually any automobile supply store. For metallic paints you will probably need to return to the dealer. Generally speaking, light colors are easier to repair than darker hues.

Before you touch up, make sure you have the right materials. First you need medium and/or fine emery cloth. Then you need a primer—light for light color cars and dark for the others. You need masking tape, newspaper or kraft paper or some other good covering. Clean the area to be touched up. If it is a scratch, first try rubbing it out with compound. If it does not respond, then you must proceed to repaint. You do the same with nicks and rust spots.

1. Use a small piece of medium emery cloth to grind off rust spots or a rusty area or the bubbly paint that signifies rusting underneath. Use it carefully and sparingly. Rub no more than you must to get the rust off.
2. Use fine emery cloth to feather around nicks and scratches and to feather areas around rust spots. Again take off as little paint as possible.

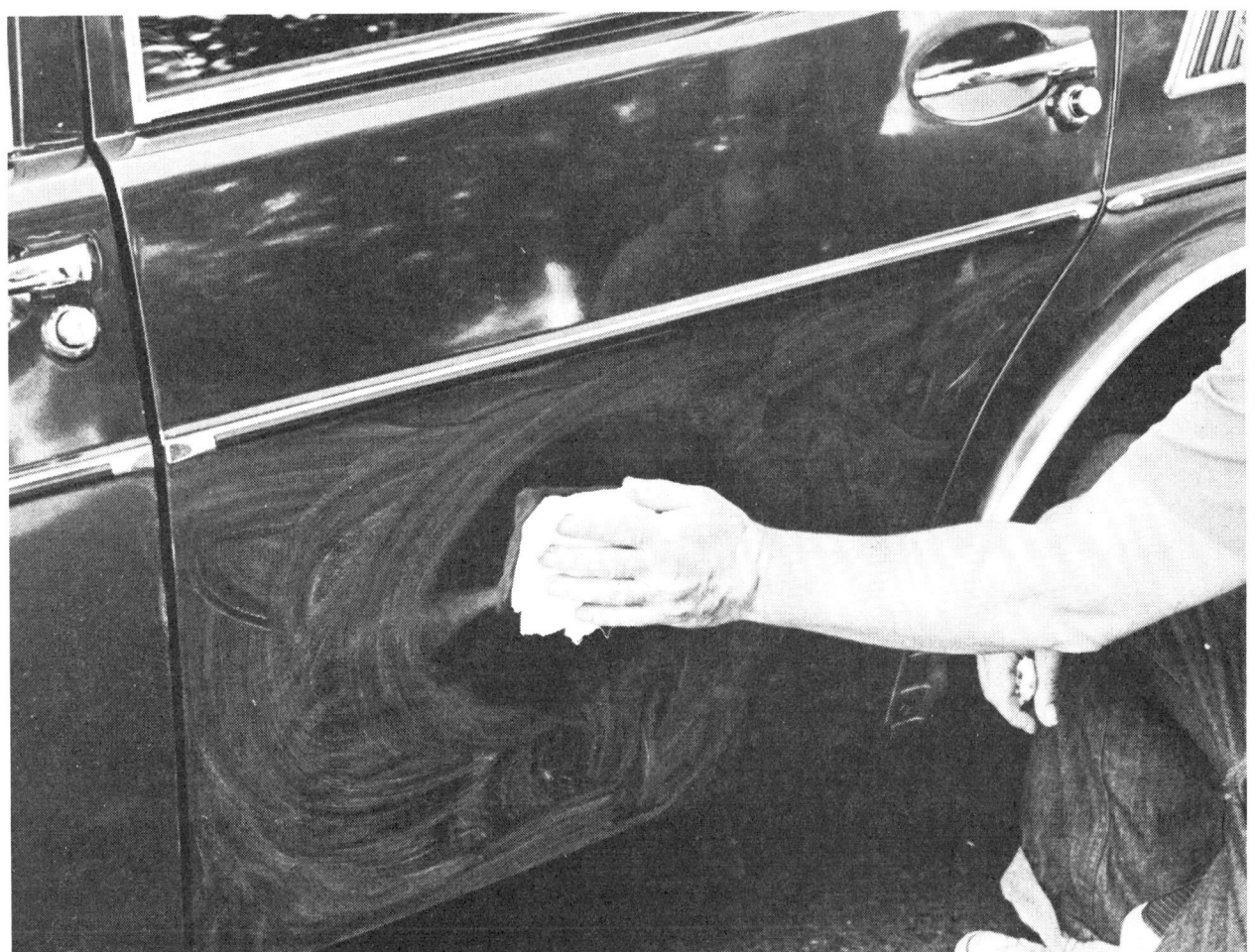

Apply polish and tar remover where needed.

Feather around large paint nicks with fine emery cloth.

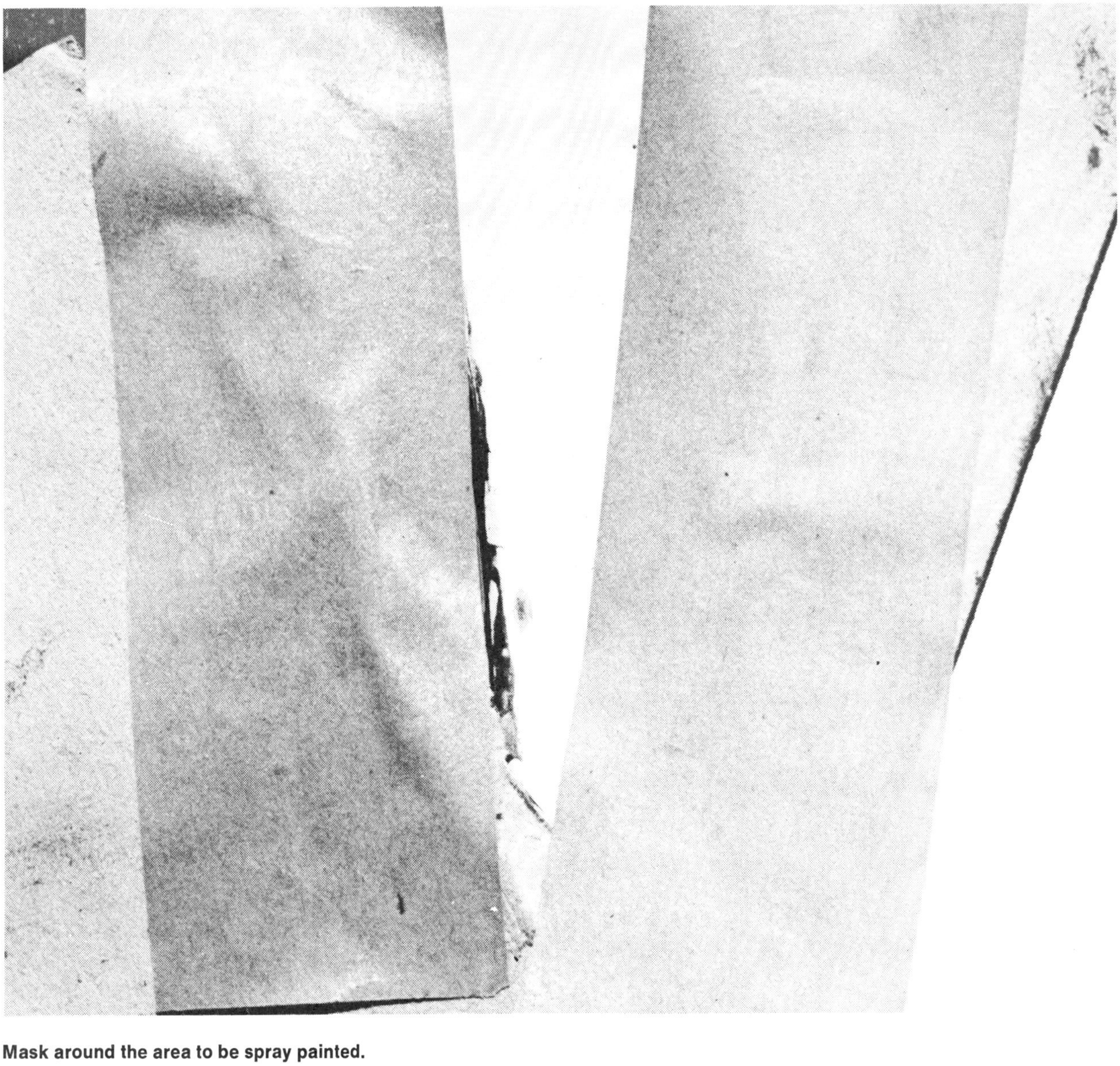

Mask around the area to be spray painted.

3. You must mask the area around where you are going to paint if you are utilizing paint spray. If you are touching up something smaller than your finger nail, it often will be easier to use a brush-on paint in one of the small bottles. You need not mask if it is a minor job. But a brush touch up usually does not come out as well as a spray.
4. After sanding the spot in question, clean it off with a soft rag or with painter's cheesecloth. If you have reached any bare metal, you need primer. Let the primer dry before proceeding to touch up.
5. When you use a spray paint, follow the directions on the can. Be patient. Apply the spray in layers rather than trying to cover the spot at once. Most spray paints dry on contact with the air. So you have no long wait. Try to avoid paint runs and indiscriminate spraying by using short bursts of paint rather than a steady stream.
6. The final finish layer should feather the crack or nick area into the surrounding paint. You should strive for a blend that is imperceptible to the eye.

MINOR BODY DINGS

Where there are dings and dents that are few enough so that you would rather do it yourself, plastic filler becomes your best friend. First sand or emery out the dent with medium emery cloth. Do it all around the ding or small dent to the bare metal. Clean the spot off. Then, with a small spatula or a tongue depressor apply the plastic filler.

Fill the dent a little above the surrounding surface. Then let the filler dry. The can will tell you how long. When the filler is dry, smooth it down to the surrounding area, clean, prime, clean again, then paint.

We must emphasize that these procedures are for tiny surface dents. For large dents or many little dents, it is probably more efficient in time and money to have a pro do it.

Let most touchup jobs dry about a week before washing the area with cold water and applying a coat of wax. For larger paint jobs, like a major portion of a door or a quarter panel, give it a fortnight.

REPAIRING WEATHERSTRIPPING

There once was a time when every car in every price class had weatherstripping around the doors and the trunk lid which were cloth covered rubber. These lasted pretty well until the cloth frayed. Today, weatherstripping is usually neoprene which is a synthetic rubber and very vulnerable to petroleum based cleaners.

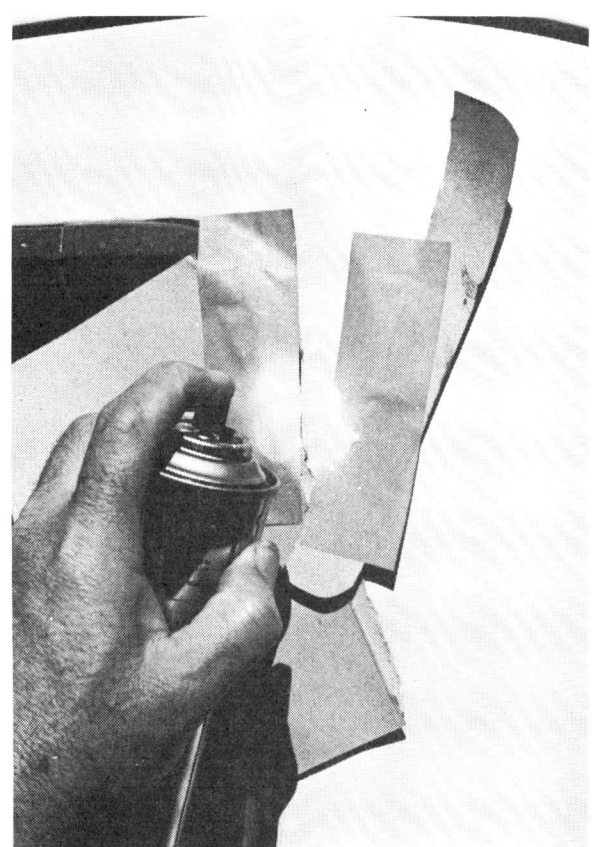

Spray the paint on in thin layers, not in globs. Small nicks are easier to do with brush touchup.

Since weatherstripping is so important to both the looks and the comfort of the car—no one likes a leaky door during a rainstorm—the best thing you can do is keep the stripping in top shape. There are rubber dressings on the market which you can use for tires, bumper guards and weatherstrips, too. An application every six months will protect the rubber from ozone degradation. Use an old toothbrush or a large artist's paint brush to apply the dressing to the weatherstrip. Be very careful not to get any on your carpeting and wipe the rubber protector off the paint as quickly as you can.

If the weatherstripping comes loose, there are a number of epoxy cements which will put it back in place. Perform this task, however, at your earliest convenience to forestall losing the whole strip.

Another method of protecting weatherstripping and also ending any squeaks or noises is to spray it with silicone spray. This often neglected product is cleaner and quicker than dressing although its effect may not last as long. It is, however, more versatile since you can use it to lubricate hinges, pulleys, door locks and other joints and small close-tolerance mechanisms. Get the kind with the long straw-type nozzle.

Cracked weatherstipping means it is time for a full replacement and that can be a messy job. You must not only remove the old strip but you must also make the surface clean before applying the new stripping. This is another of those thankless but important jobs that, for many people, should be left to a body shop. However, if you want to attempt the job, here are some tips.

If the car is five years old or less, you should be able to purchase a new strip intended for your particular model. However, it is possible to utilize the weatherstripping available in the auto departments of many stores to do an adequate job. Before you remove the old weatherstripping, find out whether your car needs the type that fits in a slot along the door opening. If this is the case, then you must get the replacement from a car dealer of the make in question. If not, then most likely you can repair the stripping with store bought materials.

There are some who only replace that part of the stripping which either is damaged or has become cracked and stiff. We agree.

Procedure

1. Cut out the stripping to be replaced, being prepared to scrape the remnants off.
2. Using medium emery cloth, sand off the surface until it is clean. The surface need not be as smooth as if you were going to paint an exterior, just clean enough that when you cover it with primer, you will get good adhesion.
3. Proceed as if you were doing the first stage of a touchup, masking surrounding paint. But you need not add a finish coat.
4. Applying the weatherstripping is simple if you obtain the kind which already is adhesive backed. We strongly recommend this kind since it saves the necessity of applying glue or cement.
5. Cut a length of stripping at least a ¼-inch larger than the gap as you have measured it.
6. Fit this length into the gap before you expose the adhesive making sure you are not stretching the rubber.
7. Once you have it fitted snugly, then strip off the backing as you press it into place carefully. If you are working with a large piece two or three feet long, the handling can get chancy if you strip the backing off all at once.

Apply vinyl top cleaner foam to one section of a vinyl roof at a time.

That is all there is to it. Do not use any kind of electrical or other tape to join the new and old strip. There is no need for it and, if you should compress the weatherstripping too much you are running the risk of giving water an entry point. Or if not water, air.

VINYL TOPS AND SEATS

We have purposely left the cleaning and renewing of vinyl seats and vinyl tops for treatment together. If the vinyl cleaner leaves your vinyl upholstery or top weathered or dull, you can buy a clear brush-on product—stick with brush-ons, they are easier to control—which will renew the sheen. If you need to renew the color or want to recolor, most companies make a product which will do that, too.

In using vinyl cleaners, it is mostly a matter of spraying or wiping it on and wiping it off. But check the label on the product you buy for specific instructions that may be important to that particular brand.

Vinyl patch kits are on the market but they apparently are very regional and vary in cost. In patching or in recoloring, leave yourself the time to do a careful, precise job. There is no reason anyone cannot get a good job if he is prepared to be careful and follow directions.

REPLACING A BROKEN RADIO ANTENNA

There is one other common job that unfortunately more and more car owners are facing. That is the replacement of a broken radio antenna. Replacement antennas come in two basic types. The difference is that the more expensive kinds have disappearing rods which are less likely to be vandalized.

For the straight replacement rod, all you need to do is remove what is left of the old stalk and attach the new rod by the ball end. It should take at most 10 minutes since you have not disturbed the lead from the radio at all. Just unscrew the set screws of the old antenna, place the new rod on the stub end, and tighten the set screws.

When antenna is broken off completely, entire assembly requires replacement.

For the disappearing version, you must read the directions carefully. You will probably have to enlarge the hole in the fender to be able to insert the housing for the disappearing version. Before you start filing away with a metal file or drilling with the router attachment you can buy for metal work with some home drills, make sure the location of the present hole is well clear of the tire. If not, you shall have to buy a cap for the present opening and drill further back on the fender.

Otherwise, measure the diameter of the aerial housing and start filing away. A small enough metal file is available at most hardware stores. A router attachment will do the job quicker, cleaner and easier.

Most disappearing aerials come with their own attachment to the radio lead and directions for attachment to a ground. If you make these attachments according to directions, you will have no problem.

CAUTION: If you get careless with the radio lead, you can get a healthy shock that will wake you up. Since the directions on each brand of antenna differs, you must read them carefully.

For a general idea of how a typical job goes, check the illustrations here.

Inspection

1. The antenna is fastened to your fender by hooks that swivel to a vertical position to fit through the hole in the fender and then flatten out horizontally to grip the metal around the hole. These hooks also serve to ground the antenna. A short threaded pipe is attached to the hooks and protrudes through the fender. A weatherproofing and cushioning gasket fits around the pipe and sits flush on top of the fender.
2. A threaded ball or fitting then screws down on the protruding pipe to the gasket. This action creates a pulling force on the hooks underneath the fender and tightens the entire assembly to the fender.
3. A heavy insulated cable, usually black in color, runs from the bottom of the antenna assembly, to which it is permanently attached, to your car's radio. This cable carries the radio signals picked up by the antenna to the radio. At the tip of this cable is a plug that pushes into a receptacle at the rear of the radio.

Tie a thin guide wire around end of antenna cable.

The easy break procedure

There are two ways in which the mast antenna usually breaks. In the first instance, a hard metal nub about an inch long remains protruding from the antenna assembly. Repair of this condition is simple as it does not involve disturbing the antenna assembly or the antenna cable. All that is needed is a replacement antenna mast.

1. The replacement mast slides over the protruding nub and is held in place by one or more set screws.
2. The set screws must be turned out before the mast is placed in position and then they are tightened. Some replacement masts also supply a small tool to tighten the set screws once the mast is on the nub.

The hard break procedure

When the protruding nub is also broken, the entire antenna assembly must be replaced. This procedure involves working under the car's dashboard in order to disconnect the antenna cable. This cable itself does not carry any electrical current, but since other wires under the dash do, it is a good idea to first disconnect one of the battery terminals to avoid an accidental short circuit.

1. Adjust the front seats all the way back so you will have enough room to lie on the floor under the dashboard.
2. Use a flashlight or droplight to locate the antenna cable running from the radio to the point where it leaves the car interior in the proximity of the antenna.
3. If the antenna is mounted on the rear fender, the cable may run under the car rug to the back of the car. After locating the antenna cable, disconnect it by pulling it straight out from the radio receptacle. Be sure to make a mental note of the receptacle's exact location to minimize the problem of reconnecting the cable from the new assembly.
4. A piece of tape or wire placed adjacent to the receptacle will aid in quickly identifying its location.
5. In order to facilitate routing the new cable through the body panels separating the outside fender from the car's interior, tie a long length of thin wire around the end of the old antenna cable.
6. The antenna assembly is removed from the fender by loosening the metal fitting on top of the fender. This is done by turning it counterclockwise with a proper size or adjustable wrench. Remove the metal fitting and the gasket taking care that the short section of threaded pipe that remains does not fall into the fender.

Antenna assembly has notches on top piece to accommodate a wrench.

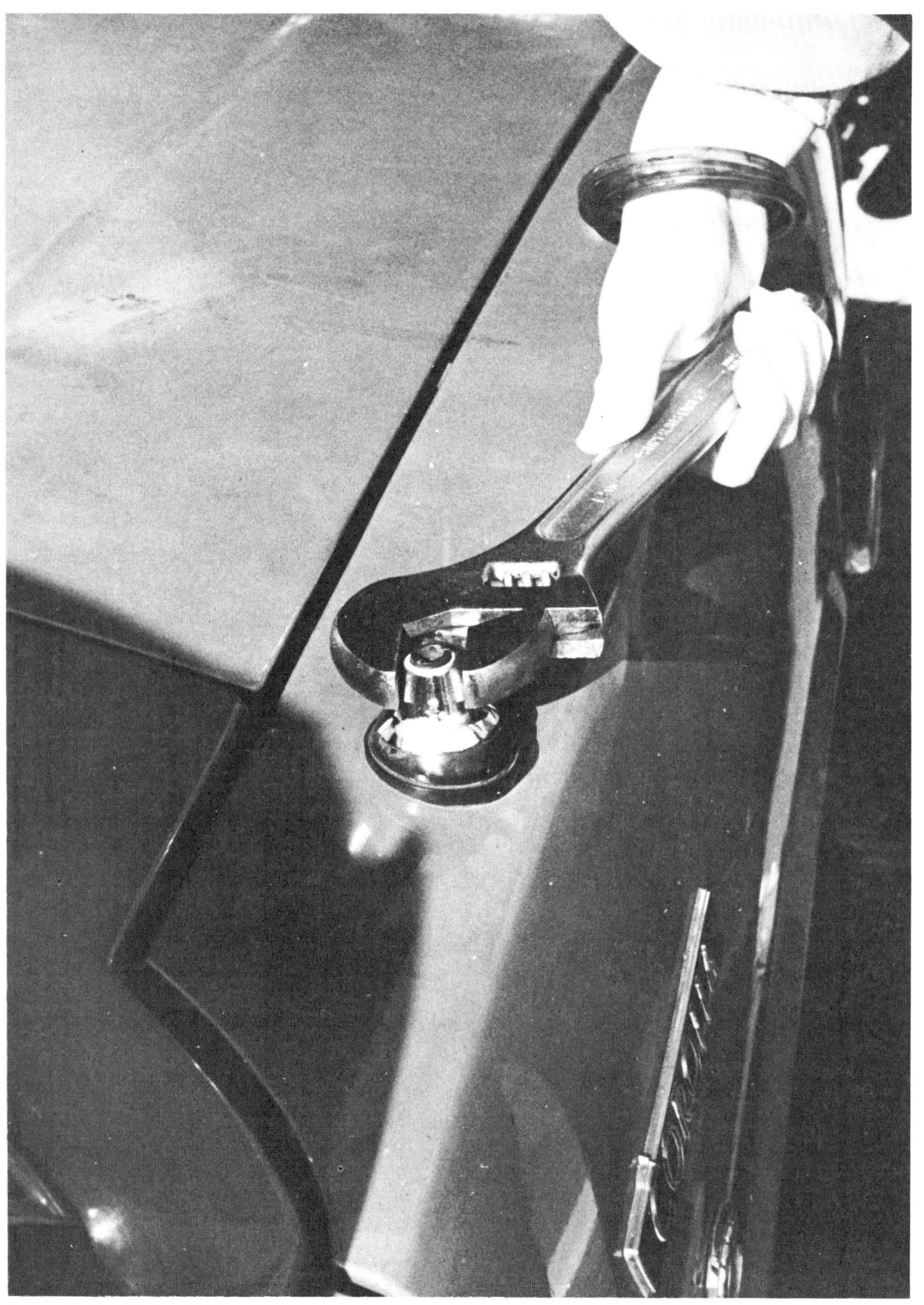
Loosen the top of the assembly.

7. Work the hooks on the bottom of this pipe into a vertical position with the aid of a small screwdriver or your finger. The old antenna assembly can now be removed.
8. Pull the antenna cable completely through the fender hole until several inches of the guide wire that you have fastened to the end also are pulled through the hole. Untie the guide wire and retie it to the end of the new antenna cable.
9. The new antenna assembly we have selected incorporates a spring on the mast which will flex and resist breaking. The mast is attached to a ball which fits into a socket. This antenna assembly is held together by two screws. The first tightens the socket assembly to the fender and is located at the bottom of the socket. It is visible when the mast/ball piece is removed. The second screw fastens the mast/ball to the socket. To install this assembly, first tie the length of guide wire that was pulled through the fender hole with the old antenna cable to the tip of the new antenna cable. Feed the cable through the fender hole while pulling on the guide wire inside the car. The antenna cable should route into the passenger compartment with ease.
10. Next, remove the screw that holds the ball and mast to the socket assembly. Then loosen the screw at the bottom of the socket all the way and then tighten only two turns. This will loosen the socket assembly sufficiently for the hooks at the bottom of the assembly to be moved to a vertical position and inserted through the fender hole. Once through the hole, they can easily be moved to the horizontal position to grip the underside of the fender. Tighten the socket screw all the way.
11. Attach the ball and mast to the socket and tighten the set screw. Extend the antenna to check that it is in the desired position. Loosening the socket and/or ball set screws will allow you to adjust the position of the antenna. Be sure to tighten the screws when the adjustment is completed.
12. Plug the antenna cable into the radio receptacle and reconnect the battery cable if it was disconnected.

Your radio is now back in action.

Remove top fitting.

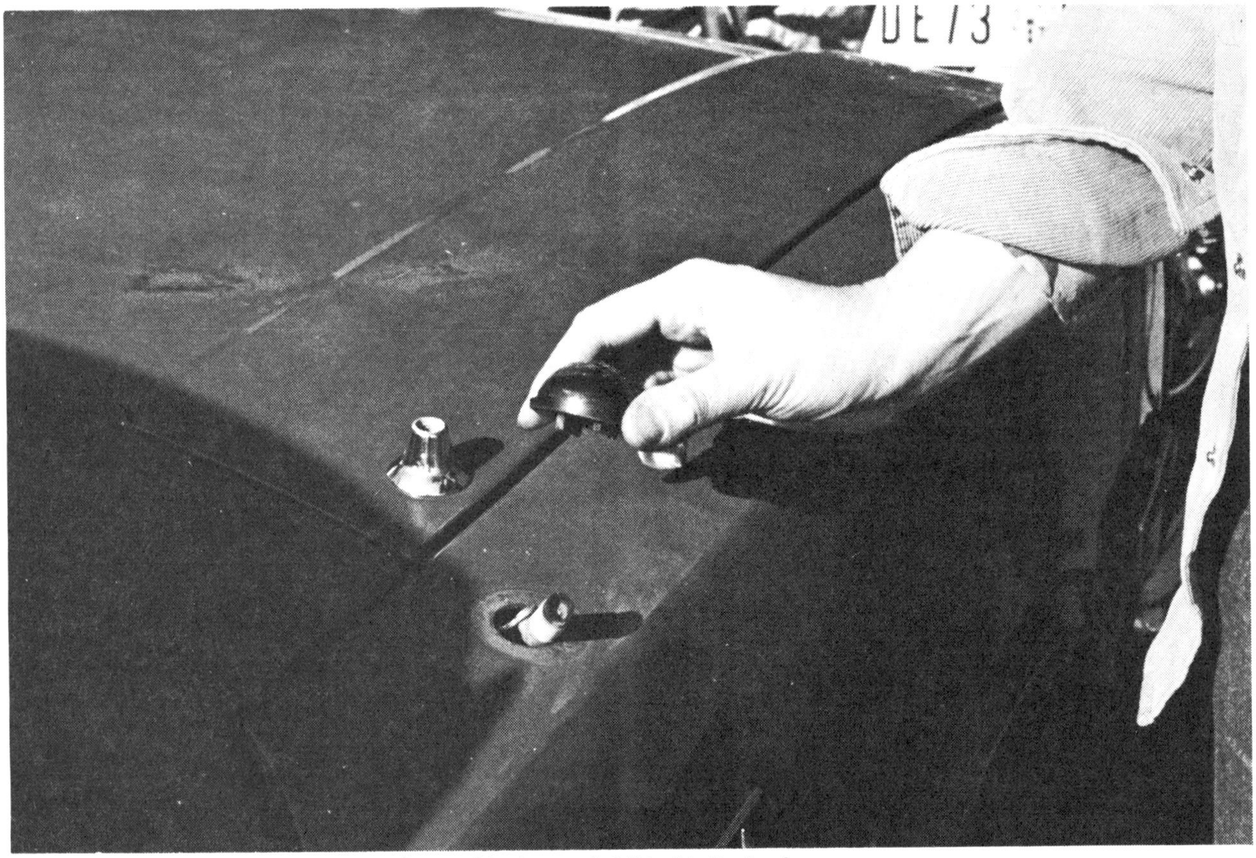

Gasket is removed next. Be sure rest of assembly does not fall inside the fender.

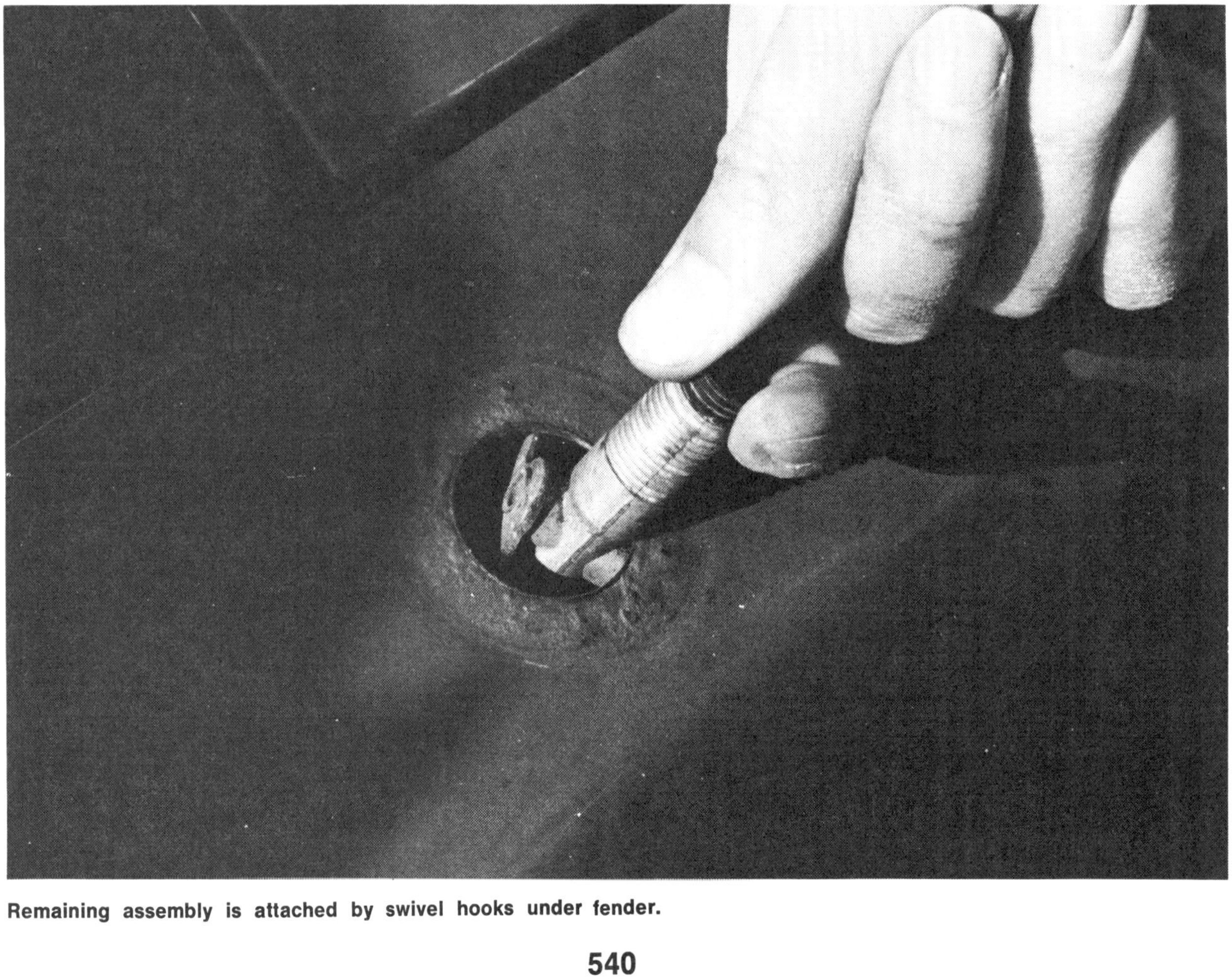

Remaining assembly is attached by swivel hooks under fender.

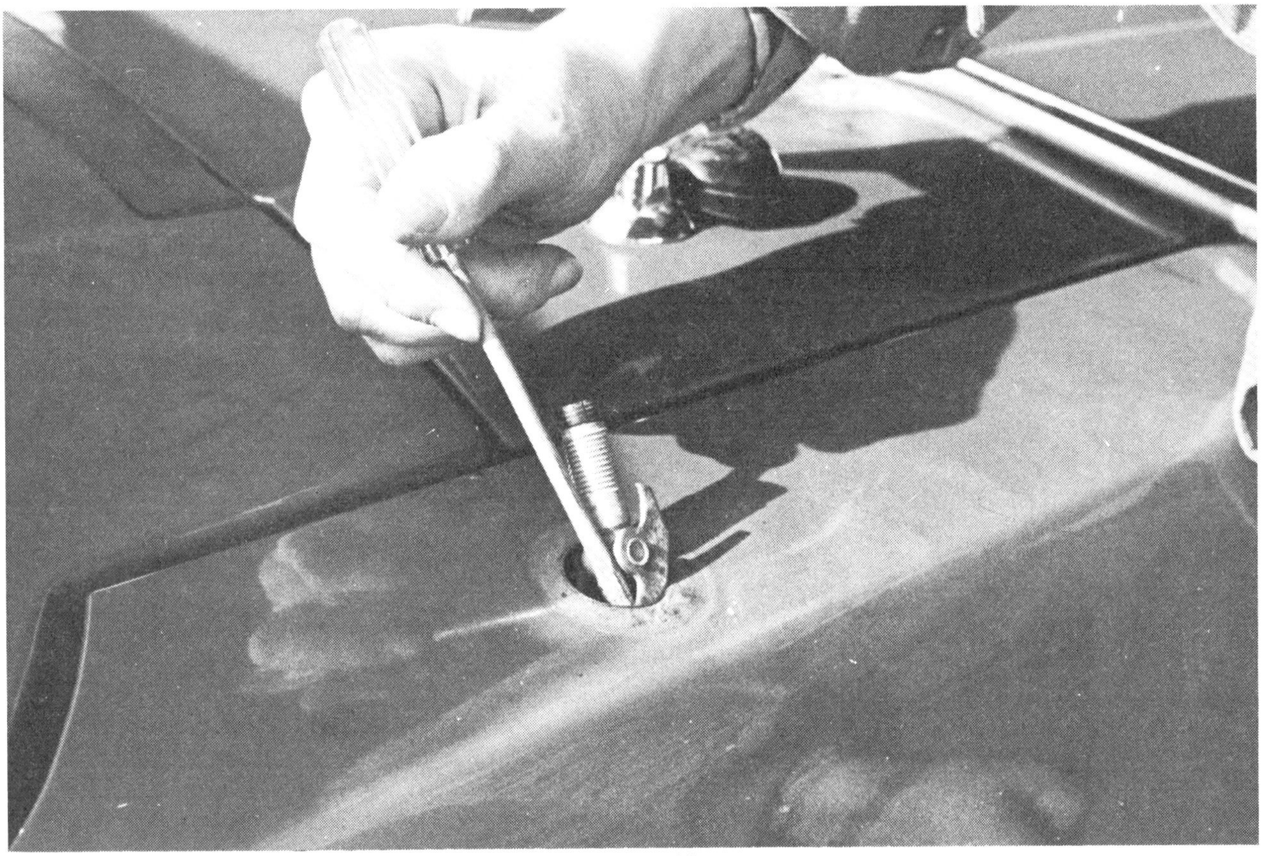

Rotate hooks to a vertical position with finger or small screwdriver.

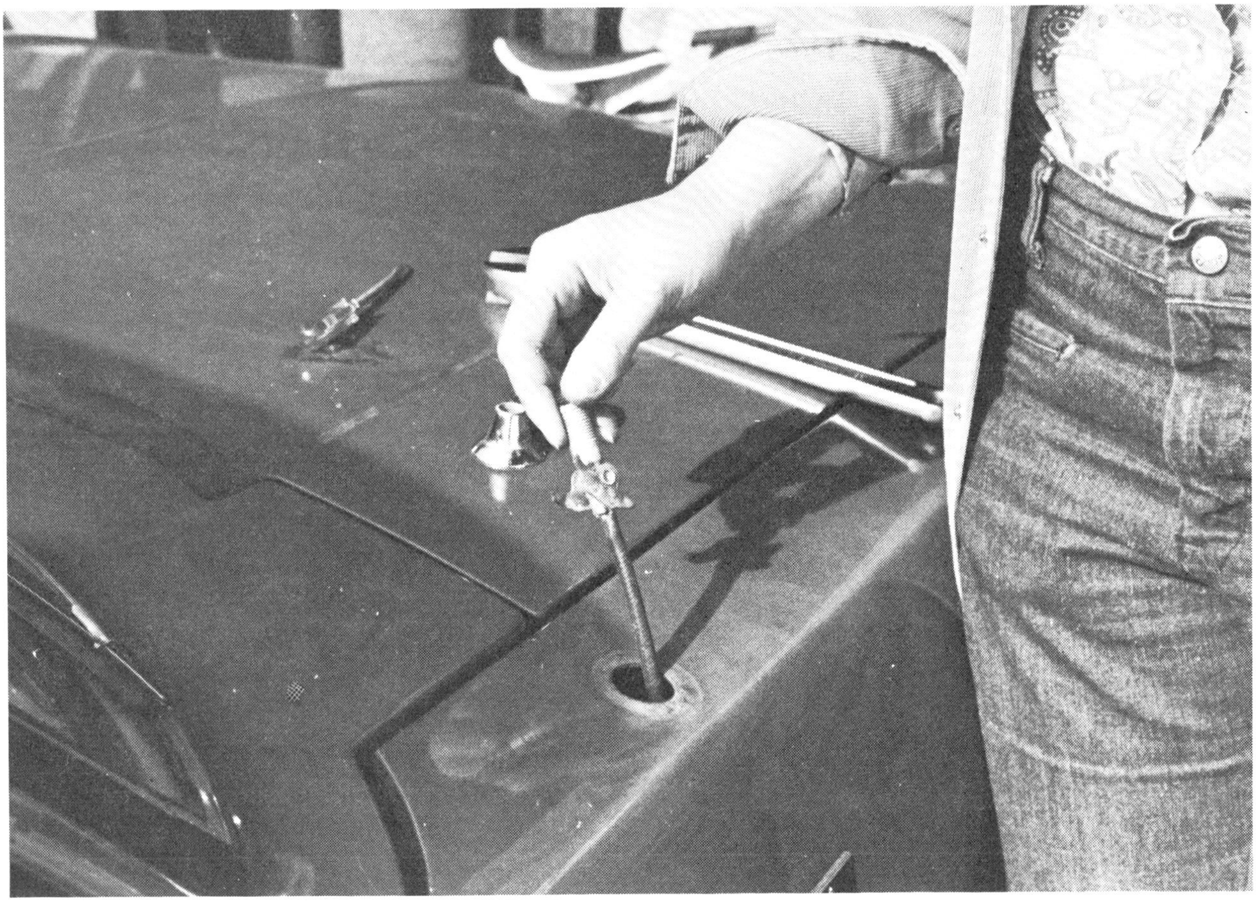

Antenna assembly can now be pulled clear.

Pull antenna cable through hole until several inches of guide wire are visible.

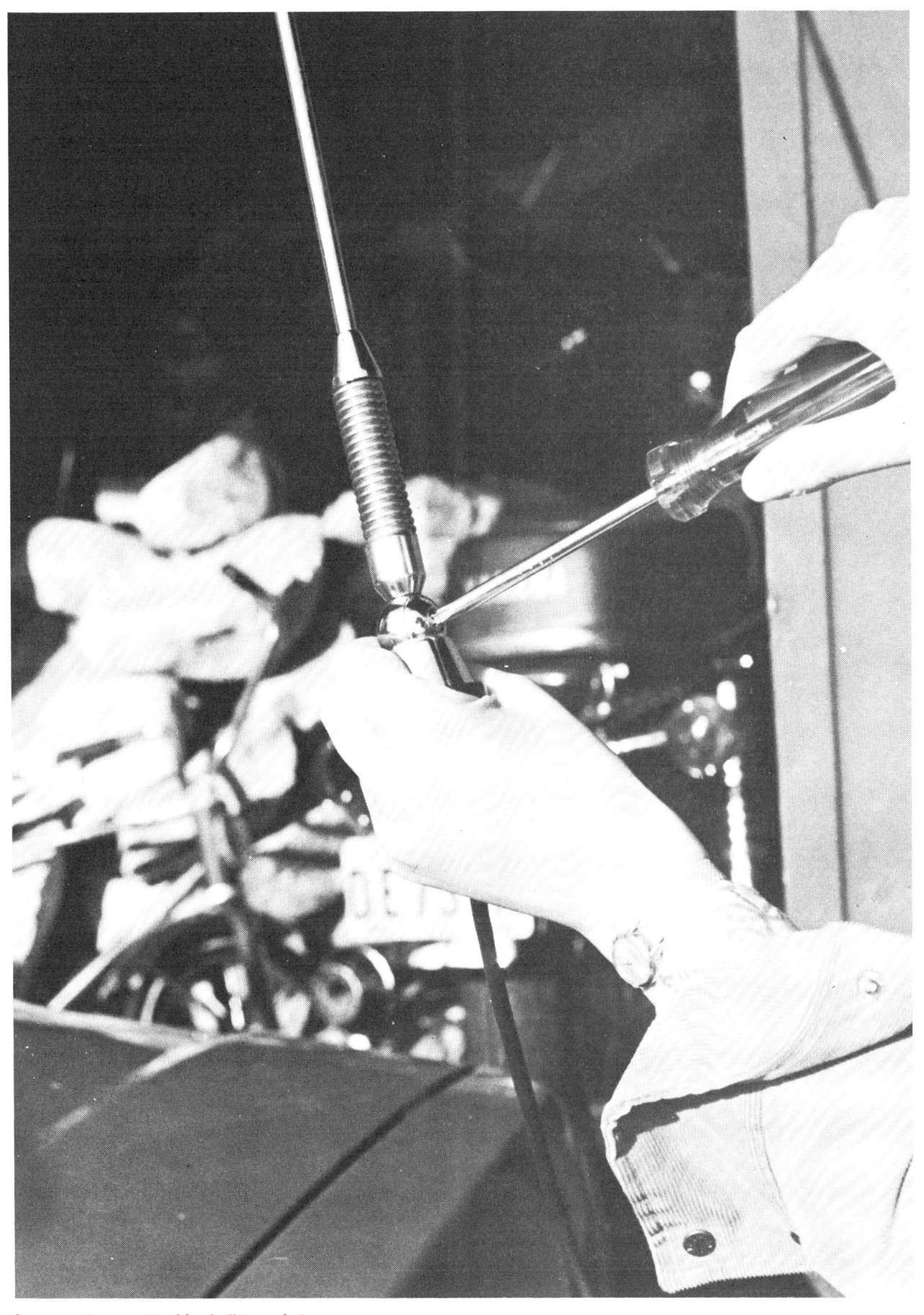

Loosen set screw attaching ball to socket.

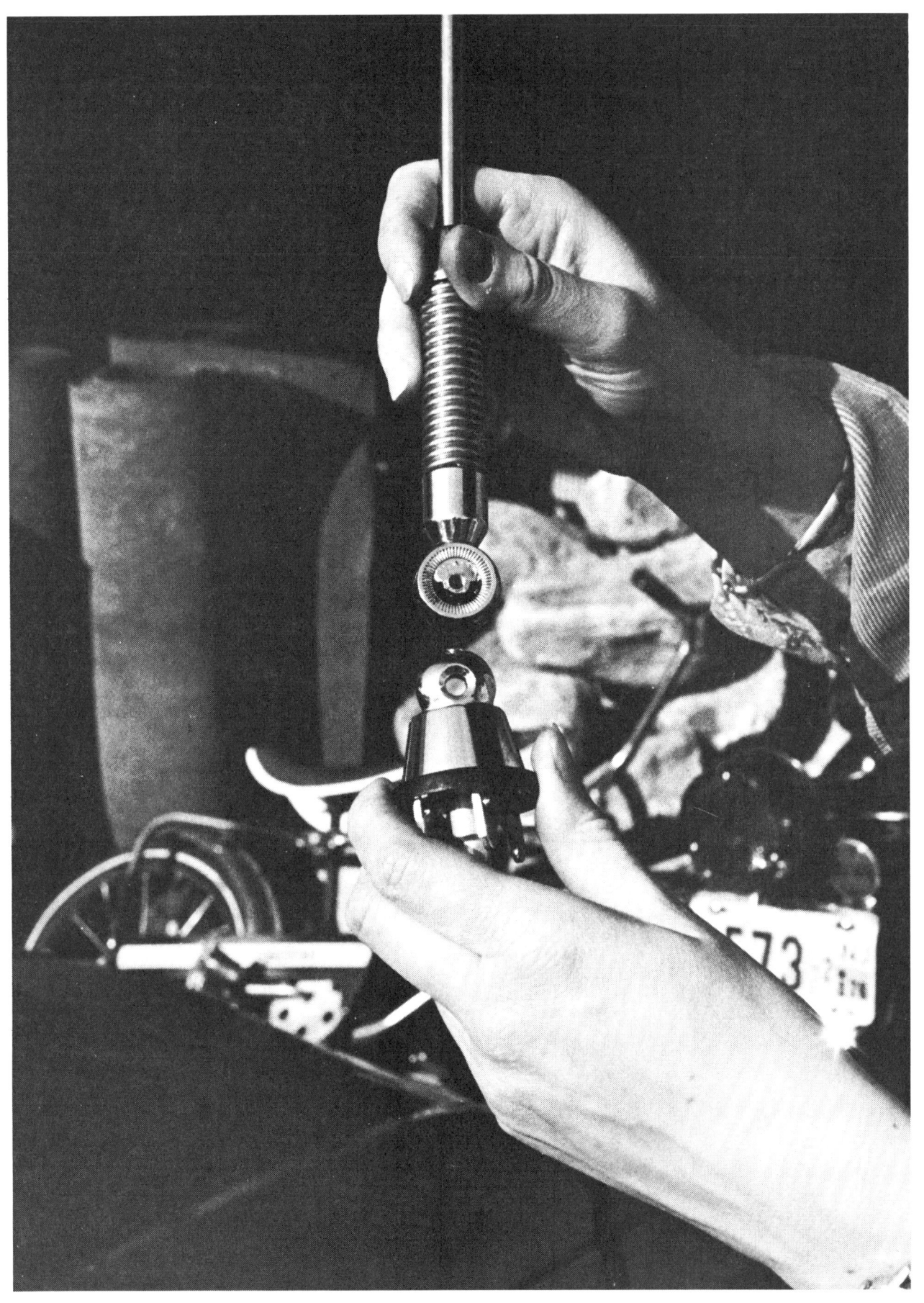

Separate the two components.

Loosen screw at bottom of socket all the way. Then tighten two more turns. This will loosen the assembly.

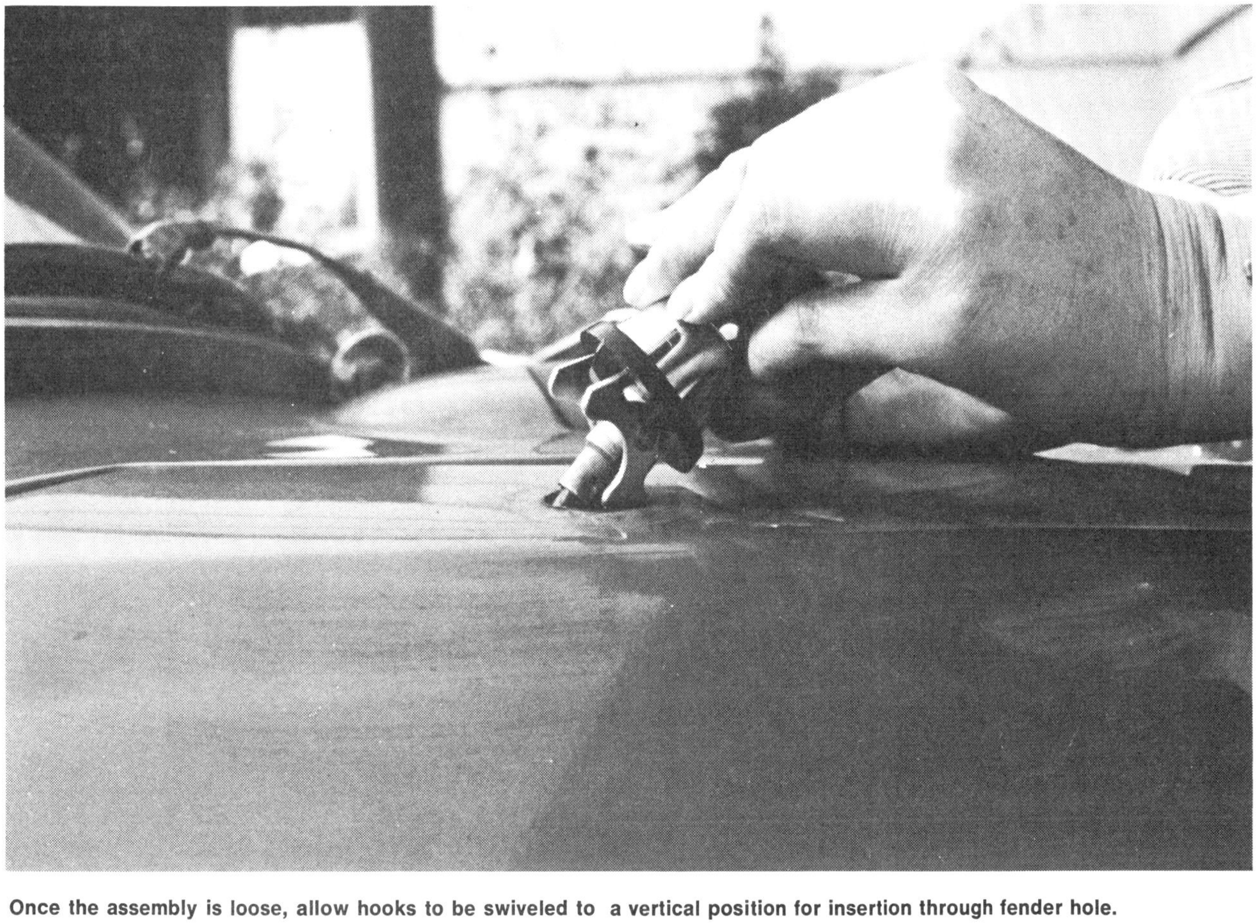

Once the assembly is loose, allow hooks to be swiveled to a vertical position for insertion through fender hole.

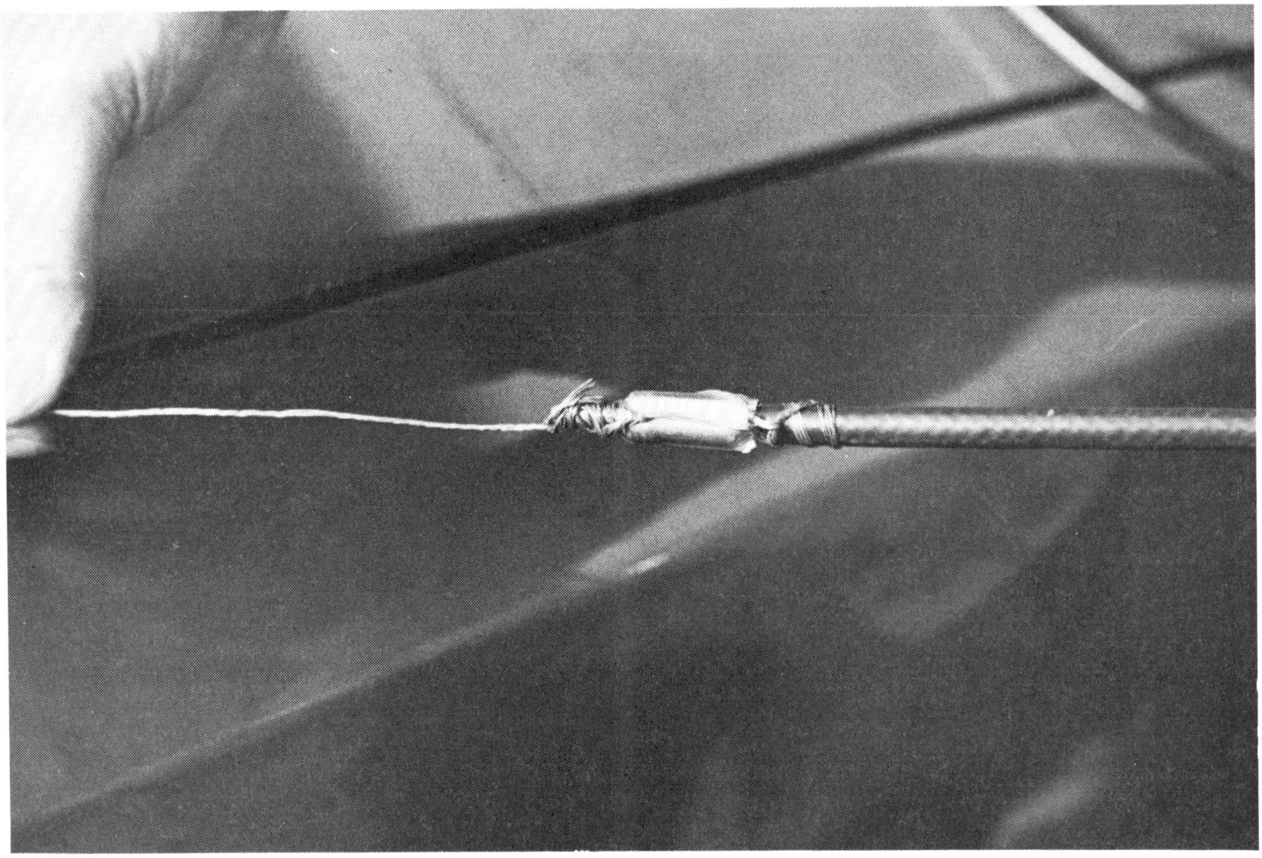

Tie guide wire around tip of antenna so it will pull at the very end of the tip.

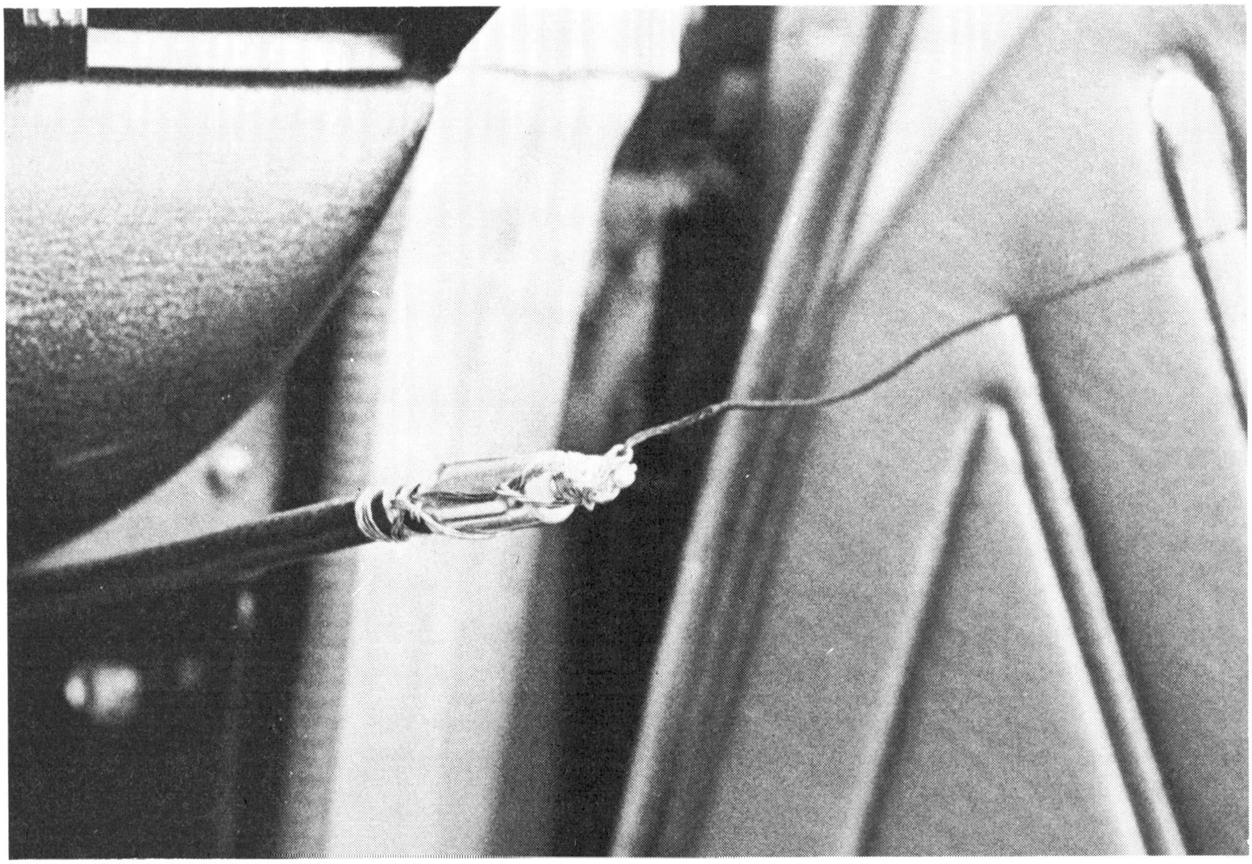

Feed the cable through the fender hole while pulling the guide wire from inside the car. This will correctly route cable.

Antenna cable plugs into radio receptacle under dash.

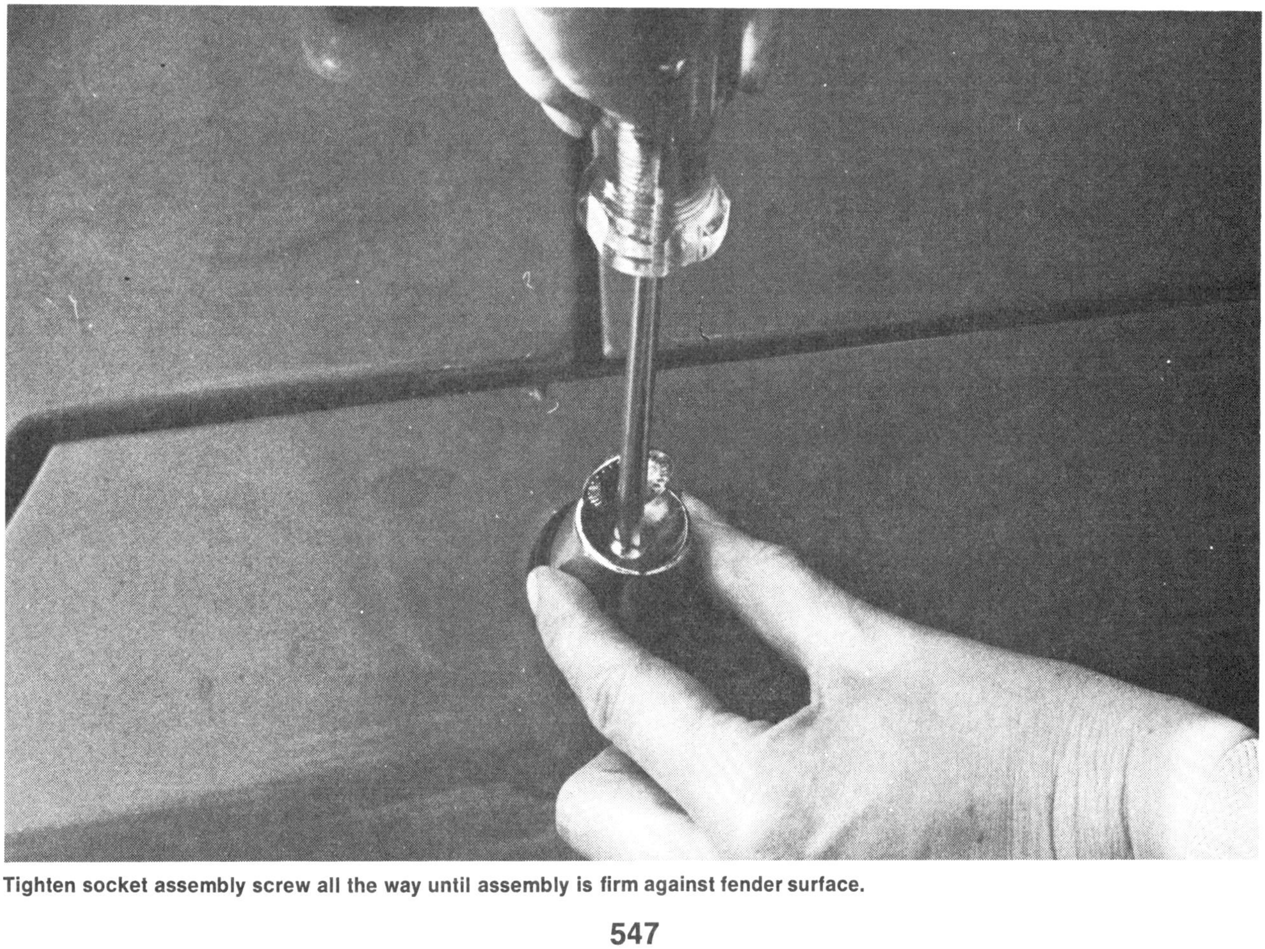

Tighten socket assembly screw all the way until assembly is firm against fender surface.

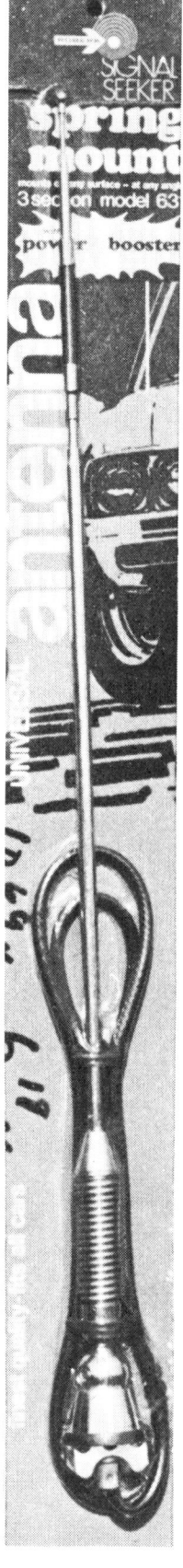

If installed carefully, a replacement antenna can look like a factory unit. Replacement antennas are available for every make and model.

INTERIOR MAINTENANCE

The ideal way to clean a car interior is to remove front and rear seats entirely for cleaning and renewal outside the vehicle, then strip the interior down to the bare metal floor. The way U.S. cars are built, this is not only difficult but not desirable if the jute padding used under carpeting in some older vehicles is glued to the metal.

But, difficult as it may be in U.S. cars, you should try it when the carpeting is showing wear spots which indicate replacement if you are going to keep the car a few years more. However, you can give your car a thorough interior cleaning without removing the seats.

Your car's interior should get a general cleaning at least once a month, and perhaps once a week when you are bringing in sand from a beach or work in construction or live anyplace where leaves, grass and dirt are going to be tracked in routinely.

Establish a cleaning routine, again starting from the top and going down. Depending upon the kind of interior headlining in the vehicle, your cleaning procedure will differ. Those that are perforated plastic or vinyl should be wiped with a damp, clean rag. Those that are cloth over firm padding can be vacuumed. Those that are cloth over little or no padding can be brushed carefully or vacuumed with a hand vacuum very carefully.

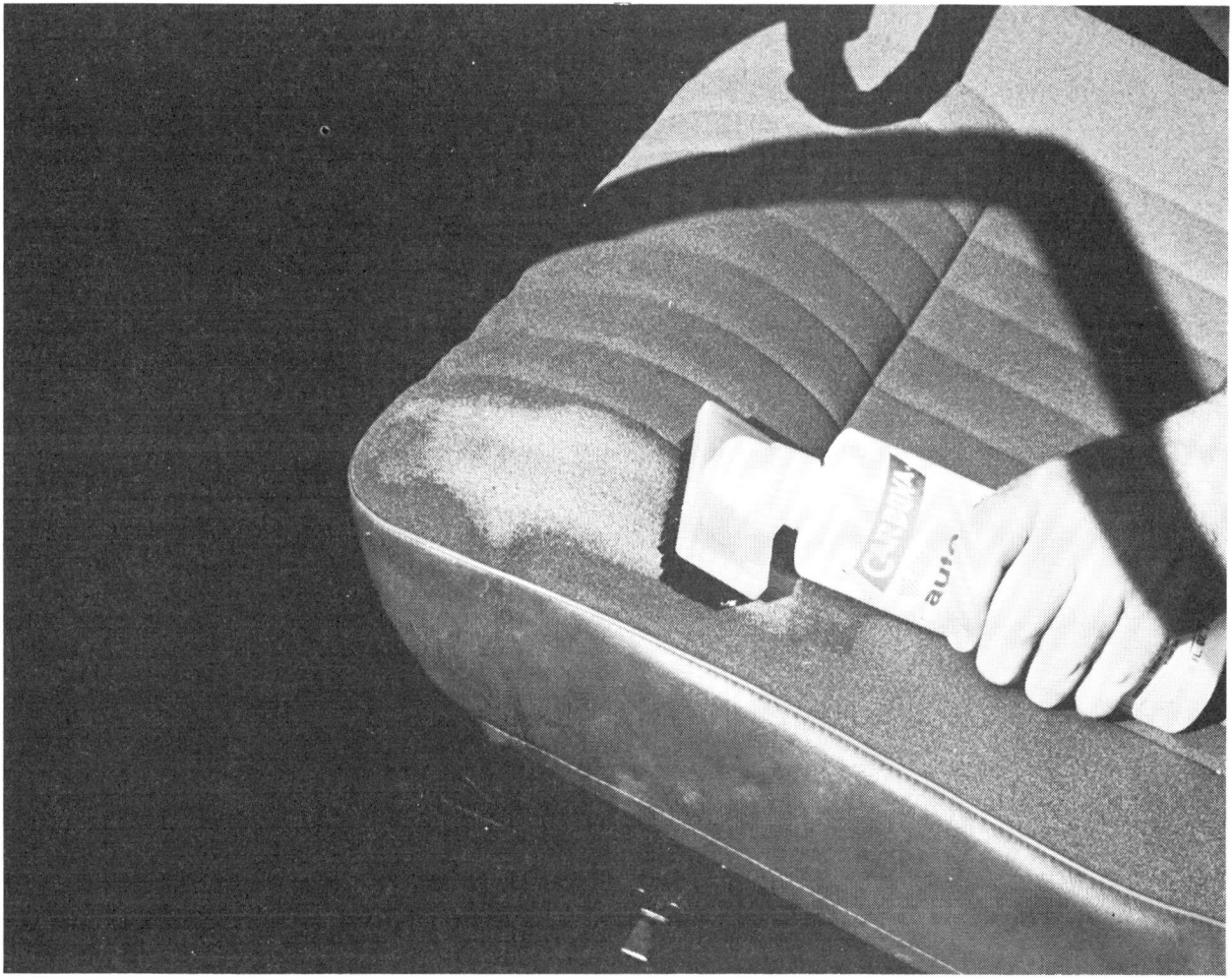

When you squirt on auto upholstery cleaner, let the cleaner do the work. Always test cleaner on unobtrusive part of seat first.

CLEANING GLASS

It is usually best to clean outside and inside the windows at the same time and that has been described earlier. But smokers and those who have some kinds of vinyl (polyvinyl chloride) upholstery may need a special cleaner to get the insides of windows cleaned of smoke film or vinyl upholstery emissions. General Motors makes a special window cleaner for this purpose carried by any Chevy, Pontiac, Olds, Buick, GMC or Cadillac dealer. This GM inside window cleaner is the quickest and the best for that purpose.

Regular window cleaner sprays containing ammonia also clean interior chrome. Also remember your rear view mirror and the glass over the instruments on your dashboard. But try not to spray it on the vinyl since the ammonia doesn't do a thing for that except take off the sheen. Clean your dashboard with a damp rag first to get the dust. Then use a vinyl cleaner. Do this before cleaning chrome stripping.

DASH AND DOORS

Use an upholstery and carpet cleaner on door panels and arm rests and door sill protectors if they are plastic. If the door sill protectors are chrome or aluminum, use your bumper chrome cleaner. Clean everything—the steering wheel, the steering wheel post, the window handles, the shift lever, the radio fascia and knobs, etc. Clean the ash trays not only by emptying them but by washing them out with an old toothbrush.

This is a good time to empty out your glove and/or console compartments and toss away the stuff you do not need. It is also a good time to check that the screws along the window posts, on the door sills and on the firewalls are present and tight. Replace them at once if they are missing.

Do the seats next to last, the floor last. Do not forget to check and clean under the seats for the usual accumulation of junk.

Unless there are specific stains on cloth fabric, your upholstery and vinyl cleaner can be sprayed directly onto the seat, worked in and allowed to dry so that is can be brushed or vacuumed off. *Every upholstery cleaner* requests in its directions that you test it on an inconspicuous place—perhaps the side of the seat nearest the center post—before using it. Do so just in case your particular fabric or vinyl reacts by stiffening (vinyl) or fading (fabric). Most post-1965

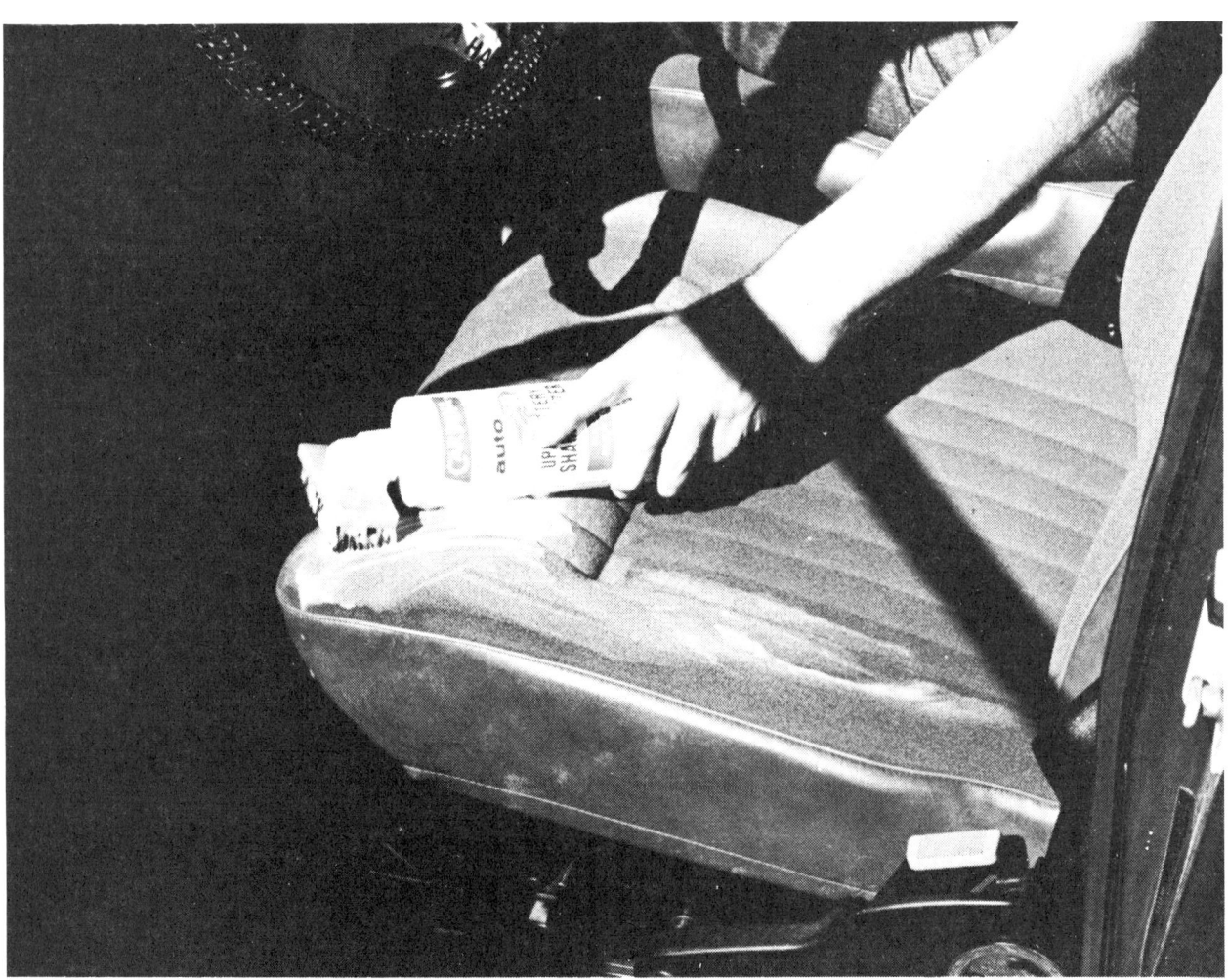

For stubborn spots, put extra cleaner and use brush applicator to work in.

cars are OK for popular upholstery cleaners. But yours may be the exception. Check first before doing large areas.

Follow the directions on the can which will probably tell you to spray the cleaner foam on and let it do most of the work of cleaning. You should help it along a little by brushing it into soiled areas.

Use as much or as little as the product directs. With vinyl that is in good condition, what you are cleaning off is a film that forms and holds the discoloring dirt on the surface. Generally, an upholstery and vinyl top cleaner will take this off before the foam dries. Just wipe it with a clean rag or paper wipe.

With fabric, let the foam dry in. Then vacuum thoroughly. Sometimes badly neglected and dirty seats need a second application with the cleaner scrubbed in. If the seats are that dirty, first wash with a scrub brush and some household clothes washing product because the dirt is too ingrained for cleaning without risking upholstery discoloration.

The overwhelming majority of car seats will respond to cleaning foams. If you have the space, take the rear seat cushion entirely out of the car to clean it. That will also give you a better chance to clean the rear compartment and the back cushion of the rear seat, often affixed to the car. And remember to clean the back of the front seat or seats.

CLEANING CARPETING

While the seats are drying, you can give the floor its first vacuuming. First remove all the debris you have accumulated underneath the front seats and take out all rubber or vinyl floor mats for cleaning outside the vehicle.

Now move the front seat as far back on the adjustment track as it will go. Vacuum, preferably with an industrial unit which can suck up small stones, gravel, chopped up leaves and other minor debris that manages to accumulate near the door sills, under the accelerator pedals and in crevices. A good home unit will do if it has the hose conversion and assorted nozzles. Vacuum anywhere on the floor you can reach. The debris that will not come out of the odd crevice or two should be brushed out to where the vacuum can gobble it up.

Vacuum off the seats before you begin to apply foam to the carpet. A hand held auto vacuum which plugs into the cigar lighter will do the job for most cars.

Then do the carpeting. Most vinyl and upholstery cleaners will clean carpeting too. But even better is a specific carpet cleaner such as you use on household carpeting. Follow directions on the can.

Either way, allow the cleaner to dry and vacuum it off. The dirt presumably has been lifted out and off the carpet fibers. If you have worn carpeting, cleaning it will not make the worn spots any less so. You will just have clean worn carpeting.

Clean rubber mats with detergent and water or even better, special rubber cleaners. Clean vinyl mats with water, simply hose blasting them.

RENEWING

When you are prepared to completely renew the interior, you can probably remove the front seats and even consider taking out the carpeting. It is more complicated in an average American automobile compared to an import.

The key is organization. For every set of screws and bolts, have a small bag marked with the origin. You will need a straight head screwdriver, a Phillips head screw driver, a ratchet wrench and socket set. If you take the seat or seats out, you will find that you also can get the seat track out.

If you have power seats, we advise against removing them. If you have a heated front seat cushion, the same caution applies. There are too many electrical connections.

There is no need to disassemble the seat itself unless, as with some American cars as well as older Volvos, the front cushion lifts out. In that case, unless you are recarpeting or repadding, you can do an excellent cleaning job without taking out the seat back.

On popular Chevrolets, Fords and MoPar products (Dodge-Plymouth-Chrysler) replacement carpeting cut to size is available from the factory. The price

Vacuuming car interior can be done very effectively with an industrial-type vacuum.

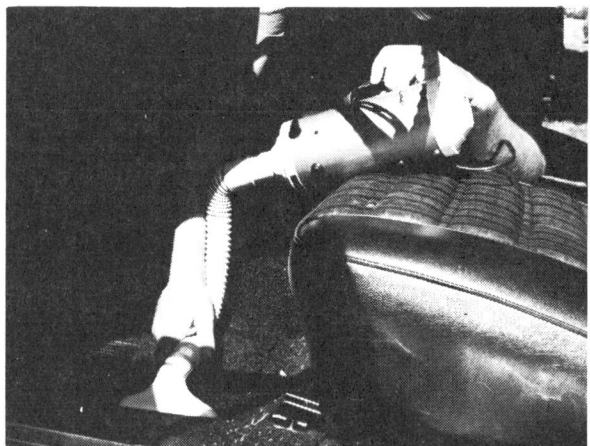

If you use a car vacuum which plugs into cigar lighter, it is easy to get at hard-to-reach carpet areas.

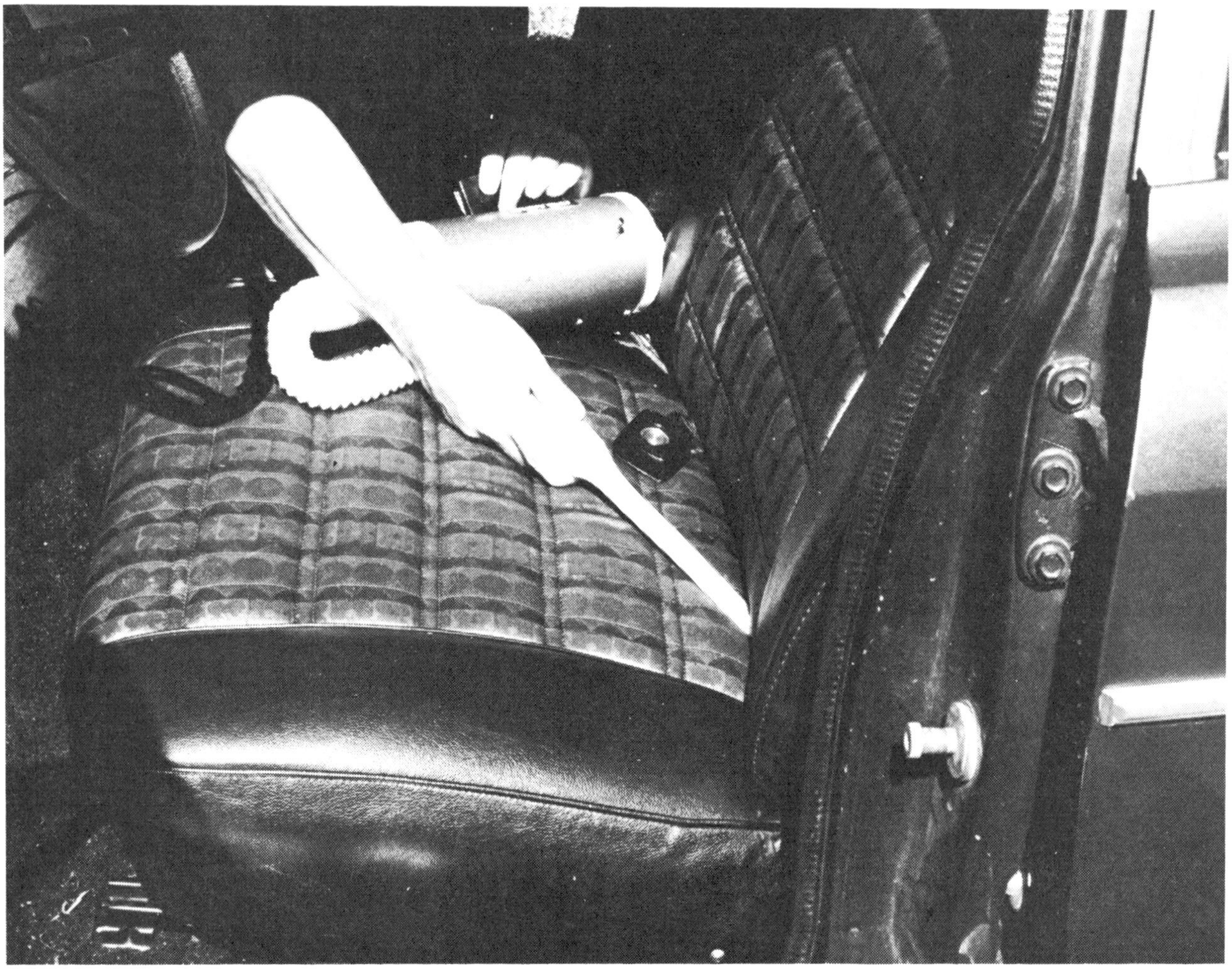

varies between dealers who invariably will have to order it. Shop two or three. Replacement with your own carpeting is easiest if you remove the old carpet carefully, then use it as a pattern. You can pick up good remnants inexpensively. But remember to get a type with a tight weave if you are trying for wear, not show.

If you replace the carpet, replace the padding, again using the old carpet as a padding. Car companies use jute padding because it deadens sound effectively and because it is cheap. You can use regulation carpet underlayment like Ozite or go to more expensive rubberized underlayments for a more luxurious feel. You buy this at a carpet store and you can ask the man who sells you the material any questions you might have.

There really should not be any unless you get the padding much thicker than the original and it will not fit under the door sills which are very important in holding down the edges. Also buy rug tape or any cloth tape in the color of your carpet to edge it off. That will make it look better and last longer. And that will really pick up the appearance of your older automobile.

The shelf under the front window of some cars and the rear window shelf are natural dust catchers and may reflect in the windows if they are shiny. If you use vinyl cleaner on them do not buff them to a shine.

Remember to vacuum in the seat creases.

Reference Data

THE SPECIFICATIONS FOR EACH CAR MAKE INCLUDE:

GENERAL ENGINE SPECIFICATIONS
- Engine identification
- Carburetor
- Bore and stroke
- Piston displacement in cubic inches
- Compression ratio
- Horsepower
- Torque
- Normal oil pressure

COOLING SYSTEM AND CAPACITY DATA
- Cooling system capacity
- Radiator cap pressure
- Thermostat opening temperature
- Fuel tank capacity
- Engine oil refill capacity
- Transmission oil capacity
- Rear axle oil capacity

TUNEUP SPECIFICATIONS
- Spark plug type
- Spark plug gap
- Ignition point gap
- Dwell angle
- Firing order
- Initial ignition timing
- Timing mark location
- Idle speed
- Air fuel ratio

TO FIND THE SPECIFICATIONS YOU REQUIRE FOR YOUR CAR, USE THE INDEX BELOW. NOTE: IF A FOOTNOTE REFERS YOU TO THE SERVICE SECTION FOR ANOTHER MAKE, THIS MEANS THAT THE ENGINE IN QUESTION IS USED IN THAT MAKE ALSO. PLEASE LOOK UP YOUR REQUIRED SPECIFICATION UNDER THAT MAKE.

AMERICAN MOTORS 554
Ambassador • American • AMX • DPL • Gremlin • Hornet • Javelin • Matador • Pacer • Rambler • Rebel • Rogue •

BUICK 558
Apollo • Centurion • Century • Electra • Gran Sport • Le Sabre • Regal • Riviera • Skylark • Special Wagons • Wildcat •

BUICK SKYHAWK 586
CADILLAC 563
CHECKER MOTORS 565
CHEVROLET 568
Bel Air • Biscayne • Camaro • Caprice • Chevelle • Impala • Monte Carlo • Nova • Wagons •

CHEVROLET CHEVETTE . . . 583
CHEVROLET MONZA 586
CHEVROLET VEGA 588
CHRYSLER 590
CORVETTE 583
DODGE 590
Aspen • Challenger • Charger Coronet • Dart • Demon • Monaco • Polara • Swinger •

FORD (Full Size) 611
Custom • Galaxie • LTD • XL • Wagons
FORD (Compact & Inter.) . . 617
Elite • Fairlane • Falcon • Granada • Maverick • Mustang • Torino •
FORD MUSTANG II 625
FORD PINTO 625
IMPERIAL 590
LINCOLN 630
Continental • Mark III-IV
MERCURY BOBCAT 625
MERCURY (Full Size) . . . 611
Brougham • Marauder • Marquis • Monterey • Wagons •
MERCURY (Compact & Inter.) . 617
Comet • Cougar • Cyclone • GT • Monarch • Montego • Wagons •
OLDSMOBILE 632
Cutlass • Delta 88 • F-85 • 4-4-2 • 98 • Omega • Royale • Super 88 • Toronado • Vista Cruiser •
OLDSMOBILE STARFIRE . . . 586

PLYMOUTH 590
Barracuda • Belvedere • Duster • Fury • GTX • Roadrunner • Satellite • Scamp • Signet • Valiant • VIP • Volaré •
PONTIAC 638
Bonneville • Catalina • Executive • Firebird • Grand Am • Grand Prix • Grand Ville • GTO • Le Mans • Sprint • Tempest • T-37 • Ventura • Wagons •
PONTIAC ASTRE 588
PONTIAC SUNBIRD 586
THUNDERBIRD 628

IMPORTED CARS
VOLKSWAGEN 646
TOYOTA 648
DATSUN 650

OTHER DATA
HOW TO PUSH AND TOW CARS WITH AUTOMATIC TRANSMISSIONS 652
METRIC/SAE EQUIVALENTS . . 654
TAP DRILL SIZES 656
CAR RIDE HEIGHTS 657

American Motors

GENERAL ENGINE SPECIFICATIONS

Year	Engine	Carburetor	Bore and Stroke	Piston Displacement, Cubic Inches	Compression Ratio	Maximum Brake H.P. @ R.P.M.	Maximum Torque Lbs. Ft. @ R.P.M.	Normal Oil Pressure Pounds
1969	128 Horsepower..............6-199	1 Barrel	3.75 x 3.00	199	8.5	128 @ 4400	182 @ 1600	75
	145 Horsepower..............6-232	1 Barrel	3.75 x 3.50	232	8.5	145 @ 4300	215 @ 1600	75
	155 Horsepower..............6-232	2 Barrel	3.75 x 3.50	232	8.5	155 @ 4400	222 @ 1600	75
	200 Horsepower..............V8-290	2 Barrel	3.75 x 3.28	290	9.0	200 @ 4600	285 @ 2800	75
	225 Horsepower..............V8-290	4 Barrel	3.75 x 3.28	290	10.0	225 @ 4700	300 @ 3200	75
	235 Horsepower..............V8-343	2 Barrel	4.08 x 3.28	343	9.0	235 @ 4400	345 @ 2600	75
	280 Horsepower..............V8-343	4 Barrel	4.08 x 3.28	343	10.2	280 @ 4800	365 @ 3000	75
	315 Horsepower..............V8-390	4 Barrel	4.165 x 3.574	390	10.2	315 @ 4600	425 @ 3200	75
1970	128 Horsepower..............6-199	1 Barrel	3.75 x 3.00	199	8.5	128 @ 4400	182 @ 1600	75
	145 Horsepower..............6-232	1 Barrel	3.75 x 3.50	232	8.5	145 @ 4300	215 @ 1600	75
	155 Horsepower..............6-232	2 Barrel	3.75 x 3.50	232	8.5	155 @ 4400	222 @ 1600	75
	210 Horsepower..............V8-304	2 Barrel	3.75 x 3.44	304	9.0	210 @ 4400	305 @ 2800	75
	245 Horsepower..............V8-360	2 Barrel	4.08 x 3.44	360	9.0	245 @ 4400	365 @ 2400	75
	290 Horsepower..............V8-360	4 Barrel	4.08 x 3.44	360	10.0	290 @ 4800	395 @ 3200	75
	325 Horsepower..............V8-390	4 Barrel	4.156 x 3.574	390	10.0	325 @ 5000	420 @ 3200	75
	340 Horsepower①..............V8-390	4 Barrel	4.165 x 3.574	390	10.0	340 @ 5100	430 @ 3600	75
1971	135 Horsepower..............6-232	1 Barrel	3.75 x 3.50	232	8.0	135 @ 4000	210 @ 1600	75
	150 Horsepower..............6-258	1 Barrel	3.75 x 3.90	258	8.0	150 @ 3800	240 @ 1800	75
	210 Horsepower..............V8-304	2 Barrel	3.75 x 3.44	304	8.4	210 @ 4400	300 @ 2600	75
	245 Horsepower..............V8-360	2 Barrel	4.08 x 3.44	360	8.5	245 @ 4400	365 @ 2600	75
	285 Horsepower..............V8-360	4 Barrel	4.08 x 3.44	360	8.5	285 @ 4800	390 @ 3200	75
	330 Horsepower..............V8-401	4 Barrel	4.17 x 3.68	401	9.5	330 @ 5000	430 @ 3400	75
1972	100 Horsepower②..............6-232	1 Barrel	3.75 x 3.50	232	8.0	100 @ 3600	185 @ 1800	75
	110 Horsepower②..............6-258	1 Barrel	3.75 x 3.895	258	8.0	110 @ 3500	195 @ 2000	75
	150 Horsepower②..............V8-304	2 Barrel	3.75 x 3.44	304	8.3	150 @ 4200	245 @ 2500	75
	175 Horsepower②..............V8-360	2 Barrel	4.08 x 3.44	360	8.3	175 @ 4000	285 @ 2400	75
	195 Horsepower②..............V8-360	4 Barrel	4.08 x 3.44	360	8.3	195 @ 4400	295 @ 2900	75
	220 Horsepower②③..............V8-360	4 Barrel	4.08 x 3.44	360	8.3	220 @ 4400	315 @ 3100	75
	255 Horsepower②..............V8-401	4 Barrel	4.165 x 3.68	401	8.5	255 @ 4600	345 @ 3300	75
1973	100 Horsepower②..............6-232	1 Barrel	3.75 x 3.50	232	8.0	100 @ 3600	185 @ 1800	75
	110 Horsepower②..............6-258	1 Barrel	3.75 x 3.895	258	8.0	110 @ 3500	195 @ 2000	75
	150 Horsepower②..............V8-304	2 Barrel	3.75 x 3.44	304	8.4	150 @ 4200	245 @ 2500	75
	175 Horsepower②..............V8-360	2 Barrel	4.08 x 3.44	360	8.5	175 @ 4000	285 @ 2400	75
	195 Horsepower②..............V8-360	4 Barrel	4.08 x 3.44	360	8.5	195 @ 4400	295 @ 2900	75
	220 Horsepower②③..............V8-360	4 Barrel	4.08 x 3.44	360	8.5	220 @ 4400	315 @ 3100	75
	255 Horsepower②..............V8-401	4 Barrel	4.165 x 3.68	401	8.5	255 @ 4600	345 @ 3300	75
1974	100 Horsepower②..............6-232	1 Barrel	3.75 x 3.50	232	8.0	100 @ 3600	185 @ 1800	75
	110 Horsepower②..............6-258	1 Barrel	3.75 x 3.90	258	8.0	110 @ 3500	195 @ 2000	75
	150 Horsepower②..............V8-304	2 Barrel	3.75 x 3.44	304	8.4	150 @ 4200	245 @ 2500	75
	175 Horsepower②..............V8-360	2 Barrel	4.08 x 3.44	360	8.5	175 @ 4000	285 @ 2400	75
	195 Horsepower②..............V8-360	4 Burerol	4.08 x 3.44	360	8.5	195 @ 4400	295 @ 2900	75
	220 Horsepower②③..............V8-360	4 Barrel	4.08 x 3.44	360	8.5	220 @ 4400	315 @ 3100	75
	255 Horsepower②..............V8-401	4 Barrel	4.165 x 3.68	401	8.5	235 @ 4600	335 @ 3200	75
1975	100 Horsepower②..............6-232	1 Barrel	3.75 x 3.50	232	8.0	90 @ 3050	163 @ 2200	37–75
	110 Horsepower②..............6-258	1 Barrel	3.75 x 3.90	258	8.0	95 @ 3050	179 @ 2100	37–75
	150 Horsepower②..............V8-304	2 Barrel	3.75 x 3.44	304	8.4	150 @ 4200	245 @ 2500	37–75
	175 Horsepower②..............V8-360	2 Barrel	4.08 x 3.44	360	8.25	175 @ 4000	285 @ 2400	37–75
	195 Horsepower②..............V8-360	4 Barrel	4.08 x 3.44	360	8.25	195 @ 4400	295 @ 2900	37–75
	220 Horsepower②..............V8-360	4 Barrel	4.08 x 3.44	360	8.25	220 @ 4400	315 @ 3100	37–75
1976	90 Horsepower②..............6-232	1 Barrel	3.75 x 3.50	232	8.0	90 @ 3050	163 @ 2200	37–75
	95 Horsepower②..............6-258	1 Barrel	3.75 x 3.90	258	8.0	95 @ 3050	179 @ 2100	37–75
	120 Horsepower②..............6-258	2 Barrel	3.75 x 3.90	258	8.0	120 @ 3600	200 @ 2000	37–75
	120 Horsepower②..............V8-304	2 Barrel	3.75 x 3.44	304	8.4	120 @ 3200	220 @ 2000	37–75
	140 Horsepower②..............V8-360	2 Barrel	4.08 x 3.44	360	8.25	140 @ 3300	251 @ 1600	37–75
	180 Horsepower②..............V8-360	4 Barrel	4.08 x 3.44	360	8.25	180 @ 3600	280 @ 2800	37–75

①—Rebel Machine.   ②—Ratings are net (as installed in the vehicle).   ③—With dual exhausts.

American Motors

TUNEUP SPECIFICATIONS

The following specifications are published from the latest information available. This data should be used only in the absence of a decal affixed in the engine compartment.

★ When using a timing light, disconnect vacuum hose or tube at distributor and plug opening in hose or tube so idle speed will not be affected.

● When checking compression, lowest cylinder must be within 80 percent of highest.

▲ Before removing wires from distributor cap, determine location of the No. 1 wire in cap, as distributor position may have been altered from that shown at the end of this chart.

Year	Spark Plug		Distributor		Ignition Timing ★			Carb. Adjustments					
	Type	Gap Inch	Point Gap Inch	Dwell Angle Deg.	Firing Order Fig. ▲	Timing BTDC ①	Mark Fig.	Hot Idle Speed ③		Air Fuel Ratio		Idle CO%	
								Std. Trans.	Auto. Trans. ②	Std. Trans.	Auto. Trans.	Std. Trans.	Auto. Trans.
1969													
6-199, 232 Std. Tr.	N14Y	.035	.016	31–34	A	TDC	D	600⑤	—	—	—	—	—
6-199, 232 Auto. Tr.	N14Y	.035	.016	31–34	A	5°	D	—	525D⑤	—	—	—	—
V8-290, 343, 390	N12Y	.035	.016	29–31	B	TDC	C	650⑤	550D⑤	—	—	—	—
1970													
6-199, 232	N14Y	.035	.016	31–34	A	3°	D	600	550D	14.0 to 1	14.0 to 1	—	—
V8-304, 360, 390	N12Y	.035	.016	29–31	B	5°④	C	650	600D	14.0 to 1	14.0 to 1	—	—
1971													
6-232 Std. Tr.	N12Y	.035	.016	31–34	A	3°	D	700	—	14.0 to 1	14.0 to 1	—	—
6-232 Auto. Tr.	N12Y	.035	.016	31–34	A	5°	D	—	600D	14.0 to 1	14.0 to 1	—	—
6-258	N12Y	.035	.016	31–34	A	5°	D	700	600D	14.0 to 1	14.0 to 1	—	—
V8-304, 360, 401	N12Y	.035	.016	29–31	B	2½°	C	750	650D	14.0 to 1	14.0 to 1	—	—
1972													
6-232 Exc. Calif.	N12Y	.035	.016	31–34	A	5°	D	600	550D	14.0 to 1	14.0 to 1	—	—
6-232 Calif.	N12Y	.035	.016	31–34	A	3°	D	700	600D	14.0 to 1	14.0 to 1	—	—
6-258 Exc. Calif.	N12Y	.035	.016	31–34	A	5°	D	600	550D	14.0 to 1	14.0 to 1	—	—
6-258 Calif.	N12Y	.035	.016	31–34	A	3°	D	700	600D	14.0 to 1	14.0 to 1	—	—
V8-304 Exc. Calif.	N12Y	.035	.016	29–31	B	5°	C	750	650D	13.5 to 1	14.0 to 1	—	—
V8-304 Calif.	N12Y	.035	.016	29–31	B	5°	C	750	700D	13.5 to 1	14.0 to 1	—	—
V8-360	N12Y	.035	.016	29–31	B	5°	C	750	700D	14.0 to 1	14.0 to 1	—	—
V8-401 Exc. Calif.	N12Y	.035	.016	29–31	B	5°	C	700	650D	13.5 to 1	13.5 to 1	—	—
V8-401 Calif.	N12Y	.035	.016	29–31	B	5°	C	700	700D	14.0 to 1	14.0 to 1	—	—
1973													
6-232	N12Y	.035	.016	31–34	A	5°	D	700⑦	600D⑧	—	—	⑨	⑨
6-258	N12Y	.035	.016	31–34	A	3°	D	700⑦	600D⑧	—	—	⑨	⑨
V8-304	N12Y	.035	.016	29–31	B	5°	C	750	700D	—	—	0.5–1.0	0.5–1.0
V8-360	N12Y	.035	.016	29–31	B	5°	C	750	700D	—	—	0.5–1.0	0.5–1.0
V8-401	N12Y	.035	.016	29–31	B	5°	C	750	700D	—	—	0.5–1.0	0.5–1.0
1974													
6-232 L/EGR	N12Y	.035	.016	31–34	A	5°	D	700	600D	—	—	⑨	⑨
6-232 W/EGR	N12Y	.035	.016	31–34	A	5°	D	600	550D	—	—	⑨	⑨
6-232 Calif.	N12Y	.035	.016	31–34	A	5°	D	600	700D	—	—	⑨	⑨
6-258 L/EGR	N12Y	.035	.016	31–34	A	3°	D	550	700D	—	—	⑨	⑨
6-258 W/EGR	N12Y	.035	.016	31–34	A	3°	D	550	600D	—	—	⑨	⑨
6-258 Calif.	N12Y	.035	.016	31–34	A	3°	D	600	700D	—	—	⑨	⑨
V8-304	N12Y	.035	.016	29–31	B	⑩	C	750	700D	—	—	0.5–1.0	0.5–1.0
V8-360	N12Y	.035	.016	29–31	B	5°	C	750	700D	—	—	0.5–1.0	0.5–1.0
V8-401	N12Y	.035	.016	29–31	B	5°	C	750	700D	—	—	0.5–1.0	0.5–1.0

American Motors

TUNEUP SPECIFICATIONS/continued

The following specifications are published from the latest information available. This data should be used only in the absence of a decal affixed in the engine compartment.

★When using a timing light, disconnect vacuum hose or tube at distributor and plug opening in hose or tube so idle speed will not be affected.

●When checking compression, lowest cylinder must be within 80 percent of highest.

▲Before removing wires from distributor cap, determine location of the No. 1 wire in cap, as distributor position may have been altered from that shown at the end of this chart.

Year	Spark Plug		Distributor		Ignition Timing★			Carb. Adjustments					
	Type	Gap Inch	Point Gap Inch	Dwell Angle Deg.	Firing Order Fig. ▲	Timing BTDC ①	Mark Fig.	Hot Idle Speed③		Air Fuel Ratio		Idle CO%	
								Std. Trans.	Auto. Trans.②	Std. Trans.	Auto. Trans.	Std. Trans.	Auto. Trans.
1975													
6-232	N12Y	.035	—	—	A	5°	E	600	⑥	—	—	—	⑪
6-258 Calif.	N12Y	.035	—	—	A	3°	E	600	⑥	—	—	—	⑪
V8-304	N12Y	.035	—	—	B	5°	C	750	700D	—	—	—	—
V8-360	N12Y	.035	—	—	B	5°	C	—	700D	—	—	—	—
1976													
6-232	N12Y	.035	—	—	A	8°	E	850	⑥	—	—	⑫	⑬
6-258 Std. Tr.	N12Y	.035	—	—	A	6°	E	⑭	—	—	—	⑫	⑬
6-258 Auto. Tr.	N12Y	.035	—	—	A	8°	E	—	⑮	—	—	⑫	⑬
V8-304	N12Y	.035	—	—	B	⑯	C	750	700D	—	—	—	—
V8-360	N12Y	.035	—	—	B	⑯	C	—	700D	—	—	—	—
V8-401⑰	N12Y	.035	—	—	B	⑯	C	—	700D	—	—	—	—

①—BTDC: Before top dead center.
②—D: Drive. N: Neutral.
③—Where two speeds are listed, lower speed indicates idle solenoid disconnected.
④—V8-390 with distributor 1111948 set at TDC.
⑤—If air conditioned turn A/C switch full on.
⑥—Exc. Calif., 550D; Calif., 700D.
⑦—Set Matador wagon at 600 R.P.M.
⑧—Set Matador at 650D.
⑨—W/Air Guard 0.5-1.0%. W/O Air Guadr 1.0-1.5%.
⑩—Exc. Calif. auto. trans., 5° BTDC; Calif. auto. trans., 2½° BTDC.
⑪—W/Air Guard, 0.8% maximum; Less Air Guard, 1.0% maximum.
⑫—Exc. Gremlin, 0.5% maximum; Gremlin, 1.0% maximum.
⑬—Exc. Matador, 1.0% maximum; Matador, 0.8% maximum.
⑭—W/Idle solenoid & all Calif., 850 RPM; Less idle solenoid, 600 RPM.
⑮—Exc. Calif. & 2 bbl. carb., 550D; Calif. & 2 bbl. carb., 700D.
⑯—Exc. Calif. auto. tr. & all std. tr., 10° BTDC; Calif. & all std. tr., 5° BTDC.
⑰—Police.

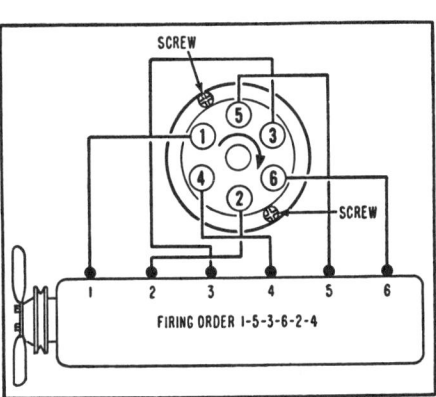

Fig. A

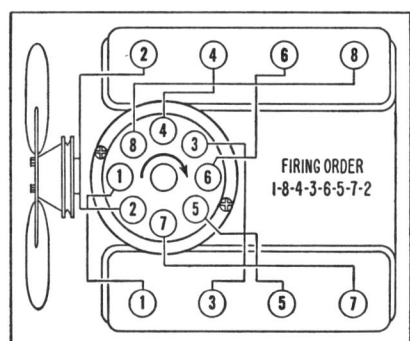

Fig. B

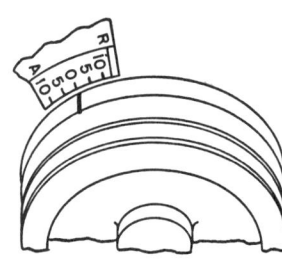

Fig. C

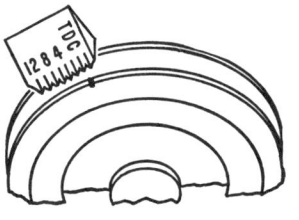

Fig. D

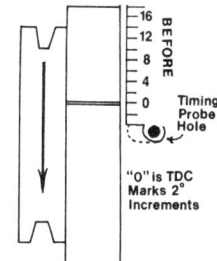

Fig. E

COOLING SYSTEM & CAPACITY DATA

Year	Model or Engine	Cooling Capacity, Qts. No Heater	Cooling Capacity, Qts. With Heater	Cooling Capacity, Qts. With A/C	Radiator Cap Relief Pressure, Lbs. With A/C	Radiator Cap Relief Pressure, Lbs. No. A/C	Thermo. Opening Temp. (1)	Fuel Tank Gals.	Engine Oil Refill Qts. (2)	Transmission Oil 3 Speed Pints	Transmission Oil 4 Speed Pints	Transmission Oil Auto. Trans. Qts. (10)	Rear Axle Oils Pint
1969	6-199, 232	9½	10½	10½	14	14	195(11)	(12)	4	1½(13)	—	9	3
	V8-290	13	14	14	14	14	195	(12)	4	3	2½	(14)	4
	V8-343, 390	12	13	13	14	14	195	(12)	4	—	2½	11	4
1970	6-199, 232	9½	10½	10½	14	14	195	(15)	4	1½(13)	—	9½	3
	V8-304	13	14	14	14	14	195	(15)	4	3	2½	9½	4
	V8-360, 390	12	13	13	14	14	195	(15)	4	—	2½	10	4
1971	6-232	9½	10½	10½	14	14	205	(3)	4	1½(13)	—	9½	(4)
	6-258	9½	10½	10½	14	14	205	(3)	4	2½	—	9½	(4)
	V8-304	13	14	14	14	14	195	(3)	4	2½	2½	9½	4
	V8-360, 401	12	13	13	14	14	195	(3)	4	3	2½	10	4
1972	6-232	9½	10½	10½	14	14	205	(5)	4	1½(13)	—	8½	(4)
	6-258	9½	10½	10½	14	14	205	(5)	4	1½(13)	—	8½	(4)
	V8-304	13	14	14	14	14	195	(5)	4	3	2½	9½	4
	V8-360, 401	12	13	13	14	14	195	(5)	4	3	2½	9½	4
1973	6-332, 258	9½	10½	10½	14	14	205	(6)	4	2½	2½	8½	(7)
	V8-304	13	14	14	14	14	195	(6)	4	2½	2½	9½	(7)
	V8-360, 401	12	13	13	14	14	195	(6)	4	2½	2½	9½	(7)
1974	6-232, 258	10	11	11½	14	14	205	(16)	4	2½	—	8½	(7)
	6-232, 258 Mat. 2 Dr. Coupe	10	11	13½(17)	14	14	205	(16)	4	2½	—	8½	(7)
	V8-304 Hornet, Gremlin	15	16	16	14	14	195	(16)	4	2½	—	8½	(7)
	V8-304 Mat., Amb.	15½	16½	16½	14	14	195	(16)	4	2½	—	8½	(7)
	V8-304, Mat. 2 Dr. Coupe	17½	18½(17)	18½(17)	14	14	195	(16)	4	2½	—	8½	(7)
	V8-304 Javelin	—	15	15½	14	14	195	(16)	4	1½	—	8½	(7)
	V8-360 Hornet	14	15	15	14	14	195	(16)	4	1½	—	9½	(7)
	V8-360, 401 Matador	14½	15½	15½(17)	14	14	195	(16)	4	—	—	9½	(7)
	V8-360, 401 Mat. 2 Dr. Coupe	16½	17½(17)	17½(17)	14	14	195	(16)	4	1½	—	9½	(7)
	V8-360, 401 Javelin	14	15	15	14	14	195	(16)	4	—	2½	9½	(7)
	V8-360, 401 Ambassador	14½	15½	15½	14	14	195	(16)	4	1½	—	9½	(7)
1975	6-232-258	—	(18)	(6)	14	14	195	(9)	4	3½(19)	—	8½	(7)
	Gremlin, Hornet V8-304	—	16	16	14	14	195	(9)	4	3½	—	8½	(7)
	Matador(20) V8-304	—	16½	16½	14	14	195	(9)	4	3½	—	8½	(7)
	Matador(21) V8-304	—	18½(17)	18½(17)	14	14	195	24½	4	3½	—	8½	(7)
	Matador(20) V8-360	—	15½	15½	14	14	195	(9)	4	3½	—	9½	(7)
	Matador(21) V8-360	—	17½(17)	17½(17)	14	14	195	24½	4	3½	—	9½	(7)
1976	6-232, 258	—	(22)	(23)	14	14	195	(24)	4	(25)	—	8½	(7)
	V8-304 Gremlin, Hornet	—	(16)	(16)	14	14	195	(24)	4	3½	—	9½	4
	V8-304 Matador(20)	—	16½(17)	16½(17)	14	14	195	(24)	4	3½	—	9½	4
	V8-304 Matador(21)	—	18½	18½	14	14	195	24½	4	3½	—	9½	4
	V8-360 Matador(20)	—	15½(17)	15½(17)	14	14	195	(24)	4	—	—	9½	4
	V8-360 Matador(21)	—	17½	17½	14	14	195	24½	4	—	—	9½	4

(1)—With permanent type anti-freeze.
(2)—Add one quart with filter change.
(3)—Gremlin, 21; Hornet & Javelin, 16; Ambassador wagons & Matador 3 seat wagon, 17; all others, 19½.
(4)—Matador & Ambassador, 4; all others, 3.
(5)—Hornet, 16; Gremlin, 21; Javelin; 16; Matador & Ambassador sedans, 19½; Matador 2 seat wagons, 19½; Matador 3 seat wagons, 21½; Ambassdor wagons, 21½.
(6)—Hornet, 16; Gremlin, 21; Javelin, 16; Matador & Amb. sedans, 19½; Matador 2 seat wagon, 19½; Matador 3 seat wagon, 20; Ambassador wagon, 20.
(7)—7⁹⁄₁₆″ axle, 3 pints. 8⅞″ axle, 4 pints.
(8)—Matador 2 dr. coupe 13½ qts., all others 11½ qts.
(9)—Gremlin, 21 gals.; Hornet, early 17 gals.; late 22 gals.; Matador exc. wagon, 24½ gals.; wagon, 21 gals.; Pacer, 22 gals.
(10)—Approximate. Make final check with dipstick.
(11)—Rambler Rogue with 6-232 uses 205°.
(12)—Rambler 16.
AMX and Javelin 19.
Rebel 3-seat wagon and Amb. wagon 19.
All Others 21½.
(13)—Fully synchronized 2½.
(14)—With 2 barrel carb. 9; with 4 barrel carb. 11.
(15)—Rebel and Ambassador sedans, 21½, Rebel 2 seat wagons, 21½. All others 19. California vehicles about 2 gal. less.
(16)—Hornet & Javelin, 16; Gremlin, 21; Matador Sedan & 2 Dr. Coupe, 24¾; Ambassador Sedan, 24¾; Mat. & Amb. Wagons, 21.
(17)—Add two quarts with coolant recovery system.
(18)—Exc. Pacer, 11 qts.; Pacer, 10½ qts.
(19)—With overdrive exc. Pacer, add 1 pt.; Pacer with overdrive, add ½ pt.
(20)—Sedan & wagon.
(21)—2 dr. coupe.
(22)—Exc. Pacer, 11 qts.; Pacer, 14 qts.
(23)—Exc. Pacer & Matador 2 dr. coupe, 11½ qts.; Pacer, 14 qts.; Matador 2 dr. coupe, 13½ qts.
(24)—Gremlin, 21 gals.; Hornet, 22 gals.; Matador exc. wagon, 24½ gals.; Wagon, 21 gals.; Pacer, 22 gals.
(25)—Exc. Pacer, Matador & overdrive, 2½ pts.; Pacer & Matador, 3½ pts.; all models with overdrive, 4 pts.

Buick/Exc. Skyhawk

GENERAL ENGINE SPECIFICATIONS

Year	Engine	Carburetor	Bore and Stroke	Piston Displacement, Cubic Inches	Compression Ratio	Maximum Brake H.P. @ R.P.M.	Maximum Torque Lbs. Ft. @ R.P.M.	Normal Oil Pressure Pounds
1970	155 Horsepower..............①6-250	1 Barrel	3.875 x 3.53	250	8.5	155 @ 4200	235 @ 1600	30-45
	260 Horsepower...............V8-350	2 Barrel	3.800 x 3.85	350	9.0	260 @ 4600	360 @ 2600	37
	285 Horsepower...............V8-350	4 Barrel	3.800 x 3.85	350	9.0	285 @ 4600	375 @ 3000	37
	315 Horsepower...............V8-350	4 Barrel	3.800 x 3.85	350	10.25	315 @ 4800	410 @ 3200	37
	350 Horsepower...............V8-455	4 Barrel	4.3125 x 3.90	455	10.00	350 @ 4600	510 @ 2800	40
	360 Horsepower...............V8-455	4 Barrel	4.3125 x 3.90	455	10.00	360 @ 4600	510 @ 2800	40
	370 Horsepower...............V8-455	4 Barrel	4.3125 x 3.90	455	10.00	370 @ 4600	510 @ 2800	40
1971	145 Horsepower..............①6-250	1 Barrel	3.875 x 3.53	250	8.5	145 @ 4000	235 @ 2400	30-45
	230 Horsepower...............V8-350	2 Barrel	3.800 x 3.85	350	8.5	230 @ 4400	350 @ 2400	37
	260 Horsepower...............V8-350	4 Barrel	3.800 x 3.85	350	8.5	260 @ 4600	360 @ 3000	37
	315 Horsepower...............V8-455	4 Barrel	4.3125 x 3.90	455	8.5	315 @ 4400	450 @ 2800	40
	330 Horsepower...............V8-455	4 Barrel	4.3125 x 3.90	455	8.5	330 @ 4600	455 @ 2800	40
	345 Horsepower...............V8-455	4 Barrel	4.3125 x 3.90	455	8.5	345 @ 5000	460 @ 3000	40
1972	150 Horsepower②...............V8-350	2 Barrel	3.800 x 3.85	350	8.5	150 @ 3800	265 @ 2400	37
	155 Horsepower②...............V8-350	2 Barrel	3.800 x 3.85	350	8.5	155 @ 3800	270 @ 2400	37
	175 Horsepower②...............V8-350	4 Barrel	3.800 x 3.85	350	8.5	175 @ 3800	270 @ 2400	37
	180 Horsepower②...............V8-350	4 Barrel	3.800 x 3.85	350	8.5	180 @ 3800	275 @ 2400	37
	190 Horsepower②...............V8-350	4 Barrel	3.800 x 3.85	350	8.5	190 @ 4000	285 @ 2800	37
	195 Horsepower②...............V8-350	4 Barrel	3.800 x 3.85	350	8.5	195 @ 4000	290 @ 2800	37
1972	225 Horsepower②...............V8-455	4 Barrel	4.3125 x 3.90	455	8.5	225 @ 4000	360 @ 2600	40
	250 Horsepower②...............V8-455	4 Barrel	4.3125 x 3.90	455	8.5	250 @ 4000	375 @ 2800	40
	260 Horsepower②...............V8-455	4 Barrel	4.3125 x 3.90	455	8.5	260 @ 4400	380 @ 2800	40
	270 Horsepower②...............V8-455	4 Barrel	4.3125 x 3.90	455	8.5	270 @ 4400	390 @ 3000	40
1973	100 Horsepower②..............6-250①	1 Barrel	3.875 x 3.53	250	8.25	100 @ 3600	175 @ 1600	40
	150 Horsepower②...............V8-350	2 Barrel	3.800 x 3.85	350	8.5	150 @ 3800	265 @ 2400	37
	175 Horsepower②...............V8-350	4 Barrel	3.800 x 3.85	350	8.5	175 @ 3800	270 @ 2400	37
	190 Horsepower②...............V8-350	4 Barrel	3.800 x 3.85	350	8.5	190 @ 4000	285 @ 2800	37
	225 Horsepower②...............V8-455	4 Barrel	4.3125 x 3.90	455	8.5	225 @ 4000	360 @ 2600	40
	250 Horsepower②...............V8-455	4 Barrel	4.3125 x 3.90	455	8.5	250 @ 4000	375 @ 2800	40
	260 Horsepower②...............V8-455	4 Barrel	4.3125 x 3.90	455	8.5	260 @ 4400	380 @ 2800	40
	270 Horsepower②...............V8-455	4 Barrel	4.3125 x 3.90	455	8.5	270 @ 4400	390 @ 3000	40
1974	100 Horsepower②..............6-250①	1 Barrel	3.875 x 3.53	250	8.25	100 @ 3600	175 @ 1600	40
	150 Horsepower②...............V8-350	2 Barrel	3.800 x 3.85	350	8.5	150 @ 3600	270 @ 2000	37
	165 Horsepower②...........V8-350③	2 Barrel	3.800 x 3.85	350	8.5	165 @ 3800	285 @ 2000	37
	175 Horsepower②...............V8-350	4 Barrel	3.800 x 3.85	350	8.5	175 @ 3800	260 @ 2000	37
	195 Horsepower②...........V8-350③	4 Barrel	3.800 x 3.85	350	8.5	195 @ 4000	280 @ 2000	37
	175 Horsepower②...............V8-455	2 Barrel	4.3125 x 3.90	455	8.5	175 @ 3400	355 @ 2000	40
	190 Horsepower②...........V8-455③	2 Barrel	4.3125 x 3.90	455	8.5	190 @ 3600	370 @ 2000	40
	210 Horsepower②...............V8-455	4 Barrel	4.3125 x 3.90	455	8.5	210 @ 3600	335 @ 2200	40
	230 Horsepower②...........V8-455③	4 Barrel	4.3125 x 3.90	455	8.5	230 @ 3800	355 @ 2200	40
	245 Horsepower②...........V8-455④	4 Barrel	4.3125 x 3.90	455	8.5	245 @ 4000	360 @ 2400	40
	255 Horsepower②...........V8-455④	4 Barrel	4.3125 x 3.90	455	8.5	255 @ 4400	370 @ 2800	40
1975	105 Horsepower②..............6-250①	1 Barrel	3.875 x 3.53	250	8.25	105 @ 3800	185 @ 1200	40
	110 Horsepower②...............V6-231	2 Barrel	3.80 x 3.40	231	8.0	110 @ 4000	175 @ 2000	37
	110 Horsepower②...........V8-260⑤	2 Barrel	3.50 x 3.385	260	8.0	110 @ 3400	205 @ 1600	35
	145 Horsepower②...............V8-350	2 Barrel	3.80 x 3.85	350	8.0	145 @ 3200	270 @ 2000	37
	165 Horsepower②...............V8-350	4 Barrel	3.80 x 3.85	350	8.0	165 @ 3800	260 @ 2200	37
	190 Horsepower②...........V8-400⑥	4 Barrel	4.12 x 3.75	400	7.6	190 @ 3400	350 @ 2400	55-60
	205 Horsepower②...............V8-455	4 Barrel	4.3125 x 3.90	455	7.9	205 @ 3800	345 @ 2000	40

Exc. Skyhawk/Buick

GENERAL ENGINE SPECIFICATIONS/continued

Year	Engine	Carburetor	Bore and Stroke	Piston Displacement, Cubic Inches	Compression Ratio	Maximum Brake H.P. @ R.P.M.	Maximum Torque Lbs. Ft. @ R.P.M.	Normal Oil Pressure Pounds
1976	110 Horsepower②............V6-231	2 Barrel	3.80 x 3.40	231	8.0	110 @ 4000	175 @ 2000	37
	110 Horsepower②..........V8-260⑤	2 Barrel	3.50 x 3.385	260	8.5	110 @ 3400	210 @ 1600	—
	145 Horsepower②..........V8-350⑦	2 Barrel	3.80 x 3.85	350	8.0	145 @ 3200	270 @ 2000	37
	160 Horsepower②..........V8-350⑧	4 Barrel	3.80 x 3.85	350	8.0	160 @ 3800	260 @ 2200	37
	165 Horsepower②............V8-350	4 Barrel	3.80 x 3.85	350	8.0	165 @ 3800	260 @ 2200	37
	Horsepower②..............V8-455	4 Barrel	4.3125 x 3.90	455	7.9	—	—	40
	Horsepower②..............V8-455	4 Barrel	4.3125 x 3.90	455	7.9	—	—	40
	Horsepower②..............V8-455	4 Barrel	4.3125 x 3.90	455	7.9	—	—	40

①—See Chevrolet chapter for service procedures on this engine.
②—Net Rating—As installed in vehicle.
③—Dual exhaust.
④—Stage 1.
⑤—See Oldsmobile chapter for service procedures on this engine.
⑥—See Pontiac chapter for service procedure on this engine.
⑦—Except California.
⑧—California.

TUNEUP SPECIFICATIONS

The following specifications are published from the latest information available. This data should be used only in the absence of a decal affixed in the engine compartment.

★When using a timing light, disconnect vacuum hose or tube at distributor and plug opening in tube or hose so idle speed will not be affected.

●When checking compression, lowest cylinder must be within 80 percent of highest.

▲Before removing wires from distributor cap, determine location of the No. 1 wire in cap, as distributor position may have been altered from that shown at the end of this chart.

Year	Spark Plug		Distributor		Ignition Timing ★			Carb. Adjustments					
								Hot Idle Speed		Air Fuel Ratio		Idle CO %	
	Type	Gap Inch	Point Gap Inch	Dwell Angle Deg.	Firing Order Fig. ▲	Timing BTDC ①	Mark Fig.	Std. Trans.	Auto. Trans. ②	Std. Trans.	Auto. Trans.	Std. Trans.	Auto. Trans.
1969													
6-250⑧ Std. Tr.	R46N	.035	.019	32	A	TDC	C	700	—	—	—	—	—
6-250⑧ Auto. Tr.	R46N	.035	.019	32	A	4°	C	—	500D④	—	—	—	—
V8-350	R45TS	.030	.016	30	B	TDC⑨	E	700	600D	—	—	—	—
V8-400 Std. Tr.	R44TS	.030	.016	30	B	2½° ATDC	E	700	—	—	—	—	—
V8-400 Auto. Tr.	R44TS	.030	.016	30	B	TDC	E	—	600D	—	—	—	—
V8-400 G.S. Stage 1	R44TS	.030	.016	30	B	10°	E	700	600D	—	—	—	—
V8-430	R44TS	.030	.016	30	B	TDC	E	—	550D	—	—	—	—
1970													
6-250⑧	R46N	.035	.019	32	A	⑥	C	700	550D	—	—	—	—
V8-350	R45TS	.030	.016	30	B	6°	G	700	600D	—	—	—	—
V8-455	R44TS	.030	.016	30	B	6°⑩	G	700	600D	—	—	—	—
1971													
6-250⑧	R46TS	.035	.019	32	A	4°	D	550	500D	—	—	—	—
V8-350 Std. Tr.	R45TS	.030	.016	30	B	6°	F	800	—	—	—	—	—
V8-350 Auto. Tr.	R45TS	.030	.016	30	B	⑪	F	—	600D	—	—	—	—
V8-455 Std. Tr.	R44TS	.030	.016	30	B	6°	F	700	—	—	—	—	—
V8-455 Auto. Tr.	R44TS	.030	.016	30	B	4°	F	—	600D	—	—	—	—
V8-455 Stage 1	R44TS	.030	.016	30	B	10°	F	700	600D	—	—	—	—

Buick/Exc. Skyhawk

TUNEUP SPECIFICATIONS/continued

The following specifications are published from the latest information available. This data should be used only in the absence of a decal affixed in the engine compartment.

OLD CAR SPECIFICATIONS: For 1946–68 Tune Up Specifications see main index.

★When using a timing light, disconnect vacuum hose or tube at distributor and plug opening in tube or hose so idle speed will not be affected.

●When checking compression, lowest cylinder must be within 80 percent of highest.

▲Before removing wires from distributor cap, determine location of the No. 1 wire in cap, as distributor position may have been altered from that shown at the end of this chart.

Year	Spark Plug		Distributor		Ignition Timing ★			Carb. Adjustments					
	Type	Gap Inch	Point Gap Inch	Dwell Angle Deg.	Firing Order Fig. ▲	Timing BTDC ①	Mark Fig.	Hot Idle Speed		Air Fuel Ratio		Idle CO %	
								Std. Trans.	Auto. Trans. ②	Std. Trans.	Auto. Trans.	Std. Trans.	Auto. Trans.
1972													
V8-350	R45TS	.040	.016	30	B	4°	F	800	650D	—	—	—	—
V8-455	R45TS	.040	.016	30	B	4°	F	900	650D	—	—	—	—
V8-455 Stage 1	R45TS	.040	.016	30	B	⑦	F	900	650D	—	—	—	—
1973													
6-250 ⑧	R46T	.035	.019	31–34	A	6°	D	700	600D	—	—	—	—
V8-350	R45TS	.040	.016	30	B	4°	F	800	650D	—	—	—	—
V8-455	R45TS	.040	.016	30	B	4°	F	900	650D	—	—	—	—
V8-455 Stage I	R45TS	.040	.016	30	B	10°	F	900	650D	—	—	—	—
1974													
6-250 ⑧	R46T	.035	.019	31–34	A	③	D	950	600D	—	—	—	—
V8-350	R45TS	.040	.016	29–31	⑭	4°	F	—	650D	—	—	—	—
V8-455	R45TS	.040	.016	29–31	⑭	⑤	F	—	650D	—	—	—	—
1975													
6-250 ⑧	R46TX	.060	—	—	I	10°	D	800	⑮	—	—	—	—
V6-231	R44SX	.060	—	—	J	12°	K	800	700D	—	—	—	—
V8-260 ⑫	R46SX	.080	—	—	L	16°	M	—	650D	—	—	—	—
V8-350	R45TSX	.060	—	—	H	12°	F	—	600D	—	—	—	—
V8-400 4 B. Carb. ⑬	R45TSX	.060	—	—	N	16°	O	—	650D	—	—	—	—
V8-455	R45TSX	.060	—	—	H	12°	F	—	600D	—	—	—	—
1976													
V6-231	R44SX	.060	—	—	J	12°	K	800	600D	—	—	—	—
V8-260 ⑫	R46SX	.080	—	—	L	⑯	M	—	650D⑰	—	—	—	—
V8-350	R45TSX	.060	—	—	H	12°	F	—	600D	—	—	—	—
V8-455	R45TSX	.060	—	—	H	12°	F	—	600D	—	—	—	—

①—BTDC: Before top dead center.
②—D: Drive. N: Neutral.
③—Manual trans., 8° BTDC; auto. trans., 6° BTDC.
④—If air conditioned, turn A/C switch to "Full On" position.
⑤—Exc. intermediate model Stage 1 eng., 4° BTDC; intermediate model Stage 1 eng., 10° BTDC.
⑥—Std. trans. TDC: Auto. Trans. 4°.
⑦—Manual trans., 8°; Automatic trans., 10°.
⑧—See Chevrolet chapter for service procedures on this engine.
⑨—5° BTDC for LeSabre.
⑩—Early Gran Sport models set at TDC.
⑪—4 Barrel carburetors and all LeSabres 4°; All others 10°.
⑫—See Oldsmobile chapter for service procedures on this engine.
⑬—See Pontiac chapter for service procedures on this engine.
⑭—Exc. H.E.I., Fig. B; H.E.I., Fig. H.
⑮—Exc. Calif., 550D with A/C On & compressor clutch wires disconnected; Calif. 600D.
⑯—Exc. Calif., 18° BTDC; Calif., 14° BTDC. At 1100 RPM.
⑰—Calif. models with A/C ON & compressor clutch wires disconnected.

Exc. Skyhawk/Buick

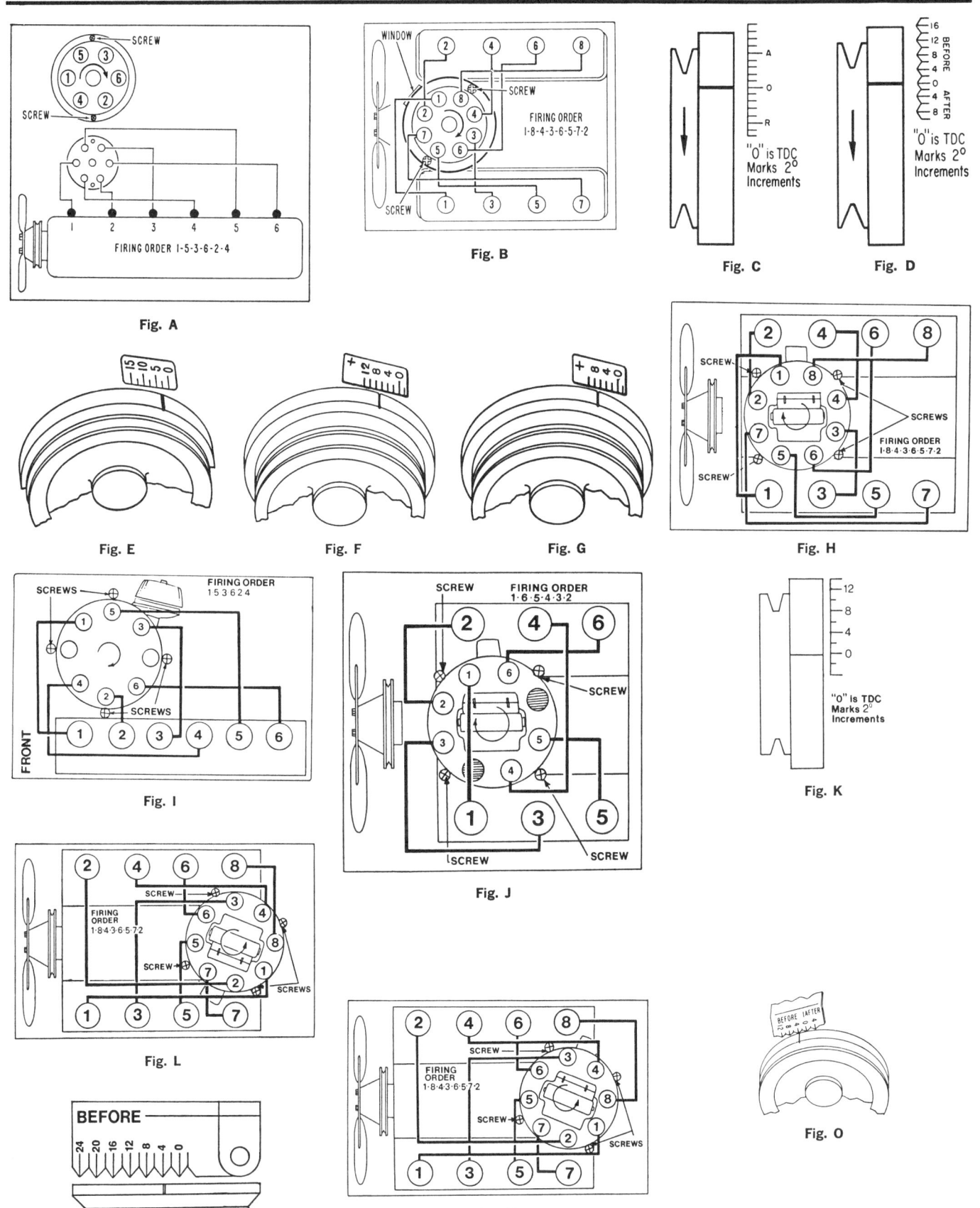

Buick/Exc. Skyhawk

COOLING SYSTEM & CAPACITY DATA

Year	Model or Engine	Cooling Capacity, Qts.			Radiator Cap Relief Pressure, Lbs.		Thermo. Opening Temp.	Fuel Tank Gals.	Engine Oil Refill Qts. ①	Transmission Oil			Rear Axle Oil Pints
		No Heater	With Heater	With A/C	With A/C	No A/C				3 Speed Pints	4 Speed Pints	Auto. Trans. Qts. ⑬	
1969	6-250	10.0	11.3	13.0	15	15	195	20	4	3 3/8	—	⑫	2.9
	V8-350⑪	12.6	13.5	13.5	15	15	190	20	4	3 3/8	—	⑭	2.9
	GS-350	12.6	13.5	13.5	15	15	190	20	4	3.4	3	⑮	2.9
	GS-400	15.3	16.2	16.7	15	15	190	20	4	3.5	3	⑯	2.9
	V8-350⑩	12.3	13.2	13.6	15	15	190	25	4	3.5	—	⑰	2.9
	V8-430	16.0	16.7	17.0	15	15	190	25	4	—	—	⑯	4 1/4
	Riviera	16.0	16.7	17.0	15	15	190	21	4	—	—	⑯	4 1/4
1970	6-250	—	16.04	16.04	15	15	190	20	4	3 1/2	3	⑮	3
	V8-350⑪	—	16.45	16.52	15	15	190	20⑱	4	3 1/2	3	⑮	3
	GS-455	—	19.17	19.67	15	15	190	20	4	4	3	⑯	3
	V8-350⑩	—	16.20	16.55	15	15	190	25⑲	4	3 1/2	—	⑮	3
	V8-455	—	19.70	20.0	15	15	190	25⑲	4	3 1/2	—	⑯	4 1/4
	Riviera	—	19.70	20.0	15	15	190	21	4	—	—	⑯	4 1/4
1971	6-250	—	16.04	16.04	15	15	195	20	4	3 1/2	—	⑮	4 1/4
	V8-350⑪	—	16.5	16.5	15	15	190	20⑱	4	3 1/2	3	⑮	4 1/4
	GS-455	—	19.0	19.5	15	15	190	20	4	3 1/2	3	⑯	4 1/4
	V8-350⑩	—	16.2	16.55	15	15	190	25⑲	4	3 1/2	—	⑮	4 1/4
	V8-455	—	19.7	20.0	15	15	190	25⑲	4	3 1/2	—	⑯	5 1/2
	Riviera	—	19.7	20.0	15	15	190	21	4	—	—	⑯	5 1/2
1972	V8-350⑪	—	16.45	16.85	15	15	190	20⑱	4	3 1/2	3	⑮	②
	V8-350⑩	—	18.9	19.3	15	15	190	25	4	—	—	⑮	②
	GS-455	—	16.2	16.3	15	15	190	20	4	3 1/2	3	⑯	②
	V8-455	—	18.7	19.0	15	15	190	25⑲	4	—	—	⑯	②
1973	6-250	—	14.0	14.0	15	15	195	21	4	3 1/2	—	⑮	②
	V8-350 Apollo	—	19.5	20.0	15	15	190	21	4	3 1/2	—	⑮	②
	V8-350⑪	—	16.45	16.85	15	15	190	22	4	3 1/2	—	⑮	②
	V8-350⑩	—	18.9	19.3	15	15	190	26	4	—	—	⑮	②
	GS-455	—	16.2	16.6	15	15	190	22	4	3 1/2	—	⑯	②
	V8-455	—	18.7	19.0	15	15	190	26③	4	—	—	⑯	②
1974	6-250	—	14.0	14.0	15	15	195	21	4	3 1/2	—	⑮	②
	V8-350 Apollo	—	16.5	17.0	15	15	190	21	4	3 1/2	—	⑮	②
	V8-350⑪	—	17.3	④	15	15	190	22	4	—	—	⑮	②
	V8-350⑩	—	17.3	17.2	15	15	190	26	4	—	—	⑮	②
	V8-455⑪	—	19.4	19.9	15	15	190	22	4	—	—	⑯	②
	V8-455⑥	—	19.6	19.8⑤	15	15	190	26③	4	—	—	⑯	②
1975	6-250	—	16.3	16.4	15	15	190	21	4	3 1/2	—	⑮	4.25
	V6-231⑦	—	16.5	16.6	15	15	190	21	4	3 1/2	—	⑮	4.25
	V6-231⑪	—	15.3	15.3	15	15	190	22	4	3 1/2	—	⑮	4.25
	V8-260⑦	—	22.4	22.9	—	—	195	21	4	3 1/2	—	⑮	4.25
	V8-350⑦	—	17.9	18.6	15	15	190	21	4	—	—	⑮	4.25
	V8-350⑪	—	16.9	17.2	15	15	190	22	4	3 1/2	—	⑮	⑳
	V8-350⑩	—	16.9	17.2	15	15	190	26	4	—	—	⑮	4.25
	V8-400	—	23.6⑧	⑨	15	15	190	26③	4	—	—	—	⑳
	V8-455	—	19.6	20⑤	15	15	190	26③	4	—	—	⑯	⑳

562

Exc. Skyhawk/Buick

COOLING SYSTEM & CAPACITY DATA/continued

Year	Model or Engine	Cooling Capacity, Qts.			Radiator Cap Relief Pressure, Lbs.		Thermo. Opening Temp.	Fuel Tank Gals.	Engine Oil Refill Qts. ①	Transmission Oil			Rear Axle Oil Pints
		No Heater	With Heater	With A/C	With A/C	No A/C				3 Speed Pints	4 Speed Pints	Auto. Trans. Qts. ⑬	
1976	V6-231⑦	—	16.6	16.7	15	15	195	21	4	3½	—	⑮	3.5
	V6-231⑪	—	15.5	15.4	15	15	195	22	4	3½	—	⑮	4.25
	V8-260⑦	—	22.4	22.9	15	15	195	21	4	3½	—	⑮	3.5
	V8-350⑦	—	17.9	18.5	15	15	195	21	4	—	—	⑮	3.5
	V8-350⑪	—	16.9	17.2	15	15	195	22	4	—	—	⑮	4.25
	V8-350⑩	—	16.9	17.2	15	15	195	26③	4	—	—	⑮	4.25
	V8-455	—	19.7	20①	15	15	195	26	4	—	—	⑥	5.4

①—Add one quart with filter change.
②—8½ inch axle, 4¼ pts.; 8⅞ inch axle, 5¼ pts.; 9⅜ inch axle, 5½ pts.
③—Estate Wagon 22 gallons.
④—With 20 inch fan shroud, 17.6 qts.; with 22 inch fan shroud, 17.2 qts.
⑤—With heavy duty cooling system 21.6 qts.
⑥—Estate Wagon, Electra & Riviera.
⑦—Apollo & Skylark.
⑧—With heavy duty cooling system, 25.6 qts.
⑨—Exc. wagon & heavy duty, 24.4 qts;. wagon & heavy duty, 26.1 qts.
⑩—LeSabre.
⑪—Intermediates
⑫—Total 9½ qts. Oil pan only 2½ qts.
⑬—Approximate. Make final check with dipstick.
⑭—Two speed unit 9½ qts. total. Oil pan only 2½ qts. Three speed unit 10 qts. total. Oil pan only 3 qts.
⑮—Total 10 qts. pan only 3 qts.
⑯—Total 11½ qts. Oil pan only 3½ qts.
⑰—Two speed unit 9½ qts. total. Oil pan only 2½ qts. Three speed unit 11½ qts. total. Oil pan only 3½ qts.
⑱—Sportwagon 23 gallons.
⑲—Estate Wagon 24 gallons.
⑳—Exc. wagon, 4¼ pts.; wagon, 5.4 pts.
㉑—With heavy duty cooling system, 21.45 qts.

Cadillac

GENERAL ENGINE SPECIFICATIONS

Year	Engine	Carburetor	Bore and Stroke	Piston Displacement, Cubic Inches	Compression Ratio	Maximum Brake H.P. @ R.P.M.	Maximum Torque Lbs. Ft. @ R.P.M.	Normal Oil Pressure Pounds
1969	375 Horsepower..............V8-472	4 Barrel	4.3000 x 4.060	472	10.50	375 @ 4400	525 @ 3000	30-35
1970	375 Horsepower..............V8-472	4 Barrel	4.3000 x 4.060	472	10.00	375 @ 4400	525 @ 3000	35-40
	400 Horsepower..............V8-500	4 Barrel	4.3000 x 4.304	500	10.00	400 @ 4400	550 @ 3000	35-40
1971	345 Horsepower..............V8-472	4 Barrel	4.3000 x 4.060	472	8.50	345 @ 4400	500 @ 2800	35-40
	365 Horsepower..............V8-500	4 Barrel	4.3000 x 4.304	500	8.50	365 @ 4400	535 @ 2800	35-40
1972-73	220 Horsepower①..............V8-472	4 Barrel	4.300 x 4.060	472	8.50	220 @ 4000	365 @ 2400	35-40
	235 Horsepower①..............V8-500	4 Barrel	4.300 x 4.304	500	8.50	235 @ 3800	385 @ 2400	35-40
1974	205 Horsepower①..............V8-472	4 Barrel	4.300 x 4.060	472	8.25	205 @ 3600	365 @ 2000	35-40
	210 Horsepower①..............V8-500	4 Barrel	4.300 x 4.304	500	8.25	210 @ 3600	380 @ 2000	35-40
1975-76	190 Horsepower①..............V8-500	4 Barrel	4.300 x 4.304	500	8.5	190 @ 3600	360 @ 2000	35-40
1976	180 Horsepower①..............V8-350	Fuel Inj.	4.057 x 3.385	350	8.0	180 @ 4400	275 @ 2000	30-45
	215 Horsepower①..............V8-500	Fuel Inj.	4.300 x 4.304	500	8.5	215 @ 3600	400 @ 2000	35

①—Net rating—as installed in the vehicle.

Cadillac

TUNEUP SPECIFICATIONS

The following specifications are published from the latest information available. This data should be used only in the absence of a decal affixed in the engine compartment.

★ When using a timing light, disconnect vacuum hose or tube at distributor and plug opening in hose or tube so idle speed will not be affected.

● When checking compression, lowest cylinder must be within 80 percent of highest.

▲ Before removing wires from distributor cap, determine location of No. 1 wire in cap, as distributor position may have been altered from that shown at the end of this chart.

Year	Spark Plug		Distributor		Ignition Timing ★			Carb. Adjustments					
	Type	Gap Inch	Point Gap Inch	Dwell Angle Deg.	Firing Order Fig. ▲	Timing BTDC ①	Mark Fig.	Hot Idle Speed		Air Fuel Ratio		Idle "CO" %	
								Std. Trans.	Auto. Trans. ②	Std. Trans.	Auto. Trans.	Std. Trans.	Auto. Trans.
1969	R44N	.035	③	30	C	5°	B	—	550D④	—	—	—	—
1970	R46N	.035	③	30	C	7½°	A	—	600D④	—	—	—	—
1971–72	R46N	.035	③	30	C	8°	D	—	600D④	—	—	—	—
1973	R46N	.035	③	30	C	8°	D	—	600D④	—	—	—	—
1974	R45NS	.035	③	30	⑤	10°	D	—	600D④	—	—	—	.5
1975–76 V8-500⑥	R45NSX	.060	—	—	E	6°	F	—	600D	—	—	—	.4
V8-500⑦	R45NSX	.060	—	—	E	12°	F	—	600D	—	—	—	—
1976 V8-350	R46SX	.080	—	—	G	10°	H	—	—	—	—	—	—

①—BTDC: Before top dead center.
②—D: Drive. N: Neutral.
③—Turn adjusting screw in (clockwise) until engine begins to misfire; then back screw out ½ turn.
④—When making adjustments, air conditioner must be turned off (if equipped). Also, hose must be disconnected at vacuum release cylinder. The hot idle compensator must be closed; this can be done by pressing finger or eraser end of pencil on compensator.
⑤—Exc. H.E.I., Fig. C; H.E.I., Fig. E.
⑥—Exc. Electronic Fuel Injection models.
⑦—Electronic Fuel Injection models.

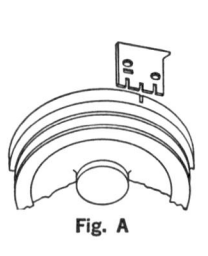

Fig. A

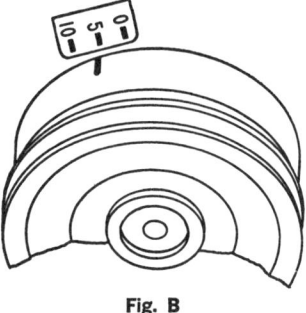

Fig. B

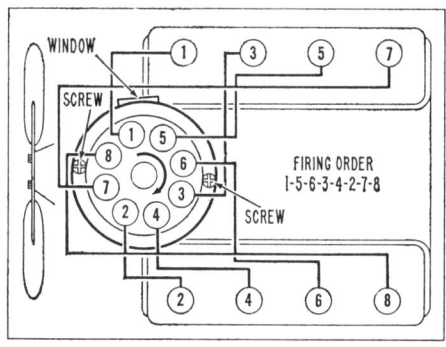

Fig. C

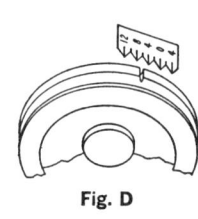

Fig. D

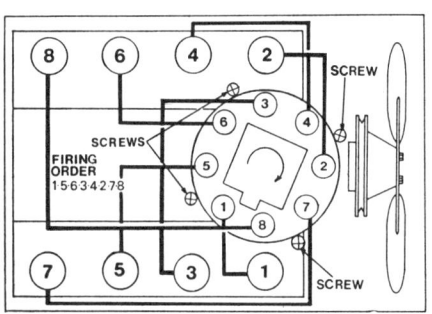

Fig. E

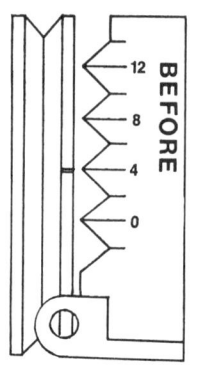

Fig. F

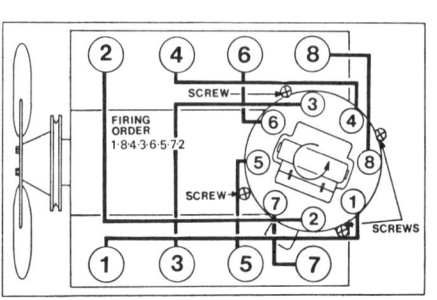

Fig. G

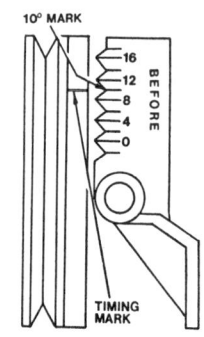

Fig. H

Cadillac

COOLING SYSTEM & CAPACITY DATA

Year	Model or Engine	Cooling Capacity, Qts. No Heater	Cooling Capacity, Qts. With Heater	Cooling Capacity, Qts. With A/C	Radiator Cap Relief Pressure, Lbs. With A/C	Radiator Cap Relief Pressure, Lbs. No. A/C	Thermo. Opening Temp. ①	Fuel Tank Gals.	Engine Oil Refill Qts. ③	Transmission Oil 3 Speed Pints	Transmission Oil 4 Speed Pints	Transmission Oil Auto. Trans. Qts. ⑦	Rear Axle Oil Pints
1969	Eldorado	—	21.3	21.8	15	15	195	24	5	—	—	⑥	4½⑨
	Series 75	—	24.8	24.8	15	15	195	20	4	—	—	⑤	5
	Others	—	21.3	21.8	15	15	195	26	4	—	—	⑤	5
1970	Eldorado	—	21.3	21.3	15	15	180	24⑨	5	—	—	⑩	4½⑧
	Series 75	—	21.8	21.8	15	15	180	26⑨	4	—	—	⑪	5
	Others	—	21.3	21.3	15	15	180	26⑨	4	—	—	⑪	5
1971–72	Eldorado	—	21.3	21.8	15	15	180	27	5	—	—	⑩	4⑧
	Series 75	—	—	24.8	15	15	180	27	4	—	—	⑪	5
	Others	—	21.3	21.8	15	15	180	27	4	—	—	⑪	5
1973–74	Eldorado	—	21.3	23.8	15	15	180	27	5	—	—	⑩	4⑧
	Series 75	—	—	26.8	15	—	180	27	4	—	—	⑪	5
	Others	—	21.3	23.8	15	15	180	27	4	—	—	⑪	5
1975	Eldorado	—	23	23	15	15	180	27½	5	—	—	⑥	4⑧
	Series 75	—	25.8	25.8	15	15	180	27½	4	—	—	⑪	5
	Others	—	23	23	15	15	180	27½	4	—	—	⑪	5
1976	Eldorado	—	23	23	15	15	180	27½	5	—	—	②	4④⑧
	Series 75	—	25.8	25.8	15	15	180	27½	4	—	—	⑪	4④
	Seville	—	18.9	18.9	15	15	180	21	4	—	—	⑪	4¼
	Others	—	23	23	15	15	180	27½	4	—	—	⑪	4④

①—For permanent anti-freeze.
②—Oil pan 5¾ qts. Total capacity 13½ qts.
③—Add one quart with filter change.
④—Exc. 3.15:1 ratio axle; 3.15:1 ratio axle, 5 pts.
⑤—Oil pan 2 qts. Total capacity 12½ qts.
⑥—Oil pan 5 qts. Total capacity 13 qts.
⑦—Approximate. Make final check with dipstick.
⑧—Front drive axle.
⑨—California vehicles approx. 2 gallons less.
⑩—Oil pan 6 qts. Total capacity 13½ qts.
⑪—Oil pan 4 qts. Total capacity 12½ qts.

Checker Motors

GENERAL ENGINE SPECIFICATIONS

Note: See Chevrolet chapter for engine service procedures.

Year	Engine	Carburetor	Bore and Stroke	Piston Displacement, Cubic Inches	Compression Ratio	Maximum Brake H.P. @ R.P.M.	Maximum Torque Lbs. Ft. @ R.P.M.	Normal Oil Pressure Pounds
1969	155 Horsepower..........6-250	1 Barrel	3.875 x 3.53	250	8.5	155 @ 4200	235 @ 1600	30–45
	235 Horsepower..........V8-327	2 Barrel	4.001 x 3.25	327	9.0	235 @ 4800	325 @ 2800	30–45
	215 Horsepower..........V8-350	2 Barrel	4.001 x 3.48	350	8.1	215 @ 4400	320 @ 2400	30–45
	300 Horsepower..........V8-350	4 Barrel	4.001 x 3.48	350	10.25	300 @ 4800	380 @ 3200	30–45
1970	155 Horsepower..........6-250	1 Barrel	3.875 x 3.53	250	8.5	155 @ 4200	235 @ 1600	30–45
	215 Horsepower..........V8-350	2 Barrel	4.001 x 3.48	350	8.1	215 @ 4400	320 @ 2400	30–45
	250 Horsepower..........V8-350	2 Barrel	4.001 x 3.48	350	9.0	250 @ 4800	345 @ 2800	30–45
1971	145 Horsepower..........6-250	1 Barrel	3.875 x 3.53	250	8.5	145 @ 4200	230 @ 1600	30–45
	215 Horsepower..........V8-350	2 Barrel	4.001 x 3.48	350	8.1	215 @ 4000	335 @ 2800	30
	245 Horsepower..........V8-350	2 Barrel	4.001 x 3.48	350	8.5	245 @ 4800	350 @ 2800	35–45
1972	110 Horsepower①..........6-250	1 Barrel	3.875 x 3.53	250	8.5	110 @ 3800	185 @ 1600	30–45
	165 Horsepower①..........V8-350	2 Barrel	4.001 x 3.48	350	8.5	165 @ 4000	280 @ 2400	35–45
	175 Horsepower①..........V8-350	4 Barrel	4.001 x 3.48	350	8.5	175 @ 4000	280 @ 2400	35–45
1973	100 Horsepower①..........6-250	1 Barrel	3.875 x 3.53	250	8.25	100 @ 3800	175 @ 1600	40
	145 Horsepower①..........V8-350	2 Barrel	4.001 x 3.48	350	8.5	145 @ 4000	255 @ 2400	40
	155 Horsepower①..........V8-350	4 Barrel	4.001 x 3.48	350	8.5	155 @ 4000	255 @ 2400	40
1974	100 Horsepower①..........6-250	1 Barrel	3.875 x 3.53	250	8.25	100 @ 3600	175 @ 1800	40
	145 Horsepower①..........V8-350	2 Barrel	4.000 x 3.48	350	8.5	145 @ 3800	250 @ 2200	40
	160 Horsepower①..........V8-350	4 Barrel	4.000 x 3.48	350	8.5	160 @ 3800	250 @ 2400	40

Checker Motors

GENERAL ENGINE SPECIFICATIONS/continued

Note: See Chevrolet chapter for engine service procedures.

Year	Engine	Carburetor	Bore and Stroke	Piston Displacement, Cubic Inches	Compression Ratio	Maximum Brake H.P. @ R.P.M.	Maximum Torque Lbs. Ft. @ R.P.M.	Normal Oil Pressure Pounds
1975	105 Horsepower①..........6-250	1 Barrel	3.875 x 3.53	250	8.25	105 @ 3800	185 @ 1200	40
	145 Horsepower①..........V8-350	2 Barrel	4.000 x 3.48	350	8.5	145 @ 3800	250 @ 2200	40
1976	105 Horsepower①..........6-250	1 Barrel	3.875 x 3.53	250	8.25	105 @ 3800	185 @ 1200	40
	145 Horsepower①..........V8-350	2 Barrel	4.000 x 3.48	350	8.5	145 @ 3800	250 @ 2200	40

①—Ratings are net—As installed in vehicle.

TUNEUP SPECIFICATIONS

★ When using a timing light, disconnect vacuum hose or tube at distributor and plug opening in hose or tube so idle speed will not be affected.
● When checking compression, lowest cylinder must be within 80 percent of highest.
▲ Before removing wires from distributor cap, determine location of the No. 1 wire in cap, as distributor position may have been altered from that shown at the end of this chart.

Year	Spark Plug Type	Gap Inch	Distributor Point Gap Inch	Dwell Angle Deg.	Firing Order Fig. ▲	Timing BTDC ①	Mark Fig.	Hot Idle Speed Std. Trans.	Hot Idle Speed Auto. Trans.②	Air Fuel Ratio Std. Trans.	Air Fuel Ratio Auto. Trans.	Idle "CO" % Std. Trans.	Idle "CO" % Auto. Trans.
1969													
6-250③	R46N	.035	⑤	31–34	A	TDC	C	700	—	—	—	—	—
6-250④	R46N	.035	⑤	31–34	A	4	C	—	500D	—	—	—	—
V8-327③	R44	.035	⑤	28–32	B	2 ATC	C	700	—	—	—	—	—
V8-327④	R44	.035	⑤	28–32	B	2	C	—	600D	—	—	—	—
V8-350⑥	CR43	.035	⑤	28–32	B	4	C	—	600D	—	—	—	—
V8-350⑦	R44	.035	⑤	28–32	B	4	C	—	600D	—	—	—	—
1970													
6-250	R46T	.035	⑤	31–34	A	4	C	700	600D	—	—	—	—
V8-350	R44	.035	⑤	28–32	B	4	C	—	600D	—	—	—	—
1971													
6-250	R46TS	.035	⑤	31–34	A	4	D	700	600D	—	—	—	—
V8-350⑧	R44TS	.035	⑤	29–31	B	6	D	—	550D	—	—	—	—
V8-350⑨	R44T	.035	⑤	29–31	B	4	D	—	550D	—	—	—	—
1972													
6-250	R46T	.035	⑤	31–34	A	4	D	—	600D	—	—	—	—
V8-350⑧	R44T	.035	⑤	29–31	B	6	D	—	600D	—	—	—	—
V8-350⑨	R44T	.035	⑤	29–31	B	8	D	—	600D	—	—	—	—
1973													
6-250	R46T	.035	⑤	31–34	A	6	D	—	600D	—	—	—	—
V8-350⑧	R44T	.035	⑤	29–31	B	8	D	—	600D	—	—	—	—
V8-350⑨	R44T	.035	⑤	29–31	B	12	D	—	600D	—	—	—	—
1974													
6-250	R46T	.035	⑤	31–34	A	6	D	—	600D	—	—	—	—
V8-350	R44T	.035	⑤	29–31	B	8	D	—	600D	—	—	—	—

Checker Motors

TUNEUP SPECIFICATIONS/continued

★When using a timing light, disconnect vacuum hose or tube at distributor and plug opening in hose or tube so idle speed will not be affected.
●When checking compression, lowest cylinder must be within 80 percent of highest.
▲Before removing wires from distributor cap, determine location of the No. 1 wire in cap, as distributor position may have been altered from that shown at the end of this chart.

Year	Spark Plug		Distributor		Ignition Timing ★			Carb. Adjustments					
								Hot Idle Speed		Air Fuel Ratio		Idle "CO" %	
	Type	Gap Inch	Point Gap Inch	Dwell Angle Deg.	Firing Order Fig. ▲	Timing BTDC ①	Mark Fig.	Std. Trans.	Auto. Trans.②	Std. Trans.	Auto. Trans.	Std. Trans.	Auto. Trans.
1975													
6-250	R46TX	.060	—	—	E	10	D	—	550D⑩	—	—	—	—
V8-350	R44TX	.060	—	—	F	6	D	—	600D	—	—	—	—
1976													
6-250	R46TS	.035	—	—	E	10	D	—	550D⑩	—	—	—	—
V8-350	R45TS	.045	—	—	F	6	D	—	600D	—	—	—	—

① —BTDC: Before top dead center.
② —D: Drive. N: Neutral.
③ —Std. Trans.
④ —Auto. Trans.
⑤ —New points, .019", used, .016". On V8's, turn adjusting screw in (clockwise) until engine misfires, then back off ½ turn.
⑥ —215 H.P.
⑦ —300 H.P.
⑧ —Marathon & Taxicab.
⑨ —Aerobus.
⑩ —Calif. 600D RPM.

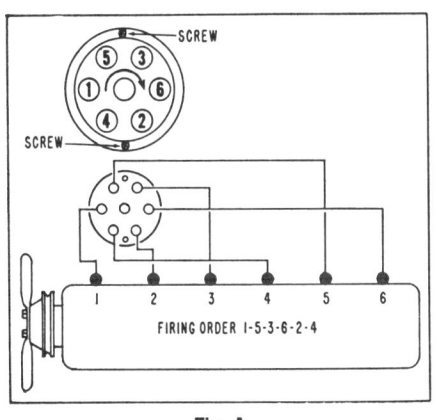

Fig. A

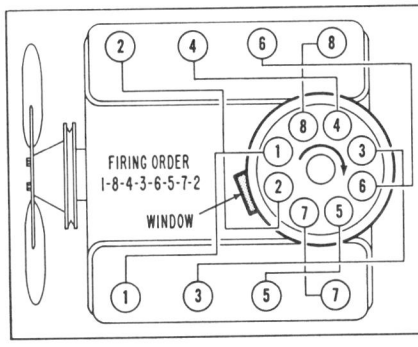

Fig. B

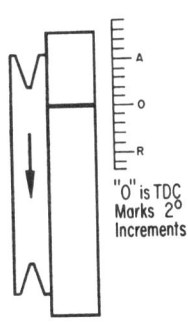

Fig. C

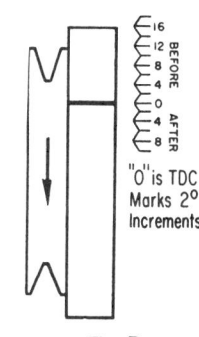

Fig. D

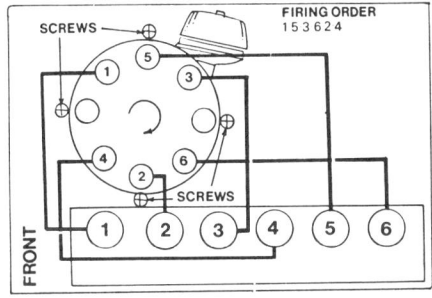

Fig. E

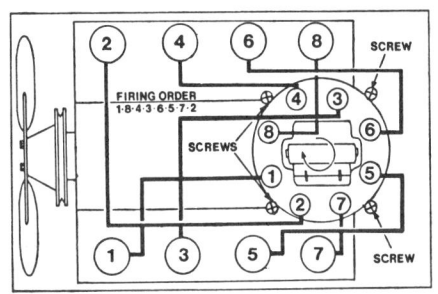

Fig. F

Checker Motors

COOLING SYSTEM & CAPACITY DATA

Year	Model or Engine	Cooling Capacity, Qts.			Radiator Cap Relief Pressure, Lbs.		Thermo. Opening Temp. ①	Fuel Tank Gals.	Engine Oil Refill Qts. ②	Transmission Oil			Rear Axle Oil Pints
		No Heater	With Heater	With A/C	With A/C	No A/C				3 Speed Pints	4 Speed Pints	Auto. Trans. Qts.③	
1969	6-250	11	12	12	13	13	195	23	4	2.6	—	8½	3
1969	V8-350④	16	17	17	13	13	195	23	4	2.6	—	8½	3
1969	V8-350⑤	—	17⑥	17⑥	13	13	180	23	4	2.6	—	8½	6
1970	6-250	11	12	12	13	13	195	23	4	—	—	8½	3
1970	V8-350④	16	17	17	13	13	195	23	4	—	—	8½	3
1970	V8-350⑤	—	17	17	13	13	180	23	4	—	—	8½	6
1971	6-250	—	12	12	13	13	195	21½	4	—	—	8½	3
1971	V8-350④	—	17	17	13	13	195	21½	4	—	—	8½	3
1971	V8-350⑤	—	21	21	13	13	195	23	4	—	—	8½	6
1972-76	6-250	—	12	12	15	15	195	21½	4	—	—	⑦	3
1972-76	V8-350④	—	17	17	15	15	195	21½	4	—	—	⑦	3
1972-76	V8-350⑤	—	21	21	15	15	195	21½	4	—	—	⑦	6

①—For permanent type anti-freeze.
②—Add one quart with filter change.
③—Approximate. Make final check with dipstick.
④—Marathon & Taxicab.
⑤—Aerobus.
⑥—Add 9 qts. with underseat heaters.
⑦—Exc. late 1973, 8½ qts. Late 1973, Turbo Hydra-Matic, 9 qts.

Chevrolet/Exc. Chevette/Monza/Vega

GENERAL ENGINE SPECIFICATIONS

Year	Engine	Carburetor	Bore and Stroke	Piston Displacement, Cubic Inches	Compression Ratio	Maximum Brake H.P. @ R.P.M.	Maximum Torque Lbs. Ft. @ R.P.M.	Normal Oil Pressure Pounds
1969	90 Horsepower............4-153	1 Barrel	3.875 x 3.25	153	8.50	90 @ 4000	152 @ 2400	30-45
	140 Horsepower............6-230	1 Barrel	3.875 x 3.25	230	8.50	140 @ 4400	220 @ 1600	30-45
	155 Horsepower............6-250	1 Barrel	3.875 x 3.53	250	8.50	155 @ 4200	235 @ 1600	30-45
	290 Horsepower............V8-302	4 Barrel	4.000 x 3.00	302	11.00	290 @ 5800	290 @ 4200	30-45
	200 Horsepower............V8-307	2 Barrel	3.875 x 3.25	307	9.00	200 @ 4600	300 @ 2400	30-45
	210 Horsepower............V8-327	2 Barrel	4.001 x 3.25	327	9.00	210 @ 4600	320 @ 2400	30-45
	235 Horsepower............V8-327	2 Barrel	4.001 x 3.25	327	9.00	235 @ 4800	325 @ 2800	30-45
	255 Horsepower............V8-350	4 Barrel	4.001 x 3.48	350	9.00	255 @ 4800	365 @ 3200	30-45
	300 Horsepower............V8-350	4 Barrel	4.001 x 3.48	350	10.25	300 @ 4800	380 @ 3200	30-45
	350 Horsepower............V8-350	4 Barrel	4.001 x 3.48	350	11.00	350 @ 5600	380 @ 3600	30-45
	370 Horsepower............V8-350	4 Barrel	4.001 x 3.48	350	11.00	370 @ 5800	380 @ 4000	30-45
	265 Horsepower............V8-396	2 Barrel	4.094 x 3.76	396	9.00	265 @ 4800	400 @ 2800	30-35
	325 Horsepower............V8-396	4 Barrel	4.094 x 3.76	396	10.25	325 @ 4800	410 @ 3200	30-35
	350 Horsepower............V8-396	4 Barrel	4.094 x 3.76	396	10.25	350 @ 5200	415 @ 3400	30-35
	375 Horsepower............V8-396	4 Barrel	4.094 x 3.76	396	11.00	375 @ 5600	415 @ 3600	30-35
	335 Horsepower............V8-427	4 Barrel	4.251 x 3.76	427	10.25	335 @ 4800	470 @ 3200	30-35
	390 Horsepower............V8-427	4 Barrel	4.251 x 3.76	427	10.25	390 @ 5400	460 @ 3600	30-35
	400 Horsepower............V8-427	4 Barrel	4.251 x 3.76	427	10.25	400 @ 5400	460 @ 3600	30-35
	425 Horsepower............V8-427	4 Barrel	4.251 x 3.76	427	11.00	425 @ 5600	460 @ 4000	30-35
	430 Horsepower............V8-427	4 Barrel	4.251 x 3.76	427	12.00	430 @ 5200	450 @ 4400	30-35
	435 Horsepower............V8-427	3 Carbs.	4.251 x 3.76	427	11.00	435 @ 5800	460 @ 4000	30-35

Exc. Chevette/Monza/Vega/Chevrolet

GENERAL ENGINE SPECIFICATIONS/continued

Year	Engine	Carburetor	Bore and Stroke	Piston Displacement, Cubic Inches	Compression Ratio	Maximum Brake H.P. @ R.P.M.	Maximum Torque Lbs. Ft. @ R.P.M.	Normal Oil Pressure Pounds
1970	90 Horsepower............4-153	1 Barrel	3.875 x 3.25	153	8.50	90 @ 4000	152 @ 2400	30–45
	140 Horsepower............6-230	1 Barrel	3.875 x 3.25	230	8.50	140 @ 4400	220 @ 1600	30–45
	155 Horsepower............6-250	1 Barrel	3.875 x 3.53	250	8.50	155 @ 4200	235 @ 1600	30–45
	200 Horsepower............V8-307	2 Barrel	3.875 x 3.25	307	9.00	200 @ 4600	300 @ 2400	30–45
	250 Horsepower............V8-350	2 Barrel	4.001 x 3.48	350	9.00	250 @ 4800	345 @ 2800	30–45
	300 Horsepower............V8-350	4 Barrel	4.001 x 3.48	350	10.25	300 @ 4800	380 @ 3200	30–45
	350 Horsepower............V8-350	4 Barrel	4.001 x 3.48	350	11.00	350 @ 5600	380 @ 3600	30–45
	360 Horsepower............V8-350	4 Barrel	4.001 x 3.48	350	11.00	360 @ 6000	380 @ 4000	35–45
	370 Horsepower............V8-350	4 Barrel	4.001 x 3.48	350	11.00	370 @ 6000	380 @ 4000	30–45
	350 Horsepower............V8-396	4 Barrel	4.125 x 3.76	①	10.25	350 @ 5200	415 @ 3400	30–35
	375 Horsepower............V8-396	4 Barrel	4.125 x 3.76	①	11.00	375 @ 5600	415 @ 3600	30–35
	265 Horsepower............V8-400	2 Barrel	4.125 x 3.75	400	9.00	265 @ 4400	400 @ 2400	30–35
	330 Horsepower............V8-400	4 Barrel	4.125 x 3.75	400	10.25	330 @ 4800	410 @ 3200	30–35
	345 Horsepower............V8-454	4 Barrel	4.251 x 4.00	454	10.25	345 @ 4400	500 @ 3000	30–35
	360 Horsepower............V8-454	4 Barrel	4.251 x 4.00	454	10.25	360 @ 4400	500 @ 3200	30–35
	390 Horsepower............V8-454	4 Barrel	4.251 x 4.00	454	10.25	390 @ 4800	500 @ 3400	30–35
	450 Horsepower............V8-454	4 Barrel	4.251 x 4.00	454	11.25	450 @ 5600	500 @ 3600	30–35
	460 Horsepower............V8-454	4 Barrel	4.251 x 4.00	454	11.25	460 @ 5600	490 @ 3000	30–35
1971	145 Horsepower............6-250	1 Barrel	3.875 x 3.53	250	8.50	145 @ 4200	230 @ 1600	30–45
	200 Horsepower............V8-307	2 Barrel	3.875 x 3.25	307	8.50	200 @ 4600	300 @ 2400	30–45
	245 Horsepower............V8-350	2 Barrel	4.00 x 3.48	350	8.50	245 @ 4800	350 @ 2800	35–45
	270 Horsepower............V8-350	4 Barrel	4.00 x 3.48	350	8.50	270 @ 4800	360 @ 3200	35–45
	330 Horsepower............V8-350	4 Barrel	4.00 x 3.48	350	9.0	330 @ 5600	360 @ 4000	35–45
	255 Horsepower............V8-400	2 Barrel	4.125 x 3.76	400	8.50	255 @ 4400	390 @ 2400	35–45
	300 Horsepower............V8-396	4 Barrel	4.126 x 3.76	①	8.50	300 @ 4800	400 @ 3200	35–45
	365 Horsepower............V8-454	4 Barrel	4.251 x 4.00	454	8.50	365 @ 4800	465 @ 3200	35–45
	425 Horsepower............V8-454	4 Barrel	4.251 x 4.00	454	9.0	425 @ 5600	475 @ 4000	35–45
1972	110 Horsepower②............6-250	1 Barrel	3.875 x 3.53	250	8.50	110 @ 3800	185 @ 1600	30–45
	130 Horsepower②............V8-307	2 Barrel	3.875 x 3.25	307	8.50	130 @ 4000	230 @ 2400	30–45
	165 Horsepower②............V8-350	2 Barrel	4.00 x 3.48	350	8.50	165 @ 4000	280 @ 2400	35–45
	175 Horsepower②............V8-350	4 Barrel	4.00 x 3.48	350	8.50	175 @ 4000	280 @ 2400	35–45
	200 Horsepower②............V8-350	4 Barrel	4.00 x 3.48	350	8.50	200 @ 4400	300 @ 2800	35–45
	255 Horsepower②............V8-350	4 Barrel	4.00 x 3.48	350	9.0	255 @ 5600	280 @ 4000	35–45
	170 Horsepower②............V8-400	2 Barrel	4.126 x 3.75	400	8.50	170 @ 3400	325 @ 2000	35–45
	210 Horsepower②............V8-402	4 Barrel	4.126 x 3.76	402	8.50	210 @ 4400	320 @ 2400	35–45
	240 Horsepower②............V8-402	4 Barrel	4.126 x 3.76	402	8.50	240 @ 4400	345 @ 3200	35–45
	230 Horsepower②............V8-454	4 Barrel	4.251 x 4.00	454	8.50	230 @ 4000	360 @ 3200	35–45
	270 Horsepower②............V8-454	4 Barrel	4.251 x 4.00	454	8.50	270 @ 4000	390 @ 3200	35–45
1973	100 Horsepower②............6-250	1 Barrel	3.875 x 3.53	250	8.25	100 @ 3800	175 @ 1600	40
	115 Horsepower②............V8-307	2 Barrel	3.875 x 3.25	307	8.50	115 @ 4000	205 @ 2000	40
	145 Horsepower②............V8-350	2 Barrel	4.00 x 3.48	350	8.50	145 @ 4000	255 @ 2400	40
	175 Horsepower②............V8-350	4 Barrel	4.00 x 3.48	350	8.50	175 @ 4000	270 @ 2400	40
	190 Horsepower②............V8-350	4 Barrel	4.00 x 3.48	350	8.50	190 @ 4400	270 @ 2800	40
	245 Horsepower②............V8-350	4 Barrel	4.00 x 3.48	350	9.0	245 @ 5200	280 @ 4000	40
	250 Horsepower②............V8-350	4 Barrel	4.00 x 3.48	350	9.0	250 @ 5200	285 @ 4000	40
	150 Horsepower②............V8-400	2 Barrel	4.126 x 3.75	400	8.50	150 @ 3200	295 @ 2000	40
	215 Horsepower②............V8-454	4 Barrel	4.251 x 4.00	454	8.50	215 @ 4000	345 @ 2400	40
	245 Horsepower②............V8-454	4 Barrel	4.251 x 4.00	454	8.50	245 @ 4000	375 @ 2800	40
	275 Horsepower②............V8-454	4 Barrel	4.251 x 4.00	454	8.50	275 @ 4000	395 @ 2800	40

Chevrolet/Exc. Chevette/Monza/Vega

GENERAL ENGINE SPECIFICATIONS/continued

Year	Engine	Carburetor	Bore and Stroke	Piston Displacement, Cubic Inches	Compression Ratio	Maximum Brake H.P. @ R.P.M.	Maximum Torque Lbs. Ft. @ R.P.M.	Normal Oil Pressure Pounds
1974	100 Horsepower②..............6-250	1 Barrel	3.875 x 3.53	250	8.25	100 @ 3600	175 @ 1800	40
	145 Horsepower②..............V8-350	2 Barrel	4.00 x 3.48	350	8.50	145 @ 3600	250 @ 2200	40
	160 Horsepower②..............V8-350	4 Barrel	4.00 x 3.48	350	8.50	160 @ 3800	250 @ 2400	40
	185 Horsepower②..............V8-350	4 Barrel	4.00 x 3.48	350	8.50	185 @ 4000	270 @ 2600	40
	195 Horsepower②..............V8-350	4 Barrel	4.00 x 3.48	350	8.50	195 @ 4400	275 @ 2800	40
	245 Horsepower②..............V8-350	4 Barrel	4.00 x 3.48	350	9.0	245 @ 5200	280 @ 4000	40
	250 Horsepower②..............V8-350	4 Barrel	4.00 x 3.48	350	9.0	250 @ 5200	285 @ 4000	40
	150 Horsepower②..............V8-400	2 Barrel	4.125 x 3.75	400	8.50	150 @ 3200	295 @ 2000	40
	180 Horsepower②..............V8-400	4 Barrel	4.125 x 3.75	400	8.50	180 @ 3800	290 @ 2400	40
	235 Horsepower②..............V8-454	4 Barrel	4.250 x 4.00	454	8.50	235 @ 4000	360 @ 2800	45
	270 Horsepower②..............V8-454	4 Barrel	4.250 x 4.00	454	8.50	270 @ 4400	380 @ 2800	45
1975	105 Horsepower②..............6-250	1 Barrel	3.875 x 3.53	250	8.25	105 @ 3800	185 @ 1200	36–41
	110 Horsepower②..............V8-262	2 Barrel	3.671 x 3.10	262	8.5	110 @ 3600	200 @ 2000	32–40
	145 Horsepower②..............V8-350	2 Barrel	4.00 x 3.48	350	8.5	145 @ 3800	250 @ 2200	32–40
	155 Horsepower②..............V8-350	4 Barrel	4.00 x 3.48	350	8.5	155 @ 3800	250 @ 2400	32–40
	165 Horsepower②..............V8-350	4 Barrel	4.00 x 3.48	350	8.5	165 @ 3800	255 @ 2400	32–40
	205 Horsepower②..............V8-350	4 Barrel	4.00 x 3.48	350	9.0	205 @ 4800	255 @ 3600	32–40
	175 Horsepower②..............V8-400	4 Barrel	4.125 x 3.75	400	8.5	175 @ 3600	305 @ 2000	42–46
	215 Horsepower②..............V8-454	4 Barrel	4.251 x 4.00	454	8.15	215 @ 4000	350 @ 2400	42–46
1976	105 Horsepower②..............6-250	1 Barrel	3.875 x 3.53	250	8.25	105 @ 3800	185 @ 1200	36–41
	140 Horsepower②..............V8-305	2 Barrel	3.736 x 3.48	305	8.5	140 @ 3800	245 @ 2000	32–40
	145 Horsepower②..............V8-350	2 Barrel	4.00 x 3.48	350	8.5	145 @ 3800	250 @ 2200	32–40
	165 Horsepower②..............V8-350	4 Barrel	4.00 x 3.48	350	8.5	165 @ 3800	260 @ 2400	32–40
	185 Horsepower②..............V8-350	4 Barrel	4.00 x 3.48	350	8.5	185 @ 4000	275 @ 2400	32–40
	195 Horsepower②..............V8-350	4 Barrel	4.00 x 3.48	350	8.5	195 @ 4400	275 @ 2800	32–40
	210 Horsepower②..............V8-350	4 Barrel	4.00 x 3.48	350	9.0	210 @ 5200	255 @ 3600	32–40
	270 Horsepower②..............V8-350	4 Barrel	4.00 x 3.48	350	8.5	270 @ 4400	380 @ 2800	32–40
	175 Horsepower②..............V8-400	4 Barrel	4.125 x 3.75	400	8.5	175 @ 3600	305 @ 2000	32–40
	235 Horsepower②..............V8-454	4 Barrel	4.251 x 4.00	454	8.5	235 @ 4000	360 @ 2800	42–46

①—Marketed as 396 cu. in. but actually 402 cu. in.   ②—Ratings are net—As installed in the vehicle.

Exc. Chevette/Monza/Vega/Chevrolet

TUNEUP SPECIFICATIONS

The following specifications are published from the latest information available. This data should be used only in the absence of a decal affixed in the engine compartment.

★ When using a timing light, disconnect vacuum hose or tube at distributor and plug opening in hose or tube so idle speed will not be affected.

● When checking compression, lowest cylinder must be within 80 percent of highest.

▲ Before removing wires from distributor cap, determine location of the No. 1 wire in cap, as distributor position may have been altered from that shown at the end of this chart.

Year	Spark Plug		Distributor		Ignition Timing ★			Carb. Adjustments					
	Type	Gap Inch	Point Gap Inch	Dwell Angle Deg.	Firing Order Fig. ▲	Timing BTDC ①	Mark Fig.	Hot Idle Speed ③		Air Fuel Ratio		Idle "CO" %	
								Std. Trans.	Auto. Trans. ②	Std. Trans.	Auto. Trans.	Std. Trans.	Auto. Trans.
CAMARO													
1969													
6-230, 250 ⑱	R46N	.035	④	31–34	D	TDC	A	700 ⑯	—	—	—	—	—
6-230, 250 ⑲	R46N	.035	④	31–34	D	4°	A	—	550D ⑯	—	—	—	—
8-302	R43	.035	④	28–32	E	4°	A	900 ⑯	—	—	—	—	—
8-307	R45S	.035	④	28–32	E	2°	A	700 ⑯	600D ⑯	—	—	—	—
8-327, 210 H.P. ⑱	R45S	.035	④	28–32	E	2° ATC	A	700 ⑯	—	—	—	—	—
8-327, 210 H.P. ⑲	R45S	.035	④	28–32	E	2°	A	—	600D ⑯	—	—	—	—
8-350, 255 H.P. ⑱	R44	.035	④	28–32	E	TDC	A	700 ⑯	—	—	—	—	—
8-350, 255 H.P. ⑲	R44	.035	④	28–32	E	4°	A	—	600D ⑯	—	—	—	—
8-350, 300 H.P. ⑱	R44	.035	④	28–32	E	TDC	A	700 ⑯	—	—	—	—	—
8-350, 300 H.P. ⑲	R44	.035	④	28–32	E	4°	A	—	600D ⑯	—	—	—	—
8-396, 325 H.P.	R44N	.035	④	28–32	E	4°	A	800 ⑯	600D ⑯	—	—	—	—
8-396, 350 H.P. ⑱	R43N	.035	④	28–32	E	TDC	A	800 ⑯	—	—	—	—	—
8-396, 350 H.P. ⑲	R43N	.035	④	28–32	E	4°	A	—	600D ⑯	—	—	—	—
8-396, 375 H.P.	R43N	.035	④	28–32	E	4°	A	750 ⑯	700D ⑯	—	—	—	—
1970													
6-250 Std. Tr.	R46T	.035	④	31–34	D	TDC	A	750	—	—	—	—	—
6-250 Auto. Tr.	R46T	.035	④	31–34	D	4°	A	—	600D/400	—	—	—	—
8-307 Std. Tr.	R43	.035	④	29–31	E	2°	A	700	—	—	—	—	—
8-307 Auto. Tr.	R43	.035	④	29–31	E	8°	A	—	600D/450	—	—	—	—
8-350, 250 H.P. ⑱	R44	.035	④	29–31	E	TDC	A	750	—	—	—	—	—
8-350, 250 H.P. ⑲	R44	.035	④	29–31	E	4°	A	—	600D/450	—	—	—	—
8-350, 300 H.P. ⑱	R44	.035	④	29–31	E	TDC	A	700	—	—	—	—	—
8-350, 300 H.P. ⑲	R44	.035	④	29–31	E	4°	A	—	600D	—	—	—	—
8-350, 360 H.P.	R43	.035	④	29–31	E	8°	A	800	750D/500	—	—	—	—
8-396, 350 H.P. ⑱㉑	R44T	.035	④	29–31	E	TDC	A	700	—	—	—	—	—
8-396, 350 H.P. ⑲㉑	R44T	.035	④	29–31	E	4°	A	—	600D	—	—	—	—
8-396, 375 H.P. ㉑	R43T	.035	④	29–31	E	4°	A	750	700D	—	—	—	—
8-454, 450 H.P.	R43T	.035	④	29–31	E	4°	A	750	700D	—	—	—	—
1971													
8-250	R46TS	.035	④	31–34	D	4°	B	550	550D	—	—	1.0	1.0
6-307 Std. Tr.	R45TS	.035	④	29–31	E	4°	B	550	—	—	—	0.5	—
8-307 Auto. Tr.	R45TS	.035	④	29–31	E	8°	B	—	550D	—	—	—	0.5
8-350, 245 H.P. ⑱	R45TS	.035	④	29–31	E	2°	B	600	—	—	—	0.5	—
8-350, 245 H.P. ⑲	R45TS	.035	④	29–31	E	6°	B	—	550D	—	—	—	0.5
8-350, 270 H.P. ⑱	R44TS	.035	④	29–31	E	4°	B	600	—	—	—	1.0	—
8-350, 270 H.P. ⑲	R44TS	.035	④	29–31	E	8°	B	—	550D	—	—	—	0.5
8-350, 330 H.P. ⑱	R43TS	.035	④	29–31	E	8°	B	700	—	—	—	—	—
8-350, 330 H.P. ⑲	R43TS	.035	④	29–31	E	12°	B	—	700D	—	—	—	—
8-396, 300 H.P.	R44TS	.035	④	29–31	E	8°	B	600	600D	—	—	1.0	1.0

Chevrolet/Exc.Chevette/Monza/Vega

TUNEUP SPECIFICATIONS/continued

The following specifications are published from the latest information available. This data should be used only in the absence of a decal affixed in the engine compartment.

★ When using a timing light, disconnect vacuum hose or tube at distributor and plug opening in hose or tube so idle speed will not be affected.

● When checking compression, lowest cylinder must be within 80 percent of highest.

▲ Before removing wires from distributor cap, determine location of the No. 1 wire in cap, as distributor position may have been altered from that shown at the end of this chart.

Year	Spark Plug		Distributor		Ignition Timing ★			Carb. Adjustments					
	Type	Gap Inch	Point Gap Inch	Dwell Angle Deg.	Firing Order Fig. ▲	Timing BTDC ①	Mark Fig.	Hot Idle Speed ③		Air Fuel Ratio		Idle "CO" %	
								Std. Trans.	Auto. Trans. ②	Std. Trans.	Auto. Trans.	Std. Trans.	Auto. Trans.
1972													
6-250	R46T	.035	④	31–34	D	4°	B	700	600D	—	—	—	—
8-307 Std. Tr.	R44T	.035	④	29–31	E	4°	B	900	—	—	—	—	—
8-307 Auto. Tr.	R44T	.035	④	29–31	E	8°	B	—	600D	—	—	—	—
8-350, 165 H.P.	R44T	.035	④	29–31	E	6°	B	900	600D	—	—	—	—
8-350, 200 H.P.⑱	R44T	.035	④	29–31	E	4°	B	800	—	—	—	—	—
8-350, 200 H.P.⑲	R44T	.035	④	29–31	E	8°	B	—	600D	—	—	—	—
8-350, 255 H.P.⑱	R44T	.035	④	29–31	E	4°	B	900	—	—	—	—	—
8-350, 255 H.P.⑲	R44T	.035	④	29–31	E	8°	B	—	700D	—	—	—	—
8-402	R44T	.035	④	29–31	E	8°	B	750	600D	—	—	—	—
1973													
6-250	R46T	.035	④	31–34	D	6°	B	700	600D	—	—	—	—
8-307 Std. Tr.	R44T	.035	④	29–31	E	4°	B	900	—	—	—	—	—
8-307 Auto. Tr.	R44T	.035	④	29–31	E	8°	B	—	600D	—	—	—	—
8-350, 145 H.P.	R44T	.035	④	29–31	E	8°	B	900	600D	—	—	—	—
8-350, 175 H.P.⑱	R44T	.035	④	29–31	E	8°	B	900	—	—	—	—	—
8-350, 175 H.P.⑲	R44T	.035	④	29–31	E	12°	B	—	600D	—	—	—	—
8-350, 245 H.P.	R44T	.035	④	29–31	E	8°	B	900	700D	—	—	—	—
1974													
6-250⑱	R46T	.035	④	31–34	D	8°	B	850	—	—	—	.3	.3
6-250⑲	R46T	.035	④	31–34	D	6°	B	—	600D	—	—	.3	.3
8-350, 145 H.P.⑱	R44T	.035	④	29–31	E	TDC	B	900	—	—	—	.5	.5
8-350, 145 H.P.⑲	R44T	.035	④	29–31	E	8°	B	—	600D	—	—	.5	.5
8-350, 160 H.P.⑱	R44T	.035	④	29–31	E	4°	B	900	—	—	—	.5	.5
8-350, 160 H.P.⑲	R44T	.035	④	29–31	E	8°	B	—	600D	—	—	.5	.5
8-350, 185 H.P.⑱	R44T	.035	④	29–31	E	8°⑥	B	900	—	—	—	.5	.5
8-350, 185 H.P.⑲	R44T	.035	④	29–31	E	8°	B	—	600D	—	—	.5	.5
8-350, 245 H.P.	R44T	.035	④	29–31	⑫	8°	B	900	700D	—	—	.5	.5
1975													
6-250	R46TX	.060	—	—	H	8°	B	850	600D	—	—	—	—
6-250⑦	R46TX	.060	—	—	H	10°	B	850	550D⑨	—	—	—	—
8-350 2 Bbl. Carb.	R44TX	.060	—	—	I	6°	B	800	600D	—	—	—	—
8-350⑱	R44TX	.060	—	—	I	6°⑥	B	800	—	—	—	—	—
8-350⑲	R44TX	.060	—	—	I	8°⑧	B	—	600D	—	—	—	—
1976													
6-250	R46TS	.035	—	—	H	6°	B	850	550D⑨	—	—	—	—
8-305⑱	R45TS	.045	—	—	I	6°	B	800	—	—	—	—	—
8-305⑲	R45TS	.045	—	—	I	8°⑬	B	—	600D	—	—	—	—
8-350 2 Bbl. Carb.	R45TS	.045	—	—	I	6°	B	800	—	—	—	—	—
8-350	R45TS	.045	—	—	I	8°⑧	B	800	600D	—	—	—	—

Exc. Chevette/Monza/Vega/Chevrolet

TUNEUP SPECIFICATIONS/continued

The following specifications are published from the latest information available. This data should be used only in the absence of a decal affixed in the engine compartment.

★ When using a timing light, disconnect vacuum hose or tube at distributor and plug opening in hose or tube so idle speed will not be affected.

● When checking compression, lowest cylinder must be within 80 percent of highest.

▲ Before removing wires from distributor cap, determine location of the No. 1 wire in cap, as distributor position may have been altered from that shown at the end of this chart.

Year	Spark Plug		Distributor		Ignition Timing ★			Carb. Adjustments					
	Type	Gap Inch	Point Gap Inch	Dwell Angle Deg.	Firing Order Fig. ▲	Timing BTDC ①	Mark Fig.	Hot Idle Speed ③		Air Fuel Ratio		Idle "CO" %	
								Std. Trans.	Auto. Trans. ②	Std. Trans.	Auto. Trans.	Std. Trans.	Auto. Trans.
CHEVELLE & MONTE CARLO													
1969													
6-230, 250 ⑱	R46N	.035	④	31–34	D	TDC	A	700 ⑯	—	—	—	—	—
6-230, 250 ⑲	R46N	.035	④	31–34	D	4°	A	—	550D ⑯	—	—	—	—
8-307	R45S	.035	④	28–32	E	2°	A	700 ⑯	600D ⑯	—	—	—	—
8-350, 255 H.P. ⑱	R44	.035	④	28–32	E	TDC	A	700 ⑯	—	—	—	—	—
8-350, 255 H.P. ⑲	R44	.035	④	28–32	E	4°	A	—	600D ⑯	—	—	—	—
8-350, 300 H.P. ⑱	R44	.035	④	28–32	E	TDC	A	700 ⑯	—	—	—	—	—
8-350, 300 H.P. ⑲	R44	.035	④	28–32	E	4°	A	—	600D ⑯	—	—	—	—
8-396, 325 H.P.	R44N	.035	④	28–32	E	4°	A	800 ⑯	600D ⑯	—	—	—	—
8-396, 350 H.P. ⑱	R43N	.035	④	28–32	E	TDC	A	800 ⑯	—	—	—	—	—
8-396, 350 H.P. ⑲	R43N	.035	④	28–32	E	4°	A	—	600D ⑯	—	—	—	—
8-396, 375 H.P.	R43N	.035	④	28–32	E	4°	A	750 ⑯	750D ⑯	—	—	—	—
1970													
6-250 ⑱	R46T	.035	④	31–34	D	TDC	A	750	—	—	—	—	—
6-250 ⑲	R46T	.035	④	31–34	D	4°	A	—	600D/400	—	—	—	—
8-307 ⑱	R43	.035	④	28–32	E	2°	A	700	—	—	—	—	—
8-307 ⑲	R43	.035	④	28–32	E	8°	A	—	600D/450	—	—	—	—
8-350 ⑱	R44	.035	④	28–32	E	TDC	A	700	—	—	—	—	—
8-350 ⑲	R44	.035	④	28–32	E	4°	A	—	600D	—	—	—	—
8-400, 265 H.P. ⑱	R44	.035	④	28–32	E	4°	A	700	—	—	—	—	—
8-400, 265 H.P. ⑲	R44	.035	④	28–32	E	8°	A	—	600D	—	—	—	—
8-400, 330 H.P.	R44T	.035	④	28–32	E	4°	A	700	600D	—	—	—	—
8-396, 350 H.P. ⑱	R44T	.035	④	28–32	E	TDC	A	700	—	—	—	—	—
8-396, 350 H.P. ⑲	R44T	.035	④	28–32	E	4°	A	—	600D	—	—	—	—
8-396, 375 H.P.	R43T	.035	④	28–32	E	4°	A	750	700D	—	—	—	—
8-454, 360 H.P.	R43T	.035	④	28–32	E	6°	A	700	600	—	—	—	—
8-454, 390 H.P.	R43T	.035	④	28–32	E	6°	A	700	600D	—	—	—	—
8-454, 450 H.P.	R43T	.035	④	28–32	E	4°	A	700	700D	—	—	—	—
1971													
6-250	R46TS	.035	④	31–34	D	4°	B	550	500D	—	—	1.0	1.0
8-307 ⑱	R45TS	.035	④	29–31	E	4°	B	550	—	—	—	0.5	—
8-307 ⑲	R45TS	.035	④	29–31	E	8°	B	—	500D	—	—	—	0.5
8-350, 245 H.P. ⑱	R45TS	.035	④	29–31	E	2°	B	600	—	—	—	0.5	—
8-350, 245 H.P. ⑲	R45TS	.035	④	29–31	E	6°	B	—	600D	—	—	—	0.5
8-350, 270 H.P. ⑱	R44TS	.035	④	29–31	E	4°	B	600	—	—	—	1.0	—
8-350, 270 H.P. ⑲	R44TS	.035	④	29–31	E	8°	B	—	600D	—	—	—	0.5
8-400	R44TS	.035	④	29–31	E	8°	B	600	600D	—	—	0.5	0.5
8-454, 365 H.P.	R43TS	.035	④	29–31	E	8°	B	600	600D	—	—	1.0	1.0
8-454, 425 H.P. ⑱	R44TS	.035	④	29–31	E	8°	B	700	—	—	—	—	—
8-454, 425 H.P. ⑲	R44TS	.035	④	29–31	E	12°	B	—	700D	—	—	—	—

Chevrolet/Exc. Chevette/Monza/Vega

TUNEUP SPECIFICATIONS/continued

The following specifications are published from the latest information available. This data should be used only in the absence of a decal affixed in the engine compartment.

★When using a timing light, disconnect vacuum hose or tube at distributor and plug opening in hose or tube so idle speed will not be affected.

●When checking compression, lowest cylinder must be within 80 percent of highest.

▲Before removing wires from distributor cap, determine location of the No. 1 wire in cap, as distributor position may have been altered from that shown at the end of this chart.

Year	Spark Plug		Distributor		Ignition Timing ★			Carb. Adjustments					
	Type	Gap Inch	Point Gap Inch	Dwell Angle Deg.	Firing Order Fig. ▲	Timing BTDC ①	Mark Fig.	Hot Idle Speed ③		Air Fuel Ratio		Idle "CO" %	
								Std. Trans.	Auto. Trans. ②	Std. Trans.	Auto. Trans.	Std. Trans.	Auto. Trans.
CHEVELLE & MONTE CARLO—Continued													
1972													
6-250	R46T	.035	④	31–34	D	4°	B	700	600D	—	—	—	—
8-307 Std. Tr.	R44T	.035	④	29–31	E	4°	B	900	—	—	—	—	—
8-307 Auto. Tr.	R44T	.035	④	29–31	E	8°	B	—	600D	—	—	—	—
8-350, 165 H.P.	R44T	.035	④	29–31	E	6°	B	900	600D	—	—	—	—
8-350, 175 H.P.⑱	R44T	.035	④	29–31	E	4°	B	800	—	—	—	—	—
8-350, 175 H.P.⑲	R44T	.035	④	29–31	E	8°	B	—	600D	—	—	—	—
8-402	R44T	.035	④	29–31	E	8°	B	750	600D	—	—	—	—
8-454	R44T	.035	④	29–31	E	8°	B	750	600D	—	—	—	—
1973													
6-250	R46T	.035	④	31–34	D	6°	B	700	600D	—	—	—	—
8-307⑱	R44T	.035	④	29–31	E	4°	B	900	—	—	—	—	—
8-307⑲	R44T	.035	④	29–31	E	8°	B	—	600D	—	—	—	—
8-350, 145 H.P.	R44T	.035	④	29–31	E	8°	B	900	600D	—	—	—	—
8-350, 175 H.P.⑱	R44T	.035	④	29–31	E	8°	B	900	—	—	—	—	—
8-350, 175 H.P.⑲	R44T	.035	④	29–31	E	12°	B	—	600D	—	—	—	—
8-454, 245 H.P.	R44T	.035	④	29–31	E	10°	B	900	600D	—	—	—	—
1974													
6-250⑱	R46T	.035	④	31–34	D	8°	B	850	—	—	—	.3	.3
6-250⑲	R46T	.035	④	31–34	D	6°	B	—	600D	—	—	.3	.3
8-350, 145 H.P.⑱	R44T	.035	④	29–31	E	TDC	B	900	—	—	—	.5	.5
8-350, 145 H.P.⑲	R44T	.035	④	29–31	E	8°	B	—	600D	—	—	.5	.5
8-350, 160 H.P.⑱	R44T	.035	④	29–31	E	4°	B	900	—	—	—	.5	.5
8-350, 160 H.P.⑲	R44T	.035	④	29–31	E	8°	B	—	600D	—	—	.5	.5
8-350, 185 H.P.⑱	R44T	.035	④	29–31	E	8°⑥	B	900	—	—	—	.5	.5
8-350, 185 H.P.⑲	R44T	.035	④	29–31	E	8°	B	—	600D	—	—	.5	.5
8-400	R44T	.035	④	29–31	E	8°	B	—	600D	—	—	.5	.5
8-454	R44T	.035	④	29–31	E	10°	B	800	600D	—	—	.5	.5
1975													
6-250	R46TX	.060	—	—	H	8°	B	850	600D	—	—	—	—
6-250⑦	R46TX	.060	—	—	H	10°	B	850	550D⑨	—	—	—	—
8-350 2 BBL. Carb.	R44TX	.060	—	—	I	6°	B	800	600D	—	—	—	—
8-350⑱	R44TX	.060	—	—	I	6°⑥	B	800	—	—	—	—	—
8-350⑲	R44TX	.060	—	—	I	8°⑧	B	—	600D	—	—	—	—
8-400	R44TX	.060	—	—	I	8°	B	—	600D	—	—	—	—
8-454	R44TX	.060	—	—	I	16°	B	—	600D	—	—	—	—
1976													
6-250	R46TS	.035	—	—	H	6°	B	850	550D9	—	—	—	—
8-305⑱	R45TS	.045	—	—	I	6°	B	800	—	—	—	—	—
8-305⑲	R45TS	.045	—	—	I	8°⑬	B	—	600D	—	—	—	—
8-350	R45TS	.045	—	—	I	6°	B	800	600D	—	—	—	—
8-400	R45TS	.045	—	—	I	8°	B	—	600D	—	—	—	—

Exc. Chevette/Monza/Vega/Chevrolet

TUNEUP SPECIFICATIONS/continued

The following specifications are published from the latest information available. This data should be used only in the absence of a decal affixed in the engine compartment.

★When using a timing light, disconnect vacuum hose or tube at distributor and plug opening in hose or tube so idle speed will not be affected.

●When checking compression, lowest cylinder must be within 80 percent of highest.

▲Before removing wires from distributor cap, determine location of the No. 1 wire in cap, as distributor position may have been altered from that shown at the end of this chart.

Year	Spark Plug		Distributor		Ignition Timing ★			Carb. Adjustments					
	Type	Gap Inch	Point Gap Inch	Dwell Angle Deg.	Firing Order Fig. ▲	Timing BTDC ①	Mark Fig.	Hot Idle Speed ③		Air Fuel Ratio		Idle "CO" %	
								Std. Trans.	Auto. Trans. ②	Std. Trans.	Auto. Trans.	Std. Trans.	Auto. Trans.
CHEVY NOVA													
1969													
4-153⑱	R46N	.035	④	31–34	F	TDC	A	750⑯	—	—	—	—	—
4-153⑲	R46N	.035	④	31–34	F	4°	A	—	600D⑯	—	—	—	—
6-230, 250⑱	R46N	.035	④	31–34	D	TDC	A	700⑯	—	—	—	—	—
6-230, 250⑲	R46N	.035	④	31–34	D	4°	A	—	550D⑯	—	—	—	—
8-307	R45S	.035	④	28–32	E	2°	A	700⑯	600D⑯	—	—	—	—
8-327, 210 H.P.⑱	R45S	.035	④	28–32	E	2° ATC	A	700⑯	—	—	—	—	—
8-350, 255 H.P.⑱	R44	.035	④	28–32	E	TDC	A	700⑯	—	—	—	—	—
8-350, 255 H.P.⑲	R44	.035	④	28–32	E	4°	A	—	600D⑯	—	—	—	—
8-350, 300 H.P.⑱	R44	.035	④	28–32	E	TDC	A	700⑯	—	—	—	—	—
8-350, 300 H.P.⑲	R44	.035	④	28–32	E	4°	A	—	600D⑯	—	—	—	—
8-396, 350 H.P.⑱	R43N	.035	④	28–32	E	TDC	A	800⑯	—	—	—	—	—
8-396, 350 H.P.⑲	R43N	.035	④	28–32	E	4°	A	—	600D⑯	—	—	—	—
8-396, 375 H.P.	R43N	.035	④	28–32	E	4°	A	750⑯	750D⑯	—	—	—	—
1970													
4-153⑱	R46N	.035	④	31–34	F	TDC	A	750	—	—	—	—	—
4-153⑲	R46N	.035	④	31–34	F	4°	A	—	650D	—	—	—	—
6-230, 250⑱	R46T	.035	④	31–34	D	TDC	A	750	—	—	—	—	—
6-230, 250⑲	R46T	.035	④	31–34	D	4°	A	—	600D/400	—	—	—	—
8-307⑱	R43	.035	④	28–32	E	2°	A	700	—	—	—	—	—
8-307⑲	R43	.035	④	28–32	E	8°	A	—	600D/450	—	—	—	—
8-350, 250 H.P.⑱	R44	.035	④	28–32	E	TDC	A	750	—	—	—	—	—
8-350, 250 H.P.⑲	R44	.035	④	28–32	E	4°	A	—	600D/450	—	—	—	—
8-350, 300 H.P.⑱	R44	.035	④	28–32	E	TDC	A	700	—	—	—	—	—
8-350, 300 H.P.⑲	R44	.035	④	28–32	E	4°	A	—	600D	—	—	—	—
8-396, 350 H.P.	R44T	.035	④	28–32	E	TDC	A	700	—	—	—	—	—
8-396, 375 H.P.⑱	R43T	.035	④	28–32	E	4°	A	750	—	—	—	—	—
8-396, 375 H.P.⑲	R43T	.035	④	28–32	E	4°	A	—	700D	—	—	—	—
1971													
6-250	R46TS	.035	④	31–34	D	4°	B	550	500D	—	—	1.0	1.0
8-307, 200 H.P.⑱	R45TS	.035	④	29–31	E	4°	B	550	—	—	—	0.5	0.5
8-307, 200 H.P.⑲	R45TS	.035	④	29–31	E	8°	B	—	550D	—	—	0.5	0.5
8-350, 245 H.P.⑱	R44TS	.035	④	29–31	E	2°	B	600	—	—	—	0.5	0.5
8-350, 245 H.P.⑲	R44TS	.035	④	29–31	E	6°	B	—	550D	—	—	0.5	0.5
8-350, 270 H.P.⑱	R44TS	.035	④	29–31	E	4°	B	600	—	—	—	1.0	—
8-350, 270 H.P.⑲	R44TS	.035	④	29–31	E	8°	B	—	550D	—	—	—	0.5
1972													
6-250	R46T	.035	④	31–34	D	4°	B	700	600D	—	—	—	—
8-307, Std. Tr.	R44T	.035	④	29–31	E	4°	B	900	—	—	—	—	—
8-307, Auto. Tr.	R44T	.035	④	29–31	E	8°	B	—	600D	—	—	—	—

575

Chevrolet/Exc. Chevette/Monza/Vega

TUNEUP SPECIFICATIONS/continued

The following specifications are published from the latest information available. This data should be used only in the absence of a decal affixed in the engine compartment.

★ When using a timing light, disconnect vacuum hose or tube at distributor and plug opening in hose or tube so idle speed will not be affected.

● When checking compression, lowest cylinder must be within 80 percent of highest.

▲ Before removing wires from distributor cap, determine location of the No. 1 wire in cap, as distributor position may have been altered from that shown at the end of this chart.

Year	Spark Plug		Distributor		Ignition Timing ★			Carb. Adjustments					
								Hot Idle Speed ③		Air Fuel Ratio		Idle "CO" %	
	Type	Gap Inch	Point Gap Inch	Dwell Angle Deg.	Firing Order Fig. ▲	Timing BTDC ①	Mark Fig.	Std. Trans.	Auto. Trans. ②	Std. Trans.	Auto. Trans.	Std. Trans.	Auto. Trans.
CHEVY NOVA—Continued													
1972													
8-350, 165 H.P.	R44T	.035	④	29–31	E	6°	B	900	600D	—	—	—	—
8-350, 200 H.P.⑱	R44T	.035	④	29–31	E	4°	B	800	—	—	—	—	—
8-350, 200 H.P.⑲	R44T	.035	④	29–31	E	8°	B	—	600D	—	—	—	—
1973													
6-250	R46T	.035	④	31–34	D	6°	B	700	600D	—	—	—	—
8-307 Std. Tr.	R44T	.035	④	29–31	E	4°	B	900	—	—	—	—	—
8-307 Auto. Tr.	R44T	.035	④	29–31	E	8°	B	—	600D	—	—	—	—
8-350, 145 H.P.	R44T	.035	④	29–31	E	8°	B	900	600D	—	—	—	—
8-350, 175 H.P.⑱	R44T	.035	④	29–31	E	8°	B	900	—	—	—	—	—
8-350, 175 H.P.⑲	R44T	.035	④	29–31	E	12°	B	—	600D	—	—	—	—
1974													
6-250⑱	R46T	.035	④	31–34	D	8°	B	850	—	—	—	.3	.3
6-250⑲	R46T	.035	④	31–34	D	6°	B	—	600D	—	—	.3	.3
8-350, 145 H.P.⑱	R44T	.035	④	29–31	E	TDC	B	900	—	—	—	.5	.5
8-350, 145 H.P.⑲	R44T	.035	④	29–31	E	8°	B	—	600D	—	—	.5	.5
8-350, 160 H.P.⑱	R44T	.035	④	29–31	E	4°	B	900	—	—	—	.5	.5
8-350, 160 H.P.⑲	R44T	.035	④	29–31	E	8°	B	—	600D	—	—	.5	.5
8-350, 185 H.P.⑱	R44T	.035	④	29–31	E	8°⑥	B	900	—	—	—	.5	.5
8-350, 185 H.P.⑲	R44T	.035	④	29–31	E	8°	B	—	600D	—	—	.5	.5
1975													
6-250	R46TX	.060	—	—	H	8°	B	850	600D	—	—	—	—
6-250⑦	R46TX	.060	—	—	H	10°	B	850	550D⑨	—	—	—	—
8-262	R44TX	.060	—	—	I	8°	G	800	600D	—	—	—	—
8-350 2 BBl. Carb.	R44TX	.060	—	—	I	6°	B	800	600D	—	—	—	—
8-350⑱	R44TX	.060	—	—	I	6°⑥	B	800	—	—	—	—	—
8-350⑲	R44TX	.060	—	—	I	8°⑧	B	—	600D	—	—	—	—
1976													
6-250	R46TS	.035	—	—	H	6°⑩	B	850	550D⑨	—	—	—	—
8-305⑱	R45TS	.045	—	—	I	6°	B	800	—	—	—	—	—
8-305⑲	R45TS	.045	—	—	I	8°⑬	B	—	600D	—	—	—	—
8-350 2 Bbl. Carb.	R45TS	.045	—	—	I	6°	B	—	600D	—	—	—	—
8-350	R45TS	.045	—	—	I	8°⑧	B	800	600D	—	—	—	—
CHEVROLET													
1969													
6-250⑱	R46N	.035	④	31–34	D	TDC	A	700⑮	—	—	—	—	—
6-250⑲	R46N	.035	④	31–34	D	4°	A	—	550D⑯	—	—	—	—
8-327, 235 H.P.⑱	R45S	.035	④	28–32	E	2° ATC	A	700⑮	—	—	—	—	—
8-327, 235 H.P.⑲	R45S	.035	④	28–32	E	2°	A	—	600D⑯	—	—	—	—

Exc. Chevette/Monza/Vega/Chevrolet

TUNEUP SPECIFICATIONS/continued

The following specifications are published from the latest information available. This data should be used only in the absence of a decal affixed in the engine compartment.

★When using a timing light, disconnect vacuum hose or tube at distributor and plug opening in hose or tube so idle speed will not be affected.

●When checking compression, lowest cylinder must be within 80 percent of highest.

▲Before removing wires from distributor cap, determine location of the No. 1 wire in cap, as distributor position may have been altered from that shown at the end of this chart.

Year	Spark Plug		Distributor		Ignition Timing ★			Carb. Adjustments					
	Type	Gap Inch	Point Gap Inch	Dwell Angle Deg.	Firing Order Fig. ▲	Timing BTDC ①	Mark Fig.	Hot Idle Speed ③		Air Fuel Ratio		Idle "CO" %	
								Std. Trans.	Auto. Trans. ②	Std. Trans.	Auto. Trans.	Std. Trans.	Auto. Trans.
CHEVROLET—Continued													
1969													
8-350, 255 H.P.⑱	R44	.035	④	28–32	E	TDC	A	700⑯	—	—	—	—	—
8-350, 255 H.P.⑲	R44	.035	④	28–32	E	4°	A	—	600D⑯	—	—	—	—
8-350, 300 H.P.⑱	R44	.035	④	28–32	E	TDC	A	700⑯	—	—	—	—	—
8-350, 300 H.P.⑲	R44	.035	④	28–32	E	4°	A	—	600D⑯	—	—	—	—
8-396, 265 H.P.⑱	R44N	.035	④	28–32	E	TDC	A	700⑯	—	—	—	—	—
8-396, 265 H.P.⑲	R44N	.035	④	28–32	E	4°	A	—	600D⑯	—	—	—	—
8-427, 335 H.P.	R44N	.035	④	28–32	E	4°	A	800⑯	600D⑯	—	—	—	—
8-427, 390 H.P.	R43N	.035	④	28–32	E	4°	A	800⑪	600D⑪	—	—	—	—
8-427, 425 H.P.	R43N	.035	④	28–32	E	4°	A	750⑯	750D⑯	—	—	—	—
1970													
6-250⑱	R46T	.035	④	31–34	D	TDC	A	750	—	—	—	—	—
6-250⑲	R46T	.035	④	31–34	D	4°	A	—	600D/400	—	—	—	—
8-350, 250 H.P.⑱	R44	.035	④	28–32	E	TDC	A	750	—	—	—	—	—
8-350, 250 H.P.⑲	R44	.035	④	28–32	E	4°	A	—	600D/450	—	—	—	—
8-350, 300 H.P.⑱	R44	.035	④	28–32	E	TDC	A	700	—	—	—	—	—
8-350, 300 H.P.⑲	R44	.035	④	28–32	E	4°	A	—	600D	—	—	—	—
8-400, 265 H.P.⑱	R44	.035	④	28–32	E	4°	A	700	—	—	—	—	—
8-400, 265 H.P.⑲	R44	.035	④	28–32	E	8°	A	—	600D/450	—	—	—	—
8-454, 345 H.P.	R44T	.035	④	28–32	E	6°	A	—	600D	—	—	—	—
8-454, 360 H.P.	R43T	.035	④	28–32	E	6°	A	700	600	—	—	—	—
8-454, 390 H.P.	R43T	.035	④	28–32	E	6°	A	700	600D	—	—	—	—
1971													
6-250	R46TS	.035	④	31–34	D	4°	B	550	550D	—	—	1.0	1.0
8-350, 245 H.P.⑱	R44TS	.035	④	29–31	E	2°	B	550	—	—	—	0.5	0.5
8-350, 245 H.P.⑲	R44TS	.035	④	29–31	E	6°	B	—	550D	—	—	0.5	0.5
8-350, 270 H.P.	R44TS	.035	④	29–31	E	8°	B	—	550D	—	—	1.0	0.5
8-400, 255 H.P.⑱	R44TS	.035	④	29–31	E	4°	B	550	—	—	—	0.5	0.5
8-400, 255 H.P.⑲	R44TS	.035	④	29–31	E	8°	B	—	550D	—	—	0.5	0.5
8-400, 300 H.P.	R44TS	.035	④	29–31	E	8°	B	—	600D	—	—	1.0	1.0
8-454, 365 H.P.	R43TS	.035	④	29–31	E	8°	B	—	600D	—	—	1.0	1.0
1972													
6-250	R46T	.035	④	31–34	D	4°	B	700	600D	—	—	—	—
8-350	R44T	.035	④	29–31	E	6°	B	—	600D	—	—	—	—
8-400	R44T	.035	④	29–31	E	6°	B	—	600D	—	—	—	—
8-402	R44T	.035	④	29–31	E	8°	B	—	600D	—	—	—	—
8-454	R44T	.035	④	29–31	E	8°	B	—	600D	—	—	—	—
1973													
6-250	R46T	.035	④	31–34	D	6°	B	700	600D	—	—	—	—
8-350, 145 H.P.	R44T	.035	④	29–31	E	8°	B	—	600D	—	—	—	—

577

Chevrolet/Exc. Chevette/Monza/Vega

TUNEUP SPECIFICATIONS/continued

The following specifications are published from the latest information available. This data should be used only in the absence of a decal affixed in the engine compartment.

★When using a timing light, disconnect vacuum hose or tube at distributor and plug opening in hose or tube so idle speed will not be affected.

●When checking compression, lowest cylinder must be within 80 percent of highest.

▲Before removing wires from distributor cap, determine location of the No. 1 wire in cap, as distributor position may have been altered from that shown at the end of this chart.

Year	Spark Plug		Distributor		Ignition Timing ★			Carb. Adjustments					
								Hot Idle Speed ③		Air Fuel Ratio		Idle "CO" %	
	Type	Gap Inch	Point Gap Inch	Dwell Angle Deg.	Firing Order Fig. ▲	Timing BTDC ①	Mark Fig.	Std. Trans.	Auto. Trans. ②	Std. Trans.	Auto. Trans.	Std. Trans.	Auto. Trans.
CHEVROLET—Continued													
1973													
8-350, 175 H.P.	R44T	.035	④	29-31	E	12°	B	—	600D	—	—	—	—
8-400	R44T	.035	④	29-31	E	8°	B	—	600D	—	—	—	—
8-454	R44T	.035	④	29-31	E	10°	B	—	600D	—	—	—	—
1974													
8-350, 145 H.P.	R44T	.035	④	29-31	E	8°	B	—	600D	—	—	.5	.5
8-350, 160 H.P.	R44T	.035	④	29-31	E	8°	B	—	600D	—	—	.5	.5
8-400	R44T	.035	④	29-31	E	8°	B	—	600D	—	—	.5	.5
8-454	R44T	.035	④	29-31	⑫	10°	B	—	600D	—	—	.5	.5
1975													
8-350 2 BBl. Carb.	R44TX	.060	—	—	I	6°	B	—	600D	—	—	—	—
8-350	R44TX	.060	—	—	I	8°⑧	B	—	600D	—	—	—	—
8-400	R44TX	.060	—	—	I	8°	B	—	600D	—	—	—	—
8-454	R44TX	.060	—	—	I	16°	B	—	600D	—	—	—	—
1976													
8-350 2 Bbl. Carb.	R45TS	.045	—	—	I	6°	B	—	600D	—	—	—	—
8-350	R45TS	.045	—	—	I	8°⑧	B	—	600D	—	—	—	—
8-400	R45TS	.045	—	—	I	8°	B	—	600D	—	—	—	—
8-454	R45TSX	.060	—	—	I	12°	B	—	550D	—	—	—	—
CORVETTE													
1969													
8-350, 300 H.P. ⑱	R44	.035	④	28-32	E	4°	A	700⑯	—	—	—	—	—
8-350, 300 H.P. ⑲	R44	.035	④	28-32	E	4°	A	—	600D⑯	—	—	—	—
8-350, 350 H.P.	R44	.035	④	28-32	E	8°	A	750⑯	—	—	—	—	—
8-350, 370 H.P.	R43	.035	④	28-32	E	⑳	A	750⑯	—	—	—	—	—
8-427, 390 H.P.	R43N	.035	④	28-32	E	4°	A	800⑪	600D⑪	—	—	—	—
8-427, 400 H.P.	R43N	.035	④	28-32	E	4°	A	800⑪	600D⑪	—	—	—	—
8-427, 425 H.P.	R43N	.035	④	28-32	E	4°	A	750⑯	750D⑯	—	—	—	—
8-427, 430 H.P.	R43XL	.035	—	—	E	12°⑤	A	1000⑯	—	—	—	—	—
8-427, 435 H.P.	R43N	.035	—	—	E	4°	A	750⑯	750D⑯	—	—	—	—
1970													
8-350, 300 H.P.	R44	.035	④	29-31	E	4°	A	700	600	—	—	—	—
8-350, 350 H.P.	R44	.035	④	29-31	E	8°	A	750		—	—	—	—
8-350, 370 H.P.	R43	.035	—	—	E	8°	A	900		—	—	—	—
8-454, 360 H.P.	R43T	.035	④	28-32	E	6°	A	700	600	—	—	—	—
8-454, 390 H.P.	R43T	.035	④	29-31	E	6°	A	700	600	—	—	—	—
8-454, 460 H.P.	R43XL	.035	—	—	E	8°	A	700	600	—	—	—	—

Exc. Chevette/Monza/Vega/Chevrolet

TUNEUP SPECIFICATIONS/continued

The following specifications are published from the latest information available. This data should be used only in the absence of a decal affixed in the engine compartment.

★When using a timing light, disconnect vacuum hose or tube at distributor and plug opening in hose or tube so idle speed will not be affected.

●When checking compression, lowest cylinder must be within 80 percent of highest.

▲Before removing wires from distributor cap, determine location of the No. 1 wire in cap, as distributor position may have been altered from that shown at the end of this chart.

Year	Spark Plug		Distributor		Ignition Timing ★			Carb. Adjustments					
	Type	Gap Inch	Point Gap Inch	Dwell Angle Deg.	Firing Order Fig. ▲	Timing BTDC ①	Mark Fig.	Hot Idle Speed ③		Air Fuel Ratio		Idle "CO" %	
								Std. Trans.	Auto. Trans. ②	Std. Trans.	Auto. Trans.	Std. Trans.	Auto. Trans.
CORVETTE—Continued													
1971													
8-350, 270 H.P.	R44TS	.035	④	29–31	E	8°	B	600	550D	—	—	1.0	0.5
8-350, 330 H.P.	R43TS	.035	—	—	E	8°	B	700	—	—	—	—	—
8-454, 365 H.P.	R43TS	.035	④	29–31	E	8°	B	600	600D	—	—	1.0	1.0
8-454, 425 H.P.⑱	R44TS	.035	—	—	E	8°	B	700	—	—	—	—	—
8-454, 425 H.P.⑲	R44TS	.035	—	—	E	12°	B	—	700D	—	—	—	—
1972													
8-350, 200 H.P.	R44T	.035	④	29–31	E	8°	B	800	600D	—	—	—	—
8-350, 255 H.P.	R44T	.035	④	29–31	E	4°	B	900	—	—	—	—	—
8-454	R44T	.035	④	29–31	E	8°	B	750	600D	—	—	—	—
1973													
8-350, 190 H.P.	R44T	.035	④	29–31	C	12°	B	900	600D	—	—	—	—
8-350, 250 H.P.	R44T	.035	④	29–31	C	8°	B	900	700D	—	—	—	—
8-454, 275 H.P.	R44T	.035	④	29–31	E	10°	B	900	600D	—	—	—	—
1974													
8-350, 195 H.P.⑱	R44T	.035	④	29–31	C	8°⑥	B	900	—	—	—	.5	.5
8-350, 195 H.P.⑲	R44T	.035	④	29–31	C	8°	B	—	600D	—	—	.5	.5
8-350, 250 H.P.	R44T	.035	④	29–31	C	8°	B	900	700D	—	—	.5	.5
8-454	R44T	.035	④	29–31	E	10°	B	800	600D	—	—	.5	.5
1975													
8-350⑱	R44TX	.060	—	—	I	6°⑥	B	800	—	—	—	—	—
8-350⑲	R44TX	.060	—	—	I	6°	B	—	600D	—	—	—	—
1976													
8-350	R45TS	.045	—	—	I	8°⑧	B	1000	700D	—	—	—	—
8-350⑭	R45TS	.045	—	—	I	12°	B	1000	700D	—	—	—	—

① —BTDC: Before top dead center.
② —D: Drive. N: Neutral.
③ —Where two speeds are listed, lower speed indicates idle solenoid disconnected.
④ —New points, .019", used .016". On V8s, turn adjusting screw in (clockwise) until engine misfires; then back off ½ turn.
⑤ —Adjust timing at 800 R.P.M.
⑥ —For California set at 4° BTDC.
⑦ —With integral intake manifold and all California models.
⑧ —For California set at 6° BTDC.
⑨ —For California 600 R.P.M.
⑩ —With Distributor 1110662 set at 8° BTDC.
⑪ —With A/C "ON".
⑫ —Exc. H.E.I., Fig. E; H.E.I., Fig. I.
⑬ —For California set at 0°.
⑭ —With dual exhaust.
⑮ —With A/C "OFF".
⑱ —With standard transmission.
⑲ —With automatic transmission.
⑳ —With distributor 1111496 set at 14°. All others set at 4°.
㉑ —Marketed as 396 but actually 402 cu. in.

Chevrolet/Exc. Chevette/Monza/Vega

TUNEUP NOTES/continued

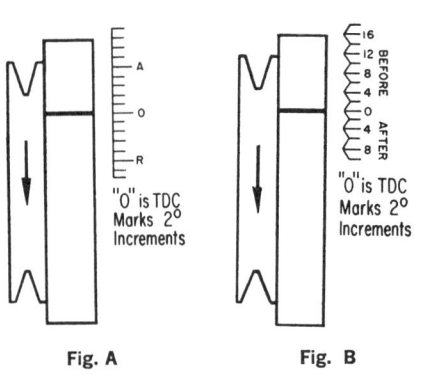

Fig. A

Fig. B

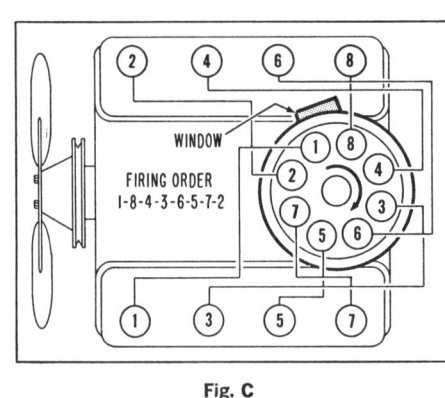

Fig. C

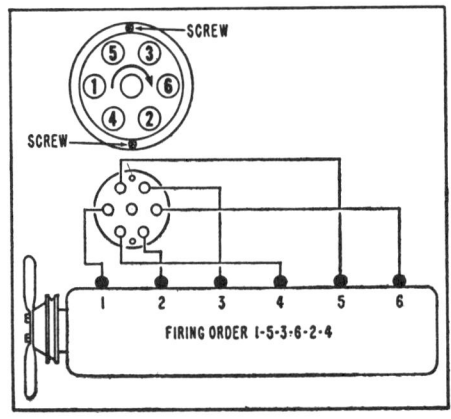

Fig. D

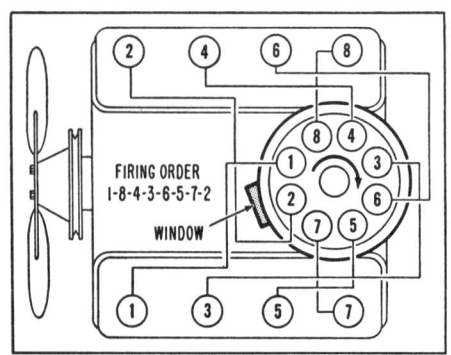

Fig. E

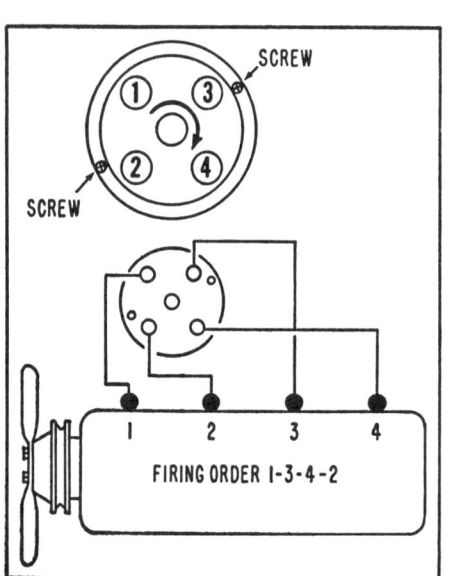

Fig. F

Fig. G

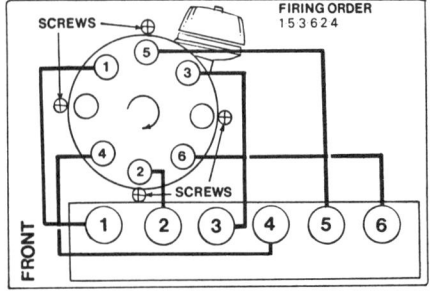

Fig. H

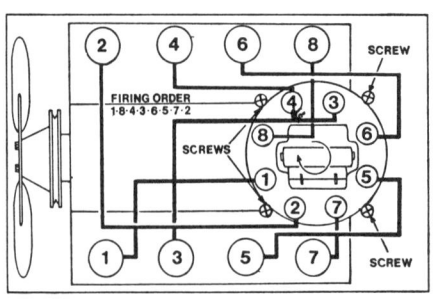

Fig. I

Exc. Chevette/Monza/Vega/Chevrolet

COOLING SYSTEM & CAPACITY DATA

Year	Model or Engine	Cooling Capacity, Qts.			Radiator Cap Relief Pressure, Lbs.		Thermo. Opening Temp. ①	Fuel Tank Gals.	Engine Oil Refill Qts. ②	Transmission Oil			Rear Axle Oil Pints
		No Heater	With Heater	With A/C	With A/C	No A/C				3 Speed Pints	4 Speed Pints	Auto. Trans. Qts. ⑮	
CAMARO													
1969	6-230, 250	11	13	13	15	15	195	18	4	3⑧	3	⑲	3½
	8-327	16	17	17	15	15	195	18	4	3⑧	3	⑲	3½
	8-350	15	16	17	15	15	195	18	4	3⑧	3	⑲	3½
	8-396	22	23	23	15	15	195	18	4	3⑧	3	⑲	4
1970	6-250	11	12	13	15	15	195	19	4	3	—	⑲	3½
	8-307	14	15	16	15	15	195	19	4	3	—	⑲	3½
	8-350 Exc. 360 H.P.	15	16	16	15	15	195	19	4	—	3	⑲	3½
	8-350, 360 H.P.	15	16	16	15	15	180	19	4	—	3	⑲	3½
	8-396㉕	22	23	23	15	15	195	19	4	—	3	⑲	3½
1971	6-250	11	12	12	15	15	195	18	4	3	—	⑲	3½
	8-307	14	15	15	15	15	195	18	4	3	—	⑲	3½
	8-350 Exc. 330 H.P.	14	15	15	15	15	195	18	4	—	3	⑲	㉖
	8-350, 330 H.P.	14	15	15	15	15	180	18	4	—	3	⑲	㉖
	8-396㉕	23	24	24	15	15	195	18	4	—	3	⑲	㉖
1972	6-250	11	12	13	15	15	195	18	4	3	—	⑲	4¼
	8-307	14	15	17	15	15	195	18	4	3	—	⑲	4¼
	8-350 Exc. 255 H.P.	15	16	17	15	15	195	18	4	—	3	⑲	4¼
	8-350, 255 H.P.	15	16	17	15	15	180	18	4	—	3	⑲	4¼
	8-402	23	24	25	15	15	195	18	4	—	3	⑲	4¼
1973	6-250	11	12	13	15	15	195	18	4	3	—	⑲	4¼
	V8-307	15	16	17	15	15	195	18	4	3	—	⑲	4¼
	V8-350, 145 H.P.	15	16	17	15	15	195	18	4	3	3	⑲	4¼
	V8-350, 175 H.P.	15	16	17	15	15	195	18	4	3	3	⑲	4¼
	V8-350, 245 H.P.	15	16	17	15	15	180	18	4	3	3	⑲	4¼
1974	6-250	14	14	—	15	15	195	21	4	3	—	⑦	4¼
	8-350, 145 H.P.	18	18	—	15	15	195	21	4	3	3	⑦	4¼
	8-350, 160 H.P.	18	18	—	15	15	195	21	4	3	3	⑦	4¼
	8-350, 185 H.P.	18	18	—	15	15	195	21	4	3	3	⑦	4¼
	8-350, 245 H.P.	18	18	—	15	15	180	21	4	3	3	⑦	4¼
1975	6-250	—	12½	12½	15	15	195	21	4	3	—	4⑥	4¼
	8-350	—	15½	16½	15	15	195	21	4	3	3	4⑥	4¼
	8-350, Z28	—	15½	16½	15	15	180	21	4	—	3	4⑥	4¼
1976	6-250	—	15	15	15	15	195	21	4	3	—	⑥	4¼
	8-305	—	17½	18½	15	15	195	21	4	3	—	⑥	4¼
	8-350	—	17½	18½	15	15	195	21	4	—	3	⑥	4¼
CHEVELLE & MONTE CARLO													
1969	6-230, 250	11	13	13	15	15	195	20⑳	4	3⑧	—	⑲	3½
	8-307	16	17	18	15	15	195	20⑳	4	3⑧	3	⑲	3½
	8-350	15	16	17	15	15	195	20⑳	4	3⑧	3	⑲	4
	8-396	22	23	23	15	15	195	20⑳	4	3⑧	3	⑲	4
1970	6-250	11	12	13	15	15	195	20㉒	4	3⑧	—	⑲	⑨
	8-307	14	15	16	15	15	195	20㉒	4	3⑧	3	⑲	⑨
	8-350	15	16	16	15	15	195	20㉒	4	3⑧	3	⑲	⑨
	8-400	22	23	24	15	15	195	20㉒	4	3⑧	3	⑲	⑨
	8-454	21	22	23	15	15	195	20㉒	4	3⑧	3	⑲	⑨
1971	6-250	11	12	12	15	15	195	18	4	3	—	⑲	㉖
	8-307	15	16	16	15	15	195	18	4	3	—	⑲	㉖
	8-350	15	16	16	15	15	195	18	4	3	3	⑲	㉖
	8-396㉕	22	23	23	15	15	195	18	4	3	3	⑲	㉖
	8-454, 365 H.P.	21	22	22	15	15	195	18	4	—	3	⑲	㉖
	8-454, 425 H.P.	21	22	22	15	15	180	18	4	—	3	⑲	㉖

Chevrolet/Exc. Chevette/Monza/Vega
COOLING SYSTEM & CAPACITY DATA/continued

Year	Model or Engine	Cooling Capacity, Qts.			Radiator Cap Relief Pressure, Lbs.		Thermo. Opening Temp. ①	Fuel Tank Gals.	Engine Oil Refill Qts. ②	Transmission Oil			Rear Axle Oil Pints
		No Heater	With Heater	With A/C	With A/C	No A/C				3 Speed Pints	4 Speed Pints	Auto. Trans. Qts. ⑮	
1972	6-250	11	12	12	15	15	195	㉘	4	3	—	⑲	㉙
	8-307	14	15	16	15	15	195	㉘	4	3	—	⑲	㉙
	8-350	15	16	17	15	15	195	㉘	4	3	3	⑲	㉙
	8-402	22	23	24	15	15	195	㉘	4	3	3	⑲	㉙
	8-454	22	23	24	15	15	195	㉘	4	—	3	⑲	㉙
1973	6-250	11	12	12	15	15	195	22	4	3	—	⑲	㉙
	8-307	15	16	17	15	15	195	22	4	3	3	⑲	㉙
	8-350, 145 H.P.	15	16	17	15	15	195	22	4	3	—	⑲	㉙
	8-350, 175 H.P.	15	16	17	15	15	195	22	4	—	4	⑲	㉙
	8-454	22	23	24	15	15	195	22	4	—	4	⑲	㉙
1974	6-250	—	14	14	15	15	195	22⑩	4	3	—	⑦	㉙
	8-350, 145 H.P.	—	18	18③	15	15	195	22⑩	4	3	—	⑦	㉙
	8-350, 160 H.P.	—	18	18③	15	15	195	22⑩	4	3	—	⑦	㉙
	8-400, 150 H.P.	—	18	18③	15	15	195	22⑩	4	—	—	⑦	㉙
	8-400, 180 H.P.	—	18	18③	15	15	195	22⑩	4	—	—	⑦	㉙
	8-454, 235 H.P.	—	24	18⑤	15	15	195	22⑩	4	—	3	⑦	㉙
1975	6-250	—	12½	12½	15	15	195	22⑩	4	3	—	4⑥	㉙
	8-350	—	16	17	15	15	195	22⑩	4	3	—	4⑥	㉙
	8-400	—	16	17	15	15	195	22⑩	4	—	—	4⑥	㉙
	8-454	—	23	24	15	15	195	22⑩	4	—	—	4½⑥	㉙
1976	6-250	—	15	17	15	15	195	22	4	3	—	⑥	4¼
	8-305	—	17½	18½	15	15	195	22	4	—	—	⑥	4¼
	8-350	—	17½	18½	15	15	195	22	4	—	—	⑥	4¼
	8-400	—	17½	18½	15	15	195	22	4	—	—	⑥	4¼

CHEVY NOVA

Year	Model or Engine	No Heater	With Heater	With A/C	With A/C	No A/C	Thermo.	Fuel Tank	Oil Refill	3 Speed	4 Speed	Auto. Trans.	Rear Axle
1969	4-153	8	9	9	15	15	195	18	4	3⑧	—	⑲	3½
	6-230, 250	11	13	13	15	15	195	18	4	3⑧	—	⑲	3½
	8-307	16	17	17	15	15	195	18	4	3⑧	3	⑲	3½
	8-350	15	16	16	15	15	195	18	4	3½	3	⑲	4
	8-396	22	23	23	15	15	195	18	4	3½	3	⑲	4
1970	4-153	8	9	9	15	15	195	18㉓	3½⑪	3	—	⑲	⑨
	6-230, 250	11	12	13	15	15	195	18㉓	4	3	—	⑲	⑨
	8-307	14	15	16	15	15	195	18㉓	4	3⑧	3	⑲	⑨
	8-350	15	16	16	15	15	195	18㉓	4	3⑧	3	⑲	⑨
1971	6-250	11	12	12	15	15	195	18	4	3	—	⑲	㉖
	8-307	15	16	16	15	15	195	18	4	3	—	⑲	㉖
	8-350	15	16	16	15	15	195	18	4	3	3	⑲	㉖
1972	6-250	11	12	12	15	15	195	16	4	3	—	⑲	4¼
	8-307	14	15	16	15	15	195	16	4	3	—	⑲	4¼
	8-350	15	16	17	15	15	195	16	4	3	3	⑲	4¼
1973	6-250	11	12	12	15	15	195	21	4	3	—	⑲	4¼
	8-307	16	15	16	15	15	195	21	4	3	—	⑲	4¼
	8-350, 145 H.P.	17	16	17	15	15	195	21	4	3	—	⑲	4¼
	8-350, 175 H.P.	17	16	17	15	15	195	21	4	—	4	⑲	4¼
1974	6-250	14	14	—	15	15	195	21	4	3	—	⑦	4¼
	8-350, 145 H.P.	18	18	—	15	15	195	21	4	3	—	⑦	4¼
	8-350, 160 H.P.	18	18	—	15	15	195	21	4	3	—	⑦	4¼
	8-350, 185 H.P.	18	18	—	15	15	195	21	4	—	3	⑦	4¼
1975	6-250	—	12½	12½	15	15	195	21	4	3	—	4⑥	4¼
	8-262	—	—	—	15	15	195	21	4	3	—	4⑥	4¼
	8-350	—	15½	16½	15	15	195	21	4	3	—	4⑥	4¼
1976	6-250	—	14	15	15	15	195	21	4	3	—	⑥	4¼
	8-305	—	17	18	15	15	195	21	4	3	—	⑥	4¼
	8-350	—	17	18	15	15	195	21	4	3	3	⑥	4¼

Exc. Chevette/Monza/Vega/Chevrolet

COOLING SYSTEM & CAPACITY DATA/continued

Year	Model or Engine	Cooling Capacity, Qts.			Radiator Cap Relief Pressure, Lbs.		Thermo. Opening Temp. ①	Fuel Tank Gals.	Engine Oil Refill Qts. ②	Transmission Oil			Rear Axle Oil Pints
		No Heater	With Heater	With A/C	With A/C	No A/C				3 Speed Pints	4 Speed Pints	Auto. Trans. Qts. ⑮	
CHEVROLET													
1969	6-250	11	12	13	15	15	195	24	4	3⑧	—	⑲	3½
	8-327	16	17	18	15	15	195	24	4	3⑧	3	⑲	3½
	8-350	14	15	16	15	15	195	24	4	3½	3	⑲	4
	8-396	22	23	23	15	15	195	24	4	3½	3	⑲	4
	8-427	21	22	22	15	15	195	24	4	3½	3	⑲	4
1970	6-250	11	12	12	15	15	195	25㉔	4	3⑧	—	⑲	⑨
	8-350, 250 H.P.	15	16	16	15	15	195	25㉔	4	3⑧	—	⑲	⑨
	8-350, 300 H.P.	15	16	17	15	15	195	25㉔	4	3⑧	—	⑲	⑨
	8-400	15	16	17	15	15	195	25㉔	4	3⑧	—	⑲	⑨
	8-454	21	22	22	15	15	195	25㉔	4	3⑧	—	⑲	⑨
1971	6-250	11	12	12	15	15	195	23㉗	4	3	—	⑲	㉖
	8-350	15	16	16	15	15	195	23㉗	4	3	—	⑲	㉖
	8-396㉕	22	23	23	15	15	195	23㉗	4	—	—	⑲	㉖
	8-400	15	16	16	15	15	195	23㉗	4	3	—	⑲	㉖
	8-454	21	22	22	15	15	195	23㉗	4	—	—	⑲	㉖
1972	6-250	11	12	12	15	15	195	23㉘	4	3	—	⑲	㉙
	8-350	15	16	17	15	15	195	23㉘	4	—	—	⑲	㉙
	8-400	15	16	17	15	15	195	23㉘	4	—	—	⑲	㉙
	8-402	22	23	24	15	15	195	23㉘	4	—	—	⑲	㉙
	8-454	21	22	23	15	15	195	23㉘	4	—	—	⑲	㉙
1973	6-250	—	12½	—	15	15	195	㉚	4	3	—	—	㉙
	8-350, 145 H.P.	—	16	17	15	15	195	㉚	4	—	—	4	㉙
	8-350, 175 H.P.	—	16	17	15	15	195	㉚	4	—	—	4	㉙
	8-400	—	16½	17	15	15	195	㉚	4	—	—	4	㉙
	8-454	—	23	24	15	15	195	㉚	4	—	—	4½	㉙
1974	8-350, 145 H.P.	—	16	17	15	15	195	26㉘	4	—	—	⑦	㉙
	8-350, 160 H.P.	—	16	17	15	15	195	26㉘	4	—	—	⑦	㉙
	8-400, 150 H.P.	—	16½	17½	15	15	195	26㉘	4	—	—	⑦	㉙
	8-400, 180 H.P.	—	16½	17½	15	15	195	26㉘	4	—	—	⑦	㉙
	8-454, 235 H.P.	—	23	24	15	15	195	26㉘	4	—	—	⑦	㉙
1975	8-350	—	16	17	15	15	195	26㉘	4	—	—	4⑥	㉙
	8-400	—	16½	17½	15	15	195	26㉘	4	—	—	4½⑥	㉙
	8-454	—	23	24	15	15	195	26㉘	4	—	—	4½⑥	㉙
1976	8-350	—	18	20	15	15	195	26㉘	4	—	—	⑥	㉙
	8-400	—	18	20	15	15	195	26㉘	4	—	—	⑥	㉙
	8-454	—	23	25	15	15	195	26㉘	4	—	—	⑥	㉙
CORVETTE													
1969	8-350	14	15	15	15	15	195	20	4	3	3	㉑	4
	8-427	21	22	22	15	15	195	20	5	3	3	㉑	4
1970	8-350 Exc. 370 H.P.	14	15	21	15	15	195	20	4	—	3	④	4
	8-350, 370 H.P.	17	18	22	15	15	180	20	4	—	3	④	4
	8-454	21	22	—	15	15	195	20	5	—	3	④	4
1971	8-350 Exc. 330 H.P.⑬	14	15	15	15	15	195	18	4	—	3	—	4
	8-350 Exc. 330 H.P.⑭	17	18	18	15	15	195	18	4	—	—	⑲	4
	8-350, 330 H.P.	17	18	18	15	15	180	18	4	—	3	⑲	4
	8-454, 365 H.P.	21	22	22	15	15	195	18	5	—	3	⑲	4
	8-454, 425 H.P.⑬	19	20	20	15	15	180	18	5	—	3	—	4
	8-454, 425 H.P.⑭	21	22	22	15	15	180	18	5	—	—	⑲	4
1972	8-350, 200 H.P.	16	17	18	15	15	195	18	4	—	3	4	4
	8-350, 255 H.P.	16	17	18	15	15	180	18	4	—	3	—	4
	8-454	22	23	24	15	15	195	18	5	—	3	4	4

Chevrolet/Exc. Chevette/Monza/Vega

COOLING SYSTEM & CAPACITY DATA/continued

Year	Model or Engine	Cooling Capacity, Qts.			Radiator Cap Relief Pressure, Lbs.		Thermo. Opening Temp. ①	Fuel Tank Gals.	Engine Oil Refill Qts. ②	Transmission Oil			Rear Axle Oil Pints
		No Heater	With Heater	With A/C	With A/C	No A/C				3 Speed Pints	4 Speed Pints	Auto. Trans. Qts. ⑲	
1973	8-350, 190 H.P.	17	18	18	15	15	195	18	4	—	3	4	4
	8-350, 250 H.P.	17	18	18	15	15	180	18	4	—	3	4	4
	8-454, 275 H.P.	23	24	24	15	15	195	18	5	—	3	4	4
1974	8-350, 195 H.P.	17	19	—	15	15	195	18	4	—	3	⑦	4
	8-350, 250 H.P.	17	19	—	15	15	180	18	4	—	3	⑦	4
	8-454, 270 H.P.	24	24	—	15	15	195	18	4	—	3	⑦	4
1975	8-350	—	18	18	15	15	180	18	4	—	3	4⑥	4
1976	8-350	—	21	21	15	15	195⑫	17	4	—	3	11	4

① —For permanent type anti-freeze.
② —Add one quart with filter change.
③ —Monte Carlo 20 qts.
④ —Refill 1½ qts. Total capacity 7½ qts.
⑤ —Monte Carlo 26 qts.
⑥ —Turbo Hydramatic 250 & 350 total capacity 10 qts., T.H. 400 total capacity 11 qts.
⑦ —Turbo Hydramatic 250 & 350 refill 2½ qts., T.H. 400 refill 3¾ qts.
⑧ —Heavy duty unit 3½.
⑨ —3¾ for 8⅛" ring gear and 4¼ for 8⅞" ring gear.
⑩ —El Camino 26 gal.
⑪ —Add one pint with filter change.
⑫ —Optional 350 engine: 180°.
⑬ —Standard trans.
⑭ —Auto. trans.
⑮ —Approximate. Make final check with dipstick.
⑲ —Powerglide & Torque Drive: Refill 3 qts. Total capacity 8½ qts. Turbo-Hydramatic 350: Refill 2½ qts. Total capacity 10 qts. Turbo-Hydramatic 400: Refill 4 qts. Total capacity 11 qts.
⑳ —Wagons 22 gallons.
㉑ —Refill 4 qts. Total capacity 11 qts.
㉒ —California vehicles about 2 gallons less.
㉓ —California vehicles about 1 gallon less.
㉔ —Wagons 22 gallons. California vehicles about 2 gallons less.
㉕ —Marketed as 396 but actually 402 cu. in.
㉖ —3½ for 8⅛" ring gear and 4 for 8⅞" ring gear.
㉗ —Wagons 20 gallons.
㉘ —Wagons 19 gallons; others 18 gallons.
㉙ —4¼ for 8⅛" and 8½" ring gears and 4.9 for 8⅞" ring gear.
㉚ —Station wagons 22 gals.; others 26 gals.

GENERAL ENGINE SPECIFICATIONS

Year	Engine	Carburetor	Bore and Stroke	Piston Displacement, Cubic Inches	Compression Ratio	Maximum Brake H.P. @ R.P.M.	Maximum Torque Lbs. Ft. @ R.P.M.	Normal Oil Pressure Pounds
1976	52 Horsepower①..........4-85	1 Barrel	3.228 x 2.606	85	8.5	52 @ 5300	67 @ 3400	55
	1400 c.c.	—	82.0 x 66.2 mm.	1.4 ltr.	—	—	97 Joules @ 3400	—
	60 Horsepower①..........4-97	1 Barrel	3.228 x 2.90	97.6	8.5	60 @ 5300	77 @ 3400	55
	1600 c.c.	—	82.0 x 75.7 mm.	1.6 ltr.	—	—	104 Joules @ 3200	—

① —Ratings are net—as installed in vehicle.

Chevrolet Chevette

TUNEUP SPECIFICATIONS

The following specifications are published from the latest information available. This data should be used only in the absence of a decal affixed in the engine compartment.

★When using a timing light, disconnect vacuum hose or tube at distributor and plug opening in hose or tube so idle speed will not be affected.

●When checking compression, lowest cylinder must be within 80 percent of highest.

▲Before removing wires from distributor cap, determine location of the No. 1 wire in cap, as distributor position may have been altered from that shown at the end of this chart.

Year	Spark Plug		Distributor		Ignition Timing ★			Carb. Adjustments					
	Type	Gap Inch	Point Gap Inch	Dwell Angle Deg.	Firing Order Fig. ▲	Timing BTDC ①	Mark Fig.	Hot Idle Speed		Air Fuel Ratio		Idle "CO" %	
								Std. Trans.	Auto. Trans.	Std. Trans.	Auto. Trans.	Std. Trans.	Auto. Trans.
1976													
4-85	R43TS	.035 (.889 mm.)	—	—	A	10	B	③	④	—	—	—	—
4-97.6	R43TS	.035 (.889 mm.)	—	—	A	②	B	③	④	—	—	—	—

①—BTDC—Before top dead center.
②—Man. trans., 8° BTDC; auto. trans., 10° BTDC.
③—All with solenoid energized—exc. Calif., 800 RPM; Calif., 1000 RPM. With solenoid de-energized—less A/C, 600 RPM; with A/C, 700 RPM.
④—All with solenoid energized—exc. Calif., 800 RPM; Calif., 850 RPM. With solenoid de-energized—all less A/C, Exc. Calif., 700 RPM; Calif., 600 RPM.

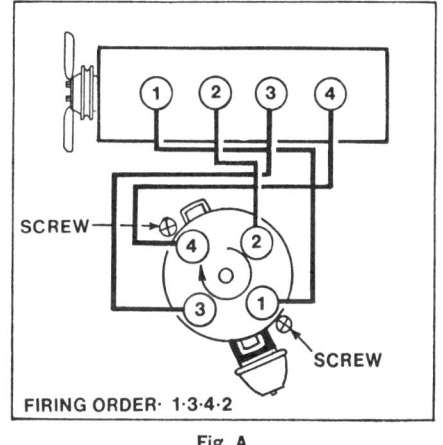

Fig. A

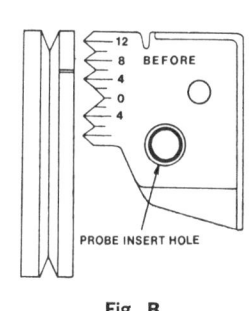

Fig. B

COOLING SYSTEM & CAPACITY DATA

Year	Model or Engine	Cooling Capacity, Qts.			Radiator Cap Relief Pressure, Lbs.		Thermo. Opening Temp. ①	Fuel Tank Gals.	Engine Oil Refill Qts. ②	Transmission Oil			Rear Axle Oils Pints
		No Heater	With Heater	With A/C	With A/C	No A/C				3 Speed Pints	4 Speed Pints	Auto. Trans. Qts. ③	
1976	4-All	—	8½	9	15	15	190	13	4	—	3	10	2
		—	8 ltr.	8.5 ltr.	—	—	—	49.2 ltr.	3.8 ltr.	—	1.5 ltr.	9.5 ltr.	.9 ltr.

①—Use with permanent type anti-freeze.
②—Add 1 qt. with filter change.
③—Approximate. Make final check with dipstick.

Monza/Skyhawk/Starfire/Sunbird

GENERAL ENGINE SPECIFICATIONS

Year	Engine	Carburetor	Bore and Stroke	Piston Displacement, Cubic Inches	Compression Ratio	Maximum Brake H.P. @ R.P.M.	Maximum Torque Lbs. Ft. @ R.P.M.	Normal Oil Pressure Pounds
1975	87 Horsepower①........4-140	2 Barrel	3.5 x 3.625	140	8.0	87 @ 4400	122 @ 2800	40
	110 Horsepower①......V6-231	2 Barrel	3.8 x 3.4	231	8.0	110 @ 4000	175 @ 2000	37
	110 Horsepower①......V8-262	2 Barrel	3.67 x 3.10	262	8.5	110 @ 3600	200 @ 2000	32–40
	125 Horsepower①......V8-350	2 Barrel	4.00 x 3.48	350	8.5	125 @ 3600	235 @ 2000	32–40
1976	69 Horsepower①........4-140	1 Barrel	3.501 x 3.625	140	8.0	69 @ 4000	113 @ 2400	27–45
	80 Horsepower①②......4-140	2 Barrel	3.501 x 3.625	140	8.0	80 @ 4000	116 @ 2800	27–45
	87 Horsepower①........4-140	2 Barrel	3.501 x 3.625	140	8.0	87 @ 4400	122 @ 2800	27–45
	110 Horsepower①......V6-231	2 Barrel	3.8 x 3.4	231	8.0	110 @ 4000	175 @ 2000	37
	110 Horsepower①......V8-262	2 Barrel	3.671 x 3.100	262	8.5	110 @ 3600	195 @ 2000	32–40

①—Ratings are net—As installed in vehicle.
②—California.

TUNEUP SPECIFICATIONS

The following specifications are published from the latest information available. This data should be used only in the absence of a decal affixed in the engine compartment.

★When using a timing light, disconnect vacuum hose or tube at distributor and plug opening in hose or tube so idle speed will not be affected.

●When checking compression, lowest cylinder must be within 80 percent of highest.

▲Before removing wires from distributor cap, determine location of No. 1 wire in cap, as distributor position may have been altered from that shown at the end of this chart.

Year	Spark Plug Type	Spark Plug Gap Inch	Distributor Point Gap Inch	Distributor Dwell Angle Deg.	Firing Order Fig. ▲	Timing BTDC ①	Mark Fig.	Hot Idle Speed Std. Trans.	Hot Idle Speed Auto. Trans.②	Air Fuel Ratio Std. Trans.	Air Fuel Ratio Auto. Trans.	Idle "CO" % Std. Trans.	Idle "CO" % Auto. Trans.
1975													
4-140	R43TSX④	.060	—	—	A	③	B	700	750D	—	—	.5	.5
V6-231	R44SX	.060	—	—	C	12°	D	800	650D	—	—	—	—
V8-262	R44TX	.060	—	—	E	8°	F	800	600D	—	—	—	—
V8-350	R44TX	.060	—	—	E	6°	G	800	600	—	—	—	—
1976													
4-140 1 Bar. Carb.	R43TS	.035	—	—	A	⑦	B	⑧	750D	—	—	—	—
4-140 2 Bar. Carb.⑤	R43TS	.035	—	—	A	⑨	B	700	750D	—	—	—	—
4-140 2 Bar. Carb.⑥	R43TS	.035	—	—	A	⑨	B	⑩	750D	—	—	—	—
V6-231	R44TSX	.060	—	—	C	12°	D	800	600D	—	—	—	—
V8-262	R45TS	.035	—	—	E	8°	F	800	600D	—	—	—	—

①—BTDC—Before Top Dead Center.
②—D—Drive.
③—Standard trans. 10°, Automatic trans. 12°.
④—If cold weather starting problems are encountered, use R43TS spark plug, gapped at .035 inch.
⑤—Exc. Calif.
⑥—California.
⑦—Man. trans., 8° BTDC; auto. trans., 10° BTDC.
⑧—Monza, 1200 RPM; Sunbird, 700 RPM.
⑨—Monza man. trans., 10° BTDC; auto. trans., 12° BTDC. Sunbird man. trans., 8° BTDC; auto. trans., 10° BTDC.
⑩—Monza; 1000 RPM; Sunbird, 700 RPM.

Monza/Skyhawk/Starfire/Sunbird

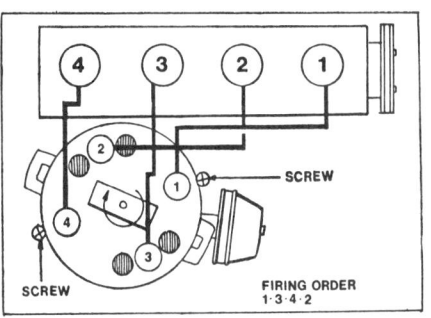
Fig. A

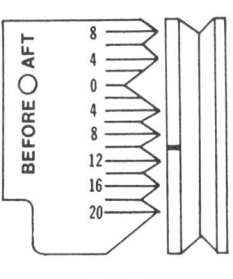
Fig. B

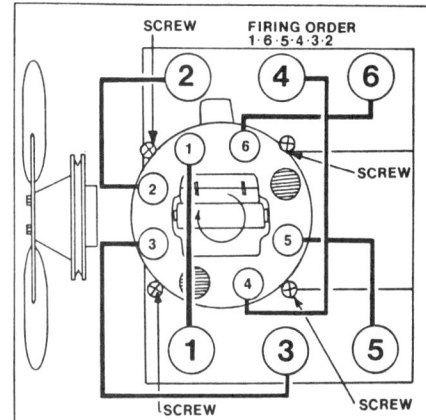
Fig. C

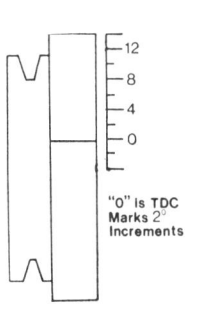
Fig. D

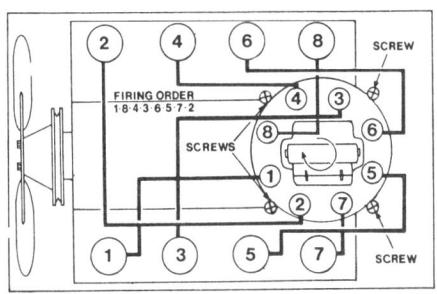
Fig. E

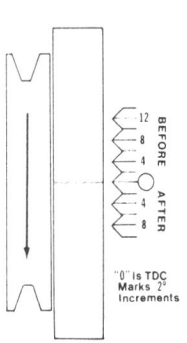
Fig. F

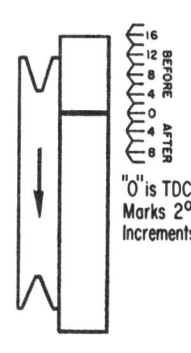
Fig. G

COOLING SYSTEM & CAPACITY DATA

Year	Model or Engine	Cooling Capacity, Qts.		Radiator Cap Relief Pressure, Lbs.		Thermo. Opening Temp. ①	Fuel Tank Gals.	Engine Oil Refill Qts. ②	Transmission Oil				Rear Axle Oil Pints
		With Heater	With A/C	With A/C	No A/C				3 Speed Pints	4 Speed Pints	5 Speed Pints	Auto. Trans. Qts.	
1975	4-140, 350	8	8	15	15	195	18½	3	—	3	—	④	2¾
	V6-231	13¼	13¾	15	15	190	18½	4	—	⑤	—	④	2¾
	V8-262, 350	18	18	15	15	195	18½	4	—	3	3½	④	2¾
1976	4-140	8½	8½	15	15	195	18½	3½	3	3	3	⑥	2¾
	V6-231	13½	14	15	15	195	18½	4	—	⑦	⑧	⑥	⑨
	V8-262	18½	18½	15	15	195	18½	4	—	3	3	④	2¾

①—For permanent type anti freeze.
②—Add 1 qt. with filter change.
③—Approximate. Make final check with dip stick.
④—Refill 3 qts., total capacity 10 qts.
⑤—Exc. Skyhawk, 2½ pts.; Skyhawk, 3½ pts.
⑥—Exc. Sunbird, refill 3 qts., total capacity 10 qts.; Sunbird, refill 2½ qts.; total capacity 10½ qts.
⑦—Skyhawk, 3½ pts.; Starfire, 2½ pts.; Sunbird, 3 pts.
⑧—Exc. Sunbird, 3½ pts.; Sunbird, 3 pts.
⑨—Exc. Sunbird, 3½ pts.; Sunbird, 2¾ pts.

Chevrolet Vega/Pontiac Astre

GENERAL ENGINE SPECIFICATIONS

Year	Engine	Carburetor	Bore and Stroke	Piston Displacement, Cubic Inches	Compression Ratio	Maximum Brake H.P. @ R.P.M.	Maximum Torque Lbs. Ft. @ R.P.M.	Normal Oil Pressure Pounds
1971–72	80 Horsepower①............4-140	1 Barrel	3.500 x 3.625	140	8.00	80 @ 4400	121 @ 2400	40
	90 Horsepower①............4-140	2 Barrel	3.500 x 3.625	140	8.00	90 @ 4800	121 @ 2800	40
1973	72 Horsepower①............4-140	1 Barrel	3.500 x 3.625	140	8.00	72 @ 4400	100 @ 2000	40
	85 Horsepower①............4-140	2 Barrel	3.500 x 3.625	140	8.00	85 @ 4800	115 @ 2400	40
1974	75 Horsepower①............4-140	1 Barrel	3.500 x 3.625	140	8.00	75 @ 4400	115 @ 2400	40
	85 Horsepower①............4-140	2 Barrel	3.500 x 3.625	140	8.00	85 @ 4400	122 @ 2400	40
1975	78 Horsepower①............4-140	1 Barrel	3.500 x 3.625	140	8.00	78 @ 4200	120 @ 2000	40
	87 Horsepower①............4-140	2 Barrel	3.500 x 3.625	140	8.00	87 @ 4400	122 @ 2800	40
1976	110 Horsepower①............4-122	②	3.500 x 3.160	122	8.50	110 @ 5600	107 @ 4800	40
	69 Horsepower①............4-140	1 Barrel	3.500 x 3.625	140	8.00	69 @ 4000	113 @ 2400	40
	80 Horsepower①③............4-140	2 Barrel	3.500 x 3.625	140	8.00	80 @ 4000	116 @ 2800	40
	87 Horsepower①............4-140	2 Barrel	3.500 x 3.625	140	8.00	87 @ 4400	122 @ 2800	40
	110 Horsepower①............4-122	②	3.500 x 3.160	122	8.50	110 @ 5600	107 @ 4800	40

①—Ratings Net—as installed in the vehicle. ②—Fuel Injection. ③—California.

TUNEUP SPECIFICATIONS

The following specifications are published from the latest information available. This data should be used only in the absence of a decal affixed in the engine compartment.

★When using a timing light, disconnect vacuum hose or tube at distributor and plug opening in hose or tube so idle speed will not be affected.

●When checking compression, lowest cylinder must be within 80 percent of highest.

▲Before removing wires from distributor cap, determine location of the No. 1 wire in cap, as distributor position may have been altered from that shown at the end of this chart.

Year	Spark Plug Type	Spark Plug Gap Inch	Distributor Point Gap Inch	Distributor Dwell Angle Deg.	Ignition Timing Firing Order Fig. ▲	Ignition Timing Timing BTDC ①	Ignition Timing Mark Fig.	Carb. Adj. Hot Idle Speed Std. Trans.	Carb. Adj. Hot Idle Speed Auto. Trans. ②	Carb. Adj. Air Fuel Ratio Std. Trans.	Carb. Adj. Air Fuel Ratio Auto. Trans.	Carb. Adj. Idle "CO" % Std. Trans.	Carb. Adj. Idle "CO" % Auto. Trans.
1971													
80 Horsepower	R42TS	.035	③	31–34	A	6°	B	850⑤	650D⑤	—	—	2.0	2.0
90 Horsepower	R42TS	.035	③	31–34	A	④	B	1200⑤	700D⑤	—	—	2.0	2.0
1972													
80 Horsepower	R42TS	.035	③	31–34	A	6°⑦	B	850⑥	700D⑤	—	—	—	—
90 Horsepower	R42TS	.035	③	31–34	A	8°	B	1200	700D⑤	—	—	—	—
1973													
72 Horsepower	R42TS	.035	③	31–34	A	8°	B	1000	750D	—	—	—	—
85 Horsepower	R42TS	.035	③	31–34	A	10°⑨	B	1200	750D⑧	—	—	—	—
1974													
All	R42TS	.035	③	31–34	A	⑩	B	700	750D	—	—	0.5	0.5
1975													
78 Horsepower	R43TSX	.060	—	—	C	⑪	D	700	550D	—	—	—	—
87 Horsepower	R43TSX⑫	.060	—	—	C	⑩	D	700	600D	—	—	—	—
Cosworth Vega	R43LTSX	.060	—	—	E	12°⑬	F	1600	—	—	—	—	—

Chevrolet Vega/Pontiac Astre

TUNEUP SPECIFICATIONS/continued

The following specifications are published from the latest information available. This data should be used only in the absence of a decal affixed in the engine compartment.

★ When using a timing light, disconnect vacuum hose or tube at distributor and plug opening in hose or tube so idle speed will not be affected.

● When checking compression, lowest cylinder must be within 80 percent of highest.

▲ Before removing wires from distributor cap, determine location of the No. 1 wire in cap, as distributor position may have been altered from that shown at the end of this chart.

Year	Spark Plug		Distributor		Ignition Timing ★			Carb. Adjustments					
	Type	Gap Inch	Point Gap Inch	Dwell Angle Deg.	Firing Order Fig. ▲	Timing BTDC ①	Mark Fig.	Hot Idle Speed		Air Fuel Ratio		Idle "CO" %	
								Std. Trans.	Auto. Trans. ②	Std. Trans.	Auto. Trans.	Std. Trans.	Auto. Trans.
1976													
1 Bar. Carb.	R43TS	.035	—	—	C	⑪	D	⑯	750D	—	—	—	—
2 Bar. Carb.⑭	R43TSX	.035	—	—	C	⑰	D	700	750D	—	—	—	—
2 Bar. Carb.⑮	R43TS	.035	—	—	C	⑰	D	⑱	750D	—	—	—	—
Cosworth Vega	R43LTS	.035	—	—	E	12°⑬	F	1600	—	—	—	—	—

① —BTDC—Before top dead center.
② —D—Drive.
③ —New points .019", used .016".
④ —With synchromesh trans. 6°; with automatic trans. 10°.
⑤ —Solenoid disconnected.
⑥ —1200 R.P.M. in California.
⑦ —4° for California vehicles w/manual trans.
⑧ —With Air Cond. 800 RPM.
⑨ —With Auto. Trans. 12°.
⑩ —Synchromesh trans. 10° BTDC; automatic trans. 12° BTDC.
⑪ —Synchromesh trans. 8° BTDC, automatic trans. 10° BTDC.
⑫ —If cold weather starting problems are encountered, use R43TS spark plug, gapped at .035 inch.
⑬ —At 1600 RPM.
⑭ —Exc. California.
⑮ —California.
⑯ —Astre 700 RPM; Vega, 1200 RPM.
⑰ —Astre man. trans., 8° BTDC; auto. trans., 10° BTDC. Vega man. trans., 10° BTDC; auto. trans., 12° BTDC.
⑱ —Astre, 700 RPM; Vega, 1000 RPM.

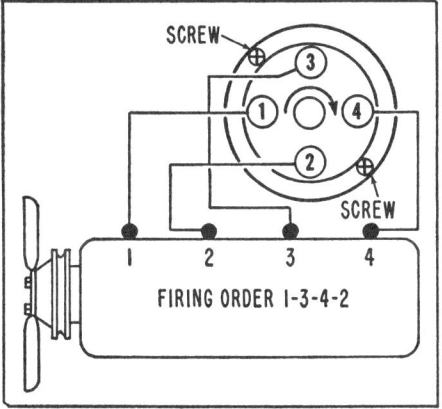

Fig. A

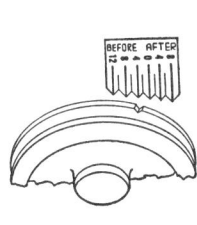

Fig. B

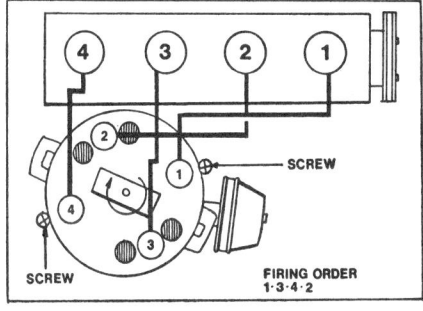

Fig. C

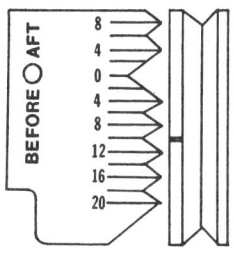

Fig. D

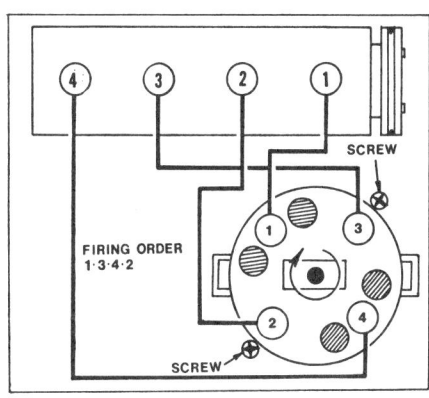

Fig. E

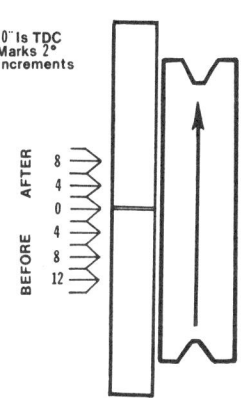

Fig. F

Chevrolet Vega/Pontiac Astre

STARTING MOTOR SPECIFICATIONS

Year	Model	Starter Number	Brush Spring Tension Oz.①	Free Speed Test			Resistance Test	
				Amps.	Volts	R.P.M.①	Amps.	Volts
1971–74	Std. Trans.	1108195	—	50–75	9	6500–10000	—	—
	Auto. Trans.	1108196	—	50–75	9	6500–10000	—	—
1975–76	Std. Trans.	1108771	—	50–75	9	6500–10000	—	—
	Auto. Trans.	1108772	—	50–75	9	6500–10000	—	—
	Cosworth Vega	1108773	—	50–75	9	6500–10000	—	—

①—Minimum.

COOLING SYSTEM & CAPACITY DATA

Year	Model or Engine	Cooling Capacity, Qts.		Radiator Cap Relief Pressure, Lbs.		Thermo. Opening Temp. ①	Fuel Tank Gals.	Engine Oil Refill Qts. ②	Transmission Oil				Rear Axle Oil Pints
		With Heater	With A/C	With A/C	No A/C				3 Speed Pints	4 Speed Pints	5 Speed Pints	Auto. Trans. Qts. ⑥	
1971–72	4-140	6.5	6.5	15	15	195	11	3	2.4	3	—	③	2.5
1973	4-140	8.6	9.0	15	15	195	11	3	3	3	—	④	2.8
1974	4-140	7.6	8.0	15	15	195	16	3	3	3	—	4	2.8
1975	4-140	7	7½	15	15	195	16	3	2.4	2.4	—	⑤	2¼
1975–76	4-122	6.8	6.8	15	15	195	16	3½	—	3	—	—	2¼
1976	4-140	8	8	15	15	195	16	3½	3	3	3	⑤	2¼

①—For permanent type anti-freeze.
②—Add 1 quart with filter change.
③—Refill 2 qts. Total capacity 8½ qts.
④—Powerglide 2½ qts.; turbo hydra-matic 4 qts.
⑤—Refill 4 qts. Total capacity 10 qts.
⑥—Approximate; make final check with dipstick.

Chrysler/Dodge/Imperial/Plymouth

GENERAL ENGINE SPECIFICATIONS

Year	Engine	Carburetor	Bore and Stroke	Piston Displacement, Cubic Inches	Compression Ratio	Maximum Brake H.P. @ R.P.M.	Maximum Torque Lbs. Ft. @ R.P.M.	Normal Oil Pressure Pounds

CHRYSLER AND IMPERIAL

Year	Engine	Carburetor	Bore and Stroke	Piston Disp.	Comp. Ratio	Max HP @ RPM	Max Torque @ RPM	Oil Press.
1969	290 Horsepower............V8-383	2 Barrel	4.25 x 3.375	383	9.2	290 @ 4400	380 @ 2400	45–65
	330 Horsepower............V8-383	4 Barrel	4.25 x 3.375	383	10.0	330 @ 5000	425 @ 3200	45–65
	350 Horsepower............V8-440	4 Barrel	4.32 x 3.75	440	10.1	350 @ 4400	480 @ 2800	45–65
	375 Horsepower............V8-440	4 Barrel	4.32 x 3.75	440	10.1	375 @ 4600	480 @ 3200	45–65
1970	290 Horsepower............V8-383	2 Barrel	4.25 x 3.375	383	8.7	290 @ 4400	380 @ 2800	45–65
	330 Horsepower............V8-383	4 Barrel	4.25 x 3.375	383	9.5	330 @ 5000	425 @ 3200	45–65
	350 Horsepower............V8-440	4 Barrel	4.32 x 3.75	440	9.7	350 @ 4400	480 @ 2800	45–65
	375 Horsepower............V8-440	4 Barrel	4.32 x 3.75	440	9.7	375 @ 4600	480 @ 3200	45–65
1971	275 Horsepower............V8-383	2 Barrel	4.25 x 3.375	383	8.7	275 @ 4400	375 @ 2800	45–65
	300 Horsepower............V8-383	4 Barrel	4.25 x 3.375	383	8.7	300 @ 4800	410 @ 3400	45–65
	190 Horsepower①..........V8-400	2 Barrel	4.342 x 3.375	400	8.2	190 @ 4400	310 @ 2400	45–65
	335 Horsepower............V8-440	4 Barrel	4.32 x 3.75	440	9.0	335 @ 4400	460 @ 3200	45–65
	370 Horsepower............V8-440	4 Barrel	4.32 x 3.75	440	9.7	370 @ 4600	480 @ 3200	45–65

Chrysler/Dodge/Imperial/Plymouth

GENERAL ENGINE SPECIFICATIONS/continued

Year	Engine	Carburetor	Bore and Stroke	Piston Displacement, Cubic Inches	Compression Ratio	Maximum Brake H.P. @ R.P.M.	Maximum Torque Lbs. Ft. @ R.P.M.	Normal Oil Pressure Pounds
1972	175 Horsepower①............V8-360	2 Barrel	4.00 x 3.58	360	8.8	175 @ 4000	285 @ 2400	45–65
	190 Horsepower①............V8-400	2 Barrel	4.342 x 3.375	400	8.2	190 @ 4400	310 @ 2400	45–65
	225 Horsepower①............V8-440	4 Barrel	4.32 x 3.75	440	8.2	225 @ 4400	345 @ 3200	45–65
	245 Horsepower①②........V8-440	4 Barrel	4.32 x 3.75	440	8.2	245 @ 4400	360 @ 3200	45–65
1973	185 Horsepower①............V8-400	2 Barrel	4.34 x 3.38	400	8.2	185 @ 3600	310 @ 2400	45–65
	215 Horsepower①............V8-440	4 Barrel	4.32 x 3.75	440	8.2	215 @ 3600	345 @ 2000	45–65
1974	185 Horsepower①............V8-400	2 Barrel	4.34 x 3.38	400	8.2	185 @ 4000	315 @ 2400	45–65
	200 Horsepower①............V8-400④	4 Barrel	4.34 x 3.38	400	8.2	200 @ 4400	310 @ 2400	45–65
	205 Horsepower①............V8-400③	4 Barrel	4.34 x 3.38	400	8.2	205 @ 4400	310 @ 2400	45–65
	220 Horsepower①............V8-440④	4 Barrel	4.32 x 3.75	440	8.2	220 @ 4000	345 @ 3200	45–65
	230 Horsepower①............V8-440③	4 Barrel	4.32 x 3.75	440	8.2	230 @ 4000	350 @ 3200	45–65
1975	135 Horsepower①............V8-318④	2 Barrel	3.91 x 3.31	318	8.5	135 @ 3600	245 @ 1600	30–80
	150 Horsepower①............V8-318③	2 Barrel	3.91 x 3.31	318	8.5	150 @ 4000	255 @ 1600	30–80
	180 Horsepower①............V8-360③	2 Barrel	4.00 x 3.58	360	8.4	180 @ 4000	290 @ 2400	30–80
	190 Horsepower①............V8-360④	4 Barrel	4.00 x 3.58	360	8.4	190 @ 4000	270 @ 3200	30–80
	165 Horsepower①............V8-400③	2 Barrel	4.34 x 3.38	400	8.2	165 @ 4000	295 @ 3200	30–80
	175 Horsepower①............V8-400③	2 Barrel	4.34 x 3.38	400	8.2	175 @ 4000	300 @ 2400	30–80
	185 Horsepower①............V8-400④	4 Barrel	4.34 x 3.38	400	8.2	185 @ 4000	285 @ 3200	30–80
	190 Horsepower①............V8-400③	4 Barrel	4.34 x 3.38	400	8.2	190 @ 4000	290 @ 3200	30–80
	195 Horsepower①............V8-400④	4 Barrel	4.34 x 3.38	400	8.2	195 @ 4000	285 @ 3200	30–80
	235 Horsepower①②........V8-400③	4 Barrel	4.34 x 3.38	400	8.2	235 @ 4000	320 @ 3200	30–80
	215 Horsepower①............V8-440	4 Barrel	4.32 x 3.75	440	8.2	215 @ 4000	330 @ 3200	30–80
1976	140 Horsepower①............V8-318④	2 Barrel	3.91 x 3.31	318	8.5	140 @ 3600	250 @ 2000	40–65
	150 Horsepower①............V8-318③	2 Barrel	3.91 x 3.31	318	8.5	150 @ 4000	255 @ 1600	40–65
	170 Horsepower①............V8-360③	2 Barrel	4.00 x 3.58	360	8.4	170 @ 4000	280 @ 2400	40–65
	175 Horsepower①............V8-360④	4 Barrel	4.00 x 3.58	360	8.4	175 @ 4000	270 @ 1600	40–65
	175 Horsepower①............V8-400③	2 Barrel	4.34 x 3.38	400	8.2	175 @ 4000	300 @ 2400	50–75
	185 Horsepower①............V8-400④	4 Barrel	4.34 x 3.38	400	8.2	185 @ 3600	285 @ 3200	50–75
	210 Horsepower①............V8-400③	4 Barrel	4.34 x 3.38	400	8.2	210 @ 4000	305 @ 3200	50–75
	240 Horsepower①②........V8-400③	4 Barrel	4.34 x 3.38	400	8.2	240 @ 4400	325 @ 3200	50–75
	200 Horsepower①............V8-440④	4 Barrel	4.32 x 3.75	440	8.2	200 @ 3600	310 @ 2400	50–75
	205 Horsepower①............V8-440③	4 Barrel	4.32 x 3.75	440	8.2	205 @ 3600	320 @ 2000	50–75

DODGE

Year	Engine	Carburetor	Bore and Stroke	Piston Displacement, Cubic Inches	Compression Ratio	Maximum Brake H.P. @ R.P.M.	Maximum Torque Lbs. Ft. @ R.P.M.	Normal Oil Pressure Pounds
1969	115 Horsepower................6-170	1 Barrel	3.40 x 3.125	170	8.5	115 @ 4400	115 @ 2400	45–65
	145 Horsepower................6-225	1 Barrel	3.40 x 4.125	225	8.4	145 @ 4000	215 @ 2400	45–65
	190 Horsepower................V8-273	2 Barrel	3.63 x 3.31	273	9.0	190 @ 4400	260 @ 2000	45–65
	230 Horsepower................V8-318	2 Barrel	3.91 x 3.31	318	9.2	230 @ 4400	340 @ 2400	45–65
	275 Horsepower................V8-340	4 Barrel	4.04 x 3.31	340	10.5	275 @ 5000	340 @ 3200	45–65
	290 Horsepower................V8-383	2 Barrel	4.25 x 3.38	383	9.2	290 @ 4400	390 @ 2800	45–65
	330 Horsepower................V8-383	4 Barrel	4.25 x 3.38	383	10.0	330 @ 5000	425 @ 3200	45–65
	335 Horsepower................V8-383	4 Barrel	4.25 x 3.38	383	10.0	335 @ 5000	425 @ 3400	45–65
	350 Horsepower................V8-440	4 Barrel	4.32 x 3.75	440	10.1	350 @ 4400	480 @ 2800	45–65
	375 Horsepower................V8-440	4 Barrel	4.32 x 3.75	440	10.1	375 @ 4600	480 @ 3200	45–65
	390 Horsepower................V8-440	Three 2 Bar.	4.32 x 3.75	440	10.5	390 @ 4700	490 @ 3200	45–65
	425 Horsepower................V8-426	Two 4 Bar.	4.25 x 3.75	426	10.25	425 @ 5000	490 @ 4000	45–65

Chrysler/Dodge/Imperial/Plymouth

GENERAL ENGINE SPECIFICATIONS/continued

Year	Engine	Carburetor	Bore and Stroke	Piston Displacement, Cubic Inches	Compression Ratio	Maximum Brake H.P. @ R.P.M.	Maximum Torque Lbs. Ft. @ R.P.M.	Normal Oil Pressure Pounds
DODGE—Continued								
1970	125 Horsepower............6-198	1 Barrel	3.40 x 3.64	198	8.4	125 @ 4400	180 @ 2000	45-65
	145 Horsepower............6-225	1 Barrel	3.40 x 4.12	225	8.4	145 @ 4000	215 @ 2400	45-65
	230 Horsepower............V8-318	2 Barrel	3.91 x 3.31	318	8.8	230 @ 4400	320 @ 2000	45-65
	275 Horsepower............V8-340	4 Barrel	4.04 x 3.31	340	10.5	275 @ 5000	340 @ 3200	45-65
	290 Horsepower............V8-383	2 Barrel	4.25 x 3.38	383	8.7	290 @ 4400	390 @ 2800	45-65
	330 Horsepower............V8-383	4 Barrel	4.25 x 3.38	383	9.5	330 @ 5000	425 @ 3200	45-65
	335 Horsepower............V8-383	4 Barrel	4.25 x 3.38	383	9.5	335 @ 5200	425 @ 3400	45-65
	425 Horsepower............V8-426	Two 4 Bar.	4.25 x 3.75	426	10.2	425 @ 5000	490 @ 4000	45-65
	350 Horsepower............V8-440	4 Barrel	4.32 x 3.75	440	9.7	350 @ 4400	480 @ 2800	45-65
	375 Horsepower............V8-440	4 Barrel	4.32 x 3.75	440	9.7	375 @ 4600	480 @ 3200	45-65
	390 Horsepower............V8-440	Three 2 Bar.	4.32 x 3.75	440	10.5	390 @ 4700	490 @ 3200	45-65
1971	125 Horsepower............6-198	1 Barrel	3.40 x 3.64	198	8.4	125 @ 4400	180 @ 2000	45-65
	145 Horsepower............6-225	1 Barrel	3.40 x 4.12	225	8.4	145 @ 4000	215 @ 2400	45-65
	230 Horsepower............V8-318	2 Barrel	3.91 x 3.31	318	8.6	230 @ 4400	320 @ 2000	45-65
	275 Horsepower............V8-340	4 Barrel	4.04 x 3.31	340	10.3	340 @ 5000	340 @ 3200	45-65
	290 Horsepower............V8-340	Three 2 Bar.	4.04 x 3.31	340	10.2	290 @ 5000	340 @ 3200	45-65
	255 Horsepower............V8-360	2 Barrel	4.00 x 3.58	360	8.7	255 @ 4400	360 @ 2400	45-65
	275 Horsepower............V8-383	2 Barrel	4.25 x 3.38	383	8.5	275 @ 4400	375 @ 2800	45-65
	300 Horsepower............V8-383	4 Barrel	4.25 x 3.38	383	8.5	300 @ 4800	410 @ 3400	45-65
	425 Horsepower............V8-426	Two 4 Bar.	4.25 x 3.75	426	10.2	425 @ 5000	490 @ 4000	45-65
	335 Horsepower............V8-440	4 Barrel	4.32 x 3.75	440	9.0	335 @ 4400	460 @ 3200	45-65
	370 Horsepower............V8-440	4 Barrel	4.32 x 3.75	440	9.7	370 @ 4600	280 @ 3200	45-65
	385 Horsepower............V8-440	Three 2 Bar.	4.32 x 3.75	440	10.5	385 @ 4700	490 @ 3200	45-65
1972	100 Horsepower[1]............6-198	1 Barrel	3.40 x 3.64	198	8.4	100 @ 4400	160 @ 2400	45-65
	110 Horsepower[1]............6-225	1 Barrel	3.40 x 4.12	225	8.4	110 @ 4000	185 @ 2000	45-65
	150 Horsepower[1]............V8-318	2 Barrel	3.91 x 3.31	318	8.6	150 @ 4000	260 @ 1600	45-65
	240 Horsepower[1]............V8-340	4 Barrel	4.04 x 3.31	340	8.5	240 @ 4800	290 @ 3600	45-65
	175 Horsepower[1]............V8-360	2 Barrel	4.00 x 3.58	360	8.8	175 @ 4000	285 @ 2400	45-65
	190 Horsepower[1]............V8-400	2 Barrel	4.34 x 3.38	400	8.2	190 @ 4400	310 @ 2400	45-65
	255 Horsepower[1][2]............V8-400	4 Barrel	4.34 x 3.38	400	8.2	255 @ 4800	340 @ 3200	45-65
	225 Horsepower[1]............V8-440	4 Barrel	4.32 x 3.75	440	8.2	225 @ 4400	345 @ 3200	45-65
	245 Horsepower[1][2]............V8-440	4 Barrel	4.32 x 3.75	440	8.2	245 @ 4400	360 @ 3200	45-65
	330 Horsepower[1]............V8-440	Three 2 Bar.	4.32 x 3.75	440	10.3	330 @ 4800	410 @ 3600	45-65
1973	95 Horsepower[1]............6-198	1 Barrel	3.40 x 3.64	198	8.4	95 @ 4000	150 @ 1600	45-65
	105 Horsepower[1]............6-225	1 Barrel	3.40 x 4.12	225	8.4	105 @ 4000	185 @ 1600	45-65
	150 Horsepower[1]............V8-318	2 Barrel	3.91 x 3.31	318	8.6	150 @ 3600	265 @ 2000	45-65
	240 Horsepower[1]............V8-340	4 Barrel	4.04 x 3.31	340	8.5	240 @ 4800	295 @ 3600	45-65
	170 Horsepower[1]............V8-360	2 Barrel	4.00 x 3.58	360	8.4	170 @ 4000	285 @ 2400	45-65
	175 Horsepower[1]............V8-400	2 Barrel	4.34 x 3.38	400	8.2	175 @ 3600	305 @ 2400	45-65
	185 Horsepower[1]............V8-400	2 Barrel	4.34 x 3.38	400	8.2	185 @ 3600	310 @ 2400	45-65
	260 Horsepower[1]............V8-400	4 Barrel	4.34 x 3.38	400	8.2	260 @ 4800	335 @ 3600	45-65
	220 Horsepower[1]............V8-440	4 Barrel	4.32 x 3.75	440	8.2	220 @ 3600	350 @ 2400	45-65
	280 Horsepower[1]............V8-440	4 Barrel	4.32 x 3.75	440	8.2	280 @ 4800	380 @ 3200	45-65
1974	95 Horsepower[1]............6-198	1 Barrel	3.40 x 3.64	198	8.4	95 @ 4000	145 @ 2000	45-65
	105 Horsepower[1]............6-225	1 Barrel	3.40 x 4.12	225	8.4	105 @ 3600	180 @ 1600	45-65
	150 Horsepower[1]............V8-318	2 Barrel	3.91 x 3.31	318	8.6	150 @ 4000	255 @ 2200	45-65
	180 Horsepower[1]............V8-360[3]	2 Barrel	4.00 x 3.58	360	8.4	180 @ 4000	290 @ 2400	45-65
	200 Horsepower[1]............V8-360[4]	4 Barrel	4.00 x 3.58	360	8.4	200 @ 4000	290 @ 3200	45-65
	245 Horsepower[1][2]............V8-360[3]	4 Barrel	4.00 x 3.58	360	8.4	245 @ 4800	320 @ 3600	45-65
	185 Horsepower[1]............V8-400[3]	2 Barrel	4.34 x 3.38	400	8.2	185 @ 4000	315 @ 2400	45-65
	200 Horsepower[1]............V8-400[4]	4 Barrel	4.34 x 3.38	400	8.2	200 @ 4400	310 @ 2400	45-65
	205 Horsepower[1]............V8-400[3]	4 Barrel	4.34 x 3.38	400	8.2	205 @ 4400	310 @ 2400	45-65
	250 Horsepower[1][2]............V8-400	4 Barrel	4.34 x 3.38	400	8.2	250 @ 4800	330 @ 3400	45-65
	230 Horsepower[1]............V8-440	4 Barrel	4.32 x 3.75	440	8.2	230 @ 4000	350 @ 3200	45-65
	220 Horsepower[1]............V8-440	4 Barrel	4.32 x 3.75	440	8.2	220 @ 4000	345 @ 3200	45-65
	275 Horsepower[1][2]............V8-440	4 Barrel	4.32 x 3.75	440	8.2	275 @ 4400	375 @ 3200	45-65

Chrysler/Dodge/Imperial/Plymouth

GENERAL ENGINE SPECIFICATIONS/continued

Year	Engine	Carburetor	Bore and Stroke	Piston Displacement, Cubic Inches	Compression Ratio	Maximum Brake H.P. @ R.P.M.	Maximum Torque H.P. @ R.P.M.	Normal Oil Pressure Pounds
DODGE—Continued								
1975	90 Horsepower①............6-225④	1 Barrel	3.40 x 3.64	225	8.4	90 @ 3600	165 @ 1600	30–70
	95 Horsepower①............6-225③	1 Barrel	3.40 x 3.64	225	8.4	95 @ 3600	170 @ 1600	30–70
	135 Horsepower①..........V8-318④	2 Barrel	3.91 x 3.31	318	8.5	135 @ 3600	245 @ 1600	30–80
	140 Horsepower①..........V8-318④	2 Barrel	3.91 x 3.31	318	8.5	140 @ 3600	255 @ 1600	30–80
	145 Horsepower①..........V8-318③	2 Barrel	3.91 x 3.31	318	8.5	145 @ 4000	255 @ 1600	30–80
	150 Horsepower①..........V8-318③	2 Barrel	3.91 x 3.31	318	8.5	150 @ 4000	255 @ 1600	30–80
	180 Horsepower①..........V8-360③	2 Barrel	4.00 x 3.58	360	8.4	180 @ 4000	290 @ 2400	30–80
	190 Horsepower①..........V8-360④	4 Barrel	4.00 x 3.58	360	8.4	190 @ 4000	270 @ 3200	30–80
	230 Horsepower①②........V8-360③	4 Barrel	4.00 x 3.58	360	8.4	230 @ 4200	320 @ 3200	30–80
	165 Horsepower①..........V8-400③	2 Barrel	4.34 x 3.38	400	8.2	165 @ 4000	295 @ 3200	30–80
	175 Horsepower①..........V8-400③	2 Barrel	4.34 x 3.38	400	8.2	175 @ 4000	300 @ 2400	30–80
	185 Horsepower①..........V8-400④	4 Barrel	4.34 x 3.38	400	8.2	185 @ 4000	285 @ 3200	30–80
	190 Horsepower①..........V8-400④	4 Barrel	4.34 x 3.38	400	8.2	190 @ 4000	290 @ 3200	30–80
	195 Horsepower①..........V8-400④	4 Barrel	4.34 x 3.38	400	8.2	195 @ 4000	285 @ 3200	30–80
	235 Horsepower①②........V8-400③	4 Barrel	4.34 x 3.38	400	8.2	235 @ 4200	320 @ 3200	30–80
	240 Horsepower①②........V8-400③	4 Barrel	4.34 x 3.38	400	8.2	240 @ 4400	325 @ 3200	30–80
	215 Horsepower①..........V8-440③	4 Barrel	4.32 x 3.75	440	8.2	215 @ 4000	330 @ 3200	30–80
	250 Horsepower①②........V8-440④	4 Barrel	4.32 x 3.75	440	8.2	250 @ 4000	350 @ 3200	30–80
	260 Horsepower①②........V8-440③	4 Barrel	4.32 x 3.75	440	8.2	260 @ 4400	355 @ 3200	30–80
1976	90 Horsepower①............6-225④	1 Barrel	3.40 x 4.12	225	8.4	90 @ 3600	165 @ 1600	40–65
	100 Horsepower①..........6-225③	1 Barrel	3.40 x 4.12	225	8.4	100 @ 3600	170 @ 1600	40–65
	140 Horsepower①..........V8-318④	2 Barrel	3.91 x 3.31	318	8.5	140 @ 3600	250 @ 2000	40–65
	150 Horsepower①..........V8-318③	2 Barrel	3.91 x 3.31	318	8.5	150 @ 4000	255 @ 1600	40–65
	170 Horsepower①..........V8-360③	2 Barrel	4.00 x 3.58	360	8.4	170 @ 4000	280 @ 2400	40–65
	175 Horsepower①..........V8-360④	4 Barrel	4.00 x 3.58	360	8.4	175 @ 4000	270 @ 1600	40–65
	220 Horsepower①②........V8-360③	4 Barrel	4.00 x 3.58	360	8.4	220 @ 4400	280 @ 3200	40–65
	175 Horsepower①..........V8-400③	2 Barrel	4.34 x 3.38	400	8.2	175 @ 4000	300 @ 2400	50–75
	185 Horsepower①..........V8-400④	4 Barrel	4.34 x 3.38	400	8.2	185 @ 3600	285 @ 3200	50–75
	210 Horsepower①..........V8-400③	4 Barrel	4.34 x 3.38	400	8.2	210 @ 4000	305 @ 3200	50–75
	240 Horsepower①②........V8-400③	4 Barrel	4.34 x 3.38	400	8.2	240 @ 4400	325 @ 3200	50–75
	200 Horsepower①..........V8-440④	4 Barrel	4.32 x 3.75	440	8.2	200 @ 3600	310 @ 2400	50–75
	205 Horsepower①..........V8-440③	4 Barrel	4.32 x 3.75	440	8.2	205 @ 3600	320 @ 2000	50–75
	250 Horsepower①②........V8-440④	4 Barrel	4.32 x 3.75	440	8.2	250 @ 4000	350 @ 3200	50–75
	255 Horsepower①②........V8-440③	4 Barrel	4.32 x 3.75	440	8.2	255 @ 4400	355 @ 3200	50–75
PLYMOUTH								
1969	115 Horsepower.............6-170	1 Barrel	3.40 x 3.125	170	8.5	115 @ 4400	155 @ 2400	45–65
	145 Horsepower.............6-225	1 Barrel	3.40 x 4.125	225	8.4	145 @ 4000	215 @ 2400	45–65
	190 Horsepower.............V8-273	2 Barrel	3.63 x 3.31	273	9.0	190 @ 4400	260 @ 2000	45–65
	230 Horsepower.............V8-318	2 Barrel	3.91 x 3.31	318	9.2	230 @ 4400	340 @ 2400	45–65
	275 Horsepower.............V8-340	4 Barrel	4.04 x 3.31	340	10.5	275 @ 5000	340 @ 3200	45–65
	290 Horsepower.............V8-383	2 Barrel	4.25 x 3.38	383	9.2	290 @ 4400	390 @ 2800	45–65
	330 Horsepower.............V8-383	4 Barrel	4.25 x 3.38	383	10.0	330 @ 5000	425 @ 3200	45–65
	335 Horsepower.............V8-383	4 Barrel	4.25 x 3.38	383	10.0	335 @ 5000	425 @ 3400	45–65
	350 Horsepower.............V8-440	4 Barrel	4.32 x 3.75	440	10.1	350 @ 4400	480 @ 2800	45–65
	375 Horsepower.............V8-440	4 Barrel	4.32 x 3.75	440	10.1	375 @ 4600	480 @ 3200	45–65
	390 Horsepower.............V8-440	Three 2 Bar.	4.32 x 3.75	440	10.5	390 @ 4700	490 @ 3200	45–65
	425 Horsepower.............V8-426	Two 4 Bar.	4.25 x 3.75	426	10.25	425 @ 5000	490 @ 4000	45–65

Chrysler/Dodge/Imperial/Plymouth

GENERAL ENGINE SPECIFICATIONS/continued

Year	Engine	Carburetor	Bore and Stroke	Piston Displacement, Cubic Inches	Compression Ratio	Maximum Brake H.P. @ R.P.M.	Maximum Torque H.P. @ R.P.M.	Normal Oil Pressure Pounds
PLYMOUTH—Continued								
1970	125 Horsepower...............6-198	1 Barrel	3.40 x 3.64	198	8.4	125 @ 4400	180 @ 2000	45–65
	145 Horsepower...............6-225	1 Barrel	3.40 x 4.12	225	8.4	145 @ 4000	215 @ 2400	45–65
	230 Horsepower..............V8-318	2 Barrel	3.91 x 3.31	318	8.8	230 @ 4400	320 @ 2000	45–65
	275 Horsepower..............V8-340	4 Barrel	4.04 x 3.31	340	10.5	275 @ 5000	340 @ 3200	45–65
	290 Horsepower..............V8-383	2 Barrel	4.25 x 3.38	383	8.7	290 @ 4400	390 @ 2800	45–65
	330 Horsepower..............V8-383	4 Barrel	4.25 x 3.38	383	9.5	330 @ 5000	425 @ 3200	45–65
	335 Horsepower..............V8-383	4 Barrel	4.25 x 3.38	383	9.5	335 @ 5200	425 @ 3400	45–65
	425 Horsepower..............V8-426	Two 4 Bar.	4.25 x 3.75	426	10.2	425 @ 5000	490 @ 4000	45–65
	350 Horsepower..............V8-440	4 Barrel	4.32 x 3.75	440	9.7	350 @ 4400	480 @ 2800	45–65
	375 Horsepower..............V8-440	4 Barrel	4.32 x 3.75	440	9.7	375 @ 4600	480 @ 3200	45–65
	390 Horsepower..............V8-440	Three 2 Bar.	4.32 x 3.75	440	10.5	390 @ 4700	490 @ 3200	45–65
1971	125 Horsepower...............6-198	1 Barrel	3.40 x 3.64	198	8.4	125 @ 4400	180 @ 2000	45–65
	145 Horsepower...............6-225	1 Barrel	3.40 x 4.12	225	8.4	145 @ 4000	215 @ 2400	45–65
	230 Horsepower..............V8-318	2 Barrel	3.91 x 3.31	318	8.6	230 @ 4400	320 @ 2000	45–65
	275 Horsepower..............V8-340	4 Barrel	4.04 x 3.31	340	10.3	340 @ 5000	340 @ 3200	45–65
	290 Horsepower..............V8-340	Three 2 Bar.	4.04 x 3.31	340	10.2	290 @ 5000	340 @ 3200	45–65
	255 Horsepower..............V8-360	2 Barrel	4.00 x 3.58	360	8.7	255 @ 4400	360 @ 2400	45–65
	275 Horsepower..............V8-383	2 Barrel	4.25 x 3.38	383	8.5	275 @ 4400	375 @ 2800	45–65
	300 Horsepower..............V8-383	4 Barrel	4.25 x 3.38	383	8.5	300 @ 4800	410 @ 3400	45–65
	425 Horsepower..............V8-426	Two 4 Bar.	4.25 x 3.75	426	10.2	425 @ 5000	490 @ 4000	45–65
	335 Horsepower..............V8-440	4 Barrel	4.32 x 3.75	440	9.0	335 @ 4400	460 @ 3200	45–65
	370 Horsepower..............V8-440	4 Barrel	4.32 x 3.75	440	9.7	370 @ 4600	280 @ 3200	45–65
	385 Horsepower..............V8-440	Three 2 Bar.	4.32 x 3.75	440	10.5	385 @ 4700	490 @ 3200	45–65
1972	100 Horsepower①...............6-198	1 Barrel	3.40 x 3.64	198	8.4	100 @ 4400	160 @ 2400	45–65
	110 Horsepower①...............6-225	1 Barrel	3.40 x 4.12	225	8.4	110 @ 4000	185 @ 2000	45–65
	150 Horsepower①..............V8-318	2 Barrel	3.91 x 3.31	318	8.6	150 @ 4000	260 @ 1600	45–65
	240 Horsepower①..............V8-340	4 Barrel	4.04 x 3.31	340	8.5	240 @ 4800	290 @ 3600	45–65
	175 Horsepower①..............V8-360	2 Barrel	4.00 x 3.58	360	8.8	175 @ 4000	285 @ 2400	45–65
	190 Horsepower①..............V8-400	2 Barrel	4.34 x 3.38	400	8.2	190 @ 4400	310 @ 2400	45–65
	255 Horsepower①②..........V8-400	4 Barrel	4.34 x 3.38	400	8.2	255 @ 4800	340 @ 3200	45–65
	255 Horsepower①..............V8-440	4 Barrel	4.32 x 3.75	440	8.2	225 @ 4400	345 @ 3200	45–65
	245 Horsepower①②..........V8-440	4 Barrel	4.32 x 3.75	440	8.2	245 @ 4400	360 @ 3200	45–65
	330 Horsepower①..............V8-440	Three 2 Bar.	4.32 x 3.75	440	10.3	330 @ 4800	410 @ 3600	45–65
1973	95 Horsepower①...............6-198	1 Barrel	3.40 x 3.64	198	8.4	95 @ 4000	150 @ 1600	45–65
	105 Horsepower①...............6-225	1 Barrel	3.40 x 4.12	225	8.4	105 @ 4000	185 @ 1600	45–65
	150 Horsepower①..............V8-318	2 Barrel	3.91 x 3.31	318	8.6	150 @ 3600	265 @ 2000	45–65
	240 Horsepower①..............V8-340	4 Barrel	4.04 x 3.31	340	8.5	240 @ 4800	295 @ 3600	45–65
	170 Horsepower①..............V8-360	2 Barrel	4.00 x 3.58	360	8.4	170 @ 4000	285 @ 2400	45–65
	175 Horsepower①..............V8-400	2 Barrel	4.34 x 3.38	400	8.2	175 @ 3600	305 @ 2400	45–65
	185 Horsepower①..............V8-400	2 Barrel	4.34 x 3.38	400	8.2	185 @ 3600	310 @ 2400	45–65
	260 Horsepower①..............V8-400	4 Barrel	4.34 x 3.38	400	8.2	260 @ 4800	335 @ 3600	45–65
	220 Horsepower①..............V8-440	4 Barrel	4.32 x 3.75	440	8.2	220 @ 3600	350 @ 2400	45–65
	280 Horsepower①..............V8-440	4 Barrel	4.32 x 3.75	440	8.2	280 @ 4800	380 @ 3200	45–65

Chrysler/Dodge/Imperial/Plymouth

GENERAL ENGINE SPECIFICATIONS/continued

Year	Engine	Carburetor	Bore and Stroke	Piston Displacement, Cubic Inches	Compression Ratio	Maximum Brake H.P. @ R.P.M.	Maximum Torque H.P. @ R.P.M.	Normal Oil Pressure Pounds
PLYMOUTH—Continued								
1974	95 Horsepower①............6-198	1 Barrel	3.40 x 3.64	198	8.4	95 @ 4000	145 @ 2000	45–65
	105 Horsepower①...........6-225	1 Barrel	3.40 x 4.12	225	8.4	105 @ 3600	180 @ 1600	45–65
	150 Horsepower①..........V8-318	2 Barrel	3.91 x 3.31	318	8.6	150 @ 4000	255 @ 2200	45–65
	170 Horsepower①②........V8-318	2 Barrel	3.91 x 3.31	318	8.6	170 @ 4000	265 @ 2600	45–65
	180 Horsepower①..........V8-360	2 Barrel	4.00 x 3.58	360	8.4	180 @ 4000	290 @ 2400	45–65
	200 Horsepower①..........V8-360④	4 Barrel	4.00 x 3.58	360	8.4	200 @ 4000	290 @ 3200	45–65
	245 Horsepower①②........V8-360③	4 Barrel	4.00 x 3.58	360	8.4	245 @ 4800	320 @ 3600	45–65
	185 Horsepower①..........V8-400	2 Barrel	4.34 x 3.38	400	8.2	185 @ 4000	315 @ 2400	45–65
	205 Horsepower①..........V8-400	4 Barrel	4.34 x 3.38	400	8.2	205 @ 4400	310 @ 2400	45–65
	250 Horsepower①②........V8-400	4 Barrel	4.34 x 3.38	400	8.2	250 @ 4800	330 @ 3400	45–65
	230 Horsepower①..........V8-440	4 Barrel	4.32 x 3.75	440	8.2	230 @ 4000	350 @ 3200	45–65
	220 Horsepower①..........V8-440	4 Barrel	4.32 x 3.75	440	8.2	220 @ 4000	345 @ 3200	45–65
	275 Horsepower①②........V8-440	4 Barrel	4.32 x 3.75	440	8.2	275 @ 4400	375 @ 3200	45–65
1975	90 Horsepower①...........6-225④	1 Barrel	3.40 x 4.12	225	8.4	90 @ 3600	165 @ 1600	30–70
	95 Horsepower①...........6-225③	1 Barrel	3.40 x 4.12	225	8.4	95 @ 3600	170 @ 1600	30–70
	135 Horsepower①.........V8-318④	2 Barrel	3.91 x 3.31	318	8.5	135 @ 3600	245 @ 1600	30–80
	140 Horsepower①.........V8-318④	2 Barrel	3.91 x 3.31	318	8.5	140 @ 3600	255 @ 1600	30–80
	145 Horsepower①.........V8-318③	2 Barrel	3.91 x 3.31	318	8.5	145 @ 4000	255 @ 1600	30–80
	150 Horsepower①.........V8-318③	2 Barrel	3.91 x 3.31	318	8.5	150 @ 4000	255 @ 1600	30–80
	180 Horsepower①.........V8-360③	2 Barrel	4.00 x 3.58	360	8.4	180 @ 4000	290 @ 2400	30–80
	190 Horsepower①.........V8-360④	4 Barrel	4.00 x 3.58	360	8.4	190 @ 4000	270 @ 3200	30–80
	230 Horsepower①②......V8-360③	4 Barrel	4.00 x 3.58	360	8.4	230 @ 4400	300 @ 3600	30–80
	165 Horsepower①.........V8-400③	2 Barrel	4.34 x 3.38	400	8.2	165 @ 4000	295 @ 3200	30–80
	175 Horsepower①.........V8-400③	2 Barrel	4.34 x 3.38	400	8.2	175 @ 4000	300 @ 2400	30–80
	185 Horsepower①.........V8-400④	4 Barrel	4.34 x 3.38	400	8.2	185 @ 4000	285 @ 3200	30–80
	190 Horsepower①.........V8-400③	4 Barrel	4.34 x 3.38	400	8.2	190 @ 4000	290 @ 3200	30–80
	195 Horsepower①.........V8-400④	4 Barrel	4.34 x 3.38	400	8.2	195 @ 4000	285 @ 3200	30–80
	235 Horsepower①②.......V8-400③	4 Barrel	4.34 x 3.38	400	8.2	235 @ 4200	320 @ 3200	30–80
	240 Horsepower①②.......V8-400③	4 Barrel	4.34 x 3.38	400	8.2	250 @ 4400	325 @ 3200	30–80
	215 Horsepower①.........V8-440	4 Barrel	4.32 x 3.75	440	8.2	215 @ 4000	330 @ 3200	30–90
	250 Horsepower①②.......V8-440④	4 Barrel	4.32 x 3.75	440	8.2	250 @ 4000	350 @ 3200	30–80
	260 Horsepower①②.......V8-440③	4 Barrel	4.32 x 3.75	440	8.2	260 @ 4400	355 @ 3200	30–80
1976	90 Horsepower①...........6-225④	1 Barrel	3.40 x 4.12	225	8.4	90 @ 3600	165 @ 1600	40–65
	100 Horsepower①..........6-225③	1 Barrel	3.40 x 4.12	225	8.4	100 @ 3600	170 @ 1600	40–65
	140 Horsepower①.........V8-318	2 Barrel	3.91 x 3.31	318	8.5	140 @ 3600	250 @ 2000	40–65
	150 Horsepower①.........V8-318	2 Barrel	3.91 x 3.31	318	8.5	150 @ 4000	255 @ 1600	40–65
	170 Horsepower①.........V8-360	2 Barrel	4.00 x 3.58	360	8.4	170 @ 4000	280 @ 2400	40–65
	175 Horsepower①.........V8-360④	4 Barrel	4.00 x 3.58	360	8.4	175 @ 4000	270 @ 1600	40–65
	200 Horsepower①②.......V8-360③	4 Barrel	4.00 x 3.58	360	8.4	220 @ 4400	280 @ 3200	40–65
	175 Horsepower①.........V8-400③	2 Barrel	4.34 x 3.38	400	8.2	175 @ 4000	300 @ 2400	50–75
	185 Horsepower①.........V8-400④	4 Barrel	4.34 x 3.38	400	8.2	185 @ 3600	285 @ 3200	50–75
	210 Horsepower①.........V8-400③	4 Barrel	4.34 x 3.38	400	8.2	210 @ 4000	305 @ 3200	50–75
	240 Horsepower①②.......V8-400③	4 Barrel	4.34 x 3.38	400	8.2	240 @ 4400	325 @ 3200	50–75
	200 Horsepower①.........V8-440④	4 Barrel	4.32 x 3.75	440	8.2	200 @ 3600	310 @ 2400	50–75
	205 Horsepower①.........V8-440③	4 Barrel	4.32 x 3.75	440	8.2	205 @ 3600	320 @ 2000	50–75
	250 Horsepower①②.......V8-440④	4 Barrel	4.32 x 3.75	440	8.2	250 @ 4000	350 @ 3200	50–75
	255 Horsepower①②.......V8-440③	4 Barrel	4.32 x 3.75	440	8.2	255 @ 4400	355 @ 3200	50–75

①—Ratings are NET—as installed in the vehicle.
②—With dual exhausts.
③—Exc. California.
④—California.

Chrysler/Dodge/Imperial/Plymouth

TUNEUP SPECIFICATIONS

The following specifications are published from the latest information available. This data should be used only in the absence of a decal affixed in the engine compartment.

★ When using a timing light, disconnect vacuum hose or tube at distributor and plug opening in hose or tube so idle speed will not be affected.

● When checking compression, lowest cylinder must be within 80 percent of highest.

▲ Before removing wires from distributor cap, determine location of the No. 1 wire in cap, as distributor position may have been altered from that shown at the end of this chart.

Year	Spark Plug Type ⑦	Spark Plug Gap Inch	Distributor Point Gap Inch	Distributor Dwell Angle Deg.	Ignition Timing★ Firing Order Fig. ▲	Ignition Timing★ Timing BTDC ①	Ignition Timing★ Mark Fig.	Carb. Adjustments Hot Idle Speed Std. Trans.	Carb. Adjustments Hot Idle Speed Auto. Trans. ②	Carb. Adjustments Air Fuel Ratio Std. Trans.	Carb. Adjustments Air Fuel Ratio Auto. Trans.	Carb. Adjustments Idle CO % ③ Std. Trans.	Carb. Adjustments Idle CO % ③ Auto. Trans.
CHRYSLER & IMPERIAL													
1969													
V8-383 Std. Tr.㉑	J14Y	.035	.017	30–35	J	TDC	F	700⑥	—	—	—	—	—
V8-383 Auto. Tr.㉑	J14Y	.035	.017	30–35	J	7½°	F	—	600⑥	—	—	—	—
V8-383 Auto. Tr.④	J11Y	.035	.017	30–35	J	5°	F	700⑥	650⑥	—	—	—	—
V8-440 Auto. Tr.	J13Y	.035	.017	30–35	J	7½°	F	—	650⑥	—	—	—	—
V8-440 Auto. Tr.㉒	J11Y	.035	.017	30–35	J	5°	F	—	650⑥	—	—	—	—
V8-440 Std. Tr.㉒	J11Y	.035	.017	⑰	J	TDC	F	700⑥	—	—	—	—	—
1970-71													
V8-360	N13Y	.035	.017	30–34	H	2½	E	750	700	14.2 to 1	14.2 to 1	—	—
V8-383 Std. Tr.㉑	J14Y	.035	.019	28½–32½	J	TDC	F	750	—	14.2 to 1	—	—	—
V8-383 Auto. Tr.㉑	J14Y	.035	.019	28½–32½	J	2½°	F	—	650N	—	14.2 to 1	—	—
V8-383 Std. Tr.④	J11Y	.035	.019	28½–32½	J	TDC	F	900	—	14.2 to 1	—	—	—
V8-383 Auto. Tr.④	J11Y	.035	.019	28½–32½	J	2½°	F	—	700N	—	14.2 to 1	—	—
V8-400 Auto. Tr.	J11Y	.035	.019	28½–32½	J	2½°	F	—	700N	—	14.2 to 1	—	—
V8-440 Auto. Tr.	J13Y	.035	.019	28½–32½	J	5°	F	—	650N	—	14.2 to 1	—	—
V8-440 Std. Tr.㉒	J11Y	.035	.019	28½–32½	J	TDC	F	900	—	14.2 to 1	—	—	—
V8-440 Auto. Tr.㉒	J11Y	.035	.019	28½–32½	J	2½°	F	—	800N	—	14.2 to 1	—	—
1972													
V8-360	N13Y	.035	.017	30–34	H	TDC	E	—	750N	14.2 to 1	14.2 to 1	—	—
V8-400	J13Y	.035	.019	28½–32½	J	5°	F	—	700N	14.2 to 1	14.2 to 1	—	—
V8-440 Chrysler	J11Y	.035	.019	28½–32½	J	10°㉗	F	—	750N㉘	14.2 to 1	14.2 to 1	—	—
V8-440 Imperial	J11Y	.035	—	—	J	10°	F	—	750N㉘	14.2 to 1	14.2 to 1	—	—
1973													
V8-400㉑	J13Y	.035	—	—	J	10°	F	—	700	—	14.2 to 1	—	—
V8-400④	J11Y	.035	—	—	J	7½°	F	—	750	—	14.2 to 1	—	—
V8-440	J11Y	.035	—	—	J	10°	F	—	700	—	14.2 to 1	—	—
1974													
V8-400㉑	J13Y	.035	—	—	J	⑨	F	—	750	—	14.3	—	—
V8-400④㉔	J13Y	.035	—	—	J	5°	F	—	750	—	14.3	—	—
V8-400④㉖	J13Y	.035	—	—	J	5°	F	—	750	—	14.1	—	—
V8-440㉔	J11Y	.035	—	—	J	10°	F	—	750	—	14.3	—	—
V8-440㉖	J11Y	.035	—	—	J	5°	F	—	750	—	14.1	—	—
1975													
V8-318⑤	N13Y	.035	—	—	H	㊱	B	—	750N	—	—	.3⑲	㉟
V8-318⑧	N13Y	.035	—	—	H	2°⑮	B	—	900N	—	—	—	.5㉚
V8-360	N12Y	.035	—	—	H	6°	B	—	750N	—	—	—	㉝
V8-400㉑	J13Y	.035	—	—	J	10°	F	—	750N	—	—	—	.3⑲
V8-400④	J13Y	.035	—	—	J	8°	F	—	750N	—	—	—	㉜
V8-400㉒	RJ87P	.035	—	—	J	6°	F	—	850N	—	—	—	.5㉚
V8-440	RJ87P	.040	—	—	J	6°	D	—	750N	—	—	—	㉞

Chrysler/Dodge/Imperial/Plymouth

TUNEUP SPECIFICATIONS/continued

The following specifications are published from the latest information available. This data should be used only in the absence of a decal affixed in the engine compartment.

★When using a timing light, disconnect vacuum hose or tube at distributor and plug opening in hose or tube so idle speed will not be affected.

●When checking compression, lowest cylinder must be within 80 percent of highest.

▲Before removing wires from distributor cap, determine location of the No. 1 wire in cap, as distributor position may have been altered from that shown at the end of this chart.

Year	Spark Plug		Distributor		Ignition Timing ★			Carb. Adjustments					
	Type ⑦	Gap Inch	Point Gap Inch	Dwell Angle Deg.	Firing Order Fig. ▲	Timing BTDC ①	Mark Fig.	Hot Idle Speed		Air Fuel Ratio		Idle "CO" % ③	
								Std. Trans.	Auto. Trans. ②	Std. Trans.	Auto. Trans.	Std. Trans.	Auto. Trans.

CHRYSLER & IMPERIAL—Continued
1976
V8-318⑤	RN12Y	.035	—	—	H	㊱	B	—	750	—	—	—	㊲
V8-318⑧	RN12Y	.035	—	—	H	2°⑮	B	—	900	—	—	—	.5⑳
V8-360㉑	RN12Y	.035	—	—	H	6°	B	—	700	—	—	—	.3⑲
V8-360④	RN12Y	.035	—	—	H	6°	B	—	750	—	—	—	2.0⑲
V8-400㉑	RJ13Y	.035	—	—	J	10°	F	—	700	—	—	—	.3⑲
V8-400④㉔	㊳	.035	—	—	J	6°	F	—	850	—	—	—	.5⑳
V8-400④㉕	RJ13Y	.035	—	—	J	8°	F	—	750	—	—	—	.5⑲
V8-440	RJ13Y	.035	—	—	J	8°	D	—	750	—	—	—	.3⑲

DODGE
1969
6-170 Std. Tr.	N14Y	.035	.020	42–47	G	5° ATC	E	750⑭	—	14.2 to 1	—	—	—
6-170 Auto. Tr.	N14Y	.035	.020	42–47	G	TDC	E	—	750N⑭	—	14.2 to 1	—	—
6-225	N14Y	.035	.020	42–47	G	TDC	E	650⑭	650N⑭	14.2 to 1	14.2 to 1	—	—
V8-273	N14Y	.035	.017	30–35	H	2½° ATC	F	700⑭	650N⑭	14.2 to 1	14.2 to 1	—	—
V8-318	N14Y	.035	.017	30–35	H	TDC	F	700⑭	650N⑭	14.2 to 1	14.2 to 1	—	—
V8-340 Std. Tr.	N9Y	.035	.017	⑰	H	TDC	F	750⑭	—	14.2 to 1	—	—	—
V8-340 Auto. Tr.	N9Y	.035	.017	30–35	H	5°	F	—	700N⑭	—	14.2 to 1	—	—
V8-383 Std. Tr.㉑	J14Y	.035	.017	30–35	J	TDC	F	700⑭	—	14.2 to 1	—	—	—
V8-383 Auto. Tr.㉑	J14Y	.035	.017	30–35	J	7½°	F	—	600N⑭	—	14.2 to 1	—	—
V8-383 Std. Tr.④	J11Y	.035	.017	30–35	J	TDC	F	700	—	14.2 to 1	—	—	—
V8-383 Auto. Tr.④	J11Y	.035	.017	30–35	J	5°	F	—	650N⑭	—	14.2 to 1	—	—
V8-383 Std. Tr.㉓	J11Y	.035	.017	⑰	J	TDC	F	700	—	14.2 to 1	—	—	—
V8-383 Auto. Tr.㉓	J11Y	.035	.017	⑰	J	5°	F	—	650N⑭	—	14.2 to 1	—	—
V8-440, 350 H.P.	J13Y	.035	.017	30–35	J	7½°	F	—	600N⑭	14.2 to 1	14.2 to 1	—	—
V8-440 Std. Tr.㉒	J11Y	.035	.017	⑰	J	TDC	F	700	—	14.2 to 1	—	—	—
V8-440 Auto. Tr.㉒	J11Y	.035	.017	30–35	J	5°	F	—	650N⑭	—	14.2 to 1	—	—
V8-426 Hemi.	N10Y	.035	.017	⑰	J	TDC	F	750	750N⑭	14.2 to 1	14.2 to 1	—	—
V8-440, 390H.P.	J11Y	.035	.017	⑰	J	5°	F	900	900	14.2 to 1	14.2 to 1	—	—

Chrysler/Dodge/Imperial/Plymouth

TUNEUP SPECIFICATIONS/continued

The following specifications are published from the latest information available. This data should be used only in the absence of a decal affixed in the engine compartment.

★ When using a timing light, disconnet vacuum hose or tube at distribtor and plug opening in hose or tube so idle speed will not be affected.
● When checking compression, lowest cylinder must be within 80 percent of highest.
▲ Before removing wires from distributor cap, determine location of the No. 1 wire in cap, as distributor position may have been altered from that shown at the end of this chart.

Year	Spark Plug		Distributor		Ignition Timing ★			Carb. Adjustments					
	Type ⑦	Gap Inch	Point Gap Inch	Dwell Angle Deg.	Firing Order Fig. ▲	Timing BTDC ①	Mark Fig.	Hot Idle Speed		Air Fuel Ratio		Idle "CO" % ③	
								Std. Trans.	Auto. Trans. ②	Std. Trans.	Auto. Trans.	Std. Trans.	Auto. Trans.
DODGE—Continued													
1970													
6-198 Std. Tr.	N14Y	.035	.020	41–46	G	2½°	C	750⑥	—	14.2 to 1	—	—	—
6-198 Auto. Tr.	N14Y	.035	.020	41–46	G	TDC	C	—	750⑥	—	14.2 to 1	—	—
6-225	N14Y	.035	.020	41–46	G	TDC	C	700⑥	650⑥	14.2 to 1	14.2 to 1	—	—
V8-318	N14Y	.035	.017	30–34	H	TDC	E	750⑥	700⑥	14.2 to 1	14.2 to 1	—	—
V8-340 Std. Tr.	N9Y	.035	.017	⑰	H	5°	E	950	—	14.2 to 1	—	—	—
V8-340 Auto. Tr.	N9Y	.035	.017	30–34	H	5°	E	—	900	—	14.2 to 1	—	—
V8-383 Std. Tr.㉑	J14Y	.035	.017	28–32	J	TDC	F	750	—	14.2 to 1	—	—	—
V8-383 Auto. Tr.㉑	J14Y	.035	.017	28–32	J	2½°	F	—	650	—	14.2 to 1	—	—
V8-383 Std. Tr.④	J11Y	.035	.017	28–32	J	TDC	F	750	—	14.2 to 1	—	—	—
V8-383 Auto. Tr.④	J11Y	.035	.017	28–32	J	2½°	F	—	750	—	14.2 to 1	—	—
V8-440, 350 H.P.	J13Y	.035	.017	28–32	J	5°	F	—	600	14.2 to 1	14.2 to 1	—	—
V8-440 Std. Tr.㉒	J11Y	.035	.017	28–32	J	TDC	F	900	—	14.2 to 1	—	—	—
V8-440 Auto. Tr.㉒	J11Y	.035	.017	28–32	J	2½°	F	—	800	—	14.2 to 1	—	—
V8-440, 390 H.P.	J11Y	.035	.017	⑰	J	5°	F	900	900	14.2 to 1	14.2 to 1	—	—
V8-426 Std. Tr.	N10Y	.035	.017	⑰	J	TDC	F	900	—	14.2 to 1	—	—	—
V8-426 Auto. Tr.	N10Y	.035	.017	⑰	J	5°	F	—	900	—	14.2 to 1	—	—
1971													
6-198	N14Y	.035	.020	41–46	G	2½°	C	800	800	14.2 to 1	14.2 to 1	—	—
6-225㉔	N14Y	.035	.020	41–46	G	TDC	C	750	750	14.2 to 1	14.2 to 1	—	—
6-225㉕	N14Y	.035	.020	41–46	G	2½°	C	750	750	14.2 to 1	14.2 to 1	—	—
V8-318	N14Y	.035	.017	30–34	H	TDC	E	750	700	14.2 to 1	14.2 to 1	—	—
1971													
V8-340 Std. Tr.④	N9Y	.035	.017	⑰	H	5°	E	900	—	14.2 to 1	—	—	—
V8-340 Auto. Tr.④	N9Y	.035	.017	30–34	H	5°	E	—	900	—	14.2 to 1	—	—
V8-340 Std. Tr.㉖	N9Y	.035	.017	⑰	H	2½°	E	1000	—	14.2 to 1	—	—	—
V8-340 Auto. Tr.㉖	N9Y	.035	.017	30–34	H	2½°	E	—	950	—	14.2 to 1	—	—
V8-340③	N9Y	.035	—	—	H	5°	E	900	—	14.2 to 1	14.2 to 1	—	—
V8-360	N13Y	.035	.017	30–34	H	2½°	E	750	700	14.2 to 1	14.2 to 1	—	—
V8-383 Std. Tr.㉑	J14Y	.035	.017	30–34	J	TDC	F	750	—	14.2 to 1	—	—	—
V8-383 Auto. Tr.㉑	J14Y	.035	.017	30–34	J	2½°	F	—	700	—	14.2 to 1	—	—
V8-383 Std. Tr.④	J11Y	.035	.017	30–34	J	TDC	F	750	—	14.2 to 1	—	—	—
V8-383 Auto. Tr.④	J11Y	.035	.017	30–34	J	2½°	F	—	700	—	14.2 to 1	—	—
V8-426 Std. Tr.	N10Y	.035	.017	⑰	J	TDC	F	900	—	14.2 to 1	—	—	—
V8-426 Auto. Tr.	N10Y	.035	.017	⑰	J	5°	F	—	900	—	14.2 to 1	—	—
V8-440	J13Y	.035	.017	28½–32½	J	5°	F	—	900	14.2 to 1	14.2 to 1	—	—
V8-440 Std. Tr.㉒	J11Y	.035	.017	28½–32½	J	TDC	F	900	—	14.2 to 1	—	—	—
V8-440 Auto. Tr.㉒	J11Y	.035	.017	28½–32½	J	2½°	F	—	900	—	14.2 to 1	—	—
V8-440㉖	J11Y	.035	.017	⑰	J	5°	F	900	900	14.2 to 1	—	—	—

Chrysler/Dodge/Imperial/Plymouth

TUNEUP SPECIFICATIONS/continued

The following specifications are published from the latest information available. This data should be used only in the absence of a decal affixed in the engine compartment.

★ When using a timing light, disconnect vacuum hose or tube at distributor and plug opening in hose or tube so idle speed will not be affected.
● When checking compression, lowest cylinder must be within 80 percent of highest.
▲ Before removing wires from distributor cap, determine location of the No. 1 wire in cap, as distributor position may have been altered from that shown at the end of this chart.

Year	Spark Plug		Distributor		Ignition Timing ★			Carb. Adjustments					
	Type ⑦	Gap Inch	Point Gap Inch	Dwell Angle Deg.	Firing Order Fig. ▲	Timing BTDC ①	Mark Fig.	Hot Idle Speed		Air Fuel Ratio		Idle "CO" % ③	
								Std. Trans.	Auto. Trans. ②	Std. Trans.	Auto. Trans.	Std. Trans.	Auto. Trans.

DODGE—Continued

1972

6-198	N14Y	.035	.020	41–46	G	2½°	C	800㉘	800N㉘	14.2 to 1	14.2 to 1	—	—
6-225	N14Y	.035	.020	41–46	G	TDC	C	750㉘	750N㉘	14.2 to 1	14.2 to 1	—	—
V8-318	N13Y	.035	.017	30–34	H	TDC	E	750	750N	14.2 to 1	14.2 to 1	—	—
V8-340	N9Y	.035	—	—	H	2½°	E	900㉙	750N	14.2 to 1	14.2 to 1	—	—
V8-360	N13Y	.035	.017	30–34	H	TDC	E	—	700N	14.2 to 1	—	—	—
V8-400㉑	J13Y	.035	.019	28½–32½	J	5°	F	—	750N	—	14.2 to 1	—	—
V8-400 Std. Tr. ④	J11Y	.035	—	—	J	2½°	F	900㉚	—	14.2 to 1	—	—	—
V8-400 Auto. Tr. ④	J11Y	.035	—	—	J	10°㉗	F	—	750N	—	14.2 to 1	—	—
V8-440	J11Y	.035	.019	28½–32½	J	10°㉗	F	—	750N㉘	14.2 to 1	14.2 to 1	—	—
V8-440 Std. Tr. ㉒	J11Y	.035	—	—	J	2½°	F	900㉚	—	14.2 to 1	—	—	—
V8-440 Auto. Tr. ㉒	J11Y	.035	—	—	J	10°㉗	F	—	900N	—	14.2 to 1	—	—
V8-440 ㉖	J11Y	.035	—	—	J	2½°	F	—	900N	14.2 to 1	—	—	—

1973

6-198	N14Y	.035	—	—	G	TDC	C	800	750N	14.2 to 1	14.2 to 1	—	—
6-225 Std. Trans.	N14Y	.035	—	—	G	2½°	C	750	—	14.2 to 1	—	—	—
6-225 Auto. Trans.	N14Y	.035	—	—	G	TDC	C	—	750N	—	14.2 to 1	—	—
8-318	N13Y	.035	—	—	H	TDC	E	750	750N	14.2 to 1	14.2 to 1	—	—
8-340 Std. Trans.	N12Y	.035	—	—	H	5°	E	900	—	14.2 to 1	—	—	—
8-340 Auto. Trans.	N12Y	.035	—	—	H	2½°⑱	E	—	750N	—	14.2 to 1	—	—
8-360	N13Y	.035	—	—	H	⑩	E	750	750N	14.2 to 1	14.2 to 1	—	—
8-400 2 Bar. Carb.	J13Y	.035	—	—	J	10°	F	700	700N	14.2 to 1	14.2 to 1	—	—
8-400 4 Bar. Carb. ㉛	J11Y	.035	—	—	J	10°	F	900	—	14.2 to 1	—	—	—
8-400 4 Bar. Carb. ⑫	J11Y	.035	—	—	J	7½°	F	—	750N	—	14.2 to 1	—	—
8-440 Std. Trans.	J11Y	.035	—	—	J	10°	F	800	—	14.2 to 1	—	—	—
8-440 Auto. Trans.	J11Y	.035	—	—	J	10°	F	—	700N	—	14.2 to 1	—	—

1974

6-198	N14Y	.035	—	—	G	2½°	C	800	750	14.3 to 1	14.3 to 1	—	—
6-225	N14Y	.035	—	—	G	TDC	C	800	750	14.3 to 1	14.3 to 1	—	—
V8-318	N13Y	.035	—	—	H	TDC	E	750	750	14.3 to 1	14.3 to 1	—	—
V8-360	N12Y	.035	—	—	H	5°⑪	E	850	850	14.3 to 1	14.3 to 1	—	—
V8-400 Auto. Trans. ㉑	J13Y	.035	—	—	J	7½°⑨	F	—	750	—	14.3 to 1	—	—
V8-400 Auto. Trans. ④	J13Y	.035	—	—	J	5°	F	—	750	—	14.3 to 1	—	—
V8-400 Std. Trans. ㉒	J11Y	.035	—	—	J	5°	F	900	—	14.3 to 1	—	—	—
V8-400 Auto. Trans. ⑯	J11Y	.035	—	—	J	5°⑬	F	—	850	—	14.3 to 1	—	—
V8-440	J11Y	.035	—	—	J	㉟	F	—	850	—	14.3 to 1	—	—

599

Chrysler/Dodge/Imperial/Plymouth

TUNEUP SPECIFICATIONS/continued

The following specifications are published from the latest information available. This data should be used only in the absence of a decal affixed in the engine compartment.

★ When using a timing light, disconnect vacuum hose or tube at distributor and plug opening in hose or tube so idle speed will not be affected.

● When checking compression, lowest cylinder must be within 80 percent of highest.

▲ Before removing wires from distributor cap, determine location of the No. 1 wire in cap, as distributor position may have been altered from that shown at the end of this chart.

Year	Spark Plug		Distributor		Ignition Timing ★			Carb. Adjustments					
	Type ⑦	Gap Inch	Point Gap Inch	Dwell Angle Deg.	Firing Order Fig. ▲	Timing BTDC ①	Mark Fig.	Hot Idle Speed		Air Fuel Ratio		Idle "CO" % ③	
								Std. Trans.	Auto. Trans. ②	Std. Trans.	Auto. Trans.	Std. Trans.	Auto. Trans.
DODGE—Continued													
1975													
6-225	BL13Y	.035	—	—	G	TDC	A	800	750N	—	—	.3⑲	㉞
V8-318⑤	N13Y	.035	—	—	H	㊱	B	750	750N	—	—	.3⑲	㉝
V8-318	N13Y	.035	—	—	H	2°⑮	B	—	900N	—	—	—	.5⑳
V8-360	N12Y	.035	—	—	H	6°	B	—	750N	—	—	—	㉝
V8-360㉒	N12Y	.035	—	—	H	2°	B	—	850N	—	—	—	.5⑳
V8-400㉑	J13Y	.035	—	—	J	10°	F	—	750N	—	—	—	.3⑲
V8-400④	J13Y	.035	—	—	J	8°	F	—	750N	—	—	—	㉜
V8-400㉒	RJ87P	.035	—	—	J	6°	F	—	850N	—	—	—	.5⑳
V8-440	RJ87P	.040	—	—	J	6°	D	—	750N	—	—	—	㉞
V8-440㉒	J11Y	.035	—	—	J	10°	D	—	750N	—	—	—	㉝
1976													
6-225 Std. Tr.	RBL13Y	.035	—	—	G	㊴	A	750㊵	—	—	—	㊲	—
6-225 Auto. Tr.	RBL13Y	.035	—	—	G	2°	A	—	750	—	—	—	㊲
V8-318⑤	RN12Y	.035	—	—	H	㊱	B	750	750	—	—	—	㊲
V8-318⑥	RN12Y	.035	—	—	H	2°⑮	B	—	900	—	—	.3⑲	㊲
V8-360㉑	RN12Y	.035	—	—	H	6°	B	—	700	—	—	—	.5⑳
V8-360④	RN12Y	.035	—	—	H	6°	B	—	750	—	—	—	.3⑲
V8-360㉒	RN12Y	.035	—	—	H	2°	B	—	850	—	—	—	2.0⑲
V8-400㉑	RJ13Y	.035	—	—	J	10°	F	—	700	—	—	—	.5⑳
V8-400④㉔	㊳	.035	—	—	J	6°	F	—	850	—	—	—	.3⑲
V8-400④㉕	RJ13Y	.035	—	—	J	8°	F	—	750	—	—	—	.5⑲
V8-440	RJ13Y	.035	—	—	J	8°	D	—	750	—	—	—	.3⑲
V8-440㉒	RJ11Y	.035	—	—	J	㊵	D	—	750	—	—	—	㉜
PLYMOUTH													
1969													
6-170 Std. Tr.	N14Y	.035	.020	42–47	G	5° ATC	E	750⑭	—	14.2 to 1	—	—	—
6-170 Auto. Tr.	N14Y	.035	.020	42–47	G	2½° ATC	E	—	750N⑭	—	14.2 to 1	—	—
6-225	N14Y	.035	.020	42–47	G	TDC	E	650⑭	650N⑭	14.2 to 1	14.2 to 1	—	—
V8-273	N14Y	.035	.017	30–35	H	2½° ATC	F	700⑭	650N⑭	14.2 to 1	14.2 to 1	—	—
V8-318	N14Y	.035	.017	30–35	H	TDC	F	700⑭	650N⑭	14.2 to 1	14.2 to 1	—	—
V8-340 Std. Tr.	N9Y	.035	.017	⑰	H	TDC	F	750⑭	—	14.2 to 1	—	—	—
V8-340 Auto. Tr.	N9Y	.035	.017	30–35	H	5°	F	—	700N⑭	—	14.2 to 1	—	—
V8-383 Std. Tr.㉑	J14Y	.035	.017	30–35	J	TDC	F	700⑭	—	14.2 to 1	—	—	—
V8-383 Auto. Tr.㉑	J14Y	.035	.017	30–35	J	7½°	F	—	600N⑭	—	14.2 to 1	—	—
V8-383 Std. Tr.④	J11Y	.035	.017	30–35	J	TDC	F	700	—	14.2 to 1	—	—	—
V8-383 Auto. Tr.④	J11Y	.035	.017	30–35	J	5°	F	—	650N⑭	—	14.2 to 1	—	—
V8-383 Std. Tr.㉓	J11Y	.035	.017	⑰	J	TDC	F	700	—	14.2 to 1	—	—	—
V8-383 Auto. Tr.㉓	J11Y	.035	.017	⑰	J	5°	F	—	650N⑭	—	14.2 to 1	—	—
V8-440, 350 H.P.	J13Y	.035	.017	30–35	J	7½°	F	—	600N⑭	14.2 to 1	14.2 to 1	—	—
V8-440 Std. Tr.㉒	J11Y	.035	.017	⑰	J	TDC	F	700	—	14.2 to 1	—	—	—
V8-440 Auto. Tr.㉒	J11Y	.035	.017	30–35	J	5°	F	—	650N⑭	—	14.2 to 1	—	—
V8-440, 390 H.P.	J11Y	.035	.017	⑰	J	5°	F	900	900⑭	14.2 to 1	14.2 to 1	—	—
V8-426 Hemi	N10Y	.035	.017	⑰	J	TDC	F	750	750⑭	14.2 to 1	—	—	—

Chrysler/Dodge/Imperial/Plymouth

TUNEUP SPECIFICATIONS/continued

The following specifications are published from the latest information available. This data should be used only in the absence of a decal affixed in the engine compartment.

★ When using a timing light, disconnect vacuum hose or tube at distributor and plug opening in hose or tube so idle speed will not be affected.

● When checking compression, lowest cylinder must be within 80 percent of highest.

▲ Before removing wires from distributor cap, determine location of the No. 1 wire in cap, as distributor position may have been altered from that shown at the end of this chart.

Year	Spark Plug		Distributor		Ignition Timing ★			Carb. Adjustments					
	Type ⑦	Gap Inch	Point Gap Inch	Dwell Angle Deg.	Firing Order Fig. ▲	Timing BTDC ①	Mark Fig.	Hot Idle Speed		Air Fuel Ratio		Idle "CO" % ③	
								Std. Trans.	Auto. Trans. ②	Std. Trans.	Auto. Trans.	Std. Trans.	Auto. Trans.
PLYMOUTH—Continued													
1970													
6-198 Std. Tr.	N14Y	.035	.020	41–46	G	2½°	C	750⑥	—	14.2 to 1	—	—	—
6-198 Auto. Tr.	N14Y	.035	.020	41–46	G	TDC	C	—	750⑥	—	14.2 to 1	—	—
6-225	N14Y	.035	.020	41–46	G	TDC	C	700⑥	650⑥	14.2 to 1	14.2 to 1	—	—
V8-318	N14Y	.035	.017	30–34	H	TDC	E	750⑥	700⑥	14.2 to 1	14.2 to 1	—	—
V8-340 Std. Tr.	N9Y	.035	.017	⑰	H	5°	E	950	—	14.2 to 1	—	—	—
V8-340 Auto. Tr.	N9Y	.035	.017	30–34	H	5°	E	—	900	—	14.2 to 1	—	—
V8-383 Std. Tr.㉑	J14Y	.035	.017	28–32	J	TDC	F	750	—	14.2 to 1	—	—	—
V8-383 Auto. Tr.㉑	J14Y	.035	.017	28–32	J	2½°	F	—	650	—	14.2 to 1	—	—
V8-383 Std. Tr.④	J11Y	.035	.017	28–32	J	TDC	F	750	—	14.2 to 1	—	—	—
V8-383 Auto. Tr.④	J11Y	.035	.017	28–32	J	2½°	F	—	750	—	14.2 to 1	—	—
V8-440, 350 H.P.	J13Y	.035	.017	28–32	J	5°	F	—	600	14.2 to 1	14.2 to 1	—	—
V8-440 Std. Tr.㉒	J11Y	.035	.017	28–32	J	TDC	F	900	—	14.2 to 1	—	—	—
V8-440 Auto. Tr.㉒	J11Y	.035	.017	28–32	J	2½°	F	—	800	—	14.2 to 1	—	—
V8-440, 390 H.P.	J11Y	.035	.017	⑰	J	5°	F	900	900	14.2 to 1	14.2 to 1	—	—
V8-426 Std. Tr.	N10Y	.035	.017	⑰	J	TDC	F	900	—	14.2 to 1	—	—	—
V8-426 Auto. Tr.	N10Y	.035	.017	⑰	J	5°	F	—	900	—	14.2 to 1	—	—
1971													
6-198	N14Y	.035	.020	41–46	G	2½°	C	800	800	14.2 to 1	14.2 to 1	—	—
6-225㉔	N14Y	.035	.020	41–46	G	TDC	C	750	750	14.2 to 1	14.2 to 1	—	—
6-225㉕	N14Y	.035	.020	41–46	G	2½°	C	750	750	14.2 to 1	14.2 to 1	—	—
V8-318	N14Y	.035	.017	30–34	H	TDC	E	750	700	14.2 to 1	14.2 to 1	—	—
V8-340 Std. Tr.④	N9Y	.035	.017	⑰	H	5°	E	900	—	14.2 to 1	—	—	—
V8-340 Auto. Tr.④	N9Y	.035	.017	30–34	H	5°	E	—	900	—	14.2 to 1	—	—
V8-340 Std. Tr.㉘	N9Y	.035	.017	⑰	H	2½°	E	1000	—	14.2 to 1	—	—	—
V8-340 Auto. Tr.㉖	N9Y	.035	.017	30–34	H	2½°	E	—	950	—	14.2 to 1	—	—
V8-340③	N9Y	.035	—	—	H	5°	E	900	—	14.2 to 1	14.2 to 1	—	—
V8-360	N13Y	.035	.017	30–34	H	2½°	E	750	700	14.2 to 1	14.2 to 1	—	—
V8-383 Std. Tr.㉑	J14Y	.035	.017	30–34	J	TDC	F	750	—	14.2 to 1	—	—	—
V8-383 Auto. Tr.㉑	J14Y	.035	.017	30–34	J	2½°	F	—	700	—	14.2 to 1	—	—
V8-383 Std. Tr.④	J11Y	.035	.017	30–34	J	TDC	F	750	—	14.2 to 1	—	—	—
V8-383 Auto. Tr.④	J11Y	.035	.017	30–34	J	2½°	F	—	700	—	14.2 to 1	—	—
V8-426 Std. Tr.	N10Y	.035	.017	⑰	J	TDC	F	900	—	14.2 to 1	—	—	—
V8-426 Auto. Tr.	N10Y	.035	.017	⑰	J	2½°	F	—	900	—	14.2 to 1	—	—
V8-440	J13Y	.035	.017	28½–32½	J	5°	F	—	900	14.2 to 1	14.2 to 1	—	—
V8-440 Std. Tr.㉒	J11Y	.035	.017	28½–32½	J	TDC	F	900	—	14.2 to 1	—	—	—
V8-440 Auto. Tr.㉒	J11Y	.035	.017	28½–32½	J	2½°	F	—	900	—	14.2 to 1	—	—
V8-440㉖	J11Y	.035	.017	⑰	J	5°	F	900	900	14.2 to 1	—	—	—

Chrysler/Dodge/Imperial/Plymouth

TUNEUP SPECIFICATIONS/continued

The following specifications are published from the latest information available. This data should be used only in the absence of a decal affixed in the engine compartment.

★ When using a timing light, disconnect vacuum hose or tube at distributor and plug opening in tube or hose so idle speed will not be affected.
● When checking compression, lowest cylinder must be within 80 percent of highest.
▲ Before removing wires from distributor cap, determide location of the No. 1 wire in cap, as distributor position may have been altered from that shown at the end of this chart.

Year	Spark Plug		Distributor		Ignition Timing★			Carb. Adjustments					
								Hot Idle Speed		Air Fuel Ratio		Idle "CO" ★ ③	
	Type ⑦	Gap Inch	Point Gap Inch	Dwell Angle Deg.	Firing Order Fig. ▲	Timing BTDC ①	Mark Fib.	Std. Trans.	Auto. Trans.②	Std. Trans.	Auto. Trans.	Std. Trans.	Auto. Trans.

PLYMOUTH—Continued

1972

6-198	N14Y	.035	.020	41–46	G	2½°	C	800㉘	800N㉘	14.2 to 1	14.2 to 1	—	—
6-225	N14Y	.035	.020	41–46	G	TDC	C	750㉘	750N㉘	14.2 to 1	14.2 to 1	—	—
V8-318	N13Y	.035	.017	30–34	H	TDC	E	750	750N㉘	14.2 to 1	14.2 to 1	—	—
V8-340	N9Y	.035	—	—	H	2½°	E	900㉙	750N	14.2 to 1	14.2 to 1	—	—
V8-360	N13Y	.035	.017	30–34	H	TDC	E	—	750N	14.2 to 1	14.2 to 1	—	—
V8-400㉑	J13Y	.035	.019	28½–32½	J	5°	F	—	700N	14.2 to 1	14.2 to 1	—	—
V8-400 Std. Tr.④	J11Y	.035	—	—	J	2½°	F	900㉚	—	14.2 to 1	—	—	—
V8-400 Auto. Tr.④	J11Y	.035	—	—	J	10°㉗	F	—	750N	—	14.2 to 1	—	—
V8-440	J11Y	.035	.019	28½–32½	J	10°㉗	F	—	750N㉘	14.2 to 1	14.2 to 1	—	—
V8-440 Std. Tr.㉒	J11Y	.035	—	—	J	2½°	F	900㉚	—	14.2 to 1	—	—	—
V8-440 Auto. Tr.㉒	J11Y	.035	—	—	J	10°㉗	F	—	900N	—	14.2 to 1	—	—
V8-440㉖	J11Y	.035	—	—	J	2½°	F	—	900N	14.2 to 1	—	—	—

1973

6-198	N14Y	.035	—	—	G	TDC	C	800	750N	14.2 to 1	14.2 to 1	—	—
6-225 Std. Trans.	N14Y	.035	—	—	G	2½°	C	750	—	14.2 to 1	—	—	—
6-225 Auto. Trans.	N14Y	.035	—	—	G	TDC	C	—	750N	—	14.2 to 1	—	—
8-318	N13Y	.035	—	—	H	TDC	E	750	750N	14.2 to 1	14.2 to 1	—	—
8-340 Std. Trans.	N12Y	.035	—	—	H	5°	E	900	—	14.2 to 1	—	—	—
8-340 Auto. Trans.	N12Y	.035	—	—	H	2½°⑱	E	—	750N	—	14.2 to 1	—	—
8-360	N13Y	.035	—	—	H	⑩	E	750	750N	14.2 to 1	14.2 to 1	—	—
8-400 2 Bar. Carb.	J13Y	.035	—	—	J	10°	F	700	700N	14.2 to 1	14.2 to 1	—	—
8-400 4 Bar. Carb.㉛	J11Y	.035	—	—	J	10°	F	900	—	14.2 to 1	—	—	—
8-400 4 Bar. Carb.⑫	J11Y	.035	—	—	J	7½°	F	—	750N	—	14.2 to 1	—	—
8-440 Std. Trans.	J11Y	.035	—	—	J	10°	F	800	—	14.2 to 1	—	—	—
8-440 Auto. Trans.	J11Y	.035	—	—	J	10°	F	—	700N	—	14.2 to 1	—	—

1974

6-198	N14Y	.035	—	—	G	2½°	C	800	750	14.3 to 1	14.3 to 1	—	—
6-225	N14Y	.035	—	—	G	TDC	C	800	750	14.3 to 1	14.3 to 1	—	—
V8-318	N13Y	.035	—	—	H	TDC	E	750	750	14.3 to 1	14.3 to 1	—	—
V8-360	N12Y	.035	—	—	H	5°⑪	E	850	850	14.3 to 1	14.3 to 1	—	—
V8-400 Auto. Trans.㉑	J13Y	.035	—	—	J	⑨	F	—	750	—	14.3 to 1	—	—
V8-400 Auto. Trans.④	J13Y	.035	—	—	J	5°	F	—	750	—	14.3 to 1	—	—
V8-400 Std. Trans.㉒	J11Y	.035	—	—	J	5°	F	900	—	14.3 to 1	—	—	—
V8-400 Auto. Trans.⑯	J11Y	.035	—	—	J	5°⑬	F	—	850	—	14.3 to 1	—	—
V8-440	J11Y	.035	—	—	J	㉟	F	—	850	—	14.3 to 1	—	—

Chrysler/Dodge/Imperial/Plymouth

TUNEUP SPECIFICATIONS/continued

The following specifications are published from the latest information available. This data should be used only in the absence of a decal affixed in the engine compartment.

★When using a timing light, disconnect vacuum hose or tube at distributor and plug opening in tube or hose so idle speed will not be affected.

●When checking compression, lowest cylinder must be within 80 percent of highest.

▲Before removing wires from distributor cap, determide location of the No. 1 wire in cap, as distributor position may have been altered from that shown at the end of this chart.

Year	Spark Plug		Distributor		Ignition Timing ★			Carb. Adjustments					
								Hot Idle Speed		Air Fuel Ratio		Idle "CO" ★ ③	
	Type ⑦	Gap Inch	Point Gap Inch	Dwell Angle Deg.	Firing Order Fig. ▲	Timing BTDC ①	Mark Fib.	Std. Trans.	Auto. Trans. ②	Std. Trans.	Auto. Trans.	Std. Trans.	Auto. Trans.

PLYMOUTH—Continued

1975

6-225	BL13Y	.035	—	—	G	TDC	A	800	750N	—	—	.3⑲	㉞
V8-318⑤	N13Y	.035	—	—	H	㊱	B	750	750N	—	—	.3⑲	㉝
V8-318	N13Y	.035	—	—	H	2°⑮	B	—	900N	—	—	—	.5⑳
V8-360	N12Y	.035	—	—	H	6°	B	—	750N	—	—	—	㉝
V8-360㉒	N12Y	.035	—	—	H	2°	B	—	850N	—	—	—	.5⑳
V8-400㉑	J13Y	.035	—	—	J	10°	F	—	750N	—	—	—	.3⑲
V8-400④	J13Y	.035	—	—	J	8°	F	—	750N	—	—	—	㉜
V8-400㉒	RJ87P	.035	—	—	J	6°	F	—	850N	—	—	—	.5⑳
V8-440	RJ87P	.040	—	—	J	6°	D	—	750N	—	—	—	㉞
V8-440㉒	J11Y	.035	—	—	J	10°	D	—	750N	—	—	—	㉝

1976

6-225 Std. Tr.	RBL13Y	.035	—	—	G	㊴	A	750㉚	—	—	—	㊲	—
6-225 Auto. Tr.	RBL13Y	.035	—	—	G	2°	A	—	750	—	—	—	㊲
V8-318⑤	RN12Y	.035	—	—	H	㊱	B	750	750	—	—	.3⑲	㊲
V8-318⑥	RN12Y	.035	—	—	H	2°⑮	B	—	900	—	—	—	.5⑳
V8-360㉑	RN12Y	.035	—	—	H	6°	B	—	700	—	—	—	.3⑲
V8-360④	RN12Y	.035	—	—	H	6°	B	—	750	—	—	—	2.0⑲
V8-360㉒	RN12Y	.035	—	—	H	2°	B	—	850	—	—	—	.5⑳
V8-400㉑	RJ13Y	.035	—	—	J	10°	F	—	700	—	—	—	.3⑲
V8-400④㉔	㊳	.035	—	—	J	6°	F	—	850	—	—	—	.5⑳
V8-400④㉕	RJ13Y	.035	—	—	J	8°	F	—	750	—	—	—	.5⑲
V8-440	RJ13Y	.035	—	—	J	8°	D	—	750	—	—	—	.3⑲
V8-440㉒	RJ11Y	.035	—	—	J	㊵	D	—	750	—	—	—	㉜

Chrysler/Dodge/Imperial/Plymouth

TUNEUP NOTES

①—BTDC: Before top dead center.
②—D: Drive. N: Neutral.
③—On 1974–76 models before adjusting idle "CO", disconnect A.I.R. pump outlet hose, if equipped.
④—Four barrel carburetor.
⑤—With catalytic converter.
⑥—Set idle speed with air conditioning compressor operating.
⑦—Champion.
⑧—With air pump.
⑨—Early production—Exc. sta. wag., 7½° BTDC; sta. wag., 5° BTDC. Late production—Exc. sta. wag., 10° BTDC; sta. wag., 7½° BTDC.
⑩—Dist. No. 3656780, TDC.
Dist. No. 3755336, 7½°.
Dist. No. 3755337 & 3755365, 5°.
⑪—Calif. V8-360 Hi Perf. Manual Trans. 2½° BTDC.
⑫—Auto. trans.
⑬—Exc. Calif. auto. trans. & Police; Calif. auto. trans. & Police, 2½°.
⑭—Adjust idle speed with headlights on. If air conditioned turn A/C switch to "Full On" position.
⑮—ATDC: after top dead center.
⑯—High performance & Police.
⑰—Each set of points 27–32°; total dwell both sets 37–42°.
⑱—Exc. Calif. late production; Calif. late production, TDC.
⑲—Measured ahead of catalytic converter.
⑳—Measured in tailpipe.
㉑—Two barrel carburetor.
㉒—High performance engine.
㉓—Formula "S" and Super Bee only.
㉔—Exc. California.
㉕—California only.
㉖—Three Carbs.
㉗—California vehicles with electronic ignition 5°.
㉘—California vehicles 700N.
㉙—California vehicles 850.
㉚—California vehicles 800.
㉛—Std. trans.
㉜—Exc. Calif., .3 (see note 19); Calif., .5 (see note 19).
㉝—Except Calif. .3 (see note 19), Calif. .5 (see note 19).
㉞—Except Calif. .3 (see note 19), Calif. 1.5 (see note 20).
㉟—Exc. Calif., 10° BTDC; Calif., 5° BTDC.
㊱—Exc. Calif., 2° BTDC; Calif., TDC.
㊲—Exc. Calif., .3 (see note 19); Calif., 1.0 (see note 19).
㊳—Exc. high performance engine, RJI3Y; high performance engine, RJ87P.
㊴—Exc. Calif., 6° BTDC; Calif., 4° BTDC.
㊵—Exc. Calif., 10° BTDC; Calif., 8° BTDC.

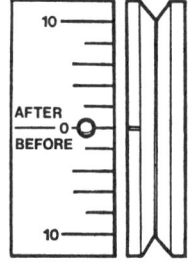

Fig. A

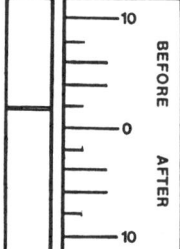

Fig. B

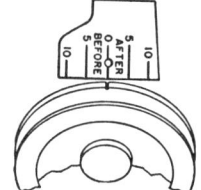

Fig. C

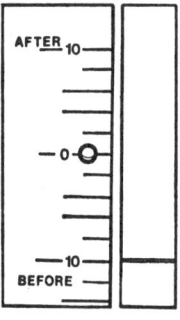

Fig. D

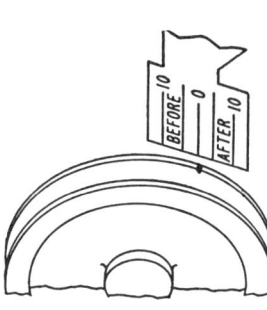

Fig. E

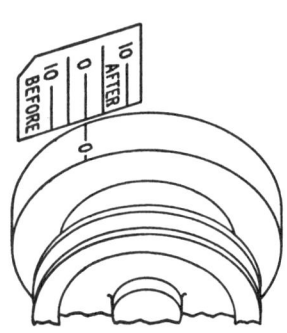

Fig. F

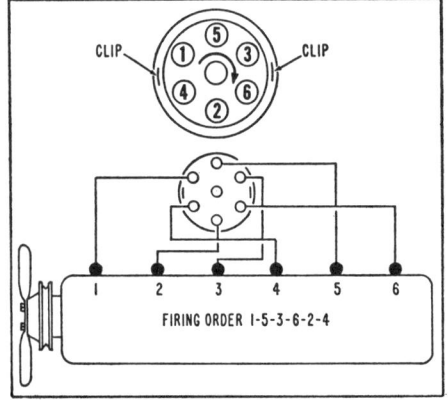

Fig. G

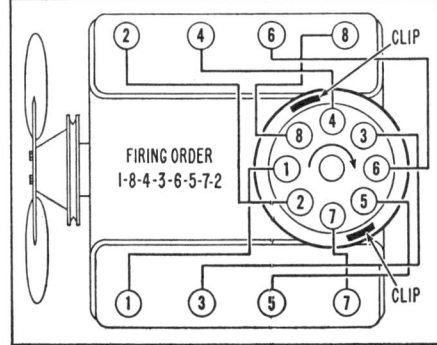

Fig. H

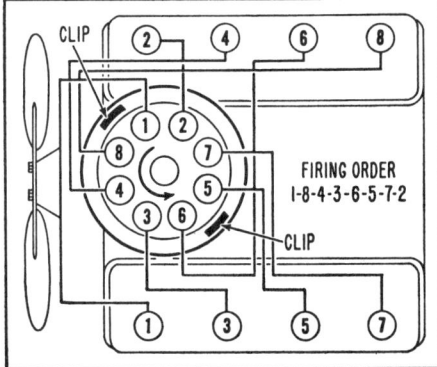

Fig. J

Chrysler/Dodge/Imperial/Plymouth

COOLING SYSTEM & CAPACITY DATA

Year	Model or Engine	Cooling Capacity, Qts.			Radiator Cap Relief Pressure, Lbs.		Thermo. Opening Temp. ①	Fuel Tank Gals.	Engine Oil Refill Qts. ②	Transmission Oil			Rear Axle Oil Pints
		No Heater	With Heater	With A/C	With A/C	No A/C				3 Speed Pints	4 Speed Pints	Auto. Trans. Qts. ⑫	
CHRYSLER													
1969	8-383	—	16⑨	17	16	16	190	24③	4	6	—	9¼	4
	8-440	—	17⑨	18	16	16	190	24③	4	6	—	9¼	4
1970	8-383, 2 B. Carb.	—	14½⑨	15	16	16	195	24⑰	4	5	—	9½	4.4
	8-383, 4 B. Carb.	—	14½⑨	16	16	16	195	24⑰	4	5	—	8	4.4
	8-440	—	15½⑨	17	16	16	195④	24⑰	4	5	—	9½	4.4
1971	8-383, 2 B. Carb.	13½	14½	15	16	16	185	23	4	4¾	—	9½	4.5
	8-383, 4 B. Carb.	13½	14½	15	16	16	185	23	4	—	—	8	4.5
	8-440	14½	15½	17	16	16	185	23	4	—	—	9½	4.5
1972	8-360	14½	15½	15	16	16	185	23	4	—	—	8	4.5
	8-400	13½	14½	14	16	16	185	23	4	—	—	9½	4.5
	8-440	14½	15½	16	16	16	185	23	4	—	—	9½	4.5
1973	8-400, 440	—	16	17	16	16	185	23	4	—	—	9½	4.4
1974	8-400, 440	—	16½	16½	16	16	195	25㉗	4	—	—	9½	4.5
1975-76	V8-318	—	16	18	16	16	195	25½	4	—	—	8½⑥	4½
	V8-360	—	16	16	16	16	195	⑤	4	—	—	9½	4½
	V8-400	—	16½	16½	16	16	195	㉑	4	—	—	9½	4½
	V8-440	—	16	16	16	16	195	26½㉗	4㉚	—	—	9½	4½
IMPERIAL													
1969	All	—	19⑨	19	16	16	190	24	4	—	—	9¼	4
1970	All	—	17½⑨	17½	16	16	195	24	4	—	—	9½	4.4
1971-72	All	16½	17½	17½	16	16	185	23	4	—	—	9½	4.5
1973	All	—	18	18	16	16	185	23	4	—	—	9½	4.4
1974	All	—	17	17	16	16	195	25	4	—	—	9½	4.5
1975	All	—	16	16	16	16	195	26½	4	—	—	9½	4½
DODGE													
1969	Dart 6-170	—	12⑮	—	—	16	200	18	4	6½	—	7¾	2
	Dart 6-225	—	13	15	16	16	190	18	4	6½	—	7¾	2
	Dart 8-273	—	17	19	16	16	190	18	4	6	7	7¾	2
	Dart 318	—	16	18	16	16	190	18	4	6	7	7¾	2⑩
	Dart 8-340	—	16	16	16	16	190	18	4	—	7	7¾	4
	Dart 8-383	—	16	16	16	16	190	18	4	—	7	7¾⑱	4
	Coronet 6-225	—	13	15	16	16	190	19	4	6½	—	7¾	2⑦
	Coro. Charger 8-318	—	16	19	16	16	190	19	4	6	—	7¾	4
	Coro. Charger 8-383	—	16	17	16	16	190	19	4	—	7½	7¾⑱	4
	Coro. Charger 8-440	—	17	18	16	16	190	19	4	—	7½	9¼	4⑬
	Coro. Charger 8-426	—	18	—	16	16	190	19	6	—	7½	8	4⑬
	Polara, Monaco 8-318	—	16	19	16	16	190	24③	4	6	—	7¾	4
	Polara, Monaco 8-383	—	16	17	16	16	190	24③	4	6	—	7¾⑱	4
	Polara, Monaco 8-440	—	17	18	16	16	190	24③	4	—	—	9¼	4⑭
1970	Dart 6 Cyl.	12	13	13	16	16	190	18	4	6½	—	8½	2
	Dart 8-318	15	16	16	16	16	195	18	4	4¾	—	8	4
	Dart 8-340	14	15	15	16	16	190	18	4	4¾	7	8	4
	Challenger 6 Cyl.	—	13	14	16	16	190	18	4	6½	—	8½	2
	Challenger 8-318	—	16	17½	16	16	195	18	4	4¾	7	8	4
	Challenger 8-340	—	15½	15½	16	16	190	18	4	4¾	7	8	4

COOLING SYSTEM & CAPACITY DATA/continued

Year	Model or Engine	Cooling Capacity, Qts.			Radiator Cap Relief Pressure, Lbs.		Thermo. Opening Temp. (1)	Fuel Tank Gals.	Engine Oil Refill Qts. (2)	Transmission Oil			Rear Axle Oil Pints
		No Heater	With Heater	With A/C	With A/C	No A/C				3 Speed Pints	4 Speed Pints	Auto. Trans. Qts. (12)	
DODGE—Continued													
1970	Challenger 8-383	—	14½	15	16	16	190	18	4	4¾	7	8(18)	4
	Challenger 8-440	—	17	17	16	16	190	18	6	—	7	9	5½
	Challenger 8-426	—	17	17	16	16	190	18	6	—	7	8½	5½
	Coro., Charger 6-225	12	13	13	16	16	190	19	4	4¾	—	8½	2
	Coro., Charger 8-318	15	16	16	16	16	195	19	4	4¾	—	8	4
	Coro., Charger 8-383	13½	14½	15	16	16	190	19	4	4¾	7	8(18)	4
	Coro., Charger 8-440	16	17	17	16	16	190	19	6	—	7	8½	5½
	Coro., Charger 8-426	16	17	17	16	16	190	19	6	—	7	8½	5½
	Polara, Monaco 8-318	16	17	17	16	16	195	24(17)	4	4¾	—	8	4
	Polara, Monaco 8-383	13½	14½	14½	16	16	195	24(17)	4	4¾	—	9½	4
	Polara, Monaco 8-440	14½	15½	15½	16	16	195	24(17)	4	—	—	9½	4
1971	Dart 6 Cyl.	12	13	13	16	16	185	17	4	6½	—	8½	2
	Dart 8-318	15	16	16½	16	16	185	17	4	4¾	—	8½	4½
	Dart 8-340	14	15	15	16	16	185	17	4	4¾	7	8	4½
	Challenger 6 Cyl.	12	13	13	16	16	185	18	4	4¾	—	8½	2
	Challenger 8-318	15	16	16½	16	16	185	18	4	4¾	—	8½	2
	Challenger 8-340	14	15	15	16	16	185	18	4	4¾	7½	8	4½
	Challenger 8-383	13½	14½	15	16	16	185	18	4	4¾	7½	8(18)	4½
	Challenger 8-440	16(19)	17(19)	17(20)	16	16	185	18	4	—	7½	9½	5½
	Challenger 8-426	14½	15½	—	16	16	185	18	6	—	7½	8	5½
	Coro., Charger 6-225	12	13	13	16	16	185	21	4	6½	—	8½	4
	Coro., Charger 8-318	15	16	16½	16	16	185	21	4	4¾	—	8½	4
	Coro., Charger 8-383	13½	14½	15	16	16	185	21	4	4¾	7½	8(18)	4
	Coro., Charger 8-440	14½	15½	17	16	16	185	21	4	—	7½	9½	5½
	Coro., Charger 8-426	14½	15½	—	16	16	185	21	6	—	7½	8	5½
	Polara, Monaco 6-225	12	13	13	16	16	185	23	4	4¾	—	8½	4½
	Polara, Monaco 8-318	15	16	16½	16	16	185	23	4	4¾	—	8½	4½
	Polara, Monaco 8-360	14	15	15	16	16	185	23	4	4¾	—	8	4½
	Polara, Monaco 8-383	13½	14½	15	16	16	185	23	4	4¾	—	8(18)	4½
	Polara, Monaco 8-440	14½	15½	17	16	16	185	23	4	—	—	9½	4½
1972	Dart 6 Cyl.	12	13	13	16	16	185	16	4	6½	—	8½	2
	Dart 8-318	15	16	16	16	16	185	16	4	4¾	—	8½	4½
	Dart 8-340	14	15	15	16	16	185	16	4	4¾	7	8	4¼
	Challenger 6 Cyl.	12	13	13	16	16	185	18	4	4¾	—	8½	2
	Challenger 8-318	15	16	16½	16	16	185	18	4	4¾	—	8½	4½
	Challenger 8-340	14	15	14½	16	16	185	18	4	4¾	7½	8	4½
	Coro., Charger 6-225	12	13	13	16	16	185	21	4	6½	—	8½	4½
	Coro., Charger 8-318	15	16	16½	16	16	185	21	4	4¾	—	8½	4½
	Coro., Charger 8-340	14	15	14½	16	16	185	21	4	—	7½	8	4½
	Coro., Charger 8-400	13½	14½	15	16	16	185	21	4	—	7½	8(18)	4½(14)
	Coro., Charger 8-440	14	15	15	16	16	185	21	4(26)	—	7½	9½	5½
	Polara, Monaco 8-318	15	16	16½	16	16	185	23	4	—	—	8½	4½
	Polara, Monaco 8-360	14½	15½	15	16	16	185	23	4	—	—	8	4½
	Polara, Monaco 8-400	13½	14½	14	16	16	185	23	4	—	—	9½	4½
	Polara, Monaco 8-440	14½	15½	16	16	16	185	23	4	—	—	9½	4½

Chrysler/Dodge/Imperial/Plymouth

COOLING SYSTEM & CAPACITY DATA/continued

Year	Model or Engine	Cooling Capacity, Qts.			Radiator Cap Relief Pressure, Lbs.		Thermo. Opening Temp. ①	Fuel Tank Gals.	Engine Oil Refill Qts. ②	Transmission Oil			Rear Axle Oil Pints
		No Heater	With Heater	With A/C	With A/C	No A/C				3 Speed Pints	4 Speed Pints	Auto. Trans. Qts. ⑫	
DODGE—Continued													
1973	Dart 6 Cyl.	12	13	13	16	16	185	16	4	6½	—	8½	2
	Dart 8-318	15	16	18	16	16	185	16	4	4¾	—	8½	2
	Dart 8-340	15	16	16	16	16	185	16	4	4¾	7	8	4½
	Challenger 6 Cyl.	12	13	13	16	16	185	18	4	4¾	—	8½	4½
	Challenger 8-318	15	16	18	16	16	185	18	4	4¾	—	8½	4½
	Challenger 8-340	14	15	16	16	16	185	18	4	4¾	7	8	4½
	Coro, Charger 6-225	12	13	13	16	16	185	21	4	6½	—	8½	2
	Coro, Charger 8-318	15	16	18	16	16	185	21	4	4¾	7½	8½	4½
	Coro, Charger 8-340	14	15	16	16	16	185	21	4	4¾	7½	8	4½
	Coro, Charger 8-400	15	16	17	16	16	185	21	4	4¾	7½	8⑱	4½
	Coro, Charger 8-440	16	17	17	16	16	185	21	4	—	—	9½	4½
	Polara, Monaco 8-318	15	16	19	16	16	185	23	4	—	—	8½	4½
	Polara, Monaco 8-360	15	16	16	16	16	185	23	4	—	—	8½	4½
	Polara, Monaco 8-400	15㉒	16㉓	17㉓	16	16	185	23	4	—	—	9½㉔	4½
	Polara, Monaco 8-440	15㉓	16㉓	17㉓	16	16	185	23	4	—	—	9½	4½
1974	Dart 6 cyl.	—	13	14	16	16	195	16	4	6½	—	8¼	2
	Dart 8-318	—	16	17½	16	16	195	16	4	4¾	7	8¼	4½
	Dart 8-360	—	16	16	16	16	195	16	4	4¾	7	8	4½
	Challenger 8-318	—	16	17½	16	16	195	18	4	4¾	—	8¼	4½
	Challenger 8-360	—	16	16	16	16	195	18	4	4¾	7½	8	4½
	Coro., Charger 6-225	—	13	15	16	16	195	19½㉘	4	4¾	—	8¼	4½
	Coro., Charger 8-318	—	16	18	16	16	195	19½㉘	4	4¾	7½	8¼	4½
	Coro., Charger 8-360	—	16½	16½	16	16	195	19½㉘	4	—	7½	8	4½
	Coro., Charger 8-400	—	16½	16½	16	16	195	19½㉘	4	—	7½	9½㉙	4½
	Coro., Charger 8-440	—	16	16	16	16	195	19½㉘	4	—	—	8	4½
	Monaco 8-360	—	16	16	16	16	195	25㉗	4	—	—	8	4½
	Monaco 8-400	—	16½	16½	16	16	195	25㉗	4	—	—	9½	4½
	Monaco 8-440	—	16	16	16	16	195	25㉗	4	—	—	9½	4½
1975	Dart 6-225	—	13	14	16	16	195	16	4	3½	—	8½	2.1
	Dart 8-318	—	16	17½	16	16	195	16	4	4¾	7	8½⑥	4½
	Dart 8-360	—	16	16	16	16	195	16	4	4¾	—	8¼	4½
	Coronet 6-225	—	13	—	16	16	195	25½	4	4¾	—	8½	4½
	Coro., Charger 8-318	—	16½	18	16	16	195	25½⑪	4	4¾	—	8½⑥	4½
	Coro., Charger 8-360	—	16	16	16	16	195	25½⑪	4	—	—	9½	4½
	Coro., Charger 8-400	—	16	16	16	16	195	25½⑪	4	—	—	9½	4½
	Coronet 8-440	—	16	16	16	16	195	25½⑪	4㉚	—	—	8¼	4½
	Monaco 8-318	—	17½	17½	16	16	195	26½㉗	4	—	—	8½⑥	4½
	Monaco 8-360	—	16	16	16	16	195	26½㉗	4	—	—	9½	4½
	Monaco 8-400	—	16½	16½	16	16	195	26½㉗	4	—	—	9½	4½
	Monaco 8-440	—	16	16	16	16	195	26½㉗	4㉚	—	—	9½	4½
1976	Aspen, Dart 6-225	—	13	14	16	16	195	㉛	4	㉜	7	8½	2
	Aspen, Dart 8-318	—	16	17	16	16	195	㉛	4	4¾	7	8½	4½
	Aspen, Dart 8-360	—	16	16	16	16	195	㉛	4	4¾	7	8½	4½
	Charger, Coronet 6-225	—	13	14½	16	16	195	25½⑪	4	4¾	—	8½	4½
	Charger, Coronet 8-318	—	16½	18	16	16	195	25½⑪	4	4¾	—	8½	4½
	Charger, Coronet 8-360	—	16	16	16	16	195	25½⑪	4	4¾	—	8½	4½
	Charger, Coronet 8-400	—	16½	16½	16	16	195	25½⑪	4	4¾	—	㉝	4½
	Coronet 8-440	—	16	16	16	16	195	25½⑪	4	4¾	—	㉝	4½
	Monaco 8-400	—	16½㉞	16½㉞	16	16	195	26½㉗	4㉚	—	—	㉝	4½
	Monaco 8-440	—	16㉞	16㉞	16	16	195	26½㉗	4㉚	—	—	㉝	4½

Chrysler/Dodge/Imperial/Plymouth

COOLING SYSTEM & CAPACITY DATA/continued

Year	Model or Engine	Cooling Capacity, Qts.			Radiator Cap Relief Pressure, Lbs.		Thermo. Opening Temp. ①	Fuel Tank Gals.	Engine Oil Refill Qts. ②	Transmission Oil			Rear Axle Oil Pints
		No Heater	With Heater	With A/C	With A/C	No A/C				3 Speed Pints	4 Speed Pints	Auto. Trans. Qts. ⑫	
PLYMOUTH													
1969	Fury, VIP 6-225	—	13	—	16	—	190	24③	4	6½	—	7¾	4
	Others 6-225	—	13	15	16	16	190	19	4	6½	—	7¾	2⑦
	Fury, VIP 8-318	—	16	19	16	16	190	24③	4	6½	—	7¾	4
	Others 8-318	—	16	19	16	16	190	19	4	6½	—	7¾	4
	Fury, VIP 8-383 2 B.C.	—	16	17	16	16	190	24③	4	—	7¾	9¼	4
	Others 8-383 2 B.C.	—	16	17	16	16	190	19	4	—	7½	9¼	4
	Fury, VIP 8-383 4 B.C.	—	16	17	16	16	190	24③	4	—	7¾	7¾	4
	Others 8-383 4 B.C.	—	16	17	16	16	190	19	4	—	7½	7¾	4
	8-426 Hemi.	—	18	—	16	—	190	19	6	—	7½	8	4⑬
	Fury, VIP 8-440	—	17	18	16	16	190	24③	4	—	7¾	9¼	4
	Others 8-440	—	17	18	16	16	190	19	4	—	7½	9¼	4⑬
1970	Fury 6-225	—	12	14	16	16	190	24③	4	4¾	—	8½	4
	Others 6-225	—	12	14	16	16	190	19	4	4¾	—	8½	2
	Fury 8-318	—	16	17½	16	16	195	24②	4	4¾	—	8	4
	Others 8-318	—	16	17½	16	16	195	19	4	4¾	—	8	4
	Fury 8-383 2 B.C.	—	14½	16	16	16	190	24③	4	4¾	—	9½	4
	Others 8-383 2 B.C.	—	14½	15	16	16	190	19	4	4¾	—	9½	4
	Fury 8-383 4 B.C.	—	14½	16	16	16	190	24③	4	—	—	8	4
	Others 8-383 4 B.C.	—	14½	16	16	16	190	19	4	4¾	7	8	4
	Fury 8-440	—	15½	17	16	16	190	24③	4	—	—	9½	4
	Others 8-440	—	15½	17	16	16	190	19	4	—	7	9½	5½
	8-426 Hemi	—	17	—	16	16	190	19	6	—	7	8½	5½
1971	Fury 6-225	12	13	13	16	16	185	23	4	6½	—	8½	4½
	Others 6-225	12	13	13	16	16	185	21	4	4¾	—	8½	4
	Fury 8-318	15	16	16½	16	16	185	23	4	4¾	—	8½	4½
	Others 8-318	15	16	16½	16	16	185	21	4	4¾	—	8½	4
	Fury 8-360	14	15	15	16	16	185	23	4	4¾	—	8	4½
	Fury 8-383	13½	14½	15	16	16	185	23	4	4¾	—	8⑱	4½
	Others 8-383	13½	14½	15	16	16	185	21	4	4¾	7½	8⑱	4
	Others 8-426	14½	15½	—	16	16	185	21	6	—	7½	8½	5½
	Fury 8-440	14½	15½	17	16	16	185	23	4	—	—	9½	4½
	Others 8-440	14½	15½	17	16	16	185	21	4	—	7½	9½	5½
1972	Satellite 6-225	12	13	13	16	16	185	21	4	6½	—	8½	4½
	Satellite 8-318	15	16	16½	16	16	185	21	4	4¾	—	8½	4½
	Satellite 8-340	14	15	14½	16	16	185	21	4	4¾	7½	8	4½
	Satellite 8-400	13½	14½	15	16	16	185	21	4	4¾	7½	8⑱	4½
	Satellite 8-440	14	15	15	16	16	185	21	4㉖	—	7½	9½	5½
	Fury 8-318	15	16	16½	16	16	185	23	4	—	—	8½	4½
	Fury 8-360	14½	15½	15	16	16	185	23	4	—	—	8	4½
	Fury 8-400	13½	14½	14	16	16	185	23	4	—	—	9½	4½
	Fury 8-440	14½	15½	16	16	16	185	23	4	—	—	9½	4½
1973	Satellite 6-225	12	13	13	16	16	185	21	4	6½	—	8½	4½
	Satellite 8-318	15	16	18	16	16	185	21	4	4¾	7.5	8½	4½
	Satellite 8-340	14	15	16	16	16	185	21	4	4¾	7.5	8	4½
	Satellite 8-400	15	16	17	16	16	185	21	4	4¾	7.5	8	4½
	Satellite 8-440	16	17	17	16	16	185	21	4	—	—	9½	4½
	Fury 8-318	15	16	19	16	16	185	23	4	—	—	8½	4½
	Fury 8-360	15	16	16	16	16	185	23	4	—	—	8	4½
	Fury 8-400	15㉒	16㉓	17㉕	16	16	185	23	4	—	—	8⑱	4½
	Fury 8-440	15㉒	16㉓	17㉕	16	16	185	23	4	—	—	9½	4½

Chrysler/Dodge/Imperial/Plymouth

COOLING SYSTEM & CAPACITY DATA/continued

Year	Model or Engine	Cooling Capacity, Qts.			Radiator Cap Relief Pressure, Lbs.		Thermo. Opening Temp. ①	Fuel Tank Gals.	Engine Oil Refill Qts. ②	Transmission Oil			Rear Axle Oil Pints
		No Heater	With Heater	With A/C	With A/C	No A/C				3 Speed Pints	4 Speed Pints	Auto. Trans. Qts. ⑫	
PLYMOUTH—Continued													
1974	Satellite 6-225	—	13	15	16	16	195	19½㉘	4	4¾	—	8½	4½
	Satellite 8-318	—	16	18	16	16	195	19½㉘	4	4¾	7½	8½	4½
	Satellite 8-360	—	16½	16½	16	16	195	19½㉘	4	—	7½	8	4½
	Satellite 8-400	—	16½	16½	16	16	195	19½㉘	4	—	7½	9㉙	4½
	Satellite 8-440	—	16	16	16	16	195	19½㉘	4	—	—	8	4½
	Fury 8-360	—	16	16	16	16	195	25㉗	4	—	—	8	4½
	Fury 8-400	—	16½	16½	16	16	195	25㉗	4	—	—	9⑱	4½
	Fury 8-440	—	16	16	16	16	195	25㉗	4	—	—	9½	4½
1975–76	Fury 6-225	—	13	—	16	16	195	25½	4	4¾	—	8½	4½
	Fury 8-318	—	16½	18	16	16	195	25½⑪	4	4¾	—	⑧	4½
	Fury 8-360	—	16	16	16	16	195	25½⑪	4	—	—	9½	4½
	Fury 8-400	—	16½	16½	16	16	195	25½⑪	4	—	—	9½	4½
	Fury 8-440	—	16	16	16	16	195	25½⑪	4㉚	—	—	8¼	4½
	Gran Fury 8-318	—	17½	17½	16	16	195	26½㉗	4	—	—	⑥	4½
	Gran Fury 8-360	—	16	16	16	16	195	26½㉗	4	—	—	9½	4½
	Gran Fury 8-400	—	16½	16½	16	16	195	26½㉗	4	—	—	9½	4½
	Gran Fury 8-440	—	16	16	16	16	195	26½㉗	4㉚	—	—	9½	4½
1976	Fury 6-225	—	13	14½	16	16	195	25½⑪	4	4¾	—	8½	4½
	Fury 8-318	—	16½	18	16	16	195	25½⑪	4	4¾	—	8½	4½
	Fury 8-360	—	16	16	16	16	195	25½⑪	4	4¾	—	8½	4½
	Fury 8-400	—	16½	16½	16	16	195	25½⑪	4	4¾	—	㉝	4½
	Fury 8-440	—	16	16	16	16	195	25½⑪	4	4¾	—	㉝	4½
	Gran Fury 8-318	—	17½	17½	16	16	195	19½	4	—	—	㉝	4½
	Gran Fury 8-360	—	16	16	16	16	195	26½㉗	4	—	—	㉝	4½
	Gran Fury 8-400	—	16½㉞	16½㉞	16	16	195	26½㉗	4	—	—	㉝	4½
	Gran Fury 8-440	—	16㉞	16㉞	16	16	195	26½㉗	4	—	—	㉝	4½
VALIANT, BARRACUDA & VOLARE													
1969	6-170	—	12	14	16	16	200	18	4	6½	—	7¾	2
	6-225	—	13	15	16	16	190	18	4	6½	—	7¾	2
	8-273	—	17	19	16	16	190	18	4	6½	7	7¾	4
	8-318	—	16	18	16	16	190	18	4	6½	7	9¼	4
	8-340	—	16	—	16	—	190	18	4	6½	7	9¼	4
	8-383 2 Bar. Carb.	—	16	—	16	—	190	18	4	6½	7	9¼	4
	8-383 4 Bar. Carb.	—	16	—	16	—	190	18	4	6½	7	7¾	4
1970	Valiant 6-198, 225	—	13	14	16	16	190	18	4	6½	—	8½	2
	Barracuda 6-225	—	13	14	16	16	190	18	4	4¾	—	8½	2
	8-318	—	16	17	16	16	195	18	4	4¾	7	8½	4
	Valiant 8-340	—	15	17	16	16	190	18	4	4¾	7	8	4
	Barracuda 8-340	—	15½	15½	16	16	190	18	4	4¾	7	8	4
	8-383 2 Bar. Carb.	—	14½	15	16	16	190	18	4	—	—	9½	4
	8-383 4 Bar. Carb.	—	14½	15	16	16	190	18	4	4¾	7	8	4
	8-440	—	17	17	16	16	190	18	6	—	7	9½	5½
	8-426	—	17	—	16	16	190	18	6	—	7	8	5½
1971	Valiant 6 Cyl.	12	13	13	16	16	185	17	4	6½	—	8½	2
	Barracuda 6 Cyl.	12	13	13	16	16	185	18	4	4¾	—	8½	2
	Valiant 8-318	15	16	16½	16	16	185	17	4	4¾	—	8½	4½
	Barracuda 8-318	15	16	16½	16	16	185	18	4	4¾	—	8½	2
	Valiant 8-340	14	15	15	16	16	185	17	4	4¾	7	8	4½
	Barracuda 8-340	14	15	15	16	16	185	18	4	4¾	7½	8	4½

Chrysler/Dodge/Imperial/Plymouth

COOLING SYSTEM & CAPACITY DATA/continued

Year	Model or Engine	Cooling Capacity, Qts.			Radiator Cap Relief Pressure, Lbs.		Thermo. Opening Temp. ①	Fuel Tank Gals.	Engine Oil Refill Qts. ②	Transmission Oil			Rear Axle Oil Pints
		No Heater	With Heater	With A/C	With A/C	No A/C				3 Speed Pints	4 Speed Pints	Auto. Trans. Qts. ⑫	

VALIANT BARRACUDA & VOLARE—Continued

Year	Model	NoH	WH	A/C	W A/C	No A/C	Thermo	Fuel	Oil	3Sp	4Sp	Auto	Rear
1971	8-383	13½	14½	15	16	16	185	18	4	4¾	7½	8⑲	4½
	8-440	16⑲	17⑲	17⑳	16	16	185	18	4	—	7½	9½	5½
	8-426	14½	15½	—	16	16	185	18	6	—	7½	8	5½
1972	Valiant 6 Cyl.	12	13	13	16	16	185	16	4	6½	—	8½	2
	Barracuda 6 Cyl.	12	13	13	16	16	185	16½	4	4¾	—	8½	2
	Valiant 8-318	15	16	16	16	16	185	16	4	4¾	—	8½	4½
	Barracuda 8-318	15	16	16½	16	16	185	16½	4	4¾	—	8½	4½
	Valiant 8-340	14	15	15	16	16	185	16	4	4¾	7	8	4½
	Barracuda 8-340	14	15	14½	16	16	185	16½	4	—	7½	8	4½
1973	Valiant 6 Cyl.	12	13	13	16	16	185	16	4	6½	—	8½	2
	Valiant 8-318	15	16	18	16	16	185	16	4	4¾	—	8½	2
	Valiant 8-340	15	16	16	16	16	185	16	4	4¾	7	8	4½
	Barracuda 6 Cyl.	12	13	13	16	16	185	16½	4	4¾	7½	8	4½
	Barracuda 8-318	15	16	18	16	16	185	16½	4	4¾	—	8½	4½
	Barracuda 8-340	14	15	16	16	16	185	16½	4	4¾	7½	8	4½
1974	Valiant 6-198	—	13	14	16	16	195	16	4	6½	—	8¼	2
	Valiant 6-225	—	13	14	16	16	195	16	4	6½	—	8¼	2
	Valiant 8-318	—	16	17½	16	16	195	16	4	4¾	7	8¼	4½
	Valiant 8-360	—	16	16	16	16	195	16	4	4¾	7	8	4½
	Barracuda 8-318	—	16	17½	16	16	195	16½	4	4¾	—	8¼	4½
	Barracuda 8-360	—	16	16	16	16	195	16½	4	4¾	7½	8	4½
1975	Valiant 6-225	—	13	14	16	16	195	16	4	3½	—	8½	2.1
	Valiant V8-318	—	16	17½	16	16	195	16	4	4¾	7	8½⑤	4½
	Valiant V8-360	—	16	16	16	16	195	16	4	—	—	8¼	4½
1976	Valiant, Volare 6-225	—	13	14	16	16	195	㉟	4	㉜	7	8½	2
	Valiant, Volare V8-318	—	16	17	16	16	195	㉟	4	4¾	7	8½	4½
	Valiant, Volare V8-360	—	16	16	16	16	195	㉟	4	4¾	7	8½	4½

①—With permanent type anti-freeze.
②—Add one qt. with filter change.
③—Wagons 22 gals.
④—440 Hi Perf. uses 190°.
⑤—Cordoba 25½ gals., Chrysler 26½, Wagon 24 gals.
⑥—With 727 transmission (heavy duty), 9½ qts.
⑦—Station Wagon 4 pints.
⑧—With 727 transmission (heavy duty), 9½ qts.; Roadrunner models 8¼ qts.
⑨—Add 1½ qts. for rear seat heater.
⑩—With manual transmission 4 pints.
⑪—Wagon 20 gals., Sedan Models with dual exhaust 20½ gals.
⑫—Approximate. Make final check with dipstick.
⑬—With manual trans. 5½ pints.
⑭—5½ pints for High Perf. engine.
⑮—Add 2 qts. for 22" radiator.
⑯—9¼ qts. for High Perf.
⑰—Wagons 23 gals.
⑱—With 2 bar. carb. 9½ qts.
⑲—Auto. Trans., 1½ qts. less.
⑳—Auto. Trans. 18 qts.
㉑—Chrysler exc. wagon, 26½ gals.; wagon, 24 gals.; Cordoba exc. dual exhaust, 25½ gals.; dual exhaust 20.5 gals.
㉒—16 quarts with 4 Bar. Carb. or Hi-Perf.
㉓—17 quarts with 4 Bar. Carb. or Hi-Perf.
㉔—8 quarts with 4 Bar. Carb. or Hi-Perf.
㉕—18 quarts with 4 Bar. Carb. or Hi-Perf.
㉖—Hi Perf. uses 6 qts. plus filter.
㉗—Wagons 24 gals.
㉘—Wagons 21 gals.
㉙—Hi Perf. 8 qts.
㉚—High performance engine 5 qts.
㉛—Aspen, 18 gals.; Dart, 16 gals.
㉜—Exc. floorshift, 3.6 pts.; floor shift, 4¾ pts.
㉝—Exc. High Perf., 9½ qts.; High Perf., 8¼ qts.
㉞—Add 1 qt. with maximum cooling or trailer towing package.
㉟—Volare, 18 gal.; Valiant, 16 gals.

Full Size Models/Ford & Mercury

GENERAL ENGINE SPECIFICATIONS

Year	Engine	Carburetor	Bore and Stroke	Piston Displacement, Cubic Inches	Compression Ratio	Maximum Brake H.P. @ R.P.M.	Maximum Torque Lbs. Ft. @ R.P.M.	Normal Oil Pressure Pounds
FORD								
1969-70	150 Horsepower............6-240	1 Barrel	4.00 x 3.18	240	9.2	150 @ 4000	234 @ 2200	35-60
	210 Horsepower............V8-302	2 Barrel	4.00 x 3.00	302	9.5	210 @ 4400	295 @ 2400	35-60
	250 Horsepower............V8-351	2 Barrel	4.00 x 3.50	351	9.5	250 @ 4600	355 @ 2600	35-60
	270 Horsepower............V8-390	2 Barrel	4.05 x 3.78	390	9.5	270 @ 4400	390 @ 2600	35-60
	320 Horsepower............V8-429	2 Barrel	4.36 x 3.59	429	10.5	320 @ 4400	460 @ 2200	35-60
	360 Horsepower............V8-429	4 Barrel	4.36 x 3.59	429	11.0	360 @ 4600	476 @ 2800	35-60
1971	140 Horsepower............6-240	1 Barrel	4.00 x 3.18	240	8.9	140 @ 4000	230 @ 2200	35-60
	210 Horsepower............V8-302	2 Barrel	4.00 x 3.00	302	9.0	210 @ 4600	296 @ 2600	35-60
	240 Horsepower............V8-351	2 Barrel	4.00 x 3.50	351	9.0	240 @ 4600	350 @ 2600	35-60
	255 Horsepower............V8-390	2 Barrel	4.05 x 3.78	390	8.6	255 @ 4400	376 @ 2600	35-60
	260 Horsepower............V8-400	2 Barrel	4.00 x 4.00	400	9.0	260 @ 4400	400 @ 2200	35-60
	320 Horsepower............V8-429	2 Barrel	4.36 x 3.59	429	10.5	320 @ 4400	460 @ 2200	35-60
	360 Horsepower............V8-429	4 Barrel	4.36 x 3.59	429	10.5	360 @ 4600	480 @ 2800	35-60
1972	103 Horsepower①............6-240	1 Barrel	4.00 x 3.18	240	8.5	103 @ 3800	170 @ 2200	35-60
	140 Horsepower①............V8-302	2 Barrel	4.00 x 3.00	302	8.5	140 @ 4000	239 @ 2000	35-60
	153 Horsepower①............V8-351	2 Barrel	4.00 x 3.50	351	8.3	153 @ 3800	266 @ 2000	35-60
	163 Horsepower①............V8-351	2 Barrel	4.00 x 3.50	351	8.6	163 @ 3800	277 @ 2000	35-60
	172 Horsepower①............V8-400	2 Barrel	4.00 x 4.00	400	8.4	172 @ 4000	298 @ 2200	35-60
	208 Horsepower①............V8-429	4 Barrel	4.36 x 3.59	429	8.5	208 @ 4400	322 @ 2800	35-60
1973	154 Horsepower①............V8-351	2 Barrel	4.00 x 3.50	351	8.0	154 @ 3800	256 @ 2400	45-65
	157 Horsepower①............V8-351	2 Barrel	4.00 x 3.50	351	8.0	157 @ 4000	246 @ 2400	45-75
	158 Horsepower①............V8-351	2 Barrel	4.00 x 3.50	351	8.0	158 @ 3800	264 @ 2400	45-65
	161 Horsepower①............V8-351	2 Barrel	4.00 x 3.50	351	8.0	161 @ 4000	254 @ 2400	45-75
	167 Horsepower①............V8-400	2 Barrel	4.00 x 4.00	400	8.0	167 @ 3600	312 @ 2200	45-75
	171 Horsepower①............V8-400	2 Barrel	4.00 x 4.00	400	8.0	171 @ 3600	314 @ 2000	45-75
	198 Horsepower①............V8-429	4 Barrel	4.36 x 3.59	429	8.0	198 @ 4400	320 @ 2800	35-65
	202 Horsepower①............V8-429	4 Barrel	4.36 x 3.59	429	8.0	202 @ 4400	320 @ 2800	35-65
	198 Horsepower①............V8-460	4 Barrel	4.36 x 3.85	460	8.0	198 @ 4400	328 @ 2800	35-65
	202 Horsepower①............V8-460	4 Barrel	4.36 x 3.85	460	8.0	202 @ 4400	330 @ 2800	35-65
1974	162 Horsepower①............V8-351	2 Barrel	4.00 x 3.50	351	8.0	162 @ 4000	275 @ 2200	45-75
	163 Horsepower①............V8-351	2 Barrel	4.00 x 3.50	351	8.0	163 @ 4200	278 @ 2000	45-65
	170 Horsepower①............V8-400	2 Barrel	4.00 x 4.00	400	8.0	170 @ 3400	330 @ 2000	45-75
	195 Horsepower①............V8-460	4 Barrel	4.36 x 3.85	460	8.0	195 @ 3800	335 @ 2600	35-65
	275 Horsepower①............V8-460	4 Barrel	4.36 x 3.85	460	8.8	275 @ 4400	395 @ 2800	35-65
1975	148 Horsepower①............V8-351	2 Barrel	4.00 x 3.50	351	8.0	148 @ 3800	243 @ 2400	50-75
	150 Horsepower①............V8-351	2 Barrel	4.00 x 3.50	351	8.0	150 @ 3800	244 @ 2800	50-75
	158 Horsepower①............V8-400	2 Barrel	4.00 x 4.00	400	8.0	158 @ 3800	276 @ 2000	50-75
	144 Horsepower①............V8-400	2 Barrel	4.00 x 4.00	400	8.0	144 @ 3600	255 @ 2200	50-75
	218 Horsepower①............V8-460	4 Barrel	4.36 x 3.85	460	8.0	218 @ 4000	369 @ 2600	40-65
1976	Horsepower①............V8-351	2 Barrel	4.00 x 3.50	351	8.0	—	—	45-65
	Horsepower①............V8-400	2 Barrel	4.00 x 4.00	400	8.0	—	—	45-65
	Horsepower①............V8-460	4 Barrel	4.36 x 3.85	460	8.0	—	—	45-65
MERCURY								
1969-70	270 Horsepower............V8-390	2 Barrel	4.05 x 3.78	390	9.5	270 @ 4400	390 @ 2600	35-60
	280 Horsepower (1969)......V8-390	2 Barrel	4.05 x 3.78	390	10.5	280 @ 4400	403 @ 2600	35-60
	320 Horsepower............V8-429	2 Barrel	4.36 x 3.59	429	10.5	320 @ 4400	460 @ 2200	35-60
	360 Horsepower............V8-429	4 Barrel	4.36 x 3.59	429	11.0	360 @ 4600	476 @ 2800	35-60
1971	240 Horsepower............V8-351	2 Barrel	4.00 x 3.50	351	9.0	240 @ 4600	350 @ 2600	35-60
	260 Horsepower............V8-400	2 Barrel	4.00 x 4.00	400	9.0	260 @ 4400	400 @ 2200	35-60
	320 Horsepower............V8-429	2 Barrel	4.36 x 3.59	429	10.5	320 @ 4400	460 @ 2200	35-60
	360 Horsepower............V8-429	4 Barrel	4.36 x 3.59	429	10.5	360 @ 4600	480 @ 2800	35-60

Ford & Mercury/Full Size Models

GENERAL ENGINE SPECIFICATIONS/continued

Year	Engine	Carburetor	Bore and Stroke	Piston Displacement, Cubic Inches	Compression Ratio	Maximum Brake H.P. @ R.P.M.	Maximum Torque Lbs. Ft. @ R.P.M.	Normal Oil Pressure Pounds
MERCURY—Continued								
1972	153 Horsepower① V8-351	2 Barrel	4.00 x 3.50	351	8.3	153 @ 3800	266 @ 2000	35–60
	163 Horsepower① V8-351	2 Barrel	4.00 x 3.50	351	8.6	163 @ 3800	277 @ 2000	35–60
	172 Horsepower① V8-400	2 Barrel	4.00 x 4.00	400	8.4	172 @ 4000	298 @ 2200	35–60
	208 Horsepower① V8-429	4 Barrel	4.36 x 3.59	429	8.5	208 @ 4400	322 @ 2800	35–60
	200 Horsepower① V8-460	4 Barrel	4.36 x 3.85	460	8.5	200 @ 4400	326 @ 2800	35–75
1973	157 Horsepower① V8-351	2 Barrel	4.00 x 3.50	351	8.0	157 @ 4000	246 @ 2400	45–75
	161 Horsepower① V8-351	2 Barrel	4.00 x 3.50	351	8.0	161 @ 4000	254 @ 2400	45–75
	167 Horsepower① V8-400	2 Barrel	4.00 x 4.00	400	8.0	167 @ 3600	312 @ 2200	45–75
	171 Horsepower① V8-400	2 Barrel	4.00 x 4.00	400	8.0	171 @ 3600	314 @ 2000	45–75
	198 Horsepower① V8-429	4 Barrel	4.36 x 3.59	429	8.0	198 @ 4400	320 @ 2800	35–65
	202 Horsepower① V8-429	4 Barrel	4.36 x 3.59	429	8.0	202 @ 4400	320 @ 2800	35–65
	198 Horsepower① V8-460	4 Barrel	4.36 x 3.85	460	8.0	198 @ 4400	328 @ 2800	35–65
	202 Horsepower① V8-460	4 Barrel	4.36 x 3.85	460	8.0	202 @ 4400	330 @ 2800	35–65
1974	170 Horsepower① V8-400	2 Barrel	4.00 x 4.00	400	8.0	170 @ 3400	330 @ 2000	45–75
	195 Horsepower① V8-460	4 Barrel	4.36 x 3.85	460	8.0	195 @ 3800	335 @ 2600	35–65
	275 Horsepower① V8-460	4 Barrel	4.36 x 3.85	460	8.8	275 @ 4400	395 @ 2800	35–65
1975	148 Horsepower① V8-351	2 Barrel	4.00 x 3.50	351	8.0	148 @ 3800	243 @ 2400	50–75
	150 Horsepower① V8-351	2 Barrel	4.00 x 3.50	351	8.0	150 @ 3800	244 @ 2800	50–75
	144 Horsepower① V8-400	2 Barrel	4.00 x 4.00	400	8.0	144 @ 3600	255 @ 2200	50–75
	158 Horsepower① V8-400	2 Barrel	4.00 x 4.00	400	8.0	158 @ 3800	276 @ 2000	50–75
	218 Horsepower① V8-460	4 Barrel	4.36 x 3.85	460	8.0	218 @ 4000	369 @ 2600	40–65
1976	Horsepower① V8-400	2 Barrel	4.00 x 4.00	400	8.0	—	—	45–65
	Horsepower① V8-400	2 Barrel	4.36 x 3.85	460	8.0	—	—	45–65

①—Ratings are NET—as installed in the vehicle.

TUNEUP SPECIFICATIONS

The following specifications are published from the latest information available. This data should be used only in the absence of a decal affixed in the engine compartment.

★ When using a timing light, disconnect vacuum hose or tube at distributor and plug opening in tube or hose so idle speed will not be affected.

● When checking compression, lowest cylinder must be within 75% of the highest.

▲ Before removing wires from distributor cap, determine location of the No. 1 wire in cap, as distributor position may have been altered from that shown at the end of this chart.

Year	Spark Plug		Distributor		Ignition Timing ★			Carb. Adjustments					
	Type ⑤	Gap Inch	Point Gap Inch	Dwell Angle Deg.	Firing Order Fig. ▲	Timing BTDC ①	Mark Fig.	Hot Idle Speed		Air Fuel Ratio		Idle "CO" %	
								Std. Trans.	Auto. Trans. ②	Std. Trans.	Auto. Trans.	Std. Trans.	Auto. Trans.
1969													
6-240	BF-42	.034	.027	35–40	C	6°	D	775/500⑭	500D	—	13.9 to 1	—	—
V8-302 Std. Tr.	BF-42	.034	.021	24–29	B	6°	F	650	—	14.0 to 1	—	1.8	—
V8-302 Auto. Tr.	BF-42	.034	.017	26–31	B	6°	F	—	550D	—	13.8 to 1	—	2.2
V8-351	BF-42	.034	.017	26–31	A	6°	F	650	550D	14.0 to 1	14.0 to 1	1.8	1.6
V8-390	BF-42	.034	.017	26–31	B	6°	E	650	550D	14.0 to 1	14.4 to 1	1.6	1.1
V8-390⑯	BF-42	.034	.021	24–29	B	6°	E	—	550D	14.0 to 1	14.4 to 1	1.8	0.5
V8-429	BF-42	.034	.017	26–31	B	6°	E	—	550D	14.0 to 1	14.4 to 1	1.8	1.2

Full Size Models/Ford & Mercury

TUNEUP SPECIFICATIONS/continued

The following specifications are published from the latest information available. This data should be used only in the absence of a decal affixed in the engine compartment.

★ When using a timing light, disconnect vacuum hose or tube at distributor and plug opening in tube or hose so idle speed will not be affected.

● When checking compression, lowest cylinder must be within 75% of the highest.

▲ Before removing wires from distributor cap, determine location of the No. 1 wire in cap, as distributor position may have been altered from that shown at the end of this chart.

Year	Spark Plug		Distributor		Ignition Timing ★			Carb. Adjustments					
								Hot Idle Speed		Air Fuel Ratio		Idle "CO" %	
	Type ⑤	Gap Inch	Point Gap Inch	Dwell Angle Deg.	Firing Order Fig. ▲	Timing BTDC ①	Mark Fig.	Std. Trans.	Auto. Trans. ②	Std. Trans.	Auto. Trans.	Std. Trans.	Auto. Trans.
1970													
6-240	BF-42	.035	⑰	⑰	C	6°	D	775/500⑭	500④	14.45 to 1	14.70 to 1	—	—
V8-302	BF-42	.035	.021	24–29	B	6°	F	775/500⑭	575④	14.0 to 1	13.8 to 1	0.34	0.44
V8-351	BF-42	.035	.021	24–29	A	6°	F	775/500⑭	575④	⑩	⑩	0.30	0.14
V8-390 Std. Tr.	BF-42	.035	.021	24–29	B	6°	E	775/500⑭	—	14.1 to 1	—	0.12	—
V8-390 Auto. Tr.	BF-42	.035	.017	26–31	B	6°	E	—	600/500⑭	—	14.4 to 1	—	0.12
V8-429⑦	BF-42	.035	.021	24–29	B	4°	E	—	600/500⑭	13.5 to 1	13.5 to 1	0.20	0.20
V8-429⑥	BF-42	.035	⑬	⑬	B	4°	E	700	600	14.5 to 1	14.5 to 1	0.75	0.75
1971													
6-240	BRF-42	.034	.027	35–40	C	6°	G	800/500⑭	500	14.5 to 1	14.5 to 1	1.0	0.5
V8-302 L/Air Cond.	BRF-42	.034	.021	24–29	B	6°	H	800/500⑭	575	12.5 to 1	12.5 to 1	0.3	0.4
V8-302 w/Air Cond.	BRF-42	.034	.021	24–29	B	6°	H	800/500⑭	600/500⑭	12.5 to 1	12.5 to 1	0.3	0.4
V8-351 L/Air Cond.⑪	BRF-42	.034	.021	24–29	A	6°	H	700/500⑭	575	13.50 to 1	13.90 to 1	1.1	0.5
V8-351 w/Air Cond.⑪	BRF-42	.034	.021	24–29	A	6°	H	700/500⑭	600/500⑭	13.50 to 1	13.90 to 1	1.1	0.5
V8-351⑫	ARF-42	.034	.021	24–29	A	6°	H	775/500⑭	600/500⑭	14.30 to 1	14.40 to 1	0.2	0.2
V8-390	BRF-42	.034	.021	24–29	B	6°	H	—	600/500⑭	—	—	—	—
V8-400	ARF-42	.034	.021	24–29	A	③	H	—	600/500⑭	14.5 to 1	14.5 to 1	—	0.7
V8-429⑦ L/Air Cond.	BRF-42	.034	.021	24–29	B	6°	H	—	590	14.5 to 1	14.5 to 1	—	0.2
V8-429⑦ w/Air Cond.	BRF-42	.034	.021	24–29	B	6°	H	—	600/500⑭	14.5 to 1	14.5 to 1	—	0.2
V8-429⑥	BRF-42	.034	.021	24–29	B	4°	H	700	600	14.50 to 1	14.50 to 1	0.2	0.2
1972													
6-240	BRF-42	.034	.027	35–39	C	6°	G	—	500	—	—	—	0.5
V8-302 w/Air Cond.	BRF-42	.034	.017	26–30	B	6°	H	800/500	600/500⑭	—	—	—	0.19
V8-302 L/Air Cond.	BRF-42	.034	.017	26–30	B	6°	H	—	575	—	—	—	0.19
V8-351 w/Air Cond.⑪	BRF-42	.034	.017	26–30	A	6°	H	—	600/500⑭	—	—	—	0.15
V8-351 L/Air Cond.⑪	BRF-42	.034	.017	26–30	A	6°	H	—	575	—	—	—	0.15
V8-351⑫	ARF-42	.034	.017	26–30	A	6°	H	—	700/500⑭	—	—	—	0.50
V8-351 Calif.⑫	ARF-42	.034	.017	26–30	A	6°	H	—	625/500⑭	—	—	—	0.50
V8-400	ARF-42	.034	.017	26–30	A	⑧	H	—	625/500⑭	—	—	—	0.10
V8-429	BRF-42	.034	.017	26–30	B	10°	H	—	600/500⑭	—	—	—	0.03
1973													
V8-351⑪	BRF-42	.034	.017	26–30	A	6°	H	—	600	—	—	—	0.5⑨
V8-351⑪	ARF-42	.034	.017	26–30	A	10°	H	—	600	—	—	0.5⑨	0.5⑨
V8-400	ARF-42	.034	.017	26–31	A	6°	H	—	625	—	—	—	0.5⑨
V8-429	ARF-42	.034	.017	26–30	B	10°	H	—	600	—	—	—	0.5⑨
V8-460	ARF-42	.034	.017	26–30	B	10°	H	—	650	—	—	—	0.4⑨
1974													
V8-351⑪	BRF-42	.044	.017	26–30	A	6°	H	—	600	—	—	—	—
V8-351⑪⑱	BRF-42	.044	—	—	A	6°	H	—	600	—	—	—	—
V8-351⑫	ARF-42	.044	.017	26–30	A	14°	H	—	650	—	—	—	—
V8-351⑫⑱	ARF-42	.044	—	—	A	14°	H	—	650	—	—	—	—
V8-400⑱	ARF-42	.044	—	—	A	12°	H	—	625	—	—	—	—
V8-460⑱	ARF-52	.054	—	—	B	⑱	H	—	⑯	—	—	—	.25

613

Ford & Mercury/Full Size Models

TUNEUP SPECIFICATIONS/continued

The following specifications are published from the latest information available. This data should be used only in the absence of a decal affixed in the engine compartment.

★ When using a timing light, disconnect vacuum hose or tube at distributor and plug opening in hose or tube so idle speed will not be affected.

● When checking compression, lowest cylinder must be within 80 percent of highest.

▲ Before removing wires from distributor cap, determine location of the No. 1 wire in cap, as distributor position may have been altered from that shown at the end of this chart.

Year	Spark Plug		Distributor		Ignition Timing ★			Carb. Adjustments					
								Hot Idle Speed ③		Air Fuel Ratio		Idle "CO" %	
	Type	Gap Inch	Point Gap Inch	Dwell Angle Deg.	Firing Order Fig. ▲	Timing BTDC ①	Mark Fig.	Std. Trans.	Auto. Trans. ③	Std. Trans.	Auto. Trans.	Std. Trans.	Auto. Trans.
1975													
V8-351	ARF-42	.044	—	—	A	14°	H	—	700D	—	—	—	—
V8-400	ARF-42	.044	—	—	A	12°	H	—	625D	—	—	—	—
V8-460	ARF-52	.044	—	—	B	14°	H	—	650D	—	—	—	—
1976													
V8-351	ARF-42	.044	—	—	A	8°	H	—	650D	—	—	—	—
V8-400	ARF-42	.044	—	—	A	10°	H	—	⑲	—	—	—	—
V8-460	ARF-52	.044	—	—	B	10°	H	—	650D	—	—	—	—

① —BTDC: Before top dead center.
② —D: Drive. N: Neutral.
③ —California vehicles 6°; all others 10°.
④ —With headlights on and A/C off.
⑤ —Autolite.
⑥ —Four barrel carburetor.
⑦ —Two barrel carburetor.
⑧ —California vehicles 6°; all others 8°.
⑨ —For Calif. 0.2%.
⑩ —With 2 Bar. Carb.—14.0 to 1, with 4 Bar. Carb.—14.5 to 1.
⑪ —Windsor engine.
⑫ —Cleveland engine.
⑬ —Dual diaphragm dist., .021 gap, 24°-29° dwell. Single diaphragm .017 gap, 26°-31° dwell.
⑭ —Higher figure is with throttle modulator energized.
⑮ —Premium fuel.
⑯ —Exc. Police Interceptor 14° at 650, Police Interceptor 10° at 700.
⑰ —Dual diaphragm dist., .027 gap, 35°-40° dwell. Single diaphragm dist., .025 gap, 37°-42° dwell.
⑱ —Breakerless distributor.
⑲ —Exc. Calif.; 650, Calif.; 625.

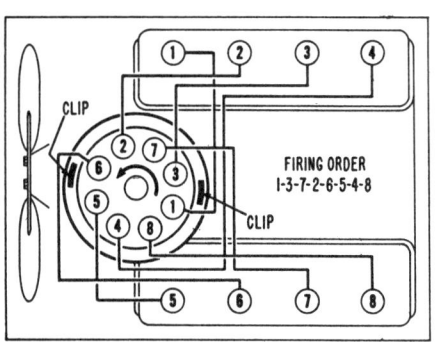

Fig. A

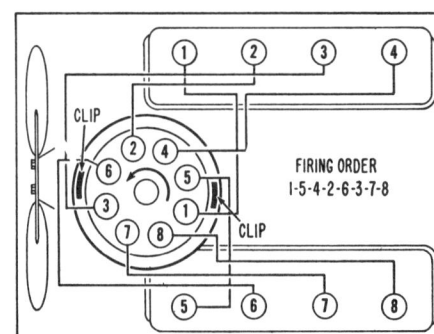

Fig. B

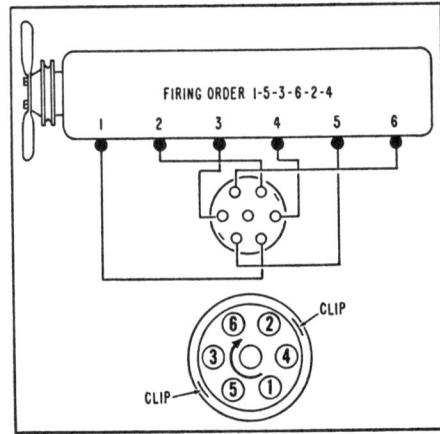

Fig. C

Full Size Models/Ford & Mercury

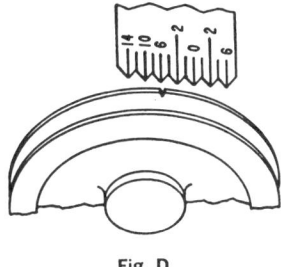

Fig. D

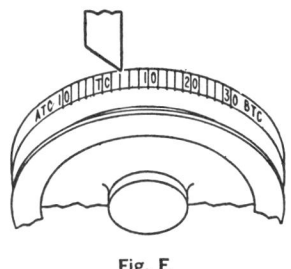

Fig. E

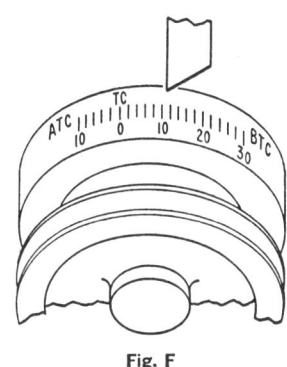

Fig. F

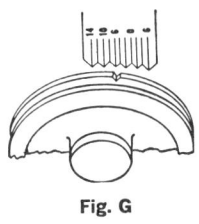

Fig. G

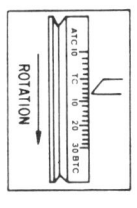

Fig. H

COOLING SYSTEM & CAPACITY DATA

Year	Model or Engine	Cooling Capacity, Qts.			Radiator Cap Relief Pressure, Lbs.		Thermo. Opening Temp. ①	Fuel Tank Gals.	Engine Oil Refill Qts. ②	Transmission Oil			Rear Axle Oil Pints
		No Heater	With Heater	With A/C	With A/C	No A/C				3 Speed Pints	4 Speed Pints	Auto. Trans. Qts. ③	
FORD													
1969	6-240	12	13	13	12-15	12-15	195	24⑥	4	3½	4	⑬	4½
	8-302	14	15	15	12-15	12-15	195	24⑥	4	3½	4	⑬	4½
	8-390	19½	20½	20½	12-15	12-15	195	24⑥	4	3½	4	⑫	5
	8-429	19½	20½	20½	12-15	12-15	195	24⑥	4	3½	4	12¾	5
1970	6-240	13½	14½	14½	12-15	12-15	195	24⑩	4	3½	4	⑬	4½
	8-302	13½	14½	14½	12-15	12-15	195	24⑩	4	3½	4	⑬	4½
	8-351	15½	16½	16½	12-15	12-15	195	24⑩	4	3½	4	⑬	5
	8-390	19	20	20	12-15	12-15	195	24⑩	4	3½	4	⑬	5
	8-429	17½	18½	18½	12-15	12-15	195	24⑩	4	3½	4	12¾	5
1971	6-240	13	14	14	12-15	12-15	195	23⑩	4	3½	4	⑬	⑤
	8-302	14	15	15	12-15	12-15	195	23⑩	4	3½	4	⑬	⑤
	8-351	15¼	16¼	16¼	12-15	12-15	195	23⑩	4	3½	4	11	5
	8-390	19	20	20	12-15	12-15	195	23⑩	4	3½	4	12¾	5
	8-400	16½	17½	18¼	12-15	12-15	195	23⑩	4	3½	4	12¾	5
	8-429	18	19	19	12-15	12-15	195	23⑩	4	3½	4	12¾	5
1972	6-240	13¼	14¼	14¼	12-15	12-15	195	22④	4	—	—	⑬	⑤
	8-302	14¼	15¼	15¼	12-15	12-15	195	22④	4	—	—	⑬	⑤
	8-351	15½	16½	16½	12-15	12-15	195	22④	4	—	—	⑬	5
	8-400	16¾	17¾	18¼	12-15	12-15	195	22④	4	—	—	12¾	5
	8-429	17¾	18¾	20	12-15	12-15	195	22④	4	—	—	12¾	5
1973	8-351⑧	14½	15½	16¼	12-15	12-15	195	22④	4	—	—	10¼	4
	8-351⑨	15½	16½	17	12-15	12-15	195	22④	4	—	—	10¼	4
	8-400	17	18	18	12-15	12-15	195	22④	4	—	—	12½	⑤
	8-429	18½	19½	19½	12-15	12-15	195	22④	4	—	—	12½	5

Ford & Mercury/Full Size Models

COOLING SYSTEM & CAPACITY DATA/continued

Year	Model or Engine	Cooling Capacity, Qts.			Radiator Cap Relief Pressure, Lbs.		Thermo. Opening Temp. ①	Fuel Tank Gals.	Engine Oil Refill Qts. ②	Transmission Oil			Rear Axle Oil Pints
		No Heater	With Heater	With A/C	With A/C	No A/C				3 Speed Pints	4 Speed Pints	Auto. Trans. Qts. ③	
FORD—Continued													
1974	8-351⑧	15.3	16½	17.2	12–16	12–16	191	22④	4	—	—	⑪	⑤
	8-351⑨	15.3	16½	16½	12–16	12–16	191	22④	4	—	—	⑭	⑤
	8-400	17	18	18½	12–16	12–16	191	22④	4	—	—	⑭	⑤
	8-460	18.4	19½	19½	12–16	12–16	191	22④	4	—	—	12½	⑤
1975	8-351	—	17.1	17.6	12–16	12–16	191	24.2④	4	—	—	⑪	⑤
	8-400	—	17.1	17.6	12–16	12–16	191	24.2④	4	—	—	⑬	⑤
	8-460	—	18.5	18.5⑮	12–16	12–16	191	24.2④	4⑯	—	—	⑬	⑤
1976	8-351	16.3	17.1	17.6	12–16	12–16	191	24.2④	4	—	—	⑪	⑤
	8-400	16.3	17.1	17.6	12–16	12–16	191	24.2④	4	—	—	⑬	⑤
	8-460	—	18.5	18.5⑮	12–16	12–16	191	24.2④	4⑯	—	—	⑬	⑤
MERCURY													
1969	All	19½	20½	20½	12–15	12–15	195	24⑥	4	3½	—	12¾	5
1970	8-390	19	20	20	12–15	12–15	195	24⑩	4	3½	—	12¾	5
	8-429	17½	18½	18½	12–15	12–15	195	24⑩	4	3½	—	12¾	5
1971	8-351	15¼	16¼	16¼	12–15	12–15	195	23⑩	4	3½	—	11	5
	8-400	16½	17½	18¼	12–15	12–15	195	23⑩	4	3½	—	12¾	5
	8-429	18	19	19	12–15	12–15	195	23⑩	4	3½	—	12¾	5
1972	8-351	15¼	16¼	16¾	12–15	12–15	195	22½⑦	4	—	—	11	5
	8-400	16.6	17.6	18.3	12–15	12–15	195	22½⑦	4	—	—	12¾	5
	8-429	17.8	18.8	19½	12–15	12–15	195	22½⑦	4	—	—	12¾	5
1973	8-351⑧	14½	15½	16¼	12–15	12–15	195	22④	4	—	—	10¼	⑤
	8-351⑨	15½	16½	17	12–15	12–15	195	22④	4	—	—	10¼	⑤
	8-400	17	18	18	12–15	12–15	195	22④	4	—	—	12½	⑤
	8-429, 460	18½	19½	19½	12–15	12–15	195	22④	4	—	—	12½	⑤
1974	8-351⑧	15.3	16½	17	12–16	12–16	191	22④	4	—	—	10½	⑤
	8-400	17	18	18½	12–16	12–16	191	22④	4	—	—	⑬	⑤
	8-460	18.4	19½	19½	12–16	12–16	191	22④	4	—	—	12½	⑤
1975	8-400	—	17.1	17.6	12–16	12–16	191	24.2④	4	—	—	⑬	⑤
	8-460	—	18.5	18.5⑮	12–16	12–16	191	24.2④	4⑯	—	—	⑬	⑤
1976	8-400	16.3	17.1	17.6	12–16	12–16	191	24.2④	4	—	—	⑬	⑤
	8-460	17.6	18.5	18.5⑮	12–16	12–16	191	24.2④	4⑯	—	—	⑬	⑤

① —With permanent type anti-freeze.
② —Add one quart with filter change.
③ —Approximate. Make final check with dipstick.
④ —Station Wagons 21 gals. Add 8 gals. with auxiliary tank.
⑤ —WER axles 4, all others 5.
⑥ —Station Wagons 20 gals.
⑦ —Station Wagons 21½ gallons.
⑧ —Cleveland engine.
⑨ —Windsor engine.
⑩ —Station Wagon 22 gals.
⑪ —C4 10½ qts., FMX 11 qts.
⑫ —Three spd. 11 qts., C6 13 qts.
⑬ —FMX 11 qts., C6 12¼ qts. C4, 10¼ qts.
⑭ —FMX 11 qts., C6 12½ qts., CW 11⅛ qts.
⑮ —Medium duty 19 qts., Heavy duty and Police 20 qts.
⑯ —Police Models 6½ qts.

Compact & Intermediate Models/Ford & Mercury

GENERAL ENGINE SPECIFICATIONS

Year	Engine	Carburetor	Bore and Stroke	Piston Displacement, Cubic Inches	Compression Ratio	Maximum Brake H.P. @ R.P.M.	Maximum Torque Lbs. Ft. @ R.P.M.	Normal Oil Pressure Pounds
1969	105 Horsepower..............6-170	1 Barrel	3.50 x 2.94	170	9.1	105 @ 4400	158 @ 2400	35-60
	120 Horsepower..............6-200	1 Barrel	3.68 x 3.13	200	8.8	120 @ 4400	190 @ 2400	35-60
	155 Horsepower..............6-250	1 Barrel	3.68 x 3.91	250	9.0①	155 @ 4000	240 @ 1600	35-60
	210 Horsepower..............V8-302	2 Barrel	4.00 x 3.00	302	9.5	210 @ 4400	295 @ 2400	35-60
	290 Horsepower "H.O."......V8-302	4 Barrel	4.00 x 3.00	302	10.5	290 @ 5800	290 @ 4300	35-60
	250 Horsepower..............V8-351	2 Barrel	4.00 x 3.50	351	9.5	250 @ 4600	355 @ 2600	35-60
	290 Horsepower..............V8-351	4 Barrel	4.00 x 3.50	351	10.7	290 @ 4800	385 @ 3200	35-60
	320 Horsepower..............V8-390	4 Barrel	4.05 x 3.78	390	10.5	320 @ 4800	427 @ 3200	35-60
	390 Horsepower..............V8-427	4 Barrel	4.23 x 3.78	427	10.9	390 @ 5600	460 @ 3200	35-60
	335 Horsepower..............V8-428	4 Barrel	4.13 x 3.98	428	10.6	335 @ 5200	440 @ 3400	35-60
	Ram Air..................V8-428	4 Barrel	4.13 x 3.98	428	10.6	—	—	35-60
1970	105 Horsepower..............6-170	1 Barrel	3.50 x 2.94	170	9.1	105 @ 4400	158 @ 2400	35-60
	120 Horsepower..............6-200	1 Barrel	3.68 x 3.13	200	8.8	120 @ 4400	190 @ 2400	35-60
	155 Horsepower..............6-250	1 Barrel	3.68 x 3.91	250	9.1	155 @ 4000	240 @ 1600	35-60
	210 Horsepower..............V8-302	2 Barrel	4.00 x 3.00	302	9.5	210 @ 4400	295 @ 2400	35-60
	290 Horsepower "BOSS"......V8-302	4 Barrel	4.00 x 3.00	302	10.5	290 @ 5800	290 @ 4300	35-60
	250 Horsepower..............V8-351	2 Barrel	4.00 x 3.50	351	9.5	250 @ 4600	355 @ 2600	35-60
	300 Horsepower..............V8-351	4 Barrel	4.00 x 3.50	351	11.0	300 @ 5400	380 @ 3400	35-60
	335 Horsepower "CJ".........V8-428	4 Barrel	4.13 x 3.98	428	10.6	335 @ 5200	440 @ 3400	35-60
	Ram Air..................V8-428	4 Barrel	4.13 x 3.98	428	10.6	—	—	35-60
	360 Horsepower..............V8-429	4 Barrel	4.36 x 3.59	429	11.0	360 @ 4600	476 @ 2800	35-60
	345 Horsepower "CJ".........V8-429	4 Barrel	4.36 x 3.59	429	11.5	345 @ 5800	450 @ 3400	35-60
	375 Horsepower "Boss".......V8-429	4 Barrel	4.36 x 3.59	429	10.5	375 @ 5200	450 @ 3400	20-60
1971	100 Horsepower..............6-170	1 Barrel	3.50 x 2.94	170	8.7	100 @ 4200	148 @ 2600	35-60
	115 Horsepower..............6-200	1 Barrel	3.68 x 3.13	200	8.7	115 @ 4000	180 @ 2200	35-60
	145 Horsepower..............6-250	1 Barrel	3.68 x 3.91	250	9.0	145 @ 4000	232 @ 1600	35-60
	210 Horsepower..............V8-302	2 Barrel	4.00 x 3.00	302	9.0	210 @ 4600	296 @ 2600	35-60
	290 Horsepower H.O..........V8-302	4 Barrel	4.00 x 3.00	302	9.4	290 @ 5800	290 @ 4300	35-60
	240 Horsepower..............V8-351	2 Barrel	4.00 x 3.50	351	9.0	240 @ 4600	350 @ 2600	35-60
	285 Horsepower..............V8-351	4 Barrel	4.00 x 3.50	351	10.7	285 @ 5400	370 @ 3400	35-60
	330 Horsepower..............V8-351	4 Barrel	4.00 x 3.50	351	11.7	330 @ 5400	370 @ 4000	35-60
	370 Horsepower "CJ".........V8-429	4 Barrel	4.36 x 3.59	429	11.3	370 @ 5400	450 @ 3400	35-60
	375 Horsepower "SCJ"........V8-429	4 Barrel	4.36 x 3.59	429	11.5	375 @ 5600	450 @ 3400	35-60
1972	82 Horsepower②..............6-170	1 Barrel	3.50 x 2.94	170	8.3	82 @ 4400	129 @ 1800	35-60
	91 Horsepower②..............6-200	1 Barrel	3.68 x 3.13	200	8.3	91 @ 4000	154 @ 2200	35-60
	95 Horsepower②..............6-250	1 Barrel	3.68 x 3.91	250	8.0	95 @ 3600	181 @ 1600	35-60
	98 Horsepower②..............6-250	1 Barrel	3.68 x 3.91	250	8.0	98 @ 3600	183 @ 1600	35-60
	99 Horsepower②..............6-250	1 Barrel	3.68 x 3.91	250	8.0	99 @ 3600	184 @ 1600	35-60
	140 Horsepower②.............V8-302	2 Barrel	4.00 x 3.00	302	8.5	140 @ 4000	230 @ 2200	35-60
	141 Horsepower②.............V8-302	2 Barrel	4.00 x 3.00	302	8.5	141 @ 4000	242 @ 2000	35-60
	143 Horsepower②.............V8-302	2 Barrel	4.00 x 3.00	302	8.5	143 @ 4200	242 @ 2000	35-60
	161 Horsepower②.............V8-351	2 Barrel	4.00 x 3.50	351	8.6	161 @ 4000	276 @ 2000	35-60
	164 Horsepower②.............V8-351	2 Barrel	4.00 x 3.50	351	8.6	164 @ 4000	276 @ 2000	35-85
	177 Horsepower②.............V8-351	2 Barrel	4.00 x 3.50	351	8.6	177 @ 4000	284 @ 2000	35-85
	248 Horsepower② "CJ".......V8-351	4 Barrel	4.00 x 3.50	351	8.6	248 @ 5400	299 @ 3800	50-70
	262 Horsepower②.............V8-351	4 Barrel	4.00 x 3.50	351	8.6	262 @ 5400	299 @ 3600	35-85
	266 Horsepower②.............V8-351	4 Barrel	4.00 x 3.50	351	8.6	266 @ 5400	301 @ 3600	35-85
	168 Horsepower②.............V8-400	2 Barrel	4.00 x 4.00	400	8.4	168 @ 4200	297 @ 2200	35-85
	205 Horsepower②.............V8-429	4 Barrel	4.36 x 3.59	429	8.5	205 @ 4400	322 @ 2600	35-60
1973	84 Horsepower..............6-200	1 Barrel	3.68 x 3.13	200	8.3	84 @ 3600	151 @ 1800	30-50
	88 Horsepower②..............6-250	1 Barrel	3.68 x 3.91	250	8.0	88 @ 3200	196 @ 1600	35-60
	92 Horsepower②..............6-250	1 Barrel	3.68 x 3.91	250	8.0	92 @ 3200	197 @ 1600	35-60
	95 Horsepower②..............6-250	1 Barrel	3.68 x 3.91	250	8.0	95 @ 3200	199 @ 1600	35-60

Ford & Mercury/Compact & Intermediate Models

GENERAL ENGINE SPECIFICATIONS/continued

Year	Engine	Carburetor	Bore and Stroke	Piston Displacement, Cubic Inches	Compression Ratio	Maximum Brake H.P. @ R.P.M.	Maximum Torque Lbs. Ft. @ R.P.M.	Normal Oil Pressure Pounds
1973	135 Horsepower②..........V8-302	2 Barrel	4.00 x 3.00	302	8.0	135 @ 4200	228 @ 2200	35-60
	136 Horsepower②..........V8-302	2 Barrel	4.00 x 3.00	302	8.0	136 @ 4200	232 @ 2200	35-60
	137 Horsepower②..........V8-302	2 Barrel	4.00 x 3.00	302	8.0	137 @ 4200	230 @ 2200	35-60
	138 Horsepower②..........V8-302	2 Barrel	4.00 x 3.00	302	8.0	138 @ 4200	234 @ 2200	35-60
	154 Horsepower②..........V8-351	2 Barrel	4.00 x 3.50	351	8.0	154 @ 4000	246 @ 2400	35-60
	156 Horsepower②..........V8-351	2 Barrel	4.00 x 3.50	351	8.0	156 @ 3800	260 @ 2400	35-60
	159 Horsepower②..........V8-351	2 Barrel	4.00 x 3.50	351	8.0	159 @ 4000	250 @ 2400	35-60
	246 Horsepower②..........V8-351	4 Barrel	4.00 x 3.50	351	8.0	246 @ 5400	312 @ 3600	35-60
	264 Horsepower②..........V8-351	4 Barrel	4.00 x 3.50	351	8.0	264 @ 5400	314 @ 3600	35-60
	163 Horsepower②..........V8-400	2 Barrel	4.00 x 4.00	400	8.0	163 @ 3800	300 @ 2000	35-60
	168 Horsepower②..........V8-400	2 Barrel	4.00 x 4.00	400	8.0	168 @ 3800	310 @ 2000	35-60
	197 Horsepower②..........V8-429	4 Barrel	4.36 x 3.59	429	8.0	197 @ 4400	320 @ 2600	35-60
	201 Horsepower②..........V8-429	4 Barrel	4.36 x 3.59	429	8.0	201 @ 4400	322 @ 2600	35-60
	274 Horsepower..........V8-460	4 Barrel	4.36 x 3.85	460	8.8	274 @ 4600	392 @ 2800	35-65
1974	84 Horsepower②..........6-200	1 Barrel	3.68 x 3.13	200	8.0	84 @ 3800	150 @ 1800	30-50
	91 Horsepower②..........6-250	1 Barrel	3.68 x 3.91	250	8.0	91 @ 3200	190 @ 1600	40-60
	140 Horsepower②..........V8-302	2 Barrel	4.00 x 3.00	302	8.0	140 @ 3800	230 @ 2600	40-60
	162 Horsepower②..........V8-351	2 Barrel	4.00 x 3.50	351	8.0	162 @ 4000	275 @ 2200	40-65
	163 Horsepower②..........V8-351	2 Barrel	4.00 x 3.50	351	8.0	163 @ 4200	278 @ 2000	45-75
	255 Horsepower②..........V8-351	4 Barrel	4.00 x 3.50	351	8.0	255 @ 5600	290 @ 3400	45-75
	170 Horsepower②..........V8-400	2 Barrel	4.00 x 4.00	400	8.0	170 @ 3400	330 @ 2000	45-75
	195 Horsepower②..........V8-460	4 Barrel	4.36 x 3.85	460	8.0	195 @ 3800	335 @ 2600	35-65
	220 Horsepower②③..........V8-460	4 Barrel	4.36 x 3.85	460	8.0	220 @ 4000	355 @ 2600	35-65
	260 Horsepower②..........V8-460	4 Barrel	4.36 x 3.85	460	8.0	260 @ 4400	355 @ 2700	35-65
1975	Horsepower②..........6-200	1 Barrel	3.68 x 3.13	200	8.3	—	—	30-50
	70 Horsepower②⑤..........6-250	1 Barrel	3.68 x 3.91	250	8.0	70 @ 2800	175 @ 1400	40-60
	72 Horsepower②④..........6-250	1 Barrel	3.68 x 3.91	250	8.0	72 @ 2900	180 @ 1400	40-60
	122 Horsepower②⑥..........V8-302	2 Barrel	4.00 x 3.00	302	8.0	122 @ 3800⑥	208 @ 1800⑦	40-60
	129 Horsepower②⑧..........V8-302	2 Barrel	4.00 x 3.00	302	8.0	129 @ 3800⑧	220 @ 1800⑨	40-60
	148 Horsepower②④..........V8-351M	2 Barrel	4.00 x 3.50	351	8.0	148 @ 3800	243 @ 2400	50-75
	150 Horsepower②⑤..........V8-351M	2 Barrel	4.00 x 3.50	351	8.0	150 @ 3800	244 @ 2800	50-75
	143 Horsepower②⑩..........V8-351W	2 Barrel	4.00 x 3.50	351	8.1	143 @ 3600⑩	255 @ 2200⑪	40-65
	154 Horsepower②⑫..........V8-351W	2 Barrel	4.00 x 3.50	351	8.1	154 @ 3800⑫	268 @ 2200	40-65
	144 Horsepower②⑤..........V8-400	2 Barrel	4.00 x 4.00	400	8.0	144 @ 3600	255 @ 2200	50-65
	158 Horsepower②④..........V8-400	2 Barrel	4.00 x 4.00	400	8.0	158 @ 4000	276 @ 2000	50-65
	216 Horsepower②④..........V8-460	4 Barrel	4.36 x 3.85	460	8.0	216 @ 4000	366 @ 2600	40-65
	217 Horsepower②⑤..........V8-460	4 Barrel	4.36 x 3.85	460	8.0	217 @ 4000	365 @ 2600	40-65
1976	Horsepower②..........6-200	1 Barrel	3.682 x 3.126	200	—	—	—	30-50
	Horsepower②..........6-250	1 Barrel	3.682 x 3.91	250	—	—	—	40-60
	Horsepower②..........V8-302	2 Barrel	4.00 x 3.00	302	—	—	—	40-60
	Horsepower②..........V8-351	2 Barrel	4.00 x 3.50	351	—	—	—	45-65⑬
	Horsepower②..........V8-400	2 Barrel	4.00 x 4.00	400	—	—	—	35-65
	Horsepower②..........V8-460	4 Barrel	4.36 x 3.85	460	—	—	—	35-65

①—Mustang "E" Model, 9.5.
②—Ratings are NET—as installed in the vehicle.
③—Cougar XR-7 requires A/C in California.
④—Except California.
⑤—California.
⑥—Comet & Maverick, California vehicles rated at 115 H.P. @ 3600 RPM.
⑦—California vehicles rated at 203 @ 1400 RPM.
⑧—Granada & Monarch, California vehicles rated at 115 H.P. @ 3600 RPM.
⑨—California vehicles rated at 203 @ 1800 RPM.
⑩—Granada, Monarch, Torino & Elite, California vehicles rated at 153 H.P. @ 3400 RPM.
⑪—California vehicles rated at 270 @ 2400 RPM.
⑫—Cougar & Montego, not available in California.
⑬—V8-351M: 45-75 pounds.

Compact & Intermediate Models/Ford & Mercury

TUNEUP SPECIFICATIONS

The following specifications are published from the latest information available. This data should be used only in the absence of a decal affixed in the engine compartment.

★ When using a timing light, disconnect vacuum hose or tube at distributor and plug opening in hose or tube so idle speed will not be affected.

● When checking compression, lowest cylinder must be within 75% of the highest.

▲ Before removing wires from distributor cap, determine location of the No. 1 wire in cap, as distributor position may have been altered from that shown at the end of this chart.

Year	Spark Plug		Distributor		Ignition Timing ★			Carb. Adjustments					
								Hot Idle Speed ③		Air Fuel Ratio		Idle "CO" %	
	Type	Gap Inch	Point Gap Inch	Dwell Angle Deg.	Firing Order Fig. ▲	Timing BTDC ①	Mark Fig.	Std. Trans.	Auto. Trans. ②	Std. Trans.	Auto. Trans.	Std. Trans.	Auto. Trans.
1969													
6-170	BF-82	.034	.027	35–40	H	6°	G	750	550D	13.80 to 1	13.60 to 1	2.2	2.6
6-200	BF-82	.034	.027	35–40	H	6°	G	750	550D	14.50 to 1	14.00 to 1	0.9	1.8
6-250 Less Air Cond.	BF-82⑱	.034	.025	37–42	H	6°	G	700	550D	14.0 to 1	13.5 to 1	1.8	2.8
6-250 With Air Cond.	BF-82⑱	.034	.025	37–42	H	6°	G	700/500	550/450D⑥	14.0 to 1	13.5 to 1	1.8	2.8
V8-302 Std. Trans.	BF-42	.034	.021	24–29	E	6°	C	650	—	14.0 to 1	—	1.8	—
V8-302 Auto. Trans.	BF-42	.034	.017	26–31	E	6°	C	—	550D	—	13.8 to 1	—	2.2
V8-302 "H.O."	AF-32	.030	.020	30–33	E	16°	C	800	—	—	—	—	—
V8-351 2 B. Carb.	BF-42	.034	.017	26–31	F	6°	C	650	550D	14.0 to 1	14.0 to 1	1.8	1.8
V8-351 4 B. Carb.	BF-32	.034	.017	26–31	F	6°	C	650	550D	14.0 to 1	14.3 to 1	1.8	1.2
V8-390 Std. Trans.	BF-42	.034	.017	26–31	E	6°	B	700	—	㉕	—	㉗	—
V8-390 Auto. Trans.	BF-32	.034	.017	26–31	E	6°	B	—	550D	—	㉖	—	㉔
V8-427	BF-32	.034	.017	26–31	E	6°	C	—	600D	—	—	—	—
V8-428	BF-32	.034	.017	26–31	E	6°	B	700	650D	14.1 to 1	14.1 to 1	1.6	1.6
1970													
6-170	BF-82	.035	.027	35–40	H	6°	G	750	550	14.45 to 1	14.45 to 1	1.0	1.0
6-200	BF-82	.035	.027	35–40	H	6°	G	750	550	14.45 to 1	14.20 to 1	1.0	1.5
6-250	BF-82	.035	.027	35–40	H	6°	G	800/500⑥	500	14.20 to 1	14.20 to 1	1.5	1.5
V8-302	BF-42	.035	.021	24–29	E	6°	C	800/500⑥	600/500D⑥	14.0 to 1	13.80 to 1	0.34	0.44
V8-302 "BOSS"	AF-32	.034	.020	30–33	E	16°	C	800/500⑥	—	13.50 to 1	—	2.80	—
V8-351⑦⑱	AF-42	.034	⑪	⑪	F	6°	C	700/500⑥	600/500D⑥	14.0 to 1	14.0 to 1	0.30	0.14
V8-351⑦⑰ Std. Tr.	BF-42	.034	⑪	⑪	F	6°	C	700/500⑥	—	14.0 to 1	—	0.30	—
V8-351⑦⑰ Auto. Tr.	BF-42	.034	⑪	⑪	F	10°	C	700/500⑥	—	—	14.0 to 1	—	0.14
V8-351⑧	AF-32	.034	⑪	⑪	F	6°	C	800/500⑥	600/500D⑥	14.44 to 1	14.45 to 1	0.90	0.75
V8-428	BF-32	.034	⑪	⑪	E	6°	B	800/500⑥	600/500D⑥	13.8 to 1	14.3 to 1	2.15	0.95
V8-429 Auto. Trans.⑧	BF-42	.034	⑪	⑪	E	4°	C	700/500⑥	700/500⑥	—	14.45 to 1	—	0.75
V8-429 "CJ"	AF-32	.034	⑪	⑪	E	10°	C	700	600	14.4 to 1	14.45 to 1	0.35	0.35
V8-429 "BOSS"	AF-32	.034	.020	30–33	E	10°	D	700	—	14.2 to 1	—	2.3	—
1971													
6-170	BRF-82	.034	.027	35–40	H	6°	A	750③	—	14.5 to 1	14.5 to 1	1.0	1.0
6-200	BRF-82	.034	.027	35–40	H	6°	A	750③	550D③	14.5 to 1	14.2 to 1	1.0	1.5
6-250	BRF-82	.034	⑤	⑤	H	6°	A	750/500⑥	600/500D⑥	14.2 to 1	14.2 to 1	1.5	1.5
V8-302	BRF-42	.034	.021	24–29	E	6°	I	800/500⑥	600/500D⑥	14.5 to 1	14.5 to 1	0.3	0.4
V8-302 H.O.	AF-32	.034	.020	30–33	E	16°	I	800/500⑥	—	14.5 to 1	—	0.3	0.4
V8-351⑦	ARF-42	.034	⑪	⑪	F	6°	I	700/500⑥	600D	14.5 to 1	14.5 to 1	0.2	0.2
V8-351⑧	ARF-42	.034	.021	24–29	F	6°	I	800/500⑥	600D	14.5 to 1	—	1.1	—
V8-429 "CJ"	AF-32	.034	.021	24–29	E	10°	C	700/500⑥	650/500D⑥	14.5 to 1	14.5 to 1	0.3	0.3
V8-429 "SCJ"	AF-32	.034	.021	24–29	E	10°	C	650/500⑥	700/500D⑥	14.5 to 1	14.5 to 1	0.3	0.3

Ford & Mercury/Compact & Intermediate Models
TUNEUP SPECIFICATIONS/continued

The following specifications are published from the latest information available. This data should be used only in the absence of a decal affixed in the engine compartment.

★When using a timing light, disconnect vacuum hose or tube at distributor and plug opening in hose or tube so idle speed will not be affected.
●When checking compression, lowest cylinder must be within 75% of the highest.
▲Before removing wires from distributor cap, determine location of the No. 1 wire in cap, as distributor position may have been altered from that shown at the end of this chart.

Year	Spark Plug		Distributor		Ignition Timing★			Carb. Adjustments					
								Hot Idle Speed③		Air Fuel Ratio		Idle "CO" %	
	Type	Gap Inch	Point Gap Inch	Dwell Angle Deg.	Firing Order Fig. ▲	Timing BTDC ①	Mark Fig.	Std. Trans.	Auto. Trans.②	Std. Trans.	Auto. Trans.	Std. Trans.	Auto. Trans.
1972													
6-170	BRF-82	.034	.027	35–39	H	6°	A	750	—	—	—	1.2	1.2
6-200 Less Air Cond.	BRF-82	.034	.027	35–39	H	6°	A	750	550D	—	—	0.8	—
6-200 With Air Cond.	BRF-82	.034	.027	35–39	H	6°	A	800/500⑥	600/500D⑥	—	—	—	1.2
6-250	BRF-82	.034	.027	35–39	H	6°	A	550	550D	—	—	1.0	1.0
6-250	BRF-82	.034	.027	35–39	H	6°	A	750/500⑥	600/500D⑥	—	—	1.0	1.0
V8-302	BRF-42	.034	.017	26–30	E	6°	I	575	575D	—	—	—	0.19
V8-302	BRF-42	.034	.017	26–30	E	6°	I	800/500⑥	600/500D⑥	—	—	—	0.19
V8-351⑦	ARF-42	.034	.017	26–30	F	6°	I	750/500⑥	575/500D⑥	—	—	0.50	0.50
V8-351⑦ Calif.	ARF-42	.034	.017	26–30	F	6°	I	—	625/500D⑥	—	—	0.50	0.50
V8-351⑧ Std. Tr.	ARF-42	.034	.020	26–30	F	16°	I	1000/500⑥	—	—	—	0.5	—
V8-351⑧ Auto. Tr.	ARF-42	.034	.017	26–30	F	16°⑬	I	—	700/500D⑥	—	—	—	0.5
V8-351⑧ Auto. Tr. Calif.	ARF-42	.034	.017	26–30	F	16°	I	—	800/500D⑥	—	—	—	0.5
V8-351 H.O.	ARF-42	.034	.020	26–30	F	10°	I	1000/500⑥	—	—	—	—	—
V8-400	ARF-42	.034	.017	26–30	F	⑫	I	—	625/500D⑥	—	—	—	0.10
V8-429	BRF-42	.034	.017	26–30	E	10°	I	—	600/500D⑥	—	—	0.3	0.3
1973													
6-200	BRF-82	.034	.027	35–39	H	6°	C	800	650D	—	—	—	—
6-250	BRF-82	.034	.025	33–39	H	6°	A	750	600D	—	—	0.5	0.5
8-302	BRF-42	.034	.017	24–30	E	6°	I	800	650D	—	—	0.5⑲	0.5⑲
8-351⑦㉓	BRF-42	.034	.017	24–30	F	6°	I	—	625D	—	—	—	0.5⑲
8-351⑦㉒	ARF-42	.034	.017	24–30	F	10°	I	—	625D	—	—	0.5⑲	0.5⑲
8-351⑧	ARF-42	.034	㉑	⑨	F	⑳	I	900	700D	—	—	0.6⑲	0.5⑲
8-400	ARF-42	.034	.017	24–30	F	6°	I	—	625D	—	—	—	0.5⑲
8-429	ARF-42	.034	.017	24–30	E	18°	I	—	600D	—	—	—	0.5⑲
8-460	ARF-42	.034	.017	24–30	E	14°	I	—	600D	—	—	—	0.4⑲
1974													
6-200	BRF-82	.034	.025	33	H	6°	A	750	550D	—	—	—	—
6-200⑭	BRF-82	.034	—	—	H	6°	A	750	550D	—	—	—	—
6-250	BRF-82	.034	.025	33	H	6°	A	600	600D	—	—	—	—
6-250⑭	BRF-82	.034	—	—	H	6°	A	600	600D	—	—	—	—
8-302	BRF-42	.034	.017	26–30	E	6°	I	850	575D	—	—	—	.5
8-302⑭	BRF-42	.034	—	—	E	6°	I	850	575D	—	—	—	.5
8-351⑦㉓	BRF-42	.034	.017	26–30	F	6°	I	—	600D	—	—	—	.4
8-351⑦㉓⑭	BRF-42	.034	—	—	F	6°	I	—	600D	—	—	—	.4
8-351⑦㉒	ARF-42	.044	.017	26–30	F	10°	I	—	650D	—	—	—	.5
8-351⑦㉒⑭	ARF-42	.044	—	—	F	10°	I	—	650D	—	—	—	.5
8-351⑧	ARF-42	.034	.017㉑	26–31	F	⑳	I	900	800D	—	—	—	—
8-351⑧⑭	ARF-42	.034	—	—	F	⑳	I	900	800D	—	—	—	—
8-400⑭	ARF-42	.044	—	—	F	⑩	I	—	625D	—	—	—	—
8-460⑭	ARF-52	.054	—	—	E	⑮	I	—	650D	—	—	—	.25
1975													
6-200⑭	BRF-82	.044	—	—	H	6°	A	750	600D	—	—	—	—
6-250⑭	BRF-82	.044	—	—	J	6°	A	750	600D	—	—	—	—
V8-302⑭	ARF-42	.044	—	—	E	6°	I	900	650D	—	—	—	—

620

Compact & Intermediate Models/Ford & Mercury

TUNEUP SPECIFICATIONS/continued

The following specifications are published from the latest information available. This data should be used only in the absence of a decal affixed in the engine compartment.

★ When using a timing light, disconnect vacuum hose or tube at distributor and plug opening in hose or tube so idle speed will not be affected.
● When checking compression, lowest cylinder must be within 75 percent of highest.
▲ Before removing wires from distributor cap, determine location of the No. 1 wire in cap, as distributor position may have been altered from that shown at the end of this chart.

Year	Spark Plug		Distributor		Ignition Timing ★			Carb. Adjustments					
								Hot Idle Speed ③		Air Fuel Ratio		Idle "CO"%	
	Type	Gap Inch	Point Gap Inch	Dwell Angle Deg.	Firing Order Fig. ▲	Timing BTDC ①	Mark Fig.	Std. Trans.	Auto. Trans. ②	Std. Trans.	Auto. Trans.	Std. Trans.	Auto. Trans.
1975—													
V8-351 ④⑭	ARF-42	.044	—	—	F	12°	I	—	650D	—	—	—	—
V8-351 ⑭㉓	ARF-42	.044	—	—	F	12°	I	—	650D	—	—	—	—
V8-400 ⑭	ARF-42	.044	—	—	F	12°	I	—	650D	—	—	—	—
V8-460 ⑭	ARF-52	.044	—	—	E	14°	I	—	650D	—	—	—	—
1976													
6-200 ⑭	BRF-82	.044	—	—	H	6°	A	800	650D	—	—	—	—
6-250 ⑭㉚	BRF-82	.044	—	—	J	㉙	A	850	600D	—	—	—	—
6-250 ⑭㉛	BRF-82	.044	—	—	J	㉜	A	850	600D	—	—	—	—
8-302 ⑭㉝㉞	ARF-42	.044	—	—	E	4°	I	—	700D	—	—	—	—
8-302 ⑭㉚㉝	ARF-42	.044	—	—	E	㉙	I	750	650D	—	—	—	—
8-302 ⑭㉚㉟	ARF-42	.044	—	—	E	㊱	I	750	650D	—	—	—	—
8-302 ⑭㉛㉞㉟	ARF-42	.044	—	—	E	8°	I	—	700D	—	—	—	—
8-351 ⑭㉓	ARF-42	.044	—	—	F	10°	I	—	650D	—	—	—	—
8-351 ⑭④	ARF-42	.044	—	—	F	8°	I	—	650D	—	—	—	—
8-400 ⑭㉚	ARF-42	.044	—	—	F	㊲	I	—	625D	—	—	—	—
8-400 ⑭㉛㉘	ARF-42	.044	—	—	F	10°	I	—	625D	—	—	—	—
8-400 ⑭㉛㉙	ARF-42	.044	—	—	F	12°	I	—	625D	—	—	—	—
8-460 ⑭	ARF-52	.044	—	—	E	㊵㉙	I	—	650D	—	—	—	—

① — BTDC: Before top dead center.
② — D: Drive.
③ — For A/C add 50 R.P.M. Set with headlamps on high beam and A/C off.
④ — Modified Engine.
⑤ — Dual diaphragm .027 gap, 35–40 dwell. Single diaphragm .025 gap, 37–42 dwell.
⑥ — Higher figure is with throttle solenoid energized.
⑦ — With two barrel carburetor.
⑧ — With four barrel carburetor.
⑨ — Manual trans. 32–35, Auto. trans. 24–30.
⑩ — Cougar 12°, all others 6°.
⑪ — Dual diaphragm .021 gap, 24°–29° dwell. Single diaphragm .017 gap, 26°–31° dwell.
⑫ — Exc. Calif. 8°, Calif. 6°.
⑬ — Cougar with 12 inch converter 10° BTDC.
⑭ — Breakerless distributor.
⑮ — Cougar 14°, all others 10°.
⑯ — Fairlane & Montego.
⑰ — Mustang & Cougar.
⑱ — Mustang "E" BF-92.
⑲ — For California 0.2%.
⑳ — Manual trans. 16° BTDC, Auto. trans. 18° BTDC.
㉑ — Manual trans. .020, Auto. trans. .017.
㉒ — Cleveland engine.
㉓ — Windsor engine.
㉔ — 2 Bar. Carb. 1.1, 4 Bar. Carb. 0.5.
㉕ — 2 Bar. Carb. 14.1 to 1, 4 Bar Carb. 14.0 to 1.
㉖ — 2 Bar. Carb. 14.4 to 1, 4 Bar. Carb. 14.8 to 1.
㉗ — 2 Bar. Carb. 1.6, 4 Bar. Carb. 1.8.
㉘ — California and Police Interceptor; 14°. All others; 10°.
㉙ — With auto. trans.; 6°. With manual trans.; 4°.
㉚ — Except Calif.
㉛ — California.
㉜ — With auto. trans.; 8°. With manual trans.; 6°.
㉝ — Granada and Monarch.
㉞ — With auto. trans.
㉟ — Comet and Maverick.
㊱ — With auto. trans.; 8°. With manual trans.; 4°.
㊲ — Cougar; 10°. Elite, Montego, Torino; 12°.
㊳ — Cougar.
㊴ — Elite, Torino and Montego.
㊵ — In drive with service and parking brake applied.

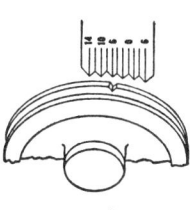

Fig. A

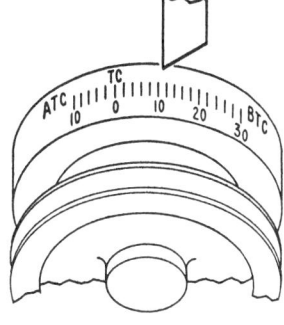

Fig. B

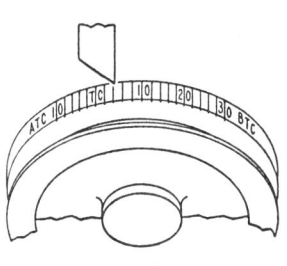

Fig. C

Ford & Mercury/Compact & Intermediate Models

TUNEUP NOTES/continued

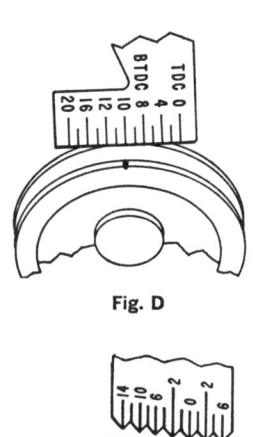

Fig. D

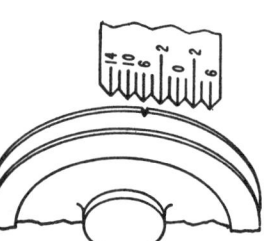

Fig. G

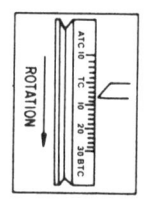

Fig. I

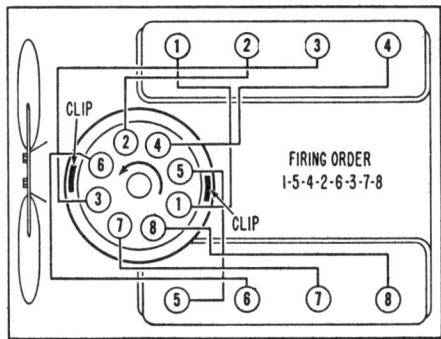

Fig. E

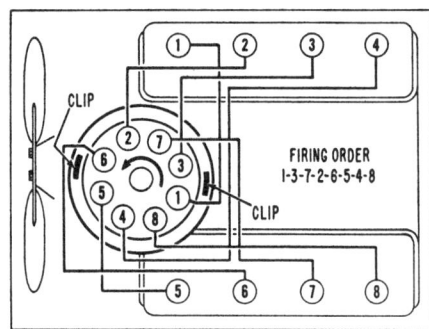

Fig. F

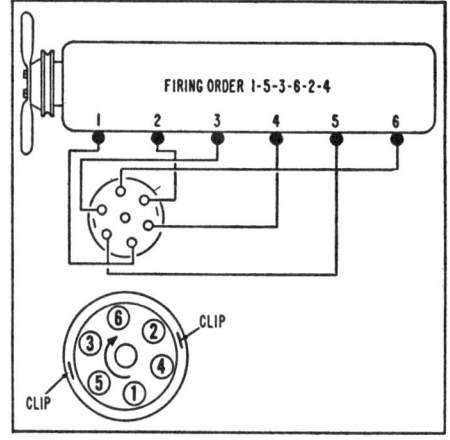

Fig. H

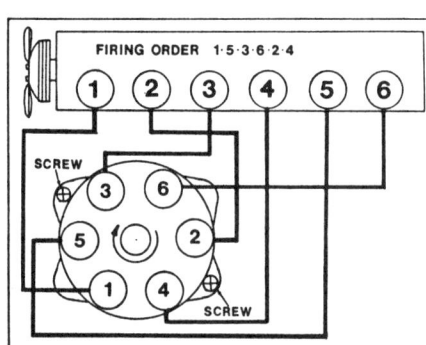

Fig. J

DISTRIBUTOR SPECIFICATIONS

★Note: If unit is checked on vehicle, double the RPM and degrees to get crankshaft figures.

Breaker arm spring tension—17–21.

Distributor Part No.①	Centrifugal Advance Degrees @ RPM of Distributor				Vacuum Advance		Distributor Retard
	Advance Starts	Intermediate Advance		Full Advance	Inches of Vacuum to Start Plunger	Max. Adv. Dist. Deg. @ Vacuum	Max. Retard Dist. Deg. @ Vacuum
1969							
C7AF-AC	0–½ @ 350	0–2 @ 500	4¾–6¾ @ 750	7¾–10 @ 1500	12¼ @ 2000	5	12½ @ 20	—
C8AF-E	0–½ @ 350	0–1¾ @ 500	4½–6¾ @ 750	8–10¼ @ 1500	12½ @ 2000	5	11 @ 25	6 @ 20
C8DF-C	0–½ @ 350	0–2 @ 500	3¼–5¼ @ 750	8¼–10½ @ 1500	12 @ 2000	5	12½ @ 25	6 @ 20
C8DF-D	0–½ @ 350	0–1¼ @ 500	2¾–4¾ @ 750	9–11¼ @ 1500	14 @ 2000	5	11 @ 25	6 @ 20
C8DF-J	0–½ @ 350	0–1½ @ 500	3¼–5¼ @ 750	9½–11¾ @ 1500	14¾ @ 2000	5	11 @ 25	6 @ 20
C8OF-H	0–½ @ 350	¾–2¾ @ 500	7½–9½ @ 750	9½–11¾ @ 1500	13½ @ 2000	5	9½ @ 25	3½ @ 20
C8OF-J	0–½ @ 350	¾–2¾ @ 500	7½–9½ @ 750	9¾–12 @ 1500	13½ @ 2000	5	11 @ 20	—

Compact & Intermediate Models/Ford & Mercury

COOLING SYSTEM & CAPACITY DATA

Year	Model or Engine	Cooling Capacity, Qts.			Radiator Cap Relief Pressure, Lbs.		Thermo. Opening Temp. ①	Fuel Tank Gals.	Engine Oil Refill Qts. ②	Transmission Oil			Rear Axle Oil Pints
		No Heater	With Heater	With A/C	With A/C	No A/C				3 Speed Pints	4 Speed Pints	Auto. Trans. Qts. ⑨	
1969	6-170, 200	8½	9½	9½	12–15	12–15	190	⑥	3½	3½	4	8	2½
	6-250	9	10	10	12–15	12–15	190	⑥	3½	3½	4	9	4
	8-302	14	15	15	12–15	12–15	190	⑥	4	3½	4	9	4
	8-351	14	15	15	12–15	12–15	190	⑥	4	3½	4	11	5
	8-390	19½	20½	20½	12–15	12–15	190	⑥	4	3½	4	12¾	5
	8-427	19½	20½	20½	12–15	12–15	190	⑥	5	3½	4	12¾	5
	8-428	19½	20½	20½	12–15	12–15	190	⑥	4	3½	4	12¾	5
1970	6-170, 200	9	10	10	12–15	12–15	190	⑫	3½	3½	4	8	2½
	6-250	10½	11½	11½	12–15	12–15	190	⑫	3½	3½	4	9	4
	8-302	14½	15½	15½	12–15	12–15	190	⑫	4	3½	4	9	4
	8-351	15½	16½	16½	12–15	12–15	190	⑫	4	3½	4	⑬	5
	8-428	19	20	20	12–15	12–15	190	⑫	4	3½	4	12¾	5
	8-429	17½	18½	18½	12–15	12–15	190	⑫	4	3½	4	12¾	5
	8-429 "CJ"	18½	19½	19½	12–15	12–15	190	⑫	4	3½	4	12¾	5
	8-429 "BOSS" ⑩	18½	19½	19½	12–15	12–15	190	⑫	4	—	4	—	5
	8-429 "BOSS" ⑪	18½	19½	19½	12–15	12–15	190	⑫	6	—	4	—	5
1971	6-170	8¼	9¼	9¼	12–15	12–15	190	16	3½	3½	—	8	4
	6-200, 250 ③	7½	8½	8½	12–15	12–15	190	16	3½	3½	—	8	4
	6-250	7½	8½	8½	12–15	12–15	190	⑭	3½	3½	—	9	4
	8-302	14	15	15	12–15	12–15	190	⑭	4	3½	4	9	4
	8-351	15¼	16¼	16¼	12–15	12–15	190	⑭	4	3½	4	⑬	5
	8-429	18½	19½	19½	12–15	12–15	190	⑭	6	3½	4	12¾	5
1972	Maverick 6-170	8¼	9¼	9¼	12–15	12–15	190	15	3½	3½	—	8	4
	Comet 6-170	8	9	9	12–15	12–15	190	15	3½	3½	—	8	4
	Maverick 6-200	8	9	9	12–15	12–15	190	15	3½	3½	—	8	4
	Comet 6-200	7¾	8¾	9	12–15	12–15	190	15	3½	3½	—	8	4
	Maverick 6-250	9	10	10	12–15	12–15	190	15	3½	3½	—	8	4
	Comet 6-250	8¾	9¾	9¾	12–15	12–15	190	15	3½	3½	—	8	4
	Torino 6-250	10½	11½	12	12–15	12–15	190	⑮	3½	3½	—	9	4
	Montego 6-250	10½	11½	11½	12–15	12–15	190	⑯	3½	3½	—	9	4
	Mustang 6-250	10¼	11¼	11¼	12–15	12–15	190	19½	3½	3½	—	9	4
	8-302 ③	12½	13½	14¼	12–15	12–15	190	15	4	3½	—	9	4
	Torino 8-302	14¼	15¼	16¼	12–15	12–15	190	⑮	4	3½	4	9	4
	Montego 8-302	14¼	15¼	15¼	12–15	12–15	190	⑯	4	3½	4	9	4
	Mustang 8-302	14¼	15¼	15½	12–15	12–15	190	19½	4	3½	4	9	4
	Torino 8-351	14½	15½	15¾	12–15	12–15	190	⑮	4	3½	4	11	5
	Montego 8-351	14½	15½	15⅞	12–15	12–15	190	⑯	4	3½	4	11	5
	Mustang 8-351	14¾	15¾	15¾	12–15	12–15	190	19½	4⑦	3½	4	11	5
	Cougar 8-351	14¾	15¾	15¾	12–15	12–15	190	16½	4	3½	4	⑧	5
	Torino 8-400	16¾	17¾	17¾	12–15	12–15	190	⑮	4	—	4	12¾	5
	Montego 8-400	16¾	17¾	17¾	12–15	12–15	190	⑯	4	—	4	12¾	5
	Torino 8-429	17¾	18¾	20	12–15	12–15	190	⑮	4	—	4	12¾	5
	Montego 8-429	17⅞	18⅞	18⅞	12–15	12–15	190	⑯	4	—	—	12¾	5
1973	Maverick 6-200	8	9	9	12–16	12–16	190	15	4	3½	—	8	4
	Maverick 6-250	8¾	9¾	9¾	12–15	12–15	190	15	3½	3½	—	8	4
	Comet 6-250	8¾	9¾	9¾	12–15	12–15	190	15	3½	3½	—	8	4
	Torino 6-250	10½	11½	11½	12–15	12–15	190	⑰	3½	3½	4	9	4
	Montego 6-250	10½	11½	11½	12–15	12–15	190	⑰	3½	3½	4	9	4
	Mustang 6-250	10¼	11¼	11¼	12–15	12–15	190	19½	3½	—	4	9	4
	8-302 ③	12½	13½	14¼	12–15	12–15	190	15	4	3½	—	9	4
	Torino 8-302	14¼	15¼	15¾	12–15	12–15	190	⑰	4	3½	4	9	4
	Montego 8-302	14¼	15¼	15¾	12–15	12–15	190	⑰	4	3½	4	9	4
	Mustang 8-302	14¼	15¼	15¼	12–15	12–15	190	19½	4	—	4	9	4

Ford & Mercury/Compact & Intermediate Models

COOLING SYSTEM & CAPACITY DATA/continued

Year	Model or Engine	Cooling Capacity, Qts.			Radiator Cap Relief Pressure, Lbs.		Thermo. Opening Temp. ①	Fuel Tank Gals.	Engine Oil Refill Qts. ②	Transmission Oil			Rear Axle Oil Pints
		No Heater	With Heater	With A/C	With A/C	No A/C				3 Speed Pints	4 Speed Pints	Auto. Trans. Qts. ⑨	
1973	Torino 8-351	14¾	15¾	16¾	12–15	12–15	190	⑰	4	3½	4	⑲	5
	Montego 8-351	14¾	15¾	16¾	12–15	12–15	190	⑰	4	3½	4	10½	5
	Mustang 8-351	14¾	15¾	15¾	12–15	12–15	190	19½	4	—	4	⑳	5
	Cougar 8-351	14¾	15¾	15¾	12–15	12–15	190	19½	4	—	4	⑳	5
	Montego 8-400	16¾	17¾	17¾	12–15	12–15	190	⑰	4	—	4	12½	5
	Torino 8-400	16¾	17¾	17¾	12–15	12–15	190	⑰	4	—	4	⑲	5
	Montego 8-429	17¾	18¾	18¾	12–15	12–15	190	⑰	4	—	4	12¾	5
	Torino 8-429	17¾	18¾	18¾	12–15	12–15	190	⑰	4	—	4	12½	5
	8-460⑩	18.5	19.5	19.5	12–16	12–16	190	⑰	6	—	—	13	5
1974	6-200③	8.0	9.0	9.0	12–16	12–16	191	15	4	3½	—	8	4
	6-250③	8.7	9½	9½	12–16	12–16	191	15	4	3½	—	9	4
	6-250⑩	—	11.9	—	12–16	12–16	191	26½	4	3½	—	10¼	4
	8-302③	12.4	13½	14¼	12–16	12–16	191	15	4	3½	—	9	4
	8-302⑩	14.2	15½	15½	12–16	12–16	191	④	4	3½	—	⑤	4
	8-351C⑩	14.8	16	16½	12–16	12–16	191	④	4	—	—	10¼	4
	Cougar 8-351C	14.9	16	16½	12–16	12–16	191	26½	4	—	—	㉓	5
	8-351 W⑩	15.3	16½	16½	12–16	12–16	191	④	4	—	—	㉓	4
	Cougar 8-351 W	15.3	16½	16½	12–16	12–16	191	26½	4	—	—	㉓	5
	8-351 "CJ"⑩	14.7	16½	16½	12–16	12–16	191	④	4	—	4	㉓	4
	Cougar 8-351 "CJ"	14.9	16½	16½	12–16	12–16	191	26½	4	—	—	㉓	5
	8-400⑩	16.7	17¾	18.3	12–16	12–16	191	④	4	—	—	㉓	4
	8-460⑩	18.4	19	19½	12–16	12–16	191	④	4	—	—	㉓	4
	Cougar 400	—	17½	18½	12–16	12–16	191	26½	4	—	—	㉓	5
	Cougar 460	—	19	19½	12–16	12–16	191	26½	6	—	—	㉓	5
1975	6-200③	8	9	9	12–16	12–16	191	19.2	4	3½	—	7.8	4
	6-250③	8	9.7	9.7	12–16	12–16	191	19.2	4	3½	—	8.8	4
	6-250⑱	—	10.5	10.7	12–16	12–16	191	19.2	4	3½	—	㉓	4
	8-302③	—	13.5	14.1	12–16	12–16	191	19.2	4	3½	—	8.8	4
	8-302⑱	—	14.4	14.6	12–16	12–16	191	19.2	4	3½	—	㉓	4
	8-351W⑱	—	15.7	16.7	12–16	12–16	191	19.2	4	3½	—	㉓	4
	8-351W㉒	—	15.9	16.2	12–16	12–16	191	④	4	—	—	㉓	5
	8-351M㉒	—	17.1	18	12–16	12–16	191	④	4	—	—	㉓	5
	8-400㉒	—	17.1	17.5	12–16	12–16	191	④	4	—	—	㉓	5
	8-460㉒	—	19.2	19.7	12–16	12–16	191	④	6	—	—	㉓	5
1976	6-200③	8.2	9	9	12–16	12–16	191	19.2	4	3½	—	8	4½
	6-200⑱	9.1	9.9	9.9	12–16	12–16	191	19.2	4	3½	—	8½	㉔
	6-250③	8.9	9.7	9.7	12–16	12–16	191	19.2	4	3½	—	9	4½
	6-250⑱	9.7	10.5	10.7	12–16	12–16	191	19.2	4	3½	—	8½	㉔
	8-302③	12.7	13.5	14.1	12–16	12–16	191	19.2	4	3½	—	9	4½
	8-302⑱	14.9	15.7	16.7	12–16	12–16	191	19.2	4	3½	—	8½	㉔
	8-351W⑱	14.9	15.7	16.7	12–16	12–16	191	19.2	4	3½	—	10	4
	8-351W㉒	15.1	15.9	16.2	12–16	12–16	191	④	4	—	—	㉑	5
	8-351㉕	16.3	17.1	17.5	12–16	12–16	191	26½	4	—	—	㉑	5
	8-351M㉒	16.3	17.1	17.5	12–16	12–16	191	④	4	—	—	㉑	5
	8-400	16.3	17.1	17.5	12–16	12–16	191	④	4	—	—	12½	5
	8-460	18.4	19.2	19.2	12–16	12–16	191	④	6	—	—	12½	5

①—Use with permanent type anti-freeze.
②—Add 1 qt. with filter change.
③—Maverick and Comet.
④—Sta. Wagons 21 gals.; others 26½ gals.
⑤—C4 9 quarts, FMX 11 quarts.
⑥—Falcon cars and Mustang 16, Cougar 17, Fairlane, Montego and Falcon Wagons 20.
⑦—H.O., 5.
⑧—12" converter, 12¾; others, 11.
⑨—Approximate. Make final check with dipstick.
⑩—Torino & Montego.
⑪—Mustang & Cougar.
⑫—Early Falcon cars & Maverick 16, Mustang, Cougar, Fairlane, Late Falcon & Montego cars 22, Fairlane, Falcon & Montego wagons 19. Subtract 2 gals. for California cars.
⑬—C4 10¼, FMX 11, C6 12¾.
⑭—Torino, Montego, Mustang & Cougar cars, 20. Station wagons, 18.
⑮—Sedans, 22½; wagons, 20½.
⑯—Sedans, 23; wagons, 21.
⑰—Sta. Wagons 20½ gals.; others 22½ gals.
⑱—Granada and Monarch.
⑲—12½" converter, 12½; others, 10½.
⑳—With 2 Bar. Carb. 11; with 4 Bar. Carb. & 10¼" converter, 10¾; others 12¾.
㉑—C4 10 quarts, FMX 11 quarts, C6 12½ quarts.
㉒—Torino, Montego and Cougar.
㉓—C4—10¼ qts., C6—10½ qts., FMX 11 qts.
㉔—With 8 inch ring gear; 4. With 9" ring gear 5.
㉕—Ford Elite.

Ford Mustang II & Pinto/Mercury Bobcat

GENERAL ENGINE SPECIFICATIONS

Year	Engine	Car-buretor	Bore and Stroke	Piston Displacement, Cubic Inches	Compression Ratio	Maximum Brake H.P. @ R.P.M.	Maximum Torque Lbs. Ft. @ R.P.M.	Normal Oil Pressure Pounds
1971	4-98①	1 Barrel	3.188 x 3.056	98①	8.4	75 @ 5000	96 @ 3000	35
	4-122②	2 Barrel	3.57 x 3.03	122②	9.0	100 @ 5600	120 @ 3600	50
1972	4-98①③	1 Barrel	3.188 x 3.056	98①	8.0	54 @ 4600	80 @ 2400	35–60
	4-122②③	2 Barrel	3.57 x 3.03	122②	8.2	86 @ 5400	103 @ 3200	35–60
1973	4-98①③	1 Barrel	3.188 x 3.056	98①	8.1	54 @ 4600	81 @ 2400	35
	4-122②③	2 Barrel	3.57 x 3.03	122②	8.2	④	98 @ 3800	50
1974	4-122②③	2 Barrel	3.575 x 3.029	122②	8.2	80 @ 5400	98 @ 3000	45–65
	4-140③⑤	2 Barrel	3.781 x 3.126	140⑤	8.4	82 @ 4600	113 @ 2600	40–60
	4-140③⑤	2 Barrel	3.781 x 3.126	140⑤	8.4	88 @ 5000	116 @ 2600	40–60
	V6-171③⑥	2 Barrel	3.66 x 2.70	171⑥	8.2	105 @ 4600	140 @ 3200	40–55
1975	4-140③⑤	2 Barrel	3.781 x 3.126	140⑤	8.4	85.5 @ 4800	113 @ 2600	40–60
	V6-171③⑥	2 Barrel	3.66 x 2.70	171⑥	8.2	110 @ 5000	135 @ 3200	40–60
	V8-302③⑦	2 Barrel	4.00 x 3.00	302	8.0	140 @ 3800	228 @ 2600	40–60
1976	4-140③⑤	2 Barrel	3.781 x 3.126	140⑤	—	—	—	—
	V6-171③⑥	2 Barrel	3.66 x 2.70	171⑥	—	—	—	—
	V8-302③⑦	2 Barrel	4.00 x 3.00	302	—	—	—	—

①—1600 cc engine.
②—2000 cc engine.
③—Net Rating—as installed in vehicle.
④—Exc. station wagon, 85 @ 5600; station wagon, 83 @ 5200.
⑤—2300 cc engine.
⑥—2800 cc engine.
⑦—Refer to the Ford & Mercury—Compact & Intermediate Chapter for Service procedures on this engine.

TUNEUP SPECIFICATIONS

The following specifications are published from the latest information available. This data should be used only in the absence of a decal affixed in the engine compartment.

★ When using a timing light, disconnect vacuum hose or tube at distributor and plug opening in hose or tube so idle speed will not be affected.

● When checking compression, lowest cylinder must be within 75 percent of highest.

▲ Before removing wires from distributor cap, determine location of the No. 1 wire in cap, as distributor position may have been altered from that shown at the end of this chart.

Year	Spark Plug Type	Spark Plug Gap Inch	Distributor Point Gap Inch	Distributor Dwell Angle Deg.	Firing Order Fig. ▲	Timing BTDC ①	Mark Fig.	Hot Idle Speed③ Std. Trans.	Hot Idle Speed③ Auto. Trans.②	Air Fuel Ratio Std. Trans.	Air Fuel Ratio Auto. Trans.	Idle "CO" % Std. Trans.	Idle "CO" % Auto. Trans.
1971													
4-98, 1600 cc	AGR-22	.030	.025	38–42	A	12°	C	800/500	—	—	—	1.2	—
4-122, 2000 cc	BRF-32	.025	.025	38–42	B	6°	D	750	650D	—	—	1.2	1.2
1972													
4-98, 1600 cc	AGR-22	.030	.025	36–40	A	12°	C	900/600	—	—	—	1.2	—
4-122, 2000 cc	BRF-42	.034	.025	36–40	B	6°④	D	750/500	650/500	—	—	1.2	1.2
1973													
4-98, 1600 cc	AGR-32	.034	.025	36–40	A	12°	C	900	—	11 to 1	—	1.5	—
4-122, 2000 cc	BRF-42	.030	.025	37–41	B	⑤	D	750	650	11 to 1	11 to 1	1.5	1.5
1974													
4-122, 2000 cc	BRF-42	.034	.025	35–41	B	6	D	750	650	⑥	⑥	—	—
4-140, 2300 cc	AGRF-52	.034	.027	35–41	G	6	E	850	750	11 to 1	11 to 1	.15	.15
V6-171, 2800 cc	AGR-42	.034	.027	35–41	H	12	F	750	650	12.7 to 1	12.7 to 1	.7	.4

Ford Mustang II & Pinto/Mercury Bobcat

TUNEUP SPECIFICATIONS/continued

The following specifications are published from the latest information available. This data should be used only in the absence of a decal affixed in the engine compartment.

★ When using a timing light, disconnect vacuum hose or tube at distributor and plug opening in hose or tube so idle speed will not be affected.

● When checking compression, lowest cylinder must be within 75 percent of highest.

▲ Before removing wires from distributor cap, determine location of the No. 1 wire in cap, as distributor position may have been altered from that shown at the end of this chart.

Year	Spark Plug		Distributor		Ignition Timing ★			Carb. Adjustments					
								Hot Idle Speed ③		Air Fuel Ratio		Idle "CO" %	
	Type	Gap Inch	Point Gap Inch	Dwell Angle Deg.	Firing Order Fig. ▲	Timing BTDC ①	Mark Fig.	Std. Trans.	Auto. Trans.②	Std. Trans.	Auto. Trans.	Std. Trans.	Auto. Trans.
1975													
4-140, 2300 cc	AGRF-52	.034	—	—	G	⑦	E	850	750D	—	—	—	—
V6-171, 2800 cc	AGR-42	.034	—	—	H	⑧	F	850	700D	—	—	—	—
V8-302 ⑨	ARF-42	.044	—	—	I	6°	J	—	700D	—	—	—	—
1976													
4-140, 2300 cc	AGRF-52	.034	—	—	G	⑦	E	750	650D	—	—	—	—
V6-171, 2800 cc	AGR-42	.034	—	—	H	⑧	F	850	700D	—	—	—	—
V8-302 ⑨	ARF-42	.044	—	—	I	6°	J	—	700D	—	—	—	—

① —BTDC: Before top dead center.
② —D: Drive.
③ —Headlamps on Hi Beam—Air Conditioner OFF. Where two speeds are listed, lower speed indicates solenoid disconnected.
④ —California vehicles with Auto. Trans. 9°.
⑤ —Auto. trans., 9°; man. trans., 6°.
⑥ —11.7:1 Except Calif.; 10:1 Calif.
⑦ —Exc. Calif. Auto. Trans., 6° BTDC; Calif. Auto. Trans., 10° BTDC.
⑧ —Manual Trans., 6° BTDC; Exc. Calif. Auto. Trans., 10° BTDC; Calif. Auto. Trans., 8° BTDC.
⑨ —Refer to the Ford & Mercury—Compact & Intermediate Chapter for service procedures on this engine.

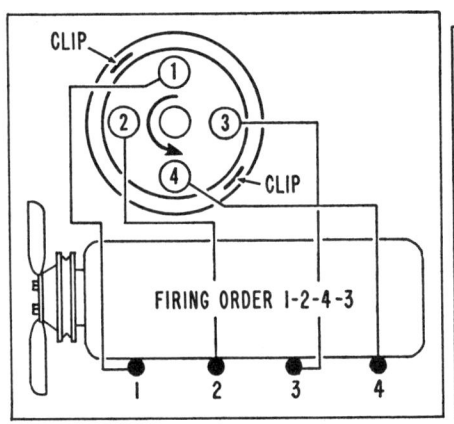

Fig. A

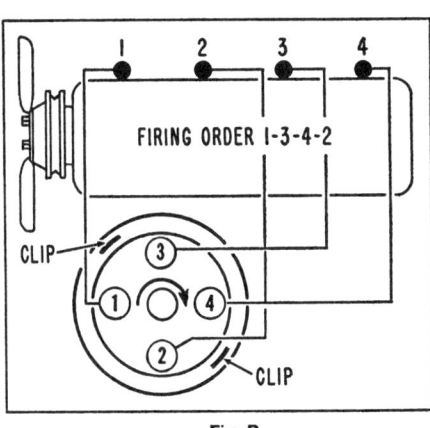

Fig. B

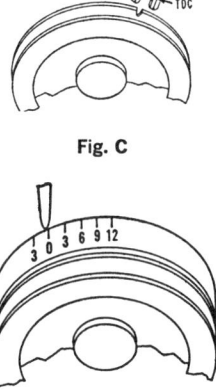

Fig. C

Fig. D

Ford Mustang II & Pinto/Mercury Bobcat

TUNEUP NOTES/continued

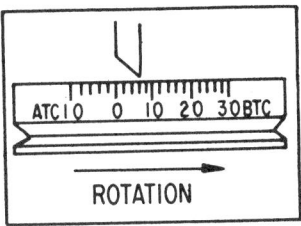

Fig. E

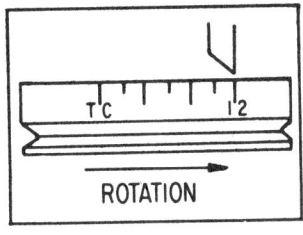

Fig. F

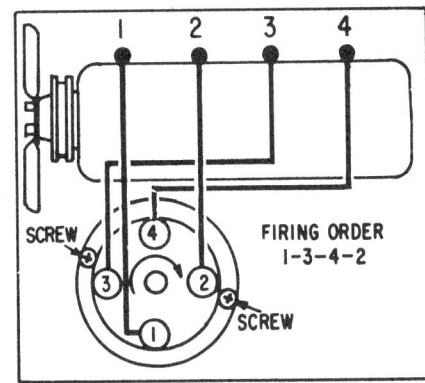

Fig. G

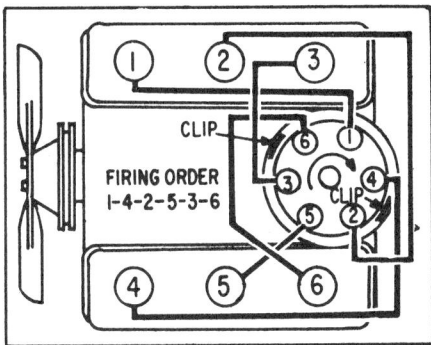

Fig. H

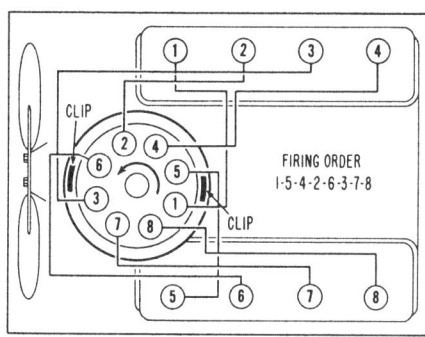

Fig. I

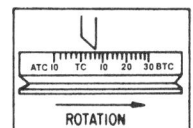

Fig. J

COOLING SYSTEM & CAPACITY DATA/continued

Year	Model or Engine	Cooling Capacity, Qts.			Radiator Cap Relief Pressure, Lbs.		Thermo. Opening Temp.	Fuel Tank Gals.	Engine Oil Refill Qts. ①	Transmission Oil			Rear Axle Oil Pints
		No Heater	With Heater	With A/C	With A/C	No A/C				3 Speed Pints	4 Speed Pints	Auto. Trans. Qts.	
1971	4-98	6	6¾	—	—	12-15	186	11	3½②	—	2½	—	2.2
	4-122	6¾	7½	7½	12-15	12-15	186	11	5	—	2½	8	2.2
1972-73	4-98	6¾	7¾	—	—	12-15	186	11	3½②	—	2½	—	2¼
	4-122	7½	8½	8½	12-15	12-15	186	11	5	—	2½	8	2¼
1974	4-122	7½	8½	8½	12-16	12-16	186	③	5	—	2.8	8	3
	4-140	7½	8½	9½	12-16	12-16	186	③	5	—	⑧	8	3
	6-171	11½	12½	12½	12-16	12-16	186	13	5②	—	4.5	8	3
1975	4-140	—	8¾	9	12-16	12-16	191	④	4½②	—	⑤	⑥	⑦
	V6-171	—	12½	13¼	12-16	12-16	186	④	5②	—	⑤	⑥	⑦
	V8-302	—	16½	16½	12-16	12-16	191	16½	5①	—	—	—	4
1976	4-140	7.9	8.7	9	12-16	12-16	191	④	4½②	—	⑤	⑥	⑦
	V6-171	11.7	12½	13.2	12-16	12-16	186	④	5②	—	⑤	⑥	⑦
	V8-302	15½	16.3	16.3	12-16	12-16	191	16½	5①	—	—	⑨	4

①—Includes 1 qt. for filter.
②—Includes ½ qt. for filter.
③—Pinto: sedan, 13; wagon, 12.
④—Exc. Sta. Wag., 13 gals.; Sta. Wag. 14 gals. Add 3½ gals. with auxiliary fuel tank.
⑤—Pinto, 2.8 pts.; Mustang II, 3½ pts.
⑥—C3 trans., 8 qts.; C4 trans., 9 qts.
⑦—Pinto, 2.2 pts.; Mustang II, 3 pts.; units with 8 inch ring gear, 4 pts.

Ford Thunderbird

GENERAL ENGINE SPECIFICATIONS

Year	Engine	Carburetor	Bore and Stroke	Piston Displacement, Cubic Inches	Compression Ratio	Maximum Brake H.P. @ R.P.M.	Maximum Torque Lbs. Ft. @ R.P.M.	Normal Oil Pressure Pounds
1969-70	360 Horsepower............V8-429	4 Barrel	4.36 x 3.59	429	11.0	360 @ 4600	476 @ 2800	35-60
1971	360 Horsepower............V8-429	4 Barrel	4.36 x 3.59	429	10.3	360 @ 4600	480 @ 2800	35-75
1972	212 Horsepower①............V8-400	2 Barrel	4.00 x 4.00	400	8.4	172 @ 4000	298 @ 2200	35-75
	212 Horsepower①............V8-429	4 Barrel	4.36 x 3.59	429	8.5	212 @ 4400	327 @ 2600	35-75
	224 Horsepower①............V8-460	4 Barrel	4.36 x 3.85	460	8.5	224 @ 4400	357 @ 2800	35-60
1973	208 Horsepower①............V8-429	4 Barrel	4.36 x 3.59	429	8.0	208 @ 4400	327 @ 2600	35-65
	208 Horsepower①............V8-460	4 Barrel	4.36 x 3.85	460	8.0	208 @ 4400	338 @ 2800	35-65
1974	220 Horsepower①............V8-460	4 Barrel	4.36 x 3.85	460	8.0	220 @ 4000	355 @ 2600	35-65
1975	216 Horsepower①............V8-460	4 Barrel	4.36 x 3.85	460	8.0	216 @ 4000	366 @ 2600	40-65
1976	Horsepower①............V8-460	4 Barrel	4.36 x 3.85	460	8.0	—	—	40-65

①—Ratings are NET—as installed in the vehicle.

TUNEUP SPECIFICATIONS

The following specifications are published from the latest information available. This data should be used only in the absence of a decal affixed in the engine compartment.

★When using a timing light, disconnect vacuum hose or tube at distributor and plug opening in hose or tube so idle speed will not be affected.
●When checking compression, lowest cylinder must be within 75 percent of highest.
▲Before removing wires from distributor cap, determine location of the No. 1 wire in cap, as distributor position may have been altered from that shown at the end of this chart.

Year	Spark Plug		Distributor		Ignition Timing ★			Carb. Adjustments					
								Hot Idle Speed		Air Fuel Ratio		Idle "CO" %	
	Type	Gap Inch	Point Gap Inch	Dwell Angle Deg.	Firing Order Fig. ▲	Timing BTDC ①	Mark Fig.	Std. Trans.	Auto. Trans.②	Std. Trans.	Auto. Trans.	Std. Trans.	Auto. Trans.
1969													
8-429	BF-42	.034	.017	26-31	A	6°⑤	B	—	550D④	—	14.3 to 1	—	1.2
1970													
8-429	BRF-42	.034	.017	26-31	A	⑬	B	—	600D⑩	—	14.5 to 1	—	0.75
1971													
8-429	BRF-42	.034	.017	26-31	A	⑬	D	—	600D	—	14.5 to 1	—	.075
1972													
8-400	ARF-42	.034	.017	26-30	C	⑦	D	—	625D⑩	—	—	—	0.10
8-429	BRF-42	.034	.017	26-30	A	10°⑧	D	—	600D⑩	—	—	—	0.3
8-460	BRF-42	.034	.017	26-30	A	⑪	D	—	600D⑩	—	—	—	0.3
1973													
8-429	ARF-42	.034	.017	26-30	A	10°	D	—	600D⑩	—	—	—	0.5⑫
8-460	ARF-42	.034	.017	26-30	A	14°	D	—	600D⑩	—	—	—	0.4⑫
1974													
8-460	ARF-52	③	⑨	—	A	14°	D	—	650D⑥	—	—	—	—
1975													
8-460	ARF-52	③	⑨	—	A	14°	D	—	650D	—	—	—	—

Ford Thunderbird

TUNEUP SPECIFICATIONS/continued

The following specifications are published from the latest information available. This data should be used only in the absence of a decal affixed in the engine compartment.

★ When using a timing light, disconnect vacuum hose or tube at distributor and plug opening in hose or tube so idle speed will not be affected.

● When checking compression, lowest cylinder must be within 80 percent of highest.

▲ Before removing wires from distributor cap, determine location of No. 1 wire in cap, as distributor position may have been altered from that shown at the end of this chart.

Year	Spark Plug		Distributor		Ignition Timing ★			Carb. Adjustments					
								Hot Idle Speed		Air Fuel Ratio		Idle "CO" %	
	Type	Gap Inch	Point Gap Inch	Dwell Angle Deg.	Firing Order Fig. ▲	Timing BTDC ①	Mark Fig.	Std. Trans.	Auto. Trans. ②	Std. Trans.	Auto. Trans.	Std. Trans.	Auto. Trans.
1976													
8-460 ⑭	ARF-52	.044	⑨	—	A	8° ⑮	D	—	650D ⑯	—	—	—	—
8-460 ⑰	ARF-52	.044	⑨	—	A	14° ⑮	D	—	650D ⑯	—	—	—	—

① —BTDC: Before top dead center.
② —D: Drive. N: Neutral.
③ —Exc. Calif., .054 inch; Calif. .044 inch.
④ —With headlights and A/C on.
⑤ —Whenever idle speed or ignition timing is adjusted, vacuum line to brake release mechanism must be disconnected and plugged, to prevent parking brake from releasing when selector is moved to Drive.
⑥ —With lights and A/C off.
⑦ —Exc. Calif. 8° BTC, Calif. 6° BTC.
⑧ —Built after Dec. 31, 1971, 14°.
⑨ —Breakerless distributor.
⑩ —With headlamp on Hi Beam—Air Conditioning OFF.
⑪ —Exc. Calif. 10° BTC, Calif 6° BTC.
⑫ —For Calif. 0.2.
⑬ —Single diaphragm 14°, Dual diaphragm 4°.
⑭ —Exc. Calif.
⑮ —In Drive with service & parking brakes applied.
⑯ —With A/C "On".
⑰ —Calif.

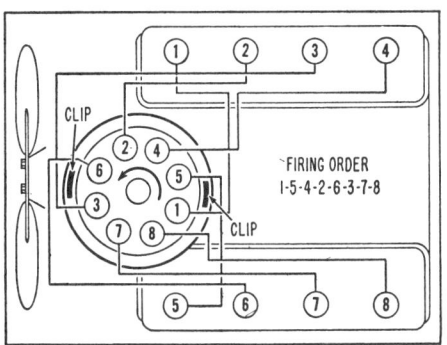

Fig. A

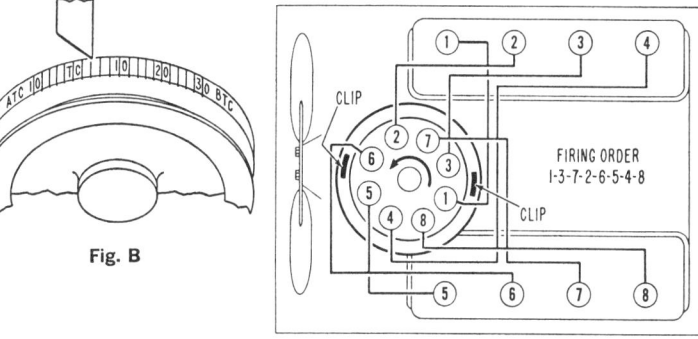

Fig. B   Fig. C 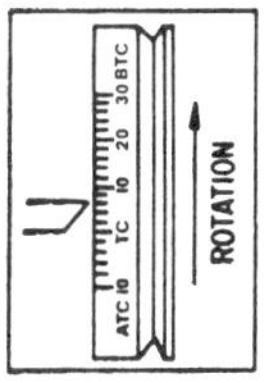   Fig. D

COOLING SYSTEM & CAPACITY DATA

Year	Model or Engine	Cooling Capacity, Qts.			Radiator Cap Relief Pressure, Lbs.		Thermo. Opening Temp. ①	Fuel Tank Gals.	Engine Oil Refill Qts. ②	Transmission Oil			Rear Axle Oil Pints
		No Heater	With Heater	With A/C	With A/C	No A/C				3 Speed Pints	4 Speed Pints	Auto. Trans. Qts. ③	
1969	V8-429	19½	20½	20½	12-15	12-15	195	24	4	—	—	12¾	5
1970	V8-429	17½	18½	18½	12-15	12-15	188	④	4	—	—	12¾	5
1971	V8-429	18½	19½	16½	12-15	12-15	188	23	4	—	—	12¾	5
1972	V8-400	16¾	17¾	18½	12-15	12-15	188	22½	4	—	—	12¾	5
	V8-429	17¾	18¾	19½	12-15	12-15	188	22½	4	—	—	12¾	5
	V8-460	19	20	20	12-15	12-15	188	22½	4	—	—	12½	5
1973	All	18½	19½	19½	12-15	12-15	188	22½	4	—	—	12½	5
1974	V8-460	—	19½	19½	12-16	12-16	191	26½	4	—	—	12½	5
1975-76	V8-460	—	19.3	19.3	12-16	12-16	191	26½	4	—	—	12½	5

① —For permanent type anti-freeze.
② —Add one quart with filter change.
③ —Approximate. Make final check with dipstick.
④ —California vehicles 22½; all others 24.

Lincoln Continental

GENERAL ENGINE SPECIFICATIONS

Year	Engine	Carburetor	Bore and Stroke	Piston Displacement, Cubic Inches	Compression Ratio	Maximum Brake H.P. @ R.P.M.	Maximum Torque Lbs. Ft. @ R.P.M.	Normal Oil Pressure Pounds
1969-70	365 Horsepower............V8-460	4 Barrel	4.3600 x 3.850	460	10.5	365 @ 4600	500 @ 2800	35-60
1971	365 Horsepower............V8-460	4 Barrel	4.3600 x 3.850	460	10.2	365 @ 4600	500 @ 2800	35-60
1972	212 Horsepower①............V8-460	4 Barrel	4.3600 x 3.850	460	8.5	212 @ 4400	342 @ 2800	35-60
	224 Horsepower①............V8-460	4 Barrel	4.3600 x 3.850	460	8.5	224 @ 4400	357 @ 2800	35-60
1973	208 Horsepower①............V8-460	4 Barrel	4.3600 x 3.850	460	8.0	208 @ 4400	338 @ 2800	35-70
	219 Horsepower①............V8-460	4 Barrel	4.3600 x 3.850	460	8.0	219 @ 4400	360 @ 2800	35-70
1974	215 Horsepower①............V8-460	4 Barrel	4.362 x 3.850	460	8.0	215 @ 4000	350 @ 2600	35-65
	220 Horsepower①............V8-460	4 Barrel	4.362 x 3.850	460	8.0	220 @ 4000	355 @ 2600	35-65
1975	253 Horsepower①............V8-460	4 Barrel	4.362 x 3.850	460	8.0	253 @ 4400	386 @ 2600	40-65
1976	Horsepower①.............V8-460	4 Barrel	4.362 x 3.850	460	8.0	—	—	40-65

①—Ratings are NET—as installed in the vehicle.

TUNEUP SPECIFICATIONS

The following specifications are published from the latest information available. This data should be used only in the absence of a decal affixed in the engine compartment.

★When using a timing light, disconnect vacuum hose or tube at distributor and plug opening in hose or tube so idle speed will not be affected.

●When checking compression, lowest cylinder must be within 75 percent of highest.

▲Before removing wires from distributor cap, determine location of No. 1 wire in cap, as distributor position may have been altered from that shown at the end of this chart.

Year	Spark Plug		Distributor		Ignition Timing ★			Carb. Adjustments					
								Hot Idle Speed		Air Fuel Ratio		Idle CO %	
	Type	Gap Inch	Point Gap Inch	Dwell Angle Deg.	Firing Order Fig. ▲	Timing BTDC ①	Mark Fig.	Std. Trans.	Auto. Trans.②	Std. Trans.	Auto. Trans.	Std. Trans.	Auto. Trans.
1969													
V8-460③	BRF-42	.034	.017	26-31	C	10°⑥	B	—	550D⑤	—	14.3 to 1	—	1.2
1970													
V8-460	BRF-42	.034	.017	26-31	C	10°⑥	A	—	600D⑦	—	14.4 to 1	—	1.0
1971													
V8-460	BRF-42	.034	.017	26-31	C	5°⑥	D	—	600D⑦	—	14.2 to 1	—	0.9
1972													
V8-460 Exc. Calif.	BF-42	.034	.017	26-30	C	10°⑥	D	—	625D⑦	—	—	—	0.3
V8-460 Calif.	BF-42	.034	.017	26-30	C	6°⑥	D	—	625D⑦	—	—	—	0.3
1973													
V8-460	ARF-42	.034	.017	24-30	C	14°	D	—	600D	—	—	—	0.4⑧
1974													
V8-460	ARF-52	.054	⑨	—	C	14°	D	—	650D	—	—	—	—
1975													
V8-460	ARF-52	.044	⑨	—	C	14°	D	—	650D	—	—	—	—

Lincoln Continental

TUNEUP SPECIFICATIONS/continued

The following specifications are published from the latest information available. This data should be used only in the absence of a decal affixed in the engine compartment.

★When using a timing light, disconnect vacuum hose or tube at distributor and plug opening in tube or hose so idle speed will not be affected.
●When checking compression, lowest cylinder must be within 80 percent of highest.
▲Before removing wires from distributor cap, determine location of the No. 1 wire in cap, as distributor position may have been altered from that shown at the end of this chart.

Year	Spark Plug		Distributor		Ignition Timing ★			Carb. Adjustments					
								Hot Idle Speed		Air Fuel Ratio		Idle CO %	
	Type	Gap Inch	Point Gap Inch	Dwell Angle Deg.	Firing Order Fig. ▲	Timing BTDC ①	Mark Fig.	Std. Trans.	Auto. Trans. ②	Std. Trans.	Auto. Trans.	Std. Trans.	Auto. Trans.
1976													
V8-460 ⑩	ARF-52	.044	⑨	—	C	8° ⑪	D	—	650D ⑫	—	—	—	—
V8-460 ⑬	ARF-52	.044	⑨	—	C	14° ⑪	D	—	650D ⑫	—	—	—	—

①—BTDC-Before top dead center.
②—D-Drive. N-Neutral.
③—With IMCO system.
⑤—With headlights on and A/C "Full On".
⑥—Whenever idle speed or ignition timing is adjusted, vacuum line to brake release mechanism must be disconnected and plugged to prevent parking brake from releasing when selector is moved to Drive.
⑦—Headlamps on Hi Beam—Air Conditioner OFF.
⑧—For California 0.2.
⑨—Breakerless distributor.
⑩—Exc. Calif.
⑪—In Drive with service & parking brakes applied.
⑫—With A/C "On".
⑬—Calif.

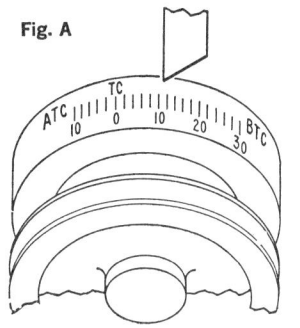

Fig. A

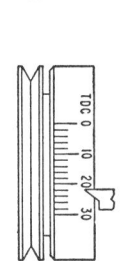

Fig. B

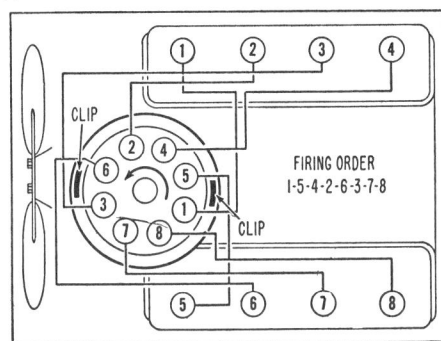

Fig. C
FIRING ORDER 1-5-4-2-6-3-7-8

Fig. D

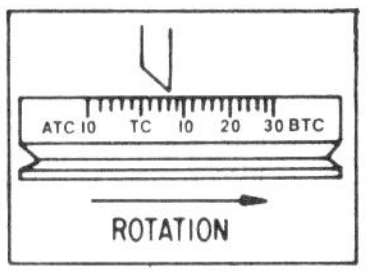

COOLING SYSTEM & CAPACITY DATA

Year	Model or Engine	Cooling Capacity, Qts.			Radiator Cap Relief Pressure, Lbs.		Thermo. Opening Temp. ①	Fuel Tank Gals.	Engine Oil Refill Qts. ③	Transmission Oil			Rear Axle Oil Pints
		No Heater	With Heater	With A/C	With A/C	No A/C				3 Speed Pints	4 Speed Pints	Auto. Trans. Qts. ②	
1969	V8-462	22½	23½	23½	12-15	12-15	185	25½	4	—	—	13½	5
	V8-460	—	22	22	12-15	12-15	185	25½	4	—	—	13½	5
1970	Lincoln	—	20½	—	12-15	12-15	188	24④	4	—	—	13	5
	Mark III	—	20½	—	12-15	12-15	188	24④	4	—	—	12¾	5
1971	Lincoln	—	19½	19½	12-15	12-15	188	23	4	—	—	13	5
	Mark III	—	19½	19½	12-15	12-15	188	23	4	—	—	12¾	5
1972-73	Lincoln	—	19½	19½	12-15	12-15	188	22	4	—	—	13⑤	5
	Mark IV	—	19½	19½	12-15	12-15	188	22½	4	—	—	12¾⑤	5
1974	Lincoln	—	20½	20½	12-16	12-16	191	22	4	—	—	12½	5
	Mark IV	—	20½	20½	12-16	12-16	191	26½	4	—	—	12½	5
1975	Lincoln	—	—	19¾	12-16	12-16	191	24¼	4	—	—	12½	5
	Mark IV	—	—	20	12-16	12-16	191	26½	4	—	—	12½	5
1976	Lincoln	—	—	19.7	12-16	12-16	191	24¼⑥	4	—	—	12	5
	Mark IV	—	—	19.8	12-16	12-16	191	26½	4	—	—	12	5

①—With permanent type anti-freeze.
②—Approximate. Make final check with dipstick.
③—Add one quart with filter change.
④—California vehicles 22½.
⑤—1973 Models 12½ quarts.
⑥—Add 8 gals. with auxiliary tank.

Oldsmobile/Exc. Starfire

GENERAL ENGINE SPECIFICATIONS

Year	Engine	Carburetor	Bore and Stroke	Piston Displacement, Cubic Inches	Compression Ratio	Maximum Brake H.P. @ R.P.M.	Maximum Torque Lbs. Ft. @ R.P.M.	Normal Oil Pressure Pounds
1969	155 Horsepower............②6-250	1 Barrel	3.875 x 3.53	250	8.50	155 @ 4200	240 @ 2000	30-45
	250 Horsepower............V8-350	2 Barrel	4.057 x 3.385	350	9.00	250 @ 4400	355 @ 2600	30-45
	310 Horsepower............V8-350	4 Barrel	4.057 x 3.385	350	10.25	310 @ 4800	390 @ 3200	30-45
	310 Horsepower............V8-455	2 Barrel	4.125 x 4.250	455	9.00	310 @ 4200	490 @ 2400	30-45
	325 Horsepower............V8-350	4 Barrel	4.057 x 3.385	350	10.50	325 @ 5400	360 @ 3600	30-45
	325 Horsepower............V8-400	4 Barrel	3.870 x 4.250	400	10.50	325 @ 4600	440 @ 3000	35-50
	350 Horsepower............V8-400	4 Barrel	3.870 x 4.250	400	10.50	350 @ 4800	440 @ 3200	35-50
	360 Horsepower............V8-400	4 Barrel	3.870 x 4.250	400	10.50	360 @ 5400	440 @ 3600	35-50
	365 Horsepower............V8-455	4 Barrel	4.125 x 4.250	455	10.25	365 @ 4600	510 @ 3000	30-45
	375 Horsepower............V8-455	4 Barrel	4.125 x 4.250	455	10.25	375 @ 4600	510 @ 3000	30-45
	390 Horsepower............V8-455	4 Barrel	4.125 x 4.250	455	10.25	390 @ 5000	500 @ 3200	30-45
	400 Horsepower............V8-455	4 Barrel	4.125 x 4.250	455	10.25	400 @ 4800	500 @ 3200	30-45
1970	155 Horsepower............②6-250	1 Barrel	3.875 x 3.53	250	8.50	155 @ 4200	240 @ 2000	30-45
	250 Horsepower............V8-350	2 Barrel	4.057 x 3.385	350	9.00	250 @ 4400	355 @ 2600	30-45
	310 Horsepower............V8-350	4 Barrel	4.057 x 3.385	350	10.25	310 @ 4800	390 @ 3200	30-45
	310 Horsepower............V8-455	2 Barrel	4.125 x 4.250	455	9.00	310 @ 4200	490 @ 2400	30-45
	320 Horsepower............V8-455	2 Barrel	4.125 x 4.250	455	10.25	320 @ 4200	500 @ 2400	30-45
	325 Horsepower............V8-350	4 Barrel	4.057 x 3.385	350	10.50	325 @ 5400	360 @ 3600	30-45
	365 Horsepower............V8-455	4 Barrel	4.125 x 4.250	455	10.50	365 @ 5000	500 @ 3200	30-45
	370 Horsepower............V8-455	4 Barrel	4.125 x 4.250	455	10.50	370 @ 5200	500 @ 3600	30-45
	375 Horsepower............V8-455	4 Barrel	4.125 x 4.250	455	10.25	375 @ 4600	510 @ 3000	30-45
	390 Horsepower............V8-455	4 Barrel	4.125 x 4.250	455	10.25	390 @ 5000	500 @ 3200	30-45
	400 Horsepower............V8-455	4 Barrel	4.125 x 4.250	455	10.25	400 @ 3200	500 @ 3200	30-45
1971	110 Horsepower①............②6-250	1 Barrel	3.875 x 3.53	250	8.10	110 @ 3800	185 @ 1600	30-45
	155 Horsepower①............V8-350	2 Barrel	4.057 x 3.385	350	8.10	155 @ 4000	275 @ 2400	30-45
	180 Horsepower①............V8-350	4 Barrel	4.057 x 3.385	350	8.10	180 @ 4000	275 @ 2400	30-45
	185 Horsepower①............V8-455	2 Barrel	4.125 x 4.250	455	8.10	185 @ 3600	355 @ 2000	30-45
	225 Horsepower①............V8-455	4 Barrel	4.125 x 4.250	455	8.10	225 @ 3600	360 @ 2600	30-45
	260 Horsepower①............V8-455	4 Barrel	4.125 x 4.250	455	8.10	260 @ 4400	370 @ 3200	30-45
	265 Horsepower①............V8-455	4 Barrel	4.125 x 4.250	455	8.10	265 @ 4200	375 @ 2800	30-45
1972	160 Horsepower①............V8-350	2 Barrel	4.057 x 3.385	350	8.50	160 @ 4000	275 @ 2400	30-45
	175 Horsepower①............V8-350	2 Barrel	4.057 x 3.385	350	8.50	175 @ 4000	295 @ 2600	30-45
	180 Horsepower①............V8-350	4 Barrel	4.057 x 3.385	350	8.50	180 @ 4000	275 @ 2800	30-45
	200 Horsepower①............V8-350	4 Barrel	4.057 x 3.385	350	8.50	200 @ 4400	300 @ 3200	30-45
	225 Horsepower①............V8-455	4 Barrel	4.125 x 4.250	455	8.50	225 @ 3600	360 @ 2600	30-45
	250 Horsepower①............V8-455	4 Barrel	4.125 x 4.250	455	8.50	250 @ 4200	370 @ 2800	30-45
	265 Horsepower①............V8-455	4 Barrel	4.125 x 4.250	455	8.50	265 @ 4200	375 @ 2800	30-45
	270 Horsepower①............V8-455	4 Barrel	4.125 x 4.250	455	8.50	270 @ 4400	370 @ 3200	30-45
	300 Horsepower①............V8-455	4 Barrel	4.125 x 4.250	455	8.50	300 @ 4700	410 @ 3200	30-45
1973	100 Horsepower①............②6-250	1 Barrel	3.875 x 3.53	250	8.25	100 @ 3600	175 @ 1600	40
	160 Horsepower①............V8-350	2 Barrel	4.057 x 3.385	350	8.5	160 @ 3800	275 @ 2400	30-45
	180 Horsepower①............V8-350	4 Barrel	4.057 x 3.385	350	8.5	180 @ 3800	275 @ 2800	30-45
	225 Horsepower①............V8-455	4 Barrel	4.125 x 4.250	455	8.5	225 @ 3600	360 @ 2600	30-45
	250 Horsepower①............V8-455	4 Barrel	4.125 x 4.250	455	8.5	250 @ 4000	375 @ 2800	30-45
	270 Horsepower①............V8-455	4 Barrel	4.125 x 4.250	455	8.5	270 @ 4200	370 @ 3200	30-45
1974	100 Horsepower①............②6-250	1 Barrel	3.87 x 3.53	250	8.5	100 @ 3600	175 @ 1800	40
	180 Horsepower①............V8-350	4 Barrel	4.057 x 3.385	350	8.5	180 @ 3800	275 @ 2800	30-45
	200 Horsepower①............V8-350	4 Barrel	4.057 x 3.385	350	8.5	200 @ 4200	300 @ 3200	30-45
	210 Horsepower①............V8-455	4 Barrel	4.126 x 4.250	455	8.5	210 @ 3600	350 @ 2400	30-45
	230 Horsepower①............V8-455	4 Barrel	4.126 x 4.250	455	8.5	230 @ 3800	370 @ 2800	30-45
	275 Horsepower①............V8-455	4 Barrel	4.126 x 4.250	455	8.5	275 @ 4200	395 @ 3200	30-45
1975	105 Horsepower①............6-250②	1 Barrel	3.87 x 3.53	250	8.25	105 @ 3800	185 @ 1200	36-41
	110 Horsepower①............V8-260	2 Barrel	3.50 x 3.385	260	8.5	110 @ 3400	205 @ 1600	30-45
	165 Horsepower①............V8-350③	4 Barrel	3.80 x 3.85	350	8.0	165 @ 3800	260 @ 2200	37
	170 Horsepower①............V8-350	4 Barrel	4.057 x 3.385	350	8.5	170 @ 3800	275 @ 2400	30-45

Exc. Starfire/Oldsmobile

GENERAL ENGINE SPECIFICATIONS/continued

Year	Engine	Carburetor	Bore and Stroke	Piston Displacement, Cubic Inches	Compression Ratio	Maximum Brake H.P. @ R.P.M.	Maximum Torque Lbs. Ft. @ R.P.M.	Normal Oil Pressure Pounds
1975	190 Horsepower①..........V8-400④	4 Barrel	4.1212 x 3.75	400	7.6	190 @ 3400	350 @ 2000	55-60
	190 Horsepower①..........V8-455⑤	4 Barrel	4.126 x 4.25	455	8.5	190 @ 3600	350 @ 2400	30-45
	215 Horsepower①..........V8-455⑥	4 Barrel	4.126 x 4.25	455	8.5	215 @ 3600	370 @ 2400	30-45
1976	105 Horsepower①...........6-250②	1 Barrel	3.87 x 3.53	250	8.5	105 @ 3800	185 @ 1200	36-41
	110 Horsepower①..........V8-260	2 Barrel	3.50 x 3.385	260	8.0	110 @ 3400	205 @ 1600	30-45
	140 Horsepower①..........V8-350③	2 Barrel	3.80 x 3.85	350	8.0	140 @ 3200	280 @ 1800	37
	155 Horsepower①..........V8-350③	4 Barrel	3.80 x 3.85	350	8.0	155 @ 3400	280 @ 1800	37
	170 Horsepower①..........V8-350	4 Barrel	4.057 x 3.385	350	8.5	170 @ 3800	275 @ 2400	30-45
	190 Horsepower①..........V8-455⑤	4 Barrel	4.126 x 4.25	455	8.5	190 @ 3400	350 @ 2000	30-45
	215 Horsepower①..........V8-455⑥	4 Barrel	4.126 x 4.25	455	8.5	215 @ 3600	370 @ 2400	30-45

①—All horsepower and torque ratings are net.
②—See Chevrolet Chapter for service procedure on this engine.
③—Omega only. See Buick Chapter for service procedures on this engine.
④—See Pontiac Chapter for service procedures on this engine.
⑤—Exc. Toronado.
⑥—Toronado.

TUNEUP SPECIFICATIONS

The following specifications are published from the latest information available. This data should be used only in the absence of a decal affixed in the engine compartment.

★When using a timing light, disconnect vacuum hose or tube at distributor and plug opening in hose or tube so idle speed will not be affected.

●When checking compression, lowest cylinder must be within 80 percent of highest.

▲Before removing wires from distributor cap, determine location of the No. 1 wire in cap, as distributor position may have been altered from that shown at the end of this chart.

Year	Spark Plug		Distributor		Ignition Timing★			Carb. Adjustments					
								Hot Idle Speed		Air Fuel Ratio		Idle "CO" %	
	Type	Gap Inch	Point Gap Inch	Dwell Angle Deg.	Firing Order Fig. ▲	Timing BTDC ①	Mark Fig.	Std. Trans.	Auto. Trans. ②	Std. Trans.	Auto. Trans.	Std. Trans.	Auto. Trans.

1969

6-250 Std. Trans.⑭	R46N	.035	③	31-34	N	TDC	B	775⑪	—	—	—	—	—
6-250 Auto. Trans.⑭	R46N	.035	③	31-34	N	4°	B	—	625D⑪	—	—	—	—
8-350, 250 H.P.	R46S	.030	.016	30	F	6°	A	675⑪	600D⑪	—	—	—	—
8-350, 310 H.P.	R45S	.030	.016	30	F	8°	A	675⑪	575D⑪	—	—	—	—
8-350, 325 H.P.	R43S	.030	.016	30	F	12°	A	675⑪	575D⑪	—	—	—	—
8-400, 325 H.P.	R44S	.030	.016	30	F	8°⑨⑮	A	—	575D⑪	—	—	—	—
8-400, 350 H.P.	R44S	.030	.016	30	F	2°⑨	A	750⑪	—	—	—	—	—
8-400, 360 H.P.	R43S	.030	.016	30	F	14°⑫	A	750⑪	650D⑪	—	—	—	—
8-455, 310 H.P.	R45S	.030	.016	30	F	6°	A	675⑪	600D⑪	—	—	—	—
8-455, 365 H.P.	R44S	.030	.016	30	F	8°⑨	A	—	575D⑪	—	—	—	—
8-455, 375 H.P.	R44S	.030	.016	30	F	8°⑨	A	—	575D⑪	—	—	—	—
8-455, 400 H.P.	R44S	.030	.016	30	F	10°⑨	A	—	575D⑪	—	—	—	—

1970

6-250 Std. Trans.⑭	R46T	.035	③	31-34	N	TDC	B	750	—	—	—	—	—
6-250 Auto. Trans.⑭	R46T	.035	③	31-34	N	4°	B	—	600D	—	—	—	—
8-350, 250 H.P.⑤	R46S	.030	.016	30	F	10°⑯	A	750	575D	—	—	—	—
8-350, 250 H.P.⑥	R46S	.030	.016	30	F	8°⑯	A	675	575D	—	—	—	—

Oldsmobile/Exc. Starfire

TUNEUP SPECIFICATIONS/continued

The following specifications are published from the latest information available. This data should be used only in the absence of a decal affixed in the engine compartment.

★ When using a timing light, disconnect vacuum hose or tube at distributor and plug opening in hose or tube so idle speed will not be affected.

● When checking compression, lowest cylinder must be within 80 percent of highest.

▲ Before removing wires from distributor cap, determine location of the No. 1 wire in cap, as distributor position may have been altered from that shown at the end of this chart.

Year	Spark Plug		Distributor		Ignition Timing ★			Carb. Adjustments					
	Type	Gap Inch	Point Gap Inch	Dwell Angle Deg.	Firing Order Fig. ▲	Timing BTDC ①	Mark Fig.	Hot Idle Speed		Air Fuel Ratio		Idle "CO" %	
								Std. Trans.	Auto. Trans. ②	Std. Trans.	Auto. Trans.	Std. Trans.	Auto. Trans.
1970—Continued													
8-350, 310 H.P.	R45S	.030	.016	30	F	10°⑯	A	650	575D	—	—	—	—
8-350, 325 H.P.	R43S	.030	.016	30	F	14°⑯	A	750	625D	—	—	—	—
8-455, 310 H.P.	R46S	.030	.016	30	F	8°⑯	A	675	575D	—	—	—	—
8-455, 320 H.P.	R45S	.030	.016	30	F	8°⑯	A	—	575D	—	—	—	—
8-455, 365 H.P.	R44S	.030	.016	30	F	8°⑨	A	750	650D	—	—	—	—
8-455, 370 H.P.	R44S	.030	.016	30	F	8°⑨	A	750	650D	—	—	—	—
8-455, 375 H.P.	R44S	.030	.016	30	F	12°⑯	A	750	600D	—	—	—	—
8-455, 390 H.P.	R45S	.030	.016	30	F	8°⑯	A	—	600D	—	—	—	—
8-455, 390 H.P.④	R44S	.030	.016	30	F	12°⑯	A	—	600D	—	—	—	—
8-455, 400 H.P.	R44S	.030	.016	30	F	12°⑯	A	—	600D	—	—	—	—
1971													
6-250⑭	R46TS	.035	③	31–34	N	4°	C	550	500D	—	—	1.0	1.0
8-350, 155 H.P.	R46S	.040	.016	30	F	10°⑯	A	750	600D	—	—	0.6	0.6
8-350, 180 H.P. S.Tr.	R45S	.040	.016	30	F	10°⑯	A	750	—	—	—	0.3	—
8-350, 180 H.P. A.Tr.	R46S	.040	.016	30	F	12°⑯	A	—	600D	—	—	—	0.3
8-350, 260 H.P.	R45S	.040	.016	30	F	10°⑯	A	750	600D	—	—	0.3	0.3
8-455, 185 H.P.	R46S	.040	.016	30	F	8°⑯	A	750	600D	—	—	0.6	0.6
8-455, 225 H.P.	R46S	.040	.016	30	F	8°⑯	A	—	600D	—	—	0.6	0.6
8-455, 260 H.P.④ S.Tr.	R45S	.040	.016	30	F	12°⑯	A	750	—	—	—	0.3	—
8-455, 260 H.P.④ A.Tr.	R45S	.040	.016	30	F	10°⑯	A	—	600D	—	—	—	0.3
8-455, 265 H.P.	R46S	.040	.016	30	F	10°⑯	A	—	600D	—	—	0.3	0.3
1972													
8-350 2 Bar. Carb.	R46S	.040	.016	30	F	8°⑯	A	750	650D	—	—	0.3	0.3
8-350 4 B. Carb. St. Tr.	R45S	.040	.016	30	F	8°⑯	A	750	—	—	—	0.3	—
8-350 4 B. Carb. A. Tr.	R46S	.040	.016	30	F	12°⑯	A	—	600D	—	—	—	0.3
8-455, 250, 270 H.P.	R46S	.040	.016	30	F	8°⑯	A	—	600D	—	—	0.3	0.3
8-455, 300 H.P.	R45S	.040	.016	30	F	10°	A	1000	650D	—	—	0.3	0.3
8-455 Others—St. Tr.	R45S	.040	.016	30	F	10°⑯	A	750	—	—	—	0.3	—
8-455 Others—A. Tr.	R46S	.040	.016	30	F	8°⑯	A	—	650D	—	—	—	0.3
1973													
6-250⑭	R46TS	.035	③	31–34	N	6°	C	700	600D	—	—	0.3	0.3
8-350 2 Bar.⑤	R46S	.040	.016	30	F	14°⑯	A	—	700D	—	—	—	0.3
8-350 2 Bar.⑥	R46S	.040	.016	30	F	12°⑯	A	—	700D	—	—	—	0.3
8-350 4 Bar. Std. Tr.	R45S	.040	.016	30	F	8°⑯	A	1100	—	—	—	0.3	—
8-350 4 Bar. Auto. Tr.	R46S	.040	.016	30	F	12°⑯⑮	A	—	650D	—	—	—	0.3
8-455⑤	R45S	.040	.016	30	F	10°⑯	A	1000	—	—	—	0.3	—
8-455⑥	R46S	.040	.016	30	F	8°⑯	A	—	650D	—	—	—	0.3

Exc. Starfire/Oldsmobile

TUNEUP SPECIFICATIONS/continued

The following specifications are published from the latest information available. This data should be used only in the absence of a decal affixed in the engine compartment.

★ When using a timing light, disconnect vacuum hose or tube at distributor and plug opening in hose or tube so idle speed will not be affected.

● When checking compression, lowest cylinder must be within 75 percent of highest.

▲ Before removing wires from distributor cap, determine location of No. 1 wire in cap, as distributor position may have been altered from that shown at the end of this chart.

Year	Spark Plug		Distributor		Ignition Timing ★			Carb. Adjustments					
	Type	Gap Inch	Point Gap Inch	Dwell Angle Deg.	Firing Order Fig. ▲	Timing BTDC ①	Mark Fig.	Hot Idle Speed		Air Fuel Ratio		Idle "CO" %	
								Std. Trans.	Auto. Trans.②	Std. Trans.	Auto. Trans.	Std. Trans.	Auto. Trans.
1974													
6-250⑭	R46TS	.035	.019	31–34	N	8°⑦	C	850	600D	—	—	0.3	0.3
8-350 4 Bar.	R46S	.040	.019	30	⑳	12°⑯	H	—	650D	—	—	0.2	0.2
8-455, 275 H.P.	R45S	.040	.019	30	⑳	14°⑯	H	—	650D	—	—	0.2	0.2
8-455 4 Bar.	R46S	.040	.019	30	⑳	8°⑯	H	—	650D	—	—	0.2	0.2
8-455 4 Bar.⑨	R46SX	.080	—	—	⑳	8°⑯	H	—	650D	—	—	0.2	0.2
8-455 4 Bar.⑬	R46S	.040	.019	30	⑳	10°⑯	H	—	650D	—	—	0.2	0.2
8-455 4 Bar.⑨⑬	R46SX	.080	—	—	⑳	10°⑯	H	—	650D	—	—	0.2	0.2
1975													
6-250⑭	R46TX	.060	—	—	I	10°	C	850	⑲	—	—	—	—
V8-260	R46SX	.080	—	—	J	⑰	G	750	650D	—	—	—	—
V8-350⑩	R45TSX	.060	—	—	K	12°	D	—	600D	—	—	—	—
V8-350	R46SX	.080	—	—	J	20°⑯	G	—	650D	—	—	—	—
V8-400⑱	R45TSX	.060	—	—	L	16°⑯	E	—	650D	—	—	—	—
V8-455	R46SX	.080	—	—	J	16°⑯	G	—	650D	—	—	—	—
V8-455⑬	R46SX	.080	—	—	J	12°⑯	G	—	650D	—	—	—	—
1976													
6-250⑭㉑	R46TS	.035	—	—	I	6°	C	850	—	—	—	—	—
6-250⑭㉒	R46TS	.035	—	—	I	10°	C	—	⑲	—	—	—	—
V8-260㉑	R46SX	.080	—	—	J	16°⑯	G	750	—	—	—	—	—
V8-260㉒㉓	R46SX	.080	—	—	J	18°⑯	G	—	650D	—	—	—	—
V8-260⑤㉔	R46SX	.080	—	—	J	16°⑯	G	—	650D	—	—	—	—
V8-260㉔㉕	R46SX	.080	—	—	J	14°⑯	G	—	650D	—	—	—	—
V8-350	R46SX	.080	—	—	J	20°⑯	G	—	⑲	—	—	—	—
V8-350⑩	R46TSX	.060	—	—	K	12°	D	—	600D	—	—	—	—
V8-455	R46SX	.080	—	—	J	16°⑯	G	—	650D	—	—	—	—
V8-455⑬㉓	R46SX	.080	—	—	J	14°⑯	G	—	650D	—	—	—	—
V8-455⑬㉔	R46SX	.080	—	—	J	12°⑯	G	—	650D	—	—	—	—

①—BTDC: Before top dead center.
②—D: Drive. N: Neutral. Add 50 R.P.M. to slow idle speed for air conditioned cars with A/C off.
③—New points .019", used points .016".
④—Air Induction.
⑤—Cutlass.
⑥—Full size cars.
⑦—At 600 rpm with auto. trans. and 850 rpm with manual trans.
⑧—With High Energy Ignition system.
⑨—At 850 R.P.M.
⑩—Omega only. See Buick Chapter for service procedures on this engine.
⑪—With A/C "OFF" and idle compensator held closed.
⑫—At 1250 R.P.M.
⑬—Toronado.
⑭—See Chevrolet Chapter for service procedures on this engine.
⑮—Vista-Cruiser 10°.
⑯—At 1100 R.P.M.
⑰—Exc. Calif., 16° BTDC; Calif., 18° BTDC. At 1100 R.P.M.
⑱—See Pontiac Chapter for service procedures on this engine.
⑲—Exc. Calif., 550D; Calif., 600D.
⑳—Exc. H.E.I., Fig. C; H.E.I., Fig. G.
㉑—Manual trans.
㉒—Auto. trans.
㉓—Exc. California.
㉔—California.
㉕—Omega.

Oldsmobile/Exc. Starfire

TUNEUP NOTES/continued

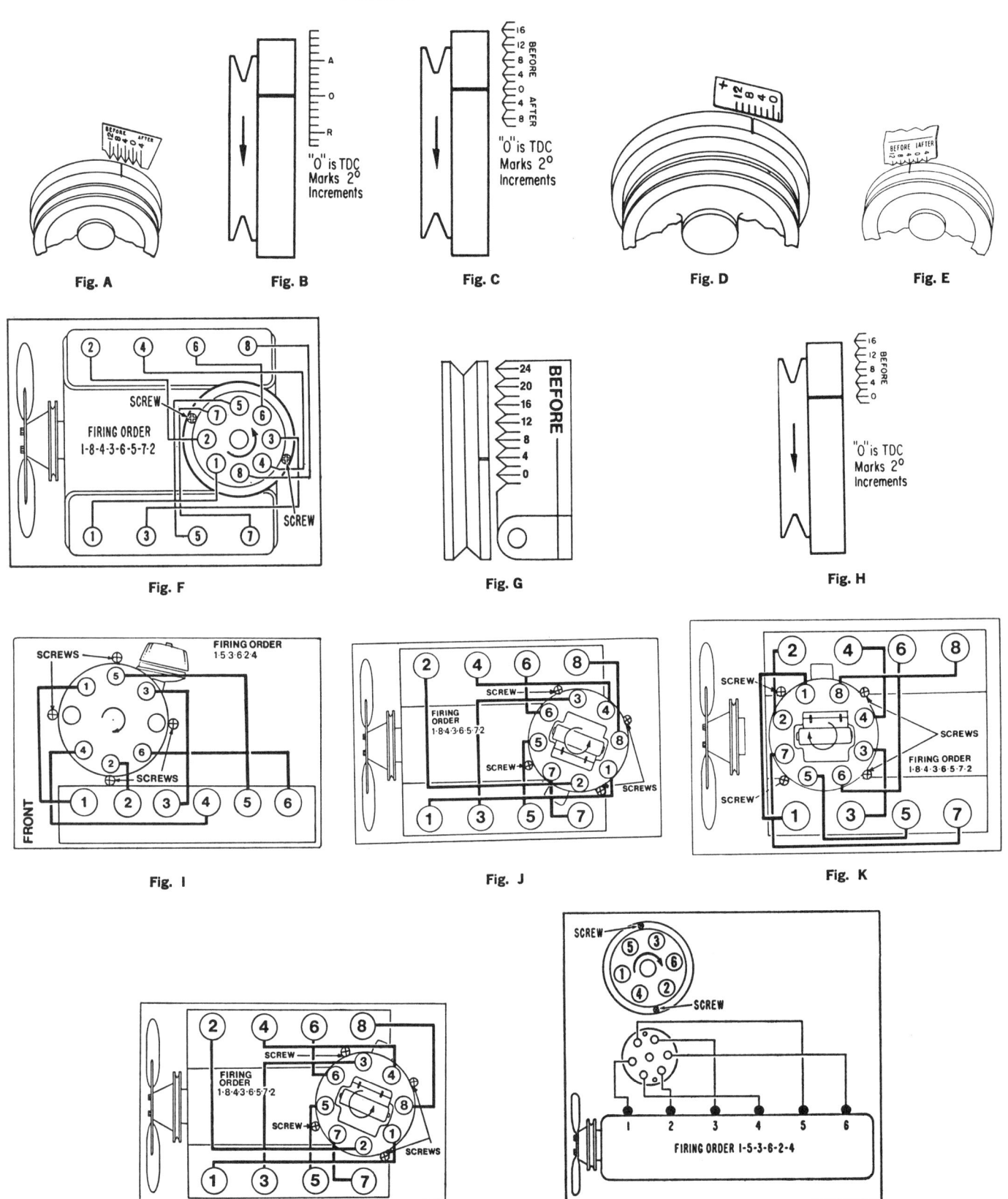

Exc. Starfire/Oldsmobile

COOLING SYSTEM & CAPACITY DATA

Year	Model or Engine	Cooling Capacity, Qts.		Radiator Cap Relief Pressure, Lbs.		Thermo. Opening Temp. ①	Fuel Tank Gals.	Engine Oil Refill Qts. ②	Transmission Oil				Rear Axle Oil Pints
		With Heater	With A/C	With A/C	No A/C				3 Speed Pints	4 Speed Pints	5 Speed Pints	Auto. Trans. Qts. ⑫	
1969	6-250	12.2	12.2	15	15	195	20	4	3½	—	—	⑩	3.69
	8-350	15.2	15.7	15	15	195	20⑬	4	3½	4.90	—	⑩	3.69
	8-400, 4-4-2	16.2	17.2	15	15	195	20	4	3½	4.90	—	⑮	3.69
	Delta, 98	17.5	18	15	15	195	25	4	4.9	—	—	⑩	5.32⑭
	Toronado	18	18.5	15	15	195	24	5	—	—	—	⑮	4
1970	6-250	12	12.0	15	15	195	20	4	3½	—	—	③	3¾
	8-350⑯	15	15.5	15	15	195	20⑬	4	3½	2¼	—	③	3¾
	8-350⑰	16.5	16.5	15	15	195	25	4	3½	2¼	—	⑩	3¾
	8-455⑯	16	16.5	15	15	195	20⑬	4	3½	2¼	—	⑩	3¾
	8-455⑰	17.5	18	15	15	195	25	4	4½	2¼	—	⑩	5⅓
	Toronado	18	18.5	15	15	195	24	5	—	—	—	⑩	4
1971	6-250	13	13	15	15	195	19⑱	4	3½	—	—	③	4¼
	8-350⑯	16	17	15	15	195	19⑮	4	⑲	2¼	—	⑩	4¼
	8-350⑰	16	17	15	15	195	24	4	3½	—	—	⑩	⑳
	8-455⑯	17	18	15	15	195	19	4	⑲	2¼	—	⑩	4¼
	8-455⑰	17	18	15	15	195	24	4	3½	—	—	⑩	⑳
	Toronado	18	19	15	15	195	24	5	—	—	—	⑩	4
1972	8-350⑯	15.2	15.7	15	15	195	19⑬	4	3½	3½	—	⑩	⑳
	8-350⑰	16.2	16.7	15	15	195	24	4	—	—	—	⑩	4¼
	8-455⑯	15.2	15.7	15	15	195	19⑬	4	3½	3½	—	⑩	4¼
	8-455⑰	17	17.5	15	15	195	24	4	—	—	—	⑩	5½
	Toronado	19.5	20	15	15	195	25	5	—	—	—	⑩	4
1973	6-250	12½	12½	15	15	195	21	4	3½	—	—	⑩	4¼
	8-350 Omega	15½	16½	15	15	195	21	4	3½	—	—	⑩	4¼
	8-350 Cutlass	16	16	15	15	195	22	4	3½	2¼	—	⑩	4¼
	8-350 "88"	16¼	16¼	15	15	195	26	4	—	—	—	⑩	5½
	8-455 Cutlass	17	18	15	15	195	22	4	—	2¼	—	⑩	4¼
	8-455⑰	17	17½	15	15	195	26㉑	4	—	—	—	⑩	5½
	Toronado	19½	20	15	15	195	26	4	—	—	—	㉒	4
1974	6-250	15½	—	15	15	195	21	4	3.5	—	—	⑩	4¼
	8-350 Omega	18½	19½	15	15	195	21	4	3.5	—	—	⑩	4¼
	8-350 Cutlass	20④	20④	15	15	195	22	4	—	—	—	⑩	4¼
	8-350⑰	21⑤	21⑤	15	15	195	26	4	—	—	—	⑩	4¼
	8-350 Sta. Wagon	20④	20④	15	15	195	22	4	—	—	—	⑩	5½
	8-455 Cutlass	21	21½⑥	15	15	195	22	4	—	—	—	⑩	4¼
	8-455⑰	21	21½⑥	15	15	195	26	4	—	—	—	⑩	5½
	8-455 Sta. Wagon	21	21½⑥	15	15	195	22	4	—	—	—	⑩	5½
	Toronado	21	21½	15	15	195	26	5	—	—	—	㉒	4
1975	6-250 Omega	15½	19½	15	15	195	21	4	3½	—	—	⑩	⑨
	6-250 Cutlass	17	17	15	15	195	22	4	3½	—	—	⑩	⑨
	8-260 Omega	18½	19½	15	15	195	21	4	3½	—	—	⑩	⑨
	8-260 Cutlass	23½	23½④	15	15	195	22	4	3½	—	—	⑩	⑨
	8-350 Omega	18½	19½	15	15	195	21	4	—	—	—	⑩	⑨
	8-350⑦	20	20④	15	15	195	26⑧	4	—	—	—	⑩	⑨
	8-400	21½	22⑥	15	15	195	26⑧	4	—	—	—	⑩	⑨
	8-455	21	21½⑥	15	15	195	26⑧	4	—	—	—	⑩	⑨
	Toronado	21	21½	15	15	195	26	5	—	—	—	㉒	4
1976	6-250 Omega	15½	16½	15	15	195	21	4	3½	—	—	⑩	㉓
	6-250 Cutlass	17	—	15	15	195	22	4	3½	—	—	⑩	㉔
	8-260 Omega	23	23½	15	15	195	21	4	3½	—	3½	⑩	㉓
	8-260 Cutlass	23½	23½④	15	15	195	22	4	3½	—	3½	⑩	㉔
	8-350 Omega	21½	22	15	15	195	21	4	—	—	—	⑩	㉓

Oldsmobile/Exc. Starfire

COOLING SYSTEM & CAPACITY DATA/continued

Year	Model or Engine	Cooling Capacity, Qts.		Radiator Cap Relief Pressure, Lbs.		Thermo. Opening Temp. ①	Fuel Tank Gals.	Engine Oil Refill Qts. ②	Transmission Oil				Rear Axle Oil Pints
		With Heater	With A/C	With A/C	No A/C				3 Speed Pints	4 Speed Pints	5 Speed Pints	Auto. Trans. Qts. ⑫	
1976	8-350 ⑦	20	20 ④	15	15	195	26 ⑧	4	—	—	—	⑩	㉔
	8-455	21	21½ ⑥	15	15	195	26 ⑧	4	—	—	—	⑩	㉔
	Toronado	21½	21½	15	15	195	26	5	—	—	—	㉒	4

①—For Be.manent type anti-freexe.
②—Add one quart with filter change.
③—Oil pan only 2 qts. After overhaul 10 qts.
④—With heavy duty cooling system add 2½ qts.
⑤—With heavy duty cooling system add 1½ qts.
⑥—With heavy duty cooling system add 2 qts.
⑦—ntermediate and full size.
⑧—Intermediate and station wagons 22 gallons.
⑨—8½" ring gear 4¼ pts., 8⅞" ring gear 5½ pts., 9⅜ ring gear 5½ pts.
⑩—Oil pan only 3 qts. After overhaul 10 qts.
⑫—Approximate; make final check with dipstick.
⑬—Vista-Cruiser 23 gallons.
⑭—With Jetaway, 3.69 pts.
⑮—Refill 4 qts.
⑯—Intermediate cars.
⑰—Full size cars.
⑱—Vista-Cruiser 22 gallons.
⑲—Standard unit 3½, heavy duty 4½.
⑳—With 10 bolt cover 4¼; with 12 bolt cover 5½.
㉑—Custom Cruiser 22 gallons.
㉒—Oil pan only 4 qts. after overhaul 12 qts.
㉓—7½" ring gear, 3½ pts.; 8½" ring gear, 4¼ pts., 8⅞" ring gear, 5½ pts.
㉔—8½" ring gear, 4¼ pts.; 8⅞" ring gear, 5½ pts.

Pontiac/Exc. Astre & Sunbird

GENERAL ENGINE SPECIFICATIONS

Year	Engine	Carburetor	Bore and Stroke	Piston Displacement, Cubic Inches	Compression Ratio	Maximum Brake H.P. @ R.P.M.	Maximum Torque Lbs. Ft. @ R.P.M.	Normal Oil Pressure Pounds
1969	175 Horsepower..............6-250	1 Barrel	3.8750 x 3.52	250	9.00	175 @ 4800	240 @ 2600	26-36
	215 Horsepower..............6-250	4 Barrel	3.8750 x 3.52	250	10.50	215 @ 5200	255 @ 3800	26-36
	230 Horsepower..............6-250	4 Barrel	3.8750 x 3.52	250	10.50	230 @ 5400	260 @ 3600	26-36
	265 Horsepower..............V8-350	2 Barrel	3.8750 x 3.75	350	9.20	265 @ 4600	355 @ 2800	30-40
	325 Horsepower..............V8-350	4 Barrel	3.8750 x 3.75	350	10.50	325 @ 5100	380 @ 3200	55-60
	330 Horsepower..............V8-350	4 Barrel	3.8750 x 3.75	350	10.50	330 @ 5100	380 @ 3200	55-60
	265 Horsepower..............V8-400	2 Barrel	4.1200 x 3.75	400	8.60	265 @ 4600	397 @ 2400	30-40
	290 Horsepower..............V8-400	2 Barrel	4.1200 x 3.75	400	10.50	290 @ 4600	428 @ 2500	30-40
	330 Horsepower..............V8-400	4 Barrel	4.1200 x 3.75	400	10.75	330 @ 4800	430 @ 3300	30-40
	335 Horsepower..............V8-400	4 Barrel	4.1200 x 3.75	400	10.75	335 @ 5000	430 @ 3400	30-40
	345 Horsepower..............V8-400	4 Barrel	4.1200 x 3.75	400	10.75	345 @ 5400	430 @ 3700	30-40
	350 Horsepower..............V8-400	4 Barrel	4.1200 x 3.75	400	10.50	350 @ 5000	445 @ 3000	55-60
	350 Horsepower..............V8-400	4 Barrel	4.1200 x 3.75	400	10.75	350 @ 5000	445 @ 3000	55-60
	366 Horsepower..............V8-400	4 Barrel	4.1200 x 3.75	400	10.75	366 @ 5100	445 @ 3600	30-40
	370 Horsepower..............V8-400	4 Barrel	4.1200 x 3.75	400	10.75	370 @ 5500	445 @ 3900	30-40
	360 Horsepower..............V8-428	4 Barrel	4.1200 x 4.00	428	10.50	360 @ 4600	472 @ 3200	30-40
	370 Horsepower..............V8-428	4 Barrel	4.1200 x 4.00	428	10.50	370 @ 4800	472 @ 3200	55-60
	390 Horsepower..............V8-428	4 Barrel	4.1200 x 4.00	428	10.75	390 @ 5200	465 @ 3400	55-60
1970	155 Horsepower..............①6-250	1 Barrel	3.875 x 3.53	250	8.50	155 @ 4200	235 @ 1600	30-45
	255 Horsepower..............V8-350	2 Barrel	3.8750 x 3.75	350	8.80	255 @ 4600	355 @ 2800	30-40
	265 Horsepower..............V8-400	2 Barrel	4.1200 x 3.75	400	8.80	265 @ 4600	397 @ 2400	30-40
	290 Horsepower..............V8-400	2 Barrel	4.1200 x 3.75	400	10.00	290 @ 4600	428 @ 2500	30-40
	330 Horsepower..............V8-400	4 Barrel	4.1200 x 3.75	400	10.00	330 @ 4800	445 @ 2900	30-40
	350 Horsepower..............V8-400	4 Barrel	4.1200 x 3.75	400	10.25	350 @ 5000	445 @ 3000	55-60
	366 Horsepower..............V8-400	4 Barrel	4.1200 x 3.75	400	10.50	366 @ 5100	445 @ 3600	30-40
	370 Horsepower..............V8-400	4 Barrel	4.1200 x 3.75	400	10.50	370 @ 5500	445 @ 3900	30-40
	360 Horsepower..............V8-455	4 Barrel	4.1510 x 4.21	455	10.00	360 @ 4300	500 @ 2700	30-40
	370 Horsepower..............V8-455	4 Barrel	4.1510 x 4.21	455	10.25	370 @ 4600	500 @ 3100	30-40

Exc. Astre & Sunbird/Pontiac

GENERAL ENGINE SPECIFICATIONS/continued

Year	Engine	Carburetor	Bore and Stroke	Piston Displacement, Cubic Inches	Compression Ratio	Maximum Brake H.P. @ R.P.M.	Maximum Torque Lbs. Ft. @ R.P.M.	Normal Oil Pressure Pounds
1971	145 Horsepower............①6-250	1 Barrel	3.875 x 3.53	250	8.50	145 @ 4200	230 @ 1600	30-45
	200 Horsepower............②V8-307	2 Barrel	3.875 x 3.25	307	8.50	200 @ 4600	300 @ 2400	30-45
	250 Horsepower............8-350	2 Barrel	3.8750 x 3.75	350	8.0	250 @ 4400	350 @ 2400	30-40
	265 Horsepower............8-400	2 Barrel	4.1200 x 3.75	400	8.2	265 @ 4400	400 @ 2400	30-40
	300 Horsepower............8-400	4 Barrel	4.1200 x 3.75	400	8.2	300 @ 4800	400 @ 3600	30-40
	280 Horsepower............8-455	2 Barrel	4.1510 x 4.21	455	8.2	280 @ 4400	455 @ 2000	30-40
	325 Horsepower............8-455	4 Barrel	4.1510 x 4.21	455	8.2	325 @ 4400	455 @ 3200	30-40
	335 Horsepower............8-455	4 Barrel	4.1510 x 4.21	455	8.4	335 @ 4800	480 @ 3600	30-40
1972	110 Horsepower③............①6-250	1 Barrel	3.875 x 3.53	250	8.50	110 @ 3800	185 @ 1600	30-45
	130 Horsepower③............②8-307	2 Barrel	3.875 x 3.25	307	8.50	130 @ 4400	230 @ 2400	30-45
	160 Horsepower③............8-350	2 Barrel	3.875 x 3.75	350	8.00	160 @ 4400	270 @ 2000	30-40
	175 Horsepower③............8-350	2 Barrel	3.875 x 3.75	350	8.00	175 @ 4400	275 @ 2000	30-40
	175 Horsepower③............8-400	2 Barrel	4.1200 x 3.75	400	8.2	175 @ 4000	310 @ 2400	30-40
	200 Horsepower③............8-400	2 Barrel	4.1200 x 3.75	400	8.2	200 @ 4000	325 @ 2400	30-40
	200 Horsepower③............8-400	4 Barrel	4.1200 x 3.75	400	8.2	200 @ 4000	295 @ 2800	30-40
	250 Horsepower③............8-400	4 Barrel	4.1200 x 3.75	400	8.2	250 @ 4400	325 @ 3200	30-40
	185 Horsepower③............8-455	2 Barrel	4.1510 x 4.21	455	8.2	185 @ 4000	350 @ 2000	30-40
	200 Horsepower③............8-455	2 Barrel	4.1510 x 4.21	455	8.2	200 @ 4000	370 @ 2000	30-40
	220 Horsepower③............8-455	4 Barrel	4.1510 x 4.21	455	8.2	220 @ 3600	350 @ 2400	30-40
	230 Horsepower③............8-455	4 Barrel	4.1510 x 4.21	455	8.2	230 @ 4400	360 @ 2800	30-40
	250 Horsepower③............8-455	4 Barrel	4.1510 x 4.21	455	8.2	250 @ 3600	370 @ 2400	30-40
	250 Horsepower③............8-455	4 Barrel	4.1510 x 4.21	455	8.2	250 @ 3600	375 @ 2400	30-40
	300 Horsepower③............8-455	4 Barrel	4.1510 x 4.21	455	8.4	300 @ 4000	415 @ 3200	30-40
1973	100 Horsepower③............①6-250	1 Barrel	3.87 x 3.53	250	8.2	100 @ 3600	175 @ 1600	30-45
	150 Horsepower③............8-350	2 Barrel	3.88 x 3.75	350	7.6	150 @ 4000	270 @ 2000	55-60
	175 Horsepower③............④8-350	2 Barrel	3.88 x 3.75	350	7.6	175 @ 4400	280 @ 2400	55-60
	170 Horsepower③............④8-400	2 Barrel	4.12 x 3.75	400	8.0	170 @ 3600	320 @ 2000	55-60
	185 Horsepower③............④8-400	2 Barrel	4.12 x 3.75	400	8.0	185 @ 4000	320 @ 2400	55-60
	200 Horsepower③............④8-400	4 Barrel	4.12 x 3.75	400	8.0	200 @ 4000	310 @ 2400	55-60
	230 Horsepower③............④8-400	4 Barrel	4.12 x 3.75	400	8.0	230 @ 4400	325 @ 3200	55-60
	215 Horsepower③............④8-455	4 Barrel	4.1510 x 4.21	455	8.0	215 @ 3600	350 @ 2400	55-60
	250 Horsepower③............④8-455	4 Barrel	4.1510 x 4.21	455	8.0	250 @ 4000	370 @ 2800	55-60
	290 Horsepower③............④8-455	4 Barrel	4.1510 x 4.21	455	8.4	290 @ 4000	395 @ 3200	75-80
	310 Horsepower③............④8-455	4 Barrel	4.1510 x 4.21	455	8.4	310 @ 4000	390 @ 3600	75-80
1974	100 Horsepower③............①6-250	1 Barrel	3.88 x 3.53	250	8.2	100 @ 3600	175 @ 1600	30-45
	155 Horsepower③............8-350	2 Barrel	3.88 x 3.75	350	7.6	155 @ 3600	275 @ 2400	55-60
	170 Horsepower③............④8-350	2 Barrel	3.88 x 3.75	350	7.6	170 @ 4000	290 @ 2400	55-60
	170 Horsepower③............④8-350	4 Barrel	3.88 x 3.75	350	7.6	170 @ 4000	280 @ 2000	55-60
	200 Horsepower③............④8-350	4 Barrel	3.88 x 3.75	350	7.6	200 @ 4400	295 @ 2800	55-60
	175 Horsepower③............8-400	2 Barrel	4.12 x 3.75	400	8.0	175 @ 3600	315 @ 2000	55-60
	190 Horsepower③............④8-400	2 Barrel	4.12 x 3.75	400	8.0	190 @ 4000	330 @ 2400	55-60
	200 Horsepower③............④8-400	4 Barrel	4.12 x 3.75	400	8.0	200 @ 4000	320 @ 2400	55-60
	225 Horsepower③............④8-400	4 Barrel	4.12 x 3.75	400	8.0	225 @ 4000	330 @ 2800	55-60
	215 Horsepower③............④8-455	4 Barrel	4.15 x 4.21	455	8.0	215 @ 3600	355 @ 2400	55-60
	250 Horsepower③............④8-455	4 Barrel	4.15 x 4.21	455	8.0	250 @ 4000	380 @ 2800	55-60
	290 Horsepower③............④8-455	4 Barrel	4.15 x 4.21	455	8.4	290 @ 4000	395 @ 3200	75-80
1975	105 Horsepower③............6-250①	1 Barrel	3.87 x 3.53	250	8.25	105 @ 3800	185 @ 1200	36-41
	110 Horsepower③..........V8-260⑤	2 Barrel	3.50 x 3.385	260	8.5	110 @ 3400	205 @ 1600	30-45
	155 Horsepower③..........V8-350	2 Barrel	3.88 x 3.75	350	7.6	155 @ 4000	—	55-60
	175 Horsepower③..........V8-350	4 Barrel	3.88 x 3.75	350	7.6	175 @ 4000	—	55-60
	145 Horsepower③..........V8-350⑥	2 Barrel	3.80 x 3.85	350	8.0	145 @ 3200	270 @ 3000	37
	165 Horsepower③..........V8-350⑥	4 Barrel	3.80 x 3.85	350	8.0	165 @ 3800	260 @ 2200	37
	170 Horsepower③..........V8-400	2 Barrel	4.12 x 3.75	400	7.6	170 @ 4000	—	55-60
	185 Horsepower③..........V8-400	4 Barrel	4.12 x 3.75	400	7.6	185 @ 3600	—	55-60
	200 Horsepower③..........V8-455	4 Barrel	4.15 x 4.21	455	7.6	200 @ 3500	—	55-60

Pontiac/Exc. Astre & Sunbird

GENERAL ENGINE SPECIFICATIONS/continued

Year	Engine	Carburetor	Bore and Stroke	Piston Displacement, Cubic Inches	Compression Ratio	Maximum Brake H.P. @ R.P.M.	Maximum Torque Ft. Lbs. @ R.P.M.	Normal Oil Pressure Pounds
1976	110 Horsepower③..........6-250①	1 Barrel	3.87 x 3.53	250	8.3	110 @ 3600	185 @ 1200	36–41
	110 Horsepower..........V8-260⑤	2 Barrel	3.50 x 3.385	260	7.5	110 @ 3400	205 @ 1600	30–45
	160 Horsepower③..........V8-350	2 Barrel	3.8762 x 3.75	350	7.6	160 @ 4000	280 @ 2000	35–40
	175 Horsepower③..........V8-350	4 Barrel	3.8762 x 3.75	350	7.6	165 @ 4000	260 @ 2400	35–40
	140 Horsepower③..........V8-350⑥	2 Barrel	3.80 x 3.85	350	8.0	140 @ 3200	280 @ 1600	37
	155 Horsepower③..........V8-350⑥	4 Barrel	3.80 x 3.85	350	8.0	155 @ 3400	280 @ 1800	37
	170 Horsepower③..........V8-400	2 Barrel	4.1212 x 3.75	400	7.6	170 @ 4000	310 @ 1600	35–40
	185 Horsepower③..........V8-400	4 Barrel	4.1212 x 3.75	400	7.6	185 @ 3600	310 @ 1600	35–40
	200 Horsepower③..........V8-455	4 Barrel	4.1522 x 4.21	455	7.6	200 @ 3500	330 @ 2000	55–60

①—For service on this engine, see Six Cylinder in Chevrolet Chapter.
②—For service on this engine, see Eight Cylinder in Chevrolet Chapter.
③—Ratings are NET—as installed in the vehicle.
④—With dual exhausts.
⑤—See Oldsmobile Chapter for service procedures.
⑥—Ventura only. See Buick Chapter for service procedures.

TUNEUP SPECIFICATIONS

The following specifications are published from the latest information available. This data should be used only in the absence of a decal affixed in the engine compartment.

★When using a timing light, disconnect vacuum hose or tube at distributor and plug opening in hose or tube so idle speed will not be affected.

♦When checking compression, lowest cylinder must be within 80% of the highest.

▲Before removing wires from distributor cap, determine location of the No. 1 wire in cap, as distributor position may have been altered from that shown at the end of this chart.

Year	Spark Plug		Distributor		Ignition Timing ★			Carb. Adjustments					
								Hot Idle Speed③		Air Fuel Ratio		Idle CO %	
	Type	Gap Inch	Point Gap Inch	Dwell Angle Deg.	Firing Order Fig. ▲	Timing BTDC ①	Mark Fig.	Std. Trans.	Auto. Trans.②	Std. Trans.	Auto. Trans.	Std. Trans.	Auto. Trans.
1969													
6-250 1 Bar. Carb.	R44NS	.035	.016	31–34	A	TDC	F	700/500	600/500D⑦	—	—	—	—
6-250 4 Bar. Carb.	R44NS	.035	.016	31–34	A	5°	F	850/600	600/500D⑦	—	—	—	—
8-350 2 Bar. Carb.	R45S	.035	.016	30	D	9°	C	850	650D⑦	—	—	—	—
8-350 4 Bar. Carb.	R45S	.035	.016	30	D	9°	C	1000	650D⑦	—	—	—	—
8-400 2 Bar. Carb.	R45S	.035	.016	30	D	9°	C	850	650D⑦	—	—	—	—
8-400 4 Bar. Carb.	⑪	.035	.016	30	D	9°	C	1000	650D⑦	—	—	—	—
8-400 Ram Air	⑪	.035	.016	30	D	15°	C	1000/650	650/500D⑦	—	—	—	—
8-428	R44S	.035	.016	30	D	9°	C	1000	650D⑦	—	—	—	—
1970													
6-250⑭ Std. Tr.	R46T	.035	.019	31–34	E	TDC	G	750/400	—	—	—	—	—
6-250⑭ Auto. Tr.	R46T	.035	.019	31–34	E	4°	G	—	600/400D	—	—	—	—
8-350 2 Bar. Carb.	R46S	.035	.016	30	D	9°	C	800	650D	—	—	—	—
8-400 2 Bar. Carb.	R46S	.035	.016	30	D	9°	C	950	650D	—	—	—	—
8-400 4 Bar. Carb.	R45S	.035	.016	30	D	15°	C	1000/650	750/500D	—	—	—	—
8-400 Ram Air	R44S	.035	.016	30	D	9°	C	950	650D	—	—	—	—
8-455	R45S⑫	.035	.016	30	D	9°	C	950	650D	—	—	—	—

Exc. Astre & Sunbird/Pontiac

TUNEUP SPECIFICATIONS/continued

The following specifications are published from the latest information available. This data should be used only in the absence of a decal affixed in the engine compartment.

★ When using a timing light, disconnect vacuum hose or tube at distributor and plug opening in hose or tube so idle speed will not be affected.

● When checking compression, lowest cylinder must be within 80% of the highest.

▲ Before removing wires from distributor cap, determine location of the No. 1 wire in cap, as distributor position may have been altered from that shown at the end of this chart.

Year	Spark Plug		Distributor		Ignition Timing ★			Carb. Adjustments					
								Hot Idle Speed ③		Air Fuel Ratio		Idle CO %	
	Type	Gap Inch	Point Gap Inch	Dwell Angle Deg.	Firing Order Fig. ▲	Timing BTDC ①	Mark Fig.	Std. Trans.	Auto. Trans. ②	Std. Trans.	Auto. Trans.	Std. Trans.	Auto. Trans.
1971													
6-250 ⑭	R46TS	.035	.019	32½	E	4°	H	850/550	650/500D	—	—	1.0	1.0
8-307 ⑭ Std. Tr.	R45TS	.035	.019	30	B	4°	H	550	—	—	—	1.0	—
8-307 ⑭ Auto. Tr.	R45TS	.035	.019	30	B	8°	H	—	550D	—	—	—	1.0
8-350 2 Bar. Carb.	R47S	.035	.016	30	D	12°	I	800	600D	—	—	1.0	1.0
8-400 2 Bar. Carb.	R47S	.035	.016	30	D	8°	I	—	600D	—	—	1.0	1.0
8-400 4 Bar. Carb.	R46S	.035	.016	30	D	12°	I	1000/600	700D	—	—	1.0	1.0
8-455	R46S	.035	.016	30	D	12°	I	—	650D	—	—	1.0	1.0
8-455 H.O.	R46S	.035	.016	30	D	12°	I	1000/600	700D	—	—	1.0	—
1972													
6-250 ⑭	R46T	.035	.019	32½	E	4°	H	850/450	650/450D	—	—	—	—
8-307 ⑭ Std. Tr.	R44T	.035	.016	30	B	4°	H	900/450	—	—	—	—	—
8-307 ⑭ Auto. Tr.	R44T	.035	.016	30	B	8°	H	—	600/450D	—	—	—	—
8-350	R46TS	.035	.016	30	D	8°	I	800	—	—	—	—	—
8-350	R46TS	.035	.016	30	D	10°	I	—	625D	—	—	—	—
8-400 2 Bar. Carb.	R46TS	.035	.016	30	D	10°	I	—	625D	—	—	—	—
8-400 4 Bar. Carb.	R45TS	.035	.016	30	D	10°	I	1000/600	700/500D	—	—	—	—
8-455 2 Bar. Carb.	R45TS	.035	.016	30	D	10°	I	—	625D	—	—	—	—
8-455 4 Bar. Carb.	R45TS	.035	.016	30	D	10°	I	—	650/500D	—	—	—	—
8-455 H.O. Std. Tr.	R45TS	.035	.016	30	D	8°	I	1000/600	—	—	—	—	—
8-455 H.O. Auto. Tr.	R45TS	.035	.016	30	D	10°	I	—	700/500D	—	—	—	—
1973													
6-250 ⑭	R46T	.035	⑮	32½	E	6°	H	700/450	600D	—	—	—	—
V8-350 Std. Tra.	R46TS	.040	.016	30	D	10°	I	900/600	—	—	—	0.2	—
V8-350 Auto. Tra.	R46TS	.040	.016	30	D	12°	I	—	650D	—	—	—	0.2
V8-400 2 Bar. Carb.	R46TS	.040	.016	30	D	⑯	I	—	650D	—	—	0.2	0.2
V8-400 4 Bar. Carb.	R45TS	.040	.016	30	D	⑯	I	1000/600	650D	—	—	0.2	0.2
V8-455	R45TS	.040	.016	30	D	⑯	I	1000	650D	—	—	0.2	0.2
V8-455 S.D.	R44TS	.040	.016	30	D	⑯	I	1000/600	750/500D	—	—	0.2	0.2
1974													
6-250 ⑭	R46T	.035	⑮	32½	E	6°	H	850	600D	—	—	0.2	0.2
V8-350 2 Bar. Carb.	R46TS	.040	⑮	30	D	⑯	I	900	650D	—	—	0.2	0.2
V8-350 2 Bar. Carb. ④	R46TS	.040	⑮	30	D	10°	I	—	625D	—	—	—	0.2
V8-350 4 Bar. Carb.	R46TS	.040	⑮	30	D	⑯	I	1000	650D	—	—	0.2	0.2
V8-350 4 Bar. Carb. ④	R46TS	.040	⑮	30	D	10°	I	—	625D	—	—	—	0.2

Pontiac/Exc. Astre & Sunbird

TUNEUP SPECIFICATIONS/continued

The following specifications are published from the latest information available. This data should be used only in the absence of a decal affixed in the engine compartment.

★ When using a timing light, disconnect vacuum hose or tube at distributor and plug opening in tube or hose so idle speed will not be affected.

● When checking compression, lowest cylinder must be within 80% of the highest.

▲ Before removing wires from distributor cap, determine location of the No. 1 wire in cap, as distributor position may have been altered from that shown at the end of this chart.

Year	Spark Plug		Distributor		Ignition Timing ★			Carb. Adjustments					
								Hot Idle Speed ③		Air Fuel Ratio		Idle CO %	
	Type	Gap Inch	Point Gap Inch	Dwell Angle Deg.	Firing Order Fig. ▲	Timing BTDC ①	Mark Fig.	Std. Trans.	Auto. Trans. ②	Std. Trans.	Auto. Trans.	Std. Trans.	Auto. Trans.
1974—Continued													
V8-400 2 Bar. Carb.	R46TS	.040	⑮	30	⑩	⑯	I	—	650D	—	—	—	0.2
V8-400 2 Bar. Carb.④	R46TS	.040	⑮	30	⑩	10°	I	—	625D	—	—	—	0.2
V8-400 4 Bar. Carb.	R45TS	.040	⑮	30	⑩	⑯	I	1000	650D	—	—	0.2	0.2
V8-400 4 Bar. Carb.④	R45TS	.040	⑮	30	⑩	10°	I	—	625D	—	—	—	0.2
V8-455	R45TS	.040	⑮	30	⑩	⑯	I	—	650D	—	—	—	0.2
V8-455④	R45TS	.040	⑮	30	⑩	10°	I	—	625D	—	—	—	0.2
V8-455 S.D.	R44TS	.040	⑮	30	⑩	12°	I	1000	750D	—	—	0.2	0.2
1975													
6-250⑭	R46TX	.060	—	—	L	10°	H	850	⑳	—	—	—	—
V8-260⑤㉑	R46SX	.080	—	—	M	16°⑨	J	750	650D	—	—	—	—
V8-260⑤㉒	R46SX	.080	—	—	M	18°⑨	J	750	650D	—	—	—	—
V8-350⑥	R45TSX	.060	—	—	N	12°	K	800	600D	—	—	—	—
V8-350㉑	R46TSX	.060	—	—	O	12°	I	775	㉓	—	—	—	—
V8-350㉒	R46TSX	.060	—	—	O	16°	I	775	㉓	—	—	—	—
V8-400㉑	㉔	.060	—	—	O	12°	I	775	㉕	—	—	—	—
V8-400㉒	㉔	.060	—	—	O	16°	I	775	㉕	—	—	—	—
V8-455㉑	R45TSX	.060	—	—	O	10°	I	—	650D	—	—	—	—
V8-455④	R45TSX	.060	—	—	O	16°	I	—	675D	—	—	—	—
1976													
6-250⑭	R46T	.035	—	—	L	㉗	H	850	㉘	—	—	—	—
V8-260⑤㉙	R46SX	.080	—	—	M	16°⑨	J	750	—	—	—	—	—
V8-260⑤㉚	R46SX	.080	—	—	M	㉛	J	—	㉘	—	—	—	—
V8-350⑥	R45TSX	.060	—	—	N	12°	K	—	600D	—	—	—	—
V8-350	R46TSX	.060	—	—	O	16°	I	—	550D	—	—	—	—
V8-400 2 Bar. Carb.	R46TSX	.060	—	—	O	16°	I	—	550D	—	—	—	—
V8-400 4 Bar. Carb.	R45TSX	.060	—	—	O	⑧	I	775	575D	—	—	—	—
V8-455㉑	R45TSX	.060	—	—	O	12°	I	775	600D	—	—	—	—
V8-455㉒	R45TSX	.060	—	—	O	16°	I	—	550D	—	—	—	—

① —BTDC: Before top dead center.
② —D: Drive. N: Neutral.
③ —Where two figures are given, the higher is with solenoid active.
④ —California.
⑤ —See Oldsmobile Chapter for service procedure.
⑥ —Ventura only. See Buick Chapter for service procedures.
⑦ —With A/C off.
⑧ —Std. Trans. 12°, Auto. Trans. 16°.
⑨ —At 1100 RPM.
⑩ —Exc. H.E.I., Fig. D; H.E.I., Fig. M.
⑪ —GTO uses R44S; all others use R45S.
⑫ —Use R44S on Ram Air option.
⑬ —All except Firebird, Gran Prix and California.
⑭ —For service on this engine, see Chevrolet Chapter.
⑮ —New points .019", used points .016".
⑯ —Std. trans. 10° BTDC. Auto trans. 12° BTDC.
⑰ —Firebird and Grand Prix except California.
⑱ —Std. Trans. 12°, Auto. Trans. 10°.
⑲ —2 BBL. Carb. 600 RPM, 4 BBL. Carb. 650 RPM.
⑳ —Exc. Calif., 550 RPM; Calif., 600 RPM.
㉑ —Std. Trans. & all California models.
㉒ —Auto. trans. exc. California.
㉓ —2 bbl. carb., 600 RPM; 4 bbl. carb.—Exc. Calif., 650 RPM; Calif., 625 RPM.
㉔ —2 bbl. carb., R46TSX; 4 bbl. carb., R45TSX.
㉕ —2 bbl. carb., 650 RPM; 4 bbl. carb.—Exc. Calif. & Grand Safari sta. wag., 650 RPM; Grand Safari sta. wag. exc. Calif., 625 RPM; All Calif. models, 600 RPM.
㉖ —Exc. California.
㉗ —Std. trans., 6° BTDC; auto. trans., 10° BTDC.
㉘ —Exc. Calif., 550D; Calif., 600D.
㉙ —Std. trans.
㉚ —Auto. trans.
㉛ —Exc. Calif., 18° BTDC; Calif., 14° BTDC. At 1100 RPM.

Exc. Astre & Sunbird/Pontiac

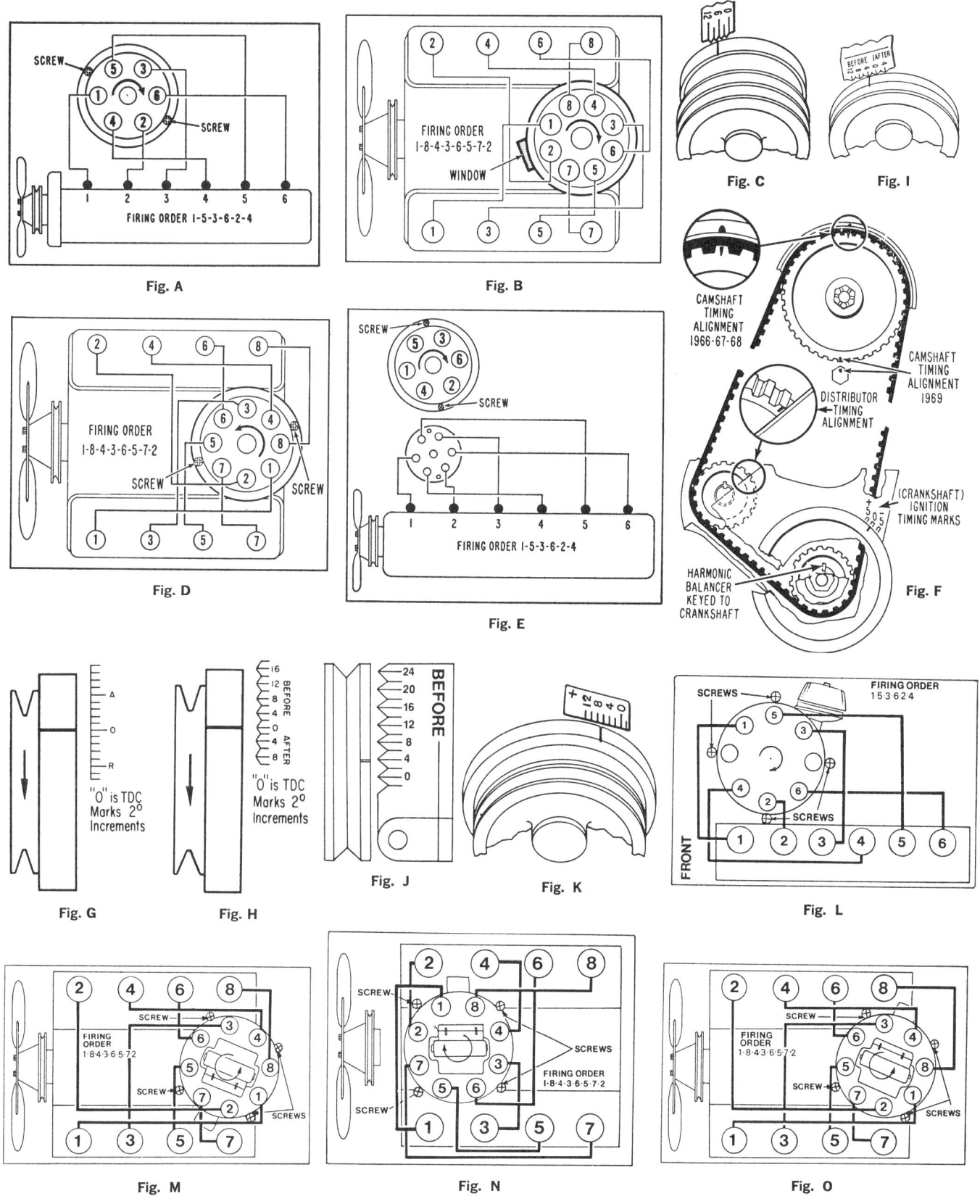

Pontiac/Exc. Astre & Sunbird

COOLING SYSTEM & CAPACITY DATA

Year	Model or Engine	Cooling Capacity, Qts.		Radiator Cap Relief Pressure, Lbs.		Thermo. Opening Temp. ①	Fuel Tank Gals.	Engine Oil Refill Qts. ②	Transmission Oil				Rear Axle Oil Pints
		With Heater	With A/C	With A/C	No A/C				3 Speed Pints	4 Speed Pints	5 Speed Pints	Auto. Trans. Qts. ⑫	
1969	6-250	12	12¼	14–17	14–17	190	21½⑮	4½⑯	3½	3½	—	⑰	3
	8-350 Tempest	20	21¼	14–17	14–17	190	21½⑮	5	3½	3½	—	⑰	3
	8-400 Tempest	18¼	19¾	14–17	14–17	190	21½⑮	5	3½	3½	—	⑰	3
	8-350 Firebird	19½	20¼	14–17	14–17	190	18½	5	3½	3½	—	⑰	3
	8-400 Firebird	18½	18¾	14–17	14–17	190	18½	5	3½	3½	—	⑰	3
	8-400 Pontiac	18	18	14–17	14–17	190	26½⑦	5	2.8	—	—	⑰	4½
	8-428 Pontiac	17¼	17¼	14–17	14–17	190	26½⑦	5	2.8	—	—	⑰	4½
	8-400 Grand Prix	18¾	21	14–17	14–17	190	21½	5	2.8	2.5	—	⑰	3
	8-428 Grand Prix	17½	17½	14–17	14–17	190	21½	5	2.8	2.5	—	⑰	3
1970	6-250	11.3	13	14–17	14–17	195	21.5	4	3.5	2½	—	3¼⑲	3
	V8-350 Tempest	19.6	19.6	14–17	14–17	190	21.5	5	⑱	2½	—	3¼⑲	3
	V8-350 Pontiac	19.6	19.6	14–17	14–17	190	26⑦	5	⑱	—	—	3¼⑲	4½
	V8-400 G.T.O.	18.3	18.3	14–17	14–17	190	21.5	5	2.8	2½	—	3¼⑲	3⑳
	V8-350 Firebird	19½	20¼	14–17	14–17	190	19½③	5	④	2½	—	⑤	3¾
	V8-400 Firebird	18½	18¾	14–17	14–17	190	19½③	5	④	2½	—	⑤	3¾
	V8-400 Pontiac	18	18	14–17	14–17	190	26⑦	5	2.8	—	—	3¼⑲	4½
	V8-400 Gr'd Prix	18.7	21.1	14–17	14–17	190	21.5	5	2.8	2½	—	3¼⑲	3⑳
	V8-455 Gr'd Prix	17.5	19.9	14–17	14–17	190	21.5	5	2.8	2½	—	3¼⑲	3⑳
	V8-455 Pontiac	17.2	17.2	14–17	14–17	190	26⑦	5	2.8	—	—	3¼⑲	4½
1971	6-250 Firebird	12	—	14–17	14–17	195	17	4	3.5	3.5	—	3⑲	4¼
	6-250 Tempest	13	12.4	14–17	14–17	195	19⑥	4	3.5	—	—	3⑲	3
	6-250 Ventura II	12.4	—	14–17	14–17	195	16	4	3.5	—	—	3⑲	3¾
	8-307 Ventura II	15.5	16.5	14–17	14–17	195	16	4	3.5	—	—	3⑲	3¾
	8-350 Firebird	19.4	20.3	14–17	14–17	195	19	5	3.5	3.5	—	3⑲	4¼
	8-350 Tempest	20.2	20.9	14–17	14–17	195	19⑥	5	3.5㉑	2.5	—	3⑲	3
	8-350 Pontiac	20.2	21	14–17	14–17	195	23.6㉒	5	2.8	—	—	3⑲	3
	8-400 Firebird	18.6	18.7	14–17	14–17	195	17	5	2.8	2.5	—	3¾⑲	4¼
	8-400 Tempest	18.6	20.8	14–17	14–17	195	19⑥	5	2.8	2.5	—	3¾⑲	3
	8-400 Pontiac	18.6	19.6	14–17	14–17	195	23.6㉒	5	2.8	2.5	—	3¾⑲	3
	8-400 Gr'd Prix	18.7	19.7	14–17	14–17	195	23.5	5	2.8	2.5	—	3¾⑲	3⑳
	8-455 Firebird	17.9	18.7	14–17	14–17	195	17	5	2.8	2.5	—	3¾⑲	4¼
	8-455 Tempest	18.6	20.8	14–17	14–17	195	19⑥	5	2.8	2.5	—	3¾⑲	3
	8-455 Pontiac	17.9	19	14–17	14–17	195	23.6㉒	5	—	2.5	—	3¾⑲	3
	8-455 Gr'd Prix	18.7	19.7	14–17	14–17	195	23.5	5	—	—	—	3¾⑲	3⑳
1972	6-250 Ventura II	12	16	14–17	14–17	195	16	4	3½	—	—	⑤	3¾
	6-250 Firebird	12	—	14–17	14–17	195	17	4	3½	—	—	⑤	4¼
	6-250 Le Mans	13	12.4	14–17	14–17	195	20㉓	4	3½	—	—	⑤	5⑳
	8-307 Ventura II	15	16	14–17	14–17	195	16	4	3	—	—	⑤	3¾
	8-350 Ventura II	19.4	20.3	14–17	14–17	195	16	5	—	—	—	⑤	3¾
	8-350 Firebird	19.4	20.3	14–17	14–17	195	17	5	2.8	2.5	—	6	4¼
	8-350 LeMans	20.2	20.9	14–17	14–17	195	20㉓	5	3½	2.5	—	6	3⑳
	8-400 Pontiac	18.6	19.6	14–17	14–17	195	25㉓	5	—	—	—	7½	5½
	8-400 Firebird	18.6	18.7	14–17	14–17	195	17	5	—	2.5	—	7½	4¼
	8-400 LeMans	18.6	20.8	14–17	14–17	196	20㉓	5	2.8	2.5	—	7½	3⑳
	8-400 Gr'd Prix	18.7	19.7	14–17	14–17	195	26	5	—	—	—	7½	3⑳
	8-455 Pontiac	17.9	19.0	14–17	14–17	195	25㉓	5	—	—	—	7½	5½
	8-455 Firebird	17.9	18.9	14–17	14–17	195	17	5	—	2.5	—	7½	4¼
	8-455 LeMans	17.9	18.9	14–17	14–17	195	20㉓	5	—	2.5	—	7½	3⑳
1973	6-250 Ventura II	12	—	14–17	14–17	195	21.5	4	3½	—	—	1½⑧	3¾
	6-250 Firebird	12.4	—	14–17	14–17	195	18	4	3½	—	—	4⑧	4¼
	6-250 Le Mans	12.4	13.4	14–17	14–17	195	22	4	3½	—	—	4⑧	3㉘
	8-350 Ventura II	19.5	20.5	14–17	14–17	195	21.5	4	3½	3½	—	4㉗	3¾
	8-350 Firebird	19.5	20.5	14–17	14–17	195	18	5	3½	3½	—	4㉗	4¼
	8-350 Le Mans	20.2	21.4	14–17	14–17	195	22	5	3½㉘	3½	—	4㉗	3㉘

Exc. Astre & Sunbird/Pontiac

COOLING SYSTEM & CAPACITY DATA/continued

Year	Model or Engine	Cooling Capacity, Qts. With Heater	Cooling Capacity, Qts. With A/C	Radiator Cap Relief Pressure, Lbs. With A/C	Radiator Cap Relief Pressure, Lbs. No A/C	Thermo. Opening Temp. ①	Fuel Tank Gals.	Engine Oil Refill Qts. ②	Transmission Oil 3 Speed Pints	Transmission Oil 4 Speed Pints	Transmission Oil 5 Speed Pints	Auto. Trans. Qts. ⑫	Rear Axle Oil Pints
1973	8-400 Pontiac	18.6	19.4	14–17	14–17	195	26⑭	5	—	—	—	3¾⑧	5½㉙
	8-400 Firebird	18.6	19.2	14–17	14–17	195	18	5	—	2½	—	3¾⑧	4¼
	8-400 Le Mans	18.6	19.8	14–17	14–17	195	22㉔	5	2¾	2½	—	3¾⑧	3㉘
	8-400 Grand Prix	18.6	19.2	14–17	14–17	195	25	5	—	—	—	3¾⑧	3㉘
	8-455 Pontiac	18.0	18.4	14–17	14–17	195	26⑭	5	—	—	—	3¾⑧	5½㉙
	8-455 Firebird	18.0	19.0	14–17	14–17	195	18	5	—	2½	—	3¾⑧	4¼
	8-455 Le Mans	18.0	19.0	14–17	14–17	195	22㉔	5	—	2½	—	3¾⑧	3㉘
1974	6-250 Ventura	13.1	—	14–17	14–17	195	21.5	4	3½	—	—	4½㉖	3¾
	6-250 Firebird	13.5	—	14–17	14–17	195	21.5	4	3½	—	—	4½㉖	4¼
	6-250 Le Mans	14.7	—	14–17	14–17	195	22	4	3½	—	—	4½㉖	3㉘
	8-350 Ventura	20.0	20.0	14–17	14–17	195	21.5	5	3½	2½	—	4½㉖	3¾
	8-350 Firebird	22.0	22.9	14–17	14–17	195	21.5	5	3½	2½	—	4½㉖	4¼
	8-350 Le Mans	21.3	23.6	14–17	14–17	195	22	5	3½㉖	2½	—	4½㉖	3㉘
	8-350 Pontiac	21.6	22.4	14–17	14–17	195	25.8	5	—	—	—	4½⑪	4¼㉙
	8-400 Firebird	21.9	22.9	14–17	14–17	195	21.5	5	—	2½	—	4½⑪	4¼
	8-400 Le Mans	21.3	22.8	14–17	14–17	195	22㉔	5	—	2½	—	4½⑪	3㉘
	8-400 Grand Prix	21.6	24.0	14–17	14–17	195	25	5	—	—	—	4½⑪	3㉚
	8-400 Pontiac	21.6	22.4	14–17	14–17	195	25.8	5	—	—	—	4½⑪	4¼㉙
	8-455 Firebird	20.3	21.3	14–17	14–17	195	21.5	5	—	2½	—	4½⑪	4¼
	8-455 Le Mans	21.1	21.6	14–17	14–17	195	22㉔	5	—	—	—	4½⑪	3㉘
	8-455 Grand Prix	20.2	22.2	14–17	14–17	195	25	5	—	—	—	4½⑪	3㉚
	8-455 Pontiac	19.8	22.3	14–17	14–17	195	25.8	5	—	—	—	4½⑪	4¼㉙
1975	6-250 Ventura	13.1	—	14–17	14–17	195	20.5	4	3½	—	—	2½㉗	3¾
	6-250 Firebird	13.1	—	14–17	14–17	195	21.5	4	3½	—	—	4⑧	4¼
	6-250 LeMans	14.7	—	14–17	14–17	195	21	4	3½	—	—	4⑧	3㉘
	V8-260 Ventura	22.4	22.9	14–17	14–17	195	20.5	4	3½	2½	—	2½㉗	3¾
	V8-350 Ventura	20	20	14–17	14–17	195	20.5	4	—	2½	—	2½㉗	3¾
	V8-350 Firebird	22	23.3	14–17	14–17	195	21.5	5	3½	2½	—	4㉗	4¼
	V8-350 LeMans	21.3	23.6	14–17	14–17	195	21	5	—	—	—	4⑧	3㉘
	V8-400 Firebird	21.3	⑨	14–17	14–17	195	21.5	5	—	2½	—	4㉗	4¼
	V8-400 LeMans	21.3	⑩	14–17	14–17	195	21⑬	5	—	—	—	3¾⑧	3㉘
	V8-400 Grand Prix	21.5	24	14–17	14–17	195	25	5	—	—	—	3¾⑧	3㉘
	V8-400 Pontiac	21.6	22.4	14–17	14–17	195	25.8	5	—	—	—	3¾⑧	5½
	V8-455 LeMans	19.9	21.6	14–17	14–17	195	21⑬	5	—	—	—	3¾⑧	3㉘
	V8-455 Grand Prix	20.2	22.5	14–17	14–17	195	25	5	—	—	—	3¾⑧	3㉘
	V8-455 Pontiac	19.8	22.3	14–17	14–17	195	25.8⑭	5	—	—	—	3¾⑧	5½
1976	6-250 Ventura	13.0	—	14–17	14–17	195	20.5	4	3.5	—	—	2½㉗	3¾
	6-250 Firebird	13.5	—	14–17	14–17	195	21.5	4	3.5	—	—	4⑧	4¼
	6-250 LeMans	15.0	—	14–17	14–17	195	21	4	3.5	—	—	4⑧	3㉘
	V8-260 Ventura	20.6	21.3	14–17	14–17	195	20.5	4	3.5	—	3.0	2½㉗	3¾
	V8-260 LeMans	23.5	26.0	14–17	14–17	195	21	4	3.5	—	3.0	4⑧	3㉘
	V8-350 Ventura	17.3	18.0	14–17	14–17	195	20.5	4	—	—	—	2½㉗	3¾
	V8-350 Firebird	21.2	21.6	14–17	14–17	195	21.5	5	—	—	—	4㉗	4¼
	V8-350 LeMans	21.4	22.0	14–17	14–17	195	21	5	—	—	—	4⑧	3㉘
	V8-350 Grand Prix	21.6	22.0	14–17	14–17	195	25	5	—	—	—	3¾⑧	3㉘
	V8-400 Firebird	21.6	23.3	14–17	14–17	195	21.5	5	—	2.5	—	4㉗	4¼
	V8-400 Le Mans	21.4	22.0	14–17	14–17	195	21⑭	5	—	—	—	3¾⑧	3㉘
	V8-400 Grand Prix	22.2	22.2	14–17	14–17	195	25	5	—	—	—	3¾⑧	3㉘
	V8-400 Pontiac	21.6	22.4	14–17	14–17	195	25.8⑭	5	—	—	—	3¾⑧	5½

Pontiac/Exc. Astre & Sunbird

COOLING SYSTEM & CAPACITY DATA/continued

Year	Model or Engine	Cooling Capacity, Qts.		Radiator Cap Relief Pressure, Lbs.		Thermo. Opening Temp. ①	Fuel Tank Gals.	Engine Oil Refill Qts. ②	Transmission Oil				Rear Axle Oil Pints
		With Heater	With A/C	With A/C	No A/C				3 Speed Pints	4 Speed Pints	5 Speed Pints	Auto. Trans. Qts. ⑫	
1976	V8-455 Firebird	23.3	23.3	14-17	14-17	195	21.5	5	—	2.5	—	4㉗	4¼
	V8-455 LeMans	21.6	21.6	14-17	14-17	195	21⑭	5	—	—	—	3¾⑧	3㉘
	V8-455 Grand Prix	22.2	22.2	14-17	14-17	195	25	5	—	—	—	3¾⑧	3㉘
	V8-455 Pontiac	22.1	22.1	14-17	14-17	195	25.8⑭	5	—	—	—	3¾⑧	5½

① —With alcohol-type anti-freeze use a 160° unit.
② —Add one quart with filter change.
③ —With Evaporative Control System 17.
④ —Saginaw 3.5, Muncie 4.
⑤ —Two speed unit; oil pan 1½ qts., complete refill 9½ qts. Turbo Hydra Matic 350; oil pan 2½ qts., complete refill 5 qts. Turbo Hydra Matic 400; oil pan 3¾ qts., complete refill 9½ qts.
⑥ —Station Wagons 21.5.
⑦ —Station Wagons 24 gals.
⑧ —Oil pan only. After overhaul 9½ qts.
⑨ —2 BBl. Carb. 22.5 qts., 4 BBl. Carb. 23.3 qts.
⑩ —2 BBl. Carb. 21.9 qts., 4 BBl. Carb. 23.6 qts.
⑪ —Oil pan only. After overhaul 12 qts.
⑫ —Approximate. Make final check with dipstick.
⑬ —Grand Am 25 gals., Sta. Wagon 22 gals.
⑭ —Station Wagons 22 gals.
⑮ —Station Wagons 20 gals.
⑯ —Add ½ qt. with filter change.
⑰ —Two speed unit; oil pan 2½ qts. and complete refill 7½ qts. Three speed unit ("J" Prefix); oil pan 3 qts. and complete refill 10 qts. Three speed unit ("P" Prefix); oil pan 3.7 qts. and complete refill 9½ qts.
⑱ —Standard unit 3.5 pints, heavy duty 2.8 pints.
⑲ —Oil pan only.
⑳ —5 pts. with 8¾" ring gear.
㉑ —Heavy duty 2.8.
㉒ —Station Wagons 22.5.
㉓ —Station Wagon 23.
㉔ —Grand Am 25 gals.
㉕ —Muncie 2¾ pints.
㉖ —Oil pan only. After overhaul 11 qts.
㉗ —Oil pan only. After overhaul 10½ qts.
㉘ —"C" Type 4.9 pints.
㉙ —"C" Type 4¼ pints.
㉚ —"C" Type 3.9 pints.
㉛ —Station Wagon 5.31 pts.
㉜ —8½" ring gear 4¼ pts.

Volkswagen

1969-74 MODEL IDENTIFICATION

Type 1—Beetle, Super Beetle and Karmann Ghia/Type 2—Station Bus, Transporter
Type 3—Fastback and Squareback/Type 4—411, 412

GENERAL ENGINE SPECIFICATIONS

★1973-76 horsepower and torque ratings are SAE net.

Model or Engine	Bore & Stroke, Inches (mm)	Piston Displacement, Cubic Inches (cc)	Compression Ratio	Maximum Brake HP @ rpm	Maximum Torque Ft. Lbs. @ rpm	Normal Oil Pressure, Pounds
1967-69						
1500① 1 carb	3.27 x 2.27 (83 x 69.0)	91.1 (1493)	7.8	54 @ 4200	82 @ 2800	28
1968-72						
1600②③	3.37 x 2.27 (85.5 x 69.0)	96.7 (1584)	7.7	65 @ 4600	87 @ 2800	28
1970						
1600① 1 carb	3.37 x 2.27 (85.5 x 69.0)	96.7 (1584)	7.5	57 @ 4400	82 @ 3000	28
1971-72						
1600①	3.37 x 2.27 (85.5 x 69.0)	96.7 (1584)	7.5	60 @ 4400	82 @ 3000	28
1700③④	3.54 x 2.60 (90.6 x 66.0)	102.5 (1679)	8.2	85 @ 5000	99 @ 3500	28
1973						
Type 1	3.37 x 2.27 (85.5 x 69.0)	96.7 (1584)	7.3	46 @ 4000	72 @ 2000	28
Type 3	3.37 x 2.27 (85.5 x 69.0)	96.7 (1584)	7.3	52 @ 4000	77 @ 2200	28
Type 4	3.54 x 2.60 (90.6 x 66.0)	103 (1679)	8.2	76 @ 4900	95 @ 2700	28

GENERAL ENGINE SPECIFICATIONS/continued

Model or Engine	Bore & Stroke, Inches (mm)	Piston Displacement, Cubic Inches (cc)	Compression Ratio	Maximum Brake HP @ rpm	Maximum Torque Ft. Lbs. @ rpm	Normal Oil Pressure, Pounds
1974						
Type 1	3.37 x 2.27 (85.5 x 69)	96.7 (1584)	7.3	46 @ 4000	72 @ 2800	28
Type 2	3.66 x 2.59 (93 x 66)	109.5 (1795)	7.3	65 @ 4200	91 @ 3000	28
Type 4	3.54 x 2.59 (90.6 x 66)	102.5 (1679)	8.2	76 @ 4900	95 @ 2700	28
Dasher	3.01 x 3.15 (76.5 x 80.0)	89.7 (1471)	8.2	75 @ 6000	79 @ 4000	28
1975						
Beetle	3.37 x 2.27 (85.5 x 69.0)	96.7 (1584)	7.3	48 @ 4200	73 @ 2800	28
Rabbit	3.01 x 3.15 (76.5 x 80.0)	89.7 (1471)	8.2	70 @ 6000	81 @ 3500	28
Scirocco	3.01 x 3.15 (76.5 x 80.0)	89.7 (1471)	8.2	70 @ 6000	81 @ 3500	28
Dasher	3.01 x 3.15 (76.5 x 80.0)	89.7 (1471)	8.2	70 @ 6000	81 @ 3500	28
181 Thing	3.37 x 2.27 (85.5 x 69.0)	96.7 (1584)	7.3	48 @ 4200	73 @ 2800	28
1976						
Beetle	3.37 x 2.27 (85.5 x 69.0)	96.7 (1584)	7.3	48 @ 4200	73 @ 2800	28
Rabbit	3.13 x 3.15 (79.5 x 80.0)	97 (1588)	8.2	71 @ 5600	82 @ 3000	28
Bus	3.70 x 2.80 (94 x 71)	120.2 (1970)	7.3	67 @ 4200	101 @ 3000	28
Dasher	3.13 x 3.15 (79.5 x 80.0)	97 (1588)	8.2	79 @ 5500	86.2 @ 3300	28
Scirocco	3.13 x 3.15 (79.5 x 80.0)	97 (1588)	8.2	71 @ 5600	82 @ 3000	28

①—Type 1.
②—Type 3.
③—Fuel injection.
④—Type 4.

TUNEUP SPECIFICATIONS

Car Model or Engine	Spark Plugs		Distributor		Firing Order	Ignition Timing		Hot Idle Speed, rpm
	Type	Gap, Inch	Point Gap, Inch	Dwell Angle, Degrees		Degrees BTDC	Mark Location	
1968-69								
1500①	Various	.026	.016	44–50	1-4-3-2	0	Pulley	850
1600②③	Various	.026	.016	44–50	1-4-3-2	0	Flywheel	850
1970-73								
1600①	Various	.028	.016	44–50	1-4-3-2	0	Pulley	850
1600②③	Various	.028	.016	44–50	1-4-3-2	5–7.5	Flywheel	850
1700	Various	.028	.017	44–50	1-4-3-2	27④	Flywheel	850

Volkswagen

TUNEUP SPECIFICATIONS/continued

Car Model or Engine	Spark Plugs Type	Spark Plugs Gap, Inch	Distributor Point Gap, Inch	Distributor Dwell Angle, Degrees	Firing Order	Ignition Timing Degrees BTDC	Ignition Timing Mark Location	Hot Idle Speed, rpm
1974								
Type 1	Bosch⑥ W145T1	.028	.016–.020	44–50	1-4-3-2	7.5⑦	Pulley	800–900 Std. 900–1000 Auto
Type 4	Bosch⑥ W145T1	.028	.016	44–50	1-4-3-2	27 @ 3500	Flywheel	800–1000
Dasher	Bosch⑥ W145T1	.028	.015	47–53	1-3-4-2	30 @ 3000⑧	Flywheel	850–1000
1975								
Beetle	Bosch W145M1	.028	.016	44–50	1-4-3-2	5 ATDC 0	Pulley	850–950 Std. 850–1000 Auto
Rabbit	Bosch W200T30	.028	.016	44–50	1-3-4-2	3 ATDC	Flywheel	900–1000
Scirocco	Bosch W200T30	.028	.016	44–50	1-3-4-2	3 ATDC	Flywheel	900–1000
Dasher	Bosch W200T30	.028	.016	44–50	1-3-4-2	3 ATDC	Flywheel	850–1000
181 Thing	Bosch W145M1	.028	.016	44–50	1-4-3-2	5 ATDC 0	Pulley	850–950 Std. 850–1000 Auto
1976								
Beetle	Bosch W145M1	.028	.016	44–50	1-4-3-2	5 ATDC	Pulley	800–950
Rabbit	Bosch W200T30	.028	.016	44–50	1-3-4-2	3 ATDC	Flywheel	850–1000
Bus	Bosch W145MZ	.028	.016	44–50	1-4-3-2	7.5 BTDC	Flywheel	900–1000
Dasher	Bosch W215T30	.028	.016	44–50	1-3-4-2	3 ATDC	Flywheel	850–1000
Scirocco	Bosch W200T30	.028	.016	44–50	1-3-4-2	3 ATDC	Flywheel	850–1000

①—Type 1.
②—Type 3.
③—Fuel injection.
④—Vacuum hoses on, at 3500 rpm.
⑤—Use of timing light is recommended. Disconnect and plug vacuum hose at distributor.
⑥—or Champion L-88-A.
⑦—Vacuum disconnected @ 800–900 rpm. Cal. M/T –5° ATDC w/vacuum connected.
⑧—Vacuum disconnected.

Toyota

VEHICLE IDENTIFICATION 1965-73

Model	Year	Engine Code
Corona	1965–69	3RC
	1970–71	8RC
	1972–73	18RC
Corolla	1968–70	K, 2K, 3K
	1971–73	3K, 2TC
Corona Mark II	1969–71	8RC
	1972	18RC
	1973	4M
Celica	1971	8RC
	1972–73	18RC
Carina	1972–73	2TC
Crown	1966–68	2M
	1969–73	4M

ENGINE IDENTIFICATION

Engine	Model
K, 2K	Corolla 1000
	Corolla 1100
3K	Corolla 1200
2TC	Corolla 1600
	Carina 1600
3RC	Corona 1900 (pushrod)
8RC	Corona 1900 (overhead cam)
	Corona Mk. II 1900
18RC	Corona 2000
	Corona Mk. II 2000
	Celica ST 2000
2M, 4M	Crown Six
	Corona Mk. II Six

GENERAL ENGINE SPECIFICATIONS
★1973-75 horsepower ratings are SAE net.

Model or Engine	Bore & Stroke, Inches (mm)	Piston Displacement, Cubic Inches (cc)	Compression Ratio	Maximum Brake HP @ rpm	Maximum Torque Ft. Lbs. @ rpm	Normal Oil Pressure, Pounds
All 1969-73						
3RC	3.46 x 3.07 (88 x 78)	115.8 (1897)	8.0	90 @ 4600	110 @ 2600	53–61
8RC	3.39 x 3.15 (86 x 80)	113.4 (1858)	9.0	108 @ 5500	117 @ 3800	57–71
18RC①	3.48 x 3.15 (88.5 x 80)	120 (1968)	8.5	97 @ 5500	106 @ 3800	57–71
K	2.95 x 2.40 (75 x 61)	65.71 (1077)	9.0	60 @ 6000	61.5 @ 3800	51–63
2K	2.95 x 2.40 (75 x 61)	65.71 (1077)	10.0	73 @ 6600	65.1 @ 4600	51–63
3K	2.95 x 2.60 (75 x 66)	71.2 (1166)	9.0	73 @ 6000	74.2 @ 3800	51–63
2TC①	3.35 x 2.76 (85 x 70)	96.9 (1588)	8.5	88 @ 6000	91.3 @ 3800	57–71
2M	2.95 x 3.35 (75 x 85)	137.5 (2250)	8.8	115 @ 5200	123 @ 3600	57–71
4M①	3.15 x 3.35 (80 x 85)	156.4 (2563)	8.5	122 @ 5200	141 @ 3600	57–71
1974						
Corolla 1200	2.95 x 2.60 (75 x 66)	71.2 (1166)	9.0	65 @ 6000	67 @ 3800	51–63
Corolla 1600	3.35 x 2.76 (85 x 70)	96.9 (1588)	8.5	88 @ 6000	91 @ 3800	57–71
Corona, Celica	3.48 x 3.15 (88.5 x 80)	120 (1968)	8.5	97 @ 5500	106 @ 3600	57–71
Mark II	3.15 x 3.35 (80 x 85)	156.4 (2563)	8.5	122 @ 5200	141 @ 3600	57–71
1975						
Corolla	3.35 x 2.76 (85 x 70)	96.9 (1588)	9.0	75 @ 5800	83 @ 3800	57–71
Corona	3.47 x 3.50 (88.4 x 88.9)	134 (2189)	8.4	96 @ 4800	120 @ 2800	57–71
Celica	3.47 x 3.50 (88.4 x 88.9)	134 (2189)	8.4	96 @ 4800	120 @ 2800	57–71
Mark II	3.15 x 3.35 (80 x 85)	156 (2563)	8.5	108 @ 5000	130 @ 2800	57–71

TUNEUP SPECIFICATIONS

Car Model or Engine	Spark Plugs Type	Spark Plugs Gap, Inch	Distributor Point Gap, Inch	Distributor Dwell Angle, Degrees	Firing Order	Ignition Timing Degrees BTDC	Ignition Timing Mark Location	Hot Idle Speed rpm
All 1969-73								
3RC	①	.028–.032	.016–.020	50–54	1-2-4-3	5	Timing cover	650
8RC	①	.030	.016–.020	50–54	1-3-4-2	②	Timing cover	650
18RC	①	.028–.032	.016–.020	50–54	1-3-4-2	7	Timing cover	650
K	①	.030	.016–.020	50–54	1-3-4-2	5	Timing cover	600
2K	①	.030	.016–.020	50–54	1-3-4-2	5	Timing cover	600
3K	①	.030	.016–.020	50–54	1-3-4-2	5	Timing cover	600
2TC	①	.030	.016–.020	50–54	1-3-4-2	5	Timing cover	750
2M	①	.030	.016–.020	39–43	1-5-3-6-2-4	0	Timing cover	750
4M	①	.030	.016–.020	39–43	1-5-3-6-2-4	5	Timing cover	750

Toyota

TUNEUP SPECIFICATIONS/continued

Car Model or Engine	Spark Plugs		Distributor		Firing Order	Ignition Timing		Hot Idle Speed, rpm
	Type	Gap, Inch	Point Gap, Inch	Dwell Angle, Degrees		Degrees BTDC	Mark Location	
1974								
Corolla 1200	①	.030	.016–.020	50–54	1-3-4-2	5	Timing cover	600
Corolla 1600	①	.030	.016–.020	50–54	1-3-4-2	5	Timing cover	750
Corona, Celica	①	.028–.032	.016–.020	50–54	1-3-4-2	7	Timing cover	650
Mark II	①	.030	.016–.020	39–43	1-5-3-6-2-4	5	Timing cover	750
1975								
Corolla	①	.030	.016–.020	50–54	1-3-4-2	10	Timing cover	850
Corona	①	.030	.016–.020	50–54	1-3-4-2	8	Timing cover	850
Celica	①	.030	.016–.020	50–54	1-3-4-2	8	Timing cover	850
Mark II	①	.030	.016–.020	50–54	1-5-3-6-2-4	10③	Timing cover	850

①—Either Denso W20EP or NGK BP6ES.
②—0° on cars before March, 1971. 10° BTDC on cars after March, 1971 with transmission controlled spark.
③—5° Calif cars.

Datsun

GENERAL ENGINE SPECIFICATIONS

Model or Engine	Bore & Stroke, Inches (mm)	Piston Displacement, Cubic Inches (cc)	Compression Ratio	Maximum Brake HP @ rpm	Maximum Torque, Ft. Lbs. @ rpm	Normal Oil Pressure, Pounds
1966-68						
J	2.87 x 3.06 (73.0 x 77.5)	79.27 (1299)	8.2	67 @ 5200	77 @ 2800	30–40
1968-71						
510	3.27 x 2.96 (83.2 x 73.7)	97.3 (1595)	8.5	96 @ 5600	100 @ 3600	54–60
240Z	3.27 x 2.96 (83.2 x 73.7)	146 (2393)	9.0	151 @ 5600	146 @ 4400	54–60
1200	2.87 x 2.76 (73.0 x 70)	71.5 (1171)	9.0	69 @ 6000	70 @ 4000	43–50
1972						
510	3.27 x 2.96 (83.2 x 73.7)	97.3 (1595)	8.5	96 @ 5600	100 @ 3600	54–60
240Z	3.27 x 2.90 (83.2 x 73.7)	146 (2393)	8.8	151 @ 5600	146 @ 4400	54–60
1200	2.87 x 2.76 (73.0 x 70)	71.5 (1171)	9.0	69 @ 6000	70 @ 4000	43–50
1973						
510	3.27 x 2.96 (83.2 x 73.7)	97.3 (1595)	8.5	81 @ 5600	88 @ 3600	54–60
610	3.35 x 3.07 (85.0 x 78.0)	108 (1770)	8.5	94 @ 5600	99 @ 3200	11–40
240Z	3.27 x 2.96 (83.2 x 73.7)	146 (2393)	8.8	129 @ 6000	127 @ 4400	54–60
1200	2.872 x 2.76 (73.0 x 70)	71.5 (1171)	8.5	61 @ 6000	65 @ 3600	43–50

Datsun

GENERAL ENGINE SPECIFICATIONS/continued

Model or Engine	Bore & Stroke, Inches (mm)	Piston Displacement, Cubic Inches (cc)	Compression Ratio	Maximum Brake HP @ rpm	Maximum Torque, Ft. Lbs. @ rpm	Normal Oil Pressure, Pounds
1974						
B210	2.87 x 3.03 (73.0 x 77.0)	78.6 (1288)	8.5	67 @ 6000	71 @ 3600	43–50
610	3.35 x 3.39 (85.0 x 86.0)	119 (1952)	8.5	97 @ 5600	102 @ 3200	11–40
710	3.35 x 3.07 (85.0 x 78.0)	108 (1770)	8.5	93 @ 6000	99 @ 3200	11–40
260Z	3.27 x 3.11 (83.0 x 79.0)	157 (2565)	8.8	139 @ 5200	137 @ 4400	11–40
1975						
B210	2.99 x 3.03 (76.0 x 77.0)	85.2 (1397)	8.5	70 @ 6000	75 @ 3600	43–50
610	3.35 x 3.39 (85.0 x 86.0)	119 (1952)	8.5	97 @ 5600	102 @ 3200	11–40
710	3.35 x 3.39 (85.0 x 86.0)	119 (1952)	8.5	97 @ 5600	102 @ 3200	11–40
280Z	3.39 x 3.11 (86.1 x 79.0)	168 (2754)	8.3	145 @ 5200	160 @ 4400	11–40

TUNEUP SPECIFICATIONS

Car Model or Engine	Spark Plugs		Distributor		Firing Order	Ignition Timing		Hot Idle Speed, rpm
	Type	Gap, Inch	Point Gap, Inch	Dwell Angle, Degrees		Degrees BTDC	Mark Location	
1966-68								
J	—	.027–.031	.018–.022	50–55	1-3-4-2	8	Pulley	600
1968-73								
L-16	—	.031–.035	.017–.022	49–55	1-3-4-2	10	Pulley	600
1970-73								
1200	—	.028–.032	.017–.022	49–55	1-3-4-2	7	Pulley	600
L-24	—	.031–.035	.016–.020	35–41	1-5-3-6-2-4	5	Pulley	750
1974								
B210 (A13)	NGK BP-5ES Hitachi L46PW	.031–.035	.017–.022	49–55	1-3-4-2	5	Pulley	800①
610 (L20B)	Hitachi CGR-600 Hanshin HR-15-1	.028–.031	.017–.022	49–55	1-3-4-2	12	Pulley	750①
710 (L18)	Hanshin HS-IS-1	.028–.031	.017–.022	49–55	1-3-4-2	12	Pulley	800①
260Z (L26)	NGK BP-6ES	.031–.035	.012–.016	—	1-5-3-6-2-4	②	Pulley	750①
1975								
B210	NGK BP-5ES Hitachi L46PW	.031–.035	.017–.022	49–55	1-3-4-2	10	Pulley	800①
610	Hitachi CGR-600 Hanshin HR-15-1	.032–.036	.017–.022	49–55	1-3-4-2	12	Pulley	750①
710	Hanshin HS-IS-1	.032–.036	.017–.022	49–55	1-3-4-2	12	Pulley	800①
280Z	NGK BP-6ES	.031–.035	.012–.016	—	1-5-3-6-2-4	7	Pulley	750①

①—Auto. trans., 650 in D. 　　②—Man. trans., 8° ATDC (retarded); Auto. Trans., 15° BTDC (advanced).

HOW TO PUSH AND TOW AUTOMATIC DRIVE CARS

Towing precautions

A disabled car must not be towed on the rear wheels with the transmission in any of the driving ranges as unnecessary damage to the transmission may result. Unless otherwise indicated in the chart, it may be towed for short distances only, with the control lever or push button in neutral (N) at a speed not in excess of 25 mph.

If for any reason the transmission is locked up, the car must not be towed on its rear wheels or serious damage to the transmission will result. If the car is to be towed for any extended distance, it should be done with the rear wheels off the ground or with the propeller shaft removed.

NOTE: Beginning with 1969 General Motors cars (1970 for others), except Corvair, if the ignition key is not available it will be necessary to tow the car with the front wheels off the ground and the rear wheels on a dolly or vice versa as the steering and shift mechanisms are also locked.

Push starting

As indicated in the chart below, a number of transmissions cannot be started by pushing. The oil circuits in these transmissions are such (no rear pumps) that the engine cannot be driven through the transmission. If the battery will not crank the engine, a fully charged battery should be installed or a jumper circuit should be used from another charged battery.
IMPORTANT: Alternator equipped cars cannot be push-started when the battery is completely dead because, unlike a generator, there is no residual magnetism in the rotor (which corresponds to the field coils in a generator).

When using jumper cables on alternator equipped cars, be sure to connect positive to positive and negative to negative to prevent damage to the alternator.

Car	Transmission	Push Starting				Towing	
		Start Pushing In	Ignition On At mph	Shift At mph	Shift To	Hold Speed At or Below mph	Maximum Distance Miles
American Motors	Flashomatic⑨	Neutral	15–20	15–20	L	40	①
	Torque Command	③	③	③	③	35	100
Chrysler Corp.	Powerflite	Neutral	0	25	L	35	100
	Torqueflite, Aluminum⑧	Neutral	0	15	L	35	100
	Torqueflite, Cast Iron	Neutral	0	15–20	L	35	100
Ford Motor Co.	Cruisematic, C4 and C6	③	③	③	③	30	①
	3 Speed⑩	Neutral	30	30	L	40	12
	2 Speed	Neutral	25	25	L	30	15
General Motors	Buick Dual Path Drive	③	③	③	③	25	①
	Buick Twin Turbine	Neutral	0	15	L	35②	①
	Corvair Powerglide	Neutral	0	20–25	L	50	①
	Dual Coupling Hydra-Matic	Neutral	30–35⑥	30–35⑥	D⑥	⑤	①
	F-85 Hydra-Matic, 1961–63	③	③	③	③	30	①
	Jetaway Hydra-Matic	③	③	③	③	45	①
	Roto Hydra-Matic	③	③	③	③	30	①
	Turbo Hydra-Matic "350" & "375B"	③	③	③	③	35①	①
	Turbo Hydra-Matic "400" & "375"	③	③	③	③	45①	①
	Powerglide, Aluminum⑨	Neutral	0	25–30	L	30①	①
	Powerglide, Cast Iron	Neutral	0	25–30	L	30	①
	Super Turbine "300"	③	③	③	③	25①	①
	Super Turbine "400"	③	③	③	③	25①	①
	Tempestorque, 1961–63	Neutral	0	20–25⑦	L	30	①
	Tempestorque, 1964	③	③	③	③	25	①
	Turboglide⑥	Neutral	25	25–30	HR or GR	30④	①
Studebaker	Flightomatic	Neutral	0	20	L	40	①

①—See Towing Precautions.
②—25 mph with air suspension.
③—Not possible to start by pushing. See Push Starting above.
④—10 mph with air suspension.
⑤—Do not tow.
⑥—Not possible to push start after 1958. See Push Starting note above.
⑦—Not possible to push start after 1962. See Push Starting note above.
⑧—Not possible to push start after 1965. See Push Starting note above.
⑨—Not possible to push start after 1966. See Push Starting note above.
⑩—Not possible to push start after 1967. See Push Starting note above.

CAR RIDE HEIGHTS

CHRYSLER CORPORATION MODELS

Chrysler Corporation cars can be adjusted for ride height and ground clearance by turning the torsion bar anchor bolts at the rear of the torsion bar. If you find that your car is not within manufacturer's specifications for ride height and ground clearance, have the torsion bars adjusted by a professional mechanic. The correct specification for each Chrysler Corporation model is given here.

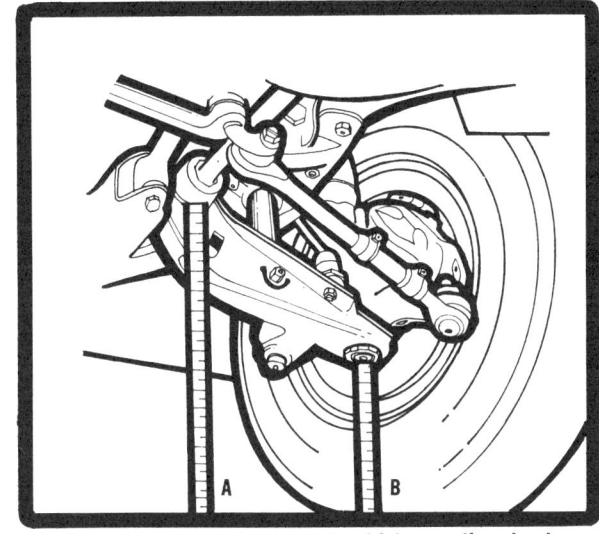

Difference between A and B should be as listed, plus or minus ⅛-inch.

CHRYSLER & IMPERIAL

Year	Model	Spec
1969-72	Chrysler	1⅛"
	Imperial	1¾"
1973	Chrysler	1¼"
	Imperial	1¾"
1974	Chrysler	1"
	Imperial	1"
1975	Cordoba	10¾" ①
	Newport & New Yorker	10⅛" ①
	Imperial	10⅛" ①

DODGE & DART

Year	Model	Spec
1969-70	Dart	2⅛"
	Challenger	1-3/16"
	Coronet, Charger	1⅞"
	Polara, Monaco	1⅜"
1971-72	Dart (2-Dr.)	1⅝"
	Dart (4-Dr.)	2⅛"
	Challenger	1"
	Coronet, Charger	1⅝"
	Polara, Monaco	1⅜"
1973	Dart (2-Dr.)	1⅞"
	Dart (4-Dr.)	2⅛"
	Challenger	1⅛"
	Coronet, Charger	1⅞"
	Polara, Monaco	1½"
1974	Dart	1⅞"
	Challenger	1⅛"
	Coronet, Charger	1⅞"
	Monaco	1"

DODGE & DART/continued

Year	Model	Spec
1975	Dart	10-15/16" ①
	Coronet & Charger SE	10¾" ①
	Monaco	10⅛" ①

PLYMOUTH

Year	Model	Spec
1969-70	Belvedere Satellite, Roadrunner	1⅞"
	Fury, V.I.P.	1⅜"
1971-72	Satellite	1⅝"
	Fury	1⅜"
1973	Satellite	1⅞"
	Fury	1½"
1974	Satellite	1⅞"
	Fury	1"
1975	Fury	10¾" ①
	Gran Fury	10⅛" ①
	Suburban	11¼" ①

VALIANT

Year	Model	Spec
1969	Barracuda	1⅜"
	Valiant	2⅛"
1970	Barracuda	1-3/16"
	Valiant	2⅛"
1971-72	Barracuda	1"
	Valiant (2-Dr.)	1⅝"
	Valiant (4-Dr.)	2⅛"
1973	Barracuda	1⅛"
	Valiant (2-Dr.)	1⅞"
	Valiant (4-Dr.)	2⅛"
1974	Barracuda	1⅛"
	Valiant	1⅞"
1975	Valiant	10-15/16"

①—Car riding height checked at "Dimension A" only.

CONVERSION TABLE

INCH FRACTIONS AND DECIMALS TO METRIC EQUIVALENTS

Fractions	Decimals	mm	Fractions	Decimals	mm	Fractions	Decimals	mm
—	.0004	.01	—	.4331	11	31/32	.96875	24.606
—	.004	.10	7/16	.4375	11.113	—	.9843	25
—	.01	.25	29/64	.4531	11.509	1	1.000	25.4
1/64	.0156	.397	15/32	.46875	11.906	—	1.0236	26
—	.0197	.50	—	.4724	12	1-1/32	1.0312	26.194
—	.0295	.75	31/64	.48437	12.303	1-1/16	1.062	26.988
1/32	.03125	.794	—	.492	12.5	—	1.063	27
—	.0394	1	1/2	.500	12.700	1-3/32	1.094	27.781
3/64	.0469	1.191	—	.5118	13	—	1.1024	28
—	.059	1.5	33/64	.5156	13.097	1-1/8	1.125	28.575
1/16	.0625	1.588	17/32	.53125	13.494	—	1.1417	29
5/64	.0781	1.984	35/64	.54687	13.891	1-5/32	1.156	29.369
—	.0787	2	—	.5512	14	—	1.1811	30
3/32	.094	2.381	9/16	.5625	14.288	1-3/16	1.1875	30.163
—	.0984	2.5	—	.571	14.5	1-7/32	1.219	30.956
7/64	.1093	2.776	37/64	.57812	14.684	—	1.2205	31
—	.1181	3	—	.5906	15	1-1/4	1.250	31.750
1/8	.1250	3.175	19/32	.59375	15.081	—	1.2598	32
—	.1378	3.5	39/64	.60937	15.478	1-9/32	1.281	32.544
9/64	.1406	3.572	5/8	.6250	15.875	—	1.2992	33
5/32	.15625	3.969	—	.6299	16	1-5/16	1.312	33.338
—	.1575	4	41/64	.6406	16.272	—	1.3386	34
11/64	.17187	4.366	—	.6496	16.5	1-11/32	1.344	34.131
—	.177	4.5	21/32	.65625	16.669	1-3/8	1.375	34.925
3/16	.1875	4.763	—	.6693	17	—	1.3779	35
—	.1969	5	43/64	.67187	17.066	1-13/32	1.406	35.719
13/64	.2031	5.159	11/16	.6875	17.463	—	1.4173	36
—	.2165	5.5	45/64	.7031	17.859	1-7/16	1.438	36.513
7/32	.21875	5.556	—	.7087	18	—	1.4567	37
15/64	.23437	5.953	23/32	.71875	18.5	1-15/32	1.469	37.306
—	.2362	6	—	.7283	18.256	—	1.4961	38
1/4	.2500	6.350	47/64	.73437	18.653	1-1/2	1.500	38.100
—	.2559	6.5	—	.7480	19	1-17/32	1.531	38.894
17/64	.2656	6.747	3/4	.7500	19.050	—	1.5354	39
—	.2756	7	49/64	.7656	19.447	1-9/16	1.562	39.688
9/32	.28125	7.144	25/32	.78125	19.844	—	1.5748	40
—	.2953	7.5	—	.7874	20	1-19/32	1.594	40.481
19/64	.29687	7.541	51/64	.79687	20.241	—	1.6142	41
5/16	.3125	7.938	13/16	.8125	20.638	1-5/8	1.625	41.275
—	.3150	8	—	.8268	21	—	1.6535	42
21/64	.3281	8.334	53/64	.8281	21.034	1-21/32	1.6562	42.069
—	.335	8.5	27/32	.84375	21.431	1-11/16	1.6875	42.863
11/32	.34375	8.731	55/64	.85937	21.828	—	1.6929	43
—	.3543	9	—	.8662	22	1-23/32	1.719	43.656
23/64	.35937	9.128	7/8	.8750	22.225	—	1.7323	44
—	.374	9.5	57/64	.8906	22.622	1-3/4	1.750	44.450
3/8	.3750	9.525	—	.9055	23	—	1.7717	45
25/64	.3906	9.922	29/32	.90625	23.019	1-25/32	1.781	45.244
—	.3937	10	59/64	.92187	23.416	—	1.8110	46
13/32	.4062	10.319	15/16	.9375	23.813	1-13/16	1.8125	46.038
—	.413	10.5	—	.9449	24	1-27/32	1.844	46.831
27/64	.42187	10.716	61/64	.9531	24.209	—	1.8504	47

INCH FRACTIONS AND DECIMALS TO METRIC EQUIVALENTS/continued

| Inches | | mm | Inches | | mm | Inches | | mm |
Fractions	Decimals		Fractions	Decimals		Fractions	Decimals	
1-7/8	1.875	47.625	—	3.0709	78	—	4.7244	120
—	1.8898	48	—	3.1102	79	4-3/4	4.750	120.650
1-29/32	1.9062	48.419	3-1/8	3.125	79.375	4-7/8	4.875	123.825
—	1.9291	49	—	3.1496	80	—	4.9212	125
1-15/16	1.9375	49.213	3-3/16	3.1875	80.963	5	5.000	127
—	1.9685	50	—	3.1890	81	—	5.1181	130
1-31/32	1.969	50.006	—	3.2283	82	5-1/4	5.250	133.350
2	2.000	50.800	3-1/4	3.250	82.550	5-1/2	5.500	139.700
—	2.0079	51	—	3.2677	83	—	5.5118	140
—	2.0472	52	—	3.3071	84	5-3/4	5.750	146.050
2-1/16	2.062	52.388	3-5/16	3.312	84.1377	—	5.9055	150
—	2.0866	53	—	3.3464	85	6	6.000	152.400
2-1/8	2.125	53.975	3-3/8	3.375	85.725	6-1/4	6.250	158.750
—	2.126	54	—	3.3858	86	—	6.2992	160
—	2.165	55	—	3.4252	87	6-1/2	6.500	165.100
2-3/16	2.1875	55.563	3-7/16	3.438	87.313	—	6.6929	170
—	2.2047	56	—	3.4646	88	6-3/4	6.750	171.450
—	2.244	57	3-1/2	3.500	88.900	7	7.000	177.800
2-1/4	2.250	57.150	—	3.5039	89	—	7.0866	180
—	2.2835	58	—	3.5433	90	—	7.4803	190
2-5/16	2.312	58.738	3-9/16	3.562	90.4877	7-1/2	7.500	190.500
—	2.3228	59	—	3.5827	91	—	7.8740	200
—	2.3622	60	—	3.622	92	8	8.000	203.200
2-3/8	2.375	60.325	3-5/8	3.625	92.075	—	8.2677	210
—	2.4016	61	—	3.6614	93	8-1/2	8.500	215.900
2-7/16	2.438	61.913	3-11/16	3.6875	93.663	—	8.6614	220
—	2.4409	62	—	3.7008	94	9	9.000	228.600
—	2.4803	63	—	3.7401	95	—	9.0551	230
2-1/2	2.500	63.500	3-3/4	3.750	95.250	—	9.4488	240
—	2.5197	64	—	3.7795	96	9-1/2	9.500	241.300
—	2.559	65	3-13/16	3.8125	96.838	—	9.8425	250
2-9/16	2.562	65.088	—	3.8189	97	10	10.000	254.000
—	2.5984	66	—	3.8583	98	—	10.2362	260
2-5/8	2.625	66.675	3-7/8	3.875	98.425	—	10.6299	270
—	2.638	67	—	3.8976	99	11	11.000	279.400
—	2.6772	68	—	3.9370	100	—	11.0236	280
2-11/16	2.6875	68.263	3-15/16	3.9375	100.013	—	11.4173	290
—	2.7165	69	—	3.9764	101	—	11.8110	300
2-3/4	2.750	69.850	4	4.000	101.600	12	12.000	304.800
—	2.7559	70	4-1/16	4.062	103.188	13	13.000	330.200
—	2.7953	71	4-1/8	4.125	104.775	—	13.7795	350
2-13/16	2.8125	71.438	—	4.1338	105	14	14.000	355.600
—	2.8346	72	4-3/16	4.1875	106.363	15	15.000	381
—	2.8740	73	4-1/4	4.250	107.950	—	15.7480	400
2-7/8	2.875	73.025	4-5/16	4.312	109.538	16	16.000	406.400
—	2.9134	74	—	4.3307	110	17	17.000	431.800
2-15/16	2.9375	74.613	4-3/8	4.375	111.125	—	17.7165	450
—	2.9527	75	4-7/16	4.438	112.713	18	18.000	457.200
—	2.9921	76	4-1/2	4.500	114.300	19	19.000	482.600
3	3.000	76.200	—	4.5275	115	—	19.6850	500
—	3.0315	77	4-9/16	4.562	115.888	20	20.000	508
3-1/16	3.062	77.788	4-5/8	4.625	117.475	21	21.000	533.400

DRILL SIZES

Letter Sizes	Drill Diam. Inches	Wire Gage Sizes	Drill Diam. Inches	Wire Gage Sizes	Drill Diam. Inches	Wire Gage Sizes	Drill Diam. Inches
Z	0.413	1	0.2280	28	0.1405	55	0.0520
Y	0.404	2	0.2210	29	0.1360	56	0.0465
X	0.397	3	0.2130	30	0.1285	57	0.0430
W	0.386	4	0.2090	31	0.1200	58	0.0420
V	0.377	5	0.2055	32	0.1160	59	0.0410
U	0.368	6	0.2040	33	0.1130	60	0.0400
T	0.358	7	0.2010	34	0.1110	61	0.0390
S	0.348	8	0.1990	35	0.1100	62	0.0380
R	0.339	9	0.1960	36	0.1065	63	0.0370
Q	0.332	10	0.1935	37	0.1040	64	0.0360
P	0.323	11	0.1910	38	0.1015	65	0.0350
O	0.316	12	0.1890	39	0.0995	66	0.0330
N	0.302	13	0.1850	40	0.0980	67	0.0320
M	0.295	14	0.1820	41	0.0960	68	0.0310
L	0.290	15	0.1800	42	0.0935	69	0.0292
K	0.281	16	0.1770	43	0.0890	70	0.0280
J	0.277	17	0.1730	44	0.0860	71	0.0260
I	0.272	18	0.1695	45	0.0820	72	0.0250
H	0.266	19	0.1660	46	0.0810	73	0.0240
G	0.261	20	0.1610	47	0.0785	74	0.0225
F	0.257	21	0.1590	48	0.0760	75	0.0210
E	0.250	22	0.1570	49	0.0730	76	0.0200
D	0.246	23	0.1540	50	0.0700	77	0.0180
C	0.242	24	0.1520	51	0.0670	78	0.0160
B	0.238	25	0.1495	52	0.0635	79	0.0145
A	0.234	26	0.1470	53	0.0595	80	0.0135
		27	0.1440	54	0.0550		

Glossary

GLOSSARY OF AUTOMOTIVE TERMINOLOGY

ABDC. After Bottom Dead Center.

A BONE. Model A Ford.

AC. Alternating current.

ACCELERATING WIND UP. See Spring Wind Up.

ACCELERATOR. The floor pedal used to control, through linkage, the throttle valve in the carburetor.

ACCELERATOR PUMP. A small pump, located in the carburetor, that sprays additional gasoline into the air stream during acceleration.

ACKERMAN PRINCIPLE. Bending the outer ends of the steering arms slightly inward so that when the car is making a turn, the inside wheel will turn more sharply than the outer wheel. This principle produces toe-out on turns.

ADDITIVE. Some solution, powder, etc., that is added to gasoline, oil, grease, etc., in an endeavor to improve the characteristics of the original product.

ADJUSTER (Starwheel, Cam, Eccentric). A device by which brake shoe-to-drum clearance may be adjusted to compensate for lining wear and maintain minimum travel during brake application without drag when brakes are unapplied.

ADVANCE (Ignition timing). To set the ignition timing so that a spark occurs earlier or more degrees before TDC.

AIR. Air Injection Reactor system of reducing objectionable exhaust emissions.

AIR FILTER (Air cleaner). Device used to filter out harmful impurities from the air drawn into the engine.

AIR FOIL. A device, similar to a stubby wing, that is mounted onto a racing car or dragster to provide high speed stability. The air foil is mounted in a horizontal position.

AIR-FUEL RATIO. The ratio by weight or by volume, between the air and gasoline that makes up the engine fuel mixture.

AIR GAP (Spark plugs). The distance between the center and side electrodes.

AIR HORN (Carburetor). Top portion of the air passageway through the carburetor.

AIR HORN (Warning). A warning horn operated by compressed air.

AIR POLLUTION. Contamination of earth's atmosphere by various natural and man-made pollutants such as smoke, gases, dust, etc.

AIR SUSPENSION (Air spring). An automotive suspension system wherein conventional steel springs are replaced by chambers filled with compressed air which supports the car's weight.

ALIGNMENT. Process of positioning separate objects (such as wheels) into a correct relationship with each other.

ALTERNATOR. A device similar to the generator but which produces AC current. The AC must be rectified before reaching the car's electrical system.

ALTERNATING CURRENT (AC). An electric current that first flows one way in the circuit and then the other.

AMMETER. An instrument used to measure the rate of current flow in amperes.

AMPERE (Amp). Unit of measurement of the rate of flow of an electrical current, named after Andre Marie Ampere, French electrical research physicist.

AMPERE HOUR CAPACITY. A measurement of storage battery ability to deliver a specified current over a specified length of time.

ANCHOR (Anchor pin, Support pin, Stop). Some point, such as a pin or slotted plate, at which brake shoes are prevented from rotating when applied against the rotating drum surface. The anchor may be fixed or adjustable, depending upon brake design.

ANODE. The positive pole in an electrical circuit.

ANTIBACKFIRE VALVE. Valve used in air injection reactor (exhaust emission control) system to prevent backfiring during the period immediately following sudden deceleration.

ANTI-BRAKE-DIP FEATURE. Arrangement of the front suspension geometry, made possible by the use of ball joints in an independent front suspension, which counters the front-end lowering effects of the apparent forward weight transfer on braking.

ANTIFREEZE. A chemical added to the cooling system to prevent the coolant from freezing in cold weather.

ANTIFREEZE HYDROMETER. Instrument for measuring the specific gravity of a coolant, and thus its antifreeze content.

ANTIPERCOLATOR. A device for venting vapors from the main discharge tube, or the well, of a carburetor.

ANTISTALL DASHPOT. Device that keeps an engine from stalling by preventing the throttle from closing too rapidly.

ARCING. Electricity leaping the gap between two electrodes.

ARMATURE (Relay, Regulator, Horn, etc.). The movable part of the unit.

ARMATURE. A rotating core, usually composed of soft iron laminations, around which is wound a coil of wire that is moved through a magnetic field in a generator or motor.

ASYMMETRICAL REAR SPRINGS. A form of rear leaf spring in which the rear axle is mounted ahead of the center of the spring. The forward portion of the spring is relatively rigid to give superior control over spring wind up while the longer rear portion is more supple to provide most of the springing action.

ATDC. After Top Dead Center.

ATMOSPHERIC VALVE (Control valve). The valve in a power brake system which controls the input of outside air to the apply side of the power brake diaphragm in proportion to the pedal pressure applied.

ATOMIZATION (Vaporization). In the carburetor and intake manifold, a fine dispersal of liquid gasoline in droplets so small and light they remain airborne. This results from the design of the fuel nozzles in the carburetor, which discharge gasoline in a spray, and the heat of the manifold, which maintains the dispersal.

AUTOMATIC CHOKE. A heat sensing device which automatically controls the choke plate in the carburetor to enrich the mixture sufficiently to keep an engine operating properly until it reaches operating temperature.

AXIS. A line or point denoting the center around which something turns or pivots.

AXLE (Rear gears). The two gears, one per axle, that are splined to the inner ends of the drive axles. They mesh with and are driven by the spider gears.

AXLE (Full-floating). An axle used to drive the rear wheels. It does not hold them on nor support them.

AXLE (Semi or one-quarter floating). An axle used to drive the wheels, hold them on, and support them.

AXLE (Three-quarter floating). An axle used to drive the rear wheels as well as hold them on. It does not support them.

AXLE (Shaft). Solid metal rod, extending from the differential, that transfers power to an automobile's drive wheel.

BACKFIRE (Intake system). Burning of the fuel mixture in the intake manifold. May be caused by faulty timing, crossed plug wires, leaky intake valve, etc.

BACKFIRE (Exhaust system). Passage of unburned fuel mixture into the exhaust system where it is ignited and causes an explosion (backfire).

BACKLASH. The amount of play between two parts. In the case of gears, it refers to how much one gear can be moved back and forth without moving the gear into which it is meshed.

BACK PRESSURE. Refers to the resistance to the flow of exhaust gases through the exhaust system.

BAFFLE. An obstruction used to slow down or divert the flow of gases, liquids, sounds, etc.

BALLAST RESISTOR. An electrical resistor in the primary circuit which is bypassed to permit a full 12-volt surge of current to facilitate engine starting and brought into the circuit to reduce voltage when the engine is running at lower speeds.

BALL JOINTS (Spherical joints, Ball-and-socket joints). A device composed of a spherical part which bears against and is retained by a matching socket, used to join two structural members. It permits rotational movement in any plane between the two joined members. Ball joints are used in front suspension control arms to support the steering knuckles, and at the ends of tie-rods to connect them to the steering arms and the center link.

BALL JOINT STEERING KNUCKLE. A steering knuckle that pivots on ball joints instead of on a kingpin.

BALL JOINT ROCKER ARMS. Rocker arms that instead of being mounted on a shaft, are mounted upon a ball-shaped device on the end of a stud.

BAND (Brake band, Lining assembly). A flexible metal strip lined with a suitable friction material, which encircles the outer diameter of a drum. When applied, the band is contracted to bring the lining material to bear against the drum, giving a braking effect similar to that of a shoe and lining assembly.

BARRELS (Bores). The air passage or passages in the carburetor through which air flows to the intake manifold, and in which fuel is added to the air.

BATTERY. A component of the automobile's electrical system which stores electrical energy for use in the system. A battery consists of a connected group of cells encased in a rectangular casing, and an acid electrolyte which supports a reversible electro-chemical reaction. When electrical energy is drawn from the battery, it is discharging. When an electrical current from the alternator is directed through the battery, the reaction is reversed and the battery is charging.

BATTERY CHARGING. The process of renewing the battery by passing an electric current through the battery in a reverse direction.

BATTERY HYDROMETER. Instrument for measuring the specific gravity of a battery's electrolyte solution and thus its state of charge.

BATTERY POSTS. Round lead posts protruding from a battery to which the battery cables are attached. See also negative terminal, positive terminal.

BEARING. A device used to support a moving component, allowing the part to move with a minimum of friction. Bearings used in automotive engines are of the ball, roller or plain types. Lubrication between moving bearing surfaces is essential to prevent metal-to-metal contact and resulting high friction.

BEARING CLEARANCE. The amount of space left between a shaft and the bearing surface. This space is for lubricating oil to enter.

BBDC. Before Bottom Dead Center.

BDC. Bottom Dead Center.

BELL HOUSING (Clutch housing). The metal covering around the flywheel and clutch, or torque converter assembly.

BELTED-BIAS TIRE. Tire with the basic body structure of a bias-ply tire that has an additional two or more layers (or belts) of material reinforced with steel or fabric between the body plies and the tread.

BELTS. Layers of material reinforced with steel or fabric within some tires that strengthen the tread and resist puncturing by sharp objects.

BENDIX TYPE STARTER DRIVE. A self-engaging starter drive gear. The gear moves into engagement when the starter starts spinning and automatically disengages when the starter stops.

BEZEL. The crimped edge of metal that secures the glass face to an instrument.

BHP. See Brake Horsepower.

BIAS-PLY TIRE. Tire in which the reinforcing cords in the body plies run in alternating directions at an angle (or bias) to the center line of the tread.

BIMETAL (Thermostatic element). A strip of two metals having appreciably different expansion characteristics under heat, bonded together. Because of the dissimilar rates of expansion, the strip will change configuration with any change in temperature.

BINDERS. Car brakes.

BLEEDING THE BRAKES. This refers to the removal of air from the hydraulic system. Bleeder screws are loosened at each wheel cylinder, one at a time, and brake fluid is forced from the master cylinder through the lines until all air is expelled.

BLOCK. That part of the engine containing the cylinders.

BLOW-BY. Leakage of combustion fumes past piston rings and into the crankcase due to high combustion chamber pressures produced during the power stroke.

BOILING POINT. The exact temperature at which a liquid begins to boil.

BONDED BRAKE LINING. Brake lining that is attached to the brake shoe by an adhesive.

BONNET. British term for car hood.

BOOSTER. A device incorporated in car system, such as brakes and steering, to increase the pressure output or decrease amount of effort required to operate, or both.

BOOT. Any flexible cover used to protect working parts from contamination by foreign material. Also, British term for trunk.

BORE. May refer to the cylinder itself or to the diameter of the cylinder.

BORE DIAMETER. The diameter of the cylinders.

BORING. Renewing the cylinders by cutting them out to a specified size. A boring bar is used to make the cut.

BORING BAR (Cylinder). A machine used to cut engine cylinders to a specific size. As used in garages, to cut worn cylinders to a new diameter.

BOX. Transmission.

BOXED ROD. Connecting rod in which the I-beam section has been stiffened by welding plates on each side of the rod.

BRAKE ANCHOR. A steel stud upon which one end of the brake shoe is either attached or rests against. The anchor is firmly affixed to the backing plate.

BRAKE BACKING PLATE. A rigid steel plate upon which the brake shoes are attached. The braking force applied to the shoes is absorbed by the backing plate.

BRAKE BAND. A band, faced with brake lining, that encircles a brake drum. It is used on several parking brake installations.

BRAKE BLEEDING. See Bleeding the Brakes.

BRAKE CYLINDER. See Wheel Cylinder.

BRAKE, DISC TYPE. A braking system that instead of using the conventional brake drum with internal brake shoes, uses a steel disc with caliper type lining application. When the brakes are applied, a section of lining on each side of the spinning disc is forced against the disc, thus imparting a braking force. This type of brake is very resistant to brake fade.

BRAKE DRUM. A cast iron or aluminum housing, bolted to the wheel, that rotates around the brake shoes. When the shoes are expanded, they rub against the machined inner surface of the brake drum and exert a braking effect upon the wheel.

BRAKE DRUM LATHE. A machine to refinish the inside of the brake drum.

BRAKE FADE. Reduction in braking force due to loss of friction between brake shoes and drum. Caused by heat buildup.

BRAKE FLUID. A special fluid used in hydraulic brake systems.

BRAKE FLUSHING. Cleaning the brake system by flushing with alcohol or brake fluid. This is done to remove water, dirt, or any other contaminant. Flushing fluid is placed in the master cylinder and forced through the lines and wheel cylinders where it exits at the cylinder bleed screws.

BRAKE HORSEPOWER (bhp). A measurement of the actual usable horsepower delivered at the crankshaft. It is commonly computed by using an engine or a chassis dynamometer.

BREAK-IN. Period of operation between the installation of new or rebuilt parts and the time in which the parts are worn to the correct fit. Driving at a reduced and varying speed for a specified mileage to permit parts to wear to the correct fit.

BRAKE LINING. A friction material fastened to the brake shoes. The brake lining is pressed against the rotating brake drum thus stopping the car.

BRAKE, PARKING. A brake used to hold the car in position while parked. One type applies the rear brake shoes by mechanical means and the other type applies a brake band to a brake drum installed in the drivetrain.

BRAKES, POWER. A conventional hydraulic brake system that utilizes engine vacuum to operate a vacuum power piston. The power piston applies pressure to the brake pedal, or in some cases, directly to the master cylinder piston. This reduces the amount of pedal pressure that the driver must exert to stop the car.

BRAKE PULL (Pull, Dive). A sudden, sometimes unpredictable tendency of the car to swerve when brakes are applied. It is an unbalanced braking condition which can be caused by contaminated linings or other malfunctions within the brake, or by any of a number of factors not directly related to the brake system.

BRAKE SHOE GRINDER. A grinder used to grind brake shoe lining so that it will be square to and concentric with the brake drum.

BRAKE SHOE HEEL. That end of the brake shoe adjacent to the anchor bolt or pin.

BRAKE SHOE TOE. The free end of the shoe. It is not attached to or resting against an anchor pin.

BRAKE SHOES. That part of the brake system, located at the wheels, upon which the brake lining is attached. When the wheel cylinders are actuated by hydraulic pressure they force the brake shoes apart and bring the lining into contact with the drum.

BRAKE WARNING SWITCH. A unit that warns the vehicle operator that one of the hydraulic systems have failed. As pressure falls in the front or rear system, the other system's normal pressure forces the piston to the inoperative side, contacting the switch terminal, causing a red warning light to light the instrument panel.

BREAKER ARM. The movable arm upon which one of the breaker points is affixed.

BREAKER POINTS (Ignition points, Point set, Points). A component of the distributor which momentarily breaks the current flow in the primary ignition circuit to create an induced high voltage current in the ignition secondary circuit. The points themselves are two small discs of metal, usually with a high tungsten content. One is attached to a stationary arm, and the other is attached to a cam-actuated moving arm which alternately opens and closes the gap between the two points.

BREATHER PIPE. A pipe opening into the interior of the engine. It is used to assist ventilation. The pipe usually extends downwards to a point just below the engine so that the passing air stream will form a partial vacuum.

BRUSH. Electrical circuit component, usually composed of graphite or carbon, used to complete the circuit between a stationary component and a moving component on an electrical part such as an alternator, generator or motor.

BTDC. Before Top Dead Center.

BUDC. Before Upper Dead Center. Same as BTDC.

BURNISH. To bring a surface to a high shine by rubbing with hard, smooth object.

BUSHING. A bearing for a shaft, spring shackle, piston pin, etc., of one piece construction which may be removed from the part.

BUTTERFLY VALVE. A valve in the carburetor that is so named due to its resemblance to the insect of the same name.

BYPASS FILTER. An oil filter that constantly filters a portion of the oil flowing through the engine.

BYPASS VALVE. A valve that can open and allow a fluid to pass through in other than its normal channel.

CABLE EQUALIZER. A device in the system of cables linking the parking brake control with the rear wheel brakes, which divides the applying force equally between the two rear wheel brakes for a more positive brake application.

CALIBRATE. As applied to test instruments, adjusting the dial needle to the correct zero or load setting.

CALIPER (Inside and outside). An adjustable measuring tool that is placed around, or within, an object and adjusted until it just contacts. It is then withdrawn and the distance measured between the contracting points.

CAM. An eccentric or lobe-shaped rotating device having one or more smoothly contoured protrusions that cause movement of an adjacent component which bears upon the cam's surface.

CAM ANGLE or DWELL (Ignition). The number of degrees the breaker cam rotates from the time the breaker points close until they open again.

CAM GROUND. A piston that is ground slightly egg-shaped. When it is heated, it becomes round.

CAMBER (Of springs, Arc, Bend). The characteristic curved appearance of automotive leaf springs.

CAMBER (Of wheels). The attitude of a wheel and tire assembly when viewed from the front of a car. If it leans outward, away from the car, at the top, the wheel is said to have positive camber. If it leans inward, it is said to have negative camber. Camber is one of the factors in front end alignment.

CAMSHAFT. In the valvetrain of an automobile engine, a rotating shaft that turns at one-half of engine speed and includes integral cams that actuate intake and exhaust valves. The camshaft is usually used to drive other engine components such as the distributor and fuel pump.

CAMSHAFT GEAR. A gear that is used to drive the camshaft.

CARBONIZE. Building up of carbon on objects such as spark plugs, pistons, heads, etc.

CARBON MONOXIDE. A deadly, colorless, odorless, and tasteless gas found in the engine exhaust. Formed by incomplete burning of hydrocarbons.

CARBURETOR (Carb). A fuel and air metering and mixing device. Automotive carburetors are of the float type, wherein air is metered by a venturi and fuel is metered by properly sized restrictions in the fuel passages. The amount of fuel-air mixture delivered to the engine is controlled by the throttle plate(s) in the carburetor.

CARBURETOR CIRCUITS. A series of passageways and units designed to perform a specific function—idle circuit, full power circuit, etc.

CARBURETOR ICING. The formation of ice on the throttle plate or valve. As the fuel nozzles feed fuel into the air horn it turns to a vapor. This robs heat from the air and when weather conditions are just right—fairly cold and quite humid—ice may form.

CARRIER BEARINGS. The bearings upon which the differential case is mounted.

CASTER. Relationship of the axis about which a steerable wheel swivels or pivots (the steering axis or king pin axis) and the point of contact between the wheel and its supporting surface (the road). Positive caster, with the axis ahead of the point of contact, will tend to pull the wheel in the direction of travel, adding directional stability. Negative caster, with the axis behind the point of contact, will tend to push the wheel to one side—an unstable condition. Caster is a factor in front end alignment.

CASTLE or CASTELLATED NUT. A nut having a series of slots cut into one end into which a cotter pin may be passed to secure the nut.

CATALYTIC CONVERTER. Device that chemically reduces harmful emissions of automobile exhaust.

CELL (Battery). The individual (separate) compartments in the battery which contain positive and negative plates suspended in electrolyte. A 6-volt battery has three cells, a 12-volt battery six cells.

CELL CONNECTOR. The lead strap or connection between battery cell groups.

CENTER STEERING LINKAGE. A steering system utilizing two tie rods connected to the steering arms and to a central idler arm. The idler arm is operated by a drag link that connects the idler arm to the pitman arm.

CENTRIFUGAL ADVANCE (Distributor). A unit designed to advance and retard the ignition timing through the action of centrifugal force.

CENTRIFUGAL CLUTCH. A clutch that utilizes centrifugal force to expand a friction device on the driving shaft until it is locked to a drum on the driven shaft.

CHARGE (Battery). Passing an electric current through a battery to restore it to the active state.

CHASSIS. Generally, chassis refers to the frame, engine, front and rear axles, springs, steering system and gas tank. Everything but the body and fenders.

CHASSIS DYNAMOMETER. See Dynamometer.

CHATTER. A low frequency vibration caused by a rapidly changing coefficient of friction between drums and linings when braking at higher speeds. This is usually caused by heat spots—small areas of the brake drums which have been drastically overheated to the point where their molecular structure has been changed from cast iron to that of steel. Steel has a different coefficient of friction than cast iron.

CHOKE (Choke plate, Choke valve). In a carburetor, a plate near the top of the air passage through the carburetor which can be closed fully or partially to restrict the amount of air admitted to the carburetor and thus cause engine vacuum to draw a richer flow of fuel from the carburetor.

CHOKE STOVE. A heating compartment in or on the exhaust manifold from which hot air is drawn to the automatic choke device.

CID. Cubic Inch Displacement.

CIRCUIT. The complete path of an electrical current, including the generating apparatus, or a distinct segment of the complete path.

CIRCUIT BREAKER. Device in an electrical circuit incorporating a bimetallic spring which, when overheated by current flow in excess of specifications, will move to separate two contact points and break the circuit to prevent damage. Some circuit breakers will reset themselves automatically when the bimetal cools, while others must be reset manually.

CLEARANCE. A given amount of space between two parts—between piston and cylinder, bearing and journal, etc.

CLOCKWISE. Rotation to the right.

CLUSTER or COUNTER GEAR. The cluster of gears that are all cut on one long gear blank. The cluster gears ride in the bottom of the transmission. The cluster provides a connection between the transmission input shaft and the output shaft.

CLUTCH. A device used to connect or disconnect the flow of power from one unit to another.

CLUTCH DIAPHRAGM SPRING. A round dish-shaped piece of flat spring steel. It is used to force the pressure plate against the clutch disc in some clutches.

CLUTCH DISC. That part of a clutch assembly that is splined to the transmission clutch or input shaft. It is faced with friction material. When the clutch is engaged, the disc is squeezed between the flywheel and the clutch pressure plate.

CLUTCH HOUSING (Bell housing). A cast iron or aluminum housing that surrounds the flywheel and clutch mechanism.

CLUTCH PEDAL FREE TRAVEL. The specific distance that the clutch pedal may be depressed before the throw-out bearing actually contacts the clutch release fingers.

CLUTCH PILOT BEARING. A small bronze bushing, or in some cases a ball bearing, placed in the end of the crankshaft or in the center of the flywheel depending on the car, that is used to support the outboard end of the transmission input shaft.

CLUTCH PRESSURE PLATE. That part of a clutch assembly that through spring pressure squeezes the clutch disc against the flywheel thereby transmitting a driving force through the assembly. To disengage the clutch, the pressure plate is drawn away from the flywheel via linkage.

CLUTCH SEMI-CENTRIFUGAL RELEASE FINGERS. Clutch release fingers that have a weight attached to them so that at high rpm the release fingers place additional pressure on the clutch pressure plate.

CLUTCH THROW-OUT FORK. The device or fork that straddles the throw-out bearing and that is used to force the throw-out bearing against the clutch release fingers.

COIL (Ignition coil). A specialized form of electrical transformer which boosts voltage supplied by the car's electrical system to an extremely high level that is adequate for the high voltage requirements of the spark plugs.

COIL SPRING. A form of spring used in automotive suspension systems. It is a steel rod wound around in a cylindrical shape, resulting in continuous coils that do not touch. When a load is placed on the coil spring, the coils draw closer together, subjecting the rod to both flexing and twisting forces.

COLLAPSED (Piston). A piston whose skirt diameter has been reduced due to heat and the forces imposed upon it during service in the engine.

COMBUSTION (Burning, Exploding). The chemical reaction of combining oxygen with another substance, resulting in the release of heat energy.

COMBUSTION CHAMBER. The portion of an engine's cylinders where combustion takes place. In general usage, the recessed portion of the cylinder head which fits over the cylinder is referred to as the combustion chamber. Although to be literally complete, the head of the piston and in some cases, the upper extreme of the cylinder should also be considered parts of the combustion chamber.

COMBUSTION CHAMBER VOLUME. Volume of combustion chamber (space above piston with piston on TDC) measured in cubic centimeters (cc).

COMMUTATOR. Axially-mounted cylindrical element at the end of an armature of a motor or generator. The cylinder is composed of copper segments separated by a thin layer of insulating material. Each segment serves as the terminal point for a coil winding of the armature. Stationary brushes contact the commutator to conduct the induced voltage from the windings to the automobile's electrical system.

COMPENSATING PORT. A small hole in a brake master cylinder to permit fluid to return to the reservoir.

COMPENSATOR VALVE (Automatic transmission). A valve designed to increase the pressure on the brake band during heavy acceleration.

COMPRESSION. In an internal combustion engine, the function of compressing the combustible mixture into a smaller volume within the cylinder so as to extract more power from the combustion that follows.

COMPRESSION CHECK. Testing the compression in all the cylinders at cranking speed. All plugs are removed, the compression gauge place in one plug hole, the throttle cracked wide open and the engine cranked until the gauge no longer climbs. The compression check is a fine way in which to determine the condition of the valves, rings and cylinders.

COMPRESSION GAUGE. A gauge used to test the compression in the cylinders.

COMPRESSION IGNITION ENGINE. A type of engine which depends upon compression of the fuel-air charge in the cylinder to generate heat sufficient to ignite the fuel spontaneously. See Diesel Engine.

COMPRESSION RATIO. The ratio of the volumes between the piston head and top of the cylinder at bottom dead center and top dead center. Generally, the higher the compression ratio (in other words, the greater the compression), the more usable power will be extracted from the fuel.

CONDENSE. Turning a vapor back into a liquid.

CONDENSATION. Moisture, from the air, deposited on a cool surface.

CONDENSER (Refrigeration). The unit in an air conditioning system that cools the hot compressed refrigerant and turns it from a vapor into a liquid.

CONDENSER. A device in the ignition distributor which absorbs the surge of current resulting when the breaker points open, and then discharges back into the primary circuit. This action protects the points from arcing and burning, and prolongs the discharge of high voltage current to the spark plugs.

CONDUCTOR. Any material through which an electrical current will flow. All materials are conductors, to a degree. In common usage, however, only those materials which conduct electricity with relatively little resistance are classed as conductors.

CONE-CLUTCH. A clutch utilizing a cone-shaped member that is forced into a cone-shaped depression in the flywheel, or other driving unit, thus locking the two together. Although no longer used on cars, the cone clutch finds some applications in small riding tractors, heavy power mowers, etc.

CONNECTING ROD (Rod, Con Rod). An engine component, usually of forged steel, which forms a structural link between the piston and the crankshaft.

CONSTANT MESH GEARS. Gears that are always in mesh with each other, driving or not.

CONSTANT VELOCITY UNIVERSAL JOINT. A universal joint so designed as to effect a smooth transfer of torque from the driven shaft to the driving shaft without any fluctuations in the speed of the driven shaft.

CONTACT POINTS (Breaker points). Two movable points or areas that when pressed together, complete a circuit. These points are usually made of tungsten, platinum or silver.

CONTINUITY LIGHT. A testing instrument with a sharp probe that can penetrate wire insulation. It is used to determine whether or not current is flowing in a circuit.

CONTROL ARMS (A-Frames). Structural members of independent front suspension which form moving links between the car's underbody structure and king pin or ball joints upon which the steering knuckle pivots.

CONTROL UNIT (Electronic ignition). A unit consisting of electronic circuitry which when triggered by the pickup coil causes the power switching transistor to interrupt the primary circuit of the ignition coil.

COOLANT. Liquid in the cooling system.

CORDS. Heavy, wound strands of reinforcing material (nylon, rayon, polyester) in the body of a tire.

COUNTERBALANCE. A weight attached to some moving part so that the part will be in balance.

COUNTERBORE. Enlarging a hole to a certain depth.

COUNTERCLOCKWISE. Rotation to the left as opposed to that of clock hands.

COUNTERSINK. To make a counterbore so that the head of a screw may set flush, or below the surface.

COUNTERWEIGHT. On a crankshaft, a mass of metal of a precise weight located opposite the connecting rod journals so as to balance out the weight of the journal and minimize unbalanced forces that cause vibrations when the engine is running.

COWL. The part of the car body between the engine firewall and the front of the dash panel.

CRANKCASE. That part of the engine that surrounds the crankshaft.

CRANKCASE DILUTION. An accumulation of unburned gasoline in the crankcase. An excessively rich fuel mixture or poor combustion will allow a certain amount of gasoline to pass down between the pistons and cylinder walls.

CRANKCASE VENTILATION SYSTEM (Crankcase breather). A system designed to remove combustion fumes and other contaminants from the crankcase and other enclosed portions of the engine.

CRANKSHAFT (Crank). Power transmitting component of an engine that converts the reciprocating motion of pistons and connecting rods to a rotary motion by means of crank throws—segments offset from the center of crankshaft rotation, to which the connecting rod is attached.

CRANKSHAFT GEAR. A gear mounted on the front of the crankshaft. It is used to drive the camshaft gear.

CROSS SHAFT (Steering). The shaft in the steering gearbox that engages the steering shaft worm. The cross shaft is splined to the pitman arm.

CRUDE OIL. Petroleum in its raw or unrefined state. It forms the basis of gasoline, engine oil, diesel oil, kerosene, etc.

CUBES. Cubic inches, or cubic inch displacement of an engine.

CU. IN. (C.I.). Cubic Inch.

CURRENT. Movement of electricity through the linked conductors of a circuit. Generally conceded to be an instantaneous displacement of electrons of the conductor from the negative pole to the positive pole, caused by the introduction of free electrons into the circuit by an electrical power source.

CYLINDER (Bore). Hollow cylindrical component of an engine, usually machined in the engine's cylinder block, in which the piston operates. Cylinder walls support and guide the piston, confine the pressures of combustion, and conduct combustion heat to engine coolant.

CYLINDER BLOCK (Engine block). The main supporting member of a liquid-cooled engine, usually of cast iron, which contains the cylinders, water jacket, crankcase, passages for engine oil and coolant, engine mounting fittings and many other components.

CYLINDER HEAD (Head). Casting and related parts used to seal the tops of an engine's cylinders. The cylinder head contains coolant passages, spark plug ports, and in the case of valve-in-head engines, the intake and exhaust valves and ports, rocker arms and associated parts.

CYLINDER HONE. A tool that uses an abrasive to smooth out and bring to exact measurements such things as engine cylinders, wheel cylinders, bushings, etc.

CYLINDER SLEEVE. A replaceable cylinder. It is made of a pipe-like section that is either pressed or pushed into the block.

DAMPING. In a hydraulic-type shock absorber, the physical control of unwanted spring vibrations that is caused by resistance to a forced flow of confined fluid through passages in the piston and base of the shock absorber.

DASHBOARD. That part of the body containing the driving instruments, switches, etc.

DASHPOT. A unit that retards or slows down the movement of some part.

DC (Electrical). Direct Current.

DC (Piston position). Dead Center. Piston at the extreme top or bottom of its stroke.

DEAD AXLE. An axle that does not rotate but merely forms a base upon which to attach the wheels.

DEAD CENTER (Engine). The point at which the piston reaches its uppermost or downmost position in the cylinder. The rod crank journal would be at 12 o'clock UDC or 6 o'clock LDC.

DE DION. A rear axle setup in which the driving wheels are attached to a curved dead axle that is attached to the frame by a central pivot. The differential unit is bolted to the frame and is connected to the driving wheels by drive axles utilizing universal joints.

DEFLECTION. In a spring, the initial movement in response to any force acting on the spring. Deflection may take the form of flexing, as with a leaf spring, or twisting, as with a torsion bar.

DEGLAZER. An abrasive tool used to remove the glaze from cylinder walls so that a new set of rings will seat.

DEGREE. 1/360 part of a circle.

DEGREE WHEEL. A wheel-like unit that is attached to the engine crankshaft. It is used to time the valves to a high degree of accuracy.

DETENT BALL AND SPRING. A spring loaded ball that snaps into a groove or notch to hold some sliding object in position.

DETERGENT. A chemical added to the engine oil to improve its characteristics (sludge control, non-foaming, etc.).

DETONATION (Knock, Ping). Virtually instantaneous combustion of fuel in the combustion chamber, resulting in the instant release of heat energy, usually with the generation of excessive pressures which can damage adjacent engine components.

DIAL GAUGE OR INDICATOR. A precision micrometer type instrument that indicates the reading via a needle moving across a dial face.

DIAPHRAGM-TYPE PUMP. A fluid moving device consisting essentially of a sealed chamber having one wall formed by a flexible diaphragm. As the diaphragm is moved out to enlarge the chamber, fluid enters past an inlet check valve. Then the diaphragm is moved inward, squeezing the fluid out of the chamber past an outlet check valve.

DIE (Thread). A tool for cutting threads.

DIE CASTING. Formation of an object by forcing molten metal, plastic, etc., into a die.

DIESEL ENGINE. An internal combustion engine that used diesel oil for fuel. The true diesel does not use an ignition system but injects diesel oil into the cylinders when the piston has compressed the air so tightly that it is hot enough to ignite the diesel fuel without a spark.

DIESELING. Condition in which fuel continues to burn after the ignition has been turned off.

DIFFERENTIAL. A unit that will drive both rear axles at the same time but will allow them to turn at different speeds when negotiating turns.

DIFFERENTIAL CASE. The steel unit to which the ring gear is attached. The case drives the spider gears and forms an inner bearing surface for the axle and gears.

DIMMER SWITCH (Beam selector switch). Two-way switch mounted on the car's floor where it can be conveniently operated by the pressure of the driver's toe to select the high beam or low beam headlight circuit.

DIODE. A cylindrical, solid-state electrical device which will allow the passage of an electrical current in one direction, but will prevent it in the other direction. Used in the alternator to convert alternating current to direct current.

DIPSTICK. The metal rod that passes into the oil sump used to determine the quantity of oil in the engine.

DIRECT CURRENT (D.C.). An electrical current which flows in only one direction. The polarity of the circuit does not change.

DIRECT DRIVE. Such as high gear when the crankshaft and drive shaft revolve at the same speed.

DIRECTIONAL STABILITY (Steering). Ability of a car to move forward in a straight line with a minimum of driver control. A car with good directional stability will not be unduly affected by side wind, road irregularities, etc.

DISCHARGE (Battery). Drawing electric current from the battery.

DISC BRAKE. See Brake (Disc).

DISC-BRAKE CALIPER. Mechanism that straddles a brake disc and contains the brake pads.

DISC WHEEL. A wheel constructed of stamped steel.

DISPLACEMENT (Piston displacement, Cubes). The volume of fuel-air mixture an engine is theoretically capable of drawing into all cylinders during one operating cycle, or the space swept through by the pistons in moving from one end of a stroke to the other. (Formula for determining Displacement: Cylinder Diameter times Cylinder Diameter times 0.7854 times Length of Stroke times Number of Cylinders; or Bore X Bore X 0.7854 X Stroke X Cylinders.)

DISTRIBUTION TUBES (Cooling system). Tubes used in the engine cooling area to guide and direct the flow of coolant to vital areas.

DISTRIBUTOR (Ignition). A unit designed to make and break the ignition primary circuit and to distribute the resultant high voltage to the proper cylinder at the correct time.

DISTRIBUTOR CAP (Ignition). An insulated cap containing a central terminal with a series (one per cylinder) of terminals that are evenly spaced in a circular pattern around the central terminal. The secondary voltage travels to the central terminal where it is then channeled to one of the outer terminals by the rotor.

DOHC. Refers to an engine with double (two) overhead camshafts.

DOUBLE FLARE. The end of the tubing, especially brake tubing, has a flare so made that the flare area utilizes two wall thicknesses. This makes a much stronger joint and from a safety standpoint, it is a must.

DOWEL PIN. A steel pin, passed through or partly through, two parts to provide proper alignment.

DOWNDRAFT CARBURETOR. A carburetor in which the air passes downward through the carburetor into the intake manifold.

DOWNSHIFT. Shifting to a lower gear.

DRAG. To accelerate a car from a standing start, over a course one-fourth mile in length. Also used by some drivers when referring to challenging another driver to an acceleration race.

DRAGGING BRAKES. A constant, relatively light contact between linings and drum when brakes are not applied, resulting in excessive lining wear and possibly other damage to linings and drums. This condition is usually due to overadjustment or other mechanical problems.

DRAG LINK. A steel rod connecting the pitman arm to one of the steering knuckles. On some installations the drag link connects the pitman arm to a center idler arm.

DRILL. A tool used to bore holes.

DRILL PRESS. A nonportable machine used for drilling.

DRIVE BELT. Any of several V-shaped belts that transfer power by means of pulleys from the crankshaft to various units as the fan and power-steering pump.

DRIVE-FIT. A fit between two parts when they must be literally driven together.

DRIVE OR PROPELLER SHAFT SAFETY STRAP. A metal strap or straps, surrounding the drive shaft to prevent the shaft from falling to the ground in the event of a universal joint or shaft failure.

DRIVE SHAFT. The shaft connecting the transmission output shaft to the differential pinion shaft.

DROP CENTER RIM. The center section of the rim being lower than the two outer edges. This allows the bead of the tire to be pushed into the low area on one side while the other side is pulled over and off the flange.

DROP FORGED. A part that has been formed by heating the steel blank red hot and pounding it into shape with a powerful drop hammer.

DRUM. Circular outer shell of the automotive brake, which rotates with the wheel and transmits braking forces to the wheel and tire when the brake shoe and lining assemblies are pressed against the inside surface of the drum rim.

DRUM RUNOUT. Term denoting the measurement of the degree of concentricity, eccentricity or ovality of drum braking surface with rotational axis of drum.

DRY CELL or DRY BATTERY. A battery like a flashlight battery, that uses no liquid electrolyte.

DRY CHARGED BATTERY. A battery with the plates charged but lacking electrolyte. When ready to be placed in service, the electrolyte is added.

DRY SLEEVE. A cylinder sleeve application in which the sleeve is supported in the block metal over its entire length. The coolant does not touch the sleeve itself.

DUAL BRAKES. Tandem or dual master cylinder to provide separate brake system for both front and rear of car.

DUAL BREAKER POINTS (Ignition). A distributor using two sets of breaker points to increase the cam angle so that at high engine speeds, sufficient spark will be produced to fire the plugs.

DUALS. Two sets of exhaust pipes and mufflers, one for each bank of cylinders.

DWELL. See Cam Angle.

DWELL METER. A precision electrical instrument used by service technicians to measure cam or dwell angle of the distributor cam as it rotates.

DYNAMIC BALANCE. A condition of stability in a moving body where no unbalanced forces are created to disturb the direction of movement. An automotive wheel and tire assembly is said to be in dynamic balance if it will revolve rapidly without showing any tendency to wobble.

DYNAMO. Another word for generator.

DYNAMOMETER. A machine used to measure the engine horsepower output. An engine dynamometer measures horsepower at the crankshaft and a chassis dynamometer measures horsepower output at the wheels.

EARTH (Electrical). British term for ground.

EARTH WIRE. British term for ground wire.

ECCENTRICITY. In a brake drum, an undesirable quality causing braking vibrations and noise. (See Drum Runout.)

ECONOMIZER VALVE. A fuel flow control device within the carburetor.

ELECTRICAL CIRCUIT. Complete path taken by electricity as it flows from a source to an electrical device, then back to the source through a ground.

ELECTRICITY. Unbalanced distribution of electrons which seek to return to a balanced condition and in so doing, release usable energy.

ELECTROCHEMICAL. Chemical (battery) production of electricity.

ELECTROCHEMICAL ENERGY. Energy available in an electrical current created by a chemical reaction.

ELECTRODE (Spark plug). The center rod passing through the insulator forms one electrode. The rod welded to the shell forms another. They are referred to as the center and side electrodes.

ELECTRODE (Welding). The metal rod that is used in arc welding.

ELECTROLYTE. Sulphuric acid and water solution in the battery.

ELEMENT (Battery). A group of plates. Three elements for a 6-volt and six elements for the 12-volt battery. The elements are connected in series.

ENGINE BLOCK. Main part of an internal-combustion engine, which contains the cylinders.

ENGINE BREATHING. A general term referring to an engine's ability to draw in, use and discharge air. See Volumetric Efficiency.

ENGINE DISPLACEMENT. The volume of the space through which the head of the piston moves in the full length of its stroke multiplied by the number of cylinders in the engine. The result is given in cubic inches.

ENGINE LUBRICATION SYSTEM. An interconnected system, consisting of a reservoir, pump, filters and necessary passages to convey oil to most moving parts requiring lubrication within the engine and then return the oil to the reservoir. A few engine parts, such as the water pump and distributor cam, are lubricated directly as needed, not by the engine lubrication system.

ENGINE TIMING. Determining the correct time, to achieve optimum ignition, for high voltage to be delivered to a spark plug in relation to its piston position.

EP LUBRICANT (Extreme pressure). A lubricant compounded to withstand very heavy loads imposed on gear teeth.

ETHYL GASOLINE. Gasoline to which ethyl fluid has been added to improve the gasoline's resistance to knocking. It slows down the burning rate thereby creating a smooth pressure curve that will allow the gasoline to be used in high compression engines.

ETHYLENE GLYCOL. A chemical solution added to the cooling system to protect against freezing.

EVAPORATION CONTROL. Pollution-control system that employs a vapor separator to collect fumes from the fuel tank and a charcoal canister to store them for burning in the engine.

EVAPORATOR. The unit in an air conditioning system used to transform refrigerant from a liquid to a gas. It is at this point that cooling takes place.

EXHAUST GAS ANALYZER. An instrument used to check the exhaust gases to determine combustion efficiency.

EXHAUST MANIFOLD (Collector). Component of the exhaust system which routes the flow of burned gases from individual exhaust ports to a common point that connects with the rest of the exhaust system.

EXHAUST MANIFOLD HEAT CONTROL VALVE (Manifold heat regulator). A thermostatically controlled valve in the exhaust system that temporarily diverts hot exhaust gases through a passage in the intake manifold to warm it before the engine reaches its normal operating temperature.

EXHAUST PIPE. Pipe connecting exhaust manifold to muffler.

EXHAUST VALVE (Engine). The valve through which the burned fuel charge passes on its way from the cylinder to the exhaust manifold.

EXPANSION TANK. A tank at the top of an automobile radiator which provides room for heated coolant to expand and give off any air that may be trapped in the coolant. It also serves to hold a reserve supply of coolant for the cooling system.

EYES (Of a spring, Loops). Open cylindrical shapes formed at the ends of the main leaf of a spring to accommodate attaching parts, usually bolts and bushings, that link the spring to the car's underbody structure.

FADE (Brake fade). A reduction in braking effectiveness as the coefficient of friction between lining and drum changes with an extreme rise in braking heat.

FEELER GAUGE. A precision-machined piece of thin, hardened steel used by service technicians to measure breaker point gap as well as other critical distances.

FIBERGLASS. A mixture of glass fibers and resin that when cured (hardened) produces a very light and strong material. It is used to build boats, car bodies, repair damaged areas, etc.

FIELD. The area covered or filled with a magnetic force.

FIELD COIL (Field windings). Closely spaced, coiled windings of insulated wire used in certain electrical devices to create a magnetic field. A specialized form of electromagnet.

FILAMENT. Component of an incandescent light bulb, normally composed of malleable tungsten, which is capable of providing such high resistance to current flow that the heat created causes the filament to glow and thus produce light.

FILLER TUBE. A tube leading from the radiator, fuel tank and either the valve cover or crankcase, and closed with a removable cap designed to provide a means of checking and/or replenishing the engine's supply of coolant, fuel and oil.

FILTER. A device designed to remove foreign substances from air, oil, gasoline, water, etc.

FINISHING STONE (Hone). A fine stone used for final finishing during honing.

FIREWALL. The metal partition between the driver's compartment and the engine compartment.

FIRING ORDER. The order in which cylinders must be fired—1, 5, 3, 6, 2, 4, etc.

FIT. Contact area between two parts.

FIXED CALIPER. The term used to define the type of disc brake that incorporates four small pistons, two on either side of the disc, to provide the necessary braking effect.

FLASHER UNIT. Specific type of automatically resetting circuit breaker in the turn signal/emergency signal circuit. It periodically interrupts the current to cause the signal lights to blink on and off when the circuit is actuated.

FLAT HEAD. An engine with all the valves in the block.

FLAT SPOT. Refers to a spot during an acceleration period where the engine seems to lose power for a second or so and will then begin to pull again.

FLOAT BOWL. That part of a carburetor that acts as a reservoir for gasoline and in which the float is placed.

FLOATING CALIPER. The term used to define the type of disc brake that incorporates only one large piston acting on one side of the disc to provide braking effect.

FLOAT LEVEL. Height of the fuel in the carburetor float bowl. Also refers to the specific float setting that will produce the correct fuel level.

FLOODING. A condition where the fuel mixture is overly rich or an excessive amount has reached the cylinders. Starting will be difficult and sometimes impossible until the condition is corrected.

FLUID COUPLING. A unit that transfers engine torque to the transmission input shaft through the use of two vaned units (called torus) operating closely together in a bath of oil. The engine drives one torus causing it to throw oil outward and into the other torus which then begins to turn the transmission input shaft. A fluid coupling cannot increase torque above that produced by the crankshaft.

FLUX (Soldering, brazing). An ingredient placed on metal being soldered or brazed, to remove and prevent the formation of surface oxidation which would make soldering or brazing difficult.

FLYWHEEL. A relatively large wheel that is attached to the crankshaft to smooth out the firing impulses. It provides inertia to keep the crankshaft turning smoothly during the periods when no power is being applied. It also forms a base for the starter ring gear and in many instances, for the clutch assembly.

FLYWHEEL RING GEAR. A gear on the outer circumference of the flywheel. The starter drive gear engages the ring gear and cranks the engine.

FOOT POUND. A measurement of the work involved in lifting one pound one foot.

FOOT POUND (Tightening). A one pound pull one foot from the center of an object.

FORGE. To force a piece of hot metal into the desired shape by hammering.

FOUR BANGER, SIX BANGER, ETC. Four-cylinder, 6-cylinder engine, etc.

FOUR-ON-THE-FLOOR. A 4-speed manual transmission with floor mounted shift.

FOUR-STROKE CYCLE (Otto Cycle). The four strokes, intake, compression, power and exhaust, which an automobile engine's piston moves through to complete one power-producing cycle.

FOUR-STROKE CYCLE ENGINE. An engine requiring two complete revolutions of the crankshaft to fire each piston once.

FREEWHEEL. Usually refers to the action of a car on a downgrade when the overdrive overrunning clutch is slipping with a resultant loss of engine braking. This condition will only occur after the overdrive unit is engaged but before the balk ring has activated the planetary gearset.

FREON-12. A gas used as the cooling medium in air conditioning and refrigeration systems.

FRICTION BEARING. A bearing made of babbitt, bronze, etc. There are no moving parts and the shaft that rests in the bearing merely rubs against the friction material in the bearing.

FRONT END ALIGNMENT (Wheel alignment, Steering alignment). The systematic procedure for checking and adjusting certain steering system factors to specifications, using a special machine designed for this purpose. Camber, caster and toe-in are set to specifications by simple adjustments, but toe-out on turns and steering axis inclination or king pin slant can be corrected only by replacing faulty parts. All of these factors must be correct to assure the steering and handling qualities that are built into the car.

FUEL-AIR MIXTURE RATIO. A numerical ratio denoting the relative proportions of fuel and air by weight that are mixed in the carburetor and delivered to the engine.

FUEL INJECTION. A system which replaces the conventional carburetor with devices that spray fuel under pressure directly into the cylinders or into the airflow just as it enters each individual cylinder.

FUEL MIXTURE. A mixture of gasoline and air. An average mixture, by weight, would contain 16 parts of air to one part of gasoline.

FUEL PUMP. A pump, usually of the diaphragm type, which supplies fuel to the carburetor.

FULL-FLOATING AXLE. A rear drive axle that does not hold the wheel on nor does it hold the wheel in line or support any weight. It merely drives the wheel. Used primarily on trucks.

FULL-FLOW OIL FILTER. An oil filter that filters all of the oil passing through the engine—before it reaches the bearings.

FUSE. Device in an electrical circuit to protect against an excessive flow of current which would overheat and damage the circuit. A fuse is a strip of soft metal that will melt at a fairly low temperature. All current in the circuit flows through this strip of metal and if current flow rises above the number of amperes the fuse is rated for, the heat that is created will cause the strip to melt, breaking the circuit. To restore the circuit, a new fuse must be inserted in place of the burned out one.

FUSE BLOCK. A special device used for holding the electrical fuses found in automobiles. They are available in single or multiple arrangements.

FUSIBLE LINK. A fuse wire used to protect the main wiring harness against overload damage. If this fuse burns out, all electrical circuits in the car are rendered inoperative.

GAL. Gallon.

GAP (Spark). Also known as spark plug gap. It is the distance the spark current jumps from the center spark plug electrode (positive) to the side electrode (ground).

GAP (Breaker point). The amount of space between the ignition point contact surfaces when they are separated to open the primary circuit.

GASKET. A material placed between two parts to insure proper sealing.

GAS TURBINE ENGINE (Jet engine). An engine in which fuel is burned continually in the combustion chambers, and which utilizes the force of the escaping burned gases to rotate a turbine wheel that drives a compressor to feed more air to the engine, making it self-sustaining.

GASOLINE (Gas). A liquid blend of volatile hydrocarbons extracted from crude oil, with certain other ingredients added to improve its qualities for use as an automobile engine fuel.

GEAR-TYPE PUMP. A fluid moving device which utilizes the rotating teeth of two meshed gears as vanes which propel fluid through a close-fitting annular passage around the perimeter of both gears.

GEAR RATIO. The relationship between the number of turns made by a driving gear to complete one full turn of the driven gear. If the driving gear turns four times to turn the gear once, the gear ratio would be 4 to 1.

GENERATOR. Device in which voltage and current are induced in the windings of a revolving armature by a magnetic field created by surrounding stationary field coils. Alternating current is generated in the armature windings but is converted to direct current by the manner in which it is picked up by the brushes on the commutator.

GLASS PACK MUFFLER. A straight-through (no baffles) muffler utilizing fiberglass packing around a perforated pipe to deaden exhaust sound.

GLAZE. A highly smooth, glassy finish on the cylinder walls.

GOVERNOR. A device designed to automatically control the speed or position of some part.

GRABBING BRAKES (Dive). A sudden increase in braking, out of proportion to pedal pressure, usually caused by contaminated linings which have an unreliable coefficient of friction.

GRID. The lead screen or plate to which the battery plate active material is affixed.

GRIND. To remove metal from an object by means of a revolving abrasive wheel, disc or belt.

GROUND. In an automobile, the practice of using the metal structure of body, engine, etc. to serve as a return path to the battery and complete the electrical circuits. The name was derived from the practice of using the earth as a return conductor for electric telegraph circuits.

GROUND (Battery). Terminal of battery that is connected to the metal framework of the car. In this country, the negative terminal is grounded.

GUDGEON PIN. British term for piston or wrist pin.

GUM. Oxidized portions of the fuel that form deposits in the fuel system or engine parts.

HARMONIC BALANCER. See Vibration Damper.

HEADERS. Special exhaust manifolds that replace the stock manifold. They are designed with smooth flowing lines to prevent back pressure caused by sharp bends, rough castings, etc.

HEAT CROSSOVER (V-8 engine). A passage from one exhaust manifold up, over and under the carburetor and on to the other manifold. This crossover provides heat to the carburetor during engine warmup.

HEAT EXCHANGER. A device, such as a radiator, either used to cool or heat by transferring heat from one object to another.

HEAT RANGE (Spark plugs). Refers to the operating temperature of a given style plug. Plugs are made to operate at different temperatures depending upon the thickness and length of the porcelain insulator.

HEAT RISER. An area, surrounding a portion of the intake manifold, through which exhaust gases can pass to heat the fuel mixture during warmup.

HEEL (Brake). The end of the brake shoe which rests against the anchor pin.

HEEL (Gear tooth). The wide end of a tapered gear tooth such as found in the differential gears.

HELICAL. A spiraling shape such as that made by a coil spring.

HELICAL GEAR. A gear that has the teeth cut at an angle to the center line of the gear.

HEMI. Engine using hemispherical-shaped combustion chambers.

HEMISPHERICAL COMBUSTION CHAMBER. A round, dome-shaped combustion chamber that is considered by many to be one of the finest shapes ever developed. The hemispherical shape lends itself to the use of large valves for improved breathing and suffers somewhat less heat loss than other shapes.

HIGH COMPRESSION HEADS. A cylinder head with a smaller combustion chamber area thereby raising the compression. The head can be custom built or can be a stock head milled (cut) down.

HIGH LIFT ROCKER ARMS. Custom rocker arms designed so that a standard lift of the push rod will depress or open the valve somewhat more than the stock lifter.

HONE. To remove metal with a fine grit abrasive stone to precise tolerances.

HORIZONTAL-OPPOSED ENGINE. An engine possessing two banks of cylinders that are placed flat or 180 degrees apart.

HORSEPOWER. Unit of measurement of mechanical power or the rate at which work is done. One horsepower equals 33,000 foot-pounds per minute.

HOTCHKISS DRIVE. The method of connecting the transmission output shaft to the differential pinion by using open driveshafts. The driving force of the rear wheels is transmitted to the frame through the rear springs or through link arms connecting the rear axle housing to the frame.

HOT ROD. A car that has been modified to produce high performance, extra power, better traction, superior gearing, better suspension, etc.

HOT SHOT BATTERY. A dry cell battery generally of six volts.

HOT WIRE. Wiring around the key switch so as to start the car without the key.

HOT WIRE. A wire connected to the battery or to some part of the electrical system in which a direct connection to the battery is present. A current-carrying wire.

HOWL (Moan). A continuous brake noise, lower in pitch but higher in volume than brake squeal. See Squeal.

HUB (Wheel). The unit to which the wheel is bolted.

HYATT ROLLER BEARING (Antifriction). Similar to a conventional roller bearing except that the rollers are hollow and are split in a spiral fashion lengthwise.

HYDRAULIC BRAKES. Brakes that are operated by hydraulic pressure that is transmitted via steel tubing to wheel cylinders that in turn apply the brake shoes to the brake drums.

HYDRAULIC LIFTER. A valve lifter that utilizes hydraulic pressure from the engine's oiling system to keep it in constant contact with both the camshaft and the valve stem. They automatically adjust to any variation in valve stem length.

HYDRAULICS. The science of liquid in motion.

HYDROCARBON. A mixture of hydrogen and carbon.

HYDROCARBON, UNBURNED. Hydrocarbons that were not burned during the normal engine combustion process. Unburned hydrocarbons make up about 0.1 percent of the engine exhaust emission.

HYDROCARBONS. Combination of hydrogen and carbon atoms. All petroleum based fuels (gasoline, kerosene, etc.) consist of hydrocarbons.

HYDROMETER. A float device for determining the specific gravity of the electrolyte in a battery. This will determine the state of charge.

HYDROPLANING. Driving phenomenon in which a car's tires ride up on a wedge of water and thereby lose contact with the road surface.

HYPOID GEARING. A system of gearing wherein the pinion gear meshes with the ring gear below the center line of the ring gear. This allows a somewhat lower drive line, thus reducing the hump in the floor of the car. For this reason hypoid gearing is used in the differential on many cars.

ID. Inside diameter.

IDLE-CIRCUIT NOZZLE. Aperture through which the fuel from the idle circuit enters the carburetor barrel.

IDLE-MIXTURE SCREW. Controlling device that adjusts the idle-circuit nozzle to control the amount of fuel reaching the cylinders during idling.

IDLE VALVE or IDLE NEEDLE. A needle used to control the amount of fuel mixture reaching the cylinders during idling. It, or they, may be adjusted by turning the exposed heads.

IDLER ARM. See Symmetrical Idler Arm.

IGNITION SYSTEM. Components which comprise two electrical circuits—the ignition primary circuit and the ignition secondary circuit. Included are the battery, coil, condenser, breaker points, distributor, spark plugs, plus the interconnecting wires and ground.

IGNITION SYSTEM. Portion of car electrical system, designed to produce a spark within the cylinders to ignite the fuel charge. Consists basically of the battery, key switch, resistor, coil, distributor, points, condenser, spark plugs and necessary wiring.

IMPACT WRENCH. An air or electrically driven wrench that tightens or loosens nuts, cap-screws, etc., with a series of sharp, rapid blows.

IMPELLER. A wheel-like device upon which fins are attached. It is whirled to pump water, move and slightly compress air, etc.

IN. Inch.

INCANDESCENT ELECTRIC BULB. Electrically energized light source, consisting of a filament enclosed within an airtight glass glove with practically all the air exhausted from its interior. When an electrical current passes through the filament, the high resistance of the filament heats it so it glows brightly.

INCLUDED ANGLE (Steering). Angle formed by center lines drawn through the steering axis (kingpin inclination) and center of the wheel (camber angle) as viewed from the front of the car. Combines both steering axis and camber angles.

INDEPENDENT SUSPENSION. A suspension system that allows each wheel to move up and down without undue influence on the other wheels.

INDICATED HORSEPOWER (ihp). Indicated horsepower is a measure of the power developed by the burning fuel within the cylinders.

INHIBITOR. A substance added to oil, water, gas, etc., to prevent action such as foaming, rusting, etc.

INJECTOR (Carburetion). Refers to the pump system (used in a fuel injection system) that squirts or injects a measured amount of gasoline into the intake manifold in the vicinity of the intake valve. In the diesel engine, fuel is injected directly into the cylinder.

INJECTOR. Nozzle and related parts used to spray a metered amount of fuel under pressure into a cylinder of a compression ignition engine.

INLET PORT. A vertical passage at the bottom of the master cylinder reservoir, positioned to allow brake fluid to enter the cylinder between the primary cup and the secondary cup. From there, it flows through a small passage in the head of the piston, past a check valve and into the forward end of the cylinder when needed. When the piston moves forward, the pressure generated ahead of the piston holds the valve closed, preventing any return flow.

IN-LINE ENGINE (Straight six, Straight eight, etc.). Engine having all its cylinders arranged in one row.

INPUT SHAFT. The shaft delivering power into a mechanism. The shaft from the clutch into the transmission is the transmission input shaft.

INSERT BEARING. A removable, precision made bearing which insures specified clearance between bearing and shaft.

INSULATOR (Electrical). A unit made of a material that will not readily conduct electricity.

INTAKE MANIFOLD. Engine component, usually a casting, which distributes the fuel-air mixture from the carburetor to the intake ports of all cylinders of an engine.

INTAKE VALVE (Engine). The valve through which fuel mixture is admitted to the cylinder.

INTERMEDIATE GEAR. Any gear in the auto transmission between 1st and high.

INTERNAL-COMBUSTION ENGINE. Engine that burns fuel inside its cylinders to product power.

JET. A small hole or orifice used to control the flow of gasoline in various parts of the carburetor.

JOUNCE. The upward movement of a wheel from its normal position, usually caused by a road bump or a weight transfer onto the wheel.

JOURNAL. That part of a rotating shaft or similar device which turns in a bearing.

KICKDOWN SWITCH. An electrical switch that will cause a transmission to shift down to a lower gear. Often used to secure fast acceleration.

KILOMETER. A metric measurement equivalent to ⅝ of a mile.

KINETIC ENERGY (Momentum). The energy of motion.

KING PIN. A pin-like component placed in a nearly vertical position, around which the steering knuckle, or front axle of single-king-pin wagons, can pivot to steer the front wheels.

KING PIN SLANT. See Steering Axis Inclination.

KNOCKING (Bearing). Noise created by part movement in a loose or worn bearing.

KNOCKING (Fuel). A condition, accompanied by an audible noise, that occurs when the gasoline in the cylinders burns too quickly. This is also referred to as detonation.

KNUCKLE (Steering knuckle). Front suspension component that acts as a hinge to support a front wheel and permit it to be turned to steer the car. The knuckle pivots on ball joints that are fitted into the outer ends of the upper and lower control arms. The wheel spindle, which provides an axle for the front wheel to rotate around, is an integral part of the knuckle. In current practice, the knuckle is bolted to the front wheel brake backing plate, keeping it stationary against braking loads.

KNURL. To roughen the surface of a piece of metal by pressing a series of cross-hatched lines into the surface, thus raising the area between these lines.

LACQUER (Paint). A fast drying automotive body paint.

LAMINATED. Something made up of many layers.

LAND (Power steering). Collar-like rings on both ends of the sliding spool which open and close the power chamber fluid ports as the steering wheel is turned.

LANDS (Ring). The piston metal between the ring grooves.

LB. Pound.

LEAD-ACID BATTERY. Battery type used almost universally in automobiles.

LEADS (Wires, Lines, Cables, etc.). Wires in an electrical circuit. Although all the terms listed here mean essentially the same thing, there can be a shade of difference between them. Leads are generally accepted to be those portions of wire that connect directly or lead to another electrical component. Lines usually are relatively long stretches of wire. Cables are heavy wires or conductors used to handle high amperage or high voltage.

LEAF SPRING. Suspension device composed of several superimposed strips of flat spring steel, which is held to the frame at one end by a shackle.

LENS. Precision-formed glass component designed to optically focus light rays so they will concentrate at a given point or in a given area.

LETTER DRILLS. A series of drills in which each drill size is designated by a letter of the alphabet.

LIMITED-SLIP DIFFERENTIAL. A differential unit designed to provide superior traction by transferring driving torque, when one wheel is spinning, to the wheel that is not slipping.

LINING. A high-friction material attached by rivets or a bonding process to the brake shoe. It can be removed when worn and replaced with a new lining.

LINKAGE. Any series of metal rods or levers that transmit motion from one unit to another.

LITER. Metric measurement of capacity equivalent to 2.11 pints. Five liters equals 1.32 gallon.

LIVE AXLE. An axle upon which the wheels are firmly affixed. The axle drives the wheels.

LIVE WIRE. See Hot Wire.

LOCKING RING. An adjustable ring on the end of the steering column that allows the driver to preset the steering wheel position according to his seating comfort.

LONG and SHORT ARM SUSPENSION. A suspension system utilizing an upper and lower control arm. The upper arm is shorter than the lower. This is done so as to allow the wheel to deflect in a vertical direction with a minimum change in camber.

LONGITUDINAL LEAF SPRING. A leaf spring that is mounted so that it is parellel to the length of the car.

LOUVER. Ventilation slots such as sometimes found in the hood of the automobile.

LOW BRAKE PEDAL. A condition where the brake pedal approaches too close to the floorboard before actuating the brakes.

LOW PIVOT SWING AXLE. A rear axle setup that attaches the differential housing to the frame via a pivot mount. A conventional type of housing and axle extend from the differential to one wheel. The other side of the differential is connected to the other driving wheel by a housing and axle that is pivoted at a point in line with the differential to frame pivot point.

LUBRICANT. Friction-reducing substance placed between moving parts.

LUG (Engine). To cause the engine to labor by failing to shift to a lower gear when necessary.

MAG. Magneto. Also, styled wheel.

MANIFOLD. Pipe that connects a series of outlets to a common opening.

MANIFOLD HEAT CONTROL VALVE. A valve placed in the exhaust manifold, or in the exhaust pipe, that deflects a certain amount of hot gas around the base of the carburetor to aid in warmup.

MANIFOLD VACUUM (Engine vacuum). Air at some pressure less than atmospheric pressure within the intake valve port, intake manifold and lower portion of the carburetor, created by the restriction to airflow to the cylinders primarily by the throttle plate or venturi in the carburetor.

MASTER CYLINDER. Unit in a hydraulic-brake system that forces brake fluid to the wheel cylinders.

METERING ROD. A movable rod used to vary the opening area through a carburetor jet.

METERING VALVE. A valve in the disc brake system that cuts off pressure to the front brakes in order to reduce front wheel braking on slippery or icy surfaces. It is sometimes called a hold-off valve.

METRIC SIZE. Units made to metric system measurements.

MICROMETER (Inside and outside). A precision measuring tool that will give readings accurate to within a fraction of one thousandth of an inch.

MIKE. Either refers to a micrometer or to using a micrometer to measure an object.

MILL. Often used to refer to the engine.

MILL. To remove metal through the use of a rotating toothed cutter.

MILLIMETER. A metric measurement equivalent to .039370 of an inch.

MILLING MACHINE. A machine that uses a variety of rotating cutter wheels to cut splines, gears, keyways, etc.

MISFIRING. Failure of a fuel charge to ignite in a cylinder of an engine.

MODULATOR (Transmission). A pressure control or adjusting valve used in the hydraulic system of the automatic transmission.

MOTOR. An electrically driven power unit (electric motor). This term is often incorrectly applied to an internal combustion engine.

MPH. Miles per hour.

MUFFLER. A device, usually of oval or round cross-section, containing tubes and baffles designed to slow the rush of exhaust gases and absorb some of their heat as they flow through the muffler.

MULTIPLE DISC CLUTCH. A clutch utilizing several clutch discs in its construction.

MULTIPLE FILAMENT BULB. Incandescent light bulb in which more than one filament is enclosed. Separate contacts on the base of the bulb allow any of the filaments to be energized selectively to provide the desired degree of illumination. Current is returned through the base of the bulb, which serves as a common ground for all filaments.

MULTIVISCOSITY OILS. Engine oils that have flow characteristics to provide adequate lubrication at both high and low temperatures.

NEEDLE BEARING (Antifriction). A roller type bearing in which the rollers have a very narrow diameter in relation to their length.

NEGATIVE. Arbitrary but commonly accepted name for one pole of a magnet or one terminal of any electric device. In an electric current, electrons are assumed to flow from the negative pole toward the positive pole.

NITROGEN OXIDES. In the combustion process, nitrogen from the air combines with oxygen to form nitrogen oxides.

NORTH POLE (Magnet). The magnetic pole from which the lines of force emanate. Travel is from north to south pole.

NUMBER DRILLS. A series of drills in which each size is designated by a number (0-80).

NUT RACK (Ball nut, Steering nut). A component of the steering gear which rides on the wormshaft and converts rotational movement of the steering wheel to linear movement which is applied to the sector gear by means of the rack gear teeth.

OCTANE RATING. Number representing a particular gasoline's ability to resist detonation, determined by the quantity of antiknock substances blended into it.

ODOMETER. Instrument, set in the speedometer, that registers the total distance traveled by a vehicle.

OHM. A unit of measurement used to indicate the amount of resistance to the flow of electricity in a given circuit.

OHMMETER. An instrument used to measure the amount of resistance in a given unit or circuit. (In ohms.)

OIL BATH AIR CLEANER. An air cleaner that utilizes a pool of oil to insure the removal of impurities from the air entering the carburetor.

OIL BURNER. An engine that consumes an excessive quantity of oil.

OIL, COMBINATION SPLASH and PRESSURE SYSTEM. An engine oiling system that uses both pressure and splash oiling to accomplish proper lubrication.

OIL FILTER. Replaceable element that removes foreign particles from circulating oil.

OIL, FULL PRESSURE SYSTEM. An engine oiling system that forces oil, under pressure, to the moving parts of the engine.

OIL GALLERY. Pipes or bored passageways in an engine that carry oil from one area to another.

OIL PUMP. Mechanism that forces lubricating oil, under pressure, through the engine.

OIL PUMPING. A condition wherein an excessive quantity of oil passes the piston rings and is consumed in the combustion chamber.

OIL SEAL. A device used to prevent oil leakage past a certain area.

OIL, SPLASH SYSTEM. An engine oiling system that depends on the connecting rods to dip into oil troughs and splash the oil to all moving parts.

OPEN CIRCUIT. A break or opening in an electrical circuit which then prohibits the passage of current.

ORIFICE (Passage). A passage between two chambers, generally precisely sized and finished to accomplish a desired degree of restriction to the flow of a fluid being forced through the orifice. Orifice connotes an engineered restriction to fluid flow to accomplish a desired control, rather than merely a simple means of conveying fluid from one point to another.

OSCILLOSCOPE. Electronic testing instrument that translates electrical-circuit performance into a pattern visible on a cathode-ray tube.

OTTO CYCLE. See Four-Stroke Cycle.

OUTLET PORT (Compensating port). A restricted passage at the bottom of the master cylinder reservoir, positioned to allow brake fluid to return to the reservoir when the brake is released, thus compensating for expansion of fluid in the lines.

OUTPUT SHAFT. Any shaft that delivers power from within a mechanism; e.g. transmission output shaft.

OVALITY (Egg-shaped). In a brake drum, an undesirable elliptical contour of the drum braking surface which can cause low-speed pulsation and other problems.

OVERDRIVE. Gear designed into some manual transmissions that, when actuated, allows the driveshaft to turn faster than the crankshaft, resulting in higher speeds with less engine effort and lower fuel consumption.

OVERHEAD CAMSHAFT. A camshaft mounted above the head. It is driven by a long timing chain.

OVERHEAD VALVES. Valves located in the head.

OVERHEAD VALVE ENGINE (OHV Engine). Engine having intake and exhaust valves mounted in the cylinder head(s) directly above the cylinders.

OVERRUNNING CLUTCH. A clutch mechanism that will drive in one direction only. If driving torque is removed or reversed, the clutch slips.

OVERRUNNING CLUTCH STARTER DRIVE. A starter drive that is mechanically engaged. When the engine starts, the overrunning clutch operates until the drive is mechanically disengaged.

OVERSQUARE ENGINE. An engine in which the bore diameter is larger than the length of the stroke.

OVERSTEER. A built-in characteristic of certain types of rear suspension geometry to cause the rear wheels to slide toward the outside of the turn.

OXIDES OF NITROGEN. Exhaust gas formed by high combustion temperatures.

PAN. Metal reservoir bolted to the bottom of a crankcase or automatic transmission that holds oil or fluid.

PANCAKE ENGINE. An engine in which the cylinders are on a horizontal plane. This reduces the overall height and enables them to be used in spots where vertical height is restricted.

PAPER AIR CLEANER. An air cleaner that makes use of special paper through which the air to the carburetor is drawn.

PARALLELOGRAM STEERING LINKAGE. A steering system utilizing two short tie rods connected to the steering arms and to a long center link. The link is supported on one end on an idler arm and the other end is attached directly to the pitman arm. The arrangement forms a parallelogram shape.

PARKING BRAKE. Hand operated brake which prevents vehicle movement while parked by locking rear wheels, or transmission output shaft.

PAWL. An arm, pivoted so that its free end can be made to engage the teeth of a shaft or gear and lock it to prevent its movement when desired. A pawl is used in a ratchet mechanism.

PCV (Positive Crankcase Ventilation). A system which prevents crankcase vapors from being discharged directly into atmosphere.

PENETRATING OIL. A special oil that is used to free rusted parts so that they can be removed.

PETROL. Gasoline.

PETROLEUM. Raw material from which gasoline, kerosene, lube oils, etc., are made. Consists of hydrogen and carbon.

PHILLIPS HEAD SCREW. A screw having a fairly deep cross slot instead of the single slot used in conventional screws.

PICKUP COIL (Electronic ignition). The coil in which voltage is induced resulting from the interaction of the reluctor and permanent magnet.

PILOT SHAFT. A dummy shaft that is placed in a mechanism as a means of aligning the parts. It is then removed and the regular shaft installed.

PINGING. A metallic rattling sound produced by the engine during heavy acceleration when the ignition timing is too far advanced for the grade of fuel being burned.

PINION CARRIER. That part of the rear axle assembly that supports and contains the pinion gear shaft.

PIPES. Exhaust system pipes.

PISTON. The movable cylindrical component of an engine whose head forms the lower extreme of the combustion chamber and which is linked by the connecting rod to the crankshaft to transmit the forces of combustion to that member.

PISTON BOSS. The built-up area around the piston pin hole.

PISTON COLLAPSE. A reduction in the diameter of the piston skirt caused by heat and constant impact stresses.

PISTON DISPLACEMENT. Amount (volume) of air displaced by a piston when moved through the full length of its stroke.

PISTON HEAD. That portion of the piston above the top ring.

PISTON LANDS. That portion of the piston which is between the ring grooves.

PISTON PIN (Wrist pin). A steel pin that is passed through the piston. It is used as a base upon which to fasten the upper end of the connecting rod. It is round and is usually hollow.

PISTON RING. A split ring installed in a groove in the piston. The ring contacts the sides of the ring groove and also rubs against the cylinder wall thus sealing the space between the piston and the wall.

PISTON RING (Compression). A ring designed to seal the burning fuel charge above the piston. Generally there are two compression rings per piston and they are located in the two top ring grooves.

PISTON RING (Oil control). A piston ring designed to scrape oil from the cylinder wall. The ring is of such a design as to allow the oil to pass through the ring and then through holes or slots in the groove. In this way the oil is returned to the pan. There are many shapes and special designs used on oil control rings.

PISTON RING END GAP. The distance left between the ends of the ring when installed in the cylinder.

PISTON RING EXPANDER. See Ring Expander.

PISTON RING GROOVE. The slots or grooves cut in the piston head to receive the piston rings.

PISTON RING SIDE CLEARANCE. The space between the sides of the ring and the ring lands.

PISTON SKIRT. That portion of the piston below the rings. (Some engines have an oil ring in the skirt area.)

PISTON SKIRT EXPANDER. A spring device placed inside the piston skirt to produce an outward pressure which increases the diameter of the skirt.

PISTON SKIRT EXPANDING. Enlarging the diameter of the piston skirt by inserting an expander, by knurling the outer skirt surface, or by peening the inside of the piston.

PITCHING (Bobbing). A fore-and-aft rocking motion of an automobile—as the front end rises, the rear end falls and vice-versa. Bobbing is usually considered as a pitching motion occurring at only one end of the car, while the other end remains relatively steady.

PITMAN ARM. A short lever arm splined to the steering gear cross shaft. The pitman arm transmits the steering force from the cross shaft to the steering linkage.

PLANET CARRIER. That part of a planetary gearset upon which the planet gears are affixed. The planet gears are free to turn on hardened pins set into the carrier.

PLANET GEARS. Those gears in a planetary gearset that are in mesh with both the ring and the sun gear. They are referred to as planet gears in that they orbit or move around the central or sun gear.

PLANETARY GEARSET. A gearing unit consisting of a ring gear with internal teeth, a sun or central pinion gear with external teeth, and a series of planet gears that are meshed with both the ring and sun gear.

PLATE. Component of a lead-acid battery cell, composed of sponge lead which is reacted upon by electrolyte to produce electric voltage.

PLATE STRAP. Electric conductor used to connect two cells of a battery so as to continue the circuit through the battery.

PLATES (Battery). Thin sections of lead peroxide or porous lead. There are two kinds of plates—positive and negative. The plates are arranged in groups, in an alternate fashion, called elements. They are completely submerged in the electrolyte.

PLAY. Movement between two parts.

PLEXIGLAS. A trade name for an acrylic plastic, made by the Rhom and Haas Co.

PLIES. Layers of rubber-coated cords that constitute the carcass of a tire.

PLUG GAPPING. Adjusting the side electrode on a spark plug to provide the proper air gap between it and the center electrode.

PLY RATING (Tires). An indication of tire strength (load carrying capacity). Does not necessarily indicate actual number of plies. A 2-ply/4-ply rating tire would have the load capacity of a four-ply tire of the same size but would have only two actual plies.

POLARITY (Battery Terminals). Indicates if the battery terminal (either one) is positive or negative (plus or minus, + or −).

POLARITY (Generator). Indicates if the pole shoes are so magnetized as to make current flow in a direction compatible with the direction of flow as set by the battery.

POLARITY (Magnet). Indicates if the end of a magnet is the north or south pole (N or S).

POLARIZING (Generator). The process of sending a quick surge of current through the field windings of the generator in a direction that will cause the pole shoes to assume the correct polarity. This will insure that the generator will cause current to flow in the same direction as normal.

POLE. One of two points at which opposite electrical qualities are concentrated, as in the two poles of a magnet.

POLE PIECE (Electronic ignition). Metal bracket around which the pickup coil is wound.

POLE SHOES. Metal pieces about which the field coil windings are placed. When current passes through the windings, the pole shoes become powerful magnets. Pole shoes are found, for example, in a generator or starter motor.

POPPET VALVE. The valve used to open and close the valve port entrances to the engine cylinders.

PORT. Openings in engine cylinder blocks for exhaust and intake, valves and water connections.

PORT. To smooth out, align and somewhat enlarge the intake passageway to the valves.

POSITIVE. Arbitrary but commonly accepted name for a pole of magnet or a terminal of an electric device. In an electric current, electrons are assumed to flow toward the positive pole from the negative pole.

POSITIVE TERMINAL. That terminal such as that on the battery, to which the current flows.

POST, TERMINAL. In a battery or other electrical device, a cylindrical protrusion at either end of the electric circuit through the device. It provides a convenient point of attachment for a wire leading to the remainder of the circuit.

POT. Carburetor.

POWER (Horsepower). A measurement of work done in a given time. A common power measuring unit is Horsepower.

POWER CHAMBERS (Power steering). The design of the piston divides the power cylinder into two chambers—one to provide power assist on left turns, and one for right turns.

POWER PACK. Term, originated in the mid-'50s but now very seldom used, to denote an engine incorporating special equipment such an an extra or larger carburetor and sometimes, special deep breathing valvetrain and exhaust components, that increase performance above that of the standard engine.

POWER STEERING. System that uses a hydraulic-pressure booster to augment the driver's steering force.

PPM (Parts-per-million). Term used in determining extent of pollution existing in given sample of air.

PREIGNITION. An undesirable early ignition of the fuel-air charge, usually due to glowing carbon deposits in the combustion chamber, which can be damaging to adjacent engine components.

PRE-LOADED BALL JOINT. A condition of tightness between the ball and socket of this type joint.

PRELOADING. Adjusting antifriction bearing so that it is under mild pressure. This prevents bearing looseness under a driving stress.

PRESS-FIT. A condition of fit (contact) between two parts that requires pressure to force the parts together. Also referred to as drive or force fit.

PRESSURE BLEEDER. A device that forces brake fluid, under pressure, into the master cylinder so that by opening the bleeder screws at the wheel cylinders, all air will be removed from the brake system.

PRESSURE CAP. A special cap for the radiator. It holds a predetermined amount of pressure on the water in the cooling system. This enables the water to run hotter without boiling.

PRESSURE RELIEF VALVE. A valve designed to open at a specific pressure. This will prevent pressures in the system from exceeding certain limits.

PRESSURE-VENT COOLING SYSTEM. Cooling system which operates at atmospheric pressure under normal conditions but becomes pressurized for more efficient cooling when high engine loads bring on added cooling requirements.

PRIMARY CELLS (Dry cells). Electrochemical power source which uses dry ingredients to generate electricity. A flashlight battery is an example of a primary cell.

PRIMARY IGNITION CIRCUIT (Primary, Low voltage circuit). The circuit in the ignition system that operates under the regular electrical system voltage (approximately 12 volts) to induce an extremely high voltage in the coil for use at the spark plugs.

PRIMARY PISTON. The rear piston in the tandem master cylinder that is actuated directly by the brake pedal or power booster.

PRIMARY SHOE. The forward shoe of the Servo-Contact Brake asembly. Its function is to absorb some of the rotating force of the drum and transmit it to the secondary shoe, forcing the secondary shoe against the drum when the brakes are applied. This reduces the pedal effort needed for braking.

PRIMARY WINDING. The outer winding of relatively heavy wire in an ignition coil. This winding carries the 12-volt flow of current from the car's battery before it is induced into the high-tension secondary winding.

PROPORTIONING VALVE. This unit operates by restricting, at a given ratio, hydraulic pressure to the rear brakes when system hydraulic pressure reaches a certain point. On light pedal application the valve allows full brake hydraulic pressure to the rear brakes.

PRIMARY WIRES. The wiring which serves the low voltage part of the ignition system. Wiring from battery to switch, resistor, coil, distributor points.

PRINTED CIRCUIT. An electrical circuit made by connecting the units with electrically conductive lines printed on a panel. This eliminates actual wire and the task of connecting it.

PRONY BRAKE. A device utilizing a friction brake to measure the horsepower output of an engine.

PROPELLER SHAFT. The shaft connecting the transmission output shaft to the differential pinion shaft.

PSI. Pounds per square inch.

PULL (Brake pull, Dive). An unbalanced braking condition at the front wheels, causing the car to swerve when the brakes are applied. Although it may be caused by a malfunctioning brake, it could also be the result of unequal caster adjustments or a lower control arm strut that is not properly tightened, allowing caster to change at one wheel when brakes are applied. A weak or broken rear spring can also cause brake pull.

PULSATION (Surge). During braking at low speeds, an out-of-round brake drum will cause a varying rate of deceleration. The driver will feel a surging or pulsating sensation in the vehicle.

PULSATION DAMPER. A device used to smooth out the pulsations or surges of fuel from the fuel pump to the carburetor.

PUMPING THE GAS PEDAL. Forcing the accelerator up and down in an endeavor to provide extra gasoline to the cylinders. This is often the cause of flooding.

PUSH ROD. The rod that connects the valve lifter to one end of the rocker arm. Used on valve-in-head installations.

QUADRANT (Gearshift). The gearshift selector indicator marked PRNDL.

RACK AND PINION GEARBOX (Steering). A type of steering gear utilizing a pinion gear on the end of the steering shaft. The pinion engages a long rack (bar with a row of teeth cut along one edge). The rack is connected directly to the steering arms via rods.

RACK AND SECTOR GEAR. Component parts of the steering gear. The rack is a series of gear teeth arranged in a straight line on the rack nut. The sector is a segment of a conventional circular gear which meshes with the teeth on the rack. Linear motion of the rack is translated into rotating motion of the sector.

RADIAL ENGINE. An engine possessing various numbers of cylinders so arranged that they form a circle around the crankshaft center line.

RADIAL TIRE. Tire in which the body cords run at right angles (radially) to the center line of the tread and that has two or more belts to strengthen the tread.

RADIATOR. Unit that dissipates engine coolant heat to the outside air by passing the fluid through finned core-pipes.

RADIUS RODS. Rods attached to the axle and pivoted on the frame. They are used to keep the axle at right angles to the frame and yet permit an up and down motion.

RANKINE-CYCLE ENGINE. External-combustion engine that utilizes the energy of expanding gases (such as steam) to drive a piston or turbine.

RATCHET. A mechanism employing a particular type of pawl that will allow movement of its associated gear in one direction while preventing movement in the opposite direction. The parking brake is held in the applied position by this type of mechanism.

RATE. A term denoting the load required to move a spring or a suspended wheel a given distance. Rate is expressed in pounds per inch. Accordingly, rate is an indicator of the softness or firmness of a given spring or suspension.

RATIO. A fixed relationship between things in number, quantity or degree. For example, if the fuel mixture contains one part of gas for fifteen parts of air, the ratio would be 15 to 1.

REAR AXLE (Banjo type). A rear axle housing from which the differential unit may be removed while the housing remains in place on the car. The housing is solid from side to side.

REAR AXLE HOUSING (Split type). A rear axle housing made up of several pieces and bolted together. The housing must be split apart to remove the differential.

REBOUND. Movement of a wheel downward from its normal position, usually due to uncontrolled over-travel of a spring as it returns after reacting to a road shock, the sudden drop of a wheel into a depression in the road or a weight transfer away from the wheel.

RECIPROCATING ACTION. Back-and-forth movement, like the action of pistons inside cylinders.

RECIRCULATING BALL WORM AND NUT. A very popular type of steering gear. It utilizes a series of ball bearings that feed through, around and back through the grooves in the worm and nut.

RED LINE. Top recommended engine rpm. If a tachometer is used, it will have a red mark indicating maximum rpm.

REFRIGERANT. The liquid used in refrigeration systems to remove heat from the evaporator coils and carry it to the condenser.

REFRIGERANT-12. The name applied to the refrigerant generally used in automotive air conditioning systems.

REGULATOR. A device used to control generator voltage and current output, or to control gas or liquid pressure.

RELIEF VALVE. Limits the power steering pump output. The valve protects the system against excessive pressure buildup.

RELUCTOR (Electronic ignition). A wheel-like rotor whose eight iron teeth vary the magnetic flux generated by the permanent magnet and act as a bridge between the permanent magnet and pickup coil for the magnetic flux.

RESISTANCE (Electrical). A measure of a conductor's ability to retard the flow of electricity.

RESISTOR. Device used in an electrical circuit to deliberately introduce added resistance to the circuit.

RESISTOR SPARK PLUG. A spark plug containing a resistor designed to shorten both the capacitive and inductive phases of the spark. This will suppress ratio interference and lengthen electrode life.

RESONATOR. A small muffler-like device that is placed into the exhaust system near the end of the tailpipe. It is used to provide additional silencing of the exhaust.

RETARD (Ignition timing). To set the ignition timing so that a spark occurs later or less degrees before TDC.

RETURNABILITY (Recovery, Return). The natural tendency of certain front end alignment factors, notably steering axis inclination, to bring the front wheels back to their straight-ahead position and hold them there following a turn.

RETURN SPRING (Pull-back spring). A spring designed to return some component to its original position after the force which moved the component has been released. In the automotive brake system, return springs are used on brake shoes, the master cylinder piston, the brake pedal mechanism, and the parking brake mechanism.

REVERSE FLUSH. Cleaning the cooling system by pumping a powerful cleaning agent through the system in a direction opposite to that of normal flow.

REVERSE IDLER GEAR. A gear used in the transmission to produce a reverse rotation of the transmission output shaft.

RIDING THE CLUTCH. Riding the clutch refers to the driver resting his foot on the clutch pedal while the car is being driven.

RING (Chrome). A ring, the outer edge of which has a thin layer of chrome plate.

RING (Pinned). A steel pin, set into the piston, is placed in the space between the ends of the ring. The ring is thus kept from moving around in the groove.

RING EXPANDER. A spring device placed under the rings to hold them snugly against the cylinder wall.

RING GEAR. May refer to the large gear that is attached to the differential carrier or to the outer gear in a planetary gear setup.

RING GROOVES. The grooves cut into the piston to accept the rings.

RING JOB. Reconditioning the cylinders and installing new rings.

RING RIDGE. That portion of the cylinder above the top limit of ring travel. In a worn cylinder, this area is of a smaller diameter than the remainder of the cylinder and will leave a ledge or ridge that must be removed.

RIVET. A metal pin used to hold two objects together. One end of the pin has a head the other end must be set or peened over.

ROAD FEEL. The feeling imparted to the steering wheel by the wheels of a car in motion. This feeling can be very important in sensing and predetermining vehicle steering response.

ROCKER ARM. A form of lever designed to transmit linear motion in a reverse direction and actuate a component, as in the valvetrain and fuel pump.

ROCKER ARM SHAFT. The shaft upon which the rocker arms are mounted.

ROCKER PANEL. That section of the car body between the front and rear fenders and beneath the doors.

RODDING THE RADIATOR. The top, and sometimes the bottom tank of the radiator is removed. The core is then cleaned by passing a cleaning rod down through the tubes. This is done when radiators are clogged with rust, scale and various mineral deposits.

ROLL (Body roll). The tendency of an automobile to lean outward, away from the direction of turn, due to the transfer of weight toward the outside wheels caused by centrifugal force.

ROLLER BEARING. A bearing utilizing a series of straight, cupped or tapered rollers engaging an inner and outer ring or race.

ROLLER CLUTCH. A clutch, utilizing a series of rollers placed in ramps, that will provide power in one direction but will slip or freewheel in the other direction.

ROTARY ENGINE. A piston engine in which the crankshaft is fixed and in which the cylinders rotate around the crankshaft.

ROTARY ENGINE (Wankel). An internal combustion engine which is not of a reciprocating (piston) engine design. One or more 3-sided rotors revolve in specially shaped chambers. In every revolution each side of the rotor performs all the functions of a 4-stroke cycle engine.

ROTARY FLOW (Torque converter). The movement of the oil as it is carried around by the pump and turbine. The rotary motion is not caused by the oil passing through the pump, to the turbine, the stator, etc., as is the case with vortex flow. Rotary flow is at right angles to the center line of the converter whereas vortex flow is parallel, depending on the ratio between the speeds of the pump and turbine.

ROTOR. A revolving part of a machine. Specifically, that portion of the alternator that revolves and carries the alternator field windings. (The ignition distributor also has a rotor which directs high tension current to the spark plug cable terminals.)

ROTOR, DISTRIBUTOR. A rotating conductor mounted on the distributor cam that carries secondary voltage to the distributor cap electrodes.

ROTOR-TYPE PUMP. A fluid moving device consisting of an inner and an outer rotor, turning on eccentric centers. As the two rotors turn, the space between their lobes expands and contracts. Fluid is introduced in the space as it expands, and is discharged as the space contracts.

ROUGHING STONE (Hone). A coarse stone used for quick removal of material during honing.

RPM. Revolutions per minute.

RUNNING FIT. A fit in which sufficient clearance has been provided to enable the parts to turn freely and to receive lubrication.

SAE. Society of Automotive Engineers.

SAE or RATED HORSEPOWER. A simple formula of long standing is used to determine what is commonly referred to as the SAE or Rated Horsepower. The formula is:

$$\frac{\text{Bore Diameter}^2 \times \text{Number of Cylinders}}{2.5}$$

This formula is used primarily for licensing purposes and is not too accurate a means of determining actual brake horsepower.

SAFETY RIM. A rim having two safety ridges, one on each lip, to prevent the tire beads from entering the drop center area in the event of a blowout. This feature keeps the tire on the rim.

SAND BLAST. Cleaning by the use of sand propelled at high speeds in an air blast.

SCALE (Cooling system). The accumulation of rust and minerals within the cooling system.

SCHEMATIC DRAWING. A drawing of an electrical circuit for a single electrical component in the simplest, most easily understood form.

SCORE. A scratch or groove on a finished surface.

SCREW EXTRACTOR. A device used to remove broken bolts, screws, etc., from holes.

SEALED BEAM HEADLIGHT. A headlight lamp in which the lens, reflector and filament are fused together to form a single unit.

SEALED BEARING. A bearing that has been lubricated at the factory and then sealed. It cannot be lubricated during service.

SEAT. A surface upon which another part rests or seats.

SEAT (Rings). Minor wearing of the piston ring surface during initial use. Rings then fit or seat properly against the cylinder wall.

SECONDARY IGNITION CIRCUIT (Secondary, High tension or High voltage circuit). The electrical circuit in the ignition system that delivers the high voltage current from the coil to the spark plugs.

SECONDARY, REVERSE, or TRAILING BRAKE SHOE. The brake shoe that is installed facing the rear of the car.

SECONDARY PISTON. The piston at the front of the tandem master cylinder and which, in normal operation, is hydraulically operated by the primary piston.

SECONDARY WINDING. The inner winding of fine wire in an ignition coil, in which a secondary or high tension voltage is created by induction.

SECONDARY WIRES. The high voltage wire from the coil to the distributor tower and from the tower to the spark plugs.

SECTOR SHAFT. Part of the power train in the power steering gear assembly, it is connected by the steering arm to the steering linkage. Its teeth mate with the teeth on the power piston. The sector shaft initiates a right or a left turn as the piston is moved upward for a left turn or downward for a right turn.

SEDIMENT. An accumulation of matter which settles to the bottom of a liquid.

SELECTOR FORKS. Devices that move the synchronizing rings in a transmission.

SELF-ENERGIZING. A brake shoe that when applied develops a wedging action that actually assists the braking force applied by the wheel cylinder.

SEMI-FLOATING AXLE. Type of axle commonly used in modern car. Outer end turns wheel and supports weight of car; inner end which is splined, floats in differential gear.

SERVO (Transmission). An oil operated device used to push or pull another part.

SERVO ACTION. Brakes so constructed as to have one end of the primary shoe bearing against the end of the secondary shoe. When the brakes are applied, the primary shoe attempts to move in the direction of the rotating drum and in so doing applies force to the secondary shoe. This action, called servo action, makes less brake pedal pressure necessary and is widely used in brake construction.

SHACKLE. A short connecting link, usually a flat plate, that is used to form a flexible connection between the eye of a leaf spring and the spring mounting point on the car's underbody structure. The flexibility is needed because a leaf spring's length changes as it flexes under deflection.

SHEAR PINS. Connecting inserts formed by injecting a plastic material into openings provided. Their purpose is to hold connected and interacting parts of an assembly in alignment under normal operating conditions, and to give way when abnormal pressure or strain is applied. In the telescoping gearshift tube, for example, if an accident causes the steering column to compress, the gearshift tube components must telescope within the column.

SHIFT FORKS. The devices that straddle slots cut in sliding gears. The fork is used to move the gear back and forth on the shaft.

SHIFT POINT. This refers to the point, either in engine rpm or road speed, at which the transmission should be shifted to the next gear.

SHIFT RAILS. Sliding rods upon which the shift forks are attached. Used for shifting automatic transmission.

SHIM. A thin, flat piece of metal, used to separate two parts by a given distance determined by the thickness of the shim or shims placed between them.

SHIMMY. A fairly violent vibration of the car's front end, sometimes strong enough to shake the steering wheel back and forth, caused by front wheels that wobble as they rotate. This condition is usually due to loose steering linkage parts, out-of-adjustment conditions of front end alignment factors, or unbalanced tires.

SHOCK ABSORBER. Hydraulic mechanism that dampens oscillation in the suspension system.

SHOE. A curved member which supports the friction material, or brake lining. It also absorbs and transmits braking forces.

SHOE KNOCK OR SLAP. A knocking noise during braking, with a frequency related to wheel speed, can be caused by spiral cutting tool marks on the drum braking surface. During braking, these fine marks pull the shoes on the left-hand brakes out until they snap back against the support plate. This condition occurs only on newly-machined drums, since usage soon wears the marks down.

SHORT CIRCUIT (Short, Shorted out). Malfunctioning condition of an electric circuit or portion thereof, in which the electric current finds a low resistance path to ground through damaged insulation or some other condition. In effect, the current takes a short cut, by-passing the higher resistance components beyond the damage or short. When this occurs, current flow is usually so high because of the greatly reduced resistance that the fuse or circuit breaker overheats and shuts off the current.

SHORT FINDER. A special testing device that pinpoints the location of a short circuit in a conductor without penetrating the insulation. The short finder detects the presence or lack of a magnetic field around a conductor.

SHRINK-FIT. A fit between two parts which is so tight, outer or encircling piece must be expanded by heating so it will fit over inner piece. In cooling, outer part shrinks and grasps inner part securely.

SIDE-DRAFT CARBURETOR. A carburetor in which the air passes through the carburetor into the intake manifold in a horizontal plane.

SILENCER. Muffler.

SILVER SOLDER. Similar to brazing except that a special silver solder metal is used.

SINGLE-BARREL, DOUBLE-BARREL and 4-BARREL CARBURETORS. This refers to the number of throttle openings or barrels from the carburetors to the intake manifold.

SKID. Sudden movement of a car, due to loss of tire traction, in which the driver loses control and the automobile slips sideways on the road.

SKIRTS. A cover for the rear fender cutout.

SLANT ENGINE. This is an in-line engine in which the cylinder block has been tilted from a vertical plane.

SLAVE CYLINDER (Wheel cylinder). A hydraulic cylinder that converts hydraulic pressure generated by a master cylinder into a mechanical force. Automotive brake wheel cylinders are slave cylinders.

SLIDING GEAR. A transmission gear that is splined to the shaft. It may be moved back and forth for shifting.

SLIDING SPOOL. Part of the power steering valve. Its sliding action controls oil flow from the oil pump.

SLIP ANGLE. The angle formed during a turn between the direction that a tire is pointed and the direction that it is actually moving. This is not an indication of tire slippage, since the tire tread flexes and twists slightly so that it moves sideways in a turn. However, it is a factor to be considered by engineers in designing suspension systems.

SLIP JOINT. A joint that will transfer driving torque from one shaft to another while allowing longitudinal movement between the two shafts.

SLIP RINGS. In an alternator, ring-like components of the rotor which take field current from brushes and convey it to the rotor field windings.

SLUDGE. Black, mushy deposits throughout the interior of the engine. Caused by a mixture of dust, oil, and water being whipped together by the moving parts.

SMOG. Fog made darker and heavier by chemical fumes and smoke.

SNAP RING. A split ring that is snapped into a groove in a shaft or in a groove in a hole. It is used to hold bearings, thrust washers, gears, etc., in place.

SNOW TIRE. Tire that has an open-tread pattern with deep grooves to provide extra traction for driving in soft snow.

SNUBBERS. An obsolete term that was originally given to the devices that are now called shock absorbers.

SOHC. Single overhead camshaft.

SOLDERING. Joining two pieces of metal together with a lead-tin mixture. Both pieces of metal must be heated to insure proper adhesion of the melted solder.

SOLENOID. An electrically operated magnetic device used to operate some unit. A movable iron core is placed inside of a coil. When current flows through the coil, the core will attempt to center itself in the coil. In so doing, the core will exert considerable force on anything it is connected to.

SOLVENT. A liquid used to dissolve or thin another material. Alcohol thins shellac, gasoline dissolves grease.

SPARK. The bridging or jumping of a gap between two electrodes by a current of electricity.

SPARK ADVANCE. Causing the spark plug to fire earlier by altering the position of the distributor breaker points in relation to the distributor shaft.

SPARK GAP. The space between the center and side electrode tips on a spark plug.

SPARK KNOCK. See Preignition.

SPARK PLUG. An electrical device used in the ignition system to provide a high-tension voltage spark for igniting the compressed fuel-air mixture.

SPECIFIC GRAVITY. The relative weight of a given volume of a specific material as compared to the weight of an equal volume of water.

SPEEDOMETER. Instrument used to determine forward speed of an auto in miles per hour.

SPIDER GEARS. Small gears mounted on a shaft pinned to the differential case. They mesh with, and drive, the axle and gears.

SPINDLE. A stub axle for a front wheel, which protrudes from the steering knuckle.

SPIRAL BEVEL GEAR. A ring and pinion setup widely used in automobile differentials. The teeth of both the ring and the pinion are tapered and cut on a spiral so that they are at an angle to the center line of the pinion shaft.

SPLINE. Metal, land, remaining between two grooves. Used to connect parts.

SPLINED JOINT. A joint between two parts in which each part has a series of splines cut along the contact area. The splines on each part slide into the grooves between the splines on the other part.

SPONGY PEDAL. When there is air in the brake lines, or shoes that are not properly centered in the drums, the brake pedal will have a springy or spongy feeling when the brakes are applied. The pedal normally will feel hard when applied.

SPOOL BALANCE VALVE (Automatic transmission). A hydraulic valve that balances incoming oil pressure against spring control pressure to produce a steady pressure to some control unit.

SPORTS CAR. Term commonly used to describe a relatively small, low slung car with a high performance engine.

SPOT WELD. Fastening parts together by fusing at various points. Heavy surge of electricity is passed through the parts held in firm contact by electrodes.

SPRAG CLUTCH. A clutch that will allow rotation in one direction but that will lock up and prevent any movement in the other direction.

SPRINGS. Primary operating components of automotive suspension systems which absorb the force of road shocks by flexing or twisting. See Coil Springs, Leaf Springs, Torsion Bars and Air Suspension.

SPRING BOOSTER. A device used to beef up sagged springs or to increase the load capacity of standard springs.

SPRING WINDUP. The curved shape assumed by the rear leaf springs during acceleration or braking.

SPRUNG WEIGHT. This refers to the weight of all parts of the car that are supported by the suspension system.

SPUR GEAR. A gear on which the teeth are cut parallel to the shaft.

SPURT (Squirt hole). A small hole in the connecting rod big end that indexes (aligns) with the oil hole in the crank journal. When the holes index, oil spurts out to lubricate the cylinder walls.

SQUARE ENGINE. An engine in which the bore diameter and stroke are of equal dimensions.

SQUEAK. A high-pitched brake noise of short duration.

SQUEAL. A continuous, high-pitched, low-volume piercing brake noise.

SQ. FT. Square Foot.

SQ. IN. Square Inch.

STABILIZER BAR (Sway bar). A specialized form of torsion bar linking both sides of an independent front suspension. It resists side sway on turns by transferring some of the added load on the suspension for one front wheel to the suspension for the other wheel. However, it also transfers road shock and vibration from one wheel to the other.

STAMPING. A sheet metal part formed by pressing between metal discs.

STARTER (Starting motor, Cranking motor). Compact, powerful electric motor that drives the engine crankshaft flywheel by means of a gear that engages mating teeth on the rim of the flywheel. It is the most powerful electric motor on the automobile and draws the most current.

STATIC BALANCE. A condition of stability in a stationary body. A wheel and tire assembly is in static balance if its weight is evenly distributed around the wheel hub axis so that it will remain in whatever position it is placed in.

STATIC PRESSURE (Brakes). A certain amount of pressure that always exists in the brake lines, even with the brake pedal released. Static pressure is maintained by a check valve.

STATOR. A small hub, upon which a series of vanes are affixed in a radial position, so placed that oil leaving the torque converter turbine strikes the stator vanes and is redirected into the pump at an angle conducive to high efficiency. The stator makes torque multiplication possible. Torque multiplication is highest at stall when the engine speed is at its highest and the turbine is standing still.

STEEL PACK MUFFLER. A straight-through (no baffles) muffler utilizing metal shavings surrounding a perforated pipe. Quiets exhaust sound.

STEERING ARM. An arm protruding from the steering knuckle, which is connected to the tie-rod and turns the steering knuckle in response to tie-rod movement.

STEERING AXIS INCLINATION. Tipping the tops of the kingpins inward towards each other. This places the center line of the steering axis nearer the center line of the tire-road contact area.

STEERING GEAR. The gears, mounted on the lower end of the steering column, that are used to multiply driver turning force.

STEERING GEAR ARM (Pitman arm, Pitman). The arm which links the cross shaft in the steering gear with the steering linkage

STEERING GEOMETRY. A term sometimes used to describe the various angles assumed by the components making up the front wheel turning arrangement, camber, caster, toe-in, etc. Also used to describe the related angles assumed by the front wheels when the car is negotiating a curve.

STEERING KNUCKLE. Device that is pivoted by the steering mechanism, causing the wheels to turn.

STEERING KNUCKLE ANGLE. The angle formed between the steering axis and the center line of the spindle. This angle is sometimes referred to as the included angle.

STICK SHIFT. This refers to a transmission that is shifted manually through the use of various forms of linkage. Often refers to the upright gearshift stick that protrudes through the floor.

STIRLING-CYCLE ENGINE. External combustion engine that uses gas that is alternately heated and cooled within a closed system to drive pistons.

STOCK CAR. A car as built by the factory.

STOVEBOLT. Generally refers to Chevrolet (GMC) 6-cylinder, in-line, valve-in-head (push rod operated) engine.

STRATIFIED-CHARGE ENGINE. Modification of the piston engine in which both lean and rich fuel mixtures are simultaneously supplied to each cylinder.

STROBOSCOPE. See Timing Light.

STROKE. The distance a piston travels from top dead center to bottom dead center.

STROKED CRANKSHAFT. A crankshaft, either a special new one or a stock crank reworked, that has the con rod throws offset increasing length of the stroke.

STRUT (Invar strut). In the controlled expansion type of aluminum piston, a steel segment cast into the piston to restrain its expansion with heat so as to nearly equal the expansion of the cast iron cylinder and maintain a more constant piston-to-cylinder wall clearance. Many struts are made of Invar- and iron-nickel alloy with desirable expansion characteristics.

STUD. A metal rod with threads on both ends.

STUD PULLER. A tool used to install or remove studs.

SUCTION. See Vacuum.

SUCTION THROTTLING VALVE. Valve placed between the air conditioning evaporator and compressor which controls evaporator pressure to provide maximum cooling without icing evaporator core.

SUMP. That part of the oil pan that contains the oil.

SUN GEAR. The center gear around which the planet gears revolve.

SUPER CAR. A car with a high horsepower engine that will provide fast acceleration and high speed.

SUPERCHARGER (Blower). An air compressor used on some high performance engines to increase volumetric efficiency by forcing a greater quantity of air into the cylinders on each intake stroke.

SUPPORT PLATE (Backing plate, Shield). A component of the brake which is attached to the car's underbody structure and supports all other brake parts except the drum.

SUPPRESSOR-TYPE CABLE. Wire or cable used for spark plug wires that resists or suppresses certain electrical signals produced in automobile ignition systems so that radio and TV signals will not be interrupted.

SUSPENSION (Suspension system). Components of a vehicle having the primary purpose of cushioning that body from the reactions of the wheels to irregularities of the surface over which the vehicle travels. Also, the supporting members for these components.

SWING AXLE. An independent rear suspension system in which each driving wheel can move up or down independently of the other. The differential unit is bolted to the frame and various forms of linkage are used upon which to mount the wheels. Drive axles, utilizing one or more universal joints, connect the differential to the drive wheels.

SWITCH. Electrical device used to control the flow of electric current. Switches normally are used either to turn a current on or off, or to route the current to one of a number of related circuits.

SYMMETRICAL IDLER ARM. A steering linkage component which supports the right side of the steering center link that operates the two tie-rods. The symmetrical idler arm is a geometric duplicate of the steering gear arm. The resulting steering linkage configuration practically eliminates front wheel toe changes during jounce and rebound caused by changes in the effective tie-rod length of earlier designs.

SYNCHROMESH TRANSMISSION. A transmission using a device that synchronizes the speed of gears that are being shifted together. This prevents gear grinding. Some transmissions use a synchromesh on all shifts, while others synchronize second and high gearshifts.

SYNCHRONIZE. To bring about a timing that will cause two or more events to occur simultaneously—a plug firing when the piston is in the correct position, the speed of two shafts being the same, a valve opening when the piston is in the correct position, etc.

SYNCHRONIZING RINGS. Devices in a synchromesh transmission that bring up the speed of the driven gear to that of the driving gear and lock the driven gear to the output shaft of the transmission.

TACHOMETER. A device used to indicate the speed of the engine in rpm.

TAILPIPE. Exhaust piping running from the muffler to the rear of the car.

TAP. To cut threads in a hole. Or the fluted tool used to cut the threads.

TAP AND DIE SET. A set of taps and dies for internal and external threading. Usually covers a range of the most popular sizes.

TAPERED ROLLER BEARING (Antifriction). A bearing utilizing a series of tapered, hardened steel rollers operating between an outer and inner hardened steel race.

TAPPET. The screw used to adjust the clearance between the valve stem and the lifter or the rocker arm.

TAPPET NOISE. Noise caused by the lash or clearance between the valve stem and rocker arm or between the valve stem and valve lifter.

TDC. Top Dead Center.

TERMINAL. A connecting point in an electric circuit. When referring to the battery, it would indicate the two battery posts.

THERMOSTAT. A temperature-sensitive device used in cooling systems to control the flow of coolant.

THICKNESS GAUGE. See Feeler Gauge.

THIRD BRUSH. A generator in which a third movable brush is used to control current output.

THROTTLE VALVE. A valve in the carburetor. It is used to control the amount of fuel mixture that reaches the cylinders.

THROW. The offset portion of the crankshaft designed to accept the connecting rod.

THROWING A ROD. When an engine throws a connecting rod from the crankshaft. Major damage is usually incurred.

THRUST BEARING. A bearing designed so as to resist side pressure.

THRUST WASHER. A bronze or hardened steel washer placed between two moving parts. The washer prevents longitudinal movement and provides a bearing surface for the thrust surfaces of the parts.

TIE ROD. A rod connecting the steering arms together. When the tie rod is moved, the wheels pivot.

TIMING CHAIN. A drive chain that operates the camshaft by engaging sprockets on the camshaft and crankshaft.

TIMING GEARS. Both the gear attached to the camshaft and the gear on the crankshaft. They provide a means of driving the camshaft.

TIMING LIGHT. A type of stroboscope used for adjusting the timing of ignition spark. One lead of the light is connected to the battery and the other to the high tension wire of the No. 1 cylinder.

TIMING MARKS (Ignition). Marks, usually located on the vibration damper, used to synchronize the ignition system so that the plugs will fire at the precise time.

TIMING MARKS (Valves). One tooth on either the camshaft or crankshaft gear will be marked with an indentation or some other mark. Another mark will be found on the other gear between two of the teeth. The two gears must be meshed so that the marked tooth meshes with the marked spot on the other gear.

TIMING THE IGNITION. Tuneup procedure in which spark plug firing is adjusted to occur at the correct instant of a given piston's cycle.

TIRE BALANCE. See Dynamic Balance and Static Balance.

TIRE BEAD. Reinforced portion of a tire that holds the tire on the wheel rim.

TIRE CASING. The main body of the tire exclusive of the tread.

TIRE PATCH AREA. The small portion of tire tread, roughly oval in shape, that provides the only contact the car has with the road at a given instant. All directional, starting and stopping control is concentrated in the tire patch areas of the four tires.

TIRE PROFILE. Ratio between a tire's tread-to-bead height and its sidewall-to-sidewall width.

TIRE PLIES. The layers of nylon, rayon, etc., that are used to form the casing. Most car tires are 2-ply with a 4-ply rating. Two-ply indicates two layers of cloth.

TIRE ROTATION. Moving the front tires to the rear and the rear to the front to equalize any wear irregularities.

TIRE SIDEWALL. That portion of the tire between the tread and the bead.

TIRE TREAD. That part of the tire that contacts the road.

TOE (Toe-in, Toe-out, Zero toe). Toe is a term denoting the comparison of the distance between the extreme front of both tires and the distance between the extreme rear of both tires, measured at the front wheels. If the front wheel tires are closer together at the front than at the rear, it is called toe-in. If farther apart at the front than at the rear, it is called toe-out And if the distance is exactly equal at front and rear, so that the wheels run parallel, it is called zero toe.

TOE-OUT ON TURNS (Front wheel turning angle). A built-in characteristic of automotive steering systems, wherein toe-out of the front wheels is increased in proportion to the degree they are turned away from the straight-ahead position. This is necessary because the inside wheel on a turn follows a path that is a tighter circle than the path of the outside wheel. Toe-out on turns is one of the factors in front end alignment.

TOGGLE SWITCH. A switch that is actuated by flipping a small lever either up and down or from side to side.

TOLERANCE. The amount of variation permitted from an exact size or measurement. The actual amount from the smallest acceptable dimensions to the largest acceptable dimension.

TOOTH HEEL (Differential ring gear). The wider outside end of the tooth.

TOOTH TOE (Differential ring gear). The narrower inside end of the tooth.

TOP DEAD CENTER (TDC). Point at which a piston reaches the top of its travel in a cylinder.

TOP OFF. Fill a container to full capacity.

TORQUE. Measurement of the force of torsion. Turning or twisting force such as the force imparted on the driveline by the engine. It is expressed as force times distance of a moment arm. (e.g. 240 foot-pounds.)

TORQUE CONVERTER. A unit, quite similar to the fluid coupling, that transfers engine torque to the transmission input shaft. Unlike the fluid coupling, the torque converter can multiply engine torque. This is accomplished by installing one or more stators between the torus members. In the torque converter, the driving torus is referred to as the pump and the driven torus as the turbine.

TORQUE MULTIPLICATION (Automatic transmission). Increasing engine torque through the use of a torque converter.

TORQUE TUBE DRIVE. The method of connecting the transmission output shaft to the differential pinion shaft by using an enclosed driveshaft. The driveshaft is enclosed in a torque tube that is bolted to the rear axle housing on one end and is pivoted through a ball joint to the rear of the transmission on the other. The driving force of the rear wheels is transferred to the frame through the torque tube.

TORQUE WRENCH. A wrench used to draw nuts, cap screws, etc., up to a specified tension by measuring the torque being applied.

TORSION. See Torque.

TORSIONAL VIBRATION. A twisting and untwisting action developed in a shaft. It is caused either by intermittent applications of power or load.

TORSION BAR. A long spring steel rod attached in such a way that one end is anchored while the other is free to twist. If an arm is attached, at right angles, to the free end, any movement of the arm will cause the rod or bar to twist. The bar's resistance to twisting provides a spring action. The torsion bar replaces both coil and leaf springs in some suspension systems.

TRACK. The distance between the front wheels or the distance between the rear wheels. They are not always the same.

TRACTION. The ability of a tire to grip the road surface, which determines the degree of effectiveness that steering, driving and braking forces will have on the car's motion.

TRACTION DIFFERENTIAL. See Limited-Slip Differential.

TRAMP. A hopping motion of the front wheels.

TRANSAXLE. A drive setup in which the transmission and differential are combined into a single unit.

TRANSFORMER. An electrical device used to increase or decrease voltage. A car ignition coil transforms the voltage from 12 volts to upward of 20,000 volts.

TRANSISTOR IGNITION. A relatively new form of ignition, this system utilizes transistors and a special coil. The conventional distributor and point setup is used. With the transistor unit, the voltage remains constant, thus permitting high engine rpm without resultant engine miss. Point life is greatly extended as the transistor system passes a very small amount of current through the points.

TRANSMISSION. A device that uses gearing or torque conversion to effect a change in the ratio between engine rpm and driving wheel rpm. When engine rpm goes up in relation to wheel rpm, more torque but less speed is produced. A reduction in engine rpm in relation to wheel rpm produces a higher road speed but delivers less torque to the driving wheels.

TRANSMISSION ADAPTER. A unit that allows a different make or year transmission to be bolted up to the original engine.

TRANSMISSION (Automatic). A transmission that automatically effects gear changes to meet varying road and load conditions. Gear changing is done through a series of oil operated clutches and bands.

TRANSMISSION (Standard, Manual, Conventional). A transmission that must be shifted manually.

TRANSVERSE LEAF SPRING. A leaf spring that is mounted so that it is at right angles to the length of the car.

TRAPS. The area over which the car is raced for timing purposes.

TREAD. The distance between the two front or two rear wheels.

TREAD (Tire). Portion of the tire which contacts the roadway.

TREAD-WEAR INDICATORS. Horizontal bands molded into a tire tread that appear across the tread grooves when only 1/16 of an inch of tread-rubber remains.

TRIP ODOMETER. An auxiliary odometer that may be reset to zero at the option of the driver. It is used for keeping track of the mileage on trips up to one thousand miles.

TROUBLESHOOTING. Diagnosing engine, transmission, and other problems by various tests.

TUBE CUTTER. A tool used to cut tubing by passing a sharp wheel around and around the tube.

TUNEUP. The process of checking, repairing and adjusting the carburetor, spark plugs, points, belts, timing, etc., in order to obtain the maximum performance from the engine.

TURBINE. A wheel upon which a series of angled vanes are affixed so that a moving column of air or liquid will impart a turning motion to the wheel.

TURBINE ENGINE. An engine that utilizes burning gases to spin a turbine, or series of turbines, as a means of propelling the car.

TURBOCHARGER. An exhaust powered supercharger.

TURBULENCE. Violent, broken movement or agitation of a fluid or gas.

TURNING RADIUS. The diameter of the circle transcribed by the outer front wheel when making a full turn.

TV ROD. This refers to the throttle valve rod that extends from the foot throttle linkage to the throttle valve in the automatic transmission.

TWIST DRILL. A metal cutting drill with spiral flutes (grooves) to permit the exit of chips while cutting.

TWO-STROKE CYCLE ENGINE. An engine requiring one complete revolution of the crankshaft to fire each piston once.

UNDERCOATING. The soft deadening material sprayed on the undersides of the car, under the hood, trunk lid, etc.

UNDERSTEER. Tendency for a car, when negotiating a turn, to resist turning and continue straight ahead.

UNDERSQUARE ENGINE. An engine in which the bore diameter is smaller than the length of the stroke.

UNITIZED BODY DESIGN (Unit body, Unibody). A method of automobile body construction which combines body and frame structures into one integrated welded assembly, instead of the previous practice of bolting the body to a separate frame.

UNIT BODY. A car body in which the body itself acts as the frame.

UNIVERSAL JOINT. A flexible joint that will permit changes in the driving angle between the driving and driven shaft.

UNSPRUNG WEIGHT. The weight of that portion of the automobile which is not supported by the springs. Included in this category are the wheels, tires, brakes, rear axle, steering knuckles and control arms.

UPDRAFT CARBURETOR. A carburetor in which the air passes upward through the carburetor into the intake manifold.

UPSET. A widening of the diameter through pounding.

UPSHIFT. Shifting to a higher gear.

VACUUM (Low pressure, Suction). Technically, a true vacuum exists only in a space where there is absolutely no matter. However, in general usage, the word is used to mean a partial vacuum, or any air pressure less than atmospheric pressure.

VACUUM ADVANCE (Distributor). A unit designed to advance and retard the ignition timing through the action of engine vacuum working on a diaphragm.

VACUUM BOOSTER. A small diaphragm vacuum pump, generally in combination with the fuel pump, that is used to bolster engine vacuum during acceleration so that the vacuum operated devices will continue to operate.

VACUUM GAUGE. A gauge used to determine the amount of vacuum existing in a chamber.

VACUUM PUMP. A diaphragm type of pump used to produce a vacuum.

VACUUM RUNOUT POINT. This refers to the point reached when a vacuum brake power piston has built up all the braking force it is capable of with the vacuum available.

VACUUM TANK. A tank in which a vacuum exists. It is generally used to provide vacuum to a power brake installation in the event engine vacuum cannot be obtained. The tank will supply several brake applications before the vacuum is exhausted.

VALVE. A device—of which there are many different types—used to either open or close an opening.

VALVE DURATION. The length of time, measured in degrees of engine crankshaft rotation, that a valve remains open.

VALVE FACE. The outer lower edge of the valve head. The face contacts valve seat when valve is closed.

VALVE FLOAT. A condition where the valves in the engine are forced back open before they have had a chance to seat. Usually brought about by extremely high rpm.

VALVE GRINDING. Renewing the valve face area by grinding on a special grinding machine.

VALVE GUIDE. The hole through which the stem of the poppet valve passes. It is designed to keep the valve in proper alignment. Some guides are pressed into place and others are merely drilled in the block or in the head metal.

VALVE-IN-HEAD ENGINE. An engine in which both intake and exhaust valves are mounted in the cylinder head and are driven by pushrods or by an overhead camshaft.

VALVE LASH. Valve tappet clearance or total clearance in the valve operating train with cam follower on camshaft base circle.

VALVE LIFT. Distance a valve moves from the fully closed to the fully opened position.

VALVE LIFTER (Cam follower). The unit that contacts the end of the valve stem and the camshaft. The follower rides on the camshaft and when the cam lobes move it upward, it opens the valve.

VALVE MARGIN. The width of the edge of the valve head between the top of the valve and the edge of the face. Too narrow a margin results in preignition and valve damage through overheating.

VALVE OIL SEAL. A neoprene rubber ring that is placed in a groove in the valve stem to prevent excess oil entering the area between the stem and the guide. There are other types of these seals.

VALVE OVERLAP. Interval at the end of the exhaust stroke and beginning of the following intake stroke when both the intake and exhaust valves are open.

VALVE PORT. The opening, through the head or block, from the intake or exhaust manifold to the valve seat.

VALVE ROTATOR. A unit that is placed on the end of the valve stem so that when the valve is opened and closed, the valve will rotate a small amount with each opening and closing. This gives longer valve life.

VALVE SEAT. The area onto which the face of the poppet seals when closed. The two common angles for this seat are forty-five and thirty degrees.

VALVE SEAT GRINDING. Renewing the valve seat area by grinding with a stone mounted upon a special mandrel.

VALVE SEAT INSERT. A hardened steel valve seat that may be removed and replaced.

VALVE SPRING. The coil spring used to keep the valves closed.

VALVE TAPPET. An adjusting screw to obtain the specified clearance at the end of the valve stem (tappet clearance). The screw may be in the top of the lifter, in the rocker arm, or in the case of the ball joint rocker arm, the nut on the mounting stud acts in place of a tappet screw.

VALVE TIMING. Adjusting the position of the camshaft to the crankshaft so that the valves will open and close at the proper time.

VALVETRAIN. A system of components within an engine, designed to actuate the intake and exhaust valves of each cylinder in the proper order. The valvetrain includes the camshaft, tappets, valves and springs, and in the case of valve-in-head engines, push rods and rocker arms.

VALVE UMBRELLA. A washer-like unit that is placed over the end of the valve stem to prevent the entry of excess oil between the stem and the guide. Used in valve-in-head installations.

VAPORIZATION. Breaking the gasoline into fine particles and mixing it with the incoming air.

VAPOR LOCK. Boiling or vaporizing of the fuel in the lines from excess heat. The boiling will interfere with the movement of the fuel and will in some cases completely stop the flow.

VAPOR SEPARATOR. A device used on cars equipped with air conditioning to prevent vapor lock by feeding vapors back to the gas tank via a separate line.

VARIABLE PITCH STATOR. A stator that has vanes that may be adjusted to various angles depending on load conditions. The van adjustment will increase or decrease the efficiency of the stator.

VARNISH. A deposit on the interior of the engine caused by the engine oil breaking down under prolonged heat and use. Certain portions of the oil deposit themselves in hard coatings of varnish.

VENTURI. In the carburetor, a streamlined constriction within the main air passage(s), designed to create a localized low pressure area in the airflow through it.

VIBRATION DAMPER. A round, weighted device attached to the front of the crankshaft to minimize the torsional vibration.

VISCOSIMETER. A device used to determine the viscosity of a given sample of oil. The oil is heated to a specific temperature and then allowed to flow through a set orifice. The length of time required for a certain amount to flow determines the oil's viscosity.

VISCOSITY. A term denoting the ability of a fluid to flow readily. A fluid with high viscosity will flow sluggishly, while one with low viscosity will flow much more readily.

VISCOSITY INDEX. A measure of an oil's ability to resist changes in viscosity when heated.

VOLATILE. Easily evaporated.

VOLATILITY. The property of gasoline, alcohol, etc., to evaporate quickly and at relatively low temperatures.

VOLT. A unit of electrical pressure or force that will move a current of one ampere through a resistance of one ohm.

VOLT (Voltage). Unit of measurement of electrical pressure. One volt is defined as the pressure or potential needed to push a current of one ampere through a resistance of one ohm.

VOLTAGE DROP. The lowering of voltage due to excess length of wire, undersize wire, etc.

VOLTAGE REGULATOR. See Regulator.

VOLTMETER. An instrument used to measure the voltage in a given circuit.

VOLUME. The measurement, in cubic inches, cubic feet, etc., of the amount of space within a certain object or area.

VOLUMETRIC EFFICIENCY. A comparison between the actual volume of fuel mixture drawn in on the intake stroke and what would be drawn in if the cylinder were to be completely filled.

VORTEX FLOW (Torque converter). The whirling motion of the oil as it moves around and around from the pump, through the turbine, through the stator and back into the pump and so on.

V-TYPE ENGINE. Internal combustion engine in which the cylinders are arranged in two banks at an angle to each other.

WALLOWING. The slow, pitching motion of a car driven over a smooth road with only slight undulations or crosswise tar strips at regular intervals. One cause of this condition is shock absorbers that exercise too little control over minor spring deflections.

WANDER (Drift). An unstable steering condition in which the car tends to steer itself slightly to both right and left, and requires repeated steering corrections. This usually indicates the need for front end alignment.

WANKEL ENGINE. See Rotary Engine.

WATER JACKET. The area around the cylinders and valves that is left hollow so that water may be admitted for cooling.

WEDGE. Engine using wedge-shaped combustion chamber.

WEDGE COMBUSTION CHAMBER. A widely-used and efficient combustion chamber utilizing a wedge shape.

WEIGHT DISTRIBUTION. The portion of the car's weight that rests on each of the four wheels. In early automobiles, as much as 70% of the car's weight was on the rear wheels. Current practice is to design cars with a weight distribution falling nearly equally on all four wheels.

WELD. To join two pieces of metal together by raising the area to be joined to a temperature hot enough for the two sections to melt and flow together. Additional metal is usually added by melting small drops from the end of a metal rod.

WET SLEEVE. A cylinder sleeve application in which the water in the cooling system contacts a major portion of the sleeve itself.

WHEEL ALIGNER. A device used to check camber, caster, toe-in, etc.

WHEEL BALANCER. A machine used to check the wheel and tire assembly for static and dynamic balance.

WHEELBASE. The distance between the center of the front wheels and the center of the rear wheels.

WHEEL CYLINDER. That part of the hydraulic brake system that receives pressure from the master cylinder and in turn applies the brake shoes to the drums.

WHEEL HOP. A hopping action of the rear wheels during heavy acceleration.

WHEELIE BARS. Short arms attached to the rear of a drag racer to prevent the front end from rising too far off the ground during heavy acceleration. Arms are usually of spring material and have small wheels attached to the ends that contact the ground.

WHEEL LUG (Lug bolt). The bolts used to fasten the wheel to the hub.

WIDE TREADS (Wide oval, etc.). Wide tires. Tire height, bead to tread surface is about 70% of the tire width across outside of casing.

WINDING THE ENGINE. Running the engine at top rpm.

WINDSCREEN. British term for windshield.

WIRING DIAGRAM. A drawing showing the various electrical units and the wiring arrangement necessary for them to function properly.

WISHBONE. The radius rod setup used in many of the older Ford cars to keep the axle square with the frame.

WITNESS MARKS. Punch marks used to position or locate some part in its proper spot.

WORM GEAR. A coarse, spiral-shaped gear cut on a shaft. It is used to engage with and drive another gear or portion of a gear. As used in the steering gearbox, it often engages the cross shaft via a roller or by a tapered pin.

WORM AND ROLLER. A type of steering gear utilizing a worm gear on the steering shaft. A roller on one end of the cross shaft engages the worm.

WORM AND SECTOR. A type of steering gear utilizing a worm gear engaging a sector (a portion of a gear) on the cross shaft.

WORM AND TAPER PIN. A type of steering gear utilizing a worm gear on the steering shaft. The end of the cross shaft engages the worm via a taper pin.

WORMSHAFT (Steering shaft, worm). A shaft in the steering gear, coupled to the shaft from the driver's steering wheel.

WRIST PIN. Round steel pin inserted through a piston to which a connecting rod is fastened.